TURBO PASCAL

Problem Solving and Program Design

THIRD EDITION

D0144550

TURBO PASCAL®

Problem Solving and Program Design

ADDISON-WESLEY PUBLISHING COMPANY, INC.
Reading, Massachusetts Menlo Park, California New York
Don Mills, Ontario Wokingham, England Amsterdam Bonn
Sydney Singapore Tokyo Madrid San Juan Milan Paris

ELLIOT B. KOFFMAN
TEMPLE UNIVERSITY

with

BRUCE R. MAXIM
UNIVERSITY OF MICHIGAN AT DEARBORN

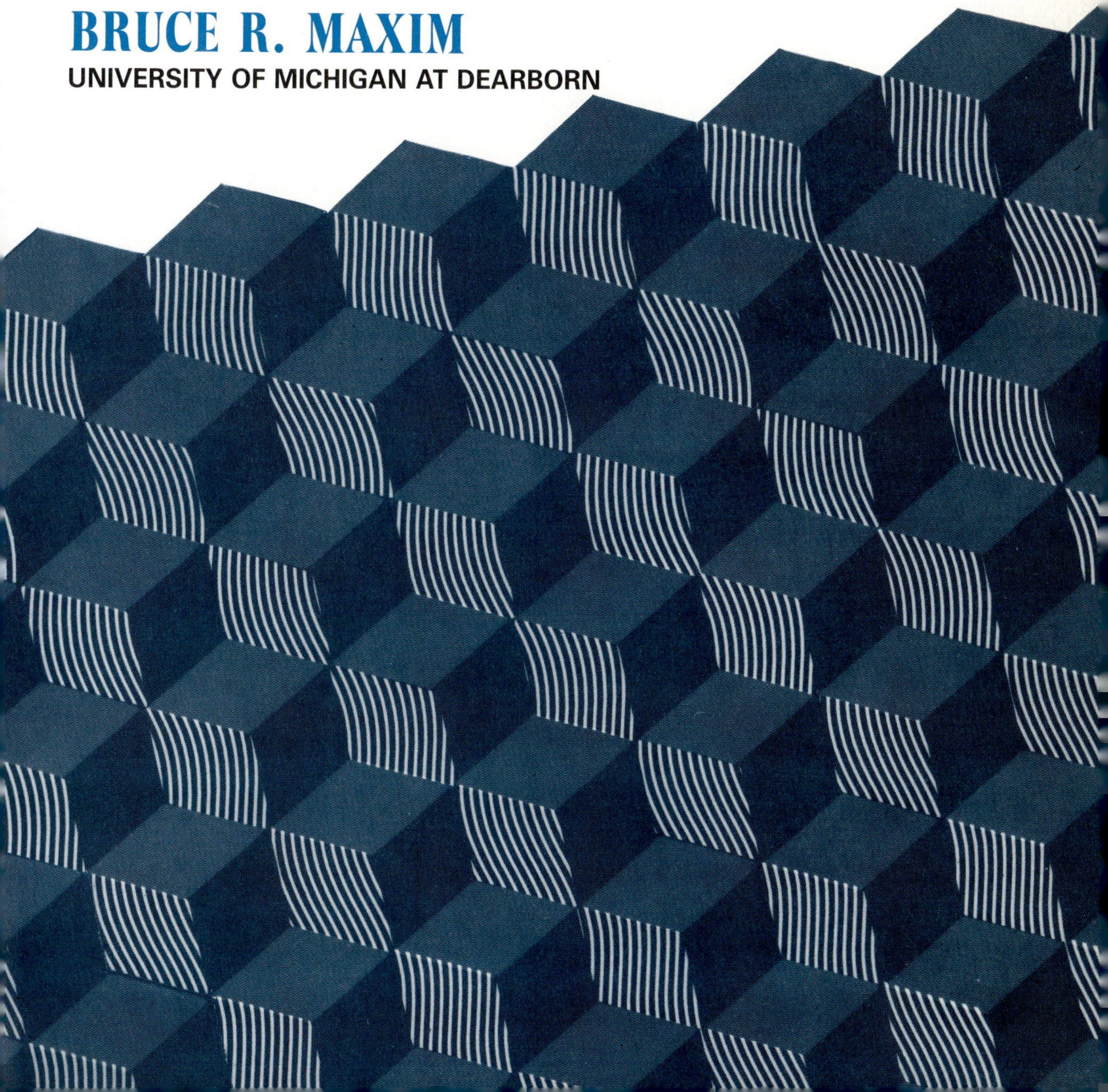

Peter Shepard, Sponsoring Editor
Loren Hilgenhurst Stevens, Production Supervisor
Nancy Benjamin, Production Editor
Joyce Cameron Weston, Text Design
Joseph Vetere, Technical Art Consultant
Tech-Graphics, Connie Hulse, Illustrations
Roy Logan, Manufacturing Supervisor
Marshall Henrichs, Cover Design

Library of Congress Cataloging-in-Publication Data

Koffman, Elliot B.
Turbo Pascal : problem solving and program design / by Elliot B. Koffman with Bruce R. Maxim.—3rd ed.
p. cm
Includes bibliographical references and index.
ISBN 0-201-53466-5
1. Pascal (Computer program language) 2. Turbo Pascal (Computer program) I. Maxim, Bruce R. II. Title.
QA76.73.P2K635 1991
005.13′3—dc20 90-49693
CIP

All screen dumps are reprinted with permission.
Copyright © 1991, 1988, 1987 Borland International, Inc.

Portions of Appendix F are reprinted with permission.
Copyright © 1991, 1988, 1987 Borland International, Inc.

Turbo Pascal is a registered trademark of Borland International, Inc.

Copyright © 1991, 1989, 1986 by Addison-Wesley Publishing Company, Inc.

All rights reserved. No part of this publication may be reproduced, stored in a retrieval system, or transmitted in any form or by any means, electronic, mechanical, photocopying, recording, or otherwise, without the prior written permission of the publisher. Printed in the United States of America.

1 2 3 4 5 6 7 8 9 10 HA 9594939291

Preface

While working on the first edition of this book, I served as chairman of a Task Force sponsored by the ACM Curriculum Committee whose purpose was to update the curricula for CS1 [1] and CS2 [2]. This was the first Turbo Pascal book to follow the recommendations and philosophy expressed in the Task Force's curriculum report for course CS1. In accordance with this philosophy, the first edition provided an early introduction to the use of procedures and taught stepwise design through procedural abstraction.

Also according to these recommendations, data abstraction and the use of abstract data types is a vital component of the second course and an important seed to plant in the first course. Users of Turbo Pascal are in a unique position to accomplish this because of the unit feature, which provides direct support for implementing abstract data types. By introducing units early in the book (Chapter 8) and integrating the use of units throughout the rest of the book, we enable instructors to properly teach these important concepts.

Prior to my starting this revision, Addison-Wesley's market research department contacted many loyal users of the previous edition to find out what they wanted to see in a new edition. Also around that time, the Joint Curriculum Task Force began to report on their work to define a computer science core and to develop course sequences in computer science [3,4]. The feedback I received from users of previous editions was that they wanted to retain the early introduction to procedures, but they also wanted to introduce the important concepts of software engineering and data abstraction in their initial programming course. Like the Joint Curriculum Task Force, they wanted to see more emphasis on theoretical aspects of computer science. They also wanted additional coverage of advanced topics. Finally, they wanted all this packaged in smaller, more digestible chapters.

---

1. Koffman, E., Miller, P., and Wardle, C., Recommended Curriculum for CS1, Communications of the ACM 27, 10 (Oct. 1984), 998-1001.

2. Koffman, E., Stemple D., and Wardle, C., Recommended Curriculum for CS2, Communications of the ACM 28, 8 (Aug. 1985), 815-818.

3. Denning, P.J. et al., Draft Report of the ACM Task Force on the Core of Computer Science (Feb. 1988).

4. Tucker, A.B. et al., Computing Curricula 1990, Draft Report of the Joint Curriculum Task Force (May, 1990).

My goal for this revision was to accomplish all these objectives so that the new edition would continue to meet the changing needs of computer science faculty. This book can be used as a text for both of the first two courses in computer science or for most of the two-semester introductory course sequences described in Appendix A of [4].

Turbo Pascal Versions

The previous edition of this book taught Turbo Pascal versions 4.0, 5.0, and 5.5. This edition focuses on version 6.0. The primary enhancements introduced in version 6.0 are the new menu-driven environment and support for object-oriented programming. The primary enhancements introduced in versions 4.0 and 5.0 are separately compilable units and the inclusion of a debugger in the integrated environment. The menu-driven environment is discussed in the body of the book and Appendix A. We discuss how units, object-oriented programming, and the debugger are treated below.

Modular Programming

This book provides an early introduction to the use of procedures. Procedures without parameters are introduced in Chapter 3 as a problem-solving tool to facilitate writing modular programs. This chapter shows how to utilize procedures to display messages and instructions to program users. In this way, students become familiar with procedures without the burden of passing parameters and without picking up bad habits such as referencing global variables from within a procedure.

Procedure parameters are introduced in Chapter 6. This material has been revised and simplified. Value parameters are now introduced first, followed by variable parameters.

The unit feature of Turbo Pascal allows programmers to create object-code libraries of reusable procedures and abstract data types. We introduce units in Chapter 8 and use them throughout the rest of the text to emphasize the importance of modular programming and reusability. We also show how to use unit `Crt` to create a user-interface consisting of a window for data entry.

Software Engineering

As recommended by the Curriculum Task Force reports, this book introduces students to the fundamentals of software engineering as they begin their formal study of programming. The complete title *Turbo Pascal: Problem Solving and Program Design* reflects the emphasis on software engineering. Problem solving is emphasized through the case study discussions.

There is a chapter on Programming in the Large (Chapter 8), which introduces the software life cycle. The important concepts of data abstraction and abstract data types are introduced in this chapter and carried throughout the rest of the book. We introduce enumerated types in this chapter and show how to encapsulate a data type and its operators as a Turbo Pascal unit.

Chapter 18 ends with two sections that describe the object-oriented approach to programming. Instructors who prefer to introduce this topic earlier should cover Section 18.7 after Chapter 11 (Records).

The important software engineering topics of program style and structured design permeate the book. Also, program documentation and verification are emphasized. Loop invariants and assertions are introduced as a tool for documenting and designing loops in Chapter 5, and preconditions and postconditions are used to document procedures starting in Chapter 6.

Finally, there is increased emphasis on testing and debugging. Each case study ends with a section on testing. Several chapters end with sections containing user screens that show how to use the Turbo Pascal integrated debugger to help debug programs that make use of the new Pascal constructs introduced in that chapter.

Organization

A major goal of the second edition was to make the material in the book more accessible to a variety of students. To this end, we made a number of important changes, which were retained in this edition. We reorganized the material so that each chapter would be shorter and introduce fewer new concepts. As an example of this, there are now separate chapters on the `if` statement (Chapter 4), on `while` loops (Chapter 5), and on procedure parameters (Chapter 6). In the first edition, these topics were covered in a single chapter on control structures.

Another organizational change was to introduce the basics of text files earlier than before. Text files are first introduced in an optional section in Chapter 2 so that students' programs can read data files prepared by their instructors. This material is reviewed in Chapter 8, which discusses the use of text files for input/output in larger programs. Finally, complete coverage of binary files, including a discussion of direct access files, appears in Chapter 14.

Pedagogical Features

To facilitate our goal of making the book more useful as a learning tool, we utilize several important pedagogical features, which are discussed below.

End of Section Exercises: Following most sections there are two kinds of exercises, self-check and programming. The answers to selected self-check exercises appear at the end of the book; the answers to the programming exercises are provided in the instructor's manual.

End of Chapter Exercises: Each chapter ends with a set of quick-check exercises with answers. There are also chapter review exercises and a set of programming projects whose solutions appear in the instructor's manual. Many new projects appear in this edition.

Examples and Case Studies: The book contains a large number and variety of programming examples. Whenever possible, examples contain small, complete programs or procedures rather than incomplete program fragments. There are also substantial case studies that help a student integrate and apply concepts studied over several chapters.

Syntax Display Boxes: The syntax display boxes describe the syntax and semantics of each new Pascal feature. The syntax displays in this edition include examples.

Program Style Displays: The program style displays discuss issues of good programming style.

Error Discussions and Chapter Review: Each chapter ends with a section that discusses common programming errors and a review section that includes a table of new Pascal constructs.

Second Course Coverage

The coverage of advanced topics includes most of the topics recommended for the second course in the Joint Curriculum Task Force's Report [4]. The inclusion of these topics provides added flexibility for instructors who wish to cover advanced material. It also allows the book to be used either as a reference by students going onto or as the primary textbook for CS2 in some courses. Topics covered include:

sets and strings (Chapter 13)
files (Chapter 14)
recursion (Chapter 15)
stacks and queues (Chapter 16)
pointers and linked lists (Chapter 17)
trees (Chapter 18)
searching and sorting (Chapter 19)
analysis of algorithms (Chapters 18 and 19)

Appendices and Supplements

There are separate appendices which cover the Turbo Pascal integrated environment, Turbo Pascal language elements, syntax diagrams, character codes, error messages, additional Turbo Pascal features, and differences between standard Pascal and Turbo Pascal.

A computerized test bank is available for this edition. Other supplements include an instructor's manual, transparency masters, and a program disk with all the programs that appear in the book. Use the reference numbers below to order these supplements from your Addison-Wesley sales representative.

Computerized Test Bank:	0-201-19477-5
Instructor's Manual:	0-201-52681-6
Transparency Masters:	0-201-52683-2
Program Disk:	0-201-52682-4

Acknowledgments

Bruce Maxim adapted this edition to take full advantage of Turbo Pascal 6.0 language extensions and special features. I am extremely grateful to Bruce for his excellent treatment of these topics.

Many people participated in the development of this book. The principal reviewers for this revision were: Taylor Binkley, Georgia State University; Richard Epstein, The George Washington University; Jacquelyn Palmer, Wright State University; Parley Robison, Brigham Young University; Kenneth Rockwood, Stevens Institute of Technology; and Major Robert Shaw, U.S. Military Academy. Other reviewers, who were most helpful in suggesting improvements, include: Robert B. Anderson, University of Houston; Robert Christiansen, University of Iowa; Denis Conrady, North Texas State University; Donald H. Cooley, Utah State University; Ed Deaton, San Diego State University; Paul L. Emerick, De Anza College; Dale Grosvenor, Iowa State University of Science and Technology; Bill Kraynek, Florida International University; Cary Laxer, Rose-Hulman Institute of Technology; Larry Neal, East Tennessee State University; Theresa M. Phinney, Texas A & M University; Keith Pierce, University of Minnesota; Howard D. Pyron, University of Missouri; Dennis E. Ray, Old Dominion University; Winifred J. Rex, Bowling Green State University; Gordon E. Stokes, Brigham Young University; Nai-Kuan Tsao, Wayne State University; R. Kenneth Walter, Weber State College.

I would also like to acknowledge the contribution of Armando Picciotto, who wrote an excellent instructor's manual for high school teachers based on a previous edition of this book. Several examples and exercises from this manual appear in the book.

A group of experienced teachers provided their comments and suggestions for changes to a proposed table of contents for this book in a series of focus group meetings. The faculty who contributed in this way included: John Buck, Indiana University, Bloomington; Philip East, University of Northern Iowa; Donald Greenwell, Eastern Kentucky University; William J. Joel, Marist College; Larry Kotman, Grand Valley State College; Masoud Milani, Florida International University; Scott Owen, Georgia State University; Terry Seethoff, Northern Michigan University; and Dawn Wilkins, Illinois College.

We are also grateful to the hundreds of teachers who participated in telephone interviews or completed course surveys organized by Addison-Wesley's market research department. The information this research provided helped to shape the book's organization and pedagogy.

The personnel at Addison-Wesley responsible for the production of this book worked diligently to meet a very demanding schedule. My editor, Peter Shepard, was closely involved in all phases of this project, starting with the initial market research. He did an excellent job of coordinating the writing and reviewing process. He was also a very valuable sounding board in helping to resolve questions raised by the reviewers. Anne King, his assistant, was very effective in contacting reviewers and keeping the review process on schedule. Bette Aaronson and Loren Hilgenhurst Stevens supervised the design and production of the book, while Nancy Benjamin coordinated the conversion of the manuscript to a finished book. Finally, I would like to thank Linda Golowka, a student at the University of Michigan, Dearborn, who was responsible for testing and debugging the programs in the book.

Philadelphia, PA E.B.K.

Contents

5 Repetition and the while Statement 125

6 Procedure Parameters 165

7 Simple Data Types 219

8 Programming in the Large 281

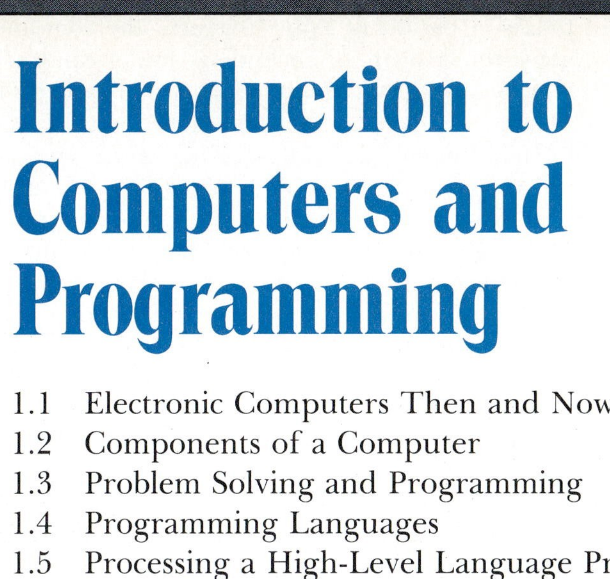

1 Introduction to Computers and Programming

From the 1940s until today—a period of only 50 years—the computer's development has spurred the growth of technology into realms only dreamed of at the turn of the century. It has also changed the way we live and how we do business. Today, we depend on computers to process our paychecks, send rockets into space, build cars and machines of all types, and help us do our shopping and banking. The computer program's role in this technology is essential; without a list of instructions to follow, the computer is virtually useless. Programming languages allow us to write those programs, and thus to communicate with computers.

You are about to begin the study of computer science using one of the most versatile programming languages available today: the Pascal language. This chapter introduces you to the computer and its components and to the major categories of programming languages.

1.1 Electronic Computers Then and Now

Computers were not always so pervasive in our society. Just a short time ago, computers were fairly mysterious devices that only a small percentage of the population knew much about. Computer know-how spread when advances in *solid-state electronics* led to cuts in the size and the cost of electronic computers. In the mid-1970s, a computer with the computational power of one of today's personal computers would have filled a nine-by-twelve-foot room and cost $100,000. Today, an equivalent personal computer (see Fig. 1.1) costs less than $3,000 and sits on a desktop.

Figure 1.1 IBM Personal Computer with Printer and Mouse

If we take the literal definition for *computer* as "a device for counting or computing," then we could consider the abacus to be the first computer. The first electronic digital computer was designed in the late 1930s by Dr. John Atanasoff at Iowa State University. Atanasoff designed his computer to perform mathematical computations for graduate students.

The first large-scale, general-purpose electronic digital computer, called the ENIAC, was built in 1946 at the University of Pennsylvania. Its design was funded by the U.S. Army, and it was used to compute ballistics tables, predict the weather, and make atomic energy calculations. The ENIAC weighed 30 tons and occupied a thirty-by-fifty-foot space (see Fig. 1.2).

Although we are often led to believe otherwise, computers cannot reason as we do. Basically, computers are devices that perform computations at incredible speeds (more than one million operations per second) and with great accuracy. However, to accomplish anything useful, a computer must be *programmed*, that is, given a sequence of explicit instructions (a *program*) to perform.

To program the ENIAC, engineers had to connect hundreds of wires and arrange thousands of switches in a certain way. In 1946, Dr. John von Neumann, of Princeton University, proposed the concept of a *stored-program computer*: a program stored in computer memory rather than set by wires and switches. Von Neumann knew programmers could easily change the contents of computer memory, so he reasoned that the stored-program concept would greatly simplify

Figure 1.2 The ENIAC Computer (Photo courtesy of Unisys Corporation)

programming a computer. Von Neumann's design was a success and is the basis of the digital computer as we know it today.

Brief History of Computing

Table 1.1 lists some of the important milestones along the path from the abacus to modern-day computers. We often use the term *first generation* to refer to

Table 1.1 Milestones in Computer Development

Date	Event
2000 BC	The abacus is first used for computations.
1642 AD	Blaise Pascal creates a mechanical adding machine for tax computations. It is unreliable.
1670	Gottfried von Leibniz creates a more reliable adding machine, which adds, subtracts, multiplies, divides, and calculates square roots.
1842	Charles Babbage designs an analytical engine to perform general calculations automatically. Ada Augusta (a.k.a. Lady Lovelace) is a programmer for this machine.
1890	Herman Hollerith designs a system to record census data. The information is stored as holes on cards which are interpreted by machines with electrical sensors. Hollerith starts a company that will eventually become IBM.
1939	John Atanasoff, with graduate student Clifford Berry, designs and builds the first electronic digital computer. His project was funded by a grant for $650.
1946	J. Presper Eckert and John Mauchly design and build the ENIAC computer. It used 18,000 vacuum tubes and cost $500,000 to build.
1946	John von Neumann proposes that a program be stored in a computer in the same way that data are stored. His proposal (called "von Neumann architecture") is the basis of modern computers.
1951	Eckert and Mauchly build the first general-purpose commercial computer, the UNIVAC.
1957	John Backus and his team at IBM complete the first FORTRAN compiler.
1958	The first computer to use the transistor as a switching device, the IBM 7090, is introduced.
1958	Seymour Cray builds the first fully transistorized computer, the CDC 1604, for Control Data Corporation.
1964	The first computer using integrated circuits, the IBM 360, is announced.
1975	The first microcomputer, the Altair, is introduced.
1975	The first supercomputer, the Cray-1, is announced.
1976	Digital Equipment Corporation introduces its popular minicomputer, the VAX 11/780.
1977	Steve Wozniak and Steve Jobs found Apple Computer.
1978	Dan Bricklin and Bob Frankston develop the first electronic spreadsheet, called VisiCalc, for the Apple computer.
1981	IBM introduces the IBM PC.
1981	Apollo Computer ships the first Domain workstation.
1982	Sun Microsystem introduces its first workstation, the Sun 100.

electronic computers that used vacuum tubes (1939–1958). The *second generation* began in 1958 with the changeover to transistors. The *third generation* began in 1964 with the introduction of integrated circuits. The *fourth generation* began in 1975 with the advent of large-scale integration.

Categories of Computers

Modern-day computers are classified according to their size and speed. The three major categories of computers are microcomputers, minicomputers, and mainframes.

Many of you have seen or used *microcomputers* such as the IBM PC (see Fig. 1.1). Microcomputers are also called personal computers or desktop computers because they are used by one person at a time and are small enough to fit on a desk. The largest microcomputers, called *workstations* (see Fig. 1.3), are commonly used by engineers to produce engineering drawings and to assist in the design and development of new products.

Minicomputers are the next larger variety of computers. They generally operate at faster speeds than microcomputers and can store larger quantities of information. Minicomputers can serve several different users simultaneously. A small- or medium-size company might use a minicomputer to perform payroll computations and to keep track of its inventory. Engineers often use minicomputers to control a chemical plant or a production process.

Figure 1.3 SUN Microsystems SPARCstation 370 (Photo Courtesy of Sun Microsystems, Inc.)

The largest computers are called *mainframes*. A large company would have one or more mainframes at its central computing facility for performing business-related computations. Mainframes are also used as "number crunchers" to generate solutions to systems of equations that characterize an engineering or scientific problem. A mainframe can solve in seconds equations that might take hours to solve on a minicomputer or even days on a microcomputer. The largest mainframes are called *supercomputers* and are used to solve the most complex systems of equations.

In the late 1950s, mainframe computers could perform only fifty instructions per second. Now it is not uncommon to have much smaller workstations that can perform over twenty million instructions per second. Obviously, there have been tremendous changes in the speed and size of computers in a relatively short time.

1.2 Components of a Computer

Despite large variations in cost, size, and capabilities, modern computers are remarkably similar to each other in a number of ways. Basically, a computer consists of the components shown in Fig. 1.4. The arrows connecting the components show the direction of information flow. These computer components are called the *hardware*.

All information that is to be processed by a computer must first be entered into the computer's *main memory* via an *input device*. The information in main memory is manipulated by the *central processor*, and the results of this manipulation are stored in main memory. Information in main memory can be displayed through an *output device*. *Secondary memory* is often used for storing large quantities of information in a semipermanent form.

Computer Memory

A computer's main memory stores information of all types: instructions, numbers, names, lists, even pictures. Picture a computer's memory as an ordered sequence of storage locations called *memory cells*. To be able to store and then *retrieve*, or access, information, we must have some way to identify the individual memory cells. Each memory cell has a unique *address* associated with it. The address indicates the cell's relative position in memory. The sample computer memory in Fig. 1.5 consists of 1,000 memory cells, with addresses 0 through 999. (Most computers have memories that consist of millions of individual cells.)

The information stored in a memory cell is called its *contents*. Every memory cell always contains some information, although we may have no idea what that information is. Whenever new information is placed in a memory cell, any information already there is destroyed and cannot be retrieved. In Fig. 1.5, the contents of memory cell 3 is the number −26, and the contents of memory cell 4 is the letter H.

The memory cells shown in Fig. 1.5 are actually aggregates, or collections, of smaller units called *bytes*. A byte is the amount of storage required to store a

Figure 1.4 Components of a Computer

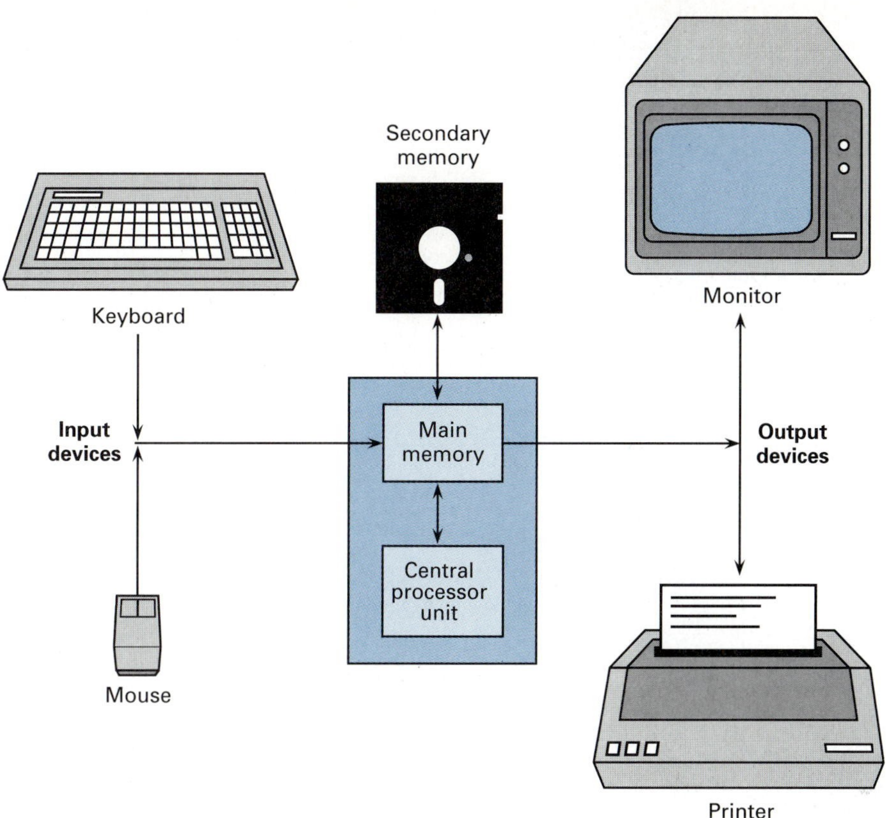

single character. The number of bytes in a memory cell varies from computer to computer. A byte is an aggregate of even smaller units of storage called *bits*, which are single binary digits (0 or 1). There are generally eight bits to a byte.

To store a value, the computer sets each bit of a selected memory cell to 0 or 1, thereby destroying what was previously in that bit. Each value is represented by a particular pattern of zeroes and ones. To retrieve a value from a memory cell, the computer copies the pattern of zeroes and ones stored in that cell to another storage area, the *memory buffer register*, where the bit pattern can be processed. The copy operation does not destroy the bit pattern currently in the memory cell.

The process just described is the same regardless of the kind of information—character, number, or program instruction—stored in a memory cell.

Central Processor Unit

The *central processor unit* (CPU) performs the actual processing and manipulation of information stored in memory. The CPU also retrieves information from memory. This information can be data or instructions for manipulating data.

Figure 1.5 A Computer Memory with 1,000 Cells

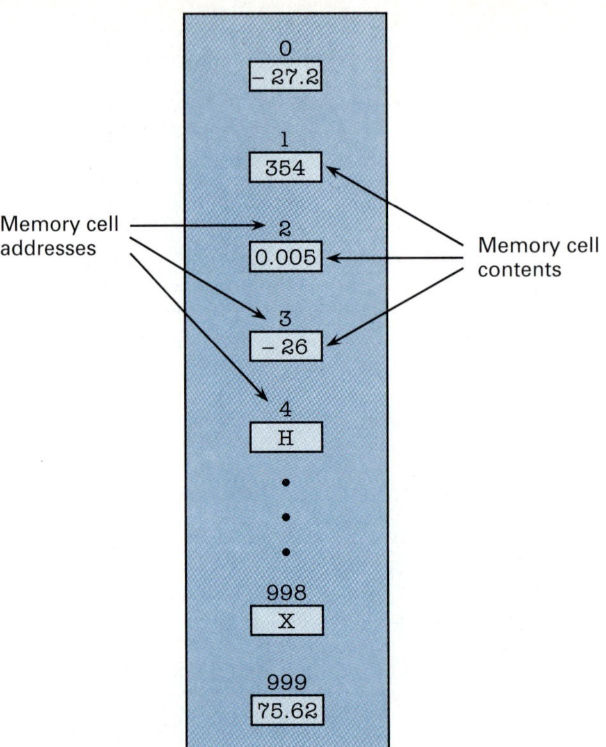

The CPU can also store the results of those manipulations back in memory for later use.

The *control unit* within the CPU coordinates all activities of the computer by determining which operations should be carried out and in what order. The control unit then transmits coordinating control signals to the computer components.

Also found within the CPU are the *arithmetic-logic unit* (ALU) and special storage locations called *registers*. The ALU consists of electronic circuitry to perform arithmetic operations (that is, addition, subtraction, multiplication, and division) and to make comparisons. The control unit copies the next program instruction from memory into the instruction register in the CPU. The ALU then performs the operation specified by the next instruction on data that are copied from memory into registers, and the computational results are copied to memory. The ALU can perform each arithmetic operation in about a millionth of a second. The ALU can also compare data stored in its registers (for example, Which value is larger? Are the values equal?); the operations that are performed next depend on the comparison results.

Input and Output Devices

Input and output (I/O) devices enable us to communicate with the computer. Specifically, I/O devices provide us with the means to enter data for a computation and to observe the results of that computation.

A common I/O device used with large computers is the computer terminal. A *computer terminal* is both an input and an output device. A terminal consists of a *keyboard* (used for entering information) and a *monitor* (used for displaying information). A computer terminal has no capability to do any local processing, so it is often called a *dumb terminal.*

Sometimes microcomputers and workstations are connected to larger computers and can be used as terminals. Because a microcomputer can also do local processing, a microcomputer connected to another computer is called a *smart terminal.*

A computer keyboard is similar to a typewriter keyboard except that it has some extra keys for performing special functions. On the IBM PC/AT–style keyboard shown in Fig. 1.6, the two columns of keys on the left (labeled F1 through F12) are *function keys.* The functions performed by pressing one of these keys depends on the program that is executing.

Most personal computers are equipped with *graphics capability* (see Fig. 1.3), which enables the output to be displayed as a two-dimensional graph or picture. With some graphics devices, the user can communicate with the computer by using a mouse to move an electronic pointer.

The only problem with using a monitor as an output device is that it leaves no written record of the computation. Once the image disappears from the monitor screen, it is lost. If you want *hard-copy output,* you have to send your computational results to an output device called a *printer* (see Fig. 1.1) or use a hard-copy terminal.

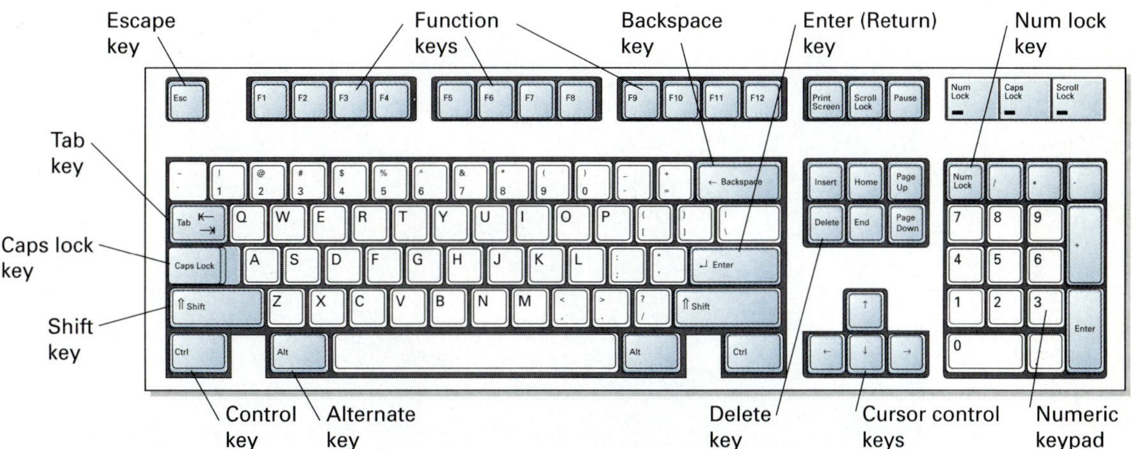

Figure 1.6 Keyboard for the IBM PC/AT

Secondary Storage

Most computers have only a limited amount of main memory. Consequently, *secondary storage* provides additional data storage capability on most computer systems. For example, a *disk drive*, which stores data on a disk, is a common secondary storage device for today's personal computers (Fig. 1.7).

There are two kinds of disks: *hard disks* and *floppy disks*, and a computer may have one or more drives of each kind. A hard disk normally cannot be removed from its drive, so the storage area on a hard disk is often shared by all the users of a computer. However, each computer user may have his or her own floppy disks that can be inserted into a disk drive as needed. Hard disks can store much more data than can floppy disks and operate much more quickly, but they are also much more expensive.

Information stored on a disk is organized into aggregates called *files*. The data for a program can be stored in a *data file* beforehand rather than being entered at the keyboard while the program is executing. Results generated by the computer can be saved as *output files* on disk. Most of the programs that you write will be saved as *program files* on disk.

Main Memory versus Secondary Memory

Main memory is much faster and more expensive than secondary memory. You must transfer data from secondary memory to main memory before it can be processed. Data in main memory is *volatile* and disappears when you switch off

Figure 1.7 Inserting a Floppy Disk into a Disk Drive

the computer. Data stored in secondary memory is *permanent* and does not disappear when the computer is switched off.

Computer Networks

Often several microcomputers in a laboratory are interconnected as a network of microcomputers (called a *local area network*) so that they can share the use of a large hard disk and high-quality printers. The microcomputers in the network can also access common programs and data stored on the disk.

Exercises for Section 1.2

Self-Check

1. What are the contents of memory cells 0 and 999 in Fig. 1.5? What memory cells contain the letter X and the fraction 0.005?
2. Explain the purpose of the arithmetic-logic unit, memory, the central processor, and the disk drive and disk. What input and output devices do you use with your computer?

1.3 Problem Solving and Programming

We mentioned earlier that a computer cannot think; therefore, to get it to do any useful work, a computer must be provided with a *program*, that is, a list of instructions. Programming a computer is a lot more involved than simply writing a list of instructions. Problem solving is a crucial component of programming. Before we can write a program to solve a particular problem, we must consider carefully all aspects of the problem and then develop and organize its solution.

Like most programming students, at first you will probably spend a great deal of time in the computer laboratory entering your programs. You will spend more time later removing the errors that inevitably will crop up in your programs.

It is tempting to rush to the computer laboratory and start entering your program as soon as you have some idea of how to write it. Resist this temptation. Instead, think carefully about the problem and its solution before you write any program instructions. When you have a potential solution in mind, plan it out beforehand (either using paper and pencil or a word processor) and modify it if necessary before you write the program.

Once you have written the program out, *desk check* your solution by carefully performing each instruction much as the computer would. To desk check a program, simulate the result of each program instruction using sample data that are easy to manipulate (for example, small whole numbers). Compare these results with the expected results and make any necessary corrections to your program. Only then should you go to the computer laboratory and enter your program. A few extra minutes spent evaluating the proposed solution using the process summarized in Fig. 1.8 often saves hours of frustration later.

Figure 1.8 Programming Strategy

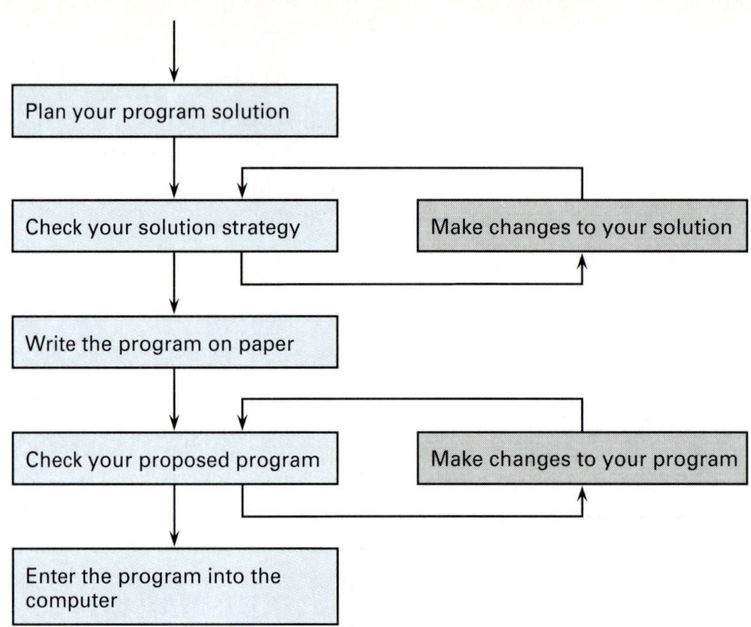

In this text, we stress a methodology for problem solving that has proved useful in helping students learn to program. This technique, called *structured programming*, should enable you to write programs that are relatively easy to read and understand and that contain fewer initial errors.

1.4 Programming Languages

Languages used for writing computer programs, called *programming languages*, fall into three broad categories: machine, assembly, and high-level languages.

High-level languages are more popular with programmers than the other two language categories. One reason for their popularity is that they are much easier to use than machine and assembly languages. Another reason is that a high-level language program is *portable*, which means that it can be used without modification on many different types of computers. An assembly language or a machine-language program, on the other hand, can be used on only one type of computer.

Some common high-level languages are FORTRAN, BASIC, COBOL, C, and Pascal. Each language was designed with a specific purpose in mind. FORTRAN is an acronym for FORmula TRANslation, and its principal users are engineers and scientists. BASIC (Beginners All-purpose Symbolic Instructional Code) was designed to be easily learned and used by students. COBOL (COmmon Business Oriented Language) is used primarily for business data-processing operations. C combines the power of an assembly language with the ease of use and portability of a high-level language. Pascal was designed for teaching structured programming.

Each of these high-level languages has a *language standard* that describes the grammatical form (*syntax*) of the language. Every high-level language instruction must conform to the syntax rules specified in the language standard. These rules are very precise—no allowances are made for instructions that are *almost* correct.

An important feature of high-level languages is that they allow us to write program instructions that resemble English. We can reference data stored in memory using easily understood descriptive names, like Name and Rate, rather than the numeric memory cell addresses discussed in Section 1.2. We can also use familiar symbols to describe operations that we want performed. For example, in several high-level languages the instruction

```
Z := X + Y
```

means add X to Y and store the result in Z. X, Y, and Z are called *variables*.

In *assembly language*, we can also use descriptive names to reference data; however, we must specify the operations to be performed on the data more explicitly. The high-level language instruction above might be written as

```
LOAD X
ADD Y
STORE Z
```

in an assembly language.

Machine language is the native tongue of a computer. Each instruction in machine language is a *binary string* (a string of zeroes and ones). Some of you may be familiar with the use of binary numbers to represent decimal integers (for example, binary 11011 corresponds to decimal 27). In an analogous way, a binary string can be used to indicate an operation to be performed and the memory cell or cells that are involved. The assembly language instructions above could be written in a machine language as

```
0010 0000 0000 0100
0100 0000 0000 0101
0011 0000 0000 0110
```

Obviously, what is easiest for a computer to understand is most difficult for a person to understand and vice versa.

A computer can understand only programs that are written in machine language. Consequently, each instruction in an assembler program or a high-level language program must first be translated into machine language. The next section discusses the steps required to process a high-level language program.

Exercises for Section 1.4

Self-Check

1. What do you think these high-level language statements mean?

```
X := A + B + C      X := Y/Z      D := C - B + A
```

2. Which high-level language was designed for teaching programming? Which was designed for business applications? Which was designed for translating scientific formulas?
3. Which type of language has instructions such as `ADD X`? Which type has instructions that are binary numbers?

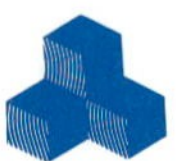

1.5 Processing a High-Level Language Program

Before the computer can process a high-level language program, the programmer must enter it into memory using an editor program (or editor). An *editor* stores lines of characters typed at the keyboard in memory and allows the user to modify (or edit) those lines. The program should also be stored on disk as a file called the program file or *source file* (see Fig. 1.9).

Once the source file is saved, it can be translated into machine language. A *compiler* program processes the source file and attempts to translate each statement.

One or more statements in the source file may contain a *syntax error*, which means that the statement does not correspond exactly to the syntax of the high-level language. In that case, the compiler causes an error message to be displayed on your monitor screen. Syntax errors are discussed in more detail in Section 2.8.

At this point, you can make changes to your source file and have the compiler process it again. If there are no more errors, the compiler creates an *object program*, which is your program translated into machine language.

In some cases, it may be necessary to load other object files into memory and link them with the object program. The linker/loader accomplishes this process. The editor, compiler, and linker/loader programs are part of your computer system. This process is shown in Fig. 1.9.

Executing a Program

To execute a program, the CPU must examine each program instruction in memory and send out the command signals required to carry out the instruction. Normally, the instructions are executed in sequence; however, as we will discuss later, it is possible to have the CPU skip over some instructions or execute some instructions more than once.

During execution, data can be entered into memory and manipulated in some specified way. There are program instructions that are used for entering or reading a program's data (called *input data*) into memory. After the input data is processed, instructions for displaying or printing values in memory can be executed to display the program results. The lines displayed by a program are called the *program output*.

Let's use the situation illustrated in Fig. 1.10—executing a payroll program stored in memory—as an example. The first step of the program enters data into memory that describe the employee's hours and pay rate. In step 2, the

Figure 1.9 Preparing a Program for Execution

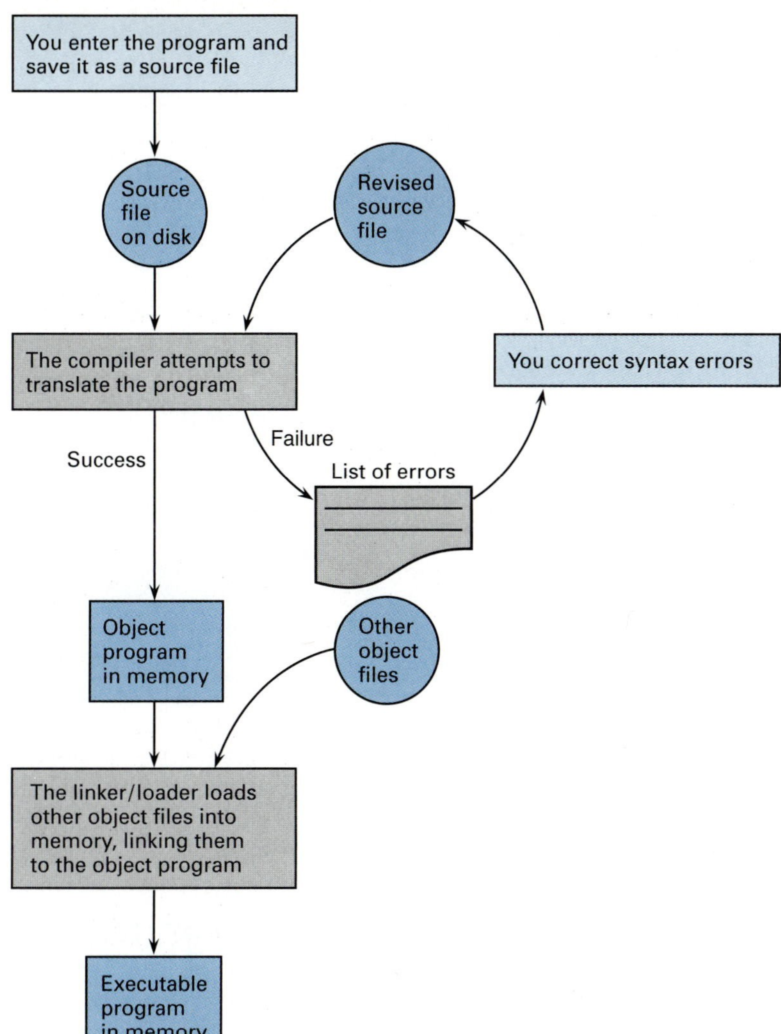

program manipulates the employee data and stores the results of the computations in memory. In the final step, the computational results are displayed as payroll reports or employee payroll checks. The next chapter takes a closer look at a program that does this.

Exercises for Section 1.5

Self-Check

1. What is the role of a compiler? What is a syntax error? In which file would a syntax error be found?

Figure 1.10 Flow of Information During Program Execution

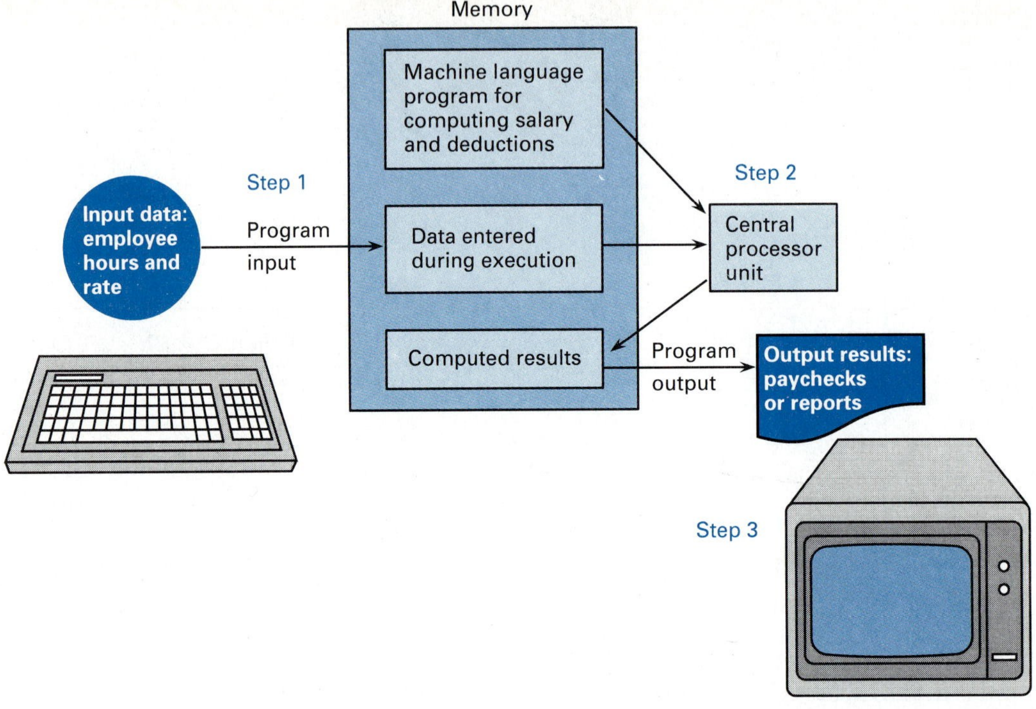

2. What is the source file? An object program? Which do you create and which does the compiler create?

1.6 Using the Turbo Pascal Integrated Environment

The mechanics of entering a program as a source file, translating it to machine language, and executing the machine language program differ on each computer system. In this text we will focus our discussion on using Turbo Pascal and a personal computer. To be able to use a computer, you will need to interact with a supervisory program, called the *operating system*. A common operating system for the IBM personal computer (PC) is MS-DOS® (Microsoft® Disk Operating System). The operating system provides several essential services to the computer user:

1. Loading and running application programs.
2. Allocating memory and processor time.
3. Providing input and output facilities.
4. Managing files of information.

Loading the Operating System

When you turn on, or *boot up*, a personal computer, the operating system is loaded into memory and begins execution. If your computer has its own hard disk, the operating system will be on drive C (the hard disk) and will issue the prompt

```
C>
```

to inform you that it is ready. You should enter the commands

```
C>CD \TP
C>Turbo
```

to enter the Turbo Pascal integrated environment. The first command (CD, for Change Directory) makes the subdirectory \TP, which contains Turbo Pascal, the active disk directory. The second command takes you into the Turbo Pascal integrated environment.

If your computer does not have a hard disk, you will have to insert your operating system disk into drive A and then turn on the power. Once booted, the operating system will display the prompt

```
A>
```

You should insert your disk containing Turbo Pascal into drive B and then use the commands

```
A>B:
B>Turbo
```

to make drive B the active drive and to enter the Turbo Pascal integrated environment.

Turbo Pascal Main Menu

Once in the Turbo Pascal integrated environment, you can create new programs, modify old ones, and compile and run these programs. You interact with the environment through the use of special display screens called *menus*.

The Turbo Pascal Main menu screen is shown in Fig. 1.11. This screen display is organized into three sections. The information displayed in the lines at the top and the bottom of the screen represent tasks that the computer can carry out. The middle area (shown in gray) is the *desktop* area, where you will open the various windows used to create and test your Pascal programs.

The tasks at the top of the screen are part of Turbo Pascal's *Main menu bar*. You can select any one of these Main menu tasks by pressing and holding the Alt key and then pressing the first letter of the task name (for example, Alt-F for File). You can also select a task by first pressing the F10 key on the keyboard, then typing the first letter of the task name (for example, F for File, E for Edit), and then pressing the Enter key. You can also select a task by moving the highlight bar over that task (using the left or right arrow key) and then pressing the Enter key. If your computer has a mouse, you can select a Main menu item by positioning the mouse cursor on the Main menu item and

Figure 1.11 Turbo Pascal 6.0 Main Menu

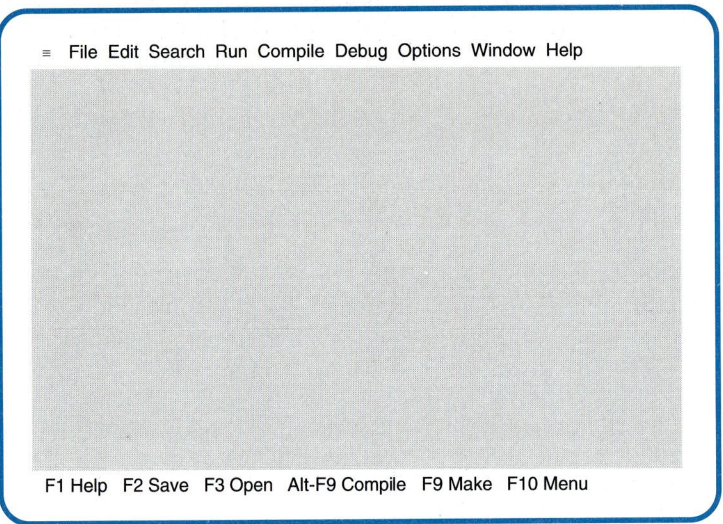

then clicking (pressing) the left mouse button. If you are using a mouse, you do not need to press the F10 key before selecting a Main menu item.

The list of tasks displayed at the bottom of the screen will change as you move from one portion of the Turbo Pascal environment to another. You select a task by pressing the indicated function key (F1 through F10) on the keyboard. For example, in the Main menu screen (or any screen), to display the Help screen relevant to your current situation within the Turbo Pascal environment, press function key F1. The Help screen provides a description of your current menu screen and its options. You press Esc (Escape) to exit the Help screen and return to your current screen.

This book describes Turbo Pascal version 6.0. Earlier versions of Turbo Pascal may perform differently. Your instructor will tell you which version of Turbo Pascal is available to you at your school.

Creating a New Program

To create a new Pascal program, you must begin with an empty Edit window on the desktop. Turbo Pascal 6.0 automatically places you in an Edit window called NONAME00.PAS when you enter the environment. However, if you wish to open a new window yourself, select the New option from the File menu as shown in Fig. 1.12. You can do this by typing the letter N, moving the highlight bar over the letter N (using the up and down arrow keys), or by using a mouse.

Once Turbo Pascal places you in the Edit window, you can begin entering your program one line at a time. You press the Enter key after typing each program line. Use the arrow keys on the keyboard to position the cursor (the

Figure 1.12 Turbo Pascal File Menu

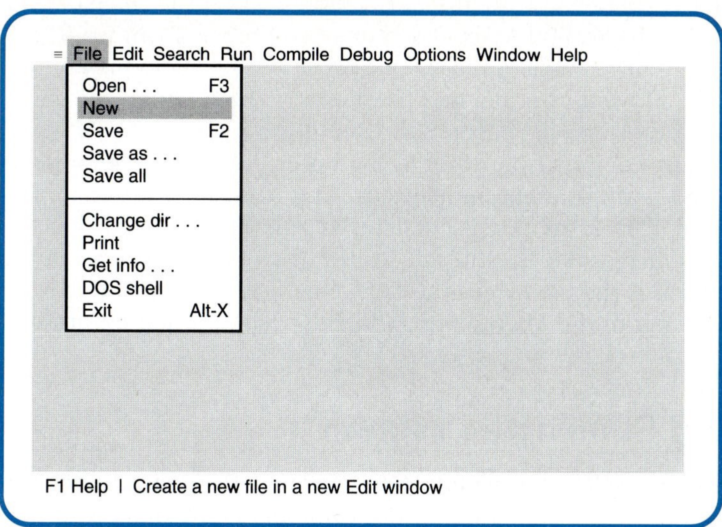

blinking line on the computer's screen) anywhere on the screen. You can correct typing errors by pressing the backspace key to erase all characters from the current cursor position back to the incorrect character. Then you can enter the correct letters in their place. Fig. 1.13 shows a complete (but incorrect) program in the Edit window NONAME00.PAS.

Figure 1.13 Incorrect Program Hello

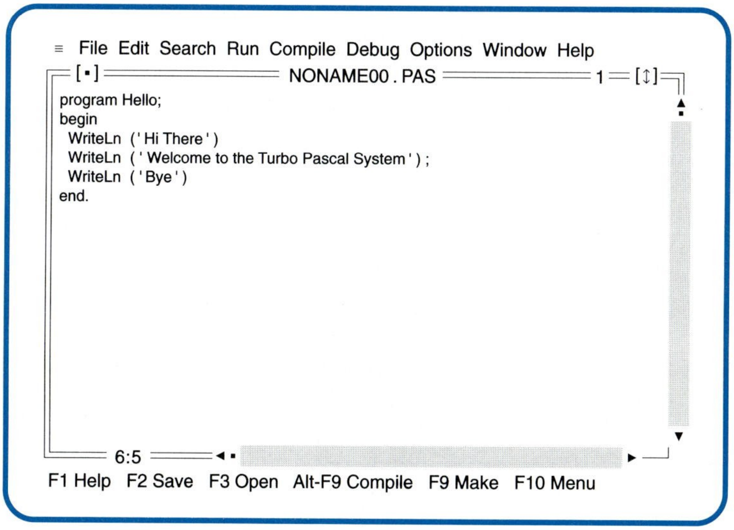

```
≡ File Edit Search Run Compile Debug Options Window Help
[•] ============ NONAME00.PAS ============ 1 =[↕]
program Hello;
begin
  WriteLn ('Hi There')
  WriteLn ('Welcome to the Turbo Pascal System');
  WriteLn ('Bye')
end.

==== 6:5 ====
F1 Help  F2 Save  F3 Open  Alt-F9 Compile  F9 Make  F10 Menu
```

After your program is complete, place a formatted disk (see Appendix A for formatting instructions) in disk drive A and save your program on the disk by pressing the F2 key (Save). Up until this point, your program has been assigned the name NONAME00.PAS by Turbo Pascal. Before saving your program with this name, Turbo Pascal gives you a chance to use a more meaningful name. For example, if you want to use the name FIRST, enter the name A:FIRST.PAS when prompted by Turbo Pascal as shown in Fig. 1.14. MS-DOS file names may be any combination of eight, or fewer, letters, digits, or some special characters (no periods or spaces allowed). The A: is the computer's disk drive designator and .PAS is an extension signifying to Turbo Pascal that this file contains Pascal source code. If you fail to include a file extension, Turbo Pascal automatically adds the file extension .PAS. Now you are ready to exit the Edit window and return to the Main menu, which is accomplished by pressing the F10 key.

Compiling and Running a Program

To compile a program, select the Compile menu from the Main menu bar. Figure 1.15 shows the choices contained in the Compile menu. Since you wish to compile your program, select the Compile option and Turbo Pascal will begin to compile the program displayed in the Edit window.

When we attempt to compile the program shown in Fig. 1.13, Turbo Pascal will display the syntax error message

```
Error 85: ";" expected
```

Figure 1.14 Saving Program as FIRST.PAS

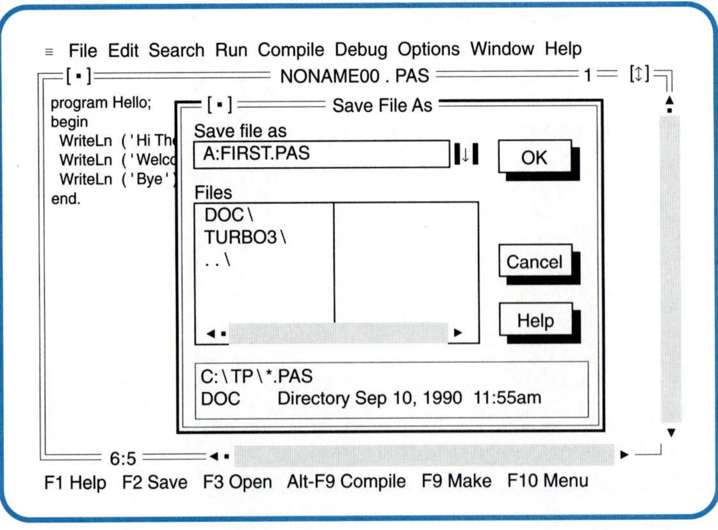

Figure 1.15 Turbo Pascal Compile Menu

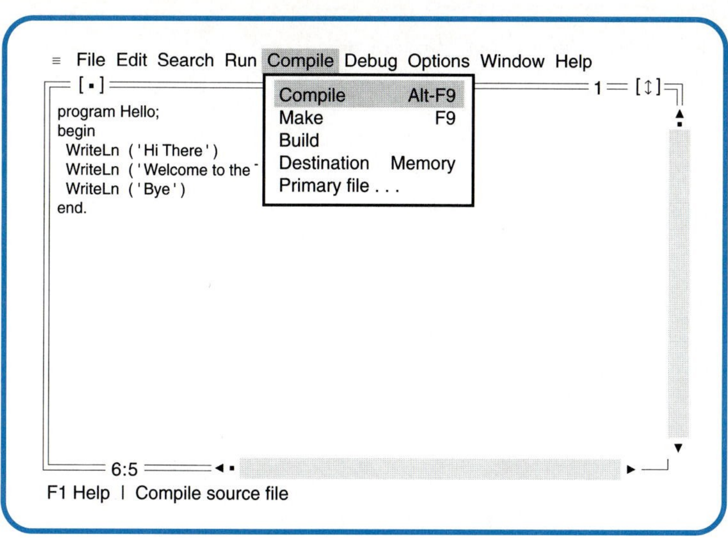

and return us to the Edit window. The cursor is positioned at the point in the program where the compilation process stopped (at `WriteLn` in the fourth line). Error 85 explains that you have forgotten to add a semicolon to the end of the third line of program text. After changing the line to

```
WriteLn ('Hi There');
```

save the revised program to disk by pressing the F2 key. You then exit the Edit window and return to the Main menu by pressing the F10 key. From the Main menu, select the Compile menu again and then select the Compile option. This time there are no errors in the program, and a *compilation status window* containing the message "Compile successful: Press any Key" will be displayed (see Fig. 1.16). You then press a key on the keyboard.

To run the program from the Main menu, after it has been compiled, select the Run menu. Figure 1.17 shows the choices contained in the Run menu. Since you want to run the program, select the Run option. Turbo Pascal begins executing the program. The main menu screen display will be replaced briefly by a *user screen* containing the program output

```
Hi There
Welcome to the Turbo Pascal System
Bye
```

and then the Main menu display will return. To review your program output, type Alt-F5 (that is, press and hold down the Alt key while pressing the F5 key). The user screen containing the program output will reappear and remain visible until you press any key on the keyboard, which returns you to the Main menu screen.

Figure 1.16 Successful Compilation

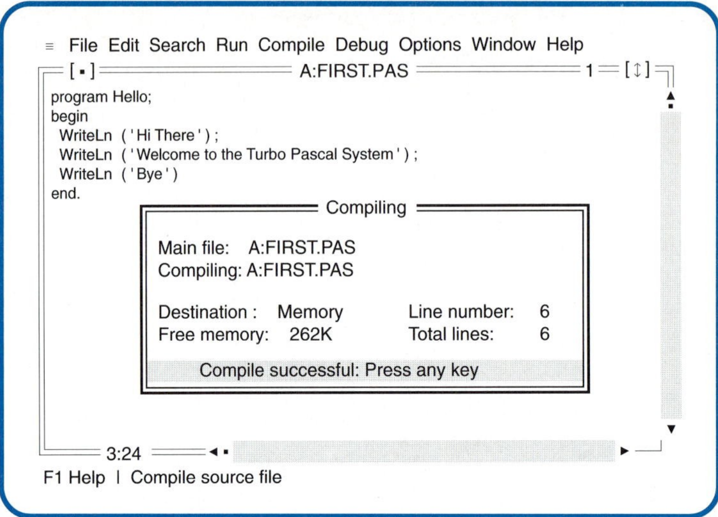

Loading a File

To load a previously saved file into an Edit window, you must get Turbo Pascal to display an "Open a File" dialog box (see Fig. 1.18). You can do this either through the File menu (select option Open) or by pressing function key F3. When the dialog box appears, either type the name of the file into the bar with label Name, or select the file name from the list shown under label Files. If you do not have a mouse, press the Tab key to access the list of files; next, use the up and down arrow keys to select the desired file.

Figure 1.17 Turbo Pascal Run Menu

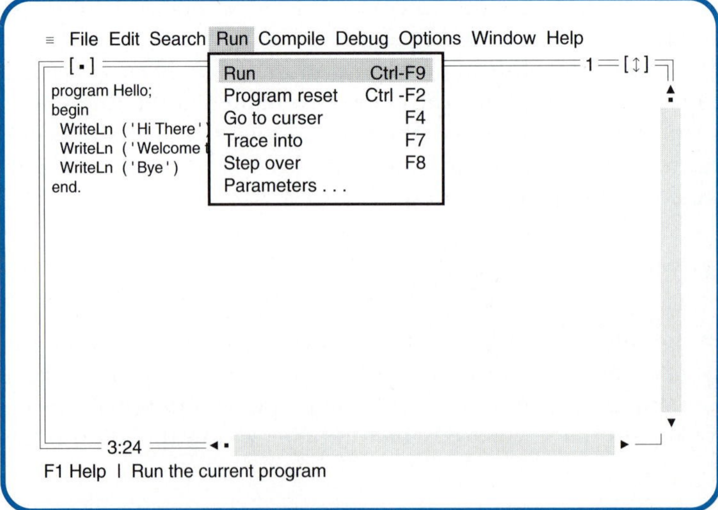

Figure 1.18 Loading Program FIRST.PAS from Disk A

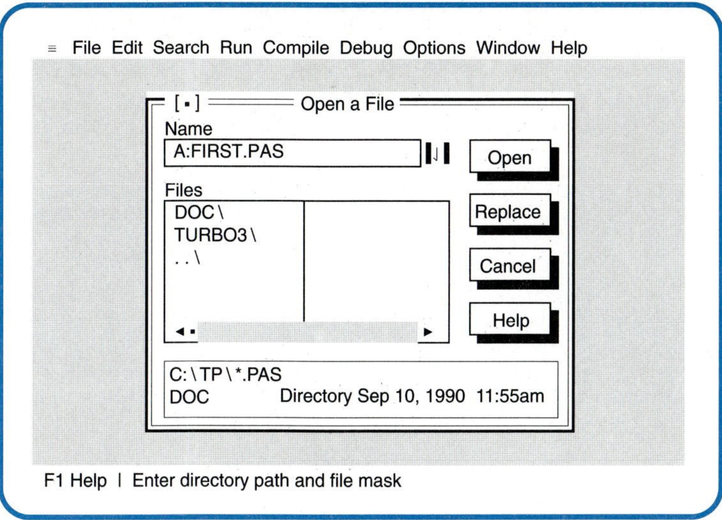

Exiting Turbo Pascal

The File menu Exit option provides you with a means of leaving Turbo Pascal and returning to the operating system. If you choose the Exit option and have made changes to your program in the Edit window, but have forgotten to save your revised program, Turbo Pascal will give you one last chance to do so by displaying a dialog box similar to that shown in Fig. 1.19.

Figure 1.19 Turbo Pascal Information Dialog Box

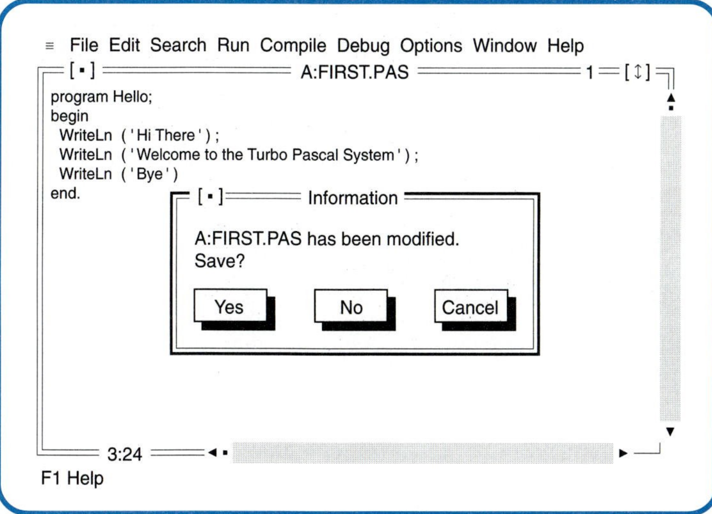

Figure 1.20 Turbo Pascal System Menu

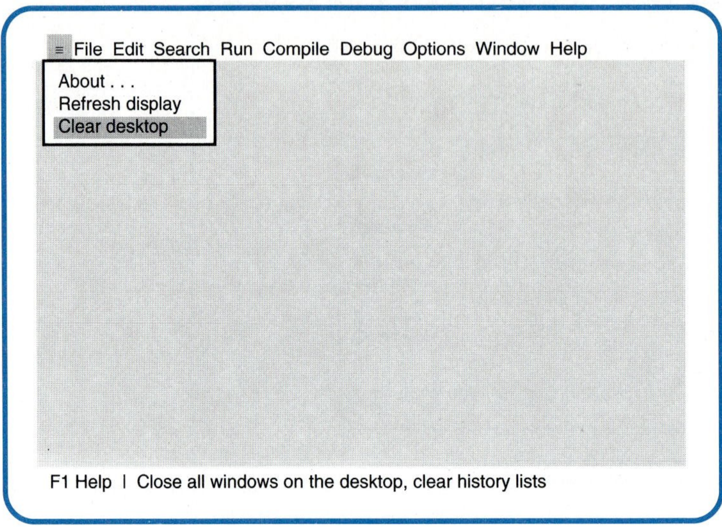

If you press the letter Y on the keyboard, your program will be saved before you exit from Turbo Pascal. To leave the File menu and return to the Main menu, press the Esc (Escape) key or F10.

It is generally a good idea to clear your Turbo Pascal desktop before quitting. You do so from the Turbo Pascal System menu (Fig. 1.20), which is the leftmost Main menu item. Then select the Clear desktop option to close all open windows and to clear all Turbo Pascal history lists.

We recommend that you examine Appendix A to learn more about using the Turbo Pascal environment. Be aware that you can get additional information regarding a Turbo Pascal task by pressing the F1 key (Help) when the highlight bar is over that task.

Turbo Pascal is distributed with a tutorial program, which can be run from the MS-DOS prompt (type TPTour). TPTour is an interactive tutorial on using the Turbo Pascal integrated environment.

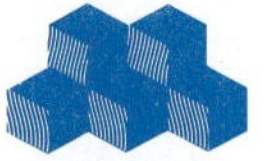

Chapter Review

This chapter described the basic components of a computer: main and secondary memory, the CPU, and input and output devices. Remember these important facts about computers:

1. A memory cell is never empty, but its initial contents may be meaningless to your program.

2. The current contents of a memory cell are destroyed whenever new information is placed in that cell.
3. Programs must be copied into the memory of the computer before they can be executed.
4. Data cannot be manipulated by the computer until they are first read into memory.
5. A computer cannot think for itself; you must use a programming language to instruct it in a precise and unambiguous manner to perform a task.
6. Programming a computer can be fun—if you are patient, organized, and careful.

✓ Quick-Check Exercises

1. The ____________ translates a ____________ language program into __________.
2. After a program is executed, all program results are automatically displayed. True or false?
3. Specify the correct order for these three operations: execution, translation, linking/loading.
4. A high-level language program is saved on disk as a ____________ file or a ____________ file.
5. The ____________ finds syntax errors in the ____________ file.
6. A machine language program is saved on disk as an ____________ file.
7. The ____________ is used to create and save the source file.
8. Computers are becoming (more/less) expensive and (bigger/smaller) in size.
9. The first large-scale, general-purpose electronic computer was the ______________. It (was/was not) a stored-program computer.

Answers to Quick-Check Exercises

1. compiler, high-level, machine language
2. false
3. translation, linking/loading, execution
4. source, program
5. compiler, source
6. object
7. editor
8. less, smaller
9. ENIAC, was not

Review Questions

1. List at least three kinds of information stored in a computer.
2. List two functions of the CPU.
3. List two input/output devices and two secondary storage devices.
4. A computer can think. True or false?
5. List the three categories of programming languages.
6. Give three advantages of programming in a high-level language such as Pascal.
7. What processes are needed to transform a Pascal program to a machine-language program that is ready for execution?
8. What are three characteristics of a structured program?

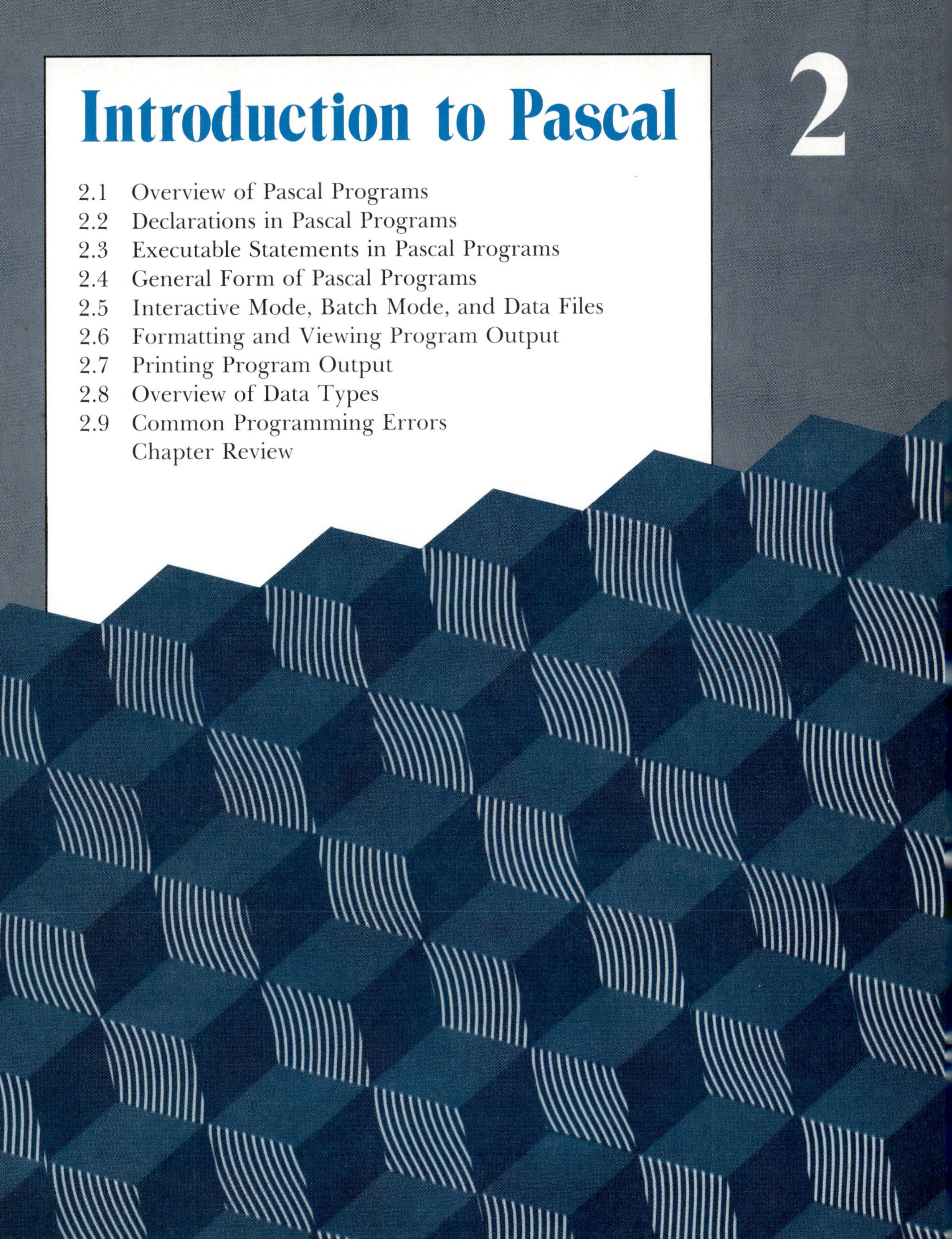

Introduction to Pascal

2

This chapter introduces the programming language Pascal, which is a high-level, general-purpose language developed in 1971 by Professor Nicklaus Wirth of Zurich, Switzerland. (A general-purpose language is one that can be put to many different applications.) Pascal is the most popular programming language for teaching programming concepts because its syntax is relatively easy to learn. Pascal also facilitates writing structured programs—programs that are relatively easy to read, understand, and keep in good working order—which is now accepted as standard programming practice. For those reasons and the fact that Pascal compilers are relatively easy to write, Pascal is also widely used in industry.

A *language standard*, which describes all Pascal language constructs and specifies their syntax, ensures that a Pascal program written on one computer will execute on another computer. This text uses Turbo Pascal, which is a dialect of Pascal that has been designed for use on personal computers. We will point out differences between Turbo Pascal and standard Pascal whenever we introduce a new language feature. Appendix G summarizes these differences.

This chapter describes Pascal statements for performing computations and statements for entering data and displaying results. Besides introducing Pascal, the chapter describes how to run Pascal programs interactively and in batch mode. In *interactive programming*, the program user enters data during program execution; in *batch mode*, the program user must prepare a data file before program execution begins. The use of data files is discussed in Section 2.5.

2.1 Overview of Pascal Programs

Before beginning our formal study of Pascal, we will examine two short programs. Don't worry about understanding the details of these programs yet; for now, concentrate on the look and the language of each program. Later we'll study them more closely.

■ Example 2.1

Figure 2.1 contains a Pascal program and a sample execution of that program (the last four lines of the figure). The program appears in the Edit window; the sample execution appears in the Output window. For easy identification, the input data typed in by the program user is in color in the Output window.

Figure 2.1 Printing a Welcoming Message

Edit Window

```
program Hello;

  var
    Name : string;

begin
  WriteLn ('Enter your name and press return>');
  ReadLn (Name);
  WriteLn ('Hello ', Name, '.');
```

```
  WriteLn ('We hope you enjoy studying Pascal!')
end.
```

Output Window

```
Enter your name and press return>
Bob
Hello Bob.
We hope you enjoy studying Pascal!
```

The program line var and the line immediately below it identify the name of a memory cell (Name) that will be used to store a person's name. The part of the program that is translated into machine language for execution follows the line begin.

Each program line that starts with the word WriteLn causes a line of program output to be displayed. The first such line

```
WriteLn ('Enter your name and press return>');
```

displays the first output line in the sample execution, which asks the user to enter his or her name.

The program instruction

```
ReadLn (Name);
```

reads the letters Bob (typed by the program user) into the memory cell Name. The next line

```
WriteLn ('Hello ', Name, '.');
```

displays Bob after the message string 'Hello '. The string '.' causes a period to be printed after the last character stored in Name is printed. Finally, the next to last line of the program displays the last line shown in the sample execution. ■

Some punctuation symbols appear in Fig. 2.1. The comma separates items in a list, and the semicolon appears at the end of several lines. We will give guidelines for the use of these symbols later.

■ Example 2.2

Suppose you are measuring shelves for a bookcase, and you want to convert inches to centimeters. You might create a program like the one shown in Fig. 2.2. The program instruction

```
ReadLn (Inches);
```

reads the number of inches to be converted (30.0 in the sample execution) into the memory cell Inches. The program instruction

```
Cent := CentPerInch * Inches;
```

computes the equivalent length in centimeters by multiplying the length in inches by 2.54 (the number of centimeters per inch); the product is stored in memory cell Cent.

Finally, the program instruction

```
WriteLn ('That equals ', Cent, ' centimeters.')
```

displays a message string, the value of Cent, and a second message string. The instruction displays the value of Cent as a real number in Pascal scientific notation (7.6200000000E+01). The value printed is equivalent to 7.62 × 10 or 76.2, as will be explained later. ■

Figure 2.2 Converting Inches to Centimeters

Edit Window

```
program InchToCent;

  const
    CentPerInch = 2.54;

  var
    Inches, Cent : Real;

begin
  WriteLn ('Enter a length in inches>');
  ReadLn (Inches);
  Cent := CentPerInch * Inches;
  WriteLn ('That equals ', Cent, ' centimeters.')
end.
```

Output Window

```
Enter a length in inches>
30.0
That equals  7.6200000000E+01 centimeters.
```

One of the nicest things about Pascal is that it lets us write programs that resemble English. At this point, you probably can read and understand the sample programs, even though you do not know how to write your own programs. In the following sections, you will learn more details about the Pascal programs we have looked at so far.

Reserved Words and Identifiers

All of the lines in the two preceding programs satisfy the syntax rules for the Pascal language. The programs contain several different elements, such as reserved words, standard identifiers, special symbols, and names for memory cells. Let's look at the first three categories. The reserved words all appear in lowercase; they have special meanings in Pascal and cannot be used for other purposes. The reserved words in Fig. 2.1 and Fig. 2.2 are

```
program, const, var, begin, end, string
```

The standard identifiers also have special meanings, but they can be used for other purposes (however, we don't recommend this practice). The standard identifiers in Fig. 2.1 and Fig. 2.2 are

```
Real, ReadLn, WriteLn
```

Some symbols (for example, =, *, :=) have special meanings in Pascal. Appendix B contains a complete list of reserved words, standard identifiers, and special symbols.

What is the difference between reserved words and standard identifiers? You cannot use a reserved word as the name of a memory cell, but you can use a standard identifier. However, once you use a standard identifier to name a memory cell, the Pascal compiler no longer associates any special meaning with that identifier. For example, you could use `WriteLn` as the name of a memory cell, but then you would not be able to use `WriteLn` for its normal purpose (to display program output). Thus, standard identifiers lose a valuable purpose.

The other identifiers appearing in the programs in Fig. 2.1 and Fig. 2.2 are described in more detail in the next sections.

PROGRAM STYLE

Use of Uppercase and Lowercase

Throughout the text, issues of good programming style are discussed in displays such as this one. Programming style displays provide guidelines for improving the appearance and the readability of your programs. Most programs are examined, studied, or used by someone other than the programmer. A program that follows consistent style conventions is easier to read and understand than one that is sloppy or inconsistent. And, although conventions make it easier for humans to understand programs, they have no effect whatsoever on the computer.

In this text, reserved words always appear in lowercase; identifiers are in mixed uppercase and lowercase. The first letter of each identifier is always capitalized. If an identifier consists of two or more words pushed together (for example, `ReadLn` is an abbreviation for Read Line), the first letter of each "word" is capitalized. We recommend that you follow this convention in your programs, so that it will be easy to distinguish reserved words from other identifiers.

The compiler does not really differentiate between uppercase and lowercase. That means you could write the reserved word `const` as `CONST` or the standard identifier `ReadLn` as `READLN`. However, `const` and `ReadLn` are preferable, according to our convention.

Because you should not redefine a standard identifier, many computer scientists emphasize this by writing standard identifiers the same as reserved words (that is, all lowercase). If your instructor prefers that you adopt this convention, you should write the standard identifier `ReadLn` as `readln`.

Exercise for Section 2.1

Self-Check

1. Why should you not use standard identifiers as names of memory cells in a program? Can you use reserved words instead?

2.2 Declarations in Pascal Programs

How do we tell the Pascal compiler what identifiers will be used in a program? One way is the *program heading*, as shown next:

```
program Hello;
```

The program heading, which begins with the reserved word `program`, identifies the name (`Hello`) of the program.

We tell the Pascal compiler the names of memory cells used in a program through constant and variable declarations. The *constant declaration*

```
const
  CentPerInch = 2.54;
```

specifies that the identifier `CentPerInch` will be used as the name of the memory cell that contains the number `2.54`; the identifier `CentPerInch` is called a *constant*. Only data values that never change (for example, the number of centimeters per inch is always `2.54`) should be associated with an identifier that is a constant. Instructions that attempt to change the value of a constant cannot appear in a Pascal program.

The *variable declaration*

```
var
  Name : string;
```

in Fig. 2.1 identifies the name of a memory cell (`Name`) that will be used to store a person's name. The variable declaration

```
var
  Inches, Cent : Real;
```

in Fig. 2.2 gives the names of two memory cells that will be used to store real numbers (for example, 30.0, 562.57). All the names listed in the preceding declarations are considered identifiers.

Identifiers listed on the left of the symbol : in a variable declaration are called *variables*. Variables are names of memory cells used in a program for storing input data and computational results. The identifier (for example, `Real`) that appears to the right of the symbol : tells the Pascal compiler the *data type* (for example, a real number) of the information stored in a particular variable. A variable that is used for storing an integer value (a number without a decimal point) has data type `Integer`. Data types are discussed in more detail in Section 2.8.

You have quite a bit of freedom in selecting the identifiers that you use in a program. The syntactic rules for Turbo Pascal are as follows:

1. An identifier must always begin with a letter.
2. An identifier must consist only of letters, digits, or the underscore symbol (_).
3. You cannot use a Pascal reserved word as an identifier.

4. If an identifier is longer than 63 characters, only the first 63 characters are used.

Some valid and invalid identifiers follow.

Valid identifiers:

```
Letter1, Letter2, Inches, Cent, CentPerInch, Hello, Cent_Per_Inch
```

Invalid identifiers:

```
1Letter, const, var, Two*Four, Joe's
```

The identifier `Cent_Per_Inch` is valid in Turbo Pascal, but not standard Pascal. For this reason, we will not use the underscore character and will write the identifier above as `CentPerInch`.

Pascal requires a declaration for every identifier used in a program unless that identifier is a standard identifier. Identifiers that are not standard identifiers are called *user-defined identifiers*. The reserved words and identifiers used in Fig. 2.1 and Fig. 2.2 are shown in Table 2.1 under their appropriate categories.

Table 2.1 Reserved Words and Identifiers in Figures 2.1 and 2.2

Reserved Words	Standard Identifiers	User-Defined Identifiers
program	Real	Hello
var	ReadLn	InchToCent
const	WriteLn	CentPerInch
begin		Inches
end		Cent
string		Name

This section introduced the program heading, constant declarations, and variable declarations; the syntactic form of each Pascal language construct is summarized in the following syntax displays. Each display describes the syntactic form of a language construct and provides an example.

SYNTAX DISPLAY

Program Heading

Form: `program` *pname*;
`program` *pname* `(Input, Output);`

Example: `program Hello;`
`program Hello (Input, Output);`

Interpretation: The name of the program is indicated by *pname*. The second form of the program heading indicates that the input data will be read from file `Input` (the keyboard); the output results will be written to file `Output` (the screen). This is the only form of the program heading that is valid in standard Pascal.

SYNTAX DISPLAY

Constant Declaration

Form: `const` *constant* = *value*;

Example: `const MyPi = 3.14159;`

Interpretation: The specified *value* is associated with the identifier *constant*. The *value* associated with *constant* cannot be changed. More than one constant declaration may follow the word `const`. A semicolon appears at the end of each constant declaration. A more complete discussion of constant declarations appears in Section 7.1.

SYNTAX DISPLAY

Variable Declaration

Form: `var` *variable list* : *type*;

Example:

```
var
   X, Y : Real;
   Me, You : Integer;
```

Interpretation: A memory cell is allocated for each variable (an identifier) in the *variable list*. The *type* of data (`Real`, `Integer`) to be stored in each variable is specified between the colon and semicolon. Commas separate the identifiers in the *variable list*. More than one list of variables can be declared after the word `var`.

PROGRAM STYLE

Choosing Identifier Names

It is important to pick meaningful names for identifiers to make it easier to understand their use. For example, the identifier `Salary` would be a good name for a variable used to store a person's salary; the identifiers `S` or `Bagel` would be a bad choice. As shown above, it is difficult to form meaningful names with fewer than three letters. On the other hand, typing errors are more likely when identifiers are too long. As a reasonable rule of thumb, use names that are between three and ten characters in length.

If you mistype an identifier, the compiler will usually detect this as a syntax error and display an *undefined identifier* error message during program translation. Sometimes mistyped identifiers resemble other identifiers, so avoid picking names that are similar to each other. Make sure you do not choose two names that are identical except for their use of case, because the compiler will not be able to distinguish between them.

Exercises for Section 2.2

Self-Check

1. Should the value of `MyPi` (3.14159) be stored in a constant or a variable?
2. Which of the following are valid Pascal identifiers?

```
MyProgram    prog2    Prog#2    2NDone    Program    'MaxScores'
```

3. Which of the following identifiers are Pascal reserved words, standard identifiers, identifiers, and invalid identifiers?

```
end       ReadLn    Bill             program   Sue's
Rate      Operate   Start            begin     const
XYZ123    123XYZ    ThisIsALongOne             Y=Z
```

Programming

1. Write a program heading for a program named `Mine` that has declarations for variables `Radius`, `Area`, and `Circumf` (all type `Real`) and the constant `MyPi` (3.14159).

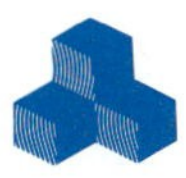

2.3 Executable Statements in Pascal Programs

One of the main functions of a computer is to perform arithmetic computations and to display the results of those computations. Such operations are specified by the *executable statements* that appear in the program body (following the reserved word `begin`). Each executable statement is translated by the Pascal compiler into one or more machine language instructions, which are copied to the object file and later executed. Declarations, on the other hand, describe the meaning and the purpose of each user-defined identifier to the Pascal compiler; they are not translated into machine language instructions and do not appear in the object file.

Assignment Statements

The *assignment statement* is used in Pascal to perform computations. The assignment statement

```
Cent := CentPerInch * Inches;
```

in Fig. 2.2 assigns a value to the variable `Cent`. In this case, `Cent` is assigned the result of the multiplication (* means multiply) of the constant `CentPerInch` by

Figure 2.3 Effect of Cent := CentPerInch * Inches;

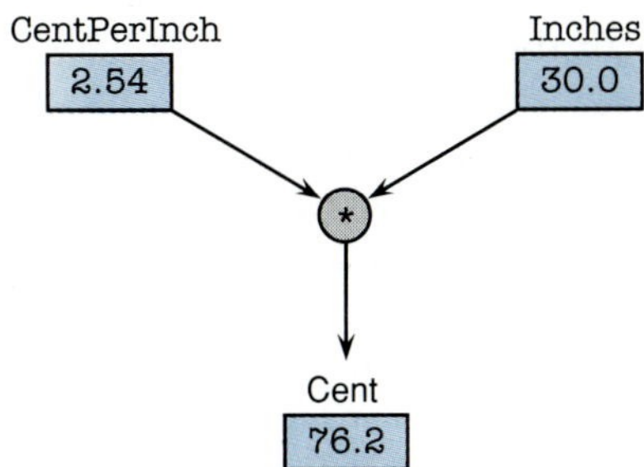

the variable `Inches`. Valid information must be stored in both `CentPerInch` and `Inches` before the assignment statement is executed. As shown in Fig. 2.3, only the value of `Cent` is affected by the assignment statement; `CentPerInch` and `Inches` retain their original values.

The symbol := is the *assignment operator* in Pascal and should be read as "becomes," "gets," or "takes the value of" rather than "equals." The : and the = must be adjacent characters with no intervening space. The general form of the assignment statement is shown in the next display.

SYNTAX DISPLAY

Assignment Statement (Arithmetic)

Form: *result* := *expression*
Example: `X := Y + Z + 2.0`
Interpretation: The variable specified by *result* is assigned the value of *expression*. The previous value of *result* is destroyed. The *expression* can be a single variable or a single constant or involve variables, constants, and the arithmetic operators listed in Table 2.2. The *expression* must be assignment compatible (described next) with the variable specified by *result*.

Table 2.2 Some Arithmetic Operators

Arithmetic Operator	Meaning
+	Addition
–	Subtraction
*	Multiplication
/	Real division

The real division operator (/) always yields a real number as its result. Chapter 7 introduces a division operator that yields an integer as its result.

An *expression* is *assignment compatible* with a *result* variable if both are the same data type, or the *result* variable is type `Real` and the *expression* is type `Integer`. This means that a type `Integer` *result* variable must be assigned a type `Integer` *expression*, but a type `Real` *result* variable may be assigned a type `Integer` or a type `Real` *expression*. We will have more to say about assignment compatible types in Chapter 7.

■ Example 2.3

In Pascal, you can write assignment statements of the form

```
Sum := Sum + Item
```

where the variable `Sum` is used on both sides of the assignment operator. Obviously this is not an algebraic equation, but it illustrates a common programming practice. This statement instructs the computer to add the current value of the variable `Sum` to the value of `Item`; the result is saved temporarily and then stored back into `Sum`. The previous value of `Sum` is destroyed in the process, as illustrated in Fig. 2.4; however, the value of `Item` is unchanged. ■

Figure 2.4 Effect of Sum := Sum + Item

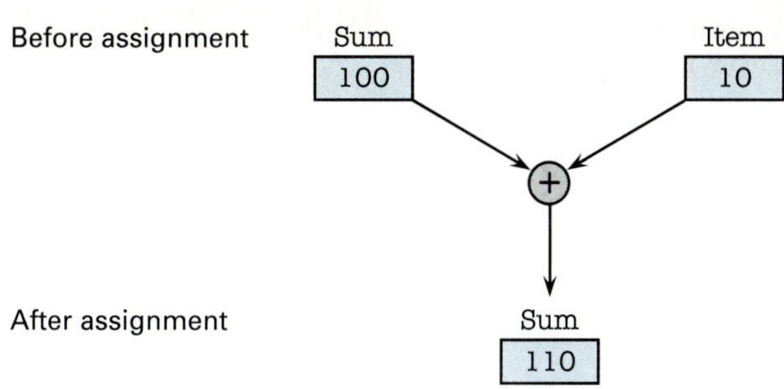

■ Example 2.4

In Pascal, you can also write assignment statements with an expression part that consists of a single variable or value. The statement

```
NewX := X
```

instructs the computer to copy the value of `X` into `NewX`. The statement

```
NewX := -X
```

instructs the computer to get the value of `X`, negate this value, and store the result in `NewX`. For example, if `X` is `3.5`, `NewX` is `-3.5`. Neither assignment statement changes the value of `X`. ■

Input/Output Operations

Data can be stored in memory in three different ways: associated with a constant, assigned to a variable, or read into a variable. We have already discussed the first two methods. The third method, reading data into a variable, is necessary if you want the program to manipulate different data each time it executes. Reading data into memory is called an *input operation.*

As it executes, a program performs computations and assigns new values to variables. These program results can be displayed to the program user by an *output operation.*

All input/output operations in Pascal are performed by executing special program units called *input/output procedures.* The input/output procedures are supplied as part of the Pascal compiler and their names are standard identifiers. The next two sections discuss how to use the input procedure named `ReadLn` and the output procedure named `WriteLn`.

Using the ReadLn Procedure

In Pascal, a *procedure call statement* calls, or activates, a procedure. Calling a procedure is analogous to asking a friend to perform an urgent task. You tell your friend what to do (but not how to do it) and wait for your friend to report back that he or she is finished. After hearing from your friend, you can go on and do something else.

In Fig. 2.2, the procedure call statement

```
ReadLn (Inches);
```

calls procedure ReadLn to read data into the variable Inches. Where does procedure ReadLn get the data that it stores in variable Inches? It reads it from the standard input device (Input). In most cases, the standard input device is the keyboard. Consequently, the computer attempts to store in Inches whatever information is typed at the keyboard by the program user. Since Inches is declared as type Real, the input operation proceeds without error only if the program user types in a real number. The program user should press the Return or Enter key after typing the number. The effect of the ReadLn operation is shown in Fig. 2.5.

The program in Fig. 2.1 reads a person's name. Each person using the program may have a different name, so the procedure call statement

```
ReadLn (Name);
```

calls the ReadLn procedure to enter data into the variable Name. Since Name is type string, up to 255 characters may be stored in the memory cell associated with Name. Figure 2.6 shows the effect of this statement when the letters Bob are entered.

Note that only three characters are actually saved, even though there is space for 255. If a name with more than 255 characters were entered, only the first 255 would be stored. The fact that the characters at the end are lost is not considered an error.

The number of characters read by the ReadLn procedure depends on the type of the variable in which the data will be stored. For variables of type Real, Turbo Pascal continues to read characters until it reaches a blank, a control character, or until the Enter key is pressed. For string variables, all characters

Figure 2.5 Effect of ReadLn (Inches);

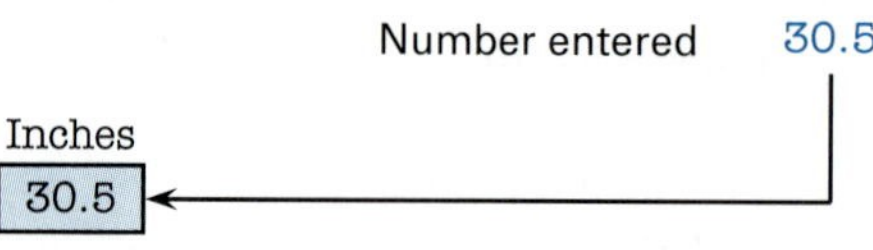

Figure 2.6 Effect of ReadLn (Name)

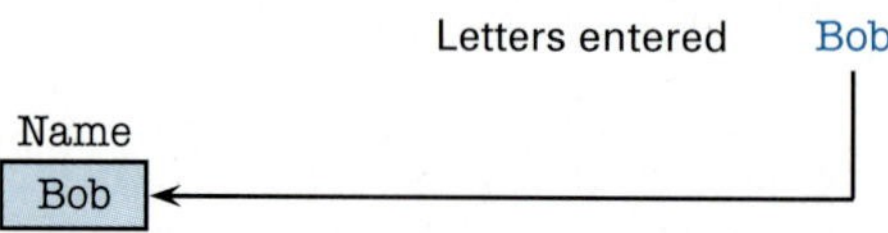

typed before the Enter key is pressed will be read, but only the first 255 characters will be saved.

How do we know when to enter the input data and what data to enter? Your program should print a prompting message that informs you what data to enter and when. (Prompting messages are discussed in more detail in the next section.) Each character entered by the program user is *echoed* on the screen and is also processed by procedure `ReadLn`.

SYNTAX DISPLAY

The ReadLn Procedure

Form: `ReadLn` (*input list*)
Example: `ReadLn (Age, NumDepend)`
Interpretation: The ReadLn procedure reads data the program user types at the keyboard into memory during program execution. The program user must enter one data item for each variable specified in the *input list*. Commas are used to separate the variable names in the *input list*.

The order of the data must correspond to the order of the variables in the *input list*. Insert one or more blank characters between consecutive numeric data items. Do not insert any blanks between consecutive character data items unless the blank character is one of the data items being read. Press the Enter key after the last data item is entered or to terminate a string data item.

The WriteLn Procedure

To see the results of a program execution, we must have some way of specifying what variable values should be displayed. In Fig. 2.2, the procedure call statement

```
WriteLn ('That equals ', Cent, ' centimeters.')
```

calls the `WriteLn` procedure to display three items: the string literal `'That equals '`, the value of `Cent`, and the string literal `' centimeters.'`. A *string literal* (or *string*) is a sequence of characters enclosed in single quotation marks or apostrophes; the characters inside the quotation marks are printed but the marks are not. The `WriteLn` procedure displays the line

```
That equals  7.6200000000E+01 centimeters.
```

Unless directed otherwise, most Pascal compilers use Pascal scientific notation to display a real value. The number `7.6200000000E+01` is 76.2 expressed in Pascal scientific notation. In normal scientific notation, 7.62×10^1 means "multiply 7.62 by 10," or move the decimal point right one digit. Because you cannot enter or display superscripts with Pascal, the letter E indicates scientific notation (sometimes called *floating-point notation*).

In Fig. 2.1, the procedure call statement

```
WriteLn ('Hello ', Name, '.');
```

displays the line

```
Hello Bob.
```

In this case, the value of `Name` (the string `'Bob'`) is printed between the strings `'Hello '` and `'.'`.

Finally, the statements

```
WriteLn ('Enter your name and press return>');
WriteLn ('Enter a length in inches>');
```

display prompts or prompting messages in Figs. 2.1 and 2.2, respectively. Always display a prompting message just before a call to procedure `ReadLn` to remind the program user to enter data. The prompt can also describe the format of the expected data. It is important to precede each `ReadLn` operation with a `WriteLn` that prints a prompt; otherwise, the program user may have no idea that the program is waiting for data or what data to enter.

The *cursor* is a moving place marker that indicates the next position on the screen where information will be displayed. After the `WriteLn` procedure is executed, the cursor advances to the start of the next line on the screen.

SYNTAX DISPLAY

The WriteLn Procedure

Form: `WriteLn` (*output list*)
Example: `WriteLn ('Hello ', Name, '.')`
Interpretation: The `WriteLn` procedure displays the value of each variable or constant in the order in which it appears in *output list*. A string is printed without the quotation marks. The cursor advances to the start of the next line after the entire output line is displayed.

Exercises for Section 2.3

Self-Check

1. Write the following numbers in normal decimal notation.

```
103E-4        1.2345E+6        123.45E+3
```

2. Correct the syntax errors in the following program and rewrite it so that it follows our style conventions. What does each statement of your corrected program do? What values are printed?

```
program SMALL VAR X, Y, X, real:
BEGIN Y = 15.0,
Z:= -Y + 3.5; Y + z =: x;
writeln (x; Y; z); end;
```

3. Show the output displayed by the following program lines when the data entered are 5 and 7.

```
WriteLn ('Enter two integers>');
ReadLn (M, N);
M := M + 5;
N := 3 * N;
WriteLn ('M = ', M);
WriteLn ('N = ', N);
```

Programming

1. Write statements that ask the user to type three numbers and that read the user's responses into `First`, `Second`, and `Third`.
2. Write a statement that displays the value of `X` in the following format:

```
The value of X is ____________
```

3. Write a program that asks the user to enter the radius of a circle and then computes and displays the circle's area and circumference. Use the formulas

$$area = MyPi \times radius \times radius$$
$$circumference = 2 \times MyPi \times radius$$

where `MyPi` is the constant 3.14159.

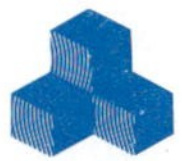

2.4 General Form of Pascal Programs

To summarize what we have discussed so far, the programs shown earlier have the general form described in Fig. 2.7. Each program begins with a program heading that identifies the name of the program.

Every identifier used in a program must be declared exactly once in the declaration part of a program unless it is a standard identifier. All constant declarations come after `const` and all variable declarations after `var`. More than one constant may be declared, and there may be more than one variable list. Commas separate identifiers in a variable list; the semicolon terminates each declaration.

In standard Pascal, the reserved words `const` and `var` can appear no more than once and must be in the order shown in Fig. 2.7. In Turbo Pascal, the reserved words `const` and `var` may appear more than once and in any order. However, it is good programming practice to follow the standard Pascal convention for their use.

The reserved word `begin` signals the start of the program body. The program body contains the statements that are translated into machine language and eventually executed. The statements we have looked at so far consist of statements that perform computations and input/output operations. The last line in a program is

```
end.
```

Figure 2.7 General Form of a Pascal Program

```
program Name;
  const
    constant = value;         ⎫
        .                     ⎪
        .                     ⎪
        .                     ⎪
    constant = value;         ⎬ Declaration part
  var                         ⎪
    variable list : type;     ⎪
        .                     ⎪
        .                     ⎪
        .                     ⎪
    variable list : type;     ⎭
begin                         ⎫
  statement;                  ⎪
      .                       ⎪
      .                       ⎬ Program body
      .                       ⎪
  statement                   ⎪
end.                          ⎭
```

Semicolons separate Pascal statements and must be inserted between statements in a program body. A semicolon is not needed before the first statement in a sequence nor after the last statement. Consequently, a semicolon should not appear after the reserved word `begin`. Most Pascal compilers allow a semicolon after the last statement in a program, but we do not recommend this practice. When present, this semicolon has the effect of inserting an "empty statement" between the last actual statement and the program terminator `end`.

As shown in Fig. 2.1, a Pascal statement can extend over more than one line. The variable and constant declarations start on one line and finish on the next. A statement that extends over more than one line cannot be split in the middle of an identifier, a reserved word, a number, or a string.

We can also write more than one statement on a line, although we recommend that you place only one statement on a line. For example, the line

```
WriteLn ('Enter two letters> ');  ReadLn (Letter1,Letter2)
```

contains a statement that displays a prompt message and a statement that reads the data requested. A semicolon separates the two statements; you would insert another semicolon at the end of the line if another statement were to follow.

PROGRAM STYLE

Use of Blank Space

The consistent and careful use of blank spaces can significantly enhance the style of a program. A blank space is required between words in a program line (for instance, between `program` and `Hello` in Fig. 2.1).

The compiler ignores extra blanks between words and symbols. You can insert spaces to improve the style and the appearance of a program. Always leave a blank space after a comma and before and after arithmetic operators such as *, –, :=. Remember to indent each line of the program except for the first and last lines and the line `begin`, and to write the reserved words `const`, `var`, and `begin` by themselves on a line so that they stand out. Indent all lines except for the first and last lines of the program and the line `begin` two or more spaces. Finally, use blank lines between sections of the program.

All these measures have the sole purpose of improving the style—and hence the clarity—of your programs. Stylistic issues have no effect whatever on the meaning of the program as far as the computer is concerned; however, they can make it easier for people to read and understand your program.

Be careful not to insert blank spaces where they do not belong. For example, there cannot be a space between the characters : and = when they form the assignment operator :=, nor can the identifier `StartSalary` be written as `Start Salary`.

Programs in Memory

Let's look at a new sample program and see what happens to memory when this program is loaded and executed.

■ Example 2.5

Figure 2.8 shows a payroll program that computes an employee's gross pay and net pay using the algebraic formulas

gross pay = *hours worked* × *hourly rate*
net pay = *gross pay* − *tax amount*

These formulas are written as the Pascal assignment statements

```
Gross := Hours * Rate;
Net := Gross - Tax;
```

in the payroll program shown in Fig. 2.8. New values of `Hours` and `Rate` are read each time the program is executed; a constant `Tax` of $25.00 is always deducted.

Figure 2.8 A Payroll Program

Edit Window

```
program Payroll;

  const
    Tax = 25.00;

  var
    Hours, Rate, Gross, Net : Real;
```

```
begin
  WriteLn ('Enter hours worked>');
  ReadLn (Hours);
  WriteLn ('Enter hourly rate>');
  ReadLn (Rate);
  Gross := Hours * Rate;
  Net := Gross - Tax;
  WriteLn ('Gross pay is $', Gross);
  WriteLn ('Net   pay is $', Net)
end.
```

Output Window

```
Enter hours worked>
40.0
Enter hourly rate>
4.50
Gross pay is $  1.8000000000E+02
Net   pay is $  1.5500000000E+02
```

The program first reads the data that represent the hours worked and the hourly rate and then computes gross pay as their product. Next, it computes net pay by deducting a constant tax amount of $25.00. Finally, it displays the computed values of gross pay and net pay.

Figure 2.9a shows the payroll program loaded into memory and the program memory area before execution of the program body. The question marks

Figure 2.9 Memory Before and After Execution of a Program

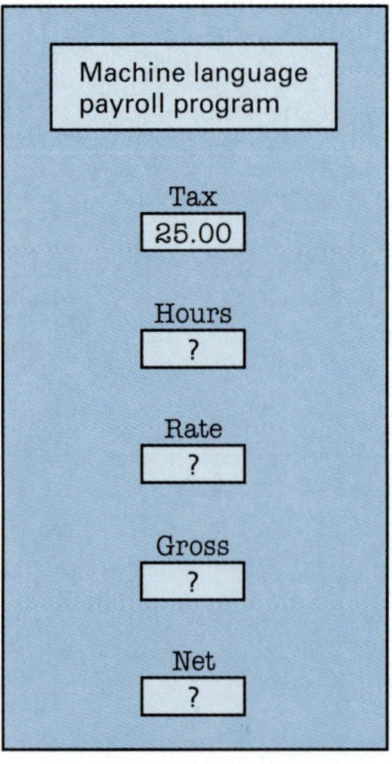

A. Memory before execution

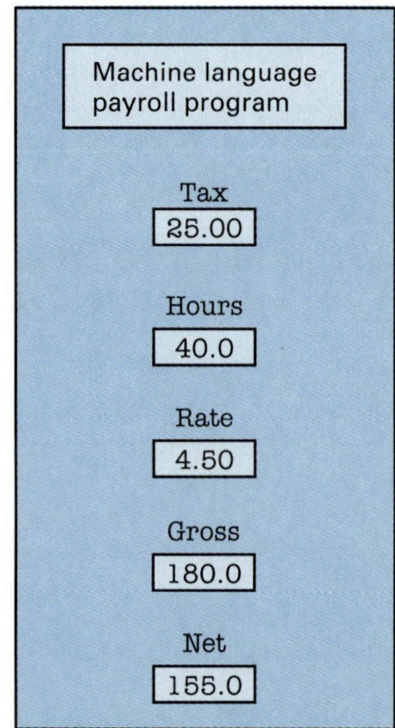

B. Memory after execution

in memory cells Hours, Rate, Gross, and Net indicate that these variables are undefined (value unknown) before program execution begins. During program execution, the data values 40.0 and 4.50 are read into the variables Hours and Rate, respectively. After the assignment statements shown earlier are used to compute values for Gross and Net, all variables are defined, as shown in Fig. 2.9b. ■

Exercise for Section 2.4

Self-Check

1. Show the contents of memory before and after execution of the program in Fig. 2.2.

2.5 Interactive Mode, Batch Mode, and Data Files

There are two basic modes of computer operation: batch and interactive. The programs we have written so far are intended to be run in *interactive mode.* In this mode, the program user can interact with the program and enter data while the program is executing.

In *batch mode,* all data must be supplied beforehand—the program user cannot interact with the program while it is executing. Batch mode is an option on most computers.

If you use batch mode, you must prepare a batch data file before executing your program. The Turbo Pascal editor may be used to create and save a batch data file in the same way in which it is used to create and save a program file. We recommend that you use the extension .DAT to denote a data file. (If you don't specify an extension, Turbo Pascal will incorrectly assume your file is a Pascal program and use the extension .PAS.)

Because a batch mode program cannot interact with its user, it makes no sense to provide prompts. Each ReadLn operation reads data items from a previously prepared data file. A WriteLn operation is used after (instead of before) each ReadLn operation to echo, or display, the data values just read into memory; otherwise, there will be no record of the data being processed.

Figure 2.10 shows the payroll program rewritten as a batch program. The program input comes from the user-defined file InData associated with the disk file B:INDATA.DAT, rather than from the standard file Input which is associated with the keyboard. A complete description of the program follows the figure.

Figure 2.10 Payroll Program as a Batch Program

Edit Window

```
program PayrollBatch;

  const
    Tax = 25.00;
```

```
   var
     InData : Text;
     Hours, Rate, Gross, Net : Real;

begin
  Assign (InData, 'B:INDATA.DAT');
  Reset (InData);

  ReadLn (InData, Hours);
  WriteLn ('Hours worked are ', Hours);
  ReadLn (InData, Rate);
  WriteLn ('Hourly rate is   ', Rate);

  Gross := Hours * Rate;
  Net := Gross - Tax;
  WriteLn ('Gross pay is $', Gross);
  WriteLn ('Net pay is   $', Net);

  Close (InData)
end.
```

Output Window

```
Hours worked are  4.0000000000E+01
Hourly rate is    4.5000000000E+00
Gross pay is $  1.8000000000E+02
Net pay is   $  1.5500000000E+02
```

Preview of Data Files (Optional)

This section previews the use of text files as data files in Pascal. A complete treatment of this topic is provided in Section 8.7. Skip this section if you will not be using data files until then.

A batch program reads its data from a data file that you created beforehand using the Turbo Pascal editor. The process used to create a data file is the same as that used to create a program, as described in Section 1.6. The `PayrollBatch` program in Fig. 2.10 reads its data from the data file `InData`, which is associated with the file `INDATA.DAT` on the diskette in drive B.

The declaration

```
var
  InData : Text;
```

indicates that `InData` has the data type `Text` (a standard identifier) and is, therefore, a *text file* (file of characters).

The statement

```
Assign (InData, 'B:INDATA.DAT');
```

associates the *internal name* of the data file (`InData`) with the *external name* (or *directory name*) of the data file (`B:INDATA.DAT`) and is the only place in the program where the external name appears. The *external name* of the data file is the name given to the data file when it was saved to disk from the editor. The statement

```
Reset (InData);
```

prepares the file InData so that it can be read.

Each of the statements

```
ReadLn (InData, Hours);
ReadLn (InData, Rate);
```

reads one real value from a line of the file InData. The statements

```
WriteLn ('Hours worked are ', Hours);
WriteLn ('Hourly rate is   ', Rate);
```

are used to echo the values read from the data file.

The sample output shown in Fig. 2.10 is generated when the file B:INDATA.DAT contains the two lines

```
40.0
4.50
```

The statement

```
Close (InData)
```

is used to indicate to the operating system that the file associated with InData is no longer being used by the program.

Exercises for Section 2.5

Self-Check

1. Explain the difference in placement of WriteLn statements used to display prompts and WriteLn statements used to echo data. Which are used in interactive programs and which are used in batch programs?

Programming

1. Rewrite the program in Fig. 2.2 as a batch program. Assume data are read from file MYDATA.DAT.

2.6 Formatting and Viewing Program Output

In the sample program output shown so far, all real numbers were printed in Pascal scientific notation. Consequently, we had little control over the appearance, or format, of each output line. This section shows you how to specify the format of an output item.

Formatting Integer Values

It is fairly easy to format program output in Pascal. This is illustrated in the next example for an integer value. An integer value in Pascal is a number without a decimal point.

■ Example 2.6

The program in Fig. 2.11 determines the value of a small collection of coins (nickels and pennies only) you receive as change for a purchase. The variables are declared to be type `Integer`, since it is impossible to have 2.5 coins. Only integer values can be stored in type `Integer` variables. The assignment statement

```
Cents := 5 * Nickels + Pennies;
```

computes the value in cents of the collection of coins in the obvious way (each nickel is worth five pennies).

The statement

```
WriteLn ('You have ', Coins :3, ' coins.')
```

causes an integer value to be printed between the two strings. The symbols `:3` after the variable `Coins` specify the *field width* (3) of the *output field* that contains the value of `Coins`. A field width of `3` indicates that we expect the output value to be `3` digits or less. If the value of `Coins` is less than `100`, it will be displayed *right justified* in its field, preceded by one or more blank spaces. This means that a single blank space will precede a two-digit number in the output field for `Coins`, or that two blank spaces will precede a one-digit number. In the output shown, there are actually three blank spaces before the digit `5` (value of `Coins`), because the string `'You have '` ends with a blank. ■

Table 2.3 shows how two integer values are printed using different format specifications. The symbol □ represents a blank character. The next to last line

Figure 2.11 Formatting an Integer Value

Edit Window

```
program CountCoins;

  var
    Nickels, Pennies, Coins, Cents : Integer;

begin
  Write ('How many nickels do you have? ');
  ReadLn (Nickels);
  Write ('How many pennies do you have? ');
  ReadLn (Pennies);
  Coins := Nickels + Pennies;
  Cents := 5 * Nickels + Pennies;
  WriteLn ('You have ', Coins :3, ' coins.');
  WriteLn ('Their value is ', Cents :4, ' cents.')
end.
```

Output Window

```
How many nickels do you have? 3
How many pennies do you have? 2
You have   5 coins.
Their value is   17 cents.
```

Table 2.3 Printing Integer Values Using Formats

Value	Format	Printed Output
234	:4	□234
234	:5	□□234
234	:6	□□□234
−234	:4	−234
−234	:5	□−234
−234	:6	□□−234
234	:Len	□□□234 (if Len is 6)
234	:1	234

shows that the width specification can be a variable (`Len`) or even an expression that has an integer value. The last line shows that when a width of 1 is used, the number is printed with no blanks preceding it, and the number of print columns actually filled varies with the size of the number (that is, the field expands as needed).

The Write Procedure

You may have noticed that the program body in Fig. 2.11 begins with two calls to an unfamiliar procedure, `Write`, that displays prompts. If you run the program in Fig. 2.11, you will see that the cursor remains positioned on the same line as the `?` after each prompt is displayed. This is because the word `Write` is used instead of `WriteLn` in the statements that print the prompting messages. Whenever we call `Write`, the cursor remains positioned after the last character displayed (a space in Fig. 2.11). In contrast, whenever we call `WriteLn`, the cursor advances to the next line after the output is displayed.

The three procedure call statements

```
Write ('You have ');
Write (Coins :3);
WriteLn (' coins.')
```

would cause the same line of output to be displayed as the single procedure call statement

```
WriteLn ('You have ', Coins :3, ' coins.')
```

It is generally more convenient to use the latter form.

SYNTAX DISPLAY

The Write Procedure

Form: `Write` (*output list*)
Example: `Write ('Enter your name >')`
Interpretation: The value of each variable or constant in the *output list* is printed. Any string in the *output list* is displayed without the quotation marks. The cursor does not advance to the next line after the output is displayed.

Formatting Real Values

Suppose you want to calculate your average speed on a trip and your gas mileage. You could do so with the program shown in Fig. 2.12, which uses the two formulas

speed = *distance* / *time*
mileage = *distance* / *gallons*

The input data consist of the trip distance, the trip time, and the number of gallons of gasoline you used.

Figure 2.12 Formatting Real Values

Edit Window

```
program Trip;

  var
    Speed, Time, Distance, Mileage, Gallons : Real;

begin
  Write ('Enter distance in miles> ');
  ReadLn (Distance);
  Write ('Enter time of trip in hours> ');
  ReadLn (Time);
  Speed := Distance / Time;
  WriteLn ('Average speed in MPH was ', Speed :5:1);
  WriteLn;

  Write ('Enter gallons used> ');
  ReadLn (Gallons);
  Mileage := Distance / Gallons;
  WriteLn ('Miles per gallon was ', Mileage :5:1)
end.
```

Output Window

```
Enter distance in miles> 100
Enter time of trip in hours> 1.5
Average speed in MPH was  66.7

Enter gallons used> 25
Miles per gallon was   4.0
```

The two statements

```
WriteLn ('Average speed in MPH was ', Speed :5:1);
WriteLn ('Miles per gallon was ', Mileage :5:1)
```

each display a string followed by a real number. The symbols `:5:1` specify that the real number should be displayed in five print positions and that there should be one digit after the decimal point. The output value displayed will be rounded to one decimal place; the decimal point accounts for one position in the field width.

The output line printed by the first call to `WriteLn` would have the form

```
Average speed in MPH was XXX.X
```

where XXX.X indicates the format of the real number (three digits, a decimal point, and a digit). A value less than or equal to 99.9 would be printed with extra blanks preceding the first digit so that the decimal point remains in the fourth print position. If the value is greater than 999.9, the field expands as needed but only one decimal digit will follow the decimal point.

Table 2.4 shows some real values that were printed using different format specifications. As shown in the table, it is possible to use a format specification of the form :*n*, where *n* is an integer expression. In this case, the real value is printed in scientific notation using a total of *n* print positions.

Table 2.4 Printing Real Values Using Formats

Value	Format	Printed Output
3.14159	:5:2	□3.14
3.14159	:4:2	3.14
3.14159	:3:2	3.14
3.14159	:5:1	□□3.1
3.14159	:5:3	3.142
3.14159	:8:5	□3.14159
3.14159	:9	□3.14E+00
0.1234	:4:2	0.12
−0.006	:4:2	-0.01
−0.006	:9	-6.00E-03
−0.006	:8:5	-0.00600
−0.006	:8:3	□□-0.006

PROGRAM STYLE

Eliminating Leading Blanks

As shown in Tables 2.3 and 2.4, a number that requires fewer print positions than specified by the format is displayed with leading blanks. To eliminate extra leading blanks, choose a format that will display the smallest value expected without leading blanks. If the actual value requires more print positions, the field width will expand to accommodate it. A format of :1 displays any integer value without leading blanks. A format of :4:2 displays any real number accurate to two decimal places without leading blanks; similarly, a format of :5:3 displays any real number accurate to three decimal places without leading blanks.

Using WriteLn without an Output List

In Fig. 2.12, the call to procedure WriteLn

```
WriteLn;
```

has no output list and causes a blank line in the middle of the program output. Execution of a WriteLn always causes the cursor to be advanced to the next line. If nothing is printed on the current line, a blank line appears in the program output.

SYNTAX DISPLAY

WriteLn Procedure (without an Output List)

Form: `WriteLn`
Interpretation: Executing the `WriteLn` procedure advances the cursor to the first column of the next line.

Formatting Strings

A string value is always printed right-justified in its field. Therefore, blank spaces precede a string if the field in which it is printed is bigger than the string. If *field width* is too small to accommodate a string value, it is expanded so that the entire string can be displayed. Table 2.5 illustrates these points.

Table 2.5 Printing String Values Using Formats

String	Format	Printed Output
'*'	:1	*
'*'	:2	□*
'*'	:3	□□*
'ACES'	:1	ACES
'ACES'	:2	ACES
'ACES'	:3	ACES
'ACES'	:4	ACES
'ACES'	:5	□ACES

Using the Output Window

Normally Turbo Pascal displays the Edit window while a program is running. Turbo Pascal momentarily switches to the user screen whenever a program pauses for data entry. Typing Alt-F5 (press and hold the Alt key while pressing the F5 key) causes the user screen to be displayed and allows you to review the program output when your program completes execution. However, some programmers prefer to view a program's output continually while the program is running.

Turbo Pascal allows you to open an Output window, which can be displayed on the screen at the same time as the Edit window. To do this, select the Output option from the Window menu, as shown in Fig. 2.13. This causes the Output window to appear at the bottom of the screen and selects it as the active window. You can use your mouse or the arrow keys to scroll through the Output window and display any output that does not appear in the Output window. To return to the Edit window and make it the active window, press the F6 key. The F6 key allows you to switch back and forth between the Edit window and the Ouput window.

When you return to the Edit window, you will notice that it now covers the Output window. To display both windows at the same time, you can reduce the size of the Edit window and uncover the Output window by using the mouse

Figure 2.13 Turbo Pascal Window Menu

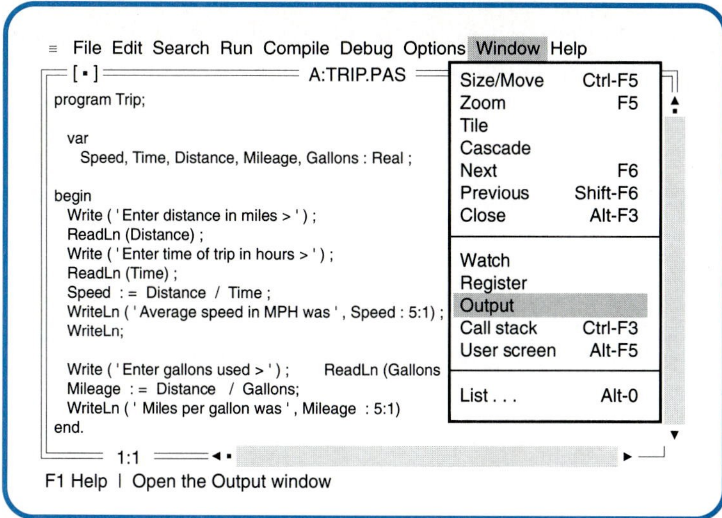

(click and drag the lower right corner of the Edit window) or by selecting the Size/Move option from the Window menu and using the arrow keys while pressing the Shift key. These operations are described in more detail in Appendix A and the Help screen from Size/Move (press F1). Figure 2.14 shows what the screen might look like with the Edit window resized and both windows displayed.

Figure 2.14 Turbo Pascal Output Window

```
≡ File Edit Search Run Compile Debug Options Window Help
[ ▪ ] A:TRIP.PAS 1 [↑]
program Trip;
  var
    Speed, Time, Distance, Mileage, Gallons : Real ;
begin
  Write ( 'Enter distance in miles > ' ) ;
  ReadLn (Distance) ;
  Write ( 'Enter time of trip in hours > ' ) ;
  ReadLn (Time) ;
  Speed : = Distance / Time;
  WriteLn ( 'Average speed in MPH was ' , Speed : 5:1) ;
1:1

Output 2
Enter distance in miles > 100
Enter time of trip in hours > 1.5
Average speed in MPH was 66.7

Enter gallons used > 25
Miles per gallon was 4.0

F1 Help  F2 Save  F3 Open  Alt-F9 Compile  F9 Make  F10 Menu
```

Exercises for Section 2.6

Self-Check

1. What is the primary difference between `Write` and `WriteLn`? When would you use `WriteLn` without an output list?
2. Correct the following statement:

```
WriteLn ("His salary is", Salary :2:10)
```

3. Show how the value `-15.564` (stored in `X`) would be printed using the following formats

```
X :8:4, X :8:3, X :8:2, X :8:1, X :8:0, X :8
```

4. Assuming `X` (type `Real`) is `12.335` and that `I` (type `Integer`) is `100`, show the output lines for the following statements. For clarity, use the symbol □ to denote a blank.

```
WriteLn ('X is ' :10, X :6:2, 'I is ' :4, I :5);
Write ('I is ' :10, I :1);
WriteLn ('X is ' :10, X :2:1);
```

Programming

1. If the variables `A`, `B`, and `C` are `504`, `302.558`, and `-12.31`, respectively, write a statement that will display the following line (for clarity, a □ denotes a space).

```
□504□□□□□302.56□□□□-12.3
```

2. Extend the program in Fig. 2.11 to handle dimes and quarters as well as nickels and pennies.

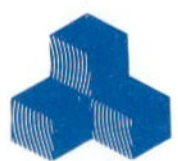

2.7 Printing Program Output

If you have a printer, you may wish to obtain a *hard copy* of your program output on paper. This can be done, as shown in Fig. 2.15. The statement

```
uses Printer;
```

must appear as the first statement following the program heading. This statement allows your program to access a previously compiled program unit named `Printer`. Unit `Printer` defines the file identifier `Lst` and associates it with the system printer. If a `Write` or `WriteLn` statement has the identifier `Lst` in front of its output list, Turbo Pascal will send the program output to the printer instead of to the video screen. To have blank lines appear in the printed output, use the statement

```
WriteLn (Lst);
```

Figure 2.15 Program Producing Output on Printer

Edit Window

```
program MilesPerHour;

  uses Printer;

  var
    Speed, Time, Distance : Real;

begin
  Write ('Enter distance in miles> ');
  ReadLn (Distance);
  Write ('Enter time of trip in hours> ');
  ReadLn (Time);
  WriteLn (Lst, 'Distance travelled is ', Distance :6:2);
  WriteLn (Lst, 'Travel time is ', Time :3:1);
  Speed := Distance / Time;
  WriteLn (Lst, 'Average speed is ', Speed :5:2)
end.
```

Output Window

```
Enter distance in miles> 100.0
Enter time of trip in hours> 1.5
```

Output to Printer

```
Distance travelled is 100.00
Travel time is 1.5
Average speed is 66.67
```

much like you would to display a blank line on the screen. We will discuss units in Chapter 8.

The Output window in Fig. 2.15 shows the prompting messages displayed by the program and the input data entered by the program user. These lines appear in the Output window, on the video screen as before. The three lines that are sent to the printer appear at the bottom of the figure. The first two lines *echo print* the data values and provide a permanent record of the input data; the last line displays the program result.

Logging Computer Output

Sometimes it is desirable to obtain a hard copy of the prompts displayed by an interactive program and the user's responses. We can do this by activating the MS-DOS *logging* feature, which causes all characters displayed on the screen to be sent to the printer as well. To activate the logging feature, press Ctrl-PrtScr (press and hold the Ctrl key and then press the PrtScr key) while in MS-DOS before you enter the Turbo Pascal integrated environment. To deactivate the logging feature, exit Turbo Pascal and press Ctrl-PrtScr again.

Exercise for Section 2.7

Self-Check

1. What changes are needed to print the results of the program in Fig. 2.10?

2.8 Overview of Data Types

Before we go any further, let's clarify exactly what is meant by a data type in a programming language. A *data type* is a set of values and a set of operations on those values. The data type of the object stored in a particular memory cell determines how the bit pattern in that cell is interpreted. For example, a bit pattern that represents a type `Integer` object is different from a bit pattern that represents a type `Char` object or a program instruction.

A *standard data type* is a data type that is predefined in the programming language (for example, `Real`, `Integer`, `Char`). Besides using standard data types, programmers can define their own data types in Pascal.

The standard data types represent familiar objects. For example, the data type `Real` is the set of real numbers (in the mathematical sense) that can be processed in Pascal. Every type `Real` object in Pascal is a real number; however, not all real numbers can be represented. Some real numbers are too large or too small, and some real numbers cannot be precisely represented because of the finite size of a memory cell (more on this in Chapter 7).

The normal arithmetic operations (+, −, *, /) for real numbers and the assignment operation (:=) can be performed on type `Real` objects in Pascal. Input/output operations are performed using procedures `Read` (described later), `ReadLn`, `Write`, and `WriteLn`.

The other common data type used to represent numbers is type `Integer`. Type `Integer` objects in Pascal correspond to the integers in mathematics (for example, −77, 0, 999, +999). However, because of the finite size of a memory cell, not all integers can be represented. Turbo Pascal supports other numeric data types, which are derived from the `Integer` and `Real` types. These will be described in Chapter 7.

The standard identifier `MaxInt` is a constant that represents the largest integer that can be represented in each Pascal system. Use the statement

```
WriteLn (MaxInt);
```

to display that value (32767 in Turbo Pascal).

The arithmetic, assignment, and input/output operations listed for type `Real` objects can also be performed on type `Integer` objects. Chapter 7 discusses the integer division operators `div` and `mod`; Appendix B lists the Pascal operators.

`Real` and `Integer` data types differ in one basic way: real objects can store a number with a decimal point and a fractional part, whereas integer variables can store only a whole number. For this reason, type `Integer` objects are more restricted in their use. We often use them to represent a count of items (for example, our count of coins), because a count must always be a whole number.

Objects of a data type may be variables, constants, or literals; a *literal* is a value that appears directly in a program. A type `Real` literal is a number that begins with a digit and contains a decimal point followed by at least one digit (for example, `0.112`, `456.0`, `123.456`). A type `Real` literal may have a *scale factor*, which is the capital letter `E` followed by an optional sign and an integer (for example, `0.112E3`, `456.0E-2`). The scale factor may also follow a string of digits without a decimal point (for example, `123E6` and `123.0E6` are equivalent `Real` literals). A scale factor means "multiply the number before the letter `E` by `10` raised to the power appearing after the letter `E`" (for example, `0.112E3` is `112.0`, `456.0E-2` is `4.56`). A `Real` literal may be preceded by a plus or a minus sign when it appears in a program. Table 2.6 shows examples of valid and invalid `Real` literals.

Table 2.6 Valid and Invalid Real Literals

Valid Real Literals	Invalid Real Literals
`3.14159`	`150` (no decimal point)
`0.005`	`.12345` (no digit before the decimal point)
`12345.0`	`16.` (no digit after the decimal point)
`15.0E-04` (value is 0.0015)	`-15E-0.3` (0.3 is an invalid power)
`2.345E2` (value is 234.5)	`12.5E.3` (.3 is an invalid power)
`12E+6` (value is 12000000)	`.123E3` (.123 is an invalid real)
`1.15E-3` (value is 0.00115)	

The last valid literal in the table, `1.15E-3`, has the same value as 1.15×10^{-3} in normal scientific notation, where the exponent $^{-3}$ causes the decimal point to be moved left three digits. A positive exponent causes the decimal point to be moved to the right; the plus sign can be omitted when the exponent is positive.

Another standard data type is type `Char`. Type `Char` variables can be used to store any single character value. A type `Char` literal must be enclosed in single apostrophes (for example, `'A'`); however, you don't use apostrophes when you enter character data at a terminal. When the `ReadLn` procedure reads character data into a type `Char` variable, the next character you enter at the terminal is stored in that variable. You can enter the blank character by pressing the space bar; a blank is written in a program as the literal `' '`.

■ Example 2.7

The program in Fig. 2.16 first reads and echos three characters entered at the keyboard. Next, it prints them in reverse order and enclosed in asterisks. Each character is stored in a variable of type `Char`; the character value `'*'` is associated with the constant `Border`.

The line

```
WriteLn (Border, Third, Second, First, Border);
```

displays the three characters in reverse order. As shown in the program output, each character value is printed in a single print position. The second character read in the sample run of Fig. 2.16 is a blank. ■

Figure 2.16 Program for Example 2.7

Edit Window

```
program Reverse;

  const
    Border = '*';

  var
    First, Second, Third : Char;

begin
  Write ('Enter 3 characters> ');
  ReadLn (First, Second, Third);
  WriteLn (Border, Third, Second, First, Border)
end.
```

Output Window

```
Enter 3 characters> E K
*K E*
```

In Fig. 2.16, the string literal `'Enter 3 characters> '` is displayed as a prompt. As in this case, strings are often used as prompts and to clarify program output. Strings cannot, however, be stored in type `Char` variables. In Turbo Pascal (but not standard Pascal), they may be stored in string variables (type `string`). String variables will be discussed in greater detail later in the text.

The fourth standard data type is type `Boolean` (named after the mathematician George Boole). `True` and `False` are the only values associated with this data type. You will see examples of Boolean expressions (expressions that evaluate to `True` or `False`) in Chapter 3.

Exercises for Section 2.8

Self-Check

1. Which of the following values are valid? Which are invalid? Identify the data types of the valid values.

```
15 'XYZ' '*' $ 25.123 15. -999 .123 'x' "x"
'9' '-5' True 'True'
```

Programming

1. Write a program that stores the values `'X'`, `'0'`, `1.345E10`, and `True` in separate memory cells. Your program should read the first three values as data items; use an assignment statement to store the last value.

2.9 Common Programming Errors

One of the first things you will discover in writing programs is that a program rarely runs correctly the first time it is executed. Murphy's Law, "If something can go wrong, it will," seems to be written with the computer programming student in mind. In fact, errors are so common that they have their own special name—*bugs*—and the process of correcting them is called *debugging a program.* To alert you to potential problems, we will provide a section on common programming errors at the end of each chapter.

When the Turbo Pascal compiler detects an error, the computer displays an *error message* indicating that you have made a mistake and what the likely cause of the error might be. You will be placed in the editor with the cursor positioned on the incorrect statement. Unfortunately, the error messages are often difficult to interpret and are sometimes misleading. Even the editor cursor position should be regarded only as indicating the approximate position of the error. If you press F1 after an error message is displayed, the Turbo Pascal Help system will provide additional information describing the error. As you gain experience you will become more proficient at locating and correcting errors.

There are two basic categories of error messages: syntax error messages and run-time error messages. *Syntax errors* are detected and displayed by the compiler as it attempts to translate your programs. If a statement has a syntax error, then it cannot be translated and your program will not be executed.

Run-time errors are detected by the computer and are displayed during the execution of a program. A run-time error occurs when the user directs the computer to perform an illegal operation, such as dividing a number by zero or manipulating undefined or invalid data.

Correcting Syntax Errors

The payroll program in Fig. 2.17 contains two syntax errors. Figure 2.17 shows the Edit window after the first attempt to compile this program. The error message suggests that the problem with the statement is an `Invalid subrange base type`, when the real problem is that the symbol : was used incorrectly in place of the symbol = in a constant declaration.

Figure 2.18 shows the Edit window after the first error is corrected and the program recompiled. In this case, the error message indicates that the compiler cannot find a declaration for the identifier `Net`. After you correct this variable declaration error, the program should compile successfully.

The process of removing syntax errors, one at a time, can be a very lengthy process. It is advisable to *desk check* (proofread) your program carefully before compiling it the first time. Two of the more common errors made by beginning programmers are forgetting to declare (or misspelling) identifier names and omitting semicolons. Both of these errors are easily discovered by careful desk checking.

Syntax errors are often caused by the improper use of apostrophes with

Figure 2.17 Bad Constant Declaration

```
≡ File Edit Search Run Compile Debug Options Window Help
[•] ═══════════════ A:PAYROLL.PAS ═══════════════ 1═[↕]
Error 27: Invalid subrange base type.

const
  Tax : 25.0 ;

var
  Hours, Rate, Gross : Real ;

begin
  WriteLn ( 'Enter hours worked' ) ;
  ReadLn (Hours) ;
  WriteLn ( 'Enter hourly rate' ) ;
  ReadLn (Rate) ;
  Gross : = Hours * Rate ;
  Net : = Gross - Tax ;
  WriteLn ( 'Gross pay is $ ' , Gross) ;
  WriteLn ( 'Net pay is   $ ' , Net)
end.
═══ 4:13 ═══◄■
F1 Help  F2 Save  F3 Open  Alt-F9 Compile  F9 Make  F10 Menu
```

strings. Make sure that you always use a single quote or apostrophe to begin and end a string; double quotes cannot be used to begin or end a string.

Another common syntax error is a missing or extra apostrophe in a string. If the apostrophe at the end of the string is missing, the Turbo Pascal compiler will display the error message `String constant exceeds line`.

Figure 2.18 Unknown Identifier

```
≡ File Edit Search Run Compile Debug Options Window Help
[•] ═══════════════ A:PAYROLL.PAS ═══════════════ 1═[↕]
Error 3 : Unknown identifier.

const
  Tax = 25.0 ;

var
  Hours, Rate, Gross : Real ;

begin
  WriteLn ( 'Enter hours worked' ) ;
  ReadLn (Hours) ;
  WriteLn ( 'Enter hourly rate' ) ;
  ReadLn (Rate) ;
  Gross : = Hours * Rate ;
  Net : = Gross - Tax ;
  WriteLn ( 'Gross pay is $ ' , Gross) ;
  WriteLn ( 'Net pay is   $ ' , Net)
end.
═══ 15:3 ═══◄■
F1 Help  F2 Save  F3 Open  Alt-F9 Compile  F9 Make  F10 Menu
```

The string below contains an internal apostrophe:

```
WriteLn ('Enter Joe's nickname> ');
```

The compiler will assume that the apostrophe used to indicate possession (`Joe's`) is terminating the string. This string must be entered as

```
WriteLn ('Enter Joe''s nickname> ');
```

where the two consecutive apostrophes are needed to indicate a single apostrophe inside a string.

Run-time Errors

Figure 2.19 shows an example of a run-time error for a program executed from within the Turbo Pascal environment. The program compiles successfully, but contains no statement assigning a value to the variable `X` before the assignment statement

```
Z := Y / X;
```

is executed. In this situation the Turbo Pascal compiler assigns the default value `0.0` to `X`. When the statement is executed, a division by zero run-time error occurs, which is indicated by the error message

```
Error 200: Division by Zero
```

You will be placed in the Turbo Pascal editor with the cursor positioned at the beginning of the assignment statement. Pressing the F1 key (for Help) causes a window to pop up showing possible causes of the run-time error. You

Figure 2.19 Program with a Run-time Error

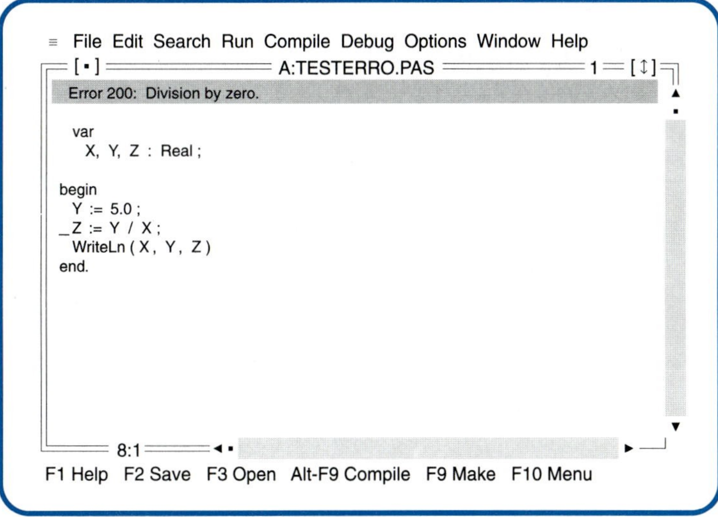

should insert a statement that assigns a non-zero value to X; it is not good programming practice to allow the compiler to assign default values to your variables.

Another common run-time error is "arithmetic overflow." This error occurs when a program attempts to store a number that is too large in the storage area allocated to a variable. Appendix F shows the code numbers and error messages for all Turbo Pascal syntax and run-time errors.

As indicated earlier, debugging a program can be very time-consuming. The best approach is to plan your programs carefully and desk check them to eliminate bugs before compiling the programs. If you are not sure of the syntax for a particular statement, look it up in the text or in the syntax guide provided inside the covers. If you follow this approach, you will save yourself much time and trouble.

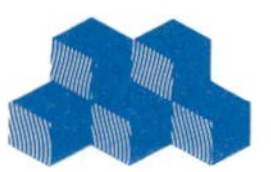

Chapter Review

You have seen how to use the Pascal programming language to perform some fundamental operations. You have learned how to instruct the computer to read information into memory, perform some simple computations, and print the results of those computations. All of this was done using symbols (punctuation marks, variable names, and special operators such as *, –, and +) that are familiar, easy to remember, and easy to use. You do not have to know very much about your computer to understand and use Pascal.

The remainder of this text introduces more features of the Pascal language and provides rules for using those features. You must remember throughout that, unlike the rules of English, the rules of Pascal are precise and allow no exceptions. The compiler cannot translate Pascal instructions that violate these rules. Remember to declare every identifier used as a variable or a constant and to separate program statements with semicolons.

New Pascal Constructs

Table 2.7 describes the new Pascal constructs introduced in this chapter.

Table 2.7 Summary of New Pascal Constructs

Construct	Effect
Program Heading	
`program Payroll;`	Identifies `Payroll` as the name of the program.
Constant Declaration	

`const`
`  Tax = 25.00;`
`  Star = '*';`
	Associates the constant `Tax` with the real value `25.00` and the constant `Star` with the type `Char` value `'*'`.

Table 2.7 Summary of New Pascal Constructs, *continued*

Construct	Effect

Variable Declaration
`var`
`  X, Y, Z : Real;`
`  Me, It   : Integer;`
	Allocates memory cells named `X`, `Y`, and `Z` for storage of real numbers and `Me` and `It` for storage of integers.

Assignment Statement `Distance := Speed * Time`	Assigns the product of `Speed` and `Time` as the value of `Distance`.
ReadLn Procedure `ReadLn (Hours, Rate)`	Enters data into the variables `Hours` and `Rate`.
Write Procedure `Write ('Net = ', Net :4:2)`	Displays the string `'Net = '` followed by the value of `Net` printed in a field of four columns and rounded to two decimal places.
WriteLn Procedure `WriteLn (X, Y)`	Prints the values of `X` and `Y` and advances the cursor to the next line.
Assign Procedure (Optional) `Assign (InData, 'B:INDATA.DAT')`	Associates internal file name `InData` with the disk file `B:INDATA.DAT`.
Reset Procedure (Optional) `Reset (InData)`	Prepares file `InData` for reading.
ReadLn with File (Optional) `ReadLn (InData, X, Y)`	Reads values of `X` and `Y` from a line of file `InData`.
Close Procedure (Optional) `Close (InData)`	Releases the disk file associated with `InData`.

Sending Output to Printer (Optional)
`Uses Printer;`
`WriteLn (Lst, 'X is ', X);`
	Indicates that program unit `Printer` will be used to send program output to file `Lst` (the printer).

✓ Quick-Check Exercises

1. What value is assigned to `X` by the following statement?

```
X := 25.0 * 3.0 / 2.5
```

2. What value is assigned to X by the following statement, assuming X is 10.0?

```
X := X - 20.0
```

3. Show the exact form of the output line displayed when X is 3.456.

```
WriteLn ('Three values of X are ', X :4:1, '*', X :5:2, '*', X: 6:3);
```

4. Show the exact form of the output line when N is 345.

```
WriteLn ('Three values of N are ', N :4, '*', N :5, '*', N :1);
```

5. What data type would you use to represent the following items: number of children at school, a letter grade on an exam, the average number of school days students are absent each year?
6. When data are entered into an interactive program, which procedure is called first, ReadLn or WriteLn?
7. When data is entered into a batch program, which procedure is called first, ReadLn or WriteLn?
8. If procedure ReadLn is reading two numbers, what character is typed after the first number? What is typed after the second number?
9. If procedure ReadLn is reading two characters, what character is typed after the first character? What is typed after the second character?
10. How does the computer determine how many data values to enter when a ReadLn operation is performed?
11. How does a program user determine how many data values to enter when a ReadLn operation is performed?
12. What kind of errors does the compiler identify?

Answers to Quick-Check Exercises

1. 30.0
2. -10.0
3. `Three values of X are  3.5* 3.46* 3.456`
4. `Three values of N are  345*  345*345`
5. Integer, Character, Real
6. WriteLn, to display a prompt
7. ReadLn, to get the data
8. a blank, the Enter key
9. the second character, the Enter key
10. It depends on the number of variables in the input list.
11. from reading the prompt
12. syntax errors

Review Questions

1. Are double or single quotation marks used as string delimiters?
2. Which of the following variables are syntactically correct?

```
Income      Two Fold
1time       C3PO
const       Income#1
Tom's       item
```

3. What is illegal about the following declarations and statement?

```
const
  MyPi = 3.14159;
var
  C, R : Real;

begin
  MyPi := C / (2 * R * R);
```

4. What computer action is required by the following statement?

```
var Cell : Real;
```

5. Write a program to read a five-character name and print the name out backward.
6. If the average size of a family is 2.8 and this value is stored in the variable `FamilySize`, provide a Pascal statement to display this fact in a readable way (leave the cursor on the same line).
7. List five standard data types of Turbo Pascal. Which is not found in standard Pascal?
8. Convert the following program statements to read and echo data in batch mode.

```
Write ('Enter three numbers separated by spaces> ');
ReadLn (X, Y, Z);
WriteLn ('Enter two characters> ');
ReadLn (Ch1, Ch2);
```

9. Write a program that reads in an integer value, doubles it, subtracts 10, and displays the result.

Programming Projects

1. Write a program to convert a temperature in degrees Fahrenheit to degrees Celsius. Use the formula

$$Celsius = (5/9) \times (Fahrenheit - 32)$$

2. Write a program that reads three data items into variables `X`, `Y`, and `Z` and then finds and prints their product and sum.
3. Write a program that reads in the weight (in pounds) of an object and then computes and prints its weight in kilograms and grams. (Hint: 1 pound equals 0.453592 kilogram and 453.59237 grams.)
4. Write a program that prints your first initial as a block letter. (Hint: Use a 6-by-6 grid for the letter and print six strings. Each string should consist of asterisks interspersed with blanks.)
5. If a human heart beats on the average of once a second for 78 years, how many times does it beat in a lifetime? (Use 365.25 for days in a year.) Rerun your program for a heart rate of 75 beats per minute.
6. Write a program that reads in the length and width of a rectangular yard and the length and width of a rectangular house situated in the yard. Your program should compute the time required to cut the grass at the rate of 2 square meters a second.
7. Write a program that reads in the numerators and denominators of two fractions and prints the numerators and denominators of the fractions that represent the sum and product of the two fractions. Your program should also print the percent equivalents of the resulting sum and product fractions.

8. The Pythagorean theorem states that the sum of the squares of the sides of a right triangle is equal to the square of the hypotenuse. For example, if two sides of a right triangle have lengths 3 and 4, then the hypotenuse must have a length of 5. The integers 3, 4, and 5 together form a *pythagorean triple*. There is an infinite number of such triples. Given two positive integers, m and n, where $m > n$, a pythagorean triple can be generated by the following formulas:

   $$side1 = m^2 - n^2$$
   $$side2 = 2mn$$
   $$hypotenuse = m^2 + n^2$$

   Write a program that reads in values for m and n and prints the values of the pythagorean triple generated by the formulas above.

3

Problem Solving and Procedures

All your life, you have been solving problems using your own intuitive strategies. Problem solving on a computer requires that you follow a more formal approach. This chapter will help you learn how to analyze a problem and devise an *algorithm*, or list of steps, to describe a possible solution. You will also learn how to verify that a proposed algorithm solves its intended problem.

In this chapter, we show you how to solve a problem by breaking it up into smaller, more manageable subproblems. We also introduce an important Pascal construct, the procedure. Procedures allow us to write each subproblem's solution as a separate group of Pascal statements.

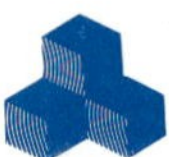

3.1 Representing and Refining Algorithms

Divide and Conquer

One of the most fundamental methods of problem solving is to break a large problem into several smaller *subproblems*. In this way, we can solve a large problem one step at a time, rather than attempt to provide the entire solution at once. This technique is often called *divide and conquer*.

As an example, let's look forward to the year 2000. Our household robot, Robbie, helps us with some simple chores. Each morning, we would like Robbie to serve us breakfast. Unfortunately, Robbie is an early production model, and to get him to perform even the simplest task, we must provide him with a detailed list of instructions. In this case, the problem to be solved is getting Robbie to serve breakfast.

Case Study: Robbie Serving Breakfast

Problem

In Fig. 3.1, Robbie is at point R (for Robbie). We want Robbie to retrieve our favorite box of cereal (at point C) and bring it to the table (at point T) in the next room.

Design Overview

We can accomplish our goal by instructing Robbie to perform the following four steps, or subproblems.

1. Move from point R to point C.
2. Retrieve the cereal box at point C.
3. Move from point C to point T.
4. Place the cereal box on the table at point T.

Solving these four subproblems will give us the solution to the original problem.

We can attack each subproblem independently. To solve any of these problems, however, we must know which basic operations Robbie can perform.

Assume that Robbie can rotate or turn to face any direction, move straight ahead, and grasp and release specified objects. Given this information, subproblems 2 and 4 are basic operations, provided Robbie is in the correct position. First, we will concentrate on moving Robbie (subproblems 1 and 3).

In solving the first subproblem,

1. Move from point R to point C

we must allow for the fact that Robbie can move in only one direction at a time, and that direction is straight ahead. Consequently, the steps required to solve subproblem 1 are

1.1 Turn to face point C.
1.2 Move from point R to point C.

Subproblem 3 can be solved in a similar way. However, since Robbie cannot walk through walls, the steps for solving subproblem 3 might be

3.1 Turn to face the doorway (point D) between the rooms.
3.2 Move from point C to point D.
3.3 Turn to face point T.
3.4 Move from point D to point T.

To summarize the process so far, we divided the original problem into four subproblems, all of which can be solved independently. We then broke up two of those subproblems into even smaller subproblems.

Now look at the complete list of the steps required to solve our problem. A list of steps to solve a problem is called an *algorithm*. The process of adding detail to a solution algorithm (for example, rewriting step 1 as steps 1.1 and 1.2) is called *stepwise refinement.*

Algorithm

1. Move from point R to point C.
   1.1 Turn to face point C.
   1.2 Move from point R to point C.
2. Retrieve the cereal box at point C.

Figure 3.1 Robbie Serving Breakfast

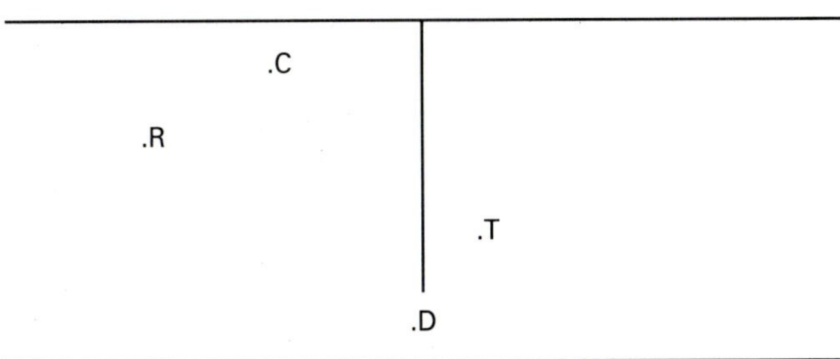

3. Move from point C to point T.
   3.1 Turn to face the doorway (point D) between the rooms.
   3.2 Move from point C to point D.
   3.3 Turn to face point T.
   3.4 Move from point D to point T.
4. Place the cereal box on the table at point T.

Algorithms in Everyday Life

Algorithms are not unique to the study of robots or computer programming. You have probably used algorithms to solve problems without being aware of it. Let's look at an everyday problem for which we can create an algorithm.

Case Study: Changing a Flat Tire

Problem

You are driving a car with two friends and suddenly get a flat tire. Fortunately, you have a spare tire and a jack in the trunk.

Design Overview

After pulling over to the side of the road, you might decide to divide the problem of changing a tire into the subproblems below.

Algorithm

1. Get the jack and jack up the car.
2. Loosen the lug nuts from the flat tire and remove it.
3. Get the spare tire, place it on the wheel, and tighten the lug nuts.
4. Lower the car.
5. Secure the jack and the flat tire in the trunk.

Since these steps are relatively independent, you might decide to assign subproblem 1 to friend A, subproblem 2 to friend B, subproblem 3 to yourself, and so on. If friend A has used a jack before, then the whole process should proceed smoothly; however, if friend A does not know how to use a jack, you need to refine step 1 further.

Step 1 Refinement

1.1 Get the jack from the trunk.
1.2 Place the jack under the car near the flat tire.
1.3 Insert the jack handle in the jack.
1.4 Place a block of wood under the car to keep it from rolling.
1.5 Jack up the car until there is enough room for the spare tire.

Step 1.4 requires a bit of decision making on your friend's part. Because the actual placement of the block of wood depends on whether the car is facing uphill or downhill, friend A needs to refine step 1.4.

Step 1.4 Refinement

1.4.1 If the car is facing uphill, place the block of wood in back of a tire that is not flat; if the car is facing downhill, place the block of wood in front of a tire that is not flat.

Finally, step 1.5 involves a repetitive action: moving the jack handle until there is sufficient room to put on the spare tire. It may take a few attempts to complete step 1.5.

Step 1.5 Refinement

1.5.1 Move the jack handle repeatedly until the car is high enough off the ground that the spare tire can be put on the wheel.

Sequential Execution, Conditional Execution, and Repetition

The algorithm for changing a flat tire has three categories of action: sequential execution, conditional execution, and repetition. *Sequential execution* simply means to carry out steps 1.1 through 1.5 in the sequence listed. Step 1.4.1 illustrates *conditional execution* in that the placement of the block of wood depends on the angle of inclination of the car. Step 1.5.1 illustrates *repetition.*

These three categories of action must be possible in a computer program as well. A program carries out its executable statements in sequence. A program also may contain *control statements* that cause conditional execution and repetition. Chapter 4 describes one Pascal statement for specifying conditional execution, and Chapter 5 describes one Pascal statement for specifying repetition.

Understanding the Problem

An important skill in human communication is the ability to listen carefully. Often we are too busy thinking about our response to really hear what the other person is saying, which can lead to a lack of understanding between the speaker and listener.

Many of us suffer from a similar difficulty when we attempt to solve problems that are presented either verbally or in writing. We do not pay close enough attention to the problem statement to determine exactly what is being asked. Consequently, either we are unable to solve the stated problem or our problem solution is incorrect because it solves the wrong problem.

This text is concerned with improving your problem-solving skills, and presents hints and techniques for problem solving. To successfully solve a problem, you must analyze the problem statement carefully before you attempt to solve it. You may need to read each problem statement two or three times. The first time, get a general idea of what is being asked. The second time, try to answer these questions:

What information should the solution provide?
What data do I have to work with?

The answer to the first question will tell you the desired results, or the *problem outputs*. The answer to the second question will tell you the data provided, or the *problem inputs*. It may be helpful to underline the phrases in the problem statement that identify the inputs and the outputs, as in the problem statement discussed in the next section.

Exercise for Section 3.1

Self-Check

1. Write an algorithm for preparing and warming a baby's formula. Make sure your algorithm prevents you from feeding the baby if the formula is too cold or too hot.

3.2 Problem Solving Illustrated

In this section we apply the problem-solving principles discussed earlier. We begin with the problem statement and finish with a computer program that solves the problem.

Case Study: Finding the Area and Circumference of a Circle

Problem

Read in the radius of a circle and compute and print its area and circumference.

Design Overview

After identifying the problem inputs and outputs, we must determine the amount and type of memory required to store those data. Clearly, one memory cell is required for the input data and two memory cells are required for the output information. All memory cells should be type `Real` because the inputs and outputs can contain fractional parts. You must also choose meaningful variable names for those cells.

Data Requirements

Problem Inputs

the radius of a circle (`Radius : Real`)

Problem Outputs
the area of the circle (`Area : Real`)
the circumference of the circle (`Circum : Real`)

Once you know the problem inputs and outputs, you should list the steps necessary to solve the problem. It is important that you pay close attention to the order of the steps. The initial algorithm follows.

Initial Algorithm

1. Read the value of `Radius`.
2. Find the area.
3. Find the circumference.
4. Print the values of the area and the circumference.

Algorithm Refinements

Next, refine any steps that do not have an obvious solution (for instance, steps 2 and 3).

Step 2 Refinement
2.1 Use the formula
`Area` $= \pi \times$ `(Radius)`^{2}

Step 3 Refinement
3.1 Use the formula
`Circum` $= 2 \times \pi \times$ `Radius`

Coding

Now you must implement the algorithm as a program by first writing the declarations for the program using the problem input and output descriptions. You must also declare any additional variables or constants introduced in the algorithm. For example, we will store the value of π (3.14159) in the constant `MyPi`. (We will see an easier way to refer to this value in Chapter 7.) Next, write the algorithm steps in Pascal, implementing refined steps where applicable.

Following this procedure gives the program shown in Fig. 3.2. Algorithm steps 1, 2.1, 3.1, and 4 are implemented in the program body following the type declarations. The purpose of the curly braces is discussed in the next section.

Figure 3.2 Finding the Area and the Circumference of a Circle

Edit Window

```
program AreaAndCircum;

{Finds and prints the area and circumference of a circle}

  const
    MyPi = 3.14159;
```

```
var
  Radius,           {input - radius of a circle}
  Area,             {output - area of a circle}
  Circum : Real;    {output - circumference of a circle}

begin {AreaAndCircum}
  {Read the value of the radius}
  Write ('Enter radius> ');
  ReadLn (Radius);

  {Find the area}
  Area := MyPi * Radius * Radius;

  {Find the circumference}
  Circum := 2.0 * MyPi * Radius;

  {Print the values of Area and Circum}
  WriteLn ('The area is ', Area :4:2);
  WriteLn ('The circumference is ', Circum :4:2)
end. {AreaAndCircum}
```

Output Window

```
Enter radius> 5.0
The area is 78.54
The circumference is 31.42
```

Exercises for Section 3.2

Self-Check

1. Describe the problem inputs and outputs and the algorithm for computing an employee's gross salary given the hours worked and the hourly rate.
2. Describe the problem inputs and outputs and the algorithm for the following problem: Read in a pair of numbers and determine the sum and average of the two numbers.

Programming

1. Write a program for question 2 in the self-check exercises.

3.3 Comments and Documentation

The program in Fig. 3.2 contains some English phrases enclosed in curly braces. Programmers use such phrases, called *comments*, to make the program easier to understand by describing the purpose of the program (see the first comment line), the use of identifiers (see the comments in the variable declarations), and the purpose of each program step (see the comments in the program body). Comments are an important part of the *documentation* of a program because they help others read and understand the program. The compiler, however, ignores comments, and they are not translated into machine language.

As shown in Fig. 3.2, a comment can appear by itself on a program line, at the end of a line after a statement, or embedded in a statement. The comment at the end of the second line

```
var
  Radius,          {input - radius of a circle}
```

is embedded within the variable declaration, which is continued following the comment. This text documents the use of most variables in that way. The next two displays describe the syntax and use of comments.

SYNTAX DISPLAY

Comment

Form: `{comment}`

Example:
```
{This is a comment}
(* and so is this *)
{One comment (* inside another *) comment}
```

Interpretation: A left curly brace indicates the start of a comment; a right curly brace indicates the end of a comment. Alternately, `(*` and `*)` can mark the beginning and the end, respectively, of a comment. Comments are listed with the program but are otherwise ignored by the Pascal compiler.

Note: Turbo Pascal (but not standard Pascal) allows comments to be nested inside one another. If the first comment begins with `{` the second must begin with `(*` and vice versa.

PROGRAM STYLE

Using Comments

Comments make a program more readable because they describe the purpose of the program and the use of each identifier. For example, the comment in the declaration

```
var
  Radius,          {input - radius of a circle}
```

describes the use of variable `Radius`.

Place comments within the program body to describe the purpose of each section of the program. Generally, you should include one comment in the program body for each major algorithm step. Make sure a comment within the program body describes what the step does rather than simply restate the step in English. For example, the comment

```
{Find the area}
Area := MyPi * Radius * Radius
```

is more descriptive than and, hence, preferable to

```
{Multiply the Radius by itself and MyPi}
Area := MyPi * Radius * Radius
```

Begin each program with a header section that consists of a series of comments specifying

- the programmer's name
- the date of the current version
- a brief description of what the program does

If you write the program for a class assignment, you should also list the class identification and your instructor's name.

Exercise for Section 3.3

Self-Check

1. Explain what is wrong with the following comments:

```
{This is a comment? *)
(* How about this one (*it seems like a comment*) doesn't it *)
```

3.4 Subproblems and Procedures

The Structure Chart

As mentioned earlier, one of the most fundamental ideas in problem solving is dividing a problem into subproblems and solving each subproblem independently of the others. In the simple problem of finding the area and the circumference of a circle, this was not a difficult task. Only two subproblems required refinement, and that was not extensive. In many situations, one or more subproblems may require significant refinement, as you will see in the next problem.

Case Study: Printing a Mother's Day Message

Problem

You would like to do something special for your mother on Mother's Day. You decide to write a Pascal program to print the message HI MOM in large capital letters.

Design Overview

You can interpret this problem in more than one way. You could simply print HI MOM as it appears here, but that would not be too impressive. It would be more unusual to use large block letters, as shown in Fig. 3.3. Because program output tends to run from the top of the screen downward, it is easier and more interesting to print the letters in a vertical column rather than across the screen.

Figure 3.3 Mother's Day Message

```
*      *
*      *
*      *
********
*      *
*      *
*      *

   **
   **
   **
   **
   **
   **
   **



*      *
**    **
* *  * *
*  **  *
*      *
*      *
*      *

  ****
 **  **
**    **
*      *
**    **
 **  **
  ****

*      *
**    **
* *  * *
*  **  *
*      *
*      *
*      *
```

Initial Algorithm

1. Print the word HI in block letters.
2. Print three blank lines.
3. Print the word MOM in block letters.

Algorithm Refinements

The obvious refinements for each step are shown next.

Step 1 Refinement

1.1 Print the letter H.
1.2 Print the letter I.

Figure 3.4 Structure Chart for Mother's Day Message

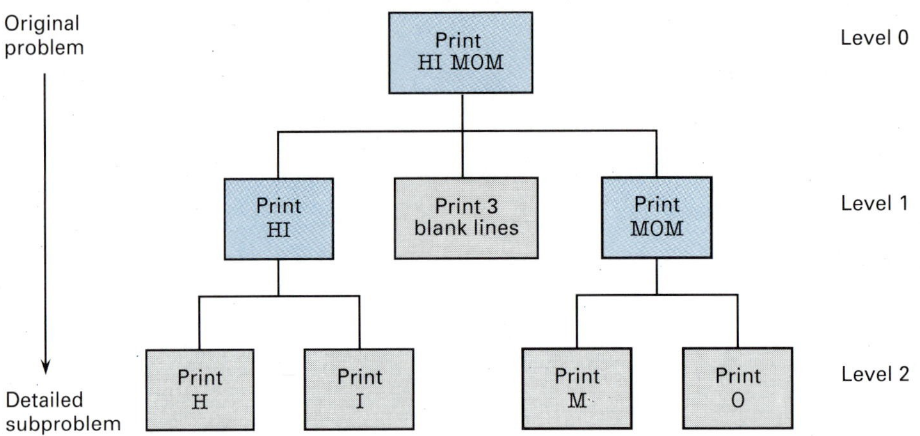

Step 3 Refinement

3.1 Print the letter M.
3.2 Print the letter O.
3.3 Print the letter M.

We can illustrate the steps in the problem-solving process with a diagram that shows the algorithm subproblems and their interdependencies. An example of such a diagram, called a *structure chart*, is shown in Fig. 3.4.

As we trace down this diagram, we go from an abstract problem to a more detailed subproblem. The original problem is shown at the top, or level 0, of the structure chart. The major subproblems appear at level 1. The different subproblems that result from the refinement of each level-1 step are shown at level 2 and are connected to their respective level-1 subproblems. The right side of the structure chart shows that the subproblem *Print MOM* (level 1) depends on the solutions to the subproblems *Print M* and *Print O* (level 2). Since the subproblem *Print 3 blank lines* is not refined further, no level-2 subproblems are connected to it.

Structure charts are intended to show the structural relationship between subproblems. The algorithm (not the structure chart) shows the order in which you must carry out each step to solve the problem.

Exercises for Section 3.4

Self-Check

1. Draw the structure chart for the case study in section 3.2.
2. Why was it all right to show the step *Print M* only once in the structure chart?

3.5 Procedures

The structure chart proceeds from the original problem at the top level down to its detailed subproblems at the bottom level. It would be convenient to follow this *top-down* approach when we code a program, and the procedure construct in Pascal enables us to do so.

A Pascal *procedure* is a grouping of program statements into a single program unit. Just like ReadLn and WriteLn, each Pascal procedure that we write can be activated through the execution of a procedure call statement. If we assume that we have procedures available that implement each of the level-2 subproblems in Fig. 3.4, we can use the following code fragment to implement the level-1 subproblem *Print HI*.

```
{Print HI.}
PrintH;
PrintI;
```

This code fragment contains two procedure call statements. During program execution, the procedure call statement

```
PrintH;
```

causes the statements contained in the body of procedure PrintH to be executed. The next section describes how to write procedure PrintH.

Figure 3.5 shows the body of the Mother's Day program, with the solution to each subproblem at level 2 in Fig. 3.4 implemented as a separate procedure. The program body (called the *main program*) implements the original algorithm. The program body begins with the code for step 1 (*Print HI*), which consists of the two procedure call statements previously listed. The code for step 2 (*Print three blank lines*) consists of three calls to procedure WriteLn. In the code for step 3 (*Print MOM*), the procedure call statement

```
PrintM
```

appears twice because the letter M must be printed twice.

Figure 3.5 Main Program Body for the Mother's Day Problem

```
begin {Mother}
  {Print HI}
  PrintH;
  PrintI;

  {Print three blank lines}
  WriteLn;
  WriteLn;
  WriteLn;

  {Print MOM}
  PrintM;
  PrintO;
  PrintM
end. {Mother}
```

SYNTAX DISPLAY

Procedure Call Statement

Form: *pname*

Example: `PrintM`

Interpretation: The procedure call statement initiates the execution of procedure *pname*. After *pname* has finished executing, the program statement that follows the procedure call is executed.

Declaring Procedures

Just like other identifiers in Pascal, a procedure must be declared before it can be referenced in a program body. Figure 3.6 shows the declaration for procedure `PrintM`.

Figure 3.6 Procedure PrintM

```
procedure PrintM;

{Prints M.}

begin {PrintM}
  WriteLn ('*       *');
  WriteLn ('**     **');
  WriteLn ('* *   * *');
  WriteLn ('*  **   *');
  WriteLn ('*       *');
  WriteLn ('*       *');
  WriteLn ('*       *');
  WriteLn
end; {PrintM}
```

A procedure declaration begins with a *procedure heading*, which consists of the word `procedure` followed by the procedure name (an identifier) and a semicolon. A comment describing the purpose of the procedure comes next, followed by the *procedure body*. The procedure body always starts with `begin` and ends with `end;`. In Fig. 3.6, the procedure body contains the seven `WriteLn` statements that cause the computer to print the block letter M, followed by an additional `WriteLn` statement that displays a blank line. The procedure call statement

```
PrintM
```

causes these `WriteLn` statements to execute.

In this text, the `begin` and `end` that bracket a procedure body are followed by a comment that identifies the procedure's name. The comment is added for clarity and is not required by Pascal. Pascal does, however, require the semicolon following `end`.

Each procedure declaration may contain declarations for its own constants, variables, and even for other procedures. These identifiers are considered *local* to the procedure; in other words, they can be referenced only within the procedure (more on this later).

SYNTAX DISPLAY

Procedure Declaration

Form:
```
procedure pname;
  local declarations
begin
  procedure body
end;
```
Example:
```
procedure SkipThree;
{Skips three lines.}
begin {SkipThree}
  WriteLn;
  WriteLn;
  WriteLn
end; {SkipThree}
```
Interpretation: The procedure *pname* is declared. Any identifiers that are declared in the *local declarations* are defined only during the execution of the procedure and can be referenced only within the procedure. The procedure body describes the data manipulation to be performed by the procedure.

Placement of Procedure Declarations in a Program

The four procedures called in Fig. 3.5 must appear in the declaration part of the program, just before the program body. It makes no difference which procedure is declared first; their order of execution is determined by the order of procedure call statements in the program body. Figure 3.7 shows the program thus far; complete the remaining procedure declarations as an exercise.

Figure 3.7 Partially Completed Mother's Day Program

```
program Mother;

{Prints a mother's day welcoming message.}


  procedure PrintM;

  {Prints M.}

  begin {PrintM}
    WriteLn ('*      *');
    WriteLn ('**    **');
    WriteLn ('* *  * *');
```

```
    WriteLn ('*  **  *');
    WriteLn ('*      *');
    WriteLn ('*      *');
    WriteLn ('*      *');
    WriteLn
  end; {PrintM}


  procedure PrintH;

  {Prints H.}

  begin {PrintH}
    {body of procedure PrintH goes here}
  end; {PrintH}


  procedure PrintI;

  {Prints I.}

  begin {PrintI}
    {body of procedure PrintI goes here}
  end; {PrintI}


  procedure Print0;

  {Prints 0.}

  begin {Print0}
    {body of procedure Print0 goes here}
  end; {Print0}


begin {Mother}
  {Print HI}
  PrintH;
  PrintI;

  {Print three blank lines}
  WriteLn;
  WriteLn;
  WriteLn;

  {Print MOM}
  PrintM;
  Print0;
  PrintM
end. {Mother}
```

PROGRAM STYLE

Use of Comments in a Program with Procedures

Figure 3.7 includes several comments. Each procedure begins with a comment that describes its purpose. The begin and the end that bracket each procedure body and the main program body are followed by a comment that identifies that procedure or program. The first and the last line of each procedure declaration is in color throughout this text to help you locate each procedure in the program listing.

Relative Order of Execution of Procedures and the Main Program

In the Mother's Day message problem, we wrote the main program body as a sequence of procedure call statements before we specified the details of all procedures. The next step is to provide the missing procedure declarations.

When we actually put the separate procedures and the main program body together, the procedures appear in the declaration part of the program just before the program body. The compiler must translate the procedure declarations before it translates the main program body. When it reaches the end of each procedure body, the compiler inserts a statement that causes a *transfer of control* back from the procedure to the calling statement. In the main program body, the compiler translates a procedure call statement as a transfer of control to the procedure.

Figure 3.8 shows the main program body and procedure `PrintH` of the Mother's Day program in separate areas of memory. Although the Pascal statements are shown in Fig. 3.8, the object code corresponding to each statement is actually stored in memory.

When the program is run, the first statement in the main program body is the first statement executed (the call to `PrintH` in Fig. 3.8). When the computer executes a procedure call statement, it transfers control to the procedure that is referenced (indicated by the colored line in Fig. 3.8). The computer allocates any memory that may be needed for the procedure's local data and then performs the statements in the procedure body. After the last statement in the

Figure 3.8 Flow of Control Between Main Program and Procedure

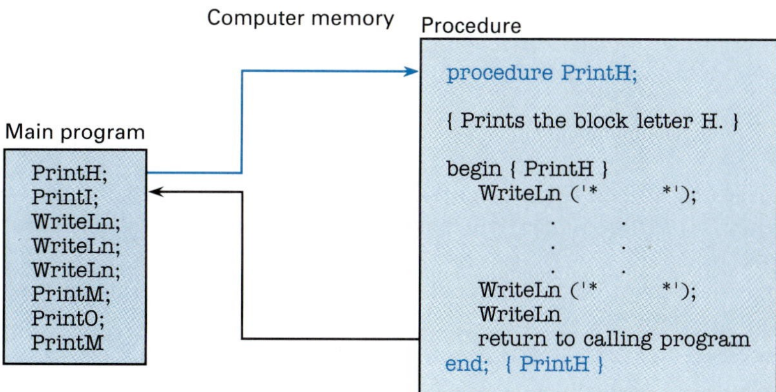

procedure body is executed, control returns to the main program (indicated by the black line in Fig. 3.8), and the computer releases any memory that was allocated to the procedure. After the return to the main program, the next statement is executed (the call to PrintI in Fig. 3.8).

Advantages of Using Procedures

Pascal procedures are convenient because they allow us to delay the detailed implementation of a complicated subproblem until a later stage. For example, we can write procedures PrintH, PrintI, and PrintO of the program Mother later. In fact, we are trying to accomplish the same goal when we divide a problem into subproblems and add details of the solution through stepwise refinement. The use of procedures enables us to implement our program in logically independent sections in the same way that we develop the solution algorithm.

Another advantage is that procedures can be executed more than once. For example, procedure PrintM is called twice in Fig. 3.7. Each time PrintM is called, the list of output statements shown in Fig. 3.6 is executed, and the letter M is printed. If we did not use procedures, those eight output statements would have to be listed twice in the program body, thereby increasing the program's length and the chance of error.

Finally, once you have written and tested a procedure, you can use it in other programs. For example, the procedures created for the program Mother could easily be used to write programs that display the message OH HIM or HI HO.

Exercises for Section 3.5

Self-Check

1. Assume you have procedures PrintH, PrintI, PrintM, and PrintO. What is the effect of executing the following main program body?

```
begin {main}
  PrintO;
  PrintH;
  WriteLn; WriteLn; WriteLn;
  PrintH;
  PrintI;
  PrintM
end. {main}
```

Programming

1. Write a procedure named Skip3 that skips three blank lines. Explain how this procedure could be used in the main program for the Mother's Day message problem.
2. Write a program to print HI HO in block letters. But first, provide a structure chart for this problem.
3. Provide procedures PrintH, PrintI, and PrintO for the Mother's Day message problem.

3.6 Displaying User Instructions

Your use of procedures is limited for the time being because you do not yet know how to pass information into or out of a procedure that you declare. (Chapter 6 describes how to use procedure parameters for that purpose.) Until you can do that, we will use procedures only to display information or instructions to a program user.

■ Example 3.1

The procedure in Fig. 3.9 displays instructions to a user of the program that computes the area and the circumference of a circle (see Fig. 3.2). If procedure `Instruct` is placed in the declaration part of the original program, the new program body can begin with the procedure call statement

```
Instruct;
```

The rest of the program body consists of the executable statements shown earlier. Figure 3.10 shows the output lines displayed by calling procedure `Instruct`. The rest of the program output will be the same as the output shown in Fig. 3.2.

Figure 3.9 Procedure Instruct

```
procedure Instruct;

{Displays instructions to a user of program AreaAndCircum.}

begin {Instruct}
  WriteLn ('This program computes the area');
  WriteLn ('and circumference of a circle.');
  WriteLn;
  WriteLn ('To use this program, enter the radius of');
  WriteLn ('the circle after the prompt: Enter radius> ');
  WriteLn;
  WriteLn ('The circumference will be computed in the');
  WriteLn ('same units of measurement as the radius. The');
  WriteLn ('area will be computed in the same units squared.');
  WriteLn
end; {Instruct}
```

Figure 3.10 Output Lines Displayed by Procedure Instruct

```
This program computes the area
and circumference of a circle.

To use this program, enter the radius of the
circle after the prompt: Enter radius>

The circumference will be computed in the
same units of measurement as the radius. The
area will be computed in the same units squared.
```

Exercises for Section 3.6

Programming

1. Show the revised program `AreaAndCircum`.
2. Write a procedure similar to `Instruct` for the program shown in Fig. 2.8.

3.7 Common Programming Errors

When using comments, you must be very careful to insert the curly braces or the combinations of parentheses and asterisks where required. If the opening `{` or `(*` is missing, the compiler will not recognize the beginning of the comment and will attempt to process the comment as a Pascal statement, causing a syntax error. If the closing `}` or `*)` is missing, the comment will simply be extended to include the program statements that follow it. If the comment is not terminated, the rest of the program will be included in the comment, and a syntax error such as `incomplete program` will be printed.

Remember to declare each procedure used in a program. The procedure declaration must precede the procedure call and is found in the declaration part of a program.

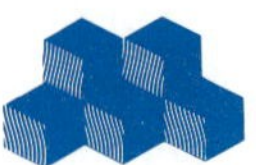

Chapter Review

The first part of this chapter outlined a method for solving problems on the computer. This method stresses six points:

1. Understand the problem.
2. Identify the input data and the output data for the problem as well as other relevant data.
3. Formulate a precise statement of the problem.
4. Develop a list of steps for solving the problem (an algorithm).
5. Refine the algorithm.
6. Implement the algorithm in Pascal.

We showed you how to divide a problem into subproblems and how to use a structure chart to indicate the relationship between subproblems. We then introduced the procedure as a means of implementing subproblems as separate program units.

By now you have absorbed several guidelines for using program comments. Well-placed and carefully worded comments and a structure chart can provide all the documentation necessary for a program.

New Pascal Constructs in Chapter 3

The new Pascal constructs introduced in this chapter are described in Table 3.1.

Table 3.1 Summary of New Pascal Constructs

Construct	Effect

Comment
`{This is a comment}`
`(* So is this! *)`
	Comments document the use of variables and statements in a program. They are ignored by the compiler.

Procedure Declaration
`procedure Display;`
`{Prints 3 lines}`
`const`
`Star = '*';`
`begin {Display}`
`WriteLn (Star);`
`WriteLn (Star);`
`WriteLn (Star)`
`end; {Display}`
	Procedure `Display` is declared and can be called to print three lines of asterisks. The local constant `Star` is defined only when `Display` is executing.

Procedure Call Statement `Display`	Calls procedure `Display` and causes it to begin execution.

✓ Quick-Check Exercises

1. Does a compiler translate comments?
2. Each statement in a program should have a comment. True or false?
3. What are two ways to denote comments?
4. Each procedure is executed in the order in which it is declared in the main program. True or false?
5. How is a procedure executed in a program?
6. List the order of the declarations in a program.
7. What is a local declaration?
8. What is a structure chart?
9. Explain how a structure chart differs from an algorithm.
10. What does the following procedure do?

```
procedure Nonsense;
begin {Nonsense}
  WriteLn ('*****');
  WriteLn ('*   *');
  WriteLn ('*****')
end; {Nonsense}
```

11. What does the following program body do?

```
begin
  Nonsense;
  Nonsense;
  Nonsense
end.
```

Answers to Quick-Check Exercises

1. no
2. false
3. using curly braces or a combination of parentheses and asterisks
4. false
5. It is called into execution by a procedure call statement.
6. constants, variables, procedures (in standard Pascal).
7. It is an identifier declared in the declaration part of a procedure.
8. A structure chart is a diagram used to show an algorithm's subproblems and their interdependence.
9. A structure chart shows the relationship between subproblems; an algorithm lists the sequence in which subproblems are performed.
10. It displays a rectangle.
11. It displays three rectangles on top of each other.

Review Questions

1. Discuss the strategy of divide and conquer.
2. Provide guidelines for the use of comments.
3. Briefly describe the steps you would take to derive an algorithm for a given problem.
4. The diagram that shows the algorithm steps and their interdependencies is called a ____________.
5. What are three advantages of using procedures?
6. Where in the final program is the main program body found and why?
7. When is a procedure executed? Where must it appear in the main program?
8. Is the use of procedures a more efficient use of the programmer's time or the computer's time? Explain.
9. Write a program that draws a rectangle made up of asterisks. Draw a structure chart for the problem. Use two procedures: `DrawSides` and `DrawLine`.

Programming Projects

1. Write three procedures: one that displays a circle, one that displays a triangle, and one that displays a rectangle. Use these procedures in a program that displays the stick figure of a woman.
2. Write procedures that display each of your initials in block letter form. Use these procedures to display your initials.
3. Write a procedure that displays a triangle. Use this procedure to display three triangles on top of each other.
4. Four track stars enter the mile race at the Penn Relays. Write a program that will read in the race time in minutes (`Minutes`) and seconds (`Seconds`) for a runner and compute and print the speed in feet per second (`FPS`) and in meters per second (`MPS`). (Hint: There are 5,280 feet in one mile and 3,282 feet in one kilometer.) Test your program on each of the times below.

Minutes	*Seconds*
3	52.83
3	59.83
4	00.03
4	16.22

Write and call a procedure that displays instructions to the program user.

5. A cyclist coasting on a level road goes from an initial velocity to a slower velocity in a certain time interval. Assuming a constant rate of deceleration, write a computer program that calculates the cyclist's rate of deceleration and determines how long it will take the cyclist to come to rest. (Hint: Use the equation

$$a = (v_f - v_i)/t$$

where a is acceleration, t is time interval, v_i is initial velocity, and v_f is the final velocity.) Write and call a procedure that displays instructions to the program user.

6. When shopping for a new house, you must consider several factors. In this problem, the initial cost of the house, the estimated annual fuel costs, and the annual tax rate are available. Write a program that will determine the total cost after a five-year period for each set of data below. Your program output should help you determine the "best buy."

Initial House Cost	*Annual Fuel Cost*	*Tax Rate*
$67,000	$2,300	0.025
$62,000	$2,500	0.025
$75,000	$1,850	0.020

To calculate the house cost, add the initial cost to the fuel cost for five years, then add the taxes for five years. Taxes for one year are computed by multiplying the tax rate by the initial cost. Write and call a procedure that displays instructions to the program user.

7. A manufacturer wishes to determine the cost of producing an open topped cylindrical container. The cost of each container will be `Cost` dollars per square centimeter of the material needed to produce the container. The surface of the container will be the sum of the area of the base, which is Pi times the radius squared, plus the area of the side, which is 2 Pi times the height of the container. Write a program to read in the radius (`Radius`) of the base, the height (`Height`) of the container, the cost per square centimeter of material (`Cost`), and the number of containers to be produced (`Quantity`). Calculate the cost of each container and the total cost of producing all the containers. Write and call a procedure that displays instructions to the user.

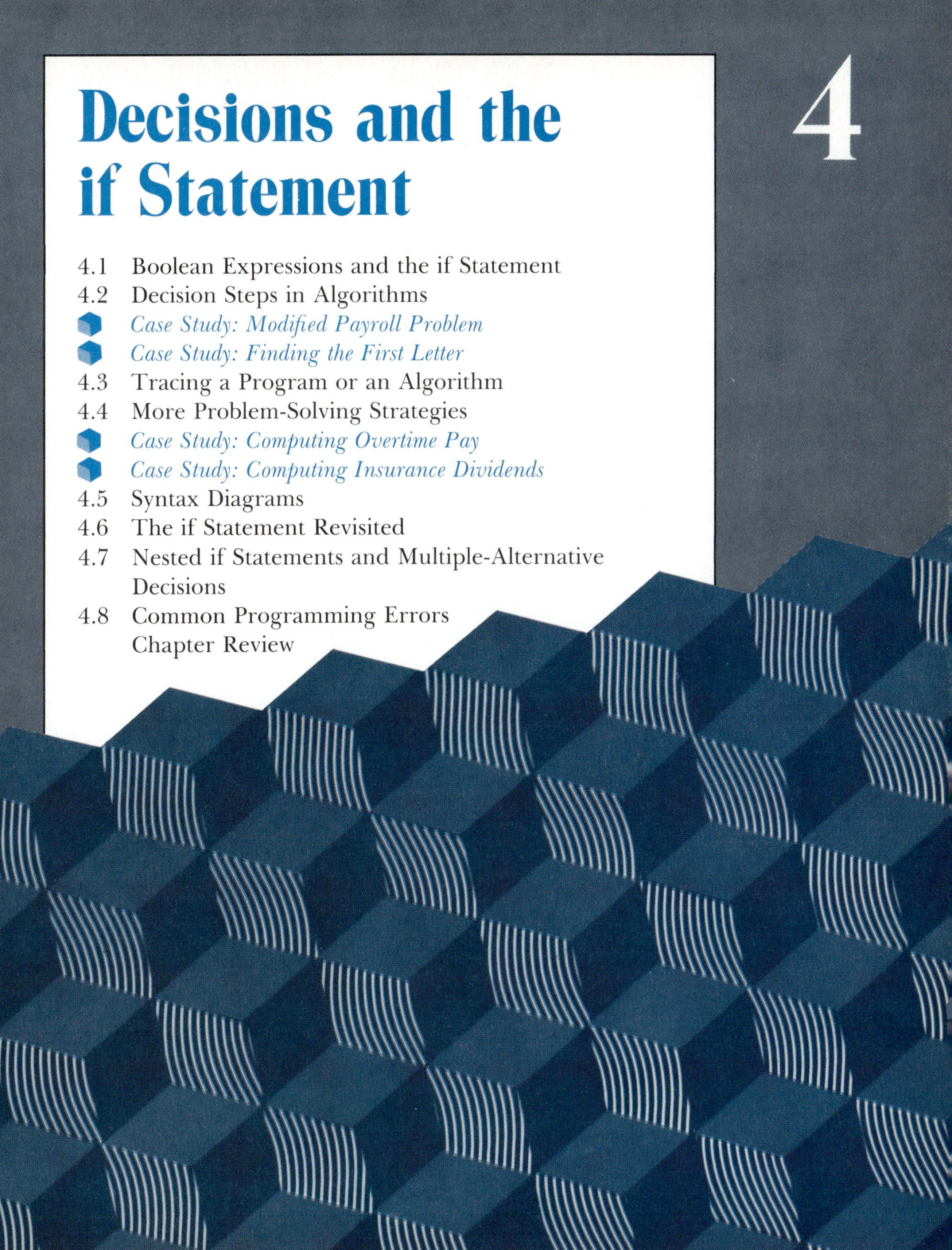

Decisions and the if Statement

4

This chapter shows you how to represent decisions in algorithms by writing steps with two or more alternative courses of action. You will see how to implement conditional execution in Pascal by using Boolean expressions and the Pascal `if` statement. This chapter provides many examples of program fragments containing `if` statements. It also introduces syntax diagrams and shows you how to use them to check the syntax of a Pascal construct.

We discuss two more problem-solving stategies: extending an existing solution and solution by analogy. We also show how to desk-check, or hand-trace, the execution of an algorithm or a program.

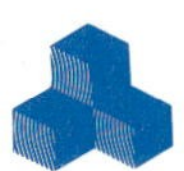

4.1 Boolean Expressions and the if Statement

In all the algorithms thus far, we executed each algorithm step exactly once in the order in which it appeared. However, we are often faced with situations in which we must provide alternative steps that may or may not be executed, depending on the input data. For example, in the simple payroll problem discussed in Chapter 2, we deducted a tax of $25 regardless of the employee's salary. It would be fairer to base the amount deducted on the employee's gross salary. For example, we might want the program to deduct a tax only if an employee's salary exceeds $100. Carrying this one step further, we might want the program to deduct one tax percentage for salaries between $100 and $300 and a higher percentage for salaries greater than $300.

Boolean Expressions and Conditions

To achieve this goal, the computer must be able to answer questions such as "Is gross salary greater than $100?" In Pascal, this is accomplished by evaluating a Boolean expression. Assuming that the employee's salary is stored in the type real variable `Gross`, the Boolean expression corresponding to that question is

```
Gross > 100.00
```

There are only two possible values for a Boolean expression: `True` or `False`. If `Gross` is greater than `100.00`, the preceding Boolean expression evaluates to `True`; if `Gross` is not greater than `100.00`, the expression evaluates to `False`. Chapter 7 examines the operators that can be used with Boolean expressions. For now, we will concentrate on learning how to write and use simple Boolean expressions called conditions.

Most conditions that we use will have one of the following forms:

variable *relational operator* *variable*
variable *relational operator* *constant*

Relational operators are the familiar symbols < (less than), <= (less than or equal to), > (greater than), >= (greater than or equal to), = (equal to), or <> (not equal to).

■ Example 4.1

Table 4.1 shows the relational operators and some sample conditions. Each condition is evaluated assuming the following variable values.

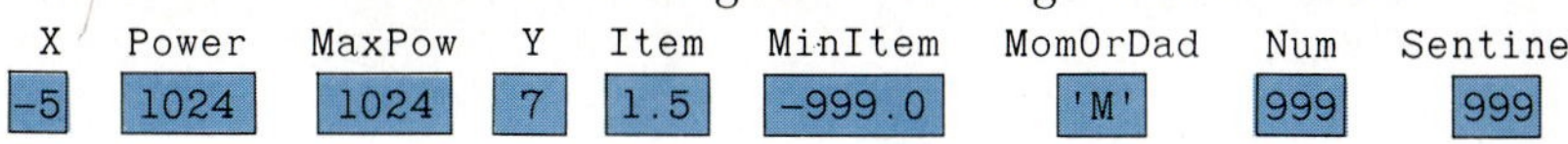

Table 4.1 Pascal Relational Operators and Sample Conditions

Operator	Condition	English Meaning	Boolean Value
`<=`	`X <= 0`	`X` less than or equal to `0`	`True`
`<`	`Power < MaxPow`	`Power` less than `MaxPow`	`False`
`>=`	`X >= Y`	`X` greater than or equal to `Y`	`False`
`>`	`Item > MinItem`	`Item` greater than `MinItem`	`True`
`=`	`MomOrDad = 'M'`	`MomOrDad` equal to `'M'`	`True`
`<>`	`Num <> Sentinel`	`Num` not equal to `Sentinel`	`False`

The if Statement

A Pascal programmer can use the `if` statement to select among several alternatives. An `if` statement always contains a Boolean expression. For example, the `if` statement

```
if Gross > 100.00 then
  Net := Gross - Tax
else
  Net := Gross
```

selects one of the two assignment statements listed. It selects the statement following `then` if the Boolean expresssion is true (that is, `Gross` is greater than `100.00`); it selects the statement following `else` if the Boolean expression is false (that is, `Gross` is not greater than `100.00`).

Figure 4.1 is a graphic description, called a *flow chart*, of the preceding `if`

Figure 4.1 Flow Chart of if Statement with Two Alternatives

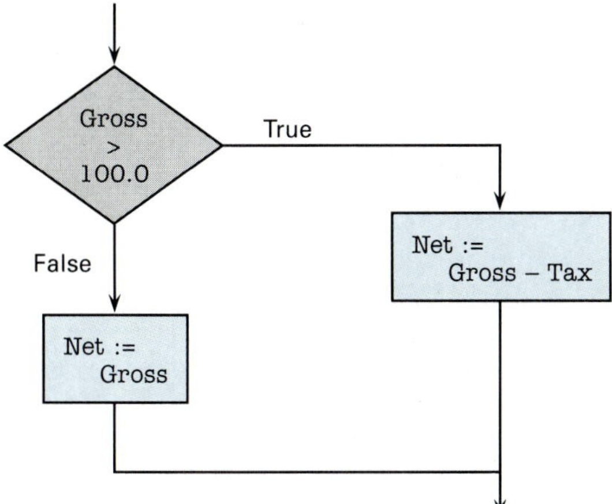

Figure 4.2 Flow Chart of if Statement with One Alternative

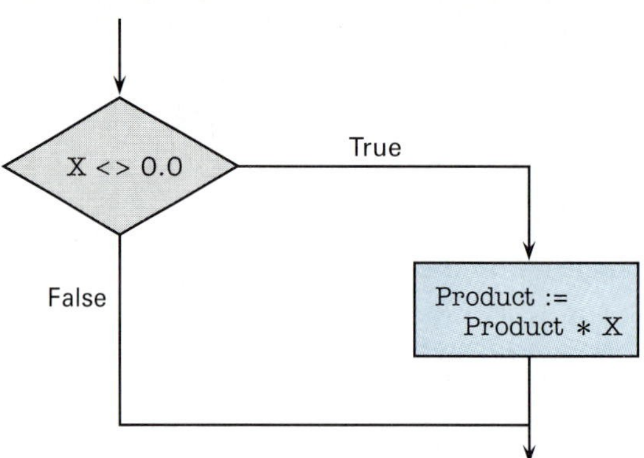

statement. Figure 4.1 shows that the condition enclosed in the diamond-shaped box (`Gross > 100.00`) is evaluated first. If the condition is true, the arrow labeled *True* is followed, and the assignment statement in the rectangle on the right is executed. If the condition is false, the arrow labeled *False* is followed, and the assignment statement in the rectangle on the left is executed.

More if Statement Examples

The preceding `if` statement has two alternatives, but only one will be executed for a given value of `Gross`. Example 4.2 illustrates that an `if` statement can also have a single alternative that is executed only when the condition is true.

■ Example 4.2

The following `if` statement has one alternative that is executed only when `X` is not equal to zero. It causes `Product` to be multiplied by `X`; the new value is then saved in `Product`, replacing the old value. If `X` is equal to zero, the multiplication is not performed. Figure 4.2 is a flow chart of this `if` statement.

```
{Multiply Product by a nonzero X only}
if X <> 0.0 then
  Product := Product * X
```

■

■ Example 4.3

The `if` statement below has two alternatives. It displays either `Hi Mom` or `Hi Dad` depending on the character stored in variable `MomOrDad` (type `Char`).

```
if MomOrDad = 'M' then
  WriteLn ('Hi Mom')
else
  WriteLn ('Hi Dad')
```

■

■ Example 4.4

The following `if` statement has one alternative; it displays the message `Hi Mom` only when `MomOrDad` has the value `'M'`. Regardless of whether or not `Hi Mom` is displayed, the message Hi Dad is always displayed. The semicolon terminates the if statement and is needed to separate the if statement from the second call to procedure WriteLn.

```
if MomOrDad = 'M' then
  WriteLn ('Hi Mom');
WriteLn ('Hi Dad')
```

The if statement that follows is incorrect because the semicolon appears before the line else. The compiler will detect a syntax error when it reaches the line else because the semicolon terminates the if statement, and a new statement cannot begin with else.

```
if MomOrDad = 'M' then
  WriteLn ('Hi Mom');
else                    {error - new statement}
  WriteLn ('Hi Dad')
```

The following displays summarize the forms of the if statement we have used so far. The next section illustrates the use of if statements and decision steps in solving problems. ■

SYNTAX DISPLAY

if Statement (Two Alternatives)

Form: if *condition* then
statement$_T$
else
statement$_F$

Example:
```
if X >= 0.0 then
  Write ('Positive')
else
  Write ('Negative')
```

Interpretation: If the *condition* evaluates to true, then *statement*$_T$ executes; otherwise, *statement*$_F$ executes.

SYNTAX DISPLAY

if Statement (One Alternative)

Form: if *condition* then
statement$_T$

Example:
```
if X > 0.0 then
  PosProd := PosProd * X
```

Interpretation: If the *condition* evaluates to true, then *statement*$_T$ executes; otherwise, it does not execute.

PROGRAM STYLE

Format of the if Statement

In all the `if` statement examples, $statement_T$ and $statement_F$ are indented. If you use the word `else`, enter it on a separate line, aligned with the word `if`. The format of the `if` statement makes its meaning apparent. Again we do this solely to improve program readability; the format used makes no difference to the compiler.

Exercises for Section 4.1

Self-Check

1. Assuming `X` is `15.0` and `Y` is `25.0`, what are the values of the following conditions?

```
X <> Y      X < X      X >= (Y - X)      X = (Y + X - Y)
```

2. What do the following statements display?

a.
```
if X < X then
  WriteLn ('Never')
else
  WriteLn ('Always')
```

b.
```
Var1 := 15.0;
Var2 := 25.12;
if Var2 <= (2 * Var1) then
  WriteLn ('O.K.')
else
  WriteLn ('Not O.K.')
```

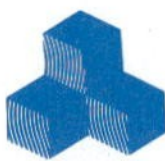

4.2 Decision Steps in Algorithms

In the problem that follows, you will see how to improve the payroll program.

Case Study: Modified Payroll Problem

Problem

Modify the simple payroll program to deduct a $25 tax only if an employee earns more than $100; otherwise, deduct no tax.

Design Overview

We will analyze this problem using the tools developed in the last chapter. We begin by listing the data requirements and the initial algorithm.

Data Requirements

Problem Constants

maximum salary without a tax deduction (`TaxBracket = 100.00`)
amount of tax deducted (`Tax = 25.00`)

Problem Inputs

hours worked (`Hours : Real`)
hourly rate (`Rate : Real`)

Problem Outputs

gross pay (`Gross : Real`)
net pay (`Net : Real`)

Unlike problem inputs, whose values may vary, problem constants have the same values for each run of the program. Each constant value is associated with an identifier (`Tax` and `TaxBracket`). The program style display following this problem describes the reason for this association.

Initial Algorithm

1. Display user instructions.
2. Enter hours worked and hourly rate.
3. Compute gross pay.
4. Compute net pay.
5. Print gross pay and net pay.

Algorithm Refinements

Figure 4.3 shows the structure chart for this algorithm. Now let's write the refinement of algorithm step 4 as a *decision step*.

Step 4 Refinement

```
4.1 if Gross > TaxBracket then
       Deduct a tax of $25
    else
       Deduct no tax
```

Figure 4.3 Structure Chart for Modified Payroll Problem

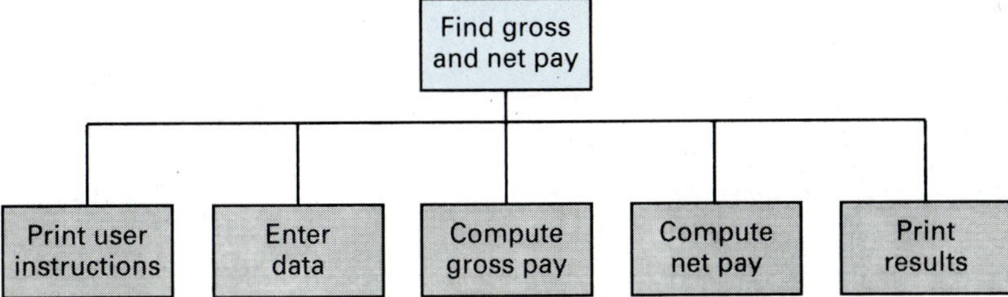

The decision step is expressed in *pseudocode*, which is a mixture of English and Pascal used to describe algorithm steps.

Coding

The modified payroll program is shown in Fig. 4.4. It begins with a multiple-line comment explaining the program purpose. Rather than surround each line of that comment with curly braces, we use the style convention of beginning and ending the comment block with an open curly brace and a close curly brace, respectively, on separate lines.

Figure 4.4 Program for Modified Payroll Problem

Edit Window

```
program ModPay;
{
 Computes and prints gross pay and net pay given an hourly
 rate and number of hours worked. Deducts a tax of $25 if
 gross salary exceeds $100; otherwise, deducts no tax.
}
   const
     TaxBracket = 100.00;        {maximum salary for no deduction}
     Tax = 25.00;                {tax amount}

   var
     Hours, Rate,                {inputs - hours worked, hourly rate}
     Gross, Net : Real;          {outputs - gross pay, net pay}

  procedure InstructModPay;

  {Displays user instructions.}

  begin {InstructModPay}
    WriteLn ('This program computes gross and net salary.');
    WriteLn ('A tax amount of $', Tax :4:2, ' is deducted');
    WriteLn ('for an employee who earns more than $', TaxBracket :4:2);
    WriteLn;
    WriteLn ('Enter hours worked and hourly rate');
    WriteLn ('on separate lines after the prompts.');
    WriteLn ('Press <Enter> after typing each number.');
    WriteLn
  end; {InstructModPay}

begin {ModPay}
  InstructModPay;                {Display user instructions}

  {Enter Hours and Rate}
  Write ('Hours worked> ');
  ReadLn (Hours);
  Write ('Hourly rate> ');
  ReadLn (Rate);

  {Compute gross salary}
  Gross := Hours * Rate;
```

```
  {Compute net salary}
  if Gross > TaxBracket then
    Net := Gross - Tax        {Deduct a tax amount}
  else
    Net := Gross;             {Deduct no tax}

  {Print Gross and Net}
  WriteLn ('Gross salary is $', Gross :6:2);
  WriteLn ('Net salary is $', Net :6:2)
end. {ModPay}
```

Output Window

```
This program computes gross and net salary.
A tax amount of $25.00 is deducted
for an employee who earns more than $100.00.

Enter hours worked and hourly rate
on separate lines after the prompts.
Press <Enter> after typing each number.

Hours worked> 40.0
Hourly rate> 5.0
Gross salary is $200.00
Net salary is $175.00
```

The program begins by calling procedure `InstructModPay` to display the user instructions (the first six lines of program output). After the input data are read, the `if` statement

```
if Gross > TaxBracket then
  Net := Gross - Tax       {Deduct a tax amount}
else
  Net := Gross;            {Deduct no tax}
```

implements the decision step (step 4). The comments on the right are embedded in the `if` statement. The semicolon in the last line separates the `if` statement from the output statements that follow.

Testing

To test this program, run it with at least two sets of data. One data set should yield a gross salary greater than \$100.00, and the other should yield a gross salary less than \$100.00. You should also test the program with a data set that yields a gross salary that is exactly \$100.00.

PROGRAM STYLE

Use of Constants

The constants `TaxBracket` and `Tax` appear in the preceding `if` statement and in Fig. 4.4. We could just as easily place the constant values (`100.00` and `25.00`) directly in the `if` statement.

The result then would be

```
if Gross > 100.00 then
  Net := Gross - 25.00        {Deduct a tax amount}
else
  Net := Gross;               {Deduct no tax}
```

However, use of constants rather than constant values provides two advantages. First, the original `if` statement is easier to understand because it uses the descriptive names `TaxBracket` and `Tax` rather than numbers, which have no intrinsic meaning. Second, a program written with constants is easier to modify than one written with constant values. For example, to use different constant values in the `ModPay` program in Fig. 4.4, we need to change only the constant declaration. If, however, we had inserted constant values directly into the `if` statement, we would have to change the `if` statement and any other statements that manipulate the constant values.

Notice that the constants also appear in two `WriteLn` statements in procedure `InstructModPay`. It is perfectly all right to reference program constants in a procedure body.

 Case Study: Finding the First Letter

Problem

Read three letters and find and print the one that comes first in the alphabet.

Design Overview

From your prior experience with conditions and decision steps, you know how to compare two numbers to see which is smaller using the relational operator `<`. We can also use this operator in Pascal to determine whether one letter precedes another in the alphabet. For example, the condition `'A' < 'F'` is true because `A` precedes `F` in the alphabet.

Data Requirements

Problem Inputs

three letters (`Ch1, Ch2, Ch3 : Char`)

Problem Outputs

the alphabetically first letter (`AlphaFirst : Char`)

Initial Algorithm

1. Read three letters into `Ch1`, `Ch2`, and `Ch3`.
2. Save the alphabetically first of `Ch1`, `Ch2`, and `Ch3` in `AlphaFirst`.
3. Print the alphabetically first letter.

Figure 4.5 Structure Chart for Finding Alphabetically First Letter

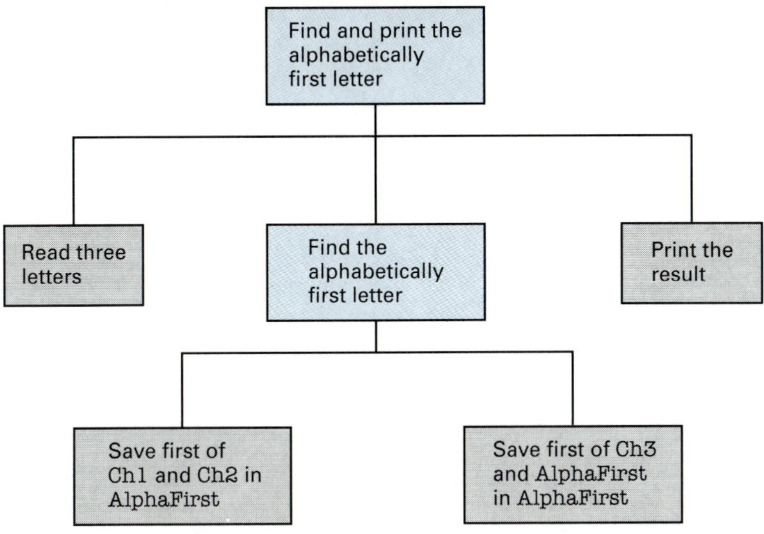

Algorithm Refinements

You can perform step 2 by first comparing `Ch1` and `Ch2` and saving the alphabetically first letter in `AlphaFirst`; the result can then be compared to `Ch3`. The refinement of step 2 follows.

Step 2 Refinement

2.1 Save the alphabetically first of `Ch1` and `Ch2` in `AlphaFirst`.
2.2 Save the alphabetically first of `Ch3` and `AlphaFirst` in `AlphaFirst`.

Figure 4.5 shows the structure chart that corresponds to the algorithm.

Coding

Program `FirstLetter` is shown in Fig. 4.6. The `if` statement with two alternatives saves either `Ch1` or `Ch2` in `AlphaFirst`. The `if` statement with one alternative stores `Ch3` in `AlphaFirst` if `Ch3` precedes the value already in `AlphaFirst`. Later in this chapter, you will see that `if` statements with more than two alternatives are also possible in Pascal.

Testing

To test this program, make sure it works when the smallest letter is in any of the three positions. Section 4.3 describes the four cases that should be tested. You should also see what happens when one of the letters is repeated, and when one or more of the letters is in lowercase.

Figure 4.6 Finding the Alphabetically First Letter

Edit Window

```
program FirstLetter;

{Finds and prints the alphabetically first letter.}

var
  Ch1, Ch2, Ch3,              {three letters read}
  AlphaFirst     : Char;      {alphabetically first letter}

begin  {FirstLetter}
  {Read three letters}
  Write ('Enter any three letters> ');
  ReadLn (Ch1, Ch2, Ch3);

  {Store the alphabetically first of Ch1 and Ch2 in AlphaFirst}
  if Ch1 < Ch2 then
    AlphaFirst := Ch1         {Ch1 comes before Ch2}
  else
    AlphaFirst := Ch2;        {Ch2 comes before Ch1}

  {Store the alphabetically first of Ch3 and AlphaFirst}
  if Ch3 < AlphaFirst then
    AlphaFirst := Ch3;        {Ch3 comes before AlphaFirst}

  {Print result}
  WriteLn (AlphaFirst, ' is the first letter alphabetically')
end. {FirstLetter}
```

Output Window

```
Enter any three letters> EBK
B is the first letter alphabetically
```

Exercises for Section 4.2

Self-Check

1. What value is assigned to X for each of the following segments given that Y is 15.0?

   a.
   ```
   X := 25.0;
   if Y <> (X - 10.0) then
     X := X - 10.0
   else
     X := X / 2.0;
   ```
   b.
   ```
   if Y < 15.0 then
     X := 5 * Y
   else
     X := 2 * Y;
   ```

Programming

1. Write Pascal statements to carry out the following steps:
   a. If Item is nonzero, then multiply Product by Item and save the result in

Product; otherwise, skip the multiplication. In either case, print the value of Product.

b. Store the absolute difference of X and Y in Z, where the absolute difference is (X − Y) or (Y − X), whichever is positive.

c. If X is zero, add 1 to ZeroCount. If X is negative, add X to MinusSum. If X is greater than zero, add X to PlusSum.

2. Modify the structure chart and program for the first-letter problem to find the first of four letters.
3. Write a structure chart and program to find the alphabetically last of three letters.

4.3 Tracing a Program or an Algorithm

A critical step in the design of an algorithm or a program is to make sure it is correct before you spend a lot of time entering or debugging it. Often a few extra minutes spent verifying the correctness of an algorithm saves hours of testing time later.

One important technique, a desk-check (also called a hand-trace) consists of a careful, step-by-step simulation on paper of how the computer would execute the algorithm or program. By using data that are relatively easy to process by hand, you should be able to simulate the effect of each step's execution.

Table 4.2 shows a trace of the program in Fig. 4.6 for the data string THE. Each program step is listed at the left in order of its execution. The values of variables referenced by a program step are shown after the step. If a program step changes the value of a variable, the table shows the new value. The effect of each step is described at the far right. For example, the table shows that the statement

```
ReadLn (Ch1, Ch2, Ch3);
```

stores the letters T, H, and E in the variables Ch1, Ch2, and Ch3.

Table 4.2 Trace of Program in Figure 4.6

Program Statement	Ch1	Ch2	Ch3	AlphaFirst	Effect
	?	?	?	?	
Write ('Enter any three...')					Prints a prompt.
ReadLn (Ch1, Ch2, Ch3)	T	H	E		Reads the data.
if Ch1 < Ch2 then					Is 'T' < 'H'? Value is false.
AlphaFirst := Ch2				H	'H' is first so far.
if Ch3 < AlphaFirst...					Is 'E' < 'H'? Value is true.
AlphaFirst := Ch3				E	'E' is first.
WriteLn (AlphaFirst...					Prints E is the first letter...

The trace in Table 4.2 clearly shows that the alphabetically first letter, `E`, of the input string is stored in `AlphaFirst` and printed. To verify that the program is correct, you would need to select other data that cause the two conditions to evaluate to different combinations of their values. Because there are two conditions and each has two possible values (true or false), there are two times two, or four, different combinations that you should try. (What are they?) An exhaustive desk-check of the program would show that it works for all of these combinations.

Besides those four cases, you should verify that the program works correctly for unusual data. For example, what would happen if two or more of the letters were the same? Would the program still provide the correct result? To complete the desk-check, you would need to show that the program handles these special situations properly.

When tracing a case, you must be careful to execute the program exactly as the computer would execute it. A desk-check in which you assume that a particular step will be executed in a certain way without explicitly testing each condition and tracing each program step is of little value.

Exercises for Section 4.3

Self-Check

1. Provide sample data and traces for the remaining three cases of the alphabetically first-letter problem. Test the special cases where two letters are the same and where all three letters are the same. What is the value of the conditions in the latter case?
2. Trace the program in Fig. 4.4 when `Hours` is `30.0` and `Rate` is `5.00`. Perform the trace when `Hours` is `20.0` and `Rate` is `4.00`.

4.4 More Problem-Solving Strategies

Often what appears to be a new problem turns out to be a variation of one you have already solved. Consequently, an important skill in problem solving is the ability to recognize that a problem is similar to one solved earlier. As you progress through this course, you will start to build up a *library* of programs and procedures. Whenever possible, try to adapt or reuse parts of successful programs.

Extending a Problem Solution

An experienced programmer usually writes programs that can be easily changed or modified to fit other situations. One reason for this is that programmers (and program users) often want to make slight improvements to a program after they have used it. If the original program is designed carefully from the beginning, the programmer can accommodate changing specifications with a minimum of effort. In the next problem, it is possible to insert a new decision step rather than rewrite the entire program.

Case Study: Computing Overtime Pay

Problem

You decide to modify the payroll program so that employees who work more than 40 hours a week are paid double for all overtime hours.

Design Overview

This problem is an extension of the modified payroll problem solved in Fig. 4.4. In this case, overtime pay must be added for eligible employees. We can solve this problem by adding a new step (step 3a) after step 3 in the original algorithm.

Data Requirements

Problem Constants

maximum salary for no tax deduction (`TaxBracket = 100.00`)
amount of tax deducted (`Tax = 25.00`)
maximum hours without overtime pay (`MaxHours = 40.0`)

Problem Inputs

hours worked (`Hours : Real`)
hourly rate (`Rate : Real`)

Problem Outputs

gross pay (`Gross : Real`)
net pay (`Net : Real`)

Initial Algorithm

1. Display user instructions.
2. Enter hours worked and hourly rate.
3. Compute gross salary.

3a. Add any overtime pay to gross salary.

4. Compute net salary.
5. Print gross salary and net salary.

Algorithm Refinements

The new step, step 3a, is refined next.

Step 3a Refinement

3a.1 `if Hours > MaxHours then`
    3a.2 Add extra pay for hours over 40 to `Gross`.

Coding

As shown in the following code segment, the `if` statement that implements step 3a should come after the statement in Fig. 4.4 that computes gross salary.

```
Gross := Hours * Rate;      {Compute gross salary}
{Add any overtime pay to gross salary}
if Hours > MaxHours then
  Gross := Gross + ((Hours - MaxHours) * Rate);
```

The assignment statement for step 3a.2 involves three arithmetic operators: +, –, and *. Chapter 7 discusses how Pascal evaluates arithmetic expressions with multiple operators. For the time being, however, you need to know that the parentheses cause the operators in the segment to be evaluated in the order of subtraction first, multiplication next, and addition last. Consequently, the overtime hours (`Hours - MaxHours`) will be multiplied by `Rate` and added to the value of `Gross` computed earlier; the result will be the new value of `Gross`.

Solution by Analogy

Sometimes a new problem is simply an old one presented in a new guise. Each time you face a problem, try to determine if you have solved a similar problem before; if you have, adapt the earlier solution. This problem-solving strategy requires a careful reading of the problem statement to detect requirements similar to those of earlier problems but worded differently.

Case Study: Computing Insurance Dividends

Problem

Each year an insurance company sends out dividend checks to its policyholders. The dividend amount is a fixed percentage (4.5%) of the policyholder's paid premium. If the policyholder has made no claims, the dividend rate for the policy is increased by 0.5%. Write a program to compute dividends.

Design Overview

This problem is similar to the overtime pay problem. You can determine the dividend amount by first computing the basic dividend, then adding the bonus dividend when applicable. (In the overtime pay problem, we followed a similar algorithm by first computing gross pay, then adding in overtime pay when earned.)

Data Requirements

Problem Constants

the fixed dividend rate of 4.5% (`FixedRate = 0.045`)
the bonus dividend rate of 0.5% (`BonusRate = 0.005`)

Figure 4.7 Structure Chart for Insurance Dividend Problem

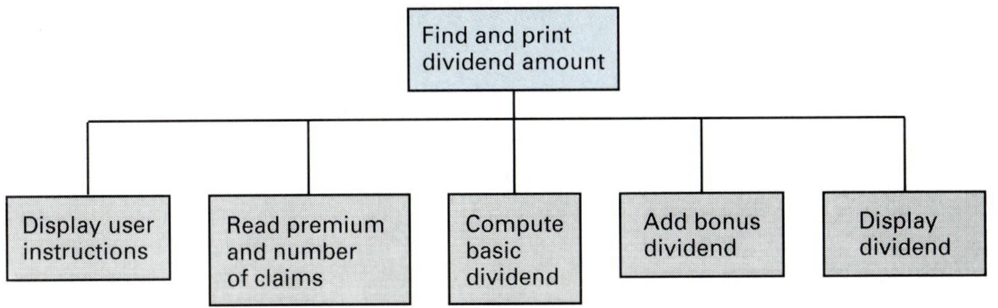

Problem Inputs

premium amount (`Premium : Real`)
number of claims (`NumClaims : Integer`)

Problem Outputs

dividend amount (`Dividend : Real`)

Initial Algorithm

1. Display user instructions.
2. Enter premium amount and number of claims.
3. Compute basic dividend.
4. Add any bonus dividend to basic dividend.
5. Print total dividend.

Algorithm Refinements

The refinement of step 4 in this problem is similar to the refinement of step 3a in the overtime pay problem. We'll look closer at this refinement next.

Step 4 Refinement

4.1 `if NumClaims = 0 then`
    4.2 Add bonus dividend to `Dividend`

Figure 4.7 shows the structure chart that corresponds to the algorithm.

Coding

The complete insurance dividend program is shown in Fig. 4.8. Because Pascal possesses no % operator, decimal fractions are required. Thus, the dividend rate, 4.5%, is written as the decimal fraction `0.045` and the bonus rate, 0.5%, is written as the decimal fraction `0.005`. Also, all real numbers must begin with a digit; therefore, a zero before the decimal point is required for a real value less than 1.0.

Case Study: Computing Insurance Dividends, continued

Figure 4.8 Insurance Company Dividend Program

Edit Window

```
program CompDividend;

{Finds and prints the insurance dividend.}

  const
    FixedRate = 0.045;          {basic dividend rate 4.5%}
    BonusRate = 0.005;          {bonus dividend rate 0.5%}

  var
    NumClaims : Integer;        {input - number of claims}
    Premium,                    {input - premium amount}
    Dividend : Real;            {output - dividend amount}

  procedure InstructDividend;

  {Displays user instructions.}

  begin {InstructDividend}
    WriteLn ('This program displays an insurance policy dividend.');
    WriteLn ('The basic dividend is ',
             FixedRate :5:3, ' times the premium.');
    WriteLn ('A bonus dividend of ',
             BonusRate :5:3, ' times the premium is paid');
    WriteLn ('for policies with no claims against them.');
    WriteLn
  end; {InstructDividend}


begin {CompDividend}
  InstructDividend;                          {Display user instructions}

  {Enter Premium and NumClaims}
  Write ('Premium amount> $');
  ReadLn (Premium);
  Write ('Number of claims> ');
  ReadLn (NumClaims);

  {Compute basic dividend}
  Dividend := Premium * FixedRate;

  {Add any bonus dividend to basic dividend}
  if NumClaims = 0 then
    Dividend := Dividend + (Premium * BonusRate);

  {Print total dividend}
  WriteLn ('Total dividend is $', Dividend :4:2)
end. {CompDividend}
```

Output Window

```
This program displays an insurance policy dividend.
The basic dividend is 0.045 times the premium.
A bonus dividend of 0.005 times the premium is paid
for policies with no claims against them.

Premium amount> $1200.00
Number of claims> 0
Total dividend is $60.00
```

Exercises for Section 4.4

Self-Check

1. Rewrite the algorithm for the overtime pay problem so that the computation of gross salary is performed in one step rather than in two (in other words, combine steps 3 and 3a). Use an `if` statement with two alternatives.
2. In Fig. 4.8, use an `if` statement with two alternatives to combine the two steps that compute `Dividend` into one step.

Programming

1. Provide the complete program for the overtime pay problem.

4.5 Syntax Diagrams

We can use a syntax diagram to describe the syntax of any Pascal language construct. The syntax diagram in Fig. 4.9 describes a Pascal *identifier*. This syntax diagram references three other syntactical elements of Pascal: *letter* (`A-Z`, `a-z`), *digit* (`0-9`) and the underscore symbol (_). You will recall that an identifier is a sequence of letters and digits starting with a letter.

To use a syntax diagram, trace through the diagram following the arrows. Start at the arrow tail on the left and finish at the arrowhead on the right. The shortest path through the diagram in Fig. 4.9 is from left to right and passing through only the top box, labeled *letter*. This means that a Pascal identifier can be any single letter (for example, `A`, `B`, `c`, `z`).

There are many other paths through this diagram. Instead of exiting at the right after passing through the top box, you can follow any path leading down and to the left. These paths go through a box labeled *digit*, another box labeled *letter* or a circle containing the underscore symbol. If you then exit the diagram, the identifier formed consists of two characters (for example, `it`, `ME`, `R2`, `D2`, `A_`).

Because there is a closed cycle, or loop, in the diagram, you can pass through the lower box labeled *letter*, the box labeled *digit*, or the underscore

Figure 4.9 Syntax Diagram Describing a Pascal Identifier

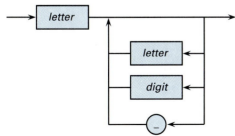

Identifier

letter

letter

digit

_

circle several times before exiting the diagram. Each time, a symbol from the box passed through (letter, digit, or _) is added to the identifier being formed. Some identifiers formed this way are `A`, `ABC`, and `A23b_4ef5`. It is impossible to trace a path that establishes `123` or `12ABC` as valid identifiers.

You can use syntax diagrams to verify that a program statement is correct before you enter it. If a syntax error occurs during debugging, you can refer to the appropriate syntax diagram to determine the correct form of the element that is incorrect. Appendix D contains all Pascal syntax diagrams.

Exercise for Section 4.5

Self-Check

1. Which of the identifiers

```
Ace    R2D2    R245    A23B    Alc    B34d5c    A23cd
```

satisfy the following syntax diagram?

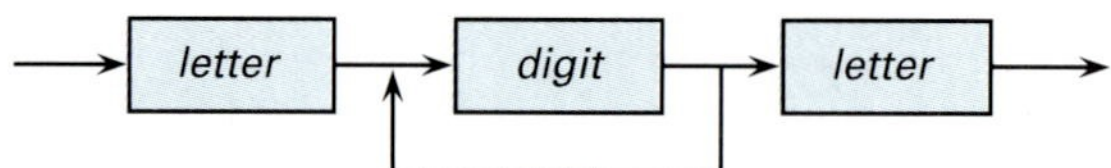

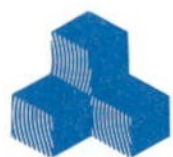

4.6 The if Statement Revisited

The syntax diagram for an `if` statement is shown in Fig. 4.10. Two kinds of boxes are in this diagram: rounded boxes (ovals) and rectangular boxes. The contents of a rounded box are taken literally, whereas, the name in a rectangular box is the label of another syntax diagram (*expression, statement*).

The reserved words (`if`, `then`, `else`) are enclosed in ovals rather than rectangular boxes. When you pass through one of these ovals, the word inside is inserted in the `if` statement being formed.

An `if` statement is completed by exiting at either arrowhead at the far right of the diagram. If the top path is followed, the `if` statement consists of only one alternative (following `then`); there is no `else` part. If the path leading

Figure 4.10 Syntax Diagram for an if Statement

if statement

if → *expression* → then → *statement*

else → *statement*

down and to the left (through `else`) is followed instead, the `if` statement consists of two alternatives.

The *statement* following the word `then` or `else` can be a single executable statement or a compound statement (described next). Some of the statements that can be used are assignment statements, procedure call statements, and other `if` statements.

More if Statement Examples

This section provides examples of `if` statements with compound statements as $statement_T$ or $statement_F$. A compound statement consists of a sequence of statements bracketed by `begin` and `end`. The body of a program or procedure is a compound statement.

■ Example 4.5

Suppose you are the manager of a clothing boutique and are planning a spring sale. You could use the following `if` statement to compute the discounted price of an item. The statement first determines the discount by multiplying the item price and the discount rate (a fraction); next, it deducts the discount. The compound statement is not executed when the discount rate is zero.

```
if DiscRate <> 0.0 then
  begin
    Discount := Price * DiscRate;     {Compute discount amount}
    Price := Price - Discount         {Deduct discount from price}
  end {if}
```

■

■ Example 4.6

In later chapters, you will see that it is useful to be able to order a pair of data values in memory so that the smaller value is stored in one variable (say, `X`) and the larger value in another (say, `Y`). The `if` statement in Fig. 4.11 rearranges any two values stored in `X` and `Y` so that the smaller number will always be in `X` and the larger number will always be in `Y`. If the two numbers are already in the proper order, the compound statement will not be executed.

Figure 4.11 if Statement to Order X and Y

```
if X > Y then
  begin {switch X and Y}
    Temp := X;              {Store old X in Temp}
    X := Y;                 {Store old Y in X}
    Y := Temp               {Store old X in Y}
  end {if}
```

The variables `X`, `Y`, and `Temp` all should be the same data type. Although the values of `X` and `Y` are being switched, an additional variable, `Temp`, is needed for storage of a copy of one of those values. Table 4.3 illustrates the need for `Temp`, assuming `X` and `Y` have original values of `12.5` and `5.0`, respectively. ■

Table 4.3 Trace of if Statement to Order X and Y

Statement Part	X	Y	Temp	Effect
	12.5	5.0	?	
`if X > Y then`				12.5 > 5.0 is true
`Temp := X;`			12.5	Store old X in Temp
`X := Y;`	5.0			Store old Y in X
`Y := Temp`		12.5		Store old X in Y

■ Example 4.7

As the manager of a clothing boutique, you want to keep records of your bank transactions. You could use the following `if` statement to process a transaction (`TransAmount`) that represents a payment for goods received (in which case, `TransType` is `'C'`) or a cash deposit. In either case, an appropriate message is printed and the account balance (`Balance`) is updated. Both the true and the false statements are compound statements.

```
if TransType = 'C' then
  begin {check}
    Write ('Check for $', TransAmount :4:2);
    Balance := Balance - TransAmount     {Deduct check amount}
  end  {check}
else
  begin {deposit}
    Write ('Deposit of $', TransAmount :4:2);
    Balance := Balance + TransAmount      {Add deposit amount}
  end {deposit and if}
```

The semicolons in the preceding `if` statement separate the individual statements in each alternative. A common error would be to insert a semicolon after the first `end` (`end; {check}`). That would terminate the `if` statement prematurely. An `Error in Statement` error message would be displayed when the compiler then tried to translate the rest of the `if` statement (beginning with `else`). ■

PROGRAM STYLE

Writing if Statements with Compound True or False Statements

Each `if` statement in this section contains at least one compound statement bracketed by `begin` and `end`. Each compound statement is indented. The purpose of the indentation is to improve our ability to read and understand the `if` statement; indentation is ignored by the Pascal compiler.

The comment after each `end` helps to associate the `end` with its corresponding `begin`. The comments are not required, but they also improve program readability.

Semicolons are required between the individual statements within a compound statement. Semicolons should not be used before or after the reserved words `then`, `else`, or `begin`. A semicolon is needed, however, after the last `end` when another statement follows the `if` statement.

Exercises for Section 4.6

Self-Check

1. Insert any necessary semicolons in the following segment and indicate how many spaces each line should be indented to improve readability.

```
if X > Y then
begin
X := X + 10.0
WriteLn ('X Bigger')
end
else
WriteLn ('X Smaller')
WriteLn ('Y is ', Y)
```

2. What would be the effect of removing the bracketing `begin` and `end` in the preceding segment?
3. What would be the effect of bracketing the last two lines in the preceding segment with `begin` and `end`?
4. Correct the following `if` statement:

```
if Num1 < 0 then
  begin
    Product := Num1 * Num2 * Num3;
    WriteLn ('Product is ', Product : 1)
  end;
else
  Sum := Num1 + Num2 + Num3;
  WriteLn ('Sum is ', Sum :1);
```

5. What syntax diagrams would you use to validate the following `if` statement? Provide the label of every syntax diagram that describes an element of this statement.

```
if X > 0 then
  begin
    X := 25.0;
    WriteLn ('Positive')
  end;
```

Programming

1. Write an `if` statement that assigns the larger of `X` and `Y` to `Larger` and the smaller to `Smaller`. Your statement should print `'X LARGER'` or `'Y LARGER'`, depending on the situation.
2. Do the same as in programming exercise 1 but print the smaller value followed by the larger value.

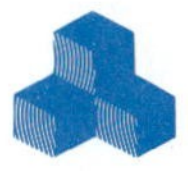

4.7 Nested if Statements and Multiple-Alternative Decisions

Until now, we used `if` statements to implement decisions involving two alternatives. In this section, you will see how the `if` statement can be used to implement decisions involving several alternatives.

A *nested* `if` statement occurs when the true or false statement of an `if` statement is itself an `if` statement. A nested `if` statement can be used to implement decisions with several alternatives, as shown in the following examples.

■ Example 4.8

The following nested `if` statement has three alternatives. It causes one of three variables (`NumPos`, `NumNeg`, or `NumZero`) to be increased by one depending on whether `X` is greater than zero, less than zero, or equal to zero, respectively.

```
{increment NumPos, NumNeg, or NumZero depending on X}
if X > 0 then
  NumPos := NumPos + 1
else
  if X < 0 then
    NumNeg := NumNeg + 1
  else  {X = 0}
    NumZero := NumZero + 1
```

The execution of this `if` statement proceeds as follows: the first condition (`X > 0`) is tested; if it is true, `NumPos` is incremented by one and the rest of the `if` statement is skipped. If the first condition is false, the second condition (`X < 0`) is tested; if the second condition is true, `NumNeg` is incremented by one; otherwise, `NumZero` is incremented. It is important to realize that the second condition is tested only if the first condition is false.

Figure 4.12 charts the execution of this statement. Each condition is shown in a diamond-shaped box. If a condition is true, its arrow labeled True is followed. If a condition is false, its arrow labeled False is followed. The diagram shows that one and only one of the statement sequences in a rectangular box will be executed. Table 4.4 traces the execution of this statement when `X` is –7. ■

Table 4.4 Trace of if Statement in Example 4.8 for X = –7

Statement Part	Effect
`If X > 0 then`	–7 `> 0` is false
`else if X < 0 then`	–7 `< 0` is true
`  NumNeg := NumNeg + 1`	Add `1` to `NumNeg`

PROGRAM STYLE

Multiple-Alternative Decisions

Nested `if` statements can become quite complex. If there are more than three alternatives and the indentation is not consistent, you may find it difficult to determine the `if` to which a given `else` belongs. (In Pascal, this is always the closest `if` without an else.) It is easier to write the nested `if` statement in Example 4.8 as the following *multiple-alternative decision*.

```
{increment NumPos, NumNeg, or NumZero depending on X}
if X > 0 then
  NumPos := NumPos + 1
```

Figure 4.12 Flow Chart of Nested if Statement in Example 4.8

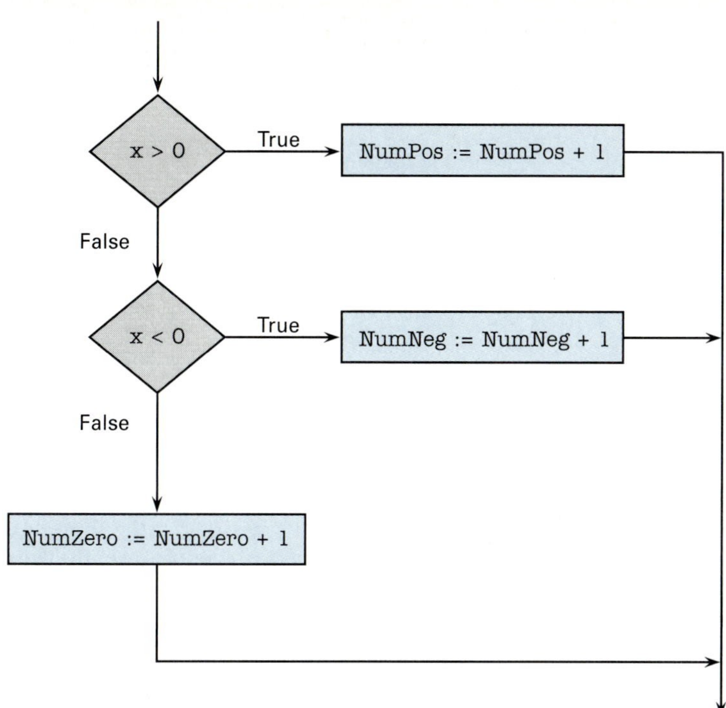


```
else if X < 0 then
  NumNeg := NumNeg + 1
else {X = 0}
  NumZero := NumZero + 1
```

In this format, the word `else` and the next condition appear on the same line. All the words `else` align, and each *dependent statement* is indented under the condition that controls its execution. The general form follows:

```
if condition₁ then
  statement₁
else if condition₂ then
  statement₂
. . .
else if conditionₙ then
  statementₙ
else
  statementₑ
```

The conditions in a multiple-alternative decision are evaluated in sequence until a true condition is reached. If a condition is true, the statement following it is executed and the rest of the multiple-alternative decision is skipped. If a condition is false, the statement following it is skipped and the next condition is tested. If all conditions are false, then *statement*$_e$ following the last `else` is executed.

Order of Conditions

Often, the conditions in a multiple-alternative decision are not *mutually exclusive*; in other words, more than one condition may be true for a given data value. If this is the case, the order of the conditions becomes important because only the statement sequence following the first true condition is executed.

■ Example 4.9

Suppose you want to match exam scores to letter grades for a large class of students. The assignment of grades is based on the exam scores, as follows:

Exam Score	*Grade Assigned*
90 and above	A
80-89	B
70-79	C
60-69	D
below 60	F

The following multiple-alternative decision prints the letter grade assigned according to the exam score. For an exam score of 85, even though the last three conditions are true, a grade of B would be assigned because the *first* true condition is `Score >= 80`.

```
{correct grade assignment}
if Score >= 90 then
  Write ('A')
else if Score >= 80 then
  Write ('B')
else if Score >= 70 then
  Write ('C')
else if Score >= 60 then
  Write ('D')
else
  Write ('F')
```

The order of conditions can also affect program efficiency. If low exam scores are more likely than high scores, it would be more efficient to test first for scores below 60, next for scores between 60 and 69, and so on (see programming exercise 1 at the end of this section). It would, however, be incorrect to write the decision as follows. *All* passing exam scores (60 or above) would be incorrectly categorized as a grade of D, because the first condition would be true and the rest would be skipped.

```
{incorrect grade assignment}
if Score >= 60 then
  Write ('D')
else if Score >= 70 then
  Write ('C')
else if Score >= 80 then
  Write ('B')
else if Score >= 90 then
  Write ('A')
else
  Write ('F')
```

■

■ Example 4.10

You can use a multiple-alternative `if` statement to implement a *decision table* that describes several alternatives. Let's say you are an accountant setting up a payroll system for a small firm. Each line of Table 4.5 indicates an employee's salary range and a corresponding base tax amount and tax percentage. Given a salary, you can calculate the tax by adding the *base tax* for that salary range to the product of the percent of excess and the amount of salary over the minimum salary for that range.

For example, the second line of the table specifies that the tax due on a salary of $2000.00 is $225.00 plus 16 percent of the excess salary over $1500.00 (that is, 16 percent of $500.00, or $80.00). Therefore, the total tax due is $225.00 plus $80.00, or $305.00.

Table 4.5 Decision Table for Example 4.10

Range	Salary	Base Tax	Percent of Excess
1	0.00-1,499.99	0.00	15
2	1,500.00-2,999.99	225.00	16
3	3,000.00-4,999.99	465.00	18
4	5,000.00-7,999.99	825.00	20
5	8,000.00-15,000.00	1425.00	25

The `if` statement in Fig. 4.13 implements the tax table. If the value of `Salary` is within the table range (0.00 to 15,000.00), exactly one of the statements assigning a value to `Tax` will be executed. A trace of the `if` statement for `Salary = 2000.00` is shown in Table 4.6. You can see that the value assigned to `Tax`, `305.00`, is correct. ■

Figure 4.13 if Statement for Table 4.5

```
if Salary < 0.0 then
  WriteLn ('Error! Negative salary $', Salary :10:2)
else if Salary < 1500.00 then                    {first range}
  Tax := 0.15 * Salary
else if Salary < 3000.00 then                    {second range}
  Tax := (Salary - 1500.00) * 0.16 + 225.00
else if Salary < 5000.00 then                    {third range}
  Tax := (Salary - 3000.00) * 0.18 + 465.00
else if Salary < 8000.00 then                    {fourth range}
  Tax := (Salary - 5000.00) * 0.20 + 825.00
else if Salary <= 15000.00 then                  {fifth range}
  Tax := (Salary - 8000.00) * 0.25 + 1425.00
else
  WriteLn ('Error! Too large salary $', Salary :10:2)
```

Table 4.6 Trace of if Statement in Figure 4.13 for Salary = $2000.00

Statement Part	Salary	Tax	**Effect**
	2000.00	?	
`if Salary < 0.0`			`2000.0 < 0.0` is false
`else if Salary < 1500.00`			`2000.0 < 1500.0` is false
`else if Salary < 3000.00`			`2000.0 < 3000.0` is true
`Tax := (Salary - 1500.00)`			Evaluates to `500.00`
`* 0.16`			Evaluates to `80.00`
`+ 225.00`		305.00	Evaluates to `305.00`

PROGRAM STYLE

Validating the Value of Variables

It is important to validate the value of a variable before you perform computations using invalid or meaningless data. Instead of computing an incorrect tax amount, the `if` statement in Fig. 4.13 prints an error message if the value of `Salary` is outside the range covered by the table (0.0 to 15,000.00). The first condition detects negative salaries; an error message is printed if `Salary` is less than zero. All conditions evaluate to False if `Salary` is greater than 15,000.00, so the alternative following `else` displays an error message.

Nested if Statements with More than One Variable

The nested `if` statements so far have all involved testing the value of a single variable; consequently, we were able to write each nested `if` statement as a multiple-alternative decision. This is not always so easy to do.

■ Example 4.11

You have just had a meeting with your parents to discuss your alternatives for next year. Your parents told you that you can apply to an Ivy League school if you can get your SAT scores above 1350 *and* earn more than $2,000 over the summer. If your SAT scores are not over 1350 but you still earn over $2,000, then you can apply to a state university and live at the dorm. If you cannot earn the necessary $2,000, you have to commute to a local community college. The following nested `if` statement summarizes the decision process you should follow; the flow chart in Fig. 4.14 diagrams it.

```
if Earnings > 2000 then
  if SAT > 1350 then
    WriteLn ('Apply to Ivy League')
  else
    WriteLn ('Apply to State University')
else
  WriteLn ('Apply to Community College')
```

Figure 4.14 Flow Chart of Nested if Statement

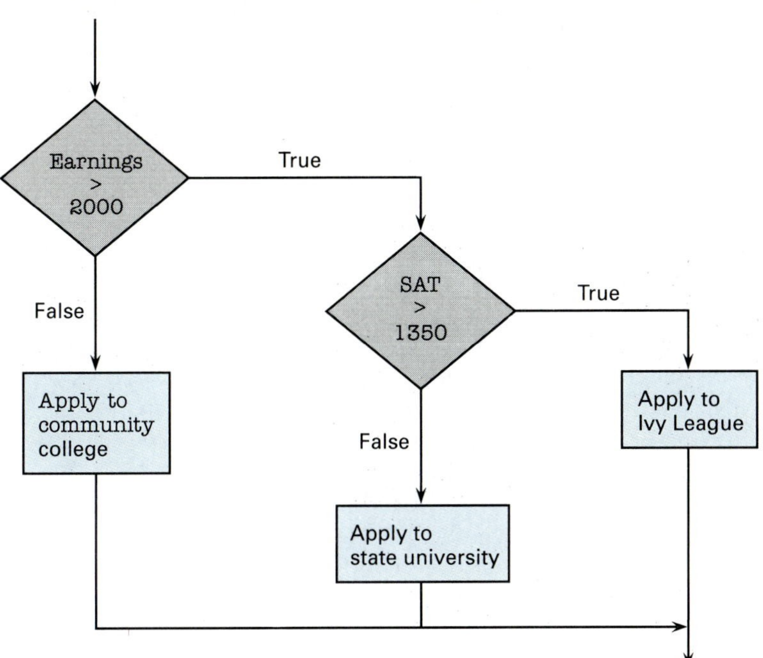

To verify that the nested `if` statement in Fig. 4.14 is correct, it is necessary to trace its execution for all possible combinations of SAT scores and summer earnings. It is clear that the rightmost rectangle is entered only when both conditions are true. The leftmost rectangle is always entered when the condition involving earnings is false. The rectangle in the middle is entered when the condition involving earnings is true, but the condition involving SAT scores is false. ■

Exercises for Section 4.7

Self-Check

1. Trace the execution of the nested `if` statement in Fig. 4.13 for `Salary = 13500.00`.
2. What would be the effect of reversing the order of the first two conditions in the `if` statement in Fig. 4.13?

Programming

1. Rewrite the `if` statement for Example 4.9 using only the relational operator `<` in all conditions.
2. Implement the following decision table using a nested `if` statement. Assume that the grade point average is within the range 0.0 through 4.0.

Grade Point Average	*Transcript Message*
0.0-0.99	`Failed semester—registration suspended`
1.0-1.99	`On probation for next semester`
2.0-2.99	(no message)
3.0-3.49	`Dean's list for semester`
3.5-4.0	`Highest honors for semester`

4.8 Common Programming Errors

Be careful with your use of semicolons inside an `if` statement. Use semicolons only to separate the statements of a compound statement within an `if` statement. A semicolon is needed after the `if` statement when more statements follow. Do not use semicolons before or after the reserved words `then` or `else` in an `if` statement.

When you are writing a nested `if` statement, try to select the conditions so that you can use the multiple-alternative format. If the conditions are not mutually exclusive (that is, more than one condition may be true), the most restrictive condition should come first.

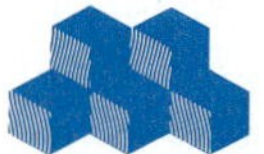

Chapter Review

This chapter discussed how to use pseudocode to represent decision steps in an algorithm. We showed you how to implement decisions with several alternatives in Pascal programs using the `if` statement.

You learned to use traces to verify that an algorithm or a program is correct. You can discover errors in logic by carefully tracing an algorithm or a program. Tracing an algorithm or a program before entering the program in the computer saves you time in the long run.

You can also use syntax diagrams to help prevent syntax errors. Refer to the syntax diagrams in Appendix D if you are unsure of the syntax of a statement. If the compiler detects a syntax error that you do not understand, refer to the syntax diagram to determine the cause of the error.

New Pascal Constructs in Chapter 4

The new Pascal constructs introduced in this chapter are described in Table 4.7.

Table 4.7 Summary of New Pascal Constructs

Construct	Effect
if Statement	
One Alternative	
`if X <> 0.0 then` `  Product := Product * X`	Multiplies `Product` by `X` only if `X` is nonzero.
Two Alternatives	

`if X >= 0.0 then`
`  WriteLn (X :4:2, ' is positive')`
`else`
`  WriteLn (X :4:2, ' is negative')`
	If `X` is greater than or equal to `0.0`, display `is positive`; otherwise, display the message `is negative`.

Multiple Alternatives	

`if X < 0.0 then`
`  begin`
`    WriteLn ('negative');`
`    AbsX := -X`
`  end`
`else if X = 0.0 then`
`  begin`
`    WriteLn ('zero');`
`    AbsX := 0.0`
`  end`
`else`
`  begin`
`    WriteLn ('positive');`
`    AbsX := X`
`  end`
	One of three messages is printed depending on whether `X` is negative, positive, or zero. `AbsX` is set to represent the absolute value or magnitude of `X`.

✓ Quick-Check Exercises

1. An `if` statement implements ____________ execution.
2. What is a compound statement?
3. What is pseudocode?
4. What values can a Boolean expression have?
5. The relational operator `<>` means ____________.
6. A ____________ is used to verify that an algorithm is correct.
7. A ____________ is used to verify that a program statement is grammatically correct.
8. Correct the following syntax errors:

```
if X > 25.0 then
  begin
      Y := X;
    else
      Y := Z
    end;
```

9. What value is assigned to Fee by the following if statement when Speed is 75?

```
if Speed > 35 then
  Fee := 20.00
else if Speed > 50 then
  Fee := 40.00
else if Speed > 75 then
  Fee := 60.00
```

10. Answer question 9 for the following if statement. Which if statement is correct?

```
if Speed > 75 then
  Fee := 60.00
else if Speed > 50 then
  Fee := 40.00
else if Speed > 35 then
  Fee := 20.00
```

11. What output line(s) are displayed by the following statements when X is 5.53? When X is 9.95?

```
if X >= 7.5 then
  begin
    X := 90.0;
    WriteLn ('X is ', X :4:2)
  end
else
  X := 25.0;
WriteLn ('X is ', X :3:1);
```

12. Explain the difference between the statements on the left and the statements on the right. For each, what is the final value of X if the initial value of X is 1?

```
if X >= 0 then              if X >= 0 then
  X := X + 1                  X := X + 1;
else if X >= 1 then         if X >= 1 then
  X := X + 2;                 X := X + 2;
```

Answers to Quick-Check Exercises

1. conditional
2. a statement bracketed by begin and end.
3. a mixture of English and Pascal used to describe algorithm steps
4. True and False
5. not equal
6. hand-trace or desk check
7. syntax diagram
8. Remove begin, end, and the first semicolon.
9. 20.00 first condition is met
10. 40.00, the one in 10
11. when X is originally 5.53:

    ```
    X is 25.0
    ```

    when X is originally 9.95:

    ```
    X is 90.00
    X is 90.0
    ```
12. A nested if statement is on the left; a sequence of if statements is on the right. X becomes 2 on the left; X becomes 4 on the right.

Review Questions

1. A decision in Pascal is actually an evaluation of a(n) __________ expression.
2. List the six relational operators discussed in this chapter.
3. What should a programmer do after writing the algorithm but before entering the program?
4. Trace the following program fragment and indicate which procedure will be called if a data value of `27.34` is entered.

```
WriteLn ('Enter a temperature> ');
ReadLn (Temp);
if Temp > 32.0 then
  NotFreezing
else
  IceForming
```

5. Write the appropriate `if` statement to compute `GrossPay`, given that the hourly rate is stored in the variable `Rate` and the total hours worked is stored in the variable `Hours`. Pay time-and-a-half for more than 40 hours worked.
6. How can syntax diagrams help a new user become comfortable with an unfamiliar programming language?
7. Given the following syntax diagram, circle the words under the diagram that are valid.

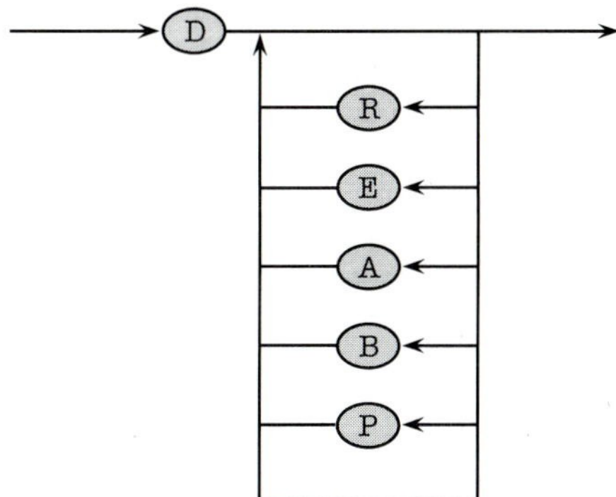

PEAR BREAD DREAR DEADEN DAD DRAB

Programming Projects

1. Write a program that displays a message that consists of three block letters, where each letter is an `X` or an `O`. The program user's data determines whether a particular letter will be an `X` or an `O`. For example, if the user enters the three letters `XOX`, the block letters `X`, `O`, and `X` will be displayed.
2. Write a program to simulate a state police radar gun. The program should read an automobile speed and print the message SPEEDING if the speed exceeds 55 mph.
3. While spending the summer as a surveyor's assistant, you decide to write a program

that transforms compass headings in degrees (0 to 360) to compass bearings. A compass bearing consists of three items: the direction you face (north or south), an angle between 0 and 90 degrees, and the direction you turn (east or west) before walking. For example, to get the bearing for a compass heading of 110.0 degrees, you would first face due south (180 degrees) and then turn 70.0 degrees east (180.0 – 110.0). The compass bearing is south 70.0 degrees east.

4. Write a program that reads in a room number, the room's capacity, and the size of the class enrolled so far and prints an output line showing the classroom number, the capacity, number of seats filled, number of seats available, and whether the class is filled. Call a procedure to display the heading below before the output line.

```
Room     Capacity     Enrollment     Empty seats     Filled/Not Filled
```

Display each part of the output line under the appropriate column heading. Test your program with the following classroom data:

Room	*Capacity*	*Enrollment*
426	25	25
327	18	14
420	20	15
317	100	90

5. Write a program that determines the additional state tax owed by an employee. The state charges a 4-percent tax on net income. Determine net income by subtracting a $500 allowance for each dependent from gross income. Your program should read gross income, number of dependents, and tax amount already deducted. It should then compute the actual tax owed and print the difference between tax owed and tax deducted followed by the message `SEND CHECK` or `REFUND`, depending on whether the difference is positive or negative.

6. The New Telephone Company has the following rate structure for long-distance calls:

   1. Any call started after 6:00 p.m. (1800 hours) but before 8:00 a.m. (0800 hours) is discounted 50 percent.
   2. Any call started after 8:00 a.m. (0800 hours) but before 6:00 p.m. (1800 hours) is charged full price.
   3. All calls are subject to a 4-percent Federal tax.
   4. The regular rate for a call is $0.40 per minute.
   5. Any call longer than 60 minutes receives a 15-percent discount (after any other discount is subtracted and before tax is added).

   Write a program that reads the start time for a call based on a twenty-four-hour clock and the length of the call. The gross cost (before any discounts or tax) should be printed followed by the net cost (after discounts are deducted and tax is added). Use a procedure to print instructions to the program user.

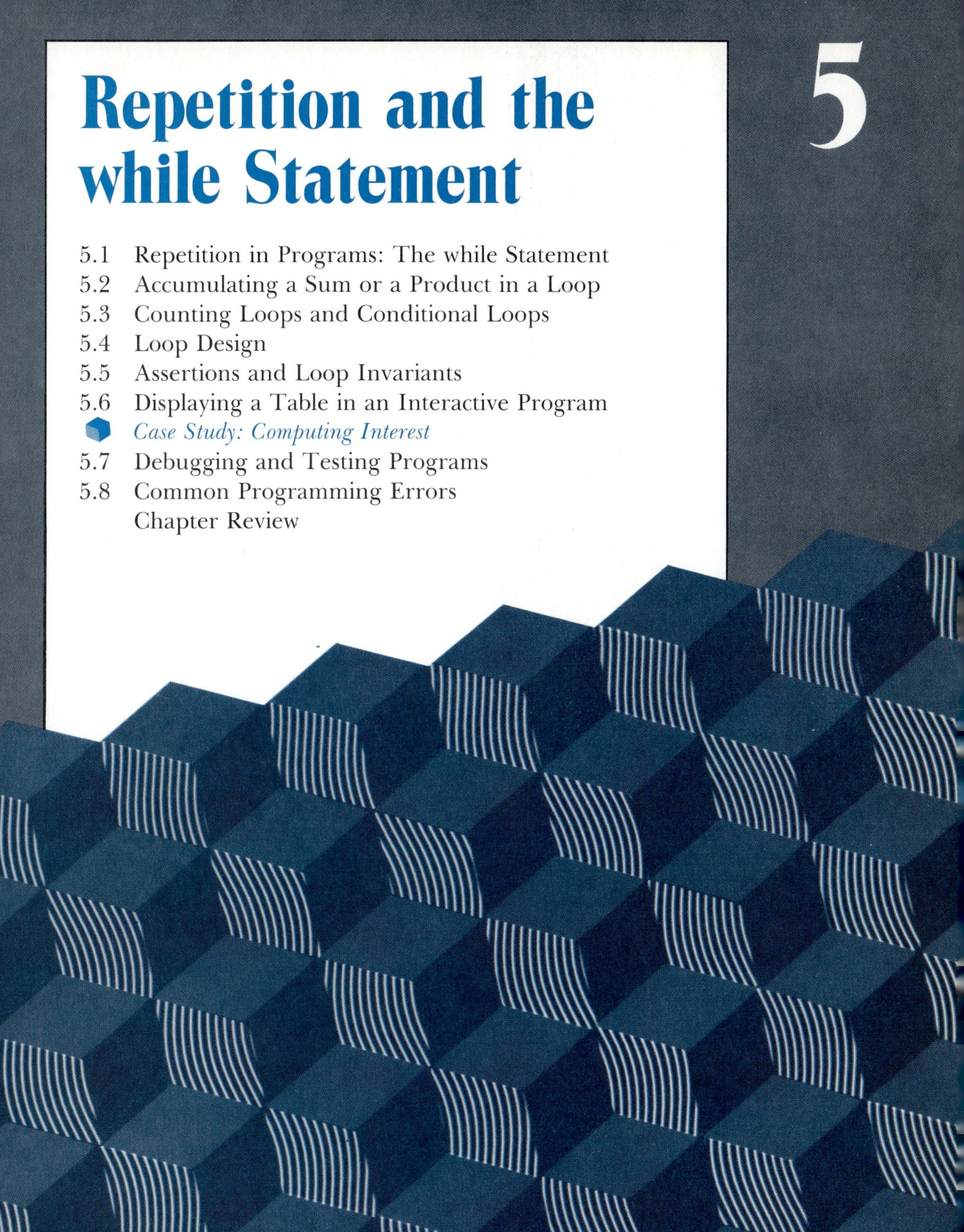

5

Repetition and the while Statement

Chapters 3 and 4 introduced you to two Pascal control statements: the procedure call statement and the if statement. The control statements of a programming language enable a programmer to control the sequence and the frequency of execution of program segments. Control statements call procedures into execution and implement decisions and repetition in programs.

In this chapter, you will see how to specify the repetition of a group of program statements (called a *loop*) using the `while` statement. You will study how to design loops in Pascal programs. This chapter describes how to verify that a loop is correct and how to use special comments, called *assertions* and *loop invariants*, that are helpful in loop design and verification.

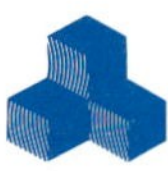

5.1 Repetition in Programs: The while Statement

Just as the ability to make decisions is an important programming tool, so is the ability to specify repetition of a group of operations. For example, a company that has seven employees will want to repeat the gross pay and net pay computations in its payroll program seven times, once for each employee.

The repetition of steps in a program is called a *loop*. The *loop body* contains the steps to be repeated. Pascal provides three control statements for specifying repetition. This chapter examines the `while` statement and previews the `for` statement. The `for` statement and the third loop form, the `repeat` statement, are examined in Chapter 9.

The while Statement

The program shown in Fig. 5.1 computes and displays gross pay for seven employees. The loop body (steps that are repeated) is the compound statement starting on the third line. The loop body reads an employee's payroll data and computes and displays that employee's salary. After seven salaries are displayed, the last statement in Fig. 5.1 calls procedure `WriteLn` to display the message `All employees processed`.

Figure 5.1 Loop to Process Seven Employees

```
CountEmp := 0;                        {no employees processed yet}
while CountEmp < 7 do                 {test value of CountEmp}
  begin
    Write ('Hours> ');
    ReadLn (Hours);
    Write ('Rate > $');
    ReadLn (Rate);
    Salary := Hours * Rate;
    WriteLn ('Salary is $', Salary :4:2);
    CountEmp := CountEmp + 1          {increment CountEmp}
  end; {while}

WriteLn ('All employees processed');
```

The three lines in color in Fig. 5.1 control the looping process. The first statement

```
CountEmp := 0;                 {no employees processed yet}
```

stores an initial value of 0 in the variable CountEmp, which represents the count of employees processed so far. The next line evaluates the Boolean expression CountEmp < 7. If the expression is true, the compound statement representing the loop body is executed, causing a new pair of data values to be read and a new salary to be computed and displayed. The last statement in the loop body

```
CountEmp := CountEmp + 1       {increment CountEmp}
```

adds 1 to the value of CountEmp. After executing the last step in the loop body, control returns to the line beginning with while, and the Boolean expression is reevaluated for the next value of CountEmp.

The loop body is executed once for each value of CountEmp from 0 to 6. Eventually CountEmp becomes 7, and the Boolean expression evaluates to false. When that happens, the loop body is not executed, and control passes to the display statement that follows the loop body.

The Boolean expression following the reserved word while is called the *loop repetition condition*. The loop is repeated when this condition is true. We say that the *loop is exited* when this condition is false.

Figure 5.2 is a flow chart of the while loop. It summarizes what we have explained so far about while loops. In the flow chart, the Boolean expression in the diamond-shaped box is evaluated first. If that expression is true, the loop body is executed, and the process is repeated. The while loop is exited when the expression becomes false.

Make sure you understand the difference between the while statement in Fig. 5.1 and the following if statement:

```
if CountEmp < 7 then
  begin
    ...
  end; {if}
```

The compound statement after the reserved word then executes at most one time. In a while statement, the compound statement after the reserved word do can execute more than once.

Syntax of the while Statement

In Fig. 5.1, variable CountEmp is called the *loop control variable* because its value determines whether the loop body is repeated. Three critical steps involve the loop control variable CountEmp:

1. CountEmp is set to an initial value of 0 (*initialized to 0*) before the while statement is reached.
2. CountEmp is tested before the start of each loop repetition (called an *iteration* or a *pass*).
3. CountEmp is updated (its value increases by 1) during each iteration.

Figure 5.2 Flow Chart of a while Loop

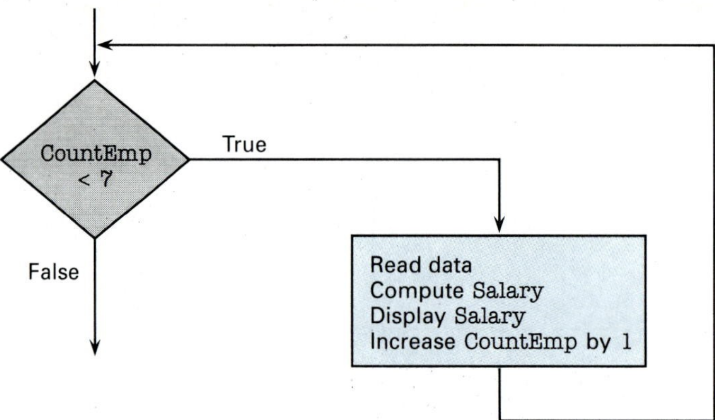

Steps similar to these three steps (initialization, test, and update) must be performed for every `while` loop. If the first step is missing, the initial test of `CountEmp` will be meaningless. The last step ensures that we progress toward the final goal (`CountEmp >= 7`) during each repetition of the loop. If the last step is missing, the value of `CountEmp` cannot change, so the loop will execute "forever" (an *infinite loop*). The syntax diagram for the `while` statement follows; it is described in the next display.

while statement

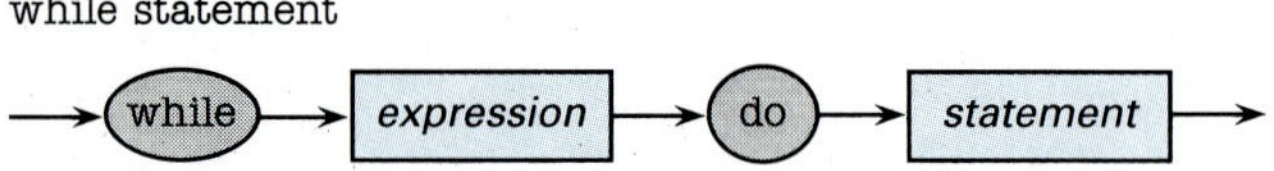

SYNTAX DISPLAY

while Statement

Form: `while` *expression* `do`
statement

Example:

```
{Display N asterisks.}
CountStar := 0;
while CountStar < N do
  begin
    Write ('*');
    CountStar := CountStar + 1
  end {while}
```

Interpretation: The *expression* (a condition to control the loop process) is tested and if it is true, the *statement* is executed and the *expression* is retested. The *statement* is repeated as long as (`while`) the *expression* is true. When the *expression* is tested and found to be false, the `while` loop is exited and the next program statement after the `while` statement is executed.

Note: If the *expression* evaluates to false the first time it is tested, the *statement* is not executed.

Formatting the while Statement

For clarity, we indent the body of a `while` loop. If the loop body is a compound statement bracketed by `begin` and `end` we terminate it with `end {while}`.

Exercises for Section 5.1

Self-Check

1. How many times is the following loop body repeated? What is printed during each repetition of the loop body?

```
X := 3;
Count := 0;
while Count < 3 do
  begin
    X := X * X;
    WriteLn (X);
    Count := Count + 1
  end {while}
```

2. Answer self-check exercise 1 if the last statement in the loop is

```
Count := Count + 2
```

3. Answer self-check exercise 1 if the last statement in the loop body is omitted.

Programming

1. Write a `while` loop that displays each integer from 1 through 5 on a separate line together with its square.

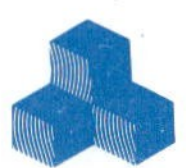

5.2 Accumulating a Sum or a Product in a Loop

Often we use loops to accumulate a sum or a product by repeating an addition or multiplication operation. The next example uses a loop to accumulate a sum.

■ Example 5.1

The program in Fig. 5.3 has a `while` loop similar to the loop in Fig. 5.1. Besides displaying each employee's salary, it accumulates the total payroll (`TotalPay`) for a company. The assignment statement

```
TotalPay := TotalPay + Salary;      {add next salary}
```

adds the current value of `Salary` to the sum being accumulated in `TotalPay`. Fig. 5.4 traces the effect of repeating this statement for the three values of `Salary` shown in the sample run.

Figure 5.3 Computing Company Payroll

Edit Window

```
program CompanyPayroll;

{Computes the payroll for a company.}

  var
    NumberEmp,                {number of employees}
    CountEmp : Integer;       {current employee}
    Hours,                    {hours worked}
    Rate,                     {hourly rate}
    Salary,                   {salary}
    TotalPay : Real;          {company payroll}

begin
  {Enter number of employees.}
  Write ('Enter number of employees >');
  ReadLn (NumberEmp);

  {Compute each employee's salary and add it to the payroll.}
  TotalPay := 0.0;
  CountEmp := 0;              {start with first employee}
  while CountEmp < NumberEmp do
    begin
      Write ('Hours> ');
      ReadLn (Hours);
      Write ('Rate > $');
      ReadLn (Rate);
      Salary := Hours * Rate;
      WriteLn ('Salary is $', Salary :4:2);
      WriteLn;
      TotalPay := TotalPay + Salary;     {add next salary}
      CountEmp := CountEmp + 1
    end; {while}

  WriteLn; WriteLn ('All employees processed');
  WriteLn ('Total payroll is ', TotalPay :4:2)
end. {CompanyPayroll}
```

Output Window

```
Enter number of employees> 3
Hours> 5
Rate > $4.00
Salary is $20.00

Hours> 6
Rate > $5.00
Salary is $30.00

Hours> 1.5
Rate > $10.00
Salary is $15.00

All employees processed
Total payroll is $65.00
```

Figure 5.4 Accumulating Partial Sums

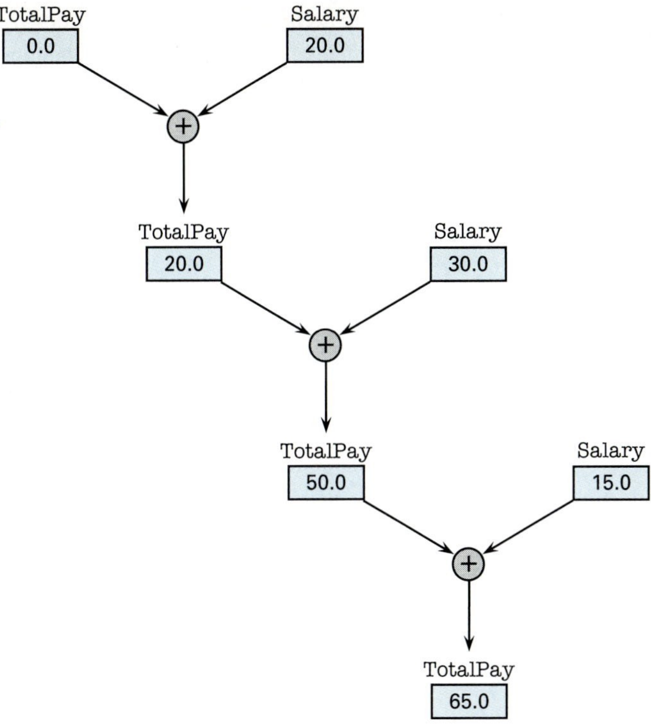

Prior to loop execution, the statement

```
TotalPay := 0.0;
```

initializes the value of `TotalPay` to zero. This step is critical; if it is omitted, the final sum will be off by whatever value happens to be stored in `TotalPay` when the program begins execution. ■

Generalizing a Loop

The first loop shown in Fig. 5.1 has a serious deficiency: it can only be used when the number of employees is exactly seven. The loop in Fig. 5.3 is much better because it can be used for any number of employees. This program begins by reading the total number of employees into variable `NumberEmp`. Before each execution of the loop body, the loop repetition condition compares the number of employees processed so far (`CountEmp`) to `NumberEmp`.

Accumulating Partial Products

In a similar way, we can use a loop to accumulate a product as shown in the next example.

■ Example 5.2

The loop below computes and displays all products of its data items that are less than 10000. It computes each new partial product by repeated execution of the statement

```
Product := Product * Item  {Compute next product}
```

Figure 5.5 traces the change in the value of Product with each execution of the above statement. If the data items are 10, 500, and 3, the partial products 1 (initial value of Product), 10, and 5000 are displayed.

```
{Display partial products less than 10000}
Product := 1;
while Product < 10000 do
  begin
    WriteLn (Product);           {Display partial product}
    Write ('Enter next item> ');
    ReadLn (Item);
    Product := Product * Item  {Compute next product}
  end {while}
```

Loop exit occurs when the value of Product is greater than or equal to 10000. Consequently, the last value assigned to Product (15000 in Fig. 5.5) is not displayed. ■

Figure 5.5 Accumulating Partial Products

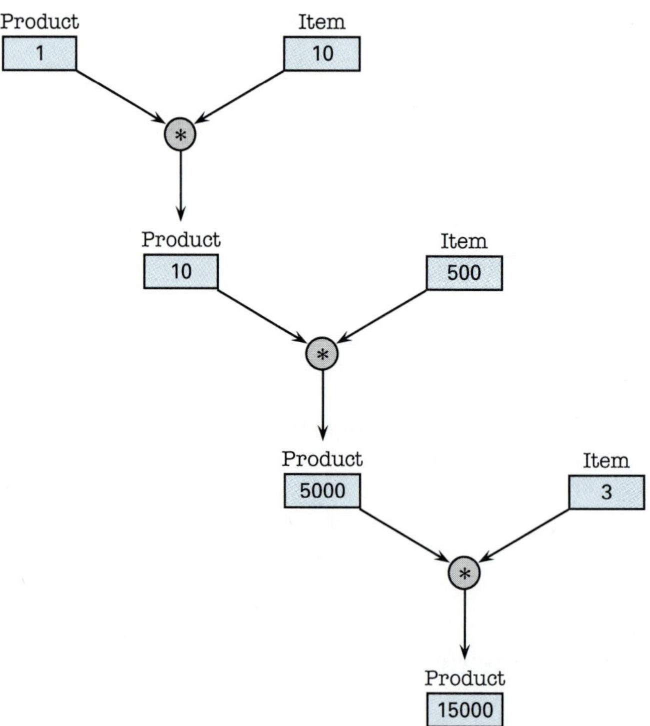

The loop in Fig. 5.5 differs from the other loops in this section. Its repetition condition involves a test of the variable `Product`. Besides controlling loop repetition, the variable `Product` also stores the result of the computation being performed in the loop. The other loops involve a test of a variable, `CountEmp`, that represents the count of loop repetitions. `CountEmp` is not directly involved in the computation being performed in the loop. We will discuss these differences further in the next section.

Exercises for Section 5.2

Self-Check

1. What is the purpose of the statement

```
WriteLn;
```

in the loop body of Fig. 5.3?

2. What output values are displayed by the following `while` loop for a data value of 5?

```
WriteLn ('Enter an integer> ');
ReadLn (X);
Product := X;
Count := 0;
while Count < 4 do
  begin
    WriteLn (Product);
    Product := Product * X;
    Count := Count + 1
  end; {while}
```

3. What values are displayed if the call to `WriteLn` comes at the end of the loop instead of the beginning?
4. What does the following segment display? Insert `begin` and `end` where needed and correct the errors. The corrected segment should read five numbers and display their sum.

```
Count := 0;
while Count <= 5 do
Count := Count + 1;
Write ('Next number> ');
ReadLn (NextNum);
NextNum := Sum + NextNum;
WriteLn (Count :1, 'numbers were added;');
WriteLn ('their sum is ', Sum:4:2)
```

Programming

1. Write a program segment that computes `1 + 2 + 3 + ... + (N - 1) + N`, where `N` is a data value. Follow the loop body with an `if` statement that compares this value to `(N * (N + 1)) / 2` and displays a message that indicates whether the values are the same or different. What message do you think will be displayed?

5.3 Counting Loops and Conditional Loops

The `while` loop shown in Fig. 5.3 is called a *counter-controlled loop* (or *counting loop*) because its repetition is controlled by a variable whose value represents a count. A counter-controlled loop follows this general format described in pseudocode.

```
Set counter variable to an initial value of 0
while counter variable < final value do
  begin
    ...
    increase counter variable by 1
  end
```

We use a counter-controlled loop when we can determine prior to loop execution exactly how many loop repetitions will be needed to solve the problem. This number should appear as the *final value* in the `while` condition.

Preview of the for Statement

Pascal provides the `for` statement as another loop form for implementing counting loops. The `for` statement is the loop form most commonly used in the BASIC programming language and may be familiar to you if you have had some prior programming experience. The `for` statement implementation of the loop in Fig. 5.3 is shown in Fig. 5.6.

Figure 5.6 Using a for Statement in a Counting Loop

```
{Process each employee starting with the first.}
TotalPay := 0.0;
for CountEmp := 1 to NumberEmp do
  begin
    Write ('Hours> ');
    ReadLn (Hours);
    Write ('Rate > $');
    ReadLn (Rate);
    Salary := Hours * Rate;
    WriteLn ('Salary is $', Salary :4:2);
    WriteLn;
    TotalPay := TotalPay + Salary
  end; {for}

WriteLn ('All employees processed');
```

The `for` statement heading

```
for CountEmp := 1 to NumberEmp do
```

contains all the control information for the loop. It specifies that the loop body will execute for each value of `CountEmp` from `1` through `NumberEmp` and combines the three loop control steps of initialization, update, and testing in one place. Consequently, separate steps to initialize and update `CountEmp` must not appear in Fig. 5.6. Note that the counter variable, `CountEmp`, is initialized to `1` (not `0`) in the `for` statement heading.

Although the `for` statement implementation of a counting loop is shorter and simpler than that of the `while` statement, the `for` statement is not as versatile as the `while` statement and can be used only to implement counting loops. For that reason, we will continue our study of loops using the `while` statement; we will cover the `for` statement in Chapter 9.

Conditional Loops

In many programming situations, you will not be able to determine the exact number of loop repetitions before loop execution begins. The number of repetitions may depend on some aspect of the data that is not known before the loop is entered, but that usually can be stated by a condition. For example, you may want to continue writing checks as long as your bank balance is positive, as indicated by the following pseudocode description:

```
while the balance is still positive do
  begin
    Read in the next transaction
    Update and print the balance
  end
```

The actual number of loop repetitions performed depends on the type of each transaction (deposit or withdrawal) and its amount.

■ Example 5.3

The program in Fig. 5.7 shows the progress of a hungry worm approaching an apple. Each time it moves, the worm cuts the distance between itself and the apple in half until the worm is close enough to enter the apple. A `while` loop is the correct looping structure to use because we have no idea beforehand how many moves the worm will need to reach the apple.

Figure 5.7 Worm Bites Apple

Edit Window

```
program WormAndApple;
{
  Prints distances between a worm and an apple.
  The worm keeps cutting the distance in half
  until it is close enough to enter the apple.
}
  const
    Close = 0.5;        {maximum distance for entry to apple}
```

```
  var
    InitialDist,      {starting distance of worm from apple}
    Distance : Real;  {distance between worm and apple}

begin {WormAndApple}
  Write ('Enter initial distance between worm and apple> ');
  ReadLn (InitialDist);
  {
   Cut the distance between the worm and the apple in half
   until the worm is close enough to enter the apple.
  }
  Distance := InitialDist;
  while Distance > Close do
    begin
      WriteLn ('The distance is ', Distance :4:2);
      Distance := Distance / 2.0         {cut Distance in half}
    end; {while}

  {Print final distance before entering the apple.}
  WriteLn;
  WriteLn ('Final distance between the worm and apple is ',
           Distance :4:2);
  WriteLn ('The worm enters the apple.')
end. {WormAndApple}
```

Output Window

```
Enter initial distance between worm and apple> 2.8
The distance is 2.80
The distance is 1.40
The distance is 0.70

Final distance between the worm and apple is 0.35
The worm enters the apple.
```

Table 5.1 traces the sample run shown in Fig. 5.7. The assignment statement just before the loop initializes the variable `Distance` to the starting distance (`2.8`), which was previously read into `InitialDist`. Next, the loop header is reached and the *loop repetition condition* (or `while` condition)

```
Distance > Close
```

is evaluated. Since this condition is true, the loop body (through `end`) is executed. The loop body displays the value of `Distance` and the statement

```
Distance := Distance / 2.0       {cut Distance in half}
```

halves the value of `Distance`, thereby bringing the worm closer to the apple. The loop repetition condition is retested with the new value of `Distance` (`1.4`); since `1.4 > 0.5` is true, the loop body displays `Distance` again, and `Distance` becomes `0.7`. The loop repetition condition is tested a third time; since `0.7 > 0.5` is true, the loop body displays `Distance` again, and `Distance` becomes `0.35`. The loop repetition condition is tested again; since `0.35 > 0.5` is false, loop exit occurs, and the statements following the loop `end` are executed.

Table 5.1 Trace of Program in Figure 5.7

Program Statement	InitialDist	Distance	Effect
	?	?	
`Write ('Enter initial ...')`	2.8		Reads the data.
`Distance := InitialDist;`		2.8	Initializes `Distance`.
`while Distance > Close do`			Is `2.8 > 0.5`? Value is `True`.
`WriteLn ('The distance ...')`			Displays `2.8`.
`Distance := Distance / 2.0`		1.4	Halves the distance.
`while Distance > Close do`			Is `1.4 > 0.5`? Value is `True`.
`WriteLn ('The distance ...')`			Displays `1.4`.
`Distance := Distance / 2.0`		0.7	Halves the distance.
`while Distance > Close do`			Is `0.7 > 0.5`? Value is `True`.
`WriteLn ('The distance ...')`			Displays `0.7`.
`Distance := / 2.0`		0.35	Halves the distance.
`while Distance > Close do`			Is `0.35 > 0.5`? Value is `False`.
`WriteLn;`			Skips a line.
`WriteLn ('Final distance ...')`			Displays `0.35`.

It is important to realize that the loop is not exited at the exact instant that `Distance` becomes `0.35`. If more statements appeared in the loop body after the assignment to `Distance`, they would be executed. Loop exit does not occur until the loop repetition condition is retested at the top of the loop and found to be false. ■

Just as in the counting loop shown earlier, there are three critical steps in Fig. 5.7 that involve the loop control variable `Distance`.

1. `Distance` is initialized to `InitialDist` before the loop header is reached.
2. `Distance` is tested before each execution of the loop body.
3. `Distance` is updated (divided by `2.0`) during each iteration.

Remember that steps similar to these must appear in every loop you write.

Exercises for Section 5.3

Self-Check

1. What is the least number of times that the body of a `while` loop can be executed?
2. What is displayed by the following segment? Correct it so that it prints all multiples of 5 from 0 through 100.

```
Sum := 0;
while Sum < 100 do
```

```
Sum := Sum + 5;
WriteLn (Sum : 1);
```

3. What values are displayed if the data value in the sample run of the program in Fig. 5.7 is `9.45`? Answer this question if the order of the statements in the loop body is reversed.
4. How would you modify the loop in Fig. 5.7 so that it also determines the number of moves (`CountMoves`) made by the worm before entering the apple? Which is the loop control variable, `Distance` or `CountMoves`?

Programming

1. There are 9,870 people in a town whose population increases by 10 percent each year. Write a loop that determines how many years (`CountYears`) it will take for the population to go over 30,000.

5.4 Loop Design

It is one thing to be able to analyze the operation of a loop and another to design your own loops. Let's consider the latter problem. The comment just before the loop in Fig. 5.7

```
{
 Cut the distance between the worm and the apple in half
 until the worm is close enough to enter the apple
}
```

summarizes the purpose of the loop. To accomplish that purpose, we must concern ourselves with loop control and loop processing. Loop control involves making sure that loop exit occurs when it is supposed to; loop processing involves making sure the loop body performs the required operations.

To help us formulate the necessary loop control and loop processing steps, it is useful to list what we know about the loop. In the worm and apple problem, if `Distance` is the distance of the worm from the apple, we can make the following observations.

1. `Distance` must be equal to `InitialDist` just before the loop begins.
2. `Distance` during pass i must be half the value of `Distance` during pass $i-1$ (for $i > 1$).
3. `Distance` must be between `Close`/2.0 and `Close` just after loop exit.

Statement 1 simply indicates that `InitialDist` is the starting distance of the worm from the apple. Statement 2 says that the distance of the worm from the apple must be cut in half during each iteration. Statement 3 derives from the fact that the worm enters the apple when `Distance <= Close`. `Distance` cannot be `<= Close`/2.0 after loop exit; if it is, the loop should have been exited at the end of an earlier pass.

Statement 1 by itself tells us what initialization must be performed. Statement 2 tells us how to process `Distance` within the loop body (that is, divide it by 2.0). Finally, statement 3 tells us when to exit the loop. Because `Distance` is decreasing, loop exit should occur when `Distance <= Close` is true. These considerations give us the following outline, which is the basis for the `while` loop shown in Fig. 5.7. The loop repetition condition, `Distance > Close`, is the opposite of the exit condition, `Distance <= Close`.

```
1. Initialize Distance to InitialDist
2. while Distance > Close do
     begin
       3. Display Distance
       4. Divide Distance by 2.0
     end {while}
```

While Loops with Zero Iterations

The body of a `while` loop is not executed if the loop repetition test fails (evaluates to false) when it is first reached. To verify that you have the initialization steps correct, make sure that the program still generates the correct results for zero iterations of the loop body. For example, if `Close` is greater than or equal to the value read into `InitialDist` (say, `0.4`), the loop body in Fig. 5.7 would not execute and the following lines would be correctly displayed.

```
Enter initial distance between worm and apple > 0.4

Final distance between the worm and apple is 0.40
The worm enters the apple.
```

Displaying a Table of Values

The next example shows you how to use a loop to display a table of values.

■ Example 5.4

Your physics professor wants you to write a program that displays the effect of gravity on a free-falling object. Your instructor would like a table that shows the height of an object dropped from a tower for every second that it is falling.

Assuming that T is the time of free fall, we can make the following observations about the height of an object dropped from a tower.

1. At $T = 0.0$, the object height is the same as the tower height.
2. While the object is falling, its height is the tower height minus the distance that the object has traveled.
3. Free fall ends when the object height is $<= 0.0$.

These considerations form the basis for the `while` loop shown in Fig. 5.8. The object height (`Height`) is initialized to the tower height (`Tower`). The `while` condition

```
Height > 0.0
```

ensures that loop exit occurs when the object hits the ground. Within the loop body, the assignment statement

```
Height := Tower - 0.5 * G * T * T
```

computes the object height where distance travelled is represented by the formula

$$distance = \frac{1}{2} GT^2$$

and G is the gravitational constant.

The number of lines in the table depends on the time interval between lines (`DeltaT`) and the tower height (`Tower`), both of which are data values. During each loop iteration, the current elapsed time, `T`, and the current object height, `Height`, are displayed and new values assigned to these variables. The message following the table is displayed when the object hits the ground. ■

Figure 5.8 Dropping an Object from a Tower

Edit Window

```
Program FreeFall;
{
  Displays the height of an object dropped
  from a tower until it hits the ground.
}

  const
    G = 9.80665;         {gravitational constant for metric units}

  var
    Height,              {height of object}
    Tower,               {height of tower}
    T,                   {elapsed time}
    DeltaT : Real;       {time interval}

begin {FreeFall}
  {Enter tower height and time interval.}
  Write ('Tower height in meters> ');
  ReadLn (Tower);
  Write ('Time in seconds between table lines> ');
  ReadLn (DeltaT); WriteLn;

  {Display object height until it hits the ground.}
  WriteLn ('Time' :10, 'Height' :10);
  T := 0.0;
  Height := Tower;
  while Height > 0.0 do
    begin
      WriteLn (T :10:2, Height :10:2);
      T := T + DeltaT;
      Height := Tower - 0.5 * G * T * T
    end; {while}

  {Object hits the ground.}
  WriteLn;
  WriteLn ('SPLATT!!!'); WriteLn
end. {FreeFall}
```

Output Window

```
Tower height in meters> 100.0
Time in seconds between table lines> 1.0
```

```
    Time     Height
    0.00     100.00
    1.00      95.10
    2.00      80.39
    3.00      55.87
    4.00      21.55

SPLATT!!!
```

PROGRAM STYLE

Displaying a Table

The program in Fig. 5.8 displays a table of output values. Before the loop is reached, the statement

```
WriteLn ('Time' :10, 'Height' :10);
```

displays the two strings that appear in the table heading. A string is printed right-justified in its field, so the rightmost character of the first string appears in column 10, and the rightmost character of the second string appears in column 20 (10 + 10).

Within the loop body, the statement

```
WriteLn (T :10:2, Height :10:2);
```

displays a pair of output values each time it is executed. The rightmost digit of the first number appears in column 10, and the rightmost digit of the second number appears in column 20. Therefore, a table consisting of two columns of numbers is displayed, and each column is right-aligned with its respective heading. Make sure that the field width (10, in this case) is large enough to accommodate the largest value that will be printed.

Working Backward to Determine Loop Initialization

It is not always so easy to come up with the initialization steps for a loop. In some cases, you will have to work backward from the results that you know are required in the first pass to determine what initial values will produce those results.

■ Example 5.5

Your little cousin is learning the binary number system and has asked you to write a program that displays all powers of 2 that are less than a certain value (say, 10000). Assuming that each power of 2 is stored in the variable `Power`, you can make the following observations about the loop.

1. `Power` during pass i is 2 times `Power` during pass $i-1$ (for $i > 1$).
2. `Power` must be between 10000 and 20000 just after loop exit.

Statement 1 derives from the fact that the powers of 2 are all multiples of 2, and statement 2 from the fact that only powers less than 10000 are displayed. From statement 1, you know that `Power` must be multiplied by 2 in the loop body. From statement 2 you know that the loop exit condition is `Power >=`

10000, so the loop repetition condition is Power < 10000. These considerations lead us to the outline below.

```
1. Initialize Power to ____
2. while Power < 10000 do
     begin
       3. Display Power
       4. Multiply Power by 2
     end
```

One way to complete step 1 is to ask what value should be displayed during the first loop repetition. The value of N raised to the power zero is one for any number N. Therefore, if we initialize Power to 1, the value displayed during the first loop repetition will be correct.

1. Initialize Power to 1 ■

Sentinel-Controlled Loops

Frequently, you will not know exactly how many data items a program will process before it begins execution. This may happen because there are too many data items to count beforehand or because the number of data items provided depends on how the computation proceeds.

One way to handle this situation is to instruct the user to enter a unique data value, called a *sentinel value*, when finished. The program then tests each data item and terminates when the sentinel value is read. You must choose the sentinel value carefully; it must be a value that could not normally occur as data.

■ Example 5.6

The following statements must be true for a sentinel-controlled loop that accumulates the sum (in Sum) of a collection of exam scores, where each score is read into the variable Score. The sentinel score must not be included in the sum.

1. Sum is the sum of all scores read so far.
2. Score contains the sentinel value just after loop exit.

From statement 1 we know that we must add each score to Sum in the loop body, and that Sum must initially be zero for its final value to be correct. From statement 2 we know that loop exit must occur after the sentinel value is read into Score. These considerations lead to the following trial loop form.

Incorrect Sentinel-Controlled Loop

```
1. Initialize Sum to zero
2. while Score is not the sentinel do
     begin
       3. Read the next score into Score
```

4. Add Score to Sum
end

Because Score has not been given an initial value, the while condition in step 2 cannot be evaluated when the loop is first reached. Another problem is that after step 3 reads the sentinel value, step 4 adds the sentinel to Sum before loop exit occurs. The solution to these problems is to read the first score as the initial value of Score before the loop is reached and to switch the order of the read and add steps in the loop body. The outline for this solution is as follows:

Correct Sentinel-Controlled Loop

1. Initialize Sum to zero
2. Read the first score into Score
3. while Score is not the sentinel do
   begin
   4. Add Score to Sum
   5. Read the next score into Score
   end

Step 2 reads in the first score, and step 4 adds this score to Sum (initial value of zero). Step 5 reads all remaining scores, including the sentinel. Step 4 adds all scores except the sentinel to Sum.

The initial read (step 2) is often called the *priming read,* because it is analogous to the priming of a pump, in which a cup of water must first be poured into a pump before it can begin to pump water out of a well. The Pascal implementation shown in Fig. 5.9 uses -1 (value of the user-defined constant Sentinel) as the sentinel because all exam scores should be nonnegative.

Figure 5.9 A Sentinel-Controlled Loop

```
Sum := 0;
WriteLn ('When done, enter -1 to stop.');
WriteString ('Enter the first score> ');
ReadLn (Score);
while Score <> Sentinel do
  begin
    Sum := Sum + Score;
    WriteLn ('Enter the next score> ');
    ReadLn (Score)
  end; {while}
WriteLn;
WriteLn ('Sum of exam scores is ', Sum :1)
```

Although it may look strange at first to see the statement

```
ReadLn (Score);
```

at two different points in the program, this is a perfectly good programming practice and causes no problems. The following sample dialogue would be used to enter the scores 55, 33, and 77.

```
When done, enter -1 to stop.
Enter the first score> 55
Enter the next score> 33
Enter the next score> 77
Enter the next score> -1

Sum of exam scores is 165
```

It is usually instructive (and often necessary) to question what happens when there are no data items to process. In this case, the sentinel value should be entered as the "first score." Loop exit would occur right after the first (and only) test of the loop repetition condition, so the loop body would not be executed (in other words, it is a loop with zero iterations). `Sum` would retain its initial value of zero, which would be correct. ■

Exercises for Section 5.4

Self-Check

1. Write statements similar to the ones shown in this section that summarize the properties of the loop in Fig. 5.3.
2. Why would it be incorrect to move the assignment statement in the loop of Fig. 5.9 to the end of the loop body?

Programming

1. Modify the loop in Fig. 5.3 so that it is a sentinel-controlled loop. Use a negative value of `Hours` as the sentinel. Read the value of `Hours` before loop repetition and at the end of the loop body.
2. Write a program segment that allows the user to enter values and prints out the number of positive and negative values entered. Use `0` as the sentinel value.
3. Write the `while` loop for a program that prints all powers of an integer, `N`, less than a specified value, `MaxPower`. On each line of a table, show the exponent (0, 1, 2, ...) and the value of the integer `N` raised to that exponent.
4. Write a loop that prints a table of equivalent Fahrenheit and Celsius temperature values. Use the formula

   $$Fahrenheit = 1.8 \times Celsius + 32.0$$

   to convert from degrees Celsius to Fahrenheit. Assume that the initial and final Celsius values are available in `InitCel` and `FinalCel` (type `Real`), respectively, and that the change in Celsius values between table entries is given by `StepCel`.

5.5 Assertions and Loop Invariants

Once a loop is designed, you should verify that it works properly. One verification method is to trace the loop's execution for a variety of different sets of data, making sure that the loop always terminates and that it produces the correct results, even when zero iterations are performed.

Exhaustive testing of a loop can be time-consuming. For this reason, computer scientists have devised techniques for quickly proving that a loop is correct. Detailed analysis of that process is beyond the scope of the text, but we will introduce some principles of loop verification that will help you design loops.

A critical part of loop verification is documentation of the loop with a special comment called an *assertion*—a logical statement that is always true. An assertion should be placed just before the loop body and just after the loop end. The assertion that precedes the loop body is called the *loop invariant.* Like the while condition, the loop invariant is evaluated just before each repetition of the loop body. The execution of the loop body may change the value of the while condition from true to false; however, the value of the loop invariant must remain true. The loop in Fig. 5.7 is rewritten in Fig. 5.10 using assertions. Remember that assertions, like all comments, are ignored by the compiler.

Figure 5.10 Worm and Apple Loop with Assertions

```
{
 Cut the distance between the worm and the apple in half
 until the worm is close enough to enter the apple
}
Distance := InitialDist;
while Distance > Close do
  {invariant:
      Distance <= InitialDist and
      Distance > Close / 2.0 and
      Distance in pass i is half Distance in pass i-1 (for i > 1)
  }
  begin
    WriteLn ('The distance is ', Distance :4:2);
    Distance := Distance / 2.0          {cut Distance in half}
  end; {while}

{assert: Distance <= Close}
```

The invariant summarizes all we know about the loop and is similar to our earlier observations:

1. Distance must be equal to InitialDist just before the loop begins.
2. Distance during pass i must be half the value of Distance during pass $i-1$ (for $i > 1$).
3. Distance must be between Close/2.0 and Close just after loop exit.

■ Example 5.7

The sentinel-controlled loop (see Fig. 5.9) is rewritten in Fig. 5.11 using assertions. Compare the loop invariant with the following statements that summarize the loop properties.

1. Sum is the sum of all scores read so far.
2. Score is the sentinel just after loop exit. ■

Figure 5.11 Sentinel-Controlled Loop with Assertions

```
Sum := 0;
WriteLn ('When done, enter -1 to stop.');
WriteLn ('Enter the first score> ');
ReadLn (Score);
while Score <> Sentinel do
  {invariant:
      Sum is the sum of all scores read and
      no prior score was the sentinel
  }
  begin
    Sum := Sum + Score;
    WriteLn ('Enter the next score> ');
    ReadLn (Score)
  end; {while}

{assert: Score is Sentinel and Sum is the sum of all scores}
```

Some computer scientists use loop invariants for loop design as well as for loop verification. By first writing the loop invariant as a comment inside the loop, they can discern from the invariant what initialization, testing, and processing steps are required.

Remembering the Previous Data Value in a Loop

In a number of situations, your program may need to remember the data value processed during the previous iteration of a loop. For example, some keyboards are "bouncy" and cause multiple occurrences of the same character when you press a key. Some faculty are forgetful and may enter the same exam score two times in succession. We can avoid errors like those by using an `if` statement nested inside a loop to check whether the current data value is the same as the last data value.

■ Example 5.8

The program in Fig. 5.12 finds the product of a collection of data values. If there are consecutive multiple occurrences of the same data value, only the first occurrence is included in the product. For example, the product of the numbers 10, 5, 5, 5, and 10 is $10 \times 5 \times 10$, or 500. Assuming that a new data value is read into `NextNum` during each loop iteration, we can make the following observations:

1. `Product` in pass i is the same as `Product` in pass $i-1$ if `NextNum` in pass i is `NextNum` in pass $i-1$; otherwise, `Product` during pass i is `NextNum` times `Product` in pass $i-1$ (for $i > 1$).
2. `NextNum` is the sentinel just after loop exit.

Statement 1 requires the loop to "remember" the value read into `NextNum` during the previous iteration. We will introduce a new program variable, `LastNum`, for that purpose. The current value of `NextNum` should be incorporated in the product only if it is different from the previous value of `NextNum` (saved in `LastNum`). A trial loop form follows.

Initial Loop Form

1. Initialize Product to _____
2. Initialize LastNum to _____
3. Read the first number into NextNum
4. while NextNum is not the sentinel do
   begin
   5. if NextNum is not equal to LastNum then
      6. Multiply Product by NextNum
   7. Set LastNum to NextNum
   8. Read the next number into NextNum
   end

For Product to be correct during the first pass, it must be initialized to 1 (step 1). We must also initialize LastNum so that the condition in step 5 can be evaluated. To ensure that the first number read into NextNum is incorporated in the product, we must pick a value for LastNum that is different from the initial data value. If we initialize LastNum to the sentinel, we know that LastNum will be different from the initial data value unless there are no actual data. These considerations lead to the revised loop form that follows:

Revised Loop Form

1. Initialize Product to 1
2. Initialize LastNum to the sentinel
3. Read the first number into NextNum
4. while NextNum is not the sentinel do
   begin
   5. if NextNum is not equal to LastNum then
      6. Multiply Product by NextNum
   7. Set LastNum to NextNum
   8. Read the next number into NextNum
   end

Within the loop, steps 7 and 8 prepare for the next iteration by saving the previous value of NextNum in LastNum before reading the next data value. What would happen if the order of those two steps was reversed? ■

Figure 5.12 Program to Multiply Nonrepeating Data

Edit Window

```
program Multiply;
{
 Finds the product of a collection of nonzero integers. If there
 are multiple consecutive occurrences of the same value, only the first
 value is included in the product.
}
 const
   Sentinel = 0;                    {sentinel value}
```

```
var
  NextNum,                        {input - new data item}
  LastNum,                        {last data item}
  Product : Integer;              {output - product of data}


procedure Instruct;

begin {Instruct}
  WriteLn ('This program computes the product of a collection');
  WriteLn ('of integer data values. If consecutive numbers');
  WriteLn ('are the same, only the first number is used.');
  WriteLn ('Enter 0 as a data value to stop the program.');
  WriteLn
end; {Instruct}


begin {Multiply}
  Instruct;                  {Display user instructions}

  {Compute product of nonzero, nonrepeating data items.}
  Product := 1;
  LastNum := Sentinel;
  Write ('Enter first number> ');
  ReadLn (NextNum);                         {read first item}
  while NextNum <> Sentinel do
    {invariant:
        No prior value of NextNum is the sentinel and
        Product in pass i is Product in pass i-1 if NextNum is
        LastNum; otherwise, Product in pass i is NextNum * Product
        in pass i-1 (for i > 1)
    }
    begin
      if NextNum <> LastNum then
        Product := Product * NextNum;     {compute next product}
      LastNum := NextNum;                 {remember last item}
      Write ('Enter next number> ');
      ReadLn (NextNum)                    {read next item}
    end; {while}

  {assert:
     NextNum is the sentinel and Product is the product of
     every value of NextNum such that NextNum <> LastNum
  }
  WriteLn ('The product is ', Product :1)
end. {Multiply}
```

Output Window

```
This program computes the product of a collection
of integer data values. If consecutive numbers
are the same, only the first number is used.
Enter 0 as a data value to stop the program.

Enter first number> 10
Enter next  number> 5
Enter next  number> 5
Enter next  number> 5
Enter next  number> 10
Enter next  number> 0
The product is 500
```

The program in Fig. 5.12 illustrates the proper form of a sentinel-controlled loop. The constant `Sentinel` has the value zero, since it is meaningless to include zero in a collection of numbers being multiplied. To determine whether or not to execute the loop, each value read into `NextNum` must be compared to `Sentinel`. For this test to make sense in the beginning, the first data value must be read before the `while` loop is reached. The next value must be read at the end of the loop so that it can be tested before starting another iteration. This general pattern is illustrated as follows:

```
Read the first data item
while current data item is not the sentinel do
  begin
    Process current data item
    Read the next data item
  end
```

Remember, in a sentinel-controlled loop, the read operation appears twice: before the `while` header (the priming read) and at the end of the loop body.

Exercises for Section 5.5

Self-Check

1. Write the loop invariant for the loop in Fig. 5.8 and the assertion following the loop.
2. What is the product computed by the program in Fig. 5.12 if only one data value besides the sentinel is supplied? What product would be computed if steps 7 and 8 of the revised algorithm were reversed and several data items were provided?

5.6 Displaying a Table in an Interactive Program

The next problem applies the ideas developed in this chapter to display a table of interest values. The tabular output is set off from the prompts and data values that also appear on the screen.

Case Study: Computing Interest

Problem

Now that you are finally graduating, your parents want to invest some money for you, and they are interested in finding out the best investment strategy. They ask you to write a program that shows how the value of a certificate of deposit increases annually. They want to use your program for fixed-rate or variable-rate certificates in which the interest rate changes at the beginning of each year. Whenever it is run, your program should display a table that shows the investment year, the annual interest, and the certificate balance at the end of each year until the balance has passed a target amount.

Design Overview

What is needed is a program that computes annual interest and new balance using the formulas

interest = *balance* * *rate*
new balance = *old balance* + *interest*

The program should display these values while the new balance is less than the target balance. You can use a single variable (`Balance`) to represent the old and the new balances, where the initial value of `Balance` is the deposit amount (`Deposit`).

Data Requirements

Problem Inputs
the deposit amount (`Deposit : Real`)
the target balance (`TargetBal : Real`)
the annual interest rate as a fraction (`Rate : Real`)
an indicator of whether the interest rate is fixed or variable
    (`FixedOrVar : Char`)

Problem Outputs
the current investment year (`Year : Integer`)
the annual balance (`Balance : Real`)
the annual interest earned (`Interest : Real`)

The type `Char` variable `FixedOrVar` indicates whether the annual interest rate is fixed (value is `'F'`) or varying (value is `'V'`).

Initial Algorithm

1. Enter the deposit amount, the value of `FixedOrVar`, and the interest rate for a fixed-rate certificate.
2. Print a table showing the year, interest earned, and account balance as long as the balance has not passed the target balance. If the interest rate is variable, read in the new rate at the start of each year before computing the annual interest.

Algorithm Refinements

Step 2 requires a loop. Since you don't know how many iterations are needed, use a `while` loop with the following properties:

1. `Year` is the number of loop iterations performed so far.
2. `Balance` is the sum of `Deposit` plus all prior values of `Interest`.

3. `Balance` is between `TargetBal` and `TargetBal + Interest` just after loop exit.

The preceding statements suggest the following refinement for step 2 of the algorithm.

Step 2 Refinement

2.1 Initialize `Year` to zero
2.2 Initialize `Balance` to `Deposit`
2.3 `while Balance < TargetBal do`
    `begin`
        2.4 Increment `Year` by 1
        2.5 `if` the interest rate is variable `then`
            2.6 Read this year's rate
        2.7 Compute the interest for this year
        2.8 Compute the new value of `Balance`
        2.9 Display the table line for the current year
    `end`

Coding

The program and a sample run are shown in Fig. 5.13. The sample run uses a variable interest rate. Using a fixed rate would eliminate the lines needed to read each annual rate.

Figure 5.13 Increasing Your Money

Edit Window

```
program GrowMoney;
{
  Prints a table of interest earned and account balance for each
  investment year for fixed or varying rate certificates.
}
  const
    Fixed = 'F';
    Variable = 'V';
    Pad = '

  var
    FixedOrVar : Char;     {input - indicates fixed or varying rate}
    Deposit,               {input - initial amount of deposit}
    Rate,                  {input - annual rate of interest}
    TargetBal,             {input - the target certificate amount}
    Balance,               {output - current certificate amount}
    Interest : Real;       {output - amount of annual interest}
    Year : Integer;        {output - year of investment}

begin {GrowMoney}
  Write ('Enter the deposit amount $');
  ReadLn (Deposit);
  Write ('Enter the desired final balance $');
  ReadLn (TargetBal);
  Write ('Is the interest rate fixed (F) or variable (V)? ');
```

```
  ReadLn (FixedOrVar);
  if FixedOrVar = Fixed then
    begin
      Write ('Enter the interest rate as a decimal fraction>');
      ReadLn (Rate)
    end
  else
    begin
      WriteLn ('Enter the interest rate as a decimal fraction');
      WriteLn ('after each prompt in the table below.')
    end; {if}

 {Display table heading}
 WriteLn;  Write (Pad);
 WriteLn ('Year' :10, 'Interest' :15, 'Balance' :15);

 {Display the certificate balance for each year.}
 Year := 0;
 Balance := Deposit;
 while Balance < TargetBal do
   {invariant:
       Balance < TargetBal + last value of Interest and
       Balance is the sum of Deposit and all values of Interest
   }
   begin
     Year := Year + 1;
     if FixedOrVar = Variable then
       begin
         Write ('Enter rate for year ', Year :2, '> ');
         ReadLn (Rate)
       end; {if}

     Interest := Balance * Rate;
     Balance := Balance + Interest;

     Write (Pad);                              {print table line}
     WriteLn (Year :10, Interest :15:2, Balance :15:2)
   end; {while}

  {assert: Balance >= TargetBal and
     Balance is the sum of Deposit and all values of Interest
  }
  WriteLn;
  Write ('Certificate amount reaches target after ');
  WriteLn (Year :1, ' years');
  WriteLn ('Final balance is $', Balance :4:2)
end. {GrowMoney}
```

Output Window

```
Enter the deposit amount $100.00
Enter the desired final balance $200.00
Is the interest rate fixed (F) or variable (V)? V
Enter the interest rate as a decimal fraction
after each prompt in the table below.

                                       Year      Interest       Balance
Enter rate for year  1> 0.075
                                          1          7.50        107.50
Enter rate for year  2> 0.080
                                          2          8.60        116.10
```

```
Enter rate for year  3> 0.085
                               3          9.87        125.97
Enter rate for year  4> 0.090
                               4         11.34        137.31
Enter rate for year  5> 0.095
                               5         13.04        150.35
Enter rate for year  6> 0.100
                               6         15.03        165.38
Enter rate for year  7> 0.150
                               7         24.81        190.19
Enter rate for year  8> 0.200
                               8         38.04        228.23

Certificate amount reaches target after 8 years
Final balance is $228.23
```

In the program output of Fig. 5.13, the lines used for data entry appear on the left, and the lines showing interest and certificate values appear on the right. This separation makes it easier to read the output table. The statement

```
Write (Pad);
```

accomplishes this separation by displaying a string of thirty blanks before each table line. The cursor remains positioned on the current output line after the blanks are displayed.

Testing

Test the program with a variable and a fixed interest rate. Use 10 percent to make it easy to check the table values. What happens if the character read into `FixedOrVar` is not `F` or `V`? You should also verify that the program works properly when the target balance is less than the initial deposit. In that case, the program should display the deposit amount as the final balance.

Suggestions for Improvement

Unfortunately, the program will not work properly if the user enters a lowercase `f` or `v` as the value of `FixedOrVar`. One solution to that problem is to insert the following multiple-alternative statement after the statement that reads the value of `FixedOrVar`. This statement changes a lowercase `f` or `v` to uppercase.

```
if FixedOrVar = 'f' then
  FixedOrVar := Fixed
else if FixedOrVar = 'v' then
  FixedOrVar := Variable;
```

Exercise for Section 5.6

Self-Check

1. What happens in the program of Fig. 5.13 if the program user enters a letter other than `F` or `V`? Explain how a `while` loop could be used to correct this problem.

5.7 Debugging and Testing Programs

Section 2.8 described the general categories of error messages that you are likely to see: syntax errors and run-time errors. It is possible for a program to execute without generating any error messages, but still produce incorrect results. Sometimes the cause of a run-time error or the origin of incorrect results is apparent and the error can be fixed easily. Often, however, the error is not obvious and may require considerable effort to locate.

The first step in attempting to find a hidden error is to try to determine what part of the program is generating incorrect results. Then insert extra `WriteLn` statements in your program to provide a trace of its execution. For example, if the loop in Fig. 5.9 is not computing the correct sum, you could insert an extra diagnostic `WriteLn` statement, as shown by the line in color in the following loop:

```
ReadLn (Score);
while Score <> Sentinel do
  begin
    Sum := Sum + Score;
    WriteLn ('***** score is ', Score, 'sum is ', Sum);
    WriteLn ('Enter the next  score> ');
    ReadLn (Score)
  end; {while}
```

The diagnostic `WriteLn` statement displays each partial sum that is accumulated and the current value of `Score`. This `WriteLn` statement displays a string of asterisks at the beginning of its output line. The asterisks make it easier to identify diagnostic output in the debugging runs and to locate the diagnostic `WriteLn` statements in the source program.

Be careful when you insert extra diagnostic `WriteLn` statements—they themselves can be a source of syntax errors. Sometimes it is necessary to add a `begin`...`end` pair if a single statement inside an `if` or `while` statement becomes a compound statement when a diagnostic `WriteLn` is added. If you insert a `WriteLn` statement after the last statement in the loop body, don't forget to separate the two statements with a semicolon.

Once it appears that you have located an error, take out the extra diagnostic statements. As a temporary measure, it is sometimes advisable to make the diagnostic statements comments by enclosing them in curly braces. If errors crop up again in later testing, it is easier to remove the braces than to retype the diagnostic statements.

Using the Debugger

Sometimes when run-time errors are difficult to locate, you may need to make use of a *debugger program.* The Turbo Pascal integrated environment contains its own debugger program, which allows you to interactively execute your program one statement at a time, while observing changes made to selected variables or expressions. The debugger also allows you to halt execution of your program when certain statements (*breakpoints*) are reached, so you can inspect or change values of selected variables before resuming execution.

To use the Turbo Pascal debugger, select the `Trace into` option (function key F7) from the Run menu. This causes an *execution bar* to appear over the `begin` line of the main program. If you press function key F7, the execution bar will advance to the first program statement. Each time you press F7, the statement under the execution bar executes, and the execution bar advances to the next statement. By repeatedly pressing function key F7, you will cause the debugger to execute your program one statement at a time.

You can view the effect of your program's execution in two ways. The first way is by examining the new program output displayed in the User screen as each `WriteLn` statement executes. At any time, you can press Alt-F5 to review the program output displayed so far. You can also open the Output window (see Section 2.6) to keep your program output displayed at all times. A better way to view the effect of each program statement is by using the Watch window.

The Watch Window

The User screen and the Output window can show the value of a variable only at the time it is displayed. You can use Turbo Pascal's *Watch window* to see how the execution of each program statement changes the value of selected program variables or expressions. In Fig. 5.14, the Watch window shows two variables and their values just before the `while` loop executes for the first time.

You can open the Watch window or add a variable or expression to it at any time during program execution. To add a new variable to the Watch window, move the Edit cursor to the first letter of that variable wherever it appears in the program. Next, select the Debug menu from the Main menu bar, pull down the Watches submenu, and choose the Add Watch option (or press Ctrl-F7), as shown in Fig. 5.14. A dialog box that contains in its `Watch`

Figure 5.14 Selecting Add Watch from the Debug Menu

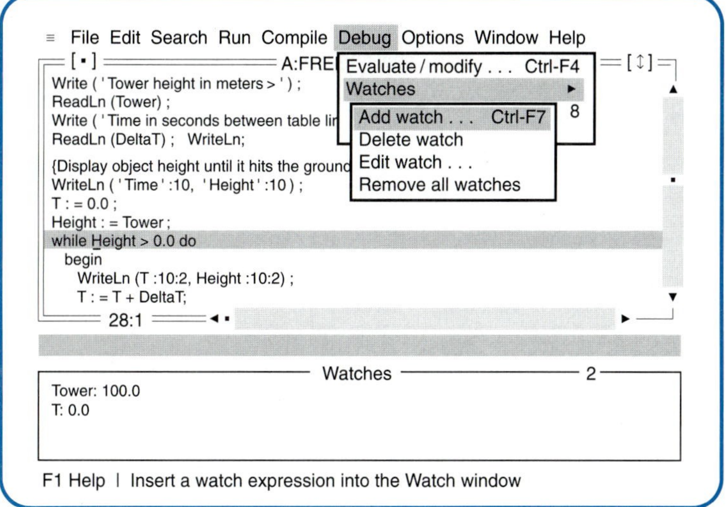

`Expression` field the variable under the Edit cursor will appear (see Fig. 5.15). If you press Enter, the variable in the `Watch Expression` field will reappear in the Watch window, along with its value. If you press the Escape key, the variable in the `Expression` field will not be added to the Watch window.

To add more variables to the Watch window, press Ctrl-F7 again, and a new Add Watch dialog box will appear. You can then type another variable name in the `Watch Expression` field and press Enter to move that variable name to the Watch window.

To add an expression to the Watch window, position the Edit cursor on the first operand of the expression and press Ctrl-F7. The Add Watch dialog box will come up on the screen, and the `Watch Expression` field will contain the operand marked by the Edit cursor. To place the remainder of the expression in the `Watch Expression` field, press the right arrow key repeatedly and then press Enter. You can also type any variable name or expression directly into the `Watch Expression` field.

You can use the F6 key to switch back and forth between the Edit window and the Watch window. To display both windows on the screen at the same time, you must reduce the size of the Edit window. First, make sure that the Edit window is the active window. Next, either use your mouse (click and drag the lower right corner of the Edit window) or select the Size/Move option from the Window menu and then use the arrow keys while pressing the Shift key. (These operations are described in more detail in Appendix A.)

To delete a single expression from the Watch window, first use the F6 key to make the Watch window the active window and then use your mouse or the up arrow and down arrow keys to highlight the expression to be deleted. Pressing the Delete key causes the highlighted expression to be removed from the Watch window. To delete all watch expressions (regardless of which window

Figure 5.15 Add Watch Dialog Box

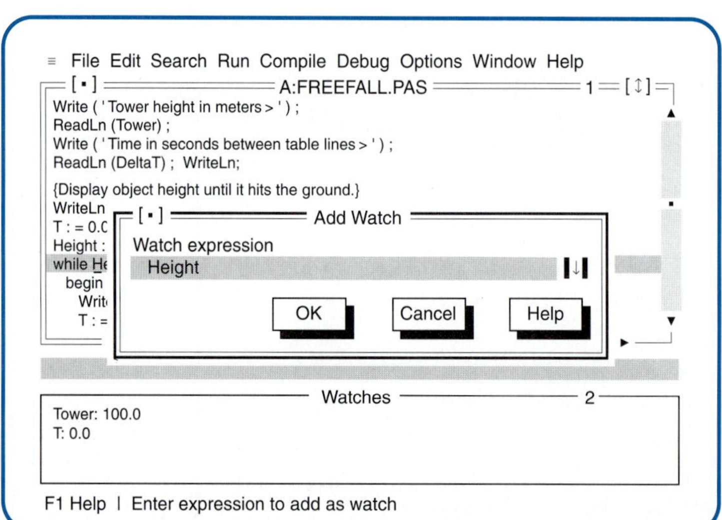

is active) from the Watch window, select the `Remove all watches` option from the Watches submenu (see Fig. 5.14).

Mixing Single-Statement and Normal Execution

If you suspect that a program bug lies in a certain section of your program, you may want to execute all statements up to this section in the normal way. To do this, move the Edit cursor to the beginning of the section where you believe the bug lies and then press F4. Turbo Pascal will execute all statements up to the one selected and pause with the Execution bar over the selected statement. At this point, you can add new variables to the Watch window and begin single-statement execution.

Breakpoints

One approach to debugging is first to separate a program into segments and then to execute all statements in a segment, pausing between segments to examine Watch window values. By doing this, you can determine which segments of a program are "buggy." Then you can rerun your program using single-statement execution within buggy segments to find the bugs. We separate a program into segments by setting *breakpoints*. After this is done, we can press Ctrl-F9 to execute all statements up to the next breakpoint or press F7 for single-statement execution.

To set a breakpoint at some program statement, position the Edit cursor on that statement and press Ctrl-F8 (Toggle breakpoint). You can also select the Toggle breakpoint option from the Debug menu. If no breakpoint exists at that statement, Turbo Pascal sets a breakpoint and marks the statement with a highlight bar. If a breakpoint already exists at that statement, Turbo Pascal removes the breakpoint and erases the highlight bar. Turbo Pascal allows you to set several breakpoints in your program and places a highlight bar over each breakpoint. If you have a color monitor, you will notice that Turbo Pascal uses different colors for breakpoints and the program execution bar.

You can view a list of the breakpoints set in your program by selecting the Breakpoints option in the Debug menu. This brings up a dialog box similar to the one shown in Fig. 5.16. You can use your mouse or the up arrow and down arrow keys to highlight any breakpoint displayed in the dialog box. By selecting the Delete button, you can remove the highlighted breakpoint from your program. Using the View button takes you to the program statement in the Edit window where the breakpoint is set, without executing your program.

The Edit button brings up the Edit Breakpoint dialog box (Fig. 5.17), which you can use to add a breakpoint or modify the condition under which execution should halt. You can use any valid Boolean expression in the `Condition` field; program execution will halt at that breakpoint only when that condition is true. The `Pass count` field is useful in monitoring the execution of loops, because you can specify the number of times a breakpoint is to be skipped before execution is halted. Using the New button when you have finished editing causes a new breakpoint to be added to your program. Using the Modify button causes the changes made to an existing breakpoint to be recorded by the debugger. If

Figure 5.16 Turbo Pascal Breakpoint Dialog Box

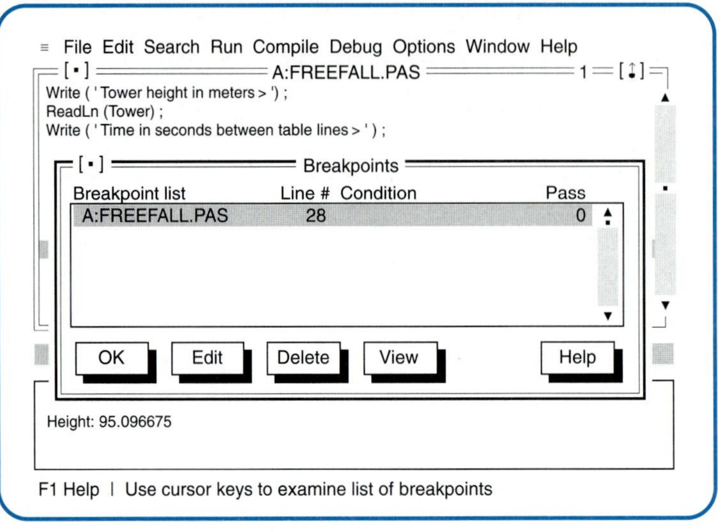

Figure 5.17 Turbo Pascal Edit Breakpoint Dialog Box

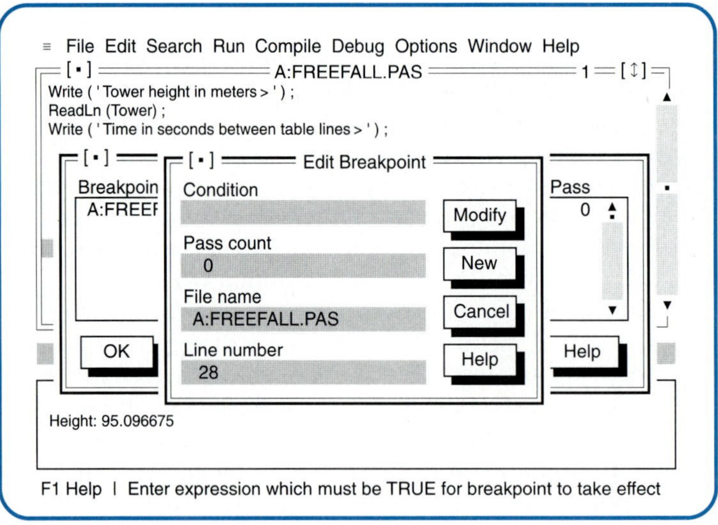

you don't have a mouse, you can move from one button to the next by pressing the Tab key.

Restarting the Debugger

If you are in the middle of a debugging session and want to start over again from the beginning of your program, press Ctrl-F2 (Program Reset). This reinitializes the debugging system and positions the execution bar over the `begin` line of the main program. It also closes any open files, clears the execution stack of any procedure calls, and releases any storage used by your program. You can also select Program Reset from the Run menu.

Prior to loading a new program into the Turbo Pascal environment after a debugging session, press Ctrl-F2 to be certain that the computer memory used by your old program is available for use by your new program. It is important to note that neither loading a new program into the Turbo Pascal system nor pressing Ctrl-F2 removes any of the expressions displayed in the Watch window or clears any of the program breakpoints. To remove watch expressions from the Watch window or to clear breakpoints, select the appropriate items from the Debug menu. You should do this prior to loading a new program into the Turbo Pascal environment.

Turbo Pascal will offer to restart the debugging session if you make any changes to a program's statements during debugging. For example, if you make a change to a program statement using an Edit command and then press one of the execution command keys (F7, F4, or Ctrl-F9), Turbo Pascal will display an Information dialog box with the message `Source has been modified. Rebuild?`. If you type Y, your program will be compiled again, the execution bar will be placed on the `begin` line of the main program, and the debugger will be reinitialized (as it would following a Program Reset). If you type N, you will continue the current debugging session and the changes made to your program will have no effect until you recompile your program.

Testing

After you have corrected all errors and the program appears to execute as expected, test the program thoroughly to make sure that it works. Earlier, we discussed tracing an algorithm and suggested that you provide enough sets of test data to ensure that all possible paths are traced. The same is true for the completed program. Make enough test runs to verify that the program works properly for representative samples of all possible data combinations.

5.8 Common Programming Errors

Beginners sometimes confuse `if` and `while` statements because both statements contain a condition. Make sure that you use an `if` statement to implement a decision step and a `while` statement to implement a conditional loop.

Be careful when you use tests for inequality to control the repetition of a `while` loop. For instance, the following loop is intended to process all transactions for a bank account while the balance is positive.

```
while Balance <> 0.0 do
  UpDate (Balance)
```

If the bank balance goes from a positive to a negative amount without being exactly 0.0, the loop does not terminate; it becomes an infinite loop. The next loop below would be safer:

```
while Balance > 0.0 do
  UpDate (Balance)
```

You should verify that the repetition condition for a `while` loop will eventually become false. If you use a sentinel-controlled loop, remember to provide a prompt that tells the program user what value to enter as the sentinel. Make sure that the sentinel value cannot be confused with a normal data item.

If the loop body contains more than one statement, remember to bracket it with `begin` and `end`. Otherwise, only the first statement will be repeated, and the remaining statements will be executed when and if the loop is exited. The following loop will not terminate because the step that updates the loop control variable is not considered part of the loop body. The program will continue to print the initial value of `Power` until you instruct the computer to terminate its execution.

```
while Power <= 10000 do
  WriteLn ('Next power of N is ', Power :6);
  Power := Power * N;
```

The same situation exists for `if` statements with a compound statement as the `True` task or `False` task. If the bracketing `begin` and `end` are missing, only the first statement will be considered part of the task, which can lead to a syntax error. In the following example, the `begin` and `end` bracket around the `True` task is missing. The compiler assumes that the semicolon at the end of the assignment statement terminates the `if` statement, so it will be unable to translate the lines that follow. This may lead to syntax errors of `; expected` (at the end of the first `WriteLn` statement) and `unexpected symbol` (the reserved word `else`).

```
if X > 0 then
  Sum := Sum + X;
  WriteLn ('Greater than zero')
else
  WriteLn ('Less than zero');
```

Finally, be sure to initialize to zero a variable used for accumulating a sum by repeated addition, and to initialize to one a variable used for accumulating a product by repeated multiplication. Omitting this step will lead to results that are inaccurate.

Chapter Review

This chapter examined the `while` statement and used it to repeat steps in a program. You learned how to implement counter-controlled loops, or loops where the number of repetitions required can be determined before the loop is entered. You also learned that the `while` statement is useful when you do not know the exact number of repetitions required before the loop begins.

In designing a `while` loop, you must consider both the loop control and the loop-processing operations that must be performed. Separate Pascal statements are needed to initialize and update the loop control variable, which is tested in the loop repetition condition.

In this chapter, you also discovered a common technique for controlling the repetition of a `while` loop: using a special sentinel value to indicate that all required data has been processed. In this case, an input variable must appear in the loop repetition condition. This variable is initialized when the first data value is read (the priming read), and it is updated at the end of the loop when the next new data value is read. Loop repetition terminates when the sentinel value is read.

The chapter discussed the importance of using assertions and loop invariants in loop verification and loop design. Throughout this text, we use loop invariants to document the processing performed by the loop body.

New Pascal Constructs

The new Pascal constructs introduced in this chapter are described in Table 5.2.

Table 5.2 Summary of New Pascal Constructs

Construct	Effect

while Statement
`Sum := 0;`
`while Sum <= MaxSum do`
`  begin`
`    Write ('Next integer> ');`
`    readln (Next);`
`    Sum := Sum + Next`
`  end`
	A collection of input data items is read and their sum is accumulated in `Sum`. This process stops when the accumulated sum exceeds `MaxSum`.

for Statement (Optional)
`for Count := 1 to 9 do`
`  WriteLn (Count, Count * Count)`
	Displays each of the digits from `1` through `9` inclusive on an output line together with its square.

✓ Quick-Check Exercises

1. A `while` loop is called a __________ loop.
2. A `while` loop is (always, sometimes, never) used for counting.
3. The priming step for a `while` loop is what kind of statement? When is it used?
4. The sentinel value is always the last value added to a sum being accumulated in a sentinel-controlled loop. True or false?
5. It is an error if a while loop body never executes. True or false?
6. What does the following segment display?

```
Product := 1;
Counter := 2;
while Counter <= 5 do
  Product := Product * Counter;
  Counter := Counter + 1;
WriteLn (Product)
```

7. What does the segment in exercise 6 display if the bracketing `begin` and `end` are inserted where intended?
8. Write the loop invariant of the segment in exercise 6.
9. Which of these may be false: loop invariant, while condition, assertion?
10. The use of loop invariants is useful for which of the following: loop control, loop design, loop verification?

Answers to Quick-Check Exercises

1. conditional
2. sometimes
3. an input operation, used in a sentinel-controlled loop
4. false—the sentinel should not be processed.
5. false
6. nothing—the loop executes "forever"
7. The value of 1 * 2 * 3 * 4 * 5, or 120.
8.
```
{invariant:
     Counter <= 6 and Product is the product of all
     integers < Counter
}
```
9. `while` condition
10. loop design, loop verification

Review Questions

1. Define a sentinel value.
2. For a sentinel value to be used properly when data are being read, where should the input statements appear?
3. Write a program called `Sum` to add and print a collection of payroll amounts entered at the terminal until a sentinel value of −1 is entered.
4. Hand-trace the following program, given the following data:

```
4 2 8 4     1 4 2 1     9 3 3 1     -22 10 8 2     3 3 4 5

program Slopes;

  const
    Sentinel = 0.0;

  var
    Slope, Y2, Y1, X2, X1 : Real;

begin {Slopes}
  WriteLn ('Enter four numbers separated by spaces');
  WriteLn ('The last two numbers cannot be the same, but');
  WriteLn ('The program terminates if the first two are.');
  WriteLn ('Enter four numbers> ');
  ReadLn (Y2, Y1, X2, X1);
  Slope := (Y2 - Y1) / (X2 - X1);
  while Slope <> Sentinel do
    begin
      WriteLn ('Slope is ', Slope :5:2);
      WriteLn ('Enter four more numbers> ');
      ReadLn (Y2, Y1, X2, X1);
      Slope := (Y2 - Y1) / (X2 - X1)
    end {while}
end. {Slopes}
```

5. Explain when it is appropriate to use semicolons within
   a. the variable declaration statement
   b. the constant declaration statement
   c. the program body
   d. an `if` statement
   e. a `while` statement

6. Which of the following statements is incorrect?
   a. Loop invariants are used in loop verification.
   b. Loop invariants are used in loop design.
   c. A loop invariant is always an assertion.
   d. An assertion is always a loop invariant.

Programming Projects

1. Write a program that finds the product of a collection of data values. Your program should ignore any negative data and should terminate when a zero value is read.
2. Write a program to read in an integer `N` and compute `Slow` = $\sum_{i=1}^{N} i = 1 + 2 + 3 + \ldots + N$ (the sum of all integers from `1` to `N`). Then compute `Fast = (N * (N + 1)) / 2` and compare `Fast` and `Slow`. Your program should print both `Fast` and `Slow` and indicate whether they are equal. (You will need a loop to compute `Slow`.) Which computation method is preferable?
3. Write a program to read a collection of integer data items and find and print the index of the first occurrence and the last occurrence of the number `12`. Your program should print index values of `0` if the number `12` is not found. The index is the sequence number of the data item `12`. For example, if the eighth data item is the only `12`, then the index value `8` should be printed for the first and last occurrence.
4. Write a program to read in a collection of exam scores ranging in value from 1 to 100. Your program should count and print the number of outstanding scores (90-100), the number of satisfactory scores (60-89), and the number of unsatisfactory scores (1-59). It should also display the category of each score. Test your program on the following data:

63	75	72	72	78	67	80	63	75
90	89	43	59	99	82	12	100	55

   Modify your program to display the average exam score (a real number) at the end of the run.
5. Write a program to process weekly employee time cards for all employees of an organization. Each employee has three data items, which indicate an identification number, the hourly wage rate, and the number of hours worked during a given week. Each employee is paid time-and-a-half for all hours worked over 40. A tax amount of 3.625 percent of gross salary is deducted. The program output should show the employee's number and net pay. Display the total payroll and the average amount paid at the end of the run.
6. Suppose you own a beer distributorship that sells Piels (ID number 1), Coors (ID number 2), Bud (ID number 3), and Iron City (ID number 4) by the case. Write a program to (a) read in the case inventory for each brand for the start of the week; (b) process all weekly sales and purchase records for each brand; and (c) print out

the final inventory. Each transaction consists of two data items. The first item is the brand identification number (an integer); the second is the amount purchased (a positive integer value) or the amount sold (a negative integer value). The weekly inventory for each brand (for the start of the week) also consists of two items: the identification number and the initial inventory for that brand. For now, you can assume that you always have sufficient foresight to prevent depletion of your inventory for any brand. (Hint: Your data entry should begin with eight values that represent the case inventory. These should be followed by the transaction values.)

7. Write a program to find the largest, smallest, and average value in a collection of N numbers, where the value of N is the first data item read.
8. Bunyan Lumber Co. needs to create a table of the engineering properties of its lumber. The dimensions of the wood are given as base and height in inches. Engineers need to know the following information about lumber:

   cross-sectional area: (base * height)
   moment of inertia: [(base * height^3)/12]
   section modulus: [(base * height^2)/6]

   The owner, Paul, makes lumber with base sizes 2, 4, 6, 8, 10, and 12 inches. The height sizes are 2, 4, 6, 8, and 10 inches. Produce a table with appropriate headings to show these values and the computed engineering properties. (Do not duplicate a 2-by-6 with a 6-by-2 board.)

6 Procedure Parameters

Chapter 3 introduced you to procedures; you learned how to use them to write separate program units corresponding to the individual steps in a problem solution. We have not used procedures extensively because we have not yet discussed how to pass information between individual procedures or between procedures and the main program. So far, our procedures can only manipulate data that are stored locally.

This chapter introduces an important concept in programming: the use of procedure parameters. In this chapter, you will see that parameters provide a convenient way to pass information between a main program and a procedure. Parameters also make procedures more versatile because they enable a procedure to manipulate different data each time it is called. For example, `WriteLn (M)` displays the value of `M`, whereas `WriteLn (N)` displays the value of `N`.

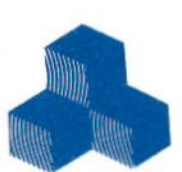

6.1 Introduction to Parameter Lists

We can make an analogy between a carefully designed program that uses procedures and a stereo system. Each stereo component is an independent device that performs a specific function. The tuner and the amplifier may contain similar electronic parts, but each component uses its own internal circuitry to perform its required function. Information in the form of electronic signals is passed back and forth between components over wires. If you look at the rear of a stereo amplifier, you will find that some plugs are marked input and others are marked output. The wires attached to the plugs marked input carry electronic signals into the amplifier, where they are processed. (These signals may come from a cassette deck, a tuner, or a compact disc player.) New electronic signals are generated. Those signals come out of the amplifier from the plugs marked output and go to the speakers or back to the tape deck for recording.

Right now, you know how to design the separate components (procedures) of a programming system, but you don't yet know how to pass data between the main program and a procedure that you write. In this chapter, you will learn how to use *parameter lists* to provide communication paths between the main program and its procedures (or between two procedures).

Actual Parameter Lists

Each procedure call statement has two parts: a procedure name and an actual parameter list. In the procedure call statement

```
WriteLn (X, Y);
```

the *actual parameter list* is `(X, Y)`, so there are two *actual parameters*, `X` and `Y`, whose values are passed into procedure `WriteLn`. We know that procedure `WriteLn` displays the values of `X` and `Y`.

In the procedure call statement

```
ReadLn (V, W);
```

the actual parameters are V and W. In this case, the procedure reads data values into these variables. The data type of each variable determines what kind of value is read.

The actual parameters are treated differently in these two procedure call statements. In the first call statement, the values of X and Y are passed into procedure WriteLn, and the procedure displays the values. Because the procedure does not change the values of X and Y, they are considered *procedure inputs*. In the second call statement, the execution of procedure ReadLn changes the contents of V and W. Because ReadLn sends values back to the calling program, V and W are considered *procedure outputs*.

Formal Parameter Lists

The system procedures WriteLn and ReadLn differ from procedures that you write in two important respects. The number of actual parameters may vary from one call to the next, and the data type of a particular actual parameter (say, the first) may also vary from one call to the next. For each procedure that you write, the number of actual parameters must be the same each time the procedure is called, and the data type of a particular parameter must be the same.

How do we tell the Pascal compiler the number of procedure parameters and the type of each parameter? The answer is through the formal parameter list.

Procedure ReportSumAve in Fig. 6.1 computes and displays the sum and average of two type Real values that are passed into the procedure as procedure inputs. The *formal parameter list*

```
(Num1, Num2 {input} : Real)
```

tells the Pascal compiler the number of parameters being processed (two), the data type of each parameter (both type Real), and the names that we will use in place of the actual parameter names in the procedure body (Num1 for the first parameter and Num2 for the second). We use the *formal parameters*, Num1 and Num2, in the procedure body to describe what we want done to the actual parameters. The actual parameters are not known when the procedure is written but are determined when the procedure call statement executes. The comment {input} identifies Num1 and Num2 as procedure inputs.

Figure 6.1 Procedure to Display Sum and Average

```
procedure ReportSumAve (Num1, Num2 {input} : Real);
{
  Displays the sum and average of Num1 and Num2.
  Pre : Num1 and Num2 are assigned values.
  Post: The sum and average value of Num1 and Num2 are displayed.
}
  var
    Sum,                  {sum of Num1, Num2}
    Average : Real;       {average of Num1, Num2}
```

```
begin {ReportSumAve}
  Sum := Num1 + Num2;
  Average := Sum / 2.0;
  WriteLn ('The sum is ', Sum :4:2);
  WriteLn ('The average is ', Average :4:2)
end; {ReportAverage}
```

PROGRAM STYLE

Preconditions and Postconditions as Comments

The declaration for procedure ReportSumAve begins with a lengthy comment that describes the procedure's operations. We use the following commenting style:

```
{
  ... comments ...
}
```

for comments that extend over multiple lines.

The comment line

```
Pre : Num1 and Num2 are assigned values.
```

describes the condition that must be true before the procedure is called; this condition is known as the *precondition*. The line

```
Post: The sum and average value of Num1 and Num2 are displayed.
```

describes the condition that must be true after the procedure execution is completed; this condition is called the *postcondition*. The use of explicit preconditions and postconditions provides valuable documentation to other programmers who might want to use the procedure. It also aids in verifying the correctness of a program that calls this procedure.

Parameter Correspondence

The body of procedure ReportSumAve begins by adding together the two values stored in its parameters Num1 and Num2 and then finds their average. For the procedure call statement

```
ReportSumAve (6.5, 3.5)
```

the formal parameter Num1 is passed the value 6.5, and the formal parameter Num2 is passed the value 3.5. The value assigned to Sum is 10.0, and the value assigned to Average is 5.0. These two values are displayed. The correspondence between the actual and the formal parameters is shown next:

Actual Parameter	*Formal Parameter*
6.5	Num1
3.5	Num2

For the procedure call statement

```
ReportSumAve (X, Y)
```

the value of X is passed to formal parameter Num1, and the value of Y is passed to formal parameter Num2. The data type of each actual parameter must be assignment compatible (see Section 2.3) with the data type of its corresponding formal parameter; otherwise, a Type mismatch syntax error occurs. Procedure ReportSumAve finds the sum and the average of its two parameter values at the time of the procedure call. Figure 6.2 shows the main program data area and the procedure data area after the procedure call statement

```
ReportSumAve (X, Y)
```

executes. The values 8.0 and 10.0 are passed into the actual parameters Num1 and Num2, respectively. The local procedure variables Sum and Average are undefined initially; the execution of the procedure body changes the values of these variables to 18.0 and 9.0, respectively.

Procedure ReportSumAve can compute and display the sum and the average of any pair of type Real numbers. We can get the procedure to operate on a different pair of numbers simply by changing the parameter list. The procedure call statement

```
ReportSumAve (Y, X)
```

would generate the same results as the previous procedure call statement; in this case, however, formal parameter Num1 corresponds to actual parameter Y and formal parameter Num2 corresponds to actual parameter X.

Figure 6.2 Data Areas at Call of ReportSumAve

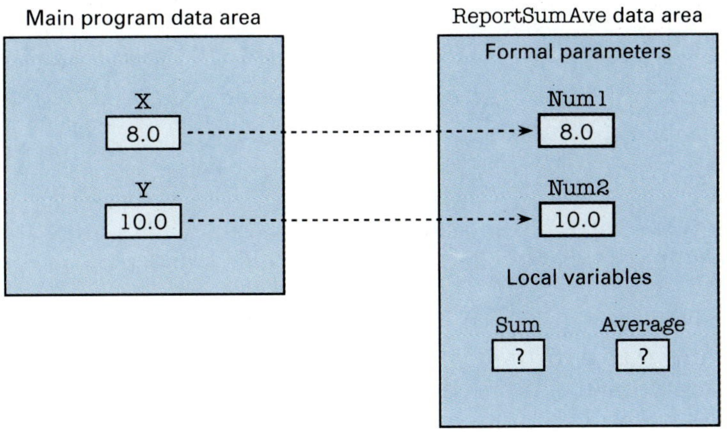

Choosing Formal Parameter Names

We have stated that the names used for formal parameters are arbitrary. Nonetheless, you should continue to follow the convention of picking names that help to document the use of the formal parameter. If a procedure is written for use in a particular program and is called only once in that program, it is reasonable to use the same name for both the formal parameter and its corresponding actual parameter. Remember that the correspondence between an actual and a formal parameter is determined solely by their position in the parameter lists, regardless of what names are used.

The Procedure Data Area

Each time a procedure call statement is executed, an area of memory is allocated for storage of that procedure's data. Included in the procedure data area are storage cells for any local variables or constants that may be declared in the procedure. The procedure data area is always erased when the procedure terminates; it is re-created empty (all values undefined) when the procedure is called again.

Exercises for Section 6.1

Self-Check

1. What is the primary purpose of procedure parameters?
2. For procedure `Cube`, which follows, what is displayed when the procedure call statement

   ```
   Cube (3)
   ```

   executes?

   ```
   procedure Cube (N : Integer);
   begin {Cube}
     Write (N :1, ' cubed is ');
     N := N * N * N;
     WriteLn (N :1)
   end; {Cube}
   ```

3. If `M` is 5, what happens when the procedure call statement

   ```
   Cube (M)
   ```

   executes? What is the value of the actual parameter `M` after the procedure executes? Where should `M` be declared and what should its data type be?

Programming

1. Write a procedure that displays the positive difference of its two formal parameters, `X` and `Y` (that is, if `X` is larger, the positive difference is `X - Y`; if `Y` is larger, the positive difference is `Y - X`.)

6.2 Value Parameters and Variable Parameters

By studying procedure ReportSumAve you learned how to pass inputs into a procedure. When a call to ReportSumAve is reached, the computer allocates memory space in the procedure data area for each formal parameter. The value of each actual parameter is stored in the memory cell(s) allocated to its corresponding formal parameter. The procedure body can manipulate this value. Next, we discuss how a procedure returns outputs to the program (or procedure) that calls it.

Procedure ComputeSumAve in Fig. 6.3 is similar to ReportSumAve. The differences are that ComputeSumAve has four parameters: two for input (Num1 and Num2) and two for output (Sum and Average). Procedure ComputeSumAve computes the sum and the average of its inputs but does not display them. Instead, those values are assigned to formal parameters Sum and Average and returned as procedure results to the calling program.

Figure 6.3 Procedure to Compute Sum and Average

```
procedure ComputeSumAve (Num1, Num2 {input} : Real;
                         var Sum, Average {output} : Real);
{
  Computes the sum and average of Num1 and Num2.
  Pre : Num1 and Num2 are assigned values.
  Post: The sum and average of Num1 and Num2 are computed
        and returned.
}

begin {ComputeSumAve}
  Sum := Num1 + Num2;
  Average := Sum / 2.0
end; {ComputeSumAve}
```

To see how this works, assume that the main program declares X, Y, Sum, and Mean as type Real variables. The procedure call statement

```
ComputeSumAve (X, Y, Sum, Mean)
```

sets up the parameter correspondence below.

Actual Parameter	*Formal Parameter*
X	Num1
Y	Num2
Sum	Sum
Mean	Average

The values of X and Y are passed into the procedure when the procedure is first called. These values are associated with formal parameters Num1 and Num2. The statement

```
Sum := Num1 + Num2;
```

stores the sum of the procedure inputs in the main program variable Sum (the third actual parameter). The statement

```
Average := Sum / 2.0
```

takes half of the value stored in the main program variable Sum and stores it in the main program variable Mean (the fourth actual parameter). The procedure execution shown in Fig. 6.4 changes the values of main program variables Sum and Mean to 18.0 and 9.0, respectively.

In Fig. 6.3, the reserved word var precedes the declaration of formal parameters Sum and Average. This tells the compiler to treat them as *variable parameters*. The compiler stores the memory address of the actual variable that corresponds to each variable parameter in the procedure data area. Through this address, the procedure can access the actual variable in the calling program and change its value or use its value in a computation. In Fig. 6.4, this relationship is shown by using a double-headed arrow to connect each variable parameter with its corresponding actual parameter. Notice that the reserved word var appears only in the formal parameter list, not in the actual parameter list.

Protection Afforded by Value Parameters

Figure 6.4 points out an important difference between formal parameters that are used as procedure inputs and those used as procedure outputs. Because they are not preceded by the reserved word var, formal parameters Num1 and Num2 are considered *value parameters*. As such, they have their own local storage cells in the procedure data area. The value passed into formal parameter Num1 is stored in the procedure data area at the time of the procedure call, and there is no further connection between formal parameter Num1 and its corresponding actual parameter. This is indicated by the dashed line in Fig. 6.4.

Figure 6.4 Data Areas after Execution of ComputeSumAve

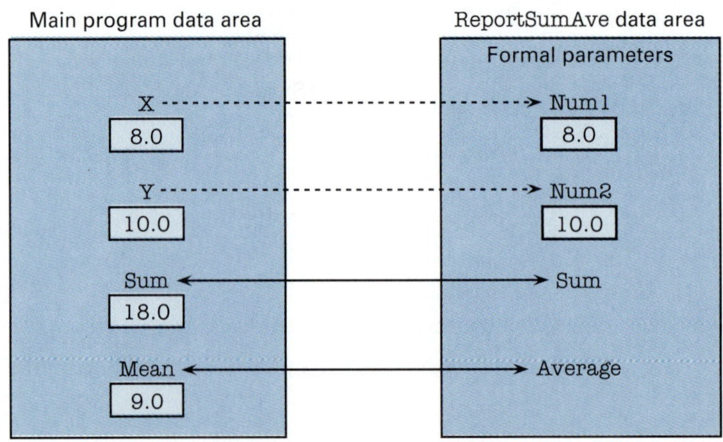

The value of formal parameter Num1 or Num2 can be used in computations or even changed by the procedure body without affecting the corresponding actual parameter. For example, if we add the statement

```
Num1 := -5.0
```

to the end of procedure ComputeSumAve, the value of formal parameter Num1 is changed to -5.0, but the value stored in the actual parameter X is still 8.0.

By making an input parameter a value parameter, we protect its value and prevent it from being changed by the procedure's execution. If we forget to declare an output parameter as a variable formal parameter, its value (not its address) will be stored locally, and any change to its value will not be returned to the calling program. This is a common source of error.

PROGRAM STYLE

Writing Formal Parameter Lists

In Fig. 6.3, the formal parameter list

```
(Num1, Num2 {input} : Real;
 var Sum, Average {output} : Real);
```

is written on two lines to improve program readability. The value parameters are written on the first line with the comment {input} inserted to document their use as procedure inputs. The variable parameters are written on the second line with the comment {output}.

Generally, this text follows the convention shown here in writing formal parameter lists. Input parameters are listed first and any output parameters are listed last. The order of the actual parameters in the procedure call must correspond to the order of the formal parameters.

Passing Information Between Procedures

So far you saw two similar procedures, ReportSumAve and ComputeSumAve, and you learned how to pass information between a main program and a procedure. Sometimes we need to pass information between procedures. For example, we might want to pass the results returned by ComputeSumAve to another procedure, say Correlate, for further processing.

Let's assume that the main program variables X and Y are passed into procedure ComputeSumAve. We can declare two more main program variables, say TempSum and TempAve, to hold the procedure results. The following procedure call statements

```
ComputeSumAve (X, Y, TempSum, TempAve);
Correlate (TempSum, TempAve)
```

pass the outputs of ComputeSumAve (TempSum and TempAve) to Correlate for further processing. Frequently, we will use main program variables to facilitate the exchange of information between procedures.

When to Use a Variable Parameter or a Value Parameter

You may be wondering how to decide when to use a variable parameter and when to use a value parameter. Some rules of thumb follow:

- If information is to be passed into a procedure and does not have to be returned or passed out of the procedure, the formal parameter representing that information should ordinarily be a value parameter (for example, Num1 and Num2 in Fig. 6.1 and Fig. 6.3). We will discuss exceptions to this rule in Section 10.4.
- If information is to be returned to the calling program from a procedure, the formal parameter representing that information must be a variable parameter (for example, Sum and Average in Fig. 6.3).
- If information is to be passed into a procedure, perhaps modified, and a new value returned, the formal parameter representing that information must be a variable parameter. We call such a parameter an *input/output* parameter.

You can use an assignment-compatible expression (or variable or constant) as an actual parameter corresponding to a value parameter. For example, the procedure call statement

```
ComputeSumAve (X + Y, 10.5, MySum, MyAve);
```

calls ComputeSumAve to compute the sum (returned in MySum) and the average (returned in MyAve) of the expression X + Y and the number 10.5. Remember, only variables can correspond to variable parameters, so MySum and MyAve must be declared as type Real variables in the calling program. This restriction is imposed because an actual parameter corresponding to a variable parameter may be modified when the procedure executes; it is illogical to allow a procedure to change the value of either a constant or an expression.

Exercises for Section 6.2

Self-Check

1. Show the output displayed by the following program in the form of a table of values for X, Y, and Z.

```
program Show;

  var
    X, Y, Z : Integer;


  procedure Sum (Num1, Num2 : Integer;
                 var Num3 : Integer);
  begin {Sum}
    Num3 := Num1 + Num2
  end; {Sum}

begin
  X := 5; Y := 3; Z := 7;
  WriteLn ('   X   Y   Z');
```

```
    Sum (X, Y, Z);
    WriteLn (X :4, Y :4, Z :4);
    Sum (Y, X, Z);
    WriteLn (X :4, Y :4, Z :4);
    Sum (Z, Y, X);
    WriteLn (X :4, Y :4, Z :4);
    Sum (Z, Z, X);
    WriteLn (X :4, Y :4, Z :4);
    Sum (Y, Y, Y);
    WriteLn (X :4, Y :4, Z :4)
  end.
```

Programming

1. Write a procedure that returns through its third parameter the positive difference of its first two parameters.
2. Write a procedure that raises its first parameter (type `Real`) to the power indicated by its second parameter (a positive integer). Use repeated multiplication. Return the result through the third parameter.

6.3 Syntax Rules for Parameter Lists

This section formally presents the syntax rules for procedure declarations and procedure call statements with parameters. The displays that follow summarize these rules.

SYNTAX DISPLAY

Procedure Declaration (Procedure with Parameters)

Form: procedure *pname* (*formal parameters*);
  declaration section
begin
  procedure body
end;

Example:

```
procedure Highlight (Ch {input} : Char;
                     var NumStars {output} : Integer);
{
  Displays Ch between two asterisks and returns the
  numbers of asterisks printed.
  Pre : Ch is defined.
  Post: Returns 3 in NumStars if Ch = Border; otherwise,
        returns 2 in NumStars.
}
  const
    Border = '*';

begin {Highlight}
  Write (Border); Write (Ch); Write (Border);
  if Ch = Border then
    NumStars := 3
  else
    NumStars := 2
end; {Highlight}
```

Interpretation: The procedure *pname* is declared. The *formal parameters* are enclosed in parentheses. The identifiers that are declared in the *declaration section* are local to the procedure and are defined only during the execution of the procedure. A formal parameter cannot be declared as a local identifier in the *declaration section*.

The *procedure body* describes the data manipulation to be performed by the procedure using the formal parameter names in the description. For a variable parameter, the procedure manipulates the corresponding actual parameter; for a value parameter, a local memory cell is initialized to the actual parameter's value, and the procedure manipulates the local copy without altering the actual parameter.

SYNTAX DISPLAY

Procedure Call Statement (Procedure with Parameters)

Form: *pname (actual parameters)*
Example: `Highlight ('A', NumAsterisks)`
Interpretation: The *actual parameters* are enclosed in parentheses. When procedure *pname* is called into execution, the first actual parameter is associated with the first formal parameter, the second actual parameter with the second formal parameter, and so on. For a value parameter, the actual parameter's value is saved in the procedure. For a variable parameter, the actual parameter's address is saved in the procedure.
Note: The *actual parameters* must satisfy the rules for parameter list correspondence, discussed later in this section.

When writing parameter lists, you must follow certain rules, as illustrated by this syntax diagram for a formal parameter list:

formal parameter list

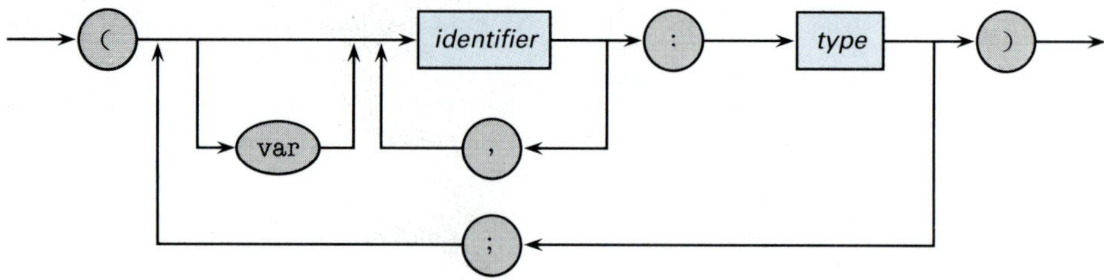

This diagram shows that a formal parameter list is always enclosed in parentheses. It consists of one or more lists of identifiers. Each list may be preceded by `var`. Identifiers are separated by commas, lists of identifiers are separated by semicolons, and each list must end with a colon followed by a data type name (for example, `Real`, `Char`, and so on).

■ Example 6.1

Two formal parameter lists follow. Each list is printed on two or more lines to improve readability.

```
(Ch3 : Char;                  (M, N, O : Integer;
 var X, Y, Z : Real)           A, B, C : Real;
                               var X, Y, Z : Real)
```

In both lists, `X`, `Y`, `Z` are declared to be type `Real` variable parameters; `Ch3`, on the left, is a type `Char` value parameter; `A`, `B`, `C`, on the right, are type `Real` value parameters; `M`, `N`, `O`, on the right, are type `Integer` value parameters. ■

The formal parameter list also determines the form of any actual parameter list that may be used to call the procedure. This form is determined during the translation of the program when the compiler processes the procedure declaration.

Later, when it reaches a procedure call statement, the compiler checks the actual parameter list for consistency with the formal parameter list. An actual parameter list can be a list of expressions, variables, or constants separated by commas. The actual parameter list must satisfy the following rules.

1. Correspondence between actual and formal parameters is determined by position in their respective parameter lists. The lists must be the same size. The names of corresponding actual and formal parameters can be different.
2. For variable parameters, the types of corresponding actual and formal parameters must be identical. For value parameters, the types of corresponding actual and formal parameters must be assignment compatible (see Section 7.8).
3. For variable parameters, an actual parameter must be a variable. For value parameters, an actual parameter can be a variable, a constant, or an expression.

■ Example 6.2

The main program contains the following declarations:

```
var
  X, Y : Real;
  M : Integer;
  Next : Char;


procedure Test (A, B : Integer;
                var C, D : Real;
                var E : Char);
```

where only the heading for procedure `Test` is shown. Procedure `Test` has two value parameters (`A` and `B`) and three variable parameters (`C`, `D`, and `E`). Any of the following procedure call statements would be syntactically correct in the main program.

```
Test (M + 3, 10, X, Y, Next);
Test (M, MaxInt, Y, X, Next);
Test (35, M * 10, Y, X, Next);
```

The correspondence specified by the first parameter list is shown in Table 6.1.

Table 6.1 Parameter Correspondence for Test (M + 3, 10, X, Y, Next)

Actual Parameter	Formal Parameter	Description
M + 3	A	Integer, value
10	B	Integer, value
X	C	Real, variable
Y	D	Real, variable
Next	E	Char, variable

The third column in Table 6.1 describes each formal parameter. The table shows that an expression (M + 3) or a constant (10) can be associated with a value parameter. The procedure call statements in Table 6.2 contain syntax errors as indicated.

Table 6.2 Invalid Procedure Call Statements

Procedure Call Statement	Error
Test (30, 10, M, X, Next)	Type of M is not Real.
Test (M, 19, X, Y)	Not enough actual parameters.
Test (M, 10, 35, Y, 'E')	Constants 35 and 'E' cannot correspond to variable parameters.
Test (M, 3.0, X, Y, Next)	Type of 3.0 is not Integer.
Test (30, 10, X, X + Y, Next)	Expression X + Y cannot correspond to a variable parameter.
Test (30, 10, C, D, E)	C, D, and E are not declared in the main program.

The last procedure call statement in Table 6.2 points out an error that programmers often make in using procedures. The actual parameter names (C, D, E) are the same as their corresponding formal parameter names. However, since these names are not declared in the main program, they cannot appear in an actual parameter list used in the main program. ■

When writing relatively long parameter lists such as the ones in Table 6.2, you must be careful not to transpose two actual parameters; that will result in a syntax error if it causes a violation of a parameter correspondence rule. Even if no syntax is violated, the procedure execution will probably generate incorrect results.

Exercises for Section 6.3

Self-Check

1. Provide a table similar to Table 6.1 for the other correct parameter lists shown in Example 6.2.
2. Correct the syntax errors in the following formal parameter lists:

```
(var A, B : Integer, C : Real)
(value M : Integer; var Next : Char)
(var Account, Real; X + Y , Real)
```

3. Assuming the declarations

```
const
  MaxInt = 32767;

var
  X, Y, Z : Real;
  M, N : Integer;

procedure Massage (var A, B : Real;
                   X : Integer);
```

what (if anything) is wrong with each incorrect procedure call statement?

a. `Massage (X, Y, Z);`
b. `Massage (X, Y, 8);`
c. `Massage (Y, X, N);`
d. `Massage (M, Y, N);`
e. `Massage (25.0, 15, X);`
f. `Massage (X, Y, M+N);`
g. `Massage (A, B, X);`
h. `Massage (Y, Z, M);`
i. `Massage (Y+Z, Y-Z, M);`
j. `Massage (Z, Y, X);`
k. `Massage (X, Y, M, 10);`
l. `Massage (Z, Y, MaxInt);`

Programming

1. Redo programming exercise 2 for section 6.2 assuming that the second parameter can be any integer value.

6.4 More Procedure Examples

This section provides more examples of procedures with parameter lists.

■ Example 6.3

Procedure `PrintStars` in Fig. 6.5 prints a row of asterisks. In the procedure heading

```
procedure PrintStars (NumStars {input} : Integer);
```

NumStars is declared to be a formal parameter of type Integer; NumStars is a value parameter (indicated by the absence of the word var).

Figure 6.5 Procedure PrintStars

```
procedure PrintStars (NumStars : Integer);
{
  Prints a row of asterisks. The number of
  asterisks printed is determined by NumStars.
  Pre : NumStars is assigned a value.
  Post: A row of asterisks is displayed.
}
  const
    Star = '*';                {symbol being printed}

  var
    CountStars : Integer;      {loop control for PrintStars}

begin {PrintStars}
  {Print a row of asterisks}
  CountStars := 1;
  while CountStars <= NumStars do
    begin
      Write (Star);
      CountStars := CountStars + 1
    end; {while}
  WriteLn
end; {PrintStars}
```

Parameter NumStars determines how many asterisks are printed. Its initial value is passed into procedure PrintStars when the procedure is called. Since there is no need for the procedure to change its parameter value, NumStars is declared to be a value parameter. The three procedure call statements

```
PrintStars (5);
PrintStars (3);
PrintStars (1)
```

would cause the following three lines to be printed:

```
*****
***
*
```

An integer value (5, 3, or 1) is assigned to NumStars when each procedure call statement is executed. ■

■ Example 6.4

Procedure Triangle in Fig. 6.6 uses procedure PrintStars to draw a triangle. This example shows that a procedure can be declared locally in another procedure and called by that procedure. In this case, the calling procedure (Triangle) passes information into procedure PrintStars each time it calls PrintStars.

Figure 6.6 Procedure Triangle

```
procedure Triangle (NumRows {input} : Integer);
{
  Prints a triangle by displaying lines of increasing length.
  The number of lines is determined by NumRows.
  Pre : NumRows is assigned a value.
  Post: A triangle is displayed.
  Requirements: Calls procedure PrintStars to display each line.
}
  var
    Row : Integer;       {loop control for Triangle}


  procedure PrintStars (NumStars : Integer);
  {
    Prints a row of asterisks. The number of
    asterisks printed is determined by NumStars.
    Pre : NumStars is assigned a value.
    Post: A row of asterisks is displayed.
  }

    const
      Star = '*';                 {symbol being printed}

    var
      CountStars : Integer;       {loop control for PrintStars}

  begin {PrintStars}
    {Print a row of asterisks}
    CountStars := 1;
    while CountStars <= NumStars do
      begin
        Write (Star);
        CountStars := CountStars + 1
      end; {while}
    WriteLn
  end; {PrintStars}


begin {Triangle}
  {Print lines of increasing length}
  Row := 1;
  while Row <= NumRows do
    begin
      PrintStars (Row);
      Row := Row + 1
    end {while}
end; {Triangle}
```

The `while` loop in the body of procedure `Triangle` repeatedly executes the procedure call statement

```
PrintStars (Row)
```

Each time `PrintStars` is called, the current value of `Row` (`1` to `NumRows`) determines how many asterisks will be displayed.

The parameter NumRows determines the number of lines in the triangle. The procedure call statement

```
Triangle (5)
```

assigns a value of 5 to NumRows and causes the following triangle to be drawn:

```
*
**
***
****
*****
```

Because procedure PrintStars is declared within procedure Triangle, PrintStars is considered a local identifier in Triangle, and PrintStars can be called only by Triangle (or by PrintStars itself). This *scope of identifiers* is discussed in detail in section 6.6. ■

■ Example 6.5

Your accountant uses the tax table shown in Table 4.5 to determine the income tax due for a particular salary. Because this table appears in many different programs, your accountant has decided to place it in procedure FindTax (see Fig. 6.7). A value is passed into input parameter Salary when the procedure is called. If Salary is within the range of the table, the tax owed is computed and assigned to output parameter Tax by the procedure execution; otherwise, -1.0 is assigned to Tax. The value assigned to Tax is returned to the calling program.

Figure 6.7 Driver Program with Procedure FindTax

Edit Window

```
program Driver;

{Tests procedure FindTax.}

  var
    MySalary,                 {input - salary}
    MyTax      : Real;        {output - tax}

  procedure FindTax (Salary {input} : Real;
                     var Tax {output} : Real);
  {
    Computes tax amount (Tax) owed for a
    salary (Salary) < $15000.
    Pre : Salary is assigned a value.
    Post: If Salary is within range, the tax owed is returned
          in Tax; otherwise, -1.0 is returned.
  }
    const
      MaxSalary = 15000.00;        {Maximum salary for table}
      OutOfRange = -1.0;           {"Tax" for an out-of-range salary}

  begin {FindTax}
    if Salary < 0.0 then
      Tax := OutOfRange                          {Salary too small}
```

```
    else if Salary < 1500.00 then              {first range}
      Tax := 0.15 * Salary
    else if Salary < 3000.00 then              {second range}
      Tax := (Salary - 1500.00) * 0.16 + 225.00
    else if Salary < 5000.00 then              {third range}
      Tax := (Salary - 3000.00) * 0.18 + 465.00
    else if Salary < 8000.00 then              {fourth range}
      Tax := (Salary - 5000.00) * 0.20 + 865.00
    else if Salary <= MaxSalary then           {fifth range}
      Tax := (Salary - 8000.00) * 0.25 + 1425.00
    else
      Tax := OutOfRange                        {Salary too large}
  end; {FindTax}

begin {Driver}
  Write ('Enter a salary less than or equal to $15000.00> $');
  ReadLn (MySalary);
  FindTax (MySalary, MyTax);
  if MyTax >= 0.0 then
    WriteLn ('The tax on $', MySalary :4:2, ' is $', MyTax :4:2)
  else
    WriteLn ('Salary $', Salary :4:2, ' is out of table range')
end. {Driver}
```

Output Window

```
Enter a salary less than or equal to $15000.00> $6000.00
The tax on $6000.00 is $1065.00
```

In Fig. 6.7, the statement

```
FindTax (MySalary, MyTax);
```

calls procedure `FindTax`. The parameter correspondence specified by this procedure call is shown in Fig. 6.8. Assuming a data value of `6000.00` was read into `MySalary` before `FindTax` was called, the value `1065.00` would be assigned to `MyTax` during the execution of procedure `FindTax`. ■

Figure 6.8 Parameter Correspondence for FindTax (MySalary, MyTax)

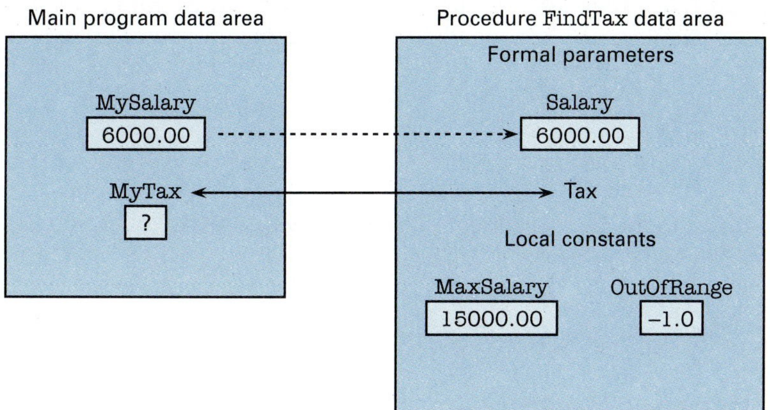

PROGRAM STYLE

Validating Input Parameters

The `if` statement in procedure `FindTax` tests for an invalid value of the input parameter `Salary` before performing the tax computation. Make sure that all procedures validate their input parameters; there are no guarantees that the values passed to an input parameter will be meaningful.

PROGRAM STYLE

Cohesive Procedures

Procedure `FindTax` is concerned only with the tax computation. It neither reads in a value for `Salary` nor displays the computed result. The result is returned to the calling program, which may display it or pass it on to another procedure that prints results. Notice that `FindTax` does not display an error message in the event that the value passed to `Salary` is out of range. It simply returns a special value (`-1.0`) to indicate this, and the calling program displays the error message.

Procedures that perform a single operation are called *cohesive procedures*. It is good programming style to write cohesive procedures, which helps to keep each procedure relatively compact and easy to read, write, and debug.

PROGRAM STYLE

Writing Driver Programs to Test Procedures

The main program body in Fig. 6.7 consists of a statement for data entry, a procedure call statement, and an `if` statement to display the procedure result. Its sole purpose is to test procedure `FindTax`. Such a program is called a *driver program*.

Experienced programmers often use driver programs to pretest procedures. Generally, the small investment in time and effort required to write a short driver program pays off by reducing the total time spent debugging a large program system that contains several procedures.

Exercises for Section 6.4

Self-Check

1. Why is the `if` statement currently in `FindTax` better than the one that follows?

```
if Salary < 0.0 then
  WriteLn (Salary :4:2, ' is out of range') {Salary too small}
...
else
  WriteLn (Salary :4:2, ' is out of range') {Salary too large}
```

Programming

1. Write a driver program that tests procedure `FindTax` for all values of `Salary` from `-100.00` to `15100.00` in increments of `500.00`.

6.5 Stepwise Design with Procedures

Now that you can pass data into and out of procedures, you can make more use of procedures in your programming. Many of the level-one subproblems shown in a structure chart will be implemented as separate procedures. In this text, if the solution to a subproblem cannot be written easily using just a few Pascal statements, it is coded as a procedure.

In this section, you will see how to add *data flow* information to a structure chart and how to practice *stepwise* design of programs.

Case Study: General Sum-and-Average Problem

Problem

Procedure `ReportSumAve` in Fig. 6.1 was used to find the sum and the average of a pair of data items. In this section, we will solve the general case of this problem by writing a program that finds and prints the sum and the average of a list of data items.

Design Overview

Figure 5.3 shows a loop that computes the total payroll for a company. We can adapt this approach to compute the sum and the average of a collection of data values.

Data Requirements

Problem Inputs

Number of data items to be summed (`NumItems : Integer`)
Each data item (`Item : Real`)

Problem Outputs

Sum of data items (`Sum : Real`)
Average of data (`Average : Real`);

Initial Algorithm

1. Read the number of items (`NumItems`).
2. Compute the sum of the data.
3. Compute the average of the data.
4. Print the sum and the average.

Algorithm Refinements

Steps 2 and 3 are the only steps that need refinement. To perform step 3, we can divide the result of step 2 by the number of data items. The average is undefined if `NumItems` is not positive. The refinement of step 3 follows.

Step 3 Refinement

3.1 `if NumItems > 0 then`
    3.2 Divide `Sum` by `NumItems`.

Rather than refine step 2 now, let's assume we have a procedure, `FindSum`, that performs this step. (We will consider how to implement `FindSum` later.)

The structure chart in Fig. 6.9 documents the data flow between subproblems. Downward-pointing arrows indicate inputs to a subproblem; upward-pointing arrows indicate outputs from a subproblem. The variables involved in the data transfer are listed inside the arrow. A label under a step contains the name of the procedure that implements the step.

Because the step "Read the number of data items" defines the value of the variable `NumItems`, `NumItems` is an output of this step. Procedure `FindSum` needs this value to know how many data items to read; consequently, `NumItems` is an input to procedure `FindSum`. The procedure result, `Sum`, is an output of `FindSum`. `Sum` must be provided as an input to the steps that compute the average (step 3) and display the program results (step 4). The main program variable `Average` is an output of step 3 and an input to step 4. For reasons that are discussed later, we will implement step 4 as procedure `PrintSumAve`.

Coding the Main Program

Once the data flow information has been added to the structure chart, the main program can be written even if the details of the procedures are not yet known.

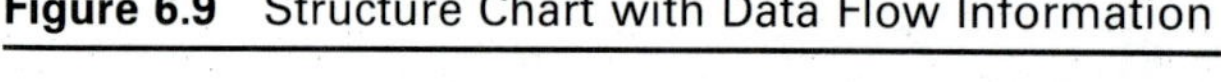
Figure 6.9 Structure Chart with Data Flow Information

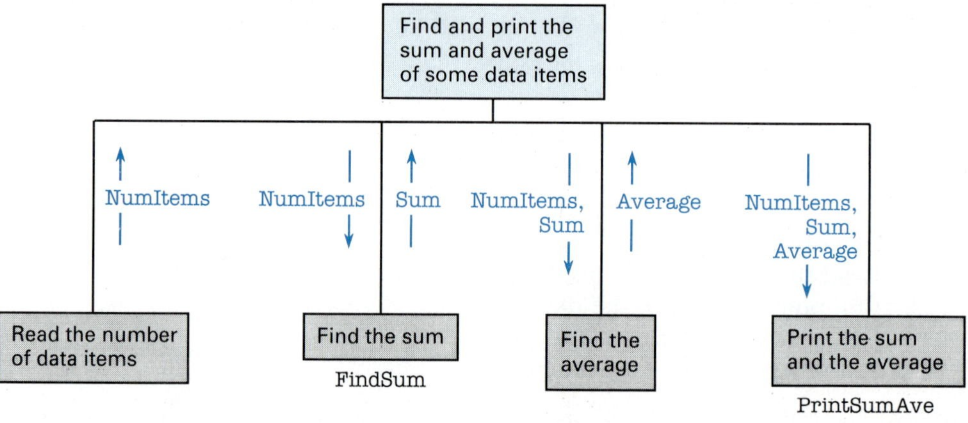

For example, we know from the data flow information in Fig. 6.9 that the procedure call statement

```
FindSum (NumItems, Sum)
```

can call `FindSum`. We also know that `NumItems` should correspond to a value parameter and `Sum` to a variable parameter. We also know that

```
PrintSumAve (NumItems, Sum, Average)
```

can call `PrintSumAve`, where all three parameters are procedure inputs.

The program, except for procedure `FindSum`, is shown in Fig. 6.10. All the variables that appear in the structure chart are declared in the main program because they store data passed to a procedure or results returned from a procedure.

Figure 6.10 Main Program with a Stub for Procedure FindSum

```
program SumItems;

{Finds and prints the sum and average of a list of data items.}

  var
    NumItems : Integer;    {input - number of items to be added}
    Sum,                   {output - sum being accumulated}
    Average : Real;        {output - average of the data}


  procedure PrintSumAve (NumItems {input} : Integer;
                         Sum, Average {input} : Real);
  {
    Displays the sum and the average of NumItems data items.
    Pre : NumItems, Sum, and Average are defined.
    Post: Displays Sum and also Average if NumItems > 0.
  }
  begin {PrintSumAve}
    if NumItems > 0 then
      begin
        WriteLn ('The sum is ', Sum :4:2);
        WriteLn ('The average is ', Average :4:2)
      end
    else
      WriteLn ('Sum and average are not defined')
  end; {PrintSumAve}


  procedure FindSum (NumItems {input} : Integer;
                     var Sum {output} : Real);
  {
    Finds the sum of a list of data items.
    Pre : NumItems is assigned a value.
    Post: NumItems data items are read; their sum is stored in Sum.
  }
  begin {FindSum stub}
    WriteLn ('Procedure FindSum entered.');
    Sum := 0.0
  end; {FindSum stub}
```

```
begin {SumItems}
  {Read the number of items to be summed}
  Write ('How many items will be summed? ');
  ReadLn (NumItems);

  {Find the sum (Sum) of a list of data items}
  FindSum (NumItems, Sum);

  {Find the average (Average) of the data}
  if NumItems > 0 then
    Average := Sum / NumItems;

  {Print the sum and average}
  PrintSumAve (NumItems, Sum, Average)
end. {SumItems}
```

Coding Procedure FindSum

The declaration for procedure `FindSum` shown in Fig. 6.10 is called a *stub*. Including this declaration enables the main program to be compiled, checked for syntax errors, and even run before `FindSum` is written. However, the program will not yet generate meaningful results because the value returned by the stub for `FindSum` is always zero.

Section 5.2 discussed accumulating a sum in a loop. We emphasized the need to initialize the sum to zero prior to loop entry. The loop control steps must ensure that the correct number of items are included in the sum being accumulated. These considerations lead to the following data requirements and algorithm for procedure `FindSum`. The completed procedure, shown in Fig. 6.11, replaces the stub in Fig. 6.10.

Procedure Inputs

The number of data items to be summed (`NumItems : Integer`)

Procedure Outputs

The sum of the data (`Sum : Real`)

Local Procedure Variables

Each data item (`Item : Real`)
Count of data items summed (`Count : Integer`)

Algorithm for FindSum

1. Read in the number of items to be summed.
2. Initialize `Sum` to zero.
3. Initialize count of items summed to zero.
4. `while` count of items < number of items `do`

   `begin`

   5. Read in the next item.
   6. Add it to `Sum`.
   7. Increment count of items.

   `end`

Figure 6.11 Procedure FindSum

```
procedure FindSum (NumItems {input} : Integer;
                   var Sum {output} : Real);
{
  Finds the sum of a list of NumItems data items.
  Pre : NumItems is assigned a value.
  Post: NumItems data items are read; their sum is stored in Sum.
}

  var
    Count : Integer;        {count of items added so far}
    Item : Real;            {the next data item to be added}

begin {FindSum}
  {Read each data item and add it to Sum}
  Sum := 0.0;
  Count := 0;
  while Count < NumItems do
    {invariant:
        Count is <= NumItems and
        Sum is the accumulated sum of data items read
    }
    begin
      Write ('Next number to be summed> ');
      ReadLn (Item);
      Sum := Sum + Item;
      Count := Count + 1
    end {while}
end; {FindSum}
```

Because `Count` and `Item` are used only within procedure `FindSum`, they are declared as local variables in `FindSum`. Figure 6.12 shows the parameter correspondence specified by the procedure call statement

```
FindSum (NumItems, Sum);
```

assuming the value `10` is read into `NumItems` just before the procedure call.

The body of the procedure begins by initializing to zero the main program variable `Sum`, which corresponds to variable parameter `Sum`. The `while` loop reads each data item into the local variable `Item` and adds it to the main program variable `Sum`. The loop and procedure exit occur after ten items are added.

Testing

In testing `SumItems`, make sure that the program displays the sum and the average correctly when `NumItems` is positive and displays a diagnostic when `NumItems` is zero or negative. The main program can be tested before and after `FindSum` is written. If it is tested before `FindSum` is completed, the values displayed for `Sum` and `Average` should be zero.

Fig 6.12 Parameter Correspondence for FindSum (NumItems, Sum)

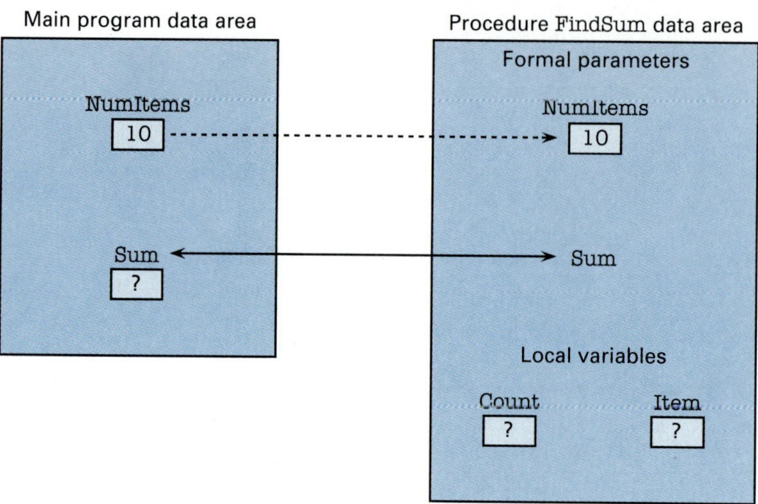

When to Use a Procedure in a Program System

The structure chart for the general sum-and-average program shown in Fig. 6.9 contains four steps, two of which are performed by procedures. We used a procedure for step 2 because its algorithm was relatively complicated, and we felt that its implementation would require several program statements. Even though it was easy to implement step 4, we used a procedure because its implementation was rather lengthy. It was obvious that the remaining steps could be implemented using just a few program statements; consequently, they were written directly in the main program. You should follow this line of reasoning in determining whether to implement a step as a separate procedure. In a large, complicated program, the main program body often consists of little more than procedure calls.

Program and Procedure Inputs and Outputs

An interesting aspect of the structure chart shown in Fig. 6.9 is that variables `Sum` and `Average` are considered problem outputs, yet they are shown as inputs to the display step (step 4). Further, they are listed as inputs in the heading for procedure `PrintSumAve`. Similarly, `NumItems`, which is a problem input, is shown as an output of step 1 in the structure chart.

Although this may seem puzzling at first, it is correct. The determination of whether a variable manipulated by a particular step is an input or an output depends solely on its usage in that step. It is permissible for a variable to be returned as an output from one step (for example, `Sum` in step 2) and passed as an input to another step (for example, `Sum` in step 4).

Including Files

In Turbo Pascal, it is possible to save the procedure `FindSum` as a separate file and use a compiler directive to instruct the compiler to insert this file in the program being compiled. A *compiler directive* is a comment beginning with the symbol `{` and having the symbol `$` as its next character. If the Pascal code for procedure `FindSum` is stored in the file `FINDSUM.PAS` on the disk contained in the B drive, the compiler directive

```
{$I B:FINDSUM.PAS}
```

causes the procedure to be inserted in the program being compiled at the point where the compiler directive occurs. The comment above would replace the stub shown in Fig. 6.10.

The use of the include file directive enables the programmer to write and save sections of a program as separate files. The compiler can then be instructed to pull these files together during compilation. Turbo Pascal also allows separate compilation of these files if they are defined as units. The use of units is discussed in Chapter 8.

SYNTAX DISPLAY

Include File Compiler Directive

Form: `{$I` *filename*`}`
Example: `{$I PROCESS.PAS}`
Interpretation: The file `PROCESS.PAS` is inserted in the source program being compiled, at the point where the comment occurs.
Note: If *filename* does not include a directory specification, the file is presumed to reside in the current directory. The file *filename* may also include file compiler directives. While the file *filename* does not need to contain the code for an entire procedure, the include file compiler directive may not appear in the middle of a statement. This means that all the statements occurring between the begin and end of a compound statement must reside in the same program file.

Case Study: Simple Sorting Problem

Next, we will write a program that uses the same procedure to process a different pair of numbers each time it is called. You will see how procedure parameters make this possible.

Problem

In many real-life and programming situations, we want to arrange a set of data so that it follows some numerical or alphabetical sequence. In programming, this is called the sorting problem. You aren't able to solve this problem for large data sets yet; however, you can write a program that reads any three numbers into the variables Num1, Num2, Num3 and rearranges the data so that the smallest number is stored in Num1, the next smallest number in Num2, and the largest number in Num3.

Design Overview

This is a special case of a sorting problem: rearranging a collection of data items so that the values are in either increasing or decreasing order. Since we have only three items to be sorted, we will solve this special case now. The general sorting problem is a bit more complicated, so we will consider it later.

Data Requirements

Problem Inputs

Three numbers (Num1, Num2, Num3 : Real)

Problem Outputs

The three numbers stored in increasing order in Num1, Num2, Num3

Initial Algorithm

1. Read the three numbers into Num1, Num2, and Num3
2. Place the smallest number in Num1, the next smallest in Num2, and the largest number in Num3.
3. Print Num1, Num2, and Num3

Algorithm Refinements

Think of the three variables Num1, Num2, Num3 as representing a list of consecutive storage cells. To perform step 2, we can compare pairs of numbers, always moving the smaller number in the pair closer to the front of the list (Num1) and the larger number closer to the end of the list (Num3). It should take three comparisons to sort the numbers in the list; one possible sequence of comparisons follows.

Step 2 Refinement

2.1 Compare Num1 and Num2 and store the smaller number in Num1 and the larger number in Num2.

2.2 Compare Num1 and Num3 and store the smaller number in Num1 and the larger number in Num3.

2.3 Compare Num2 and Num3 and store the smaller number in Num2 and the larger number in Num3.

Table 6.3 traces this refinement for the input sequence 8.0, 10.0, 6.0. The final order is correct.

Table 6.3 Trace of Step 2 Refinement for Data 8.0, 10.0, 6.0

Algorithm Step	Num1	Num2	Num3	Effect
	8.0	10.0	6.0	
2.1	8.0	10.0		Num1, Num2 are in order.
2.2	6.0		8.0	8.0 > 6.0, switch Num1 and Num3.
2.3		8.0	10.0	10.0 > 8.0, switch Num2 and Num3.

The structure chart for step 2 of this algorithm is shown in Fig. 6.13. The data flow information for step 2.1 shows that Num1 and Num2 are used as both inputs and outputs. Since steps 2.1, 2.2, and 2.3 perform the same operation on different data, it would be a waste of time and effort to write a different procedure for each step. We will use one procedure, Order, to order any pair of numbers.

Coding

The procedure call statement

```
Order (Num1, Num2)
```

can be used to perform step 2.1 of the algorithm: store the smaller number in Num1 and the larger number in Num2. The complete program is shown in Fig. 6.14. The main program body contains three statements that call procedure Order:

```
Order (Num1, Num2);       {Order the data in Num1 and Num2}
Order (Num1, Num3);       {Order the data in Num1 and Num3}
Order (Num2, Num3);       {Order the data in Num2 and Num3}
```

Because each statement contains a different actual parameter list, a different pair of variables is manipulated each time the procedure is called.

Figure 6.13 Structure Chart for Step 2 of Sorting Problem

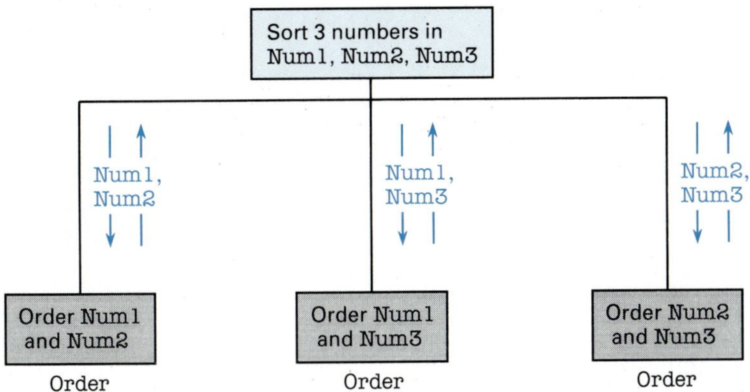

Case Study: Simple Sorting Problem, continued

Figure 6.14 Program to Order Three Numbers

Edit Window

```
program Sort3Numbers;
{
  Reads three numbers and sorts them
  so that they are in increasing order.
}
  var
    Num1, Num2, Num3 : Real;        {a list of three cells}


  procedure Order (var X, Y {input/output} : Real);
  {
    Orders a pair of numbers represented by X and Y so that the
    smaller number is in X and the larger number is in Y.
    Pre : X and Y are assigned values.
    Post: X is the smaller of the pair and Y is the larger.
  }
    var
      Temp : Real;       {copy of number originally in X}

  begin {Order}
    if X > Y then
      begin {Switch the values of X and Y}
        Temp := X;                    {Store old X in Temp}
        X := Y;                       {Store old Y in X}
        Y := Temp                     {Store old X in Y}
      end {if}
  end; {Order}


begin {Sort3Numbers}
   WriteLn ('Enter 3 numbers to be sorted separated by spaces> ');
   ReadLn (Num1, Num2, Num3);

   {Sort the numbers}
   Order (Num1, Num2);      {Order the data in Num1 and Num2}
   Order (Num1, Num3);      {Order the data in Num1 and Num3}
   Order (Num2, Num3);      {Order the data in Num2 and Num3}

   {Print the results}
   WriteLn ('The three numbers in order are:');
   WriteLn (Num1 :8:2, Num2 :8:2, Num3 :8:2)
end. {Sort3Numbers}
```

Output Window

```
Enter 3 numbers to be sorted separated by spaces>
8.0  10.0  6.0
The three numbers in order are:
    6.00    8.00    10.00
```

The body of procedure `Order` consists of the `if` statement from Fig. 4.11. The procedure heading contains the formal parameter list

```
(var X, Y {input/output} : Real)
```

which identifies X and Y as the formal parameters. X and Y are classified as input/output parameters because the procedure uses the current actual parameter values as inputs and may return new values.

The sequence of the actual parameters is important. The first actual parameter is paired with the first formal parameter, the second actual parameter is paired with the second formal parameter, and so on. If the first procedure call statement in Fig. 6.14 were written as

```
Order (Num2, Num1)
```

the smaller number would be stored in Num2 and the larger number in Num1 instead of the other way around.

Exercises for Section 6.5

Self-Check

1. Add data flow information to the structure chart shown in Fig. 4.7. Implement each subproblem as a procedure with parameters.
2. How does adding data flow information to a structure chart help you determine where variables should be declared?
3. Trace the execution of the three procedure call statements

```
Order (Num3, Num2);
Order (Num3, Num1);
Order (Num2, Num1)
```

for the data sets 8.0, 10.0, 6.0 and 10.0, 8.0, 60.0. What does this sequence do?

Programming

1. A procedure has four formal parameters: W, X, Y, and Z (all type Real). The procedure execution stores the sum of W and X in Y and the product of W and X in Z. Which parameters are inputs and which are outputs? Write the procedure.

6.6 Scope of Identifiers

Nested Procedures

In Fig. 6.10, procedures FindSum and PrintSumAve are nested or contained in program SumItems. It is also possible for one procedure to be nested within another. For example, procedure PrintStars is nested in procedure Triangle in Fig. 6.6. Nested procedures occur frequently in Pascal and are a natural consequence of the top-down design process.

Each procedure in a nest of procedures has its own declaration part and body; this is also true for the main program. A procedure's parameter list is included in its declaration part.

Figure 6.15 displays the organization of procedures in program `Nested`. Each box represents a procedure or program *block*. A block consists of the declaration part (including any parameter list) and the body of a program or procedure. The name of the block is indicated just above it.

Figure 6.15 shows procedures `Outer` and `Too` nested in the main program block. Procedure `Inner` is shown nested in the block for `Outer`.

Scope of Identifiers

The statements in each program or procedure body written so far manipulate only local identifiers. Although you have not done so yet, it is possible in Pascal to reference identifiers that are not declared locally.

The Pascal scope rules tell us where an identifier is visible and can be referenced.

Pascal Scope Rules

1. The scope of an identifier is the block in which it is declared. Therefore, an identifier declared in procedure `P` is visible in procedure `P` and in all procedures enclosed in procedure `P`.
2. If an identifier `I` declared in procedure `P` is redeclared in some inner procedure `Q` enclosed in `P`, then procedure `Q` and all its enclosed procedures are excluded from the scope of `I` declared in `P`.

According to rule 1, the *scope of an identifier* is the block in which it is declared. The scope of the parameter `Letter` and the constant `Blank` (in Fig. 6.15) is the block for procedure `Too`; therefore, `Letter` and `Blank` are visible only in procedure `Too`.

Because procedure `Inner` is nested in procedure `Outer`, the scope of an identifier declared in procedure `Outer` includes the block for procedure `Inner`. Therefore, an identifier declared in `Outer` (for example, variable `M`) is visible in the body of either procedure.

Figure 6.15 shows the scope of formal parameter `Z` as the block for procedure `Inner` only. Formal parameter `Z` is not visible in the body of procedure `Outer` or procedure `Too` or in the main program body.

Rule 2 takes effect when there are multiple declarations of the same identifier. We discuss rule 2 in the next section.

Because all procedures are nested in the main program block, an identifier declared in the main program is visible anywhere in the program system. For this reason, main program variables are called *global variables.*

Although global variables can be referenced in procedures, this is a dangerous practice. If a procedure references a global variable, it is possible for the value of that variable to change when the procedure is executed (a phenomenon called a *side effect*). Often, no documentation exists to indicate that the procedure manipulates a global variable; consequently, it may be difficult to

Figure 6.15 Procedure Nesting

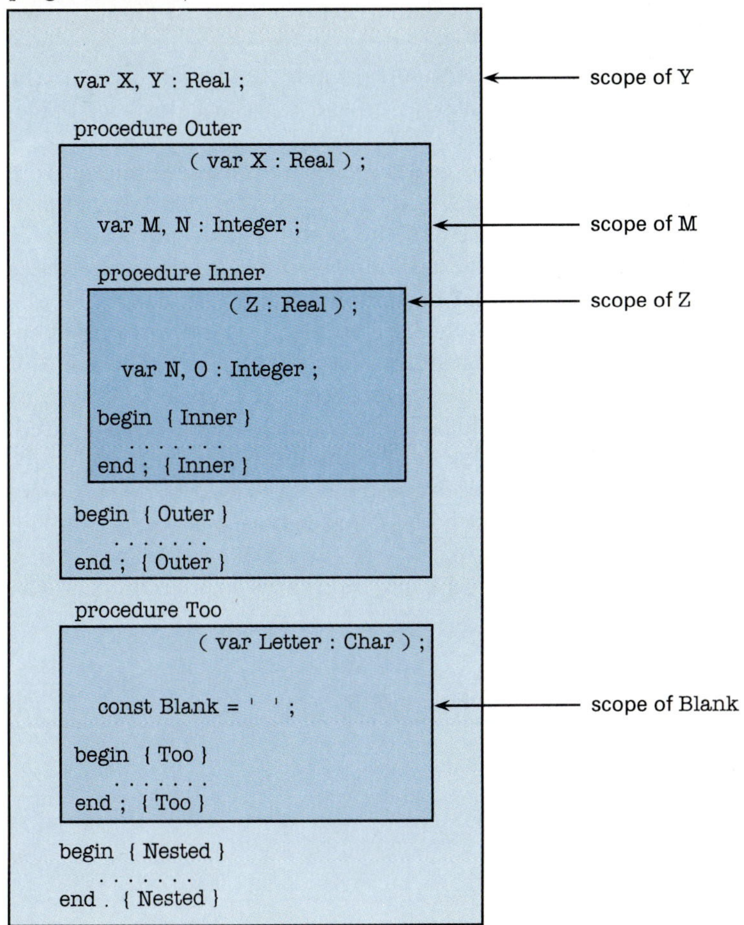
program Nested ;
var X, Y : Real ;
procedure Outer
(var X : Real) ;
var M, N : Integer ;
procedure Inner
(Z : Real) ;
var N, O : Integer ;
begin { Inner }
. . . .
end ; { Inner }
begin { Outer }
. . . .
end ; { Outer }
procedure Too
(var Letter : Char) ;
const Blank = ' ' ;
begin { Too }
. . . .
end ; { Too }
begin { Nested }
. . . .
end . { Nested }
scope of Y
scope of M
scope of Z
scope of Blank

find a statement in a procedure that is responsible for assigning an incorrect or unexpected value to a global variable. If the statement

```
Y := Y + 3.5;        {Example of a side effect}
```

appears in any procedure in Fig. 6.15, it will cause a side effect (adding `3.5` to global variable `Y`) whenever that procedure is called.

The formal parameter list and local declarations for a procedure explicitly document the data that will be manipulated. In this text, only identifiers (including parameters) that are declared locally in a procedure will be referenced in that procedure. The only exceptions are global constants and type identifiers (discussed in later chapters). It is permissible to reference a global constant in a procedure because Pascal does not allow the value of a constant to be changed. Hence, there cannot be a side effect when a global constant is referenced.

Multiple Declarations of Identifiers

An identifier can be declared only once in a given procedure; however, the same identifier can be declared in more than one procedure. In Fig. 6.15, for example, `X` is declared as a global variable in the main program and as a formal parameter in procedure `Outer`. Consequently, when `X` is referenced in the program system, some question may arise as to which declaration takes precedence.

According to scope rule 2, procedures `Outer` and `Inner` are excluded from the scope of global variable `X`, because `X` is declared as a formal parameter of `Outer`. Therefore, when `X` is referenced in the body of procedure `Outer` or `Inner`, formal parameter `X` is manipulated. When `X` is referenced anywhere else in the program system, global variable `X` is manipulated.

If an identifier is not declared locally, then scope rule 2 requires the compiler to use the closest declaration in an outer block that contains the point of reference. For example, if identifier `N` is referenced in procedure `Inner` or procedure `Outer`, the corresponding local declaration for identifier `N` is used. If identifier `M` is referenced in procedure `Inner` where it is not declared locally, the declaration for variable `M` in procedure `Outer` is used. A reference to identifier `M` in either the main program body or procedure `Too` would cause an `identifier not declared` syntax error.

Table 6.4 lists the meanings of the valid references to identifiers in the

Table 6.4 Valid Identifier References for Figure 6.15

Block	**Meaning of Each Identifier**
`Nested`	`X`, `Y` (global variables) `Outer`, `Too` (procedures declared in `Nested`)
`Outer`	`X` (parameter of `Outer`) `M`, `N` (local variables) `Inner` (local procedure) `Y` (variable declared in `Nested`) `Outer`, `Too` (procedures declared in `Nested`)
`Inner`	`Z` (parameter of `Inner`) `N`, `O` (local variables) `M` (variable declared in `Outer`) `X` (parameter of `Outer`) `Inner` (procedure declared in `Outer`) `Y` (variable declared in `Nested`) `Outer`, `Too` (procedures declared in `Nested`)
`Too`	`Letter` (parameter of `Too`) `Blank` (local constant) `X`, `Y` (global variables) `Outer`, `Too` (procedures declared in `Nested`)

blocks of Fig. 6.15. Procedure names are included with other identifiers in this table; they are discussed shortly.

Illustrating the Scope Rules

Next, we will look at a program that illustrates bad programming practice, because the identifier names are not meaningful and are unnecessarily redundant. Studying this example should help you master the Pascal scope rules.

■ Example 6.6

Figure 6.16 shows a procedure declared in a main program. W is declared as a variable in both the procedure and the main program; X is declared as a variable in the main program and as a parameter in the procedure; Y is declared as a variable in the main program only.

Figure 6.16 Example of Scope Rules

Edit Window

```
program ScopeRules;

    var
      W, X, Y : Real;


    procedure Change (var X {input/output} : Real);

      var
        W, Z : Real;

    begin {Change}
      W := 35.0;               {change local W}
      X := 6.0;                {change parameter X}
      Y := Y + 1.0;            {side effect - change global Y}
      Z := 3.0                 {change local Z}
    end; {Change}

begin {ScopeRules}
  W := 5.5;                    {change global W}
  X := 2.0;                    {change global X}
  Y := 3.0;                    {change global Y}
  Change (W);
  WriteLn ('W' :5, 'X' :5, 'Y' :5);
  WriteLn (W :5:2, X :5:2, Y :5:2)
end. {ScopeRules}
```

Output Window

```
    W    X    Y
  6.0  2.0  4.0
```

The main program begins by initializing global variables W, X, and Y. The initial values of the three main program variables are

The procedure call statement

```
Change (W);
```

calls procedure Change with main program variable W corresponding to parameter X. In Change, the assignment statement

```
X := 6.0;               {change parameter X}
```

stores 6.0 in the main program variable W, and the assignment statement

```
Y := Y + 1.0;           {side effect - change global Y}
```

increments main program variable Y (a side effect). The other two assignment statements in Change affect only its local variables W and Z. The main program variables after Change executes are as follows. Notice that main program variable X is unchanged and that the value of W is 6.0 (not 35.0).

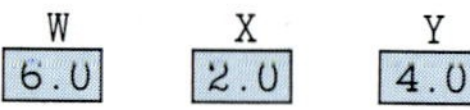

It is interesting to consider what happens if X or Y is used as the actual parameter instead of W. That question is left as an exercise. ■

Procedure Calls

Because procedure names are identifiers, the Pascal scope rules specify where a procedure can be referenced or called. Procedures Outer and Too are global identifiers (declared in the main program), so they can be called anywhere. Procedure Inner is declared in procedure Outer, so it can be called only by procedure Outer or by Inner itself (called a *recursive procedure call*).

As things stand now, a call to Inner in the body of procedure Too or the main program body would cause an identifier is undeclared syntax error. If we declare procedure Inner in the main program instead of inside procedure Outer, then both the main program and procedure Too will be able to call Inner.

The Forward Declaration

In the preceding section, we implied that procedures Outer and Inner can call procedure Too because Too is a global identifier. However, procedure Too is declared after procedure Outer, the Pascal compiler has no way of checking that a call to Too in procedure Outer (or Inner) is correct. Therefore, we must provide a *forward declaration* for procedure Too that includes the procedure heading if Too is called by a procedure declared before it. The first line that follows is a forward declaration:

```
procedure Too (var Letter : Char); forward;

procedure Outer (var X : Real);
  ......
end; {Outer}
```

```
procedure Too;
  ......
end; {Too}
```

The heading for procedure `Too` comes first, followed by the complete declaration for procedures `Outer` and `Too`. The formal parameter list for procedure `Too` appears only in the forward declaration.

Exercises for Section 6.6

Self-Check

1. Explain why variable `N` declared in `Outer` cannot be referenced by the main program, procedure `Inner`, or procedure `Too`.
2. What would be the effect of executing the body of `Inner` as follows?

```
begin {Inner}
  X := 5.5;
  Y := 6.6;
  M := 2;
  N := 3;
  O := 4
end; {Inner}
```

3. If the preceding statement sequence was the body of `Outer`, `Too`, or `Nested`, then some of the assignment statements would be syntactically incorrect. Identify the incorrect statements and indicate the effect of executing all the others in each block.
4. What kind of error would occur if the assignment statement

```
Z := 15.0;
```

was inserted into the main program in Fig. 6.16?

5. Show the new values of `W`, `X`, and `Y` if `X` is the actual parameter in the procedure call statement of Fig. 6.16. What is the answer if `Y` is the actual parameter? What would be the effect of making the formal parameter a value parameter?

6.7 Top-Down Design Illustrated

This section demonstrates the top-down design process in solving a problem. The program solution will be implemented in a stepwise manner starting at the top of the structure chart or with the main program. The problem solution makes extensive use of procedures with parameters.

Case Study: Balancing a Checkbook

Problem

You have just received a new personal computer and you want to write a program to help balance your checkbook. The program should read your initial checkbook balance and each transaction (check or deposit). It should also print the new balance after each transaction and a warning message if the balance becomes negative. At the end of the session, the starting and final balance should be printed, along with a count of the number of checks and deposits processed.

Design Overview

After the starting balance is read, each transaction is read and processed separately. We can use a simple code (`'C'` and `'D'`) to distinguish between checks and deposits. The transaction amount will be a real number. The starting balance must be available at the end, so we will save it in variable `StartBal` and use a different variable (`CurBal`) to keep track of the current balance.

Data Requirements

Problem Inputs

Starting checkbook balance (`StartBal : Real`)
Transaction data
  type of transaction (`TranType : Char`)
  amount of transaction (`Amount : Real`)

Problem Outputs

Current balance after each transaction (`CurBal : Real`)
Number of checks (`NumCheck : Integer`)
Number of deposits (`NumDep : Integer`)

Initial Algorithm

1. Display the instructions and read the starting balance.
2. For each transaction read the transaction, update and print the current balance, and increment the count of checks or deposits.

Figure 6.17 Structure Chart (Levels 0 and 1) for Checkbook Problem

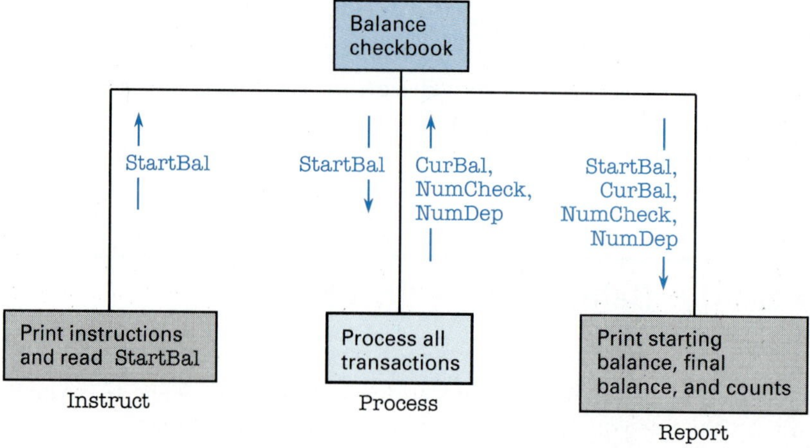

3. Print the starting and final balance and the number of checks and deposits processed.

Figure 6.17 shows the structure chart for this algorithm. The level-1 subproblems will be written as procedures `Instruct`, `Process`, and `Report`. The data flow information shows that `StartBal` is read by `Instruct` and passed to `Process`. Procedure `Process` defines the program results (`CurBal`, `NumCheck`, `NumDep`); these results are passed to `Report` and printed.

The variables shown in the structure chart should be declared in the main program, because each variable must be declared at the highest level in which it appears in the structure chart. Variables that are passed between the main program and a level-1 procedure must be declared in the main program.

Coding the Main Program

The data flow information is used to write the parameter lists in the program shown in Fig. 6.18. Procedures `Instruct` and `Report` consist of input/output statements only, so we write them now. Because procedure `Process` requires further refinement, we write it as a stub.

Figure 6.18 Checkbook-Balancing Program with Stub for Process

```
program CheckBook;
{
  Reads the starting balance for a checking account and processes
  all transactions. Prints the new balance after each transaction
  is processed. Also prints a count of the total number of checks
  and deposits processed
}
  var
    StartBal,                         {input - starting balance}
    CurBal     : Real;                {output - current balance}
    NumCheck,                         {output - number of checks}
    NumDep     : Integer;             {output - number of deposits}


  procedure Instruct (var {output} StartBal : Real);
  {
    Displays the instructions and reads the starting balance.
    Pre : None
    Post: User instructions are displayed and StartBal is read in.
  }
  begin {Instruct}
    WriteLn ('Balance your checking account!');
    WriteLn;
    WriteLn ('Enter C (Check), D (Deposit), or Q (Quit)');
    WriteLn ('after prompt C, D, or Q> ');
    WriteLn;
    WriteLn ('Enter a positive number after prompt Amount $');
    WriteLn;
    Write ('Begin by entering your starting balance $');
    ReadLn (StartBal)
  end; {Instruct}
```

```
procedure Process (StartBal {input} : Real;
                   var CurBal {output} : Real;
                   var NumCheck, NumDep {output} : Integer);
begin {Process stub}
  WriteLn ('Procedure Process entered.');
  CurBal := 0.0;  NumCheck := 0;  NumDep := 0
end; {Process}


procedure Report (StartBal, CurBal {input} : Real;
                  NumCheck, NumDep {input} : Integer);
{
  Prints the starting and final balances and the count of checks
  and deposits
  Pre : StartBal, CurBal, NumCheck, and NumDep are assigned values.
  Post: Program results are displayed.
}
begin {Report}
  WriteLn;
  WriteLn ('Starting balance was $', StartBal :10:2);
  WriteLn ('Final    balance  is $', CurBal :10:2);
  WriteLn ('Number of checks written: ', NumCheck :3);
  WriteLn ('Number of deposits made : ', NumDep :3)
end; {Report}

begin {CheckBook}
  {Display user instructions and read StartBal}
  Instruct (StartBal);

  {Process each transaction}
  Process (StartBal, CurBal, NumCheck, NumDep);

  {Print starting and final balances and count of checks/deposits}
  Report (StartBal, CurBal, NumCheck, NumDep)
end. {CheckBook}
```

Coding the Procedures

Procedure `Process` performs step 2 of the algorithm, which is repeated below.

Algorithm for Process

2. For each transaction read the transaction, update and print the current balance, and increment the count of checks or deposits.

It is obvious that a `while` loop is needed. Assuming that we do not know how many transactions will occur, we can use a sentinel-controlled loop that compares the transaction code to a sentinel value. The loop properties follow:

1. `CurBal` is `StartBal` plus all transactions that are deposits and minus all transactions that are checks.
2. `NumCheck` is the count of checks so far.

Figure 6.19 Structure Chart for Procedure Process

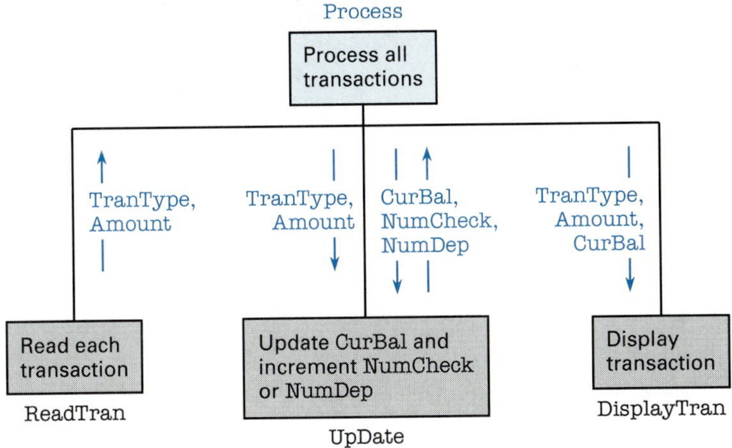

3. NumDep is the count of deposits so far.
4. The transaction code is the sentinel just after loop exit.

These statements suggest the following refinement.

Algorithm for Process

1. Initialize `NumCheck` and `NumDep` to zero.
2. Initialize `CurBal` to `StartBal`.
3. Read the first transaction.
4. `while` the transaction code is not the sentinel `do`

```
begin
   5. Update CurBal and increment NumCheck or NumDep.
   6. Display CurBal and the transaction.
   7. Read the next transaction.
end
```

The structure chart for `Process` is shown in Fig. 6.19. Procedure `ReadTran` performs steps 3 and 7 of the refined algorithm, `UpDate` performs step 5, and `DisplayTran` performs step 6. Two new variables, `TranType` and `Amount`, should be declared as local variables in procedure `Process`. Variables passed between a level-1 and a level-2 procedure should be declared in the level-1 procedure. The identifiers `CurBal`, `NumCheck`, and `NumDep` are declared already as formal parameters of `Process`.

Local Variables for Process

The transaction type (`TranType : Char`)

The transaction amount (`Amount : Real`)

The procedure nesting prescribed by this structure chart and the earlier one is summarized in Fig. 6.20. Each procedure that is subordinate to a higher-level procedure is nested in that higher-level procedure. Figure 6.20 shows that ReadTran, Update, and DisplayTran are nested in Process, which is nested in CheckBook. Procedures Instruct and Report are also nested in CheckBook.

Figure 6.20 Procedure Nesting for Checkbook Problem

```
program CheckBook
  procedure Instruct
  procedure Process
    procedure ReadTran
    procedure Update
    procedure DisplayTran
  procedure Report
```

Procedure UpDate will consist of an if statement that implements the decision table shown in Table 6.5. Procedure Process is shown in Fig. 6.21.

Table 6.5 Decision Table for UpDate

Condition	Desired Action
TranType = 'D'	Increment NumDep, add Amount to CurBal
TranType = 'C'	Increment NumCheck, subtract Amount from CurBal

Figure 6.21 Procedure Process for Checkbook Balancing Program

```
procedure Process (StartBal {input} : Real;
                   var CurBal {output} : Real;
                   var NumCheck, NumDep {output} : Integer);
{
  Processes each transaction. Reads each transaction, updates and
  prints the current balance, and increments the count of checks or
  deposits.
  Pre  : StartBal is assigned a value.
  Post : CurBal is StartBal plus deposits and minus withdrawals.
         NumCheck is the count of checks.
         NumDep is the count of deposits.
  Calls: ReadTran, Update, and DisplayTran
}
  const
    Sentinel = 'Q';         {sentinel value}
    Deposit = 'D';          {deposit code}
    Check = 'C';            {check code}

  var
    TranType : Char;        {transaction type (check or deposit)}
    Amount : Real;          {transaction amount}
```

```
procedure ReadTran (var TranType {output} : Char;
                    var Amount {output} : Real);
{
  Reads each transaction.
  Pre : None
  Post: TranType and Amount are read in.
}
begin {ReadTran}
  WriteLn;
  Write ('C, D, or Q: ');
  ReadLn (TranType);
  if TranType <> Sentinel then
    begin {Read amount}
      Write ('Amount $');
      ReadLn (Amount)
    end {if}
end; {ReadTran}


procedure UpDate (TranType {input} : Char;
                  Amount {input} : Real;
                  var CurBal {input/output} : Real;
                  var NumCheck, NumDep {input/output} : Integer);
{
  Updates CurBal and increments NumCheck for a check or
  NumDep for a deposit.
  Pre : TranType, Amount, CurBal, NumCheck, and NumDep are defined.
  Post: CurBal is increased (deposit) or decreased (check) by
        Amount. NumCheck or NumDep is increased by one.
}
begin {Update}
  if TranType = Deposit then
    begin
      CurBal := CurBal + Amount;
      NumDep := NumDep + 1
    end {if}
  else if TranType = Check then
    begin
      CurBal := CurBal - Amount;
      NumCheck := NumCheck + 1
    end {if}
end; {UpDate}


procedure DisplayTran (TranType {input} : Char;
                       Amount,
                       CurBal {input} : Real);
{
  Displays current transaction and balance.
  Pre : TranType, Amount, and Curbal are assigned values.
  Post: Transaction data are displayed.
}
begin {DisplayTran}
  if TranType = Deposit then
    begin
      Write ('Depositing $', Amount :8:2);
      WriteLn ('Balance of $', CurBal :12:2)
    end {Deposit}
  else if TranType = Check then
```

```
    begin
      Write ('Check for    $', Amount: 8:2);
      WriteLn ('    Balance of $', CurBal :12:2);
      if CurBal < 0.0 then
        WriteLn ('Warning! Your account is overdrawn.')
    end {Check}
  else {not check or deposit}
    begin
      Write ('Invalid transaction type ', TranType);
      WriteLn (' - transaction ignored.')
    end {if}
end; {DisplayTran}

begin {Process}
  {Initialize counters to zero and CurBal to StartBal}
  NumCheck := 0;  NumDep := 0;  CurBal := StartBal;

  {Read first transaction}
  ReadTran (TranType, Amount);

  {Process each transaction until done}
  while TranType <> Sentinel do
  {invariant:
     CurBal is StartBal + all deposits, - minus all checks and
     NumDep is the number of deposits so far and
     NumCheck is the number of checks so far and
     no prior value of TranType was Sentinel
  }
    begin
      UpDate (TranType, Amount, CurBal, NumCheck, NumDep);
      DisplayTran (TranType, Amount, CurBal);
      ReadTran (TranType, Amount)
    end {while}
end; {Process}
```

Procedure `Process` processes all transactions. `Process` calls `ReadTran` to read each transaction, `UpDate` to process the transaction just read, and `DisplayTran` to display the result. Because these three procedures are called by `Process` only, they are declared inside `Process`.

Procedure `DisplayTran` contains a nested `if` statement that differentiates between checks and deposits. When `TranType` is `'C'`, the inner `if` statement is executed and detects an overdrawn account (`CurBal` is negative).

Testing

A sample run of the checkbook balancing program is shown in Fig. 6.22. When you test this program, make sure you provide invalid as well as valid transaction types. Also make sure that invalid transaction types are not counted as either deposits or checks and that the amount associated with an invalid transaction type is ignored.

Figure 6.22 Sample Run of Checkbook Balancing Program

```
Balance your checking account!

Enter C (Check), D (Deposit), or Q (Quit)
after prompt C, D, or Q:

Enter a positive number after prompt Amount $

Begin by entering your starting balance    $1000.00

C, D, or Q > D
Amount $100.00
Depositing $  100.00       Balance of $    1100.00

C, D, or Q > C
Amount $1200.00
Check for  $ 1200.00       Balance of $    -100.00
Warning! Your account is overdrawn.

C, D, or Q > X
Amount $500.00
Invalid transaction type X - transaction ignored.

C, D, or Q > Q

Starting balance was $   1000.00
Final    balance  is $   -100.00
Number of checks written:   1
Number of deposits made :   1
```

PROGRAM STYLE

Stepwise Design with Procedures

The program system for the checkbook problem is a good illustration of the stepwise design process. It uses procedures to implement each of the subproblems shown in the structure chart. With the exception of procedure `Process`, each procedure is relatively short (less than one page) and has a single purpose.

The main program at the bottom of Fig. 6.18 contains three procedure call statements. The second procedure call statement

```
Process (StartBal, CurBal, NumCheck, NumDep);
```

processes all transactions. Procedure `Process` calls procedures `ReadTran`, `UpDate`, and `DisplayTran` to perform the read, update, and display operations, respectively. These level-2 procedures are declared inside procedure `Process`.

The variables `TranType` and `Amount` are declared in `Process`, because they are used only by `Process` and the level-2 procedures. Similarly, the constants `Sentinel`, `Check`, and `Deposit` are declared in `Process` and are referenced as needed in the level-2 procedures.

Exercise for Section 6.7

Programming

1. Modify the checkbook program so that a penalty amount of $15.00 is deducted for each overdrawn check, and a count of overdrawn checks is maintained and printed next to each overdrawn check. Reset the count of overdrafts to zero whenever the balance becomes positive.

6.8 Debugging and Testing a Program System

Top-Down and Bottom-Up Debugging and Testing

As the number of statements in a program system grows, the possibility of error also increases. If we keep each procedure to a manageable size, the likelihood of error is less. It is also easier to read and test each procedure. Finally, the limited use of global variables minimizes the chance of harmful side effects, which are difficult to locate.

In some of the case studies in this chapter, we inserted stubs in the main program for procedures that were not yet written. This is a common practice when a team of programmers is working on a problem. Obviously not all procedures are ready at the same time. The use of stubs enables programmers to test and debug the main program flow and those procedures that are available.

Each stub displays an identification message and assigns values to its output parameters to prevent execution errors caused by undefined values. The messages provide a trace of procedure execution. This process is called *top-down testing*.

When a complicated procedure is completed, it can be tested separately with a short driver program. It is easier to locate and correct errors when dealing with a single procedure rather than with a complete program system. The driver program should (1) contain all necessary declarations and statements that assign values to all input and input/output parameters, (2) call the procedure, and (3) display the procedure results. Once we are confident that a procedure works properly, it can be substituted for its stub in the program system. The process of separately testing individual procedures before inserting them in a program system is called *bottom-up testing*.

By following a combination of top-down and bottom-up testing, a programming team can be fairly confident that the complete program system will be relatively free of errors when it is finally put together. Consequently, the final debugging sessions should proceed quickly and smoothly. A list of suggestions for debugging a program system follows.

Debugging Tips for Program Systems

1. Carefully document each procedure parameter and local identifier using comments as you write the code. Also describe the procedure operation using comments.
2. Leave a trace of execution by printing the procedure name as you enter it.
3. Print the values of all input and input/output parameters upon entry to a procedure. Check that these values make sense.
4. Print the values of all output parameters after returning from a procedure. Hand-check these values to verify that they are correct. Make sure that all input/output and output parameters are declared as variable parameters.
5. Make sure that a procedure stub assigns a value to each of its output parameters.

It is a good idea to plan for debugging as you write each procedure rather than afterward. Include the output statements required for debugging tips 2, 3, and 4 in the original Pascal code for the procedure. When you are satisfied that the procedure works, you can remove the debugging statements. One efficient way to remove the debugging statements is to change them to comments by enclosing them in the symbol pairs (*, *). If you have a problem later, you can search for and remove these symbol pairs, thereby changing the comments to executable statements. We describe another technique for controlling the display of debugging diagnostics in Section 7.4.

Figure 6.23 demonstrates these points for procedure `FindTax` and its driver program (first shown in Fig. 6.7).

Figure 6.23 Debugging Statements for a Procedure Call

```
program Driver;

{Tests procedure FindTax.}

  var
    MySalary,                {input - salary}
    MyTax      : Real;       {output - tax}


  procedure FindTax (Salary {input} : Real;
                     var Tax {output} : Real);
  begin {FindTax}
    WriteLn ('Procedure FindTax entered');
    WriteLn ('Value of Salay is ', Salary :4:2);
    ......
  end; {FindTax}


begin {Driver}
  .....
  FindTax (MySalary, MyTax);
  WriteLn ('Value returned from FindTax is ', MyTax :4:2)
  .....
end. {Driver}
```

Using the Debugger to Trace a Procedure

In the last section, we showed how to display the initial values of a procedure's input and input/output parameters using special debugging statements. You can also use the Turbo Pascal debugger and its trace feature (function key F7) to provide this information. If the next statement to be executed is a procedure call, pressing F7 will cause the procedure to be entered. The procedure body will appear in the Edit window with its `begin` line highlighted. Then you designate the procedure parameters as Watch variables using the steps described in Section 5.7. The initial parameter values will appear in the Watch window. As you execute each statement in the procedure (by pressing F7), any new values assigned to output parameters or input/output parameters will be reflected in the Watch window.

After the procedure return occurs, you can use the debugger to see what values were returned to the calling program. This time, designate as Watch variables any actual parameters that correspond to output parameters or to input/output parameters. The values returned by the procedure will appear in the Watch window.

Using the Step Over Option

If you have thoroughly tested a procedure before using it in a new program, there is no need to execute each individual statement of that procedure when using the Turbo Pascal debugger. Whenever the next statement to be executed is a procedure call statement, you have the option of executing the complete procedure body at once, or of executing each statement in the procedure body individually. If you press F8 (Step over), the debugger will execute the whole procedure body, stopping at the first statement after the procedure call. If you wish to trace the execution of each individual statement in the procedure body, press F7 (Trace into) to enter the procedure.

Identifier Scope and Watch Window Variables

The values displayed in the Watch window are determined by the normal scope rules for Pascal identifiers. Consequently, a procedure's local variables and formal parameters will be displayed with the value `Unknown identifier` until that procedure begins execution. Upon exit from the procedure, its local variables and formal parameters will again have `Unknown identifier` displayed as their value in the Watch window.

When identifiers having the same name are declared in different parts of a program, a Watch variable may be *qualified* by prefixing it with the name of the module in which it is declared so its value can be displayed throughout the execution of the program. For the watch variables shown in Fig. 6.24, `ScopeRules.W` refers to the global identifier `W` declared in the main program `ScopeRules`, and `Change.W` refers to the local identifier `W` declared in procedure `Change`. When procedure `Change` completes execution, the value displayed for `Change.W` is `Cannot access this symbol`, while the value of `ScopeRules.W` does not change.

Figure 6.24 Qualifying Watch Variables

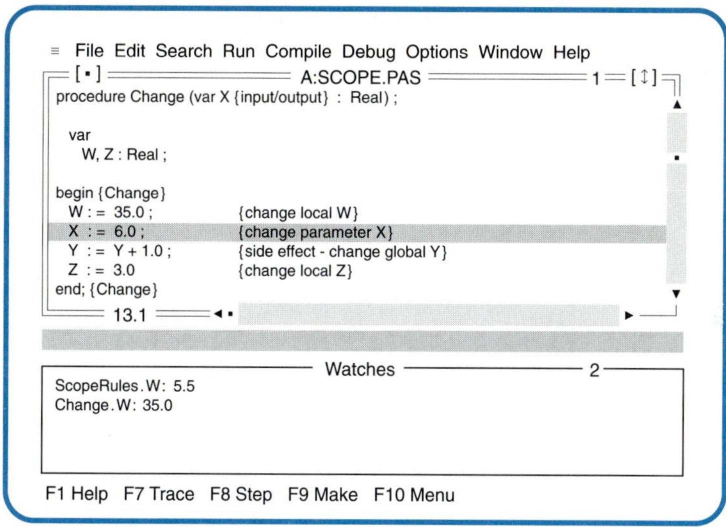
≡ File Edit Search Run Compile Debug Options Window Help
[▪] A:SCOPE.PAS 1=[↕]
procedure Change (var X {input/output} : Real) ;
var
W, Z : Real ;
begin {Change}
W := 35.0 ; {change local W}
X := 6.0 ; {change parameter X}
Y := Y + 1.0 ; {side effect - change global Y}
Z := 3.0 {change local Z}
end; {Change}
13.1
Watches 2
ScopeRules.W: 5.5
Change.W: 35.0
F1 Help F7 Trace F8 Step F9 Make F10 Menu

6.9 Common Programming Errors

The Pascal scope rules determine where an identifier can be referenced. If an identifier is referenced outside its scope, an `identifier not declared` syntax error results.

There are many opportunities for error when you use procedures with parameter lists. The proper use of parameters is difficult for beginning programmers to master. One obvious pitfall occurs in ensuring that the actual parameter list has the same number of parameters as the formal parameter list. The syntax errors `"," expected` and `")" expected` indicate this problem.

A common error made by beginning Pascal programmers is calling procedures with the actual parameters listed in the wrong order. Forgetting to use variable parameters for formal parameters intended to be used as output or as input/output parameters is another common error. Sometimes beginning programmers think that every group of parameters following the first occurrence of the reserved word `var` will be treated as variable parameters as well. This is *not* true; each group of variable parameters must be preceeded by `var`. Because these errors are not likely to be flagged as compilation errors, it often takes a bit of work with the Turbo Pascal debugger to track them down.

Each actual parameter must be assignment-compatible with its corresponding formal parameter (for a value parameter) or the same data type (for a variable parameter). An actual parameter that corresponds to a variable formal parameter must be a variable. Violation of the first rule results in a `type mismatch` syntax error; violation of the second rule results in a `variable identifier expected` syntax error.

You should return a procedure result to the calling module by assigning a

Table 6.6 Summary of New Pascal Constructs

Construct	Effect
Procedure with Parameters	

<pre>procedure A (X : Real;
             Op : Char;
             var XTo3 : Real);
 	
begin {A}
  if Op = '*' then
    XTo3 := X * X * X
  else if Op = '+' then
    XTo3 := X + X + X
  else
    WriteLn ('Invalid')
end; {A}</pre>
	Procedure `A` has two value parameters (`X` and `Op`) and one variable parameter (`XTo3`). If `Op` is `'*'`, the value returned is `X * X * X`; if `Op` is `'+'`, the value returned is `X + X + X`; otherwise, an error message is printed. A result is returned by assigning a new value to the actual parameter (a variable) that corresponds to parameter `XTo3`.

Procedure Call Statement	
`A (5.5, '+', Y)`	Calls procedure `A`. `5.5` is passed into `X`, `'+'` into `Op`, and the value `16.5` is stored in `Y`.

value to a variable parameter. Any value assigned to a value parameter will be stored locally in the procedure and will not be returned.

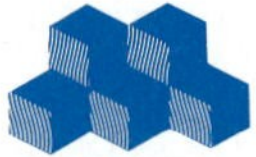

Chapter Review

This chapter focused on the use of procedure parameters for passing data to and from procedures. The parameter list provides a highly visible communication path between the procedure and the calling program. By using parameters, we can cause different data to be manipulated by a procedure each time we call it, making it easier to reuse the procedure in another program system.

There are two types of parameters: value and variable. A value parameter is used only for passing data into a procedure. A variable parameter is used to return results from a procedure. The actual parameter corresponding to a value parameter can be an expression or a constant; the actual parameter corresponding to a variable parameter must be a variable.

We also examined the scope of identifiers. An identifier can be referenced anywhere within the block that declares it. If one block is nested inside another and an identifier is declared in the outer block, then the identifier's meaning in the inner block is determined by its declaration in the outer block. If the identifer is declared in both blocks, its meaning in the inner block is determined by its declaration in the inner block.

A global variable is a variable that is declared in the main program; a local variable is declared in a procedure. A local variable is defined only during the execution of the procedure; its value is lost when the procedure is finished.

New Pascal Constructs

The new Pascal constructs introduced in this chapter are described in Table 6.6.

✓ Quick-Check Exercises

1. The ____________ parameters appear in the procedure call and the ____________ parameters appear in the procedure declaration.
2. Constants and expressions can correspond to formal parameters that are ________ parameters.
3. Formal parameters that are ____________ parameters must have actual parameters that are ____________.
4. Formal parameters that are ____________ parameters must have actual parameters that are the ____________ data type.
5. The data types of corresponding value parameters must be ____________.
6. Which is used to test a procedure, a driver or a stub?
7. Which is used to test main program flow, a driver or a stub?
8. A side effect is a change to a ____________ variable caused by execution of a procedure.
9. What are the values of main program variables X and Y after the following program executes?

```
program Nonsense;
  var X, Y : Real;

  procedure Silly (X : Real);
    var Y : Real;
  begin
    Y := 25.0;
    X := Y
  end; {Silly}

begin {Nonsense}
  Silly (X)
end. {Nonsense}
```

10. Answer exercise 9 if parameter X of `Silly` is a variable parameter.
11. Answer exercise 9 if parameter X of `Silly` is a variable parameter and the local declaration for Y is removed from `Silly`.
12. Answer exercise 9 if parameter X of `Silly` is a variable parameter, Y is a local variable in `Silly`, and the procedure call statement is changed to `Silly (Y)`.
13. Answer exercise 12 if the local declaration for Y is removed from `Silly`.

Answers to Quick-Check Exercises

1. actual; formal
2. value
3. variable; variables
4. variable; same
5. assignment-compatible
6. driver
7. stub
8. nonlocal, or global
9. both undefined
10. X is 25.0, Y is undefined
11. both 25.0
12. X is undefined, Y is 25.0
13. X is undefined, Y is 25.0

Review Questions

1. Write the procedure heading for a procedure called `Script` that accepts three parameters passed to it. The first parameter is the number of spaces to print at the beginning of a line. The second parameter is the character to print after the spaces. The third parameter is the number of times to print the second parameter on the same line.
2. Write a procedure called `LetterGrade` that has one input parameter called `Grade`, and that prints out the corresponding letter grade using a straight scale (90-100 is an A, 80-89 is a B, and so on).
3. Explain the difference between a value parameter and a variable parameter with respect to the parameter's relationship to the variables in the calling program.
4. Explain the allocation of memory cells when a procedure is called.
5. Write the procedure heading for a procedure named `Pass` that passes two integer parameters. The first parameter should be a value parameter and the second a variable parameter.
6. Explain the use of a stub in refining an algorithm.
7. In the following chart, which procedures on the right can be referenced (called) by the corresponding procedure on the left? Which procedures are inaccessible?

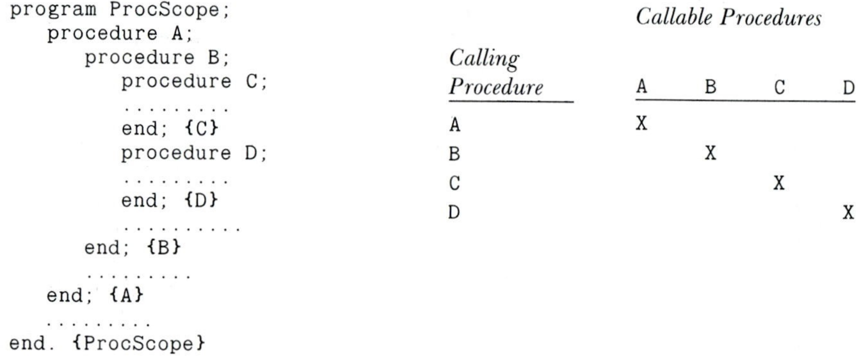

```
program ProcScope;
   procedure A;
      procedure B;
         procedure C;
         .........
         end; {C}
         procedure D;
         .........
         end; {D}
         .........
      end; {B}
      .........
   end; {A}
   .........
end. {ProcScope}
```

Calling Procedure	*Callable Procedures* A	B	C	D
A	X			
B		X		
C			X	
D				X

Programming Projects

1. a. Write a program to process a collection of savings account transactions (deposits or withdrawals). Your program should begin by reading in the previous account balance, then read and process each transaction. Enter a positive value for a deposit and a negative value for a withdrawal. For each transaction, print the message `Withdrawal` or `Deposit` and the new balance. Print an error message if a withdrawal would result in a negative balance and do not change the balance.
   b. Compute and print the number of deposits, the number of withdrawals, the number of invalid withdrawals, and the total dollar amount for each type of transaction.
2. a. Write a program that computes and prints the fractional powers of two ($\frac{1}{2}$, $\frac{1}{4}$, $\frac{1}{8}$, and so on). The program should also print the decimal value of each fraction as shown below.

Power	*Fraction*	*Decimal Value*
1	$\frac{1}{2}$	0.5
2	$\frac{1}{4}$	0.25
3	$\frac{1}{8}$	0.125

Print all values through power equal to 10.

b. Add an extra output column that shows the sum of all decimal values so far. The first three sums are 0.5, 0.75, and 0.875.

3. a. The trustees of a small college are considering voting a pay raise for the twelve faculty members. They want to grant a 5.5 percent pay raise; however, before doing so, they want to know how much this will cost. Write a program that will print the pay raise for each faculty member and the total amount of the raises. Also, print the total faculty payroll before and after the raise. Test your program for the following salaries:

$12,500	$14,029.50	$16,000	$13,250
$15,500	$12,800	$20,000.50	$18,900
$13,780	$17,300	$14,120.25	$14,000

b. Redo the program assuming that faculty earning less than $14,000 receive a 4 percent raise, faculty earning more than $16,500 receive a 7 percent raise, and all others receive a 5.5 percent raise. For each faculty member, print the raise percentage as well as the amount.

4. The assessor in your town has estimated the market value of all fourteen properties and wants a program that determines the tax owed on each property and the total tax to be collected. The tax rate is 125 mils per dollar of assessed value. (A mil is 0.1 of a penny.) The assessed value of each property is 28 percent of its estimated market value. The market values are

$50,000	$48,000	$45,500	$67,000	$37,600	$47,100	$65,000
$53,350	$28,000	$58,000	$52,250	$48,000	$56,500	$43,700

5. Patients required to take many kinds of medication often find it difficult to remember when to take their medicine. Given the following set of medications, write a program that prints an hourly table indicating what medication to take at any given hour. Use a counter variable `Clock` to go through a twenty-four-hour day. Print the table based on the following prescriptions:

Medication	*Frequency*
Iron pill	0800, 1200, 1800
Antibiotic	Every 4 hours, starting at 0400
Vitamin	0800, 2100
Calcium	1100, 2000

6. A monthly magazine wants a program that will print out renewal notices to its subscribers and cancellation notices when appropriate. Using procedures when advisable, write a program that first reads in the current month number (1 through 12) and year. For each subscription processed, read in four data items: the account number, the month and the year the subscription started, and the number of years paid for the subscription.

   Read in each set of subscription information and print a renewal notice if the current month is either the month prior to expiration or the month of expiration. Print a cancellation notice if the current month comes after the expiration month.

Sample input might be

`10, 88`	for a current month of October 1988
`1364, 4, 85, 3`	for account `1364` whose 3-year subscription began in April 1985

7. The square root of a number `N` can be approximated by repeated calculation using the formula

   NG = .5(LG + N / LG)

   where `NG` stands for next guess and `LG` stands for last guess. Write a procedure that implements this process. The first parameter will be a positive real number, the second will be an initial guess of the square root, and the third will be the computed result.

   The initial guess will be the starting value of `LG`. The procedure will compute a value for `NG` using the preceding formula. The difference between `NG` and `LG` is checked to see whether these two guesses are almost identical. If so, the procedure is exited and `NG` is the square root; otherwise, the new guess (`NG`) becomes the last guess (`LG`) and the process is repeated (that is, another value is computed for `NG`, the difference is checked, and so forth).

   For this program, the loop should be repeated until the magnitude of the difference is less than `0.005` (`Delta`). Use an initial guess of `1.0` and test the program for the numbers 4, `120.5`, 88, `36.01`, and `10,000`.
8. It was a dark and stormy night. Our secret agent (007), is behind enemy lines at a fuel depot. He walks over to a cylindrical fuel tank, which is 20 feet tall and 8 feet in diameter. He opens a 2-inch-diameter circular nozzle. He knows that the volume of the fuel leaving the tank is

   volume lost = velocity * (area of the nozzle) * time

   and that

   velocity = 8.02 * (height of fluid in the tank)$^{0.5}$

   How long will it take to empty the tank?

   Hint: Although this is really a calculus problem, we can simulate it with the computer and get a close answer. We can calculate the volume lost over a short period of time, like 60 seconds, and assume that the loss of fluid is constant. We can then subtract the volume from the tank and determine the new height of the fluid inside the tank at the end of the minute. We can then calculate the loss for the next minute. This can be done over and over until the tank is dry. Print a table showing the elapsed time in seconds, the volume lost, and the height of the fluid. At the very end, convert the total elapsed seconds to minutes. The fluid height can be negative on the last line of the table.

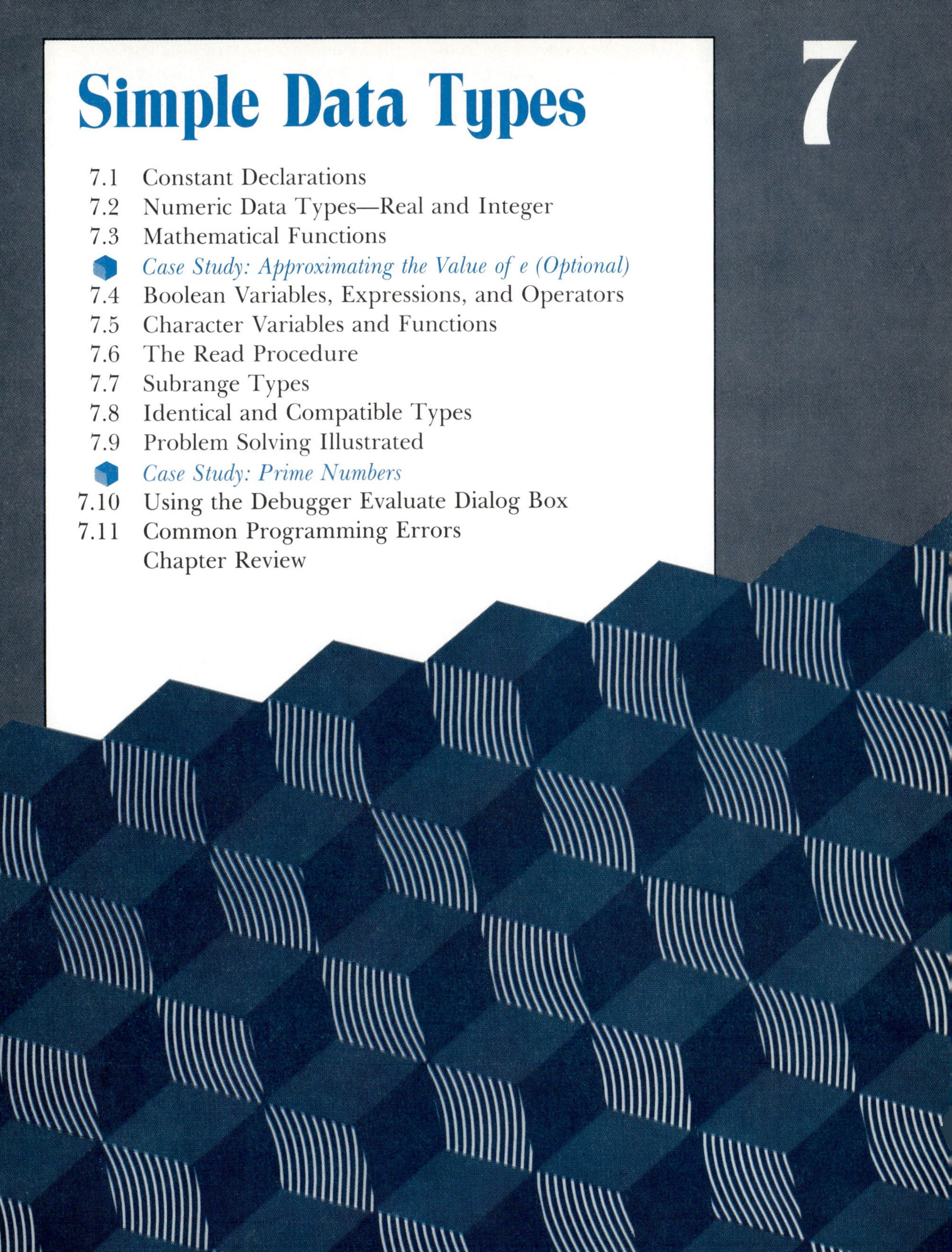

7 Simple Data Types

So far, you have used four of the standard data types of Turbo Pascal: `Integer`, `Real`, `Char`, and `Boolean` (conditions in `if` and `while` statements). This chapter takes a closer look at these data types, introduces new operators and operations that you can perform on them and introduces additional numeric types available in Turbo Pascal. We describe the standard functions of Pascal and demonstrate how they can help you simplify computations.

You'll also learn how to declare new data types, called subrange types. All of the data types in this chapter are *simple* data types—that is, only a single value can be stored in each variable. Later chapters examine variables that can be used to store multiple values.

7.1 Constant Declarations

Let's begin by reexamining constants in Turbo Pascal. The syntax diagram of a constant declaration follows:

Constant Declaration

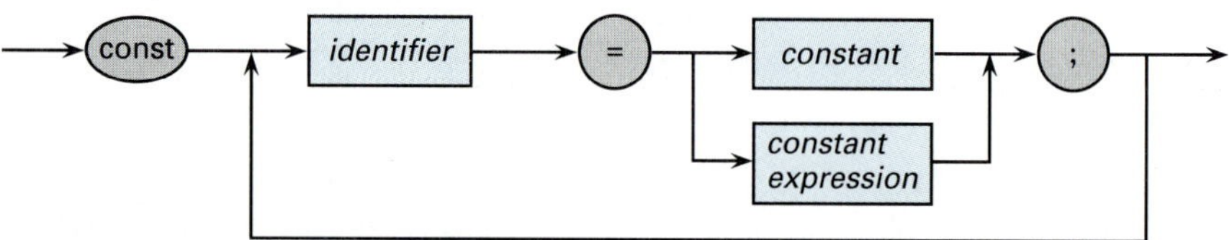

In standard Pascal, each constant definition has the form

identifier = *constant*

where *constant* is described in the next syntax diagram. Turbo Pascal also allows a constant identifier to be associated with a *constant expression*, which is an expression involving only constant operands.

Constant

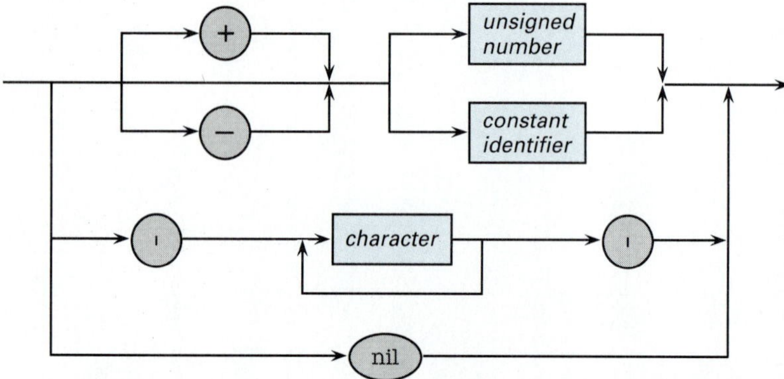

■ Example 7.1

A sample constant declaration follows.

```
const
  Max = 100;
  Min = -Max;
  SpeedOfLight = 2.998E+5;
  Debug = True;
  Name = 'Alice';
  Small = Max - 1;
```

The constant declaration for `Min` uses the previously defined constant `Max`. Because `Max` has the value `100`, `Min` has the value `-100`. The constant `SpeedOfLight` is associated with a real value (`299800.0`) expressed in scientific notation. The `Boolean` constant `Debug` is associated with the `Boolean` value `True`. The constant `Name` is associated with the *string value* `'Alice'`. (String values are discussed further in Chapter 10 and Chapter 13. The constant value `nil` is discussed in Chapter 17.) The declaration for `Small` uses a constant expression with value 99. ■

As mentioned earlier, there are two reasons for using constants. First, the name `SpeedOfLight` has more meaning to a reader of a program than the value `2.998E+5`. Second, if we change the declaration of a constant, we also change the value of that constant wherever it is referenced in the program.

Exercise for Section 7.1

Self-Check

1. Which of the following declared constants are valid and which are invalid?

```
const
  MinInt = -MaxInt;
  MaxLetter = 'Z';
  MinusZ = -MaxLetter;
  MaxSize = 50;
  MinSize = MaxSize - 10;
```

7.2 Numeric Data Types—Real and Integer

The data types `Integer` and `Real` represent numeric information. We used `Integer` variables as loop counters and to represent data, such as exam scores, that were whole numbers. In most other instances, we used type `Real` numeric data.

Differences Between Numeric Types

You may be wondering why it is necessary to have two numeric types. Can the data type `Real` be used for all numbers? The answer is yes, but on many computers, operations that involve integers are faster than those that involve real numbers. Less space is needed to store integers. Also, operations with integers are always precise, whereas there may be some loss of accuracy when you are dealing with real numbers.

These differences result from how real numbers and integers are represented internally in a computer's memory. All data are represented in memory as *binary strings*, that is, strings of zeros and ones. However, the binary string stored for the integer 13 is not the same as the binary string stored for the real number 13.0. The actual internal representation is computer-dependent; compare the integer format (called *fixed-point*) and the real format (called *floating-point*) shown in Fig. 7.1.

Figure 7.1 shows that positive integers are represented by standard binary numbers. If you are familiar with the binary number system, you know that the integer 13 is represented as the binary number 01101.

Real format is analogous to scientific notation. The storage area occupied by a real number is divided into two sections: the *mantissa* and the *exponent*. The mantissa is a binary fraction between 0.5 and 1.0 (-0.5 and -1.0 for a negative number). The exponent is a power of two. The mantissa and the exponent are chosen so that the following formula is correct:

$$\textit{real number} = \textit{mantissa} \times 2^{\textit{exponent}}$$

Because of the finite size of a memory cell, not all real numbers in the range of reals can be represented precisely. We will talk more about this later.

Besides the capability of storing fractions, the range of numbers that can be represented in real format is considerably larger than that for integer format. For example, on the IBM PC, positive real numbers range in value from 10^{-39} (a very small fraction) to 10^{38}, whereas the range of positive integers extends from 1 to approximately 32767. For the IBM PC, a real number requires three times the storage space that an integer does.

You can find the largest integer represented in your Pascal system by executing the statement

```
WriteLn ('Largest integer = ', MaxInt);
```

where `MaxInt` is a predefined constant. In Turbo Pascal the value of `MaxInt` is 32767. The range of integers represented extends from -32768 (`–MaxInt – 1`) to 32767 (`MaxInt`).

Figure 7.1 Integer and Real Formats

Fixed-point
Binary number

Floating-point	
Mantissa	Exponent

Numeric Literals

A constant value that appears in an expression is called a *literal*. The data type of a numeric literal is determined in the following way. If the literal has a decimal point, it is considered type `Real`. A type `Real` literal can also have a decimal *scale factor*. For example, in the literal `2.998E+5`, the scale factor is 10^5. A literal without a decimal point or a scale factor is considered type `Integer`.

Type of an Expression

The data type of an expression depends on the type of its operands. For example, the expression

```
Ace + Bandage
```

is type `Integer` if both `Ace` and `Bandage` are type `Integer`; otherwise, it is type `Real`. The expression

```
Ace / Bandage
```

is type `Real` because the `Real` division operator, /, always generates a type `Real` result.

All the arithmetic operators you have encountered so far (+, -, *, and /) can be used with either `Integer` or `Real` operands. Table 7.1 shows the data type of an expression with one arithmetic operator. The first two columns list the data type of the operands; the remaining columns show the data type of the expression for different operators. If one or both operands are type `Real`, the expression is always type `Real`; only when both operands are type `Integer` can the result be type `Integer`. If the operator is /, the result is type `Real`, even when both operands are type `Integer`.

Table 7.1 Data Type of an Arithmetic Expression

Operands		Operator		
Left	**Right**	`+, -, *`	`/`	`mod, div`
`Real`	`Real`	`Real`	`Real`	illegal
`Real`	`Integer`	`Real`	`Real`	illegal
`Integer`	`Real`	`Real`	`Real`	illegal
`Integer`	`Integer`	`Integer`	`Real`	`Integer`

Pascal does not allow a type `Real` expression to be assigned to a type `Integer` variable because the fractional part cannot be represented and will be lost. This means that the following assignment statements will generate syntax errors if `Count` is a type `Integer` variable. However, a type `Real` or type `Integer` expression can be assigned to a type `Real` variable.

```
Count := 3.5;          {illegal assignment of a real number to Integer}
Count := Count + 1.0;         {illegal; 1.0 is Real, so result is Real}
Count := Count / 2;               {illegal; result of division is Real}
```

Arithmetic Operators div and mod

In Table 7.1, two new operators—div and mod—can be used only with type Integer operands. The integer division operator, div, computes the integral part of the quotient that results when its first operand is divided by its second operand; the modulus operator, mod, computes the integer remainder.

The expression M div N (M and N both integers) is equal to the truncated quotient of M divided by N. For example, if M is 7 and N is 2, the value of M div N is the truncated quotient of 7 divided by 2, or 3. The result of M div N is always type Integer.

■ Example 7.2

Table 7.2 shows some examples of valid and invalid expressions involving the operator div. The result is always zero when the magnitude of the first operand is less than the magnitude of the second operand. The last example in the last column is invalid because the expression (4 / 2) is type Real. ■

Table 7.2 The div Operator

Expression	Result	Expression	Result	Expression	Result
3 div 15	0	3 div -15	0	15.0 div 3	invalid
15 div 3	5	15 div -3	-5	15.0 div 3.0	invalid
16 div 3	5	16 div -3	-5	15 div 3.0	invalid
17 div 3	5	-17 div 3	-5	15 div (4 / 2)	invalid
18 div 3	6	-18 div -3	6		

The modulus operator, mod, must also be used with integer operands. The expression M mod N (M and N both type Integer) is equal to the remainder of M divided by N. For example, 7 mod 2 is equal to the remainder of 7 divided by 2, or 1. In standard Pascal, the second operand of mod must always be greater than zero. Turbo Pascal only requires the second operand to be non-zero.

The formula

```
M = (M div N) * N + (M mod N)
```

defines the relationship between the operators div and mod. This relationship is also illustrated by the example

```
7 = (7 div 2) * 2 + (7 mod 2) =  3 * 2 + 1 = 7
```

In this example, M is 7 and N is 2, so the quotient is 3 (7 div 2) and the remainder is 1 (7 mod 2). The process of dividing 7 by 2 is shown in the following diagram.

```
7 div 2
   ↓
   3 R1 ← 7 mod 2
 2√7
   6
   1
```

■ Example 7.3

Table 7.3 illustrates the mod operator. The magnitude of the result is always less than the second operand (the divisor). The mod operation is undefined when its second operand is zero. By comparing the second and third columns, you can see that M mod N is the negation of –M mod N. ■

Table 7.3 The mod Operator

Expression	Result	Expression	Result	Expression	Result
3 mod 5	3	5 mod 3	2	-5 mod 3	-2
4 mod 5	4	5 mod 4	1	-5 mod 4	-1
5 mod 5	0	15 mod 5	0	-15 mod 5	0
6 mod 5	1	15 mod 6	3	-15 mod 6	-3
7 mod 5	2	15 mod 7	1	-15 mod -7	-1
8 mod 5	3	15 mod 8	7	15 mod 0	undefined

SYNTAX DISPLAY

Operators div and mod

Form: *operand*$_1$ div *operand*$_2$
operand$_1$ mod *operand*$_2$

Example: 15 div 7
7 mod 15

Interpretation: The operator div yields the integral part of the result of *operand*$_1$ divided by *operand*$_2$; any remainder is truncated. The operator mod yields the integer remainder of this division. Both operands must be integer constants, variables, or expressions with integer values.

Note: If *operand*$_2$ is 0, the result of the div or mod operation is undefined.

■ Example 7.4

Procedure PrintDigits in Fig. 7.2 prints each digit of its parameter Decimal in reverse order (e.g., if Decimal is 738, the digits printed are 8, 3, 7). This is accomplished by printing each remainder (0 through 9) of Decimal divided by 10; the integer quotient of Decimal divided by 10 becomes the new value of Decimal.

The parameter Decimal is the loop-control variable. Within the while loop, the mod operator assigns to Digit the rightmost digit of Decimal; the div operator assigns the rest of the number to Decimal. The loop is exited when Decimal becomes 0. Because Decimal is a value parameter, the actual parameter value is not changed by the procedure execution.

Figure 7.2 Printing Decimal Digits

```
procedure PrintDigits (Decimal {input} : Integer);
{
  Prints the digits of Decimal in reverse order.
```

```
    Pre : Decimal is assigned a value.
    Post: Each digit of Decimal is displayed, starting with the
          least significant one.
  }
    const
      Base = 10;                        {number system base}

    var
      Digit : Integer;                  {each digit}

  begin {PrintDigits}
    Decimal := Abs(Decimal);            {assert: Decimal is positive}
    {Find and print remainders of Decimal divided by Base}
    while Decimal <> 0 do
      {invariant:
         Digit in pass i is the rightmost digit of Decimal (for i >=1)
         and Decimal in pass i is Decimal in pass i-1 with its rightmost
         digit removed (for i > 1)
         and Decimal >= 0
      }
      begin
        Digit := Decimal mod Base;      {Get next digit}
        Write (Digit :1);
        Decimal := Decimal div Base     {Get next quotient}
      end; {while}

    {assert: Decimal is zero}
    WriteLn
  end; {PrintDigits}
```

Table 7.4 shows a trace of the loop execution for an actual parameter of 43. The digits 3 and 4 are printed. (Section 7.3 discusses function `Abs`.)

Expressions with Multiple Operators

To write expressions that compute the desired results, you must know the Pascal rules for evaluating expressions. For example, in the expression `A + B * C`, is

Table 7.4 Trace of Execution of PrintDigits(43)

Statement	Decimal 43	Digit	**Effect**
`while Decimal <> 0 do`			`43 <> 0` is true.
`Digit := Decimal mod Base`		3	Next digit is 3.
`Write (Digit :1)`			Print 3.
`Decimal := Decimal div Base`	4		Quotient is 4.
`while Decimal <> 0 do`			`4 <> 0` is true.
`Digit := Decimal mod Base`		4	Next digit is 4.
`Write (Digit : 1)`			Print 4.
`Decimal := Decimal div Base`	0		Quotient is 0.
`while Decimal <> 0 do`			`0 <> 0 is false.` Exit loop.

* performed before +, or vice versa? Is the expression `X / Y * Z` evaluated as `(X / Y) * Z` or as `X / (Y * Z)`?

Some expressions with multiple operators are

```
1.8 * Celsius + 32.0
(Salary - 5000.00) * 0.20 + 1425.00
```

In both these cases, the algebraic rule that multiplication or division is performed before addition or subtraction applies. The use of parentheses in the second expression ensures that subtraction is done first. The Pascal rules for expression evaluation are based on standard algebraic rules.

Rules for Expression Evaluation

a. All parenthesized subexpressions are evaluated first. Nested parenthesized subexpressions are evaluated inside out, with the innermost subexpression evaluated first.

b. *The operator precedence rule*: operators in the same subexpression are evaluated in the following order:

`*, /, div, mod`	first
`+, -`	last

c. *The left associative rule*: operators in the same subexpression and at the same precedence level (such as + and –) are evaluated left to right.

■ Example 7.5

The formula for the area of a circle

$$a = \pi r^2$$

can be written in Turbo Pascal as

```
Area := Pi * Radius * Radius
```

where `Pi` is the function returning 3.14159. Figure 7.3 shows the *evaluation tree* for this formula. In the tree, the arrows connect each operand with its operator. The number to the left of each operator shows the order of operator evaluation; the letter to the right is that of the rule that applies. ■

Figure 7.3 Evaluation Tree for Area := Pi * Radius * Radius

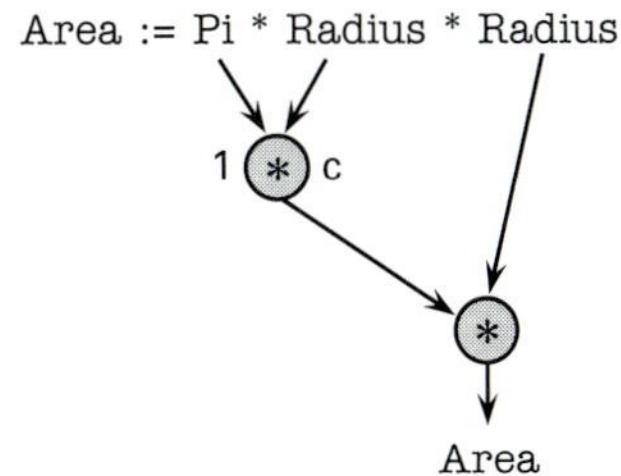

In the next section, we will see that `Pi` is a standard function returning 3.14159. We will also see another way to specify `Radius * Radius`.

■ Example 7.6

The formula for the average velocity, v, of a particle traveling on a line between points p_1 and p_2 in time t_1 to t_2 is

$$v = \frac{p_2 - p_1}{t_2 - t_1}$$

This formula can be written and evaluated in Pascal as shown in Fig. 7.4.

Inserting parentheses in an expression affects the order of operator evaluation. Use parentheses freely to clarify the order of evaluation. ■

Figure 7.4 Evaluation Tree for V := (P2 – P1) / (T2 – T1)

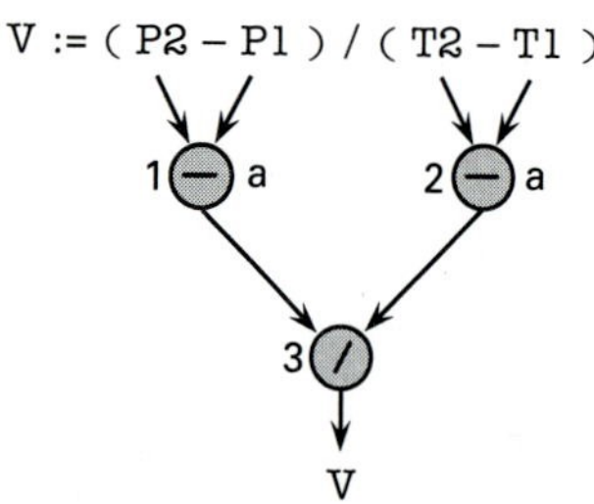

■ Example 7.7

Consider the expression

```
Z - (A + B div 2) + W * Y
```

containing integer variables only. The parenthesized subexpression `(A + B div 2)` is evaluated first (rule (a)) beginning with `B div 2` (rule (b)). Once the value of `B div 2` is determined, it can be added to `A` to obtain the value of `(A + B div 2)`. Next, the multiplication operation is performed (rule (b) and the value for `W * Y` is determined. Then the value of `(A + B div 2)` is subtracted from `Z` (rule (c)). Finally, that result is added to `W * Y`. The evaluation tree for this expression is shown in Fig. 7.5. ■

Writing Mathematical Formulas in Pascal

There are two problem areas in writing a mathematical formula in Pascal: one concerns multiplication and the other concerns division. You can imply multiplication in a mathematical formula by writing the two items to be multiplied next to each other, for example, $a = bc$. In Pascal, however, you must always use the `*` operator to indicate multiplication, as in

```
A := B * C
```

Figure 7.5 Evaluation Tree for Z − (A + B div 2) + W * Y

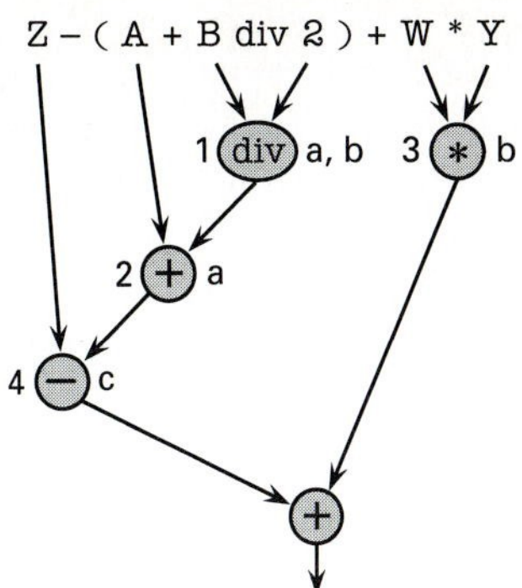

The other difficulty arises in formulas involving division. We normally write the numerator and the denominator on separate lines:

$$m = \frac{y - b}{x - a}$$

In Pascal, all assignment statements must be written in a linear form. Consequently, parentheses are often needed to separate the numerator from the denominator and to clearly indicate the order of evaluation of the operators in the expression. The preceding formula would be written in Pascal as

```
M := (Y - B) / (X - A)
```

■ Example 7.8

This example illustrates how several mathematical formulas can be written in Pascal.

Mathematical Formula	*Pascal Expression*
1. $b^2 - 4ac$	`B * B - 4 * A * C`
2. $a + b - c$	`A + B - C`
3. $\frac{a + b}{c + d}$	`(A + B) / (C + D)`
4. $\frac{1}{1 + x^2}$	`1 / (1 + X * X)`
5. $a \text{ x } - (b + c)$	`A * (-(B + C))`

The points illustrated are as follows:

- Always specify multiplication explicitly by using the operator * where needed (example 1).
- Use parentheses when required to control the order of operator evaluation (examples 3 and 4).
- Never write two arithmetic operators in succession; they must be separated by an operand or an open parenthesis (example 5). ■

Additional Numeric Types in Turbo Pascal (Optional)

There may be times when you need to use `Integer` values that are too large (or too small) to fit in the storage space allocated to type `Integer` variables. In standard Pascal, you would be forced to use type `Real` variables to store these values. Turbo Pascal contains a data type `LongInt`, which has values between `-2147483648` and `2147483647`. Turbo Pascal defines a constant `MaxLongInt` whose value is `2147483647`. Table 7.5 lists the additional `Integer` data types supported by Turbo Pascal, along with the range of values which may be stored in variables of each type. All Turbo Pascal operators that may be used with `Integer` operands may also be used with operands of the data types listed in Table 7.5.

Table 7.5 Integer Data Types

Type	Ranges
`Byte`	`0..255`
`ShortInt`	`-128..127`
`Integer`	`-32768..32767`
`Word`	`0..65535`
`LongInt`	`-2147483648..2147483647`

Turbo Pascal also provides several additional data types that may be used to declare variables for storing floating-point values of greater precision than allowed for ordinary type `Real` variables. These data types are listed in Table 7.6, along with the range of values that may be stored in variables of each type and the number of significant digits allowed. All Turbo Pascal operators that may be used with `Real` operands may also be used with operands of the data types listed in Table 7.6.

Table 7.6 Real Data Types

Type	Ranges	Significant Digits
`Single`	`1.5E-45 .. 3.4E38`	7-8
`Real`	`2.9E-39 .. 1.7E38`	11-12
`Double`	`5.0E-324 .. 1.7E308`	15-16
`Extended`	`1.9E-4951 .. 1.1E4932`	19-20

While the additional `Integer` types are always available in Turbo Pascal, you must use special compiler directives to use the extended `Real` types. The compiler directives needed depend on whether or not your computer has an 8087 numeric co-processor. (The 8087 co-processor is a computer "chip" installed on some IBM personal computers for performing floating-point computations more efficiently.) If the 8087 co-processor is installed, use the compiler directive pair {$N+,E-}, which instructs the compiler to perform floating-point numeric processing by calling procedures that utilize the 8087 co-processor. If the 8087 co-processor is not installed, use the compiler directive pair {$N+,E+}, which instructs the compiler to perform floating-point computations by calling procedures that *emulate* (simulate with software) the 8087 co-processor.

SYNTAX DISPLAY

Numeric Support Compiler Directive

Form: {$N-} or {$N+}
Default: {$N-}
Interpretation: When passive (value –), the compiler generates code to perform floating-point calculations that do not require the 8087 co-processor. When active (value +), the compiler generates code to perform floating-point calculations using the 8087 numeric co-processor. The 8087 chip may be installed or emulated in software.
Note: The {$N+} state is required to make use of the Turbo Pascal extended Real data types: Single, Double, or Extended. In Turbo Pascal version 4.0, your computer must have an 8087 co-processor to use these types.

SYNTAX DISPLAY

Emulation Compiler Directive

Form: {$E-} or {$E+}
Default: {$E+}
Interpretation: When active (value +), the 8087 numeric co-processor is emulated. When passive (value –), the numeric co-processor is used directly.

Exercises for Section 7.2

Self-Check

1. What result is generated for PrintDigits (23) and PrintDigits (64) if Base is 2? If Base is 8?
2. Evaluate the following expressions with 7 and 22 as operands.

```
22 div 7      7 div 22      22 mod 7      7 mod 22
```

Repeat this exercise for the following pairs of integers:

```
15, 16     3, 23     4, 16
```

3. Given the declarations below and assuming the function `Pi` returns 3.14159 as its value, find the value of each of the following statements that are valid. Also indicate which are invalid and why. Assume that `A` is 3, `B` is 4, and `Y` is `-1.0`.

```
const
  MaxI = 1000;

var
  X, Y : Real;
  A, B, I : Integer;
```

a. `I := A mod B`
b. `I := (990 - MaxI) div A`
c. `I := A mod Y`
d. `X := Pi * Y`
e. `I := A / B`
f. `X := A / B`
g. `X := A mod (A / B)`
h. `I := B div 0`
i. `I := A mod (990 - MaxI)`
j. `I := (MaxI - 990) div A`
k. `X := A / Y`
l. `I := Pi * A`
m. `X := Pi div Y`
n. `X := A div B`
o. `I := (MaxI - 990) mod A`
p. `I := A mod 0`
q. `I := A mod (MaxI - 990)`

4. What values are assigned by the legal statements in exercise 3, assuming `A` is 5, `B` is 2, and `Y` is `2.0`?
5. Assume that you have the following variable declarations:

```
var
  Color, Lime, Straw, Yellow, Red, Orange : Integer;
  Black, White, Green, Blue, Purple, Crayon : Real;
```

Evaluate each of the following statements given these values: `Color` is 2, `Black` is `2.5`, `Crayon` is `-1.3`, `Straw` is 1, `Red` is 3, and `Purple` is `0.3E1`.

a. `White := Color * 2.5 / Purple`
b. `Green := Color / Purple`
c. `Orange := Color div Red`
d. `Blue := (Color + Straw) / (Crayon + 0.3)`
e. `Lime : = Red div Color + Red mod Color`
f. `Purple : = Straw / Red * Color`

6. Let `A`, `B`, `C`, and `X` be the names of four type `Real` variables and let `I`, `J`, and `K` be the names of three type `Integer` variables. Each of the following statements contains a violation of the rules for forming arithmetic expressions. Rewrite each statement so it is consistent with the rules.

a. `X := 4.0 A * C`
b. `A := AC`
c. `I := 2 * -J`
d. `K := 3(I + J)`
e. `X := 5A / BC`
f. `I := 5J3`

7.3 Mathematical Functions

This section describes the use of functions in expressions. Functions are Pascal features that are helpful in specifying numeric computations. Each function performs a different mathematical operation (square root, cosine, and the like) and returns a single value. Functions are referenced directly in an expression; the value computed by the function is then substituted for the function reference.

■ Example 7.9

`Sqrt` is the name of a function that computes the square root of a positive value. If the value of `X` is `20.0`, the statement

```
Y := 5.7 + Sqrt(X + 5.0)
```

assigns a value of `10.7` to the type `Real` variable `Y`. The execution of this statement is as follows:

1. The expression argument `(X + 5.0)` is evaluated as `25.0`.
2. The function returns the square root of `25.0`, or `5.0`.
3. The sum of `5.7` and the function result (`5.0`) is assigned to `Y`, so `Y` gets `10.7`. ■

Pascal provides a number of standard mathematical functions, such as `Sqrt`, that programmers can use (see Table 7.7). The function name is always followed by its *argument* (an actual parameter) enclosed in parentheses, as shown in Example 7.9 (where the argument is `X + 5.0`). Any legal expression of the proper type can be an argument for these functions.

Table 7.7 Standard Functions

Function	**Purpose**	**Argument**	**Result**
`Abs(X)`	Returns the absolute value of its argument.	`Real` or `Integer`	Same as argument
`Arctan(X)`	Returns the angle `y` in radians, satisfying `X = tan(y)` where `-π/2 <= y <= π/2`.	`Real` or `Integer`	`Real` (radians)
`Cos(X)`	Returns the cosine of angle `X`.	`Real` or `Integer` (radians)	`Real`
`Exp(X)`	Returns e^x where $e = 2.71828\ldots$	`Real` or `Integer`	`Real`
`Ln(X)`	Returns the natural logarithm of `X` for `X > 0.0`.	`Real` or `Integer`	`Real`
`Odd(N)`	Returns `True` if its argument is an odd integer; otherwise, returns `False`.	`Integer`	`Boolean`
`Round(X)`	Returns the closest integer value to its argument.	`Real`	`LongInt`
`Sin(X)`	Returns the sine of angle `X`.	`Real` or `Integer` (radians)	`Real`
`Sqr(X)`	Returns the square of `X`.	`Real` or `Integer`	Same as argument
`Sqrt(X)`	Returns the positive square root of `X` for `X >= 0.0`.	`Real` or `Integer`	`Real`
`Trunc(X)`	Returns the integral part of its argument.	`Real`	`LongInt`

Except for Abs, Sqr, Round, and Trunc, each of the functions listed in Table 7.7 returns (computes) a Real value regardless of its parameter type (Real or Integer). The type of the result computed by a reference to Abs or Sqr is the same as the type of its parameter.

The functions Round and Trunc require type Real parameters and always return integer values. These functions determine the integral part of a real-valued expression. Consequently, the expressions

```
Trunc(1.5 * Gross)
Round(TotalScore / NumStudents)
```

have integer values and can be assigned to type Integer variables. Trunc simply *truncates*, or removes, the fractional part of its parameter; function Round *rounds* its parameter to the nearest whole number. For example, Trunc(17.5) is 17, while Round(17.5) is 18; Trunc(-3.8) is -3, while Round(-3.8) is -4.

Most of the functions in Table 7.7 perform common mathematical computations. The arguments for Ln and Sqrt must be positive. The arguments for Sin and Cos must be expressed in radians, not degrees. Arctan expresses its result in radians.

One additional function, Odd, is used only with an integer parameter. Odd determines whether an integer variable or expression evaluates to an odd number. The function Odd returns the Boolean value True or False (for example, Odd(3) is True; Odd(4) is False).

■ Example 7.10

You could use the Pascal functions Sqr and Sqrt to compute the roots of a quadratic equation in X of the form

$$AX^2 + BX + C = 0$$

The two roots are defined as

$$Root_1 = \frac{-B + \sqrt{B^2 - 4AC}}{2A} \quad \text{and} \quad Root_2 = \frac{-B - \sqrt{B^2 - 4AC}}{2A}$$

The if statement in Fig. 7.6 assigns values to Root1 and Root2 when the *discriminant* $(B^2 - 4AC)$ is greater than or equal to zero.

Figure 7.6 Roots of a Quadratic Equation

```
Disc := Sqr(B) - 4 * A * C ;           {Define discriminant}
if Disc > 0.0 then
  begin
    Root1 := (-B + Sqrt(Disc)) / (2 * A);
    Root2 := (-B - Sqrt(Disc)) / (2 * A)
  end {Disc > 0.0}
else if Disc = 0.0 then
  begin
    Root1 := -B / (2 * A);
    Root2 := Root1          {roots are equal}
  end {Disc = 0.0}
```

```
else
  WriteLn ('Roots are imaginary and were not defined.')
```

■ Example 7.11

The program in Fig. 7.7 illustrates the use of several arithmetic functions. The function references are inserted in the output list of the `WriteLn` statement. The `Abs` function finds the absolute value of `X` before the `Sqrt` function is called, because the square root of a negative number is undefined. ■

Figure 7.7 Using the Arithmetic Functions

Edit Window

```
program ArithFunc;

{Illustrates the arithmetic functions.}

   const
      Sentinel = 0.0;                          {sentinel value}

   var
      X : Real;                                {each data value}

begin  {ArithFunc}
   {Print the table heading}
   WriteLn ('After each line enter a real number or 0.0 to stop');
   WriteLn;
   WriteLn ('X', 'Trunc(X)' :16, 'Round(X)' :10, 'Abs(X)' :10,
            'Sqr(X)' :10, 'Sqrt(Abs(X))' :15);

   {Read and process each value of X}
   ReadLn (X);                                 {Get first number}
   while X <> Sentinel do
      begin
         WriteLn (Trunc(X) :17, Round(X) :10, Abs(X) :10:2,
                  Sqr(X) :10:2, Sqrt(Abs(X)) :10:2);
         ReadLn (X)                            {Get next number}
      end {while}
end. {ArithFunc}
```

Output Window

```
After each line enter a real number or 0.0 to stop
X         Trunc(X)  Round(X)    Abs(X)    Sqr(X)   Sqrt(Abs(X))
4.3
                 4         4      4.30     18.49        2.07
-24.78
               -24       -25     24.78    614.05        4.98
0.0
```

Additional Turbo Pascal Functions

Table 7.8 shows additional mathematical functions that are available in Turbo Pascal (but not standard Pascal). Functions `Frac` and `Int` can be used to extract the fractional and whole number part, respectively, of a real number. If `X` has the value `5.16123`, `Frac (X)` returns the `Real` value `0.16123` and `Int(X)` returns the `Real` value `5.0`.

Table 7.8 Turbo Pascal Mathematical Functions

Function	Purpose	Argument	Result
`Frac(num)`	Returns the fractional part of its argument.	`Real`	`Real`
`Int(num)`	Returns the whole number part of its argument.	`Real`	`Real`
`Pi`	Returns an approximation to `Pi`.	none	`Real`
`Random`	Returns real random number between `0.0` and `1.0`.	none	`Real`
`Random(int)`	Returns a random integer greater than or equal to `0` and less than `int`.	`Integer`	`Integer`

The function `Pi` is unusual as it has no arguments. It always returns an approximation to the value of `Pi` (3.1415926...); the precision of this value depends on the state of the numeric support compiler option (`N`).

The function `Random` generates a random number. A *random number* is a number that is selected at random from a specified range of numbers. Each of the numbers in the range is equally likely to be selected. `Random` may be called with or without an argument. The procedure `Randomize` should be called prior to the first call to function `Random`. Random numbers may be used to simulate the toss of a coin (two possible values) or a die (six possible values).

■ Example 7.12

Procedure `MultQuest` in Fig. 7.8 could be part of a program that provides drill in arithmetic. In `MultQuest`, the function `Random` is called twice. Each time an integer between `0` and `Limit` is selected. These random values are used to generate the operands (`Mult1`, `Mult2`) in a multiplication question. If `7` and `80` are the values returned by `Random` the question

```
What is the value of 7 * 80?
```

is printed. If the correct answer is read into `Response`, the Boolean assignment statement

```
Correct := Response = (Mult1 * Mult2)
```

sets the output parameter `Correct` to `True`; otherwise, it is set to `False`. Boolean assignment statements are explained in Section 7.4.

Figure 7.8 Procedure MultQuest

```
procedure MultQuest (Limit {input} : Integer;
                     var Correct {output} : Boolean);
{
 Asks a multiplication question and checks student's response.
 Pre : Limit defines the upper bound for the
       multiplicand or multiplier.
 Post: If question is answered correctly, returns True through
       Correct; otherwise, returns False.
}
  var
    Mult1, Mult2,                          {the two operands}
    Response      : Integer;               {student response}

  begin {MultQuest}
    Mult1 := Random(Limit + 1);           {get first operand}
    Mult2 := Random(Limit + 1);          {get second operand}

    WriteLn ('What is the value of ',
             Mult1 :1, '*', Mult2 :1, '?');
    ReadLn (Response);
    Correct := Response = (Mult1 * Mult2)    {evaluate answer}
  end; {MultQuest}
```

Advanced Mathematical Functions (Optional)

This section and the problem that follows discuss more advanced concepts of mathematics, including logarithms, exponents, trigonometric functions, and series approximations. You may want to skip some of this material if you do not have the appropriate mathematical background.

■ Example 7.13

There is no exponentiation operator in Pascal. This means that it is not possible to write u^v directly when u and v are type `Real`. However, from the study of logarithms we know that

$$\ln(u^v) = v \times \ln(u)$$

and

$$z = e^{\ln(z)}$$

where e is 2.71828.... So we can derive that

$$u^v = e^{(v \times \ln(u))}$$

This formula can be implemented in Pascal as

```
UToPowerV := Exp(V * Ln(U))
```

■

■ Example 7.14

The program in Fig. 7.9 draws a sine curve. It uses the Pascal function `Sin`, which returns the trigonometric sine of its parameter, an angle expressed in radians.

Figure 7.9 Plotting a Sine Curve

Edit Window

```
program SineCurve;

{Plots a sine curve.}

  const
    Star = '*';                              {symbol being plotted}
    Scale = 20;                              {scale factor for plot}
    MinAngle = 0;                            {smallest angle}
    MaxAngle = 360;                          {largest angle}
    StepAngle = 18;                          {increment in degrees}

  var
    Theta,                                   {angle in degrees}
    Indent : Integer;                        {column of each *}
    Radian : Real;                           {angle in radians}
    RadPerDegree : Real;                     {radians per degree}


begin {SineCurve}
  RadPerDegree := Pi / 180.0;
  WriteLn ('Theta', 'Sine curve plot' :28);
  Theta := MinAngle;                        {initial value of Theta}
  while Theta <= MaxAngle do
    begin
      Radian := Theta * RadPerDegree;              {Compute radians}
      Indent := 1 + Round(Scale * (1.0 + Sin(Radian)));
      Write (Theta :4, '|');
      Write (Star : Indent);                 {Plot * in column Indent}
      WriteLn (Sin(Radian) :20);                  {Print sine value}
      Theta := Theta + StepAngle                    {Get next angle}
    end {while}
end. {SineCurve}
```

Output Window

```
Theta               Sine curve plot
   0|                    *    0.0000000000E+00
  18|                          *    3.0901699437E-01
  36|                                *    5.8778525229E-01
  54|                                    *    8.0901699437E-01
  72|                                       *    9.5105651630E-01
  90|                                        *    9.9999999999E-01
 108|                                       *    9.5105651629E-01
 126|                                    *    8.0901699438E-01
 144|                                *    5.8778525229E-01
 162|                          *    3.0901699438E-01
 180|                    *    0.0000000000E+00
 198|              *    -3.0901699438E-01
 216|        *    -5.8778525229E-01
 234|    *    -8.0901699438E-01
 252| *    -9.5105651629E-01
 270|*    -9.9999999999E-01
 288| *    -9.5105651629E-01
 306|    *    -8.0901699437E-01
 324|        *    -5.8778525229E-01
 342|              *    -3.0901699437E-01
 360|                    *    0.0000000000E+00
```

The while loop is executed for values of Theta equal to 0, 18, 36, . . . , 360 degrees. For each Theta, the first assignment statement below

```
Radian := Theta * RadPerDegree;              {Compute radians}
Indent := 1 + Round(Scale * (1.0 + Sin(Radian)));
```

computes the number of radians corresponding to Theta. Then the variable Indent is assigned a value based on Sin(Radian). This value increases from 1 when Sin(Radian) is -1.0 to 41 (1 + Scale * 2.0) when Sin(Radian) is 1.0. Finally, the statement

```
Write (Star :Indent);        {Plot * in column Indent}
```

plots an asterisk somewhere in columns 1 through 41 as determined by the value of Indent. Remember, a string (or a character) is printed right-justified in its field; the value of Indent determines the size of the output field. ■

PROGRAM STYLE

Checking Boundary Values

The discussion for Example 7.13 states that the value of Indent ranges from 1 to 41 as the sine value goes from -1 to 1. It is a good idea to check the accuracy of those assumptions; you can usually do so by checking the boundaries of the range, as follows:

```
Sin(Radian) is -1.0, Indent := 1 + Round(Scale * (1.0 + (-1.0))
                     Indent := 1 + Round(20 * 0.0)
                     Indent := 1

Sin(Radian) is +1.0, Indent := 1 + Round(20 * (1.0 + 1.0))
                     Indent := 1 + Round(20 * 2.0)
                     Indent := 41
```

Case Study: Approximating the Value of e (Optional)

Problem

A number of mathematical quantities can be represented using a series approximation where a series is represented by a summation of an infinite number of terms. For example, the base of the natural logarithms, e (value is 2.71828...), can be determined by evaluating the expression

$$1 + 1/1! + 1/2! + 1/3! + \ldots + 1/n! + \ldots$$

where $n!$ is the factorial of n, defined as follows:

$$0! = 1$$
$$n! = n \times (n-1)! \text{ (for } n > 1\text{)}$$

Design Overview

We can get an approximation to the value of e by summing the series for a finite value of n. Usually, the larger the value of n, the more accurate the computed result. This expression can be represented, using *summation notation*, as

$$\sum_{i=0}^{n} 1/i!$$

where the first term is obtained by substituting 0 for i (1/0! is 1/1), the second term is obtained by substituting 1 for i (1/1!), and so on. A counting loop can be used to easily implement the preceding formula.

Data Requirements

Problem Inputs
The number of terms, n, in the sum (`N : Integer`)

Problem Outputs
The approximate value of e (`E : Real`)

Program Variable
The `ith` term of the series (`IthTerm : Real`)
Loop-control variable (`I : Integer`)

Algorithm

1. Read in the value of `N`.
2. Initialize `E` to `1.0`.
3. Initialize `IthTerm` to `1.0`.
4. `for` each `I` from `1` to `N do`
   `begin`
   5. Compute the ith term in the series
   6. Add the ith term to `E`
   `end`
7. Print the value of `E`.

The program is shown in Fig. 7.10. Inside the loop, the statement

```
IthTerm := IthTerm / I;
```

computes the value of the ith term in the series by dividing the previous term by the loop-control variable `I`. The following formula shows that this division does indeed produce the next term in the series.

$$(1 / (i - 1)!) / i = 1 / (i \times (i - 1)!) = 1 / i!$$

Because 0! is 1, `IthTerm` must be initialized to `1.0`. The statement

```
E := E + IthTerm
```

adds the new value of IthTerm to the sum being accumulated in E. Trace the execution of this loop to satisfy yourself that IthTerm takes on the values 1/1!, 1/2!, 1/3!, and so on, during successive loop iterations.

Figure 7.10 Series Approximation to e

Edit Window

```
program ESeries;

{Computes the value of e by a series approximation.}

   var
     E,                       {the value being approximated}
     IthTerm : Real;          {ith term in series}
     N,                       {number of terms in series}
     I : Integer;             {loop control variable}

begin {ESeries}
  Write ('Enter the number of terms in the series> ');
  ReadLn (N);

  {Compute each term and add it to the accumulating sum.}
  E := 1.0;                 {initial sum}
  IthTerm := 1.0;           {first term}
  I := 1;
  while I <= n do
    begin
      IthTerm := IthTerm / I;
      E := E + IthTerm;
      I := I + 1
    end; {while}

  {Print the result.}
  WriteLn ('The approximate value of e is ', E :20)
end. {ESeries}
```

Output Window

```
Enter the number of terms in the series> 15
The approximate value of e is    2.7182818284E+00
```

Numerical Inaccuracies

One of the problems in processing real numbers is that sometimes an error occurs in the representation of real data. Just as certain numbers cannot be represented exactly in the decimal number system (for example, the fraction ⅓ is 0.333333...), so some numbers cannot be represented exactly in real format. The *representational error* depends on the number of binary digits (bits) used in the mantissa: the more bits, the smaller the error.

The number 0.1 is an example of a real number that has a representational error. The effect of a small error is often magnified through repeated computations. Therefore, because the result of adding 0.1 ten times is not exactly 1.0, the following loop may fail to terminate on some computers.

```
Trial := 0.0;
while Trial <> 1.0 do
  begin
    ...

    Trial := Trial + 0.1
  end {while}
```

If the loop repetition test is changed to `Trial < 1.0`, the loop may execute ten times on one computer and eleven times on another. For this reason, it is best to use integer variables whenever possible in loop repetition tests.

Other problems occur during the manipulation of very large and very small real numbers. When a large number and a small number are added, the larger number may cancel out the smaller number, resulting in a *cancellation error*. If `X` is much larger than `Y`, then `X + Y` may have the same value as `X` (e.g., `1000.0 + 0.0001234` is equal to `1000.0` on some computers).

For this reason, you can sometimes obtain more accurate results by carefully selecting the order in which computations are performed. For example, in computing the value of `e` in the preceding case study, the terms of the series

$$1 + 1/1! + 1/2! + ... + 1/n!$$

were generated in left-to-right order and added to a sum being accumulated in `E`. When `n` is large, the value of `1/n!` is very small; thus, the effect of adding a very small term to a sum larger than `2.0` may be lost. If the terms are generated and summed in right-to-left order instead, the computation result might be more accurate.

If two very small numbers are multiplied and the result is too small to be represented accurately, it will be represented as zero. This phenomenon is called *floating-point underflow*. Similarly, if two very large numbers are multiplied, the result may be too large to be represented. This phenomenon, called *floating-point overflow*, causes Turbo Pascal to halt program execution and display a `floating-point Overflow` error message. *Integer overflow* occurs when an `Integer` result is too large to be stored in an `Integer` variable; Turbo Pascal does not flag this as a run-time error.

Exercises for Section 7.3

Self-Check

1. Rewrite the following mathematical expressions using Pascal functions.
   a. $\sqrt{U + V} \times W^2$ b. $\log_n (X^Y)$
   c. $\sqrt{(X - Y)^2}$ d. $|XY - W/Z|$

2. Evaluate the following:
   a. `Trunc(-15.8)` b. `Round(-15.8)`
   c. `Round(6.8) * Sqr(3)` d. `Sqrt(Abs(Round(-15.8)))`

Programming

1. Write a procedure that computes

   $e^{a \times \ln(b)}$

   Call this procedure with several different values of a and b and display the results. Verify for yourself that the results are correct.
2. Using the `Round` function, write a Pascal statement to round any real value `X` to the nearest two decimal places. Hint: You have to multiply by `100.0` before rounding.
3. The value of e^x is represented by the series

   $1 + x + x^2/2! + x^3/3! + ... + x^n/n! + ...$

   Write a program to compute and print the value of this series for any x and any n. Compare the result to `Exp(x)` and print a message `O.K` or `Not O.K.`, depending on whether the difference between these results exceeds `0.001`.

7.4 Boolean Variables, Expressions, and Operators

Chapter 1 introduced the data type `Boolean`. Since then we have used Boolean expressions (expressions that evaluate to true or false) to control loop repetition and to select one of the alternatives in an `if` statement. Some examples of Boolean expressions follow:

```
Gross > TaxBrak
Item <> Sentinel
TranType = 'C'
```

The simplest Boolean expression is a Boolean variable or constant that has one of the Boolean values, `True` or `False`. The statement

```
const
  Debug = True;
```

specifies that the Boolean constant `Debug` has the value `True`; the statement

```
var
  Switch, Flag : Boolean;
```

declares `Switch` and `Flag` to be Boolean variables—variables that can be assigned only the values `True` and `False`.

Boolean Operators

A Boolean variable or constant is the simplest form of a Boolean expression (for example, `Switch`). We have used the relational operators (<, =, >, and so on) with numeric data to form conditions or Boolean expressions (for example, `Salary < MinSal`).

There are three Boolean operators in standard Pascal: `and`, `or`, and `not`. These operators work in conjunction with operands that are Boolean expressions, for example,

```
(Salary < MinSal) or (NumDepend > 5)
(Temp > 90.0) and (Humidity > 0.90)
WinningRecord and (not Probation)
```

The first Boolean expression determines whether an employee pays no income tax. It evaluates to true if either condition in parentheses is true. The second Boolean expression describes an unbearable summer day, with temperature and humidity both above 90. The expression evaluates to true only when both conditions are true. The third Boolean expression manipulates two Boolean variables (`WinningRecord`, `Probation`). A college team for which this expression is true may be eligible for the postseason tournament.

The Boolean operators, are described in Table 7.9, Table 7.10, and Table 7.11.

Table 7.9 and Operator

Operand1	**Operand2**	**Operand1** `and` **Operand2**
`True`	`True`	`True`
`True`	`False`	`False`
`False`	`True`	`False`
`False`	`False`	`False`

Table 7.10 or Operator

Operand1	**Operand2**	**Operand1** `or` **Operand2**
`True`	`True`	`True`
`True`	`False`	`True`
`False`	`True`	`True`
`False`	`False`	`False`

Table 7.11 not Operator

Operand1	`not` **Operand1**
`True`	`False`
`False`	`True`

Table 7.9 shows that the `and` operator yields a True result only when both its operands are true; Table 7.10 shows that the `or` operator yields a False result only when both its operands are False. The `not` operator has a single operand;

Table 7.11 shows that the `not` operator yields the *logical complement*, or negation, of its operand.

The precedence of an operator determines its order of evaluation. Table 7.12 shows the precedence of all operators in Pascal, including the relational operators.

Table 7.12 Operator Precedence

Operator	Precedence
`not`	Highest (evaluated first)
`*, /, div, mod, and`	↓
`+, -, or`	
`<, <=, =, <>, >=, >`	Lowest (evaluated last)

As you can see, the `not` operator has the highest precedence, followed by the multiplicative operators (including `and`), the additive operators (including `or`), and, last, the relational operators. Because the relational operators have the lowest precedence, you should generally use them with parentheses to prevent syntax errors.

■ Example 7.15

The expression

```
X < Y + Z
```

involving the real variables `X`, `Y`, and `Z` is interpreted correctly as

```
X < (Y + Z)
```

because + has higher precedence than <. However, the expression

```
X < Y or Z < Y
```

causes the syntax error `invalid type of operands`. It is interpreted as

```
X < (Y or Z) < Y
```

because `or` has higher precedence than <. This is an error because the type `Real` variables `Y` and `Z` cannot be operands of the Boolean operator `or`.

This error is quite common; however, you can avoid it and similar errors by using parentheses freely. The following parentheses prevent a syntax error.

```
(X < Y) or (Z < Y)
```

■

■ Example 7.16

The following are all legal Boolean expressions if `X`, `Y`, and `Z` are type `Real` and `Flag` is type `Boolean`. The value of each expression, shown in brackets, assumes that `X` is `3.0`, `Y` is `4.0`, `Z` is `2.0`, and `Flag` is `False`.

1. `(X > Z) and (Y > Z)` [True]
2. `(X + Y / Z) <= 3.5` [False]

3. `(Z > X) or (Z > Y)` [False]
4. `not Flag` [True]
5. `(X = 1.0) or (X = 3.0)` [True]
6. `(0.0 < X) and (X < 3.5)` [True]
7. `(X <= Y) and (Y <= Z)` [False]
8. `not Flag or ((Y + Z) >= (X - Z))` [True]
9. `not (Flag or ((Y + Z) >= (X - Z)))` [False]

Expression 1 gives the Pascal form of the relationship "X and Y are greater than Z." You may be tempted to write expression 1 as

```
X and Y > Z
```

However, that is an illegal Boolean expression because the real variable X cannot be an operand of the Boolean operator and. Similarly, expression 5 shows the correct way to express the relationship "X is equal to 1.0 or to 3.0."

Expression 6 is the Pascal form of the relationship 0.0 < X < 3.5 (that is, "X is in the range 0.0 to 3.5"). Similarly, expression 7 shows the Pascal form of the relationship X <= Y <= Z (that is, "Y is in the range X to Z, inclusive").

Finally, expression 8 is evaluated in Fig. 7.11; the values given at the beginning of Example 7.16 are shown above the expression.

The expression in Fig. 7.11 is rewritten as follows with parentheses enclosing the term not Flag. Although the parentheses are not required, they do clarify the meaning of the expression.

```
(not Flag) or ((Y + Z) >= (X - Z))
```

Short-Circuit Evaluation of Boolean Expressions

When evaluating Boolean expressions, we often employ a technique called *short-circuit evaluation*. This means that we can stop evaluating a Boolean expression as soon as its value can be determined. For example, if the value of Flag is False, then not Flag is True, so the expression in Fig. 7.11 must evaluate to

Figure 7.11 Evaluation Tree for not Flag or ((Y + Z) >= (X − Z))

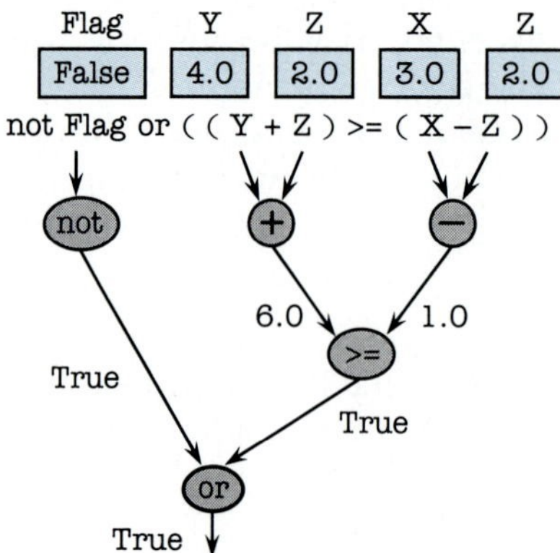

True regardless of the value of the parenthesized expression following or (that is, True or (...) must always be True). Consequently, there is no need to evaluate the parenthesized expression following or when not Flag is True. By similar reasoning, we can show that False and (...) must always be False, so there is no need to evaluate the parenthesized expression following the and operator. By default, Turbo Pascal uses short-circuit evaluation of Boolean expressions; standard Pascal does not.

■ Example 7.17

If X is zero, the if condition

```
if (X <> 0.0) and (Y / X > 5.0) then
```

is False, because (X <> 0.0) is False so False and (...) must always be False. Consequently, there is no need to evaluate the subexpression (Y / X > 5.0) when X is zero. However, if this expression is evaluated, a division by zero run-time error occurs because the divisor X is zero.

To prevent this run-time error for programs compiled by Pascal compilers that do not use short-circuit Boolean evaluation, the above if condition should be split as shown next.

```
if (X <> 0.0) then
  if (Y / X > 5.0) then
```

The first condition *guards* the second and prevents the latter from being evaluated when X is zero. The result of evaluating these conditions is the same for short-circuit or complete evaluation. ■

Be wary of short-circuit evaluation and avoid writing Boolean expressions that rely on it. The compiler directive {$B+} can be used to have the Turbo Pascal compiler generate code that causes complete evaluation of all Boolean expressions. The {$B+} directive should precede the first Boolean expression for which complete evaluation is desired. Once enabled, complete Boolean evaluation remains in effect until the {$B-} directive is encountered.

SYNTAX DISPLAY

Boolean Evaluation Compiler Directive

Form: {$B-} or {$B+}
Default: {$B-}
Interpretation: In the default state, Turbo Pascal uses short-circuit Boolean evaluation. Use of the compiler directive {$B+} causes the compiler to generate code for complete evaluation of every operand of a Boolean expression.
Note: Writing a Boolean expression whose value changes depending on whether short-circuit or complete evaluation is used is not good programming practice. This may cause run-time errors when you attempt to compile and run your programs on different computers.

Boolean Assignment Statements

We can write assignment statements that assign a Boolean value to a Boolean variable. The statement

```
Same := X = Y
```

assigns the value True to the Boolean variable Same when X and Y are equal; otherwise, the value False is assigned. This assignment is more efficient than the if statement

```
if X = Y then
  Same := True
else
  Same := False
```

which has the same effect.

■ Example 7.18

Either of the following assignment statements assigns the value True to Even if N is an even number.

```
Even := not Odd(N)        |        Even := (N mod 2) = 0
```

The statement on the left assigns to Even the complement of the value returned by the Boolean function Odd; the one on the right assigns a value of True to Even when the remainder of N divided by 2 is 0. (All even numbers are divisible by 2.) ■

Using Boolean Variables as Program Flags

Boolean variables are often used as *program flags*, which signal whether or not a special event occurs in a program. The fact that such an event occurs is important to the future execution of the program. A Boolean variable that is a program flag is initialized to one of its two possible values (True or False) and reset to the other as soon as the event being monitored occurs.

■ Example 7.19

Procedure ReadPos in Fig. 7.12 continues to read integer values until an integer greater than 0 is entered. The first value greater than 0 is returned as the procedure result.

The Boolean variable Positive acts as a program flag to signal whether the event data entry of a positive integer has occurred. Positive is initialized to False when the procedure is entered. Inside the while loop, the assignment statement

```
Positive := N > 0
```

resets Positive to True when an integer greater than 0 is entered. The loop is repeated as long as Positive is still False. ■

Figure 7.12 Procedure ReadPos

```
procedure ReadPos (var N {output} : Integer);
{
  Reads a positive integer into N.
  Pre : None
  Post: Returns in N the next data value greater than 0.
}
  var
    Positive : Boolean;           {program flag - loop control}

begin  {ReadPos}
  {Keep reading until a valid number is read}
  Positive := False;            {Assume valid number not read}
  while not Positive do
    {invariant:
       No prior value of N was greater than zero.
    }
    begin
      Write ('Enter an integer greater than 0> ');
      ReadLn (N);                {Read next integer into N}
      Positive := N > 0          {Set Positive to True if N > 0}
    end  {while}
end; {ReadPos}
```

Reading and Writing Boolean Values

Procedure `WriteLn` displays Boolean values, but procedure `ReadLn` cannot be used to read a Boolean value. Procedure `ReadLnBool` (see Fig. 7.13) "reads" a Boolean value. It does this by assigning a Boolean value to output parameter `BoolVal` based on the next data character. The statement

```
BoolVal := (NextChar = 'T') or (NextChar = 't');
```

assigns `True` to `BoolVal` if the data character read into `NextChar` is `T` or `t`; otherwise, it assigns `False` to `BoolVal`.

Figure 7.13 Procedure ReadLnBool

```
procedure ReadLnBool (var BoolVal {output} ,
                          Success {output} : Boolean);
{
  Reads a Boolean value (represented by T or F) into BoolVal and
  sets the flag Success.
  Pre : None
  Post: BoolVal is set to True if T or t is read; otherwise,
        BoolVal is set to False. Success is set to True only
        if one of the four characters T, t, F, or f is read.
}
  var
    NextCh : Char;             {a data character}
```

```
begin {ReadLnBool}
  ReadLn (NextCh);
  BoolVal := (NextCh = 'T') or (NextCh = 't');
  Success := BoolVal or (NextCh = 'F') or (NextCh = 'f')
end; {ReadLnBool}
```

Using a Boolean Parameter as a Flag

The second parameter of ReadLnBool is used as a flag to signal whether a valid data character was read. In ReadLnBool, the assignment statement

```
Success := BoolVal or (NextCh = 'F') or (NextCh = 'f')
```

assigns True to Success if the character read was T, t, F, or f. If the value returned in Success is False, the calling program should call ReadLnBool again. Assuming the calling program contains the variable declarations

```
var
  NextBool,              {input - next Boolean data value}
  ReadDone : Boolean;    {flag -- True if read succeeds; }
                         {              otherwise, False}
```

the following while loop could be used to read a Boolean value into NextBool.

```
ReadDone := False;       {no value read yet}
while not ReadDone Do
  begin
    Write ('Enter T or F> ');
    ReadLnBool (NextBool, ReadDone)
  end; {while}
```

The while loop body executes until procedure ReadLnBool sets ReadDone to True.

Using a Global Boolean Constant for Debugging

As mentioned earlier, a programmer should plan for debugging by including diagnostic print statements in the original code. One way to prevent the diagnostic print statements from executing during production runs is to declare a global Boolean constant (say Debug) whose value is True during debugging and False during production runs. The declaration part of the main module contains the constant declaration

```
const
  Debug = True;      {turn debugging diagnostics on}
```

during debugging runs and the constant declaration

```
const
  Debug = False;     {turn debugging diagnostics off}
```

during production runs. The following diagnostic print statements are executed only when Debug is True (that is, during debugging runs). Sections 5.7 and 6.8 discuss where to place diagnostic print statements.

```
if Debug then
  begin
    WriteLn ('Procedure ProcessGoods entered');
    WriteLn ('Input parameter Salary is ', Salary :12:2)
  end; {if}
```

Exercises for Section 7.4

Self-Check

1. Draw the evaluation tree for expression 9 of Example 7.16.
2. Write the following Boolean assignment statements:
   a. Assign a value of True to Between if the value of N lies between –K and +K, inclusive; otherwise, assign a value of False.
   b. Assign a value of True to UpperCase if Ch is an uppercase letter; otherwise, assign a value of False.
   c. Assign a value of True to Divisor if M is a divisor of N; otherwise, assign a value of False.

Programming

1. Write a procedure that returns a Boolean flag indicating whether or not its first parameter is divisible by its second parameter.

7.5 Character Variables and Functions

Pascal provides a character data type that can store and manipulate the individual characters that make up a person's name, address, and other personal data. Character variables are declared using the data type Char in a declaration. A type Char literal consists of a single character (a letter, a digit, a punctuation mark, or the like) enclosed in apostrophes. A character value can be assigned to a character variable or associated with a constant identifier, as shown in the following examples:

```
const
  Star = '*';

var
  NextLetter : Char;

begin
  NextLetter := 'A'
```

The character variable NextLetter is assigned the character value 'A' by the assignment statement. A single character variable or value can appear on the right side of a character assignment statement. Character values can also be compared, read, and printed.

Using Relational Operators with Characters

Assuming `Next` and `First` are type `Char`, the Boolean expressions

```
Next = First
Next <> First
```

determine whether two character variables have the same or different values. Order comparisons can also be performed on character variables using the relational operators <, <=, >, >=.

To understand the result of an order comparison, you must know something about how characters are represented internally in your computer. Each character has its own unique numeric code; the binary form of this code is stored in a memory cell that has a character value. These binary numbers are compared by the relational operators in the normal way.

The character code used by Turbo Pascal is called ASCII (American Standard Code for Information Interchange) and is shown in Appendix E. (Other Pascal systems may use different codes.)The digit characters are an increasing sequence of consecutive characters in ASCII. The digit characters `'0'` through `'9'` have code values of `48` through `57` (decimal). The following order relationship holds for the digit characters (that is, `'0' < '1'`, `'1' < '2'`, and so on).

```
'0'<'1'<'2'<'3'<'4'<'5'<'6'<'7'<'8'<'9'
```

The uppercase letters are also an increasing sequence of consecutive characters in ASCII. The uppercase letters have the decimal code values `65` through `90`. The following order relationship holds for uppercase letters.

```
'A'<'B'<'C'< ... <'X'<'Y'<'Z'
```

The lowercase letters are included in the ASCII character set. They are also an increasing, consecutive sequence of characters. In ASCII, the lowercase letters have the decimal code values `97` through `122`, and the following order relationship holds.

```
'a'<'b'<'c'< ... <'x'<'y'<'z'
```

In ASCII, the *printable characters* have codes from `32` (for a blank or a space) to `126` (for the symbol ~). The other codes represent normally nonprintable *control characters*, although Turbo Pascal does have printable symbols for these codes when they are displayed on the screen. Sending a control character to an output device causes the device to perform a special operation, such as returning the cursor to column one, advancing the cursor to the next line, or ringing a bell.

The Ordinal Functions: Ord, Pred, and Succ

The data types `Integer`, `Boolean`, and `Char` are considered *ordinal types*. With ordinal data types, each value (except the first) has a unique predecessor; each value (except the last) has a unique successor. For example, the predecessor of 5 is 4; the successor of 5 is 6. The data type `Real` is not an ordinal type because a real number like 3.1415 does not have a unique successor. (Is its successor 3.1416 or 3.14151?)

The order or sequence of an ordinal data type is well defined. For example, `-MaxInt-1` is the smallest integer, and the positive integers follow the sequence `1, 2, 3, ..., MaxInt`. The order of the Boolean values is `False, True`.

The Pascal function `Ord` determines the *ordinal number*, or relative position, of an ordinal value in its sequence of values. If the parameter of `Ord` is an integer, the ordinal number returned is the integer itself. For all other ordinal types, the ordinal number of the first value in the sequence is zero, the ordinal number of the second value is one, and so on. Thus, `Ord(False)` is zero and `Ord(True)` is one. If `A` and `B` belong to the same ordinal type and `A < B` is true, then `Ord(A) < Ord(B)` must also be true.

The Pascal function `Pred` returns the predecessor of its parameter, and the Pascal function `Succ` returns the successor. These functions, like `Ord`, can be used only with parameters that are ordinal types.

■ Example 7.20

Table 7.13 shows the results of using the `Ord`, `Succ`, and `Pred` functions with an integer or a Boolean parameter. As shown in Table 7.13, one value in each ordinal type does not have a successor (`MaxInt, True`). The Boolean value that does not have a predecessor is `False`. The integer value that does not have a predecessor is `-MaxInt-1`. Although you can use these functions with any of the ordinal types, they are most often used with type `Char` and the enumerated types discussed in Chapter 8. ■

Table 7.13 Results of Ord, Succ, and Pred

Parameter	Ord	Succ	Pred
15	15	16	14
0	0	1	-1
-30	-30	-29	-31
MaxInt	MaxInt	undefined	MaxInt-1
-MaxInt-1	-MaxInt-1	-MaxInt	undefined
False	0	True	undefined
True	1	undefined	False

■ Example 7.21

The following table is for ASCII.

Table 7.14 Results of Ord, Succ, and Pred Functions for ASCII

Parameter	Ord	Succ	Pred
'C'	67	D	B
'7'	55	8	6
'y'	121	z	x
' '	32	!	nonprintable

Table 7.14 shows that the digit 7 has the ordinal number 55 in ASCII. The expression

```
Ord('7') - Ord('0') = 7
```

is true because the digit characters are in consecutive sequence.

Table 7.14 also shows that the character 'C' has the ordinal number 67 in ASCII. Because the character 'D' is the successor of the character 'C', it must have an ordinal number of 68. Because the letters are in consecutive sequence in ASCII, the Boolean expression

```
Ord('C') - Ord('A') = 2
```

is `True`. In ASCII, the lowercase letters follow the uppercase letters, and the difference in code values for both cases of the same letter is 32 (for example, `Ord('a') - Ord('A')` is 32). ■

The Function Chr

The function `Chr` returns a character as its result. The character returned is the one whose ordinal number is the function argument. Therefore, the result of the function reference `Chr(67)` is the character with ordinal number 67 (the letter `C` in the ASCII code).

If `Ch` is a type `Char` variable, the *nested function reference*

```
Chr(Ord(Ch))
```

has the same value as `Ch`. Therefore, the function `Chr` is the *inverse* of the `Ord` function for the characters.

■ Example 7.22

The following `if` statement sets `LowCase` to the lowercase form of a capital letter stored in `NextChar`, where `NextChar` and `LowCase` are both type `Char`. If `NextChar` does not contain a capital letter, `LowCase` is assigned the same value as `NextChar`.

```
if ('A' <= NextChar) and (NextChar <= 'Z') then
  LowCase := Chr(Ord(NextChar) - Ord('A') + Ord('a'))
else
  LowCase := NextChar
```

If `NextChar` has the value 'C', the Boolean expression is `True` and the assignment statement is evaluated as follows, assuming the letters are consecutive characters.

```
LowCase := Chr(Ord('C') - Ord('A') + Ord('a'))
           Chr(2 + Ord('a'))
           Chr(99) = 'c'
```

If the ASCII code is used, we can write the first assignment statement in the previous `if` statement as

```
LowCase := Chr(Ord(NextChar) + 32)
```

If `NextChar` is 'C', `Ord(NextChar)` is 67 so 'c' is assigned to `LowCase`. ■

■ Example 7.23

A *collating sequence* is a sequence of characters arranged by ordinal number. The program in Fig. 7.14 prints part of the Pascal collating sequence. It lists the characters with ordinal numbers 32 through 90, inclusive. The sequence shown is for the ASCII code; the first character printed is a blank (ordinal number 32). ■

Figure 7.14 Printing Part of a Collating Sequence

Edit Window

```
program Collate;
{Prints part of the collating sequence.}
  const
    Min = 32;                        {smallest ordinal number}
    Max = 90;                        {largest ordinal number}

  var
   NextOrd : Integer;                {each ordinal number}

begin {Collate}
   {Print characters Chr(32) through Chr(90)}
   NextOrd := Min;
   while NextOrd <= Max do
     begin
       Write (Chr(NextOrd));         {Print next character}
       NextOrd := NextOrd + 1
     end; {while}
   WriteLn
end. {Collate}
```

Output Window

```
 !"#$%&'()*+,-./0123456789:;<=>?@ABCDEFGHIJKLMNOPQRSTUVWXYZ
```

Function UpCase

Another useful function provided in Turbo Pascal (but not standard Pascal) is `UpCase`. Function `UpCase` returns the uppercase equivalent of its `Char` argument (if one exists). For example, `UpCase('a')` returns `'A'`. Table 7.15 summarizes the functions introduced in this section.

Table 7.15 Functions for Ordinal and Character Types

Function	Purpose	Argument	Result
`Chr(N)`	Returns the character whose ordinal number is `N`.	`Integer`	`Char`
`Ord(N)`	Returns the ordinal number of its argument.	Any ordinal type	`Integer`
`Pred(N)`	Returns the predecessor of its argument.	Any ordinal type	Same as argument
`Succ(N)`	Returns the successor of its argument.	Any ordinal type	Same as argument
`UpCase(Ch)`	Returns uppercase equivalent of argument.	`Char`	`Char`

Exercises for Section 7.5

Self-Check

1. Evaluate the following:
   a. `Ord(True)`
   b. `Pred(True)`
   c. `Succ(False)`
   d. `Ord(True) - Ord(False)`

2. Evaluate the following; assume the letters are consecutive characters.
   a. `Ord('D') - Ord('A')`
   b. `Ord('d') - Ord('a')`
   c. `Succ(Pred('a'))`
   d. `Chr(Ord('C'))`
   e. `Chr(Ord('C') - Ord('A') + Ord('a'))`
   f. `Ord('7') - Ord('6')`
   g. `Ord('9') - Ord('0')`
   h. `Succ(Succ(Succ('d')))`
   i. `Chr(Ord('A') + 5)`
   j. `UpCase ('b')`

7.6 The Read Procedure

So far, we have used the `ReadLn` procedure to read data into a program. Pascal also provides the `Read` procedure for data entry. We often use `Read` in a loop to read a sequence of data characters into a single input variable, as shown next.

■ Example 7.24

The program in Fig. 7.15 reads a sentence ending in a period and counts the number of blanks in the sentence. Each character entered after the prompting message is read into the variable `Next` and tested to see if it is a blank.

The statement

```
Read (Next)
```

which appears twice in the program, reads one character at a time from the data line because `Next` is type `Char`. The `while` loop exit occurs after the sentinel character (.) is read. The `ReadLn` statement that appears after the loop is used to "read" the Enter key. ■

Figure 7.15 Counting Blanks in a Sentence

Edit Window

```
program BlankCount;

{Counts the number of blanks in a sentence.}
```

```
  const
    Blank = ' ';                  {character being counted}
    Sentinel = '.';               {sentinel character}

  var
    Next  : Char;                 {next character in sentence}
    Count : Integer;              {number of blank characters}

begin  {BlankCount}
  Count :=  0;                    {Initialize Count}
  WriteLn ('Enter a sentence ending with a "', Sentinel, '"');

  {Process each input character up to the sentinel}
  Read (Next);                              {Get first character}
  while Next <> Sentinel do
    {invariant:
        Count is the count of blanks so far and
        no prior value of Next is the sentinel
    }
    begin
      if Next = Blank then
        Count := Count + 1;         {Increment blank count}
      Read (Next)                   {Get next character}
    end;  {while}
  ReadLn;
  {assert: Count is the count of blanks and Next is the sentinel}
  WriteLn;
  WriteLn ('The number of blanks is ', Count :1)
end. {BlankCount}
```

Output Window

```
Enter a sentence ending with a "."
There was an old woman who lived in a shoe.
The number of blanks is 9
```

The Read Procedure

The program in Fig. 7.15 uses the Pascal `Read` procedure to read individual characters from a data line. Like the `ReadLn` procedure, the `Read` procedure causes input data to be stored in the variables specified in its input list. Both statements

```
Read (Next)        |       ReadLn (Next)
```

cause one data character to be read into the character variable `Next`, but with one important difference. After the `ReadLn` statement is executed, the computer automatically empties the input buffer when Enter is pressed; any additional characters typed on the current data line before the Enter key is pressed are not processed. The input buffer is not emptied after a `Read` statement is executed; therefore, any additional characters typed on the current line are processed by the next `Read` or `ReadLn`. Section 8.7 further details the differences between procedures `Read` and `ReadLn`.

SYNTAX DISPLAY

Read Procedure with ReadLn

Form: `Read` (*input list*);
`ReadLn;`

Example: `Read (Next, N, Dummy, Ch);`
`ReadLn;`

Interpretation: Data are entered into each variable specified in the *input list*. There must be one data item for each variable in the *input list*, and the order of the data must correspond to the order of the variables in the *input list*. Insert one or more blank characters between numeric data items. If a character or string data item is being read after a number, insert a single blank character between the number and the character data. You must read the blank character into a dummy character variable (for example, `Dummy`) before reading the actual character data. Do not insert any extra blanks between consecutive character data items. The first character that follows the last one read will be processed when the next `Read` or `ReadLn` statement is executed. Press the Enter key after you have entered all data items.

The `ReadLn` without a parameter is used to "read" the Enter key. If the `Read` statement appears in a loop, the `ReadLn` statement should follow the loop `end`.

Note: `Read` is system dependent. On some Pascal systems, data characters are processed as they are entered; in Turbo Pascal, the data characters are not processed until after the Enter key is pressed, so you can edit the data line (using the backspace key) before you press Enter on the PC keyboard.

■ Example 7.25

It is sometimes desirable to read a number as a string of individual characters. This enables the program to detect and ignore data entry errors. For example, if the program user enters a letter instead of a number, the error is detected and the program prompts again for a data value. Similarly, if the program user types in `$15,400` instead of the number `15400`, the extra characters are ignored.

Procedure `ReadLnInt` in Fig. 7.16 reads in a string of characters ending with a sentinel (the character `%`) and ignores any character that is not a digit. It also computes the value of the number (an integer) formed by the digits only. For example, if the characters `$15,43AB0%` are entered, the value returned through `NumData` is `15430`.

Figure 7.16 Reading a Number as a String of Characters

```
procedure ReadLnInt (var NumData {output} : Integer);
{
  Reads consecutive characters ending with the symbol %. Computes
  the integer value of the digit characters, ignoring nondigits.
  Pre : None
```

```
  Post: Returns in NumData the numeric value of the digit
        characters read.
}
  const
    Base = 10;                          {the number system base}
    Sentinel = '%';                     {the sentinel character}

  var
    Next : Char;                        {each character read}
    Digit : Integer;     {the value of each numeric character}

begin {ReadLnInt}
  {Accumulate the numeric value of the digits in NumData}
  NumData := 0;                               {initial value is zero}
  Read (Next);                                 {Read first character}
  while Next<> Sentinel do
    {invariant:
        No prior value of Next is the sentinel and
        NumData is the accumulated numeric value of all prior digit
        characters read into Next
    }
    begin
      if ('0' <= Next) and (Next <= '9') then
        begin {digit}
          Digit := Ord(Next) - Ord('0');       {Get digit value}
          NumData := Base * NumData + Digit    {Add digit value}
        end;  {digit}
      Read (Next)                       {Read next character}
    end;  {while}
  ReadLn;
  {assertion:
     Next is the sentinel and
     NumData is the number formed from the digit
     characters read as data
  }
end; {ReadLnInt}
```

In Fig. 7.16, the statements

```
Digit := Ord(Next) - Ord('0');          {Get digit value}
NumData := Base * NumData + Digit       {Add digit value}
```

assign to Digit an integer value between 0 (for character value '0') and 9 (for character value '9'). The number being accumulated in NumData is multiplied by 10, and the value of Digit is added to it. Table 7.16 traces the procedure execution for the input characters 3N5%; the value returned is 35. ■

Table 7.16 Trace of Execution of Procedure ReadLnInt for Data 3N5%

Statement	Next	Digit	NumData	Effect
NumData := 0			0	Initialize NumData.
Read (Next)	3			Get character.
while Next <> Sentinel do				'3' <> '%' is true.
if ('0'<=Next) and (Next<='9')				'3' is a digit.
Digit := Ord(Next) - Ord ('0')		3		Digit value is 3.

Table 7.15 *continued*

Statement	Next	Digit	NumData	Effect
`NumData := Base*NumData+Digit`			3	NumData gets 3.
`Read (Next)`	N			Get character.
`while Next <> Sentinel do`				`'N'<> '%'` is true.
`if ('0'<=Next) and (Next<='9')`				`'N'` is not a digit.
`Read (Next)`	5			Get character.
`while Next <> Sentinel do`				`'5' <> '%'` is true.
`if ('0'<=Next) and (Next<='9')`				`'5'` is a digit.
`Digit := Ord(Next) - Ord ('0')`		5		Digit value is 5.
`NumData := Base*NumData+Digit`			35	NumData gets `10 * 3 + 5`.
`Read (Next)`	%			Get character.
`while Next<> Sentinel do`				`'%' <> '%'` is false.
`ReadLn`				Empty input buffer.

7.7 Subrange Types

One of the most important features of Pascal is that it permits the declaration of new data types. Many of these data types are discussed in later chapters. This section focuses on new data types that are subranges of the ordinal types, where a *subrange* defines a subset of the values associated with a particular ordinal type (the *host type*). Subranges make a program more readable and enable Pascal to detect when a variable is given a value that is unreasonable in the problem environment.

■ Example 7.26

Type declarations begin with the reserved word `type` and are used to declare a new data type. The Pascal scope rules for identifiers apply to names of data types. Declarations of two subrange types and a variable of each new type follow.

```
type
  Letter = 'A'..'Z';
  DaysInMonth = 1..31;

var
  NextChar : Letter;
  InDay : DaysInMonth;
```

The first subrange, `Letter`, has the host type `Char`. Any character value from `'A'` to `'Z'`, inclusive, can be stored in a variable of type `Letter`. Attempting to store any other character in a variable of type `Letter` is a *range error* and may be detected during program compilation or execution. For the assignment statement

```
NextChar := 'a'
```

Turbo Pascal detects a constant out of range error during compilation.

`DaysInMonth` is a subrange with host type `Integer`. A variable of type `DaysInMonth` can be used to keep track of the current date, a value between `1` and `31`, inclusive. The statement

```
ReadLn (InDay)
```

reads a data value into `InDay (type DaysInMonth)`. Turbo Pascal will detect a run-time `range check` error if a data value less than `1` or greater than `31` is entered when range checking is enabled. ■

SYNTAX DISPLAY

Subrange Type Declaration

Form: `type` *subrange type* = *minvalue* .. *maxvalue*;
Example: `type LowCase = 'a' .. 'z';`
Interpretation: A new data type named *subrange type* is defined. A variable of type *subrange type* can be assigned a value from *minvalue* through *maxvalue*, inclusive. The values *minvalue* and *maxvalue* must belong to the same ordinal type (called the host type), and `Ord(`*minvalue*`)` must be less than or equal to `Ord(`*maxvalue*`)`. *minvalue* and *maxvalue* can be constant identifiers of the same data type.

The scope rules for a subrange-type identifier are the same as for other Pascal identifiers. The operations that can be performed on a variable whose type is a subrange are the same as for the host type of the subrange. The host type can be a standard ordinal type (`Integer`, `Char`, or `Boolean`) or any previously declared enumerated type (discussed in Section 8.7). The host type is determined by the pair of values that define the subrange; the ordinal number of the first value must be less than the ordinal number of the second value.

The `type` declaration must come before a variable of that type is declared in a Pascal block. The form of the declaration part for standard Pascal is summarized as follows:

constant declarations
type declarations
variable declarations
procedure declarations

In Turbo Pascal, this order does not have to be followed but every identifier must be declared before its first reference.

Enabling Range Checking

Although subrange types provide the capability for detecting a value that is out of range during program execution, Turbo Pascal (unlike standard Pascal) does not automatically perform range checking. Range checking is controlled by the `R` compiler option, which is passive by default (value is −). Using the compiler directive `{$R+}` causes the Turbo Pascal compiler to generate range checking code.

SYNTAX DISPLAY

Range Checking Compiler Directive

Form: `{$R-}` or `{$R+}`
Default: `{$R-}`
Interpretation: In the `{$R-}` state, Turbo Pascal does not check for subrange errors during program execution. The compiler directive `{$R+}` enables the generation of range checking code and should be used while debugging programs. When this option is active, all assignments to ordinal and subrange variables are checked to be within range.

PROGRAM STYLE

Motivation for Using Subranges and Range Checking

You may be wondering, "Why bother with subranges? They don't seem to provide any new capabilities." Subranges do, however, provide additional opportunity for your program to "bomb," because attempting to store an out-of-range value in a variable whose type is a subrange stops program compilation or execution. This should happen only as the result of an error by the programmer or program user and prevents the error from going undetected.

For example, if `InDay` is type `Integer` (instead of `DaysInMonth`), the program continues to execute regardless of what value is assigned to `InDay`. Assigning an overly large value (say, `1000`) to `InDay` may cause a later statement to fail or the program to generate incorrect results. In the former case, the program user may have difficulty finding the statement that was actually at fault (that is, the statement that assigned the out-of-range value). In the latter case, the program user may not even be aware that an error has occurred if program execution is completed in a normal manner. The use of subranges and range checking ensures the immediate detection of an out-of-range value.

For these reasons, you should always use the compiler directive `{$R+}` when you are debugging a program. Also, use it during normal production runs. The range-checking code generated by the compiler will make your program slightly longer. Consequently, you may want to disable range-checking in production runs if time and space efficiency are critical concerns.

Exercise for Section 7.7

Self-Check

1. Identify which of the following subranges are illegal.

a. `1..MaxInt`	d. `'A'..'z'`
b. `'A'..'Z'`	e. `'c'..'c'`
c. `-15..15`	f. `0..'9'`

g. `15..-15`
h. `'ACE'..'HAT'`
i. `'a'..'Z'`
j. `-MaxInt..-MaxInt + 5`

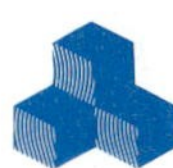

7.8 Identical and Compatible Types

In Turbo Pascal, two types are considered to be *type identical* (the same type) only when they are declared to be equivalent to one another, or each type is declared to be equivalent to a third type identifier. The type declarations below

```
type
  Numbers   = Integer;
  PosAndNeg = Numbers;
  IntType   = PosAndNeg;
```

have the effect of making `Numbers`, `PosAndNeg`, `IntType`, and `Integer` identical types. However, `Percent` and `Hundred` declared below are not identical types, because `1..100` is not a type identifier.

```
type
  Percent = 1..100;
  Hundred = 1..100;
```

Two variables declared with the same type declaration are always considered to be of identical types. The variables `Score1` and `Score2` declared below are the same type.

```
var
  Score1, Score2 : 1..100;
```

Variables declared separately are considered to have identical types only when declared using the same type identifier. For the declarations

```
var
  Score1 : 1..50;
  Score2 : 1..50;
  Score3 : Percent;
  Score4 : Percent;
```

variables `Score3` and `Score4` have identical types, but variables `Score1` and `Score2` do not have identical types. In a procedure call, the type of each variable that corresponds to a variable formal parameter must be identical to that of its corresponding formal parameter.

Type Compatible

Two data types are considered *type compatible* in Turbo Pascal if they are type identical, if both are integer types (`Byte`, `ShortInt`, `Integer`, `Word`, `LongInt`) though not necessarily the same integer type, if both are `Real` types (`Single`, `Real`, `Double`, `Extended`), if one type is a subrange of the other (for example, `Letter` and `Char` in Example 7.26, or both are subranges of the same host type.

Operands that are type compatible may be manipulated by the same operator. For example, the expression

```
NextCh <> '3'
```

is syntactically correct as long as NextCh is type Char or Letter. On the other hand, the expression

```
NextCh <> 3
```

causes a syntax error because the integer 3 is not type compatible with NextCh.

The variable InDay declared in Example 7.26 may be manipulated like any other Integer variable. It can be used as an actual parameter that corresponds to a formal value parameter that is of type Integer, type DaysInMonth, or any other subrange with host type Integer. However, as discussed previously, InDay may only correspond to a formal variable parameter that is type identical to DaysInMonth.

Assignment Compatible

An expression is considered *assignment compatible* with a variable in Turbo Pascal if any of the following holds.

- their types are type identical
- they are compatible ordinal types and the value of the expression falls within the range of possible values for the variable
- they are Real types (Single, Real, Double, Extended) and the value of the expression falls within the range of possible values for the variable
- the variable has one of the Real types and the expression has one of the Integer types (Byte, ShortInt, Integer, Word, LongInt)

If a variable and an expression are assignment compatible, then the expression may be assigned to the variable without error.

Assuming the declarations

```
type
  Letter = 'A'..'Z';

var
  NextCh : Letter;
```

the assignment statement

```
NextCh := '3';
```

causes the syntax error Constant out of range because the constant '3' is not assignment compatible with the variable NextCh (type Letter). If Ch is of type Char, and range checking is enabled using {$R+}, the assignment statement

```
NextCh := Ch;
```

will compile, but it may cause a Range check error at run-time. This error occurs if the character stored in Ch is not an uppercase letter.

We will discuss more issues of type compatibility and assignment compatibility in later chapters.

Exercise for Section 7.8

Self-Check

1. Assuming that I is type 0..10, J is type Integer, and K is type Real, indicate whether each expression below is assignment compatible with the variable on the left and whether any constraints are necessary to avoid an out of range error.
   a. K := 3 * I + J
   b. I := 15
   c. J := Trunc(K) + 2 * I
   d. I := I div J
   e. I := I / J
   f. I := J mod 11
   g. J := 2 * K + 3

7.9 Problem Solving Illustrated

The case study for Chapter 7 involves the manipulation of type Integer and Char data. It also illustrates the use of Boolean variables as program flags.

Case Study: Prime Numbers

Problem

A prime number is an integer that has no divisors other than 1 and itself. Examples of prime numbers are the integers 2, 3, 5, 7, and 11. Your mathematics professor wants you to write a program that tests a positive integer to determine whether or not it is a prime number.

Design Overview

A number cannot be prime if it has a divisor, other than itself, that is greater than 1. Even numbers cannot be prime because they have 2 as a divisor. To determine whether an odd number, say N, is prime, you must test whether it is divisible by any integer from 2 through N − 1. Your program should either print a message indicating that an integer is a prime number or print the smallest divisor of the number if it is not prime.

Data Requirements

Problem Inputs

The number to be tested for a prime number (N : Integer)

Problem Outputs

The smallest divisor if N is not prime (FirstDiv : Integer)

Case Study: Prime Numbers, continued

Initial Algorithm

1. Read in the number to be tested for a prime number.
2. Find the smallest divisor > 1 or determine that the number is prime.
3. Print a message that the number is prime or print its smallest divisor

Algorithm Refinements and Structure Chart

Use the Boolean variable `Prime`, described below, as a program flag to indicate whether `N` is prime. The structure chart is shown in Fig. 7.17.

Additional Program Variables
Program flag that will be set to `True` if `N` is prime and will be set to `False` if `N` is not prime (`Prime : Boolean`)

Step 2 of the algorithm is performed by procedure `TestPrime` which is described after the main program. `TestPrime` returns the value of `Prime` and `FirstDiv`.

Step 3 of the algorithm is relatively simple; it is included in the main program. The refinement for step 3 follows.

Step 3 Refinement

```
3.1 if N is prime then
        3.2 Print a message that N is prime
    else
        3.3 Print the first divisor of N
```

Coding the Main Program

The main program consists of calls to procedure `EnterInt`, which performs step 1, and procedure `TestPrime`, which performs step 2. A stub is provided

Figure 7.17 Structure Chart for Prime Number Problem

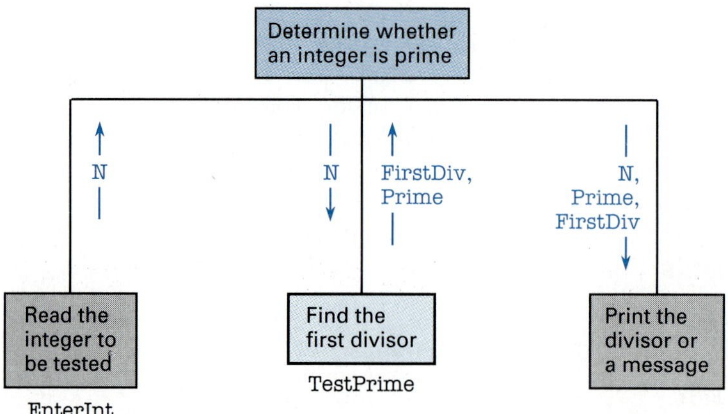

for TestPrime, but EnterInt is included with the main program shown in Fig. 7.18. Procedure EnterInt returns the first data value that lies between its two input parameter values. (EnterInt is used in other programming examples in this text.)

Figure 7.18 Main Program to Test for a Prime Number

```
{$R+}
program PrimeNumber;
{
  Prints the smallest divisor (other than 1) of the integer N if
  a divisor exists; otherwise, prints a message that N is prime.
}
  const
    Maximum = 1000;          {largest prime candidate}

  type
    SmallInt = 2..Maximum;   {range of values for N}

  var
    N : Integer;          {input - number being tested as a prime}
    FirstDiv : SmallInt;  {output - first divisor if found}
    Prime    : Boolean;   {flag - signals whether N is prime
                           (True) or not prime (False)       }



  procedure EnterInt (MinN, MaxN {input} : Integer;
                      var N {output} : Integer);
  {
    Reads an integer between MinN and MaxN into N.
    Pre : MinN and MaxN are assigned values.
    Post: Returns in N the first data value between MinN and MaxN
          if MinN <= MaxN is true; otherwise, N is not defined.
  }
    var
      InRange : Boolean;      {program flag - loop control}

  begin {EnterInt}
    if MinN <= MaxN then
      InRange := False        {no valid value in N as yet}
    else
      begin
        WriteLn ('Error - empty range for EnterInt');
        InRange := True                {skip data entry loop}
      end; {if}

    {Keep reading until a valid number is read into N.}
    while not InRange do
      {invariant:
          No prior value of N is in the range MinN through MaxN
      }
      begin
        Write ('Enter an integer between ');
        Write (MinN :1, ' and ', MaxN :1, '> ');
        ReadLn (N);
        InRange := (MinN <= N) and (N <= MaxN)
      end {while}
```

```
    {assert: N is in the range MinN to MaxN if MinN <= MaxN}
  end; {EnterInt}

  procedure TestPrime (N {input} : Integer;
                       var FirstDiv {output} : SmallInt;
                       var Prime {output} : Boolean);
  {
   Finds first divisor (FirstDiv) of N if it exists.
   Pre : N is assigned a value.
   Post: FirstDiv is the first divisor of N besides 1 and N.
         Prime is True if a divisor is not found; otherwise,
         Prime is False.
  }
  begin {TestPrime stub}
    WriteLn ('Procedure TestPrime entered');
    FirstDiv := 2;
    Prime := True
  end; {TestPrime stub}

begin {PrimeNumber}
  {Enter an integer to test for a prime number}
  WriteLn ('Enter a number that you think is a prime.');
  EnterInt (2, Maximum, N);

  {
   Find smallest divisor FirstDiv or determine that N is prime.
   Set Prime to indicate whether or not N is a prime number.
  }
  TestPrime (N, FirstDiv, Prime);

  {Print first divisor or a message that N is prime}
  if Prime then
    WriteLn (N :1, ' is a prime number')
  else
    WriteLn (FirstDiv :1, ' is the smallest divisor of ', N :1)
end. {PrimeNumber}
```

Coding the Procedures

EnterInt begins with an if statement that verifies that its two input parameters, MinN and MaxN, satisfy the condition MinN <= MaxN. If this condition is true, the program flag InRange is set to False and the while loop executes until a valid data value is read (InRange becomes True). If this condition is false, the program flag InRange is set to True and an error message is displayed. Setting InRange to True ensures that the while loop will be skipped. This is critical because the while loop will execute forever if it is entered when MinN is greater than MaxN.

It is unlikely that a caller of EnterInt will pass it two integer values that do not satisfy the condition MinN <= MaxN. However, it is a good idea to practice *defensive programming* and display an error message just in case the improbable occurs.

Procedure TestPrime determines whether N has any divisors other than 1 and itself. If N is an even integer, then it is divisible by 2. Therefore, 2 is the only even integer that can be prime, and 2 is the smallest divisor of all other even integers.

If `N` is an odd integer, its only possible divisors are the odd integers less than `N`. In fact, it can be proven that a number is prime if it is not divisible by any odd integer less than or equal to its square root. These considerations form the basis for the following algorithm.

Algorithm for Procedure TestPrime

1. `if` `N` = 2 `then`
    2. `N` is a prime number

   `else if` `N` is even `then`
    3. 2 is the smallest divisor and `N` is not prime

   `else`
    4. Test each odd integer between 3 and the square root of `N` to see whether it is a divisor of `N`

Step 4 must test each odd integer as a possible divisor of `N` until a divisor is found. We will write a separate procedure (`TestOdd`) to accomplish this. `TestOdd` should contain a `while` loop with the following loop invariant:

```
{invariant:
    FirstDiv during pass i is 1 + 2 * i (i.e., 3, 5, 7, ... ) and
    no prior value of FirstDiv is a divisor of N or
    is greater than the square root of N
}
```

This invariant suggests the `while` loop shown in the following algorithm; the structure chart for `TestPrime` and `TestOdd` is shown in Fig. 7.19.

Algorithm for TestOdd

1. Assume `N` is a prime number (i.e., set `Prime` to `True`).
2. Initialize `FirstDiv` to 3.

Figure 7.19 Structure Chart for TestPrime and TestOdd

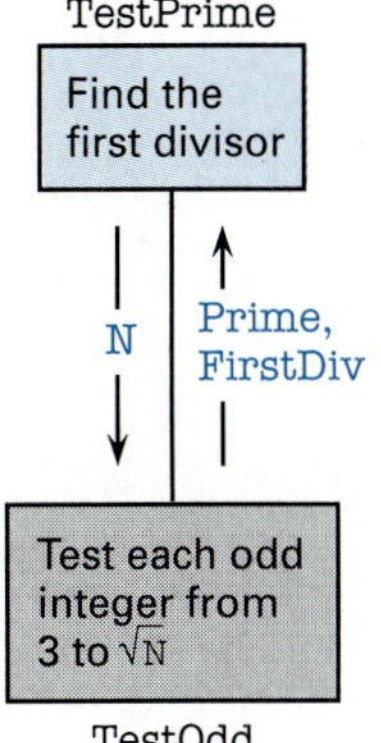

Case Study: Prime Numbers, continued

3. `while` N is still prime and `FirstDiv <= Sqrt(N) do`
   4. `if FirstDiv` is a divisor of N `then`
      5. `Set Prime` to `False` (N is not prime).

      `else`

      6. Set `FirstDiv` to the next odd number.

The nesting of procedures for the entire program system is shown in Fig. 7.20. Procedure `TestPrime` (with nested procedure `TestOdd`) is shown in Fig. 7.21.

Figure 7.20 Nesting of Procedures in Program PrimeNumber

```
program PrimeNumber
  procedure EnterInt
  procedure TestPrime
    procedure TestOdd
```

Figure 7.21 Procedure TestPrime with TestOdd

```
procedure TestPrime (N {input} : SmallInt;
                     var FirstDiv {output} : SmallInt;
                     var Prime {output} : Boolean);
{
 Finds first divisor (FirstDiv) of N if it exists.
 Pre : N is assigned a value.
 Post: FirstDiv is the first divisor of N besides 1 and N.
       Prime is True if a divisor is not found; otherwise,
       Prime is False.
}

  procedure TestOdd (N {input} : SmallInt;
                     var FirstDiv {output} : SmallInt;
                     var Prime {output} : Boolean);
  {
    Tests each odd integer from 3 to the square root of N as a
    divisor of N.
    Pre : N is odd.
    Post: FirstDiv is the smallest divisor if one is found.
          Prime is True if a divisor is not found; otherwise,
          Prime is False.
  }
    var
      MaxPossibleDiv : SmallInt; {largest possible divisor}

  begin {TestOdd}
    Prime := True;                     {Assume that N is prime}
    FirstDiv := 3;                                {Try 3 first}
    MaxPossibleDiv := Trunc(Sqrt(N));
    while Prime and (FirstDiv <= MaxPossibleDiv) do
      {invariant:
          FirstDiv during pass i is 1 + 2 * i (3, 5, 7, ... ) and
```

```
        no prior value of FirstDiv is a divisor of N or
        is greater than the square root of N
    }
    if (N mod FirstDiv) = 0 then
      Prime := False                      {N is not prime}
    else
      FirstDiv := FirstDiv + 2         {Try next odd number}

  {assertion:
     Prime is True and FirstDiv > Sqrt(N) or
     Prime is False and FirstDiv is the smallest divisor of N
  }
  end; {TestOdd}


begin {TestPrime}
  if N = 2 then
    Prime := True                         {2 is a prime number}
  else if not Odd(N) then
    begin  {N is even}
      Prime := False;
      FirstDiv := 2                       {2 is first divisor}
    end {N is even}
  else  {N is odd}
    TestOdd (N, FirstDiv, Prime)          {Test for a divisor}
end; {TestPrime}
```

The program flag Prime is set within TestOdd or TestPrime to indicate whether N is a prime number. In TestOdd, Prime is initialized to True before any candidate divisors are tested. If a divisor is found, Prime is reset to False and the while loop is exited. If no divisors are found, Prime remains True and the loop is exited when FirstDiv becomes greater than Sqrt(N). The values of Prime and FirstDiv are returned to the main program.

PROGRAM STYLE

Removing Unnecessary Computation from Loops

In procedure TestOdd, the local variable MaxPossibleDiv is used to hold the maximum possible divisor ($\sqrt{N}$) and is assigned its value by the statement

```
MaxPossibleDiv := Trunc(Sqrt(N));
```

just before the while loop. The Trunc function returns the integral part of the square root of N.

If MaxPossibleDiv was not declared as a local variable, the preceding expression would be included in the while loop condition and would be reevaluated each time the loop was repeated. This is not necessary, since the expression value never changes. You should examine loops carefully and remove any computations that always generate the same results.

Planning for Reuse

The parameter N represents the prime number candidate in all procedures described earlier. N is declared as type Integer in the main program and procedure EnterInt and as type SmallInt (the subrange 2..Maximum) in TestPrime and TestOdd. This is permissible, because N is a value parameter in TestPrime and TestOdd and SmallInt is a subrange of type Integer.

There are two reasons why N cannot be declared type SmallInt in procedure EnterInt. First, if an out-of-range value is read into N, a run-time error might occur. Second, we are planning to reuse EnterInt in other program systems. Because N is a variable parameter, its data type must be the same as the data type of its corresponding actual parameter. It is easier to use the standard type Integer than to redefine type SmallInt in each program that calls EnterInt.

Testing

You should test the complete program for both small and large numbers that are prime numbers. You should be able to find a table of primes to help you select sample cases. Make sure you test nonprimes that are odd numbers and nonprimes that are even numbers. Also, test procedure EnterInt using data values that are not in range.

Several sample runs of the prime number program are shown in Fig. 7.22. The test values used for N were selected to exercise all parts of the program and to verify that the program works for prime numbers as well as nonprime numbers. The operation of the program at the boundaries (2 and 1000) was also checked, as well as the operation of the program for invalid data values (0 and 1001). A very large prime number (997) was used as a test case, as well as odd and even numbers that are not prime. Although many valid data values were not tested, the sample selected is representative and provides a fair indication that the program is correct.

Figure 7.22 Four Sample Runs of the Prime Number Program

```
Enter a number that you think is a prime.
Enter an integer between 2 and 1000> 1000
2 is the smallest divisor of 1000


Enter a number that you think is a prime.
Enter an integer between 2 and 1000> 997
997 is a prime number


Enter a number that you think is a prime.
Enter an integer between 2 and 1000> 35
5 is the smallest divisor of 35
```

```
Enter a number that you think is a prime.
Enter an integer between 2 and 1000> 0
Enter an integer between 2 and 1000> 1001
Enter an integer between 2 and 1000> 2
2 is a prime number
```

Use a similar strategy when you select test data to exercise your programs. Avoid choosing sample test data that are similar. Also, select test data that are at or near any boundary values.

Exercise for Section 7.9

Programming

1. Modify `TestPrime` to print all divisors of `N` where `N` may be any positive integer (odd or even). If `N` is prime, the only divisors printed should be `1` and `N`.

7.10 Using the Debugger Evaluate and Modify Dialog Box

You can use the Turbo Pascal debugger to verify that a complicated expression in your program is correct. To do this, select the Evaluate option from the Debug menu after halting your program. This brings up three windows labeled Evaluate, Result, and New Value with the cursor in the Evaluate window. If you type in the expression you wish evaluated and press Enter, the value of this expression at the current location in your program will appear in the Value window.

Initially, the `Expression` field will contain a default expression consisting of the identifier under the Edit window cursor, or it will be blank if the Edit window cursor is not over an identifier. This expression can be edited or replaced by another expression. When you have finished editing, press the Enter key to evaluate the contents of the `Expression` field. The value of this expression at the current location in your program will be displayed in the `Result` field.

Another way to enter an expression in the `Expression` field is to place the Edit cursor on the first operand of the expression you want to check just before bringing up the Evaluate and Modify dialog box (Fig. 7.23). This identifier will appear in the `Expression` field when the dialog box pops up. You can use the right arrow key to add additional operands and operators to the `Expression` field. Press the Enter key to evaluate the final expression.

If the `Expression` field contains a single variable, you can modify its value. First, move the cursor to the `New value` field using the Tab key or the mouse and type in a new value or expression for the variable. Pressing the Enter key will cause the contents of the `New value` field to be evaluated and displayed in

Figure 7.23 Turbo Pascal Evaluate and Modify Dialog Box

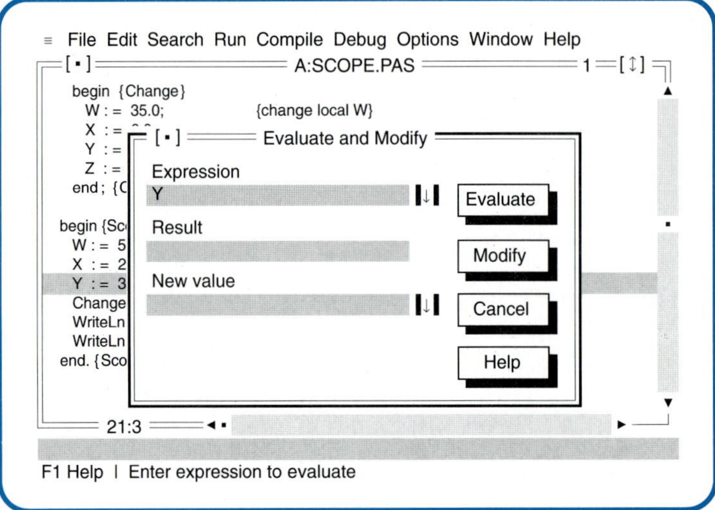

the `Result` field. The expression entered in the `New value` field must be type compatible with the variable displayed in the `Expression` field.

The new value assigned to the variable is retained by the Turbo Pascal debugger if you select the Modify button when the Evaluate and Modify dialog box is closed (by pressing the Esc key or using the mouse). The Evaluate button is selected automatically when the dialog box cursor is on the `Expression` field. The Modify button is selected automatically when the cursor is on the `New value` field. You can select either button by using the Tab key or the mouse.

7.11 Common Programming Errors

A good deal of care is required when you work with complicated expressions. It is easy to inadvertently omit parentheses or operators. If an operator or a single parenthesis is omitted, a syntax error will be detected. If a pair of parentheses is omitted, the expression, although syntactically correct, will compute the wrong value.

Sometimes it is beneficial to break a complicated expression into subexpressions that are separately assigned to *temporary variables* and then to manipulate those temporary variables. For example, it is easier to write correctly the three assignment statements

```
Temp1 := Sqrt(X + Y);
Temp2 := 1 + Temp1;
Z := Temp1 / Temp2
```

than the single assignment statement

```
Z := Sqrt(X + Y) / (1 + Sqrt(X + Y))
```

which has the same effect. Using three assignment statements is also more efficient, because the square root operation is performed only once; it is performed twice in the single assignment statement.

Be careful that you use the correct type of operator with each operand. The arithmetic operators can be used only with type `Integer` or type `Real` operands. The operators `div` and `mod` can be used only with type `Integer` operands.

The only operators that you can use with type `Char` data are the relational operators. The Boolean expression

```
3 <> '3'
```

is invalid because one of its operands is an integer and the other is a character value.

You can use the Boolean operators, `and`, `or`, and `not`, only with Boolean expressions. In the expression

```
Flag and (X <= Y)
```

the variable `Flag` must be type `Boolean`. This statement would be invalid without the parentheses unless `X` and `Y` are type `Boolean`.

Syntax or run-time errors may occur when you use the built-in functions. The argument of the functions `Chr` and `Odd` must be type `Integer` or a subrange of `Integer`; the argument of the functions `Ord`, `Succ`, and `Pred` must be an ordinal type (not type `Real`).

If the argument of `Sqrt` or `Ln` is negative, an error will occur. The result of the functions `Succ`, `Pred`, and `Chr` will be undefined for certain arguments.

Using the `{$R+}` compiler directive and subranges can help you detect erroneous computations or data. If a value being assigned is outside the subrange, an `out of range` error occurs. The operations that can be performed on a variable with a subrange type are determined by the host type for that subrange. However, a variable whose type is a subrange type cannot correspond to a formal variable parameter whose type is the host type for that subrange.

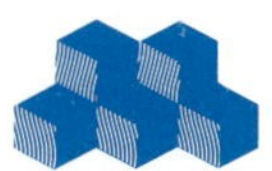

Chapter Review

This chapter described how to write arithmetic expressions involving several operators and the built-in functions of Pascal. It also discussed the manipulation of other simple data types, including the standard types—`Boolean` and `Char`—and programmer-defined subranges. Several new numeric data types and operators were introduced, including the operators `div` and `mod` for manipulating integer data and the operators `and`, `or`, and `not` for manipulating Boolean data.

This chapter also discussed the concept of an ordinal number and introduced the functions `Pred`, `Succ`, and `Ord` for the manipulation of ordinal data types. We used the function `Chr`, the inverse of `Ord`, to find the character corresponding to a given ordinal number.

New Pascal Constructs

Table 7.17 describes the new Pascal constructs introduced in this chapter.

Table 7.17 Summary of New Pascal Constructs

Construct	Effect
Arithmetic Assignment `I := J div K + (L + 5) mod N;`	Adds the result (an integer) of `J div K` to the result (an integer) of `(L + 5) mod N`. `J`, `K`, `L`, and `N` must be type `Integer`.
Character Assignment `NextCh := 'A';`	Assigns the character value `'A'` to `NextCh`.

Constant Expression
`const`
`FahrenheitToCelsius := 9/5;`
	Turbo Pascal allows the use of constant expressions in constant declarations.

Boolean Assignment `Even := not Odd(N);`	If `N` is an even number, assigns the value `True` to `Even`; otherwise, assigns the value `False` to `Even`.

Subrange Declaration
`type`
`Digit = '0'..'9';`
	A subrange of the characters is declared. This subrange (named `Digit`) consists of the character values `'0'` though `'9'`.

✓ Quick-Check Exercises

1. The operator ____________ means real division, the operator ____________ means integer division, and the operator ____________ yields the remainder of ____________ division.
2. Complete the following formula for integers `N` and `M`.
   `N = (N ____________ M) ____________ M + (N ____________ M)`
3. Write a condition that is `True` if `N` divides `M`.
4. Evaluate the Boolean expression

   ```
   True and ((30 mod 10) = 0)
   ```

   Is the outer pair of parentheses required? What about the inner pair?
5. Evaluate the Boolean expression

   ```
   False and (((30 mod 10) div 0) = 0)
   ```

   What error can occur when this expression is evaluated? When would this error not occur?

6. In ASCII, what is the value of `Chr(Ord('a'))`? Of `Chr(Ord('a') + 3)`? Of `Chr(Ord('z') - 26)`? `Chr(Ord('z') - 32)`?
7. What is the value of `Ord('9') - Ord('0')`? Is this answer the same for all Pascal compilers? What about `Ord('z') - Ord('a')`?
8. Can a variable whose type is a subrange type correspond to a formal variable parameter whose type is the host type? What if the formal parameter is a value parameter?
9. If two variables are type compatible, can one always be assigned to the other?
10. Under what condition can one variable be assigned to another when they are not type compatible?

Answers to Quick-Check Exercises

1. /, `div`, `mod`, `integer`
2. `N = (N div M) * M + (N mod M)`
3. `(M mod N) = 0`
4. `True`, outer needed, inner not needed
5. `False`, attempted division by zero, not detected if compiler uses short-circuit evaluation
6. `'a'`, `'d'`, `'a'`, `'Z'`
7. `9`, yes, `26`, no
8. No, yes
9. Yes, if they are the same type or the one getting a new value is the host type and the other is a subrange of that host. If the one getting a new value is a subrange type, the value of the variable being assigned should be in range.
10. A variable whose type is `Integer` or a subrange type whose host type is `Integer` can be assigned to a type `Real` variable.

Review Questions

1. What are the advantages of data type `Integer` over data type `Real`?
2. Given the following declarations, indicate the data type of the result of each expression below.

```
var
  X, Y : Real;
  A, B : Integer;
```

	Type
`X * Y`	________
`A * B`	________
`B / Y`	________
`B div A`	________
`X / Y`	________
`A mod B`	________
`X mod Y`	________

3. What is the answer to each of the following operations?

`11 mod 2`	________	`11 div 2`	________
`12 mod -3`	________	`12 div -3`	________
`27 mod 4`	________	`-25 div 4`	________
`18 mod 6`	________	`-18 div -5`	________

4. What is the result of the expression `(3 + 4 / 2) + 8 - 15 mod 4`?
5. Write an assignment statement that rounds a real variable `Num1` to two digits after the decimal point, leaving the result in `Num1`.
6. Write a procedure called `Change` that has one real parameter `C` and four integer parameters `Q`, `D`, `N`, and `P`. `C` is a value parameter; the others are variable parameters. The procedure returns the number of quarters in `Q`, the number of dimes in `D`, the number of nickels in `N`, and the number of pennies in `P` to make change with the minimum number of coins. `C` (the change amount) is less than $1.00. Hint: Use the `mod` and `div` operators.
7. List and explain three computational errors that may occur in type `Real` expressions.
8. Write an `if` statement that writes out `True` or `False` according to the following conditions: either `Flag` is `True` or `Color` is `'R'`, or both `Money` is `'P'` and `Time` is `1230`.
9. Write the statement to assign a value of `True` to the Boolean variable `OverTime` only if a worker's weekly `Hours` are greater than `40`.
10. Write a Boolean expression using the `Ord` function that determines whether the ordinal value for `'a'` is greater than the ordinal value for `'Z'`. What is the value of this expression in ASCII?
11. Write the Pascal statements necessary to enter an integer between 0 and 9, inclusive, and convert it to an equivalent character value (for example, `0` to `'0'`, `1` to `'1'`) to be stored in a character variable `Num`.

Programming Projects

1. A company has ten employees, many of whom work overtime (more than forty hours) each week. The company accountant wants a payroll program that reads each employee's name, hourly rate (`rate`), and hours worked (`hours`). The program must compute the gross salary and net pay as follows:

$$\text{gross} = \begin{cases} \text{hours} \times \text{rate (if hours} <= 40) \\ 1.5 \times \text{rate} \times (\text{hours} - 40) + 40 \times \text{rate (if hours} > 40) \end{cases}$$

$$\text{net} = \begin{cases} \text{gross (if gross} <= \$65) \\ \text{gross} - (15 + 0.45 \times \text{gross) (if gross} > \$65) \end{cases}$$

The program should print each employee's gross salary and net pay. The total amount of the payroll, which can be computed by adding the gross salaries for all employees, should be printed at the end. Test your program on the following data:

Name	*Rate*	*Hours*
Ivory Hunter	6.50	35
Track Star	4.50	10
Smokey Bear	3.25	80
Oscar Grouch	6.00	10
Jane Jezebel	4.65	25
Fat Eddie	8.00	40
Pumpkin Pie	9.65	35
Sara Lee	5.00	40
Human Eraser	6.25	52

2. A number is said to be perfect if the sum of its divisors (except for itself) is equal to itself. For example, 6 is a perfect number because the sum of its divisors (1 + 2 +

3) is 6. The number 8 is said to be deficient if the sum of its divisors (1 + 2 + 4) is only 7. 12 is said to be abundant if the sum of its divisors (1 + 2 + 3 + 4 + 6) is 16. Write a program that lists the factors of the numbers between 1 and 100 and classifies each number as perfect, deficient, or abundant.

3. Let `n` be a positive integer consisting of up to ten digits, $d_{10}d_9...d_1$. Write a program to list in one column each of the digits in the number `n`. The rightmost digit, d_1, should be listed at the top of the column. Hint: If `n = 3704`, what is the value of `digit` as computed according to the following formula?

```
digit = n mod 10
```

Test your program for values of `n` equal to `6, 3704`, and `17498`.

4. An integer `N` is divisible by `9` if the sum of its digits is divisible by `9`. Use the algorithm developed for project 3 to determine whether the following numbers are divisible by `9`.

```
N = 154368
N = 621594
N = 123456
```

5. Redo project 4 by reading each digit of the number to be tested into the type `Char` variable `Digit`. Form the sum of the numeric values of the digits. Hint: The numeric value of `Digit` (type `Char`) is `Ord(Digit) - Ord('0')`.

6. The interest paid on a savings account is compounded daily. This means that if you start with `StartBal` dollars in the bank, at the end of the first day you will have a balance of

```
StartBal * (1 + rate/365)
```

dollars, where `rate` is the annual interest rate (`0.10` if the annual rate is 10 percent). At the end of the second day, you will have

```
StartBal * (1 + rate/365) * (1 + rate/365)
```

dollars, and at the end of `N` days you will have

$$\texttt{StartBal * (1 + rate/365)}^{\texttt{N}}$$

dollars. Write a program that processes values for `StartBal`, `rate`, and `N`, and computes the final account balance.

7. Compute the monthly payment and the total payment for a bank loan, given:
   a. the amount of the loan
   b. the duration of the loan in months
   c. the interest rate for the loan

   Your program should read in one loan at a time, perform the required computation, and print the values of the monthly payment and the total payment.

   Test your program with at least the following data (and more if you want).

Loan	*Months*	*Rate*
16000	300	12.50
24000	360	13.50
30000	300	15.50
42000	360	14.50
22000	300	15.50
300000	240	15.25

Hints: The formula for computing monthly payment is

$$\text{monthpay} = \frac{\text{ratem} \times \text{expm}^{\text{months}} \times \text{loan}}{\text{expm}^{\text{months}} - 1.0}$$

where

$$\text{ratem} = \text{rate} \,/\, 1200.0$$
$$\text{expm} = (1.0 + \text{ratem})$$

and you will need a loop to multiply `expm` by itself `months` times.
The formula for computing the total payment is

$$\text{total} = \text{monthpay} \times \text{months}$$

8. Write a program that allows the user to play the game of Battleship. Your program should use the Random function to generate two numbers between 0 and 20 representing the coordinates of a battleship position within a 20 by 20 grid. The user should be prompted to guess the coordinates of the battleship. If the user guesses correctly, she wins the game. If she guesses incorrectly, the computer uses the distance formula to tell her how close she was with her guess and prompts her to guess again. Your program should display instructions and keep track of the number of guesses it takes to win the game.

$$\text{distance} = \text{sqrt}((x1 - x2)^2 + (y1 - y2)^2)$$

9. Experiments that are either too expensive or dangerous to perform are often simulated on the computer when the computer is able to provide a good representation of the experiment. Write a program that uses the Random function to simulate the dropping of glass rods which break into three pieces. The purpose of the experiment is to estimate the probability that the lengths of the three pieces are such that they might form the sides of a triangle.

   For the purposes of this experiment you may assume that the glass rod always breaks into three pieces. If you use the line segment 0 to 1 (on the real number line) as a mathematical model of the glass rod, the Random function can generate two numbers between 0 and 1 representing the coordinates of the breaks. The triangle inequality (the sum of the lengths of two sides of a triangle are always greater than the length of the third side) may be used to test the length of each piece against the lengths of the other two pieces.

   To estimate the probability that the pieces of the rod form a triangle, you will need to repeat the experiment many times and count the number of times a triangle can be formed from the pieces. The probability estimate is the number of successes divided by the total number of rods dropped. Your program should prompt the user for the number of rods to drop and allow the experiment to be repeated. Use a sentinel value of -1 to halt execution of the program.

8

Programming in the Large

Up to this point, this book has been primarily concerned with the writing of small, "throwaway" programs that solve particular programming problems, but that otherwise have little general use. In this chapter, you will begin to consider large-scale programming, called *programming in the large*. The discussion will focus on some principles of software engineering that have proved useful for designing large program systems. You will also learn more about abstraction and its use in programming.

To make large programs more readable, you can declare new data types whose values—which depend on the problem domain—you specify. You can then combine these data types with relevant operator procedures in library modules or units that can be compiled and reused.

Finally, you will learn how to use files of data with your programs. You will be able to enter program data from data files and save program output on output files. Using data files frees you from having to continually reenter test data while debugging a program. Using output files enables you to save output on disk rather than simply view it on the screen.

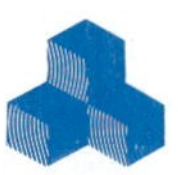

8.1 The Software Life Cycle

Programming in college is somewhat different from programming in the real world. In college, you are generally given the problem specification by an instructor. Sometimes the problem specification is ambiguous or incomplete, and interaction between the instructor and the class is necessary so the students can pin down the details.

In the real world, the initial specification for a software product (a large program system) may also be incomplete. The specification is clarified through extensive interaction between the prospective users of the software and its designers (called *system analysts*). Through this interaction, the software designers determine precisely what the users want the proposed software to do, and the users determine what to expect from the software product. Although it may seem like common sense to proceed in this manner, very often a "final" software product does not perform as expected. The reason is usually a communication gap between those responsible for the product's design and its eventual users; generally, both parties are at fault when the software fails to meet expectations.

One cause of the communication gap is that software users often are not familiar enough with computers and their capabilities to know if their requests are reasonable or how to specify what they want. Software designers, on the other hand, often assume that they are the best judges of what the user really wants; they are quick to interpret a user's incomplete or unclear specification as a "blank check" to do what they think best. To avoid these problems, it is imperative that a complete, written description of the *requirements specification* for a new software product be generated at the beginning of the project and that both users and designers sign the document.

Following the requirements specification, a detailed *analysis* of several different approaches to solving the problem is undertaken, including an estimate of the costs and the anticipated benefits of each approach. The culmination of this analysis is the selection of the best solution method.

The *design* process begins as soon as the analysis is completed. A major part of the software design process is decomposing the complete software system into a set of subsystems. Each subsystem is further decomposed into a set of smaller program modules and procedures. It is important to determine whether any procedures from existing systems can be reused in the new system. The software design should be carefully documented in a report that contains structure charts and high-level pseudocode.

Another critical part of the design process is determining the software's internal data representation. In college programming, the instructor often recommends or requires a particular data type or data structure. In the real world, the programmer must choose the internal representation that will lead to the most efficient and effective solution.

Once the design is complete, it is *coded*, that is, implemented as a program in a particular programming language. Nowadays, it is rare for a large software project to be implemented by a single programmer. Most often, a large project is assigned to a team of programmers. Some programmers may have been involved with the design; others, however, are new to the project. It is important for team members to coordinate beforehand the overall organization of the project.

Each team member is responsible for a set of procedures, some of which are accessed by other team members. After the initial organization meeting, each team member provides the others with a specification for each procedure that he or she is implementing. The specification is similar to the documentation provided for each procedure in this text. It consists of a brief statement of the purpose of the procedure, its preconditions and postconditions, and its formal parameter list. This information is all that a potential user of the procedure needs to know to call it correctly.

Normally, one team member acts as "librarian" by assuming responsibility for determining the status of each procedure in the system. Initially, the *library of procedures* consists of a stub for each procedure. As a new procedure is completed and tested, its updated version replaces the version currently in the library. The librarian keeps track of the date that each new version of a procedure was inserted in the library and makes sure that all programmers are using the latest version of any procedure.

Part of the coding task involves removing all apparent program bugs (debugging) and performing preliminary tests on each procedure, module, subsystem, and system. Once the bugs are removed, the coding and debugging phase is complete, and it is time to exhaustively test the software product.

In college programming, you design, code, debug, and test your programs. Testing a program in a college environment often consists of making several sample runs. Since you are the programmer and also do the testing and are responsible for correcting any bugs, the testing process often is not as complete as it should be. Once you are satisfied that the program is correct, you hand it in to the instructor and go on to something else.

In the real world, testing is a more rigorous process that is usually performed by a group other than the programmers; the users of the software product should be involved in the testing phase. It is important to identify all bugs early, because the software that controls a rocket or processes payroll checks must be absolutely free of errors before its first use. Also, a software product usually must continue to perform effectively over a long period, sometimes in a changing environment. This requirement may cause periodic updating, or *maintenance*, of the program to correct new errors or to incorporate changes, for example, revised tax laws.

The *software life cycle* described above consists of at least the following phases:

1. Requirements specification
2. Analysis
3. Design
4. Coding and debugging
5. Testing
6. Operation and maintenance

This cycle is iterative. During the design phase, problems may arise that make it necessary to modify the requirements specification. Any such changes require approval of the users. Similarly, during coding it may become necessary to reconsider decisions made in the design phase. Again, any changes must be approved by the system designers and users.

Estimates vary as to the percentage of time spent in each phase. For example, a typical system may require a year to proceed through the first four phases, three months of testing, then four years of operation and maintenance. So you can see why it is important to design and document software in such a way that it can be easily understood and maintained by a variety of users.

You may be wondering what relevance all of this has to your current course. Those of you who are majoring in computer science will begin to participate in the design of large program systems in your next course. Consequently, a major goal of the Pascal course is to prepare you to work on increasingly larger and more complex problems. Some of the techniques may seem out of place or unnecessary to solve the simpler problems assigned in this class, but it is important that you learn and practice these techniques now so you will be able to apply them later.

Exercise for Section 8.1

Self-Check

1. Name the six phases of the software life cycle. Which phase is the longest?

8.2 Using Abstraction to Manage Complexity

Beginning programmers often find it difficult to get started on a problem. They are often reluctant to start writing the code for a program until they have worked out the solution to every detail. Of course, preplanning and concern for detail are commendable, but these normally positive work habits can be overdone to the extent that they block the problem-solving process. To make problem solving flow as smoothly as possible, use the strategy of "divide and conquer" to decompose a problem into more manageable subproblems.

Procedural Abstraction

Abstraction is a powerful technique that helps programmers deal with complex issues in a piecemeal fashion. The dictionary defines *abstraction* as the act or process of separating the inherent qualities or properties of something from the actual physical object to which they belong. An example of the use of abstraction is our description in Chapter 1 of a memory cell as a storage location for a data value. We are not concerned with the details of the physical structure of memory and memory cells; we don't need to know them to use a memory cell in programming.

So far, you have practiced *procedural abstraction*, which is the philosophy that procedure development should separate the concern of *what* is to be achieved by a procedure from the details of *how* it is to be achieved. In other words, you can specify what you expect a procedure to do, then use that procedure in the design of a problem solution before you know how to implement the procedure. You have even been able to perform a preliminary test of overall design by using procedure stubs. Of course, each procedure stub must be replaced by an actual procedure before you can execute the final program.

Turbo Pascal enables you to more fully realize the potential of procedural abstraction than does standard Pascal. Once you have designed and implemented a procedure that has some general use, Turbo Pascal (but not standard Pascal) allows you to encapsulate that procedure with others in your own library module or *unit*. You can then import that procedure into another program that needs the same operation performed and call it to carry out the operation. In this way, you can truly separate the *what* from the *how*. You can use a procedure as long as you know what it does and how to call it even if you have no idea how the procedure is implemented.

You can use your own units in much the same way you use predefined units that are part of the Turbo Pascal system (e.g., `Printer` and `Crt`). You can compile each unit individually and later Turbo Pascal can link the object code for a procedure in a compiled unit to a program that calls it. The next section discusses how to create and use your own units.

8.3 Turbo Pascal Units

As you progress through this course, you will write many Pascal programs and procedures. You should try to keep each new procedure as general as possible so that you can reuse it in other applications. You will eventually build up a sizeable library of your own procedures. Reusing tried and tested procedures is always much more efficient than starting from scratch. Each new procedure that you write has to be thoroughly tested and debugged, whereas the procedures in your personal library already have been tested, saving time as you use these procedures over and over again.

As an example, it would be useful to have a set of procedures available for performing data entry operations. Since procedure `ReadLn` cannot be used to read Boolean values, it would be useful to have our own procedure for this purpose. Procedure `ReadLnBool`, shown in Fig. 7.13, reads a character value and returns either `True` or `False` based on the data character. `ReadLnBool` should certainly be included in your programming library.

In many situations, you want a data value to lie within a specific subrange of values. For example, you might want to enter an integer in the range `-10` to `+10`. Procedure `EnterInt` (see Fig. 7.18) accomplishes this operation. You could easily write similar procedures, called `EnterChar` and `EnterReal`, for the other standard data types found in Pascal. These procedures might also be useful additions to a programmer's library.

The uses Statement

Turbo Pascal allows the programmer to create and access disk files containing collections of previously compiled constants, data types, variables, procedures, and functions. These files are called *units* in Turbo Pascal, and may be accessed by a program or another unit by placing a `uses` statement at the start of a program or appropriate unit section. For example, the statement

```
uses MyStuff, NewUtilities, Printer;
```

specifies the names of three units, `MyStuff`, `NewUtilities`, and `Printer`, whose object code will be linked to the program containing the `uses` statement.

Turbo Pascal assumes that the object code for a user-defined unit is stored in a disk file whose name consists of the unit name followed by the extension `TPU`. If the unit name is longer than 8 characters (for example, unit `NewUtilities`), Turbo Pascal will look for a disk file whose name consists of the first 8 characters of the unit name (`NEWUTILI.TPU`).

There are several advantages to using previously compiled units.

1. The object code for procedures in units is accessible, thereby saving compilation time.
2. The new programs you write will be simpler and more concise because they do not have to contain declarations for identifiers defined in previously compiled units.
3. It is easier to debug a program system that uses tried and tested procedures contained in a library unit instead of new, untested procedures.
4. It is easier to apportion a large project to individual programming team members.
5. You can change the details of a unit's code without having to recompile the modules that use it.

As you develop and debug new program systems, you will have to compile only the main program and any new procedures not already in a unit. This speeds up the program development process considerably. The new program system will also be more concise and more readable because you do not have to redeclare procedures contained in a unit that is used by the new program system.

SYNTAX DISPLAY

uses Statement

Form: `uses` *unitlist*;

Examples: `uses Printer, Crt, EnterData;`

Interpretation: The Turbo Pascal compiler must include portions of the object code for units listed in *unitlist* when generating the object code for a program or another unit containing the `uses` statement.

Note 1: The units contained in the Turbo Pascal run-time library (`Printer`, `Crt`, `Dos`, etc.) are stored in the disk file `TURBO.TPL`. All other units are assumed to reside in the disk files whose names are derived from the first 8 characters of the unit name with the extension `.TPU`.

Note 2: Turbo Pascal first looks in the current directory to find the object code file for a given unit. If the file is not found, the directory specified in the Unit directories item of the Turbo Pascal Directories submenu of the Options menu is searched next (see Fig. 8.5).

8.4 User Interfaces and Windows

Turbo Pascal comes with several predefined units. We showed how to use the Turbo Pascal unit `Printer` in Section 2.7, and we discuss other predefined units in Appendix B. In this section, we illustrate how to use some features of the Turbo Pascal unit called `Crt`. This unit contains a number of functions and procedures that allow you to develop *user-friendly interfaces* for your programs that resemble the menus found in the Turbo Pascal integrated environment.

■ Example 8.1

Section 6.7 contains a case study involving a program that processes a number of different checkbook transactions (checks and deposits). The main program calls procedure `ReadTran` (see Fig. 6.21) to read a character code indicating the type of transaction (`C` for check, `D` for deposit, or `Q` for quit) and the transaction amount.

If the first line of the main program is

```
uses Crt;
```

we can utilize constants and procedures defined in unit `Crt` to read this information in a more user-friendly fashion. Figure 8.1 shows a new procedure, `ReadTran`, which uses the following procedures from unit `Crt`: `ClrScr` (clear screen), `Window` (create a window), `TextColor` (set text color), `TextBackground` (set background color), and `GotoXY` (move cursor).

Figure 8.1 Procedure ReadTran Using Unit Crt

```
procedure ReadTran (var TranType {output} : Char;
                    var Amount   {output} : Real);
{
  Reads each transaction type and amount.
  Pre   : None
  Post  : TranType and Amount are read in.
  Calls: Window, ClrScr, TextColor, TextBackground
         from unit CRT.
}
begin {ReadTran}
  {Define data entry window}
  Window (5, 10, 30, 20);   {window from (5, 10) to (30, 20)}
  TextColor (Black);            {Reverse text and background}
  TextBackground (White);
  ClrScr;

  {Get transaction type}
  WriteLn ('Enter a letter code from');
  WriteLn ('the blinking line below');
  GotoXY (1, 5);
  WriteLn ('check  deposit  quit');
  WriteLn ('--------------------');
  TextColor (128 + Black);          {start of blinking text}
  WriteLn ('  C       D      Q');
  TextColor (Black);                  {end of blinking text}
  GotoXY (1, 9);
  Write ('Code >');
  ReadLn (TranType);

  {Get transaction amount}
  if TranType <> Sentinel then
    begin
      GotoXY (1, 11);
      Write ('Amount $');
      ReadLn (Amount)
    end; {if}

  {Restore window to full screen - normal display mode}
  Window (1, 1, 80, 25);   {window from (1, 1) to (80, 25)}
  TextColor (White);            {Normal text and background}
  TextBackground (Black);
  ClrScr
end; {ReadTran}
```

Figure 8.2 shows a sample execution of procedure `ReadTran`. The data read are `C` (value of `TranType`) and `300.00` (value of `Amount`). The procedure output is shown as black text within a white *window*. The location of this window is determined by considering the display screen as an X, Y coordinate system with 80 columns (1 <= X <= 80) and 25 rows (1 <= Y <= 25). The top left corner of the entire screen is the point (1, 1), and the bottom right corner of the screen is the point (80, 25). The statement

```
Window (5, 10, 30, 20);    {window from (5, 10) to (30, 20)}
```

defines a rectangular window with the top left corner at (5, 10) and the bottom right corner at (30, 20).

Figure 8.2 Sample Execution of ReadTran

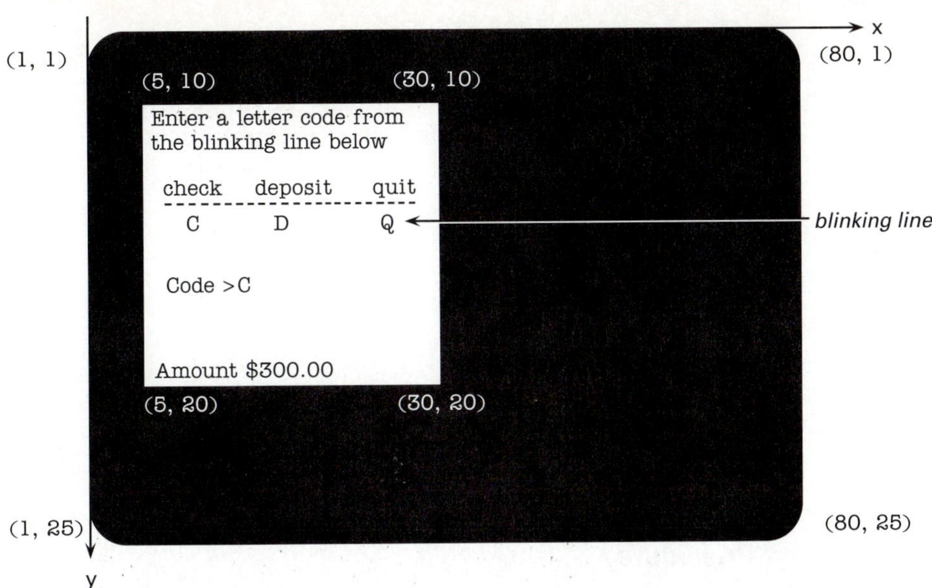

The first two statements below

```
TextColor (Black);                {Reverse text and background}
TextBackground (White);
ClrScr;                                     {Clear the screen}
```

define the background color (`White`) of the active window and the color (`Black`) of any text displayed in that window. These statements cause any subsequent `WriteLn` statements to display black text inside a white background instead of vice versa. The constants `Black` and `White` are both defined in unit `Crt`. Procedure `ClrScr` sets all character positions in the active window to blanks and displays the active window in the background color (`White`).

Procedure `GotoXY` moves the cursor within the active window. The actual parameters used with procedure `GotoXY` define the cursor position relative to the active window. For example,

```
GotoXY (1, 1);
```

would move the cursor to the character position in the top left corner of the active window (absolute coordinates (5, 10) if the white window is the active window). In procedure `ReadTran`, the first call to `GoToXY`

```
GotoXY (1, 5);
```

moves the cursor to column 1, row 5 of the active window (X is 1, Y is 5). Note that the X, Y coordinates of the new cursor position are relative to the active window, not the screen.

The first two statements below

```
TextColor (128 + Black);                  {start of blinking text}
WriteLn ('  C       D       Q');
TextColor (Black);                          {end of blinking text}
```

cause a line of character codes (C, D, Q) to be displayed in black text that blinks on and off. Adding 128 to the text color value causes the subsequently displayed characters to blink. The third statement resets the text color to black (no blinking).

After the data entry is completed, the statements

```
Window (1, 1, 80, 25);      {window from (1, 1) to (80, 25)}
TextColor (White);               {Normal text and background}
TextBackground (Black);
ClrScr
```

reset the active window to the full screen and restore the text color and background to their normal values (white text in a black background). The cursor appears at the top left corner of an empty screen. ■

SYNTAX DISPLAY

The ClrScr Procedure

Form: `ClrScr`
Interpretation: The `ClrScr` procedure clears the currently active window and places the cursor in the top left corner of the window. Procedure `ClrScr` is defined in unit `Crt`.

SYNTAX DISPLAY

The GotoXY Procedure

Form: `GotoXY (`*XPos*`,` *YPos*`)`
Example: `GotoXY (5, 10)`
Interpretation: The `GotoXY` procedure moves the cursor to the position indicated by *XPos* and *YPos* relative to the active window. *XPos* indicates the column position, and *YPos* indicates the row position of the cursor relative to the active window. If *XPos* and *YPos* are 1, the cursor is moved to the top left corner of the active window. Procedure `GotoXY` is defined in unit `Crt`.

SYNTAX DISPLAY

The TextBackground Procedure

Form: `TextBackground (`*color*`)`
Example: `TextBackground (Black)`
Interpretation: The `TextBackground` procedure sets the background of the active window as determined by *color*, where *color* is one of the color

constants: Black, Blue, Green, Cyan, Red, Magenta, Brown, LightGray, DarkGray, LightBlue, LightGreen, LightCyan, LightRed, LightMagenta, Yellow, White. The normal background color is Black. The color constants and procedure TextBackground are defined in unit Crt.

SYNTAX DISPLAY

The TextColor Procedure

Form: `TextColor (`*color*`)`
Example: `TextColor (White)`
Interpretation: The TextColor procedure sets the color of subsequent text as determined by *color*. If *color* is the expression 128 + *colorval* and *colorval* is a color constant, the subsequent text will blink. The normal text color is White. Procedure TextColor is defined in unit Crt.

SYNTAX DISPLAY

The Window Procedure

Form: `Window (`*X1*, *Y1*, *X2*, *Y2*`)`
Example: `Window (5, 10, 30, 20)`
Interpretation: The Window procedure defines the rectangle with top left coordinate (*X1*, *Y1*) and bottom right coordinate (*X2*, *Y2*) as the active window. To define the entire screen as the active window, use (1, 1, 80, 25) as the actual parameter list. The cursor is positioned at the top left character position in the active window when a new active window is defined. Procedure Window is part of unit Crt.

8.5 Writing New Units

Unit EnterData shown in Fig. 8.3 contains the data entry procedures described at the start of this section. The structure of a unit is quite similar to the structure of a Turbo Pascal program. The first line of a unit begins with the reserved word unit instead of program, and the last line of a unit is end..

Figure 8.3 Unit EnterData

```
unit EnterData;
{
 Contains procedures for reading a Boolean value and
 for reading an integer value within a prescribed range.
}
interface
  procedure ReadLnBool (var BoolVal, Success {output} : Boolean);
  {
    Reads a Boolean value (represented by a T or F) into
```

```
    BoolVal and sets the flag Success.
    Pre : None
    Post: BoolVal is set to True if T or t is read; otherwise,
          BoolVal is set to False. Success is set to True only
          if one of the four characters T, t, F, or f is read.
  }

  procedure EnterInt (MinN, MaxN {input} : Integer;
                      var N {output} : Integer);
  {
   Reads an integer between MinN and MaxN into N.
   Pre : MinN and MaxN are assigned values.
   Post: Returns in N first data value between MinN and MaxN
         if MinN <= MaxN is True; otherwise, N is not defined.
   }

implementation
  procedure ReadLnBool (var BoolVal, Success {output} : Boolean);
    var
      NextChar    : Char;         {data character}
  begin {ReadLnBool}
    WriteLn ('Type T or F> ');
    ReadLn (NextChar);
    BoolVal := (NextChar = 'T') or (NextChar = 't')
    Success := BoolVal or (NextChar = 'F') or (NextChar = 'f')
  end: {ReadLnBool}

  procedure EnterInt (MinN, MaxN {input} : Integer;
                      var N {output} : Integer);
    var
      InRange : Boolean;        {program flag -- loop control}

  begin {EnterInt}
    if MinN <= MaxN then
      InRange := False            {no valid value in N as yet}
    else
      begin
        WriteLn ('Error - empty range for EnterInt');
        InRange := True                        {skip entry loop}
      end; {if}

    {Keep reading until valid number is read}
    while not InRange do
      begin
        Write ('Enter an integer between ');
        Write (MinN :3, ' and ', MaxN :3, '> ');
        ReadLn (N);
        InRange := (MinN <= N) and (N <= MaxN)
       end {while}
    end; {EnterInt}

  end. {EnterData}
```

A unit consists of two required sections, interface and implementation, and one optional section, initialization. The *interface section* of a unit begins with the reserved word `interface`. The interface section is called the *public part* of a unit because it contains all the information that a programmer needs to know in order to use the unit. It also contains all declarations required by the Turbo Pascal compiler to check that a unit is being used correctly by a program or another unit (called a *client module*).

The identifiers declared in the interface section can be referenced by a client of the unit so they are considered *visible*. Any constant, type, and variable declarations are written using the usual Pascal syntax. However, only procedure headings and documentation appear in the interface section; procedure bodies appear in the implementation section. Forward declarations for procedures are neither necessary nor allowed.

The *implementation section* contains complete declarations for procedures and functions whose headings appear in the interface section. There may also be some new identifiers declared in the implementation section. Because the new identifiers cannot be accessed outside the unit, the implementation section is called the *private part* of the unit and the new identifiers and procedure bodies are said to be *hidden* from a user.

When writing the implementation section, you do not need to repeat the parameter lists for procedures first listed in the interface section. However, if parameter lists are included for these procedures, they must be identical to those appearing in the interface section. We recommend that you include the parameter lists.

The end of a unit is indicated by the line

```
end.
```

There is no need to have a corresponding `begin` unless the unit has an initialization section. The *initialization section* assigns initial values to any variables declared in the unit and is always executed before a client module.

SYNTAX DISPLAY

Unit Definition

Form:

```
unit unit name;

interface
  public declarations

implementation
  private declarations
  public procedure and function declarations
  initialization section
end.
```

Example:

```
unit TwoItems;

interface
  procedure SwapTwo (var X, Y {input/output} : Real);
  {
   Swaps two real values.
   Pre : X, Y are defined.
   Post: X is old Y and Y is old X.
  }

implementation
  procedure SwapTwo (var X, Y, {input/output} : Real);
    var Temp : Real;
```

```
        begin {SwapTwo}
          Temp := X;
          X := Y;
          Y := Temp
        end; {SwapTwo}

      end. {TwoItems}
```

Interpretation: Unit *unit name* is a separate program module which can be compiled to disk and then used by other units or programs. The interface part contains *public declarations*. The public identifiers may be referenced by any program or unit that lists *unit name* in its `uses` statement. Only procedure and function headings appear in the interface part; their complete declarations appear in the implementation part.

The implementation part contains *private declarations* as well as declarations for public procedures and functions. Any private identifiers declared in the implementation part cannot be referenced outside unit *unit name*.

If present, the *initialization section* starts with the reserved word `begin` and it is used to initialize any variables declared in the unit. It executes before the client program.

Notes: A `uses` statment may come after either the `interface` line or the `implementation` line. If a unit is listed after the `interface` line, its public identifiers may be referenced anywhere in unit *unit name*. If a unit name is listed after the `implementation` line, its publice identifiers may be referenced only in the implementation part of unit *unit name*.

PROGRAM STYLE

Validating a Library Procedure's Parameters

Procedure `EnterInt` begins by checking whether its user correctly entered its input parameters, `MinN` and `MaxN`. If the parameters define an empty range, an error message is displayed and the read operation is skipped. Make sure that you carefully validate input parameters for procedures that are candidates for inclusion in a library. Since library procedures can be reused many times and by many different programmers, this extra effort can pay valuable dividends.

Compiling and Using Units

Before you can use unit `EnterData` in a program, you must compile it to disk. To compile a program or unit to disk, first load the source file into the Edit window, and then select the Compile menu. When the Compile menu is displayed, press the letter D key to change the storage destination for the object code from Memory to Disk. (To change the destination back to Memory, simply press the letter D key again.) After changing the destination to Disk, you can compile your unit. (You can also compile a program to disk, create an .EXE file, which can be executed from the MS-DOS prompt.)

The Turbo Pascal compiler will expect to find the object code for a unit used by a client module in a file that has a name derived from the first eight characters of the unit name followed by the extension .TPU. If the source code for unit EnterData is stored in file ENTERDAT.PAS, the Turbo Pascal compiler will create a unit object file with the name ENTERDAT.TPU. This will enable proper linking with any clients that make use of unit EnterData.

Once EnterData has been compiled to disk, you can use it just as you would the predefined unit Printer. However, since a client program may be on a different disk or directory than the .TPU files it imports, you may need to use the Options menu to tell the Turbo Pascal compiler where your .TPU files reside before you compile a client program or unit. To do this, select the Options menu, then highlight and select the Directories option as shown in Fig. 8.4. This will cause the Directories dialog box to appear on screen.

Figure 8.4 Turbo Pascal Options Menu

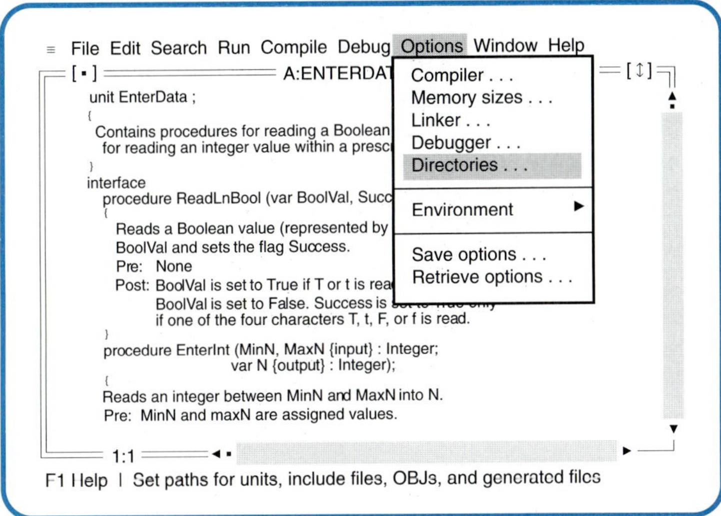

The Directories dialog box is shown in Fig. 8.5. The EXE & TPU field will be selected by default. You should type an MS-DOS path specification telling Turbo Pascal where your .TPU files are located. A path specification may consist of a disk drive name (e.g., A:), a disk drive name followed by a subdirectory name (e.g., C:\PASCAL), or a subdirectory name by itself (e.g., \TP\TOOLS). If your .TPU files reside in several disk locations, you can give a list of path specifications with the items separated by semicolons (e.g., A:;C:\PASCAL;\TP\TOOLS). Pressing the Enter key after typing a path specification closes the dialog box. The Directories dialog box can also indicate the location of any Include files used by a client program or unit when it is compiled.

Figure 8.5 Turbo Pascal Directories Dialog Box

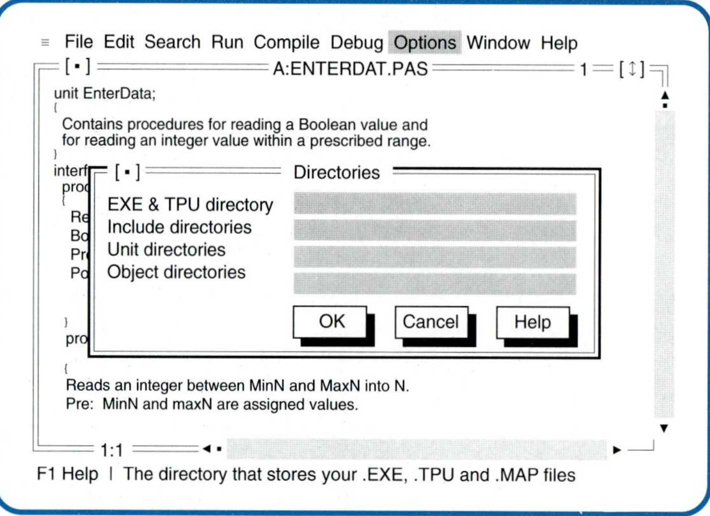

■ Example 8.2

A program that uses the unit `EnterData` is shown in Fig. 8.6. This program can be compiled and run in the normal way. Procedure `ReadLnBool` displays the prompt shown on the second line of the output window, reads the data character, and returns its Boolean representation to variable `NextBool`. ■

Figure 8.6 Program TestEnterData

Edit Window

```
program TestEnterData;

{Tests procedure ReadLnBool in unit EnterData.}

  uses EnterData;                {imports ReadLnBool}

  var
    NextBool,                    {input - next Boolean data value}
    ReadDone  : Boolean;         {Flag -- True if read succeeds;
                                           otherwise, False}
begin {TestEnterData}
  ReadDone := False;             {no value read yet}
  while not ReadDone do
    begin
      WriteLn ('Enter a Boolean value:');
      ReadLnBool (NextBool, ReadDone)
    end; {while}

  if ReadDone then
    WriteLn ('Boolean value read was ', NextBool)
  else
    WriteLn ('Invalid data character read')
end. {TestEnterData}
```

Output Window

```
Enter a Boolean value:
Type T or F> T
Boolean value read was True
```

Exercises for Section 8.5

Self-Check

1. Discuss what changes are required for the program in Fig. 7.18 to use procedure `EnterInt` declared in unit `EnterData`.

Programming

1. Write procedure `EnterChar` that returns a data character that lies within a specified range of characters. Your procedure should display an error message if the specified range is invalid.
2. Redo exercise 1 for a procedure that reads a real data value between a specified range of real numbers.

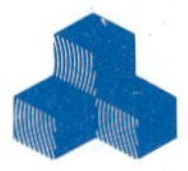

8.6 Additional Features of Units (Optional)

This section discusses additional features of units. You may prefer to skip this section initially. These features are introduced through the next example.

■ Example 8.3

Unit `Errors` in Fig. 8.7 illustrates how a compiler might handle the printing of error messages. The unit contains a procedure, `ProcessError`, which is called whenever the compiler detects an error. `ProcessError` has a single parameter that represents the error code.

Figure 8.7 Unit Errors

```
unit Errors;

interface                          {public part}
  var
    TooBuggy : Boolean;            {error flag}

  procedure ProcessError (ErrorCode {input} : Integer);
  {
   Increments error count and displays error message.
   Pre  : ErrorCount and ErrorCode are defined.
   Post : ErrorCount is incremented and an error message
          is displayed.  TooBuggy is set to True if
          ErrorCount exceeds ErrorLimit.
   Calls: ShowError in unit Display.
  }
```

```
implementation                              {private part}
  uses Display;                             {imports ShowError}

  const
    ErrorLimit = 10;                        {private constant}

  var
    ErrorCount : Integer:                   {private error counter}

  procedure ProcessError (ErrorCode {input} : Integer);
  begin {ProcessError}
    ErrorCount := ErrorCount + 1;
    Display.ShowError (ErrorCode);          {Print a message}
    TooBuggy := (ErrorCount > ErrorLimit)
  end; {ProcessError}

begin {Errors initialization}
  TooBuggy := False;
  ErrorCount := 0
end. {Errors}
```

Besides procedure `ProcessError`, three other identifiers are declared in unit `Errors`. There is a public variable, `TooBuggy`, and a private variable, `ErrorCount`. There is also a private constant, `ErrorLimit`. The initialization section of unit `Errors` initializes `TooBuggy` to `False` and `ErrorCount` to zero when the unit is first loaded into memory.

After every error, `ProcessError` increments the count of errors (`Error-Count`) and calls procedure `ShowError` (declared in unit `Display`) to display the error message corresponding to the error code. Also, `ProcessError` sets `TooBuggy` to `True` if the count of errors exceeds the value of `ErrorLimit`.

To illustrate how we might use unit `Errors`, assume program `TestError` begins with the lines

```
program TestError;

  uses Errors;

  var
    ErrorCode : Integer;
```

The procedure call statement

```
ProcessError (ErrorCode)
```

could be used in program `TestError` to call `ProcessError`. Also in `TestError`, the `while` loop header

```
while not TooBuggy do
```

tests the value of `TooBuggy`, causing loop exit to occur when `TooBuggy` becomes `True` (after the count of errors exceeds `ErrorLimit`). Variable `TooBuggy` must not be declared in program `TestError` because its scope is global, as discussed next. ■

Unit Variables

Unit variables can be declared in the interface section (variable TooBuggy) or implementation section (variable ErrorCount) of a unit. Normally, a unit variable is initialized by the code in the optional initialization section of its unit. The unit's initialization code executes before its client module. If multiple units are listed in the uses statement of a client module, they execute in the order in which they are listed.

A public variable (for example, TooBuggy) has global scope within the unit in which it is declared and within any client of that unit. A private variable has global scope within the unit but cannot be referenced outside the unit.

A unit variable is considered a *statically allocated variable*, which means that its storage remains allocated throughout the execution of the main program. In contrast, a local variable declared in a procedure is allocated only while the procedure itself is executing, and its value is lost on exit from the procedure.

Units Using Other Units

It is possible for one unit to be a client of another. For example, unit Errors shown in Example 8.3 calls procedure ShowError declared in unit Display.

In Fig. 8.7, unit Display is listed in a uses statement after the implementation line. This means that procedure ShowError and any other identifiers declared in unit Display can be referenced only in the implementation section of unit Errors.

Because unit Errors uses unit Display, unit Display must be compiled to disk before unit Errors can be compiled. If program TestError uses unit Errors, then both units Display and Errors must be compiled to disk before TestError can be compiled. If you forget to compile either one, the compiler displays the error message File not found followed by the name of the object code file that is missing.

Module Dependency Diagram

The *module dependency diagram* in Fig. 8.8 summarizes the control flow between program TestError and units Errors and Display.

A module dependency diagram resembles a system structure chart. The difference is that a system structure chart shows both control flow and data flow between the procedures of a single module or program system, whereas a module dependency diagram shows control flow between units and the main program.

Qualified Identifiers in Units

A client module can reference any of the public identifiers declared in the units listed in its uses statement. If the same identifier is declared in two or more units used by a module, you need to qualify each reference to that identifier in

Figure 8.8 Module Dependency Diagram

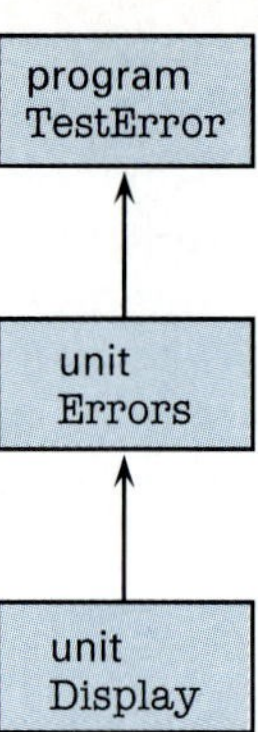

the module. To qualify an identifier, prefix it with its unit name followed by a period. In unit `Errors`, the line

```
Display.ShowError (ErrorNum)
```

contains a qualified reference to procedure `ShowError` declared in unit `Display`. Some programmers prefer to qualify all references to public identifiers appearing in a program.

Recompilation of Units

If you change the interface section of a unit, all clients of that unit must also be recompiled. For example, if you change the interface section of unit `Display` (stored in source file `DISPLAY.PAS`), you must also recompile unit `Errors`. This will be done automatically in Turbo Pascal when you run program `TestError` because `TestError` uses unit `Errors`. If you do not want to rerun `TestError`, you can still get any necessary recompilations performed by choosing the Make option from the Compile menu with file `TESTERROR.PAS` in the Edit window.

If you change only the implementation section of a unit but not its interface section, there is no need to recompile its clients that are themselves units. This means that you can change the body of a procedure that is declared in a unit without having to recompile all clients of that unit. However, if you change the procedure's parameter list then you must recompile all the unit's clients. A client program will always need to be recompiled to link in the new object code for a unit that is changed.

Exercise for Section 8.6

Self-Check

1. Explain the reasons for qualifying an identifier. If all references to unit identifier `TooBuggy` in program `TestError` were qualified, could `TooBuggy`

be redeclared in program `TestError`? Rewrite the `while` loop heading

```
while not TooBuggy do
```

with a qualified reference to `TooBuggy`.

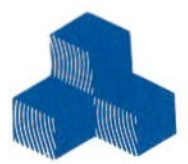

8.7 Enumerated Types

This section introduces a feature of Pascal that improves the readability of large programs. In many programming situations, the standard data types and their values are inadequate. For example, in a budget program you might want to distinguish among the following categories of expenditures: entertainment, rent, utilities, food, clothing, automobile, insurance, miscellaneous. Pascal allows you to create *enumerated types*, each with its own set of values.

For example, the following enumerated type, `Expenses`, has eight possible values enclosed in parentheses.

```
type
  Expenses = (Entertainment, Rent, Utilities, Food,
              Clothing, Automobile, Insurance, Miscellaneous);

var
  ExpenseKind : Expenses;
```

The variable `ExpenseKind` (type `Expenses`) can contain any of the eight values. The following `if` statement tests the value stored in `ExpenseKind`.

```
if ExpenseKind = Entertainment then
  WriteLn ('Postpone until after your payday.')
else if ExpenseKind = Rent then
  WriteLn ('Pay before the first of the month!')
.....
```

■ Example 8.4

The following enumerated type `Day` has the values `Sunday`, `Monday`, and so on.

```
type
  Day = (Sunday, Monday, Tuesday, Wednesday,
         Thursday, Friday, Saturday);        {days of the week}
```

The values associated with an enumerated type must be identifiers; they cannot be numeric, character, or string literals (for example, `'Sunday'` cannot be a value for an enumerated type). ■

The scope rules for identifiers apply to enumerated types and their values. Each enumerated type value is treated as a constant identifier in the block containing the type-declaration statement. The type declaration must precede any variable declaration that references it.

SYNTAX DISPLAY

Enumerated Type Declaration

Form: `type` *enumerated type* `=` `(`*identifier list*`);`

Example: `type Class = (Freshman, Sophomore, Junior, Senior);`

Interpretation: A new data type named *enumerated type* is declared. The values associated with this type are specified in the *identifier list*. Each value is defined as a constant identifier in the block containing the type declaration statement.

Note: A particular identifier can appear in only one *identifier list* in a given block.

An identifier cannot appear in more than one enumerated type declaration. If type Day is already declared, the type declaration

```
type
  TDay = (Tuesday, Thursday);
```

is invalid.

Enumerated Type Operators

Like the standard types Integer, Boolean, and Char, each enumerated type is considered an ordinal type, so the order relationship between its values is fixed when the enumerated type is declared. For type Day, the first value in its list (Sunday) has ordinal number 0, the next value (Monday) has ordinal number 1, and so on. The only operators that can accompany ordinal types are the relational and assignment operators. The following order relations are all true:

```
Sunday < Monday
Wednesday <> Tuesday
Wednesday = Wednesday
Wednesday >= Tuesday
Entertainment < Rent
```

The order relation

```
Entertainment < Wednesday
```

would cause a syntax error, because the values shown are associated with two different enumerated types.

The assignment operator can define the value of a variable whose type is an enumerated type. The variable declaration

```
var
  Today,              {current day of the week}
  Tomorrow : Day;     {day after Today}
```

specifies that Today and Tomorrow are type Day; therefore, they can be assigned any of the values listed in the declaration for type Day. Consequently, the assignment statements

```
Today := Friday;
Tomorrow := Saturday;
```

assign the value Friday to variable Today and Saturday to variable Tomorrow. After the assignments, the following order relations are all true.

```
Today = Friday
Tomorrow = Saturday
Today < Tomorrow
Today <> Wednesday
Today >= Sunday
```

We can use functions Succ, Pred, and Ord (see Section 7.5) with enumerated types. Some examples follow, assuming that Today is Friday and Tomorrow is Saturday.

```
Ord(Today) is 5
Ord(Tomorrow) is 6
Succ(Today) is Saturday
Pred(Today) is Thursday
Succ(Tomorrow) is undefined
Pred(Tomorrow) is Friday
```

The next-to-last example above is undefined because no value of type Day follows Saturday. Similarly, if Today is Sunday, the value of Pred(Sunday) is undefined. Succ or Pred operations leading to undefined results may cause a range error or overflow error during program execution.

■ Example 8.5

The following if statement reassigns the value of Today (type Day) to the next day of the week.

```
if Today = Saturday then
  Tomorrow := Sunday
else
  Tomorrow := Succ(Today)
```

Because the days of a week are cyclical, the if statement assumes that Sunday is the day after Saturday. The last value (Saturday) in the enumerated type Day is treated separately, because Succ(Today) is undefined when Today is Saturday. ■

Type Conversion

The Ord function converts from any ordinal type to type Integer; the Chr function converts from type Integer to type Char. Consequently, Chr is the inverse of the Ord function for the data type Char.

In standard Pascal it is not possible to convert from type Integer to any other data type except type Char. However, in Turbo Pascal it is possible to convert from one ordinal data type to another. The types do not need to be assignment compatible. These conversions are accomplished by using the data type we wish to convert to as a "function" or *value typecast.*

Table 8.1 shows the values of some type conversion "functions." As shown in the first four lines, the "function" Integer is equivalent to the function Ord. Both functions convert their arguments to an integer value that represents the

Table 8.1 Type Conversion "Functions"

Typecast	Value
`Ord(Monday)`	`1`
`Integer(Monday)`	`1`
`Ord('7')`	`55`
`Integer('7')`	`55`
`Boolean(0)`	`False`
`Boolean(1)`	`True`
`Boolean(2)`	`True`
`Boolean(Monday)`	`True`
`Boolean(Tuesday)`	`True`
`Day(0)`	`Sunday`
`Day(False)`	`Sunday`
`Day(1)`	`Monday`
`Day(True)`	`Monday`

ordinal number of the argument (e.g., `Integer(Sunday)` is `0` and `Integer(Monday)` is `1`).

The "function" `Boolean` converts its argument to a value of type `Boolean` (`False` or `True`). Since both `1` and `Monday` have an ordinal value of `1` in their respective type (`Integer` and `Day`), they yield the same result (`True`) when passed as arguments to "function" `Boolean`. The result is `True` because `True` has an ordinal value of `1`. However, the value of `Boolean(Tuesday)` is also `True` although the ordinal value of `Tuesday` is `2`. Turbo Pascal does not seem to check typecast arguments for range errors, even when range checking is enabled using `{$R+}`. The "function" `Day` converts its argument to a value of type `Day`.

SYNTAX DISPLAY

Value Typecasts (Type Conversion Functions)

Form: *type identifier* (*argument*)
Example: `Integer('5')`
Interpretation: If *type identifier* is an ordinal data type and the value of *argument* is of another ordinal data type, then the function designator returns a value associated with data type *type identifier*.

Subranges of Enumerated Types

We can declare subranges of enumerated types. The following declarations specify that `WeekDay` (values `Monday` through `Friday`) is a subrange of type `Day` and variable `SchoolDay` is type `WeekDay`.

```
type
  Day = (Sunday, Monday, Tuesday, Wednesday,
         Thursday, Friday, Saturday);     {days of the week}
  WeekDay = Monday..Friday;               {week days only}

var
  SchoolDay : WeekDay;
```

The assignment statement

```
SchoolDay := Monday;
```

is valid; however, the assignment statement

```
SchoolDay := Sunday;
```

causes a `constant out of range` syntax error.

Reading and Writing Enumerated Type Values

The programmer defines the enumerated types; thus, their values are not known in advance. The Pascal input/output procedures cannot read or write enumerated type values. However, you can write your own procedures for this purpose.

■ Example 8.6

Given the declarations

```
type
  Color = (Red, Green, Blue, Yellow);

var
  Eyes : Color;
```

the statement

```
Write (Ord(Eyes) :1)
```

can be used for diagnostic printing during debugging. It does not print the value of `Eyes`, but it does display the ordinal number of the value, that is, an integer from `0` (for `Red`) to `3` (for `Yellow`).

Procedure `WriteColor` in Fig. 8.9 prints a string that represents a value of type `Color`. If the value of `Eyes` is defined, the statement

```
WriteColor (Eyes)
```

displays the value of `Eyes` as a string. Make sure you understand the difference between the string `'Blue'` and the constant identifier `Blue`. ■

Figure 8.9 Procedure to Print a Value of Type Color

```
procedure WriteColor (InColor {input} : Color);
{
   Displays the value of InColor.
   Pre : InColor is assigned a value.
   Post: The value of InColor is displayed as a string.
}
begin {WriteColor}
  if InColor = Red then
    WriteLn ('Red')
  else if InColor = Green then
    WriteLn ('Green')
  else if InColor = Blue then
    WriteLn ('Blue')
```

```
  else if InColor = Yellow then
    WriteLn ('Yellow')
end; {WriteColor}
```

It is slightly more difficult to read the value of an enumerated type variable than it is to display it. The next example shows one method.

■ Example 8.7

Procedure `ReadLnColor` in Fig. 8.10 returns one value of type `Color` and one of type `Boolean`. If `Eyes` is type `Color` and `ValidColor` is type `Boolean`, the procedure call statement

```
ReadLnColor (Eyes, ValidColor)
```

attempts to read the value of `Eyes` and sets `ValidColor` to indicate the success (`ValidColor` is `True`) or failure (`ValidColor` is `False`) of this operation. `ReadLnColor` reads a single color value from each data line, ignoring all but the first letter on the line. If `Black` and `Brown` are added to the list of values for `Color`, it becomes necessary to read additional characters when the first letter read is `B` (see programming exercise 1 at the end of this section).

Figure 8.10 Procedure ReadLnColor

```
procedure ReadLnColor (var ItemColor  {output} : Color;
                       var ValidColor {output} : Boolean);
{
  Assigns a value to ItemColor based on an input character. Sets
  ValidColor to indicate whether the assignment was made.
  Pre : None
  Post: ItemColor is defined if the character read is 'R', 'G',
        'B', or 'Y'.
        ValidColor is set to True if ItemColor is defined;
        otherwise, ValidColor is set to False.
}
  var
    ColorChar : Char;          {first letter of color name}

begin  {ReadLnColor}
  Write ('Enter first letter of color> ');
  ReadLn (ColorChar);
  ColorChar := UpCase(ColorChar);    {Convert to uppercase}

  {Assign the color value}
  ValidColor := True;                  {Assume valid color}
  if (ColorChar = 'R') then
    ItemColor := Red
  else if (ColorChar = 'G') then
    ItemColor := Green
  else if (ColorChar = 'B') then
    ItemColor := Blue
  else if (ColorChar = 'Y') then
    ItemColor := Yellow
  else
    ValidColor := False          {valid color was not read}
end; {ReadLnColor}
```

Using Typecasting to Read Enumerated Values

In Turbo Pascal, the procedure ReadLnColor shown in Fig. 8.11 could also be used to "read" a value into parameter ItemColor. This version of the procedure uses the typecasting facility of Turbo Pascal. The WriteLn statements print a menu indicating which integer value to enter for each color. The statement

```
ItemColor := Color(ColorNum);
```

converts an integer from 0 to 3 (value of ColorNum) to its corresponding Color value.

Figure 8.11 Procedure ReadLnColor Using Typecasting

```
procedure ReadLnColor (var ItemColor  {output} : Color;
                       var ValidColor {output} : Boolean);
{
  Pre  : None
  Post : Returns the color value corresponding to the first data
         value between 0 and 3.
  Calls: EnterInt in EnterData
}
  var
    ColorNum : Integer;            {menu position of color name}

begin {ReadLnColor}
  ValidColor := True;                       {Assume valid color}
  WriteLn ('Enter 0 for Red');
  WriteLn ('Enter 1 for Green');
  WriteLn ('Enter 2 for Yellow');
  WriteLn ('Enter 3 for Blue');
  Write ('Enter a color value> ');
  EnterInt (0, 3, ColorNum);              {Get the color number}
  ItemColor := Color(ColorNum)              {Assign color value}
end; {ReadLnColor}
```

The last line in the documentation for procedure ReadLnColor is

```
Calls: EnterInt in EnterData
```

This line indicates that ReadLnColor calls library procedure EnterInt which is imported from library unit EnterData. This reminds a user of this procedure that the line

```
uses EnterData;
```

must appear in any program that calls procedure ReadLnColor.

Motivation for Using Enumerated Types

At this point you may have a legitimate concern: Is it worth using enumerated types, considering that it is so much trouble to read and write their values? Also, if we need to use a letter code to enter the value of an enumerated type variable, why not use that code throughout the program? The fact is that enumerated types in a program make that program considerably easier to read and understand.

■ Example 8.8

The if statement

```
if DayNum = 1 then
  PayFactor = 2.0        {double pay for Sunday}
else if DayNum = 7 then
  PayFactor := 1.5       {time and a half for Saturday}
else
  PayFactor := 1.0       {regular pay}
```

might appear in a payroll program without enumerated types if Sunday and Saturday are "coded" as the integers 1 and 7, respectively. If we use the enumerated type Day and variable Today (type Day), we can write this statement as

```
if Today = Sunday then
  PayFactor := 2.0
else if Today = Saturday then
  PayFactor := 1.5
else
  PayFactor := 1.0
```

The latter form is obviously more readable because, instead of an obscure code, it uses values (Saturday and Sunday) that are meaningful to the problem. Consequently, the comments in the first statement are not needed. ■

In a lengthy program, the extra overhead required to implement procedures for reading and writing the values associated with an enumerated type are insignificant. If you place these procedures in your programming library, it is easy to reuse them.

Another advantage to using enumerated types is that the creation of an enumerated type automatically limits the range of values that can be assigned to a variable. With an integer code, any integer value can be assigned unless you take the trouble to declare a subrange type. When you declare an enumerated type, you explicitly declare the set of values that can be assigned to a variable of that type. In the preceding example, any integer value can be assigned to variable DayNum; however, only one of the seven values listed in the declaration for enumerated type Day can be assigned to variable Today.

Exercises for Section 8.7

Self-Check

1. Evaluate each of the following, assuming that Today (type Day) is Thursday.
   a. Ord(Monday)
   b. Ord(Today)
   c. Today < Tuesday
   d. Succ(Wednesday)
   e. Pred(Succ(Today))
   f. Succ(Today)
   g. Pred(Today)
   h. Today >= Thursday
   i. Pred(Sunday)
   j. Ord(Succ(Succ(Today)))

2. Which of the following type declarations are valid? Which are invalid? What is wrong with each invalid type declaration?
   a. `type Letters = ('A', 'B', 'C');`
   b. `type Letters = (A, B, C);`
      `TwoLetters = (A..B);`
   c. `type Letters = ('A'..'Z');`
   d. `type Boolean = (True, False);`
   e. `type Day = (Sun, Mon, Tue, Wed, Thu, Fri, Sat);`
      `WeekDay = Mon..Fri;`
      `WeekEnd = Sat..Sun;`
      `TDay = (Tue, Thu);`
3. Declare an enumerated type `Month` and rewrite the following `if` statement, assuming that `CurMonth` is type `Month` instead of type `Integer`.

```
if CurMonth = 1 then
  WriteLn ('Happy new year')
else if CurMonth = 6 then
  WriteLn ('Summer begins')
else if CurMonth = 9 then
  WriteLn ('Back to school')
else if CurMonth = 12 then
  WriteLn ('Happy Holidays');
```

Programming

1. Rewrite procedure `ReadLnColor` (see Fig. 8.10), assuming that `Black` and `Brown` are also values for enumerated type `Color`.
2. Write procedure `WriteMonth` for enumerated type `Month` in exercise 3.

8.8 Data Abstraction and Abstract Data Types

To analyze the solution to a case study, we first list its data requirements and the algorithm. Then, we use procedural abstraction to design and implement the algorithm. The next step is to analyze a problem's data requirements.

Data abstraction is a powerful programming tool. It is the conceptual approach of combining a data type with a set of operations on that data type. Furthermore, data abstraction is the philosophy that we can use such data types without knowing the details of the underlying computer system representation. Just as procedural abstraction enables us to focus on *what* a procedure does without worrying about *how* it does it, data abstraction enables us to consider the data objects needed and the operations that must be performed on those objects, without being concerned with unnecessary details.

You have already practiced data abstraction—you have used the `Real` data type to represent certain numbers, without knowing much about the internal representation of that data type on a computer. The specification for the Pascal data type `Real` is shown in the following display.

Specification for Data Type Real

Elements: The elements are real numbers whose range depends on the number of bits used for storage. For example, for the IBM Personal Computer, the range of positive real numbers is 0.29E−38 to 1.70E38. Because of the nature of the representation, not all real numbers in this range are included. Type `Real` literals may be written with an optional scale factor. There must be a decimal point and at least one digit before and after the decimal point in each `Real` literal.

Operators: The arithmetic operators are `+`, `-`, `*`, and `/`. The relational operators are `<=`, `<`, `=`, `<>`, `>`, and `>=`. The assignment operator is `:=`. The functions `Abs`, `Exp`, `Ln`, `Sqr`, `Round`, `Trunc`, `Arctan`, `Cos`, `Sin`, `Frac`, and `Int` can be used with type `Real` arguments. Also, procedures `Read`, `ReadLn`, `Write`, and `WriteLn` can be passed type `Real` parameters.

Abstract Data Types

The combination of a data type and its operators is called an *abstract data type* (ADT). Through its type declaration facility, Pascal enables you to create your own abstract data types. You can declare a new data type and write operators for that type in the form of procedures. You can encapsulate the data type and procedures (operators) together in a unit. Whenever you want to use the data type in a client program, you can access it by including a `uses` statement at the beginning of the client program.

Exercise for Section 8.8

Self-Check

1. Write the specifications for the data types `Integer`, `Char`, and `Boolean`.

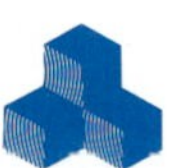

8.9 Abstract Data Type Day

In many programming problems, you need to process information relating to the day of the week. To facilitate this processing, you can implement an ADT containing data type `Day` and the operators for reading and writing the days of the week.

The ADT should contain declarations for the enumerated type `Day` and procedures `ReadLnDay` and `WriteDay`. The ADT shown in Fig. 8.12 has been implemented as the Turbo Pascal unit `DayADT`. Programmers who want to use unit `DayADT` should read the interface section of the unit because it contains all the information they need to know.

The specification of the ADT begins with the type declaration for `Day`. Users of the ADT must know about the data type `Day`, so its declaration appears in the interface section of the unit. Next come the headings for procedures `ReadLnDay` and `WriteDay`, along with comments documenting each procedure.

Figure 8.12 Unit DayADT


```
unit DayADT;
{
  Abstract data type Day: contains declarations for enunerated
  type Day and procedures for reading and displaying values of
  type Day.
}
interface                                {type specification}

  type
    Day = (Sunday, Monday, Tuesday, Wednesday,
           Thursday, Friday, Saturday);

  procedure ReadLnDay (Var OneDay    {output} : Day;
                       var ValidDay {output} : Boolean);
  {
    Reads a value into OneDay.
    Pre : None
    Post: OneDay is assigned a value if the two characters
          read are SU, MO, TU, WE, TH, FR, or SA;
          otherwise, OneDay is undefined.
          ValidDay is set to True if OneDay is defined;
          otherwise, ValidDay is set to False.
  }

  procedure WriteDay (OneDay {input} : Day);
  {
    Displays the value of OneDay
    Pre : OneDay is defined
    Post: Display OneDay as a string
  }

implementation                      {procedure definitions }

  procedure ReadLnDay (var OneDay    {output} : Day;
                       var ValidDay {output} : Boolean);
    var
      DayCh1,             {input - first letter in day}
      DayCh2  : Char;     {input - second letter in day}

  begin {ReadLnDay}
    Write ('Enter first two letters of the day name> ');
    ReadLn (DayCh1, DayCh2);
    DayCh1 := UpCase(DayCh1);
    DayCh2 := UpCase(DayCh2);

    {Convert to day of week}
    ValidDay := True;                        {assume valid day}
    if (DayCh1 = 'S') and (DayCh2 = 'U') then
      OneDay := Sunday
    else if (DayCh1 = 'M') and (DayCh2 = 'O') then
      OneDay := Monday
    else if (DayCh1 = 'T') and (DayCh2 = 'U') then
      OneDay := Tuesday
    else if (DayCh1 = 'W') and (DayCh2 = 'E') then
      OneDay := Wednesday
    else if (DayCh1 = 'T') and (DayCh2 = 'H') then
      OneDay := Thursday
    else if (DayCh1 = 'F') and (DayCh2 = 'R') then
      OneDay := Friday
    else if (DayCh1 = 'S') and (DayCh2 = 'A') then
      OneDay := Saturday
```

```
    else
      ValidDay := False                              {day is not valid}
  end; {ReadLnDay}

  procedure WriteDay (OneDay {input} : Day);
  begin {WriteDay}
    if  OneDay = Sunday then
      Write ('Sunday')
    else if OneDay = Monday then
      Write ('Monday')
    else if OneDay = Tuesday then
      Write ('Tuesday')
    else if OneDay = Wednesday then
      Write ('Wednesday')
    else if OneDay = Thursday then
      Write ('Thursday')
    else if OneDay = Friday then
      Write ('Friday')
    else if OneDay = Saturday then
      Write ('Saturday')
  end; {WriteDay}

end.  {DayADT}
```

The details of the procedure implementations are provided in the unit implementation section, which follows the interface section. Because of space limitations, we have omitted the procedure documentation, which already appears in the unit interface section.

Using Abstract Type Day

You should save the source file for unit DayADT in the disk file DAYADT.PAS and have the compiler write the object code for the unit disk file DAYADT.TPU. When you use unit DayADT in a new program or unit, you must place the statement

```
uses DayADT;
```

after the program heading or after the interface or implementation line of a client unit. As we discussed earlier, this will cause the compiler to link the object code contained in file DAYADT.TPU to the object code version of your Pascal program.

■ Example 8.9

The program shown in Fig. 8.13 uses unit DayADT. It reads and displays a day of the week.

Figure 8.13 Testing Unit DayADT

Edit Window

```
program TestDay;
{
  Test abstract data type DayADT.
  Imports: Day, ReadLnDay, WriteDay from DayADT (see Fig 8.12)
```

```
}
  uses DayADT;

  var
    Today : Day;              {input - day being read}
    GoodDay : Boolean;        {program flag}

begin {TestDay}
  WriteLn ('What day is Today?');
  ReadLnDay (Today, GoodDay);
  WriteLn;
  if not GoodDay then
    WriteLn ('Error - no day read')
  else
    begin
      Write ('Today is ');
      WriteDay (Today);
      WriteLn;
      if Today = Sunday then
        WriteLn ('Today is the first day of the week')
    end {outer if}
end. {TestDay}
```

Output Window

```
What day is today?
Enter the first two letters of the day name> SU
Today is Sunday
Today is the first day of the week
```

The module dependency diagram in Fig. 8.14 summarizes the interaction between `TestDay` and unit `DayADT`.

Figure 8.14 Module Dependency Diagram

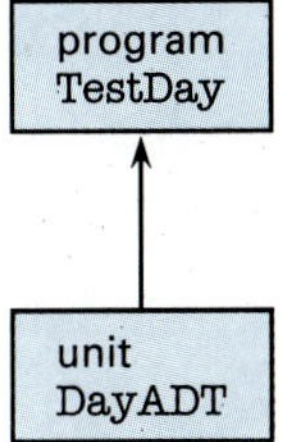

Exercise for Section 8.9

Programming

1. Write an abstract data type containing the declaration for type `Color` and procedures `ReadLnColor` and `WriteColor` (Example 8.6 and Example 8.7, respectively).

 8.10 Text Files

Up to this point, we have written most programs as interactive programs; in other words, each program reads all input data from the keyboard and displays all outputs on the screen. This mode of operation is fine for small programs. However, as you begin to write larger programs, you will see that there are many advantages to using disk files for program input and output.

You can create a data file using a text editor in the same way you create a program file. Once the data file is entered in computer memory, you can carefully check and edit each line before you save it as a disk file. When you enter data interactively, you do not have the opportunity to examine and edit the data.

After the data file is saved on disk, you can instruct your program to read data from the data file rather than from the keyboard. Recall from Chapter 2 that this mode of program execution is called batch mode. Because the program data are supplied before execution begins, prompting messages are not required in batch programs. Instead, batch programs must contain display statements that echo print data values, thereby providing a record of the data that are read and processed in a particular run.

Besides giving you the opportunity to check for errors in your data, using data files has another advantage. Because a data file can be read many times, during debugging you can rerun the program as often as you need to, without retyping the test data each time.

You can also instruct your program to write its output to a disk file rather than display it on the screen. When output is written to the screen, it disappears after it scrolls off the screen and cannot be retrieved. However, if program output is written to a disk file, you can use an operating system command such as

`TYPE` *filename*

to display file *filename* as often as you wish. You can also get a hard copy of a disk file by sending it to the printer.

Finally, you can use the output file generated by one program as a data file for another program. For example, a payroll program may compute employee salaries and write each employee's name and salary to an output file. A second program that prints employee checks could use the output of the payroll program as its data file.

Text Files

This section shows you how to get a Pascal program to read from a data file and to write program results to an output file. In Pascal, these files are called text files.

The text file is the first data structure we will examine. A *data structure* is a collection of data stored in the computer under one name. A *text file* is a collection of characters stored under the same name in secondary memory (that is, on a disk). A text file has no fixed size. To mark the end of a text file, the computer places a special character, called the *end-of-file* character (denoted as `<eof>`), following the last character in a text file.

As you create a text file using an editor program, you press the Enter key to separate the file into lines. Each time you press Enter, another special character, called the *end-of-line* character (denoted as `<eoln>`), is placed in the file.

Figure 8.15 shows a text file that consists of two lines of letters, blank characters, an exclamation point, and a period. Each line ends with `<eoln>`, and `<eof>` follows the last `<eoln>` in the file. For convenience in scanning the file's contents, we have listed each line of the file as a separate line. In the actual file stored on disk, the characters are stored in consecutive storage locations, with each character occupying a single storage location. The first character of the second line (the letter `I`) occupies the next storage location following the first `<eoln>`.

Figure 8.15 A Text File

```
This is a text file!<eoln>
It has two lines.<eoln><eof>
```

A text file can also contain numeric data or mixed numeric and character data. Figure 8.16 shows a text file that consists of numeric data and blank characters. Each number is stored on disk as a sequence of digit characters; blank characters separate numbers on the same line.

Figure 8.16 A Text File of Numbers

```
1234 345<eoln>
999 -17<eoln><eof>
```

The Keyboard and Screen as Text Files

In interactive programming, Pascal treats data entered at the keyboard as if it were read from the system file `Input`. This data is placed in an *input buffer* (a storage area) and held there until you press the Enter key. This allows you to use the normal editing features of your keyboard before allowing Turbo Pascal to process your data line. Pressing the Enter key causes the `<eoln>` character (Ctrl-M in MS-DOS) to be added to the end of your data line. Normally in interactive mode, you use a sentinal value to indicate the end of data, rather than attempting to enter the `<eof>` character in the system file `Input`; however, the `<eof>` character (Ctrl-Z in MS-DOS) could be used.

In a similar way, displaying characters on the screen is equivalent to writing characters to system file `Output`. The `WriteLn` procedure places the `<eoln>` character in this file, thereby moving the cursor to the start of the next line of the screen. Both Input and Output may be treated as text files because their individual components are characters, with each line terminated by the <eoln> character.

The EOLN and EOF Functions

<eoln> and <eof> are different from the other characters in a text file because they are not data characters. A program can read <eoln> into a type Char variable; however, the character value Ctrl-M (carriage return) will be stored in that variable, and its value prints as a blank. If a program attempts to read <eof>, an attempt to read beyond end of file run-time error results.

If we can't read or write these characters in the normal way, how do we process them? Pascal provides two functions that enable us to determine whether the next character is <eoln> or <eof>. The function EOLN returns a value of True if the next character is <eoln>; the function EOF returns a value of True if the next character is <eof>. The algorithm in Fig. 8.17 uses the EOLN and EOF functions to control the processing of a data file.

Figure 8.17 Using EOF and EOLN to Process a File

```
while not EOF(data file) do
  begin
    while not EOLN(data file) do
      Process each data character in the current line;

    {assert: the next character is <eoln> }
    Process the <eoln> character
  end; {while}

{assert: the next character is <eof> }
```

If the data file is not empty, the initial call to EOF returns a value of False (not EOF is True), and the computer executes the inner while loop. This loop processes each character in a line up to (but not including) the <eoln>. For the data file shown in Fig. 8.15, the first execution of the while loop processes the first line of characters:

```
This is a text file!
```

When the next character is <eoln>, the EOLN function returns True, so the inner while loop is exited. The <eoln> is processed immediately after loop exit, and the outer while loop is repeated.

Each repetition of the outer while loop begins with a call to the EOF function to test whether the next character is the <eof> character. If it is, the EOF function returns True (not EOF is False), so the outer loop is exited. If the next character is not <eof>, the EOF function returns False (not EOF is True), so the inner loop executes again and processes the next line of data up to <eoln>. For the file in Fig. 8.15, the second execution of the inner `while` loop processes the second line of characters:

```
It has two lines.
```

After the second <eoln> is processed, the next character is <eof>, so the `EOF` function returns `True`, and the outer `while` loop is exited. We use this algorithm later in a program that duplicates a file by copying all its characters to another file.

SYNTAX DISPLAY

EOLN Function (for Text Files)

Form: `EOLN(`*filename*`)`
Interpretation: The function result is `True` if the next character in file *filename* is <eoln>; otherwise, the function result is `False`.
Note: If *filename* is omitted, the file is assumed to be the system file `Input`. In standard Pascal, it is an error to call the `EOLN` function if `EOF(`*filename*`)` is `True`.

SYNTAX DISPLAY

EOF Function (for Text Files)

Form: `EOF(`*filename*`)`
Interpretation: The function result is `True` if the next character in file *filename* is <eof>; otherwise, the function result is `False`.
Note: If *filename* is omitted, the file is assumed to be the system file `Input`. If a read operation is attempted in standard Pascal when `EOF` (*filename*) is `True`, `an attempt to read past the end of the input file error` occurs and the program stops.

Declaring a Text File

Before we can reference a text file in a program, we must declare it just like any other data object. For example, the declaration

```
var
  InData, OutData : Text;
```

identifies `InData` and `OutData` as variables of type `Text`. `Text` is the predefined data type for a text file; therefore, `InData` and `OutData` are names of text files in any program that contains the preceding declaration.

Directory Names for Files

To access a text file created using the Turbo Pascal editor or created by another Pascal program, you must know its *directory name*, which is the name used to identify it in a disk's directory. A disk directory contains the names of all files stored on the disk. The `Assign` procedure is used in Turbo Pascal to associate a file variable with a permanent file that is saved on disk.

The procedure call statements

```
Assign (Infile, 'B:INFILE.DAT');
Assign (Students, 'CLASS.DAT');
```

associate the file variables `Infile` with the permanent file `INDATA.DAT` and the file Students with the permanent file `CLASS.DAT`. The file `INDATA.DAT` resides on the B disk drive and the file `CLASS.DAT` resides on the default disk drive.

The `Assign` statement is the only place where the directory name of the file appears. The file variable is used exclusively to refer to the file in all program statements.

SYNTAX DISPLAY

Assign Procedure

Form: `Assign` (*filevar*, *dirname*)
Example: `Assign (Infile, 'B:INFILE.DAT');`
Interpretation: The permanent file whose directory name is specified by the string *dirname* is associated with the file identifier *filevar*.
Notes: `Assign` must never be used on an open file. If *dirname* is the null string (`''`), *filevar* becomes associated with the standard `Input` or standard `Output` file, depending on whether *filevar* is later opened for input (by `Reset`) or output (by `Rewrite`). `Assign` is not part of standard Pascal.

Preparing a File for Input or Output

Before a program can use a file, the file must be prepared for input or output. At any given time, a file can be used for either input or output, but not both simultaneously. If a file is being used for input, then its components can be read as data. If a file is being used for output, then new components can be written to the file.

The procedure call statement

```
Reset (InData)
```

prepares file `InData` for input by moving its file position pointer to the beginning of the file. The *file position pointer* selects the next character to be processed in the file. After the `Reset` operation is performed, the next character to be read is always the first character in the file. The `Reset` operation must be done before any characters are read from file `InData`. The `Reset` operation fails if file `InData` was not previously saved on disk.

The procedure call statement

```
Rewrite (OutData)
```

prepares file `OutData` for output. If no file `OutData` is saved on disk, a file that is initially empty (that is, OutData has no characters) is created. If a file OutData is already saved on disk, its file position pointer moves to the beginning of the file. Any program output replaces the old data associated with file OutData and all old data are lost. You do not have to prepare the system files Input or Output for processing.

To read and process a file a second time in the same program run, perform the Reset operation again. A program can also read and echo print (to the screen) an output file it creates by calling the Reset procedure with the newly created file as its parameter. The Reset operation prepares this file for input, and your program can then read data from that file and display it. Make sure that you call procedure Assign to associate the file variable with its directory name before the initial call to Reset or Rewrite. If you neglect to call Assign first, a File not assigned run-time error will occur.

SYNTAX DISPLAY

Reset Procedure

Form: Reset (*infile*)
Interpretation: File *infile* is prepared for input and the file position pointer for *infile* is moved to the first file component. The Reset operation is automatically performed on system file Input, so Reset (Input) is not required.

SYNTAX DISPLAY

Rewrite Procedure

Form: Rewrite (*outfile*)
Interpretation: File *outfile* is prepared for output and *outfile* is initialized to an empty file. Any data previously associated with file *outfile* are lost. The Rewrite operation is automatically performed on system file Output, so Rewrite (Output) is not required.

Reading and Writing a Text File

You've learned how to declare a text file and how to prepare one for processing. All that remains is to find out how to instruct the computer to read data from an input file or to write program results to an output file.

If NextCh is a type Char variable, we know that the procedure call statement

```
Read (NextCh)
```

reads the next data character typed at the keyboard into NextCh. This is really an abbreviation for the procedure call statement

```
Read (Input, NextCh)
```

which has the same effect. The first parameter for a Read (or ReadLn) operation should be a file name. However, the file name may be omitted if it is the file `Input`.

The statement

```
Read (InData, NextCh)
```

reads the next character from file `InData` into `NextCh`, where the next character is the one selected by the file position pointer. The computer automatically advances the file position pointer after each read operation. Remember to prepare `InData` for input using `Reset` before the first read operation.

In a similar manner, the procedure call statements

```
Write (Ch)        |        Write (Output, Ch)
```

display the value of `Ch` on the screen. The statement

```
Write (OutData, Ch)
```

writes the value of `Ch` to the end of file `OutData`. Remember to prepare `OutData` for output using `Rewrite` before the first call procedure `Write`.

■ Example 8.10

It is a good idea to have a backup or duplicate copy of a file in case the original file data are lost. Even though many operating systems provide a command that copies a file, we will write our own Pascal program to do this. Program `CopyFile` in Fig. 8.18 copies each character in file `InData` to file `OutData`. ■

Figure 8.18 Program to Copy a File

Edit Window

```
program CopyFile;

{Copies file InData to file OutData.}

  var
    InData,              {data file}
    OutData : Text;      {output file}
    NextCh : Char;       {each data character}

begin {CopyFile}
  {Prepare the text files for input/output.}
  Assign (InData, 'B:OLD.DAT');
  Assign (OutData, 'B:NEW.DAT');
  Reset (InData);
  Rewrite (OutData);

  {Copy each character from InData to OutData.}
  while not EOF(InData) do
    begin
      {Copy the next data line.}
      while not EOLN(InData) do
        begin
          Read (InData, NextCh);
          Write (OutData, NextCh)
        end; {inner while}
```

```
      {assertion: next character is <eoln> }
      ReadLn (InData);
      WriteLn (OutData)
    end; {outer while}

  {assertion: next character is <eof> }
  Close (InData);
  Close (OutData);
  WriteLn (Output, 'File InData copied to file OutData.')
end. {CopyFile}
```

Output Window

```
File InData copied to file OutData.
```

The nested `while` loops in Fig. 8.18 implement the algorithm first shown in Fig. 8.17. The data file, `InData`, is the argument in the calls to functions `EOLN` and `EOF`. As long as the next character is not `<eoln>`, the statements

```
Read (InData, NextCh);
Write (OutData, NextCh)
```

read the next character of file `InData` into `NextCh`, then write that character to file `OutData`.

If the next character is `<eoln>`, the inner `while` loop is exited and the statements

```
ReadLn (InData);
WriteLn (OutData)
```

are executed. The data file, `InData`, is the only parameter in the call to `ReadLn`. In this case, the `ReadLn` procedure does not read any data, but simply advances the file position pointer for `InData` past the `<eoln>` to the first character of the next line. The second statement writes the `<eoln>` to file `OutData`. After the `<eoln>` is processed, function `EOF` is called again to test whether there are more data characters left to be copied.

Figure 8.19 shows the result of executing the preceding statement pair after the end of the first line of file `InData`. The next character in file `InData` is in color.

Figure 8.19 Effect of First ReadLn and WriteLn

File InData	File OutData
`This is a text file! <eoln>` `It has two lines.<eoln><eof>`	`This is a text file!`

a) Before `ReadLn` and `WriteLn`

File InData	File OutData
`This is a text file!<eoln>` `It has two lines.<eoln><eof>`	`This is a text file!<eoln>`

b) After `ReadLn` and `WriteLn`

It is interesting to contemplate the effect of omitting either of the preceding statements. If `WriteLn (OutData)` is deleted, the `<eoln>` will not be written to file `OutData` whenever the end of a line is reached in file `InData`. Consequently, `OutData` will contain all the characters in file `InData`, but on one line. If `ReadLn (InData)` is omitted, the file position pointer will not be advanced and the `<eoln>` will still be the next character. Consequently, `EOLN (InData)` will remain `True`, the inner loop is exited immediately, and another `<eoln>` is written to file `OutData`. This continues "forever," or until the program is terminated by its user.

Figure 8.20 shows the effect of executing the statement pair after the end of the second line of file `InData`. After the pair executes, the `<eof>` is the next character in file `Indata`, so the `EOF` function returns `True` and the outer loop is exited.

The procedure call statements

```
Close (InData);
Close (OutData);
```

at the end of the program close the files that were processed. The last statement above causes any file data that may be saved in memory to be written to file `OutData`. While it is not required that you explicitly close input files, it is a good idea to close any file you process in Turbo Pascal, whether it is used for input or output.

After the files are closed, the statement

```
WriteLn (Output, 'File InData copied to file OutData.')
```

writes a message to file `Output` (the screen). (We have included the file parameter `Output` for the sake of consistency with the other calls to Pascal's input/output procedures.) After closing the file `OutData`, the computer automatically writes the `<eof>` at the end of file `OutData`.

Figure 8.20 Effect of Second ReadLn and WriteLn

File `InData`	File `OutData`
`This is a text file!<eoln>` `It has two lines.<eoln><eof>`	`This is a text file!<eoln>` `It has two lines.`

a) Before `ReadLn` and `WriteLn`

File `InData`	File `OutData`
`This is a text file!<eoln>` `It has two lines.<eoln><eof>`	`This is a text file!<eoln>` `It has two lines.<eoln>`

b) After `ReadLn` and `WriteLn`

SYNTAX DISPLAY

Close Procedure

Form: `Close (`*filevar*`)`
Example: `Close (InData)`

Interpretation: The file denoted by *filevar* is closed. If *filevar* is an output file, any data remaining in memory is written to the file associated with *filevar*.
Note: If *filevar* is already closed when passed to `Close`, a run-time error occurs. `Close` is not part of standard Pascal.

Omitting the File Parameter in an Input/Output Operation

A common source of error is forgetting to use a file name with `EOLN` or `EOF`. In this case, the system uses file `Input`. A similar error is forgetting to use a file name with `Read`/`ReadLn` (file `Input` used) or `Write`/`WriteLn` (file `Output` used). Normally, no error diagnostic is displayed, so the cause of the error is not obvious.

Reading and Writing Numeric Data

When a value is being read into a type `Char` variable, only a single character is read, regardless of what that character might be (for example, a letter, a digit, a blank, or an `<eoln>`). Consequently, the file position pointer is advanced one character position. When a value is being read into a numeric variable (type `Integer` or type `Real`), a group of characters is read, and the file position pointer is advanced past all characters in the group.

When it reads a numeric value, the computer skips over any leading blanks, control characters, or `<eoln>` characters until it encounters a character that is not a blank, a control character, or `<eoln>`. That character must be a sign or a digit; if it is not, an execution error such as `non-digit found while reading number` occurs, and the program stops. If the first character is valid, the computer continues reading characters until it encounters a terminating character. The terminating character must be a blank, a control character, or an `<eoln>`. The file position pointer is then advanced to the terminating character. The next `Read` or `ReadLn` will process this character.

Although you have not yet done so in interactive programming, it is possible to read more than one number at a time or a mixture of numeric and character data. If several variables are listed in the parameter list for `Read` or `ReadLn`, the computer reads data into each variable in the order in which it appears. The file position pointer advances after each value is entered. When procedure `Read` is used, the file position pointer advances to the first character that was not read. When `ReadLn` is used, the file position pointer advances past any characters at the end of the current data line to the start of the next data line (that is, past the next `<eoln>` character). Any characters skipped over in this way are not processed.

Table 8.2 shows several examples of `Read` and `ReadLn` statements and their effects. Assume that `X` is type `Real`, `N` is type `Integer`, `C` is type `Char`, and the first character processed is the first character in the file. The position of the file

Table 8.2 Effects of Read/ReadLn

Statement and Effect	Next Character after Read
`Read (InData, X, N, C)` X is 1234.56, N is 789, C is ' '	1234.56□789□A345.67<eoln> W<eoln><eof>
`ReadLn (InData, X, N, C)` X is 1234.56, N is 789, C is ' '	1234.56□789□A345.67<eoln> W<eoln><eof>
`Read (InData, X, C, N)` X is 1234.56, C is ' ', N is 789	1234.56□789□A345.67<eoln> W<eoln><eof>
`ReadLn (InData, X, C, N)` X is 1234.56, C is ' ', N is 789	1234.56□789□A345.67<eoln> W<eoln><eof>
`Read (InData, C, X, N)` C is '1', X is 234.56, N is 789	1234.56□789□A345.67<eoln> W<eoln><eof>
`ReadLn (InData, C, X, N)` C is '1', X is 234.56, N is 789	1234.56□789□A345.67<eoln> W<eoln><eof>

`ReadLn (InData, X, N);`
`Read (InData, C);`
X is 1234.56, N is 789, C is 'W'
	1234.56□789□A345.67<eoln>
	W<eoln><eof>

`ReadLn (InData, X);`
`ReadLn (InData, C);`
X is 1234.56, C is 'W'
	1234.56□789□A345.67<eoln>
	W<eoln><eof>

position pointer after each read operation is shown in color to the right. The symbol □ denotes a blank character.

Writing a numeric value to a file is similar to writing a numeric value to the screen. The computer writes the number as a sequence of digit characters. The character - precedes a negative number. The character . is inserted in a type `Real` value. You can specify the number of characters that represent a numeric value by using a format specification; otherwise, the Pascal system controls this specification.

■ Example 8.11

A friend has a text file that contains numeric data (all integers) and wants you to write a program that finds the sum and the average of all numbers in that file. Because your friend has not been very careful in preparing the data file, some lines contain more numbers than others. A sample file, `InNumbers`, follows:

```
20  50<eoln>
100<eoln>
80  42  60<eoln><eof>
```

Program `SumFile` in Fig. 8.21 computes the sum and the average requested and displays them on the screen. To simplify later processing of the data, it also creates a new file, `OutNumbers`, that contains a single number per line. The following output file corresponds to the preceding data file:

```
 20<eoln>
 50<eoln>
100<eoln>
 80<eoln>
 42<eoln>
 60<eoln><eof>
```

Figure 8.21 Adding Numbers in a Text File

Edit Window

```
program SumFile;
{
  Finds the sum of a file of integers and writes
  each integer on a separate line of the output file.
}
  var
    InNumbers,                 {input file}
    OutNumbers : Text;         {output file}
    NextNum,                   {input - each integer}
    Sum,                       {output - sum of integers}
    Count : Integer;           {output - count of integers}
    Average : Real;            {output - average of integers}

begin
  {Prepare files InNumbers and OutNumbers.}
  Assign (InNumbers, 'NUM.DAT');
  Assign (OutNumbers, 'OUT.DAT');
  Reset (InNumbers);
  Rewrite (OutNumbers);

  {Accumulate sum of integers.}
  Sum := 0;
  Count := 0;
  while not EOF(InNumbers) do
    begin
      {Process each integer on the current line.}
      while not EOLN(InNumbers) do
        begin
          Read (InNumbers, NextNum);        {get the number}
          WriteLn (OutNumbers, NextNum);    {copy it to file}
          Sum := Sum + NextNum;
          Count := Count + 1
        end; {inner while}

      {assertion: next character is <eoln> }
      ReadLn (InNumbers)
    end; {outer while}

  {assertion:
     next character is <eof> and
     Sum is the sum of all integers read
  }
  if Count <> 0 then
    begin
      Average := Sum / Count;
      WriteLn (Output, 'The sum is ', Sum :1);
```

```
      WriteLn (Output, 'The average is ', Average :3:1)
    end
  else
   WriteLn (Output, 'Data file is empty');

  Close (InNumbers);
  Close (OutNumbers)
end.  {SumFile}
```

Output Window

```
The sum is 352
The average is 58.7
```

Within the inner `while` loop, the first statement below

```
Read (InNumbers, NextNum);                    {get the number}
WriteLn (OutNumbers, NextNum)                 {copy it to file}
```

reads the next number from file `InNumbers` into `NextNum`. The integer value corresponding to the string of digits read is stored in `NextNum`. The `WriteLn` procedure writes this value as a string of digit characters to `OutNumbers` and writes an `<eoln>` after each number. Each value of `NextNum` is also added to `Sum`.

The inner `while` loop is exited after the last number in a line is read because the next character is `<eoln>`. The statement

```
ReadLn (InNumbers)
```

advances the file position pointer for `InNumbers` to the start of the next line. After the last line of `InNumbers` is processed, the next character is the `<eof>`, so the outer `while` loop is exited and the program results are displayed on the screen. ■

SYNTAX DISPLAY

Read, ReadLn Procedures (for Text Files)

Form: `Read` (*infile, input list*)
`ReadLn` (*infile, input list*)

Example: `Read (InData, X, Y, Z);`
`ReadLn (InData, Ch1, Ch2)`

Interpretation: A sequence of characters is read from file *infile* into the variables specified in *input list*. The type of each variable in *input list* must be `Char`, `Integer`, a subrange of `Char` or `Integer`, or `Real`. If the data type of a variable is `Char`, only a single character is read into that variable; if the data type of a variable is `Integer` or `Real`, a sequence of numeric characters is read, converted to a binary value, and stored in that variable. If `Read` is used, the file position pointer for *infile* is advanced past the last character read. If `ReadLn` is used, the file position pointer for *infile* is advanced to the start of the next line.

Notes: If *infile* is omitted, the file is assumed to be the system file `Input`. File *infile* must first be prepared for input with `Reset (`*infile*`)`, except when *infile* is `Input`. An error results if `EOF(`*infile*`)` is true before the read operation.

SYNTAX DISPLAY

Write, WriteLn Procedures (for Text files)

Form: `Write (`*outfile*, *output list*`)`
`WriteLn (`*outfile*, *output list*`)`

Example:
```
Write (MyResult, Salary);
WriteLn (MyResult, Hours :3:1, ' $', Salary :4:2)
```

Interpretation: The characters specified by *output list* are written to the end of file *outfile*. The type of each expression in *output list* must be one of the standard data types (`Boolean`, `Char`, `Integer`, `Real`), a subrange of a standard data type, or a character string. If an expression is type `Char`, a single character is written to file *outfile*; otherwise, a sequence of characters may be written. If `WriteLn` is used, an `<eoln>` is written as the last character in *outfile*. The file position pointer for *outfile* is at the end of the file.

Notes: If *outfile* is omitted, the file is assumed to be the system file `Output`. File *outfile* must first be prepared for output with `Rewrite (`*outfile*`)` except when *outfile* is `Output`.

Exercises for Section 8.10

Self-Check

1. Let `X` be type `Real`, `N` type `Integer`, and `C` type `Char`. Indicate the contents of each variable after each read operation is performed, assuming that the file consists of the following lines and that the `Reset` operation occurs before each read.

```
123 3.145 XYZ<eoln>
35 Z<eoln>
```

a. `ReadLn (InData, N, X);  Read (Indata, C)`
b. `Read (InData, N, X, C);`
c. `Read (InData, N, X, C, C);`
d. `ReadLn (InData, N);  Read (InData, C);`
e. `ReadLn (InData, X);  Read (InData, C, N);`
f. `ReadLn (InData, C, N, X);  Read (InData, C);`
g. `ReadLn (InData, C, C, C, X);  Read (InData, N);`
h. `Read (InData, N, X, C, C, C, C, N);`
i. `Read (InData, N, X, C, C, C, C);`

2. What would be the effect, if any, of trailing blanks at the end of data lines in the data file for the program in Fig. 8.21? What would be the effect of blank lines?

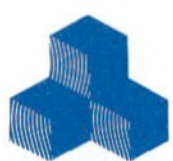

8.11 Using Text Files

If one program writes its output to a disk file rather than to the screen, a second program may use this output file as its own data file. In this way, the two programs communicate with each other through the disk file. This case study is an example of a program whose output file is intended for later use as an input data file.

Case Study: Preparing a Payroll File

Problem

Your company's accountant wants you to write two programs for processing the company's payroll. The first program will read a data file consisting of employee salary data. The data for each employee are stored on two consecutive lines: the first line is the employee's name, and the second line contains that employee's hours worked and hourly rate. A sample data file follows.

```
Peter Liacouras<eoln>
40.0  50.00<eoln>
Caryn Koffman<eoln>
20.0  10.00<eoln><eof>
```

The first program echoes each employee's name to an output file, followed by a line that contains the employee's computed gross salary. It also computes and displays the total payroll amount. The output file corresponding to the data file is shown next. The second line of the output file contains the product of the two values read from the second line of the data file.

```
Peter Liacouras<eoln>
2000.00<eoln>
Caryn Koffman<eoln>
200.00<eoln><eof>
```

The second program will read the output file and print payroll checks based on the contents of this file. For example, the first check issued should be a check for $2,000.00 made out to Peter Liacouras.

Design Overview

We will write the first program now and leave the second one as a programming project at the end of this chapter. The program must copy each employee's name to the output file. It must also compute each employee's salary, copy it to the output file, and add it to the payroll total.

Data Requirements

Problem Inputs (from Data File InEmp)
Each employee's name
Each employee's hours worked (`Hours : Real`)
Each employee's hourly rate (`Rate : Real`)

Problem Outputs (to Output File OutEmp)
Each employee's name
Each employee's salary (`Salary : Real`)

Problem Outputs (to System File Output)
The payroll total (`Payroll : Real`)

Initial Algorithm

1. Prepare files `InEmp` and `OutEmp`.
2. Initialize payroll total to `0.0`.
3. `while` there are more employees `do`
   `begin`
   4. Read next employee's name from `InEmp` and write it to `OutEmp`.
   5. Read next employee's salary data.
   6. Compute next employee's salary.
   7. Write next employee's salary to `OutEmp` and add it to payroll total.

   `end`
8. Display payroll total on screen.

Algorithm Refinements

We will use procedure `CopyLine` to perform step 4. The algorithm for `CopyLine` follows.

Algorithm for CopyLine

1. `while` the next character is not the `<eoln>` character `do`
   Copy the next character from `InEmp` to `OutEmp`.
2. Advance past the `<eoln>` in the input file.
3. Write the `<eoln>` to the output file.

Coding

The main program and procedure `CopyLine` are shown in Fig. 8.22. The program uses three text files: `Output`, `InEmp`, and `OutEmp`.

Figure 8.22 Writing a Payroll File

Edit Window

```
program PreCheck;
{
  Writes each employee's name and gross salary to an
  output file and computes total payroll amount.
```

```
}
  var
    InEmp,              {data file}
    OutEmp : Text;      {output file}
    Hours,              {input - hours worked}
    Rate,               {input - hourly rate}
    Salary,             {output - gross salary}
    Payroll : Real;     {output - total payroll}


  procedure CopyLine (var InFile, {input file}
                          OutFile {output file} : Text);
  {
    Copies one line of file InFile to file OutFile.

    Pre : InFile and OutFile are prepared for input/output.
    Post: Next line of InFile is copied to OutFile.
  }
    var
      NextCh : Char;                  {each data character}

  begin {CopyLine}
    {Copy all data characters up to <eoln>}
    while not EOLN(InFile) do
      begin
        Read (InFile, NextCh);
        Write (OutFile, NextCh)
      end; {while}

    {assertion: next character is <eoln>}
    ReadLn (InFile);
    WriteLn (OutFile)
  end; {CopyLine}


begin {PreCheck}
  {Prepare InEmp and OutEmp}
  Assign (InEmp, 'B:INEMP.DAT');
  Assign (OutEmp, 'B:OUTEMP.DAT');
  Reset (InEmp);
  Rewrite (OutEmp);

  {Compute each individual salary and total payroll amount.}
  Payroll := 0.0;
  while not EOF(InEmp) do
    begin
      CopyLine (InEmp, OutEmp);        {copy employee name}
      ReadLn (InEmp, Hours, Rate);     {get salary data}
      Salary := Hours * Rate;
      WriteLn (OutEmp, Salary :4:2);
      Payroll := Payroll + Salary
    end; {while}

  {assertion: at end of file}
  Close(InEmp);
  Close(OutEmp);

  {Display result}
  WriteLn (Output, 'Total payroll is $', Payroll :4:2)
end. {PreCheck}
```

Output Window

```
Total payroll is $2200.00
```

The while loop in the main program tests whether the next character is the <eof>. If it is not, procedure CopyLine copies an employee's name from its input file (InEmp) to its output file (OutEmp). CopyLine processes every other line of file InEmp, starting with the first line.

After CopyLine processes the <eoln> following an employee's name, the statement

```
ReadLn (InEmp, Hours, Rate);        {get salary data}
```

reads that employee's salary data from InEmp and advances the file position pointer to the first letter of the next employee's name. Next, the statement

```
WriteLn (OutEmp, Salary :4:2);
```

writes the salary for the current employee to file OutEmp. After the current employee's salary is added to the payroll total, the next employee is processed.

The Importance of Advancing Past the <eoln>

It is easy to make an error when you are reading character data mixed with numeric data. Many problems are caused by not advancing past the <eoln>. For example, consider what would happen if we attempt to use the statement

```
Read (InEmp, Hours, Rate);        {get salary data}
```

to read the first employee's salary data instead of the call to ReadLn shown in Fig. 8.18. The difficulty is that the Read procedure advances the file position pointer for file InEmp up to the <eoln>, but not past it.

```
40.0 50.00<eoln>
```

When CopyLine is called to copy the second employee's name, the while loop exit occurs immediately, without reading the name, because the next character is the <eoln>. The <eoln> is processed just before CopyLine returns to the main program, and the next character is now the first letter of an employee's name. When

```
Read (InEmp, Hours, Rate);        {get salary data}
```

executes again, a non-digit found while reading number error occurs and the program stops.

File Parameters

Procedure CopyLine has two variable parameters, InFile and OutFile. It may seem strange to declare file parameter InFile as variable, since this parameter represents an input file. However, Pascal requires all file parameters to be variable because it is not possible to make a local copy of a complete file in memory.

Exercise for Section 8.11

Programming

1. Rewrite CopyFile (see Fig. 8.18) as a procedure where the input file and output file are parameters.

8.12 Debugging with Units and Files

Using units and text files can make debugging easier. All procedures in a unit should be carefully debugged and tested before they become a permanent part of your programming library. Since it is not possible to execute a unit's source file directly, you will need to write a driver program to test its procedures. Once a unit's procedures have been tested thoroughly, it is safe to assume that their execution in future programs will be error free.

Turbo Pascal's integrated debugger lets you use the F8 key (Run/Step Over) when the next statement is a call to a library procedure in a unit. The F7 key (Run/Trace Into) can be used to step through each statement in a procedure defined in a unit if the unit's source code resides in the same directory as its .TPU file. Unit names, followed by a period, can be used to qualify Watch variable expressions if variables with the same name have been declared in different units.

When you are debugging a large program that makes use of several program units and include files, it is often difficult to keep track of where you are in the program. If your source program makes use of several files, you can use the Search menu Find procedure to help you locate the source code for a particular procedure. To do this, first select the Search menu and then the Find procedure option, as shown in Fig. 8.23.

This causes the Find Procedure dialog box to appear on the screen (Fig. 8.24). If you type the name of a procedure in the Procedure name field, the debugger will search the various source files used by your program. If the search is successful, the debugger will load the appropriate source file into a new Edit window. You may use a unit name to qualify the procedure name if the same procedure name has been declared in more than one unit.

It is important to note that the Find procedure command does not change the current debugging state. This means that the next line to be executed in your program will be the same before and after the use of Find procedure. To have your program execute up to the first line of the procedure located by Find procedure, press function key F4 (Go to Cursor).

Figure 8.23 Turbo Pascal Search Menu

```
≡ File Edit Search Run Compile Debug Options Window Help
[•]          Find . . .                NTE.PAS                1=[↕]
program Tes  Replace . . .
{Tests proce Search again              Data.}
  uses Ente  Go to line number . . .   orts ReadLnBool}
  var        Find procedure . . .
    NextBoo  Find error . . .          t - next Boolean data value}
    ReadDone  :  Boolean;              {flag -- True if read succeeds;
                                          otherwise, False}
begin {TestEnterData}
  ReadDone := False;                   {no value read yet}
  while not ReadDone do
    begin
      WriteLn ('Enter a Boolean value:');
      ReadLnBool (NextBool, ReadDone);
    end; {while}
  if ReadDone then
    WriteLn ('Boolean value read was ', NextBool)
  else
    WriteLn ('Invalid data character read')
      16:1
F1 Help | Search for a procedure or function declaration while debugging
```

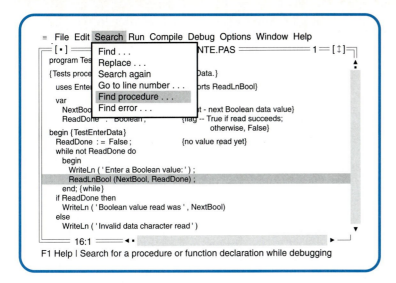

Preparing a data file that contains a representative set of test data for a new program will make it easier to debug the program. Each time it is run, the program can read the test data from this file, saving you the trouble of having to retype the data items. After the program has been debugged, replace the MS-DOS file directory name in the `Assign` statement with the null string (''), so Turbo Pascal will read data from the keyboard in subsequent runs.

Figure 8.24 Turbo Pascal Find Procedure Dialog Box

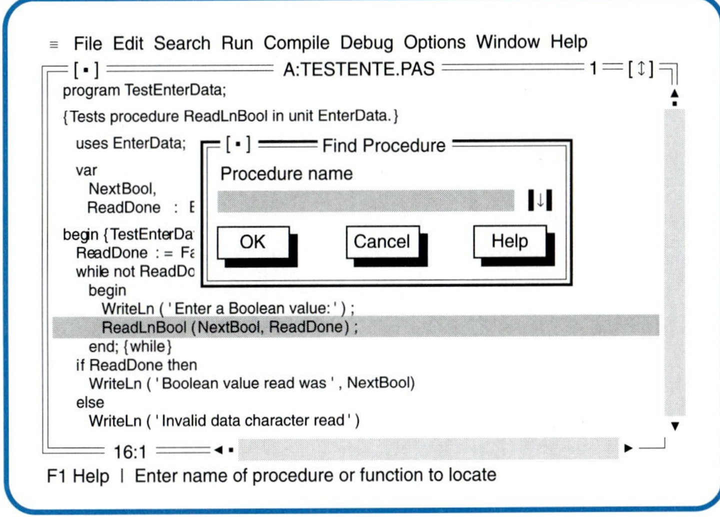

You can use file identifiers as Watch variables. The value displayed in the Watch window for a file identifier will be a parenthesized list that contains the MS-DOS file directory name associated with the file identifier by `Assign`. The value will also indicate whether the file is open for input, open for output, or closed.

8.13 Common Programming Errors

When writing user-defined units, insert only the procedure headings in the unit's interface section; the complete procedure declarations must appear in the unit's implementation section. Any constant, type, variable, or procedure that is intended for use by client modules must be declared in the unit's interface section.

Any time a change is made to the interface section of a unit, the client units using that unit must be recompiled. If you forget to recompile any of the client units, a `Unit version mismatch` error results when you attempt to compile a program or unit which uses one of these client units. If only the unit's implementation or initialization sections are changed, client units do not need to be recompiled. However, client programs must always be recompiled whenever a change is made to a unit.

When you are declaring enumerated types, remember that only identifiers can appear in the list of values for an enumerated type. Strings, characters, and numbers are not allowed. Make sure that the same constant identifier does not appear in more than one enumerated type declaration in a given block. It is permissible for a given constant identifier to appear in more than one subrange type declaration. Remember that there are no standard procedures available to read or write the values of an enumerated type.

File processing in any programming language tends to be difficult to master; Pascal is no exception. The name, which will be used as a file variable in the program, may differ from the actual directory name of the associated disk file. All file names must be declared as variables (type `Text`), except for system files `Input` and `Output`.

Do not forget to associate a file variable with its directory name using the `Assign` procedure before opening the file. You must then prepare the file for input or output using the `Reset` or `Rewrite` procedure (except for system files `Input` and `Output`). If you rewrite an existing file, the data on that file may be lost. Make sure you do not inadvertently place the `Reset` or `Rewrite` statement in a loop. If you do, a read operation in the loop will repeatedly read the first file component; a write operation in the loop will repeatedly write the first file component.

The `Read/ReadLn` procedure can be used only after a file has been prepared for input. Similarly, the `Write/WriteLn` procedure can be used only after a file has been prepared for output. Be sure to specify the file name as the first Be careful not to try to read data when the file position pointer for a file is at the `<eof>`. Also, when you use function `EOLN` or `EOF` to control data entry, don't forget to include the data file name as the function argument.

Chapter Review

This chapter discussed programming in the large. It introduced many techniques that are useful in writing larger program systems, such as the use of procedure libraries, enumerated types, abstract data types, and text files for input and output.

This chapter described how to write user-defined units. You saw that the unit's interface section contains all the information required for a client program or another unit to make use of the unit. Each identifier that is visible outside the unit is declared in the unit's interface section. The procedure headings are also contained in the unit's interface section, although their code bodies are hidden in the unit's implementation section.

You saw that there are many advantages to creating and using your own procedure libraries or units. Units are the building blocks of larger programs. The use of units makes it easier to apportion pieces of a large project to different members of a programming team. Once a unit has been completed, it can be compiled and its procedures can be imported and reused by other units. You can change a client module without having to recompile the unit being imported. If you rewrite the body of a procedure in a unit implementation section, then you have to recompile only that unit, not its client units. As long as you don't change the interface section of a unit, its client units do not need to be recompiled.

This chapter also described how to declare enumerated types with a list of values tailored to a particular application. The use of enumerated types makes large programs more readable. You saw how to encapsulate an enumerated type, together with its operators, as an abstract data type (ADT).

You learned how to instruct a program to read its data from a data file rather than from the keyboard and how to save the output generated by a program as a file on disk. Both features make it easier to debug large programs.

The file type `Text` is predefined as a file of characters. The `<eoln>` character breaks a text file into lines. The `EOLN` function can test for an `<eoln>`, and the `WriteLn` statement places one in a `Text` file.

When `Text` files are processed, sequences of characters are transferred between main memory and disk storage. The data type of a variable used in an input list must be `Char`, `Integer`, a subrange of `Char` or `Integer`, `Real`, or `string`. The data type of an expression used in an output list must be `Char`, `Integer`, a subrange of `Char` or `Integer`, `Boolean`, `Real`, or `string`.

Use the `Reset` procedure to move the file position pointer for an input file to the first character in the file. Use the `Rewrite` procedure to prepare an output file before writing to it. While you are reading a file, the `EOF` function can test whether the end of the file has been reached.

New Pascal Constructs

Table 8.3 describes the new Pascal constructs introduced in this chapter.

Table 8.3 Summary of New Pascal Constructs

Construct	Effect

Enumerated Type Declaration
`type`
`  BColor = (Blue, Black, Brown)`
	An enumerated type `BColor` is declared with values `Blue`, `Black`, and `Brown`.

Table 8.3 *continued*

Construct	Effect

File Declaration
`var`
`  MoreChars,`
`  MoreDigits : Text;`
`  I : Integer,`
`  NextCh : Char;`
	`MoreChars` and `MoreDigits` are text files.

Assign Procedure `Assign (MoreDigits, 'B:DIGITS.DAT');`	Internal file `MoreDigits` is associated with disk file `DIGITS.DAT`, located on drive B.

Reset and Rewrite Procedures
`Reset (MoreDigits);`
`Rewrite (MoreChars);`
	`MoreDigits` is prepared for input, and `MoreChars` is prepared for output.

Read and Write Procedures
`Read (MoreDigits, I);`
`WriteLn (MoreChars, 'number: ', I);`
	The next integer is read from file `MoreDigits` into variable `I` (type `Integer`). The string `'number: '` is written to `MoreChars` followed by the value of `I`.

EOF Function
`Reset (MoreDigits);`
`Rewrite (MoreChars);`
`while not EOF(MoreDigits) do`
`  begin`
`    ReadLn (MoreDigits, I);`
`    WriteLn (MoreChars, I)`
`  end; {while}`
	File `MoreDigits` is prepared for input and file `MoreChars` for output. The first integer value on each line of file `MoreDigits` is written to a separate line of file `MoreChars`.

EOLN Function
`Reset (MoreDigits);`
`while not EOLN(MoreDigits) do`
`  begin`
`    Read (MoreDigits, NextCh);`
`    Write (Output, NextCh)`
`  end;  {while}`
`ReadLn (MoreDigits);`
	File `MoreDigits` is prepared for input. Each character on the first line is read into `NextCh` and displayed on the terminal screen. The file position pointer for `MoreDigits` is advanced to the first character of the second line.

Close Procedure `Close (MoreChars);`	File `MoreChars` is closed, and is no longer associated with a permanent file.

✓ Quick-Check Exercises

1. The six phases of the software life cycle follow, listed in arbitrary order. Place them in their correct order.

testing, design, requirements specification, operation and maintenance, coding and debugging, analysis

2. In which phases are the users of a software product likely to be involved?
3. In which phases are the programmers and the analysts likely to be involved?
4. Which phase lasts the longest?
5. Explain the difference between a subrange type and an enumerated type.
6. Can you declare a subrange whose host type is an enumerated type?
7. What is wrong with the following enumerated type declaration?

```
type Prime = (2, 3, 5, 7, 9, 11, 13);
```

8. Name the two sections of an abstract data type. Where is the data type declaration found? Where are the procedure declarations found?
9. The ____________ operation prepares a file for input, and the ____________ operation prepares it for output.
10. A ____________ separates a ____________ file into lines, and the ____________ appears at the end of a file.
11. Correct the following segment:

```
Reset (Number);
while not EOF do
  Read (InFile, Number);
```

Answers to Quick-Check Exercises

1. Requirements specification, analysis, design, coding and debugging, testing, operation and maintenance
2. Requirements specification, testing, operation and maintenance
3. All phases
4. Operation and maintenance
5. A subrange type is a subset of values of a previously declared ordinal type; an enumerated type is an ordinal type whose values are identifiers not previously declared.
6. Yes
7. Integers cannot be used as enumerated type values.
8. Interface and implementation sections, interface, implementation
9. `Reset`, `Rewrite`
10. `<eoln>`, text, `<eof>`
11.

```
Reset (InFile);
while not EOF(InFile) do
  Read (InFile, Number);
```

Review Questions

1. Write an enumerated type declaration for `Fiscal` as the months from `July` through `June`. Declare the subrange `Winter` as `December` through `February`.
2. Write an abstract data type for the positions on a baseball team (pitcher, catcher, infield, outfield) and operators to read and write those positions.
3. List three advantages to using files for input and output as opposed to the standard input and output you have used thus far in this course.
4. Where are files stored?
5. Explain why a file may have two distinct names. What conventions are followed for choosing each name? Which name appears in the file variable declaration? Which name appears in an operating system command?

6. Write a loop that reads up to `10` integer values from a data file and displays them on the screen. If there are not `10` integers in the file, the message `That's all, folks` should be displayed after the last number.
7. Define the terms *procedural abstraction* and *data abstraction*.
8. Which of the following are likely to occur in a programmer's library of procedures? Explain your answer.
   a. A procedure that raises a number to a specified power
   b. A procedure that writes the user instructions for a particular program
   c. A procedure that displays the message `HI MOM` in block letters
   d. A procedure that displays the block letter `M`

Programming Projects

1. Write an abstract data type that consists of data type `MyColor` and operators for reading and writing the colors (Red, Yellow, Green, Blue, Black, and White).
2. Make use of the Crt unit and modify the user interface developed in project 7 from Chapter 7, so that the user is prompted for information inside a window as we did in procedure `ReadTran` (Fig. 8.1). Have your program display the values input for the loan amount, duration, interest, and the values computed for the monthly and total payments in a second window.
3. Each month, a bank customer deposits $50 into a savings account. The account earns 6.5 percent interest, calculated on a quarterly basis (one-fourth of 6.5 percent every three months). Write a program to compute the total investment, total amount in the account, and the interest accrued for each of the 120 months of a 10-year period. Assume that the rate is applied to all funds in the account at the end of a quarter, regardless of when the deposits were made.

   Print all values accurate to two decimal places. The table printed by your program should begin as follows:

```
MONTH      INVESTMENT      NEW AMOUNT      INTEREST      TOTAL SAVINGS
  1           50.00           50.00          0.00            50.00
  2          100.00          100.00          0.00           100.00
  3          150.00          150.00          2.44           152.44
  4          200.00          202.44          0.00           202.44
  5          250.00          252.44          0.00           252.44
  6          300.00          302.44          4.91           307.35
  7          350.00          357.35          0.00           357.35
```

4. Create a Turbo Pascal unit containing at least four procedures that may be used to determine the following for an integer input parameter:
   a. Is it a multiple of 7, 11, or 13?
   b. Is the sum of its digits even or odd?
   c. Its square root.
   d. Is it a prime number?

   Write a client program to test your unit using the following values:

```
104   3772   12   121   77   3075
```

5. Write a program that reads several lines from a data file and prints each word of the file on a separate line of an output file, followed by a count of the number of letters in that word. After all lines are processed, the program should display the number of words processed. Assume that words are separated by one or more blanks. Include

a procedure, `SkipBlanks`, that skips over a sequence of blanks between words. Modify your solution to display the number of data lines read.

6. Whatsamata U. offers a service to its faculty in computing grades at the end of each semester. A program processes three weighted test scores and calculates a student's average and letter grade (an A is 90-100, a B is 80-89, etc.). Read the student data from a file and write each student's ID number, test score, average, and grade to an output file.

   Write a program to provide this valuable service. The data will consist of the three test weights followed by three test scores and a student ID number (four digits) for each student. Calculate the weighted average for each student and the corresponding grade. This information should be printed along with the initial three test scores. The weighted average for each student is equal to:

   ```
   weight1 * score1 + weight2 * score2 + weight3 * score3
   ```

   For summary statistics, print the highest average, the lowest average, the average of the averages, and the total number of students processed.

   Sample data:

   ```
   0.35  0.25  0.40        Test weights
   100   76    88   1014   Test scores and id
   ```

7. An employee time card is represented as one long string of characters. Write a program that processes a collection of these strings stored on a data file and writes the results to an output file.

   a. Compute gross pay using the formula

   $$gross = regular\ hours \times rate + overtime\ hours \times 1.5 \times rate$$

   b. Compute net pay by subtracting the following deductions:

   federal tax = .14 × (*gross* − 13 × *dependents*)
   Social Security = 0.052 × *gross*
   city tax = 4% of *gross* if employee works in the city
   union dues = 6.75% of *gross* for union member

   The data string for each employee takes up forty-two positions:

Positions	*Data*
1-10	Employee's last name
11-20	Employee's first name
21	C for city office or S for suburban office
22	U for union or N for nonunion
23-26	Employee's identification number
27	Blank
28-29	Number of regular hours (a whole number)
30	Blank
31-36	Hourly rate (dollars and cents)
37	Blank
38-39	Number of dependents
40	Blank
41-42	Number of overtime hours (a whole number)

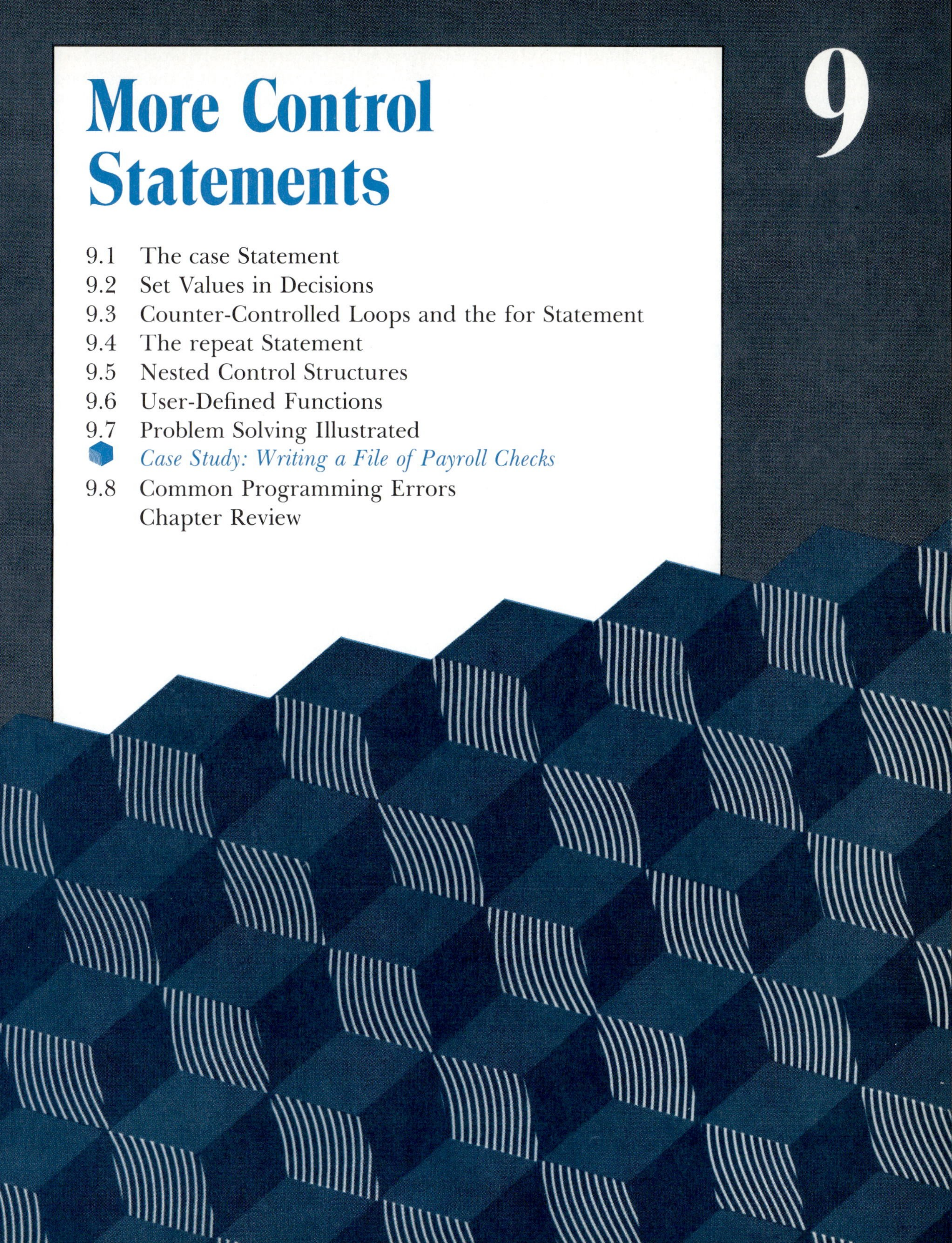

More Control Statements

9

This chapter introduces more control statements. You are already familiar with how to use the `if` statement to implement decisions; the `case` statement is another way to select among several alternative tasks.

We also introduce two new loop forms: the `for` loop and the `repeat` loop. We discuss the relative advantages of each of the three loop forms (`while`, `for`, and `repeat`) and determine when it is best to use each form. We also reexamine nested control structures, especially nested loops, and demonstrate how to use them.

So far, you have used the standard Pascal functions to simplify computations. In this chapter, you will see how to declare and use your own functions.

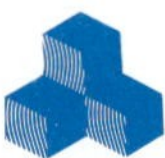

9.1 The case Statement

The `case` statement is used in Pascal to select one of several alternatives. It is especially useful when the selection is based on the value of a single variable or a simple expression. This variable or expression must be an ordinal type.

■ Example 9.1

The `case` statement

```
case MomOrDad of
  'M', 'm' : WriteLn ('Hello Mom - Happy Mother''s Day');
  'D', 'd' : WriteLn ('Hello Dad - Happy Father''s Day')
end  {case}
```

behaves the same as the following `if` statement when the character stored in `MomOrDad` is one of the four letters listed (`M`, `m`, `D`, or `d`).

```
if (MomOrDad = 'M') or (MomOrDad = 'm') then
  WriteLn ('Hello Mom - Happy Mother''s Day')
else if (MomOrDad = 'D') or (MomOrDad = 'd') then
  WriteLn ('Hello Dad - Happy Father''s Day')
```

The message displayed by the `case` statement depends on the value of the *case selector* `MomOrDad` (type `Char`). If the case selector value is `'M'` or `'m'`, the first message is displayed. If the *case selector* value is `'D'` or `'d'`, the second message is displayed. The lists `'M', 'm'` and `'D', 'd'` are called *case labels.* ■

■ Example 9.2

Procedure `WriteDay` in Fig. 9.1 uses a `case` statement to print a string that indicates the value of a variable whose type is the enumerated type `Day`. This procedure is more readable and efficient than the one shown in Fig. 8.8.

Figure 9.1 Procedure WriteDay

```
procedure WriteDay (OneDay {input} : Day);
{
  Displays the value of OneDay.
  Pre : OneDay is defined.
```

```
  Post: Displays OneDay as a string.
}
begin {WriteDay}
  case OneDay of
    Sunday    : WriteLn ('Sunday');
    Monday    : WriteLn ('Monday');
    Tuesday   : WriteLn ('Tuesday');
    Wednesday : WriteLn ('Wednesday');
    Thursday  : WriteLn ('Thursday');
    Friday    : WriteLn ('Friday');
    Saturday  : WriteLn ('Saturday')
  end {case}
end; {WriteDay}
```

Seven alternatives are shown in Fig. 9.1; the value of `OneDay` (type `Day`) is used to select one of those alternatives for execution. The seven possible values of `OneDay` are listed as case labels to the left of each colon; the task for that case label follows the colon. After the `WriteLn` statement selected is executed, the `case` statement and the procedure are exited. ■

A common error is the use of a string such as `'Sunday'` as a `case` label. This causes the syntax error `constant and case type do not match`. It is important to remember that only ordinal values (that is, characters or integers) or ordinal constants (that is, identifiers) may appear in case labels.

■ Example 9.3

The following `case` statement could be used to compute the numeric value of the hexadecimal digit stored in `HexDigit` (type `Char`). In the hexadecimal number systems, the valid "digits" are the character values `0` through `9` and `A` through `F`. The character values `0` through `9` have the numeric values 0 through 9; the character values `A` through `F` have the numeric values 10 (for `A`) through 15 (for `F`).

```
case HexDigit of
   '0','1','2','3','4','5','6','7','8','9' :
              Decimal := Ord(HexDigit) - Ord('0');
   'A','B','C','D','E','F' :
              Decimal := Ord(HexDigit) - Ord('A') + 10
end {case}
```

This `case` statement causes the first assignment statement to be executed when `HexDigit` is one of the digits `0` through `9`. The assignment statement

```
Decimal := Ord(HexDigit) - Ord('A') + 10
```

executes when `HexDigit` is one of the letters `A` through `F`. Assuming that the letters are consecutive characters (as in the ASCII character set), this statement assigns to `Decimal` a value from 10 (for `A`) to 15 (for `F`).

In Turbo Pascal (but not standard Pascal), you can use subrange notation to abbreviate case labels. The last case statement is rewritten below using subranges.

```
case HexDigit of
  '0'..'9' : Decimal := Ord(HexDigit) - Ord('0');
  'A'..'F' : Decimal := Ord(HexDigit) - Ord('A') + 10
end  {case}
```

■ Example 9.4

Your professor uses the case statement in Fig. 9.2 in a student transcript program that computes grade point average (GPA). For each case shown, the total points (`Points`) earned toward the GPA increase by an amount based on the letter grade (`Grade`); the total credits earned towards graduation (`GradCredits`) increase by one if the course is passed. The compound statement bracketed by a `begin . . . end` pair executes when `Grade` is `A` through `D`. Assuming that the letters are in consecutive order, the expression

```
Ord('A') - Ord(Grade) + 4
```

evaluates to 4 when `Grade` is `A`; 3 when `Grade` is `B`, and so on.

Figure 9.2 case Statement for Student Transcript Program

```
case Grade of
  'A'..'D' :
        begin
          Points := Points + (Ord('A') - Ord(Grade) + 4);
          GradCredits := GradCredits + 1
        end;
  'P' : GradCredits := GradCredits + 1;
  'F', 'I', 'W' : {no points or credits}
end; {case}
```

In Fig. 9.2, grades of A through D earn variable numbers of points (4 for an A, 3 for a B, etc.) and 1 graduation credit each. A grade of P (Pass) earns 1 graduation credit, and grades of F (Fail), I (Incomplete), or W (Withdrawal) earn no graduation credit and no points. ■

What happens if the program user enters a grade that is not listed in a case label? In standard Pascal a run-time error occurs. However, in Turbo Pascal nothing happens and the next statement following the end `{case}` is executed. Turbo Pascal also allows the use of an `else` clause to print an error message or take some corrective action if the `case` selector has an unexpected data value. In the `case` statement in Fig. 9.3, the `else` clause prints the message `Invalid grade` if an unexpected value is stored in `Grade`. The `else` clause may not be used in standard Pascal.

Figure 9.3 case Statement with else Clause

```
case Grade of
  'A'..'D' :
        begin
          Points := Points + (Ord('A') - Ord(Grade) + 4);
          GradCredits := GradCredits + 1
        end;
```

```
  'P' : GradCredits := GradCredits + 1;
  'F', 'I', 'W' : {no points or credits}
else
  WriteLn ('Invalid grade ', Grade, ' entered.')
end; {case}
```

The case statement is described in the next display.

SYNTAX DISPLAY

case Statement

Form: case *selector* of
label$_1$: *statement*$_1$;
label$_2$: *statement*$_2$;
.
.
.
label$_n$: *statement*$_n$
else
label$_e$: *statement*$_e$
end

Example:

```
case N of
  1, 2 : WriteLn ('Buckle my shoe');
  3, 4 : WriteLn ('Shut the door');
  5, 6 : WriteLn ('Pick up sticks')
else
  WriteLn (N,'is bad value for N')
end
```

Interpretation: The *selector* expression is evaluated and compared to each case label. Each *label*$_i$ is a subrange or a list of one or more possible values for the *selector*. Only one *statement*$_i$ is executed; if the *selector* value is listed in *label*$_i$, *statement*$_i$ is executed. Control is then passed to the first statement following end. Each *statement*$_i$ may be a single or a compound Pascal statement.

Note 1: If the value of the *selector* is not listed in any case label, the next statement is executed unless an else clause is provided. If present, the else clause is executed. In standard Pascal, a run-time error occurs when the selector value fails to match any case label.

Note 2: A particular *selector* value may appear in, at most, one case label.

Note 3: The type of each *selector* value must correspond to the type of the selector expression.

Note 4: Any ordinal data type is permitted as the *selector* type.

If no action is to be performed for a particular case label, this is indicated by placing the semicolon, or end (for the last case), immediately following the colon. Each *statement*$_i$, except the last one, should be followed by a semicolon; the last statement is followed by the word end. There is no corresponding begin for a case statement.

Comparison of Nested if Statements and the case Statement

You can use nested `if` statements, more general than the `case` statement, to implement a multiple-alternative decision. The `case` statement, however, is more readable and should be used whenever practical. `Case` labels that contain type `Real` values or strings are not permitted.

You should use the `case` statement when each `case` label contains a list of values of reasonable size (ten or less). However, if the number of values in a `case` selector is large or there are large gaps in those values, use a nested `if` statement. You should also use a nested `if` statement when there are a large number of values that require no action to be taken.

Exercises for Section 9.1

Self-Check

1. Write an `if` statement that corresponds to the following `case` statement:

```
case X > Y of
  True  : WriteLn ('X greater');
  False : WriteLn ('Y greater or equal')
end
```

2. If type `Color` is described as the list of identifiers (`Red`, `Green`, `Blue`, `Brown`, `Yellow`), write a `case` statement that assigns a value to `Eyes` (type `Color`), given that the first two letters of the color name are stored in `Letter1` and `Letter2`.

Programming

1. Rewrite the `case` statement in Fig. 9.1 as a nested `if` statement.
2. Write a `case` statement that prints a message indicating whether `NextCh` (type `Char`) is an operator symbol (+, –, *, =, <, >, /), a punctuation symbol (comma, semicolon, parenthesis, brace, or bracket), or a digit. Your statement should print the category selected. Write the equivalent `if` statement.

9.2 Set Values in Decisions

Many of you have studied sets in a mathematics course. In mathematics, a *set* is represented by a list of *set elements* enclosed in curly braces. In Pascal, set elements are enclosed in square brackets. For example, the set of odd integers from 1 through 9 is written as {1, 3, 5, 7, 9} in mathematics and as `[1, 3, 5, 7, 9]` in Pascal. The order in which elements are listed in a set is immaterial; the Pascal set `[9, 5, 7, 1, 3]` is equivalent to `[1, 3, 5, 7, 9]`.

■ Example 9.5

The `case` statement in Example 9.3 is rewritten as the following nested `if` statement:

```
if HexDigit in ['0'..'9'] then
  Decimal := Ord(HexDigit) - Ord('0')
```

```
else if HexDigit in ['A','B','C','D','E','F'] then
  Decimal := Ord(HexDigit) - Ord('A') + 10
else
  WriteLn (HexDigit, ' is an invalid Hexadecimal digit.')
```

This statement uses the set `['A','B','C','D','E','F']` to represent the letters A through F. The set membership operator `in` is used to test whether `HexDigit` is one of the elements of this set. The Boolean expression

```
HexDigit in ['A','B','C','D','E','F']
```

evaluates to `True` if `HexDigit` is one of the set elements listed; otherwise, the Boolean expression evaluates to `False`.

The Boolean expression

```
HexDigit in ['0'..'9']
```

uses subrange notation to describe a set whose elements are the digits `'0'` through `'9'`. The following set describes the set of characters that may appear in a real number (the digits and the characters +, –, `E`, and .).

```
['0'..'9', '+', '-', 'E', '.']
```

■

SYNTAX DISPLAY

Set Values

Form: [*list of elements*]
Example: `['+', '-', '*', '/', '<', '>', '=']`
Interpretation: A set is defined whose set elements are the *list of elements* enclosed in brackets. The elements of a set must belong to the same ordinal type or to compatible ordinal types. Commas separate elements in the *list of elements.* A group of consecutive elements may be specified using subrange notation [(that is, *minval* . . *maxval,* where *minval* and *maxval* are type-compatible expressions and `Ord(`*minval*`)` <= `Ord(`*maxval*`)`].
Note: In Turbo Pascal, no more than 256 values may be contained in a set, `Ord(`*minval*`)` must be >= 0, and `Ord(`*maxval*`)` must be <= 255.

SYNTAX DISPLAY

Set Membership Operator in

Form: *element* `in` [*list of elements*]
Example: `NextCh in ['+','-','*','/','<','>','=']`
Interpretation: The set membership operator `in` describes a condition that evaluates to `True` when *element* is included in *list of elements*; otherwise, the condition evaluates to `False`. The data type of *element* must be compatible with the set elements.

Guarding a case Statement

In standard Pascal, an `out of range` error occurs if the value of the `case` selector variable does not match one of the `case` labels. Standard Pascal does not allow the use of an `else` clause as a means of trapping the `out of range` error. However, the set membership test can be used in conjunction with an `if` statement to *guard* the `case` statement. If you add an `else` clause to the `if` statement, you can achieve the same effect as with the Turbo Pascal `case` statement.

■ Example 9.6

The `if` statement below has a `case` statement as its `True` alternative.

```
if HexDigit in ['0'..'9', 'A'..'F'] then
  case HexDigit of
    '0','1','2','3','4','5','6','7','8','9' :
             Decimal := Ord(HexDigit) - Ord('0');
    'A','B','C','D','E','F' :
             Decimal := Ord(HexDigit) - Ord('A') + 10
  end  {case}
else
  WriteLn (HexDigit, ' is an invalid Hexadecimal digit.')
```

Now the `case` statement is executed only when `HexDigit` has a valid integer value; an error message is printed when `HexDigit` is not valid. ■

Exercises for Section 9.2

Self-Check

1. Which of the following sets are valid and which are invalid? What are the elements of the valid sets?
   a. `[1, 3, 1..5]`
   b. `['1', '3', '1'..'5']`
   c. `[1, 3, '1'..'5']`
   d. `['1', '3', 'A'..'C']`
2. Write a set that consists of the special characters used for punctuation in Pascal or to denote operators.

Programming

1. Guard a `case` statement with an `if` statement so that the `case` statement displays the category of `NextCh` as a vowel, as a digit, or as a Pascal operator. Otherwise, the `else` clause of the `if` statement should print a message indicating that `NextCh` is not one of the characters being checked for.

9.3 Counter-Controlled Loops and the for Statement

So far, you have used the `while` statement to implement repetition in programs. Pascal provides another loop form, the `for` statement, that is more efficient for implementing counter-controlled loops. You will recall from Chapter 5 that a counter variable controls the repetition of a counter-controlled loop, and that a counter-controlled loop is of the following general format described in pseudocode:

```
Set counter variable to initial value
while counter variable <= final value do
  begin
    . . .
    increment counter variable to its next value
  end
```

The next pseudocode describes a `for` statement that has the same behavior as the preceding `while` statement.

```
for counter variable := initial value to final value do
  begin
    . . .
  end
```

All manipulation of the *counter variable* is specified in the `for` statement header. These three operations are

1. Initializing the *counter variable* to *initial value*
2. Testing if *counter variable* <= *final value*
3. Incrementing *counter variable* to its next value before each test

■ Example 9.7

The following statements behave in the same way.

```
{Print N blank lines}
Line := 1;
while Line <= N do
  begin
    WriteLn;
    Line := Line + 1
  end {while}
```

```
{Print N blank lines}
for Line := 1 to N do
  WriteLn
```

If `Line` and `N` are type `Integer` variables, the `for` statement on the right causes the `WriteLn` operation to be performed `N` times. The `while` loop implementation shown on the left is longer because of the assignment statements

```
Line := 1;
Line := Line + 1
```

which are needed to initialize and update the counter variable. ■

■ Example 9.8

The `for` statement in Fig. 9.4 reads salary data for seven employees and computes and displays each employee's gross salary. (Compare it with the `while` statement shown in Fig. 5.1.)

Figure 9.4 for Loop for Seven Employees

```
for EmpNumber := 1 to 7 do
  begin
    Write ('Hours >');
    ReadLn (Hours);
    Write ('Rate  > $');
    ReadLn (Rate);
    Salary := Hours * Rate;
```

```
    WriteLn ('Salary is $', Salary :4:2);
    WriteLn
  end; {for}

WriteLn ('All employees processed')
```

Read the first line of Fig. 9.4 as "for each value of EmpNumber from 1 to 7 do." There is no need to provide additional Pascal statements to set EmpNumber to an initial value or to update the value of EmpNumber; these two operations are automatically performed in a for loop. ■

■ Example 9.9

We can write procedure PrintI for the Mother's Day problem in Fig. 3.7 using the for statement shown in Fig. 9.5. This procedure prints seven lines that contain asterisks in columns 4 and 5. A blank line is printed just before the return from the procedure.

Figure 9.5 Procedure PrintI

```
procedure PrintI;

{Prints the block letter I.}

   var
     NextLine : Integer;  {Loop control variable -
                                 from 1 to 7          }

begin {PrintI}
  for NextLine := 1 to 7 do
    WriteLn ('   **');
  WriteLn
end; {PrintI}
```

The for statement in Fig. 9.5 specifies that the counter variable NextLine should take on each of the values in the range 1 to 7 during successive loop repetitions. This means that the value of NextLine is 1 during the first loop repetition, 2 during the second loop repetition, and 7 during the last loop repetition. ■

PROGRAM STYLE

Counter Variables as Local Variables

In Fig. 9.5, the counter variable NextLine is declared as a local variable in procedure PrintI. All counter variables should be declared as local variables.

The counter variable can also be referenced in the loop body, but its value should not be changed. In standard Pascal, changing the value of the counter variable results in a run-time error. In Turbo Pascal, changing the value of the counter variable may cause an infinite loop. The next example illustrates a for statement which references the counter variable in the loop body.

■ Example 9.10

The program in Fig. 9.6 uses a for loop to print a list of integer values and their squares. During each repetition of the loop body, the statement

```
Square := Sqr(I);
```

calls function Sqr to compute the square of the counter variable I; then the value of I and Square are displayed. Table 9.1 traces the loop execution.

Figure 9.6 Printing a Table of Integers and Their Squares

Edit Window

```
program Squares;

{Displays a table of integers and their squares.}

  const
    MaxI = 4;              {largest integer in table}

  var
    I,                     {counter variable}
    Square : Integer;      {output - square of I}

begin {Squares}
  {Prints a list of integer values and their squares.}
  WriteLn ('I' :10, 'I * I' :10);
  for I := 1 to MaxI do
    begin
      Square := Sqr(I);
      WriteLn (I :10, Square :10)
    end {for}
end. {Squares}
```

Output Window

```
         I     I * I
         1         1
         2         4
         3         9
         4        16
```

Table 9.1 Trace of Program in Figure 9.6

Statement	I	Square	Effect
	?	?	
for I := 1 to MaxI	1		Initialize I to 1.
Square := Sqr(I)		1	Assign 1 * 1 to Square.
WriteLn (I, Square)			Print 1, 1.
Increment and test I	2		2 <= 4 is True.
Square := I * I		4	Assign 2 * 2 to Square.
WriteLn (I, Square)			Print 2, 4.

Table 9.1 *continued*

Statement	I	Square	Effect
`Increment and test I`	3		3 <= 4 is `True`.
`Square := I * I`		9	Assign `3 * 3` to `Square`.
`WriteLn (I, Square)`			Print `3, 9`.
`Increment and test I`	4		4 <= 4 is `True`.
`Square := I * I`		16	Assign `4 * 4` to `Square`.
`WriteLn (I, Square)`			Print `4, 16`.
`Increment and test I`	4		Exit loop.

The trace in Table 9.1 shows that the counter variable `I` is initialized to `1` when the `for` loop is reached. After each loop repetition, `I` is incremented by one and tested to see whether its value is still less than or equal to `MaxI` (4). If the test result is `True`, the loop body is executed again, and the next values of `I` and `Square` are printed. If the test result is `False`, the loop is exited.

`I` is equal to `MaxI` during the last loop repetition and in Turbo Pascal, `I` retains its last value when the loop is exited. In standard Pascal, `I` becomes undefined upon exit from a `for` loop and `I` may not be referenced before it is assigned a new value. ■

Syntax of a for Statement

The syntax diagram for a `for` statement is shown next.

for Statement

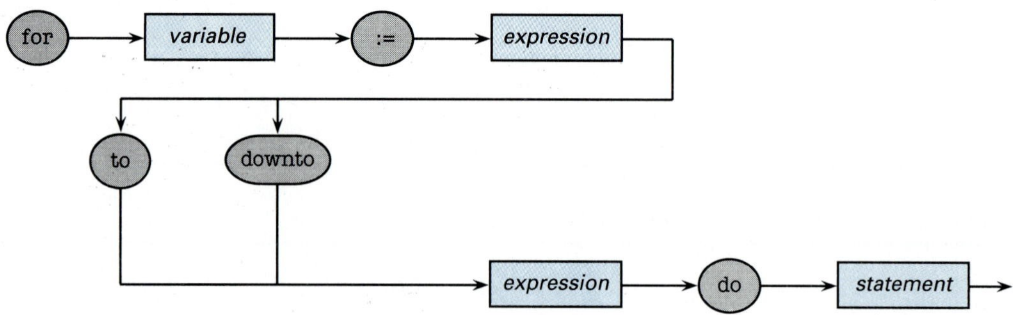

SYNTAX DISPLAY

for Statement

Form: `for` *counter* := *initial* `to` *final* `do`
statement

for *counter* := *initial* downto *final* do
statement

Example:
```
for I := 1 to 5 do
  begin
    ReadLn (Indata, NextNum);
    Sum := Sum + NextNum
  end;

for CountDown := 10 downto 0 do
  WriteLn (CountDown :2)
```

Interpretation: The statement that comprises the loop body is executed once for each value of *counter* between *initial* and *final*, inclusive. *initial* and *final* can be constants, variables, or expressions of the same ordinal type as *counter*.

Note 1: The value of *counter* should not be modified in *statement*.

Note 2: The value of *final* is computed once, just before loop entry. If *final* is an expression, any change in the value of that expression has no effect on the number of iterations performed.

Note 3: After loop exit, the value of *counter* retains its last value.

Note 4: *statement* is not executed if *initial* is greater than *final*. (In the downto form, *statement* is not executed if *initial* is less than *final*.)

More for Loop Examples

The for loop can be used with other ordinal types besides Integer. The examples that follow use counter variables of type Char and the enumerated type Day.

■ Example 9.11

The following for loop prints each uppercase letter and its ordinal number. The counter variable, Next, must be type Char.

```
for Next := 'A' to 'Z' do
  WriteLn (Next, Ord(Next))
```

■ Example 9.12

The for loop in Fig. 9.7 reads hours worked during each week day for an employee and accumulates the sum of the hours worked in WeekHours. Assuming that the counter variable Today is declared as the enumerated type Day (see Fig. 8.8), the loop executes for Today equal to Monday through Friday. During each iteration, the calls to Write, WriteDay (see Fig. 9.1), and WriteLn display a prompt such as

```
Enter hours for Monday>
```

where WriteDay fills in the day name. Next, each value read into DayHours is added to WeekHours. After loop exit, the final value of WeekHours is displayed. ■

Figure 9.7 Accumulating Hours Worked

```
WeekHours := 0.0;
for Today := Monday to Friday do
  begin
    Write ('Enter hours for ');
    WriteDay (Today);
    Write ('> ');
    ReadLn (DayHours);
    WeekHours := WeekHours + DayHours
  end; {for}

WriteLn ('Total weekly hours are ', WeekHours :4:2)
```

The examples so far use the reserved word to and increase the value of the counter variable after each loop repetition. If the reserved word downto is used instead, the value of the counter variable decreases after each loop repetition.

■ Example 9.13

A student wants a fast way to compute and print the Fahrenheit temperature that corresponds to each integer Celsius (C) temperature from 5 degrees C downto -10 degrees C. She could use the following for loop.

```
for Celsius := 5 downto -10 do
  begin
    Fahrenheit := 1.8 * Celsius + 32;
    WriteLn (Celsius :10, Fahrenheit :15:1)
  end {for}
```

Exercises for Section 9.3

Self-Check

1. Trace the following program segments.

a.
```
J := 10;
for I := 1 to 5 do
  begin
    WriteLn (I, J);
    J := J - 2
  end; {for}
```

b.
```
for Ch := 'A' to 'Z' do
  WriteLn (Chr(Ord(Ch) + Ord('a') - Ord('A')), Ch)
```

2. Write for loop headers that process all value of Celsius (type Integer) in the following ranges:

-10 through +10
100 through 1
15 through 50
50 through -75

Programming

1. Write a `for` statement that prints each digit character and its ordinal number on a separate output line.
2. Write a `for` loop that computes the sum of the first `N` integers, where `N` is a data value. After loop exit, compare the sum with the value of the algebraic formula

$$\frac{N(N + 1)}{2}$$

and print a message indicating whether or not the sum equals this value.

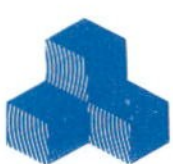

9.4 The repeat Statement

The `repeat` statement specifies a conditional loop that is repeated `until` its condition becomes true. Such a loop is called a `repeat-until` loop.

■ Example 9.14

Both program segments in Fig. 9.8 print the powers of 2 whose values lie between `1` and `1000`.

Figure 9.8 while and repeat Statements

```
Power := 1;
while Power < 1000 do
  begin
    Write (Power :5);
    Power := Power * 2
  end {while}
```

a) `while` statement

```
Power := 1;
repeat
  Write (Power :5);
  Power := Power * 2
until Power >= 1000
```

b) `repeat` statement

The test used in the `repeat-until` loop (`Power >= 1000`) is the *complement*, or opposite, of the test used in the `while` loop. The loop body is repeated until the value of `Power` is greater than or equal to `1000`. ■

Because loop repetition stops when the condition is `True`, the test is called a *loop-termination test* rather than a loop-repetition test. There is no need for a `begin/end` bracket around the loop body because the reserved words `repeat` and `until` perform that function.

SYNTAX DISPLAY

Repeat Statement (repeat-until Loop)

Form: `repeat`
loop body
`until` *termination condition*

Example: `repeat`
```
         Write ('Enter a digit: ');
         Read (Ch)
       until ('0' <= Ch) and (Ch <= '9')
```
Interpretation: After each execution of *loop body*, *termination condition* is evaluated. If *termination condition* is `True`, loop exit occurs and the next program statement is executed. If *termination condition* is `False`, *loop body* is repeated.

■ Example 9.15

You can use the `repeat` statement in a loop that attempts to read a valid data item from the keyboard. Procedure `ReadBool` in Fig. 9.9 is an improved version of a procedure that reads a Boolean value. `ReadBool` uses a `repeat-until` loop to read in a letter (`T` or `F`) that represents a Boolean value (`True` or `False`). Compare this to procedure `ReadLnBool` (see Fig. 7.13) which needed a second Boolean parameter to signal whether a valid data character was read. This parameter is not needed here because loop exit cannot occur unless a valid character is read.

Figure 9.9 Procedure ReadBool with repeat-until Loop

```
procedure ReadBool (var BoolVal {output} : Boolean);
{
  Reads a Boolean value (represented by T or F) into BoolVal.
  Pre : None
  Post: BoolVal is set to True if T or t is read, and to False
        if F or f is read.
}
  var
    NextCh : Char;             {a data character}

begin {ReadBool}
  repeat
    {invariant:
       No prior value of NextCh was 'T','t','F','f'.
    }
    Write ('Enter T or F> ');
    Read (NextCh)
  until NextCh in ['T','t','F','f'];

  {assertion:  NextCh is valid}
  BoolVal := (NextCh = 'T') or (NextCh = 't')
end; {ReadBool}
```

Figure 9.9 shows the loop invariant for a `repeat-until` loop as a comment following the word `repeat`. A set value is used to simplify the `until` condition. ■

■ Example 9.16

To play the children's game Rock, Scissors, Paper, each player must enter the letter `R` (rock), `S` (scissors), or `P` (paper). In Fig. 9.10, if `PlayerNum` is `1`, the `repeat` statement in procedure `EnterMove` continues to display the prompt

```
Player number 1, enter your move>
```

and to read a data character until a valid letter is entered. ■

Figure 9.10 Procedure EnterMove for Rock, Scissors, Paper Game

```
procedure EnterMove (PlayerNum {input} : Integer;
                     var Move {output} : Char);
{
  Enters a valid move for the Rock, Scissors, Paper game.
  Pre : PlayerNum is the number (1 or 2) of the current player.
  Post: A valid move is returned through Move.
}
begin {EnterMove}
  repeat
    Write ('Player number ', PlayerNum :1);
    Write (', enter your move> ');
    ReadLn (Move)
  until Move in ['r', 'R', 's', 'S', 'p', 'P']
end; {EnterMove}
```

■ Example 9.17

A `repeat` statement is often used to control a *menu-driven program*, which prints a list of choices from which the program user selects a program operation. For example, procedure `DisplayMenu` might display the following menu for a statistics program.

```
1. Compute an average.
2. Compute a standard deviation.
3. Find the median.
4. Find the smallest and largest value.
5. Plot the data.
6. Exit the program.
```

The main control routine for such a program would follow the pseudocode

```
repeat
  Display the menu.
  Read the user's choice.
  Perform the user's choice.
until choice is exit
```

In the program fragment in Fig. 9.11, procedures `DisplayMenu`, `EnterInt` (see Fig. 7.18) and `DoChoice` are repeated until the value read into `Choice` is `ExitChoice` (a constant). Recall that `EnterInt` returns in its third parameter an integer value bounded by its first two parameters. ■

Figure 9.11 Main Control Loop for Menu-Driven Program

```
repeat
  DisplayMenu;
  EnterInt (1, ExitChoice, Choice);
  DoChoice (Choice)
until Choice = ExitChoice
```

Complementing a Condition

Figure 9.8 showed a simple Boolean expression (`Power < 1000`) and its complement (`Power >= 1000`). To switch from one loop form to the other, we need to know how to complement a condition.

We can complement a simple condition by changing the relational operator, as follows:

Operator	*Operator in Complement*
<	>=
<=	>
>	<=
>=	<
=	<>
<>	=

For example, the complement of `X <= Y` is `X > Y`. If the expression begins with `not`, remove the `not` (for example, the complement of `not Flag` is `Flag`).

DeMorgan's theorem explains how to complement a compound Boolean expression: write the complement of each individual Boolean expression and change each `and` to `or` and each `or` to `and`. Another way to complement a Boolean expression is to precede the entire expression with `not`. Table 9.2 shows the complements of some Boolean expressions.

SYNTAX DISPLAY

DeMorgan's Theorem

Form: `not (`$expression_1$` and `$expression_2$`) =`
`(not `$expression_1$`) or (not `$expression_2$`)`
`not (`$expression_1$` or `$expression_2$`) =`
`(not `$expression_1$`) and (not `$expression_2$`)`

In Table 9.2, `Flag` is a Boolean variable, `Next` is type `Char`, and `X`, `Y`, `M`, and `N` are type `Integer`. In the complement of the expression on the first line, the relational operators are reversed (for example, `>=` is changed to `<`) and the operator `and` is changed to `or`. The last two lines show two complements of the same expression. In the last line, the expression is complemented by simply

Table 9.2 Complements of Boolean Expressions

Expression	Complement
`(X >= 1) and (X <= 5)`	`(X < 1) or (X > 5)`
`(not Flag) or (X <= Y)`	`Flag and (X > Y)`
`Flag and (not Switch)`	`(not Flag) or Switch`
`(N mod M = 0) and Flag`	`(N mod M <> 0) or (not Flag)`
`Next in ['A','B','C']`	`not (Next in ['A','B','C'])`
`(Next = 'A') or (Next = 'a')`	`(Next <> 'A') and (Next <> 'a')`
`(Next = 'A') or (Next = 'a')`	`not((Next = 'A') or (Next = 'a'))`

inserting the Boolean operator `not` in front of the entire condition. Any Boolean expression can be complemented in this way.

Table 9.2 also shows how to form the complement of a test for set membership (third line from bottom). Programmers often make the common error of writing an expression of the form `Next not in [...]`, which is invalid because it contains two consecutive operators (`not in`).

Review of for, while, and repeat Loops

Pascal contains three kinds of loops: `for`, `while`, and `repeat`. Use the `for` loop as a counting loop, a loop for which the number of iterations required can be determined at the beginning of loop execution. The counter variable of a `for` loop must belong to an ordinal type.

The `while` and `repeat` loops are both conditional loops; their numbers of iterations depend on whether the value of a condition is `True` or `False`. The `while` loop is repeated as long as its loop repetition condition is `True`; the `repeat` loop is repeated until its loop-termination condition becomes `True`. It is relatively easy to rewrite a `repeat` loop as a `while` loop by complementing the condition. Not all `while` loops can be written as `repeat` loops, however, because a `repeat` loop always executes at least once, whereas a `while` loop body may be skipped entirely. For this reason, a `while` loop is preferred over a `repeat` loop, unless you are certain that at least one loop iteration must always be performed.

Figure 9.12 illustrates, with a simple counting loop, the three loop forms. (The dotted lines represent the loop body.) The `for` loop is the best to use in this situation. The `repeat` loop must be nested in an `if` statement to prevent it from being executed when `StartValue` is greater than `StopValue`. For this reason, the `repeat-until` version of a counting loop is least desirable.

Figure 9.12 Comparison of Three Loop Forms

```
for Count := StartValue to StopValue do
  begin
    ......

  end  {for}
```

```
Count := StartValue
while Count <= StopValue do
  begin
    ......

    Count := Succ(Count)
  end {while}
```

```
Count := StartValue;
if StartValue <= StopValue then
  repeat
    ......

    Count := Succ(Count)
  until Count > StopValue
```

In Fig. 9.12, `Count`, `StartValue`, and `StopValue` must be compatible ordinal types. The successor function (`Succ`) is used in both the `while` and the `repeat` loops to update the loop-control variable `Count`, although `Count := Count + 1` can be used if `Count` is type `Integer`. `Count` is equal to `Succ(StopValue)` after the `while` or `repeat` loops are executed; `Count` is equal to `StartValue` if those loops are skipped. If an enumerated type is used and `StopValue` is the largest value of this type, the value of `Succ(StopValue)` is undefined. This could lead to a run-time error in the `while` and `repeat` versions.

Exercises for Section 9.4

Self-Check

1. What are the complements of the following conditions?
   a. `(X <= Y) and (X <> 15)`
   b. `(X <= Y) and (X <> 15) or (Z = 7.5)`
   c. `(X <> 15) or (Z = 7.5) and (X <= Y)`
   d. `Flag or (X <> 15.7)`
   e. `not Flag and (NextCh in ['A'..'H'])`

2. What does the following `while` statement display? Rewrite it as a `for` statement and as a `repeat` statement.

```
Num := 10;
while Num <= 100 do
  begin
    WriteLn (Num);
    Num := Num + 10
  end {while}
```

3. What does the following `for` statement display? Rewrite it as a `while` statement and as a `repeat` statement.

```
for Ch := 'a' to 'z' do
  begin
    NumSpaces := Ord(Ch) - Ord('a') + 1;
```

```
    WriteLn ('*' :NumSpaces, Ch)
  end {for}
```

Programming

1. Write a procedure that reads the next character that is not a letter or a digit from a data line. Write two versions: one using `repeat` and one using `while`.

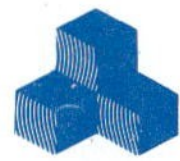

9.5 Nested Control Structures

This section examines nested control structures. You have seen examples of nested `if` statements in earlier programs. It is also possible to nest `case` statements, as shown next.

■ Example 9.18

Figure 9.10 shows a procedure that enters a valid move for the Rock, Scissors, Paper game. Assuming that the two players' moves are stored in `Move1` and `Move2`, procedure `CheckWin` (see Fig. 9.13) displays the result for one play of the game. The value of `Move1` determines which of the three inner `case` statements executes; the value of `Move2` selects the message that is displayed. For example, if `Move1` is `'r'` and `Move2` is `'p'`, the line in color executes and displays the message

```
Paper covers rock
```

which implies that player 2 (`Move2` is `'p'`) wins this time. ■

Figure 9.13 Procedure CheckWin

```
Procedure CheckWin (Move1, Move2 {input} : Char);
{
  Displays the result of one play of "Rock, Scissors, Paper".
  Pre : Move1 and Move2 contain valid moves.
  Post: Displays the result of the current play.
}
begin {CheckWin}
  case Move1 of
    'r', 'R' : {Check second player's move}
               case Move2 of
                 'r', 'R' : WriteLn ('Rock ties rock');
                 's', 'S' : WriteLn ('Rock crushes scissors');
                 'p', 'P' : WriteLn ('Paper covers rock')
               end; {case Move2}
    's', 'S' : {Check second player's move}
               case Move2 of
                 'r', 'R' : WriteLn ('Rock crushes scissors');
                 's', 'S' : WriteLn ('Scissors ties scissors');
                 'p', 'P' : WriteLn ('Scissors cuts paper')
               end; {case Move2}
    'p', 'P' : {Check second player's move}
               case Move2 of
```

```
                'r', 'R' : WriteLn ('Paper covers rock');
                's', 'S' : WriteLn ('Scissors cuts paper');
                'p', 'P' : WriteLn ('Paper ties paper')
              end {case Move2}
  end {case Move1}
end; {CheckWin}
```

Nested Loops

This section examines nested loops. You have seen examples of nested loops in earlier programs; however, the nesting was not apparent because the inner loop was contained in a procedure. Nested loops consist of an outer loop with one or more inner loops. Each time the outer loop is repeated, the inner loops are reentered, their loop control parameters reevaluated, and all required iterations performed.

■ Example 9.19

Figure 9.14 shows a sample run of a program with two nested `for` loops. The outer loop is repeated three times (for `I` equals `1`, `2`, and `3`). Each time the outer loop is repeated, the statement

```
WriteLn ('Outer' :5, I :7);
```

displays the string `'Outer'` and the value of `I` (the outer loop-control variable). Next, the inner loop is entered, and its loop control variable `J` is reset to `1`. The number of times the inner loop is repeated depends on the current value of `I`. Each time the inner loop is repeated, the statement

```
WriteLn ('Inner' :7, J :10)
```

displays the string `'Inner'` and the value of `J`.

Figure 9.14 Nested for Loop Program

Edit Window

```
program NestLoop;
{Illustrates a pair of nested for loops.}

  type
    SmallInt = 1..3;

  var
    I, J : SmallInt;             {loop control variables}

begin  {NestLoop}
  WriteLn ('I' :12, 'J' :5);     {Print heading}
  for I := 1 to 3 do
    begin  {outer loop}
      WriteLn ('Outer' :5, I :7);
      for J := 1 to I do
        WriteLn ('Inner' :7, J :10)
    end  {outer loop}
end. {NestLoop}
```

Output Window

```
            I    J
Outer       1
  Inner          1
Outer       2
  Inner          1
  Inner          2
Outer       3
  Inner          1
  Inner          2
  Inner          3
```

A compound statement executes each time the outer `for` loop is repeated. This statement displays the value of the outer loop-control variable and then executes the inner `for` loop. The body of the inner `for` loop is a single statement that displays the value of the inner loop-control variable. This statement executes `I` times, where `I` is the outer loop-control variable. ■

In Fig. 9.14, the outer loop-control variable `I` is the loop parameter that determines the number of repetitions of the inner loop. Although this is perfectly valid, you cannot use the same variable as the loop-control variable of both an outer and an inner `for` loop in the same nest.

■ Example 9.20

Program `Triangle` in Fig. 9.15 prints an isosceles triangle. The program contains an outer loop (loop-control variable `Row`) and two inner loops. Each time the outer loop is repeated, two inner loops are executed. The first inner loop prints the leading blank spaces; the second inner loop prints one or more asterisks.

Figure 9.15 Isosceles Triangle Program

Edit Window

```
program Triangle;

{Draws an isosceles triangle.}

  const
    NumLines = 5;                {number of rows in triangle}
    Blank = ' ';   Star = '*';   {output characters}

  var
    Row,                           {loop control for outer loop}
    LeadBlanks,              {loop control for first inner loop}
    CountStars : Integer;   {loop control for second inner loop}

begin {Triangle}
  for Row := 1 to NumLines do
    begin                                    {Draw each row}
      for LeadBlanks := NumLines - Row downto 1 do
        Write (Blank);                 {Print leading blanks}
```

```
      for CountStars := 1 to 2 * Row - 1 do
        Write (Star);                          {Print asterisks}
      WriteLn                                   {Terminate line}
    end  {for Row}
end. {Triangle}
```

Output Window

```
    *
   ***
  *****
 *******
*********
```

The outer loop is repeated five times; the number of repetitions performed by the inner loops is based on the value of Row. Table 9.3 lists the inner loop-control parameters for each value of Row. As shown in Table 9.3, four blanks and one asterisk are printed when Row is 1, three blanks and three asterisks are printed when Row is 2, and so on. When Row is 5, the first inner loop is skipped and nine (2 * 5 - 1) asterisks are printed. ■

Table 9.3 Inner Loop-Control Parameters

Row	LeadBlanks	CountStars	Effect
1	4 downto 1	1 to 1	Displays 4 blanks and 1 star.
2	3 downto 1	1 to 3	Displays 3 blanks and 3 stars.
3	2 downto 1	1 to 5	Displays 2 blanks and 5 stars.
4	1 downto 1	1 to 7	Displays 1 blank and 7 stars.
5	0 downto 1	1 to 9	Displays 0 blanks and 9 stars.

■ Example 9.21

The program in Fig. 9.16 prints the addition table for integer values between 0 and 9 (type SmallInt). For example, the table line beginning with the digit 9 shows the result of adding to 9 each of the digits 0 through 9. The initial for loop prints the table heading, which is the operator +, and the list of digits from 0 through 9.

The nested for loops are used to print the table body. The outer for loop (loop-control variable AddEnd1) first prints the current value of AddEnd1. In the inner for loop, each value of AddEnd2 (0 through 9) is added to AddEnd1 and the individual sums are printed. Each time the outer loop is repeated, 10 additions are performed; a total of 100 sums are printed. ■

Figure 9.16 Printing an Addition Table

Edit Window

```
program AddTable;
{Prints an addition table.}

  const
    Maxdigit = 9;                                {largest digit}
```

```
  type
    SmallInt = 0..Maxdigit;                    {range of digits}

  var
    AddEndl,                                   {first addend}
    AddEnd2   : SmallInt;                      {second addend}
    Sum       : Integer;                       {sum of addends}

begin  {AddTable}
  {Print the table heading.}
  Write ('+');
  for AddEnd2 := 0 to Maxdigit do
    Write (AddEnd2: 3);            {Print each digit in heading}
  WriteLn;                                     {Terminate heading}

  {Print the table body.}
  for AddEndl := 0 to Maxdigit do
    begin                          {Print each row of the table}
      Write (AddEndl :1);                {Identify first addend}
      for AddEnd2 := 0 to Maxdigit do
        begin
          Sum := AddEndl + AddEnd2;
          Write (Sum :3)                    {Print sum of addends}
        end;  {for AddEnd2}
      WriteLn                               {Terminate table row}
    end  {for AddEndl}
end. {AddTable}
```

Output Window

```
+  0  1  2  3  4  5  6  7  8  9
0  0  1  2  3  4  5  6  7  8  9
1  1  2  3  4  5  6  7  8  9 10
2  2  3  4  5  6  7  8  9 10 11
3  3  4  5  6  7  8  9 10 11 12
4  4  5  6  7  8  9 10 11 12 13
5  5  6  7  8  9 10 11 12 13 14
6  6  7  8  9 10 11 12 13 14 15
7  7  8  9 10 11 12 13 14 15 16
8  8  9 10 11 12 13 14 15 16 17
9  9 10 11 12 13 14 15 16 17 18
```

■ Example 9.22

The program in Fig. 9.17 contains a pair of nested `while` loops that can be used to read and echo-print the data on an existing data file. The inner loop reads a line of the data file and displays it on the screen. The outer loop is repeated as long as there are more lines to read.

Figure 9.17 Reading and Echoing a File

```
program EchoText;

{Reads and echos an existing data file.}

  var
    NextChar : Char;               {each character in the file}
    InData : Text;                 {input - the data file}
```

```
begin  {EchoText}
  Assign (InData, 'B:ECHO.DAT');
  Reset (InData);
  while not EOF(InData) do
    begin                           {Echo each line}
      while not EOLN(InData) do
        begin                       {Echo each character}
          Read (InData, NextChar);
          Write (NextChar)
        end;  {of line}
      ReadLn (InData);               {Skip <eoln> character}
      WriteLn                        {Terminate output line}
    end; {of file}
  Close (InData)
end. {EchoText}
```

It is interesting to contemplate the effect of omitting the `ReadLn` statement. Exit from the inner loop occurs when the `<eoln>` at the end of the first line is the next character to be read (`not EOLN` is `False`). The outer loop is repeated because there are more data on the file (`not EOF` is `True`); however, the inner loop is then skipped because the next character is still the `<eoln>`. An endless loop results because the outer loop is repeated again and the inner loop skipped again, *ad infinitum*. If your program reads lines of character data, remember to use the `ReadLn` statement to skip over each `<eoln>`. ■

Exercises for Section 9.5

Self-Check

1. What is displayed by the following program segments assuming `M` is 3 and `N` is 5?

   a.
   ```
   for I := 1 to N do
     begin
       for J := 1 to I do
         Write ('*');
       WriteLn
     end; {for I}
   ```

   b.
   ```
   for I := 1 to N do
     begin
       for J := 1 to M do
         Write ('*');
       WriteLn
     end; {for I}
   ```

2. Show the output printed by the following nested loops:

```
for I := 1 to 2 do
  begin
    WriteLn ('Outer' :5, I :5);
    for J := 1 to 3 do
      WriteLn ('Inner' :7, I :3, J :3);
    for K := 2 downto 1 do
      WriteLn ('Inner' :7, I :3, K :3)
  end; {for I}
```

Programming

1. Write a main program for playing the Rock, Scissors, Paper game. Use procedures `EnterMove` (see Fig. 9.10) and `CheckWin` (see Fig. 9.13).
2. Rewrite the nested `case` statement in `CheckWin` as a nest of multiple-alternative `if` statements.
3. Write a program that prints the multiplication table. Use separate procedures to print the table heading and the table body.
4. Write a nest of loops that causes the following output to be printed.

```
1
1 2
1 2 3
1 2 3 4
1 2 3
1 2
1
```

9.6 User-Defined Functions

Chapter 7 introduced some Pascal functions, such as `Abs`, `Sqrt`, and `Ord`. You can also declare your own functions in much the same way you declare procedures. Think of a function as a special type of procedure—a procedure that returns exactly one result. Generally, the parameters of a function are value parameters that cannot be modified by the function execution.

■ Example 9.23

Function `Cube` in Fig. 9.18 returns the cube of its argument. The function heading

```
function Cube (X : Real) : Real;
```

identifies the function name and its parameter list. The formal parameters for a function are generally input parameters, so we did not insert the comment `{input}` after `X`. A type identifier after the parameter list indicates the type of the result returned by the function. The result can be any previously defined simple data type, including `Real`, `Integer`, `Boolean`, `Char`, an enumerated type, or a subrange type. Turbo Pascal also allows strings and extended numeric types as function results.

Figure 9.18 Function Cube

```
function Cube (X : Real) : Real;
{
  Returns the cube of its argument.
  Pre : X is assigned a value.
  Post: X * X * X is returned.
}
begin {Cube}
  Cube := X * X * X
end; {Cube}
```

Unlike a procedure, which returns a result by modifying a variable parameter, a function result is defined by the assignment of a value to the function name. Within the function body, the statement

```
Cube := X * X * X
```

defines the function result.

A user-defined function is called in the same way as a standard Pascal function: by reference to it in an expression. If Y and Z are type Real variables in the main program, the assignment statement

```
Z := Cube(Y)
```

stores the value of Y cubed in Z. The *function designator* Cube(Y) calls function Cube with Y as its argument. The function result is assigned to Z. A function must always be called by including a function designator in an expression; a procedure call statement cannot be used to call a function. Notice that there is no space between the function name Cube and the parameter list (Y). ■

■ Example 9.24

Function Powers in Fig. 9.19 raises its first parameter, X, to the integer power indicated by its second parameter, N. This is accomplished by multiplying X by itself N times and accumulating the product in Product. The function designator Abs(N) ensures that the required number of multiplications are performed, even when N is negative.

Figure 9.19 Function Powers

```
function Powers (X : Real; N : Integer) : Real;
{
  Computes the value of X raised to the power N.
  Pre : X and N are assigned values.
  Post: Returns X raised to the power N.
}
  var
     Product : Real;                  {the accumulated product}
     Count   : Integer;               {loop control variable}

begin {Powers}
  if X = 0.0 then
    Powers := 0.0
  else
    begin {X <> 0.0}
      Product := 1.0;                    {Initialize Product}
      for Count := 1 to Abs(N) do
        Product := Product * X; {Multiply X by itself N times}

      {Define function result}
      if N >= 0 then
        Powers := Product          {function result when N >= 0}
      else
        Powers := 1.0 / Product   {function result when N < 0}
    end {X <> 0.0}
end; {Powers}
```

If X is zero, the function result is 0.0. If X is nonzero, the for loop in function Powers multiplies X by itself N times, saving the partial products in local variable Product. The for loop limit expression, Abs(N), ensures that the required number of multiplications are performed, even when N is negative.

After loop exit, the if statement defines the function result. If N is positive, the statement

```
Powers := Product
```

defines the function result as the last partial product; if N is negative, the statement

```
Powers := 1.0 / Product
```

defines the function result as a fraction. ■

Be careful when you use a function name inside its function declaration. Normally, a function name should not appear in an expression inside the function. For example, the assignment statement

```
Powers := Powers * X
```

would be illegal inside function Powers. Later, in Chapter 15, we remove this restriction and see that the expression in the assignment statement

```
Powers := Powers(X, N-1) * X
```

contains a valid *recursive call* to function Powers.

Suppose you want to calculate the amount of money that accumulates in your savings account over a certain period of time. The following assignment statement computes the actual amount, Amount, in the savings account after N days have passed. Deposit is the initial amount deposited at a daily interest rate of DailyRate.

```
Amount := Deposit * Powers(1 + DailyRate, N)
```

This statement is derived from the formula

$$amount = deposit \times (1 + daily\ rate)^N$$

The function designator

```
Powers(1 + DailyRate, N)
```

calls function Powers to raise the expression 1 + DailyRate to the power N. After execution of the function body, the function result replaces the function designator in the calling expression. That result is then multiplied by the value of Deposit, and the product is stored in Amount.

SYNTAX DISPLAY

Function Declaration

Form: function *fname* (*formal parameters*) : *result type*;

local declaration section

```
begin
  function body
end;
```

Example:

```
function Hypotenuse (A, B : Real) : Real;
begin {Hypotenuse}
  Hypotenuse := Sqrt(Sqr(A) + Sqr(B))
end; {Hypotenuse}
```

Interpretation: The function *fname* is declared. The list of *formal parameters* is enclosed in parentheses. The data type of the function result is indicated by the identifier *result type*. Any identifiers declared in the *local declaration section* are defined only during the execution of the function.

function body describes the data manipulation to be performed by the function. At least one statement that gives a value to *fname* must be executed each time the function is called. The last value given to *fname* is returned as the function result upon completion of *function body*. This value replaces the function reference in the expression that calls the function.

Note 1: The identifier *result type* must be the name of a standard data type (`Boolean`, `Integer`, `Real`, or `Char`), a previously defined enumerated type, a subrange type, or a pointer type (described in Chapter 17). Turbo Pascal allows strings and extended numeric types as result types, as well.

Note 2: If there are no parameters, omit the *formal parameters* and the parentheses.

SYNTAX DISPLAY

Function Designator

Form: *fname (actual parameters)*

Example: `Hypotenuse(X, Y)`

Interpretation: The function *fname* is executed, and its result replaces the function designator. During the function execution, the first actual parameter is associated with the first formal parameter, the second actual parameter with the second formal parameter, and so on.

Note: The *actual parameters* are separated by commas. The number of actual and formal parameters must be the same. Each actual parameter that is an expression is evaluated when *fname* is called; this value is assigned to the corresponding formal parameter. Each actual parameter must be assignment compatible with its corresponding formal parameter. If there are no formal parameters, omit the *actual parameters* and enclosing parentheses.

PROGRAM STYLE

Checking Special Cases

What happens in function `Powers` if the value of `X` or `N` happens to be zero? If `X` is zero, the statement

```
Powers := 0.0
```

executes and the function exit occurs. If N is zero, the statement

```
Product := 1.0;
```

executes and the for loop is skipped. In this case, the if statement following the for loop correctly assigns a value of 1.0 as the function result.

Often a procedure or function fails for special cases such as these. It is important to identify special cases and verify that they are handled properly.

Functions with Nonnumeric Results

A function can return a value belonging to any of the standard types, an enumerated type, a subrange type, an extended numeric type, a string, or a pointer type (discussed in Chapter 17). This section provides examples of functions with different result types.

■ Example 9.25

Function Cap (see Fig. 9.20) is similar to the Turbo Pascal function UpCase and returns a result that is type Char. If its argument is a lowercase letter, it returns the corresponding uppercase letter; otherwise, it returns its argument.

Figure 9.20 Function Cap

```
function Cap (Ch : Char) : Char;
{
  Returns the uppercase letter corresponding to Ch.
  Pre : Ch is defined.
  Post: If Ch is lowercase, returns the corresponding uppercase
        letter; otherwise, returns Ch.
}
begin {Cap}
  if Ch in ['a'..'z'] then
    Cap := Chr(Ord(Ch) - Ord('a') + Ord('A'))
  else
    Cap := Ch
end; {Cap}
```

If the argument passed to Cap is a lowercase letter, the assignment statement

```
Cap := Chr(Ord(Ch) - Ord('a') + Ord('A'))
```

executes. If Ch is 'c' and the letters are in consecutive order, then the argument of function Chr is 2 + Ord('A') and the value 'C' is assigned to Cap. If the ASCII code is used, we can write this statement as

```
Cap := Chr(Ord(Ch) - 32)
```

■ Example 9.26

Function DayConvert in Fig. 9.21 converts a number representing the day of the week (0 through 6) to a value of enumerated type Day (Sunday through Saturday). The case statement performs the conversion. In the event that DayNum is outside the range 0 through 6, the function returns to the calling expression without defining the function result. The fact that the function result is undefined may cause an execution error in standard Pascal but not in Turbo Pascal. ■

Figure 9.21 Function DayConvert

```
function DayConvert (DayNum : Integer) : Day;
{
  Converts a day number to a value of type Day.
  Pre : DayNum is assigned an integer value between 0 and 6.
  Post: Returns the corresponding value of type Day using
        0 for Sunday, 1 for Monday, etc.
}
begin {DayConvert}
  case DayNum of
    0 : DayConvert := Sunday;
    1 : DayConvert := Monday;
    2 : DayConvert := Tuesday;
    3 : DayConvert := Wednesday;
    4 : DayConvert := Thursday;
    5 : DayConvert := Friday;
    6 : DayConvert := Saturday
  end {case}
end; {DayConvert}
```

■ Example 9.27

Janice and Guy are arguing about the number of days that will be in the month of February in year 1995. They could use the function in Fig. 9.22 to determine the number of days in any month of the twentieth century. The data types Month, YearRange, and DayRange are defined as follows.

```
type
   Month = (January, February, March, April, May, June, July,
            August, September, October, November, December);
   YearRange = 1900..1999;
   DayRange = 1..31;
```

Figure 9.22 Function DaysInMonth

```
function DaysInMonth (CurMonth : Month;
                      ThisYear : YearRange) : DayRange;
{
  Determines the number of days in a given month and year.
  Pre : CurMonth and ThisYear are assigned values.
  Post: Returns an integer between 28 and 31 representing
        the number of days in month CurMonth for year ThisYear.
}
   var
     LeapYear : Boolean;        {Is ThisYear a leap year?}
```

```
begin {DaysInMonth}
  case CurMonth of
    April, June, September, November :
                 DaysInMonth := 30;
    January, March, May, July, August, October, December :
                 DaysInMonth := 31;
    February : begin
                 LeapYear := (ThisYear <> 1900) and
                             ((ThisYear mod 4) = 0);
                 if LeapYear then
                   DaysInMonth := 29
                 else
                   DaysInMonth := 28
               end {February}
  end {case}
end; {DaysInMonth}
```

If `CurMonth` is `February`, the Boolean variable `LeapYear` is set to indicate whether `ThisYear` is a leap year. The leap years in the twentieth century are 1904, 1908, 1912, and so on. If `ThisYear` is a leap year, `DaysInMonth` is set to `29`; otherwise, `DaysInMonth` is set to `28`. An example of a function designator that calls the function `DaysInMonth` is

```
DaysInMonth(May, 1942)
```

The value returned is `31`. ■

■ Example 9.28

Boolean functions are often used to make Boolean expressions more readable. The Boolean function `LowerCase` in Fig. 9.23 determines whether its argument is a lowercase letter (returns `True`) or not (returns `False`). Function `LowerCase` is referenced in the following loop, which reads a sequence of lowercase letters and stops reading after a character that is not a lowercase letter is read.

```
Read (Ch);
while LowerCase(Ch) do
  Read (Ch);
```

A similar function called `UpperCase` is left as an exercise at the end of this section. ■

Figure 9.23 Function LowerCase

```
function LowerCase (Ch : Char) : Boolean;
{
  Determines whether Ch is a lowercase letter.
  Pre : Ch is assigned a value.
  Post: Returns True if Ch is a lowercase letter;
        otherwise, returns False.
}
begin {LowerCase}
  LowerCase := Ch in ['a'..'z']
end; {LowerCase}
```

All the function examples in this section can transform one or more input values into a single output value. A variety of result types are illustrated: `Real`, `Char`, `Boolean`, enumerated type `Day`, and subrange type `DayRange`. Because a function should not return a result by modifying its parameters, all the function parameters were value parameters.

PROGRAM STYLE

When to Use a Function Instead of a Procedure

Some of the procedures that we wrote earlier can also be implemented as functions. Any procedure that returns a single result can be rewritten as a function.

A general rule of thumb is to always use a procedure when more than one result is returned. If a single result is returned, use a function when a pure computation is performed that requires no data beyond what is provided through the parameter list.

If input or output operations are also performed, use a procedure instead of a function, even if only a single result is returned. The reason is that a function call can be inserted in an expression, and it is generally not useful to read or display information as part of an expression evaluation.

Unlike a procedure, a function should not return a result by modifying a parameter. When a function changes a parameter's value during execution, a *side effect* is said to have occurred. For now, make sure you protect all function parameters from modification by making them value parameters. (In later chapters, you will see that variable parameters can be used under certain circumstances.)

Exercises for Section 9.6

Self-Check

1. What does the following function do? Does it have any side effects? Remove any side effects and correct the errors in the function declaration.

```
function MyTest (var X, Y : Real;
                 var Result : Real) : Real;
{
  Returns the sum of the square roots of X and Y.
  Pre : X and Y defined.
  Post: Returns square root of X + square root of Y.
}
begin {MyTest}
  X := Abs(X);
  Y := Abs(Y);
  Result := Sqrt(X) + Sqrt(Y)
end;  {MyTest}
```

2. Rewrite function `DayConvert` using Turbo Pascal's typecasting feature.

Programming

1. Write a function that computes the absolute difference of its two arguments, where the absolute difference of `A` and `B` is `A - B` if `A` is greater than `B` and `B - A` if `B` is greater than `A`.
2. Write a function that computes the tuition you owe for a specified number of credit hours at a university. Assume the charge per credit hour is $100 for up to twelve credit hours, and a flat fee of $1,200 is charged for twelve to sixteen credit hours. An additional fee of $100 is charged for each credit hour over sixteen.
3. Function `Powers` in Fig. 9.19 works perfectly well for an integer exponent; however, the exponent cannot be type `Real`. Write a new function that will handle type `Real` exponents. Hint: Use the `Ln` and `Exp` functions of Pascal.
4. Write a program that uses function `Powers` to compute and print a table showing the powers of 2.
5. Write function `UpperCase`.
6. Rewrite function `Cap` using function `LowerCase`.

9.7 Problem Solving Illustrated

This problem illustrates most of the concepts discussed in the last two chapters. The problem involves writing a file of payroll checks where the amount of each check is written in words.

Case Study: Writing a File of Payroll Checks

Problem

In the last chapter, we implemented a program that created a payroll file consisting of an employee's name and salary amount on consecutive lines of the file. Now, we will consider how to implement a program that processes this file, writing a new file of checks for each employee. For instance, if the first employee's name is Sam Johnson and his salary is $35.67, the lines

```
PAY TO THE ORDER OF: Sam Johnson
thirty-five dollars and sixty-seven cents       $35.67
```

should be written to the output file.

Design Overview

When you write a check, you indicate the amount in both figures and words. As part of a check writing program, we would need a procedure, `WriteWords`, that writes a check amount in words. Our program will read each employee's name and salary amount from file `Payroll` and write a check for each employee to an output file.

Data Requirements

Problem Inputs

The employee data file (`Payroll : Text`)
Each employee's name
Each employee's salary (`Salary : Real`)

Problem Outputs

A file of checks, one for each employee (`Checks : Text`)

Initial Algorithm

1. `while` there are more employees `do`
   `begin`
   2. Copy the next employee's name from file `Payroll` to file `Checks`.
   3. Write the next employee's salary in words.
   4. Write the next employee's salary.

   `end`

Coding the Main Program

We can use procedure `CopyLine` in Fig. 8.18 to perform step 2, and procedure `WriteWords` to perform step 3. The main program is shown in Fig. 9.24. Because we are reading and writing from text files, each call to an input/output procedure has a file name as its first parameter. The main program displays a message on the screen when it finishes writing file `Checks`. We will discuss unit `WriteDigits` later.

Figure 9.24 Check Writing Program

Edit Window

```
program WriteChecks;

{Writes a check for each employee to file Checks.}

uses WriteDigits;

  var
    Salary : Real;              {input - current salary}
    Payroll,                    {input - file of employees}
    Checks   : Text;            {output - file of checks}

  {Insert procedures WriteWords and CopyLine (see Fig. 8.18)}

  {$I WriteWords.PAS}
  {$I CopyLine.PAS}

begin {WriteChecks}
  {Prepare text files.}
  Assign (Payroll, 'PAYROLL.DAT');
  Assign (Checks, 'CHECKS.DAT');
```

```
  Reset (Payroll);
  Rewrite (Checks);

  {Write each employee name and check amount to file Checks.}
  while not EOF(Payroll) do
    begin
      Write (Checks, 'PAY TO THE ORDER OF: ');
      CopyLine (Payroll, Checks);                    {Write name}
      WriteLn (Checks);
      ReadLn (Payroll, Salary);

      WriteWords (Checks, Salary);        {Write amount in words}
      WriteLn (Checks, '     $', Salary :4:2);
      WriteLn (Checks); WriteLn (Checks)             {Skip lines}
    end;  {while}

  Close (Payroll);
  Close (Checks);
  WriteLn (Output, 'File of checks completed.')
end. {WriteChecks}
```

Output Window

```
File of checks completed.
```

Procedure WriteWords

Next we focus on procedure `WriteWords`, which writes a check amount in words. Some examples of the desired procedure output follow.

Amount	*Amount in Words*
43.55	forty-three dollars and fifty-five cents
62.05	sixty-two dollars and five cents
15.20	fifteen dollars and twenty cents
0.95	zero dollars and ninety-five cents
35.00	thirty-five dollars and zero cents

`WriteWords` must separate the check amount into two integers, `Dollars` and `Cents`. Once this is done, `Dollars` can be written, followed by the string `' dollars and '`, the value of `Cents`, and the string `' cents'`. For the sake of simplicity, we restrict the check writing procedure to amounts less than $100.

Data Requirements for WriteWords

Procedure Inputs

The output file name (`Checks : Text`)

Check amount as a real number (`Amount : Real`)

Procedure Outputs

Description of check amount in words

Figure 9.25 Structure Chart for Procedure WriteWords

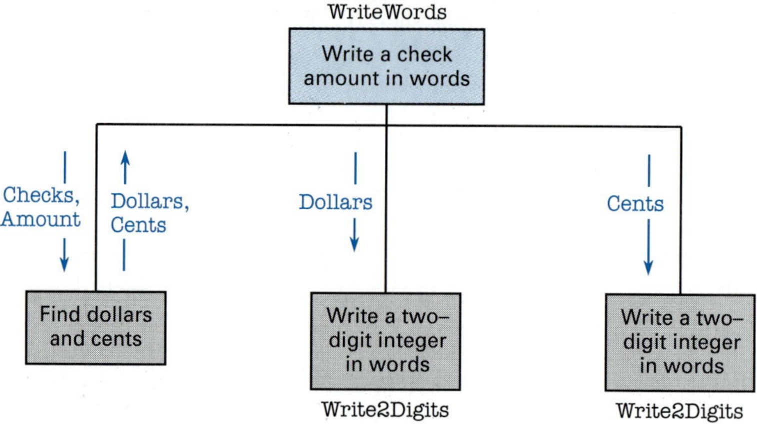

Local Variables for WriteWords
Dollar amount (`Dollars : 0..99`)
Number of cents (`Cents : 0..99`)
Total check amount in pennies (`CheckPennies : Integer`)

Algorithm for WriteWords

```
1. if check amount is invalid then
      2. Print an error message
   else
     begin
       3. Separate check amount into Dollars and Cents.
       4. Write Dollars in words.
       5. Write ' dollars and '.
       6. Write Cents in words.
       7. Write ' cents'.
     end
```

Coding Procedure WriteWords

The structure chart for procedure `WriteWords` is shown in Fig. 9.25. Procedure `Write2Digits` is called twice: first to write the value of `Dollars` in words (step 4), then to write the value of `Cents` in words (step 6). Because the operation of writing a two-digit number in words is fairly general and may be needed by other programs that we develop, we include procedure `Write2Digits` in library unit `WriteDigits`. For reasons that will become clear, we also need to insert procedure `Write1Digit` (a procedure that writes a single-digit number in words) in unit `WriteDigits`. Figure 9.26 shows procedure `WriteWords`.

Figure 9.26 Procedure WriteWords

```
procedure WriteWords (var Checks {input} : Text;
                      Amount {input} : Real);
{
  Writes a check amount in words to file Checks.
  Pre  : Amount is assigned a value between 0.0 and 99.99.
  Post : Writes the value of Check in words.
  Calls: Write2Digits in WriteDigits
}
  const
    MaxInteger = 99;         {Maximum dollar value of check}
    CentsPerDollar = 100;    {Number of cents in a dollar}

  type
    SmallInt = 0..MaxInteger;     {range of check amount}

  var
    Dollars,                      {the dollar amount}
    Cents     : SmallInt;         {the cents amount}
    CheckPennies : Integer;       {total check in pennies}

begin {WriteWords}
  if (Amount <= 0.0) or (Trunc(Amount) > MaxInteger) then
    WriteLn (Output, 'Check amount ', Amount, ' is invalid.')
  else
    begin {valid amount}
      CheckPennies := Round(CentsPerDollar * Amount);
      Dollars := CheckPennies div CentsPerDollar;
      Cents := CheckPennies mod CentsPerDollar;
      Write2Digits (Checks, Dollars);     {Write dollar amount}
      Write (Checks, ' dollars and ');
      Write2Digits (Checks, Cents);       {Write cents amount}
      Write (Checks, ' cents')
    end {valid amount}
end; {WriteWords}
```

WriteWords displays an error message on the screen if the check amount is invalid. Otherwise, the assignment statements

```
CheckPennies := Round(CentsPerDollar * Amount);
Dollars := CheckPennies div CentsPerDollar;
Cents := CheckPennies mod CentsPerDollar;
```

determine the value of Dollars and Cents (for instance, if Amount is 95.63 then CheckPennies is 9563, Dollars is 95, and Cents is 63).

Coding Unit WriteDigits

Procedure Write2Digits writes in words an integer value less than 100. Its parameter value is separated into a tens digit (stored in Tens) and a units digit (stored in `Units`). Once this separation is performed, the two digits are written in words. The data requirements and algorithm for `Write2Digits` follow.

Procedure Inputs
The output file name (`OutFile : Text`)
A number less than 100 (`TwoDigitNum : Integer`)

Procedure Outputs
A two-digit integer written in words

Local Variables for Write2Digits
The tens digit (`Tens : 0..9`)
The units digit (`Units : 0..9`)

Algorithm for Write2Digits

1. Separate `TwoDigitNum` into `Tens` and `Units` digits.
2. Write `Tens` digit and `Units` digit in words.

Step 2 of `Write2Digits` must be able to write integers that are less than `10` (`Tens` is `0`), in the teens (`Tens` is `1`), and above the teens (`Tens >= 2`). If `Tens` is `0`, only the `Units` digit is written. If `Tens` is `1`, then the string for a number between `10` (`'ten'`) and `19` (`'nineteen'`) is written. If `Tens` is between `2` and `9`, then a string (`'twenty'` through `'ninety'`) representing the `Tens` digit is written, followed by a string for the `Units` digit, provided the latter is not `0`. The refinement of step 2 follows.

Refinement of Step 2 of Write2Digits

```
2.1    case Tens of
          0 : Write the Units digit
          1 : Select and write a string based on the Units digit
          2 : Write 'twenty' and a nonzero Units digit
          3 : Write 'thirty' and a nonzero Units digit
          4 : Write 'forty' and a nonzero Units digit
          5 : Write 'fifty' and a nonzero Units digit
          8 : Write 'eighty' and a nonzero Units digit
          6, 7, 9 : Write the Tens digit followed by 'ty'
                    and a non-zero Units digit
       end
```

The preceding case alternatives are similar for values of `Tens` (the case selector) between `2` and `8`. After a string is written, procedure `Write1Digit` is called to write the value of `Units`. If `Tens` is `6`, `7`, or `9`, procedure `Write1Digit` is called once to write the value of `Tens` and a second time to write the value of `Units`. If `Tens` is `0`, `Write1Digit` is called to display the value of `Units` only. Finally, if `Tens` is `1`, a second `case` statement with selector `Units` is needed to determine which of the strings `'ten'`, `'eleven'`, `'twelve'`, and so on, is written. This case statement is shown in the code for procedure Write2Digits (see Fig. 9.27).

Figure 9.27 Unit WriteDigits

```
unit WriteDigits;
{
 Procedures for writing two-digit and
 one-digit integers in words
}
interface

  procedure Write1Digit (var OutFile {input} : Text;
                         InDigit {input} : Integer);

  procedure Write2Digits (var OutFile {input} : Text;
                          TwoDigitNum {input} : Integer);

implementation

  procedure Write1Digit (var OutFile {input} : Text;
                         InDigit {input} : Integer);
  {
    Writes InDigit in words to OutFile.
    Pre : InDigit is assigned a value between 0 and 9.
    Post: InDigit is written in words.
  }
  begin {Write1Digit}
    if not (InDigit in [0..9]) then
      WriteLn (Output, 'error in Write1Digit parameter')
    else
      case InDigit of
        0 : Write (OutFile, 'zero');
        1 : Write (OutFile, 'one');
        2 : Write (OutFile, 'two');
        3 : Write (OutFile, 'three');
        4 : Write (OutFile, 'four');
        5 : Write (OutFile, 'five');
        6 : Write (OutFile, 'six');
        7 : Write (OutFile, 'seven');
        8 : Write (OutFile, 'eight');
        9 : Write (OutFile, 'nine')
      end {case}
  end; {Write1Digit}


  procedure Write2Digits (var OutFile {input} : Text;
                          TwoDigitNum {input} : Integer);
  {
    Writes its two-digit parameter in words to OutFile.
      Pre  : TwoDigitNum is assigned a value between 0 and 99.
      Post : TwoDigitNum is written in words.
      Calls: Write1Digit
    }
      type
        Digit = 0..9;
```

```
  var
    Tens,                                             {tens digit}
    Units : Digit;                                    {units digit}


  procedure CalllDigit (var OutFile {input} : Text;
                        Units {input} : Digit);
  {
    Writes a dash to file OutFile and calls procedure
    WritelDigit if Units is not zero.
    Pre : Units is assigned a value between 0 and 9.
    Post: Calls WritelDigit if Units is not 0.
  }
  begin {CalllDigit}
    if Units <> 0 then
      begin
        Write (OutFile, '-');
        WritelDigit (OutFile, Units)
      end {if}
  end; {CalllDigit}


begin  {Write2Digits}
  Tens := TwoDigitNum div 10;
  Units := TwoDigitNum mod 10;
  if not (TwoDigitNum in [0..99]) then
    WriteLn (Output, 'invalid parameter for Write2Digits')
  else
    case Tens of
      0 : WritelDigit (OutFile, Units);   {Write units digit only}
      1 : case Units of              {Write the special case teens}
            0 : Write (OutFile, 'ten');
            1 : Write (OutFile, 'eleven');
            2 : Write (OutFile, 'twelve');
            3 : Write (OutFile, 'thirteen');
            5 : Write (OutFile, 'fifteen');
            8 : Write (OutFile, 'eighteen');
            4, 6, 7, 9 : begin {Write ...teen}
                           WritelDigit (OutFile, Units);
                           Write (OutFile, 'teen')
                         end {Write ...teen}
          end; {case Units}
      2 : begin                                  {Write twenty ... }
            Write (OutFile, 'twenty');
            CalllDigit (OutFile, Units)
          end; {2}
      3 : begin                                  {Write thirty ... }
            Write (OutFile, 'thirty');
            CalllDigit (OutFile, Units)
          end; {3}
      4 : begin                                  {Write forty ... }
            Write (OutFile, 'forty');
            CalllDigit (OutFile, Units)
          end; {4}
      5 : begin                                  {Write fifty ... }
            Write (OutFile, 'fifty');
            CalllDigit (OutFile, Units)
          end; {5}
      8 : begin                                  {Write eighty ... }
            Write (OutFile, 'eighty');
```

```
            CalllDigit (OutFile, Units)
          end; {8}
      6, 7, 9 : begin                             {Write ...ty ...}
                  WritelDigit (OutFile, Tens);
                  Write (OutFile, 'ty');
                  CalllDigit (OutFile, Units)
                end {6, 7, 9}
    end  {case Tens}
  end;  {Write2Digits}
end.  {WriteDigits}
```

Write2Digits introduces a new procedure, CalllDigit, whose purpose is to "screen" calls to WritelDigit. CalllDigit is called when Tens is between 2 and 9; CalllDigit calls WritelDigit to write the value of Units only if Units is nonzero. The reason for this is so that a number such as 80 (Tens is 8, Units is 0) will be written as eighty rather than as eighty-zero.

The subrange Digit is declared in procedure Write2Digits and is used as the data type of the formal parameter for CalllDigit. A common error in using a programmer-defined data type is specifying the type declaration in the procedure heading. The procedure heading

```
procedure CalllDigit (var OutFile {input} : Text;
                      Units {input} : 0..9);
```

causes a syntax error because the type of parameter Units must be an identifier, not a subrange.

PROGRAM STYLE

Validating Case Selectors

In procedure Write2Digits, an if statement tests the value of the case selector Tens before the case statement is executed. In a similar manner, an if statement in procedure WritelDigit tests the value of the case selector InDigit. Both conditions involve a test for membership in the set [0..9].

Each if statement displays an error message on the screen if the case selector value is outside its expected range. Although this is unlikely, it is a good idea to include these tests as a precaution, particularly since both procedures are candidates for inclusion in a procedure library.

Exercises for Section 9.7

Self-Check

1. Show by example that the assignment statements in Write2Digits that assign values to Tens and Units are correct. Do the same for the assignment statements in WriteWords that assign values to Dollars and Cents.

Programming

1. A salary amount of $1.01 is written as `one dollars and one cents` to file `Checks`. How could this error be fixed? What procedure block should be changed?

9.8 Common Programming Errors

When you use a `case` statement, make sure the `case` selector and labels are of the same ordinal type. Remember that only lists of ordinal values can be used as `case` labels and that no value can appear in more than one `case` label. Be sure to insert the `end {case}`; there is no matching `begin`.

A `repeat-until` loop always executes at least once. Use a `repeat` statement only if you are certain that there is no possibility of zero loop iterations; otherwise, use a `while` loop.

Be sure to trace each nest of loops carefully, checking all loop parameter values. A loop-control variable for a `for` statement should not be changed inside the loop body. It is illegal to use the same loop-control variable for two `for` statements within the same nest.

When you are using functions, make sure that the function result is defined for all valid parameter values. Do not use the function name in an expression inside the function body. Avoid using variable parameters and returning a result by modifying a function parameter (a function side effect).

Chapter Review

This chapter introduced the `case` statement as a convenient means of implementing decisions with several alternatives. You saw how to use the `case` statement to implement decisions that are based on the value of a variable or a simple expression (the `case` selector). The `case` selector must have an ordinal data type.

We completed our discussion of loops by introducing the `for` statement (`for` loop) and `repeat` statement (`repeat-until` loop). We used the `for` statement to implement counting loops in which the exact number of loop iterations could be determined before loop repetition begins. The counter variable may increase in value (`to` form) or decrease in value (`downto` form) after each loop iteration.

We used the `repeat` statement to implement conditional loops. With the `repeat` statement, you can implement a loop that will always execute at least one time.

We also analyzed nested loops. Every inner loop of a nest is reentered and executed to completion each time an outer loop is repeated.

We used functions to implement modules that return a single result. The parameters of a function should be value parameters. Usually, you define a function result by assigning a value to the function name inside the function body. You call a function by using it in an expression in the calling program; the function name and actual parameters (function arguments) are inserted directly in the expression.

New Pascal Constructs

Table 9.4 shows the new Pascal constructs introduced in this chapter.

Table 9.4 Summary of New Pascal Constructs

Construct	Effect

case Statement
`case NextCh of`
`  'A', 'a' : WriteLn ('Excellent');`
`  'B', 'b' : WriteLn ('Good');`
`  'C', 'c' : WriteLn ('O.K.');`
`  'D', 'd', 'F', 'f' :`
`            begin`
`              WriteLn ('Poor');`
`              Probation (IDNum)`
`            end`
`else`
`  WriteLn ('Bad Value')`
`end; {case}`
	Prints one of five messages based on the value of `NextCh` (type `Char`). If `NextCh` is `'D'`, `'d'` or `'F'`, `'f'`, procedure `Probation` is also called with `IDNum` as an actual parameter; A `Bad Value` message is printed for all other values of `NextCh`.

Set Values and Operator in
`if CurMonth in [Dec, Jan, Feb] then`
`  WriteLn ('Winter storm watch')`
	The message `'Winter storm watch'` is printed if the value of `CurMonth` is one of the three constants listed. `CurMonth` and the constants must belong to the same enumerated data type.

for Statement
`for CurMonth := Mar to Jul do`
`  begin`
`    Read (MonthSales);`
`    YearSales := YearSales +`
`                 MonthSales`
`  end; {for}`
	The loop body is repeated for each value of `CurMonth` from `Mar` through `Jul`, inclusive. For each month, the value of `MonthSales` is read and added to `YearSales`.

Repeat Statement
`repeat`
`  Write ('Enter a digit >');`
`  ReadLn (Ch)`
`until ('0' <= Ch) and (Ch <= '9');`
	The user is prompted to press a single numeric key on the keyboard, until a valid key is pressed.

Declaring a Function
`function Sign (X : Real) : Char;`
`begin {Sign}`
`  if X > 0.0 then`
`    Sign := '+'`
`  else`
`    Sign := '-'`
`end; {Sign}`
	Returns a character value that indicates the sign (`'+'` or `'-'`) of its type `Real` argument.

✓ Quick-Check Exercises

1. A case statement is often used instead of ____________.
2. Which of the following can appear in a case label? In a set value?

   a subrange of integers, a list of integers, a real value, a Boolean value, a type Char value, a string value, an enumerated type value

3. Explain how to use a set value to guard a case statement and prevent a case value out of range error in standard Pascal.
4. Which loop form always executes at least one time? Which loop form is the most general? Which loop form should you use to implement a counting loop? Which loop form should you use in a menu-driven program?
5. How many times does the following Write statement execute? How many times does the WriteLn execute? What is the last value displayed?

```
for I := 1 to 10 do
  begin
    for J := 1 to I do
      Write (I * J);
    WriteLn
  end
```

6. How many times does the following Write statement execute? How many times does the WriteLn execute? What is the last value displayed?

```
for I := 1 to 10 do
  begin
    for J := 1 to 5 do
      Write (I * J);
    WriteLn
  end
```

7. How does a function return its value? How many values should be returned by a user-defined function?
8. A ____________ occurs when a function assigns a value to one of its variable parameters.
9. The parameters of a function generally should be ____________ parameters.

Answers to Quick-Check Exercises

1. Nested if statements or a multiple-alternative if statement
2. In a case label: a list of integers, a subrange of integers, a Boolean value, a Char value, an enumerated type value. In a set value: a list of integers, a Boolean value, a Char value, an enumerated type value, and a small subrange of integers.
3. A set value can be used in an if condition that permits the case statement to be executed only when the case selector matches one of the elements in the set. All case label values should appear in the set value.
4. repeat, while, for, repeat
5. 1 + 2 + 3 + . . . + 9 + 10, or 55, for Write, 10 for WriteLn, last value displayed is 100
6. 50 for Write, 10 for WriteLn, last value displayed is 50
7. Returns one value by assigning a value to the function name, one
8. side effect
9. value

Review Questions

1. When should a nested `if` statement be used instead of a `case` statement?
2. Write a `case` statement to select an operation based on `Inventory`. Increment `TotalPaper` by `PaperOrder` if `Inventory` is `'B'` or `'C'`; increment `TotalRibbon` by `RibbonOrder` if `Inventory` is `'L'`, `'T'`, or `'D'`; increment `TotalLabel` by `LabelOrder` if `Inventory` is `'A'` or `'X'`. Do not take any action if `Inventory` is `'M'`.
3. Write the `for` statement that displays the character values of the ordinal numbers 32 through 126, inclusive. Use `OrdNum` as the loop control variable. What is the value of `OrdNum`, after completion of the loop?
4. Write a `repeat` statement that will accept only a valid response to a menu. A valid response would be any of the following: `'A'`, `'a'` or `'B'`, `'b'`.
5. Write the complement of each of the following Boolean expressions

```
Flag and (I < 20)
(Ord(NextCh) = 0) or EOLN(InData)
not (Vowel and Consonant)
(Round(N) = N) or (N < Sqr(M))
```

6. Write an `if` statement that tests to see if `Today` is a working day. Print either the message `'Workday'` or `'Weekend'`. Assume that `Today` is type `Day`, an enumerated type that has the days of the week as its values.
7. Write an equivalent `case` statement for exercise 6.
8. Write a `for` statement that runs from `'Z'` to `'A'` and prints only the consonants. Test each character against the set of vowels.
9. Write a nested loop that prints the first six letters of the alphabet on a line, the next five letters on the next line, the next four letters on the next line, and so on, down to and including one letter (the letter U) on the last line. Use either uppercase or lowercase letters.
10. Write a function called `FindNet` that computes a worker's weekly net pay given `Hours` (an `Integer`) and `Rate` (a `Real`) as input parameters. Pay time-and-a-half for any hours worked over forty and subtract 30 percent for taxes. For thirty or more hours but less than forty, subtract 20 percent for taxes. For twenty or more hours but less than thirty, subtract 10 percent for taxes. Do not deduct any taxes for less than twenty hours. Be sure to check for a valid number of hours (`0 <= Hours <= 168`).

Programming Projects

1. Write a program that reads in a positive real number and finds and prints the number of digits to the left of the decimal point. Hint: Find the whole part and repeatedly divide by 10 until the number becomes less than 1. Test the program with the following data:

```
4703.62     0.01     0.47     5764     10.12     40000
```

2. Write a program that finds the largest value, the smallest value, and the sum of the input data. After all data are processed, call two functions to find the average value and the range of values in the data collection. Print the results.
3. Each year the state legislature rates the productivity of the faculty of each of the state-supported colleges and universities. The rating is based on reports submitted by the faculty members indicating the average number of hours worked per week

during the school year. Each faculty member is ranked, and the university receives an overall rank.

The faculty productivity ranks are computed as follows:

a. Faculty members averaging over fifty-five hours per week are considered highly productive.
b. Faculty members averaging between thirty-five and fifty-five hours a week, inclusive, are considered satisfactory.
c. Faculty members averaging fewer than thirty-five hours a week are considered overpaid.

The productivity rating of each school is determined by first computing the faculty average for the school, then comparing the faculty average to the category ranges.

Write a program to rank the following faculty:

Name	*Hours*
Herm	63
Flo	37
Jake	20
Maureen	55
Saul	72
Tony	40
Al	12

Your program should print a three-column table giving the name, hours, and productivity rank of each faculty member. It should also compute and print the school's overall productivity ranking.

4. Write a savings account transaction program that will process the following set of data:

```
Adam      1054.37 ┐
W           25.00 │
D          243.35 ├ group 1
W          254.55 │
Z                 ┘

Eve       2008.24 ┐
W           15.55 ├ group 2
Z                 ┘

Mary       128.24 ┐
W           62.48 │
D           13.42 ├ group 3
W           84.60 │
Z                 ┘

Sam          7.77 ┐
Z                 ┘ group 4

Joe         15.27 ┐
W           16.12 │
D           10.00 ├ group 5
Z                 ┘

Beth     12900.00 ┐
D         9270.00 ├ group 6
Z                 ┘
```

The first record in each group (header) gives the name for an account and the starting balance in the account. All subsequent records show the amount of each withdrawal (W) and deposit (D) made for that account, followed by a sentinel value (Z). Print out the final balance for each account processed. If a balance is negative, print an appropriate message and take whatever corrective steps you deem proper. If there are no transactions for an account, print a message so indicating.

5. Write a program to print a table of the following form.

```
Home Loan Mortgage Interest Payments per $1000.00
Rate (Percent)      Duration (Years)     Monthly Payment      Total Payment
10.00               20                   _______________      _____________
10.00               25                   _______________      _____________
10.00               30                   _______________      _____________
10.25               20                   _______________      _____________
```

where the formula for monthly payment and total payment is given in programming project 7 of Chapter 7.

Your program should print a table that shows the monthly and total payments on a loan of \$1,000 for interest rates from 10% to 14% with increments of 0.25%. The loan duration should be 20, 25, and 30 years. Your program should contain nested loops, some of which may be inside separate procedures, depending on your solution. Make sure you remove all redundant computations from inside your loops.

6. Write a program to read in a string of characters that represent a Roman numeral and then convert it to Arabic form (an integer). The character values for Roman numerals are as follows:

M	1000
D	500
C	100
L	50
X	10
V	5
I	1

Test your program on the following data: LXXXVII (87), CCXIX (219), MCCCLIV (1354), MMDCLXXIII (2673), MCDLXXVI (1476).

7. Newton's method for finding roots of an equation

$$f(x) = 0$$

starts with an initial guess, x_0, and then generates successive guesses $x_1, x_2, x_3, \ldots, x_n, x_{n+1}, \ldots$ using the iterative formula:

$$x_{n+1} = x_n - f(x_n)/f'(x_n)$$

where x_{n+1} is the new guess generated from the previous guess, x_n, and f' is a function that is the derivative of f.

Write a program that will find roots of equations using Newton's method. Your program should contain user-defined functions for both f and f'. The stopping criteria will be when successive guesses are very close, that is, when

$$|x_{n+1} - x_n| < \text{Epsilon}$$

and Epsilon is some small user-defined constant. For the function f use

$$f(x) = x^2 - 4$$

over the x interval [0, 20].

8. Generate a graph that indicates the rainfall for the city of Bedrock and that can be used to compare the average rainfall with the previous year's rainfall. Assume a maximum monthly rainfall of 15 inches. In addition, provide some summary statistics that will indicate (1) annual rainfall for last year, (2) average annual rainfall, and (3) the difference between the two. The input data will consist of twelve pairs of numbers. The first number in each pair will be the average rainfall for a month, and the second number will be what fell the previous year. The first data pair will represent January, the second February, and so forth. The output should resemble the following:

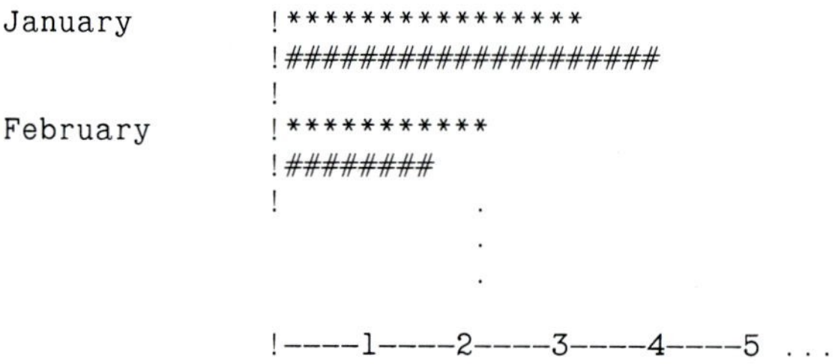

```
January         !****************
                !####################
                !
February        !***********
                !########
                !
                        .
                        .
                        .

                !----1----2----3----4----5 ...

* - average rainfall for a given month

# - previous year's rainfall for a given month
```

The data for the chart above begins with 3.2 4.0 (for January) 2.2 1.6 (for February).

9. Write a client program that uses procedure `GotoXY` from the `CRT` unit to plot two functions (`Y = F(X)` and `Y = G(X)`) on the same axes for the `X` interval `[ InitialX, FinalX ]`. The definitions for the functions (`F` and `G`) and the constants (`InitialX` and `FinalX`) should be imported from a Turbo Pascal unit. Use different symbols for the plots of `F` and `G`. Use a third plotting symbol to mark any points where the two functions intersect one another. Test your program using the functions

$$f(x) = 2 * x + 10$$
$$g(x) = 1.0 + x^2$$

over the interval `[-5, 5]`. You may find it desirable to scale the `X` and `Y` values (see Fig. 7.9) to allow more of the graph to fit on the screen (which can have at most 25 lines of 80 characters each).

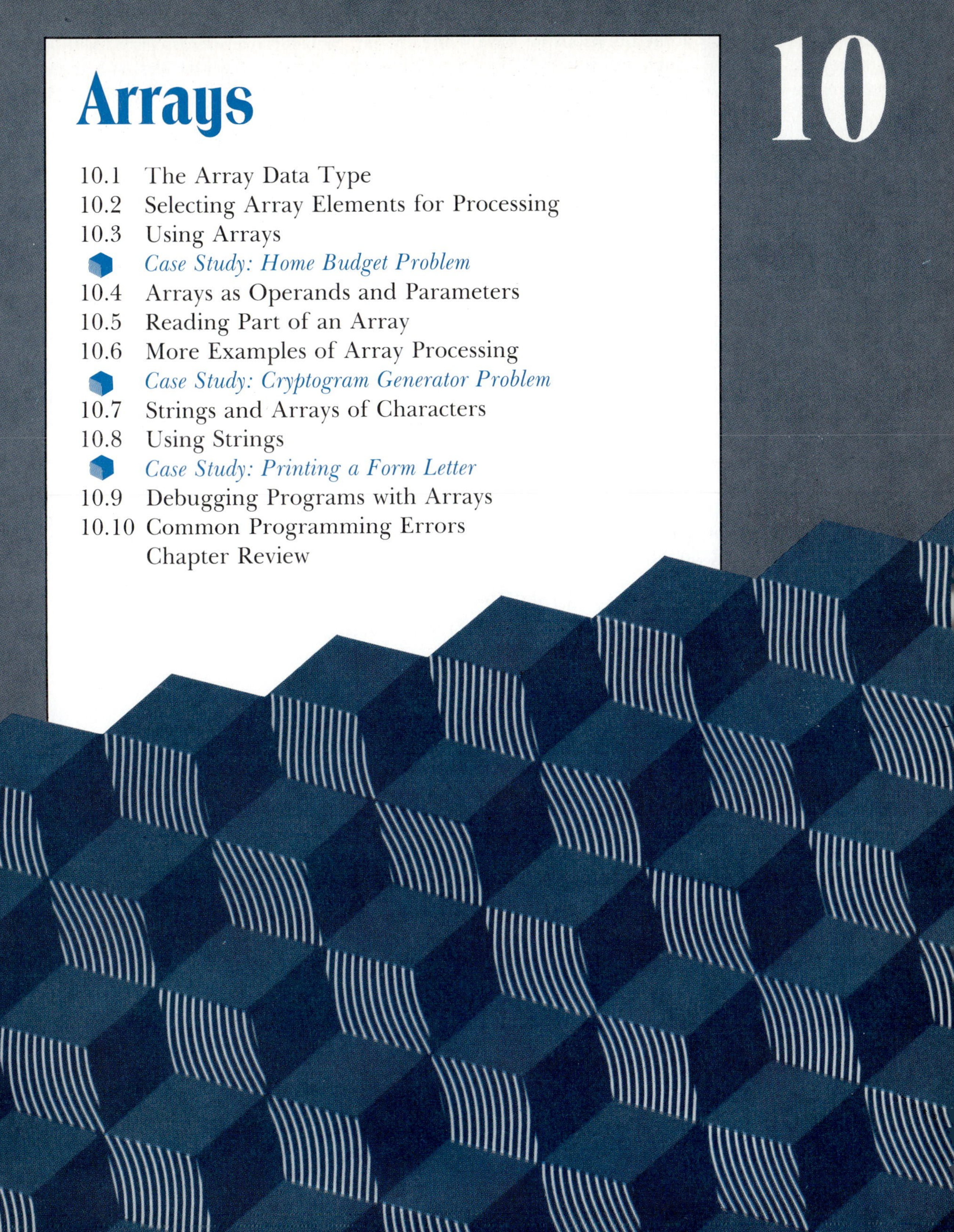

10 Arrays

In the programs we have written so far, each variable was associated with a single memory cell. These variables are called simple variables, and their data types are simple ones. The only exceptions were file variables, which were associated with a collection of characters stored on disk.

In this chapter, you will study *structured variables*, or data structures. A structured variable represents a grouping of related data items in main memory. The items in a structured variable can be processed individually, although some operations can be performed on the structure as a whole.

Pascal provides *type constructors*, which can be used to form new data types from simpler objects. The type constructor `array` is described in this chapter. The type constructors `record` and `set` are discussed in later chapters.

The *array* is a data structure in which we store a collection of data items of the same type (for example, all the exam scores for a class). By using an array, we can associate a single variable name (for example, `Scores`) with the entire collection of data. This association enables us to save the entire collection of data in main memory (one item per memory cell) and to reference individual items easily. To process an individual item, we specify the array name and indicate the array element being manipulated (for example, `Scores[3]` references the third item in the array `Scores`).

Because each score is saved in a separate cell in main memory, we can process the individual items more than once and in any order. In previous programs, we reused the same cell to store each exam score. Consequently, we could not access the third score after the fourth score was read.

The use of string variables makes it easier to store character strings in memory. String variables or strings are introduced for that purpose, and you will see how to read textual data into strings.

10.1 The Array Data Type

This section illustrates the basic operations that can be performed on an array. We begin by showing how to allocate memory space for an array in Pascal.

Array Type Declaration

Normally, we first describe the structure of an array in an *array type declaration*. Then we can allocate storage for one or more arrays of that type. The array type `RealArray`, declared next, is followed by the declaration of array `X` of type `RealArray`. The array type declaration uses subrange type `IndexRange`.

```
type
  IndexRange = 1..8;
  RealArray = array [IndexRange] of Real;

var
  X : RealArray;
```

Pascal associates eight memory cells with the name `X`. Each element of array `X` can contain a single real value. So a total of eight real values can be stored and referenced using the array name `X`.

Figure 10.1 The Eight Elements of the Array X

Array X

X[1]	X[2]	X[3]	X[4]	X[5]	X[6]	X[7]	X[8]
16.0	12.0	6.0	8.0	2.5	12.0	14.0	- 54.5
First element	Second element	Third element					Eighth element

To process the data stored in an array, we must be able to reference each individual element. The *array subscript* differentiates among elements of the same array. For example, if `X` is the array with eight elements, we can refer to the elements of array `X` as shown in Fig. 10.1.

The *subscripted variable* `X[1]` (read as "`X` sub `1`") references the first element of the array `X`, `X[2]` the second element, and `X[8]` the eighth element. The number enclosed in brackets is the array subscript. Later, you will see that the subscript can be an expression of any ordinal type.

■ Example 10.1

Let `X` be the array shown in Fig. 10.1. Some statements that manipulate this array are shown in Table 10.1.

Table 10.1 Statements that Manipulate Array X

Statement	Explanation
`WriteLn (X[1])`	Displays the value of `X[1]`, or `16.0`.
`X[4] := 25.0`	Stores the value `25.0` in `X[4]`.
`Sum := X[1] + X[2]`	Stores the sum of `X[1]` and `X[2]`, or `28.0`, in the variable `Sum`.
`Sum := Sum + X[3]`	Adds `X[3]` to `Sum`. The new `Sum` is `34.0`.
`X[4] := X[4] + 1.0`	Adds `1.0` to `X[4]`. The new `X[4]` is `26.0`.
`X[3] := X[1] + X[2]`	Stores the sum of `X[1]` and `X[2]` in `X[3]`. The new `X[3]` is `28.0`.

The contents of array `X` after execution of these statements are shown next. Notice that only `X[3]` and `X[4]` have changed. ■

Array X

X[1]	X[2]	X[3]	X[4]	X[5]	X[6]	X[7]	X[8]
16.0	12.0	28.0	26.0	2.5	12.0	14.0	- 54.5
First element	Second element	Third element					Eighth element

■ Example 10.2

The declaration section for a plant operations program is shown next. The type declaration declares two simple types, `EmpRange` and `Day`, and two array types, `EmpArray` and `DayArray`. Two arrays, `Vacation` and `PlantHours`, are declared in the variable declaration section.

```
const
  NumEmp = 10;                       {Number of employees}

type
  EmpRange = 1..NumEmp;              {subscript range}
  EmpArray = array [EmpRange] of Boolean;
  Day = (Sunday, Monday, Tuesday, Wednesday,
         Thursday, Friday, Saturday);
  DayArray = array [Day] of Real;

var
  Vacation : EmpArray;
  PlantHours : DayArray;
```

The array `Vacation` has ten elements (subscripts `1` through `NumEmp`); each element of array `Vacation` can store a Boolean value. The contents of this array could indicate which employees are on vacation (`Vacation[I]` is `True` if employee `I` is on vacation). If employees `1`, `3`, `5`, `7`, and `9` are on vacation, the array would have the values shown in Fig. 10.2.

The array `PlantHours` has seven elements (subscripts `Sunday` through `Saturday`). The array element `PlantHours[Sunday]` could indicate how many hours the plant was operating on Sunday of the past week. The array shown in Fig. 10.3 indicates that the plant was closed on the weekend and operated a single shift on Monday and Thursday, double shifts on Tuesday and Friday, and a triple shift on Wednesday. ■

It is possible to eliminate the declarations for the constant `NumEmp` and data types `EmpRange` and `EmpArray` and just declare the array `Vacation`, as shown next.

```
var
  Vacation : array [1..10] of Boolean;
```

Figure 10.2 Array Vacation

Vacation[1]	True
Vacation[2]	False
Vacation[3]	True
Vacation[4]	False
Vacation[5]	True
Vacation[6]	False
Vacation[7]	True
Vacation[8]	False
Vacation[9]	True
Vacation[10]	False

Figure 10.3 Array PlantHours

PlantHours[Sunday]	0.0
PlantHours[Monday]	8.0
PlantHours[Tuesday]	16.0
PlantHours[Wednesday]	24.0
PlantHours[Thursday]	8.0
PlantHours[Friday]	16.0
PlantHours[Saturday]	0.0

There are three advantages to the original set of declarations. First, it is easy to change the declared size of array `Vacation`. By simply redefining the constant `NumEmp`, we change the array size. Second, the data types `EmpArray` and `DayArray` can be used as type identifiers elsewhere in the program. And third, the constant `NumEmp` can be referenced in the program body.

Because a type identifier is not used in the revised declaration of array `Vacation`, its type is said to be *anonymous*. In general, you should avoid using anonymous types (unnamed types).

SYNTAX DISPLAY

Array Type Declaration

Form:
```
type
  array type = array [subscript type] of element type;
```

Example:
```
type
  IndexRange = 1..5;
  SmallArray = array [IndexRange] of Char;
```

Interpretation: The identifier *array type* describes a collection of array elements; each element can store an item of type *element type*. The *subscript type* can be either of the standard ordinal types `Boolean` or `Char`, an enumerated type, or a subrange type. There is one array element for each value in the *subscript type*.

The *element type* describes the type of each element in the array. All elements of an array are the same type.

Note 1: The standard types `Real` and `Integer` cannot be used as a *subscript type*; however, a subrange of the integers may be a *subscript type*.

Note 2: The *element type* can be any standard or user-defined type.

Note 1 in the preceding display states that the standard types `Integer` and `Real` cannot be used as subscript types. Type `Integer` is not allowed because an array of type `Integer` would have an excessive number of elements. Type `Real` is not allowed because it is not an ordinal type.

It is important to realize that an array type declaration does not require allocation of storage space in memory. The array type describes the structure of an array only. Only variables actually store information and require storage. Storage space is not allocated until a variable of this type is declared.

Abstract Array

We can summarize what we have discussed so far about arrays in the following specification for an abstract array.

Specification for Abstract Array

Structure: An array is a collection of elements of the same data type. For each array, an ordinal subscript type is specified. There is an array element that corresponds to each value in the ordinal type. The ordinal type `Integer` cannot be a subscript type; however, a subrange of type `Integer` can be a subscript type.

Operators: Two basic operations act on the elements of an array: *store* and *retrieve*. The store operation inserts a value into the array. If `A` is an array and `C` is a variable that is assignment compatible (defined in Section 7.8) with the element type of `A`, the statement

```
A[I] := C
```

stores the contents of `C` in element `I` of array `A`. If the element type of `A` is assignment compatible with the type of variable `D`, the statement

```
D := A[I]
```

retrieves element `I` of array `A` and copies its value into `D`. For both of these statements, the value of subscript `I` must be in the range of the array subscript type; otherwise, a run-time error may occur.

The assignment operator can also be used to copy the contents of one array to another of the same type. If arrays `A` and `B` are the same type, the statement

```
A := B
```

copies all values associated with array `B` to array `A`.

The preceding display summarizes all the information you need to know to use an array. You do not need to know how Pascal stores the elements of an array in memory or how it implements the `retrieve` and `store` operators.

Exercises for Section 10.1

Self-Check

1. What is the difference between the expressions `X3` and `X[3]`?
2. For the following declarations, how many memory cells are reserved for data and what type of data can be stored there? When is the memory allocated: after the type declaration or after the variable declaration?

```
type
  AnArray = array [1..5] of Char;
```

```
var
  Grades : AnArray;
```

3. Write the variable and type declarations for the valid array descriptions that follow.
   a. subscript type `Boolean`, element type `Real`
   b. subscript type `'A'..'F'`, element type `Integer`
   c. subscript type `Char`, element type `Boolean`
   d. subscript type `Integer`, element type `Real`
   e. subscript type `Char`, element type `Real`
   f. subscript type `Real`, element type `Char`
   g. subscript type `Day` (enumerated type), element type `Real`

10.2 Selecting Array Elements for Processing

Using a Subscript as an Index to an Array

Each array reference includes the array name and a subscript enclosed in brackets; the subscript determines which array element is processed. The subscript (sometimes called an *index*) used in an array reference must be an expression that is assignment compatible with the *subscript type* specified in the array declaration. Very often, the *subscript type* is a subrange whose host type is `Integer`. In this case, the subscript must be an integer expression whose value is in the range specified by the *subscript type*. For the array `Vacation` declared in Example 10.2, the allowable subscript values are the integers 1 through 10.

■ Example 10.3

Table 10.2 shows some sample statements involving the array `X` shown in Fig. 10.1. `I` is assumed to be a type `Integer` variable with value `6`. Make sure you understand each statement.

Table 10.2 Some Sample Statements for Array X in Figure 10.1

Statement	Effect
`Write (4, X[4])`	Displays `4` and `8.0` (value of `X[4]`).
`Write (I, X[I])`	Displays `6` and `12.0` (value of `X[6]`).
`Write (X[I] + 1)`	Displays `13.0` (value of `12.0 + 1`).
`Write (X[I] + I)`	Displays `18.0` (value of `12.0 + 6`).
`Write (X[I+1])`	Displays `14.0` (value of `X[7]`).
`Write (X[I+I])`	Illegal attempt to display `X[12]`.
`Write (X[2*I])`	Illegal attempt to display `X[12]`.
`Write (X[2*I-4])`	Displays `-54.5` (value of `X[8]`).
`Write (X[Trunc(X[5])])`	Displays `12.0` (value of `X[2]`).
`X[I] := X[I+1]`	Assigns `14.0` (value of `X[7]`) to `X[6]`.
`X[I-1] := X[I]`	Assigns `14.0` (new value of `X[6]`) to `X[5]`.
`X[I] - 1 := X[I-1]`	Illegal assignment statement.

You can see two attempts to display element X[12], which is not in the array. In standard Pascal, these attempts result in an index expression out of bounds run-time error. This means there is no array element with the current subscript, or index, value. Turbo Pascal does not check for invalid array subscript references unless range checking is enabled using the {$R+} compiler directive. Range checking should always be enabled during program development and testing.

The last Write statement in Table 10.2 uses Trunc(X[5]) as a subscript expression. Because this evaluates to 2, the value of X[2] (and not X[5]) is printed. If the value of Trunc(X[5]) is outside the range 1 through 8 and range checking is enabled, a run-time error occurs.

Two different subscripts are used in the last three assignment statements in the table. The first assignment statement copies the value of X[7] to X[6] (subscripts I+1 and I); the second assignment statement copies the value of X[6] to X[5] (subscripts I and I-1). The last assignment statement causes a syntax error because there is an expression to the left of the assignment operator. ■

SYNTAX DISPLAY

Array Reference

Form: *name*[*subscript*]
Example: X[3 * I - 2]
Interpretation: The *subscript* must be an expression that is assignment compatible with the subscript type specified in the declaration for array *name*. If the expression is the wrong data type, the syntax error index type is not compatible with declaration is detected. If the expression value is not in range and range checking is enabled using {$R+}, the run-time error Range check error occurs.

Using for Loops with Arrays

Frequently, we want to process the elements of an array in sequence, starting with the first element, for example, entering data into the array or printing its contents. We can accomplish this sequential processing using a for loop whose loop-control variable (I) is also the array subscript (X[I]). Increasing the value of the loop-control variable by 1 causes the next array element to be processed.

■ Example 10.4

The array Cube, declared as follows, stores the cubes of the first ten integers (for example, Cube[1] is 1, Cube[10] is 1000).

```
type
  IndexRange = 1..10;
  IntArray = array [IndexRange] of Integer;

var
  Cube : IntArray;                        {array of cubes}
  I : Integer;                            {loop control variable}
```

The for statement

```
for I := 1 to 10 do
  Cube[I] := I * I * I
```

initializes this array as follows. ■

Array Cube

[1]	[2]	[3]	[4]	[5]	[6]	[7]	[8]	[9]	[10]
1	8	27	64	125	216	343	512	729	1000

■ Example 10.5

For array PlantHours (see Example 10.2), the enumerated type Day is the declared subscript type. The assignment statements

```
PlantHours[Sunday] := 0.0;
PlantHours[Monday] := 8.0;
PlantHours[Tuesday] := 16.0;
PlantHours[Wednesday] := 24.0
```

assign the values shown in Fig. 10.3 to the first four elements of PlantHours. Assuming that Today is type Day, the following statements have the same effect.

```
PlantHours[Sunday] := 0.0;
for Today := Monday to Wednesday do
  PlantHours[Today] := PlantHours[Pred(Today)] + 8.0
```

The assignment statement in the for loop executes for three values of Today (Monday through Wednesday). Table 10.3 shows the effect of the assignment statement for each value of Today. ■

Table 10.3 Assigning Values to Array PlantHours

Today	Pred(Today)	**Effect**
Monday	Sunday	Assigns 8.0 to PlantHours[Monday].
Tuesday	Monday	Assigns 16.0 to PlantHours[Tuesday].
Wednesday	Tuesday	Assigns 24.0 to PlantHours[Wednesday].

■ Example 10.6

In Fig. 10.4, the declarations

```
const
  MaxItems = 8;                          {number of data items}

type
  IndexRange = 1..MaxItems;
  RealArray = array [IndexRange] of Real;
```

```
var
  X : RealArray;                          {array of data}
  I : IndexRange;                         {loop-control variable}
```

allocate storage for an array X of Real elements with subscripts in the range 1..8. The program uses three for loops to process the array X. The loop-control variable I (1 <= I <= 8) is also the array subscript in each loop. The first for loop

```
for I := 1 to MaxItems do
  Read (X[I]);
```

reads one data value into each array element (the first item is stored in X[1], the second item in X[2], and so on). The Read statement is repeated for each value of I from 1 to 8; each repetition causes a new data value to be read and stored in X[I]. The subscript I determines the array element that receives the next data value. The data line shown in the sample run causes the array to be initialized, as in Fig. 10.1.

The second for loop accumulates (in Sum) the sum of all values stored in the array. (We trace this loop later.) The last for loop

```
for I := 1 to MaxItems do
  WriteLn (I :4, X[I] :8:2, X[I]-Average :14:2)
```

displays a table that shows each array element, X[I], and the difference between that element and the average value, X[I]-Average.

Figure 10.4 Table of Differences

Edit Window

```
{$R+}
program ShowDiff;
{
  Computes the average value of an array of data and
  prints the difference between each value and the average.
}
  const
    MaxItems = 8;                        {number of data items}

  type
    IndexRange = 1..MaxItems;
    RealArray = array [IndexRange] of Real;

  var
    X : RealArray;                       {array of data}
    I : IndexRange;                      {loop-control variable}
    Average,                             {average value of data}
    Sum      : Real;                     {sum of the data}

begin {ShowDiff}
  {Enter the data.}
  Write ('Enter ', MaxItems :1, ' numbers> ');
  for I := 1 to MaxItems do
    Read (X[I]);

  {Compute the average value.}
  Sum := 0.0;                                   {Initialize Sum}
```

```
  for I := 1 to MaxItems do
    Sum := Sum + X[I];                    {Add each element to Sum}
  Average := Sum / MaxItems;                     {Get average value}
  WriteLn ('Average value is ', Average :3:1); WriteLn;
  {Display the difference between each item and the average.}
  WriteLn ('Table of differences between X[I] and the average');
  WriteLn ('I' :4, 'X[I]' :8, 'Difference' : 14);
  for I := 1 to MaxItems do
    WriteLn (I :4, X[I] :8:1, X[I]-Average :14:1)
end. {ShowDiff}
```

Output Window

```
Enter 8 numbers> 16.0  12.0  6.0  8.0  2.5  12.0  14.0  -54.5
The average value is 2.0

Table of differences between X[I] and the average
   I    X[I]    Difference
   1    16.0          14.0
   2    12.0          10.0
   3     6.0           4.0
   4     8.0           6.0
   5     2.5           0.5
   6    12.0          10.0
   7    14.0          12.0
   8   -54.5         -56.5
```

The program fragment

```
Sum := 0.0;                                 {Initialize Sum}
for I := 1 to MaxItems do
  Sum := Sum + X[I];               {Add each element to Sum}
```

accumulates the sum of all eight elements of array X in the variable Sum. Each time the for loop is repeated, the next element of array X is added to Sum. The execution of this program fragment is traced in Table 10.4 for the first three repetitions of the loop.

Table 10.4 Partial Trace of for Loop

Statement Part	I	X[I]	Sum	Effect
Sum:= 0.0;			0.0	Initializes Sum.
for I := 1 to MaxItems do	1	16.0		Initializes I to 1;
Sum := Sum + X[I]			16.0	add X[1] to Sum.
increment and test I	2	12.0		2 <= 8 is True;
Sum := Sum + X[I]			28.0	add X[2] to Sum.
increment and test I	3	6.0		3 <= 8 is True;
Sum := Sum + X[I]			34.0	add X[3] to Sum.

In Fig. 10.4, the subscripted variable `X[I]` is an actual parameter for the standard Pascal `Read` or `WriteLn` procedure. You always have to read data into an array one element at a time, as shown in this example. In most instances, you also have to display one array element at time; however, Section 10.7 shows that this requirement may be waived when you are dealing with strings.

Exercises for Section 10.2

Self-Check

1. If an array is declared to have ten elements, must the program use all ten of them?
2. The following sequence of statements changes the initial contents of array `X` displayed in Fig. 10.4. Describe what each statement does to the array and show the final contents of array `X` after all statements execute.

```
I := 3;
X[I] := X[I] + 10.0;
X[I - 1] := X[2 * I - 1];
X[I + 1] := X[2 * I] + X[2 * I + 1];
for I := 5 to 7 do
  X[I] := X[I + 1];
for I := 3 downto 1 do
  X[I + 1] := X[I]
```

3. Write program statements that will do the following to array `X` shown in Fig. 10.4.
   a. Replace the third element with `7.0`.
   b. Copy the element in the fifth location into the first one.
   c. Subtract the first element from the fourth and store the result in the fifth element.
   d. Increase the sixth element by 2.
   e. Find the sum of the first five elements.
   f. Multiply each of the first six elements by 2 and place each product in an element of the array `AnswerArray`.
   g. Display all even-numbered elements on one line.

10.3 Using Arrays

This section illustrates the use of an array. It demonstrates two different methods for array access: sequential access and random access. We discuss their differences after the case study.

Case Study: Home Budget Problem

Problem

Your parents want a program that keeps track of their monthly expenses in each of several categories. The program should read each expense amount, add it to the appropriate category total, and print the total expenditure by category. The input data consist of the category and the amount of each purchase made during the past month.

Design Overview

Your parents have selected these budget categories: entertainment, food, clothing, rent, tuition, insurance, and miscellaneous. Seven separate totals must be accumulated; each total can be associated with a different element of a seven-element array. The program must read each expenditure, determine to which category it belongs, and then add that expenditure to the appropriate array element. When finished with all expenditures, the program should print a table that shows each category and its accumulated total. As in all programs that accumulate a sum, each total must be initialized to zero.

Data Requirements

We could simply use an array with subscripts 1 through 7; however, the program would be more readable if we declare a data type `BudgetCat` and use this data type as the array subscript type.

Data Type

```
BudgetCat = (Entertainment, Food, Clothing, Rent,
             Tuition, Insurance, Miscellaneous);
```

Problem Inputs

Each expenditure and its category

Problem Outputs

The array of seven expenditure totals (`Budget`)

Initial Algorithm

1. Initialize all category totals to zero.
2. Read each expenditure and add it to the appropriate total.
3. Print the accumulated total for each category.

Structure Chart and Refinements

The structure chart in Fig. 10.5 shows the relationship between the three steps. The array `Budget` is manipulated by all three procedures in the program solution. Procedures `Initialize` and `Post` store information in this array; this information is displayed by procedure `Report`.

Coding the Main Program

Figure 10.6 shows the program. The main program contains declarations for the data type `BudgetCat` and the array `Budget`. The array `Budget` (type `BudgetArray`) appears in each parameter list and is passed between each procedure and the main program. When an entire array is passed, no subscript is used.

Figure 10.5 Structure Chart for Home Budget Problem

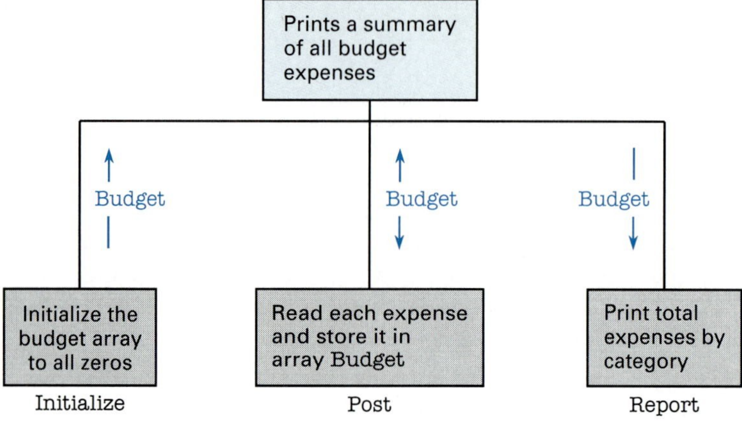

Figure 10.6 Home Budget Program

```
{$R+}
program HomeBudget;

{Prints a summary of all expenses by budget category.}

  type
    BudgetCat = (Entertainment, Food, Clothing, Rent,
                 Tuition, Insurance, Miscellaneous);
    BudgetArray = array [BudgetCat] of Real;    {array type}

  var
    Budget : BudgetArray;          {output - array of totals}


  procedure Initialize (var Budget {output} : BudgetArray);
  {
    Initializes array Budget to all zeros.
    Pre : None
    Post: Each element of Budget is 0.0
  }
    var
      NextCat : BudgetCat;         {loop-control variable }
                                           array subscript}
  begin  {Initialize}
    for NextCat := Entertainment to Miscellaneous do
      Budget[NextCat] := 0.0
  end;  {Initialize}


  procedure Post (var Budget {input/output} : BudgetArray);
  {
    Reads each expenditure amount and adds it to the appropriate
    element of array Budget.
```

```
    Pre : Each array element Budget[i] is 0.0
    Post: Each array element Budget[i] is the sum of expense
          amounts for category i.
  }
  begin  {Poststub}
    WriteLn ('Procedure Post entered')
  end;  {Poststub}


  procedure Report (Budget {input} : BudgetArray);
  {
    Prints the expenditures in each budget category.
    Pre : Array Budget is defined.
    Post: Displays each budget category name and amount.
  }
    var
      NextCat : BudgetCat;              {loop control-variable }
                                            array subscript    }

    procedure PrintCat (NextCat {input} : BudgetCat);
    {
      Displays budget category.
      Pre : Nextcat is a budget category.
      Post: Displays NextCat as a string.
    }
    begin  {PrintCat}
      case NextCat of
        Entertainment : Write ('Entertainment' :15);
        Food          : Write ('Food         ' :15);
        Clothing      : Write ('Clothing     ' :15);
        Rent          : Write ('Rent         ' :15);
        Tuition       : Write ('Tuition      ' :15);
        Insurance     : Write ('Insurance    ' :15);
        Miscellaneous : Write ('Miscellaneous' :15)
      end  {case}
    end; {PrintCat}


  begin  {Report}
    WriteLn;
    WriteLn ('Category     ' :15,  'Expenses' :15):  {heading}
    {Print each category name and the total}
    for NextCat := Entertainment to Miscellaneous do
      begin
        PrintCat (NextCat);
        WriteLn (Budget[NextCat] :15:2)
      end {for}
  end;  {Report}

begin  {HomeBudget}
  {Initialize array Budget to all zeros.}
  Initialize (Budget);

  {Read and process each expenditure.}
  Post (Budget);

  {Print the expenditures in each category.}
  Report (Budget)
end. {HomeBudget}
```

The loop-control variable NextCat (type BudgetCat) is declared as a local variable in each procedure. In procedure Initialize, the assignment statement

```
Budget[NextCat] := 0.0
```

is repeated once for each value of NextCat and sets each element of Budget to zero. In procedure Report, the statements

```
PrintCat (NextCat);
WriteLn (Budget[NextCat] :15:2)
```

call PrintCat to display a budget category name and WriteLn to display the category total.

Procedure Post must read each expenditure and add it to the appropriate array element. The total of all entertainment expenditures is accumulated in Budget[Entertainment], all food expenditures are accumulated in Budget[Food], and so forth.

Coding Procedure Post

Procedure Post is shown in Fig. 10.7; it uses procedure EnterCat to read the budget category as an integer value and typecasting to convert this value to type BudgetCat.

Figure 10.7 Procedure Post for Home Budget Problem

```
procedure Post (var Budget {input/output} : BudgetArray);
{
  Reads each expenditure amount and adds it to the appropriate
  element of array Budget.
  Pre : Each array element Budget[i] is 0.0
  Post: Each array element Budget[i] is the sum of expense
        amounts for category i.
}
  const
    Quit = 7;                         {sentinel category number}
    MaxCategory = 7;                  {number of budget categories}

  var
    Choice  : Integer;             {next category as an integer}
    NextCat : BudgetCat;           {next category as type BudgetCat}
    Expense : Real;                {expenditure amount}


  procedure EnterCat (var Choice {output} : Integer);
  {
    Reads the budget category as an integer value.
    Pre : None
    Post: Choice is an integer from 0 to 7.
  }
  begin
    repeat
      WriteLn ('0 - Entertainment');
      WriteLn ('1 - Food');
      WriteLn ('2 - Clothing');
```

```
      WriteLn ('3 - Rent');
      WriteLn ('4 - Tuition');
      WriteLn ('5 - Insurance');
      WriteLn ('6 - Miscellaneous');
      WriteLn ('7 - Quit program');
      WriteLn ('Enter the category number> ');
      ReadLn (Choice)
    until Choice in [0..Quit]
  end; {EnterCat}


begin  {Post}
  {Read each budget category and expense and add it to Budget.}
  EnterCat (Choice);
  while Choice <> Quit do
    {invariant:
        no prior value of Choice is Quit
        and Budget[NextCat] is the sum of prior budget entries
        for category NextCat.
    }
    begin
      NextCat := BudgetCat(Choice);  {Convert to type BudgetCat}
      Write ('Enter the expenditure amount $');
      ReadLn (Expense); WriteLn;
      Budget[NextCat] := Budget[NextCat] + Expense;
      EnterCat (Choice)
    end {while }
end; {Post}
```

Procedure `Post` begins by calling `EnterCat` to read an integer representing the category into `Choice`. The `while` loop body is executed for each value of `Choice` that is not zero. "Function" `BudgetCat` assigns a value to `NextCat` (type `BudgetCat`) based on the value of `Choice`. The assignment statement

```
Budget[NextCat] := Budget[NextCat] + Expense;
```

adds the expense amount to whatever element of array `Budget` is selected by `NextCat`.

Testing

A sample run of the home budget program is shown in Fig. 10.8. For the sake of brevity, we display the list of categories just once. As indicated in this run, it is not necessary for the input data to be in order by category. You should verify that all budget categories without purchases remain zero. Also, verify that out-of-range category values do not cause the program to terminate prematurely.

Figure 10.8 Sample Run of Home Budget Program

```
0 - Entertainment
1 - Food
2 - Clothing
```

Case Study: Home Budget Problem, continued

```
3 - Rent
4 - Tuition
5 - Insurance
6 - Miscellaneous
7 - Quit program
Enter the category number> 2
Enter the expenditure amount $25.00

Enter the category number> 6
Enter the expenditure amount $25.00

Enter the category number> 2
Enter the expenditure amount $15.00

Enter the category number> 0
Enter the expenditure amount $675.00

Enter the category number> 7

  Category        Expenses
  Entertainment    675.00
  Food               0.00
  Clothing          40.00
  Rent               0.00
  Tuition            0.00
  Insurance          0.00
  Miscellaneous     25.00
```

Sequential versus Random Access to Arrays

The home budget program illustrates two common ways of selecting array elements for processing. Often, we need to manipulate all elements of an array in some uniform manner (for instance, we might want to initialize them all to zero). In such situations, it makes sense to process the array elements in sequence (*sequential access*), starting with the first and ending with the last. In procedures `Initialize` and `Report`, we accomplish that by using a `for` loop whose loop-control variable is also the array subscript.

In procedure `Post`, the order in which the array elements are accessed depends completely on the order of the data. The value assigned to `NextCat` determines the element to be incremented. This approach is called *random access* because the order is not predictable.

Exercise for Section 10.3

Self-Check

1. What happens if the user of the budget program enters the category `-1` by mistake?

10.4 Arrays as Operands and Parameters

The Pascal operators (for example, <, =, >, +, and –) can manipulate only one array element at a time (provided the element type is an appropriate simple type). Consequently, an array name in an expression is generally followed by its subscript.

Copying an Array

One exception to the preceding rule is the *array copy* operation. It is possible to copy the contents of one array to another array, provided the arrays are the same array type. Given the declarations

```
const
  MaxSize = 100;

type
  Index = 1..MaxSize;
  TestArray = array [Index] of Real;

var
  W, X, Y : TestArray;
  Z : array [Index] of Real;
```

the assignment statements

```
X := Y                        {valid array copy}
W := Y                        {valid array copy}
```

copy each value in array `Y` to the corresponding element of arrays `X` and `W` (that is, `Y[1]` is copied to `X[1]` and `W[1]`, `Y[2]` to `X[2]` and `W[2]`, and so forth.

It is important to realize that the assignments

```
Z := Y;                       {invalid array copy}
X := Z                        {invalid array copy}
```

are invalid. Even though array `Z` has the same structure as arrays `W`, `X`, and `Y`, the type of array `Z` is anonymous and is not considered the same as the named type `TestArray`. Therefore, you must either declare array `Z` as type `TestArray` or use a loop to copy each element individually. This is another reason to avoid the use of anonymous or unnamed types (see Section 10.1).

Arrays as Parameters

If several elements of an array are being manipulated by a procedure, it is generally better to pass the entire array of data instead of individual array elements. In Fig. 10.6, the procedure call statements

```
Initialize (Budget);
Post (Budget);
Report (Budget)
```

pass the entire array `Budget` to each procedure. `Budget` is declared as a variable parameter in procedures Initialize and Post and as a value parameter in procedure Report.

In all three procedures, the formal parameter is declared as type BudgetArray. This is necessary because the formal and the actual parameter must be the same array type. The procedure heading

```
procedure Initialize (var Budget : array [BudgetCat] of Real);
```

is invalid because the parameter type must be an identifier.

When an array is used as a variable parameter, Pascal passes the address of the first actual array element into the procedure data area. Because the array elements are stored in adjacent memory cells, the entire array of data can be accessed. The procedure directly manipulates the actual array.

When an array is used as a value parameter, a local copy of the array is made when the procedure is called. The local array is initialized so that it contains the same values as the corresponding actual array. The procedure manipulates the local array, and any changes made to the local array are not reflected in the actual array.

The next two examples illustrate the use of arrays as parameters, assuming the following declarations.

```
const
  MaxSize = 5;

type
  IndexType = 1..MaxSize;
  TestArray = array [IndexType] of Real;

var
  X, Y, Z : TestArray;
```

■ Example 10.7

Although it is possible to use a single assignment statement to copy one array to another, the assignment statement

```
Z := X + Y      {illegal addition of arrays}
```

is invalid because the operator + cannot have an array as an operand. You might use procedure AddArray (Fig. 10.9) to add two arrays of type TestArray.

Figure 10.9 Procedure AddArray

```
procedure AddArray (A, B  {input}  : TestArray;
                    var C {output} : TestArray);

{
  Stores the sum of A[i] and B[i] in C[i]. Array elements
  with subscripts 1..MaxSize are summed, element by element.
  Pre : A[i] and B[i] (1 <= i <= MaxSize) are assigned values
  Post: C[i] := A[i] + B[i] (1 <= i <= MaxSize).
}
```

```
  var
    I : IndexType;          {loop control and array subscript}

begin  {AddArray}
  {Add corresponding elements of each array}
  for I := 1 to MaxSize do
    C[I] := A[I] + B[I]
end;  {AddArray}
```

The parameter correspondence for arrays established by the procedure call statement

```
AddArray (X, Y, Z)
```

is shown in Fig. 10.10. Arrays `A` and `B` in the procedure data area are local copies of arrays `X` and `Y`. As indicated by the solid arrow, the address of the first element of array `Z` is stored in parameter `C`. The procedure results are stored directly in array `Z`. After execution of the procedure, `Z[1]` will contain the sum of `X[1]` and `Y[1]`, or `3.5`; `Z[2]` will contain `6.7`; and so on. Arrays `X` and `Y` will be unchanged. ■

Figure 10.10 Parameter Correspondence for AddArray (X, Y, Z)

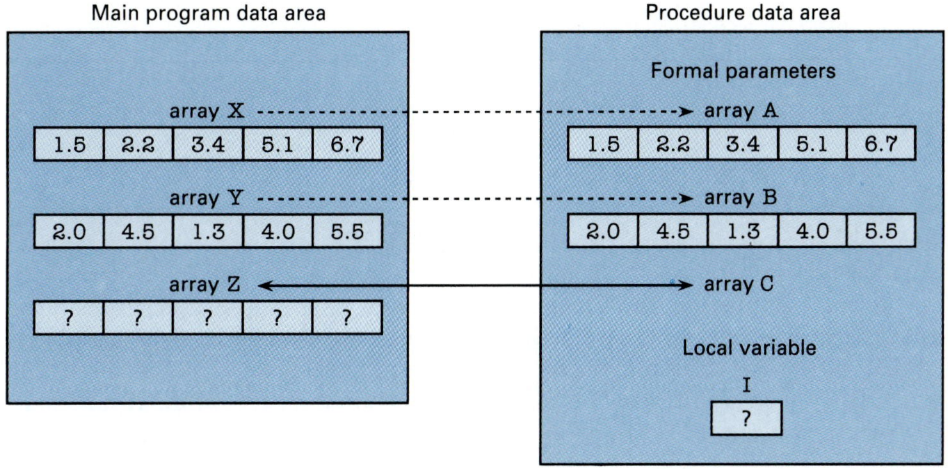

■ Example 10.8

Function `SameArray` in Fig. 10.11 determines whether two arrays (of type `TestArray`) are identical. Two arrays are considered identical if the first element of one is the same as the first element of the other, the second element of one is the same as the second element of the other, and so forth.

We can determine that the arrays are not identical by finding a single pair of unequal elements. Consequently, the `while` loop may be executed anywhere from one time (first elements unequal) to `MaxSize - 1` times. Loop exit occurs when a pair of unequal elements is found or just before the last pair is tested.

Figure 10.11 Function SameArray

```
function SameArray (A, B : TestArray) : Boolean;
{
  Returns a value of True if the arrays A, B are identical;
  otherwise, returns a value of False.
  Pre : A[i] and B[i] (1 <= i <= MaxSize) are assigned values.
  Post: Returns True if A[i] = B[i] for all i in range
            1..MaxSize; otherwise, returns False.
}
   var
     I : Integer;                            {Array subscript}

begin
  I := 1;                                    {Start with first pair}

  {Test corresponding elements of arrays A and B.}
  while (I < MaxSize) and (A[I] = B[I]) do
    {invariant:
        1 <= I <= MaxSize and
        A[I] = B[I] for all prior values of I
    }
    I := I + 1;                              {Advance to next pair}

  {assert:
     an unequal pair was found or all but the
     last pair were compared
  }
  SameArray := A[I] = B[I]                   {Define result}
end;  {SameArray}
```

After loop exit, the Boolean assignment statement

```
SameArray := A[I] = B[I]    {Define result}
```

defines the function result. If loop exit occurs because the pair of elements with subscript I is unequal, the function result is False. If loop exit occurs because the last pair of elements is reached, the function result is True if this pair is equal; otherwise, the function result is False.

As an example of how you might use function SameArray, the if statement

```
if SameArray(X, Y) then
  Z := X
else
  AddArray (X, Y, Z)
```

either copies array X to array Z (when X and Y are identical) or stores the sum of arrays X and Y in array Z (when X and Y are not identical).

Because the arrays have MaxSize elements, a common error is to use the condition

```
(I <= MaxSize) and (A[I] = B[I])
```

as the while condition in Fig. 10.11, which causes all element pairs to be tested by the while condition if the arrays are equal. When I is MaxSize + 1, the first part of this condition evaluates to `False`; however, the second part must still be evaluated unless short-circuit evaluation is used. This leads to an `index expression out of bounds` run-time error because array element `A[MaxSize+1]` does not exist.

PROGRAM STYLE

Efficiency of Variable Parameters versus Protection of Value Parameters

Parameters `A` and `B` in Fig. 10.11 are declared as value parameters because they only store data passed into procedure `AddArray` and their values should not be changed by `AddArray`. Pascal must create a local copy of these two arrays each time procedure `AddArray` is called. This copying uses valuable computer time and memory space. If the arrays being copied are very large, the program may terminate with an error because all of its memory space has been used.

To conserve time and memory space, experienced programmers sometimes declare arrays that are used only for input as variable parameters rather than as value parameters. This means, however, that the corresponding actual array is directly manipulated by the procedure and is no longer protected from accidental modification by the procedure. Any changes (either by accident or by design) made to the actual array are an undesirable side effect of the function's execution. If an array corresponds to a value parameter, the changes are made to a local copy, and the actual array is unaffected.

Finding the Minimum or Maximum Value in an Array

A common operation is to determine the minimum or maximum value stored in an array. In Chapter 4, we wrote a program to find the smallest of three characters (see Fig. 4.6). The approach taken to finding the minimum or maximum value in an array is similar. The algorithm for finding the maximum value follows.

Algorithm for Finding the Maximum Value in an Array

1. Assume that the first element is the largest so far and save its subscript as the subscript of the largest so far.
2. `for` each array element `do`
    3. `if` the current element is > than the largest so far `then`
        4. Save the subscript of the current element as the subscript of the largest so far.

Function `MaxBudget` in Fig. 10.12 implements this algorithm for the array `Budget` displayed in Fig. 10.8. The function returns the subscript (type `Category`) of the largest value in array `Budget`.

Figure 10.12 Function MaxBudget

```
function MaxBudget (Budget {input} : BudgetArray) : BudgetCat;
{
  Returns the subscript of the largest element in array Budget.
  Pre : Array Budget is defined.
  Post: Budget[MaxIndex] is the largest value in the array.
}
  var
    MaxIndex,                  {Index of largest so far}
    NextIndex : BudgetCat;  {Index of current element}

begin {MaxBudget}
  MaxIndex := Entertainment;  {Assume first element is largest}
  for NextIndex := Entertainment to Miscellaneous do
    if Budget[NextIndex] > Budget[MaxIndex] then
      MaxIndex := NextIndex;

  {assertion:
     All elements are examined and
     MaxIndex is the index of the largest element
  }
  MaxBudget := MaxIndex           {Define result}
end; {MaxBudget}
```

It is important to realize that function MaxBudget returns the subscript (or index) of the largest value, not the largest value itself. Assuming NextCat is type BudgetCat, the following statements display the largest value.

```
NextCat := MaxBudget(Budget);
WriteLn ('The largest expenditure is $', Budget[NextCat] :4:2)
```

Although not as easy to read, the single statement that follows is equivalent; it uses the function designator as the subscript expression.

```
WriteLn ('The largest expenditure is $',
         Budget[MaxBudget(Budget)] :4:2)
```

Individual Array Elements as Parameters

It is acceptable practice to use a single array element as an actual parameter. For example, the expression

```
Round(Budget[5])
```

rounds the value stored in the fifth element of array Budget, where the subscripted variable Budget[5] is the actual parameter passed to function Round.

■ Example 10.9

Procedure Exchange in Fig. 10.13 exchanges the values of its two type Real parameters.

Figure 10.13 Procedure Exchange

```
procedure Exchange (var P, Q {input/output} : Real);
{
  Exchanges the values of P and Q.
  Pre : P and Q are assigned values.
  Post: P has the value passed into Q and vice-versa.
}
  var
    Temp : Real;            {temporary variable for the exchange}

begin {Exchange}
  Temp := P;  P := Q;  Q := Temp
end; {Exchange}
```

The procedure call statement

```
Exchange (X[2], X[1])
```

uses this procedure to exchange the contents of the first two elements (type `Real`) of array `X`. The identifier `X` is the name of an array in the calling program. The actual parameter `X[2]` corresponds to formal parameter `P`; the actual parameter `X[1]` corresponds to formal parameter `Q`. This correspondence is shown in Fig. 10.14 for a particular array `X`. ■

It is illegal to use a subscripted variable as a formal parameter. For example, the procedure declaration

```
procedure Exchange (var X[I], X[J] {input/output} : Real);
```

would cause a syntax error.

Figure 10.14 Parameter Correspondence for Exchange (X[2], X[1])

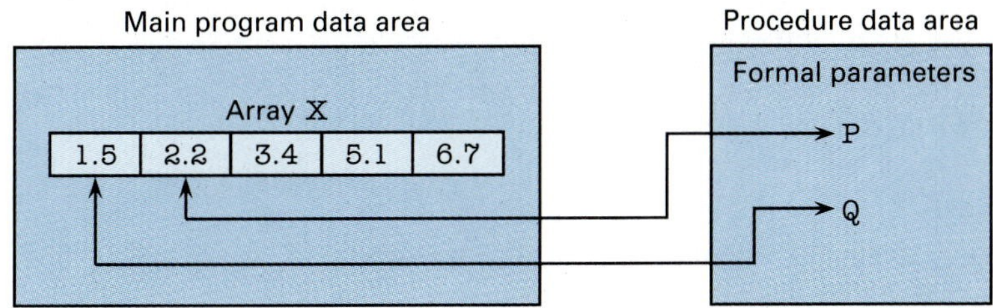

Exercises for Section 10.4

Self-Check

1. When is it better to pass an entire array of data to a procedure rather than individual elements?

2. When is a copy of an entire array made for an array that is a procedure parameter? What happens to the copy after the procedure executes?
3. In function SameArray, what will be the value of I when the statement

```
SameArray := A[I] = B[I]
```

executes if array A is equal to array B? If the third elements do not match?
4. Describe how to modify function MaxBudget to get a new function, Min-Budget, that returns the smallest array element.

Programming

1. Write a procedure that assigns a value of True to element I of the output array if element I of one input array has the same value as element I of the other input array; otherwise, assign a value of False. If the input arrays have subscript type IndexType, the output array should have the following type.

```
type
  BoolArray = array [IndexType] of Boolean;
```

2. Write a procedure that copies each value stored in one array to the corresponding element of another array. (For example, if the arrays are InArray and OutArray, copy InArray[1] to OutArray[1], then copy InArray[2] to OutArray[2], and so on.)
3. Write a procedure that reverses the values stored in an array. If array X has N elements, then X[1] becomes X[N], X[2] becomes X[N-1], and so forth. Hint: Make a local copy of the array before you start to reverse the elements.

10.5 Reading Part of an Array

Usually, we don't know in advance exactly how many elements will be stored in an array. For example, if a professor is processing exam scores, there might be 150 students in one class, 200 in the next, and so on. In this situation, we should declare an array that can accommodate the largest class. Only part of this array will actually be processed for a smaller class.

■ Example 10.10

The array Scores, declared as follows, can accommodate a class of up to 250 students. Each array element can contain an integer value between 0 and 100.

```
const
  MaxSize = 250;
  MaxScore = 100;

type
  ClassIndex = 1..MaxSize;
  ScoreRange = 0..MaxScore;
  ScoreArray = array [ClassIndex] of ScoreRange;
  ClassRange = 0..MaxSize;
```

```
var
  Scores : ScoreArray;
  ClassSize : ClassRange;
```

Procedure ReadScores in Fig. 10.15 reads up to 250 exam scores and prints a warning message when the array is filled. The actual number of scores read is returned as the value of ClassSize. It calls EnterInt declared in unit EnterData (see Fig. 8.3) to read each exam score.

Figure 10.15 Reading Part of an Array

```
procedure ReadScores (var Scores {output} : ScoreArray;
                      var ClassSize {output} : ClassRange);

{
  Reads an array of exam scores (Scores)
  for a class of up to MaxSize students.
  Pre  : None
  Post : The data values are stored in array Scores.
         The number of values read is stored in
         ClassSize (0 <= ClassSize <= MaxSize)
  Calls: Procedure EnterInt in EnterData
}
  const
    Sentinel = -1;              {Sentinel value}

  var
    TempScore : Integer;        {Temporary storage for a score}

begin
  Write ('Enter next score after the prompt or enter ');
  WriteLn (Sentinel :1, ' to stop.');

  {Read each array element until done.}
  ClassSize := 0;                           {initial class size}
  EnterInt (Sentinel, MaxScore, TempScore);
  while (TempScore <> Sentinel) and (ClassSize < MaxSize) do
    {invariant:
       No prior value of TempScore is Sentinel and
       ClassSize <= MaxSize
    }
    begin
      ClassSize := ClassSize + 1;          {Increment ClassSize}
      Scores[ClassSize] := TempScore;      {Save the score}
      EnterInt (Sentinel, MaxScore, TempScore);
    end;  {while}

  {Assert:  Sentinel was read or array is filled.}
  if ClassSize = MaxSize then
    WriteLn ('Array is filled.')
end;  {ReadScores}
```

In any subsequent processing of array Scores, use the variable ClassSize to limit the number of array elements processed. Only the subarray with subscripts 1..ClassSize contains meaningful data; consequently, array elements with subscripts larger than ClassSize should not be manipulated. ClassSize should be passed as a parameter to any procedure that processes the partially filled array.

Exercises for Section 10.5

Self-Check

1. In procedure `ReadScores`, what prevents the user from entering more than `MaxSize` scores?
2. What is the range of data values that can be entered? What is the range of data values that can be stored in the array?
3. Rewrite the `while` loop in `ReadScores` as a `repeat-until` loop. Why is the `while` loop better? Why can't we use a `for` loop?

10.6 More Examples of Array Processing

Many of the arrays processed so far had subscript types that were subranges of the integers. This, of course, is not required in Pascal, because a subscript type can be any ordinal type (except `Integer`). A number of different array types are described in Table 10.5.

Table 10.5 Some Array Types and Applications

Array Type	Application
`type NameArray = array [1..10] of Char;` `var Name : NameArray;`	`Name[1] := 'A';` stores a person's name (up to 10 letters).
`type Temperatures = array [-10..10] of Real;` `var Fahrenheit : Temperatures;`	`Fahrenheit[0] := 32.0;` stores Fahrenheit temperatures corresponding to -10 through 10 degrees Celsius.
`type Counters = array ['A'..'Z'] of Integer;` `var LetterCount : Counters;`	`LetterCount['A'] := 0;` stores the number of times each uppercase letter occurs.
`type Flags = array ['A'..'Z'] of Boolean;` `var LetterFound : Flags;`	`LetterFound['X'] := False;` stores a set of flags indicating which letters occur and which do not.
`type BoolCounts = array [Boolean] of Integer;` `var Answers : BoolCounts;`	`Answers[True] := 15;` stores the number of `True` answers and `False` answers to a quiz.

The array Name has ten elements and can store the letters of a person's name. The array Fahrenheit, with twenty-one elements, can store the Fahrenheit temperature corresponding to each Celsius temperature in the range −10 through +10 degrees Celsius. For example, Fahrenheit[0] would be the Fahrenheit temperature, 32.0, corresponding to 0 degrees Celsius. Arrays LetterCount and LetterFound have the same subscript type (that is, the uppercase letters) and are discussed in the next section. The array Answers has only two elements, with subscript values True and False.

Arrays with Subscripts of Type Char

An array with subscript type Char (or a subrange of Char) is a useful data structure, as shown in the next example.

■ Example 10.11

The arrays LetterCount and LetterFound described in Table 10.5 have the subscript type ['A'..'Z']. Thus, there is an array element for each uppercase letter. The program in Fig. 10.16 displays the number of occurrences of each letter in a line of text. It uses LetterCount['A'] to store the number of occurrences of the letter 'A'. If the letter A occurs, LetterFound['A'] is True; otherwise, LetterFound['A'] is False. Function UpCase converts the case of each letter read into NextChar to uppercase so that both t and T cause the count for letter T to be incremented.

Figure 10.16 Counting Letters in a Line

Edit Window

```
{$R+}
program Concordance;
{
  Finds and prints the number of occurrences of each letter.
  The case of each letter is immaterial. Letters with counts
  of zero are not displayed.
}
  const
    Sentinel = '*';                {sentinel character}

  type
    Letter = 'A'..'Z';
    CountArray = array [Letter] of Integer;
    FoundArray = array [Letter] of Boolean;

  var
    LetterCount : CountArray;        {output -- array of counts}
    LetterFound : FoundArray;        {array of flags}
    NextChar : Char;                 {input - each input character}

begin  {Concordance}
  {Initialize LetterCount and LetterFound.}
  for NextChar := 'A' to 'Z' do
    begin
      LetterCount[NextChar] := 0;      {Initialize counts}
      LetterFound[NextChar] := False   {Initialize flags}
    end; {for}
```

```
  {Count the letters in a line.}
  WriteLn ('Type in a line of text ending with ', Sentinel);
  repeat
    Read (NextChar);                     {Get next character}
    NextChar := UpCase(NextChar);        {Convert to uppercase}
    if NextChar in ['A'..'Z'] then
      begin  {letter}
        LetterCount[NextChar] := LetterCount[NextChar] + 1;
        LetterFound[NextChar] := True          {Set letter flag}
      end  {letter}
  until NextChar = Sentinel;

  {Print counts of letters that are in the line.}
  WriteLn;
  WriteLn ('Letter', 'Occurrences' :16);
  for NextChar := 'A' to 'Z' do
    if LetterFound[NextChar] then
      WriteLn (NextChar :6, LetterCount[NextChar] :16)
end. {Concordance}
```

Output Window

```
Type in a line ending with *
This is it!*

Letter      Occurrences
     H                1
     I                3
     S                2
     T                2
```

In the last `if` statement, the condition

```
LetterFound[NextChar]
```

is true if there are one or more occurrences of the letter `NextChar`. This `if` statement ensures that only counts greater than zero are printed. This condition can also be written as

```
LetterCount[NextChar] > 0
```

Doing this is more efficient, because it allows us to eliminate the array `LetterFound`.

Case Study: Cryptogram Generator Problem

Problem

Your local intelligence agency needs a program to encode messages. One approach is to use a program that generates cryptograms. A cryptogram is a coded message that is formed by substituting a code character for each letter of the original message. The substitution is performed uniformly throughout the original message—for instance, every A is replaced by an S, every B is replaced by a P, and so forth. All punctuation (including spaces between words) remains unchanged.

Design Overview

The program must examine each character in the message and replace each character that is a letter by its code symbol. We can store the code symbols in an array `Code` with subscript type `'A'..'Z'` and element type `Char`. The character stored in `Code['A']` will be the code symbol for the letter `'A'`. This enables us to simply look up the code symbol for a letter by using that letter as an index to the array `Code`.

Data Requirements

Problem Inputs

The array of code symbols `(Code : array ['A'..'Z'] of Char)`
Each message character

Problem Outputs

Each character of the cryptogram

Initial Algorithm

1. Read in the code symbol for each letter.
2. Read each message character and display the cryptogram.

Algorithm Refinements and Structure Chart

As shown in the structure chart (see Fig. 10.17), procedure `ReadCode` performs step 1 and procedure `Encrypt` performs step 2. The data requirements and algorithms for these procedures follow the structure chart.

Local Variable for ReadCode

Loop control variable for accessing array `Code`
    `(NextLetter : 'A'..'Z')`

Figure 10.17 Structure Chart for Cryptogram Generator

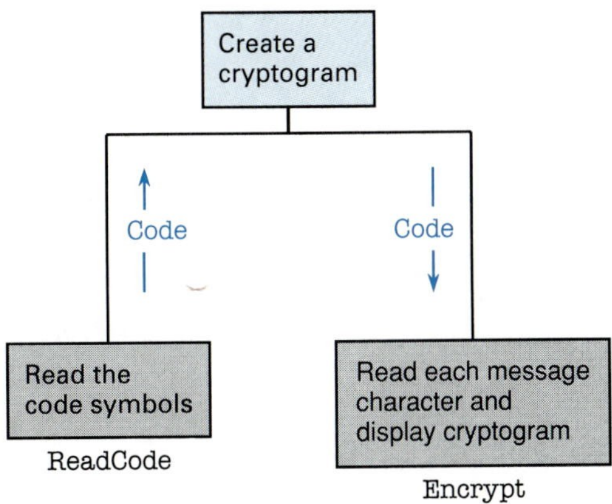

Algorithm for ReadCode

1. Display the alphabet.
2. `for` each letter `do`
    3. Read in the code symbol and store it in array `Code`.

Local Constant for Encrypt

The sentinel character for the message (`Sentinel = '#'`)

Local Variable for Encrypt

Each message character (`NextChar : Char`)

Algorithm for Encrypt

1. `repeat`
    2. Read the next message character.
    3. Display the message character or its code symbol.

    `until` the message is complete

Coding

The program in Fig. 10.18 assumes that the uppercase letters are consecutive characters, as they are in the ASCII character set.

Figure 10.18 Cryptogram Generator

Edit Window

```
{$R+}
program Cryptogram;

{Generates cryptograms corresponding to input messages.}

  type
    Letter = 'A'..'Z';
    CodeArray = array [Letter] of Char;

  var
    Code : CodeArray;            {input - array of code symbols}


  procedure ReadCode (var Code {output} : CodeArray);
  {
    Reads in the code symbol for each letter.
    Pre : None
    Post: 26 data values are read into array Code.
  }
    var
      NextLetter : Letter;            {each letter}

  begin {ReadCode}
    WriteLn ('First specify the code.');
    WriteLn ('Enter a code symbol under each letter.');
    WriteLn ('ABCDEFGHIJKLMNOPQRSTUVWXYZ');
    {Read each code symbol into array Code.}
    for NextLetter := 'A' to 'Z' do
      Read (Code[NextLetter]);
    ReadLn;                           {Terminate input line}
```

```
    WriteLn                            {Skip a line}
  end;  {ReadCode}


  procedure Encrypt (Code {input} : CodeArray);
  {
    Reads each character and prints it or its code symbol.
    Pre : Array Code is defined.
    Post: Each character read was printed or its code
          symbol was printed and the sentinel was just read.
  }
    const
      Sentinel = '#';                        {sentinel character}

    var
      NextChar : Char;       {input - each message character}

  begin  {Encrypt}
    WriteLn ('Enter each character of your message;');
    WriteLn ('terminate it with the symbol ', Sentinel);
    repeat
      Read (NextChar);
      NextChar := UpCase(NextChar);    {convert to uppercase}
      if NextChar in ['A'..'Z'] then
        Write (Code[NextChar])           {Print code symbol}
      else
        Write (NextChar)                 {Print non-letter}
    until NextChar = Sentinel
  end;  {Encrypt}


begin  {Cryptogram}
  {Read in the code symbol for each letter.}
  ReadCode (Code);

  {Read each character and print it or its code symbol.}
  Encrypt (Code)
end. {Cryptogram}
```

Output Window

```
First specify the code you wish to use.
Enter a code symbol under each letter.
ABCDEFGHIJKLMNOPQRSTUVWXYZ
BCDEFGHIJKLMNOPQRSTUVWXYZA


Enter each character of your message;
terminate it with the symbol #
A tiny one!#
B UJOZ POF!#
```

Testing

In the preceding sample run, the code symbol for each letter is entered directly beneath that letter and read by procedure ReadCode. The sample run ends with two lines of output: the first contains the message; the second contains its cryptogram. For a simple test, try using each letter as its own code symbol. In that case, both lines should be the same. Make sure the program encodes lowercase letters as well as uppercase letters. Characters that are not letters should not be changed.

Exercises for Section 10.6

Self-Check

1. Describe the following array types:
   a. `array [1..20] of Char`
   b. `array ['0'..'9'] of Boolean`
   c. `array [-5..5] of Real`
   d. `array [Boolean] of Char`

2. Provide array type declarations for representing the following:
   a. A group of rooms (living room, dining room, kitchen, etc.) that have a given area.
   b. Elementary school grade levels with a given number of students per grade.
   c. A group of colors with letter values assigned according to the first letter of their name (for example, `'B'` for blue).

3. Why is it that spaces and commas are not encoded in the cryptogram program?

Programming

1. Make changes to the cryptogram program to encode the blank character and the punctuation symbols `, ; : ? ! .` . Hint: Use subscript type `Char`.

10.7 Strings and Arrays of Characters

Until now, our use of character data has been quite limited. We have used variables of type `Char` to hold single character values. We have read sequences of characters into variables of type `string`. In this section, we discuss character arrays and compare them to Turbo Pascal string type variables. String variables are discussed more fully in Chapter 13.

The Pascal declarations

```
const
  Size = 10;

type
  IndexRange = 1..Size;
  CharArray = array [IndexRange] of Char;

var
  Name : CharArray;
  I : Integer;
```

declare a character array `Name` with ten elements; a single character can be stored in each array element.

The program in Fig. 10.19 first reads a sequence of characters into the array Name, then prints the characters stored in Name. For the data shown in Fig. 10.19, the array Name would be defined as shown below. Name[9] contains the blank character.

Array Name

[1]	[2]	[3]	[4]	[5]	[6]	[7]	[8]	[9]	[10]
J	o	n	a	t	h	a	n	□	B

Figure 10.19 Program StoreChars

Edit Window

```
{$R+}
program StoreChars (Input, Output);

{Reads a string of characters into an array.}

  const
    Size = 10;

  type
    IndexRange = 1..Size;
    CharArray = array [IndexRange] of Char;

  var
    Name : CharArray;
    I : Integer;

begin {StoreChars}
  Write ('Enter your first name and an initial ');
  WriteLn ('using 10 characters> ');
  for I := 1 to Size do
    Read (Name[I]);
  ReadLn;

  WriteLn;
  Write ('Hello ');
  for I := 1 to Size do
    Write (Name[I]);
  WriteLn ('!')
end. {StoreChars}
```

Output Window

```
Enter your first name and initial using 10 characters> Jonathan B
Hello Jonathan B!
```

As with any other array, a loop must be used to print all the data stored in a character array. In Turbo Pascal, it is possible to use string variables to simplify operations on character arrays.

Declaring String Variables

A string variable can be thought of as a special kind of character array. Two kinds of data are associated with a string variable, its contents and its length. The length of a string variable is dynamic (changeable) and is determined by the string value currently stored in it. The length of a string variable may range from 0 (no characters stored) to its declared maximum size called its *capacity* (not to exceed 255).

The declarations

```
type
  String10 = string[10];
var
  MyName : String10;
```

identify `MyName` as a string variable that can contain up to 10 characters. The assignment statement

```
MyName := 'Koffman';
```

specifies both the contents (`'Koffman'`) of a string variable `MyName` and its current length (7). The assignment statement

```
MyName := '*';
```

changes the contents of `MyName` to `'*'` and its current length to 1.

SYNTAX DIAGRAM

String Type Declaration

Form: `type`
string type = `string[`*size*`];`

Example: `type`
`String10 = string[10];`

Interpretation: The identifier *string type* denotes a string type that can be used to declare a string variable of capacity *size*.

Note: *size* must be in the range 1 to 255. If *size* is omitted, it is assumed to be 255.

Function Length

The function `Length` can be used to determine the length of a string. If the string `'abc'` is stored in `MyName`, the value of `Length(MyName)` is 3. The value of `Length(MyName)` becomes 1 when the assignment statement

```
MyName := '*';
```

is executed.

SYNTAX DIAGRAM

Length Function (for String Variables)

Form: `Length(`*string*`)`

Example: `Length(Name)`

Interpretation: The function returns an integer indicating the number of characters currently stored in *string*.

The program StoreChars can be shortened considerably if Name is declared using the string data type. This is because the characters to be stored in Name can be read all at one time using a single ReadLn and the contents of Name can be displayed using a single WriteLn statement. A version of program StoreChars, which uses a string variable, appears in Fig. 10.20.

Figure 10.20 Program StoreChars Using String Variable

```
program StoreChars;

{Reads a string of characters into a string.}

  const
    Size = 10;

  type
    String10 = string[Size];

  var
    Name : String10;

begin {StoreChars}
  WriteLn ('Enter your first name and an initial ');
  WriteLn ('using 10 characters> ');
  ReadLn (Name);

  WriteLn ('Hello ', Name, '!')
end. {StoreChars}
```

Referencing Individual Characters in a String

We can manipulate individual characters in a string variable in the same way that we manipulate the individual elements of an array of characters. For example, if MyName is a string variable (type string[10]), then the statement

```
WriteLn (MyName);
```

prints the contents of MyName (up to 10 characters) whereas the statement

```
WriteLn (MyName[1], MyName[Length(MyName)]);
```

displays the first and last characters only. The subscript Length(MyName) selects the last character currently stored in MyName.

The assignment statement

```
MyName[1] := '*';
```

replaces the first character stored in MyName with an asterisk. The for statement

```
for I := 1 to Length(MyName) do
  if MyName[I] = ' ' then
    MyName[I] := '*';
```

replaces all blank characters currently stored in MyName with asterisks. The use of the Length function to define the upper limit of a for loop is very common.

This ensures that only characters currently in the string will be processed by the loop. It makes no sense to manipulate a string position that is beyond its current length.

Reading and Writing Strings

When Read or ReadLn is called with a string variable as its parameter, the number of data characters read is limited by the capacity of the string variable. However, if either an <eoln> or <eof> is reached, before the string variable is filled, the actual string read will be shorter than the capacity of the string variable. The ReadLn procedure advances past the <eoln>.

On output, only the characters currently assigned to a string are displayed. This means that the number of characters written for a string variable may be less than its capacity. Format specifications may be used with string variables to cause additional blanks to precede the contents of the string variable. For example, the statement

```
WriteLn (MyName :12);
```

causes the string

```
'     Koffman'
```

to be written if the value of MyName is 'Koffman'.

If the field width is smaller than the length of the string variable, it is ignored. This means that

```
WriteLn (MyName :7);
```

and

```
WriteLn (MyName :5);
```

both display seven characters (the length of 'Koffman').

String Variables and Type Char Variables

Type Char variables may be assigned to string variables, but string variables may not be assigned to type Char variables. However, it is permissible to assign individual characters from a string to variables of type Char, and conversely.

■ Example 10.12

If NextChar is of type Char, the statment

```
NextChar := MyName[2];
```

copies the second character of string variable MyName into NextChar. The statement

```
MyName[3] := NextChar;
```

redefines the third character of MyName to be the same as the second character. The statement

```
MyName := NextChar;
```

redefines `MyName` as a string of length `1` (value `NextChar`). The statement

```
NextChar := MyName;
```

is not allowed, even if the capacity of `MyName` is `1`. ■

String Assignment

A string variable can be assigned a string literal or the contents of another string variable. The length and capacity of the string operands do not have to be the same. Let's assume that a string variable with capacity *n* (that is, `string[`*n*`]`) is being assigned; only the first *n* characters will be stored in the string variable. If *n* is larger than the length of the string being assigned (say, *m*), then all *m* characters will be stored in the string variable.

■ Example 10.13

Assume the following declarations

```
type
  String3 = string[3];
  String5 = string[5];
var
  X : String3;
  Y : String5;
```

The assignment statements

```
X := '1234567890';
Y := X;
```

store the string `'123'` in both `X` and `Y` because `X` has the smaller capacity and receives its value first. However, the assignment statements

```
Y := '1234567890';
X := Y;
```

store the string `'12345'` in `Y` and `'123'` in `X`. This time the strings stored are different because `Y` receives its value first. ■

Comparing Strings

Function `SameArray` in Fig. 10.11 determines whether two arrays of real numbers are identical. It is much easier to make this determination for strings because Pascal allows them to be operands of the relational operators. Assuming the declarations

```
type
  String3 = string[3];

var
  AlphaStr, BetaStr : String3;        {strings being compared}
  Same, Differ : Boolean;             {Boolean flags}
```

the statement

```
Same := AlphaStr = BetaStr          {Are strings identical?}
```

assigns the value `True` to `Same` when `AlphaStr` and `BetaStr` contain the same string. The assignment statement

```
Differ := AlphaStr <> BetaStr       {Are strings different?}
```

assigns the value `True` to `Differ` when `AlphaStr` and `BetaStr` contain different strings. The assignment statement

```
Same := AlphaStr = 'Rob'            {Is string Rob?}
```

assigns the value `True` to `Same` when `AlphaStr` contains the string `'Rob'`. Finally, the assignment statement

```
Differ := AlphaStr = 'Robert'
```

always assigns the value `True` to `Differ` because the string `'Robert'` is too long to be stored in `AlphaStr`.

Using the relational operators `<`, `<=`, `>`, and `>=`, it is also possible to compare strings for *lexicographic*, or alphabetical, order. The result of such a comparison is based on the collating sequence (order of characters).

For example, the condition

```
AlphaStr < BetaStr
```

is true if the string stored in `AlphaStr` is considered less than the string stored in `BetaStr`. This is determined by comparing corresponding characters in both strings starting with the first pair. If the characters are the same, the next pair is checked. If the characters in position `i` are the first different pair, then `AlphaStr` is less than `BetaStr` if `AlphaStr[i]` is less than `BetaStr[i]`. If two strings of different lengths are compared and all characters of the shorter string match the corresponding characters of the longer string, then the shorter string will be treated as being less than the longer string.

The conditions shown in Table 10.6 are true for the ASCII character codes shown in Appendix E. The reason each condition is true is explained in the last column.

The last line of Table 10.6 shows the curious result that `'30 ' >= '123'` is true. It is true, because the condition result is based solely on the relationship between the first pair of different characters, `'3'` and `'1'`. To avoid these funny results, replace any blanks in numeric strings with zeros. The condition

```
'300' >= '123'
```

is true while the condition

```
'030' >= '123'
```

is false, as expected.

Table 10.6 Some True String Comparisons

AlphaStr	Operator	BetaStr	Reason Condition Is True
'AAA'	<	'ZZZ'	'A' < 'Z'
'AZZ'	<	'ZZZ'	'A' < 'Z'
'ZAZ'	<	'ZZA'	'A' < 'Z'
'AZZ	<	'BAA'	'A' < 'B'
'B11'	>	'A99'	'B' > 'A'
'B11'	<	'B12'	'1' < '2'
'ACE'	<	'AID'	'C' < 'I'
'AB'	<	'ABC'	AlphaStr is shorter
'BA'	>	'ABC'	'B' > 'A'
'123'	>	'103'	'2' > '0'
'123'	>=	'123'	All characters equal
'30 '	>=	'123'	'3' > '1'

Strings as Parameters

In Turbo Pascal, the type of an actual parameter used in a procedure call must be identical to the type of its corresponding variable formal parameter. However, actual parameters used in procedure calls need only be assignment compatible with their corresponding value parameters. This is true for string type parameters, as well.

Assume the declarations

```
type
  String10 = string[10];

var
  ShortStr : String10;

procedure One (var St : string);
 . . .
procedure Two (St : string);
 . . .
```

appear in a Turbo Pascal program. The procedure call

```
Two (ShortStr);
```

is allowed because procedure Two has a value parameter, but the procedure call

```
One (ShortStr);
```

causes a `Type mismatch` syntax error.

However, it is possible to use actual string parameters whose types are not identical to their corresponding variable formal parameters. This is accomplished by disabling the `Var String Checking` compiler option using the compiler directive {$V-}. Once the V compiler option is disabled, the compiler will allow the procedure call

```
One (ShortStr);
```

even though the types of the actual and formal string parameters are not the same.

Using the compiler directive {$V-} in your program will make it easier to access string procedure libraries, because the parameter types do not have to be identical. However, as we pointed out in our discussion of string assignments, you should be aware that characters may be lost if the total number of characters in the string being passed exceeds the declared capacity of either the actual or formal parameter.

SYNTAX DISPLAY

Var String Checking Compiler Directive

Default: {$V+}

When active, the V option causes strict type checking to be performed on strings passed as variable parameters. Strict type checking requires that formal and actual parameters be identical string types. In the {$V-} state, any string type variable is allowed as an actual parameter, even if its capacity is not the same as that of the formal parameter.

A summary of the properties of strings and arrays is provided below. More string operations are discussed in Chapter 13.

- The length of a string variable is dynamic (changeable) and is determined by the data stored in it. This length cannot be less than 0, nor more than the capacity of the string variable (a maximum of 255). The size of an array is fixed.
- A string variable can be read or written by executing a single `ReadLn` (`Read`) or `WriteLn` (`Write`) statement. An array must be read (or written) one element at a time using a loop.
- String variables and string data of different types and lengths may be manipulated together as operands of the assignment operator or the relational operators. Only arrays of the same type may be manipulated together.

Exercises for Section 10.7

Self-Check

1. If an assignment statement is used to store a string, what must be true about the length of the string? What can be done if this is not the case?
2. What is the difference in determining whether two arrays of real numbers are the same as opposed to determining if two strings are the same?

Programming

1. Write a procedure that finds the working length of a string that is padded with blanks. Do not include the blank padding in the working length.
2. Write a procedure that stores the reverse of an input string parameter in its output parameter (for example, if the input string is `'happy'`, the output string should be `'yppah'`.)
3. Write a program that uses the procedure in the preceding exercise to determine whether a string is a palindrome. (A palindrome is a string that reads the same way left to right as it does right to left, for example, `'level'`.)

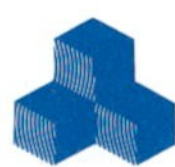

10.8 Using Strings

Now that we have a way to store character strings in memory, we can improve our capability to manipulate textual data. Suppose that during the spring semester you begin thinking about a summer job. One thing you might want to do is write a program that prints form letters so you can do a mass mailing to inquire about summer job opportunities in a variety of fields.

Case Study: Printing a Form Letter

Problem

You want a program that can help you write job application letters. Each letter will be sent to an output file for printing.

Design Overview

A letter consists of a heading, a salutation, the body, and a closing. The heading, salutation, and first line of the body will be different for each letter, but the body and the closing will be the same. First, you'll use an editor to create the letter body and closing and save it as a text file (`BodyFile`). To individualize each letter, you want to enter data for the first part of the letter at the keyboard and then write the first part of the letter to the output file (`Letter`). Next, you can write the rest of the letter from file `BodyFile` to the output file.

An example of the data entry process for the first part of the letter follows. The information you'll enter is in color.

```
Today's date          > July 27, 1990
Employer name         > Peter Liacouras
Company name          > Temple University
Address               > Broad and Montgomery Streets
City, state, and zip> Philadelphia, PA 19122
```

This data would be inserted in the first several lines written to the output file, as shown in Fig. 10.21.

Figure 10.21 First Lines of File Letter

```
                                             July 27, 1990

Peter Liacouras
Temple University
Broad and Montgomery Streets
Philadelphia, PA  19122

Dear Peter Liacouras:

     I am interested in applying for a job at Temple University.
```

Data Requirements

Problem Inputs

The body of the letter (`BodyFile : Text`)
Today's date (`Date : StringType`)
Employer's name (`Employer : StringType`)
Company name (`Company : StringType`)
Company address (`Address : StringType`)
City, state, and zip (`CityStZip : StringType`)

Problem Outputs

The complete letter (`Letter : Text`)

Initial Algorithm

1. Read the preamble data from the keyboard and write it to `Letter`.
2. Copy the letter body to `Letter`.

Algorithm Refinement and Structure Chart

From the structure chart in Fig. 10.22, you can see that procedures `Preamble` and `WriteBody` perform steps 1 and 2, respectively.

Figure 10.22 Structure Chart for Form Letter Program

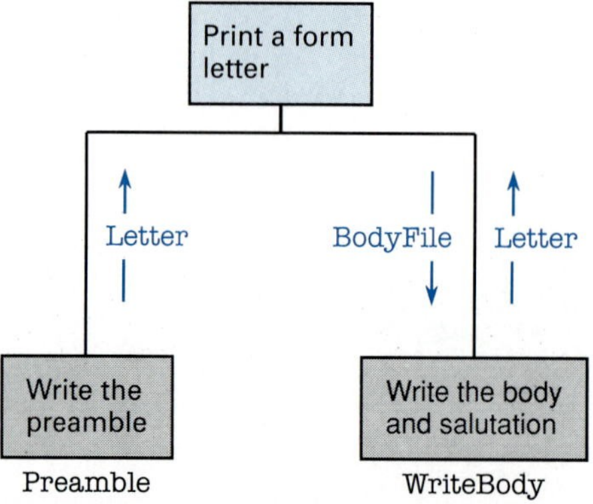

Coding the Main Program

The main program body, shown in Fig. 10.23, prepares both text files and calls procedures `Preamble` and `WriteBody`. The main program displays a message before data entry begins and a message after the letter is completed.

Figure 10.23 Form Letter Writing Program

```
{$R+}
program FormLetter;
{
  Writes a job application letter to an output file. The data
  for the letter preamble is read from the keyboard; the letter
  body is copied from a data file to the output file.
}
  const
    StrLength = 65;

  type
    StringType = string [StrLength];

  var
    BodyFile,                       {input - body of letter}
    Letter    : Text;               {output - completed letter file}


  {Insert procedures Preamble and WriteBody here.}

begin {FormLetter}
  Assign (BodyFile, 'BODY.DAT');
  Assign (Letter, 'LETTER.DAT');
  Reset (BodyFile);
  Rewrite (Letter);
  WriteLn (Output, 'Writing job application letter.');
  Preamble (Letter);
  WriteBody (BodyFile, Letter);
  Close (BodyFile);
  Close (Letter);
  WriteLn (Output, 'Letter copied to output file.')
end. {FormLetter}
```

Coding the Procedures

Procedure `Preamble` (see Fig. 10.24) reads, from the keyboard the strings needed for the letter heading and the salutation. After data entry, the strings read into `DateString`, `Employer`, `Company`, `Address`, `CityStZip` are written to file `Letter`.

Figure 10.24 Procedure Preamble

```
procedure Preamble (var Letter {output} : Text);
{
  Writes a preamble for a job application letter to an output file.
  Pre : The output file is opened.
  Post: Writes the heading, salutation, and first sentence of a
        job application letter using data entered at the keyboard.
}
```

Case Study: Printing a Form Letter, continued

```
  const
    PageWidth = 50;                         {padding for date}

  var
    DateString,                             {input - data strings}
    Employer, Company,                      {        "           }
    Address, CityStZip : StringType;        {        "           }

begin {Preamble}
  {Enter all data}
  Write ('Today''s date         > ');
  ReadLn (DateString);
  Write ('Employer name        > ');
  ReadLn (Employer);
  Write ('Company name         > ');
  ReadLn (Company);
  Write ('Address              > ');
  ReadLn (Address);
  Write ('City, state, and zip> ');
  ReadLn (CityStZip);

  {Write letter preamble.}
  WriteLn (Letter, ' ' :PageWidth, DateString);
  WriteLn (Letter);
  WriteLn (Letter, Employer);
  WriteLn (Letter, Company);
  WriteLn (Letter, CityStZip);
  WriteLn (Letter);
  WriteLn (Letter, 'Dear ', Employer, ':');
  WriteLn (Letter);
  Write (Letter, '     I am interested in applying for a job at ');
  WriteLn (Letter, Company, '.');
  WriteLn (Letter)
end; {Preamble}
```

Procedure `WriteBody` copies the body of the letter (not shown) from the input file to the output file. Procedure `WriteBody` is shown in Fig. 10.25. The `while` loop copies each line of the data file to the output file.

Figure 10.25 Procedure WriteBody

```
procedure WriteBody (var BodyFile {input},
                         Letter   {output} : Text);
{
   Copies the body of a job application letter from a data file
   to an output file.
   Pre : The input file and output file are opened.
   Post: Writes the letter body to the output file.
}
   var
     OneLine : StringType;          {next data line}

    begin {WriteBody}
      {Copy each line until done}
```

```
  while not EOF(BodyFile) do
    begin
      ReadLn (BodyFile, OneLine);
      WriteLn (Letter, OneLine)
    end {while}
end; {WriteBody}
```

Testing

Try to read strings from the keyboard as well as from a data file. See what happens when the data lines are longer than the length of the receiving string variable and when the data line is exactly the same length as the string variable. When you run the form letter program, try using an empty file `BodyFile`.

Exercise for Section 10.8

Programming

1. Write a procedure `WriteString` that displays characters `1` through `StrLen` of a string where the string and `StrLen` are passed as parameters.

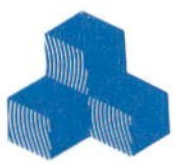

10.9 Debugging Programs with Arrays

During debugging, it is best to use array sizes that are relatively small. If constants are used in array size declarations, then associate these constants with small values. After your program is error free, you can change the constants to their normal values. Also, make sure you enable range checking by using the `{$R+}` compiler directive.

If a variable or expression is used as an array subscript, then you can use the Watch window to observe the subscript value as the program executes. You can place an array element (a subscripted variable) or an entire array in a Watch window. If an array element is in a Watch window, the value displayed will be determined by the current subscript value. If `X` is the array shown in Fig. 10.1 and `X[I]` is placed in the Watch window, the value displayed for `X[I]` is `16.0` when the value of `I` is `1`. When the value of `I` becomes `2`, the value displayed for `X[I]` is `12.0`. The `{$R+}` compiler directive should be used to ensure that `X[I]` is a valid array reference.

If the array name is placed in the Watch window, the entire array will be displayed with the array element values separated by commas and enclosed in parentheses. If `X` is the array shown in Fig. 10.1 and the identifier `X` is placed in the Watch window, the Watch window will contain

```
X: (16.0,12.0,6.0,8.0,2.5,12.0,14.0,-54.5)
```

Strange looking values may be displayed for array elements that have not been assigned values.

If the array is too large to fit in the Watch window, you can use the F6 key to move to the Watch window. Then use the left and right arrow keys (or your mouse and the Watch window's horizontal scroll bar) to scan through the array.

Alternatively, you can display a portion of the array in the Watch window by entering a subscripted variable followed by a comma and a repeat count as a Watch expression. For example, the Watch expression

```
X[3],4
```

causes the following line to be displayed in the Watch window

```
X[3],4: 6.0,8.0,2.5,12.0
```

This line represents the values of four array elements: `X[3]`, `X[4]`, `X[5]`, and `X[6]`. Similarly, a subscripted variable followed by a repeat count could be used to display a portion of a string.

If a loop processes individual array elements, you might prefer to place breakpoints before and after the loop rather than trace each statement in the loop body as its executes. This is particularly true for a loop that reads data into an array; it makes little sense to watch each value being stored. The use of breakpoints allows you to compare the array contents before and after loop execution.

10.10 Common Programming Errors

The most common error in the use of arrays is a subscript expression whose value goes outside the allowable range during program execution. If this happens when range checking is not being performed (the default in Turbo Pascal), storage locations outside the array or even program instructions could be modified without your knowledge. For this reason it is very important that you enable range checking using the `{$R+}` compiler directive when testing and debugging programs. You should also keep range checking enabled during normal production runs unless the execution speed of your program is of critical concern.

Subscript range errors are most often caused by an incorrect subscript expression, a nonterminating loop, or a loop that executes one more time than required. The last situation often arises when the mode of Boolean expression evaluation is changed from short-circuit evaluation to complete evaluation (compiler directive `{$B+}`). A nonterminating loop may occur if the loop control update is erroneously placed outside the loop body.

Subscript range errors are most likely for subscript values at the loop boundaries. If these values are in range, it is likely that all other subscript references in the loop are in range as well.

As with all Pascal data types, make sure there are no type inconsistencies. The subscript type and element type used in all array references must correspond to the types specified in the array declaration.

Similarly, the types of two arrays used in an array copy statement or as corresponding parameters must be the same. Remember to use only identifiers without subscripts as formal array parameters and to specify the types of all array parameters using identifiers.

A variable of type `string[N]` is a string variable of capacity `N` (a constant). Such a string variable can store a string value of up to `N` characters. If you attempt to read or assign a string whose length is longer than `N`, the extra characters will not be stored and no error message will be displayed.

The contents of a string variable can be treated as a single entity or as an array of characters. If your program references individual string characters, be sure to enable range checking (use `{$R+}`).

When using variable parameters that are string types, remember that corresponding actual and formal parameters must be the same string type. However, you can use the compiler directive `{$V-}` to disable type checking of string parameters. Be aware that this may result in some strings being truncated without warning. For value parameters, it is never necessary for corresponding parameters to be the same string type, but strings will be truncated when the capacity of the variable receiving the data is smaller than the string being passed.

Chapter Review

This chapter introduced a data structure called an array, which is a convenient facility for naming and referencing a collection of like items. We discussed how to declare an array type and how to reference an individual array element by placing a subscript in brackets following the array name.

The `for` statement enables us to easily reference the elements of an array in sequence. We can use `for` statements to initialize arrays, to read and print arrays, and to control the manipulation of individual array elements in sequence.

We also examined how to allocate storage for a string variable and how to store a string value in a string variable. You saw that operations such as comparison, assignment, and display are performed more easily on a string variable because the entire string can be processed as a unit rather than element by element.

New Pascal Constructs

Table 10.7 describes the new Pascal constructs introduced in this chapter.

Table 10.7 Summary of New Pascal Constructs

Construct	Effect

Array Declaration
`type`
`  IndexRange = 1..10;`
`  IntArray = array [IndexRange] of Integer;`
 	
`var`
`  Cube, Count : IntArray;`
	The data type `IntArray` describes an array with 10 type `Integer` elements. `Cube` and `Count` are arrays with this structure.

String Declaration
`type`
`  String10 = string[10];`
 	
`var`
`  Name : String10;`
	The data type `String10` describes a string type with capacity for 10 characters. `Name` is a string variable of type `String10`.

Array References
`for I := 1 to 10 do`
`  Cube [I] := I * I * I`
	Saves `I` cubed in the `I`th element of array `Cube`.

`if Cube[5] > 100 then`	Compares `Cube[5]` to `100`.
`Write (Cube[1], Cube[2])`	Displays the first two cubes.
Array Copy `Count := Cube`	Copies contents of array `Cube` to array `Count`.
Operations on Strings `Name := 'R. Koffman'`	Saves `'R. Koffman'` in `Name`.
`WriteLn (Name)`	Displays `'R. Koffman'`.
`WriteLn (Name[4]);`	Displays `'K'`.
`Name[1] := 'E';`	Changes the first character of `Name` to `E`.
`if Name > 'Daffy Duck' then`	Compares `Name` to `'Daffy Duck'`.

✓ Quick-Check Exercises

1. What is a data structure?
2. Which standard types cannot be array subscript types? Array element types?
3. Can values of different types be stored in an array?
4. If an array is declared to have ten elements, must the program use all ten?

5. When can the assignment operator be used with an array as its operands? Answer the same question for the equality operator.
6. The two methods of array access are ____________ and ____________.
7. The ____________ loop allows us to access the elements of an array in ________ order.
8. Can the variable declared as follows be used to store a string of length five using an assignment statement? If not, why not?

```
var
  AString : string[6];
```

9. Explain why variable parameters are a more efficient use of memory when passing arrays to a procedure.
10. Declare variables `First` and `Last` that can be used to enter a person's first name and last name (maximum of twenty characters each) into separate strings.

Answers to Quick-Check Exercises

1. A data structure is a grouping of related values in main memory.
2. `Real` and `Integer`; all can be element types.
3. No
4. No
5. If the arrays are the same type. Never.
6. random and sequential
7. `for`, sequential
8. Yes
9. A local copy of each array used as a value parameter is made when a procedure is called.
10.
```
type
  AString = string[20];

var
  First, Last : AString;
```

Review Questions

1. Identify the error in the following code segment. When will the error be detected?

```
program Test;
  type
    AnArray = array [1..8] of Integer;

  var
    X : AnArray;
    I : Integer;

begin {Test}
  for I := 1 to 9 do
    X[I] := I
end. {Test}
```

2. Declare an array of reals called `Week` that can be referenced by using any day of the week as a subscript, where `Sunday` is the first subscript.
3. Identify the error in the following segment of Pascal statements.

```
type
  AnArray = array [Char] of Real;

var
  X : AnArray;
  I : Integer;

begin
  I := 1;
  X[I] := 8.384
end.
```

4. Is the last statement in the following Pascal program segment a valid Pascal statement?

```
type
  RealArray = array [1..8] of Real;

var
  X : RealArray;
  I : Integer;

begin
  I := 1;
  X(I) := 8.384
end.
```

5. What are two common ways of selecting array elements for processing?
6. Write a Pascal program segment to print out the index of the smallest and the largest numbers in an array `X` of 20 integers with values from `0` to `100`. Assume array `X` already has values assigned to each element.
7. The parameters for a procedure are two arrays (type `RealArray`) and an integer that represents the length of the arrays. The procedure copies the first array in the parameter list to the other array in reverse order using a loop structure. Write the procedure.
8. List three advantages to using strings.
9. What would be a valid reason for not passing an array that provides input to a procedure as a value parameter?

Programming Projects

1. Write a program to read `N` data items into two arrays `X` and `Y` of size `20`. Store the product of corresponding elements of `X` and `Y` in a third array `Z`, also of size `20`. Print a three-column table displaying the arrays `X`, `Y`, and `Z`. Then compute and print the square root of the sum of the items in `Z`. Make up your own data, with `N` less than `20`.
2. Write a program for the following problem. You are given a collection of scores for the last exam in your computer course. You are to compute the average of these scores and then assign grades to each student according to the following rule.

   If a student's score is within 10 points (above or below) of the average, assign a grade of `Satisfactory`. If the score is more than 10 points higher than the average, assign a grade of `Outstanding`. If the score is more than 10 points below the average, assign a grade of `Unsatisfactory`.

   Hint: The output from your program should consist of a labeled three-column list containing the ID number, exam score, and grade of each student.

3. Assume for a moment that your computer has the very limited capability of being able to read and write only single integer digits and to add together two integers consisting of one decimal digit each. Write a program that can read in two integers of up to 30 digits each, add these digits together, and display the result. Test your program using pairs of numbers of varying lengths.

   Hints: Store the two numbers in two integer arrays of size 30, one digit per array element. If the number is less than 30 digits in length, enter enough leading zeros (to the left of the number) to make the number 30 digits long.

   You will need a loop to add the digits in corresponding array elements starting with subscript 30. Don't forget to handle the carry digit if there is one! Use a Boolean variable to indicate whether the sum of the last pair of digits is greater than 9.
4. The results of a true-false exam given to a computer science class have been coded for input to a program. The information available for each student consists of a student identification number and the student's answers to ten true or false questions. The available data are as follows:

Student Identification	*Answer String*
0080	FTTFTFTTFT
0340	FTFTFTTTFF
0341	FTTFTTTTTT
0401	TTFFTFFTTT
0462	TTFTTTFFTF
0463	TTTTTTTTTT
0464	FTFFTFFTFT
0512	TFTFTFTFTF
0618	TTTFFTTFTF
0619	FFFFFFFFFF
0687	TFTTFTTFTF
0700	FTFFTTFFFT
0712	FTFTFTFTFT
0837	TFTFTTFTFT

   Write a program that first reads in the answer string representing the ten correct answers (use `FTFFTFFTFT` as data). Next, read each student's data and compute and store the number of correct answers for each student in one array and store the student ID number in the corresponding element of another array. Determine the best score, `Best`. Then print a three-column table that displays the ID number, the score, and the grade for each student. The grade should be determined as follows: if the score is equal to `Best` or `Best-1`, give an `A`; if it is `Best-2` or `Best-3`, give a `C`. Otherwise, give an `F`.
5. The results of a survey of the households in your township are available for public scrutiny. Each record contains data for one household, including a four-digit integer identification number, the annual income for the household, and the number of members of the household. Write a program to read the survey results into three arrays and perform the following analyses:
   a. Count the number of households included in the survey and print a three-column table displaying the data read in. (Assume that no more than twenty-five households were surveyed.)
   b. Calculate the average household income and list the identification number and income of each household that exceeds the average.
   c. Determine the percentage of households that have incomes below the poverty level. Compute the poverty level income using the formula

$$p = \$6500.00 + \$750.00 * (m - 2)$$

where m is the number of members of each household. This formula shows that the poverty level depends on the number of family members, m, and the poverty level income increases as m gets larger.

Test your program on the following data.

Identification Number	*Annual Income*	*Household Members*
1041	12,180	4
1062	13,240	3
1327	19,800	2
1483	22,458	8
1900	17,000	2
2112	18,125	7
2345	15,623	2
3210	3,200	6
3600	6,500	5
3601	11,970	2
4725	8,900	3
6217	10,000	2
9280	6,200	1

6. Assume that a set of sentences is to be processed. Each sentence consists of a sequence of words, separated by one or more blank spaces. Write a program that will read these sentences and count the number of words with one letter, the number of words with two letters, and so on, up to ten letters.
7. Write an interactive program that plays the game of Hangman. Read the word to be guessed into string `Word`. The player must guess the letters belonging to `Word`. The program should terminate when either all letters have been guessed correctly (player wins) or a specified number of incorrect guesses have been made (computer wins). Hint: Use a string variable `Solution` to keep track of the solution so far. Initialize `Solution` to a string of symbols `'*'`. Each time a letter in `Word` is guessed, replace the corresponding `'*'` in `Solution` with that letter.
8. Write a program to simulate a game called Reversi. The game begins by displaying the digits 1 to 9 in a scrambled order. The user is then prompted for the number of digits to reverse starting from the left. The order of these digits is reversed and the new list of digits is displayed. For example, if the initial order of the numbers is

```
5  4  6  2  1  7  9  8  3
```

and the user requests reversal of the first 5 digits, the new list displayed would be

```
1  2  6  4  5  7  9  8  3
```

By continuing this process, it is possible to arrange the digits in ascending numerical order. The object of Reversi is to do this with the fewest number of turns. Some thought must be given to generating the digits 1 to 9 in scrambled order, since simply calling Random 9 times may generate duplicate values.

11

Records

The previous chapter introduced the array, a data structure that is fundamental to programming and included in almost every high-level programming language. This chapter examines another data structure, the record (available in Pascal but not in all other high-level languages). Records make it easier to organize and represent information in Pascal, a major reason for the popularity of the Pascal language.

Like an array, a record is a collection of related data items. Unlike an array, however, the individual components of a record can contain data of different types. We can use a record to store a variety of information about a person, such as the name, marital status, age, and date of birth. Each data item is stored in a separate record field; we can reference each data item stored in a record through its field name.

In this chapter, we also develop an abstract data type for complex arithmetic, consisting of a record type and associated operators.

11.1 The Record Data Type

A *data base* is a collection of information stored in a computer memory or a disk file. A data base is subdivided into records, which normally contain information regarding particular data objects. For example, the description of a person, place, or thing would be stored as a record.

Record Type Declaration

Before a record can be created or saved, the record format must be specified through a record type declaration.

■ Example 11.1

The staff of our small software firm is growing rapidly. To keep the records more accessible and organized, we decide to store relevant data, such as the following descriptive information, in an employee data base.

```
ID  : 1234
Name: Caryn Jackson
Sex : Female
Number of Dependents: 2
Hourly Rate: 3.98
Taxable Salary (for 40 hour week): 130.40
```

We can declare a record type `Employee` to store this information. There must be six *fields* in the record type, one for each data item. We must specify the name of each field and the type of information stored in each field. We choose the names in the same way we choose all other identifiers: the names describe the nature of the information represented. The contents of each field determines the appropriate data type. For example, the employee's name should be stored in a string field.

The record type `Employee` has six distinct fields. One is a string type, two are type `Real`, one is type `Integer`, one is a subrange type, and one (`Sex`) is an enumerated type (`Gender`).

```
const
  StrLength = 20;

type
  IDRange = 1111..9999;
  StringType = string[StrLength];
  Gender = (Female, Male);

  Employee = record
               ID : IDRange;
               Name : StringType;
               Sex : Gender;
               NumDepend : Integer;
               Rate, TaxSal : Real
             end; {Employee}
```

The record type is a template that describes the format of each record and the name of each data element. A variable declaration is required to allocate storage space for a record. The record variables `Clerk` and `Janitor` are declared next.

```
var
  Clerk, Janitor : Employee;
```

The record variables `Clerk` and `Janitor` both have the structure specified in the declaration for record type `Employee`. Thus, the memory allocated for each consists of storage space for six distinct values. The record variable `Clerk` is pictured as follows, assuming the values shown earlier are stored in memory. ■

Record variable Clerk

ID	1234
Name	Caryn□Jackson
Sex	Female
NumDepend	2
Rate	3.98
TaxSal	130.40

As illustrated in the type declaration for `Employee`, each field of a record can be a standard data type or a user-defined simple or structured data type. The record type declaration is described in the next display.

SYNTAX DISPLAY

Record Type Declaration

Form: `type`
rec type = `record`

id list$_1$: *type*$_1$;
id list$_2$: *type*$_2$;
.
.
.
id list$_n$: *type*$_n$
`end;`

Example:
```
type
  Complex = record
              RealPart, ImaginaryPart : Real
            end;
```

Interpretation: The identifier *rec type* is the name of the record structure being described. Each *id list*$_i$ is a list of one or more field names separated by commas; the data type of each field in *id list*$_i$ is specified by *type*$_i$.
Note: *type*$_i$ can be any standard or user-defined data type, including a structured type. If *type*$_i$ is a user-defined data type, it can be defined either before the record or as part of the record description.

Manipulating Individual Fields of a Record

We can reference a record field by using a *field selector*, which consists of the record variable name followed by the field name. A period separates the field name and the record name.

■ Example 11.2

Figure 11.1 is an example of the record variable `Clerk`. The data shown earlier could be stored in `Clerk` through the sequence of assignment statements in the figure.

Figure 11.1 Record Variable Clerk

```
Clerk.ID := 1234;
Clerk.Name := 'Caryn Jackson';
Clerk.Sex := Female;
Clerk.NumDepend := 2;
Clerk.Rate := 3.98;
Clerk.TaxSal := Clerk.Rate * 40.0 - Clerk.NumDepend * 14.40;
```

Once data are stored in a record, they can be manipulated the same as other data in memory. For example, the last assignment statement in Fig. 11.1 computes the clerk's taxable salary by deducting $14.40 for each dependent from the gross salary (`Clerk.Rate * 40.0`). The computed result is saved in the record field `Clerk.TaxSal`.

The statements

```
Write ('The clerk is ');
case Clerk.Sex of
  Female : Write ('Ms. ');
  Male   : Write ('Mr. ')
end; {case}
Write (Clerk.Name)
```

display the clerk's name after an appropriate title (`'Ms.'` or `'Mr.'`); the output line follows.

```
The clerk is Ms. Caryn Jackson
```

■

Abstract Record

We can summarize what we have discussed about records in the following specification for an abstract record.

Specification for Abstract Records

Structure: A record is a collection of related data values of different types. Each data value is stored in a separate field of the record.
Operators: Two basic operators act on fields of a record: *store* and *retrieve*. The store operator inserts a value into the record field. If `A` is a record with a field named `B`, and `C` is an expression that is assignment compatible with the type of field `B`, the statement

```
A.B := C
```

stores the contents of `C` in field `B` of record `A`. If field `B` of record `A` is assignment compatible with the type of variable `C`, the statement

```
C := A.B
```

retrieves the value in field `B` of record `A` and copies it into `C`.

The assignment operator can also be used to copy the contents of one record to another record of the same type. If `A` and `D` are record variables of the same type, the statement

```
A := D
```

copies all values associated with record `D` to record `A`.

Exercises for Section 11.1

Self-Check

1. Each part in an inventory is represented by its part number, a descriptive name, the quantity on hand, and the price. Define a record type `Part`.
2. A catalog listing for a textbook consists of the author's name, the title, the publisher, and the year of publication. Declare a record type `CatalogEntry`

and variable Book and write assignment statements that store the relevant data for this textbook in Book.

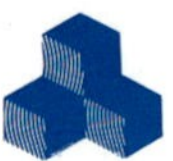

11.2 The with Statement

It is tedious to write the complete field selector each time you reference a field of a record. You can use the with statement to shorten the field selector.

```
with Clerk do
  begin
    Write ('The clerk is ');
    case Sex of
      Female : Write ('Ms. ');
      Male   : Write ('Mr. ')
    end;  {case}
    WriteLn (Name);

    TaxSal := 40.0 * Rate - 14.40 * NumDepend;
    WriteLn ('The clerk''s taxable salary is $', TaxSal :4:2)
  end; {with}
```

As you can see, you don't need to specify both the record variable and the field names inside a with statement. The record variable Clerk is identified in the with statement header; consequently, only the field name is needed, not the complete field selector (for example, Rate instead of Clerk.Rate). The with statement is particularly useful when you are manipulating several fields of the same record variable, as in this example.

SYNTAX DISPLAY

with Statement

Form: with *record var* do
statement

Example:
```
with Clerk do
  if NumDepend > 3 then
    Rate := 1.5 * Rate
```

Interpretation: *Statement* can be a single statement or a compound statement. *record var* is the name of a record variable. Anywhere within *statement*, you can reference a field of *record var* by specifying only its field name.

■ Example 11.3

The program in Fig. 11.2 computes the distance from an arbitrary point on the *x*-*y* plane to the origin (intersection of the *x*-axis and the *y*-axis). The values of the *x*-coordinate and the *y*-coordinate are entered as data and stored in the fields X and Y of the record variable Point1. The formula used to compute the distance, *d*, from the origin to an arbitrary point (*X*, *Y*) is

$$d = \sqrt{X^2 + Y^2}$$

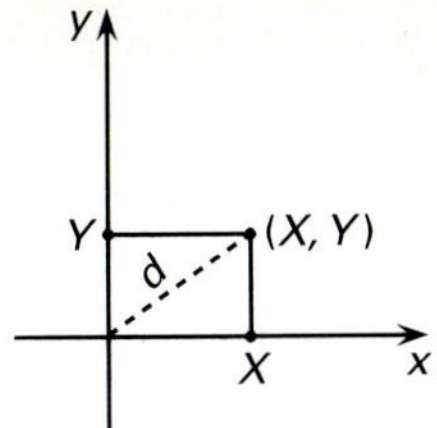

Because the record variable `Pointl` is specified in the `with` statement header, we need only the field names `X` and `Y` to reference the coordinates of the data point. Each coordinate is read separately, because it is illegal to use a record variable as a parameter of a `ReadLn` or `WriteLn` procedure (i.e., only individual fields of a record variable may be read or displayed at a terminal, not the entire record). ■

Figure 11.2 Distance from Point to Origin

Edit Window

```
program DistOrigin;

{Finds the distance from a point to the origin.}

  type
    Point = record
              X, Y : Real
            end;  {Point}

  var
    Pointl : Point;          {input - the data point}
    Distance : Real;         {output - its distance from the origin}

begin
  with Pointl do
    begin
      Write ('X> ');
      ReadLn (X);
      Write ('Y> ');
      ReadLn (Y);
      Distance := Sqrt(Sqr(X) + Sqr(Y));
      WriteLn ('Distance to origin is ', Distance :4:2)
    end {with}
end.
```

Output Window

```
X> 3.00
Y> 4.00
Distance to origin is 5.00
```

PROGRAM STYLE

A Word of Caution About the with Statement

Although the `with` statement is helpful in reducing the length of program statements that manipulate record components, it also can reduce the clarity of these statements. For example, in Fig. 11.2 it is not obvious that the statement

```
Distance := Sqrt(Sqr(X) + Sqr(Y));
```

is passing to the function Sqr two record fields (Point.X and Point.Y) and not two variables.

The possibility of confusion and error increases when you are manipulating two record variables (say, Point1 and Point2). In that case, if the field name X is referenced by itself, it is not apparent whether we mean Point1.X or Point2.X. Pascal uses the record variable specified in the closest with statement header.

Exercises for Section 11.2

Self-Check

1. Write the Pascal statements, using a with statement, required to print the values stored in Clerk in the form shown in Fig. 11.1.

Programming

1. Modify program DistOrigin to find the distance between two points. Use the formula

$$Distance = \sqrt{(X_1 - X_2)^2 + (Y_1 - Y_2)^2}$$

Store the points in two record variables of type Point.

11.3 Records as Operands and Parameters

Because arithmetic and logical operations can be performed only on individual memory cells, record variables cannot be used as the operands of arithmetic and relational operators. Arithmetic and logical operators must be used with individual fields of a record, as shown in the previous section. This is also true at this point for the standard procedures Read/ReadLn and Write/WriteLn. (Chapter 14 examines how to read and write entire record variables to certain types of files.)

Record Assignment

We can copy all the fields of one record variable to another record variable of the same type using a record copy (assignment) statement. If Clerk and Janitor are both record variables of type Employee, the statement

```
Clerk := Janitor        {copy Janitor to Clerk}
```

copies each field of Janitor into the corresponding field of Clerk.

Records as Parameters

A record can be passed as a parameter to a function or procedure, provided the actual parameter is the same type as its corresponding formal parameter. The use of records as parameters can shorten parameter lists considerably, because one parameter (the record variable) can be passed instead of several related parameters.

■ Example 11.4

In a grading program, the summary statistics for an exam might consist of the average score, the highest and lowest scores, and the standard deviation. In previous problems, we would have stored these data in separate variables; now, however, it makes sense to group them together as a record.

```
type
  ExamStats = record
                Low, High : 0..100;
                Average, StandardDev : Real;
              end;  {ExamStats}

var
  Exam : ExamStats;
```

A procedure that computes one of these results (for example, `Average`) could be passed a single record field (for example, `Exam.Average`). A procedure that manipulates more than one field could be passed the entire record. An example is procedure `PrintStat`, shown in Fig. 11.3. ■

Figure 11.3 Procedure PrintStat

```
procedure PrintStat (Exam {input} : ExamStats);
{
  Prints the exam statistics.
  Pre : The fields of record variable Exam are assigned values.
  Post: Each field of Exam is displayed.
}
begin {PrintStat}
  with Exam do
    begin
      WriteLn ('High score: ', High :1);
      WriteLn ('Low score: ', Low :1);
      WriteLn ('Average: ', Average :3:1);
      WriteLn ('Standard deviation: ', StandardDev :3:1)
    end  {with}
end;  {PrintStat}
```

■ Example 11.5

Before performing a potentially dangerous or costly experiment in the laboratory, we can often use a computer program to simulate the experiment. In computer simulations, we need to keep track of the time of day as the experiment progresses. Normally, the time of day is updated after a certain period has elapsed. The record type `Time` is declared as follows, assuming a twenty-four-hour clock.

```
type
  Time = record
    Hour : 0..23;
    Minute, Second : 0..59
  end;  {Time}
```

Procedure `ChangeTime` in Fig. 11.4 updates the time of day, `TimeOfDay` (type `Time`), after a time interval, `ElapsedTime`, which is expressed in seconds. Each statement that uses the `mod` operator updates a particular field of the record represented by `TimeOfDay`. The `mod` operator ensures that each updated value is within the required range; the `div` operator converts multiples of sixty seconds to minutes and multiples of sixty minutes to hours. ■

Figure 11.4 Procedure ChangeTime

```
procedure ChangeTime (ElapsedTime {input} : Integer;
                      var TimeOfDay {input/output} : Time);
{
  Updates the time of day, TimeOfDay, assuming a 24-hour clock
  and an elapsed time of ElapsedTime in seconds.
  Pre : ElapsedTime and record TimeOfDay are assigned values.
  Post: TimeOfDay is incremented by ElapsedTime.
}

  var
    NewHour, NewMin, NewSec : Integer; {temporary values}

begin {ChangeTime}
  with TimeOfDay do
    begin
      NewSec := Second + ElapsedTime;              {total seconds}
      Second := NewSec mod 60;                    {seconds mod 60}
      NewMin := Minute + (NewSec div 60);          {total minutes}
      Minute := NewMin mod 60;                    {minutes mod 60}
      NewHour := Hour + (NewMin div 60);             {total hours}
      Hour := NewHour mod 24                        {hours mod 24}
    end {with}
end;  {ChangeTime}
```

Reading a Record

Normally, we use a procedure to read data into a record. Procedure `Read-Employee` in Fig. 11.5 could be used to read data into the first five fields of a record variable of type `Employee`. Because we are passing a record variable to `ReadEmployee`, only one parameter is needed, not five. The procedure call statement

```
ReadEmployee (Clerk)
```

causes the data read to be stored in record variable `Clerk`.

Figure 11.5 Procedure ReadEmployee

```
procedure ReadEmployee (var OneClerk {output} : Employee);
{
  Reads one employee record into OneClerk.
  Pre : None
  Post: Data are read into record OneClerk.
}
  var
    SexChar : Char;              {letter indicating sex}

begin {ReadEmployee}
  with OneClerk do
    Write ('ID> ');
    ReadLn (ID);
    Write ('Name> ');
    ReadLn (Name);
    Write ('Sex (F or M)> ');
    ReadLn (SexChar);
    case SexChar of
      'F', 'f' : Sex := Female;
      'M', 'm' : Sex := Male
    end; {case}

    Write ('Number of dependents> ');
    ReadLn (NumDepend);
    Write ('Hourly rate> ');
    ReadLn (Rate)
  end  {with}
end; {ReadEmployee}
```

Exercises for Section 11.3

Self-Check

1. What does the following program segment do? Provide the declarations for variables `Exam1` and `Exam2`.

```
PrintStat (Exam1);
Exam2 := Exam1;
Exam2.High := Exam2.High - 5.0;
PrintStat (Exam2)
```

2. If all fields of variable `Now` (type `Time`) are initially zero, how is `Now` changed by the execution of the following program segment?

```
ChangeTime (3600, Now);
ChangeTime (7125, Now)
```

Programming

1. Write a procedure that initializes all fields of a variable of type `Time` to zero.
2. Write a procedure to read in the data for a record variable of type `CatalogEntry`. (See exercise 2 at the end of Section 11.1).
3. Write a procedure that reads in the coordinates of a point (type `Point`) on the *x*-*y* plane.

11.4 Abstract Data Types Revisited

Abstraction is a powerful tool in programming. Procedural abstraction enables us to focus on the operations that we want to perform without having to provide immediately the details of how each operation will be implemented.

Data abstraction is the technique of focusing on the data and the operations to be performed without being concerned about how the data are actually represented in memory. Chapter 8 showed you how to implement an abstract data type (ADT) consisting of a data type and its relevant operators. An ADT can be saved as a separate file and inserted into a Pascal program as needed.

The program that uses an ADT is called the *client program*. A client program can declare and manipulate objects of this data type and use the data type's operators without knowing the details of the internal representation of the data type or the implementation of its operators; the details are hidden from the client program (called *information hiding*). In this way, we separate the use of the data and the operators (by the client program) from the representation and the implementation (by the ADT).

Data abstraction provides several advantages. It allows us to implement the client program and the ADT relatively independent of each other. If we decide to change the implementation of an operator (procedure) in the ADT, we can do so without affecting the client program. Finally, because the internal representation of a data type is hidden from its client program, we can even change the internal representation at a later time without modifying the client program.

Case Study: Abstract Data Type for Complex Arithmetic

This section explains how to specify and implement an ADT for complex arithmetic.

Problem

An engineering professor wants us to write a set of procedures that can be used to perform arithmetic on complex numbers. A complex number is a number with a real part and an imaginary part. For example, the complex number $a + ib$ [also written as (a, b)] has a real part of a and an imaginary part of b, where the symbol i represents $\sqrt{-1}$. The professor wants us to provide a module for creating, defining, reading, and displaying a complex number. The module should also contain procedures for performing complex arithmetic (for example, addition, subtraction, multiplication, and division of complex numbers). There should also be operators for extracting real and imaginary parts and finding the absolute value (magnitude) of the complex number.

Design Overview

We will implement an ADT to represent the data structure for a complex number with operators for each of the tasks listed. The specification of the abstract data type `ComplexNumber` follows.

Specification of ComplexNumber

Structure: A complex number is an object of type `Complex` that consists of a pair of `Real` values.

Operators: In the following descriptions, assume these parameters:

`A`, `B`, and `C` represent complex numbers

`X` and `Y` represent type `Real` values

```
procedure InitialComplex (var C {output} : Complex);
{Creates a complex number C and initializes it to (0.0, 0.0).}

procedure SetComplex (X, Y {input} : Real;
                      var C {output} : Complex);
{Sets C to the complex number (X, Y).}

procedure ReadComplex (var C {output} : Complex);
{Reads a pair of values into complex number C.}

procedure WriteComplex (C {input} : Complex);
{Displays complex number C.}

procedure AddComplex (A, B  {input}  : Complex;
                      var C {output} : Complex);
{Complex number C is the sum of complex numbers A and B.}

procedure SubtractComplex (A, B  {input}  : Complex;
                           var C {output} : Complex);
{Complex number C is the difference of complex numbers A and B.}

procedure MultiplyComplex (A, B  {input}  : Complex;
                           var C {output} : Complex);
{Complex number C is the product of complex numbers A and B.}

procedure DivideComplex (A, B  {input}  : Complex;
                         var C {output} : Complex);
{Complex number C is the quotient of complex numbers A and B.}

function GetReal (A : Complex) : Real;
{Returns the real part of complex number A.}

function GetImaginary (A : Complex) : Real;
{Returns the imaginary part of complex number A.}

function AbsComplex (A : Complex) : Real;
{Returns the absolute value of complex number A.}
```

The first operator listed is `InitialComplex`, which initializes a variable of type `Complex` to `(0.0, 0.0)`. The remaining operators are procedures that define the value of a complex number (`SetComplex` and `ReadComplex`), display a complex number (`WriteComplex`), perform complex arithmetic operations (`AddComplex`, etc.), extract the real and imaginary parts (`GetReal`, `Get-Imaginary`), and find the absolute value (`AbsComplex`).

After the specification is written, programmers can implement client programs that use the ADT `ComplexNumber`. If stubs are available for the operator procedures, the client programs can be compiled and executed to test the overall flow of control. Once the ADT is completed, the client programs can be executed in a meaningful way. Figure 11.6 is a partially completed implementation of the ADT.

Figure 11.6 Abstract Data Type Complex

```
unit ComplexNumber;
{Abstract data type for complex numbers}

interface
  type                                {data type specification}
    Complex = record
                RealPart, ImaginaryPart : Real
              end; {Complex}

  procedure InitialComplex (var C {output} : Complex);
  {
    Creates a complex number C and initializes it to (0.0, 0.0).
    Pre : None
    Post: C is initialized to (0.0, 0.0)
  }

  procedure SetComplex (X, Y  {input}  : Real;
                        var C {output} : Complex);
  {
    Sets the complex number C to (X, Y).
    Pre : None
    Post: C is the complex number (X, Y).
  }

  procedure ReadComplex (var C {output} : Complex);
  {
    Reads a pair of values into complex number C.
    Pre : None
    Post: The first real number read is the real part of C;
          the second real number read is the imaginary part of C.
  }

  procedure WriteComplex (C {input} : Complex);
  {
    Displays complex number C.
    Pre : C is assigned a value.
    Post: Print the real and imaginary parts of C.
  }

  procedure Addcomplex (A, B  {input}  : Complex;
                        var C {output} : Complex);
  {
    Complex number C is the sum of complex numbers A and B.
    Pre : A and B are assigned values.
    Post: C is the complex sum of A and B.
  }
  procedure SubtractComplex (A, B  {input}  : Complex;
                             var C {output} : Complex);
```

```
  {
    Complex number C is the difference of complex numbers A and B.
    Pre : A and B are assigned values.
    Post: C is the complex difference of A and B.
  }

  procedure MultiplyComplex (A, B  {input}  : Complex;
                             var C {output} : Complex);
  {
    Complex number C is the product of complex numbers A and B.
    Pre : A and B are assigned values.
    Post: C is the complex product of A and B.
  }

  procedure DivideComplex (A, B  {input}  : Complex;
                           var C {output} : Complex);
  {
    Complex number C is the quotient of complex numbers A and B.
    Pre : A and B are assigned values.
    Post: C is the complex quotient of A and B.
  }

  function GetReal (A : Complex) : Real;
  {
    Returns the real part of complex number A.
    Pre : A is assigned a value.
    Post: The real part of A is returned.
  }

  function GetImaginary (A : Complex) : Real;
  {
    Returns the imaginary part of complex number A.
    Pre : A is assigned a value.
    Post: The imaginary part of A is returned.
  }

  function AbsComplex (A : Complex) : Real;
  {
    Returns the absolute value of complex number A.
    Pre : A is assigned a value.
    Post: The absolute value of A is returned.
  }

implementation                        {operator procedures}

  procedure InitialComplex (var C {output} : Complex);
  begin {InitialComplex}
     C.RealPart := 0.0;
     C.ImaginaryPart := 0.0
  end; {InitialComplex}

  procedure SetComplex (X, Y  {input}  : Real;
                        var C {output} : Complex);
  begin {SetComplex}
     C.RealPart := X;
     C.ImaginaryPart := Y
  end; {SetComplex}

  procedure ReadComplex (var C {output} : Complex);
  begin {ReadComplex}
```

```
    Write ('Real part> ');
    ReadLn (C.RealPart);
    Write ('Imaginary part> ');
    ReadLn (C.ImaginaryPart)
  end; {ReadComplex}

  procedure WriteComplex (C {input} : Complex);
  begin {WriteComplex}
    Write ('(', C.RealPart :4:2);
    WriteLn (', ', C.ImaginaryPart :4:2, ')');
  end; {WriteComplex}

  procedure AddComplex (A, B  {input}  : Complex;
                        var C {output} : Complex);
  begin {AddComplex}
    C.RealPart := A.RealPart + B.RealPart;
    C.ImaginaryPart := A.ImaginaryPart + B.ImaginaryPart
  end; {AddComplex}

  procedure SubtractComplex (A, B, {input}  : Complex;
                             var C {output} : Complex);
  begin {SubtractComplex}
    C.RealPart := A.RealPart - B.RealPart;
    C.ImaginaryPart := A.ImaginaryPart - B.Imaginary Part
  end; {SubtractComplex}

  procedure MultiplyComplex (A, B, {input}  : Complex;
                             var C {output} : Complex);
  begin {MultiplyComplex}
    WriteLn ('Procedure MultiplyComplex called.')
  end; {MultiplyComplex}

  procedure DivideComplex (A, B, {input}  : Complex;
                           var C {output} : Complex);
  begin {DivideComplex}
    WriteLn ('Procedure DivideComplex called.')
  end; {DivideComplex}

  function GetReal (A {input} : Complex);
  begin {GetReal}
    GetReal := A.RealPart
  end; {GetReal}

  function GetImaginary (A {input} : Complex);
  begin {GetImaginary}
    GetImaginary := A.ImaginaryPart
  end; {GetImaginary}

  function AbsComplex (A {input} : Complex);
  begin {AbsComplex}
    AbsComplex := Sqrt(A.RealPart * A.RealPart +
                       A.ImaginaryPart * A.ImaginaryPart)
  end; {AbsComplex}
end. {ComplexNumber}
```

The complex addition and subtraction operators are implemented as procedures AddComplex and SubtractComplex, respectively. From these procedures, we see that the sum (or difference) of two complex numbers is obtained by adding (or subtracting) the real and imaginary parts separately. Function `AbsComplex` computes the absolute value of a complex number according to the following formula (the multiply and divide procedures are left as an exercise).

$$|a + ib| = \sqrt{(a + ib) * (a - ib)} = \sqrt{a^2 + b^2}$$

The engineering professor can now execute client programs that use the ADT for complex arithmetic. Each client program must contain the statement

```
uses ComplexNumber;
```

Figure 11.7 is a client module that uses ADT `ComplexNumber`.

Figure 11.7 Using ADT ComplexNumber

Edit Window

```
program TestComplex;
{
   Reads two complex numbers and displays their sum and difference.
   Also displays the absolute value of one of the numbers.
   Uses the abstract data type ComplexNumber.

  Imports:  Complex, ReadComplex, AddComplex, SubtractComplex,
            WriteComplex, AbsComplex from unit ComplexNumber
}

   uses ComplexNumber;

   var
     A, B, C : Complex;               {three complex numbers}

begin {TestComplex}
  {Read in complex numbers A and B.}
  WriteLn ('Enter the first complex number.');
  ReadComplex (A);
  WriteLn;
  WriteLn ('Enter the second complex number.');
  ReadComplex (B);

  AddComplex (A, B, C);                         {form the sum}
  Write ('The complex sum is ');
  WriteComplex (C);                          {display the sum}
  SubtractComplex (A, B, C);             {form the difference}
  Write ('The complex difference is ');
  WriteComplex (C);                   {display the difference}

  Write ('The absolute value of the first complex number is ');
  WriteLn (AbsComplex(A) :4:2)
end. {TestComplex}
```

Output Window

```
Enter the first complex number.
Real part> 3.5
Imaginary part> 5.2
```

Case Study: Abstract Data Type for Complex Arithmetic, continued

```
Enter the second complex number.
Real part> 2.5
Imaginary part> 1.2

The complex sum is (6.00, 6.40)
The complex difference is (1.00, 4.00)
The absolute value of the first complex number is 6.27
```

Figure 11.8 Module Dependency for TestComplex

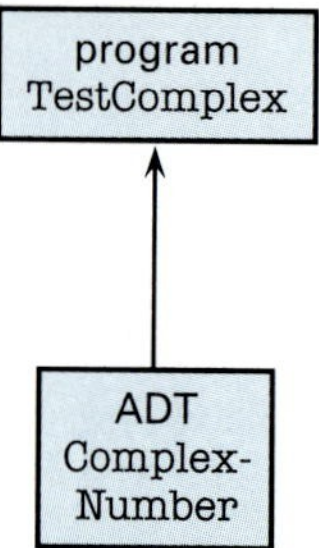

Module `TestComplex` uses the data type `Complex` and five of its operators. The body of `TestComplex` begins by reading data into complex numbers `A` and `B`. Next, the sum and the difference of these complex numbers are saved in `C` and displayed. Finally, the absolute value of complex number `A` is displayed. Figure 11.8 shows the module dependency.

A client program that uses ADT `ComplexNumber` does not need to know the actual internal representation of data type `ComplexNumber` (that is, a record with two `Real` fields). The client program can call an operator procedure of ADT `ComplexNumber` to perform an operation (for example, complex addition) without having this knowledge. In fact, it is better to hide this information from the client program, to prevent the client from directly manipulating the individual fields of a complex variable.

Referencing a Data Structure Declared in an ADT

The client program in Fig. 11.7 could use the statements

```
AddComplex (A, B, C);        {form the sum}
Write ('The real part of the sum is ');
WriteLn (C.RealPart :4:2);
```

to display the real part only of the sum of `A` and `B`. This is a bad programming practice, however, because the field name `C.RealPart` is based on a particular internal representation (record with fields `RealPart` and `ImaginaryPart`) of the data type `Complex`. If we later decide to use a different internal representation (for example, an array of two elements) for data type `Complex`, the field name `C.RealPart` would no longer be correct, and the client program would have to be modified.

It would be much better to replace the last line with the line

```
WriteLn (GetReal(C) :4:2);
```

In this case, procedure `GetReal` (an operator of `ComplexNumber`) would extract the real part of complex number `C` before it is displayed. Now the client program will always be correct regardless of the internal representation used for data type `Complex`.

Exercises for Section 11.4

Self-Check

1. What does the program segment below display?

```
SetComplex (3.5, 5.0, A);
SetComplex (-5.0, 6.5, B);
SubtractComplex (A, B, C);
WriteComplex (C);
SetComplex (GetReal(A), -GetImaginary(A), C);
AddComplex (A, C, B);
WriteComplex (B);
WriteLn (AbsComplex(B) :4:2)
```

Programming

1. Write additional procedures `MultiplyComplex` and `DivideComplex` to implement the operations of multiplication and division of complex numbers defined as follows:

$$(a, b) \times (c, d) = (ac - bd, ad + bc)$$

$$(a, b) / (c, d) = \left(\frac{ac + bd}{c^2 + d^2}, \frac{bc - ad}{c^2 + d^2}\right)$$

11.5 Hierarchical Records

To solve any programming problem, we must select data structures that enable us to efficiently represent a variety of information. The selection of data structures is an important part of the problem-solving process. The data structures we use can profoundly affect the efficiency and the simplicity of the completed program.

The data-structuring facilities in Pascal are powerful and general. In the previous examples, all record fields were simple types or strings. It is possible to declare a record type with fields that are other structured types. We call a record type with one or more fields that are record types a *hierarchical record.*

We began our study of records by introducing the record type Employee. In this section, we modify that record by adding new fields for storage of the employee's address, starting date, and date of birth. The record type NewEmployee is declared in Fig. 11.9, along with two additional record types, Date and Address.

Figure 11.9 Declaration of a Hierarchical Record

```
const
  StrLength = 20;          {length of all strings except zipcode}
  ZipStringSize = 5;       {length of zipcode string}

type
  IDRange = 1111..9999;
  StringType = string[StrLength];
  ZipString = string[ZipStringSize];
  Month = (January, February, March, April, May, June,
           July, August, September, October, November, December);
  Gender = (Female, Male);

  Employee = record
               ID : IDRange;
               Name : StringType;
               Sex : Gender;
               NumDepend : Integer;
               Rate, TaxSal : Real
             end; {Employee}

  Address = record
              Street, City, State : StringType;
              ZipCode : ZipString
            end; {Address}

  Date = record
           ThisMonth : Month;
           Day : 1..31;
           Year : 1900..1999
         end;  {Date}

  NewEmployee = record
                  PayData : Employee;
                  Home : Address;
                  StartDate, BirthDate : Date
                end;  {NewEmployee}

var
   Programmer : NewEmployee;
```

If Programmer is a record variable of type NewEmployee, the hierarchical structure of Programmer can be sketched as shown in Fig. 11.10. This diagram provides a graphic display of the record form.

The diagram in Fig. 11.10 shows that Programmer is a record with fields PayData, Home, StartDate, and BirthDate. Each of these fields is itself a record (called a *subrecord* of Programmer). The fields of each subrecord are indicated under that subrecord.

Figure 11.10 Record Variable Programmer (Type NewEmployee)

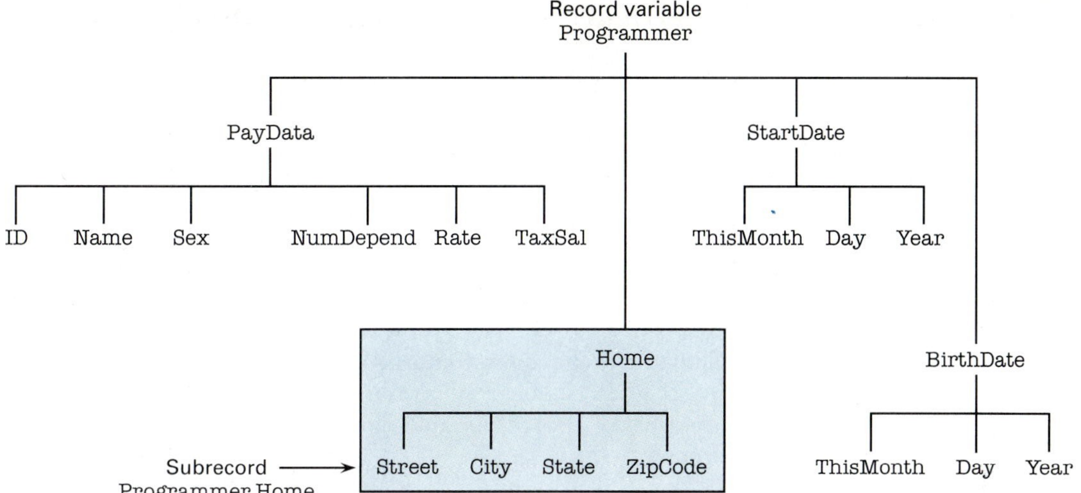

To reference a field in this diagram, we must trace a complete path to it starting from the top of the diagram. For example, the field selector

```
Programmer.StartDate
```

references the subrecord `StartDate` (type `Date`) of the variable `Programmer`. The field selector

```
Programmer.StartDate.Year
```

references the `Year` field of the subrecord `Programmer.StartDate`. The field selector

```
Programmer.Year
```

is incomplete (which `Year` field?) and would cause a syntax error.

The record copy statement

```
Programmer.StartDate := DayOfYear
```

is legal if `DayOfYear` is a record variable of type `Date`. This statement copies each field of `DayOfYear` into the corresponding field of the subrecord `Programmer.StartDate`.

In many situations, we can use the `with` statement to shorten the field selector. The statement

```
with Programmer.StartDate do
  WriteLn ('Year started: ', Year:4, ', day started: ', Day:1)
```

displays two fields of the subrecord `Programmer.StartDate`. The computation for taxable salary could be written as

```
with Programmer.PayData do
  TaxSal := Rate * 40.0 - NumDepend * 14.40
```

The `with` statement

```
with Programmer do
  WriteLn (PayData.Name, ' started work in ', StartDate.Year :4)
```

displays an output line of the form

```
Caryn Jackson started work in 1976
```

It is also possible to nest `with` statements. The following nested `with` statement also displays the preceding output line.

```
with Programmer do
  with PayData do
    with StartDate do
      WriteLn (Name, ' started work in ', Year :4)
```

The record variable name (`Programmer`) must precede the subrecord names, as shown. The order of the field names `PayData` and `StartDate` is not important.

We can also use a list of record variable names and field names in a `with` statement. The statement

```
with Programmer, PayData, StartDate do
  WriteLn (Name, ' started work in ', Year :4)
```

is equivalent to the ones just discussed.

Procedure `ReadNewEmp` in Fig. 11.11 could be used to read in a record of type `NewEmployee`. It calls procedures `ReadEmployee` (see Fig. 11.5), `Read-Address`, and `ReadDate` (see programming exercise).

Figure 11.11 Procedure ReadNewEmp

```
procedure ReadNewEmp (var NewEmp {output} : NewEmployee);
{
   Reads a record into record variable NewEmp.
   Pre  : None
   Post : Reads data into all fields of record NewEmp.
   Calls: Procedures ReadEmployee (see Fig. 11.5),
          ReadAddress, and ReadDate (see exercises below)
}
begin {ReadNewEmp}
  with NewEmp do
    begin
      ReadEmployee (PayData);
      ReadAddress (Home);
      ReadDate (StartDate);
      ReadDate (BirthDate)
    end {with}
end; {ReadNewEmp}
```

Exercises for Section 11.5

Self-Check

1. What must be the type of `NewAddress` if the following statement is correct?

```
Programmer.Home := NewAddress
```

2. Write the field selector needed to reference each of the following fields.
   a. the programmer's salary
   b. the programmer's street address
   c. the programmer's month of birth
   d. the month the programmer started working

Programming

1. Write procedures `ReadAddress` and `ReadDate`.

11.6 Variant Records (Optional)

All record variables of type `NewEmployee` have the same form and structure. It is possible, however, to define record types that have some fields that are the same for all variables of that type (fixed part) and some fields that may be different (variant part).

For example, we might want to include additional information about an employee based on the employee's marital status. For all married employees, we might want to know the spouse's name and the number of children. For all divorced employees, we might want to know the date of the divorce. For all single employees, we might want to know whether the employee lives alone.

This new employee type, `Executive`, is declared in Fig. 11.12 and uses several data types declared earlier in Fig. 11.9.

Figure 11.12 Record Type Executive and Record Variable Boss

```
const
  StrLength = 20;          {length of all strings except zipcode}
  ZipStringSize = 5;       {length of zipcode string}

type
  IDRange = 1111..9999;
  StringType = string[StrLength];
  ZipString = string[ZipStringSize];
  Month = (January, February, March, April, May, June,
           July, August, September, October, November, December);

  Gender = (Female, Male);

  Employee = record
               ID : IDRange;
               Name : StringType;
               Sex : Gender;
               NumDepend : Integer;
               Rate, TaxSal : Real
             end; {Employee}

  Address = record
              Street, City, State : StringType;
              ZipCode : ZipString
            end; {Address}

  Date = record
           ThisMonth : Month;
```

```
          Day : 1..31;
          Year : 1900..1999
        end;  {Date}

  NewEmployee = record
                  PayData : Employee;
                  Home : Address;
                  StartDate, BirthDate : Date
                end;  {NewEmployee}

  MaritalStatus = (Married, Divorced, Single);
  Executive = record
                PayData : Employee;
                Home : Address;
                StartDate, BirthDate : Date;
              case MS : MaritalStatus of
                Married  : (SpouseName : StringType;
                            NumberKids : Integer);
                Divorced : (DivorceDate : Date);
                Single   : (LivesAlone : Boolean)
              end; {Executive}

var
  Boss : Executive;
```

The fixed part of a record always precedes the variant part. The fixed part of record type `Executive` has the form of record type `NewEmployee`. The variant part begins with the *tag field*

```
case MS : MaritalStatus of
```

which defines a special field `MS`, of type `MaritalStatus`. The value of the tag field `MS` (`Married`, `Divorced`, or `Single`) indicates the form of the remainder of the record. If the value of the tag field is `Married`, there are two additional fields, `SpouseName` (type `StringType`) and `NumberKids` (type `Integer`); otherwise, there is only one additional field, `DivorceDate` (type `Date`) or `LivesAlone` (type `Boolean`).

Figure 11.13 Three Variants of Record Variable Boss

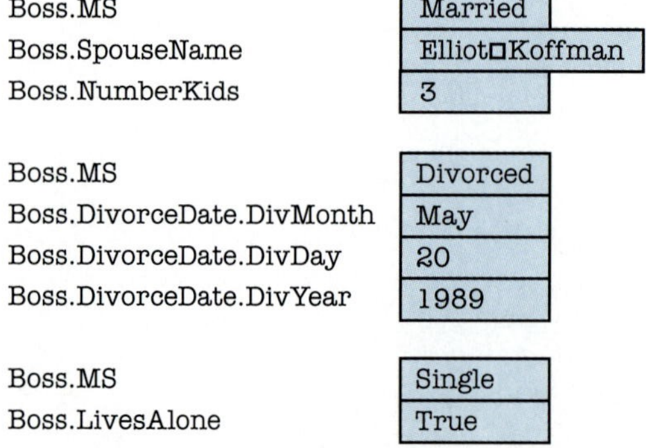

Figure 11.13 shows three variants of record variable `Boss`, starting with the tag field. The fixed parts of all these records (not shown) have the same form.

For each variable of type `Executive`, the compiler allocates sufficient storage space to accommodate the largest of the record variants. However, only one variant is defined at any given time and that particular variant is determined by the tag field value.

The amount of storage required for each variant depends on how many bytes are used to store integer values and enumerated type values on a particular computer. The first variant in Fig. 11.13 requires more than twenty bytes of storage (one byte per character of the spouse's name) and should be the largest.

■ Example 11.6

If the value of `Boss.MS` is `Married`, then only the variant fields `SpouseName` and `NumberKids` can be correctly referenced; all other variant fields are undefined. Assuming the first variant shown in Fig. 11.14 is stored in record `Boss`, the program fragment

```
with Boss do
  begin
    WriteLn ('The spouse''s name is ', SpouseName, '.');
    WriteLn ('They have ', NumberKids :1, ' children.')
  end {with}
```

displays the line

```
The spouse's name is Elliot Koffman.
They have 3 children.
```

We must ensure that the variant fields that are referenced are consistent with the current tag field value. The compiler and run-time system do not normally check this. If the value of `Boss.MS` is not `Married` when the preceding fragment is executed, the information displayed will be meaningless. For that reason, a `case` statement is often used to process the variant part of a record. By using the tag field as the `case` selector, we can ensure that only the currently defined variant is manipulated. ■

■ Example 11.7

The fragment in Fig. 11.14 displays the data stored in the variant part of record `Boss`. The value of `Boss.MS` determines what information is displayed. ■

Figure 11.14 Displaying a Variant Record

```
{Display the variant part}
with Boss do
  case MS of
    Married :
        begin
          WriteLn ('The spouse''s name is ', SpouseName, ',');
          WriteLn ('They have ', NumberKids :1, ' children.')
        end; {Married}
    Divorced :
        with DivorceDate do
```

```
      WriteLn ('Divorced on ', Ord(ThisMonth) + 1 :2,
               '/', Day :2, '/', Year :4);
  Single :
    if LivesAlone then
      WriteLn ('Lives alone')
    else
      WriteLn ('Does not live alone')
end {case}
```

The syntax for a record with fixed and variant parts is described in the following syntax display.

SYNTAX DISPLAY

Record Type with Variant Part

Form: type

rec type = record

$\left.\begin{array}{l} \textit{id list}_1 : \textit{type}_1; \\ \textit{id list}_2 : \textit{type}_2; \\ \quad . \\ \quad . \\ \quad . \\ \textit{id list}_n : \textit{type}_n; \end{array}\right\}$ *fixed part*

$\left.\begin{array}{l} \texttt{case}\ \textit{tag}: \textit{tag type}\ \texttt{of} \\ \textit{label}_1 : (\textit{field list}_1); \\ \textit{label}_2 : (\textit{field list}_2); \\ \quad . \\ \quad . \\ \quad . \\ \textit{label}_k : (\textit{field list}_k) \end{array}\right\}$ *variant part*

end;

Example:

```
type
  Face = record
           Eyes : Color;
         case Bald : Boolean of
           True  : (WearsWig  : Boolean);
           False : (HairColor : Color)
         end;
```

Interpretation: The *field list* for the fixed part is declared first. The variant part starts with the reserved word case. The identifier *tag* is the name of the tag field of the record; the tag field name is separated by a colon from its type (*tag type*), which must be type Boolean, an enumerated type, or a subrange of an ordinal type.

The case labels ($label_1$, $label_2$,..., $label_k$) are lists of values of the tag field as defined by *tag type*. $Field\ list_i$ describes the record fields associated with $label_i$. Each element of $field\ list_i$ specifies a field name and its type; the elements in $field\ list_i$ are separated by semicolons. $Field\ list_i$ is enclosed in parentheses.

Note 1: All field names must be unique. The same field name may not appear in the fixed and variant parts or in two field lists of the variant part.
Note 2: An empty field list (no variant part for that `case` label) is indicated by an empty pair of parentheses, `( )`.
Note 3: It is possible for a field list to also have a variant part. If it does, the variant part must follow the fixed part of the field list.
Note 4: There is only one `end` for the record type declaration; there is no separate `end` for the `case`.

When you initially store data in a record with a variant part, the tag field value should be read first. Once the value of the tag field is defined, data can be read into the variant fields associated with that value.

Case Study: Areas and Perimeters of Different Figures

Problem

We want to write a program that determines the area and the perimeter for a variety of geometric figures.

Design Overview

To solve this problem, we will create an abstract data type that represents a geometric figure and contains operators for entering the figure's characteristics, computing its perimeter, computing its area, and displaying its characteristics. Because the characteristics for a figure are related, we want to save them in a record. However, the characteristics for each figure shape are different, so we must use a record with a variant part. The record declared next has two fixed fields for storing the figure's area and perimeter; the variant part is used for storing the figure's characteristics.

Data Requirements

Data Types

```
FigKind = (Circle, Rectangle, Square, Other);
Figure = record
           Area, Perimeter : Real;
         case Shape : FigKind of
           Circle    : (Radius : Real);
           Rectangle : (Width, Height : Real);
           Square    : (Side : Real);
           Other     : ()
         end; {Figure}
```

Problem Inputs

A letter representing the kind of figure (`FigChar : Char`)
The relevant characteristics for the figure selected

Problem Outputs
The figure Area (`Area : Real`)
The figure perimeter (`Perimeter : Real`)

Initial Algorithm

1. Determine the type of the figure.
2. Read in the figure characteristics.
3. Compute the area of the figure.
4. Compute the perimeter of the figure.
5. Display the complete record for the figure.

Coding the Main Program

We will write a procedure to perform each algorithm step. The main program (Fig. 11.15) consists of a sequence of calls to these procedures.

Figure 11.15 Program Geometry

Edit Window

```
program Geometry;
{
  Finds perimeters and areas of various kinds of figures.

  Imports: Figure, FigKind, GetFigureType, ReadFigure,
           DisplayFigure, ComputeArea, ComputePerim
           from unit FigureADT

}
  uses FigureADT;

  var
    MyFig : Figure;                {a figure}

begin {Geometry}
  GetFigure (MyFig);
  ReadFigure (MyFig);
  ComputeArea (MyFig);
  ComputePerim (MyFig);
  DisplayFig (MyFig)
end. {Geometry}
```

Output Window

```
Enter the object's shape.
Enter C (Circle), R (Rectangle), S (Square)> R
Enter width > 5.0
Enter height> 6.5

Figure shape is Rectangle
Width is 5.00
Height is 6.50
Area is 32.50
Perimeter is 23.00
```

Coding the Procedures

Procedure `GetFigure` reads in the character that denotes the kind of figure and saves the corresponding value of type `FigKind` in the tag field `Shape`. If the character entered is not one of the letters (C, R, or S), the value Other is stored in the tag field. ReadFigure must read the data required for the kind of figure indicated by the tag field. The other operator procedures are straightforward and are shown in Fig. 11.16.

Figure 11.16 Unit FigureADT

```
unit FigureADT;
{
  Abstract data type Figure with procedures for reading
  and displaying the characteristics of type Figure.
}

interface

  type                              {data type specification}
    FigKind = (Circle, Rectangle, Square, Other);
    Figure = record
               Area, Perimeter : Real;
             case Shape : FigKind of
               Circle    : (Radius : Real);
               Rectangle : (Width, Height : Real);
               Square    : (Side : Real);
               Other     : ()
             end; {Figure}
  procedure GetFigure (var OneFig {output}  : Figure);
  {
    Defines tag field of OneFig.
    Pre : None
    Post: The tag field value corresponds to the next data character.
  }

  procedure ReadFigure (var Onefig {input/ouput} : Figure);
  {
    Enters data into OneFig.
    Pre : The tag field of OneFig is defined.
    Post: The characteristics of OneFig are defined.
  }

  procedure ComputePerim (var OneFig {input/output} : Figure);
  {
    Defines Perimeter field of OneFig.
    Pre : The tag field and characteristics of OneFig are defined.
    Post: Assigns value to Perimeter field.
  }

  procedure ComputeArea (var OneFig {input/output} : Figure);
  {
    Defines Area field of OneFig.
    Pre : The tag field and characteristics of OneFig are defined.
    Post: Assigns value to Area field.
  }

  procedure DisplayFig (OneFig {input} : Figure);
  {
    Displays the characteristics of OneFig.
    Pre : All fields of OneFig are defined.
    Post: Displays each field of OneFig.
  }
```

Case Study: Areas and Perimeters of Different Figures, continued

```
implementation                        {operator procedures}

  procedure GetFigure (var OneFig {output}  : Figure);
    var
      FigChar : Char;        {input - data character for figure shape}

  begin {GetFigure}
    WriteLn ('Enter the kind of object');
    Write ('Enter C (Circle), R (Rectangle), or S (Square)> ');
    Read (FigChar);
    with OneFig do
      case FigChar of
        'c', 'C' : Shape := Circle;
        'r', 'R' : Shape := Rectangle;
        's', 'S' : Shape := Square;
        else
          Shape := Other
      end {case}
  end; {GetFigure}


  procedure ReadFigure (var OneFig {input/output} : Figure);
  begin {ReadFigure}
    with OneFig do
      {Select the proper variant and read pertinent data}
      case Shape of
        Circle    : begin
                      Write ('Enter radius> ');
                      ReadLn (Radius)
                    end; {Circle}
        Rectangle : begin
                      Write ('Enter width > ');
                      ReadLn (Width);
                      Write ('Enter height> ');
                      ReadLn (Height)
                    end; {Rectangle}
        Square    : begin
                      Write ('Enter length of side> ');
                      ReadLn (Side)
                    end; {Square}
        Other     : WriteLn ('Characteristics are unknown')
      end {case}
  end; {ReadFigure}


  procedure ComputePerim (var OneFig {input/output} : Figure);
  begin {ComputePerim}
    with OneFig do
      case Shape of
        Circle    : Perimeter := 2.0 * Pi * Radius;
        Rectangle : Perimeter := 2.0 * (Width + Height);
        Square    : Perimeter := 4.0 * Side;
        Other     : Perimeter := 0.0;
      end {case}
  end; {ComputePerim}


  procedure ComputeArea (var OneFig {input/output} : Figure);
  begin {ComputeArea}
```

```
    with OneFig do
      case Shape of
        Circle    : Area := Pi * Radius * Radius;
        Rectangle : Area := Width * Height;
        Square    : Area := Side * Side;
        Other     : Area := 0.0;
      end {case}
  end; {ComputeArea}


  procedure DisplayFig (OneFig {input} : Figure);
  begin {DisplayFig}
    with OneFig do
      {Display shape and characteristics}
      begin
        WriteLn;
        Write ('Figure shape is ');
        case Shape of
          Circle    : begin
                        WriteLn ('Circle');
                        WriteLn ('Radius is ', Radius :4:2)
                      end; {Circle}
          Rectangle : begin
                        WriteLn ('Rectangle');
                        WriteLn ('Height is ', Height :4:2);
                        WriteLn ('Width is ',  Width :4:2)
                      end; {Rectangle}
          Square    : begin
                        WriteLn ('Square');
                        WriteLn ('Side is ', Side :4:2)
                      end; {Square}
          Other     : WriteLn ('No characteristics for figure')
        end; {case}

        {Display area and perimeter}
      WriteLn ('Area is ', Area :4:2);
      WriteLn ('Perimeter is ', Perimeter :4:2)
    end {with}
  end; {DisplayFig}
end. {FigureADT}
```

In each procedure, a `case` statement controls the processing of the data in the variant part. Procedures `ComputePerim` and `ComputeArea` define their respective fields in the data structure.

Exercises for Section 11.6

Self-Check

1. Determine how many bytes are needed to store each variant for a record of type `Executive`, assuming two bytes for an integer or an enumerated type value and one byte for a character or a Boolean value. Don't include the tag field in your calculations.

2. Write a statement that displays `Boss.SpouseName` if defined or the message `Not married.`

Programming

1. Write a procedure to display a record of type `Face` as declared in the syntax display in this section.
2. Add the variant

```
RightTriangle : (Base, Height : Real);
```

to `Figure` and modify the operator procedures to include triangles. Use the formulas

$$area = \frac{1}{2}\, base \times height$$
$$hypotenuse = \sqrt{base^2 + height^2}$$

where *base* and *height* are the two sides that form the right angle and *hypotenuse* is the side opposite the right angle.

11.7 Debugging Programs with Records

To display the value of a record field in the Watch window, you must use the fully qualified field name as a Watch expression. To display the value of field `ID` of the record variable `Clerk` shown in Fig. 11.1, you would use `Clerk.ID` as a Watch expression. The `with` statement has no effect on field identifiers used in Watch expressions.

To display all fields of a record variable, the record identifier is used as a Watch expression. Like an array, the record's field values will be displayed in the Watch window as a list enclosed in parentheses. If `Clerk` is used as a Watch expression with the field values shown in Fig. 11.1, the Watch window will display

```
Clerk: (1234,'Caryn Jackson',FEMALE,2,3.98,130.4)
```

Strange looking values may be displayed for record fields that have not been assigned values.

If the field list is too long to fit in the Watch window, you can use the F6 key to move to the Watch Window. Then use either the left or the right arrow key (or your mouse and the Watch window horizontal scroll bar) to scan through the field list.

If you use the Watch expression

```
Clerk,R
```

the Watch window will display each field name of `Clerk` followed by its value:

```
Clerk,R: (ID:1234,NAME:'Caryn Jackson',SEX:FEMALE,NUMDEPEND:2,
          RATE:3.98,TAXSAL:130.4)
```

The *Debug expression format character* `R` causes this to happen.

Hierarchical records are displayed in the Watch window as nested, parenthesized lists of values. The same is true for records containing arrays as fields. Subrecords and record fields that are arrays can be displayed in the Watch window if you use their fully qualified names as Watch expressions. Subrecords and array type record fields will displayed as a list of values enclosed in parentheses.

11.8 Common Programming Errors

When programmers use records, their most common error is incorrectly specifying the record field to be manipulated. The full field selector (record variable and field name) must be used unless the record reference is nested inside a `with` statement or the entire record is to be manipulated. So far, we have discussed the latter option only for record copy statements and for records passed as parameters. When reading or writing records at the terminal, you must process each field separately.

If a record variable name is listed in a `with` statement header, only the field name is required to reference fields of that record inside the `with` statement. You must still use the full field selector to reference fields of any other record variable.

For variant records, remember that the value of the tag field determines the form of the variant part that is currently defined. Manipulating any other variant will cause unpredictable results. You must ensure that the correct variant is being processed—the computer does not check this. So always manipulate a variant record in a `case` statement with the tag field as the `case` selector to ensure that the proper variant part is being manipulated.

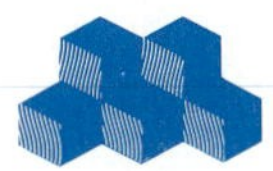

Chapter Review

This chapter examined the record data structure. Records were shown to be useful for organizing a collection of related data items of different types. Using hierarchical records and variant records, we created some very general data structures to model our "real world" data organization.

In processing records, we discussed how to reference each individual component through the use of a field selector consisting of the record variable name and field name separated by a period. We introduced the `with` statement as a means of shortening the field selector. If a record variable name is specified in a `with` statement header, then the field name may be used by itself inside the `with` statement.

Each individual component of a record must be manipulated separately in an input or an output operation or in an arithmetic expression. However, it is permissible to assign one record variable to another record variable of the same type (record copy statement) or to pass a record as a parameter to a procedure or function.

New Pascal Constructs

The Pascal constructs introduced in this chapter are described in Table 11.1.

Table 11.1 Summary of New Pascal Constructs

Construct	Effect

Record Declaration
`type`
`  Part = record`
`           ID : [1111..9999];`
`           Quantity : Integer;`
`           Price : Real`
`         end; {Part}`
`var`
`  Nuts, Bolts : Part;`
	A record type `Part` is declared with fields that can store two integers and a real number. `Nuts` and `Bolts` are record variables of type `Part`.

Record Variant Declaration
`type`
`  ChildKind = (Girl, Boy);`
`  Child = record`
`            First, Last : Char;`
`            Age : Integer;`
`          case Sex : ChildKind of`
`            Girl : (Sugar, Spice :`
`                    Real);`
`            Boy : (Snakes, Snails,`
`                   Tails : Integer)`
`          end; {Child}`
`var`
`  Kid : Child;`
	A record type with a variant part is declared. Each record variable can store two characters and an integer. One variant part can store two real numbers, and the other can store three integers. The record variable `Kid` is type `Child`.

Record Reference
`TotalCost := Nuts.Quantity`
`             * Nuts.Price`
	Multiplies two fields of `Nuts`.

`WriteLn (Bolts.ID :4)`	Prints `ID` field of `Bolts`.
Record Copy `Bolts := Nuts`	Copies record `Nuts` to `Bolts`.

with Statement
`with Bolts do`
`  Write (ID :4, Price :8:2)`
	Prints 2 fields of `Bolts`.

Referencing a Record Variant
`with Kid do`
`  case Sex of`
`    Girl :`
	Uses a `case` statement to read data into the variant part of record variable `Kid`.

Construct	Effect

<pre>   begin
        Write (Pounds of sugar> ');
        ReadLn (Sugar)
      end; {Girl}
    Boy :
      begin
        Write ('Number of snakes> ');
        ReadLn (Snakes)
      end {boy}
  end; {case}</pre>
	If tag field `Sex` is `Girl`, reads a value into the field `Sugar`. If tag field `Kind` is `Boy`, reads a value into the field `Snakes`.

✓ Quick-Check Exercises

1. What is the primary difference between a record and an array? Which would you use to store the catalog description of a course? Which would you use to store the names of the students in the course?
2. What is a field selector?
3. Why do we use a `with` statement? What is a disadvantage of using the `with` statement?
4. If you use nested `with` statements to reference fields of a hierarchical record, what identifier should appear in the outermost `with` statement header?
5. When can you use the assignment operator with record operands? When can you use the equality operator?
6. For `AStudent` declared as follows, provide a statement that displays the initials of `AStudent`.

```
type
  StringType = string[StrLength];
  Student = record
              FirstName, LastName : StringType;
              Age, Score : Integer;
              Grade : Char
            end; {Student}

var
  AStudent : Student;
```

7. How many fields are there in a record of type `Student`?
8. If an `Integer` uses two bytes of storage, a character one, and `StrLength` is 20, how many bytes of storage are occupied by `AStudent`?
9. Write a procedure that displays a variable of type `Student`.
10. When should you use a record variant?

Answers to Quick-Check Exercises

1. The values stored in an array must all be the same type; the values stored in a record do not have to be the same type. Record for catalog item; array for list of names.

2. A field selector is used to select a particular record field for processing.
3. A `with` statement allows us to abbreviate field selectors. It is helpful when we must reference several fields of the same record. Its disadvantage is that it makes the program less readable because it separates the record variable name from the field name. It is particularly confusing when there are multiple records of the same type or when a record has nested subrecords.
4. The record variable name.
5. When the records are the same type. Never.
6. `WriteLn (AStudent.First[1], AStudent.Last[1])`
7. Five.
8. Forty-five.
9.
```
procedure WriteStudent (OneStu {input} : Student);
begin
   WriteLn ('Student is ', OneStu.FirstName,
            ' ', OneStu.LastName);
   WriteLn ('Age is ', OneStu.Age :1);
   WriteLn ('Score is ', OneStu.Score :1);
   WriteLn ('Grade is ', OneStu.Grade)
end;
```
10. When an object has some fields that are always the same and some fields that may be different.

Review Questions

1. Declare a record called `Subscriber` that contains the fields `Name`, `StreetAddress`, `MonthlyBill` (how much the subscriber owes), and which paper the subscriber receives (`Morning`, `Evening`, or `Both`).
2. Write a Pascal program to enter and then print out the data in record `Competition` declared as follows:

```
const
  StrLength = 20;

type
  StringType = string[StrLength];
  OlympicEvent = record
                   Event,
                   Entrant,
                   Country : StringType;
                   Place : Integer
                 end; {OlympicEvent}

var
  Competition: OlympicEvent;
```

3. Explain the use of the `with` statement.
4. Identify and correct the errors in the following program.

```
program Report;

  type
    String15 = string[15];
```

```
  SummerHelp = record
                 Name : String15;
                 StartDate : String15;
                 HoursWorked : Real
               end; {SummerHelp}

 var
   Operator : SummerHelp;
begin {Report}
  with SummerHelp do
    begin
      Name := 'Stoney Viceroy';
      StartDate := 'June 1, 1984';
      HoursWorked := 29.3
    end; {with}
  WriteLn (Operator)
end. {Report}
```

5. Declare the proper data structure to store the following student data: `GPA`, `Major`, `Address` (consisting of `StreetAddress`, `City`, `State`, `ZipCode`), and `ClassSchedule` (consisting of up to six class records, each of which has `Description`, `Time`, and `Days` fields). Use whatever data types are most appropriate for each field.
6. Write the variant declaration for `Supplies`, which consists of `Paper`, `Ribbon`, or `Labels`. For `Paper`, the information needed is the number of sheets per box and the size of the paper. For `Ribbon`, the size, color, and kind (`Carbon` or `Cloth`) are needed. For `Labels`, the size and number per box are needed. For each supply, the cost, number on hand, and the reorder point must also be stored. Use whatever data types are appropriate for each field.
7. Write the declaration for `Vehicle`. If the vehicle is a `Truck`, then `BedSize` and `CabSize` are needed. If the vehicle is a wagon, then third seat or not is needed (`Boolean`). If the vehicle is a `Sedan`, then the information needed is `TwoDoor` or `FourDoor`. For all vehicles, you need to know whether the transmission is `Manual` or `Automatic`; if it has `AirConditioning`, `PowerSteering`, or `PowerBrakes` (all `Boolean`); and the `Gas Mileage`. Use whatever data types are appropriate for each field.

Programming Projects

1. Implement an abstract data type that consists of the data structure described in review question 5 and procedures for reading and displaying an object of that type.
2. Implement an abstract data type that consists of the data structure described in review question 6 and procedures for reading and displaying an object of that type.
3. Implement an abstract data type that consists of the data structure described in review question 7 and procedures for reading and displaying an object of that type.
4. A number expressed in scientific notation is represented by its mantissa (a fraction) and its exponent. Write a procedure that reads two character strings that represent numbers in Pascal scientific notation and stores each number in a record with two fields. Write a procedure that prints the contents of each record as a real value. Also write a procedure that computes the sum, the product, the difference, and the quotient of the two numbers. Hint: The string `-0.1234E20` represents a number in scientific notation. The fraction `-0.1234` is the mantissa and the number `20` is the exponent.
5. At a grocery store, the food has been categorized, and those categories are to be

computerized. Write a procedure to read and store information into a variant record with appropriate data types.

The first letter read will be M, F, or V (indicating meat, fruit, or vegetable, respectively). The second set of information (until a blank is encountered) will be the name of the food (maximum of twenty letters). The third item read will be the unit cost. The fourth item read will be the unit (O, for ounces, or P for pounds).

The last field read will be one character that indicates information based on the M, F, or V read earlier. For meat, the valid input values are R for red meat, P for poultry, and F for fish. For fruit, the valid input values are T for tropical and N for nontropical. For vegetables the valid input values are B for beans, P for potatoes, O for other.

The procedure should check that each data item is valid before assigning a value to the record parameter. Also write a procedure to print the data stored for a food object.

6. Standard Pascal does not have the `string` data type found in Turbo Pascal. One way to allow access to strings in standard Pascal is to define your own `string ADT` using the following declarations:

```
const
  StrLength = 80;

type
  StrRange = 1..StrLength;
  StringType = record
                 Len : 0..StrLength;
                 Contents : array [StrRange] of Char
               end;
```

Write a Turbo Pascal unit containing operators for reading and writing `StringType` variables, for computing their length, for checking string equality, and for checking whether one string is lexically less than a second string.

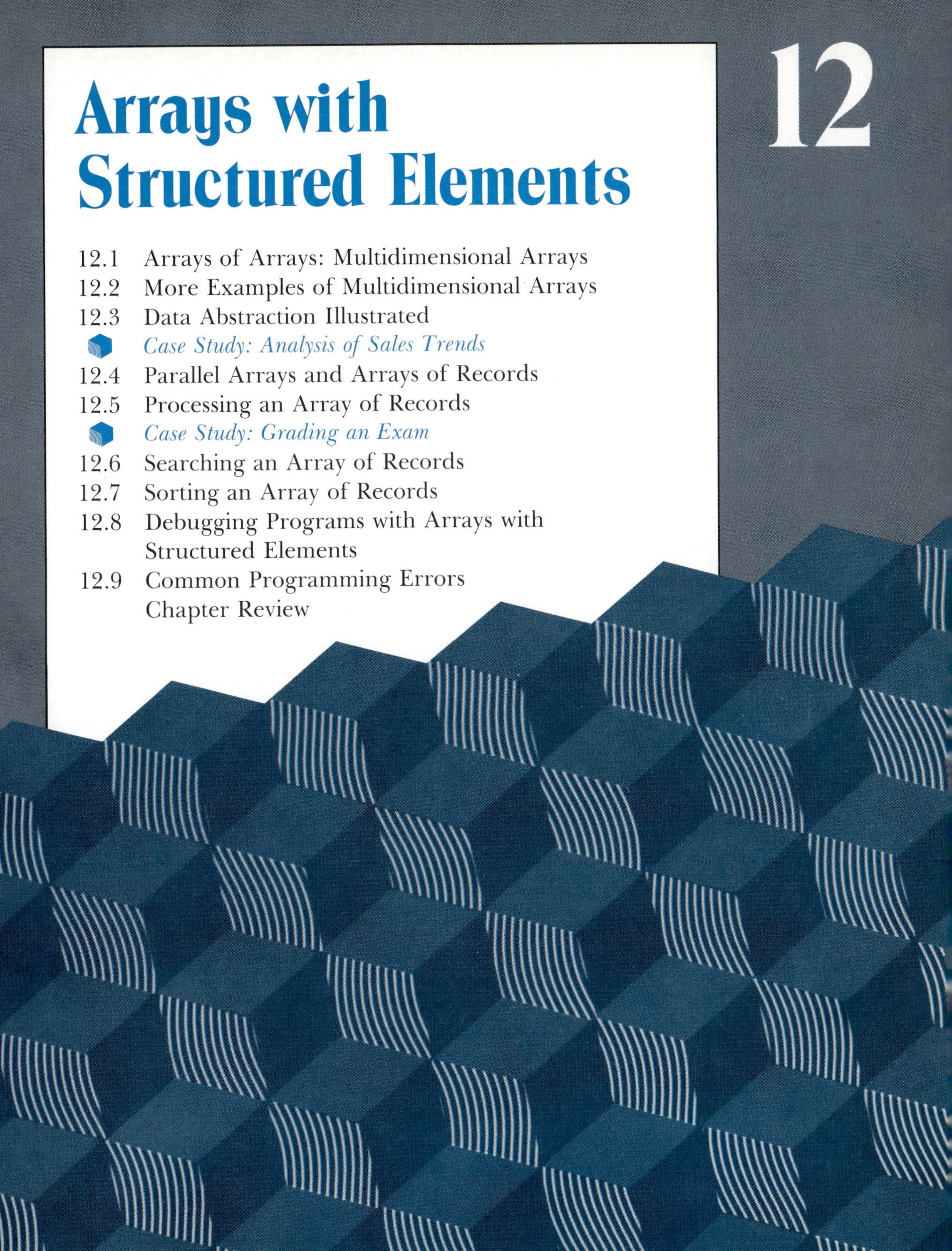

12 Arrays with Structured Elements

So far, you have seen programs that use arrays with many different subscript and element types. All the arrays we have discussed to this point have had individual elements that were simple types. This chapter examines arrays whose elements are structured types.

We begin by examining arrays with elements that are themselves arrays. These arrays of arrays are called *multidimensional arrays* and are often used to store tables of data or to represent multidimensional objects.

We also examine arrays with elements that are records. Arrays of records are useful data structures that can represent many real-world objects. For example, it is convenient to use an array of records to represent a class of students or the members of a baseball team.

Finally, we show you how to perform some common operations on arrays of records. These operations include searching for a particular record in an array and ordering the array elements according to the values in a particular field (sorting the array).

12.1 Arrays of Arrays: Multidimensional Arrays

So far, we have used array elements to store single data values. But array elements can also be data structures. One application is an array whose elements are strings.

Arrays of Strings

In earlier examples, we wrote programs with enumerated types. One drawback to using enumerated types is that their values cannot be read or written directly. By using arrays of strings, we can simplify printing enumerated type values, as shown next.

■ Example 12.1

In Fig. 12.1, the names of the twelve months are saved in an array, `MonthName`, declared as follows.

```
type
  Month = (January, February, March, April, May, June, July,
           August, September, October, November, December);
  String9 = string[9];
  MonthArray = array [Month] of String9;

var
  MonthName : MonthArray;      {array of strings}
```

The elements of array `MonthName` are strings. After the statements in the unit's initialization section execute, each month name is stored as a string in its respective array element. Each string is right-justified, which means that it begins with leading blanks if necessary (for example, `MonthName[January]` is `'  January'`).

Figure 12.1 Operators for ADT Month

```
unit MonthADT;
{
  Abstract data type MonthADT: contains declarations for enumerated type
  Month and procedures for reading and displaying values of type Month.
  Exports: Month, ReadMonth, WriteMonth
  Imports: EnterInt from unit EnterData (see Fig. 8.3)
}
interface
  uses EnterData;

  type
    Month = (January, February, March, April, May, June, July, August,
             September, October, November, December);

  procedure ReadMonth (var OneMonth {output} : Month);
  {
    Reads an integer from 1 to 12 and converts it to a month.
    Pre  : None
    Post : Returns in OneMonth the month value corresponding to the inte-
           ger value read.
    Calls: EnterInt from unit EnterData
  }

  procedure WriteMonth (OneMonth {input} : Month);
  {
    Displays the name string corresponding to OneMonth.
    Pre : Global array MonthName is initialized.
    Post: A string is displayed.
  }

implementation
  type
    String9 = string[9];
    MonthArray = array [Month] of String9;

  var
    MonthName : MonthArray;        {hidden array of names}

  procedure ReadMonth (var OneMonth {output} : Month);
    var
      MonthInt : Integer;          {input - number of month}

  begin {ReadMonth}
    EnterInt (1, 12, MonthInt);
    OneMonth := Month(MonthInt - 1)     {Convert to month}
  end; {ReadMonth}

  procedure WriteMonth (OneMonth {output} : Month);
  begin {WriteMonth}
    Write (MonthName[OneMonth])
  end; {WriteMonth}

begin {MonthADT initialization}
  MonthName[January]   := '  January';
  MonthName[February]  := ' February';
  MonthName[March]     := '    March';
  MonthName[April]     := '    April';
  MonthName[May]       := '      May';
  MonthName[June]      := '     June';
  MonthName[July]      := '     July';
```

```
  MonthName[August]    := '   August';
  MonthName[September] := 'September';
  MonthName[October]   := '  October';
  MonthName[November]  := ' November';
  MonthName[December]  := ' December'
end. {MonthADT}
```

Procedure WriteMonth in Fig. 12.1 displays the month name selected by its parameter. For example, the procedure call statement

```
WriteMonth (February)
```

displays the array element MonthName[February], which contains the string ' February'. Procedure ReadMonth reads an integer from 1 to 12 (using EnterInt) and converts it to a month value. The two procedures in Fig. 12.1, together with data type Month, form an abstract data type (MonthADT).

Identifiers Month, WriteMonth, and ReadMonth are visible to users of this ADT; identifiers MonthArray, String9, and MonthName are hidden. Once array MonthName is initialized, it retains its values.

Multidimensional Arrays

Because a string can be treated like an array of characters, the array type MonthArray can be considered an array of arrays. Such a data structure is called a *two-dimensional array*.

■ Example 12.2

A two-dimensional object we are all familiar with is a tic-tac-toe board. The declarations

```
type
  BoardRange = 1..3;
  BoardRow = array [BoardRange] of Char;
  BoardArray = array [BoardRange] of BoardRow;

var
  TicTacToe : BoardArray;
```

allocate storage for the array TicTacToe. This array has nine storage cells arranged in three rows and three columns. A single character value can be stored in each cell.

In the preceding declarations, BoardRow is declared as an array type with three elements of type Char, and BoardArray is declared as an array type with three elements of type BoardRow. Consequently, the variable TicTacToe (type BoardArray) is an array of arrays, or a two-dimensional array, as pictured in Fig. 12.2. ■

It is generally clearer to use a single-type declaration to declare a multidimensional-array type. The declarations

Figure 12.2 A Tic-Tac-Toe Board Stored as Array TicTacToe

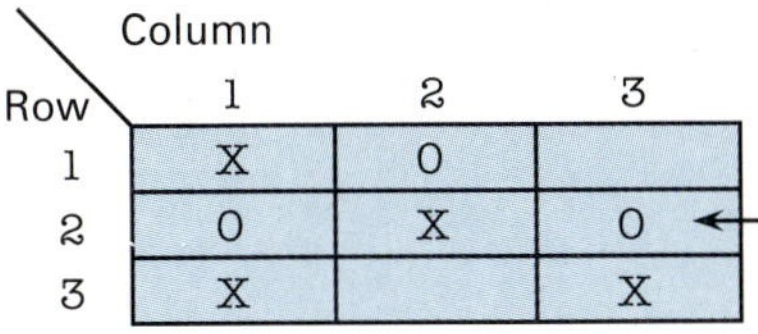

Row \ Column	1	2	3
1	X	0	
2	0	X	0
3	X		X


```
type
  BoardRange = 1..3;
  BoardArray = array [BoardRange, BoardRange] of Char;

var
  TicTacToe : BoardArray;
```

are equivalent to the ones at the beginning of this example in that they allocate storage for a two-dimensional array (`TicTacToe`) with three rows and three columns. This array has nine elements, each of which must be referenced by specifying a row subscript (`1`, `2`, or `3`) and a column subscript (`1`, `2`, or `3`). Each array element contains a character value. The array element `TicTacToe[2,3]` (or `TicTacToe[2][3]`) pointed to in Fig. 12.2 is in row 2, column 3 of the array; it contains the character `0`. The diagonal line consisting of array elements `TicTacToe[1,1]`, `TicTacToe[2,2]`, and `TicTacToe[3,3]` represents a win for player `X`, because each cell contains the character `X`.

SYNTAX DISPLAY

Array Type Declaration (Multidimensional)

Form: `type`
  multidim = `array` [$subscript_1$] `of array` [$subscript_2$]...
    `of array` [$subscript_n$] `of` *element type;*

or

  `type`
  multidim =
    `array` [$subscript_1$, $subscript_2$, ... , $subscript_n$]
      `of` *element type;*

Example:
```
type
  YearRange = 1900..1999;
  YearByMonth = array [YearRange, Month] of Real;
  Election = array [Candidate] of array [Precinct]
               of Integer;
```

Interpretation: $Subscript_i$ represents the subscript type of dimension *i* of array type *multidim*. The subscript type can be `Boolean`, `Char`, an enumerated type, or a subrange type with host type `Integer` or any other ordinal type. The *element type* can be any standard data type or a previously defined simple or structured data type.

Although we are focusing our discussion on arrays with two and three dimensions, there is no limit on the number of dimensions allowed in Pascal. Be aware that the amount of memory space allocated for storage of a multidimensional array can be quite large. For this reason, avoid passing multidimensional arrays as value parameters.

■ Example 12.3

The array `Table` declared as

```
var
  Table : array [1..7, 1..5, 1..6] of Real;
```

consists of three dimensions: the first subscript can take on values from `1` to `7`; the second, from `1` to `5`; and the third, from `1` to `6`. A total of 7 x 5 x 6, or 210, real numbers can be stored in the array `Table`. All three subscripts must be specified in each reference to array `Table` (for example, `Table[2,3,4]`). ■

Storage of Multidimensional Arrays

Most Pascal compilers store multidimensional arrays in adjacent memory cells to simplify accessing the individual elements. The elements of a two-dimensional array are normally stored in order by row (that is, first row 1, then row 2, and so on). This is called *row-major order*. To access a particular array element, the compiler computes the *offset* of that element from the first element stored. To perform this computation, the compiler must know the size of each element in bytes and the number of elements per row. Both values are available from the array type declaration.

For example, the array `TicTacToe` would be stored as shown in Fig. 12.3. There are three elements per row, and each element occupies one byte of storage. The offset for element `TicTacToe[`i,j`]` is computed from the formula

$$offset = (i-1) \times 3 + (j-1)$$

This formula gives a value of `0` as the offset for element `TicTacToe[1,1]` and a value of `5` as the offset for element `TicTacToe[2,3]`.

Figure 12.3 Array TicTacToe in Memory

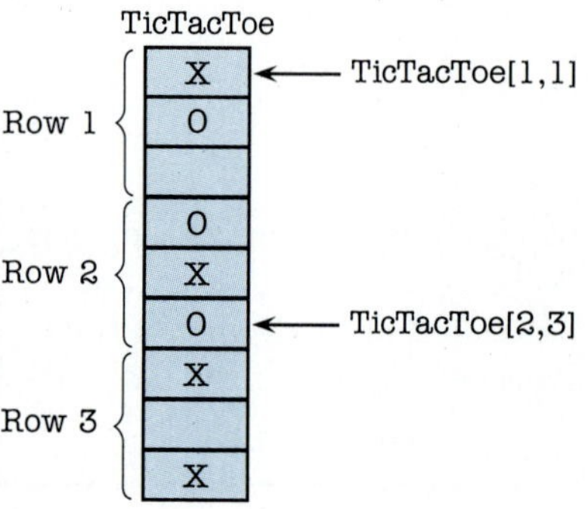

Manipulation of Two-Dimensional Arrays

We must specify a row subscript and a column subscript to reference an element of a two-dimensional array. The type of each subscript must be compatible with the corresponding subscript type specified in the array declaration.

If I is type Integer, the statement

```
for I := 1 to 3 do
  Write (TicTacToe[1,I])
```

displays the first row of array TicTacToe (TicTacToe[1,1], TicTacToe[1,2], and TicTacToe[1,3]) on the current output line. The statement

```
for I := 1 to 3 do
  WriteLn (TicTacToe[I,2])
```

displays the second column of TicTacToe (TicTacToe[1,2], TicTacToe[2,2], and TicTacToe[3,2]) in a vertical line.

We can use nested loops to access all elements in a multidimensional array in a predetermined order. In the next three examples, the outer loop-control variable determines the row being accessed, and the inner loop-control variable selects each element in that row.

■ Example 12.4

Procedure PrintBoard in Fig. 12.4 displays the current status of a tic-tac-toe board. A sample output of this procedure is also shown. ■

Figure 12.4 Procedure PrintBoard with Sample Output

```
procedure PrintBoard (TicTacToe {input} : BoardArray);
{
  Displays the status of a tic-tac-toe board.
  Pre : Array TicTacToe is defined.
  Post: Displays each element of array TicTacToe.
}
  var
    Row, Column : BoardRange;

begin {PrintBoard}
  WriteLn ('-------');
  for Row := 1 to 3 do
    begin
      {Print all columns of current row}
      for Column := 1 to 3 do
        Write ('|', TicTacToe [Row,Column]);
      WriteLn ('|');
      WriteLn ('-------')
    end {Row}
end; {PrintBoard}
```

```
-------
|X|O| |
-------
|O|X|O|
-------
|X| |X|
-------
```

■ Example 12.5

Function `IsFilled` in Fig. 12.5 returns a value of `True` if a tic-tac-toe board is all filled up; it returns a value of `False` if there is at least one cell that contains the constant `Empty`. Assume that all cells are initialized to `Empty` before the game begins. To move to a particular cell, a player replaces the constant `Empty` in that cell with an `X` or an `O`. A player can call function `IsFilled` before making a move to determine if there are any possible moves left. The `if` statement

```
if IsFilled(TicTacToe) then
  WriteLn ('Game is a draw!')
```

prints an appropriate message when there are no moves. ■

Figure 12.5 Function IsFilled

```
function IsFilled (TicTacToe : BoardArray) : Boolean;
{
  Tests whether the array TicTacToe is filled.
  Pre : All elements of array TicTacToe are assigned values.
  Post: Returns False if any cell contains the constant
        Empty; otherwise, returns True (array is filled).
}
  const
    Empty = ' ';

  var
    Row, Column : BoardRange;     {row and column subscripts}

begin {IsFilled}
  IsFilled := True;              {Assume the array is filled.}
  {Reset IsFilled to False if any cell is empty.}
  for Row := 1 to 3 do
    for Column := 1 to 3 do
      if TicTacToe[Row,Column] = Empty then
        IsFilled := False                {array is not filled}
end; {IsFilled}
```

■ Example 12.6

Procedure `EnterMove` in Fig. 12.6 is used to enter a move into the array `TicTacToe`. `EnterMove` calls procedure `EnterInt` (see Fig. 7.18) twice to enter a pair of values into the move coordinates, `MoveRow` and `MoveColumn`. If the cell selected by these coordinates is empty, its value is reset to the character stored in `Player` (`X` or `O`). ■

Figure 12.6 Procedure EnterMove

```
procedure EnterMove (Player {input} : Char;
                     var TicTacToe {input/output} : BoardArray);
{
  Stores an X or O (identity of Player) in the array TicTacToe.
  Pre  : Player is X or O and array TicTacToe has at least
         one empty cell.
  Post : The value of Player is stored in the empty cell of
```

```
         TicTacToe whose coordinates are read in; the rest
         of array TicTacToe is unchanged.
  Calls: Procedure EnterInt from unit EnterData
}
  const
    Empty = ' ';                {contents of an empty cell}

  var
    MoveRow, MoveColumn : Integer;      {coordinates of
                                            selected cell}

begin {EnterMove}
  repeat
    WriteLn ('Enter your move row and then the column');
    EnterInt (1, 3, MoveRow);
    EnterInt (1, 3, MoveColumn);
    if TicTacToe[MoveRow, MoveColumn] <> Empty then
      WriteLn ('Cell is occupied - try again')
  until TicTacToe[MoveRow, MoveColumn] = Empty;

  {assertion: A valid move is entered}
  TicTacToe[MoveRow, MoveColumn] := Player      {Define cell }
end; {EnterMove}
```

Exercises for Section 12.1

Self-Check

1. Declare a three-dimensional array type in which the first subscript consists of letters from `'A'` to `'F'`, the second subscript consists of integers from `1` to `10`, and the third consists of the user-defined type `Day`. Real numbers will be stored in the array. How many elements can be stored in an array with this type?
2. Assuming the following declarations

```
type
  MatrixType = array [1..5, 1..4] of Real;
var
  Matrix : MatrixType,
```

answer these questions:

a. How many elements in array `Matrix`?
b. Write a statement to display the element in row 3, column 4.
c. What is the offset for this element?
d. What formula is used to compute the offset for `Matrix[`i, j`]`?
e. Write a loop that computes the sum of the elements in row 5.
f. Write a loop that computes the sum of the elements in column 4.
g. Write nested loops that compute the sum of all the array elements.
h. Write nested loops that display the array elements in the following order: display column 4 as the first output line, column 3 as the second output line, and so on.

Programming

1. Write a function that determines who has won a game of tic-tac-toe. The function should first check all rows to see if one player occupies all the cells

in that row, then check all columns, and then check the two diagonals. The function should return a value from the enumerated type (`NoWinner`, `XWins`, `OWins`).

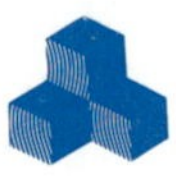

12.2 More Examples of Multidimensional Arrays

The subscript type for each dimension of the multidimensional array `TicTacToe` is a subrange of type `Integer`. It is not necessary for all the subscript types to have the same host type. The arrays in the next example have a different subscript type for each dimension.

■ Example 12.7

A university offers fifty courses at each of five campuses. The registrar's office can conveniently store the enrollments of these courses in the array `Enroll`, declared as follows:

```
const
  MaxCourse = 50;                    {maximum number of courses}

type
  CourseIndex = 1..MaxCourse;
  Campus = (Main, Ambler, Center, Delaware, Montco);
  ClassArray = array [CourseIndex, Campus] of Integer;

var
  Enroll : ClassArray;
```

This array consists of 250 elements, as shown in Fig. 12.7. `Enroll[1, Center]` represents the number of students in course 1 at Center campus.

Figure 12.7 Two-Dimensional Array Enroll

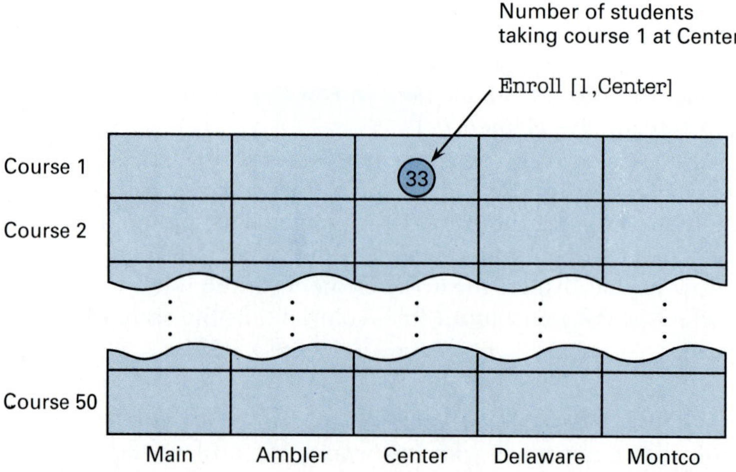

If the registrar wants to break down enrollment information according to student rank, it would require a three-dimensional array with 1,000 elements. This array is declared as follows and is shown in Fig. 12.8.

```
const
  MaxCourse = 50;           {maximum number of courses}

type
  CourseIndex = 1..MaxCourse;
  Campus = (Main, Ambler, Center, Delaware, Montco);
  Rank = (Freshman, Sophomore, Junior, Senior);
  BigClassArray = array [CourseIndex, Campus, Rank] of Integer;

var
  ClassEnroll : BigClassArray;                  {class enrollment}
  CurCampus : Campus;                           {current campus}
  ClassRank : Rank;                             {current rank}
  Total : Integer;                              {student totals}
```

The subscripted variable `ClassEnroll[1, Center, Senior]` represents the number of seniors taking course 1 at Center campus. ■

■ Example 12.8

The program segment

```
Total :=  0;
for ClassRank := Freshman to Senior do
  Total := Total + ClassEnroll[1, Center, ClassRank]
```

computes the total number of students of all ranks in course 1 at Center campus.

Figure 12.8 Three-Dimensional Array ClassEnroll

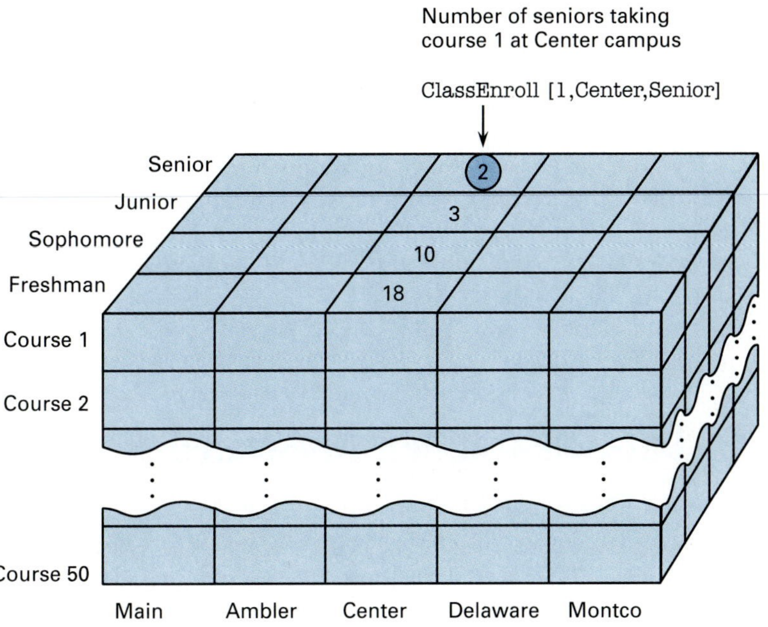

The program segment

```
Total := 0;
for CurCampus := Main to Montco do
  for ClassRank := Freshman to Senior do
    Total := Total + ClassEnroll[1, CurCampus, ClassRank]
```

computes the total number of students in course 1 (regardless of rank or campus). ■

Exercises for Section 12.2

Self-Check

1. Declare a three-dimensional array that can keep track of the number of students in the math classes (`Math1`, `Algebra`, `Geometry`, `Algebra2`, `Trigonometry`, `Calculus`) at your old high school according to the grade level and the sex of the students. How many elements are in this array?
2. Extend row-major order to three dimensions and show how the array `ClassEnroll` might be stored. What would be the offset for the array element `ClassEnroll[1, Center, Senior]` and the general formula for `ClassEnroll[i, j, k]`?

Programming

1. Redefine `MaxCourse` as `5` and write program segments that perform the following operations:
   a. Enter the enrollment data.
   b. Find the number of juniors in all classes at all campuses. Count students once for each course in which they are enrolled.
   c. Find the number of sophomores on all campuses who are enrolled in course 2.
   d. Compute and print the number of students at Main campus enrolled in each course and the total number of students at Main campus in all courses. Count students once for each course in which they are enrolled.
   e. Compute and print the number of upperclass students in all courses at each campus, as well as the total number of upperclass students enrolled. (Upperclass students are juniors and seniors.) Again, count students once for each course in which they are enrolled.

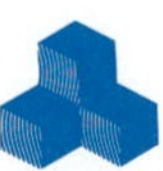

12.3 Data Abstraction Illustrated

By this time, you have learned quite a lot about Pascal and programming. Your knowledge of arrays and records will enable you to write fairly sophisticated programs. This section develops a general program that might be used by a company to analyze sales figures. We will use data abstraction, focusing on the data structures and their operators, to solve this problem.

Case Study: Analysis of Sales Trends

Problem

The HighRisk Software Company has employed us to develop a general sales analysis program that they can market to a number of different companies. This program will be used to enter and display sales figures in a variety of formats. The program will be *menu driven*, which means that users choose from a number of different options. The menu format is shown in Fig. 12.9.

Figure 12.9 Menu for Sales Analysis Program

```
Menu for Sales Analysis Program

 0. Get help.
 1. Enter sales data.
 2. Update sales data.
 3. Display sales data as a two-dimensional table.
 4. Compute annual sales totals.
 5. Tabulate monthly sales totals.
 6. Display annual sales totals.
 7. Display monthly sales totals.
 8. Display largest annual sales amount and year sold.
 9. Display largest monthly sales amount and month sold.
10. Graph annual sales data by year.
11. Graph monthly sales data by month.
12. Exit the program.
```

Design Overview

The operations to be performed are listed in the menu shown in Fig. 12.9. The main program will repeatedly display this menu and then perform the user's choice. The most difficult part of the problem is selecting the appropriate data structures and writing operators to perform each of the menu operations.

Data Requirements

Problem Inputs

The selected option (`Choice : Integer`)
The table of sales data (`Sales`)

Problem Outputs

The updated sales table displayed as a matrix (`Sales`)
The annual sales totals displayed in a table and as a bar graph (`SumByYear`)
The monthly sales totals displayed in a table and as a bar graph (`SumByMonth`)

There are three major data structures: a table of sales data organized by year and month, a collection of annual sales totals, and a collection of monthly sales totals. Menu choices 1 through 5 are performed on the complete table of sales data; menu choices 6, 8, and 10 are performed on the annual sales totals; and menu choices 7, 9, and 11 are performed on the monthly sales totals.

Abstract Data Type Specification

We can consider each data object and its associated operators as an abstract data type. We provide specifications for the sales table and annual sales totals next; the specification for monthly sales totals would be similar to the specification for annual sales totals.

Specification of Sales Table Abstract Data Type

Structure: The sales table, type `SalesRecord`, consists of a collection of `Real` values organized by year and month. There is one value for each month in the range of years covered. There are also two integer values that represent the starting year and the ending year.
Operators: Assume `Sales` is type `SalesRecord`.

`EnterSales (var Sales)`: Reads and saves the range of years covered and one sales amount for each month of the year.

`UpdateSales (var Sales)`: Modifies one or more entries in the sales table.

`DisplaySales (Sales)`: Displays the data in the sales table.

`TabYear (Sales, var SumByYear)`: Computes and stores the annual totals.

`TabMonth (Sales, var SumByMonth)`: Computes and stores the monthly totals.

Specification of Annual Sales Totals Abstract Data Type

Structure: The record for annual sales totals, type `YearSums`, consists of a collection of `Real` values, one for each year. There are also two integer values that represent the starting and the ending year.
Operators: Assume `SumByYear` is type `YearSums`.

`DisplayYear (SumByYear)`: Displays the annual sales total for each year of the range covered.

`MaxByYear (SumByYear, var LargeAmount, var LargeYear)`: Finds the largest annual sum (`LargeAmount`) and its year (`LargeYear`).

`GraphYear (SumByYear)`: Displays the annual sums in a bar graph.

The complete sales table stores a sales amount (type `Real`) for each month of a given year range (`MinYear..MaxYear`). The sales data can be stored in a two-dimensional array organized by year and month. This array will be part of a record, `Sales`, which also stores the first year (`First`) and the last year (`Last`) for which sales data are available (`MinYear <= First <= Last <= MaxYear`). Figure 12.10 shows the declarations for record `Sales`.

Figure 12.10 Declarations for Record Sales

```
const
  MinYear = 1985;
  MaxYear = 1999;

type
  YearRange = MinYear..MaxYear;
  SalesArray = array [YearRange, Month] of Real;
  SalesRecord = record
                  First, Last : YearRange;
                  Volume : SalesArray
                end; {SalesRecord}

var
  Sales : SalesRecord;
```

An object of type `SalesRecord` will accommodate sales data for the number of years in the subrange `YearRange`. For simplicity, we have chosen a rather small range.

Figure 12.11 shows a sketch of the memory area allocated to the record variable `Sales`. There is storage space for two `Integer` values (`Sales.First` and `Sales.Last`) and an array of `120` (10 rows by 12 columns) type `Real` values. As shown, array element `Sales.Volume[1989,December]` has the value `5549.00`.

The collection of annual sales totals can be stored in a record `SumByYear`. This record has an array field, `Sums`, with type `Real` elements and subscript type `YearRange`. For instance, `SumByYear.Sums[1989]` will contain the total of all sales in 1989. It also has two integer fields, `First` and `Last`, that specify the range of years covered (`MinYear <= First <= Last <= MaxYear`).

Figure 12.11 Record Sales

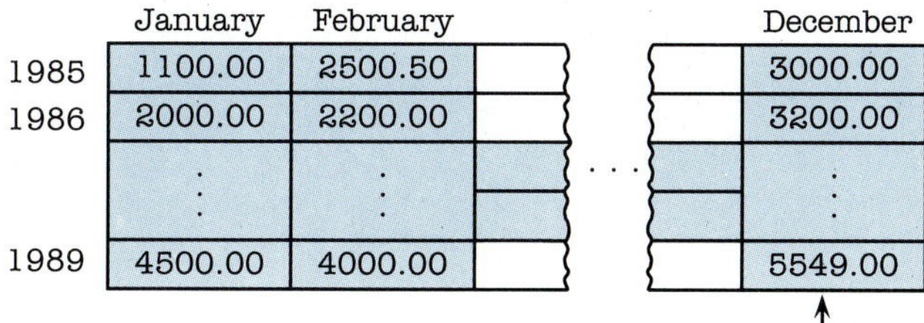

The collection of monthly sales totals can be stored in a one-dimensional array, `SumByMonth`, of type `Real` elements with subscript type `Month`. For instance, `SumByMonth[January]` will contain the total of all sales in January. Figure 12.12 shows the declarations and the memory layout for the record `SumByYear`; Fig. 12.13 shows the same for the array `SumByMonth`.

Figure 12.12 Record SumByYear

```
type
  YearArray = array [YearRange] of Real;
  YearSums = record
               First, Last : YearRange;
               Sums : YearArray
             end; {YearSums}

var
  SumByYear : YearSums;
```

Record SumByYear

SumByYear.First	1985
SumByYear.Last	1989

Array SumByYear.Sums

1985	17500.00	
1986	19000.00	← SumByYear.Sums[1986]
.	.	
.	.	
.	.	
1989	22455.00	

Figure 12.13 Array SumByMonth

```
type
  MonthSums = array [Month] of Real;

var
  SumByMonth : MonthSums;
```

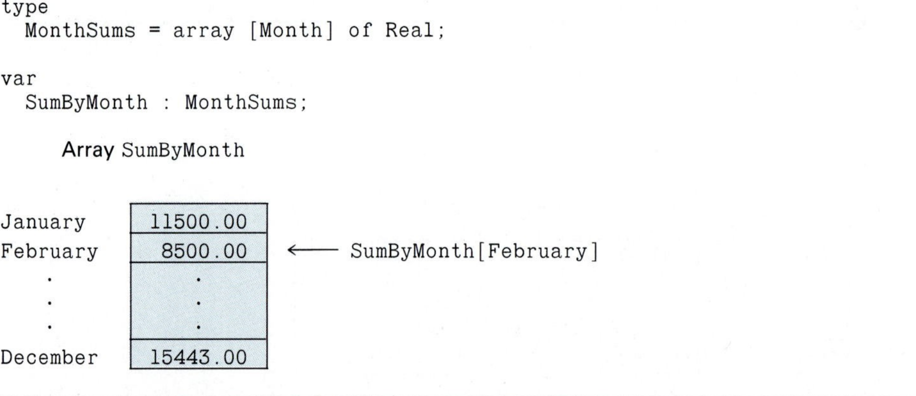

Design of Main Program

Now that we know the form of the major data objects and their operators, we can proceed with the design of the main program. The main program must allocate storage space for the data structures being manipulated, display the menu of choices, read each choice, and call the relevant operator procedure(s). Because certain operations must be performed before others, the main program must maintain the status of program flags that indicate which operations have been performed. The additional data requirements for the main program follow.

Program Variables

A program flag indicating whether sales data are read
(`ReadDone : Boolean`)

A program flag indicating whether annual sums are computed
(`YearDone : Boolean`)

A program flag indicating whether monthly sums are computed
(`MonthDone : Boolean`)

Algorithm for Main Program

1. Set status flags `ReadDone`, `YearDone`, and `MonthDone` to `False`.
2. `repeat`
    3. Display the menu.
    4. Read the user's choice.
    5. Perform the user's choice, updating `Sales`, `SumByYear`, `SumByMonth`, and the program flags.

   `until` user is done

Coding the Main Program

`ReadDone`, `YearDone`, and `MonthDone` (type `Boolean`) indicate whether the records `Sales` and `SumByYear` and array `SumByMonth` are defined. They are all initialized to `False`; `ReadDone` is set to `True` when `Sales` is defined, `YearDone` is set to `True` when `SumByYear` is defined, and `MonthDone` is set to `True` when `SumByMonth` is defined. The main program is shown in Fig. 12.14.

Figure 12.14 Program SalesAnalysis

```
{$R+}
program SalesAnalysis;
{
 Analyzes data provided for a sales table organized by year and month.
 Tabulates, displays, and graphs sales totals by year and month as di-
 rected by the program user.
 Imports: Month, WriteMonth, ReadMonth from ADT Month (Fig. 12.1)
          EnterInt from EnterData (Fig. 8.1)
          SalesRecord, EnterSales, UpdateSales, DisplaySales,
            TabYear, TabMonth from sales table ADT (Fig. 12.17)
          YearSums, DisplayYear, MaxByYear, GraphYear, YearRange,
            MinYear, MaxYear, from annual totals ADT (Fig. 12.18)
```

```
        MonthSums, DiplayMonth, MaxByMonth, GraphMonth
          from monthly totals ADT.
}
  uses EnterData, MonthADT, SalesTable, MonthlyTotals, AnnualTotals;
  const
    ExitChoice = 12;

  var
    Sales : SalesRecord;        {input/output - table of sales data}
    SumByYear : YearSums;       {output - sales totals for each year}
    SumByMonth : MonthSums;     {output - sales totals for each month}
    Choice : Integer;           {input - option selected}
    ReadDone,                   {flag for Sales defined}
    YearDone,                   {flag for SumByYear defined}
    MonthDone : Boolean;        {flag for SumByMonth defined}

  {Insert DisplayMenu}
  {$I DoChoice}

begin {SalesAnalysis}
  {Set program flags.}
  ReadDone := False;
  MonthDone := False;
  YearDone := False;

  {Perform user's choice until done}
  repeat
    DisplayMenu;
    EnterInt (0, ExitChoice, Choice);
    DoChoice (Choice, Sales, SumByYear, SumByMonth,
              ReadDone, YearDone, MonthDone)
  until Choice = ExitChoice
end. {SalesAnalysis}
```

Figure 12.15 is the module dependency diagram for the sales analysis program. It shows the interaction between the various modules used in the program system. Each high-level unit must import the lower level units that are connected to it. For example, procedure `EnterInt` in unit `EnterData` is called by operators in `MonthADT` and ADT `SalesTable` so unit `EnterData` must be imported by both of these units.

Coding DisplayMenu and DoChoice

Procedure `DisplayMenu` consists of the collection of `WriteLn` statements needed to print the menu and is left as an exercise at the end of this section. Procedure `DoChoice` (see Fig. 12.16) calls one or more of the operator procedures that are imported from the ADTs; the value of `Choice` determines which procedure(s) are called. If the preconditions are not met for a procedure, `DoChoice` displays an error message.

If the value of `Choice` is zero, `DoChoice` calls procedure `DisplayHelp` to print help messages to the user. `DisplayHelp` should provide information regarding any of the operations that the user wants clarified; `DisplayHelp` is also left as an exercise.

Figure 12.15 Module Dependency Diagram for Sales Analysis Program

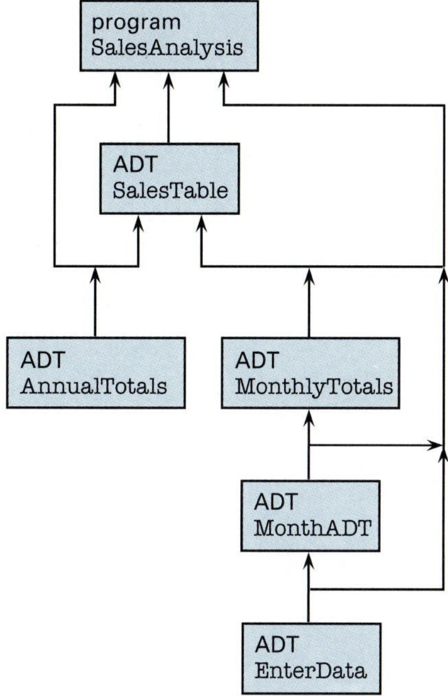

Figure 12.16 Procedure DoChoice

```
procedure DoChoice (var Choice {input/output} : Integer;
                    var Sales {input/output} : SalesRecord;
                    var SumByYear {input/output} : YearSums;
                    var SumByMonth {input/output} : MonthSums;
                    var ReadDone, YearDone,
                        MonthDone  {input/output} : Boolean);
{
   Performs the option selected by Choice.
   Pre  : Choice, ReadDone, YearDone, and MonthDone are defined.
   Post : Performs operation selected by Choice on Sales,
          SumByYear, and SumByMonth and resets flags ReadDone,
          YearDone, and MonthDone as required.
   Calls: DisplayHelp, EnterSales, UpdateSales, DisplaySales,
          TabYear, TabMonth, DisplayYear, DisplayMonth, MaxByYear,
          MaxByMonth, GraphYear, GraphMonth
}
   var
     ExitChar : Char;      {used to validate exit request}
     LargeAmount : Real;   {the largest plotted value}
     LargeYear : Integer;  {year with largest annual amount}
     LargeMonth : Month;   {month with largest monthly amount}

  {Insert DisplayHelp}
```

Case Study: Analysis of Sales Trends, continued

```
begin {DoChoice}
  {
   Make sure that EnterSales is done first and that TabYear
   is performed before operations on SumByYear and that
   TabMonth is performed before operations on SumBymonth.
  }
  if (choice > 1) and (not ReadDone) then
    WriteLn ('Read sales data first - enter 1')
  else if (Choice in [6, 8, 10]) and (not YearDone) then
    WriteLn ('Tabulate annual sums first - enter 4')
  else if (Choice in [7, 9, 11]) and (not MonthDone) then
    WriteLn ('Tabulate monthly sums first - enter 5')
  else
    case Choice of
       0 :  DisplayHelp;
       1 :  begin
              EnterSales (Sales);
              ReadDone := True; YearDone := False; MonthDone := False
            end; {1}
       2 :  begin
              UpdateSales (Sales);
              YearDone := False;  MonthDone:= False
            end; {2}
       3 :  DisplaySales (Sales);
       4 :  begin
              TabYear (Sales, SumByYear);
              YearDone := True
            end; {4}
       5 :  begin
              TabMonth (Sales, SumByMonth);
              MonthDone := True
            end; {5}
       6 :  DisplayYear (SumByYear);
       7 :  DisplayMonth (SumByMonth);
       8 :  begin
              MaxByYear (SumByYear, LargeAmount, LargeYear);
              WriteLn ('Largest annual sum is $',
                       LargeAmount :4:2, ' in year ', LargeYear)
            end; {8}
       9 :  begin
              MaxByMonth (SumByMonth, LargeAmount, LargeMonth);
              WriteLn ('Largest monthly sum is $',
                       LargeAmount :4:2, ' in month ');
              WriteMonth (LargeMonth)
            end; {9}
      10 :  GraphYear (SumByYear);
      11 :  GraphMonth (SumByMonth);
      12 :  begin
              Write ('Exit program? Enter Y (Yes) or N (No) > ');
              Read (ExitChar);
              if (ExitChar = 'Y') or (ExitChar = 'y') then
                WriteLn ('Sales analysis completed.')
              else
                Choice := 0         {cancel exit request}
            end {12}
    end {case}
end;  {DoChoice}
```

PROGRAM STYLE

Verifying an Exit Request

The case statement in procedure DoChoice requires program users to verify that they want to exit the sales analysis program when Choice is ExitChoice (value is 12). Without this verification step, all data entry and analysis may have to be repeated if the program user selects the exit option by mistake.

Coding the Sales Table ADT

Figure 12.17 shows unit SalesTable containing data type SalesRecord and the operators for the sales table ADT. Procedure EnterSales reads data into array Sales.Volume. EnterSales first calls EnterInt twice to read in the range of years covered. Next, a pair of nested for loops enters the sales data. Procedure WriteMonth displays the current month name as a prompt.

Procedure UpdateSales can be used to change an incorrect sales table value or to add new values at a later time. The program user must enter the year, month, and sales amount for each table entry being updated. ReadMonth enters an integer from 1 to 12 and converts it to a value of type Month.

Most screens are not wide enough to display the sales data for all twelve months of a year. Consequently, DisplaySales calls ShowHalf twice: first to print the sales figures for the first six months and then to print the figures for the last six months. ShowHalf begins by displaying six months as column headings. Next, a pair of nested for loops displays the sales figures for those six months of each year.

Procedure TabYear accumulates the sum of each row of the sales table and stores it in the appropriate element of array SumByYear. (Procedure TabMonth is left as an exercise at the end of this section.) Notice that record Sales is declared as a variable parameter in DisplaySales and TabYear even though it is used only for input. We have done this to save the time and memory that would be needed to make a local copy of this rather sizable record.

Figure 12.17 Sales Table ADT

```
unit SalesTable;
{
 Abstract data type SalesTable: contains declarations for record type
 SalesRecord and procedures for manipulating sales data.
 Exports: SalesRecord, SalesArray, EnterSales,
          UpdateSales, DisplaySales, TabYear, TabMonth

 Imports: EnterInt from unit EnterData (Fig. 8.3)
          Month, ReadMonth, WriteMonth from MonthADT
          MonthSums, DisplayMonth, MaxByMonth, GraphMonth
            from MonthlyTotals
```

```
          YearRange, MinYear, MaxYear, YearSums, DisplayYear,
            MaxByYear, GraphYear from AnnualTotals (Fig. 12.18)
}
interface
  uses EnterData, MonthADT, MonthlyTotals, AnnualTotals;

  type
    SalesArray = array [YearRange, Month] of Real;
    SalesRecord = record
                    First, Last : YearRange;
                    Volume : SalesArray
                  end; {SalesRecord}

  procedure EnterSales (var Sales {output} : SalesRecord);
  {
    Reads the sales data into the record Sales.
    Pre  : None
    Post : The fields First and Last are defined and
           sales data are read into array Volume for each month of
           years First..Last.
    Calls: EnterInt, WriteMonth
  }

  procedure UpdateSales (var Sales {input/output} : SalesRecord);
  {
    Changes one or more values in array Sales.Volume.
    Pre  : Record Sales is defined.
    Post : Reads year, month, and value for each update
           and stores the new value in array Sales.Volume.
    Calls: EnterInt, ReadMonth
  }

  procedure DisplaySales (var Sales {input} : SalesRecord);
  {
    Displays the sales data.
    Pre  : Record Sales is defined.
    Post : Displays a two-dimensional table of sales volume
           by month for years First..Last.
    Calls: ShowHalf to display table in chunks of 6 months.
  }

  procedure TabYear (var Sales {input} : SalesRecord;
                     var SumByYear {output} : YearSums);
  {
    Tabulates sales totals by year. Sums are stored in array SumByYear.
    Pre : Record Sales is defined.
    Post: SumByYear.First and SumByYear.Last are defined and elements
          SumByYear.Sums[First] through SumByYear.Sums[Last] are
          tabulated.
  }

  procedure TabMonth (var Sales {input} : SalesRecord;
                      var SumByMonth {output} : MonthSums);
  {
    Tabulates sales totals by month. Sums are stored in array SumByMonth.
    Pre : Record Sales is defined.
    Post: SumByMonth[January] through SumByMonth[December] are
          tabulated.
  }

implementation
```

```
procedure EnterSales (var Sales (output) : SalesRecord);
   var
     CurMonth : Month;            {current month}
     CurYear : YearRange;         {current year}
     TempYear : Integer;          {holds data value for year}

begin {EnterSales}
  {Enter first and last years of sales data.}
  WriteLn ('Enter first year of sales data.');
  EnterInt (MinYear, MaxYear, TempYear);
  Sales.First := TempYear;
  WriteLn ('Enter last year of sales data.');
  EnterInt (Sales.First, MaxYear, TempYear);
  Sales.Last := TempYear;

  {Enter sales table data.}
  for CurYear := Sales.First to Sales.Last do
    begin
      WriteLn;
      Write ('For year ', CurYear :4);
      WriteLn (', enter sales amount for each month or 0.0');
      for CurMonth := January to December do
        begin
          WriteMonth (CurMonth);
          Write (' $');
          ReadLn (Sales.Volume[CurYear, CurMonth])
        end {for CurMonth}
    end {for CurYear}
end; {EnterSales}


procedure UpdateSales (var Sales {input/output} : SalesRecord);
  var
    NewYear : Integer;         {Year of entry being updated.}
    NewMonth : Month;          {Month of entry being updated.}
    NewAmount : Real;          {Updated value}
    MoreChar : Char;           {More changes ('Y' or 'N')}

begin {UpdateSales}
  WriteLn ('Enter year, month, and amount for each update.');
  repeat
    Write ('For year - ');
    EnterInt (Sales.First, Sales.Last, NewYear);
    Write ('For month - ');
    ReadMonth (NewMonth);
    Write ('Enter amount $');
    ReadLn (NewAmount);
    Sales.Volume[NewYear, NewMonth] := NewAmount;
    Write ('Any more changes?  Enter Y (Yes) or N (No) > ');
    Read (MoreChar)
  until (MoreChar = 'N') or (MoreChar = 'n')
end; {UpdateSales}


procedure DisplaySales (var Sales {input} : SalesRecord);

   procedure ShowHalf (var Sales {input} : SalesRecord;
                       FirstMonth, LastMonth {input} : Month);
   {
      Displays the sales amounts by year for each of the months from
      FirstMonth to LastMonth.
```

```
      Pre  : Record Sales and FirstMonth and LastMonth are defined.
      Post : Displays sales volumes in a table whose rows are
             Sales.First..Sales.Last and whose columns are
             FirstMonth..LastMonth.
      Calls: WriteMonth
   }
      var
        CurMonth : Month;                    {loop-control variable}
        CurYear : YearRange;                 {loop-control variable}

   begin {ShowHalf}
     {Print table heading for the months displayed.}
     Write ('Year');
     for CurMonth := FirstMonth to LastMonth do
       begin
         Write (' ');                             {Leave a space}
         WriteMonth (CurMonth)                 {Print month name}
       end; {for}
     WriteLn;                                   {End the heading}

     {Print sales figures for each month of each year.}
     for CurYear := Sales.First to Sales.Last do
       begin
         Write (CurYear :4);
         for CurMonth := FirstMonth to LastMonth do
           Write (Sales.Volume[CurYear, CurMonth] :10:2);
         WriteLn
       end {for CurYear}
   end; {ShowHalf}

begin {DisplaySales}
  {Display first 6 months and last 6 months of array Sales.}
  ShowHalf (Sales, January, June);   WriteLn;
  ShowHalf (Sales, July, December);  WriteLn
end; {DisplaySales}


procedure TabYear (var Sales {input} : SalesRecord;
                   var SumByYear {output} : YearSums);
   var
     CurMonth : Month;                        {loop-control variable}
     CurYear : YearRange;                     {loop-control variable}
     Sum : Real;                              {sum for each year}

begin {TabYear}
  {Store range of years covered.}
  SumByYear.First := Sales.First;
  SumByYear.Last := Sales.Last;

  {Find each annual total.}
  for CurYear := Sales.First to Sales.Last do
    begin
      {Accumulate sum for 12 months}
      Sum := 0.0;
      for CurMonth := January to December do
        Sum := Sum + Sales.Volume[CurYear, CurMonth];
      SumByYear.Sums[CurYear] := Sum         {Store sales total}
    end; {for CurYear}
  WriteLn ('Annual sums tabulated')
  end;  {TabYear}
end. {SalesTable}
```

Coding the Annual Totals ADT

Figure 12.18 shows unit AnnualTotals containing data type SalesTable and the operators for the annual totals ADT. Procedure DisplayYear simply displays the values in array field Sums (a one-dimensional array) and is left as an exercise at the end of this section.

Procedure MaxByYear returns through LargeAmount the largest value in the array field Sums. It does this by saving the largest value found so far (starting with Sums[SumByYear.First]) in parameter LargeAmount. Each time an array element containing a larger value is found, its value is stored in LargeAmount and its subscript is stored in LargeYear.

Procedure GraphYear draws a bar chart of the values stored in array field Sums. First, GraphYear calls MaxByYear to determine the largest annual sales total. Next, it divides this value by the constant ScreenWidth (value is 50) to get the value represented by each point plotted. For each year being displayed, the while loop in GraphYear continues to plot points until the value plotted exceeds the sales total for that year. Hence, the largest value will be plotted as a bar of length ScreenWidth; all other bars will be smaller.

Figure 12.18 Annual Totals ADT

```
unit AnnualTotals;
{
  Abstract data type AnnualTotals: contains declarations for
  record type YearSums and procedures for manipulating annual
  sales data.
  Exports: YearRange, MinYear, MaxYear, YearSums,
           DisplayYear, MaxByYear, GraphYear
  Imports: Month, ReadMonth, WriteMonth from MonthADT
}
interface

  const
    MinYear = 1985;
    MaxYear = 1999;

  type
    YearRange = MinYear..MaxYear;
    YearArray = array [YearRange] of Real;
    YearSums = record
                 First, Last : YearRange;
                 Sums : YearArray
               end; {YearSums}

  procedure DisplayYear (SumByYear {input} : YearSums);
  {
    Displays sales totals by year. Sums are retrieved from array
    SumByYear.
    Pre : SumByYear.Sums[i] contains sales totals for the year i.
    Post: SumByYear.First and SumByYear.Last are defined and elements
          SumByYear.Sums[First] through SumByYear.Sums[Last] are
          displayed.
  }
  procedure MaxByYear (var SumByYear {input} : YearSums;
                       var LargeAmount {output} : Real;
```

```
                     var LargeYear {output} : Integer);
{
  Finds the largest value in array SumByYear.Sums
  Pre  : Record SumByYear is defined.
  Post : Returns the largest value in array SumByYear.Sums
         through LargeAmount and its corresponding
         year through LargeYear.
}

procedure GraphYear (var SumByYear {input} : YearSums);
{
  Displays a graph of array SumByYear.Sums.
  Pre : Record SumByYear is defined.
  Post: Displays a bar graph such that the size of the bar drawn for
        each element of array SumByYear.Sums is proportional to its
        value.
  Calls: MaxByYear
}

implementation

{Insert procedure DisplayYear}

procedure MaxByYear (var SumByYear {input} : YearSums;
                     var LargeAmount {output} : Real;
                     var LargeYear {output} : Integer);
  var
    CurYear : YearRange;        {loop control variable}

begin {MaxByYear}
  {First year's amount is largest so far.}
  with SumByYear do
    begin
      LargeYear := First;
      LargeAmount := Sums[First];

      {Find the largest value in array field Sums.}
      for CurYear := First + 1 to Last do
        {invariant:
           LargeAmount contains largest amount so far and
           Sums[LargeYear] is equal to LargeAmount.
        }
        if Sums[CurYear] > LargeAmount then
          begin
            {Save new largest amount so far.}
            LargeAmount := Sums[CurYear];
            LargeYear := CurYear
          end {if}
    end {with}
end; {MaxByYear}


procedure GraphYear (var SumByYear {input} : YearSums);
  const
    Star = '*';                {symbol plotted}
    ScreenWidth = 50;          {longest bar length}

  var
    LargeAmount,               {the largest value plotted}
    Increment,                 {the amount represented by each point}
```

```
      PlotVal : Real;           {the amount plotted so far}
      LargeYear : Integer;      {the year of largest annual amount}
      CurYear : YearRange       {loop control variable}

  begin {GraphYear}
    {Define the scale for the horizontal axis.}
    MaxByYear (SumByYear, LargeAmount, LargeYear);
    Increment := LargeAmount / ScreenWidth;

    {Plot the bar graph.}
    WriteLn;
    WriteLn ('Year|      Sales in Dollars');   {Print heading}
    {Print a bar for each element of array field SumByYear.Sums}
    with SumByYear do
      for CurYear := First to Last do
        begin
          Write (CurYear :4, '|');                  {Print the year}
          {Plot points until value plotted exceeds element value.}
          PlotVal := Increment;           {Initialize sum plotted}
          while PlotVal <= Sums[CurYear] do
            begin
              Write (Star);                    {Plot a new point}
              PlotVal := PlotVal + Increment  {Add to sum plotted}
            end {while}
        end; {for}

    {Draw horizontal scale}
    WriteLn ('0.00^         ^          ^          ^',
                   '         ^          ^', LargeAmount :4:2);
    WriteLn ('     Each point represents ', Increment :4:2)
    end;  {GraphYear}
  end. {AnnualTotals}
```

Testing the Sales Analysis Program

A sample run of the sales analysis program is shown in Fig. 12.19. To save space, only part of the data entry process and only the first menu display are shown. The options selected are 1, 2, 4, 6, 8, 10, and 12.

To test this program completely, you should select options whose preconditions are not satisfied. For instance, selecting option 7, 9, or 11 should display the error message `Tabulate monthly sums first - enter 5`. You should also enter year values that are outside the expected range to make sure that they do not cause a fatal program error. Finally, provide the missing procedures and verify that they perform their intended operations.

Figure 12.19 Sample Run of the Sales Analysis Program

```
Menu for Sales Analysis Program

 0. Get help.
 1. Enter sales data.
 2. Update sales data.
 3. Display sales data as a two-dimensional table.
 4. Compute annual sales totals.
```

```
 5. Tabulate monthly sales totals.
 6. Display annual sales totals.
 7. Display monthly sales totals.
 8. Display largest annual sales amount and year sold.
 9. Display largest monthly sales amount and month sold.
10. Graph annual sales data by year.
11. Graph monthly sales data by month.
12. Exit the program.

Choose an option - Enter a number between 0 and 12> 1
Enter first year of sales data.
Enter a number between 1985 and 1999> 1987
Enter last year of sales data.
Enter a number between 1987 and 1999> 1988


For year 1987, enter sales amount for each month or 0.0
  January $1000.00
 February $600.00
    March $700.00
          .
          .
          .

For year 1988, enter sales amount for each month or 0.0
  January $500.00
 February $400.00
    March $400.00
          .
          .
          .

Choose an option - Enter a number between 0 and 12> 2
Enter year, month, and amount for each update.
For year - Enter a number between 1987 and 1988> 1987

For month - Enter a number between 1 and 12 > 2
Enter amount $600.00
Any more changes?  Enter Y (Yes) or N (No) > N

Choose an option - Enter a number between 0 and 12> 3
Table of Sales Volume by Year and Month

Year  January      February  March     April       May      June
1987  1000.00      600.00    700.00    800.00    950.00   1000.00
1988   500.00      400.00    400.00    900.00   1000.00     55.00

Year     July      August September   October November  December
1987   500.00      500.00    900.00    600.00   950.50   1000.00
1988   300.00      800.00    750.00    900.00   600.00    300.00

Choose an option - Enter a number between 0 and 12> 4
Annual sums tabulated.

Choose an option - Enter a number between 0 and 12> 6
Table of Sales Totals by Year

      Year     Sales
      1987   9500.50
      1988   6905.00
```

```
Choose an option - Enter a number between 0 and 12> 8
Largest annual sum is $9500.50 in year 1987
Choose an option - Enter a number between 0 and 12> 10

Year|     Sales in Dollars
1987|**************************************************
1988|************************************
0.00^         ^         ^         ^         ^         ^9500.50
     Each point represents 190.00

Choose an option - Enter a number between 0 and 12> 12
Exit program? Enter Y (Yes) or N (No) > Y
Sales analysis completed.
```

Exercises for Section 12.3

Self-Check

1. Explain why the variable `TempYear` is needed in procedure `EnterSales`.
2. Why is it necesary for `DisplaySales` to call `ShowHalf` twice?

Programming

1. Write procedures `DisplayMenu`, `DisplayHelp`, and `DisplayYear`.
2. Write unit `MonthlyTotals` containing declarations for type `MonthSums` and procedures `DisplayMonth`, `MaxByMonth`, and `GraphMonth` for the monthly totals ADT.

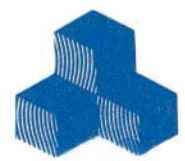

12.4 Parallel Arrays and Arrays of Records

Often a data collection contains items of different types. For example, the data that represent the performance of a class of students on an exam consist of the students' names, their exam scores, and their grades.

Parallel Arrays

One approach to organizing these data would be to declare separate arrays with identical subscript types for the names, scores, and grades, as follows:

```
const
  MaxClass = 200;
  StrLength = 20;

type
  ClassIndex = 1..MaxClass;
  StringType = string[StrLength];
  NameArray = array [ClassIndex] of StringType;
```

```
    ScoreArray = array [ClassIndex] of Integer;
    GradeArray = array [ClassIndex] of Char;

var
    Names  : NameArray;
    Scores : ScoreArray;
    Grades : GradeArray;
```

These three arrays are called *parallel arrays*, because all the data items with the same subscript (say, *i*) pertain to a particular student (the *i*th student). Related data items are in the same shade of color in Fig. 12.20. The data for the first student are stored in `Names[1]`, `Scores[1]`, and `Grades[1]`. A better way to organize the student data is shown next.

Declaring an Array of Student Records

A more natural and more convenient organization of the class performance data is to group all the information pertaining to a particular student in a record. The data structure declared next represents the class data as a single array of records named `Class`. A sample array `Class` is shown in Fig. 12.21.

```
const
  MaxClass = 200;
  StrLength = 20;

type
  ClassIndex = 1..MaxClass;
  StringType = string[StrLength];
  Student = record
              Name  : StringType;
              Score : Integer;
              Grade : Char
            end; {Student}
  StudentArray = array [ClassIndex] of Student;

var
  Class : StudentArray;
```

In Fig. 12.21, the data for the first student are stored in record `Class[1]`. The individual data items are `Class[1].Name`, `Class[1].Score`, and `Class[1].Grade`. As shown, `Class[1].Grade` is `A`.

Figure 12.20 Three Parallel Arrays

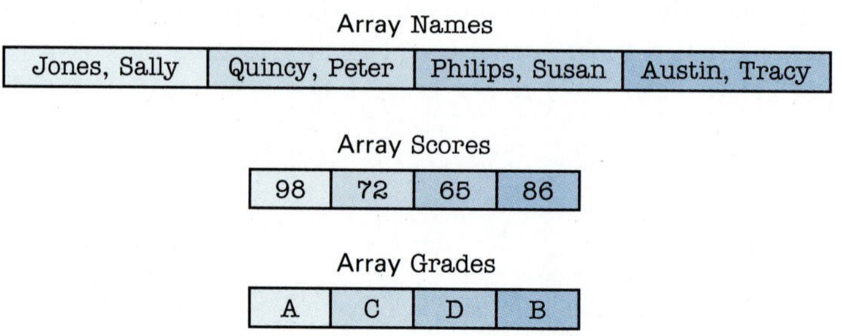

Figure 12.21 Array of Records

Array Class

	Name	Score	Grade
Class[1]	Jones, Sally	98	A ← Class[1].Grade
Class[2]	Quincy, Peter	72	C
Class[3]	Philips, Susan	65	D
Class[4]	Austin, Tracy	86	B

If procedure `ReadOneStudent` is available to read a single student record, the following `for` statement can be used to fill the entire array `Class` with data.

```
for I := 1 to MaxClass do
  ReadOneStudent (Class[I]);
```

Each time `ReadOneStudent` is called, the record returned will be stored as the ith element (`1 <= I <= MaxClass`) of array `Class`. The following `for` statement can be used to display all the names read.

```
for I := 1 to MaxClass do
  WriteLn (Class[I].Name)
```

Using the with Statement with an Array of Records

Be careful when you use a `with` statement to process an array of records. For example, the `with` statement that begins

```
with Class[I] do
```

uses the subscripted variable `Class[I]` as its record variable. The particular array element referenced depends on the value of `I`. If `I` is undefined or is out of range, a run-time error will result.

If `I` is updated inside the `with` statement, the array element referenced will not change. For example, the following statements display the first student's name `MaxClassSize` times. Because `I` is `1` when the `with` statement is reached, `Class[1]` is the record referenced in the `with` statement body. Even though the `for` loop changes the value of `I`, `Class[1]` is still the record referenced, so `Class[1].Name` will be displayed repeatedly.

```
I := 1;
{incorrect attempt to display all student names}
with Class[I] do
  for I := 1 to MaxClass do
    WriteLn (Name)
```

The correct way to sequence these statements is shown next.

```
{Display all student names}
for I := 1 to MaxClass do
  with Class[I] do
    WriteLn (Name)
```

Now all student names will be printed, because `I` is changed by the `for` statement external to the `with` statement. Each time the `with` statement is reached, it references a new record. Whenever a `for` statement accesses an array of records in sequential order, the `with` statement should be nested inside the `for` statement and not vice versa.

Exercises for Section 12.4

Self-Check

1. For the array of records `Class`, what value is displayed by each of the following valid statements?

   a. `WriteLn (Class[3].Name[4]);`
   b. `WriteLn (Class[3].Grade[4]);`
   c. `WriteLn (Class.Grade[3]);`
   d. `WriteLn (Class[4].Name);`
   e. `WriteLn (Class[4].Name[4].Grade)`
   f. `WriteLn (Class[3].Grade)`
   g. `WriteLn (Class[3]);`
   h. `WriteLn (Class.Name[4]);`

2. Write a `for` loop that could be used to read data into the three parallel arrays declared in this section. Assume that the number of students, `NumStu`, is known before loop execution begins.
3. Does storage of an array of records require more or less memory space than storage of parallel arrays?

Programming

1. Write procedure `ReadOneStudent`. Read each student's name and score; leave the grade field undefined.

12.5 Processing an Array of Records

This problem illustrates the use of an array of records. It processes the array of students declared earlier.

Case Study: Grading an Exam

Problem

Your computer science professor wants a program that will assist her in assigning grades for an exam. The program should read and display each student's name and exam score, compute and display all exam statistics (that is, the number of students who took the exam, the lowest score, the highest score, average score, median score, and standard deviation), and assign letter grades based on the class average and standard deviation.

Design Overview

Currently your professor stores the information for her classes in a gradebook. Each gradebook page lists the students on the left and has a column on the right for storing the exam scores and the corresponding letter grades. The exam statistics appear at the bottom of the page. A sample entry for one exam is shown in Fig. 12.22. The student names and numeric scores are provided as input data; the letter grades, the number of students, and the exam statistics are all undefined initially.

Figure 12.22 Sample Gradebook Entry

```
Name                   Score/Grade
Sally Adams              80     ?
Robert Baker             70     ?
Jane Cohen               60     ?
William Dooley           73     ?
     .
     .
     .

Number of Students        ?

Lowest Score              ?
Highest Score             ?
Median Score              ?
Average Score             ?
Standard Deviation        ?
```

Data Requirements

Problem Inputs

The name of each student taking the exam (a string)
The score of each student taking the exam (an integer)

Problem Outputs

Each student's name, score, and letter grade (a character)
The number of students taking the exam (an integer)
The exam statistics, including the lowest score, the highest score, and median score (integers) and the average and standard deviation (real numbers)

Data Type Specification

We can store the student data and exam statistics shown in Fig. 12.22 in two separate data structures. The first is a single record with two fields: an array of student records and the number of students. The second data structure is a record for storing the exam statistics. Figure 12.23 shows the declarations for these data structures; Fig. 12.24 sketches their layout in memory.

Specification of Gradebook Abstract Data Type

Structure: Consists of a record of data (a string, an integer, and a character) for each student who took the exam and a count of students (all stored in record `Test`). Also, consists of a collection of `Real` values that represent the exam statistics (stored in record `Stats`).

Operators: `ReadStudents (var Test)`: Reads and saves the student names and exam scores. Also counts the number of students who took the exam.

`DisplayStudents (Test)`: Displays the name, numeric score, and letter grade for each student who took the exam.

`ComputeStats (Test, var Stats)`: Computes and stores the exam statistics.

`DisplayStats (Stats)`: Displays the exam statistics.

`AssignGrades (var Test, Stats)`: Assigns and stores the letter grade for each student.

Figure 12.23 Declarations for a Gradebook Entry

```
const
  StrLength = 20;                  {length of each name string}
  MaxClass = 200;                  {maximum number of students}

type
  StringType = string[StrLength];
  Student = record                          {one student record}
              Name : StringType;
              Score : Integer;
              Grade : Char
            end; {Student}

  ClassRange = 0..MaxClass;
  ClassIndex = 1..MaxClass;
  StudentArray = array [ClassIndex] of Student; {array of records}

  Exam = record
           Class : StudentArray;
           NumStu : ClassRange
         end; {Exam}

  Statistics = record
                 LowScore, HighScore,
                 Median : Integer;
                 Average,
                 StandardDev : Real
               end; {Statistics}
var
  Test  : Exam;                {the student data and count}
  Stats : Statistics;          {the exam statistics}
```

Figure 12.24 Records Test and Stats in Memory

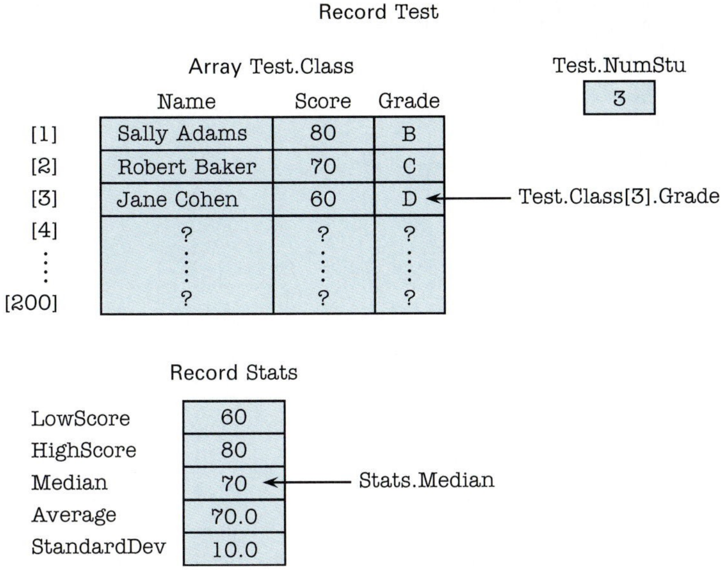

Record Test

Array Test.Class

	Name	Score	Grade
[1]	Sally Adams	80	B
[2]	Robert Baker	70	C
[3]	Jane Cohen	60	D ← Test.Class[3].Grade
[4]	?	?	?
⋮	⋮	⋮	⋮
[200]	?	?	?

Test.NumStu: 3

Record Stats

LowScore	60
HighScore	80
Median	70 ← Stats.Median
Average	70.0
StandardDev	10.0

Design of Main Program

The main program for the student grading program uses the operators in the gradebook entry ADT to process the data structures `Test` and `Stats` in the appropriate sequence. The main program algorithm is shown next.

Main Program Algorithm

1. Read the student data.
2. Compute the exam statistics.
3. Print the exam statistics.
4. Assign letter grades to each student.
5. Print each student's final record.

Coding the Main Program

The main program is shown in Fig. 12.25. The record types `Exam` and `Statistics` (see Fig. 12.23) are referenced in the declaration part. Figure 12.26 is the module dependency diagram.

Figure 12.25 Student Grading Program

```
{$R+}
program Grader;
{ Computes and displays the exam statistics, assigns letter
  grades, and displays each student's record.
```

```
  Imports:  MaxClass, Student, ClassRange, ClassIndex, StudentArray,
              Exam, Statistics, ReadStudents, DisplayStudents,
              ComputeStats, DisplayStats, AssignGrades from
              GradeBook ADT (see Fig. 12.27).
}
  uses GradeBook;

  var
    Test  : Exam;                  {the student data and count}
    Stats : Statistics;            {the exam statistics}

begin {Grader}
  ReadStudents (Test);
  ComputeStats (Test, Stats);
  DisplayStats (Stats);
  AssignGrades (Test, Stats);
  DisplayStudents (Test)
end. {Grader}
```

Coding the GradeBook ADT

The type declarations and operators for the gradebook ADT are shown in Fig. 12.27. Procedure `ReadStudents` calls procedure `ReadOneStudent` once for each student who took the exam. `ReadOneStudent` returns the next student's name and score through its parameter `NextStudent`. Entering a blank name (by pressing the Return key) indicates that there are no more students. If a nonblank name is read, the count of students processed (`I`) is incremented by one, and the statement

```
Test.Class[I] := NextStudent
```

copies the input data into the next element of the array `Test.Class`. The number of students is stored in `Test.NumStu` and displayed just before the procedure finishes.

Procedure `DisplayStudents` displays a table of student records, one student record per output line. The statements

```
for I := 1 to Test.NumStu do
  with Test.Class[I] do
    WriteLn (Name :20, Score :10, Grade :10)
```

Figure 12.26 Module Dependency Diagram for Student Grading Program

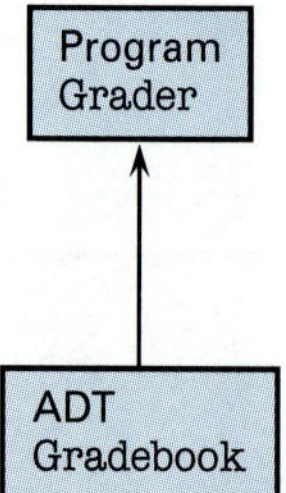

display the next student record, Test.Class[I]. Because the with statement is nested inside the for statement, a different student's record is printed on each output line.

Procedure AssignGrades assigns a letter grade to each student. The grade can be determined by comparing the student's score to the class average and the standard deviation. Table 12.1 describes the desired grade assignments.

Table 12.1 Decision Table for Assigning Letter Grades

Score Range	Grade
>= Average + 1.5 * StandardDev	A
>= Average + 0.5 * StandardDev	B
>= Average - 0.5 * StandardDev	C
>= Average - 1.5 * StandardDev	D
< Average - 1.5 * StandardDev	F

The if statement in procedure AssignGrades implements the decision table. The for loop causes the if statement to be repeated once for each student. Because the if statement is also nested inside the with statement, the fields Score and Grade reference fields of the record variable Test.Class[I] (that is, the current student record).

Finally, procedure ComputeStats computes the exam statistics and stores the results in the subrecord Test.Stats. ComputeStats calls a different function to compute each statistic. Function FindAverage returns the average score and is shown in Fig. 12.27. Function FindStandardDev is discussed after the figure, and function FindMedian is discussed in Section 12.7. The rest of the statistical functions are left as exercises. Procedure DisplayStats displays the contents of record Stats and is also left as an exercise.

Figure 12.27 GradeBook ADT

```
unit GradeBook;
{
  Abstract data type GradeBook: contains declarations for record
  types Student, Exam, and Statistics and procedures for reading
  and displaying student data and computing exam statistics.
  Exports: MaxClass, Student, ClassRange, ClassIndex,
           StudentArray, Exam, Statistics, ReadStudents,
           DisplayStudents, ComputeStats, DisplayStats,
           AssignGrades
}
interface

  const
    StringLen = 20;                 {capacity of each name string}
    MaxClass = 200;                 {maximum number of students}

  type
    StringType = string[StringLen];
    Student = record
```

```
                Name : StringType;
                Score : Integer;
                Grade : Char
              end; {Student}

  ClassRange = 0..MaxClass;
  ClassIndex = 1..MaxClass;
  StudentArray = array [ClassIndex] of Student; {array of records}

  Exam = record
           Class : StudentArray;
           NumStu : ClassRange
         end; {Exam}

  Statistics = record
                 LowScore,
                 HighScore,
                 Median      : Integer;
                 Average,
                 StandardDev : Real
               end; {Statistics}

procedure ReadStudents (var Test {output} : Exam);
{
  Reads in the student records for one exam and counts the
  number of students who took the exam.
  Pre  : None
  Post : Name and score of each student is stored in Test.Class and
         a count of students is displayed and stored in
         Test.NumStu.
  Calls: ReadOneStudent
}

procedure DisplayStudents (var Test {input} : Exam);
{
  Displays the student records.
  Pre  : Record Test is defined.
  Post: Displays exam performance data for each student.
}

procedure ComputeStats (var Test {input} : Exam;
                        var Stats {output} : Statistics);
{
  Compute all exam statistics.
  Pre  : Students scores are read and record Test is defined.
  Post : Stores low, high, and median scores, and
         average and standard deviations in record Stats.
  Calls: FindLow, FindHigh, FindMedian, FindAverage,
         and FindStandardDev
}

procedure AssignGrades (var Test {input/output} : Exam;
                        Stats {input} : Statistics);
{
  Assigns letter grade to each student based on the exam score,
  class average, and standard deviation.
  Pre : All exam scores are stored in Test.Class and Average and
        StandardDev are defined (part of record Stats).
  Post: The letter grade for each student is stored in
        Test.Class.
}
```

```
  procedure DisplayStats (Stats {input} : Statistics);
  {Displays the statistics for an exam.}

implementation

  procedure ReadStudents (var Test {output} : Exam);

    const
      Sentinel = '';                         {sentinel name}

    var
      NextStudent : Student;                 {current student record}
      I : ClassRange;              {loop control and array subscript}


    procedure ReadOneStudent (var NextStudent {output} : Student);
    {
      Enters the Name and Score for one student.
      Pre : None
      Post: A string is read into NextStudent.Name. If the string
            is not blank, an integer is read into NextStudent.Score.
    }
    begin {ReadOneStudent}
      with NextStudent do
        begin
          WriteLn;  Write ('Name > ');
          ReadLn (Name);
          if Name <> Sentinel then
            begin
              Write ('Score> ');
              ReadLn (Score)
            end {if}
         end {with}
     end; {ReadOneStudent}

  begin {ReadStudents}
    WriteLn ('Enter the data requested for each student.');
    WriteLn ('Press return (after prompt Name >) when done.');

    I := 0;                       {initial count of students}
    repeat
      {invariant:
         The sentinel name was not read and
         I < MaxClass
      }
      ReadOneStudent (NextStudent);     {Read next student}
      if NextStudent.Name <> Sentinel then
        begin
          I := I + 1;           {Increase count}
          Test.Class[I] := NextStudent
        end {if}
    until (NextStudent.Name = Sentinel) or (I = MaxClass);

    {assert:  no more students or array is filled}
    Test.NumStu := I;
    WriteLn (I :1, ' student records were stored in memory.');
    if I = MaxClass then
      WriteLn ('Student array is completely filled.')
  end; {ReadStudents}

  procedure DisplayStudents (var Test {input} : Exam);
```

```
  var
    I : ClassIndex;          {loop-control variable}

begin {DisplayStudents}
  WriteLn;
  WriteLn ('The individual student data follow:');
  {Print heading}
  WriteLn ('Name' :20, 'Score' :10, 'Grade' :10);

  {Print each student's data.}
  for I := 1 to Test.NumStu do
    with Test.Class[I] do
      WriteLn (Name :20, Score :10, Grade :10)
end; {DisplayStudents}


procedure AssignGrades (var Test {input/output} : Exam;
                        Stats {input} : Statistics);
  var
    I : ClassIndex;             {loop control variable}

begin  {AssignGrades}
  with Test, Stats do
    for I := 1 to NumStu do
      with Class[I] do
        if Score >= Average + 1.5 * StandardDev then
           Grade := 'A'
        else if Score >= Average + 0.5 * StandardDev then
          Grade := 'B'
        else if Score >= Average - 0.5 * StandardDev then
          Grade := 'C'
        else if Score >= Average - 1.5 * StandardDev then
          Grade := 'D'
        else
          Grade := 'F'
end; {AssignGrades}


procedure ComputeStats (var Test {input}  : Exam;
                        var Stats {output} :Statistics);

{Insert FindLow, FindHigh, FindMedian, FindStandardDev}

  function FindAverage (var Test : Exam) : Real;
  {
    Returns the average of the scores stored in array Test.Class.
    Pre : Student scores are stored in Test.Class.
    Post: Returns the average of the scores in Test.Class
  }
    var
      Sum : Real;             {the accumulating sum of scores}
      I : ClassIndex;       {loop control variable and subscript}

  begin {FindAverage}
    {Accumulate the sum of all scores}
    Sum := 0;
    for I := 1 to Test.NumStu do
      Sum := Sum + Test.Class[I].Score;

    {Return the average score or 0.0}
```

```
      if Test.NumStu <> 0 then
        FindAverage := Sum / Test.NumStu
      else
        FindAverage := 0.0
    end; {FindAverage}

  begin {ComputeStats}
    with Stats do
      begin
        Average := FindAverage(Test);
        LowScore := FindLow(Test);
        HighScore := FindHigh(Test);
        Median := FindMedian(Test);
        StandardDev := FindStandardDev(Test, Average)
      end {with}
  end; {ComputeStats}

  procedure DisplayStats (Stats {input} : Statistics);
  begin {DisplayStats stub}
    WriteLn ('Procedure DisplayStats entered.')
  end {DisplayStats}
end; {GradeBook}
```

One of the functions called by `ComputeStats` is function `FindStandardDev`. This function implements the formula

$$\textit{standard deviation} = \sqrt{\frac{\sum_{i=1}^{N} (\textit{score}_i - \textit{average})^2}{N - 1}}$$

which is a measure of the spread, or dispersion, of the grades around the average grade. Statistical theory states that for a bell curve, 68.34 percent of the grades lie within one standard deviation of the average grade. Function `FindStandardDev` in Fig. 12.28 implements the formula for standard deviation.

Figure 12.28 Function FindStandardDev

```
function FindStandardDev (var Test {input} : Exam;
                              Average  {input} : Real) : Real;
{
  Returns the standard deviation of the scores in array
  Test.Class.
  Pre : The score fields are defined and Average was computed.
  Post: Returns the standard deviation if defined; otherwise,
        returns zero.
}
  var
    SumSquares : Real;            {Sum of squares}
    I : ClassIndex;               {loop control and subscript}

begin {FindStandardDev}
```

Case Study: Grading an Exam, continued

```
  SumSquares := 0;
  with Test do
    for I := 1 to NumStu do
      SumSquares := Sqr(Class[I].Score - Average)
                    + SumSquares;

  if Test.NumStu > 1 then
    FindStandardDev := Sqrt(SumSquares / (Test.NumStu - 1))
  else
    FindStandardDev := 0.0
end; {FindStandardDev}
```

Testing the Program

A sample run of the student grading program is shown in Fig. 12.29. We should verify that the program works correctly when the array `Test.Class` is completely filled (`MaxClass` students took the exam).

Figure 12.29 Sample Run of Student Grading Program

```
Enter the data requested for each student.
Press return (after prompt Name >) when done.

Name > Joe Costa
Score> 80

Name > Lee Hayes
Score> 70

Name > Bill Titcomb
Score> 60

Name >
3 student records were stored in memory.

Low   High   Median   Average   Standard deviation
 60    80      70       70.0           10.0

The individual student data follow:
                  Name  Score     Grade
             Joe Costa     80         B
             Lee Hayes     70         C
          Bill Titcomb     60         D
```

Exercises for Section 12.5

Self-Check

1. For the data in Fig. 12.29, what value is displayed by each of the following valid statements?
   a. `WriteLn (Test.Class.NumStu);`
   b. `WriteLn (Exam.NumStu);`

c. `with Test, Class[1] do`
`     WriteLn (Score, Grade, Name);`

d. `WriteLn (Test.NumStu);`

e. `WriteLn (Class.NumStu);`

f. `WriteLn (Test.Class.Name[2]);`

g. `WriteLn (Test[1].Class.Name[2]);`

h. `WriteLn (Test.Class[1].Name[2]);`

i. `WriteLn (Test.Class[1].Name);`

j. `WriteLn (Statistics.Average);`

Programming

1. Write procedure `DisplayStats`.
2. Write functions `FindLow` and `FindHigh`.

12.6 Searching an Array of Records

A common problem in processing arrays is *searching* an array to determine whether it contains a particular data item. If the array elements are records, then we must compare a particular field of each record, called the *record key*, to the data item we are seeking. Once we have located the item in question, we can display or modify the record. In this section, we will write a procedure that searches for a particular student's record.

■ Example 12.9

Function `Search` (Fig. 12.30) searches the array `Test.Class` for a record whose `Name` field matches the *target name,* `StuName`. If the target name is located, `Search` returns the index of the student record with that name. Otherwise, it returns a value of zero. For the array field `Class` shown in Fig. 12.24, the value returned would be `2` for the target name `'Robert Baker'` the value returned would be `0` for the target name `'Bob Baker'`.

Figure 12.30 Function Search

```
function Search (var Test : Exam;
                 StuName : StringType) : Integer;
{
  Searches for StuName in the Name field of array Test.Class.
  Pre : Test is defined and 1 <= Test.NumStu <= MaxClass.
  Post: Returns the subscript of StuName if found;
        otherwise, returns zero.
}
  var
    CurStu : Integer;          {array subscript}

begin  {Search}
  {Compare the Name field of each record to StuName until done.}
  CurStu := 1;                {Start with the first record}
  with Test do
    begin
```

```
      while (CurStu < NumStu) and (Class[CurStu].Name <> StuName) do
        {invariant:
            CurStu is <= NumStu and
            no prior Name field contains StuName
        }
        CurStu := CurStu + 1;                         {Check next record}

      {assertion: StuName is found or last element is reached.}
      {Define the function result.}
      if Class[CurStu].Name = StuName then
        Search := CurStu                    {Return target subscript}
      else
        Search := 0                         {Return 0}
    end {with}
end; {Search}
```

The while condition compares the student name selected by CurStu to the target name. If they are equal, loop exit occurs. If they are unequal and the last record has not been reached, CurStu advances to the next student record.

Loop exit occurs when the target name is found or the last element is reached. After loop exit, the if statement returns the location of the current student (CurStu) if StuName was found; otherwise, it returns zero. ■

■ Example 12.10

Your computer science professor wants us to modify the grading program in Fig. 12.25 so that it is menu driven. Besides the operators shown in Fig. 12.27, she wants to be able to display a particular student's record and to change a particular student's record.

Procedure DisplayOne in Fig. 12.31 performs the first of these two new operations. It reads the target name, calls Search to locate the target name in the array Test.Class, and then displays the complete student record. Procedure ChangeRecord reads the target name, calls Search to locate the target name in the array Test.Class, and then reads and stores the new score and grade in the array. ■

Figure 12.31 Procedures DisplayOne and ChangeRecord

```
procedure DisplayOne (var Test {input} : Exam);
{
  Displays a selected record of array Test.Class
  Pre  : Test is defined.
  Post : Displays the record for the student whose name is read.
  Calls: Function Search
}
  var
    Target : StringType;        {data for record being updated}
    Index : ClassRange;         {subscript of target record or 0}

begin {DisplayOne}
  Write ('Enter student name> ');
  ReadLn (Target);
  Index := Search (Test, Target);        {Find Target}
```

```
  {Display record or error message.}
  if Index <> 0 then
    with Test.Class[Index] do
      WriteLn ('Score is ', Score :3, '; Grade is ', Grade)
  else
    WriteLn ('No record for student ', Target)
end; {DisplayOne}


procedure ChangeRecord (var Test {input/output} : Exam);
{
  Changes a selected record of array Test.Class
  Pre  : Test is defined.
  Post : Changes the record for the student whose name is read.
  Calls: Function Search
}
  var
    Target : StringType;        {data for record being updated}
    Index : ClassRange;         {subscript of target record or 0}

begin {ChangeRecord}
   {Enter and search for the target name.}
   Write ('Enter name of target student> ');
   ReadLn (Target);
   Index := Search (Test, Target);

   {If target name is found, update the record.}
   if Index <> 0 then
     with Test.Class[Index] do
       begin
         Write ('New score> ');
         ReadLn (Score);
         Write ('New Grade> ');
         ReadLn (Grade)
       end {with}
   else
     WriteLn ('Student ', Target, ' did not take the exam. ')
end;  {ChangeRecord}
```

Exercises for Section 12.6

Self-Check

1. What happens in function `Search` if the last student name matches the target name? Why can't we use the condition `CurStu <= NumStu` in the `while` condition?
2. Another technique for searching an array is to introduce a program flag, say `Found`, that is initially `False` and that is set to `True` inside a search loop if the target value is found. Loop repetition continues as long as `Found` is `False` and all elements have not been tested. After loop exit, the value of `Found` determines whether the current subscript or zero is returned as the function result. Write the procedure body.

Programming

1. Write a procedure to count the number of students who scored a passing grade (D or higher) on an exam.

2. Rewrite the main program for the grading program as a menu-driven program. Provide as menu choices all the operations discussed in this section and Section 12.5.

12.7 Sorting an Array of Records

In Section 6.5 we discussed a simple sort operation that involved three numbers. We performed the sort by examining pairs of numbers and exchanging them if they were out of order. There are many times when we would like to sort the elements in an array, for example, to print a grade report in alphabetical order or in order by score.

This section discusses a fairly intuitive (but not very efficient) algorithm called the *selection sort.* To perform a selection sort of an array with `N` elements (subscripts `1..N`), we locate the largest element in the array and then switch the largest element with the element at subscript `N`, thereby placing the largest element at position `N`. Then we locate the largest element remaining in the subarray with subscripts `1..N-1` and switch it with the element at subscript `N-1`, thereby placing the second largest element at position `N-1`. Then we locate the largest element remaining in subarray `1..N-2` and switch it with the element at subscript `N-2`, and so on.

Figure 12.32 traces the operation of the selection sort algorithm. The diagram on the left shows the original array. Each subsequent diagram shows the array after the next largest element is moved to its final position in the array. The subarray in the darker color represents the portion of the array that is sorted after each exchange occurs. Note that it requires at most `N-1` exchanges to sort an array with `N` elements. The algorithm follows.

Selection Sort Algorithm

1. `for I := N downto 2 do`
    2. Find the largest element in subarray `1..I`.
    3. `if` the largest element is not at subscript `I` `then`
       Switch the largest element with the one at subscript `I`.

The refinement of step 2 also contains a `for` loop and is shown next.

Figure 12.32 Trace of Selection Sort

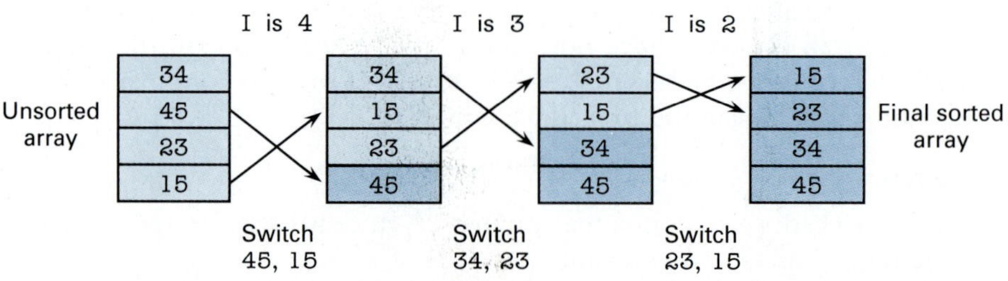

Step 2 Refinement

2.1 Save `I` as the position of the largest so far in the subarray
2.2 `for J := I-1 downto 1 do`
    2.3 `if` the element at `J` is bigger than largest so far `then`
        Save `J` as the position of the largest so far.

Procedure `SelectSort` in Fig. 12.33 implements the selection sort algorithm for the array field `Class` of parameter `Test`. Local variable `IndexOfMax` holds the location of the largest exam score found so far in the current subarray. After each execution of the inner `for` loop, procedure `Switch` is called to exchange the elements with subscripts `IndexOfMax` and `I`, provided that the element at `I` is not the next largest element. After the execution of procedure `SelectSort`, the student records will be ordered by exam score (record with smallest score first).

Figure 12.33 Selection Sort Procedure

```
procedure SelectSort (var Test {input/output} : Exam);
{
  Orders the data in array Test.Class by exam score.
  Pre : Record Test is defined.
  Post: The records in array Test.Class are ordered by score.
}
  var
    I,                {subscript of last element in subarray}
    J,           {subscript of element being compared to max}
    IndexOfMax : ClassIndex;              {index of max so far}

  procedure Switch (var Stu1, Stu2 {input/output} : Student);

  {Switches records Stu1 and Stu2.}

    var
      TempStu : Student;          {temporary student record}

  begin  {Switch}
    TempStu := Stu1;  Stu1 := Stu2;  Stu2 := TempStu
  end; {Switch}


begin {SelectSort}
  with Test do
    {Order array Test.Class according to Score field.}
    for I := NumStu downto 2 do
      begin
        {Find the element in subarray 1..I with largest Score}
        IndexOfMax := I;
        for J := I-1 downto 1 do
          if Class[J].Score > Class[IndexOfMax].Score then
           IndexOfMax := J;

        {assert: element at IndexOfMax is largest in subarray}
        {Switch element at I with element at IndexOfMax}
        if IndexOfMax <> I then
          Switch (Class[I], Class[IndexOfMax])
       end {for I}
end; {SelectSort}
```

Analysis of Selection Sort

As mentioned earlier, at most N-1 exchanges are needed to sort an array of N elements. Each exchange occurs after exit from the inner for loop. An exchange is not performed, however, if the largest element is already at position I of subarray 1..I (that is, IndexOfMax = I).

For an array of N elements, there are N-1 comparisons of Score fields during the first execution of the inner loop, N-2 comparisons during the second execution, and so on. The number of Score field comparisons, therefore, is represented by the series

```
1 + 2 + 3 + ... + N-2 + N-1
```

The value of this series is expressed in the closed form

$$\frac{N \times (N-1)}{2}$$

Therefore, to sort an array of 10 elements requires 10 x 9/2, or 45, Score field comparisons and, at most, 9 exchanges.

Finally, there is an additional comparison after each exit from the inner for loop (I is compared to IndexOfMax). This comparison takes less time to perform because no array reference is required. We could eliminate these N-1 comparisons and always perform the exchange (even when the largest element was already at position I). However, this would be less efficient generally because it would take more time to perform an exchange of records than to do the comparisons. ■

Coding Function FindMedian

Procedure ComputeStats (see Fig. 12.27) uses function FindMedian to compute the median score on an exam. It is relatively easy to determine the median score once the student records are in order by score. If there are an odd number of records, the median score is found in the middle element of array Test.Class where the subscript expression (NumStu div 2) + 1 selects the middle element. If there are an even number of records, the median score is the average of the two middle scores. As an example, for a sorted array with four scores, the median is the average of the second and third scores.

Function FindMedian is shown in Fig. 12.34. Notice that record Test is declared as a value parameter so that only the local copy of array Test.Class will be sorted, not the actual array.

Figure 12.34 Function FindMedian

```
function FindMedian (Test : Exam) : Integer;
{
  Returns the median score found in array Test.Class.
  Pre  : Student scores are stored in Test.Class.
  Post : Returns the middle score if there are an odd number
         of scores; otherwise, returns the average of the
         middle two scores.
```

```
  Calls: SelectSort
}
  var
    Middle : Integer;          {index to middle element}

begin {FindMedian}
  SelectSort (Test);
  with Test do
    begin
      Middle := (NumStu div 2) + 1;
      if Odd(NumStu) then
        FindMedian := Class[Middle].Score
      else
        FindMedian := (Class[Middle - 1].Score +
                       Class[Middle].Score) div 2
    end {with}
end; {FindMedian}
```

Exercises for Section 12.7

Self-Check

1. Trace the execution of the selection sort on the following list of scores. Show the array after each exchange occurs. How many exchanges are required? How many comparisons?

   `10 55 34 56 76 5`

2. How could you get the scores in descending order (largest score first)? What changes would be needed to sort the array field `Class` by student name instead of by score?
3. Because we are ordering the array by `Score` field, we propose changing procedure `Switch` to exchange only the `Score` fields. Describe the effect of this proposal.
4. Trace function `FindMedian` for the list of scores in exercise 1.
5. When you are looking for the largest element in subarray `1..I-1`, why is it more efficient to start the search with the last element (that is, `IndexOfMax := I-1`) rather than the first element?

Programming

1. Another method of performing the selection sort is to place the smallest element in position `1`, the next smallest in position `2`, and so on. Write this version.

12.8 Debugging Programs with Arrays with Structured Elements

You can use the Watch window to display single elements of multidimensional arrays, several adjacent array elements, or entire multidimensional arrays. Multidimensional arrays are displayed in the Watch window as nested, parenthesized lists. To display all of the two-dimensional array shown in Fig. 12.2, use the Watch expression

```
TicTacToe
```

The Watch window will display the contents of the array `TicTacToe` as

```
TicTacToe: (('X','O',' '),('O','X','O'),('X',' ','X'))
```

The elements of `TicTacToe` appear in row-major order, with row 1 followed by rows 2 and 3. If you use the Watch expression

```
TicTacToe[2]
```

elements of the second row of array `TicTacToe` will appear in the Watch window as

```
TicTacToe[2]: ('O','X','O')
```

Repeat counts can be used in Watch expressions to display several adjacent elements of array `TicTacToe` or to display several adjacent rows of array `TicTacToe`. The Watch expression

```
TicTacToe[2,1],2
```

causes the first and second elements of row 2 in array `TicTacToe` to be displayed in the Watch window as

```
TicTacToe[2,1],2: 'O','X'
```

Some caution should be used, since adjacent array elements are not necessarily in the same row. The watch expression

```
TicTacToe[2,3],2
```

causes the display of array elements `TicTacToe[2,3]` and `TicTacToe[3,1]` in the Watch window. The Watch expression

```
TicTacToe[1],2
```

causes the first and second rows of array `TicTacToe` to be displayed in the Watch window as

```
TicTacToe[1],2: ('X','O',' '),('O','X','O')
```

You can also use the Watch window to display all or portions of arrays whose elements are record types. Arrays of records are displayed as nested, parenthesized lists of values. If we assume that the values shown in Fig. 12.21 represent the entire contents of the array `Class` for `MaxClass = 4`, then typing the array name `Class` as a Watch expression causes the Watch window to display

```
Class: (('Jones, Sally',98,'A'),('Quincy, Peter',72,'C'),
       ('Philips, Susan',65,'D'),('Austin, Tracy',86,'B'))
```

Both repeat counts and Debug expression format characters can be used in Watch expressions involving arrays of record type elements. The Watch expression

```
Class[2]
```

causes the second record of array Class to be displayed in the Watch window. The Watch expression

```
Class[2],2
```

causes the second and third records of Class to be displayed, while the Watch expression

```
Class[2],R
```

causes the field names and values of the second record of array Class to be displayed in the Watch window, as we discussed in Section 11.7. As a final example, the Watch expression

```
Class[2],2R
```

causes the field names and values for the second and third records of the array Class to be displayed in the Watch window.

12.9 Common Programming Errors

When you use multidimensional arrays, make sure the subscript for each dimension is consistent with its declared type. If any subscript value is out of range, a run-time error will be detected.

If you use nested for loops to process the array elements, make sure that loop-control variables used as array subscripts are in the correct order. The order of the loop-control variables determines the sequence in which the array elements are processed.

When an array of records is processed, the array name and the subscript must be included as part of the field selector (for example X[I].Key references field Key of the Ith record). If you use a for statement to process all array elements in sequence, then you must nest any with statement that references the array records inside the for statement, as shown next.

```
for I := 1 to N do
  with X[I] do
    ...
```

As the loop-control variable I changes, the next array record is processed by the with statement. If the nesting order is reversed, as in

```
with X[I] do
  for I := 1 to N do
    ...
```

then the same array record is processed N times. The record that is processed is determined by the value of I when the with statement is first reached. Changing the value of I inside the with statement has no effect.

Chapter Review

In this chapter, arrays of arrays, or multidimensional arrays, were used to represent tables of information and game boards. We used nested loops to manipulate the elements of a multidimensional array in a systematic way. The correspondence between the loop-control variables and the array subscripts determines the order in which the array elements are processed.

You also saw how to manipulate arrays of records. Arrays of records can be used to represent many real-world data collections. We also introduced a technique for searching and a technique for sorting arrays of records.

New Pascal Constructs

The Pascal constructs introduced in this chapter are described in Table 12.2.

Table 12.2 Summary of New Pascal Constructs

Construct	Effect
Declaring Multidimensional Arrays	

`type`
`  WeekIndex = 1..52;`
`  Day = (Sunday,Monday,Tuesday,Wednesday,`
`         Thursday,Friday,Saturday);`
`  Matrix = array [WeekIndex, Day] of Real;`
 	
`var`
`  Sales : Matrix;`
	Matrix describes a two-dimensional array with 52 rows and 7 columns (days of the week). `Sales` is an array of this type and can store 364 real numbers.

Array References	
`Write (Sales[3, Monday])`	Displays the element of `Sales` for `Monday` of week 3.

`for Week := 1 to 52 do`
`  for Today := Sunday to Saturday do`
`    Sales[Week, Today] := 0.0`
	Initializes each element of `Sales` to zero.

`ReadLn (Sales[1, Sunday])`	Reads the value for the first `Sunday` into `Sales`.
Declaring Arrays of Records	

`type`
`  IndexRange = 1..10;`
`  AElement = record`
`               Data : Real;`
`               Key : Integer`
`             end; {AElement}`
`  DataArray = array [IndexRange] of AElement;`
	`DataArray` is an array type with ten elements of type `AElement` (a record). Each element has fields named `Data` and `Key`.

`var` `  MyData : DataArray`	`MyData` is a variable of type `DataArray`.

Table 12.2 *continued*

Construct	Effect

Referencing an Array of Records
`MyData[1].Data := 3.14159;`
`MyData[10].Key := 9999;`
	The real value `3.14159` is stored in the first `Data` field of array `MyData`; the value `9999` is stored in the last `Key` field.

✓ Quick-Check Exercises

1. In Pascal, how many subscripts can an array have?
2. What is the difference between row-major and column-major order? Which does Pascal use?
3. What does row-major order mean when an array has more than two subscripts?
4. What control structure is used to process all the elements in a multidimensional array?
5. Write a program segment to display the sum of the values (type `Real`) in each column of a two-dimensional array, `Table`, with data type `array [1..5, 1..3] of Real`. How many column sums will be displayed? How many elements are included in each sum?
6. Write the type declaration for an array that stores the batting averages by position (`Catcher`, `Pitcher`, `FirstBase`, etc.) for each of ten baseball teams in two leagues (`American` and `National`).
7. Write the type declaration for a data structure that stores a player's name, salary, position, batting average, fielding percentage, number of hits, runs, runs batted in, and errors.
8. Write the type declaration for a data structure that stores the information in exercise 7 for a team of twenty-five players.
9. If the array `Team` has the structure described in exercise 8, write a program segment that displays the first two categories of information for the first five players.

Answers to Quick-Check Exercises

1. There is no specific limit; however, the size of the array is limited by the memory space available, and multidimensional arrays can require considerable memory.
2. In row-major order, the first row of the array is placed at the beginning of the memory area allocated to the array. It is followed by the second row, and so on. In column-major order, the first column is placed at the beginning of the array memory area. Pascal uses row-major order.
3. If an array `Table` has `N` subscripts, the array elements are placed in memory in the order `Table[1,1,...,1,1]`, `Table[1,1,...,1,2]`, `Table[1,1,...,1,3]`, and so on. Then the next-to-last subscript is changed and the elements `Table[1,1,...,2,1]`, `Table[1,1,...,2,2]`, `Table[1,1,...,2,3]` ... are placed. The first subscript will be the last one that changes.
4. Nested `for` loops
5.
```
for Column := 1 to 3 do
  begin
    ColumnSum := 0.0;
    for Row := 1 to 5 do
```

```
      ColumnSum := ColumnSum + Table[Row,Column];
    WriteLn ('Sum for column ', Column :1, ' is ', ColumnSum)
  end {for Column}
```

Three column sums; five elements added per column

6.
```
type
  IndexRange = 1..10;
  Position = (Pitcher, Catcher, FirstBase, SecondBase, ThirdBase,
              ShortStop, LeftField, CenterField, RightField);
  League = (American, National);
  BAArray = array [League, IndexRange, Position] of Real;
```

7.
```
type
   StringType = string[20];
   Player = record
               Name : StringType;
               Salary : Real;
               Place : Position;
               BatAve, FieldPct : Real;
               Hits, Runs, RBIs, Errors : Integer
             end; {Player}
```

8.
```
type
   IndexRange = 1..25;
   StringType = ...
   Player = ...
   TeamArray = array [IndexRange] of Player;
```

9.
```
for I : = 1 to 5 do
   WriteLn (Team[I].Name, Team[I].Salary)
```

Review Questions

1. Define row-major order.
2. Declare an array that can be used to store each title of the `Top40` hits for each week of the year given that the `TitleLength` will be twenty characters.
3. Write the declaration of the array `YearlyHours` to store the hours each of five employees works each day of the week, each week of the year.
4. Write the declarations for the array `CPUArray` that will hold twenty records of type `CPU`. The record `CPU` has the following fields: `IDNumber` (eleven characters in length), `Make` (five characters), `Location` (fifteen characters), and `Ports` (integer).
5. Use the following declarations for this exercise and exercises 6 through 9.

```
const
  TotalEmployees = 20;

type
  IndexRange = 1..TotalEmployees;
  Employee = record
               ID: Integer;
               Rate,
               Hours : Real
             end; {Employee}
  EmpArray = array [IndexRange] of Employee;

var
  Employees : EmpArray;
```

Write the function `TotalGross` that will return the total gross pay given the data stored in array `Employees`.

6. Explain what is wrong with the following fragment and fix it.

```
I := 1;
with Employees[I] do
  while I <= TotalEmployees do
    begin
      WriteLn (Hours :12:2);
      I := I + 1
    end {while}
```

7. Explain what is wrong with the following fragment and fix it.

```
I := 1;
while (Employees[I].ID <> 999) and (I <= TotalEmployees) do
  I := I + 1
```

8. Write a fragment that displays the ID number of each employee who works between ten and twenty hours per week.
9. Write a fragment that displays the ID number of the employee who works the most hours.
10. How many exchanges are required to sort the following list of integers using selection sort? How many comparisons are performed?

```
20 30 40 25 60 80
```

11. Procedure `SelectSort` in Figure 12.33 placed the elements of an array in order by `Score` field. Change the condition in the procedure so that records with the same `Score` value are ordered by name (smaller name first). The field `Score` is called the *primary key*, and the field `Name` is called the *secondary key*.

Programming Projects

1. Write a program that generates the Morse code for a sentence that ends with a period and contains no characters besides letters and blanks. First, read the Morse code for each letter of the alphabet and save it in an array of strings. Next, read each word and display its Morse equivalent on a separate line. The Morse code is as follows:
   A .-, B -..., C -.-., D -.., E ., F ..-., G --., H ...., I .., J .---, K -.-, L .-.., M --, N -., O ---, P .--., Q --.-, R .-., S ..., T -, U ..-, V ...-, W .--, X -..-, Y -.--, Z --..
2. Write a set of procedures to manipulate a pair of matrices. Provide procedures for addition, subtraction, and multiplication. Each procedure should validate its input parameters (that is, check all matrix dimensions) before performing the required data manipulation.
3. The results from the mayor's race have been reported by each precinct as follows:

Precinct	*Candidate A*	*Candidate B*	*Candidate C*	*Candidate D*
1	192	48	206	37
2	147	90	312	21
3	186	12	121	38
4	114	21	408	39
5	267	13	382	29

Write a program to do the following:

a. Print out the table with appropriate headings for the rows and columns.
b. Compute and print the total number of votes received by each candidate and the percent of the total votes cast.
c. If any one candidate received over 50 percent of the votes, the program should print a message declaring that candidate the winner.
d. If no candidate received 50 percent of the votes, the program should print a message declaring a run-off between the two candidates who received the highest number of votes; the two candidates should be identified by their letter names.
e. Run the program once with the preceding data and once with candidate C receiving only 108 votes in precinct 4.

4. Many supermarkets make use of computer equipment at their checkout counters, which allows the clerk to drag the item purchased across a sensor that reads the bar code on the product container. After reading the bar code, the store inventory database is examined, the item's price and product description are located, counts are reduced, and a receipt is printed. Your task is to write a program that simulates this process.

   Your program will need to read the inventory information from the data file on disk into an array of records. The data in the inventory file is written one item per line, beginning with a 2-digit product code, followed by a 30-character product description, its price, and the quantity of that item in stock. Your program will need to copy the revised version of the inventory to a new data file after all purchases are processed.

   Processing customers' orders involves reading a series of product codes representing each person's purchases from a second data file. A zero product code marks the end of each customer order. As each product code is read, the inventory list is searched to find a matching product code. Once located, the product price and description may be printed on the receipt and quantity on hand reduced by one. At the bottom of the receipt, you are to print the total for the goods purchased by the customer.
5. An array of records can contain descriptions of people, including name, height, weight, sex, color of hair, color of eyes, and religion. Write a program that reads and stores data into this array, sorts the array in alphabetical order by name, and prints its contents.
6. Write a program that searches an array of records of type `Employee` (see Section 11.1) to find and print the data stored for all employees who match a target description. The array of employee data should be read in first and then the target data. A blank target name indicates that the name field should be ignored during the matching process. Add a third category (`Unknown`) for the sex field. Enter a range of values for each numeric target field. A lower bound of `-1` indicates that a particular numeric field should be ignored.
7. The inventory for a warehouse is stored on an inventory file and shipments into and from the warehouse (transactions) are to be processed. Each file line will contain an ID number (three digits), name (maximum of ten characters), initial quantity on hand, and cost per item. Write a procedure that will read and store the file data into an appropriate array of records. At that point, write the initial contents of the warehouse.

   Now process the transactions, which consist of the ID number for the item and the quantity of items shipped or received (if negative, the items were shipped; if positive, the items were received). Read each transaction from the keyboard.

   After transaction is processed, display a message indicating the item name, the quantity shipped or received, and the new quantity on hand. The program should check to make sure that more items are not shipped than are on hand and that the ID number requested for a transaction matches those in the warehouse.

After all transactions are processed, print a list of all items in the warehouse. Show how many of each remain and the approximate total value of each item in the inventory.

A sample inventory file might be

```
376      BOLTS      350     0.05
142      NUTS       425     0.03
261      HAMMERS    100     10.45
```

8. Write a program that reads names and addresses from a data file and outputs the names and addresses reformatted as mailing labels. Your program should prompt the user for the number of columns of labels (1, 2, or 3) to produce, as well as the number of lines on each label and width of the label expressed as the number of characters allowed on a line. Two blank lines should separate each row of labels from one another. Here is a row of labels printed using two columns. Each label contains 3 lines of 24 characters each.

```
JOHN A SMITH              JOAN B. SMITH
123 S MAIN                456 MICHIGAN AVE
ANN ARBOR, MI 48103       DEARBORN, MI 48128
```

Hint: Define an input record and copy each new label to some output data structure (possibly an array of records). When the output data structure contains one label for each column (or when EOF becomes true) write a row of labels and repeat the process.

9. Write a program that simulates the movement of radioactive particles in a 20 by 20 two-dimensional shield around a reactor. Particles enter the shield at some random position in the shield coordinate space. Once a particle enters the shield, it can move in one of four directions. The direction for the next second of travel is determined by a random number between 1 and 4 (forward, backward, left, right). A change in direction is interpreted as a collision with another particle, which results in a dissipation of energy. Each particle can have only a limited number of collisions before it dies. A particle exits the shield if its position places it outside the shield coordinate space before K collisions occur. Determine the percentage of particles that exit the shield where K and the number of particles are input as data items. Also compute the average number of times a particle's path crosses itself during travel time within the shield.

Hint: Mark each array position occupied by a particle before it dies or exits the shield.

13 Sets and Strings

In this chapter, we complete the study of the set data type. We first looked at sets in Chapter 9; since then, we have used sets and the set membership operator `in` to simplify conditions. In this chapter, you will learn how to perform the operations of set union, set intersection, and set difference in Pascal and how to test for subsets, supersets, and set equality. These operations make it easier to use sets in programming.

The string data type is the second topic covered in this chapter. Strings are used in programs that process textual data (for example, word processors, text editors, and business data-processing applications). Turbo Pascal provides a dynamic string data type, along with several functions and procedures that allow us to work with string variables. In Section 10.7 we introduced the Turbo Pascal string data type and compared it to an array of characters. In this chapter, we will complete our discussion of the Turbo Pascal string data type and operators for string variables.

13.1 Set Data Type

Chapter 9 discussed set values in conditional statements. Until now, we have used the set membership operator `in` only with set values. This section examines the other set operators and shows you how to declare and manipulate set variables.

■ Example 13.1

The following statements define a set type `Digit` and two set variables, `Odds` and `Evens`. Each set variable of type `Digit` can contain between zero and ten elements chosen from the integers in the subrange `0..9`. The set variables `Odds` and `Evens` represent the set of odd digits and even digits in the range `0` through 9. ■

```
type
   Digit = set of 0..9;

var
   Odds, Evens : Digit;

begin
   Odds := [1, 3, 5, 7, 9];
   Evens := [0, 2, 4, 6, 8]
```

The set type declaration is described in the following display.

SYNTAX DISPLAY

Set Type Declaration

Form: `type`
set type = `set of` *base type*;

Example: `type`
```
            Uppercase = set of 'A'..'Z';
```
Interpretation: The identifier *set type* is defined over the values specified in *base type*. A variable declared to be of type *set type* is a set whose elements are chosen from the values in *base type*. The *base type* must be an ordinal type.
Notes: Most implementations impose a limit on the number of values in the *base type* of a set. In Turbo Pascal, this limit is the same as the number of values in the data type `Char (256)`. This allows you to declare `set of Char` as a set type. Given this limitation, you may not use the data type `Integer` as a *base type*; however, a suitable subrange of type `Integer` is allowed.

Set Assignment, Empty Set, and Universal Set

You can modify an existing set by using the set operators discussed in the next section. Before you can manipulate a set, however, you must define its initial elements with a set assignment statement, as shown in the next example.

■ Example 13.2

The following statements specify three set variables defined over the base type `Cars`.

```
type
  Cars = (Dodge, Ford, Lincoln, Cadillac, Fiesta, Pontiac,
          Corvette, Buick, Chevrolet, Mercury, Mustang);
  CarSet = set of Cars;

var
  Avis, Hertz, Merger : CarSet;

begin
  Avis := [Dodge, Lincoln, Fiesta];
  Hertz := [Dodge..Cadillac, Mercury];
```

Each assignment statement consists of a set variable on the left and a set value on the right. A pair of brackets and a list of values from the base type of the set being defined indicate a set value. As shown in the assignment statement for `Hertz`, a list of consecutive values can be denoted as a subrange (see Section 9.2). The set `Avis` consists of the three elements listed; the set `Hertz` consists of five elements (what are they?).

It is also possible to have a set variable on the right of the assignment statement, provided both set variables have compatible base types. The value of the set variable on the right would be assigned to the set variable on the left.

```
Merger := Hertz;
```

Often, we want to denote that a set is empty or has no elements. An *empty set* is indicated by an empty pair of brackets ([ ]).

```
Merger := []
```

A set variable must always be initialized before it can be used with any of the set operators. A set variable often is initialized to the empty set or to the *universal set*, which is the set that consists of all values of the base type. For instance, the universal set for a set of type `CarSet` would be denoted as `[Dodge..Mustang]`. ■

The set-assignment statement is shown in the following display. As the display indicates, it is possible to write set expressions that involve set manipulation operators. These operators are described in the next section.

SYNTAX DISPLAY

Set Assignment

Form: *set var* := *set expression*
Example: `Uppercase := ['A'..'Z']  {set of uppercase letters}`
Interpretation: The variable, *set var*, is defined as the set whose elements are determined by the value of *set expression*. The *set expression* may be a set value or another set variable. Alternatively, a *set expression* may specify the manipulation of two or more sets using the set operators. The base type of *set var* and *set expression* must be type compatible, and all the elements in *set expression* must be included in the base type of *set-var*.

Set Union, Intersection, and Difference

The set operators union, intersection, and difference require as operands two sets of the same type. The *union* of two sets (set operator +) is the set of elements that are contained in either set or both sets.

```
[1,3,4] + [1,2,4] is [1,2,3,4]
[1,3] + [2,4] is [1,2,3,4]
['A','C','F'] + ['B','C','D','F'] is ['A','B','C','D','F']
['A','C','F'] + ['A','C','D','F'] is ['A','C','D','F']
Avis + Hertz is [Dodge, Ford, Lincoln, Cadillac, Fiesta, Mercury];
```

The *intersection* of two sets (set operator *) is the set of all elements that are common to both sets.

```
[1,3,4] * [1,2,4] is [1,4]
[1,3] * [2,4] is []
['A','C','F'] * ['B','C','D','F'] is ['C','F']
['A','C','F'] * ['A','C','D','F'] is ['A','C','F']
Avis * Hertz is [Dodge, Lincoln]
```

The *difference* of set A and set B (set operator –) is the set of elements that are in set A but not in set B.

```
[1,3,4] - [1,2,4] is [3]
[1,3] - [2,4] is [1,3]
```

```
['A','C','F'] - ['B','C','D','F'] is ['A']
['A','C','F'] - ['A','C','D','F'] is []
['A','C','D','F'] - ['A','C','F'] is ['D']
Avis - Hertz is [Fiesta]
Hertz - Avis is [Ford, Cadillac, Mercury]
```

The set operator – is not *commutative*. This means that `A - B` and `B - A` can have different values. The set operators + and *, however, are commutative.

The operators +, *, and – are treated as set operators when their operands are sets. The compiler determines which operation is intended from its context (this is called *operator overloading*). You can use these operators to combine two sets to form a third set. If more than one set operator appears in an expression, the normal precedence rules for the operators +, *, and – apply (see Table 7.12). When in doubt, use parentheses to specify the intended order of evaluation.

Often, we need to insert a new element into an existing set. You perform the insertion by forming the union of the existing set and the *unit set*, which contains only the new element. The set `[2]`, which follows, is a unit set.

```
[1,3,4,5] + [2] is [1,2,3,4,5]
```

It makes no difference how many times we insert an element into a set:

```
[1,2,3,4,5] + [2] is [1,2,3,4,5]
```

Avoid the common error of omitting the brackets around a unit set. For example, the expressions

```
[1,3,4,5] + 2
Avis + Cadillac
```

are invalid because one operand is a set and the other is a constant. The correct forms of these expressions follow.

```
[1,3,4,5] + [2]
Avis + [Cadillac]
```

Likewise, the expression

```
[Avis] + [Cadillac]
```

is invalid; the brackets around `Avis` are not needed because `Avis` is a set.

■ Example 13.3

Procedure `BuildSets` in Fig. 13.1 returns a set of odd numbers (`Odds`) and a set of even numbers (`Evens`) in the range `0` to `MaxNum`. Procedure `BuildSets` uses the set operators + (union) and – (difference). Given the declarations

```
const
  MaxNum = 60;

type
  IntSet = set of 0..MaxNum;

var
  OneSet, TwoSet : IntSet;
```

the procedure call statement

```
BuildSets (OneSet, TwoSet)
```

stores the set [1, 3, 5, ... , 57, 59] in OneSet and the set [0, 2, 4, 6, ... , 58, 60] in TwoSet. ■

Figure 13.1 Procedure BuildSets

```
procedure BuildSets (var Odds, Evens {output} : IntSet);
{
  Builds a set of odd integers (Odds) and a set of even
  integers (Evens) in the range 0 to MaxNum.
  Pre : None
  Post: Odds contains the odd integers <= MaxNum and
        Evens contains the even integers <= MaxNum
}
  var
    I : Integer;                    {loop-control variable}

begin  {BuildSets}
  Odds := [];                 {initialize Odds to the empty set}

  {Build a set of odd integers.}
  I := 1;                  {initialize I to first odd integer}
  while I <= MaxNum do
    {invariant:
        all prior values of I are <= MaxNum and
        Odds contains each prior value of I that is an odd number
    }
    begin
      Odds := Odds + [I];       {union next odd integer to Odds}
      I := I + 2              {get next odd integer}
    end; {while}

  {assertion:
     I is greater than MaxNum and Odds contains all
     odd numbers <= MaxNum
  }
  {Define set Evens.}
  Evens := [0..MaxNum] - Odds
end;  {BuildSets}
```

Set Relational Operators

You can also compare sets through the use of the relational operators =, <>, <=, and >=. Both operands of a set relational operator must have the same base type. The operators = and <> test whether two sets contain the same elements.

[1,3] = [1,3] is True	[1,3] <> [1,3] is False
[1,3] = [2,4] is False	[1,3] <> [2,4] is True
[1,3] = [3,1] is True	[1,3] <> [3,1] is False
[] = [1] is False	[] <> [1] is True

As indicated by the next-to-last line, the order in which the elements of a set are listed is not important ([1,3] and [3,1] denote the same set). However, we normally list the elements of a set in increasing ordinal sequence.

Other relational operators determine subset and superset relationships.

- Set A is a *subset* of set B (A <= B) if every element of A is also an element of B.

```
[1,3]      <=[1,2,3,4] is True
[1,3]      <=[1,3]     is True
[1,2,3,4]  <=[1,3]     is False
[1,3]      <=[]        is False
[]         <=[1,3]     is True
```

As indicated in the last line, the empty set, [], is a subset of every set.

- Set A is a *superset* of set B (A >= B) if every element of B is also an element of A.

```
[1,3]      >= [1,2,3,4] is False
[1,3]      >= [1,3]     is True
[1,2,3,4]  >= [1,3]     is True
[1,3]      >= []        is True
[]         >= [1,3]     is False
```

The set relations A >= B and B <= A are equivalent for any two sets A and B.

The set operators are summarized in Table 13.1.

Table 13.1 Set Operators

Operator	Meaning	Example
+	Set union	['A'] + ['B'] is ['A', 'B']
–	Set difference	['A', 'B'] – ['A'] is ['B']
*	Set intersection	['A', 'B'] * ['A'] is ['A']
=	Set equality	['A', 'B'] = ['B', 'A'] is True
<>	Set inequality	['A', 'B'] <> ['A'] is True
<=	Subset	['A', 'B'] <= ['A'] is False
>=	Superset	['A', 'B'] >= ['B'] is True

Reading and Writing Sets

Like most other data structures, a set cannot be a parameter of the standard Read or Write procedures. Data items to be stored in a set must be read individually and inserted in an initially empty set using the set union operator.

■ Example 13.4

Procedure ReadSet in Fig. 13.2 reads a sequence of uppercase letters terminated by * and inserts them in the set represented by parameters Letters (set type LetterSet). Given the declarations

```
type
  LetterSet = set of 'A'..'Z';
```

```
var
  MyLetters : LetterSet;
```

you could use the procedure call statement

```
ReadSet (MyLetters)
```

to enter data in the set `MyLetters`. ■

Figure 13.2 Procedure ReadSet

```
procedure ReadSet (var Letters {output} : LetterSet);
{
  Reads a set of uppercase letters terminated by *
  and stores them in Letters.
  Pre : None
  Post: Returns through Letters all the uppercase letters read
        before the character *.
}
  const
    Sentinel = '*';                       {sentinel character}

  var
    NextChar : Char;                      {next input character}

begin  {ReadSet}
  Letters := [];                      {initialize Letters}
  Write ('Enter a set of uppercase letters');
  WriteLn (' ending with the symbol ', Sentinel);
  Read (NextChar);                    {read first data item}
  while NextChar <> Sentinel do
    {invariant:
       No prior value of NextChar is the sentinel and
       Letters contains each uppercase letter read so far
    }
    begin
      if NextChar in ['A'..'Z'] then
        Letters := Letters + [NextChar];   {insert next letter}
      Read (NextChar)                      {read next character}
    end  {while}

  {assertion: last character read was the sentinel}
end;  {ReadSet}
```

To print a set, you need to test every value in the base type to see whether it is a set element. Only values that are set elements should be printed.

■ Example 13.5

Procedure `PrintSet` in Fig. 13.3 prints the uppercase letters in the set represented by its parameter `Letters`. ■

Figure 13.3 Procedure PrintSet

```
procedure PrintSet (Letters {input} : LetterSet);
{
  Prints the uppercase letters in set Letters.
  Pre : Letters is defined.
```

```
  Post: Each uppercase letter in Letters is displayed.
}
  var
    NextLetter : 'A'..'Z';           {loop-control variable}

begin {PrintSet}
  for NextLetter := 'A' to 'Z' do
    if NextLetter in Letters then
      Write (NextLetter)             {print a set member}
end;  {PrintSet}
```

Exercises for Section 13.1

Self-Check

1. Given that `A` is the set `[1,3,5,7]`, `B` is the set `[2,4,6]`, and `C` is the set `[1,2,3]`, evaluate the following set expressions.
   a. `A + (B - C)`
   b. `A + (B * C)`
   c. `A + B + C`
   d. `(C - A) <= B`
   e. `[] <= A * B * C`
   f. `A + B <> [1..7]`
   g. `C + (A - C)`
   h. `C - (A - B)`
   i. `(C - A) - B`
   j. `(B + C) = (A + C)`
   k. `A - C - [5,7] = []`
   l. `A + B >= [1..7]`

Programming

1. Modify `PrintSet` to print a set of type `Digit`.

13.2 Sets in Computer Graphics

In picture processing, we want to write programs that can find and analyze patterns of characters that appear in a picture that is displayed on a screen. Each screen position is called a *pixel,* or picture element. A pixel has a grey level associated with it that determines whether it is considered dark or light.

One approach to representing the screen is to store it as a two-dimensional array of pixel values; another approach is to store it as an array of sets. In the latter representation, each array element is the set of darkened pixels for a line, and there is one set for each line of the screen.

Figure 13.4 shows a section (called a *window*) of a monitor screen. There is a diagonal line on the left and a vertical bar on the right.

The type declarations for a picture displayed on a screen window consisting of ten rows and twenty columns follow.

```
const
  ScreenHeight = 10;        {# of rows}
  ScreenWidth = 20;         {# of columns}

type
  PixelValue = (Dark, Light);
  HeightIndex = 1..ScreenHeight;
  Line = set of 1..Screen Width;
  Screen = array [HeightIndex] of Line;
```

Figure 13.4 Monitor Screen with Window

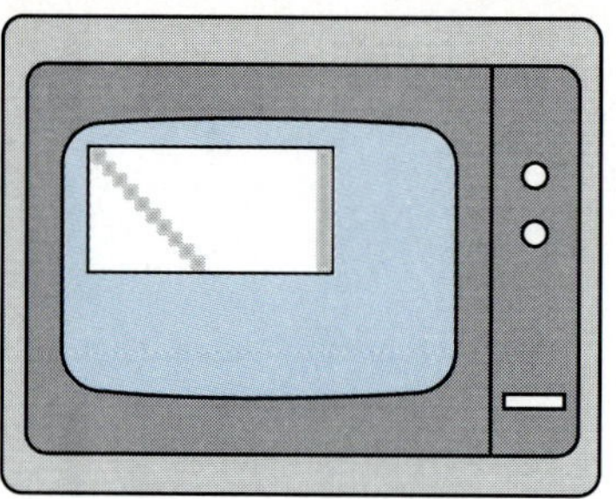

```
var
  Picture : Screen;
```

For the picture in Fig. 13.4, `Picture[1]` represents the set of darkened elements in the first line and is the set `[1, 2, 18, 19, 20]`. `Picture[2]` is the set `[2, 3, 18, 19, 20]` and `Picture [3]` is the set `[3, 4, 18, 19, 20]`. The intersection of these three sets is `[18, 19, 20]`. This implies that there is a vertical bar on the right. The union of these three sets is `[1, 2, 3, 4, 18, 19, 20]`. This implies that there is also a diagonal bar on the left.

■ Example 13.6

Procedure `SetPicture` (Fig. 13.5) is called by a picture-processing program to define array `Picture`. For each pixel, the procedure reads an integer value that represents the grey level (darkness) of that pixel. If the grey level value is greater than `Threshold` (a parameter), that pixel is inserted in the appropriate set of darkened pixels. As an example, if the value passed to `Threshold` is `6`, the dialogue that follows defines `Picture[1]` as `[1, 2, 18, 19, 20]`. ■

```
Enter the grey level (0 - 9) for row 1
Enter 20 values starting with column 1.
7 8 6 5 4 3 3 4 3 4 5 3 4 4 5 5 6 7 8 9
```

Figure 13.5 Procedure SetPicture

```
procedure SetPicture (Threshold {input} : Integer;
                      var Picture {output} : Screen);
{
  Defines the array Picture representing a computer image by
  reading in the grey level value for each pixel.
  Pre : Threshold is defined.
  Post: Picture[i] is the set of columns in row i with
        grey level value greater than Threshold
        (1 <= i <= ScreenHeight).
}
  var
    Row : 1..ScreenHeight;
    Column : 1..ScreenWidth;
    GreyLevel : 0..9;
```

```
begin {SetPicture}
  {Define array Picture.}
  for Row := 1 to ScreenHeight do
    begin
      WriteLn ('Enter the grey level (0 - 9) for row ', Row :1);
      Write ('Enter ', ScreenWidth :1);
      WriteLn (' values starting with column 1.');
      Picture[Row] := [];            {Initialize row set}
      for Column := 1 to ScreenWidth do
        begin
          Read (GreyLevel);
          if GreyLevel > Threshold then
            Picture[Row] := Picture[Row] + [Column]
        end; {for Column}
      ReadLn;
      WriteLn
    end {for Row}
end; {SetPicture}
```

Exercises for Section 13.2

Self-Check

1. What is the purpose of the `ReadLn` and `WriteLn` statements in procedure `SetPicture`?
2. Assuming `MyPic` is type `Screen`, what is the value of `MyPic[1]` for the procedure call statement

   ```
   SetPicture (5, MyPic)
   ```

   when the first data line is: `3 4 5 6 7 8 9 8 7 6 5 4 9 8 7 3 4 9 7 5`?

Programming

1. Write procedure `ShowPicture` that displays the picture on a screen by writing the character @ in each pixel that is considered dark.

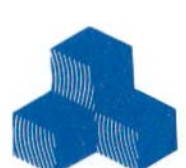

13.3 Variable-Length Strings

Many computer applications are concerned with the manipulation of character strings or textual data rather than numerical data. For example, a word processor was used in writing this text; computerized typesetters are used extensively in the publishing of books and newspapers; "personalized" junk mail is computer generated; and computers are used to analyze great works of literature. Basically, a Pascal program is a sequence of words and symbols that are interpreted by a compiler.

If you have ever used a word processor, you are familiar with the kinds of operations we might want to perform on string data. For example, we frequently want to insert one or more characters into an existing string, delete a portion of a string (called a *substring*), overwrite or replace one substring of a string with another, search for a target substring, or join two strings together to form a longer string.

The Null String

As we have seen, the working length of a string variable is dynamic and is determined by the data stored in it. This length cannot exceed the declared maximum for that variable. A string with zero characters is called a *null string*. If `Name` is a string variable, the statements below

```
Name := '';
WriteLn ('Length is ', Length(Name) :1);
```

would assign the null string to `Name` and display the message

```
'Length is 0'.
```

Converting Between Strings and Numbers

Two procedures in Turbo Pascal are used to convert a string to a number (procedure `Val`) and a number to a string (procedure `Str`). The string involved in the conversion must be a numeric string. A *numeric string* is a string that satisfies the syntax requirements for a valid Pascal number (for example, `'1234'`, `'0.12E5'`).

Assuming that `IntNum` and `Error` are type `Integer`, the procedure (call) statement

```
Val ('1234', IntNum, Error);
```

causes the `Integer` value `1234` to be stored in `IntNum` and `0` in `Error`. The procedure (call) statement

```
Val ('12#34%', IntNum, Error);
```

causes the value `3` to be returned to `Error` to indicate that the character in position `3` is not numeric; the value of `IntNum` is undefined.

■ Example 13.7

Table 13.2 shows the results for several calls to `Val`, assuming that `RealNum` is type `Real` and `IntNum` and `Error` are type `Integer`. The type of the second parameter determines whether an `Integer` or `Real` value will be returned. As shown by the last two lines, a blank cannot appear in the numeric string being converted. ■

Table 13.2 Using the Val Procedure

Call to Val	Values Returned
`Val ('-3507', IntNum, Error)`	`IntNum` is –3507, `Error` is 0
`Val ('-3507', RealNum, Error)`	`RealNum` is –3507.0, `Error` is 0
`Val ('1.23E3', RealNum, Error)`	`RealNum` is 1230.0, `Error` is 0
`Val ('1.23E3', IntNum, Error)`	`IntNum` is undefined, `Error` is 2
`Val ('1.23E 3', RealNum, Error)`	`RealNum` is undefined, `Error` is 6
`Val ('  1.2E3', RealNum, Error)`	`RealNum` is undefined, `Error` is 1

■ Example 13.8

The program fragment

```
repeat
  Write ('Enter an integer value> ');
  ReadLn (NumStr);
  Val (NumStr, IntNum, Error)
until Error = 0;
```

can be used to store an integer value in `IntNum`. If a valid numeric string is read into `NumStr` (string type), procedure `Val` returns its numeric value in `IntNum` (type `Integer`). If an invalid numeric string is read, procedure `Val` returns a non-zero value in `Error` (type `Integer`) and the loop is repeated. The purpose of this loop is to prevent an `Invalid numeric format` error. If the value of `IntNum` is read directly using the statement

```
ReadLn (IntNum);
```

program execution would terminate when an invalid integer value is entered by mistake.

The `Str` procedure performs the inverse of the operation performed by `Val`; that is, it converts a number to a numeric string. The procedure call statement

```
Str (345 :5, NumStr);
```

stores the string `'  345'` in `NumStr` (a string type) where the format specification `:5` causes the result string to have a field width of `5`. The procedure call statement

```
Str (345.126 :7:2, NumStr);
```

causes the string `' 345.12'` to be stored in `NumStr`. The procedure call statement

```
Str (345.126 :3:1, NumStr)
```

causes the string `'345.1'` to be stored in `NumStr`.

SYNTAX DISPLAY

Val Procedure

Form: `Val` (*numeric string*, *number*, *error*)
Example: `Val ('-5', N, E)`
Interpretation: A *numeric string* is converted to a numeric value which is returned in *number*. The data type of the number passed into *numeric string* must match the data type (`Real` or `Integer`) of *number*. The value returned for *error* indicates the position of the first invalid character (`0` if *numeric string* satisfies the syntax for a number). The parameter *error* must be type `Integer`.
Notes: If range-checking is enabled using `{$R+}`, out-of-range values will generate a run-time error. If range-checking is disabled (default), the value returned in *number* may contain the result of an overflow computation even though the value returned in *error* is `0`.

SYNTAX DISPLAY

Str Procedure

Form: `Str` (*number* : *format*, *numeric string*)
Example: `Str (N :1, S)`
Interpretation: The value passed to *number* is converted to a *numeric string*. The *format* specification determines the form and length of *numeric string*, as it would if used with the `Write` procedure.

Substrings and the Copy Function

It is often necessary to manipulate segments, or *substrings*, of a larger character string. For example, we might want to examine the three components (month, day, year) of the string `'Jun 25, 1990'`. Procedure `Copy` can be used to do this, as shown next.

■ Example 13.9

Assume that a date string (stored in `Date`) always has the form `'MMM DD, YYYY'`, where the characters represented by `MMM` are the month name, `DD` the day of the month, and `YYYY` the year. Assuming `Date`, `MonthStr`, `Day`, and `Year` are variable-length strings, the statement

```
MonthStr := Copy(Date, 1, 3);
```

assigns to `MonthStr` the substring of `Date` starting at position `1` and consisting of the first three characters. The statement

```
Day := Copy(Date 5, 2);
```

assigns to `Day` the two characters that represent the day of the month (positions five and six). Finally, the statement

```
Year := Copy(Date, 9, 4);
```

assigns to `Year` the four characters that represent the year (positions `9` through `12`). If the contents of `Date` are `'Jun 25, 1986'`, the contents of the variable length strings `MonthStr`, `Day`, and `Year` become `'Jun'`, `'25'`, and `'1990'`, respectively. ■

■ Example 13.10

Procedure `PrintWords` in Fig. 13.6 displays each word found in its parameter `Sentence` on a separate line. It assumes that there is always a single blank character between words.

The variable `First` always points to the start of the current word and is initialized to 1. During each execution of the `for` loop, the Boolean expression

```
Sentence[Next] = WordSeparator
```

tests whether the next character is a blank. If so, the substring occupying positions `First` through `Next-1` in `Sentence` is copied to `Word` by the statement

```
Word := Copy(Sentence, First, Next-First);   {get word}
```

The values of First and Next are shown below just before the fourth word of a string stored in Sentence is displayed. The value of Next–First is 5, so the substring short is displayed.

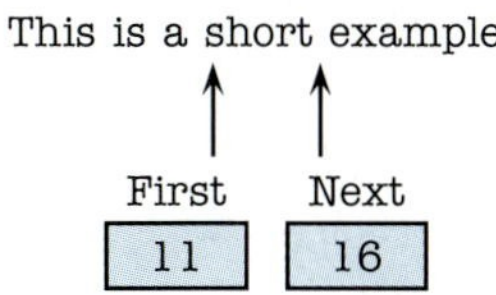

After each word is printed, First is reset to Next + 1, the position of the first character of the next word. After loop exit, the statement

```
Word := Copy(Sentence, First, SentLen-First+1);
```

stores the last word of Sentence in Word. For the sentence above, the value of First is 17 and the value of the third parameter is 7 $(23 - 17 + 1)$, so the last word displayed is example.

Figure 13.6 Procedure PrintWords

```
procedure PrintWords (Sentence {input} : string);
{
  Displays each word of a sentence on a separate line.
  Pre : Variable length string Sentence is defined.
  Post: Each word in sentence is displayed on a separate line.
}
  const
    WordSeparator = ' ';

  var
    Word : string;              {each word}
    SentLen,                    {length of Sentence}
    First,                      {first character in each word}
    Next   : Integer;           {position of next character}

begin {PrintWords}
  {Display each word of Sentence on a separate line.}
  First := 1;            {first word starts at position 1}
  SentLen := Length(Sentence);
  for Next := 1 to SentLen do
    begin
      if Sentence[Next] = WordSeparator then
        begin
          Word := Copy(Sentence, First, Next-First);   {get word}
          WriteLn (Word);
          First := Next + 1
        end {if}
    end; {for}

  {Display last word.}
  Word := Copy(Sentence, First, SentLen-First+1);
  WriteLn (Word)
end; {PrintWords}
```

SYNTAX DISPLAY

Copy Function

Form: `Copy (`*source, index, size*`)`

Interpretation: The function returns the substring of *source* at position *index* and consisting of *size* characters. The parameter souce must be a string variable or value; *index* and *size* must be type `Integer`.

Notes: If *index* is larger than the length of *source*, an empty string is returned. If *size* specifies more characters than remain following position *index*, only the remainder of the string is returned.

Concatenating Strings

The `Copy` procedure is used to reference a substring of a longer string. You can use the `Concat` procedure to combine two or more strings to form a new string.

■ Example 13.11

The following statements join together, or *concatenate*, their string arguments. The string result is stored in `Name`. For the string contents (the symbol □ denotes a blank)

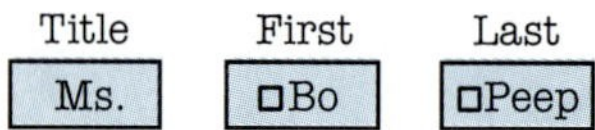

the statement

```
Name := Concat(Title, Last);
```

stores the string `'Ms. Peep'` in `Name`. The statement

```
Name := Concat(Title, First, Last);
```

stores the string `'Ms. Bo Peep'` in `Name`. The statement

```
Name := Concat(Last, ',', First, ' ', Title);
```

stores the string `'Peep, Bo Ms.'` in `Name`.

In Turbo Pascal, the operator + can also be used to concatenate strings. The assignment statement above can be written as

```
Name := Last + ',' + First + ' ' + Title;
```

When the operands are strings, Turbo Pascal interprets the operator + as concatenate instead of add.

■ Example 13.12

Function `Reverse` in Fig. 13.7 uses the `Concat` function. This function reverses the string passed to its argument string `InString`. The string being formed is saved in `TempString`. `TempString` is initialized to the null string. Characters are taken one at a time from `InString`, starting with the last character, and joined to the end of TempString. The first character of InString is the last character joined to TempString. Table 13.3 traces the execution of this function when InString is 'Turbo'. ■

Table 13.3 Trace of for Loop When InString Is 'Turbo'

I	InString[I]	TempString
5	'o'	'o'
4	'b'	'ob'
3	'r'	'obr'
2	'u'	'obru
1	'T'	'obruT'

Figure 13.7 Function for Reversing a String

```
function Reverse (InString : string) : string;

{Reverses the string stored in InString.}

var
   I           :Integer;             {loop control variable}
   TempString  :string;              {temporary reversed string}

begin {Reverse}
  TempString := '';                  {initialize TempString}

  for I := Length(InString) downto 1 do
    TempString := Concat(TempString, InString[I]);

  Reverse := TempString              {define result}
end; {Reverse}
```

SYNTAX DISPLAY

Function Concat

Form: Concat (*string list*)
Example: Concat('Bo', 'Diddly')
Interpretation: The string arguments in *string list* are joined together in the order in which they are listed.
Note: If the resulting string is longer than 255 characters, it is truncated after the 255th character.

String Search

In processing string data, we often need to locate a particular substring. For example, we might want to know if the string 'and ' appears in a sentence, and if so, where? If Target is a string of length 4 with contents 'and ', the statement

```
PosAnd := Pos(Target, Sentence)
```

assigns to PosAnd the starting position of the first occurrence of 'and ' in string Sentence. If the string 'Birds and bees fly all day' is stored in Sentence, the value assigned to PosAnd is 7. If the string 'and ' is not in Sentence, the Pos function returns zero.

■ Example 13.13

A compiler can determine the form of many statements by checking whether the statement begins with a reserved word. If leading blanks are removed from Statement and if Target is a string of length four with contents 'for ', the condition

```
Pos(Target, Statement) = 1
```

is true when Statement is a for statement.

Another task of the compiler is to extract the syntactic elements of each statement. A for statement may have the syntactic form

for *counter* := *initial* to *final* do *statement*

The first two statements that follow use the Pos function to locate the strings 'for ' (contents of Target1) and ':=' (contents of Target2). The if statement copies the substring between these symbols into the string Counter.

```
PosFor := Pos(Target1, Statement);
PosAssign := Pos(Target2, Statement);
if (PosFor > 0) and (PosAssign > PosFor) then
  Counter := Copy(Statement, Posfor + 4, PosAssign - PosFor - 4)
```

Because the string 'for ' has four characters, the starting position of the *counter* is at position PosFor + 4. The number of characters in the *counter* is determined by the expression PosAssign - PosFor - 4. If the string 'for ID := 1 to N do X := X + 1' is stored in Statement, then PosFor gets 1, PosAssign gets 8, and the contents of Counter is the string 'ID ' (length is 8 - 1 - 4, or 3).

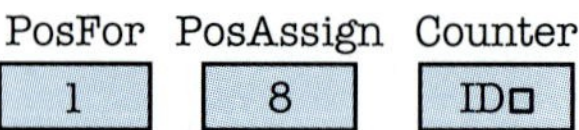

SYNTAX DISPLAY

Pos Function

Form: Pos (*pattern*, *source*)
Example: Pos('you', 'Me/you')
Interpretation: The string *source* is examined from left to right to determine the location of the first occurrence of the substring *pattern*. If *pattern* is found, the value returned is the position in *source* of the first character of *pattern*; otherwise, the value returned is zero.

Procedures Delete and Insert

Besides the string-manipulation functions described so far, there are procedures to insert and delete substrings. They are illustrated next.

■ Example 13.14

Assume that Sentence contains the string 'This is the example.' before the first procedure call. The procedure call statement

```
Delete (Sentence, 1, 5);
```

deletes the first five characters from string Sentence. The new contents of Sentence become 'is the example'.

If Target is the string of length four with contents 'the ', the procedure call statement

```
Delete (Sentence, Pos(Target, Sentence), 4);
```

deletes the first occurrence of the string 'the ' from Sentence. The new contents of Sentence becomes 'is example'. Finally, the statements

```
PosTarg := Pos(Target, Sentence);
if PosTarg > 0 then
  Delete (Sentence, PosTarg, Length(Target))
```

delete the first occurrence of string Target from Sentence, provided Target is found. If Target is the string 'ex', the new contents of Sentence become 'is ample'. ■

■ Example 13.15

Assume that the contents of Sentence is the string 'is the stuff?' and the contents of NewString is 'Where '. The procedure call statement

```
Insert (NewString, Sentence, 1)
```

inserts the string 'Where ' at the beginning of string Sentence, changing its contents to 'Where is the stuff?'.

Assume the contents of Target is 'stuff' and the contents of NewString is '*#@! ', the statements

```
PosStuff := Pos(Target, Sentence);
if PosStuff > 0 then
  Insert (NewString, Sentence, PosStuff)
```

insert the string '*#%! ' in front of the string 'stuff' in Sentence. The new contents of Sentence becomes 'Where is the *#%! stuff'. ■

■ Example 13.16

Procedure Replace in Fig. 13.8 replaces a specified target string (Target) in a source string (Source) with a new string (Pattern). It uses function Pos to locate Target, Delete to delete it, and Insert to insert Pattern in place of Target. An error message is displayed if Target is not found.

Figure 13.8 Procedure Replace

```
procedure Replace (Target, Pattern : string;
                   var source : string);
{
  Replaces first string Target in Source with Pattern if found.
```

```
    Pre : Target, Pattern, and Source are defined.
    Post: Source is modified.
}
    var
      PosTarg : Integer;                {position of Target}

begin  {Replace}
  PosTarg := Pos(Target, Source);      {locate Target}
  if PosTarg > 0 then
    begin
      Delete (Source, PosTarg, Length(Target));
      Insert (Pattern, Source, PosTarg)
    end
  else
    WriteLn ('No replacement -- string ', Target, ' not found.')
end; {Replace}
```

SYNTAX DISPLAY

Delete Procedure

Form: `Delete` (*source*, *index*, *size*)

Example: `Delete ('He**llo', 3, 2)`

Interpretation: The next *size* characters are removed from string *source* starting with the character at position *index*. The parameter *source* must be a string and *size* and *index* must be type `Integer`.

Notes: If *index* is greater than `Length` (*source*), no characters are deleted. If *size* specifies more characters than remain, beginning with position *index*, the remainder of the string is deleted.

SYNTAX DISPLAY

Insert Procedure

Form: `Insert` (*pattern*, *destination*, *index*)

Example: `Insert ('bb', 'Buly', 3)`

Interpretation: The string *pattern* is inserted before the character currently in position *index*. The parameters *pattern* and *destination* must be strings and *index* must be type `Integer`.

Note: If resulting string is longer than 255 characters, it is truncated after the 255th character.

Exercises for Section 13.3

Self-Check

1. Determine the result of the following procedure calls and function designators. Assume that the string variables below are type `string[20]`, and that the initial contents of `Templ` are `'Abra'` and for `Temp2` are `'cadabra'`.
   a. `Magic := Concat(Templ, Temp2)`
   b. `Length(Magic)`
   c. `HisMagic := Copy(Magic, 1, 8)`

d. `Delete (HisMagic, 4, 3)`
e. `Insert (Templ, HisMagic, 3)`
f. `Pos(Temp2, Magic)`
g. `Pos(Templ, Magic)`
h. `Val ('1.234', RealNum, Error)`
i. `Str (1.234 :3:1, RealStr)`

2. `Source`, `Target`, and `Destin` are three variables of type `string` with capacity 20. Assume that `Source` begins with a person's last name and has a comma and one space between the last and first names (that is, *last name, first name*). Use `Pos` and `Copy` to store the first name in `Destin` and the second name in `Target`.

Programming

1. Write a program that calls `PrintWords` to read in a sentence and then display each word on a separate line. Insert the necessary declarations and procedure calls.

13.4 String Processing Illustrated

You have been using a text editor to create and edit Pascal programs. This is a fairly sophisticated *screen-oriented* editor in which special commands move the cursor around the video screen and specify edit operations. Although you cannot develop such an editor yet, you can write a less sophisticated one.

Case Study: Text Editor

Problem

We need an editor to perform some editing operations on a line of text. The editor should be able to locate a specified target string, delete a substring, insert a substring at a specified location, and replace one substring with another.

Design Overview

We can use Turbo Pascal's string manipulation functions and procedures to perform the editing operations relatively easily. We will write a program that enters a string and then processes a series of edit commands for that string.

Data Requirements

Problem Inputs

The source string (`Source : string`)
Each edit command (`Command : Char`)

Problem Outputs

The modified source string (`Source : string`)

Initial Algorithm

1. Read the string to be edited into `Source`.
2. `repeat`
    3. Read an edit command.
    4. Perform each edit operation.

   `until` done

Refinements and Program Structure

Step 4 is performed by procedure `DoEdit`. `DoEdit` is responsible for calling the appropriate string operators to read any data strings and to perform the required operations. A portion of the structure chart for the text editor is shown in Fig. 13.9; the local variables and algorithm for procedure `DoEdit` follow.

Local Variables

A substring to be found, replaced, or deleted (`OldStr : string`)
A substring to be inserted (`NewStr : string`)
An index to the string `Source` (`Index : Integer`)

Figure 13.9 Structure Chart for Text Editor Program

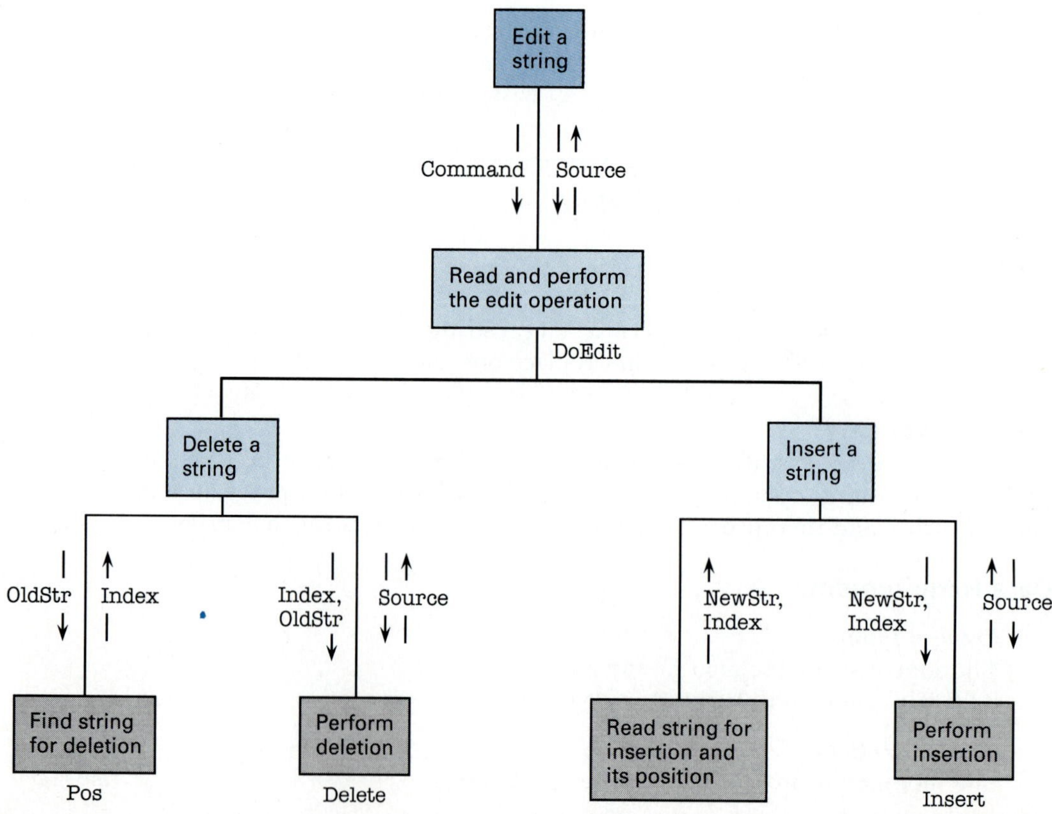

Algorithm for DoEdit

1. `case Command of`
   - `'D'`: Read the substring to be deleted and delete it.
   - `'I'`: Read the substring to be inserted and its position and insert it.
   - `'F'`: Read substring to be found and print its position if found.
   - `'R'`: Read substring to be replaced and replace it.

   `end {case}`

The complete program is shown in Fig. 13.10, along with a sample run.

Figure 13.10 Text Editor Program and Sample Run

Edit Window

```
program TextEdit;
  {Performs text editing operations on a source string.}

  const
    Sentinel = 'Q';       {sentinel command}
    Capacity = 80;        {predefined maximum length}

  type
    StringType = string[Capacity];

  var
    Source : StringType;          {the string being edited}
    Command : Char;               {each edit command}

  {$I Replace}

  procedure DoEdit (Command {input} : Char;
                    var Source : StringType);
  {
    Performs the edit operation specified by Command.
    Pre : Command and Source are defined.
    Post: One or more data strings are read and
          Source is modified if Command is
          'D','I','F', or 'R'. If Command is 'Q',
          a message is displayed; otherwise, nothing
          is done.
  }
    var
      NewStr, OldStr : StringType; {work strings}
      Index : Integer;             {index to string Source}

   begin {DoEdit}
     {Perform the operation.}
     if Command in ['D', 'I', 'F', 'R', 'Q'] then
       case Command of
         'D' : begin {Delete}
                 Write ('Delete what string? ');
                 ReadLn (OldStr);
                 Index := Pos(OldStr, Source);
                 if Index > 0 then
                   Delete (Source, Index, Length(OldStr))
```

Case Study: Text Editor, continued

```
                else
                  begin
                    Write (OldStr);
                    WriteLn (' not found')
                  end {if}
              end; {delete}
        'I' : begin {Insert}
                Write ('Insert what string? ');
                ReadLn (NewStr);
                Write ('At what position? ');
                ReadLn (Index);
                Insert (NewStr, Source, Index)
              end; {Insert}
        'F' : begin {Find}
                Write ('Find what string? ');
                ReadLn (OldStr);
                Index := Pos(OldStr, Source);
                if Index > 0 then
                  begin
                    Write (OldStr);
                    WriteLn (' found at position ', Index :3)
                  end
                else
                  begin
                    Write (OldStr);
                    WriteLn (' not found')
                  end {if}
              end; {Find}
        'R' : begin {Replace}
                Write ('Replace old string? ');
                ReadLn (OldStr);
                Write ('With new string? ');
                ReadLn (NewStr);
                Replace (OldStr, NewStr, Source)
              end; {Replace}
        'Q' : WriteLn ('Quitting text editor.')
      end {case}
    else
      WriteLn ('Invalid edit character')
  end; {DoEdit}

begin {TextEdit}
  {Read in the string to be edited.}
  WriteLn ('Enter the source string:');
  ReadLn (Source);

  {Perform each edit operation until done.}
  repeat
    {Get the operation symbol.}
    WriteLn;
    Write ('Enter D (Delete), I (Insert), ');
    Write ('F (Find), R (Replace), Q (Quit): ');
    ReadLn (Command);
    Command := UpCase(Command);      {convert to uppercase}

    {Perform operation}
    DoEdit (Command, Source);

    {Display latest string}
    Write ('New source: ');
    WriteLn (Source)
```

```
  until Command = Sentinel
end. {TextEdit}
```

Output Window

```
Enter the source string:
Mary had a cute little lamb.

Enter D (Delete), I (Insert), F (Find), R (Replace), Q (Quit): f
Find what string? cute
cute  found at position 12
New source: Mary had a cute little lamb.

Enter D (Delete), I (Insert), F (Find), R (Replace), Q (Quit): i
Insert what string? very
At what position? 12
New source: Mary had a very cute little lamb.

Enter D (Delete), I (Insert), F (Find), R (Replace), Q (Quit): R
Replace old string? lamb
With new string? lamb chop
New source: Mary had a very cute little lamb chop.

Enter D (Delete), I (Insert), F (Find), R (Replace), Q (Quit): D
Delete what string? very cute little
New source: Mary had a lamb chop.

Enter D (Delete), I (Insert), F (Find), R (Replace), Q (Quit): q
Quitting text editor.
New source: Mary had a lamb chop.
```

Exercise for Section 13.4

Self-Check

1. Draw the program structure chart for replacing a string.

13.5 Common Programming Errors

Remember that a set variable, like any variable, must be initialized before it can be manipulated. It is tempting to assume that a set is empty and then to begin processing it without initializing it to the empty set, [], through an explicit assignment.

Many of the Pascal operators can be used with sets. The meaning of the operator is, of course, different when its operands are sets and not numbers. Remember to use a unit set (a set of one element) when you insert or delete a set element. The set union operation in the expression

```
['A','E','O','U'] + 'I'          {incorrect set union}
```

is incorrect and should be rewritten as

```
['A','E','O','U'] + ['I']          {correct set union}
```

It is not possible to use a set as an operand of the standard `Read` or `Write` procedure. You must read in the elements of a set individually and insert them into an initially empty set using the set union operator. To print a set, you must test each value in the base type of a set for set membership. Only those values that are in the set should be printed.

You should use the string operators provided by Turbo Pascal, but remember that they are not available in standard Pascal. In standard Pascal, you would need to implement your own string ADT.

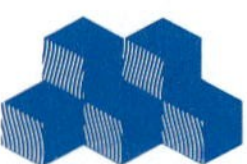

Chapter Review

The set data type can store a collection of elements of the same type (called the base type). Each value in the base type of a set is either a member of the set or it is not. Unlike an array, a value can be saved only once in a set, and there is no way to determine the sequence in which the values were stored in the set (for example, `[1,5,2,4]` is the same set as `[1,2,4,5]`).

String operators can simplify the processing of textual data. Standard Pascal does not provide a variable-length string data type. We described Turbo Pascal's string function and procedures in this chapter.

New Pascal Constructs

The Pascal constructs introduced in this chapter are described in Table 13.4.

Table 13.4 Summary of New Pascal Constructs

Construct	Effect
Set Type Declaration	

`type`
`  DigitSet = set of 0..9;`
 	
`var`
`  Digits, Primes : DigitSet;`
	Declares a set type `DigitSet` whose base type is the set of digits from `0` through `9`. `Digits` and `Primes` are set variables of type `DigitSet`.

Set Assignment	
`Digits := [];`	`Digits` is the empty set.
`Primes := [2,3,5] + [7];`	`Primes is the set [2,3,5,7].`
`Digits := Digits + [1..3];`	`Digits` is the set `[1,2,3]`.
`Digits := [0..9] - [1,3,5,7,9];`	`Digits` is the set `[0,2,4,6,8]`.
`Digits := [1,3,5,7,9] * Primes`	`Digits` is the set `[3,5,7]`.
Set Relations	
`Primes <= Digits`	`True` if `Primes` is a subset of `Digits`.

Table 13.4 *continued*

Construct	Effect
`Primes >= []`	Always `True`.
`Primes <> []`	`True` if `Primes` contains any element.
`[1,2,3] = [3,2,1]`	`True` because order does not matter.
String Declaration	

`const Capacity = 10;`
`type StringType = string[Capacity];`
`var FirstName, LastName, TempName :`
`  StringType;`
	`FirstName`, `LastName`, and `TempName` are variable-length strings (string capacity is ten characters).

String Assignment	

`FirstName := 'Daffy';`
`LastName := 'Duck';`
`TempName := LastName;`
	Saves `'Daffy'` in `FirstName` and `'Duck'` in `LastName` and `TempName`.

String Length	
`Length(FirstName);`	Returns the current length (5) of `FirstName`.
String Copy	
`TempName := Copy(FirstName, 1, 3);`	Copies `'Daf'` to `TempName`.
String Concatenation	
`TempName := Concat(FirstName, LastName);`	Stores `'DaffyDuck'` in `TempName`.
String Search	
`Pos('Du', FirstName);`	Returns `0` (`'Du'` not found).
`Pos('Du', LastName);`	Returns `1` (`'Du'` found at `1`).
`Pos('Du', TempName);`	Returns `6` (`'Du'` found at `6`).
String Deletion	
`Delete (TempName, 7, 2);`	Changes `TempName` to `'DaffyDk'`.
String Insertion	
`Insert ('uc', TempName, 7);`	Changes `TempName` to `'DaffyDuck`.

✓ Quick-Check Exercises

1. What is the universal set?
2. Which can have the most elements: a set union, an intersection, or a difference? Which of these operators is not commutative?
3. Can you have a set whose base type is `Integer` or `Char`? How about a subrange type with host type `Integer` or `Char`?

4. Does it make any difference in which order the elements of a set are inserted? Does it make any difference if an element is inserted more than once into the same set?
5. Given that `Set1` is `[1..3]`, what are the contents of the following sets?
   a. `Set2 := Set1 + [4, 5, 6];`
   b. `Set3 := Set1 - Set2;`
   c. `Set4 := Set3 + [4, 7];`
   d. `Set5 := Set4 + [4, 6]`
   e. `Set6 := Set5 * Set2`
6. What is the advantage of storing a string in a variable of type `string` instead of using an array of characters?
7. Is it easier to compare two strings stored in variables of type `string` or in arrays of characters? Explain your answer.
8. Assuming `S1`, `S2`, and `S3` are type `string`, what is the effect of the following statements when `Pos` returns a nonzero value?
   a. `S3 := Copy(S1, 1, 6);`
      `S3 := Concat (S3, S2, S3);`
   b. `S3 := Copy (S2, 1, Pos(S1, S2) -1);`
   c. `S3 := Copy (S2, Pos(S1, S2), Length(S2));`
   d. `S3 := Copy (S2, Pos(S1, S2), Length(S1));`
   e. `Delete (S2, Pos(S1, S2), Length(S1));`
   f. `Insert (S1, S2, Pos(S1, S2));`
9. Answer exercise 8 when `Pos` returns `0`.
10. Write procedure `PadString` that pads a variable-length string with blanks.

Answers to Quick-Check Exercises

1. The set containing all the values in the base type.
2. The union of two sets. Set difference (operator –) is not commutative.
3. You cannot use `Integer` as a base type, but you can use `Char`. A subrange of `Integer` or `Char` can be the base type.
4. No; no
5. a. `[1..6]` b. `[]` c. `[4,7]` d. `[4,6,7]` e. `[4,6]`
6. The actual length is also stored. Turbo Pascal's string functions and procedures can be used to assist in processing the string data.
7. It is easier to compare two strings because you can use the relational operators. Two arrays can be compared element by element, but there may be some problems if the arrays don't contain the same number of elements.
8. a. The substring consisting of the first six characters in `S1` is concatentated with `S2`; the result is stored in `S3`.
   b. The substring of `S2` that precedes the first occurrence of `S1` in `S2` is assigned to `S3`.
   c. The substring of `S2` starting at the first occurrence of `S1` in `S2` is assigned to `S3`.
   d. The substring `S1` is assigned to `S3`.
   e. The first occurrence of `S1` is deleted from `S2`.
   f. The string `S1` is inserted in `S2` just before its first occurrence.
9. a. not affected
   b, c, d. The null string is stored in `S3`.
   e, f. `S2` should not be changed.
10.

```
procedure PadString (var AString {input/output} : StringType);
  const
    Pad = ' ';
  var
```

```
    I : Integer
  begin {PadString}
   for I := Length(AString) + 1 to Capacity do
     AString := Concat(AString, Pad);
end; {PadString}
```

Review Questions

1. Why may we be unable to declare a set whose base type is Char?
2. Write the declarations for a set, Oysters, whose values are the months of the year (enumerated type Month). Initialize Oysters to the set of all months that contain the letter r in their name. Write an assignment statement that inserts the month May in this set and deletes the month September.
3. The following for loop prints each member of a set whose elements are values of enumerated type Day. Write the declaration for set TestSet. Rewrite the loop as a while loop whose repetition condition is TestSet <> []. Use the set operator - to delete each set element after it is displayed.

```
for Today := Sunday to Saturday do
  if Today in TestSet then
    WriteDay (Today)
```

4. Provide the declarations for the two sets below. What are the intersection and union of sets Vowel and Letter? What are the two set differences?

```
Vowel := ['Y','U','O','I'];
Letter := ['A'..'P'];
```

5. What is the difference between the current length of a string and the capacity of a string? Which does function Length return?
6. Indicate whether each of the following identifiers is a procedure or function. Describe the type of result returned by each.

```
Length, Concat, Pos, Copy, Insert, Delete
```

7. Write the declarations and statements for a program segment that first reads a data line into a variable of type StringType and stores all of the symbols in the subrange '!'..'/' that appear in the string in a set Symbols1. Assume the ASCII character set and test each of the characters in this subrange using function Pos to determine whether it appears in the string. If so, insert it in the set Symbols1. Next, write a new search loop that scans the string, testing each character in the string for membership in the set ['!'..'/']. Insert each character that qualifies in set Symbols2. When you are done, test whether Symbols1 and Symbols2 are identical sets.

Programming Projects

1. Write a program that removes all the blanks from a character string.
2. Write a program that reads in a sequence of lines and displays a count of the total number of words in those lines and counts of the number of words with one letter, two letters, and so on.
3. Write a program that reads in a sequence of lines and displays each line read with all four-letter words replaced with asterisks.

4. Write a program that reads in a sequence of lines and rewrites each line in a simplified form of "pig latin." If the word begins with a consonant, strip off the first letter and place it at the end of the word followed by the string `'ay'`.
5. Write a procedure that reads in an array of cards and stores it in an array of sets, one set for each suit. Use an enumerated type for the suits and one for the card face values. The data for each card will be presented in the form of a character representing the suit and a character representing the card face value (`'2'..'9'`, `'T'`, `'J'`, `'Q'`, `'K'`, `'A'`).
6. Write a Pascal program to play the Taxman game. In this game the user plays against the computer. The object is to accumulate the most points. During the course of the game, the user selects from the numbers 1 to 40. If the number is still available, the user is credited with points equal to the number chosen and the number is removed from the set of available numbers. After a number is chosen, the computer is credited with points equivalent to the sum of the unclaimed factors of the number chosen. The user may not choose a number with no factors. The computer gets all unclaimed numbers added to its score when the game ends.

   As an example, consider the game played with only the numbers 1 to 6 in the set. If the user selects 6, the computer gets all divisors of 6, namely 3, 2, 1, and the score is tied. But now only 4 and 5 are left to choose from and neither has any factors left, so the computer wins 15 to 6. To win, the user should have chosen 5 first, then 4, and then 6. This time he or she wins 15 to 7.
7. Revise the text editor discussed in Section 13.4 so that it will edit a "page" of text. Store each line of the page in a separate element of an array of strings. Maintain a pointer (index) to the line currently being edited. In addition to the edit commands, include commands that move the index to the top of the page, the bottom of the page, and up or down a specified number of lines. Your program should also be able to delete an entire line, insert a new line preceding the current line, and replace the current line with another. The first two of these new operations will require moving a portion of the array of strings up or down by one element.
8. Write a program that will read 400 characters into a 20-by-20 array. Afterward, read in a character string of a maximum of ten characters that will be used to search the "table" of characters. Indicate how many times the second string occurs in the 20-by-20 array. This should include horizontal, vertical, and right-diagonal occurrences. (Right-diagonal means going down and to the right for the search.)
9. Write a program to scan a line of characters containing an equation and calculate the result. Assume all operands are integers. Make tests to determine if the equation is valid.

   Valid operations are +, −, /, *, and ^, where +, −, /, and * have their typical functions and ^ indicates the left value is raised to the power of the right operand (which must be positive).

   Numbers may be negative. All operations are done in left-to-right order (no operator precedence). For example,

   ```
   2 + 3 ^ 2 + 36 * 1
   ```

   would be

   ```
   5 ^ 2 + 36 * 1 = 25 + 36 * 1 = 61 * 1 = 61
   ```

   Use sets to verify the equations' operations and ignore all blanks. Output should consist of an equal sign (=) and then the answer. If an equation is invalid, display the message `** INVALID **`.

14

Files

We introduced files in Chapter 8. Like an array, a file is a collection of elements that are all the same type. Because files are located in secondary memory (that is, on a disk) rather than in main memory, they can be much larger than arrays. The elements of an array can be accessed in arbitrary, or *random order*; files in standard Pascal can be accessed only in *sequential order*. This means that file component 1, component 2, ..., component *n*-1 must be accessed before file component *n* can be accessed. Turbo Pascal allows both *direct* (random) access and sequential access to file components.

This chapter reviews text files. We also study other file types whose components are records. Finally, we discuss how Turbo Pascal allows a file to be accessed in random order, just like an array.

14.1 Review of Text Files

This section reviews what you learned about text files in Section 8.8. Files can store large quantities of data on disk. All components of a file are the same type. A text file is a file whose components are characters from the Pascal character set. A special character, the end-of-line mark, separates sequences of adjacent characters into lines. Associated with each file is a file-position pointer, which indicates the next file component to be processed.

If `InFile` is the name of a file variable and `B:NEWDATA.DAT` is the directory name of a file stored on a disk in the B drive, the statement

```
Assign (InData, 'B:NEWDATA.DAT');
```

associates the file variable `InData` with the disk file `B:NEWDATA.DAT`. The `Assign` procedure must be called prior to opening the file with either the `Reset` or `Rewrite` procedures and may not be called if `InData` is already open for input or output.

You can use a file for input or for output, but not both simultaneously. If you're using a file for input, then its components can be read as data. If you're using a file for output, then new components can be written to the file.

If `InFile` is the name of a file, the statement

```
Reset (InFile)
```

calls the standard procedure `Reset` to prepare (*open*) file `InFile` for input. The file-position pointer is moved to the beginning of file `InFile`, so that the first file component is read by the next `Read` operation. The file-position pointer is automatically advanced after each `Read` operation.

If `OutFile` is the name of a file, the statement

```
Rewrite (OutFile)
```

calls the standard procedure `Rewrite` to prepare file `OutFile` for output. If `OutFile` is a new file, it is initialized to an empty file. If `OutFile` is an existing file in disk storage, its file-position pointer is returned to the beginning. In this way, `OutFile` becomes an empty file, and the data previously associated with the file are lost.

■ Example 14.1

Assume that `InFile` and `OutFile` are both text files. The statements

```
Reset (InFile);
Rewrite (OutFile);
```

open `InFile` for input and `OutFile` for output, as shown next. If file `OutFile` is non-empty, the `Rewrite` operation still returns the file-position pointer to the beginning, causing the existing file data to be lost. ■

After Reset and Rewrite

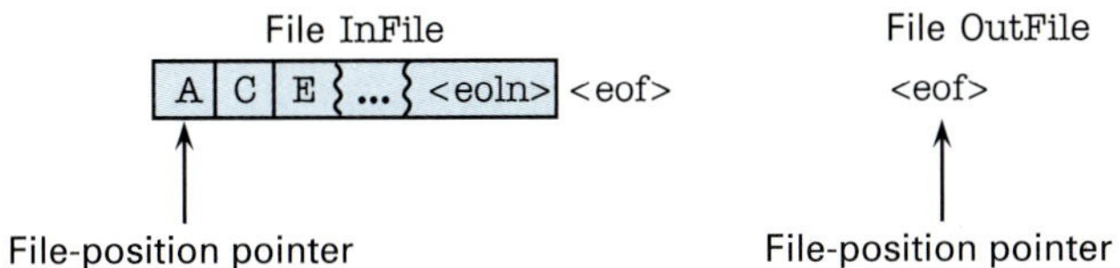

Procedures `Read` and `ReadLn` can be used with system file `Input` (the keyboard) or any other text file that has been opened for input. Similarly, procedures `Write` and `WriteLn` can be used with system file `Output` (the screen) or any other text file that has been opened for output. The file to be processed is determined by the first parameter in a call to any of these procedures. If the first parameter is not a file variable, system file `Input` (for `Read` and `ReadLn`) or system file `Output` (for `Write` and `WriteLn`) is processed.

The `EOF` and `EOLN` functions test for the end of a file and the end of a line of a text file, respectively. The function parameter indicates which input file is being tested. If there is no parameter, system file `Input` is assumed. The function designator `EOF(InFile)` evaluates to `True` when the next character in file `InFile` is the `<eof>`. The function designator `EOLN(InFile)` evaluates to `True` when the next character in file `InFile` is an `<eoln>`.

In Turbo Pascal, the procedure call statement

```
Close (InData);
```

closes the open file `InData`. Its effect is to release the disk file previously associated with `InData`. It is especially critical that you close an output file. When an output file is closed, any file components that have not yet been written to the file by the operating system are appended to the end of the file. If the file is not closed, these remaining file components may be lost.

The specification for the abstract data type text file follows.

Specification for Text File Abstract Data Type

Structure: A text file is an ordered collection of characters stored on disk. A special character, the end-of-line mark, segments the file into lines.

Operators:

`Assign (F,`*disk file*`)`: Associates internal file `F` with the disk file named *disk file*.

`Reset (F)`: Opens file `F` for input.

`Rewrite (F)`: Opens file `F` for output.

`Read (F,` *input list*`)`: Reads data from file `F` into the variables specified in *input list*. If `F` is missing, it reads data from system file `Input`.

`ReadLn (F,` *input list*`)`: Same as `Read` except that it advances the file-position pointer for file `F` to the start of the next line after performing the data entry.

`Write (F,` *output list*`)`: Writes data values in *output list* to file `F`. If `F` is missing, it writes data to system file `Output`.

`WriteLn (F,` *output list*`)`: Same as `Write` except that it writes an `<eoln>` to file `F` after all data values.

`EOF (F)`: Returns `True` if the `<eof>` is the next character in file `F`; otherwise, it returns `False`.

`EOLN (F)`: Returns `True` if an `<eoln>` is the next character in file `F`; otherwise, it returns `False`.

`Close (F)`: Releases disk file associated with file `F`.

■ Example 14.2

Procedure `CopyFile` in Fig. 14.1 reviews the use of the file operators. It copies each character of its input file to its output file. (Procedure `CopyFile` is based on an earlier program; see Fig. 8.14.) ■

Figure 14.1 Procedure CopyFile

```
procedure CopyFile (var InFile  {input},
                       OutFile {output} : Text);
{
  Copies file InFile to file OutFile.
  Pre : File InFile is defined.
  Post: File OutFile is a copy of InFile. The file-position
        pointers for both files are advanced to the <eof>
        character.
}
  var
    NextCh : Char;              {next character}

begin
  Reset (InFile);               {prepare input file}
  Rewrite (OutFile);            {prepare output file}
  while not EOF(InFile) do
    begin
      While not EOLN(InFile) do
        begin
          Read  (InFile, NextCh);
          Write (OutFile, NextCh)    {copy character}
        end; {line}
```

```
      {assertion: <eoln> reached}
      ReadLn (InFile);                  {skip <eoln>}
      WriteLn (OutFile)                 {insert <eoln>}
    end {file}

  {assertion: <eof> reached}
end; {CopyFile}
```

Exercises for Section 14.1

Self-Check

1. Rewrite procedure `CopyFile` so that it uses procedures `ReadLn` and `WriteLn` to enter a data line as a string instead of using the inner `while` loop.
2. What does the following program do? What happens if a data line does not contain enough characters to satisfy the input list?

```
program Mystery;
  var
    InData : Text;
    Ch1, Ch2, Ch3 : Char;
begin
  Assign (InData, 'INDATA.DAT')
  Reset (InData);
  while not EOF(InData) do
    begin
      ReadLn (InData, Ch1, Ch2, Ch3);
      WriteLn (Ch1, Ch2, Ch3)
    end; {while}
  Close(InData)
end. {Mystery}
```

Programming

1. Write procedure `CompressFile` that copies all nonblank characters in its input file to its output file.

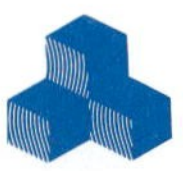

14.2 File Processing Illustrated

In the game show called "Wheel of Fortune," three contestants attempt to guess a phrase. The contestants select consonants that they think are in the phrase. If a contestant picks a consonant that does occur in the phrase, the letter is inserted wherever it belongs. Contestants can also "buy" vowels; if the chosen vowel occurs in the phrase, it too is inserted.

Case Study: Wheel of Fortune Problem

Problem

The game show producers want a computer program that can help them select phrases. Because the consonants are key, it would help the producers if the program can show them what the phrase looks like without vowels. The program should read a phrase entered at the keyboard, then display that phrase with a minus sign inserted in place of every vowel. A list of vowels and consonants occurring in the phrase should be printed underneath the phrase. For example, the phrase

```
THIS IS A SAMPLE
PHRASE WITH
VOWELS REMOVED
```

would generate the output

```
TH-S -S - S-MPL-
PHR-S- W-TH
V-W-LS R-M-V-D
The consonants are: DHLMPRSTVW
The vowels are: AEIO
```

Design Overview

We will read each line of the phrase, substitute a minus sign for each vowel, and write each converted line to a text file (`Scratch`). Each individual character in a line will be added to a set of consonants or vowels. After the phrase is completed, file `Scratch` will be echo printed.

Data Requirements

Problem Inputs

Phrase to be processed (uppercase letters)

Problem Outputs

Phrase with vowels removed (`Scratch : Text`)
Set of consonants in the phrase (`Consonants : set of 'A'..'Z'`)
Set of vowels in the phrase (`Vowels : set of 'A'..'Z'`)

Figure 14.2 Structure Chart for Wheel of Fortune Problem

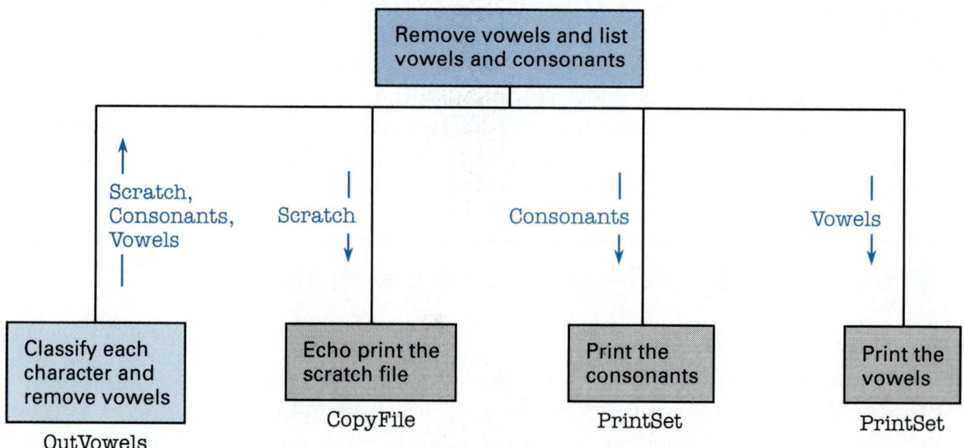

Initial Algorithm

1. Classify each character as a consonant or a vowel, substitute a minus sign for each vowel, and write the phrase to a scratch file.
2. Echo print the scratch file.
3. Print the set of consonants.
4. Print the set of vowels.

Program Structure

In the structure chart in Fig. 14.2, separate procedures accomplish steps 1 through 4. Step 1 is the only one that we have not yet solved; we will discuss procedure `OutVowels` later. Procedure `CopyFile` performs step 2, and procedure `PrintSet` (see Fig. 13.3) performs steps 3 and 4.

Coding the Main Program

The main program for the Wheel of Fortune problem appears in Fig. 14.3.

Figure 14.3 Main Program for Wheel of Fortune Problem

```
program Wheel;
{
  Displays a phrase with vowels removed. Also
  lists the consonants and vowels in the phrase.
  Imports: CopyFile (see Fig. 14.1)
           PrintSet (see Fig. 13.3)
}
  const
    Capacity = 80;            {string capacity}

  type
    StringType = string[Capacity];
    LetterSet = set of 'A'..'Z';         {set of letters}

  var
    Consonants,                          {set of consonants}
    Vowels      : LetterSet;             {set of vowels}
    Scratch : Text;                      {a scratch file}

  {Insert OutVowels, CopyFile, PrintSet}

begin {Wheel}
  {
   Classify each character as a consonant or vowel, substitute
   - for each vowel, and write the scratch file.
  }
  Assign (Scratch, 'SCRATCH.DAT');
  OutVowels (Scratch, Consonants, Vowels);
  Close (Scratch);

  {Echo print the scratch file.}
  CopyFile (Scratch, Output);
  Erase (Scratch);
```

```
  {Print the set of consonants.}
  Write ('The consonants are: ');
  PrintSet (Consonants);
  WriteLn;

  {Print the set of vowels.}
  Write ('The vowels are: ');
  PrintSet (Vowels)
end. {Wheel}
```

Coding Procedure OutVowels

Procedure `OutVowels` creates the file `Scratch` and defines the sets `Vowels` and `Consonants`. The local variables and algorithm for `OutVowels` follow.

Local Variables for OutVowels
A line of the phrase (`NextLine : StringType`)

Algorithm for OutVowels
1. Prepare `Scratch` for output.
2. Initialize `Consonants` and `Vowels` to empty sets.
3. Read the first line of the phrase.
4. `while` there are more lines in the phrase `do`
   `begin`
   5. Replace each vowel in the current line with – and add the vowel to `Vowels`. Add each consonant to `Consonants`.

Figure 14.4 Structure Chart for Procedure OutVowels

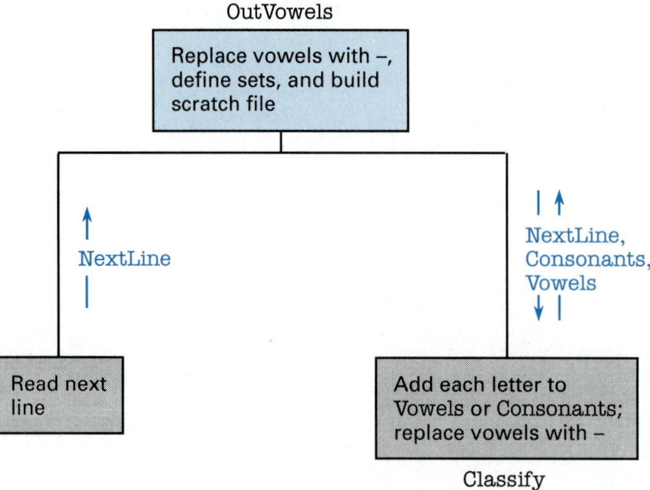

6. Write the modified line to file `Scratch`.
7. Read the next line of the phrase.

`end`

Procedure `ReadLnStrVar` enters each line of the phrase into string variable `NextLine`. Procedure `Classify` performs step 5. The structure chart for `OutVowels` is shown in Fig. 14.4; procedure `OutVowels` is shown in Fig. 14.5.

Figure 14.5 Procedure OutVowels

```
procedure OutVowels (var Scratch   {output} : Text;
                     var Consonants {output},
                         Vowels     {output} : LetterSet);
{
  Classifies each character as a consonant or vowel, substitutes
  - for each vowel, and writes the scratch file.
  Pre : None.
  Post: File Scratch is an echo of the input except each vowel
        is replaced by -, Consonants is the set of all consonants
        entered, and Vowels is the set of all vowels entered.
}
  var
    NextLine : StringType;          {the next data line}


  procedure Classify (var NextLine  {input/output} : StringType;
                      var Consonants {input/output},
                          Vowels     {input/output} : LetterSet);
  {
    Adds each letter in NextLine to the set Consonants or Vowels.
    Replaces each vowel in NextLine with -.
    Pre : NextLine, Consonants, and Vowels are defined.
    Post: Each vowel in NextLine is inserted in set Vowels and
          each consonant in NextLine is inserted in Consonants.
  }
    const
      NewChar = '-';                  {replacement character}

    var
      AllVowels,                      {set of all vowels}
      AllConsonants : LetterSet;      {set of all consonants}
      NextChar : Char;                {each character in the line}
      I : 1..Capacity;                {loop-control variable}

  begin  {Classify}
    {Initialize AllVowels and AllConsonants}
    AllVowels := ['A','E','I','O','U'];
    AllConsonants := ['A'..'Z'] - AllVowels;  {rest of alphabet}

    {Replace each vowel with -; update vowel and consonant sets.}
    for I := 1 to Length(NextLine) do
      begin
        NextChar := NextLine[I];          {Get next character}
        NextChar := UpCase(NextChar);
        if NextChar in AllVowels then
```

Case Study: Wheel of Fortune Problem, continued

```
        begin  {vowel}
          Vowels := Vowels + [NextChar];        {insert vowel}
          NextLine[I] := NewChar                {replace vowel}
        end  {vowel}
      else if NextChar in AllConsonants then
        Consonants := Consonants + [NextChar]   {add consonant}
    end  {for}
  end;  {Classify}

begin  {OutVowels}
  Rewrite (Scratch);                     {prepare Scratch for output}
  Consonants := [];   Vowels := [];                  {initialize sets}

  {Print user instructions.}
  WriteLn ('Enter each line of the text phrase.');
  WriteLn ('Press an extra return when done.');

  {Read each line, convert it, and write it to Scratch.}
  ReadLn (NextLine);                      {get the first line}
  while Length(NextLine) <> 0 do
    begin
      {Replace vowels with - and update Consonants and Vowels.}
      Classify (NextLine, Consonants, Vowels);

      {Write converted line to scratch file.}
      WriteLn (Scratch, NextLine);        {insert <eoln>}
      ReadLn (NextLine)                   {get the next line}
    end  {while}
end;  {OutVowels}
```

The length of the input line controls repetition of the `while` loop in procedure `OutVowels`. A length of zero indicates that the Enter key was pressed twice. Each line is written to file `Scratch` after it is processed by procedure `Classify`.

The sets `AllVowels` and `AllConsonants` are defined in `Classify` as the set of all vowels and consonants, respectively. The assignment statement

```
AllConsonants := ['A'..'Z'] - AllVowels;    {rest of alphabet}
```

defines `AllConsonants` properly when the letters are consecutive characters.

In `Classify`, the statements

```
Vowels := Vowels + [NextChar];        {insert vowel}
NextLine[I] := NewChar                {replace vowel}
```

insert a letter (`NextChar`) that is a vowel in the set `Vowels` and replace that letter with a minus sign in the string `NextLine`. A letter that is a consonant is inserted into the set `Consonants` by the statement

```
Consonants := Consonants + [NextChar]     {add consonant}
```

Use of Scratch Files

File `Scratch` is created by procedure `OutVowels` and echo printed by procedure `CopyFile`. Because it is completely processed during the execution of program `Wheel`, you don't need to retain file `Scratch` in secondary storage after `Wheel` is finished. The procedure call statement

```
Erase (Scratch)
```

frees up the disk storage used by `Scratch`. `Erase` is not part of standard Pascal. `Files` that are defined only during the execution of a program are called *scratch,* or temporary, files. The space used by a scratch file on a disk can be reallocated after the program is finished.

It would have been just as easy to use an array of strings instead of a scratch file to store each line of the phrase being processed. We used a scratch file for two reasons: first, to demonstrate its use; second, because the number of lines in the input phrase is unknown. Because of limitations on available memory, it might be impossible to store a very long phrase in an array of strings; however, this is no problem if we use a scratch file.

Exercises for Section 14.2

Self-Check

1. In program `Wheel`, where are the vowels and consonants that are in the data phrase stored? How are they printed to the screen?
2. For program `Wheel`, discuss the changes that would be needed to save the phrase in an array of strings instead of a scratch file.

14.3 User-Defined File Types and Binary Files

In a text file, the individual components are characters from the Pascal character set. We can use the type constructor `file` to declare new file types whose components are any type, simple or structured, except for another file type.

■ Example 14.3

Program `EchoFile` in Fig. 14.6 creates and echo prints a file of integer values from `1` to `1000`. The file type declaration

```
type
  NumberFile = file of Integer;
```

identifies NumberFile as a file type whose components are integer values. The file that is created, named Numbers, follows.

file Numbers

Figure 14.6 Program EchoFile

```
program EchoFile;

{Creates a file of integer values and echo prints it.}

  const
    NumInt = 1000;              {number of integers in the file}

  type
    NumberFile = file of Integer;

  var
    Numbers : NumberFile; {file of integers}
    I,                    {loop control variable}
    NextInt : Integer;    {each integer read from file Numbers}

begin {EchoFile}
  {Create a file of integers.}
  Assign (Numbers, 'B:NUMBERS.DAT');
  Rewrite (Numbers);     {initialize Numbers to an empty file}
  for I := 1 to NumInt do
    Write (Numbers, I); {write each integer to Numbers}
  Close (Numbers);

  {Echo print file Numbers.}
  Reset (Numbers);                    {prepare Numbers for input}
  while not EOF(Numbers) do
    begin
      Read (Numbers, NextInt); {read next integer into NextInt}
      WriteLn (Output, NextInt :4)                 {display it}
    end;  {while}

  Close (Numbers)
end. {EchoFile}
```

EchoFile begins by preparing file Numbers for output (the Rewrite statement). The for loop with loop-control variable I creates a file of integer values. The statement

```
Write (Numbers, I);            {write each integer to Numbers}
```

copies each value of I (1 to 1000) to file Numbers.

Next, file Numbers is closed and then prepared for input (the Reset statement). The while loop echo prints each value stored in Numbers until the end of file Numbers is reached (EOF(Numbers) is True). Within the loop, the statement

```
Read (Numbers, NextInt);  {read next integer into NextInt}
```

reads the next file component (an integer value) into variable NextInt. The statement

```
WriteLn (Output, NextInt :4)                    {display it}
```

displays this value on a separate line of the screen (system file Output). ■

Comparison of Binary Files and Text Files

File Numbers is called a binary file. A *binary file* is a file that is created by the execution of a program and in which the internal representation of each component is stored directly. It is faster to process a binary file than a text file. For example, if the variable NextInt has the value 244, the statement

```
Write (Numbers, NextInt)
```

copies the internal binary representation of NextInt from memory to file Numbers. If your computer uses two bytes to store an integer value, the byte that stores the highest-order bits would contain all zeros and the byte that stores the lowest-order bits would contain the binary string 11110100 (244 = 128 + 64 + 32 + 16 + 4). Both bytes would be written to disk as the next file component.

Assuming OutFile is a text file, the statement

```
Write (OutFile, NextInt :4)
```

writes the value of NextInt to OutFile using four characters (four bytes). To do this, the computer must first convert the binary number in NextInt to the character string ' 244' and then write the binary code for the characters blank, 2, 4, and 4 to file OutFile. Obviously, it takes more time to do the conversion and copy each character than it does to copy the internal binary representation to disk. It also requires twice as much disk space to store four characters as it does to store the internal binary representation of the integer value (four bytes versus two).

There is another advantage to a binary file. Each time we write a Real value to a text file, the computer must convert this value to a character string, whose precision is determined by the format specification. This may result in a loss of accuracy.

As shown in Fig. 14.4, you can use the standard procedures Read and Write with binary files. The file name must be the first parameter. For the Read procedure, all variables in the input list must be the same type as the file components. For the Write procedure, each output expression must be the same type as the file components.

The Pascal system uses an <eof> to denote the end of a binary file; however, we will not show this indicator when we sketch a binary file. We can use the EOF function to test for the end of a binary file in the same way that it tests for the end of a text file. The file name must be passed as a parameter to the EOF function (for example, EOF(Numbers)).

Unlike text files, binary files cannot be segmented into lines. Consequently, the standard procedures ReadLn, WriteLn, and EOLN cannot be used with binary files.

In the next section, you will see that complete data structures (that is, records and arrays) can be read from binary files and written to binary files with a single `Read` or `Write` operation. This simplifies input/output considerably and makes it much more efficient. This, of course, is not possible with text files; each array element or record field must be read or written separately. The only exception for text files is writing a string.

SYNTAX DISPLAY

File Type Declaration

Form: `type` *file type* `= file of` *component type*;

Example:

```
type
  Item = record
           ID : Integer;
           Salary : Real
         end; {Item}
  ItemFile = file of Item;
```

Interpretation: A new type *file type* is declared whose components must be type *component type*. Any standard or previously declared data type, except for another file type or a structured type with a file type as one of its constituents, can be the component type.

SYNTAX DISPLAY

Read Procedure (for Binary Files)

Form: `Read` (*infile*, *input list*)

Example: `Read (NumberFile, NextInt)`

Interpretation: The `Read` procedure reads one component of file *infile* into each variable in *input list* and then advances the file-position pointer to the next unread file component. The type of each variable must correspond to the component type for *infile*. The value of `EOF` (*infile*) must be `False` before the `Read` operation occurs.

SYNTAX DISPLAY

Write Procedure (for Binary Files)

Form: `Write` (*outfile*, *output list*)

Example: `Write (Numbers, NextInt, 500)`

Interpretation: The `Write` procedure appends the value of each expression in *output list* to file *outfile*. The type of each expression must correspond to the component type for *outfile*.

Exercises for Section 14.3

Self-Check

1. Assume your computer uses four bytes to store a type `Real` value in memory. How many bytes would be required to store six `Real` numbers in a binary file? Answer the same question for a text file in which each number is written

using the format specification :4:2. Are there any circumstances under which either of your answers might change?

2. Complete the following program. What does it do?

```
program Mystery;
  type
    NumberType = file of _______;

  var
    Data : _______;
    OutData : _______;
    Next : Integer;

begin
  Assign (Data, 'DATA.DAT');
  Assign (OutData, 'OUT.DAT');
  _______ (Data);
  _______ (OutData);
  while not EOF (_______) do
    begin
      Read (_______, Next);
      if Next < 50 then
        begin
          Write (_______, Next);
          WriteLn (_______, Next :2, ' Failed')
        end {if}
    end; {while}

  Close (Data);
  Close (OutData)
end. {Mystery}
```

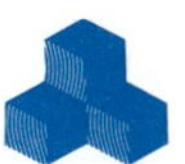

14.4 Files of Records

The components of a binary file can be any type, simple or structured, except for another file type. Often, the components of a binary file are records. This section looks at ways to create a binary file of records.

Creating a Binary File

Unlike a text file, a binary file cannot be created using an editor program. To create a binary file, we must write and run a program that repeats the following steps until the binary file is completed.

1. Read the data for the next file component from a text file (or the keyboard) and save it in memory.
2. Copy the internal binary representation from memory to the binary file.

After the program executes, the binary file is stored on disk and is available for further processing.

The process of creating a binary file with two records is illustrated in Fig. 14.7. The text file `InData` is read by program `MakeBinary` (see Fig. 14.8) which creates the binary file `Employee`. The data for each employee consisting of an ID number, hourly rate, and hours worked, appears on two lines of file `InData`.

Figure 14.7 Creating a Binary File with Two Records

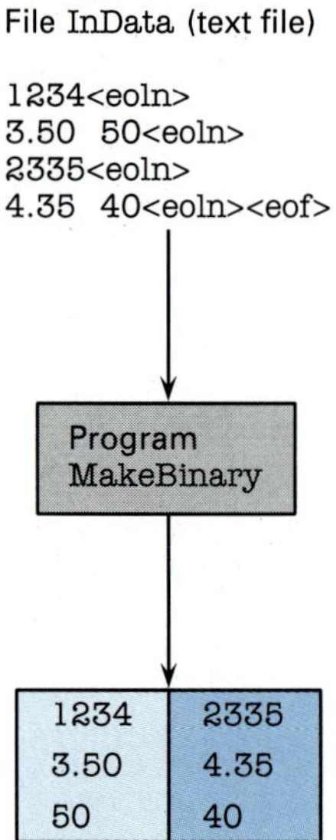

After `MakeBinary` reads an employee's data from `InData` into record `OneEmp`, the statement

```
Write (Employee, OneEmp)          {Write it to Employee}
```

writes the resulting record to file `Employee`. Because `InData` is type `Text`, it has 26 components (all characters) and terminates with an `<eof>` (not counted). File `Employee` has only two components; each component is a record with three fields.

Figure 14.8 Program MakeBinary

```
program MakeBinary;

{Creates a binary file of records.}

  type
    Item = record
             ID : Integer;
             Rate : Real;
             Hours : Integer
           end; {Item}
    ItemFile = file of Item;

  var
    InData : Text;            {input - text file}
    Employee : ItemFile;      {output - binary file}
    OneEmp : Item;            {each record}
```

```
begin
  Assign (InData, 'INDATA.DAT');
  Assign (Employee, 'EMPLOYEE.DAT');
  Reset (InData);
  Rewrite (Employee);
  while not EOF(InData) do
    begin
      {Read next record}
      with OneEmp do
        begin
          ReadLn (InData, ID);
          ReadLn (InData, Rate, Hours)
        end; {with}
      Write (Employee, OneEmp)        {Write it to Employee}
    end; {while}

  Close (InData);
  Close (Employee)
end. {MakeBinary}
```

■ Example 14.4

The program in Fig. 14.9 creates a binary file, `Inventory`, that represents the inventory of a bookstore. Each file component is a record of type `Book`, because `Inventory` is declared as type `BookFile` (file of `Book`). The information saved in each component consists of a four-digit stock number, the book's author and title (strings), the price, and the quantity on hand. The program also computes and prints the total value of the inventory.

The main program calls procedure `ReadBook` to enter the data for each book from the terminal into record variable `OneBook`. `ReadBook` first reads the book's stock number. If the stock number is not the sentinel, `ReadBook` calls procedure `ReadLn` to read the author and title strings. After `OneBook` is defined, the statements

```
Write (Inventory, OneBook);    {Copy the book to Inventory}
InvValue := InvValue + OneBook.Price * OneBook.Quantity;
```

copy the internal, binary form of the entire record `OneBook` to file `Inventory` and update the inventory value. ■

Figure 14.9 Creating a Bookstore Inventory File

Edit Window

```
program BookInventory;
{
 Creates an inventory file, Inventory, from data entered at the
 terminal. Also computes and prints the total inventory value.
}
  const
    StrLength = 20;                       {size of each string}
    Sentinel = 9999;                      {sentinel stock number}

  type
    StockRange = 1111..9999;              {range of stock numbers}
    StringType = string[StrLength];
```

```
    Book = record
             StockNum : StockRange;
             Author,
             Title   : StringType;
             Price : Real;
             Quantity : Integer
           end;  {Book}
    BookFile = file of Book;

  var
    Inventory : BookFile;                    {the new inventory file}
    OneBook : Book;                          {each book}
    InvValue : Real;                         {value of inventory}


  procedure ReadBook (var OneBook {output} : Book);
  {
    Reads a book from the keyboard into OneBook.
    Pre : None
    Post: Data are read from the keyboard into each field of the
          record represented by parameter OneBook.
  }

  begin  {ReadBook}
    with OneBook do
      begin
        Write ('Stock number> ');    ReadLn (StockNum);
        if StockNum <> Sentinel then
          begin
            Write ('Author> ');
            ReadLn (Author);
            Write ('Title> ');
            ReadLn (Title);
            Write ('Price $');
            ReadLn (Price);
            Write ('Quantity> ');
            ReadLn (Quantity)
          end {if}
      end; {with}
    WriteLn
  end;  {ReadBook}


begin  {BookInventory}
  Assign (Inventory, 'INVEN.DAT');
  Rewrite (Inventory);          {Prepare Inventory for output}
  InvValue := 0.0;              {Initialize inventory value}

  {Read and copy each book until done.}
  WriteLn ('Enter the data requested for each book.');
  WriteLn ('Enter a stock number of 9999 when done.');
  ReadBook (OneBook);                             {Read first book}
  while OneBook.StockNum <> Sentinel do
    begin
      Write (Inventory, OneBook);    {Copy the book to Inventory}
      InvValue := InvValue + OneBook.Price * OneBook.Quantity;
      ReadBook (OneBook)                          {Read next book}
    end;  {while}

  Write (Inventory, OneBook);     {write sentinel record to file}
  Close (Inventory);
  {Print inventory value.}
```

```
  WriteLn ('Inventory value is $', InvValue :4:2)
end. {BookInventory}
```

Output Window

```
Enter the data requested for each book.
Enter a stock number of 9999 when done.
Stock Number> 1234
Author> Robert Ludlum
Title> The Parsifal Mosaic
Price $17.95
Quantity> 10

Stock Number> 7654
Author> Blaise Pascal
Title> Pascal Made Easy
Price $50.00
Quantity> 1

Stock Number> 9999

Inventory value is $229.50
```

The binary file created when the program in Fig. 14.9 is run is shown next. The last record serves as a sentinel. The `StockNum` field (value is `9999`) is the only field of the sentinel record that has its value defined.

File Inventory

1234	7654	9999
Robert Ludlum	Blaise Pascal	?
The Parsifal Mosaic	Pascal Made Easy	?
17.95	50.00	?
10	1	?

Exercises for Section 14.4

Self-Check

1. Assume a real number uses four bytes and an integer uses two bytes. How many bytes are processed when a component of file `Inventory` is read or written? Answer the same question for file `Employee` in Fig. 14.7.
2. Why does it not matter that some of the fields of the sentinel record are not defined? Under what circumstances might this present a problem?
3. Write all the declarations necessary for a file whose components are student records, where each record consists of a student ID number and an array of five scores. Write a loop that reads each student's record from the file and displays the student's ID number and first score.
4. Redo exercise 3 assuming that there are ten students and each student record is an element of the array `Class`, which is stored as the only component of a binary file.

Programming

1. Write a procedure that resets file `Inventory` and displays each inventory record on the screen. Call procedure `WriteOneRecord` to display each record.
2. Write procedure `WriteOneRecord`.

14.5 File Merge Illustrated

Like most data structures, a file frequently needs to be modified or updated after it has been created. You may want to modify one or more fields of an existing record, delete a record, insert a new record, or simply display the current field values for a record.

Unlike a text file, a binary file cannot be modified with an editor. Instead, we must create a new file whose records are based on the original file. To do this, we must read each existing record, perhaps modify it, and then write it to the new file.

One kind of update operation is a *file merge*. In a file merge, we combine two files of the same type into a third file. If the records in the two original files are ordered according to a key field, the records in the new file must also be in order by key field.

Case Study: Merging Files

Problem

Whenever our bookstore receives a new shipment of books, a file (`Update`) is prepared that describes the new shipment. To keep our inventory file (`Inventory`) up to date, we need a program to combine or merge the information on these two files, assuming the records on both files are the same type (`Book`).

Design Overview

Merging two files is a common data-processing operation. To perform this task efficiently (and most other tasks involving sequential files), we assume that the records on both files are in order by stock number. We also reserve the largest stock number (9999) as a special sentinel record always found at the end of each file.

Our task is to create a third file (`NewInven`) that contains all data appearing on the two existing files. If a stock number appears on only one of the files, then its corresponding record will be copied directly to `NewInven`. If a stock number appears on both files, then the data from file `Update` will be copied to `NewInven`, because that is the most recent information; however, the `Quantity` field of the record written to `NewInven` must be the sum of both `Quantity` fields (the quantity shipped plus the quantity on hand). The records on the new file must be in order by stock number.

Figure 14.10 illustrates the result of merging two small sample files. For simplicity, only the `Stock` and `Quantity` fields of all three files are shown. The only stock numbers appearing on all three files are 4234 and the sentinel stock

Figure 14.10 Sample File Merge Operation

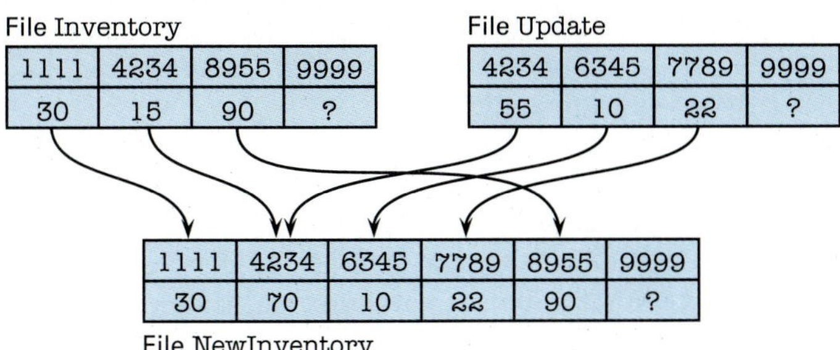

number (9999). The original inventory file (`Inventory`) and the update file (`Update`) each contains four records (including the sentinel); the new inventory file (`NewInven`) contains six records (including the sentinel), in order by stock number. Records 1111 and 8955 are copied directly from file `Inventory`; records 6345 and 7789 are copied directly from file `Update`; and record 4234 is a combination of the data on files `Inventory` and `Update`.

The data requirements and algorithm for a `Merge` procedure are described next. Because we are writing a procedure, the type declarations, which should appear in the main program, would be similar to those in Fig. 14.9.

Data Requirements

Problem Inputs

The current inventory file (`Inventory : BookFile`)
The file of new books received (`Update : BookFile`)

Problem Outputs

The new inventory file (`NewInven : BookFile`)

Local Variables

The current record from `Inventory` (`InvenBook : Book`)
The current record from `Update` (`UpdateBook : Book`)

Initial Algorithm

1. Prepare files `Inventory` and `Update` for input and file `NewInven` for output.
2. Read the first record from `Inventory` into `InvenBook` and from `Update` into `UpdateBook`.
3. Copy all records that appear on only one input file to `NewInven`. If a record appears on both input files, sum both `Quantity` values before copying record `UpdateBook` to `NewInven`.

Refinements and Program Structure

Step 3 compares each pair of records stored in `InvenBook` and `UpdateBook`. Because the records on file `NewInven` must be in order by stock number, the record with the smaller stock number is written to `NewInven`. Another record is then read from the file containing the record just written, and the comparison process is repeated. If the stock numbers of `UpdateBook` and `InvenBook` are the same (a record appears on both files), the new value of `UpdateBook.Quantity` is computed, the modified record is written to `NewInven`, and the next records are read from both input files.

Step 3 Refinement

```
3.1 while there are more records to copy do
      3.2 if InvenBook.StockNum < UpdateBook.StockNum then
            3.3 Write InvenBook to NewInven and read the next
                record of Inventory into InvenBook.
          else if InvenBook.StockNum > UpdateBook.StockNum then
            3.4 Write UpdateBook to NewInven and read the next
                record of Update into UpdateBook.
          else
            3.5 Modify the Quantity field of UpdateBook, write
                UpdateBook to NewInven, and read the next record
                from Inventory and Update.
3.6 Write the sentinel record to NewInven.
```

Let's trace this step assuming `InvenBook` and `UpdateBook` initially contain the first file records.

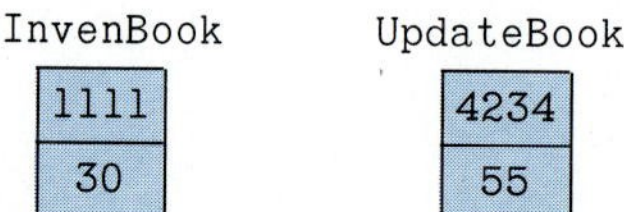

Because `1111` is less than `4234`, record `InvenBook` is copied to file `NewInven` (step 3.3) and the next record is read into `InvenBook`.

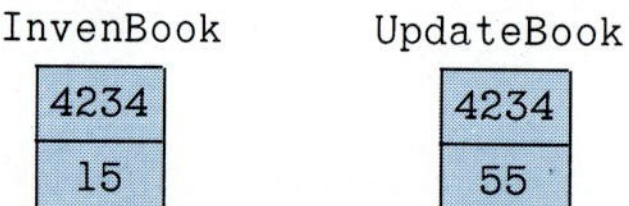

Now the stock numbers are equal, so the quantity fields are summed (step 3.5), the new record with stock number `4234` is written to file `NewInven`, and the next records are read into `InvenBook` and `UpdateBook`.

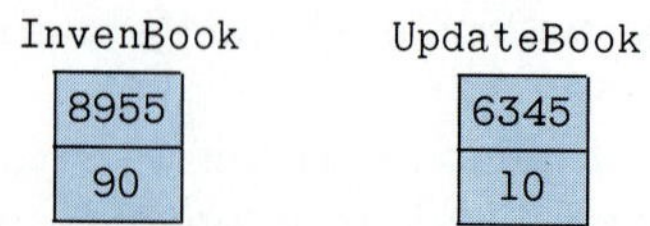

This time the record in `UpdateBook` is copied to `NewInven` (step 3.4), the next record is read into `UpdateBook`, and the merge continues.

What happens when the end of one input file is reached? The stock number for the current record of that file will be `9999` (the maximum), so each record read from the other input file will be copied directly to file `NewInven`. When

Figure 14.11 Structure Chart for Procedure Merge

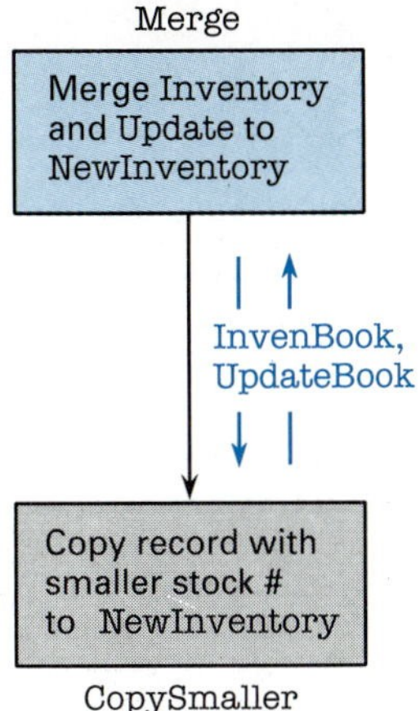

the ends of both input files are reached, the `while` loop is exited and the sentinel record is written to file `NewInven` (step 3.6).

Procedure `CopySmaller` implements step 3.2 above. The structure chart for the `Merge` procedure is shown in Fig. 14.11.

Coding Procedure Merge

Procedure `Merge` is shown in Fig. 14.12. The only output displayed on the screen as a result of executing procedure `Merge` is the message `File merge completed`. After the procedure's execution, you may want to echo print file `NewInven`. You could do this by resetting file `NewInven` and then writing individual fields of each record to the screen. Once you are certain file `NewInven` is correct, you can use an operating system command to rename it `Inventory`. You could then use `Inventory` as the input inventory file and merge it with another `Update` file at a later time.

Figure 14.12 Procedure Merge

```
procedure Merge (var Inventory, Update {input} : BookFile;
                 var NewInven {output} : BookFile);
{
  Merges the data on files Inventory and Update to file NewInven.
  Pre : Files Inventory and Update are existing files ordered by
        stock number and ending with a sentinel stock number.
  Post: Each record appearing in only Inventory or Update
        is copied to NewInventory. If a stock number appears in
        both files, the Quantity fields are summed and the
        remaining fields are copied from Update. File NewInven
        is in order by stock number and ends with the sentinel.
}
  var
    InvenBook,             {current record of file Inventory}
```

Case Study: Merging Files, continued

```
    UpdateBook : Book;      {current record of file Update}

  procedure CopySmaller (var InvenBook,
                             UpdateBook {input/output} : Book;
                         var Inventory, Update, {input}
                             NewInventory {output} : BookFile);
  {
   Writes the next record to file NewInven using data in
   InvenBook and UpdateBook. Also reads a new record from
   Inventory into InvenBook or from Update into UpdateBook or both
   to replace the record(s) that were written.
   Pre : InvenBook and UpdateBook are defined, and files
         Inventory and Update are opened for input and file
         NewInven is opened for output.
   Post: The record with the smaller StockNum field is written to
         NewInven and new data are read into that record. If both
         records have the same StockNum value, the Quantity fields
         are summed in UpdateBook, the modified record is written,
         and new records are read from both input files.
  }
  begin  {CopySmaller}
    if InvenBook.StockNum < UpdateBook.StockNum then
      begin {<}
        Write (NewInven, InvenBook);       {copy InvenBook}
        Read (Inventory, InvenBook)
      end  {<}
    else if InvenBook.StockNum > UpdateBook.StockNum then
      begin {>}
        Write (NewInven, UpdateBook);      {copy UpdateBook}
        Read (Update, UpdateBook)
      end {>}
    else
      begin {=}
        UpdateBook.Quantity := UpdateBook.Quantity +
                               InvenBook.Quantity;
        Write (NewInven, UpdateBook);      {copy new UpdateBook}
        Read (Inventory, InvenBook);       {read both records}
        Read (Update, UpdateBook)
      end  {=}
  end;  {CopySmaller}


begin {Merge}
  Assign (Inventory, 'INVEN.DAT');
  Assign (UpDate   , 'UPDATE.DAT');
  Assign (NewInven , 'NEWINVEN.DAT');

  {Prepare Inventory and Update for input, NewInven for output.}
  Reset (Inventory);  Reset (Update);  Rewrite (NewInven);

  {Read the first record from Inventory and Update.}
  Read (Inventory, InvenBook);  Read(Update, UpdateBook);

  {Copy all records from file Inventory and Update to NewInven.}
  while (InvenBook.StockNum <> Sentinel) or
        (UpdateBook.StockNum <> Sentinel) do
    CopySmaller (InvenBook, UpdateBook, Inventory,
                 Update, NewInven);

  {Write the sentinel record to NewInven.}
  Write (NewInven, InvenBook);
```

```
  WriteLn ('File merge completed')
  Close (Inventory);
  Close (UpDate);
  Close (NewInven)
end;  {Merge}
```

You can adapt the merge procedure to perform other update operations. For example, you could merge a file that represents the daily sales of all books (file Sales) with file Inventory to generate an updated inventory file at the end of each day. If the quantity field of each record in file Sales is subtracted from the quantity field of the corresponding record in file Inventory, the difference would represent the quantity remaining in stock. You could even delete records whose quantity fields became negative or zero by simply not copying such records to NewInven.

PROGRAM STYLE

Analysis of the Merge Procedure

A number of questions arise about the merge procedure shown in Fig. 14.12. For example, what happens if an input file is empty or contains only the sentinel record? Because procedure Merge always reads at least one record, an execution error will occur if either input file is empty. If a file contains only the sentinel record, then only the sentinel record will be read from that file, and all the records in the other file will be copied directly to file NewInven. If both input files contain only the sentinel record, the while loop will be exited immediately, and only the sentinel record will be copied to file NewInven after loop exit.

Finally, we must ask about the efficiency of the merge procedure when the end of one file is reached much sooner than the other. This imbalance would result in the stock number 9999 being repeatedly compared to the stock numbers on the file that is not yet finished. It would be more efficient to exit the while loop when the end of one file is reached, then copy all remaining records on the other file directly to file NewInven. This modification is left as an exercise at the end of this section.

Testing

To test the merge procedure, provide files that contain only the sentinel record as well as files with one or more actual records. Make sure that the merge procedure works properly regardless of which of the two input files has all its records processed first. Also make sure that there is exactly one sentinel record on the merged file.

Exercises for Section 14.5

Self-Check

1. In procedure `Merge`, what three important assumptions are made about the two files that are merged? Must the two input files have the same number of records?
2. What happens if a record from one input file has the same stock number as a record from the other input file? What happens if one input file has two consecutive records with the same stock number?

Programming

1. Modify procedure `Merge` assuming that its input files do not contain a sentinel record. In this case, there should not be a sentinel record on the merged file. Exit from the merge loop when the end of either file is reached and then copy the remaining records from the unfinished file.

14.6 Searching a Data Base

Computerized matching of data against a file of records is becoming a common practice. For example, many real estate companies maintain a large file of property listings; a realtor can process the file to locate desirable properties for a client. Similarly, computerized dating services maintain a file of clients from which compatible matches can be made.

These large files of data are called *data bases*. In this section we will write a program that searches a data base to find all records that match a proposed set of requirements.

Case Study: Data Base Inquiry

Problem

One reason for storing the bookstore inventory as a computer file is to facilitate answering questions regarding that data base. Some questions of interest might be

- What books by Robert Ludlum are in stock?
- What books in the price range $5.95 to $8.00 are in stock?
- What is the stock number of the book *Pascal Made Easy* and how many copies are in stock?
- What books costing more than $25 are in stock in quantities greater than 10?

These questions and others can be answered if we know the correct way to ask them.

Design Overview

A data base inquiry program has two phases: setting the search parameters and searching for records that satisfy the parameters. In our program, we will assume that all the record fields can be involved in the search. The program user must enter low and high bounds for each field. Let's illustrate how we might set the search parameters to answer this question:

> What are the books by Tennyson that cost less than $11 and for which two or more copies are in stock?

Assuming that there are never more than 5,000 copies of a book in stock and that the price of any book does not exceed $1,000, we can use this sample dialogue to set the search parameters.

```
Enter the low bound for stock number or 1111: 1111
Enter the high bound for stock number or 9999: 9999
Enter the low bound for author name or AAA: Tennyson
Enter the high bound for author name or zzz: Tennyson
Enter the low bound for title or AAA: AAA
Enter the high bound for title or zzz: zzz
Enter the low bound for price or $0: $0
Enter the high bound for price or $1000: $10.99
Enter the low bound for quantity or 0: 2
Enter the high bound for quantity or 5000: 5000
```

Data Requirements

Problem Inputs

The search parameter bounds (`Params : SearchParams`)
The inventory file (`Inventory : BookFile`)

Problem Outputs

All books that satisfy the search parameters

Initial Algorithm

1. Prepare file `Inventory` for input.
2. Enter the search parameters.
3. Display all books that match the parameters.

Refinements and Program Structure

To simplify parameter passing between the procedures that implement steps 1 and 2, we store the search parameters in record variable `Params` (type `SearchParams`). The structure chart for the data base inquiry problem is shown in Fig. 14.13.

Coding the Main Program

The main program is shown in Fig. 14.14.

Coding the Procedures

Procedure `EnterParams` is left as an exercise at the end of this section. Procedure `DisplayMatch` must examine each file record with a stock number between the low and high bounds for stock numbers. If a record satisfies the search parameters, it is displayed. `DisplayMatch` should also print a message if no

Figure 14.13 Structure Chart for Data Base Inquiry Problem

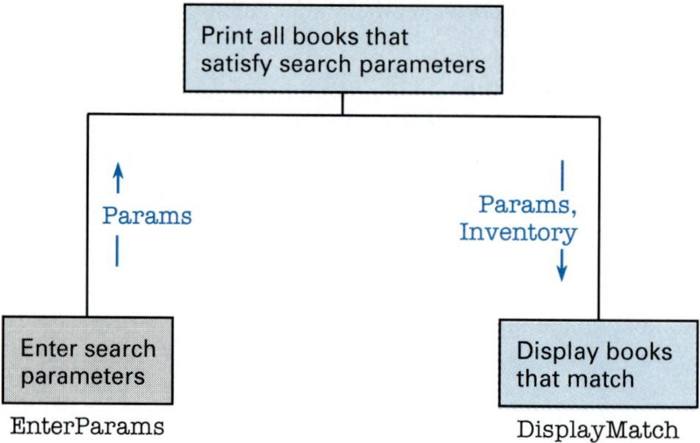

Figure 14.14 Main Program for Data Base Inquiry Problem

```
program Inquire;
{
  Prints all books that satisfy the search parameters specified
  by the program user.
}

  const
    StrLength = 20;                         {size of each string}
    MaxQuantity = 5000;                     {maximum quantity}
    MaxPrice = 1000.00;                     {maximum book price}
    MinStock = 1111;                        {minimum stock number}
    MaxStock = 9999;                        {maximum stock number}

  type
    StringType = string[StrLength];
    StockRange = MinStock..MaxStock;
    Book = record
             StockNum : StockRange;     {four digit stock number}
             Author,
             Title   : StringType;
             Price : Real;
             Quantity : Integer
           end;  {Book}

    BookFile = file of Book;

    SearchParams = record             {search parameter bounds}
                     LowStock, HighStock : StockRange;
                     LowAuthor, HighAuthor,
                     LowTitle, HighTitle    : StringType;
                     LowPrice, HighPrice : Real;
                     LowQuant, HighQuant : Integer
                   end; {SearchParams}
  var
    Inventory : BookFile;                   {the inventory file}
    Params : SearchParams;                  {the search parameters}
```

```
  procedure EnterParams (var Params {output} : SearchParams);
  {
   Enters the search parameters and validates them.
   Pre : None
   Post: Returns the low bound and high bound for each search
         parameter though Params. The low bound for a parameter
         must be <= the high bound and both bounds must be in
         range.
  }
  begin  {EnterParams stub}
    WriteLn ('Procedure EnterParams entered.')
  end;  {EnterParams}

  procedure DisplayMatch (var Inventory {input} : BookFile;
                          Params {input} : SearchParams);
  {
   Displays all records of Inventory that satisfy search
   parameters.
   Pre : File Inventory is opened for input and Params is defined.
   Post: An inventory record is displayed if its field values are
         within the bounds specified by record Params.
  }
  begin  {DisplayMatch}
    WriteLn ('Procedure DisplayMatch entered.')
  end;  {DisplayMatch}


begin  {Inquire}
  Assign (Inventory, 'INVEN.DAT');
  Reset (Inventory);

  {Enter the search parameters.}
  EnterParams (Params);

  {Display all books that match the search parameters.}
  DisplayMatch (Inventory, Params);
  Close (Inventory)
end. {Inquire}
```

---

matches are found. The local variables and algorithm for procedure `DisplayMatch` follow.

Local Variables for DisplayMatch

The current book (`NextBook : Book`)
A program flag indicating whether or not there are any matches (`NoMatches : Boolean`)

Algorithm for DisplayMatch

1. Advance to the first record whose stock number is within range.
2. Initialize `NoMatches` to `True`.
3. `while` the current stock number is still in range `do`
   `begin`
      4. `If` the search parameters match `then`

Figure 14.15 Structure Chart for DisplayMatch

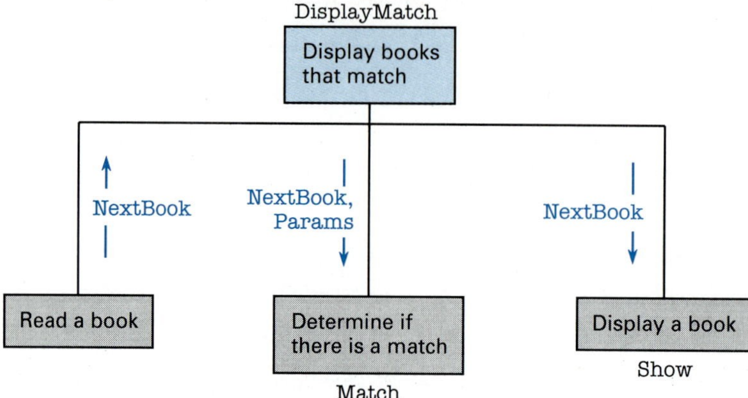

5. Display the book and set `NoMatches` to `False`.
6. Read the next book record.

`end`

7. `if` there are no matches `then`
   8. Print a `no books available` message

The structure chart for `DisplayMatch` is shown in Fig. 14.15. The Boolean function `Match` implements step 3; procedure `Show` implements step 4. The program is shown in Fig. 14.16.

Figure 14.16 Procedure DisplayMatch

```
procedure DisplayMatch (var Inventory {input} : BookFile;
                        Params {input} : SearchParams);
{
  Displays all records of Inventory that satisfy search
  parameters.
  Pre : File Inventory is opened for input and Params is defined.
  Post: An inventory record is displayed if its field values are
        within the bounds specified by record Params.
}
  var
    NextBook : Book;       {the current record}
    NoMatches : Boolean;   {indicates if there were any matches}


  function Match (NextBook : Book;
                  Params : SearchParams) : Boolean;
  {
   Determines whether record NextBook satisfies all search
   parameters.
   Pre : NextBook and Params are defined.
   Post: Returns True if all parameters are matched; otherwise,
         returns False.
  }
```

```
    var
      Matched : Boolean;                    {local Boolean flag}

  begin  {Match}
    with Params do
      begin
        Matched := (LowAuthor <= NextBook.Author)
                    and (NextBook.Author <= HighAuthor);
        Matched := Matched and (LowTitle <= NextBook.Title)
                     and (NextBook.Title <= HighTitle);
        Matched := Matched and (LowPrice <= NextBook.Price)
                     and (NextBook.Price <= HighPrice);
        Matched := Matched and (LowQuant <= NextBook.Quantity)
                     and (NextBook.Quantity <= HighQuant)
      end;  {with}

    {Define function result.}
    Match := Matched
  end;  {Match}

  procedure Show (NextBook {input} : Book);
  {
    Displays each field of NextBook at the terminal. Leaves a
    line space after each book.
    Pre : NextBook is defined.
    Post: All fields of NextBook are displayed.
  }
  begin  {Show stub}
    WriteLn ('Procedure Show entered.');
    WriteLn ('Stock number is ', NextBook.StockNum :1)
  end;  {Show}


begin  {DisplayMatch}
  {
   Advance to first record with a stock number greater than
   or equal to the lower bound.
  }
  Read (Inventory, NextBook);
  while not EOF(Inventory) and
       (Params.LowStock > NextBook.StockNum) do
    Read (Inventory, NextBook);

  {assert: end of file reached or NextBook.StockNum in range}
  {Display each book that satisfies the search parameters.}
  NoMatches := True;            {assume no matches to start}
  WriteLn ('Books that satisfy the search parameters follow.');
  while (NextBook.StockNum <= Params.HighStock)
          and not EOF(Inventory) do
    {invariant:
        each record that matches the parameters is displayed and
        no record with stock number > Params.HighStock was
        processed and the file position pointer has not passed
        the end of file.
    }
    begin
      if Match(NextBook, Params) then
        begin
          NoMatches := False;       {signal a match}
          Show (NextBook)        {print matched record}
        end; {if}
```

Case Study: Data Base Inquiry, continued

```
      Read (Inventory, NextBook)     {read the next record}
    end;  {while}

  {assert: all records in range searched or at end of file}
  if NoMatches then
    WriteLn ('Sorry, no books are available.')
end;  {DisplayMatch}
```

In function Match, a local Boolean variable, Matched, indicates whether or not each search parameter is satisfied. Four assignment statements—one for each parameter except stock number—assign a value to Matched. If a search parameter is not satisfied, its corresponding assignment statement sets Matched to False. Because Matched is "anded" with the result of each parameter test, once Matched is set to False, it remains False. Consequently, for the function result to be True, NextBook must satisfy all search parameters.

Testing

Before you can test the data base program, you have to create a binary file using program BookInventory (see Fig. 14.9). Make sure you provide search requests that are not satisfied by any file records as well as requests that are. If you specify the maximum range for each search parameter, the program should display all records of the binary file. After a request is satisfied, verify that you can eliminate one or more of the records displayed by narrowing the search parameters.

Exercises for Section 14.6

Self-Check

1. Write the search parameters needed to answer the questions listed at the beginning of this section.
2. Which procedure or function determines whether a particular record matches the search parameters? What procedure or function displays each record that matches the search parameters?
3. How does Boolean variable Matched work in function Match? Why is it not necessary to test field StockNum in function Match?

Programming

1. Write procedures EnterParams and Show described in the data base inquiry problem.

14.7 Direct-Access Files

The files processed so far in this chapter have been sequential files. This means that each operation is performed on every file component and that the components are processed in order, starting with the first one. Sequential files are perfectly adequate whenever a file-processing operation involves most of the components in a file. However, if we want to modify only a few components in a large file, it is wasteful and time-consuming to have to process every component in the file.

For this reason, Turbo Pascal, but not standard Pascal, provides operators that enable *direct access* or *random access* to a file. Direct access means that a program can access any file component at any time. A direct-access file is analogous to a large array stored on disk in that the components can be accessed in either sequential order or arbitrary order. With direct access, we can intermix read and write operations on the same file. With sequential access, we can either read all the components of a file or write all its components.

We cannot use an editor program to create a direct-access file. We must write a program that reads the data for a direct-access file from a text file (or the keyboard), stores this data in memory, and copies the data from memory to the direct-access file. To access a particular file component, we must first move the file-position pointer to that component. Once the file-position pointer has been moved, a read or write operation can be performed.

In Turbo Pascal, direct access is supported for any binary file but not for text files. If binary file `Inventory` (see Fig. 14.9) has been opened for input, the procedure call statement

```
Seek (Inventory, 9);
```

advances the file-position pointer for `Inventory` to record number `9`. This is actually the tenth record, because the first record has record number `0`. Function `FileSize` returns the number of records in a binary file. If there are twenty records in file `Inventory` (record numbers `0` through `19`), the function designator `FileSize(Inventory)` returns `20`.

■ Example 14.5

Procedure `UpdateBook` in Fig. 14.17 updates the record of file `Inventory` selected by parameter `RecNum`. The condition

```
(RecNum >= 0) and (RecNum < FileSize(Inventory))
```

is true if `RecNum` is in range. The statement

```
Seek (Inventory, RecNum);
```

moves the file-position pointer to record number `RecNum` just before the `Read` operation and just before the `Write` operation. It is necessary to execute this statement twice because the `Read` operation advances the file-position pointer to record `RecNum + 1`. ■

Figure 14.17 Procedure UpdateBook in Turbo Pascal

```
procedure UpdateBook (var Inventory {input/output} : BookFile;
                      RecNum,
                      Sales {input} : Integer);
{
  Updates record RecNum of file Inventory by subtracting the
  amount sold (Sales) from the Quantity field.
```

```
  Pre : Inventory is opened for input (using Reset)
        and RecNum and Sales are defined.
  Post: Quantity field of record RecNum is decremented by Sales.
}
  var
    OneBook : Book;      {record being updated}

begin {UpdateBook}
  if (RecNum >= 0) and (RecNum < FileSize(Inventory)) then
    begin
      Seek (Inventory, RecNum);        {Move to record RecNum}
      Read (Inventory, OneBook);
      OneBook.Quantity := OneBook.Quantity - Sales;   {Update}
      Seek (Inventory, RecNum);      {Return to record RecNum}
      Write (Inventory, OneBook)        {Write updated record}
    end
  else
    WriteLn ('Record number is out of range.')
end; {UpdateBook}
```

SYNTAX DISPLAY

Seek Procedure

Form: `Seek` (*iofile*, *recnum*)
Example: `Seek (Inventory, 10)`
Interpretation: The file-position pointer for binary file *iofile* is moved to file component number *recnum*, where the first component has number `0`. Unpredictable results will occur if the value of *recnum* is less than `0` or greater than *n* for a file of *n* components. It is not advisable to perform two `Seek` operations without an intervening `Read` or `Write`.
Note: The file *iofile* must have been opened for input using the `Reset` procedure, prior to the first call to the `Seek` procedure. `Seek` is not part of standard Pascal.

SYNTAX DISPLAY

FileSize Function

Form: `FileSize(`*iofile*`)`
Example: `FileSize(Inventory)`
Interpretation: The `FileSize` function returns the number of components in binary file *iofile*.
Note: The file *iofile* must have been opened for input using the `Reset` procedure. `FileSize` is not part of standard Pascal.

Appending a Record in Turbo Pascal

In Turbo Pascal, the function designator `FileSize(Inventory)` returns the number of records in file `Inventory`. The statements

```
Seek (Inventory, FileSize(Inventory));
Write (Inventory, NewBook)
```

can be used to append a new record, NewBook, to the end of file Inventory. If there are n records in file Inventory, function FileSize returns n. Procedure Seek advances the file-position pointer to record number n or just past the last record (record number $n-1$) in the current file. Procedure Write then writes NewBook to the end of the file.

14.8 Common Programming Errors

File processing in any programming language tends to be difficult to master, and Pascal is no exception. Remember to declare a file variable for each file you process (except Input or Output). All file types (except Text) must be declared.

Do not forget to prepare a file for input or output using the Assign procedure, followed by either the Reset or Rewrite procedure (except for system files Input and Output). If you rewrite an existing file, the data in that file will be lost. If you forget to close a file that was open for output, part of the data written to that file may be lost. Make sure you do not inadvertently place the Reset or Rewrite statement in a loop. If you do, a Read operation in the loop will repeatedly read the first file component; a Write operation in the loop will repeatedly write the first file component.

You can use the Read or ReadLn procedure only after you have prepared a file for input. Similarly, you can use the Write or WriteLn procedure only after you have prepared a file for output. Be sure to specify the file name as the first procedure parameter; otherwise, the system file Input or Output is assumed. An attempt to read beyond end of file error occurs if a Read operation is performed when the file-position pointer for a file has passed the last file component. When you are using the EOF function to control a loop that is reading data from a file, don't forget to pass the file name to function EOF.

You can perform a number of operations with text files that you cannot perform with binary files, because binary files are not segmented into lines. You cannot use the EOLN function and ReadLn and WriteLn procedures with binary files. Also, you cannot create or modify a binary file using an editor program. A binary file must be created by running a program before it can be used.

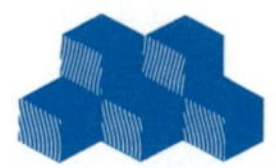

Chapter Review

The components of a file can be any simple or structured type except for another file type. The file type Text is predefined. Its components are the Pascal characters and a special character, <eoln>. The EOLN function can test for an <eoln>, and the WriteLn statement places one in a text file. If an <eoln> is read into a type Char variable, it is stored as a blank character.

When you process text files, sequences of characters are transferred between main memory and disk storage. The data type of a variable in an input list must be Char,

Integer, Real, a string type, or a subrange of Char or Integer. The data type of an expression in an output list must be Char, Integer, Real, Boolean, a string type, or a subrange of Char or Integer. Structured variables cannot appear in an input list or an output list for a text file.

In this chapter, you learned how to declare and manipulate binary files whose components may be any simple or structured type (except for another file type). We created a file of records and merged two files of records into a third file. We also searched a data base to retrieve file records that matched a specified set of search parameters.

Binary files do have an advantage in that an entire file component can be transferred between a binary file and a variable in main memory. The variable involved in the data transfer must be the same type as the components of the binary file.

Finally, we discussed Turbo Pascal procedures that permit direct access to files. We also showed you how to append a component to the end of a file.

New Pascal Constructs

The Pascal constructs introduced in this chapter are summarized in Table 14.1.

Table 14.1 Summary of New Pascal Constructs

Construct	Effect
File-Type Declaration	

`type`
`  DigitFile = file of Integer;`
 	
`var`
`  MoreDigits : DigitFile;`
`  MoreChars : Text;`
`  I : Integer;`
`  NextCh : Char;`
	Declares a file type DigitFile whose components are integers.
	MoreDigits is a file of type DigitFile.
	MoreChars is a file of type Text.

Assign Procedure	
`Assign (MoreDigits, 'B:NUM.DAT');`	File variable MoreDigits is associated with the disk file B:NUM.DAT.
`Assign (MoreChars, '');`	File variable MoreChars is associated with system file Output.
Reset and Rewrite Procedures	
`Reset (MoreDigits).` `Rewrite (MoreChars);`	MoreDigits is prepared for input. MoreChars is prepared for output.
Read and Write Procedures	
`Read (MoreDigits, I);` `WriteLn (MoreChars, 'number: ', I)`	The next integer is read from file MoreDigits into variable I (type Integer). A sequence of characters representing a string and the value of I are written to file MoreChars.

Table 14.1 *continued*

Construct	Effect

EOF Function
`while not EOF(MoreDigits) do`
`  begin`
`    Read (MoreDigits, I);`
`    WriteLn (MoreChars, I)`
`  end {while}`
	Every integer value on file `MoreDigits` is written as a sequence of characters on a separate line of file `MoreChars`.

EOLN Function
`Reset (MoreChars);`
`while not EOLN(MoreChars) do`
`  begin`
`    Read (MoreChars, NextCh);`
`    Write (NextCh)`
`  end {while}`
	File `MoreChars` is prepared for input. Each character on the current line of file `MoreChars` is read into `NextCh` and displayed on the screen.

Seek Procedure `Seek (MoreDigits, 5);`	Positions the file-position pointer to the sixth component of binary file `MoreDigits`.
FileSize Function `FileSize (MoreDigits);`	Returns the number of components stored in binary file `MoreDigits`.
Close Procedure `Close (MoreDigits);`	Closes the disk file associated with file variable `MoreDigits`.

✓ Quick-Check Exercises

1. What data types can be read or written to a text file?
2. What data types can be read or written to a binary file?
3. Under what circumstances can a file variable not appear in the variable declarations? Under what circumstances can a file type not appear in the type declarations?
4. When is it appropriate to pass a file as a value parameter to a procedure?
5. Comment on the correctness of this statement: It is more efficient to use a text file because the computer knows that each component is a single character that can be copied into a single byte of main memory; with a binary file, however, the size of the components may vary.
6. What limits the number of records that can be written to a file?
7. What limits the number of records that can be read from a file? How do you know when you have read them all?
8. What happens if the `Reset` operation is performed on a file that has just been created in a program? What happens if the `Rewrite` operation is performed on the same file?

Answers to Quick-Check Exercises

1. A string type or any of the standard data types (or a subrange thereof) except type Boolean can be read; any of the standard data types (or a subrange thereof) plus strings can be written.
2. The file's component type, which is any simple or structured type that does not have a file type as one of its constituents.
3. When the file is system file `Input` or `Output`. When the file type is type `Text`.
4. Never
5. The statement is not correct. It is true that two binary files may have components of different sizes, but the components of a particular file must all be the same data type and the same size. This size can be determined from the type declarations. Because no data conversions are necessary when you use binary files, binary files are more efficient than text files.
6. The only limit is the available space on disk.
7. The number of records that were written to the file when it was created. Use the `EOF` function to test for the end-of-file marker.
8. `Reset` prepares the file for input so we can echo print it if we want to check the records that were written. `Rewrite` causes the data in the file to be lost.

Review Questions

1. What are three advantages to using files for input and output as opposed to the standard input (keyboard) and output (screen)?
2. Where are files stored?
3. Modify procedure `CopyFile` to write data to both the file `OutFile` and the system file `Output`.
4. Consider an `EmpStat` file (type `Text`) that contains records for up to fifteen employees. The data for each employee consist of the employee's name (maximum length, twenty characters), social security number (maximum length, eleven characters), gross pay for the week (real), taxes deducted (real), and the net pay (real) for the week. Each data item is on a separate line of file `EmpStat`. Write a program called `PayReport`, which will create a text file `ReportFile` with the heading line

   ```
   NAME                SOC.SEC.NUM          GROSS      TAXES      NET
   ```

   followed by two blank lines, then the pertinent information under each column heading. `ReportFile` should contain up to eighteen lines of information after `PayReport` is executed.
5. What is a scratch file?
6. What are the characteristics of a binary file?
7. Imagine for a moment that you are a college professor who uses a computerized system to maintain student records. Write the type and variable declaration for a file that will consist of multiple records of type `StudentStats`. The statistics kept on each student are the `GPA`, `Major`, `Address` (consisting of `Name`, `StreetAddress`, `City`, `State`, and `ZipCode`), and `ClassSchedule` (consisting of up to six records of `Class`, each containing `Description`, `Time`, and `Days` fields). Use whatever variable types are appropriate for each field.

Programming Projects

1. Assume you have a file of records, each containing a person's last name, first name, birth date, and sex. Create a new file of records containing only first names and sex.

Also print out the complete name of every person whose last name begins with the letter A, C, F, or P through Z and who was born in a month beginning with the letter J.

2. Create separate files of saleswomen and salesmen in your furniture store. For each employee on these files, include an employee number (four digits), a name, and a salary. Each file should be in order by employee number. Merge these two files into a third file that also has a gender field containing one of the values in the type (`Female, Male`). After the file merge operation, find the average salary for all employees. Then search the new file and print a list of all female employees earning more than the average salary and a separate list of all male employees earning more than the average. Hint: You will have to search the new file once for each list.
3. Write a procedure that will merge the contents of three sorted files by ID number and write the merged data to an output file. The parameters to the procedure will be the three input files and the one output file. Data will be of the form

```
Data = record
         ID : Integer;
         Name : StringType;
         Length : Integer;
         Salary : Real
       end;
```

Assume there is no sentinel record. Test your procedure with some sample data.

4. Cooking recipes can be stored on a computer and, with the use of files, can be quickly referenced.

a. Write a procedure that will create a text file of recipes from information entered at the terminal. The format of the data to be stored is

(1) recipe type (`Dessert`, `Meat`, etc.)
(2) subtype (for `Dessert`, use `Cake`, `Pie`, or `Brownies`)
(3) name (for cake, `German Chocolate`)
(4) number of lines in the recipe to follow
(5) the actual recipe

Items 1, 2, 3, and 4 should be on separate lines.

b. Write a procedure that will accept as parameters a file and a record of search parameters that will cause all recipes of a type, all recipes of a subtype, or a specific recipe to be written.

5. College football teams need a service to keep track of records and vital statistics. Write a program that will maintain this information on a file. An update file will be "posted" weekly against the master file of all team statistics to date, and all the records will be updated. All of the information in both files will be stored in order by ID number. Each master record will contain the team's ID number; team name; number of games won, lost, and tied; total yards gained by the team's offense; total yards gained by the other teams against this one; total points scored by this team; and total points scored by the other teams against this one.

For this program, use the master file `Teams` and update `Teams` from file `Weekly`. Write the updated information to a file called `NewTeams`. In addition, each record of the weekly file should be echo printed. At the completion of processing the files, write a message indicating the number of weekly scores processed, the team that scored the most points, and the team with the most offensive yardage for this week.

6. Write a program that takes a master file of college football information and prints out teams that match a specified set of search parameters. The bounds on the search parameters could be presented in the format described in Section 14.6. Some infor-

mation you might want to print: all teams with a won/lost percentage in a certain range; all teams within a certain range of points scored or scored upon; all teams with a certain range of yardage gained or given up; all teams with a certain number of games won, tied, or lost. (Note: The won/lost percentage is calculated by dividing number of games won by total games played; ties count as half a game won.)

7. Write a program that updates a file of type `Inventory` (see Section 14.4). Your program should be able to modify an existing record, insert a new record, and delete an existing record. Assume that the update requests are in order by stock number and that they have the form

```
type
  ChangeKind = (Delete, Insert, Modify);
  UpdateReq = record
                case Change : ChangeKind of
                  Delete : (StockNumber : StockRange);
                  Insert : (NewBook : Book);
                  Modify : (ModBook : Book)
                end; {UpdateReq}
```

   Each update request should be read from a binary file. Only the stock number appears in an update request for a deletion. The new book record is supplied for a request to insert a record or to modify an existing record. Your program should also print an error message for invalid requests, such as an attempt to delete a record that does not exist, an attempt to insert a new record with the same stock number as an existing record, or an attempt to modify a record that does not exist.

8. Do project 4 from Chapter 12 using a direct-access data file in place of the array of records to house the store inventory. Your program should first create and initialize a direct-access binary file to house up to 100 inventory records (record numbers 0 to 99). Once the direct-access file has been initialized, the file containing the customers' purchases would then be processed, using the item product code as the record number to locate the appropriate inventory file record. Since the inventory is housed in a data file and is updated as each new purchase is made, it is not necessary to make another copy of the inventory file when all purchases have been processed.

   To initialize the direct-access data file, write 100 dummy records (records where each field value is some missing data code) to a new binary file. Then read a sequential version of the inventory file one record at a time and call `Seek` to determine its location in the direct-access file.

9. Do project 7 as a menu-driven program using a direct-access file to house the inventory data. Assume that the `Stocknumber` is used as the record number to access the inventory file. The subrange `Stockrange` should be redefined to be `0..99` (to avoid having 1000 record positions that are never used in the inventory file). Menu options to support are: creating a blank file, inserting records, updating records, deleting records, displaying selected records, displaying all active records.

   Since records cannot be physically deleted from the direct-access inventory file, a Boolean field (`DeletedRec`) should be added to each inventory record. Deleting a record then simply involves setting field `DeletedRec` to `True` and copying the modified record back to the inventory file. Likewise, adding a record involves setting the `DeletedRec` field to `False`, in addition to assigning values to each of the other fields.

15 Recursion

A recursive procedure or function is one that calls itself. This ability enables a recursive procedure to be repeated with different parameter values. You can use recursion as an alternative to iteration (looping). Generally, a recursive solution is less efficient, in terms of computer time, than an iterative one because of the overhead for the extra procedure calls. In many instances, however, the use of recursion enables us to specify a natural, simple solution to a problem that would otherwise be difficult to solve. For this reason, recursion is an important and powerful tool in problem solving and programming.

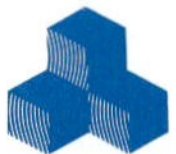

15.1 The Nature of Recursion

Problems that lend themselves to a recursive solution have the following characteristics:

- One or more simple cases of the problem (called *stopping cases*) have a simple, nonrecursive solution.
- The other cases of the problem can be reduced (using recursion) to problems that are closer to stopping cases.
- Eventually the problem can be reduced to stopping cases only, which are relatively easy to solve.

The recursive algorithms that we write generally consist of an `if` statement with this form:

```
if the stopping case is reached then
  Solve it
else
  Reduce the problem using recursion
```

Figure 15.1 illustrates this approach. Let's assume that for a particular problem of size N, we can split the problem into a problem of size 1, which we can solve (a stopping case), and a problem of size $N-1$. We can split the problem of size $N-1$ into another problem of size 1 and a problem of size $N-2$, which we can split further. If we split the problem N times, we end up with N problems of size 1, all of which we can solve.

Figure 15.1 Splitting a Problem into Smaller Problems

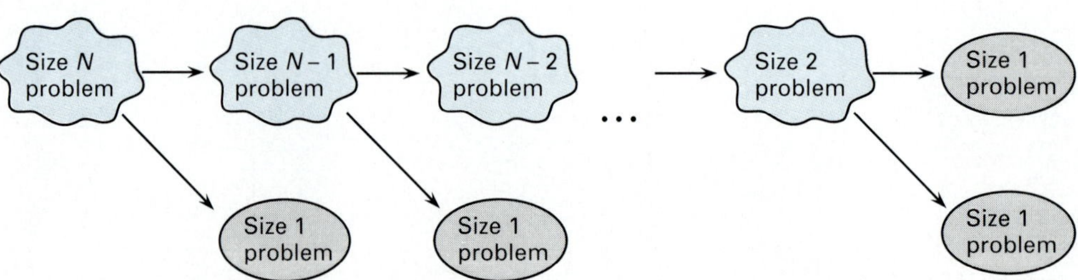

■ Example 15.1

Consider how we might solve the problem of multiplying 6 by 3, assuming that we know the addition tables but not the multiplication tables. The problem of multiplying 6 by 3 can be split into the two problems:

1. Multiply 6 by 2.
2. Add 6 to the result of problem 1.

Because we know the addition tables, we can solve problem 2 but not problem 1. Problem 1, however, is simpler than the original problem. We can split it into two problems, 1.1 and 1.2, leaving us three problems to solve, two of which are additions.

1.1 Multiply 6 by 1.
1.2 Add 6 to the result.

Even though we don't know the multiplication tables, we are familiar with the simple rule that, for any M, $M \times 1$ is M. By solving problem 1.1 (the answer is 6) and problem 1.2, we get the solution to problem 1 (the answer is 12). Solving problem 2 gives us the final answer, 18.

Figure 15.2 implements this approach to doing multiplication as the recursive Pascal function `Multiply` which returns the product, `M` × `N`, of its two arguments. The body of function `Multiply` implements the general form of a recursive algorithm shown earlier. The stopping case is reached when the condition `N = 1` is true. In this case, the statement

```
Multiply := M                          {stopping case}
```

executes, so the answer is `M`. If `N` is greater than `1`, the statement

```
Multiply := M + Multiply(M, N-1)       {recursive step}
```

executes, splitting the original problem into the two simpler problems:

1. Multiply `M` by `N-1`.
2. Add `M` to the result.

The first of these problems is solved by calling `Multiply` again with `N-1` as its second argument. If the new second argument is greater than `1`, there will be additional calls to function `Multiply`.

Figure 15.2 Recursive Function Multiply

```
function Multiply (M, N : Integer) : Integer;
{
  Performs multiplication using + operator.
  Pre : M and N are defined and N > 0.
  Post: Returns M * N
}
begin {Multiply}
  if N = 1 then
     Multiply := M                     {stopping case}
  else
     Multiply := M + Multiply(M, N-1)  {recursive step}
end; {Multiply}
```

Note the two different uses of the identifier `Multiply` in the recursive step in Fig. 15.2. The first one assigns a value to `Multiply` representing the function result, while the second calls the function recursively. ■

For now, you will have to take our word that function `Multiply` performs as desired. We will see how to trace the execution of a recursive function or procedure in the next section.

The next example illustrates how we might solve a difficult problem just by splitting it into smaller problems. You will see how to solve this problem after you have more experience using recursion.

■ Example 15.2

The Towers of Hanoi problem involves moving a specified number of disks that are all different sizes from one tower (or peg) to another. Legend has it that the world will come to an end when the problem is solved for sixty-four disks. In the version of the problem shown in Fig. 15.3, there are five disks (numbered 1 through 5) and three towers or pegs (lettered A, B, and C). The goal is to move the five disks from peg A to peg C subject to the following rules:

1. Only one disk may be moved at a time, and this disk must be the top disk on a peg.
2. A larger disk can never be placed on top of a smaller disk.

The stopping cases of the problem involve moving only one disk (for example, "move disk 2 from peg A to peg C"). Simpler problems than the original would be to move four disks subject to the conditions above, to move three disks, and so on. Therefore, we want to split the original five-disk problem into one or more problems involving fewer disks. Let's consider splitting the original problem into three problems:

1. Move four disks from peg A to peg B.
2. Move disk 5 from peg A to peg C.
3. Move four disks from peg B to peg C.

Step 1 moves all disks but the largest to tower B, an auxiliary tower not mentioned in the original problem. Step 2 moves the largest disk to the goal tower, tower C. Step 3 then moves the remaining disks from B to the goal tower, where they will be placed on top of the largest disk. Let's assume that we can perform step 1 and step 2 (a stopping case); Fig. 15.4 shows the status of the

Figure 15.3 Towers of Hanoi

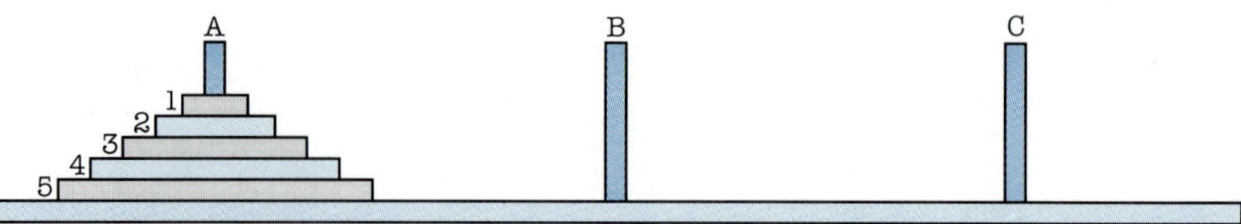

Figure 15.4 Towers of Hanoi after Steps 1 and 2

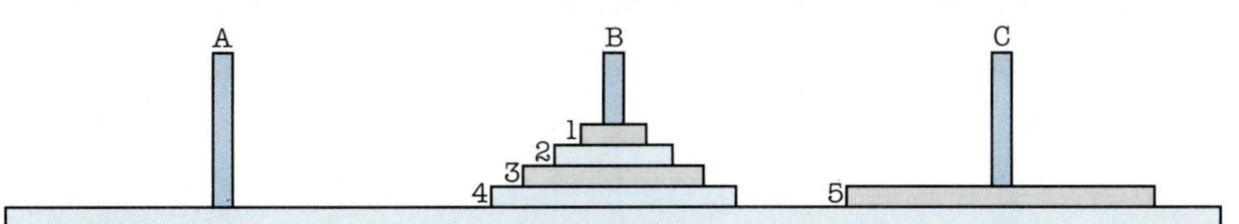

three towers after completion of these steps. At this point, it should be clear that we can solve the original five-disk problem if we can complete step 3.

Unfortunately, we still don't know how to perform step 1 or step 3. Both steps, however, involve four disks instead of five, so they are easier than the original problem. We should be able to split them into even simpler problems. Step 3 involves moving four disks from tower B to tower C, so we can split it into two three-disk problems and one one-disk problem:

3.1 Move three disks from peg B to peg A.
3.2 Move disk 4 from peg B to peg C.
3.3 Move three disks from peg A to peg C.

Figure 15.5 shows the towers after completion of steps 3.1 and 3.2. The two largest disks are now on peg C. Once we complete step 3.3, all five disks will be on peg C.

By splitting each *N*-disk problem into two problems involving *N*-1 disks and a one-disk problem, we eventually reach the point where all the cases involve only one disk, cases that we know how to solve. Later, we will write a Pascal program that solves the Towers of Hanoi problem. ■

Exercises for Section 15.1

Self-Check

1. Show the problems that are generated by the function designator `Multiply(5, 4)`. Use a diagram similar to Fig. 15.1.
2. Show the problems that are generated when you attempt to solve the problem "Move two disks from peg A to peg C." Answer the same question for the problem "Move three disks from peg A to peg C." Draw a diagram similar to Fig. 15.1.

Figure 15.5 Towers of Hanoi after Steps 1, 2, 3.1, and 3.2

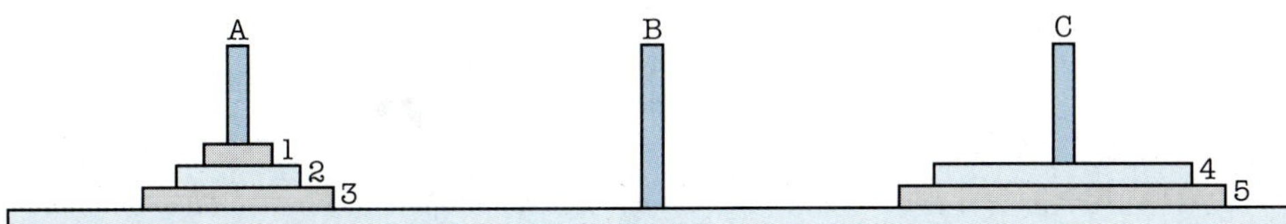

15.2 Tracing a Recursive Procedure or Function

Hand-tracing an algorithm's execution provides us with valuable insight as to how that algorithm works. We can also trace the execution of a recursive procedure or function. We illustrate how to do this with a recursive function and procedure.

Tracing a Recursive Function

In the last section, we wrote the recursive function `Multiply`. We can trace the execution of the function designator `Multiply(6, 3)` by drawing an *activation frame* that corresponds to each call of the function. An activation frame shows the parameter values for each call and summarizes its execution.

The three activation frames generated to solve the problem of multiplying 6 by 3 are shown in Fig. 15.6. The part of each activation frame that executes before the next recursive call is in color; the part that executes after the return from the next call is in gray. The darker the color of an activation frame, the greater the depth of recursion.

The value returned from each call is shown alongside each black arrow. The return arrow from each function call points to the operator +, because the addition is performed just after the return.

Figure 15.6 Trace of Function Multiply

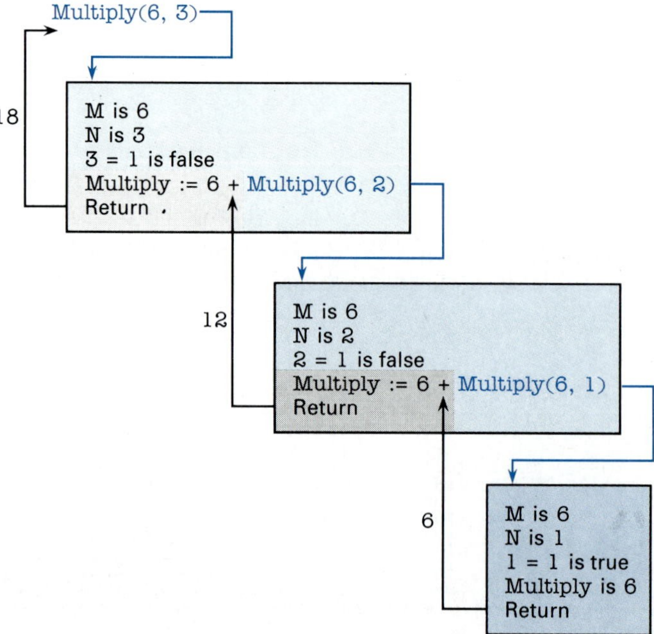

The figure shows that there are three calls to function Multiply. Parameter M has the value 6 for all three calls; parameter N has the values 3, 2, and finally 1. Because N is 1 in the third call, the value of M (6) is returned as the result of the third and last call. After the return to the second activation frame, the value of M is added to this result, and the sum (12) is returned as the result of the second call. After the return to the first activation frame, the value of M is added to this result, and the sum (18) is returned as the result of the original call to function Multiply.

Tracing a Recursive Procedure

■ Example 15.3

Procedure Palindrome in Fig. 15.7 is a recursive procedure that reads in a string of length N and prints it out backward. (A *palindrome* is a string of characters that reads the same backward and forward.) If the procedure call statement

```
Palindrome (5)
```

is executed, the five characters entered at the screen are printed in reverse order. If the characters abcde are entered when this procedure is called, the lines

```
abcde
edcba
```

appear on the screen. The letters in color are entered as data and the letters in black are printed. If the procedure call statement

```
Palindrome (3)
```

is executed instead, only three characters are read, and the lines

```
abc
cba
```

appear on the screen.

Figure 15.7 Procedure Palindrome

```
procedure Palindrome (N : Integer);
{
  Displays a string of length N in
  reverse of the order in which it is entered.
  Pre : N is greater than or equal to one.
  Post: Displays N characters.
}
  var
    Next : Char;     {next data character}

begin {Palindrome}
  if N <= 1 then
    begin {stopping case}
      Read (Next);
```

```
      Write (Next)
    end {stopping case}
  else
    begin {recursion}
      Read (Next);
      Palindrome (N-1);
      Write (Next)
    end {recursion}
end; {Palindrome}
```

Like most recursive procedures, the body of procedure `Palindrome` consists of an `if` statement that evaluates a *terminating condition*, `N <= 1`. When the terminating condition is true, the problem has reached a stopping case: a data string of length `1`. If `N <= 1` is true, the `Read` and `Write` statements are executed.

If the terminating condition is false (`N > 1`), the recursive step (following `else`) is executed. The `Read` statement enters the next data character. The procedure call statement

```
Palindrome (N-1);
```

calls the procedure recursively, with the parameter value decreased by one. The character just read is not displayed until later. This is because the `Write` statement comes after the recursive procedure call; consequently, the `Write` statement cannot be performed until after the procedure execution is completed and control is returned back to the `Write` statement. For example, the character that is read when `N` is `3` is not displayed until after the procedure execution for `N` equal to `2` is done. Hence, this character is displayed after the characters that are read when `N` is `2` and `N` is `1`.

To fully understand this, trace the execution of the procedure call statement

```
Palindrome (3)
```

The trace shown in Fig. 15.8 assumes the letters `abc` have been entered as data.

The trace shows three separate activation frames for procedure `Palindrome`. Each activation frame begins with a list of the initial values of `N` and `Next` for that frame. The value of `N` is passed into the procedure when it is called, because `N` is a value parameter; the value of `Next` is initially undefined, because `Next` is a local variable.

Figure 15.8 Trace of Palindrome (3)

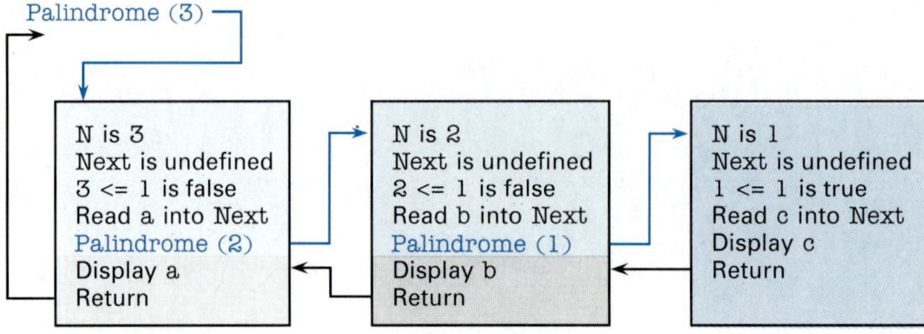

The statements that are executed for each frame are shown next. The statements in color are recursive procedure calls and result in a new activation frame, as indicated by the colored arrows. A procedure return occurs when the procedure end statement is reached. This is indicated by the word `Return` and a black arrow that points to the statement in the calling frame to which the procedure returns. Tracing the colored arrows and then the black arrows in Fig. 15.8 gives us the sequence of events listed in Fig. 15.9. To help you understand this list, all the statements for a particular activation frame are indented to the same column.

Figure 15.9 Sequence of Events for Trace of Palindrome (3)

Call `Palindrome` with `N` equal to `3`.
    Read the first character (`a`) into `Next`.
    Call `Palindrome` with `N` equal to `2`.
        Read the second character (`b`) into `Next`.
        Call `Palindrome` with `N` equal to `1`.
            Read the third character (`c`) into `Next`.
            Display the third character (`c`).
            Return from third call.
        Display the second character (`b`).
        Return from second call.
    Display the first character (`a`).
    Return from original call.

As shown, there are three calls to procedure `Palindrome`, each with a different parameter value. The procedure returns always occur in the reverse order of the procedure calls; that is, we return from the last call first, then we return from the next to last call, and so on. After we return from a particular execution of the procedure, we display the character that was read into `Next` just prior to that procedure call. ■

Parameter and Local Variable Stacks

You may be wondering how Pascal keeps track of the values of `N` and `Next` at any given point. Pascal uses a special data structure called a *stack*, which is analogous to a stack of dishes or trays. Think of the countless times you have stood in line in a cafeteria. Recall that clean dishes are always placed on top of a stack of dishes. When we need a dish, we always remove the one most recently placed on the stack. This causes the next to last dish placed on the stack to move to the top of the stack. (The stack data structure is discussed further in Chapter 16.)

Similarly, whenever a new procedure call occurs, the parameter value associated with that call is placed on the top of the parameter stack. Also, a new cell whose value is initially undefined is placed on top of the stack that is maintained for the local variable `Next`. Whenever `N` or `Next` is referenced, the value at the top of the corresponding stack is always used. When a procedure return occurs, the value currently at the top of each stack is removed, and the value just below it moves to the top.

As an example, let's look at the two stacks right after the first call to `Palindrome`. There is one cell on each stack, as follows.

After first call to Palindrome

```
 N       Next
| 3 |    | ? |
```

The letter `a` is read into `Next` just before the second call to `Palindrome`.

```
 N       Next
| 3 |    | a |
```

After the second call to `Palindrome`, the number `2` is placed on top of the stack for `N`, and the top of the stack for `Next` becomes undefined again, as shown next. The value in color is at the top of each stack.

After second call to Palindrome

```
 N       Next
| 2 |    | ? |
| 3 |    | a |
```

The letter `b` is read into `Next` just before the third call to `Palindrome`.

```
 N       Next
| 2 |    | b |
| 3 |    | a |
```

However, `Next` becomes undefined again right after the third call.

After third call to Palindrome

```
 N       Next
| 1 |    | ? |
| 2 |    | b |
| 3 |    | a |
```

During this execution of the procedure, the letter `c` is read into `Next`, and `c` is echo printed immediately because `N` is `1` (the stopping case).

```
 N       Next
| 1 |    | c |
| 2 |    | b |
| 3 |    | a |
```

The procedure return causes the values at the top of the stack to be removed, as shown next.

After first return

N	Next
2	b
3	a

Because control is returned to a `Write` statement, the value of `Next` (b) at the top of the stack is then displayed. Another return occurs, causing the values currently at the top of the stack to be removed.

After second return

Again, control is returned to a `Write` statement, and the value of `Next` (a) at the top of the stack is displayed. The third and last return removes the last pair of values from the stack, and `N` and `Next` both become undefined.

After third return

Chapter 16 shows you how to declare and manipulate stacks yourself. Because these steps are all done automatically by Pascal, we can write recursive procedures without worrying about the stacks.

Implementation of Parameter Stacks in Pascal

For illustrative purposes, we have used separate stacks for `N` and `Next` in our discussion; the compiler, however, actually maintains a single stack. Each time a call to a procedure or function occurs, all its parameters and local variables are pushed onto the stack along with the memory address of the calling statement. The latter gives the computer the return point after execution of the procedure or function. Although multiple copies of a procedure's parameters may be saved on the stack, only one copy of the procedure body is in memory.

Exercises for Section 15.2

Self-Check

1. Why is `N` a value parameter in Fig. 15.7?
2. Assume the characters `*+-/` are entered for the procedure call statement

   ```
   Palindrome (4)
   ```

   What output line would appear on the screen? Show the contents of the stacks immediately after each procedure call and return.

3. Trace the execution of `Multiply(5, 4)` and show the stacks after each recursive call.

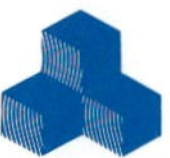

15.3 Recursive Mathematical Functions

Many mathematical functions are defined recursively. An example is the factorial of a number n ($n!$).

- $0!$ is 1
- $n!$ is $n \times (n-1)!$, for $n > 0$

Thus, $4! = 4 \times 3! = 4 \times 3 \times 2!$, and so on. It is easy to implement this definition as a recursive function in Pascal.

■ Example 15.4

Function `Factor` in Fig. 15.10 computes the factorial of its argument `N`. The recursive step

```
Factor := N * Factor(N-1)
```

implements the second line of the factorial definition. This means that the result of the current call (argument `N`) is determined by multiplying the result of the next call (argument `N-1`) by `N`.

Figure 15.10 Recursive Function Factor

```
function Factor (N : Integer) : Integer;
{
  Computes the factorial of N (N!).
  Pre : N is defined and N >= 0.
  Post: Returns N!
}
begin {Factor}
  if N = 0 then
    Factor := 1
  else
    Factor := N * Factor(N-1)
end;  {Factor}
```

A trace of

```
Fact := Factor(3)
```

is shown in Fig. 15.11. The value returned from the original call, `Factor(3)`, is 6, and this value is assigned to `Fact`. Be careful when you use the factorial function; its value increases rapidly and could lead to an integer-overflow error (for example, `10!` is 3628800). ■

Although the recursive implementation of function `Factor` follows naturally from its definition, this function can be implemented easily using iteration. The iterative version is shown in Fig. 15.12.

Figure 15.11 Trace of Fact := Factor(3)

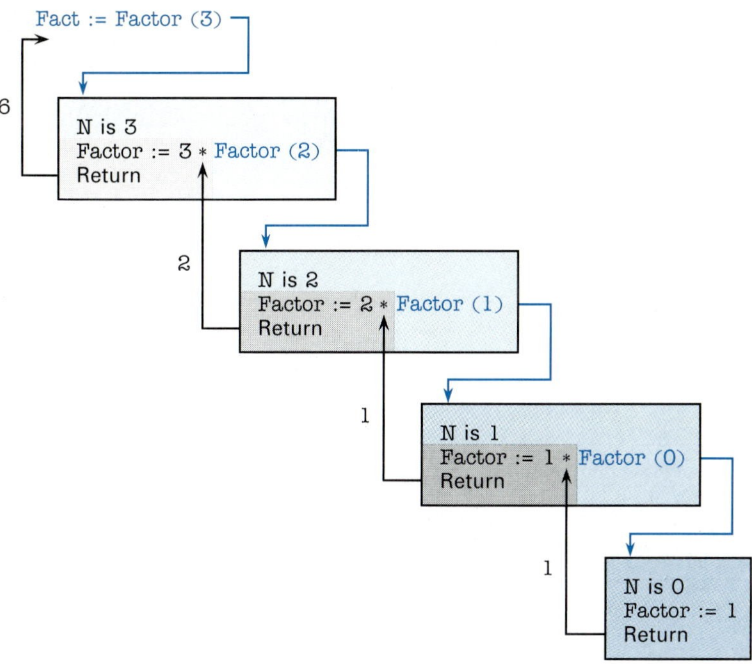

Figure 15.12 Iterative Function Factor

```
function Factor (N : Integer) : Integer;
{
  Computes the factorial of N (N!).
  Pre : N is defined and N >= 0.
  Post: Returns N!
}
  var
    I,                        {loop-control variable}
    Factorial : Integer;      {storage for accumulating product}

begin {Factor}
  Factorial := 1;
  for I := 2 to N do
    Factorial := Factorial * I;

  Factor := Factorial         {Define result}
end; {Factor}
```

Notice that the iterative version contains a loop as its major control structure, whereas the recursive version contains an `if` statement. Also, a local variable, `Factorial`, is needed in the iterative version to hold the accumulating product.

■ Example 15.5

The Fibonacci numbers are a sequence of numbers that have many varied uses. They were originally intended to model the growth of a rabbit colony. We will not go into details of the model here, but you can see that the Fibonacci sequence 1, 1, 2, 3, 5, 8, 13, 21, 34, ... increases rapidly. The fifteenth number in the sequence is 610 (that's a lot of rabbits!). The Fibonacci sequence is defined as follows:

- Fib_1 is 1.
- Fib_2 is 1.
- Fib_n is $Fib_{n-2} + Fib_{n-1}$, for $n > 2$.

Verify for yourself that the sequence of numbers shown in the preceding paragraph is correct.

A recursive function that computes the Nth Fibonacci number is shown in Fig. 15.13. Although easy to write, the Fibonacci function is not very efficient, because each recursive step generates two calls to function Fibonacci. ■

Figure 15.13 Recursive Function Fibonacci

```
function Fibonacci (N : Integer) : Integer;
{
  Computes the Nth Fibonacci number.
  Pre : N is defined and N > 0
  Post: Returns the Nth Fibonacci number.
}
begin  {Fibonacci}
  if (N = 1) or (N = 2) then
    Fibonacci := 1
  else
    Fibonacci := Fibonacci(N-2) + Fibonacci(N-1)
end;  {Fibonacci}
```

■ Example 15.6

Euclid's algorithm for finding the greatest common divisor (GCD) of two positive integers, (M and N), is defined recursively as follows. The *greatest common divisor* of two integers is the largest integer that divides them both.

- GCD(M,N) is N if N <= M and N divides M
- GCD(M,N) is GCD(N,M) if M < N
- GCD(M,N) is GCD(N, remainder of M divided by N)

This algorithm states that the GCD is N if N is the smaller number and N divides M. If M is the smaller number, then the GCD determination should be performed with the arguments transposed. If N does not divide M, the answer is obtained by finding the GCD of N and the remainder of M divided by N. The declaration and use of the Pascal function GCD is shown in Fig. 15.14. ■

Figure 15.14 Function GCD

Edit Window

```
program FindGCD;

{Prints the greatest common divisor of two integers.}
  var
    M, N : Integer;              {two input items}

  function GCD (M, N : Integer) : Integer;
  {
    Finds the greatest common divisor of M and N.
    Pre : M and N are defined and both are > 0.
    Post: Returns the greatest common divisor of M and N.
  }
  begin {GCD}
    if (N <= M) and (M mod N = 0) then
      GCD := N
    else if M < N then
      GCD := GCD(N, M)
    else
      GCD := GCD(N, M mod N)
    end; {GCD}

begin {FindGCD}
  Write ('Enter two positive integers separated by a space: ');
  ReadLn (M, N);
  WriteLn ('Their greatest common divisor is ', GCD (M, N) :1)
end. {FindGCD}
```

Output Window

```
Enter two positive integers separated by a space: 24 84
Their greatest common divisor is 12
```

Exercises for Section 15.3

Self-Check

1. Complete the following recursive function, which calculates the value of a number (Base) raised to a power (Power). Assume that Power is positive.

```
function PowerRaiser (Base, Power : Integer) : Integer;
begin
  if Power = ____________ then
    PowerRaiser := ____________
  else
    PowerRaiser := ____________ * ____________
end;
```

2. What is the output of the following program? What does function Strange compute?

```
program TestStrange;

  function Strange (N : Integer) : Integer;
  begin
    if N = 1 then
      Strange := 0
```

```
    else
      Strange := 1 + Strange (N div 2)
  end;  {Strange}

begin
  WriteLn (Strange(8))
end. {TestStrange}
```

3. What would happen if the terminating condition for function `Fibonacci` is just `(N = 1)`?

Programming

1. Write a recursive function, `FindSum`, that calculates the sum of successive integers starting at `1` and ending at `N` (for example, `FindSum(N) = 1 + 2 + ... + (N-1) + N`).
2. Write an iterative version of the Fibonacci function.
3. Write an iterative function for the greatest common divisor.

15.4 Recursive Procedures with Array Parameters

This section examines three familiar problems and implements recursive procedures to solve them. All three problems involve processing an array.

Case Study: Printing an Array Backward

Problem

Provide a recursive solution to the problem of printing the elements of an array in reverse order.

Design Overview

If the array `X` has elements with subscripts `1..N`, then the element values should be printed in the sequence `X[N], X[N-1], X[N-2], ..., X[2], X[1]`. The stopping case is printing an array with one element (`N` is `1`); the solution is to print that element. For larger arrays, the recursive step is to print the last array element (`X[N]`) and then print the subarray with subscripts `1..N-1` backward.

Data Requirements

Problem Inputs

An array of integer values (`X : IntArray`)
The number of elements in the array (`N : IndexRange`)

Problem Outputs

The array values in reverse order (`X[N], X[N-1], ... , X[2], X[1]`)

Initial Algorithm

```
1. if N is 1 then
      2. Print X[1]
   else
     begin
       3. Print X[N]
       4. Print the subarray with subscripts 1..N-1
     end
```

Coding

Procedure `PrintBack` in Fig. 15.15 implements the recursive algorithm.

Figure 15.15 Procedure PrintBack

```
procedure PrintBack (var X {input} : IntArray;
                     N {input} : IndexRange);
{
  Prints an array of integers (X) with subscripts 1..N.
  Pre : Array X and N are defined and N > 0.
  Post: Displays X[N], X[N-1], ... , X[2], X[1]
}
begin {PrintBack }
  if N = 1 then
    WriteLn (X[1])                    {stopping case}
  else
    begin {recursive step}
      WriteLn (X[N]);
      PrintBack (X, N-1)
    end  {recursive step}
end;  {PrintBack }
```

Testing

Given the declarations

```
type
  IndexRange = 1..20;
  IntArray = array [IndexRange] of Integer;

var
  Test : IntArray;
```

and the procedure call statement

```
PrintBack (Test, 3)
```

three `WriteLn` statements will be executed in the following order, and the elements of `Test` will be printed backward.

```
WriteLn (Test[3]);
WriteLn (Test[2]);
WriteLn (Test[1])
```

Case Study: Printing an Array Backward, continued

Figure 15.16 Trace of PrintBack (Test, 3)

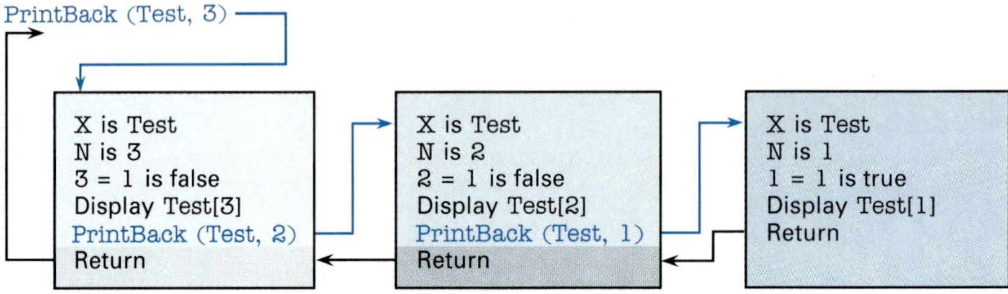

To verify this, in Fig. 15.16 we trace the execution of the original call to `PrintBack`. Tracing the colored arrows and then the black arrows leads to the sequence of events listed in Fig. 15.17.

Figure 15.17 Sequence of Events for Trace of PrintBack (Test, 3)

Call `PrintBack` with parameters `Test` and `3`.
  Print `Test[3]`.
  Call `PrintBack` with parameters `Test` and `2`.
    Print `Test[2]`.
    Call `PrintBack` with parameters `Test` and `1`.
      Print `Test[1]`.
      Return from third call.
    Return from second call.
  Return from original call.

As shown in Fig. 15.17, there are three calls to procedure `PrintBack`, each with different parameters. This time, there are no statements left to execute after the returns, because the recursive call

```
PrintBack (X, N-1)
```

occurs at the end of the recursive step.

Case Study: Printing an Array in Normal Order

Problem

Provide a recursive procedure that prints the elements of an array in normal order.

Design Overview

We can use the approach we just followed in the preceding problem to print the elements of an array in normal order. Again, the stopping case is an array with just one element.

Data Requirements

Problem Inputs

An array of integer values (`X : IntArray`)
The number of elements in the array (`N : IndexRange`)

Problem Outputs

The array values in normal order (`X[1], X[2], ... , X[N-1], X[N]`)

Initial Algorithm

1. `if` `N` is `1` `then`
    2. Print `X[1]`

   `else`

   `begin`
    3. Print the subarray with subscripts `1..N-1`
    4. Print `X[N]`

   `end`

The only difference between this algorithm and the one shown earlier is that steps 3 and 4 are transposed.

Coding

Procedure `PrintNormal` is shown in Fig. 15.18.

Figure 15.18 Procedure PrintNormal

```
procedure PrintNormal (var X {input} : IntArray;
                       N {input} : IndexRange);
{
  Prints an array of integers (X) with subscripts 1..N.
  Pre : Array X and N are defined and N > 0.
  Post: Displays X[1], ... , X[N-1], X[N]
}
begin {PrintNormal }
  if N = 1 then
    WriteLn (X[1])                     {stopping case}
  else
    begin {recursive step}
      PrintNormal (X, N-1);
      WriteLn (X[N])
    end  {recursive step}
end;  {PrintNormal}
```

Case Study: Printing an Array in Normal Order, continued

Figure 15.19 Trace of PrintNormal (Test, 3)

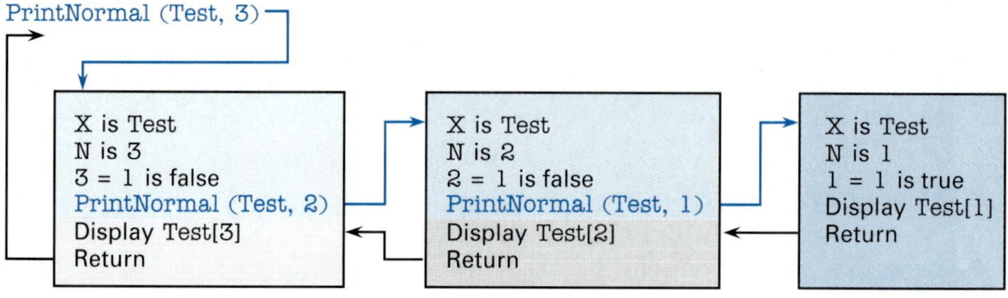

Testing

The trace of `PrintNormal (Test, 3)` is shown in Fig. 15.19. Following the colored arrows and then the black arrows results in the sequence of events listed in Fig. 15.20. This time, there are no statements that precede the recursive calls; a display operation is performed after each return.

Figure 15.20 Sequence of Events for Trace of PrintNormal (Test, 3)

Call `PrintNormal` with parameters `Test` and `3`.
  Call `PrintNormal` with parameters `Test` and `2`.
    Call `PrintNormal` with parameters `Test` and `1`.
      Print `Test[1]`.
      Return from third call.
    Print `Test[2]`.
    Return from second call.
  Print `Test[3]`.
  Return from original call.

PROGRAM STYLE

Avoiding Value Array Parameters in Recursive Procedures

`X` is declared as a variable parameter in procedures `PrintBack` and `PrintNormal`, even though it is used for input only. If `X` was a value parameter instead, each recursive call would generate a local copy of the actual array corresponding to `X` in each activation frame. This could result in a tremendous waste of time and memory space. For example, if `X` corresponds to an array with ten elements and we want to print the entire array (`N` is 10), there will be 10 activation frames and storage space will be needed for 100 integer values. If `N` is 100, then storage space will be needed for 100 x 100, or 10,000, integer values.

Case Study: Recursive Selection Sort

Problem

We have discussed selection sort and implemented an iterative selection sort procedure. Because the selection sort first finds the largest element in an array and places it where it belongs, then finds and places the next largest element, and so on, it is a good candidate for a recursive solution.

Design Overview

The selection sort algorithm follows from the preceding description. The stopping case is an array of length 1, which is sorted by definition. Review Fig. 12.32 to see how the elements of an array are placed in their final positions by a selection sort.

Recursive Algorithm for Selection Sort

```
1. if N is 1 then
     2. The array is sorted.
   else
     begin
       3. Place the largest array element in X[N].
       4. Sort the subarray with subscripts 1..N-1.
     end
```

Coding

The algorithm is implemented as a recursive procedure at the end of Fig. 15.21. Procedure `PlaceLargest` performs step 3 of the algorithm. The recursive procedure `SelectSort` is simpler to understand than the one shown in Fig. 12.33 because it contains a single `if` statement instead of nested `for` loops. The recursive procedure executes more slowly, however, because of the extra overhead due to the recursive procedure calls.

Figure 15.21 PlaceLargest and Recursive SelectSort

```
procedure PlaceLargest (var X {input/output} : IntArray;
                        N {input} : IndexRange);
{
  Finds the largest element in array X[1]..X[N] and exchanges
  it with the element at X[N].
  Pre : Array X and N are defined and N > 0.
  Post: X[N] contains the largest value.
}
  var
    Temp,                   {temporary copy for exchange}
    J,                      {array subscript and loop control}
    MaxIndex : Integer;     {index of largest so far}
```

Case Study: Recursive Selection Sort, continued

```
begin {PlaceLargest}
  {Save subscript of largest element in MaxIndex}
  MaxIndex := N;                    {assume X[N] is largest}
  for J := N-1 downto 1 do
    if X[J] > X[MaxIndex] then
      MaxIndex := J;                {X[J] is largest so far}

  {assertion: MaxIndex is subscript of largest element}
  if MaxIndex <> N then
    begin {exchange X[N] and X[MaxIndex]}
      Temp := X[N];  X[N] := X[MaxIndex];  X[MaxIndex] := Temp
    end {if}
end; {PlaceLargest}


procedure SelectSort (var X {input/output} : IntArray;
                      N {input} : IndexRange);
{
  Sorts an array of integers (X) with subscripts 1..N.
  Pre : Array X and N are defined and N > 0.
  Post: The array elements are in numerical order.
}
begin {SelectSort}
  if N > 1 then
    begin {recursive step}
      {Place largest value in X[N] and sort subarray 1..N-1.}
      PlaceLargest (X, N);
      SelectSort (X, N-1)
    end {recursive step}
end; {SelectSort}
```

If `N = 1`, procedure `SelectSort` returns without doing anything. This behavior is correct because a one-element array is always sorted.

Exercises for Section 15.4

Self-Check

1. Trace the execution of `SelectSort` on an array that has the integers `5`, `8`, `10`, and `1` stored in consecutive elements.
2. For the array in exercise 1, trace the execution of `PrintNormal` and `PrintBack`.

Programming

1. Provide an iterative procedure that is equivalent to `PrintBack` in Fig. 15.15.
2. Write a recursive procedure that reverses the elements in an array `X[1..N]`. The recursive step should shift the subarray `X[2..N]` down one element into the subarray `X[1..N-1]` (for example, `X[1]` gets `X[2]`, `X[2]` gets `X[3]`, ... `X[N-1]` gets `X[N]`), store the old `X[1]` in `X[N]`, and then reverse the subarray `X[1..N-1]`.

15.5 Problem Solving with Recursion

The next case study is considerably more complicated than the preceding ones. It leads to a recursive procedure that solves the Towers of Hanoi problem you encountered in Section 15.1.

Case Study: Towers of Hanoi Problem

Problem

Solve the Towers of Hanoi problem for N disks, where N is a parameter.

Design Overview

The solution to the Towers of Hanoi problem consists of a printed list of individual disk moves. We need a recursive procedure that can be used to move any number of disks from one peg to another, using the third peg as an auxiliary.

Data Requirements

Problem Inputs

The number of disks to be moved (`N : Integer`)
The *from* peg (`FromPeg : 'A'..'C'`)
The *to* peg (`ToPeg : 'A'..'C'`)
The *auxiliary* peg (`AuxPeg : 'A'..'C'`)

Problem Outputs

A list of individual disk moves

Initial Algorithm

1. `if N is 1 then`
    2. Move disk `1` from the *from* peg to the *to* peg
   `else`
    `begin`
      3. Move `N-1` disks from the *from* peg to the *auxiliary* peg using the *to* peg.
      4. Move disk `N` from the *from* peg to the *to* peg.
      5. Move `N-1` disks from the *auxiliary* peg to the *to* peg using the *from* peg.
    `end`

If `N` is `1`, a stopping case is reached. If `N` is greater than `1`, the recursive step (following `else`) splits the original problem into three smaller subproblems, one of which is a stopping case. Each stopping case displays a move instruction. Verify that the recursive step generates the three problems listed before Fig. 15.3 when `N` is `5`, the *from* peg is `A`, and the *to* peg is `C`.

The implementation of this algorithm is shown as procedure `Tower` in Fig. 15.22. Procedure `Tower` has four parameters. The procedure call statement

```
Tower ('A', 'C', 'B', 5)
```

solves the problem posed earlier of moving five disks from tower `A` to tower `C` using `B` as an auxiliary.

In Fig. 15.22, the stopping case (move disk 1) is implemented as a call to procedure `WriteLn`. Each recursive step consists of two recursive calls to `Tower`, with a call to `WriteLn` sandwiched between them. The first recursive call solves the problem of moving `N-1` disks to the *auxiliary* peg. The call to `WriteLn` displays a message to move disk `N` to the *to* peg. The second recursive call solves the problem of moving the `N-1` disks back from the *auxiliary* peg to the *to* peg.

Figure 15.22 Recursive Procedure Tower

```
procedure Tower (FromPeg,
                 ToPeg,
                 AuxPeg {input} : Char;
                 N      {input} : Integer);
{
  Moves N disks from FromPeg to ToPeg
  using AuxPeg as an auxiliary.
  Pre : FromPeg, ToPeg, AuxPeg, and N are defined.
  Post: Displays a list of move instructions that transfer
        the disks.
}
begin  {Tower}
  if N = 1 then
    WriteLn ('Move disk 1 from peg ', FromPeg,
             ' to peg ', ToPeg)
  else
    begin {recursive step}
      Tower (FromPeg, AuxPeg, ToPeg, N-1);
      WriteLn ('Move disk ', N :1, ' from peg ', FromPeg,
               ' to peg ', ToPeg);
      Tower (AuxPeg, ToPeg, FromPeg, N-1)
    end {recursive step}
end;  {Tower}
```

Testing

The procedure call statement

```
Tower ('A', 'C', 'B', 3)
```

solves a simpler three-disk problem: move three disks from peg `A` to peg `C`. Its execution is traced in Fig. 15.23; the output generated is shown in Fig. 15.24. Verify for yourself that this list of steps does indeed solve the three-disk problem.

Figure 15.23 Trace of Tower ('A', 'C', 'B', 3)

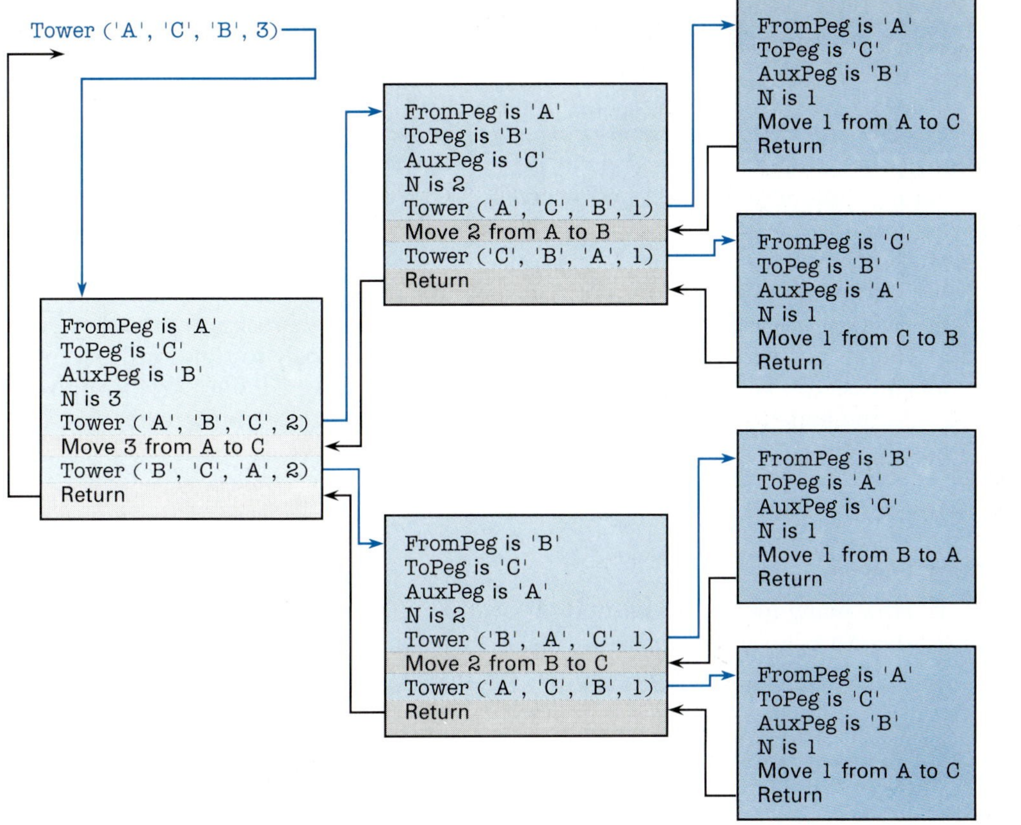

Figure 15.24 Output Generated by Tower ('A', 'C', 'B', 3)

```
Move disk 1 from A to C
Move disk 2 from A to B
Move disk 1 from C to B
Move disk 3 from A to C
Move disk 1 from B to A
Move disk 2 from B to C
Move disk 1 from A to C
```

Comparison of Iteration and Recursive Procedures

It is interesting to consider that procedure `Tower` in Fig. 15.22 will solve the Towers of Hanoi problem for any number of disks. The three-disk problem results in a total of seven calls to procedure `Tower` and is solved by seven disk moves. The five-disk problem would result in a total of thirty-one calls to procedure `Tower` and is solved in thirty-one moves. In general, the number of moves required to solve the n-disk problem is $2^n - 1$. Because each procedure call requires the allocation and initialization of a local data area in memory, the computer time increases exponentially with the problem size. For this reason, be careful about running the program with a value of `N` larger than 10.

The dramatic increase in processing time for larger towers is a function of the problem, not of recursion. In general, however, if there are recursive and iterative solutions to the same problem, the recursive solution requires more time and space because of the extra procedure calls. We discuss algorithm efficiency later.

Although recursion was not really needed to solve the simpler problems in this section, it was extremely useful in formulating an algorithm for the Towers of Hanoi. For certain problems, recursion leads naturally to solutions that are much easier to read and understand than their iterative counterparts. In those cases, the benefits gained from increased clarity far outweigh the extra cost in time and memory of running a recursive program.

Exercises for Section 15.5

Self-Check

1. How many moves are needed to solve the six-disk problem?
2. Write a main program that reads in a data value for `N` (the number of disks) and calls procedure `Tower` to move `N` disks from `A` to `B`.

15.6 Recursive Functions with Array Parameters

We can follow the process described in the previous sections to write recursive functions with array parameters. That process involves identifying the stopping cases of a problem. For other cases, we must be able to reduce the problem to one that is closer to a stopping case.

Case Study: Summing the Values in an Array

Problem

We want to write a recursive function that finds the sum of the values in an array `X` with subscripts `1..N`.

Design Overview

The stopping case occurs when `N` is `1`, that is, the sum is `X[1]`. If `N` is not `1`, then we must add `X[N]` to the sum we get when we add the values in the subarray with subscripts `1..N-1`.

Data Requirements

Problem Inputs

An array of integer values (`X : IntArray`)

The number of elements in the array (`N : IndexRange`)

Problem Outputs

The sum of the array values

Initial Algorithm

```
1. if N is 1 then
     2. The sum is X[1]
   else
     begin
       3. Add X[N] to the sum of values in the subarray with
          subscripts 1..N-1
     end
```

Coding

Function `FindSum` in Fig. 15.25 implements this algorithm. The result of calling `FindSum` for a small array (`N` is 3) is also shown.

Figure 15.25 Using Recursive Function FindSum

Edit Window

```
program TestFindSum;

{Tests function FindSum.}

  type
    IndexRange = 1..20;
    IntArray = array [IndexRange] of Integer;

  var
    N : IndexRange;
    X : IntArray;


  function FindSum (var X : IntArray;
                    N : IndexRange) : Integer;
  {
    Finds the sum of the values in elements 1..N of array X.
    Pre : Array X and N are defined and N > 0.
    Post: Returns sum of first N elements of X.
  }
  begin {FindSum}
    if N = 1 then
      FindSum := X[1]
    else
      FindSum := X[N] + FindSum(X, N-1)
  end;  {FindSum}
```

```
begin {TestFindSum}
  N := 3;
  X[1] := 5;  X[2] := 10;  X[3] := -7;
  WriteLn ('The array sum is ', FindSum(X, 3) :1)
end. {TestFindSum}
```

Output Window

```
The array sum is 8
```

Testing

Figure 15.26 shows a trace of the function call `FindSum(X, 3)`. As before, the colored part of each activation frame executes before the next recursive function call, and each colored arrow points to a new activation frame. The gray part of each activation frame executes after the return from a recursive call, and each black arrow indicates the return point (the operator +) after a function execution. The value returned is indicated alongside the arrow. The value returned for the original call, `FindSum(X, 3)`, is 8, which is printed.

Functions that return Boolean values (`True` or `False`) can also be written recursively. These functions do not perform a computation; however, the function result is still determined by evaluating an expression (type Boolean) con-

Figure 15.26 Trace of FindSum(X, 3)

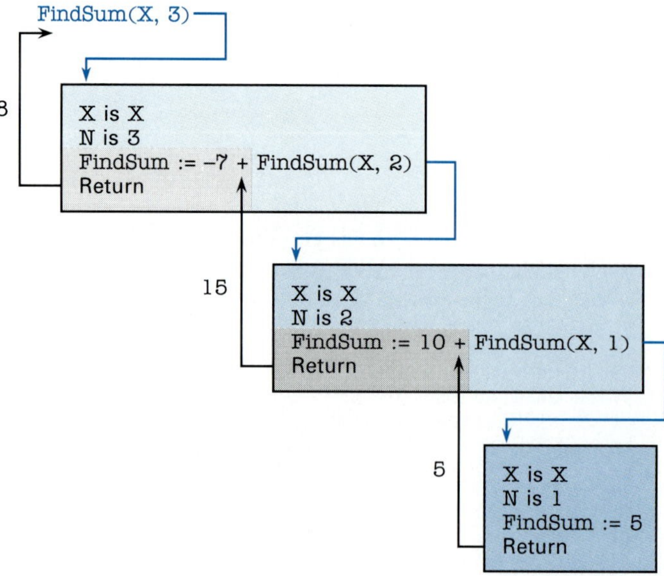

taining a recursive call. We will write recursive functions that search an array and compare two arrays.

■ Example 15.7

The Boolean function `Member` in Fig. 15.27 returns the value `True` if the argument `Target` is in the array `X` with subscripts `1..N`; otherwise, it returns the value `False`. If `N` is `1` (the stopping case), the result is determined by comparing `X[1]` and `Target`. If `N` is not `1` (the recursive step), then the result is true if either `X[N]` is `Target` or `Target` occurs in the subarray with subscripts `1..N-1`. The recursive step is implemented as the assignment statement

```
Member := (X[N] = Target) or Member(X, Target, N-1)
```

in Fig. 15.27.

Figure 15.27 Recursive Function Member

```
function Member (var X : IntArray;
                 Target : Integer;
                 N : IndexRange) : Boolean;
{
  Searches for Target in array X with subscripts 1..N.
  Pre : Target, N and array X are defined and N > 0.
  Post: Returns True if Target is located in array X; otherwise,
        returns False.
}
begin {Member}
  if N = 1 then
    Member := (X[1] = Target)
  else
    Member := (X[N] = Target) or Member(X, Target, N-1)
end; {Member}
```

The function designator `Member(X, 10, 3)` is traced in Fig. 15.28 for the array `X` defined in Fig. 15.25. The value returned is `True`, because the expression `X[N] = Target` is `True` when `N` is `2` (the second activation frame). ■

■ Example 15.8

The Boolean function `Equal` returns the value `True` if two arrays, say `X` and `Y`, of `N` elements are the same (for example, `X[1] = Y[1]`, `X[2] = Y[2]`,..., `X[N] = Y[N]`). This function (see Fig. 15.29) looks similar to function `Member`. For the stopping case, single-element arrays, the function result depends on whether or not `X[1] = Y[1]`. For larger arrays, the result is `True` if `X[N] = Y[N]` and the subarrays with subscripts `1..N-1` are equal. ■

Figure 15.28 Trace of Function Member

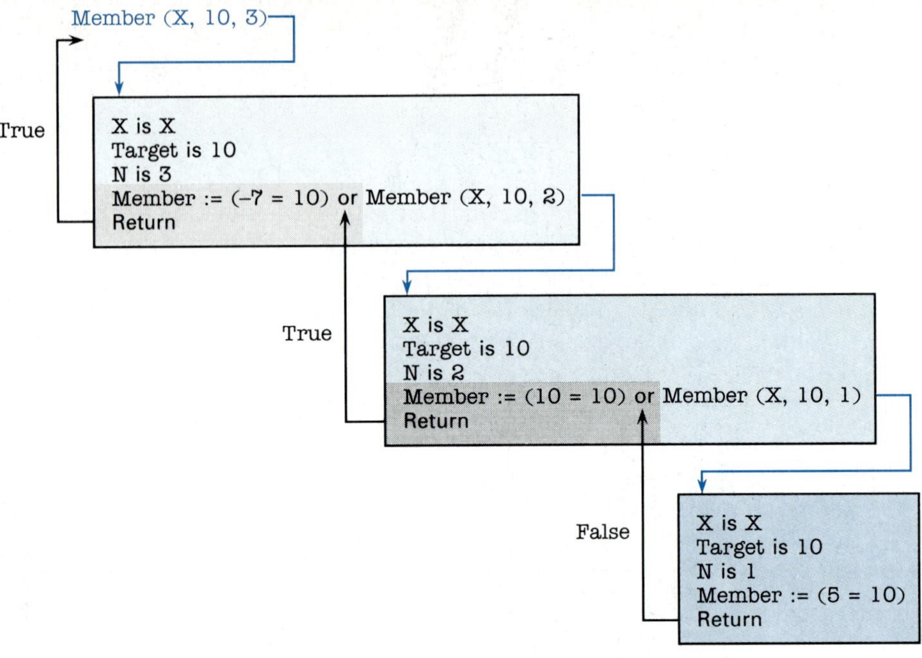

Figure 15.29 Recursive Function Equal

```
function Equal (var X, Y : IntArray;
                N : IndexRange) : Boolean;
{
  Compares arrays X and Y with elements 1..N.
  Pre : Arrays X and Y are defined and N > 0.
  Post: Returns True if arrays X and Y are equal; otherwise,
        returns False.
}
begin {Equal}
  if N = 1 then
    Equal := X[1] = Y[1]
  else
    Equal := (X[N] = Y[N]) and Equal(X, Y, N-1)
end; {Equal}
```

Comparison of Iterative and Recursive Functions

Consider the iterative version of function `Member` shown in Fig. 15.30. A `for` loop is needed to examine each array element. Without recursion, it is not possible to use the function name in an expression, so a local variable, `Found`, is needed to represent the result so far. Before returning from the function, the final value of `Found` is assigned as the function result.

Figure 15.30 Iterative Function Member

```
function Member (var X : IntArray;
                 Target : Integer;
                 N : IndexRange) : Boolean;
{
  Compares arrays X and Y with elements 1..N.
  Pre : Arrays X and Y are defined and N > 0.
  Post: Returns True if arrays X and Y are equal; otherwise,
        returns False.
}
var
  Found : Boolean;               {local flag}
  I : Integer;                   {loop-control variable}

begin {Member}
  Found := False;              {assume Target not found}
  {Search array X for Target.}
  for I := 1 to N do
    Found := Found or (X[I] = Target);

  Member := Found                          {define result}
end; {Member}
```

This is a little different from the iterative array search shown in Chapter 12 (see Fig. 12.30). We could make it more efficient by using a `while` loop and exiting from the loop when `Found` becomes `True`; however, the version shown in Fig. 15.30 would still execute faster than the recursive version.

Many programmers would argue that the recursive version is esthetically more pleasing. It is certainly more compact (a single `if` statement) and requires no local variables. Once you are accustomed to thinking recursively, the recursive form is somewhat easier to read and understand than the iterative form.

Some programmers like to use recursion as a conceptual tool. Once they have written the recursive form of a function or procedure, they can always translate it into an iterative version if run-time efficiency is a major concern.

Exercises for Section 15.6

Self-Check

1. Trace the execution of recursive function `Equal` for the three-element arrays `X` (element values `1`, `15`, `10`) and `Y` (element values `1`, `5`, `7`). Write out completely in one equivalent Boolean expression the values that function `Equal` is assigned through all three recursive calls for array `X`. Spell out all the values that are being compared.
2. Answer exercise 1 for the recursive function `Member` and array `X`.
3. What does the following recursive function do? Trace its execution on array `X` in exercise 1.

```
function Mystery (X : IntArray;
                  N : IndexRange) : Integer;
  var
    Temp : Integer;
```

```
begin
  if N = 1 then
    Mystery := X[1]
  else
    begin
      Temp := Mystery(X, N-1);
      if X[N] > Temp then
        Mystery := X[N]
      else
        Mystery := Temp
    end {if}
end; {Mystery}
```

Programming

1. Write a recursive function that finds the product of the elements in an array X of N elements.
2. Write a recursive function that finds the index of the smallest element in an array.

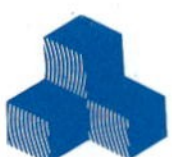

15.7 Picture Processing with Recursion

Case Study: Counting Cells in a Blob

This problem illustrates the power of recursion. The problem would be much more difficult without using recursion, but its solution is relatively easy to write recursively.

Problem

We have a two-dimensional grid of cells, each of which may be empty or filled. The filled cells that are connected form a blob. There may be several blobs on the grid. We want a function that accepts as input the coordinates of a particular cell and returns the size of the blob containing that cell.

There are three blobs in the sample grid in Fig. 15.31. If the function parameters represent the X and Y coordinates of a cell, the result of BlobCount(3, 4) is 5; the result of BlobCount(1, 2) is 2; the result of BlobCount(5, 5) is 0; the result of BlobCount(5, 1) is 4.

Design Overview

Function BlobCount must test the cell specified by its arguments to see if it is filled. There are two stopping cases: the cell (X, Y) is not on the grid, or the cell (X, Y) is empty; in either case, the value returned by BlobCount is 0. If the cell is on the grid and is filled, the value returned is 1 plus the size of the blobs containing each of its neighbors. To avoid counting a filled cell more than once, we mark it as empty once we have visited it.

Figure 15.31 Grid with Three Blobs

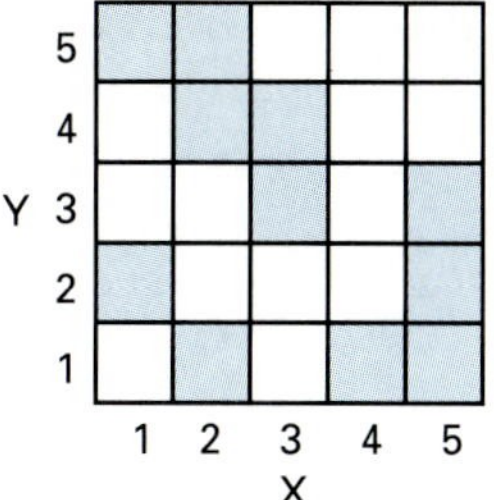

Data Requirements

Problem Inputs

The grid (`Grid : BlobArray`)

The X and Y coordinates of the point being visited
 (`X, Y : Integer`)

Problem Outputs

The number of the cells in the blob containing point (`X, Y`)

Initial Algorithm

```
1. if cell (X, Y) is not in the array then
     2. Return a count of 0
   else if cell (X, Y) is empty then
     3. Return a count of 0
   else
     begin
       4. Mark cell (X, Y) as empty
       5. Add 1 and see whether the blob contains any of
          the 8 neighbors of cell (X, Y)
     end
```

Coding

Function `BlobCount` is shown in Fig. 15.32. The array type `BlobArray` has element values `Filled` or `Empty`. The constants `MaxX` and `MaxY` represent the largest `X` and `Y` coordinate, respectively.

Figure 15.32 Function BlobCount

```
const
  MaxX = 100;
  MaxY = 100;

type
  RowIndex = 1..MaxX;
  ColIndex = 1..MaxY;
  Contents = (Filled, Empty);
  BlobArray = array [RowIndex, ColIndex] of Contents;
```

Case Study: Counting Cells in a Blob, continued

```
function BlobCount (Grid : BlobArray;
                    X, Y : Integer) : Integer;
{
  Counts the number of filled cells in the blob containing
  point (X, Y).
  Pre  : Array Grid and point (X, Y) are defined.
  Post : Returns the size of the blob containing the point (X, Y).
  Calls: Blob to perform the counting operation.
}


  function Blob (var Grid {input/output} : BlobArray;
                 X, Y : Integer) : Integer;
  {
   Performs counting operation for BlobCount.
   Pre : Array Grid and point (X, Y) are defined.
   Post: Returns the size of the blob containing the point (X, Y).
         Resets the status of each cell in the blob to Empty.
  }
  begin {Blob}
    if (X < 1) or (X > MaxX) or (Y < 1) or (Y > MaxY) then
      Blob := 0                    {cell not in grid}
    else if Grid[X, Y] = Empty then
      Blob := 0                    {cell is empty}
    else {cell is filled}
      begin {recursive step}
        Grid[X, Y] := Empty;
        Blob := 1 + Blob(Grid, X-1, Y+1) + Blob(Grid, X, Y+1) +
                Blob(Grid, X+1, Y+1) + Blob(Grid, X+1, Y) +
                Blob(Grid, X+1, Y-1) + Blob(Grid, X, Y-1) +
                Blob(Grid, X-1, Y-1) + Blob(Grid, X-1, Y)
      end {recursive step}
  end; {Blob}


begin {BlobCount}
  {Call Blob and return its result.}
  BlobCount := Blob(Grid, X, Y)
end; {BlobCount}
```

Function `Blob` in Fig. 15.32 implements the counting algorithm; function `BlobCount` simply calls the recursive function `Blob`, passes on its arguments, and returns the count computed by function `Blob` as its own result. The reason we use two functions instead of one is to protect the actual array from being modified when filled cells are reset to empty by function `Blob`. We will come back to this point shortly.

If the cell being visited is off the grid or is empty, a value of zero is returned immediately. Otherwise, the recursive step executes, causing function `Blob` to call itself eight times; each time, a different neighbor of the current cell is visited. The cells are visited in a clockwise manner, starting with the neighbor above and to the left. The function result is the sum of all values returned from these recursive calls plus 1 (for the current cell).

The sequence of operations performed in function `Blob` is important. The `if` statement tests whether the cell (`X, Y`) is on the grid before testing whether (`X, Y`) is empty. If the order was reversed, an `index out of bounds` run-time error would occur whenever (`X, Y`) was off the grid.

Also, the recursive step resets `Grid[X, Y]` to `Empty` before visiting the neighbors of point (`X, Y`). If this was not done first, then cell (`X, Y`) would be counted more than once, because it is a neighbor of all its neighbors. A worse problem is that the recursion would not terminate. When each neighbor of the current cell is visited, `Blob` is called again with the coordinates of the current cell as arguments. If the current cell is `Empty`, an immediate return occurs. If the current cell was still `Filled`, the recursive step would be executed erroneously. Eventually the program would run out of time or memory space (the latter is often indicated by a `stack overflow` run-time error).

A side effect of the execution of function `Blob` is that all cells that are part of the blob being processed are reset to `Empty`. This is the reason for using two functions. Because the array is passed as a value parameter to function `BlobCount`, a local copy is saved when `BlobCount` is first called. Only this local array, not the actual array, is changed by function `Blob`. If the counting operation was performed in function `BlobCount` instead of function `Blob`, eight copies of this array would be made each time the recursive step was executed, and we would soon run out of memory.

Exercise for Section 15.7

Self-Check

1. Trace the execution of function `BlobCount` for the coordinate pairs `(1, 1)` and `(1, 2)` in the sample grid.
2. Is the order of the two tests performed in function `Blob` critical? What happens if we reverse them or combine them into a single condition?

Programming

1. Write the recursive function `FindMin` that finds the smallest value in an integer array `X` with subscripts `1..N`.

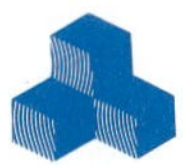

15.8 Debugging Recursive Subprograms

You can use the Turbo Pascal debugger to aid in debugging a recursive function or procedure. If you place a value parameter in the Watch window, you can see how that parameter's value changes during successive calls to the recursive subprogram. If your subprogram's local variables are in a Watch window, you can observe their values as you single-step through the subprogram using the F7 function key.

The Call Stack window can help trace the execution of a recursive subprogram. Each time a procedure or function is called, the Turbo Pascal debugger remembers the call by placing a record on the Call Stack. This record contains the subprogram name along with the values of the actual parameters used in the subprogram call. When the procedure or function is exited, its record is removed from the Call Stack. Whenever execution pauses during a debugging session, you can view the contents of the Call Stack by pressing Ctrl-F3. This opens a window similar to that shown in Fig. 15.33.

Figure 15.33 Call Stack Window

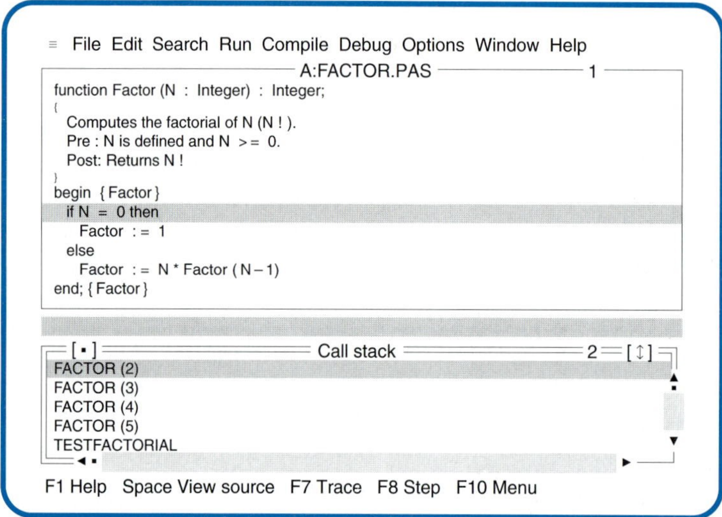

The Call Stack window contains a list of the calls to the currently active subprograms. If this list is too long to fit on the screen, use the F6 key to move to the Call Stack window and then use the arrow keys (or the mouse) to scroll through the list of calls.

You can also determine the statement currently executing in any of the active calls. Normally, the most recent call is highlighted in the Call Stack window, and its currently executing statement is highlighted in the Edit window. If you select another call in the Call Stack window (using the arrow keys or the mouse), the Call Stack window will disappear and the Edit window cursor will be positioned at the statement currently executing in that call. You can bring back the Call Stack window by pressing Ctrl-F3 again.

15.9 Common Programming Errors

The most common problem with a recursive procedure is that it may not terminate properly. For example, if the terminating condition is not correct or is incomplete, then the procedure may call itself indefinitely or until all available memory is used up. Normally, a `stack overflow` run-time error indicates that a recursive procedure is not terminating. Make sure you identify all stopping cases and provide a terminating condition for each one. Also be sure that each recursive step leads to a situation that is closer to a stopping case and that repeated recursive calls eventually lead to stopping cases only.

The use of large arrays or other data structures as value parameters can quickly consume all available memory. Unless absolutely essential for data protection, arrays should be passed as variable parameters. Any expression such as `N-1` must be passed as a value parameter.

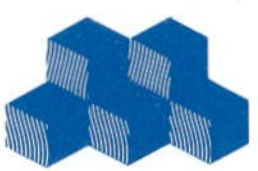

Chapter Review

This chapter provides several examples of recursive procedures and functions. Studying them should give you some appreciation of the power of recursion as a problem-solving and programming tool and provide you with valuable insight regarding its use. It may take you some time to feel comfortable thinking in this new way, but it is certainly worth the effort.

✓ Quick-Check Exercises

1. Explain the use of a stack in recursion.
2. Which is generally more efficient, recursion or iteration?
3. Which control statement is always in a recursive procedure or function?
4. What are the two uses of the function name in a recursive function?
5. How many times does the function name appear in a recursive function? In a recursive procedure?
6. Why would a programmer use recursion to conceptualize a problem solution but use iteration to implement it?
7. What is the problem with value array parameters in recursion?
8. In a recursive problem involving `N` items, why must `N` be a value parameter?
9. What causes a `stack overflow` error?
10. What can you say about a recursive algorithm that has the following form?
    `if` *condition* `then`
        Perform recursive step.

Answers to Quick-Check Exercises

1. The stack is used to hold all parameter and local variable values and the return point for each execution of a recursive procedure.
2. Iteration
3. `if` statement
4. To assign a value to the function and to call it recursively
5. At least three or more times in a function: once to assign a value for the stopping case, once to assign a value for the recursive step, and once to call the function recursively. There may be more than one recursive call, as in function `Fibonacci`. At least once in a procedure.

6. When its solution is much easier to conceptualize using recursion but its implementation would be too inefficient.
7. A copy of the array must be pushed onto the stack each time a call occurs. All available stack memory could be exhausted.
8. If N was a variable parameter, it would not be possible to use the expression N-1 as an actual parameter in a recursive call.
9. Too many recursive calls.
10. Nothing is done when the stopping case is reached.

Review Questions

1. Explain the nature of a recursive problem.
2. Discuss the efficiency of recursive procedures.
3. Differentiate between stopping cases and a terminating condition.
4. Write a recursive procedure that prints the accumulating sum of ordinal values corresponding to each character in a string. For example, if the string value is 'a boy', the first value printed would be the ordinal number of a, then the sum of ordinals for a and the space character, then the sum of ordinals for a, space, b, and so on.
5. Write a recursive function that returns the sum of ordinal values corresponding to the characters stored in a string; however, this time exclude any space characters from the sum.
6. Convert the following program from an iterative process to a recursive function that calculates an approximate value for e, the base of the natural logarithms, by summing the series

   $1 + 1/1! + 1/2! + \ldots 1/N!$

   until additional terms do not affect the approximation.

```
program ELog;

  var
    ENL, Delta, Fact : Real;
    N : Integer;

begin {ELog}
  ENL := 1.0;
  N := 1;
  Fact := 1.0;
  Delta := 1.0;
  repeat
    ENL := ENL + Delta;
    N := N + 1;
    Fact := Fact * N;
    Delta := 1 / Fact
   until ENL = (ENL + Delta);
   Write ('The value of e is ', E :18:15)
 end. {ELog}
```

Programming Projects

1. Write a procedure that reads each row of an array as a string and converts it to a row of Grid (see Fig.15.31). The first character of row 1 corresponds to Grid[1,1],

the second character to `Grid[1,2]`, and so on. Set the element value to `Empty` if the character is blank; otherwise, set it to `Filled`. The number of rows in the array should be read first. Use this procedure in a program that reads in cell coordinates and prints the number of cells in the blob containing each coordinate pair.

2. The expression for computing $C(n,r)$, the number of combinations of n items taken r at a time is

$$c(n,r) = \frac{n!}{r!(n-r)!}$$

Write and test a function for computing $c(n,r)$, given that $n!$ is the factorial of n.

3. A palindrome is a word that is spelled exactly the same when the letters are reversed, for example, level, deed, and mom. Write a recursive function that returns the Boolean value `True` if a word, passed as a parameter, is a palindrome.
4. Write a recursive function that returns the value of the following recursive definition:

```
F(X,Y) = X - Y, if X or Y < 0
F(X,Y) = F(X-1,Y) + F(X,Y-1), otherwise
```

5. Write a recursive procedure that lists all the pairs of subsets for a given set of letters. For example:

```
['A', 'C', 'E', 'G'] => ['A', 'C'], ['A', 'E'], ['A', 'G'],
                        ['C', 'E'], ['C', 'G'], ['E', 'G']
```

6. Write a procedure that accepts an 8-by-8 array of characters that represents a maze. Each position can contain either an `'X'` or a blank. Starting at position `[1,1]`, list any path through the maze to get to location `[8,8]`. Only horizontal and vertical moves are allowed (no diagonal moves). If no path exists, write a message indicating such.

   Moves can be made only to locations that contain a blank. If an `'X'` is encountered, that path is blocked and another must be chosen. Use recursion.

7. One method of solving a continuous numerical function for a root is the *bisection method* described next. Given a numerical function, defined as f(X), and two values of X that are known to bracket one of the roots, an approximation to this root can be determined through a method of repeated division of this bracket.

   For a set of values of X to bracket a root, the value of the function for one X must be negative and the other must be positive. This is illustrated in the diagram, which plots f(X) for values of X between $X1$ and $X2$.

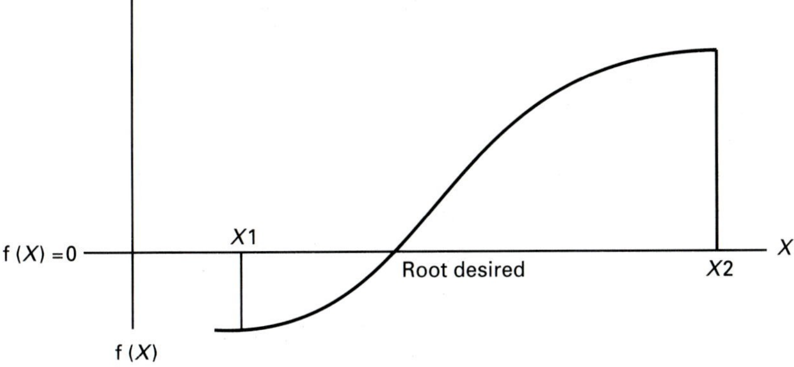

The algorithm requires that the midpoint between the left X and the right X be evaluated in the function. If the midpoint equals zero, the root is found; otherwise, the left X ($X1$) or the right X ($X2$) is set to this midpoint. To determine whether to replace $X1$ or $X2$, the sign of the midpoint is compared against the signs of the values of $f(X1)$ and $f(X2)$. The midpoint replaces the X ($X1$ or $X2$) whose function value has the same sign as the function value at the midpoint.

This routine can be written recursively. The terminating conditions are true when either the midpoint evaluated in the function is zero or the absolute value of the left X minus the right X is less than some small predetermined value (for example, 0.0005). If the second condition occurs, the root is said to be approximately equal to the midpoint of the last set of left and right Xs.

8. The Eight Queens problem is a famous chess problem that has as its goal the placement of 8 queens on a single chess board so that no queen will be able to attack any other queen. A queen may move any number of squares vertically, horizontally, or diagonally. A chess board may be represented as a two-dimensional array with 8 rows and 8 columns. Write a program containing a recursive routine that solves the Eight Queens problem.

   Hint: Arbitrarily choose a location for the first queen, then attempt to place a second queen in the next available open row. This process continues as long as it is possible to place queens. If a dead-end is reached, the last placed queen is removed from the board and repositioned. To do this, the algorithm would need to backtrack to a previous activation of the recursive routine and attempt to place the queen in a different location.

9. We can use a merge technique to sort two arrays. The *mergesort* begins by taking adjacent pairs of array values and ordering the values in each pair. It then forms groups of four elements by merging adjacent pairs (first pair with second pair, third pair with fourth pair, etc.) into another array. It then takes adjacent groups of four elements from this new array and merges them back into the original array as groups of eight, etcetera. The process terminates when a single group is formed that has the same number of elements as the array. The following illustration is of a mergesort for an array with eight elements. Write a `MergeSort` procedure.

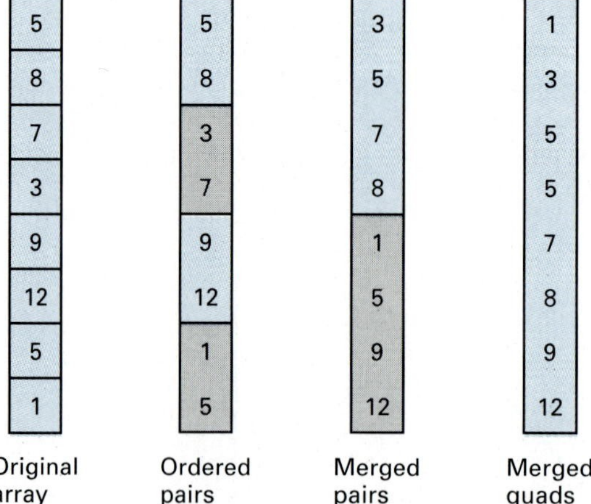

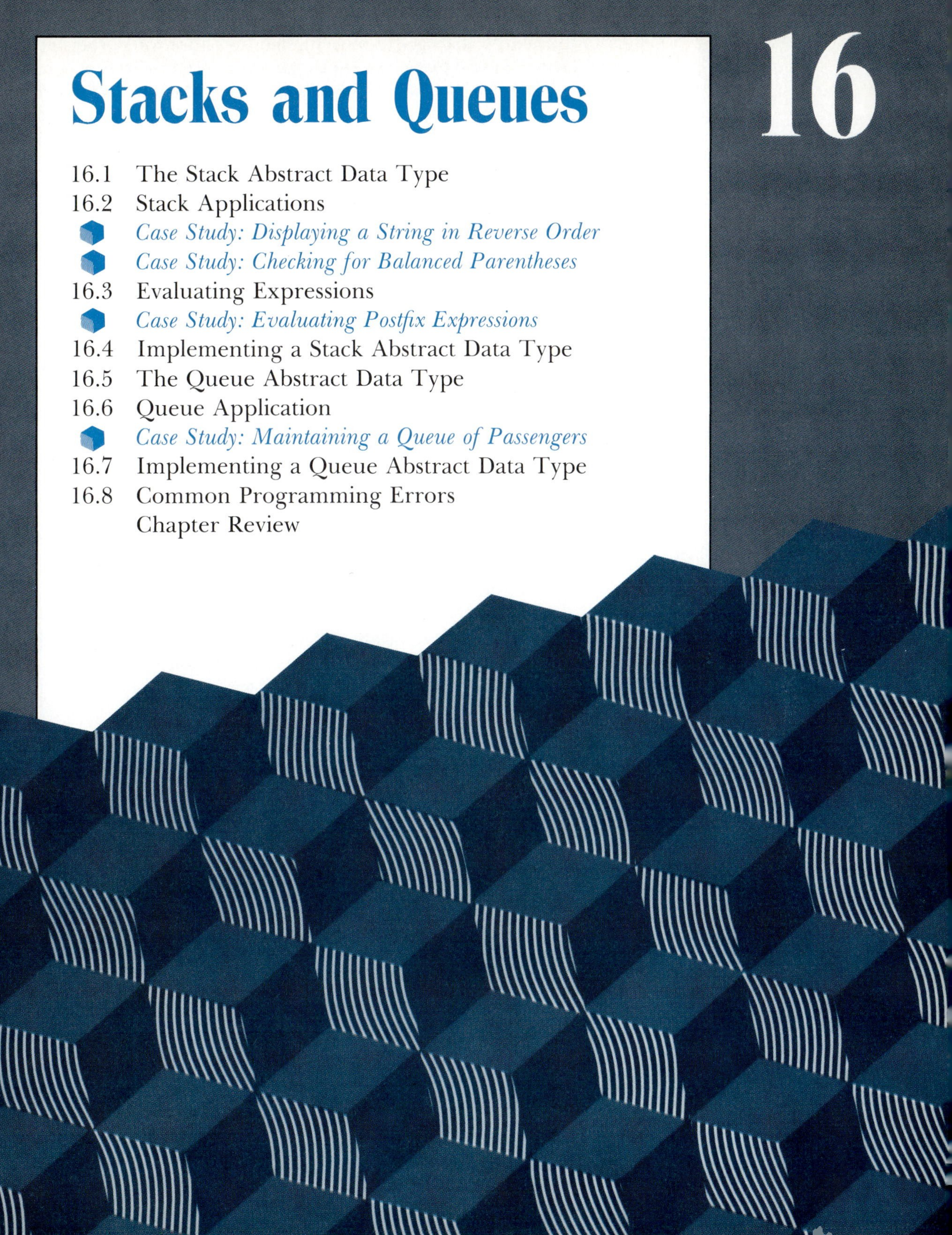

16 Stacks and Queues

Chapter 15 introduced the stack as a useful data structure for storing the actual parameters passed in each call to a recursive procedure or function. A stack is a convenient mechanism for storing information (or dishes in a cafeteria); we can access only the top item in a stack. The first part of this chapter illustrates how to use a stack and how to implement an abstract data type for a stack.

The rest of the chapter discusses a related data structure, the queue. The British people don't "wait in line," they "queue up." We will use a queue to represent a list of airline passengers waiting to see a ticket agent. We will also implement an abstract data type for a queue.

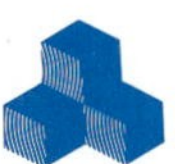

16.1 The Stack Abstract Data Type

In this section, we discuss a data abstraction, the stack, that is useful in computer science applications such as writing compilers. A stack is characterized by the property that at any one time only the top element of the stack is accessible. Some of the operations that we might want to perform on a stack are summarized in the following specification.

Specification of Abstract Data Type Stack

Elements: A stack consists of a collection of elements that are all the same data type.

Structure: The elements of a stack are ordered according to when they were placed on the stack. Only the element that was last inserted onto the stack can be removed or examined. New elements are inserted at the top of the stack.

Operators: The following descriptions assume these parameters:

`S` represents the stack.
`X` has the same data type as the stack elements.
`Success` is type `Boolean` and indicates whether or not the operation succeeds.

`CreateStack (var S)`: Creates an empty stack.

`Push (var S, X, var Success)`: If stack `S` is not full, the value in `X` is placed on the top of the stack and `Success` is set to `True`. Otherwise, the top of the stack is not changed and `Success` is set to `False`.

`Pop (var S, var X, var Success)`: If stack `S` is not empty, the value at the top of the stack is removed, its value is placed in `X`, and `Success` is set to `True`. If the stack is empty, `X` is not defined and `Success` is set to `False`.

`Retrieve (S, var X, var Success)`: If stack `S` is not empty, the value at the top of the stack is copied into `X`, and `Success` is set to `True`. If the stack is empty, X is not defined and Success is set to False. In either case, the stack is not changed.

IsEmpty(S): Returns True if stack S is empty; otherwise, returns False.

IsFull(S): Returns True if stack S is full; otherwise, returns False.

We can illustrate how these operators work and use them in a client program without worrying about the details of how the stack is represented in memory. We discuss an internal representation for a stack (ADT Stack) and implement the stack operators in Section 16.4. Because we want to be able to manipulate different types of data objects using a stack, we use the identifier StackElement to represent the type of each stack element. Each client program must import data types StackElement and Stack from ADT Stack.

A client program can allocate multiple stacks by declaring several variables of type Stack. Because StackElement can only be declared once in a program, all stacks used in a particular program must have the same type of element.

Procedure CreateStack must be called before a stack can be processed. CreateStack creates a stack that is initially empty. If S is declared as type Stack, the statements

```
CreateStack (S);
if IsEmpty(S) then
  WriteLn ('Stack is empty')
```

display the message Stack is empty.

■ Example 16.1

A stack S of character elements is shown in Fig. 16.1. The stack has four elements; the first element placed on the stack was '2', and the last element placed on the stack was '*'.

For stack S in Fig. 16.1, the value of IsEmpty(S) is False. The value of IsFull(S) is False if stack S can store more than four elements; otherwise, the value of IsFull(S) is True. The procedure call statement

```
Retrieve (S, X, Success)
```

stores '*' in X (type Char) without changing S. The procedure call statement

```
Pop (S, X, Success)
```

Figure 16.1 Stack S

```
| * |
| C |
| + |
| 2 |
 ---
  S
```

Figure 16.2 Stack S after Pop Operation

```
| C |
| + |
| 2 |
 ---
  S
```

removes '*' from S and stores it in X. The new stack S contains three elements and is shown in Fig. 16.2.

The procedure call statement

```
Push (S, '/', Success)
```

pushes '/' onto the stack; the new stack S contains four elements and is shown in Fig. 16.3. The value of Success (type Boolean) after each of the operations should be True. ■

Exercise for Section 16.1

Self-Check

1. Assume that the stack S is defined as in Fig. 16.3. Perform the following sequence of operations. Indicate the result of each operation and the new stack if it is changed. Rather than draw the stack each time, use the notation |2+C/ to represent the stack in Fig. 16.3 where the last symbol on the right (/) is at the top of the stack.

```
Push (S, '$', Success);
Push (S, '-', Success);
Pop (S, NextCh, Success);
Retrieve (S, NextCh, Success);
IsEmpty (S);
IsFull (S)
```

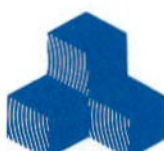

16.2 Stack Applications

This section examines some client programs that use stacks. These programs should give you some idea of the importance of the stack data type.

Figure 16.3 Stack S after Push Operation

```
| / |
| C |
| + |
| 2 |
 ---
  S
```

Case Study: Displaying a String in Reverse Order

Program

A reading instructor is studying dyslexia and wants a program that displays a word or a sentence in reverse order.

Design Overview

A stack of characters is a good data structure for such a program. If we first push each data character onto a stack and then pop each character and display it, the characters will be displayed in reverse order. The sequence of characters is displayed in reverse order because the last character pushed onto the stack is the first one popped. For example, the diagram in Fig. 16.4 shows the stack `S` after the letters in the string `'house'` are processed. The first letter popped and displayed is `e`, the next letter is `s`, and so on.

Data Requirements

Problem Inputs
Each data character

Problem Outputs
Each character on the stack

Program Variables
The stack of characters (`S : Stack`)

Algorithm

1. Create an empty stack of characters.
2. Push each data character onto a stack.
3. Pop each character and display it.
4. Indicate whether the stack is empty or full.

Program Structure

The structure chart (Fig. 16.5) shows that procedure `CreateStack` performs step 1, procedure `FillStack` performs step 2, and procedure `DisplayStack` performs step 3. `FillStack` and `DisplayStack` call procedures `Push` and `Pop`

Figure 16.4 Pushing 'house' onto a Stack

```
| e |
| s |
| u |
| o |
| h |
+---+
  S
```

Figure 16.5 Structure Chart for PrintReverse

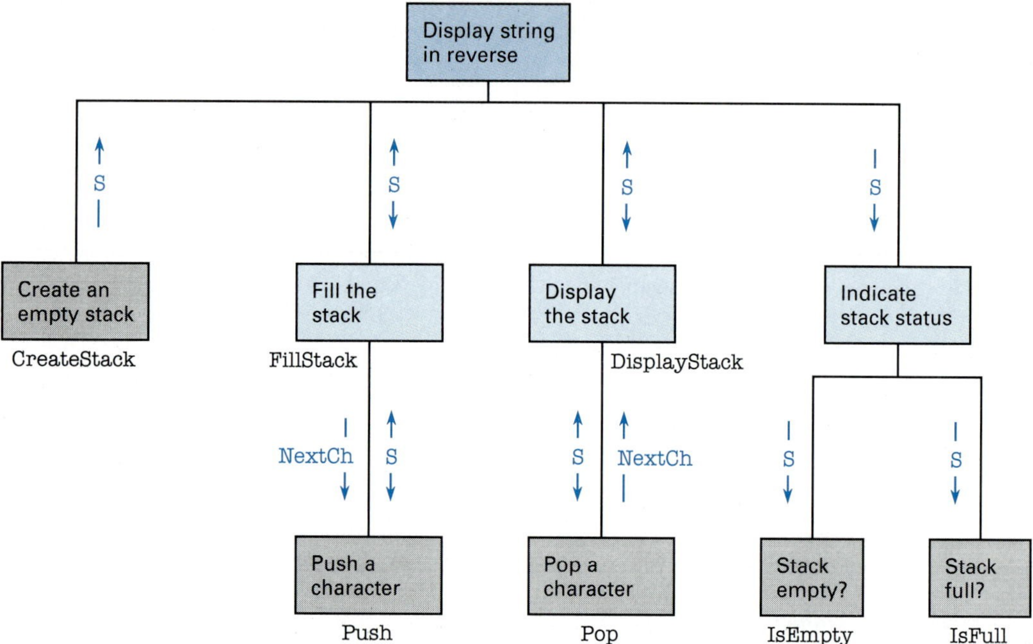

from StackADT. Functions IsEmpty and IsFull (from StackADT) are called to perform step 4.

Coding the Main Program

The main program and its procedures are shown in Fig. 16.6. The type declarations for StackElement (type is Char) and Stack must be imported from StackADT along with the stack operators. Procedures FillStack and DisplayStack are described after the program.

Figure 16.6 Program PrintReverse

Edit Window

```
program PrintReverse;
{
  Reads a sequence of characters and displays it in reverse
  order.

  Imports: Stack, StackElement, CreateStack, Push, Pop,
           IsFull, IsEmpty from StackADT (see Section 16.4)
}
  uses StackADT;

  var
    S : Stack;                    {the stack of characters}
```

```
  {$I FillStack (* see Fig. 16.7 *)}
  {$I DisplayStack (* see Fig. 16.8 *)}


begin {PrintReverse}
  CreateStack (S);               {start with an empty stack}

  {Fill the stack.}
  FillStack (S);

  {Display the characters in reverse order.}
  DisplayStack (S);

  {Display status of stack S.}
  if IsEmpty(S) then
    WriteLn ('Stack is empty - operation succeeds')
  else if IsFull(S) then
    WriteLn ('Stack is full - reversal failed')
end. {PrintReverse}
```

Output Window

```
Enter a string of one or more characters.
Press return when done.
This is a short string.
.gnirts trohs a si sihT
Stack is empty - operation succeeds
```

Coding the Procedures

The `repeat-until` loop in procedure `FillStack` (Fig. 16.7) reads each data character (at least one) into `NextCh` and pushes it onto the stack. The `if` statement displays an error message when the input string is too long (if the user enters more characters than the stack capacity before pressing the return key).

Figure 16.7 Procedure FillStack

```
procedure FillStack (var S {in/out} : Stack);
{
  Reads data characters and pushes them onto the stack.
  Pre  : S is a stack.
  Post : Each data character read is pushed onto stack S.
  Calls: Push
}
  var
    NextCh : Char;               {the next character}
    Success : Boolean;           {flag}

begin {FillStack}
  WriteLn ('Enter a string of one or more characters.');
  WriteLn ('Press return when done.');

  repeat
    Read (NextCh);                 {read next character}
    Push (S, NextCh, Success)      {push it onto stack}
  until Eoln(Input) or not Success;
```

```
  {Print an error if stack overflows.}
  if not Success then
    WriteLn ('Stack overflow error - string too long')
end; {FillStack}
```

The while loop in procedure DisplayStack (Fig. 16.8) pops each character from the stack into NextCh and then displays it. The loop is repeated as long as there are characters remaining on the stack (Success is True). After DisplayStack is finished, the stack should be empty.

Figure 16.8 Procedure DisplayStack

```
procedure DisplayStack (var S {in/out} : Stack);
{
  Pops each stack character and displays it.
  Pre  : Stack S is defined.
  Post : Each character is displayed and S is empty.
  Calls: Pop
}

  var
    NextCh : Char;                    {the next character}
    Success : Boolean;                {flag}

begin {DisplayStack}
  Pop (S, NextCh, Success);
  while Success do
    begin
      Write (NextCh);
      Pop (S, NextCh, Success)
    end; {while}
  WriteLn
end; {DisplayStack}
```

Testing

It is a good idea to see what happens when the stack overflows. This can be done by setting MaxStack to a small value (for example, 10).

Case Study: Checking for Balanced Parentheses

One application of a stack is to determine whether an expression is balanced with respect to parentheses. For example, the expression

```
(a + b * (c / (d - e))) + (d / e)
1        2    3      321   1     1
```

is balanced. We can solve this problem without using a stack by ignoring all characters except the symbols (and). We add 1 to a counter for each open parenthesis that follows another open parenthesis and subtract 1 for each close parenthesis that follows another close parenthesis. Because we are ignoring all other symbols, the parentheses being considered do not have to be consecutive characters. Assuming the initial count is 1, for a balanced expression the count ends at 1, and is never less than one.

This task becomes more difficult if we use different types of enclosure symbols as parentheses. For example, the expression

```
(a + b * {c / [d - e]}) + (d / e)
```

is balanced, but the expression

```
(a + b * {c / [d - e}]) + (d / e)
```

is not because the subexpression `[d - e}` is incorrect.

Problem

The set of open parentheses includes `{`, `[`, `(`. An expression is balanced if each subexpression that starts with the symbol `{` ends with the symbol `}`; the same is true for the symbol pairs `[,]` and `(,)`. Another way of saying this is that the unmatched open parenthesis that is nearest to each close parenthesis must have the correct shape (for example, if `}` is the close parenthesis in question, the symbol `{` must be the nearest unmatched open parenthesis.)

Design Overview

Without stacks it would be fairly difficult to solve this problem, but with stacks it becomes easy. First, we scan the expression from left to right, ignoring all characters except for parentheses. Then we push each open parenthesis onto a stack of characters. When we reach a close parenthesis, we see if it matches the symbol on the top of the stack. If the characters don't match or the stack is empty, there is an error in the expression. If they do match, we continue the scan.

Data Requirements

Problem Inputs

The expression to be checked for balanced parentheses
(`Expression : String`)

Problem Outputs

The function result indicating whether the parentheses in `Expression` are balanced

Program Variables

The stack of open parentheses (`ParenStack : Stack`)
A flag indicating whether parentheses are balanced
(`Balanced : Boolean`)
The next character in `Expression` (`NextCh : Char`)

The index of the next character (`Index : Integer`)
The open parenthesis at the top of the stack (`Open : Char`)
The close parenthesis being matched (`Close : Char`)

Algorithm

```
1. Create an empty stack of characters.
2. Assume that the expression is balanced (Balanced is True).
3. while the expression is balanced and still in the string do
     begin
       4. Get the next character in the data string.
       5. if the next character is an open parenthesis then
            6. Push it onto the stack
          else if the next character is a close parenthesis then
            begin
              7. Pop the top of the stack
              8. if stack was empty or its top was incorrect then
                   Set Balanced to False.
            end
     end
9. if the expression is balanced then
     10. There is an error if the stack is not empty.
```

The `if` statement at step 5 tests each character in the expression, ignoring all characters except for open and close parentheses. If the next character is an open parenthesis, it is pushed onto the stack. If the next character is a close parenthesis, the nearest unmatched open parenthesis is retrieved (by popping the stack) and compared to the close parenthesis (steps 7 and 8).

Coding

Figure 16.9 shows a function that determines whether its input parameter (an expression) is balanced. The `if` statement in the `while` loop tests for open and close parentheses. Each open parenthesis is pushed onto stack `ParenStack`. For each close parenthesis, procedure `Pop` retrieves the nearest unmatched open parenthesis from the stack. If the stack was empty, `Pop` sets `Balanced` to `False`, causing the `while` loop exit. Otherwise, the case statement sets `Balanced` to indicate whether the character popped matches the current close parenthesis. After loop exit occurs, the function result is defined. It is true only when the expression is balanced and the stack is empty.

Figure 16.9 Function IsBalanced

```
function IsBalanced (Expression : string) : Boolean;
{
  Determines whether Expression is balanced with respect
  to parentheses.
```

```
  Pre     : Expression is defined.
  Post    : Returns True if Expression is balanced; otherwise,
            returns False.
  Imports: Stack, Push, Pop and IsEmpty from ADT Stack.
}
  var
    ParenStack : Stack;        {the stack of open parentheses}
    NextCh,                    {the next character in Expression}
    CloseParen,                {close parenthesis to be matched}
    OpenParen : Char;          {open parenthesis at top of stack}
    Index : Integer;           {index to Expression}
    Balanced : Boolean;        {program flag}

begin {IsBalanced}
  CreateStack (ParenStack);          {Create an empty stack}
  Balanced := True;
  Index := 1;
  while Balanced and (Index <= Length(Expression)) do
    {invariant:
        All closing parentheses so far were matched and
        Index <= Length(Expression) + 1
    }
    begin
      NextCh := Expression[Index];             {access next
                                                character}
      if NextCh in ['(', '[', '{'] then
        Push (ParenStack, NextCh, Balanced) {stack parenthesis}
      else if NextCh in [')', ']', '}'] then
        begin {close paren}
          CloseParen := NextCh;
          {Get nearest unmatched open parenthesis}
          Pop (ParenStack, OpenParen, Balanced);
          if Balanced then
            {Check for matching parentheses.}
            case CloseParen of
              ')' : Balanced := OpenParen = '(';
              ']' : Balanced := OpenParen = '[';
              '}' : Balanced := OpenParen = '{'
            end {case}
          end; {close paren}
        Index := Index + 1      {access next character}
      end; {while}

    {Define function result}
    if Balanced then
      IsBalanced := IsEmpty(ParenStack)
    else
      IsBalanced := False
  end; {IsBalanced}
```

Testing

You have to write a driver program to test function IsBalanced. The driver program has to import the type declarations for StackElement (type is Char) and Stack (from StackADT). It also has to import the stack operators that are called by `IsBalanced`. Make sure you use a variety of balanced and unbalanced expressions to test `IsBalanced`, as well as an expression without parentheses.

Exercises for Section 16.2

Self-Check

1. Trace the execution of function `IsBalanced` for each of the following expressions. Your trace should show the stack after each `Push` or `Pop` operation. Also show the values of `Balanced`, `Open`, and `Close` after each close parenthesis is processed.

```
(a + b * {c / [d - e]}) + (d / e)
(a + b * {c / [d - e}}) + (d / e)
```

Programming

1. Write a main program to test function `IsBalanced`.

16.3 Evaluating Expressions

One task of a compiler is to evaluate arithmetic expressions. This section discusses one approach to expression evaluation.

Some of you may use calculators that evaluate postfix expressions. A *postfix expression* is an expression in which each operator follows its operands. We discuss postfix expressions further in Chapter 18; for the time being, however, you can get a pretty good idea of what a postfix epression is by studying the examples in Table 16.1. The grouping marks under each expression should help you visualize the operands for each operator. The more familiar *infix expression* corresponding to each postfix expression is also shown.

The advantage of postfix form is that there is no need to group subexpressions in parentheses or to consider operator precedence. The grouping marks in Table 16.1 are only for our convenience and are not required. Next, we write a program that evaluates a postfix expression.

Table 16.1 Table of Postfix Expressions

Example	Infix Expression	Value
`5 6 *`	`5 * 6`	30
`5 6 1 + *`	`5 * (6 + 1)`	35
`5 6 * 10 -`	`(5 * 6) - 10`	20
`4 5 6 * 3 / +`	`4 + ((5 * 6) / 3)`	14

Case Study: Evaluating Postfix Expressions

Problem

Simulate the operation of a calculator by reading an expression in postfix form and displaying its result. Each data character will be a blank, a digit character, or one of the operator characters from the set `[+, -, *, /]`.

Design Overview

Using a stack of integer values makes it easy to evaluate the expression. Our program will push each integer operand onto the stack. When an operator is read, the top two operands are popped, the operation is performed on its operands, and the result is pushed back onto the stack. The final result should be the only value remaining on the stack when the end of the expression is reached.

Data Requirements

Problem Inputs

The expression to evaluate (`Expression`)

Problem Outputs

The expression value (`Result : Integer`)

Program Variables

The stack of integer operands (`OpStack : Stack`)
Program flag indicating result of a stack operation (`Success : Boolean`)
The next character in `Expression` (`NextCh : Char`)
The index to the next character (`Index : Integer`)
The next integer value in `Expression` (`NewOp : Integer`)
The two operands of an operator (`Op1, Op2 : Integer`)

Algorithm

```
1. Read the expression string.
2. Create an empty stack of integers.
3. Set Success to True.
4. while Success is True and not at the end of the expression do
     begin
       5. Get the next character.
       6. if the character is a digit then
            begin
              7. Get the integer that starts with this digit.
              8. Push the integer onto the stack.
            end
          else if the character is an operator then
            begin
              9. Pop the top two operands.
```

```
            10. Evaluate the operation.
            11. Push the result onto the stack.
         end
      end
12. Display the result
```

Table 16.2 shows the evaluation of the third expression in Table 16.1 using this algorithm. The arrow under the expression points to the character being processed; the stack diagram shows the stack after this character is processed.

Table 16.2 Evaluating a Postfix Expression

Expression	Action	Stack
`5 6 * 10 -` `↑`	Push 5.	5
`5 6 * 10 -` `  ↑`	Push 6.	6 5
`5 6 * 10 -` `    ↑`	Pop 6 and 5; evaluate `5 * 6`; push 30.	30
`5 6 * 10 -` `      ↑`	Push 10.	10 30
`5 6 * 10 -` `         ↑`	Pop 10 and 30; evaluate `30 - 10`, push 20.	20
`5 6 * 10 -` `         ↑`	Pop 20; stack is empty; result is 20.	

Refinements and Program Structure

The stack operators perform algorithm steps 2, 8, 9, 11, and 12. Steps 7 and 10 are the only algorithm steps that require refinement. Step 7 is performed by procedure `GetInteger` and step 10 by function `Eval`. The structure chart in Fig. 16.10 shows the data flow between these two subprograms and the main program.

Coding the Main Program

The main program is shown in Fig. 16.11. Besides the operators mentioned earlier, data types `StackElement` (type is `Integer`), `Stack`, and `String` must all be imported into the main program.

Each time stack `S` is manipulated, the Boolean flag `Success` is set to indicate the success or failure of that operation. If `Success` is `False`, the program displays an error message and terminates the expression evaluation. If the final value of `Success` is `True` and the stack is empty, the result is displayed.

Figure 16.10 Structure Chart for Program PostFix

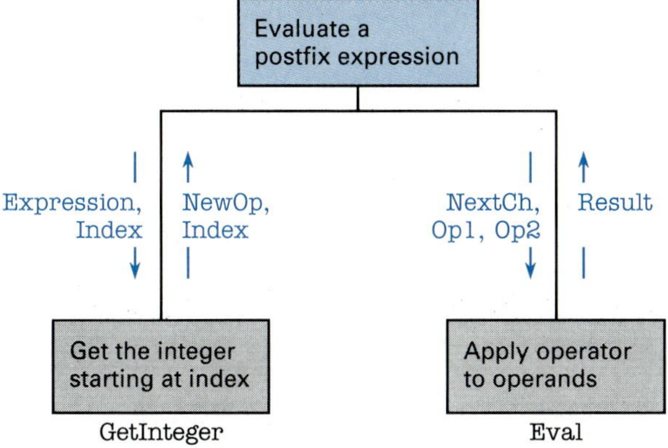

Figure 16.11 Program PostFix and Sample Run

Edit Window

```
program PostFix;
{
  Evaluates a postfix expression.

  Imports : Stack, CreateStack, Pop, Push,
            IsEmpty from StackADT (see Section 16.4)
}
  uses StackADT;

  var
    OpStack : Stack;               {a stack of integers}
    Expression : string;           {expression to be evaluated}
    NextCh : Char;                 {the next data character}
    Index : Integer;               {index of next character}
    Op1, Op2,                      {operand values from stack}
    NewOp,                         {new operand for the stack}
    Result : Integer;              {result of operator evaluation}
    Success : Boolean;             {flag for stack operation}

  {$I GetInteger (* see Fig. 16.12 *)}
  {$I Eval (* see Fig. 16.13 *)}
begin {Postfix}
  Write ('Enter your expression> ');
  ReadLn (Expression);

  CreateStack (OpStack);                         {Create an empty stack}
  Index := 1;
  Success := True;
  while Success and (Index <= Length(Expression)) do
    {invariant:
        OpStack contains all unprocessed operands and results and
        Index <= Length(Expression) + 1
    }
```

```
    begin
      NextCh := Expression[Index];                    {Get the next character}
      if NextCh in ['0'..'9'] then
        begin {digit}
          GetInteger(Expression, Index, NewOp);       {Get integer value}
          Push (OpStack, NewOp, Success);             {Push integer value}
          if not Success then
            WriteLn ('Stack overflow error')
        end {digit}
      else if NextCh in ['+','-','*','/'] then
        begin {operator}
          Pop (OpStack, Op2, Success);                {Get last operand}
          Pop (OpStack, Op1, Success);                {Get first operand}
          if not Success then
            WriteLn ('Invalid expression')
          else
            begin {evaluate operator}
              Result := Eval(NextCh, Op1, Op2);
              Push (OpStack, Result, Success);        {Push result}
              if not Success then
                WriteLn ('Stack overflow')
            end {evaluate operator}
        end; {operator}
      Index := Index + 1                              {Go to next character}
    end; {while}

  if Success then
    Pop (OpStack, Result, Success);                   {Get the result}
  if Success and IsEmpty(OpStack) then
    WriteLn ('Expression value is ', Result :1)       {Print it}
  else
    WriteLn ('Invalid expression')
end. {Postfix}
```

Output Window

```
Enter your expression> 5 6 * 10 -

Expression value is 20
```

Coding the Subprograms

Procedure `GetInteger` (Fig. 16.12) accumulates the integer value of a string of consecutive digit characters and returns this value through parameter `NewOp`. The assignment statement

```
NewOp := (10 * NewOp) + Ord(NextCh) - Ord('0');
```

adds the numeric value of the digit character in `NextCh` to the numeric value being accumulated in `NewOp`. For example, if the current value of `NewOp` is `15` and `NextCh` is `'3'`, `NewOp` gets the value `153`. When `GetInteger` returns to the main program, `Index` points to the last digit of the number just processed.

Figure 16.12 Procedure GetInteger

```
procedure GetInteger (Expression {input} : string;
                      var Index {input/output},
                      NewOp {output} : Integer);
```

```
{
  Returns in NewOp the integer whose first digit is at position
  Index.
  Pre : Expression and Index are defined and the character at Index
        is a digit.
  Post: Index points to the last digit of the number whose first digit
        is pointed to by the initial value of Index.
        NewOp is the value of that number.
}
begin {GetInteger}
  NewOp := 0;
  NextCh := Expression[Index];
  while (NextCh in ['0'..'9']) and (Index <= Length(Expression)) do
    {invariant:
       Prior character in NextCh was a digit and
       Index <= Length(Expression) + 1 and
       NewOp is the numerical value of all digits processed so far
    }
    begin
      NewOp := (10 * NewOp) + Ord(NextCh) - Ord('0');
      Index := Index + 1;
      NextCh := Expression[Index]
    end; {while}

  {assert:
    NewOp is the numerical value of the substring processed and
    Index is at the end of the substring or just past it.
  }
  if not (NextCh in ['0'..'9']) then
    Index := Index - 1                {point to the last digit}
end; {GetInteger}
```

Whenever an operator is encountered, the main program pops its two operands off the stack and calls function `Eval` (Fig. 16.13) to compute the result of applying the operator (passed through `NextCh`) to its operands (passed through `Op1`, `Op2`). The case statement in function `Eval` selects the appropriate operation and performs it.

Figure 16.13 Function Eval

```
function Eval (NextCh : Char;
               Op1, Op2 : Integer) : Integer;
{
  Applies operator NextCh to operands Op1, Op2.
  Pre : NextCh is an operator and Op1, Op2 are defined.
  Post: If NextCh is '+', returns Op1 + Op2, and so on.
}
begin {Eval}
  if NextCh in ['+', '-', '*', '/'] then
    case NextCh of
      '+' : Eval := Op1 + Op2;
      '-' : Eval := Op1 - Op2;
      '*' : Eval := Op1 * Op2;
      '/' : Eval := Op1 div Op2      {integer division}
    end {case}
```

Case Study: Evaluating Postfix Expressions, continued

```
  else
    WriteLn ('Error in operator symbol')
end; {Eval}
```

Testing

You have to import the necessary data types and procedures to test program `PostFix`. See what happens when the expression is not a valid postfix expression or when it contains characters other than those expected.

Exercises for Section 16.3

Self-Check

1. Trace the evaluation of the last expression in Table 16.1. Show the stack each time it is modified and how the values of `NewOp` and `Result` change as the program executes.

Programming

1. Modify program `PostFix` to handle the exponentiation operator, indicated by the symbol `^`. Assume that the first operand is raised to the power indicated by the second operand.

16.4 Implementing a Stack Abstract Data Type

This section discusses how we might implement a stack in Pascal. We begin with the internal representation for a stack.

Declaration for Type Stack

The data type `Stack` declared in the interface section for `StackADT` (Fig. 16.14) has two fields, `Top` and `Items`. The array field `Items` provides storage for the stack elements. `Top` is an index to this array and selects the element at the top of the stack. We can store up to `MaxStack` (value is `100`) elements in an object of type `Stack`.

Figure 16.14 Interface Section for Unit StackADT

```
unit StackADT;

{
 Abstract data type Stack: contains declarations for record
```

```
 type Stack and operator procedures for an object of type Stack.
  Exports: Stack, StackElement, CreateStack, Push, Pop,
           Retrieve, IsEmpty, IsFull
}
interface

   const
      MaxStack = 100;

   type
     {Insert declaration for StackElement}

     StackRange = 1..MaxStack;
     Stack = record
               Top : 0..MaxStack;
               Items : array [StackRange] of StackElement
             end; {Stack}

   procedure CreateStack (var S {output} : Stack);
   {
     Creates an empty stack.
     Pre : None
     Post: S is an empty stack.
   }

   procedure Push (var S {input/output} : Stack;
                   X {input} : StackElement;
                   var Success {output} : Boolean);
   {
     Pushes X onto stack S.
     Pre : X is defined and S is a stack that has been created.
     Post: Sets Success to indicate success (True) or failure (False) of
           push operation.
   }

   procedure Pop (var S {input/output} : Stack;
                  var X {output} : StackElement;
                  var Success {output} : Boolean);
   {
     Pops the top of stack S into X.
     Pre : S is a stack that has been created.
     Post: Contents of X is character at top of stack S which is then re-
           moved from S. Sets Success to indicate success (True) or failure
           (False) of pop operation.
   }

   procedure Retrieve (S {in} : Stack;
                       var X {out} : StackElement;
                       var Success {out} : Boolean);
   {
     Copies the value at the top of the stack into X.
     Pre : S is a stack.
     Post: Contents of X is character at top of stack S; S is unchanged.
           Sets Success to indicate success (True) or failure (False).
   }

   function IsEmpty (S : Stack) : Boolean;
   {
     Pre : S is a stack.
     Post: Returns True if stack S is empty;
           otherwise, returns False.
   }
```

```
function IsFull (S : Stack) : Boolean;
{
  Pre : S is a stack.
  Post: Returns True if stack S is full;
        otherwise, returns False.
}
```

The comment

```
{Insert declaration for StackElement}
```

reminds us that we must declare data type `StackElement` before we can declare record type `Stack`. If we use the declaration

```
StackElement = Char;
```

a variable of type `Stack` will be able to store up to 100 characters.

As always, storage is not allocated until a variable of type `Stack` is declared. Assuming `StackElement` is type `Char`, the variable declaration

```
var
  S : Stack;
```

allocates storage for a stack, `S`, of up to 100 characters. Notice that the storage space for the entire stack is allocated at one time, even though there will not be any items on the stack initially.

The following abstract stack `S` (on the left) would be represented in memory by the record shown on the right. `S.Top` is `3`, and the stack consists of the subarray `S.Items[1..3]`; the subarray `S.Items[4..100]` is currently undefined.

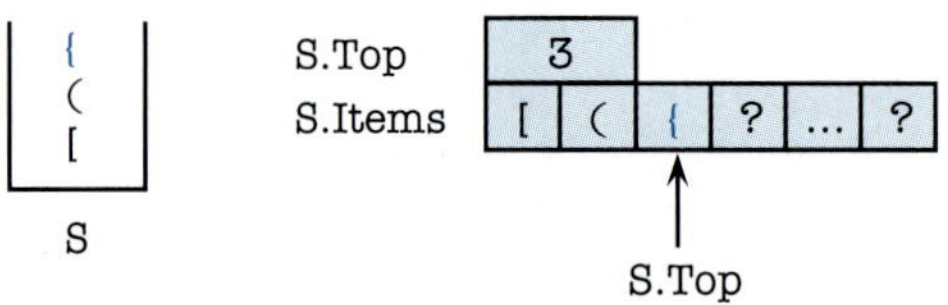

The array element `S.Items[S.Top]` contains the character value `'{'`, which is the value at the top of the stack.

We can change the capacity of a stack by redefining the constant `MaxStack`. Also, we can change the stack elements to another simple type or a structured type by changing the declaration for `StackElement`. If we use the declaration

```
StackElement = Integer;
```

a variable of type `Stack` will be able to store up to 100 integer values.

■ Example 16.2

Figure 16.15 shows the effect of the statement

```
Push (S, '(', Success)
```

Figure 16.15 Pushing '(' onto Stack S

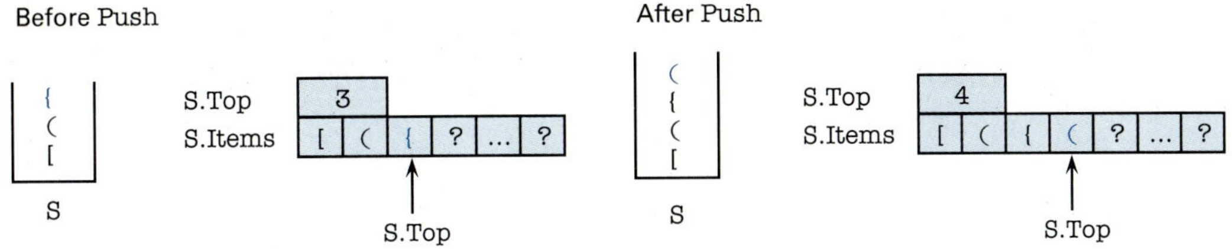

where the initial stack `S` is shown on the left. Before `Push` is executed, `S.Top` is 3, so `S.Items[3]` is the element at the top of the stack. Procedure `Push` must increment `S.Top` to 4 so the new item (`'('`) will be stored in `S.Items[4]`, as shown on the right of the figure. ■

Stack Operators

The stack operators manipulate the array field `Items` using the `Integer` field `Top` as an index to the array. Their implementation is fairly straightforward. You should have little difficulty in reading and understanding the stack operators shown in the implementation section of `StackADT` (Fig. 16.16).

Figure 16.16 Implementation Section for Unit StackADT

```
{$R+}
implementation

procedure CreateStack (var S {output} : Stack);
begin {CreateStack}
  S.Top := 0              {stack is empty}
end; {CreateStack}


procedure Push (var S {in/out} : Stack;
                X {in} : StackElement;
                var Success {out} : Boolean);
begin {Push}
  if S.Top >= MaxStack then
    Success := False      {no room on stack}
  else
    begin
      S.Top := S.Top + 1;     {increment top of stack pointer}
      S.Items[S.Top] := X;    {push X onto stack}
      Success := True
    end {if}
end; {Push}


procedure Pop (var S {in/out} : Stack;
               var X {out} : StackElement;
               var Success {out} : Boolean);
begin {Pop}
  if S.Top <= 0 then
    Success := False
```

```
    else
      begin
        X := S.Items[S.Top];        {pop top of stack into X}
        S.Top := S.Top - 1;         {decrement top of stack pointer}
        Success := True
      end {if}
  end; {Pop}


  procedure Retrieve (S {in} : Stack;
                      var X {out} : StackElement;
                      var Success {out} : Boolean);
  begin {Retrieve}
    if S.Top <= 0 then
      Success := False
    else
      begin
        X := S.Items[S.Top];        {copy top of stack into X}
        Success := True
      end {if}
  end; {Retrieve}


  function IsEmpty (S : Stack) : Boolean;
  begin {IsEmpty}
    IsEmpty := S.Top <= 0
  end; {IsEmpty}


  function IsFull (S : Stack) : Boolean;
  begin {IsFull}
    IsFull := S.Top >= MaxStack
  end; {IsFull}

  end. {StackADT}
```

Procedure `CreateStack` must be called before the stack can be manipulated. In `CreateStack`, the statement

```
S.Top := 0                  {stack is empty}
```

initializes a stack by setting its top-of-stack pointer to zero.

Procedure `Push` increments the top-of-stack pointer before it pushes a new value onto the stack. Procedure `Pop` copies the value at the top of the stack (denoted by `S.Items[S.Top]`) into `X` before decrementing the top-of-stack pointer. Procedure `Retrieve` copies the value at the top of the stack into `X` without changing the top-of-stack pointer. Functions `IsFull` and `IsEmpty` test the top-of-stack pointer to determine the stack status.

PROGRAM STYLE

Efficiency versus Readability

Procedure `Push` in Fig. 16.16 uses the condition `S.Top >= MaxStack` to determine whether the stack represented by `S` is full. It would be more readable, but less efficient, to use the function designator `IsFull(S)` to test whether stack `S` is full. You should use the function designator `IsFull(S)` for this purpose in any client program that manipulates the stack, because the stack's internal representation may be hidden from a client program. It is perfectly reasonable, however, for another stack operator to directly manipulate internal fields of a stack.

Exercises for Section 16.4

Self-Check

1. Declare a stack of fifty student records, where each record consists of a student's name `string[20]`, an exam score, and a letter grade. Can you use the stack operators to manipulate this stack?

Programming

1. Write an operator `SizeOfStack` that returns the number of elements currently on the stack.

16.5 The Queue Abstract Data Type

A *queue* is a data abstraction that can be used, for example, to model a line of customers waiting at a checkout counter or a stream of jobs waiting to be printed by a printer in a computer center. A queue differs from a stack in that new elements are inserted at one end (the rear of the queue) and existing elements are removed from the other end (the front of the queue). In this way, the element that has been waiting longest is removed first. In contrast, stack elements are inserted and removed from the same end (the top of the stack). A queue is called a *first-in, first-out* structure (FIFO), while a stack is called a *last-in, first-out* (LIFO) structure.

A queue of three passengers waiting to see an airline ticket agent is shown in Fig. 16.17. The name of the passenger who has been waiting the longest is

Figure 16.17 A Passenger Queue

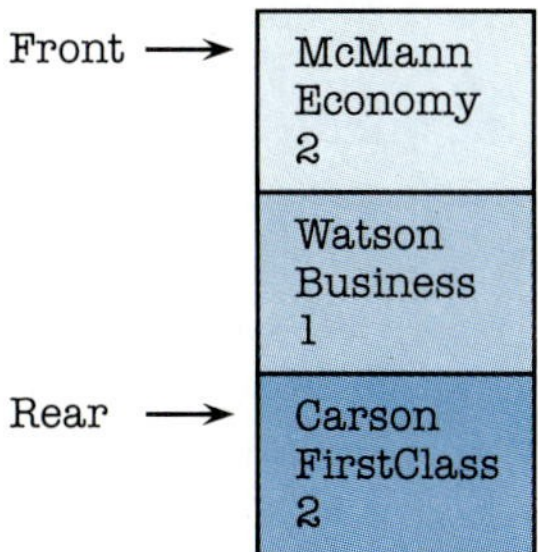

McMann (pointed to by Front); the name of the most recent arrival is Carson (pointed to by Rear). Passenger McMann will be the first one removed from the queue when an agent becomes available, and pointer Front will be moved to passenger Watson. Any new passengers will follow passenger Carson in the queue, and pointer Rear will be adjusted accordingly.

The specification for the abstract data type Queue follows; compare it with the earlier specification for an abstract stack.

Specification of Queue Abstract Data Type

Elements: A queue consists of a collection of elements that are all the same data type.

Structure: The elements of a queue are ordered according to time of arrival. The element that was first inserted into the queue is the only one that may be removed or examined. Elements are removed from the front of the queue and inserted at the rear of the queue.

Operators: The following descriptions assume these parameters:

Q represents the queue.
El (pronounced el) has the same data type as the queue elements.
Success is type Boolean and indicates whether the operation succeeds.

CreateQueue (var Q): Creates an empty queue Q.

Insert (var Q, El, var Success): If queue Q is not full, the value in El is inserted at the rear of the queue, and Success is set to True. Otherwise, the queue is not changed, and Success is set to False.

Remove (var Q, var El, var Success): If queue Q is not empty, the element at the front of the queue is removed and copied to El, and Success is set to True. If the queue is empty, El is not changed, and Success is set to False.

Retrieve (Q, var El, var Success): If queue Q is not empty, the element at the front of the queue is copied into El, and Success is set to True. If the queue is empty, El is not defined, and Success is set to False. In either case, the queue is not changed.

IsEmpty(Q): Returns True if queue Q is empty; otherwise, returns False.

IsFull(Q): Returns True if queue Q is full; otherwise, returns False.

SizeOfQueue(Q): Returns the number of elements in the queue.

We implement unit QueueADT in section 16.7. As before, we assume that the identifier QueueElement represents the type of each queue element. Each client program must import type declarations for QueueElement and Queue.

Exercise for Section 16.5

Self-Check

1. Draw the queue in Fig. 16.17 after the insertion of first-class passenger `Harris` (3 seats reserved) and the removal of one passenger from the queue. Which passenger is removed? How many passengers are left?

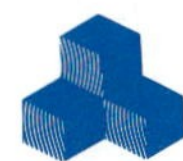

16.6 Queue Application

Our application is a program that processes a queue of airline passengers.

Case Study: Maintaining a Queue of Passengers

Problem

Write a menu-driven program that maintains a queue of passengers waiting to see a ticket agent. The program user should be able to insert a new passenger at the rear of the queue, display the passenger at the front of the queue, and remove the passenger at the front of the queue. Just before it terminates, the program should display the number of passengers left in the queue.

Design Overview

We can use the queue abstract data type and operators `Insert`, `Retrieve`, and `Remove` to process the queue. We can simplify the program by using an abstract data type, `Passenger`, that contains type declarations for an airline passenger and provides its input/output operators (`ReadPass` and `WritePass`). We will implement this abstract data type later.

Data Requirements

Problem Inputs

The operation to be performed (`Choice : Char`)
The next passenger's data (`NextPass : Passenger`)

Problem Outputs

The passenger at the front of the queue (`FirstPass : Passenger`)

Program Variables

The queue of passengers (`PassQueue : Queue`)
A flag for storing the result of a queue operation
(`Success : Boolean`)

Algorithm

1. Initialize the queue.

2. `repeat`
    3. Display the menu.
    4. Read the operation selected.
    5. Perform the operation selected.

   `until` user is done or a queue operation fails
6. Display the number of passengers left in the queue.

Coding the Main Program

The main program (Fig. 16.18) imports the type declarations for `Passenger` (from `PassengerADT`) and for `QueueElement` and `Queue` (both from `QueueADT`). Procedure `CreateQueue` (from `QueueADT`) initializes the passenger queue to an empty queue. In the main program body, the statement

```
Write ('Enter I(nsert), R(emove), D(isplay), or Q(uit)> ');
```

displays the menu of choices (step 3). After the selection is read into `Choice`, the main program calls procedure `ModifyQueue` to perform step 5. Procedure `ModifyQueue` is discussed next.

Figure 16.18 Program UseQueue

```
program UseQueue;
{
  Manipulates a queue of airline passenger.

  Import: Passenger, ReadPass, WritePass from PassengerADT
          (see Fig. 16.21)
          Queue, CreateQueue, Insert,
          Remove, and Retrieve from QueueADT (see Section 16.7).
}

  uses QueueADT, PassengerADT;

  var
    PassQueue : Queue;          {a passenger queue}
    Choice : Char;              {operation request}
    Success : Boolean;          {program flag}

  {$I ModifyQueue (* see Fig. 16.19 *)}

begin {UseQueue}
  CreateQueue (PassQueue);             {start with an empty queue}

  {Process all requests until done.}
  repeat
    Write ('Enter I(nsert), R(emove), D(isplay), or Q(uit)> ');
    ReadLn (Choice);
    {Process current request.}
    ModifyQueue (PassQueue, Choice, Success);
    WriteLn
  until (Choice = 'Q') or (not Success)
end. {UseQueue}
```

Coding ModifyQueue

For each selection, procedure `ModifyQueue` (Fig. 16.19) calls the operators required to manipulate the `Queue` (from `QueueADT`) and the operators needed to read or display a passenger record (from `PassengerADT`). The main control structure is a case statement that determines which operators are called.

Figure 16.19 Procedure ModifyQueue

```
procedure ModifyQueue (var Q {in/out} : Queue;
                       Choice {input} : Char;
                       var Success {output} : Boolean);
{
  Performs the operation indicated by Choice on the queue Q.
  Pre  : Q has been created.
  Post : Q is modified based on Choice and Success indicates
         whether requested operation was performed.
  Calls: ReadPass, WritePass, Insert, Remove, Retrieve
}
  var
    NextPass,                   {new passenger}
    FirstPass : Passenger;      {passenger at front of queue}

begin {ModifyQueue}
  if Choice in ['I', 'R', 'D', 'Q'] then
    case Choice of
      'I' : begin {insert}
              WriteLn ('Enter passenger data.');
              ReadPass (NextPass);
              Insert (Q, NextPass, Success);
              if not Success then
                WriteLn ('Queue is full - no insertion');
            end; {insert}
      'R' : begin {remove}
              Remove (Q, FirstPass, Success);
              if Success then
                begin
                  WriteLn ('Passenger removed from queue follows.');
                  WritePass (FirstPass)
                end
              else
                WriteLn ('Queue is empty - no deletion')
            end; {remove}
      'D' : begin {display}
              Retrieve (Q, FirstPass, Success);
              if Success then
                begin
                  WriteLn ('Passenger at head of queue follows.');
                  WritePass (FirstPass)
                end
             else
               WriteLn ('Queue is empty - no passenger')
             end; {display}
       'Q' : begin
               WriteLn ('Leaving passenger queue.');
               WriteLn ('Number of passengers in the queue is ',
                        SizeOfQueue(Q) :1)
```

```
        end {quit}
      end {case}
    else
      WriteLn ('Incorrect choice - try again.')
end; {ModifyQueue}
```

Testing

You can store the initial passenger list in the queue by selecting a sequence of insert operations. In the sample run of program `UseQueue`, shown in Fig. 16.20, passenger `Brown` is inserted first, followed by passenger `Watson`. After passenger `Brown` is removed from the queue, the new passenger at the front of the queue (`Watson`) is displayed.

To test the program thoroughly, you have to try to display or remove a passenger after the queue is empty. Either attempt should cause the error message `Queue is empty` – to be displayed before the program terminates. To check that there is no insertion after the queue is full, it is necessary to redefine the queue capacity (part of the declaration for type `Queue`) so that the message `Queue is full - no insertion` appears after a small number of passenger insertions takes place.

Figure 16.20 Sample Run of Program UseQueue

```
Enter I(nsert), R(emove), D(isplay), or Q(uit)> I
Enter passenger data.
Passenger Name> Brown
Class (F, B, E, S)> E
Number of seats - Enter an integer between 1 and 30> 2

Enter I(nsert), R(emove), D(isplay), or Q(uit)> I
Enter passenger data.
Passenger Name> Watson
Class (F, B, E, S)> B
Number of Seats - Enter an integer between 1 and 30> 1

Enter I(nsert), R(emove), D(isplay), or Q(uit)> I
Enter passenger data.
Passenger Name> Dietz
Class (F, B, E, S)> E
Number of Seats - Enter an integer between 1 and 30> 3

Enter I(nsert), R(emove), D(isplay), or Q(uit)> R
Passenger removed from queue follows.
Brown
Economy Class
  2 Seats

Enter I(nsert), R(emove), D(isplay), or Q(uit)> D
Passenger at head of queue follows.
Watson
Business Class
  1 Seat
```

```
Enter I(nsert), R(emove), D(isplay), or Q(uit)> Q
Leaving passenger queue.
Number of passengers in the queue is 2
```

Coding the Passenger Abstract Data Type

Figure 16.21 shows an ADT that contains a declaration for record type `Passenger`. Procedure `ReadPass` and `WritePass` read and write a single passenger's record. (The completion of `WritePass` is left as an exercise.)

Figure 16.21 Unit PassengerADT

```
unit PassengerADT;

{
  Abstract data type Passenger: contains declarations for record
  type Passenger and procedures for reading and displaying values of
  type Passenger.
  Exports: Passenger, ReadPass, WritePass
  Imports: EnterInt from unit EnterData (Fig. 8.3)
}
interface
  uses EnterData;

  const
    MaxSeats = 30;
    StringSize = 20;

  type
    ClassType = (FirstClass, Business, Economy, StandBy, Undesignated);
    StringType = string[StringSize];
    Passenger = record
                  Name : StringType;
                  Class : ClassType;
                  NumSeats : Integer
                end; {Passenger}

  procedure ReadPass (var OnePass {output} : Passenger);
  {
    Reads one record of type Passenger.
    Pre : None
    Post: Data are read into all fields of OnePass
  }

  procedure WritePass (OnePass : Passenger);
  {Displays one record of type Passenger.}

implementation

  procedure ReadPass (var OnePass {output} : Passenger);
    var
      ClassCh : Char;           {input - character for class type}

    function ClassConvert (ClassCh : Char) : ClassType;
```

```
    {
      Converts a character to a class type.
    }
    begin {ClassConvert stub}
      ClassConvert := Economy
    end; {ClassConvert}

  begin {ReadPass}
    with OnePass do
      begin
        Write ('Passenger name> ');
        ReadLn (Name);
        Write ('Class (F, B, E, S)> ');
        ReadLn (ClassCh);
        Class := ClassConvert(ClassCh);
        Write ('Number of Seats - ');
        EnterInt (1, 30, NumSeats)
      end {with}
  end; {ReadPass}


  procedure WritePass (OnePass : Passenger);
  begin {WritePass stub}
    Write ('Name: ');
    WriteLn (OnePass.Name)
  end; {WritePass stub}

end. {PassengerADT}
```

At this point, we can draw the module-dependency diagram for program UseQueue (Fig. 16.22). As shown, both UseQueue and QueueADT use unit PassengerADT. We will implement unit QueueADT next.

Figure 16.22 Module-Dependency Diagram for UseQueue

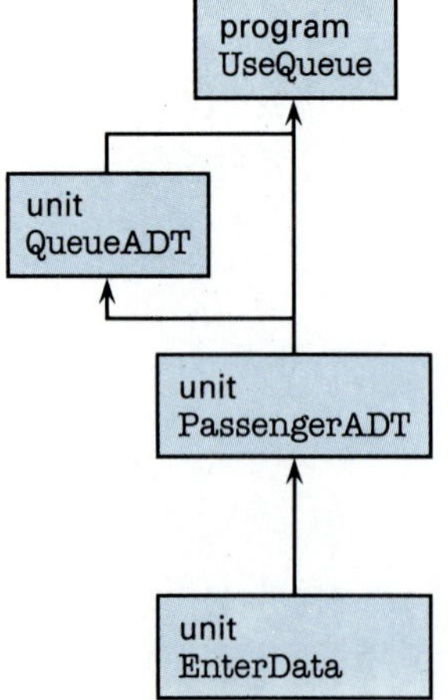

Exercises for Section 16.6

Self-Check

1. Draw the queue after the completion of the sample run in Fig. 16.20.

Programming

1. Complete procedure `WritePass`.
2. Complete function `ClassConvert` (in procedure `ReadPass`).

16.7 Implementing a Queue Abstract Data Type

To represent a queue, we will use a record structure that consists of three `Integer` fields (`Front`, `Rear`, `NumItems`) and an array field, `Items`, that provides storage for the queue elements. The declarations for a queue whose capacity is 100 elements is shown in the interface section for `QueueADT` (Fig. 16.23).

Figure 16.23 Interface Section for Unit QueueADT

```
unit QueueADT;
{
  Abstract data type Queue: contains declarations for record
  type Queue and operator procedures for an object of type Queue.
  Exports: Queue, QueueElement, CreateQueue, Insert, Remove,
           Retrieve, IsEmpty, IsFull, SizeOfQueue
}

interface

  const
    MaxQueue = 100;

  type
    {insert declaration for QueueElement}

    QueueRange = 1..MaxQueue;
    Queue = record
              Front, Rear : QueueRange;
              NumItems : 0..MaxQueue;
              Items : array [QueueRange] of QueueElement
            end; {Queue}

  procedure CreateQueue (var Q {output} : Queue);
  {
    Creates an empty queue.
    Pre : None
    Post: Q is initialized to a queue of zero elements.
  }

  procedure Insert (var Q {input/output} : Queue;
                    El {input} : QueueElement;
                    var Success {output} : Boolean);
```

```
{
  Inserts El in queue Q.
  Pre : Q has been created.
  Post: If Q is not full, increments Rear and inserts El.
        Sets Success to indicate success or failure.
}

procedure Remove (var Q {input/output} : Queue;
                  var El {output} : QueueElement;
                  var Success {output} : Boolean);
{
  Removes the element at the front of queue Q and copies it into El.
  Pre : Q has been created.
  Post: If Q is not empty, El contains its first element,
        Front is decremented,
        and Success indicates success or failure.
}

procedure Retrieve (Q {in} : Queue;
                    var El {out} : QueueElement;
                    var Success {out} : Boolean};
{
  Copies the value at the front of queue Q into El without
  removing it.
  Pre : Q has been created
  Post: If Q is not empty, El contains its first element
        and Success indicates success or failure.
}

function IsEmpty (Q : Queue) : Boolean;
{
  Tests for an empty queue.
  Pre : Q has been created.
  Post: Returns True if queue Q is empty; otherwise, returns False.
}

function IsFull (Q : Queue) : Boolean;
{
  Tests for a full queue.
  Pre : Q has been created.
  Post: Returns True if queue Q is full; otherwise, returns False.
}

function SizeofQueue (Q : Queue) : Integer;
{
  Finds the number of elements in a queue.
  Pre : Q has been created.
  Post: Returns the number of elements in the queue.
}
```

The `Integer` fields `Front` and `Rear` are pointers to the queue elements at the front and the rear of the queue, respectively. The `Integer` field `NumItems` keeps track of the actual number of items in the queue and allows us to easily determine if the queue is `Empty` (`NumItems` is `0`) or `Full` (`NumItems` is `MaxQueue`). The comment

```
{insert declaration for QueueElement}
```

reminds us that we must declare data type QueueElement before we can declare record type Queue.

If we use the type declaration

```
type
  QueueElement = Char;
```

a variable of type Queue can store up to 100 characters. If we insert the statement

```
uses PassengerADT;
```

and use the declaration

```
type
  QueueElement = Passenger;
```

a variable of type Queue can store up to 100 airline passengers.

It makes sense to store the first queue record in element 1, the second queue record in element 2, and so on. After a queue is filled with data, Front has a value of 1 and Rear points to the last record inserted in the queue (Rear <= MaxQueue). Fig. 16.24 shows a queue, Q, that is filled to its capacity (Numitems is MaxQueue). The queue contains the symbols &, *, +, /, − in that order.

Because Q is filled to capacity, we cannot insert a new character. We can remove a queue element by decrementing NumItems and incrementing Front to 2, thereby removing Q.Items[1] (the symbol &). However, we still cannot insert a new character, because Rear is at its maximum value. One way to solve this problem is to represent the array field Items as a circular array. In a *circular array*, the elements wrap around so that the first element actually follows the last. This allows us to "increment" Rear to 1 and store a new character in Q.Items[1].

■ Example 16.3

Figure 16.25 shows the effect of inserting a new element in the queue just described. As shown on the left of the figure, three characters are currently in this queue (stored in Q.Items[3..5]). The question marks in Q.Items[1..2] indicate that the values stored in these elements have been removed from the queue. The two elements that are currently unused are shown in gray.

The right side of Fig. 16.25 shows the queue after insertion of a new character ('$'). The value of Rear is "incremented" to 1, and the next element is inserted in Q.Items[1]. This queue element follows the character '-' in

Figure 16.24 A Queue Filled with Characters

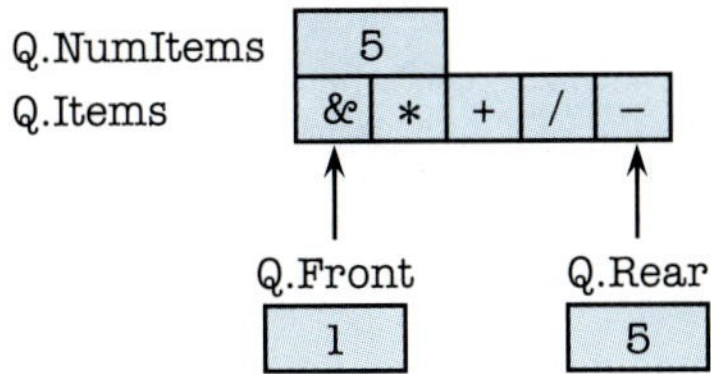

Figure 16.25 A Queue as a Circular Array

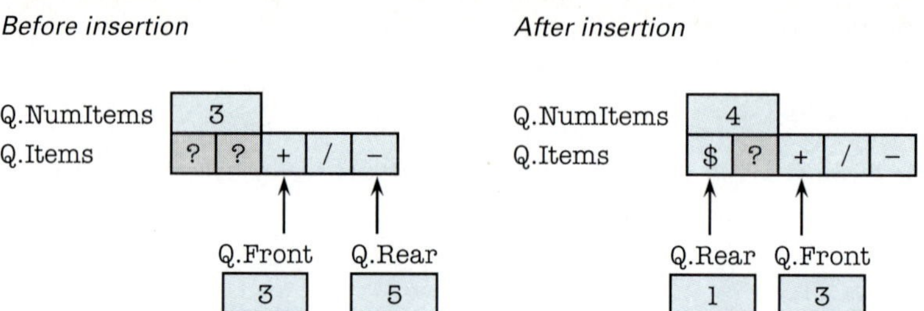

`Q.Items[5]`. The value of `Q.Front` is still 3 because the character `'+'` at `Q.Items[3]` has been in the queue the longest. `Q.Items[2]` is now the only queue element that is unused. The new queue contains the symbols +, /, −, $ in that order.

Figure 16.26 shows the operators for the queue abstract data type. ■

Figure 16.26 Operators for Unit Queue ADT

```
{$R+}
implementation


procedure CreateQueue (var Q {output} : Queue);
begin {CreateQueue}
  Q.NumItems := 0;             {queue is empty}
  Q.Front := 1;
  Q.Rear := MaxQueue           {queue is circular}
end; {CreateQueue}


procedure Insert (var Q {in/out} : Queue;
                  El {in} : QueueElement;
                  var Success {out} : Boolean);
begin {Insert}
  if Q.NumItems = MaxQueue then
    Success := False         {queue is full}
  else
    begin {insert El}
      Q.Rear := (Q.Rear mod MaxQueue) + 1;     {increment Rear}
      Q.Items[Q.Rear] := El;
      Q.NumItems := Q.NumItems + 1;
      Success := True
    end {insert El}
end; {Insert}


procedure Remove (var Q {in/out} : Queue;
                  var El {out} : QueueElement;
                  var Success {out} : Boolean);
begin {Remove}
  if Q.NumItems = 0 then
    Success := False           {queue is empty}
```

```
  else
    begin
      {Remove the element at the front of the queue.}
      El := Q.Items[Q.Front];
      Q.Front := (Q.Front mod MaxQueue) + 1; {increment Front}
      Q.NumItems := Q.NumItems - 1;
      Success := True
    end {if}
end; {Remove}


procedure Retrieve (Q {in} : Queue;
                    var El {out} : QueueElement;
                    var Success {out} : Boolean);
begin {Retrieve}
  if Q.NumItems = 0 then
    Success := False          {queue is empty}
  else
    begin
      {Retrieve the item at the front of the queue.}
      El := Q.Items[Q.Front];
      Success := True
    end {if}
end; {Retrieve}

function IsEmpty (Q : Queue) : Boolean;
begin {IsEmpty}
  IsEmpty := Q.NumItems = 0
end; {IsEmpty}

function IsFull (Q : Queue) : Boolean;
begin {IsFull}
  IsFull := Q.NumItems = MaxQueue
end; {IsFull}

function SizeOfQueue (Q : Queue) : Integer;
begin {SizeOfQueue}
  SizeOfQueue := Q.NumItems
end; {SizeOfQueue}

end. {QueueADT}
```

Procedure `CreateQueue` must be called before any of the other operators. `CreateQueue` sets `Q.NumItems` to `0` and `Q.Front` to `1`, because array element `Q.Items[1]` is considered the front of the empty queue. `Q.Rear` is initialized to `MaxQueue` because the queue is circular.

In procedure `Insert`, the statement

```
Q.Rear := (Q.Rear mod MaxQueue) + 1;          {increment Rear}
```

is used to increment the value of `Q.Rear`. When `Q.Rear` is less than `MaxQueue`, this statement simply increments its value by 1. But when `Q.Rear` is equal to `MaxQueue`, this statement sets `Q.Rear` to `1` (`MaxQueue mod MaxQueue` is `0`), thereby wrapping the last element of the queue around to the first element. Because `CreateQueue` initializes `Q.Rear` to `MaxQueue`, the first queue element will be placed in `Items[1]`, as desired.

In procedure Remove, the element currently stored in Items[Front] is copied into El before Q.Front is incremented. In procedure Retrieve, the element at Items[Front] is copied into El, but Q.Front is not changed.

The number of elements in the queue is changed by procedures Insert and Remove, so Q.NumItems must be incremented by 1 in Insert and decremented by 1 in Remove. The value of Q.NumItems is tested in both IsFull and IsEmpty to determine the status of the queue. Function SizeOfQueue simply returns the value of Q.NumItems.

Exercises for Section 16.7

Self-Check

1. What are the final values of Q.Front, Q.Rear, and the Name fields of Q.Items[1..3] after the sample run of UseQueue in Fig. 16.20?
2. Provide the algorithm for the operator in programming exercise 1, which follows. If program UseQueue calls this operator, how does it affect the module dependency diagram in Fig. 16.22?

Programming

1. Write an operator that displays the entire queue contents, from Front to Rear, inclusive.

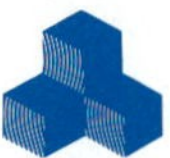

16.8 Common Programming Errors

In this chapter, we used an array field to store the contents of a stack or a queue. Consequently, all stack and queue operators manipulated an array subscript. The errors you are likely to encounter are the same errors discussed at the end of Chapter 10. The most common error when using arrays is an out-of-range subscript. For this reason, you should use the compiler directive {$R+} to enable range-checking.

The client programs in this chapter all used one or more abstract data types. Make sure that the abstract data types are available in your procedure library and that all necessary uses statements are inserted where they belong.

Chapter Review

This chapter introduced two data structures, stacks and queues. Stacks are used to implement recursion and expression translation. A stack is a last-in, first-out data structure. This means that the last item inserted is the first one removed. In contrast, a queue is a first-in, first-out data structure. Queues are used to implement waiting lists.

We showed how to use these abstractions to perform many useful operations. In particular, we used stacks to check for balanced parentheses and to evaluate arithmetic expressions. We also showed how to implement stacks and queues using arrays.

✓ Quick-Check Exercises

1. A stack is a ____________ data structure; a queue is a ____________ data structure.
2. Would a compiler use a stack or a queue in a program that converts regular arithmetic expressions to postfix form?
3. Would a time-sharing system use a stack or a queue in a program that determines which job should be executed next?
4. Would a compiler use a stack or a queue to keep track of return addresses for procedure calls?
5. Draw the array representation of the following stack. What is `S.Items[1]`? What is the value of `S.Top`? What is the value of `S.Items[S.Top-1]`?

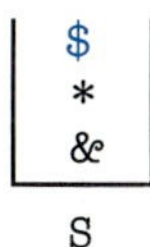

6. Why should the statement `S.Top := S.Top - 1` not appear in a client program of unit `StackADT`?
7. Write a program segment that removes the element just below the top of the stack from the stack. Use the stack operators.
8. Write a stack operator called `PopNextTop` that performs the operation in exercise 7. Do not use the stack operators.
9. Assume that a circular queue `Q` of capacity `6` contains the five characters +, *, -, &, #, where + is stored in the front of the queue. In the array representation, what is the value of `Q.Front`? What is the value of `Q.Rear`? What is the value of `Q.Items[Q.Rear-1]`?
10. Delete the character at the front of the queue in exercise 9 and insert the character \ and then %. Draw the new queue. What is the value of `Q.Front`? What is the value of `Q.Rear`? What is the value of `Q.Items[Q.Rear-1]`?
11. Can you have two stacks of real numbers in the same client program? Can you have a stack of integers and a stack of characters in the same client program?

Answers to Quick-Check Exercises

1. Last-in, first-out; first-in, first-out
2. Stack
3. Queue—give priority to the job waiting the longest to execute.
4. Stack
5. &, `S.Top` is 3, *

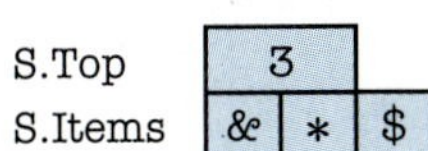

6. The client program should not be aware of the internal representation of the stack.

7.
```
Pop (S, X, Success);
Pop (S, Y, Success);
Push (S, X, Success)
```

8.
```
procedure PopNextTop (var S {input/output} : Stack;
                      var Ch {output} : Char;
                      var Success {output} : Boolean);
begin
  S.Items[Top-1] := S.Items[S.Top];
  S.Top := S.Top - 1
end; {PopNextTop}
```

9. `Q.Front` is 1; `Q.Rear` is 5; &
10. `Q.Front` is 2; `Q.Rear` is 1; \

Q.Items	%	*	–	&	#	\
	↑ Q.Rear	↑ Q.Front				

11. Yes; no

Review Questions

1. Show the effect of each of the following operations on stack `S`. Assume that `Y` (type `Char`) contains the character `'&'`. What are the final values of `X` and `Success` (type `Boolean`) and the contents of stack `S`? Ignore any statements with syntax errors.

```
CreateStack (S);
Push (S, '+', Success);
Pop (S, X, Success);
Pop (S, X, Success);
Push (S, '(', Success);
Push (S, Y, Success);
Pop (S, '&', Success)
```

2. Assuming stack `S` is implemented in an array, answer exercise 1 by showing the values of integer field `Top` and array field `Items` after each operation.
3. Write a stack operator called `PopTwo` that removes the top two stack elements and returns them as procedure results. Use procedure `Pop`.
4. Answer exercise 3 without using `Pop`.
5. Answer exercise 1 for a queue `Q` of characters. Replace `CreateStack` with `CreateQueue`, `Push` with `Insert`, and `Pop` with `Remove`.
6. Assuming queue `Q` is implemented in an array with five elements, answer exercise 2 by showing the values of integer fields `Front` and `Rear` and array field `Items` after each operation.
7. Write a queue operator called `MoveToRear` that moves the element currently at the front of the queue to the rear of the queue. The element that was second in line will be at the front of the queue. Do this using `Insert` and `Remove` operators.
8. Answer exercise 7 without using `Insert` and `Remove` operators. Manipulate the internal queue fields directly.
9. Write a queue operator called `MoveToFront` that moves the element at the rear of the queue to the front of the queue. Do this using `Insert` and `Remove`.
10. Answer exercise 9 without using `Insert` and `Remove`.

Programming Projects

1. Extend the queue abstract data type to include an operator that displays a queue. Change `QueueElement` to represent a customer at a bank. Store the customer's name, transaction type, and amount in the customer record. Write a client module that simulates a typical session for a bank teller. After every five customers are processed, display the size of the queue and the names of the customers who are waiting.
2. Carry out project 1 using a stack instead of a queue.
3. Write a program to monitor the flow of an item into and out of a warehouse. The warehouse will have numerous deliveries and shipments for this item (a widget) during the time period covered. A shipment out is billed at a profit of 50 percent over the cost of a widget. Unfortunately, each shipment received may have a different cost associated with it. The accountants for the firm have instituted a last-in, first-out system for filling orders. This means that the newest widgets are the first ones sent out to fill an order. This method of inventory can be represented using a stack. The `Push` procedure will insert a shipment received. The `Pop` procedure will delete a shipment out. Each data record will consist of

   `S` or `O`: shipment received or an order to be sent
   `#`: quantity received or shipped out
   `Cost`: cost per widget (for a shipment received only)
   `Vendor`: character string that names company sent to or received from

   Write the necessary procedures to store the shipments received and to process orders. The output for an order will consist of the quantity and the total cost for all the widgets in the order. Hint: Each widget price is 50 percent higher than its cost. The widgets used to fill an order may come from multiple shipments with different costs.
4. Redo project 3 assuming the widgets are shipped using a first-in, first-out strategy. Use a queue to store the widget orders.
5. Write a client program for the stack abstract data type that can be used to compile a simple arithmetic expression without parentheses. For example, the expression

```
A + B * C - D
```

should be compiled as the table

Operation	Operand1	Operand2	Result
*	B	C	Z
+	A	Z	Y
–	Y	D	X

The table shows the order in which the operations are performed (*, +, –) and the operands for each operator. The result column gives the name of an identifier (working backward from `Z`) chosen to hold each result. Assume the operands are the letters `A` through `F` and the operators are (+, –, *, /).

Your program should read each character and process it as follows. If the character is a blank, ignore it. If it is an operand, push it onto the operand stack. If the character is not an operator, display an error message and terminate the program. If it is an operator, compare its precedence with that of the operator on top of the stack (* and / have higher precedence than + and –). If the new operator has higher precedence than the one currently on top (or if the stack is empty), it should be pushed onto the stack.

If the new operator has the same or lower precedence, the operator on the top of the stack must be evaluated next. This is done by popping it off the operator stack along with a pair of operands from the operand stack and writing a new line of the output table. The character selected to hold the result should then be pushed onto the operand stack. Next, the new operator should be compared to the new top of the operator stack. Continue to generate output table lines until the top of the operator stack has lower precedence than the new operator or the stack is empty. At this point, push the new operator onto the top of the stack and examine the next character in the data string. When the end of the string is reached, pop any remaining operators along with its operand pair as just described. Remember to push the result character onto the operand stack after each table line is generated.

6. A *dequeue* might be described as a double-ended queue, that is, a structure in which elements can be inserted or removed from either end. Write a Turbo Pascal unit containing the declarations and operators necessary to implement a dequeue.

17

Dynamic Data Structures

This chapter discusses how Pascal can be used to create *dynamic data structures*. Dynamic data structures are data structures that expand and contract as a program executes. A dynamic data structure is a collection of elements (called *nodes*) that are records. Unlike an array, which always contains storage for a fixed number of elements, the number of records stored in a dynamic data structure changes as the program executes.

Dynamic data structures are extremely flexible. It is relatively easy to add new information by creating a new node and inserting it between two existing nodes. It is also relatively easy to delete a node.

In this chapter, we examine several examples of dynamic data structures. These include lists, stacks, queues, and circular lists. You will learn how to store information in these data structures and how to process that information.

17.1 Pointers and the New Statement

Before discussing dynamic data structures, we will introduce the pointer data type. We can declare variables (called *pointer variables*) whose types are pointer types. We can store the memory address of a data object in a pointer variable and, in this way, reference or access the data object through the pointer variable that points to it.

For example, the type declaration

```
type
  RealPointer = ^Real;

var
  P : RealPointer;
```

identifies `RealPointer` as the name of a data type. Read `^Real` as "pointer to `Real`." The variable declaration specifies that `P` is a pointer variable of type `RealPointer`. This means that we can store the memory address of a type `Real` variable in `P`.

The statement

```
New (P);
```

calls the Pascal procedure `New`, which allocates storage for a type `Real` value and places the address of this memory cell in pointer variable `P`. Once storage is allocated for the type `Real` value pointed to by `P`, we can store a value in that memory cell and manipulate it. The exact location in memory of this particular cell is immaterial.

We can represent the value of a pointer variable by an arrow drawn to a memory cell. The diagram

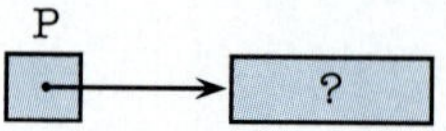

shows that pointer variable `P` points to a memory cell whose contents are unknown. This is the situation that exists just after `New(P)` is executed.

Notice that the two memory cells shown in the diagram are allocated storage at different times. Storage is allocated for the cell on the left during compilation when the variable declaration is reached. Storage is allocated for the cell on the right during run-time when the `New` statement is executed.

The symbol `P^` or `P↑` references the memory cell pointed to by pointer variable `P`. The ^ (caret) or ↑ (uparrow) is called the *dereferencing operator*. (Don't confuse the symbol ↑ with a cursor movement key.) The assignment statement

```
P^ := 15.0
```

stores the `Real` value `15.0` in memory cell `P^` (the cell pointed to by `P`), as shown next.

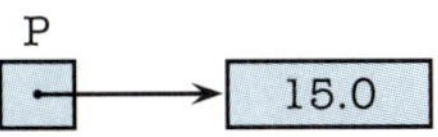

The statement

```
Write (P^ :12:1)
```

displays the value (`15.0`) stored in memory cell `P^`. The statements

```
P := 15.0;              {invalid assignment}
Write (P :12:1)         {invalid address display}
```

are both invalid because we cannot store a type `Real` value in pointer variable `P` nor can we display the value (an address) of a pointer variable.

We are introducing pointer variables and pointer types now because they are used to create and access dynamic data structures. Later in this chapter, you will see how to use a pointer variable to reference a dynamic data structure and how to use pointer fields to connect the nodes of a dynamic data structure.

SYNTAX DIAGRAM

Pointer Type Declaration

Form: `type` *ptype* = ^*dtype;*
Example: `type RealPointer =^Real;`
Interpretation: Pointer type *ptype* is a data type whose values are memory cell addresses. A data object whose address is stored in a variable of type *ptype* must be type *dtype*.

SYNTAX DIAGRAM

New Procedure

Form: `New (`*pvar*`)`
Example: `New (P)`
Interpretation: Storage for a new data object is allocated, and the address of this data object is stored in pointer variable *pvar*. If *pvar* is type *ptype*, the internal representation and size of the new data object is determined from the declaration for *ptype*. *pvar*^ (or *pvar* ↑) references this data object.

Records with Pointer Fields

Because we don't know beforehand how many nodes will be in a dynamic data structure, we cannot allocate storage for a dynamic data structure in the conventional way, that is, through a variable declaration. Instead, we must allocate storage for each node as needed and, somehow, join that node to the rest of the structure.

We can connect two nodes if we include a pointer field in each node. The declarations

```
type
  NodePointer = ^Node;
  Node = record
           Current : string[2];
           Volts : Integer;
           Link : NodePointer
         end; {Node}

var
  P, Q, R : NodePointer;
```

identify NodePointer as a pointer type. A pointer variable of type NodePointer points to a record of type Node with three fields: Current, Volts, and Link. The Link field is also type NodePointer. We can use this field to point to the "next" node in a dynamic data structure. We illustrate how to connect two nodes in the next section.

Notice that the type declaration for NodePointer makes reference to the identifier Node, which is not yet declared. The declaration of a pointer type is the only situation in which Pascal allows us to reference an undeclared identifier.

Variables P, Q, and R are pointer variables and can be used to reference records of type Node (denoted by P^, Q^, and R^). An address can be stored in a pointer variable in one of two ways. The statements

```
New (P);  New (Q);
```

allocate storage for two records of type Node. The memory address of the first of these records is stored in P, and the memory address of the second of these records is stored in Q. All three fields of these two nodes are initially undefined.

The assignment statements

```
P^.Current := 'AC';  P^.Volts := 115;
Q^.Current := 'DC';  Q^.Volts := 12;
```

define two fields of these nodes, as shown in Fig. 17.1. The Link fields are still undefined. It makes no difference where the arrow representing the value of a pointer variable touches its node.

Besides using a New statement, we can also use an assignment statement to store an address in a pointer variable. The *pointer assignment statement*

```
R := P;
```

copies the value of pointer variable P into pointer variable R. This means that pointers P and R contain the same memory address and, therefore, point to the same node, as shown in Fig. 17.2.

Figure 17.1 Nodes P^ and Q^

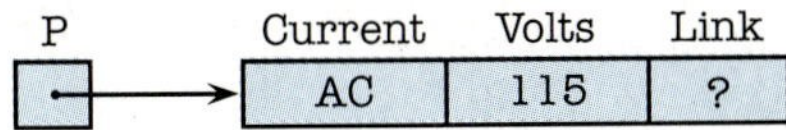

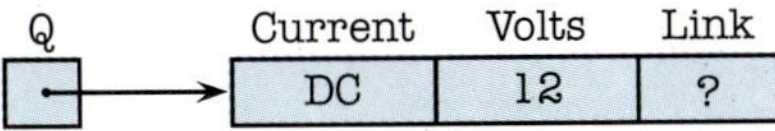

Figure 17.2 Nodes (R^, P^) and Q

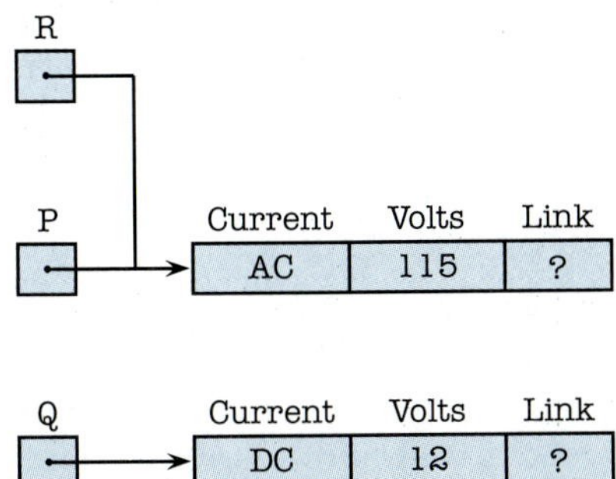

We can compare two pointer variables using the relational operators = and <>. The following conditions are all true for pointer variables P, Q, and R above. We cannot use any of the other relational operators with pointer variables.

```
P = R
P <> Q
R <> Q
```

The pointer assignment statements

```
P := Q;   Q := R;
```

would have the effect of exchanging the nodes pointed to by P and Q, as shown in Fig. 17.3.

Figure 17.3 Nodes (R^, Q^) and P^

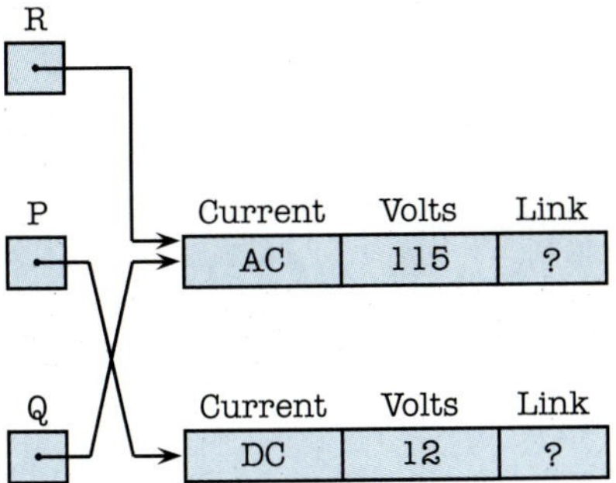

The statement

```
WriteLn (Q^.Current, P^.Current);
```

displays the `Current` fields of the records pointed to by `Q` and `P`. For the situation depicted in Fig. 17.3, the line

```
ACDC
```

would be displayed.

The statement

```
New (Q)
```

changes the value of `Q` to the address of a new node, thereby disconnecting `Q` from its previous node. The new values of pointer variables `P`, `Q`, and `R` are shown in Fig. 17.4. The data fields of the new node pointed to by `Q` are initially undefined.

Pointers `P`, `Q`, and `R` are analogous to subscripts in that they select a particular node, or element, of a data structure. Unlike subscripts, however, their range of values is not declared and their values (memory cell addresses) cannot be printed.

It is important that you understand the difference between using `P` and `P^` in a program. `P` is a pointer variable (type `NodePointer`) and is used to store the address of a data structure of type `Node`. `P` can be assigned a new value through a pointer assignment or execution of a `New` statement. `P^` is the name of the record pointed to by `P` and can be manipulated like any other record in Pascal. The field selectors `P^.Current` and `P^.Volts` can be used to reference data (a string and an integer) stored in this record.

Connecting Nodes

One purpose of dynamically allocated nodes is to enable us to grow data structures of varying size. We accomplish this by connecting individual nodes. If you look at the nodes allocated in the last section, you will see that their `Link` fields

Figure 17.4 Nodes R^, P^, and Q^

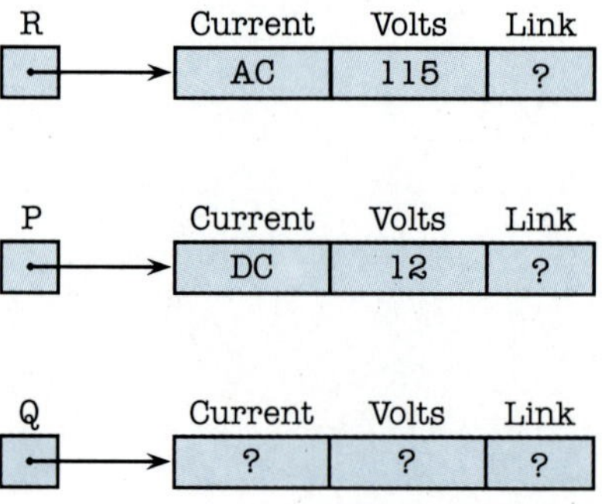

Figure 17.5 Connecting Nodes

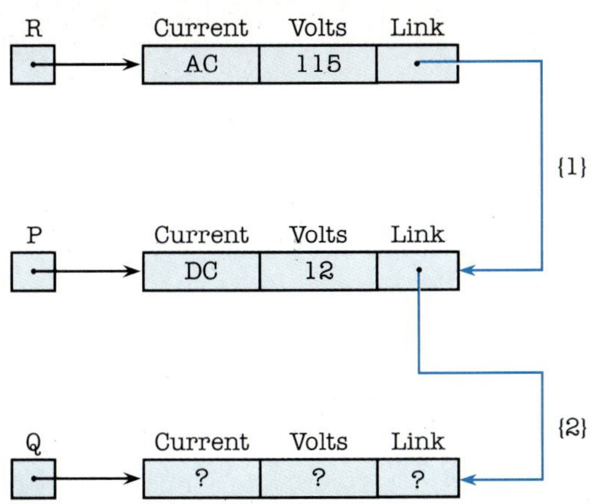

are undefined. Because the `Link` fields are type `NodePointer`, they can be used to store a memory cell address. The pointer assignment statement

```
{1} R^.Link := P;
```

copies the address stored in `P` into the `Link` field of `Node R^`, thereby connecting node `R^` to `Node P^`. Similarly, the pointer assignment statement

```
{2} P^.Link := Q
```

copies the address stored in pointer variable `Q` into the `Link` field of node `P^`, thereby connecting node `P^` to node `Q^`. The situation after execution of these two assignment statements is shown in Fig. 17.5. The arrows that represent the new values of `R^.Link` and `P^.Link` are shown in color. The label next to the arrow denotes one of the pointer assignments.

The data structure pointed to by `R` has now grown to include all three nodes. The first node is referenced by `R^`. The second node can be referenced by `P^` or `R^.Link^`. Finally, the third node can be referenced by `Q^`, `P^.Link^`, or even `R^.Link^.Link^`.

Exercises for Section 17.1

Self-Check

1. For Fig. 17.5, explain the effect of each of the following assignment statements:

   a. `R^.Current := 'CA'`
   b. `P^ := R^`
   c. `P.Current := 'HT'`
   d. `P := 54`
   e. `R^.Link^.Volts := 0`
   f. `P := R`
   g. `R^.Link^.Link^.Current := 'XY'`
   h. `Q^.Volts := R^.Volts`

2. The assignment statements

```
R := P;   P := Q;   Q := R
```

exchange the values of pointer variables P and Q (type NodePointer). What do the following assignment statements do?

```
R^.Current := P^.Current;
P^.Current := Q^.Current;
Q^.Current := R^.Current
```

Programming

1. Write a program segment that creates a collection of nodes and stores the musical scale (do, re, mi, fa, so, la, ti, do) in those nodes. Connect the nodes so that do is stored in the first node, re in the second, and so on.

17.2 Manipulating the Heap

In the last section, you saw that a new record is created whenever the New procedure is executed. You may be wondering where in memory the new record is stored. Pascal maintains a storage pool of available memory cells called a *heap*; memory cells from this pool are allocated whenever procedure New is executed.

Effect of the New Statement on the Heap

If P is a pointer variable of type NodePointer (declared in the last section), the statement

```
New (P)
```

allocates memory space for the storage of two characters, an integer variable, and an address. These cells are originally undefined (they retain whatever data was last stored in them) and the memory address of the first cell allocated is stored in P. Allocated cells are no longer considered part of the heap. The only way to reference allocated cells is through pointer variable P (for example, P^.Current, P^.Volts, or P^.Link).

Figure 17.6 shows the pointer variable P and the heap before and after the execution of New (P). The *before* diagram shows pointer variable P as undefined

Figure 17.6 Heap before and after New (P)

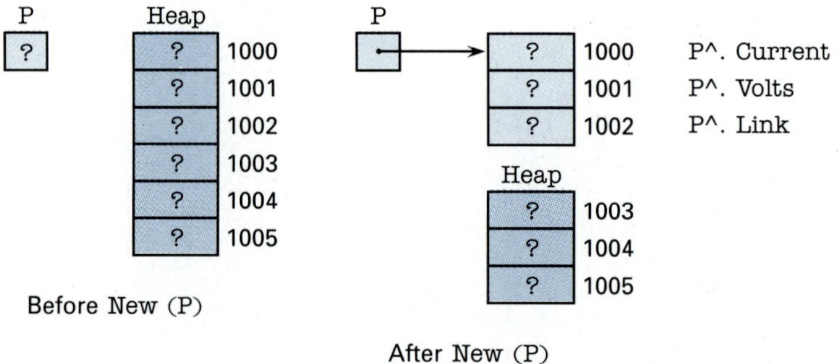

before the execution of `New (P)`. The *after* diagram shows `P` pointing to the first of three memory cells allocated for the new record (assuming that three memory cells can accommodate a record of type `Node`). The cells still considered part of the heap are in the darker color.

For example, if the memory cells with addresses `1000` through `1005` were originally in the heap, after the execution of `New (P)` only the memory cells with addresses `1003` through `1005` would be considered still part of the heap. The address `1000` would be stored in pointer variable `P`, and that cell would be named `P^.Current`; memory cells `1001` and `1002` would be named `P^.Volts` and `P^.Link`, respectively.

Returning Cells to the Heap

The procedure call statement

```
Dispose (P)
```

returns the memory cells pointed to by `P` to the heap. The value of pointer variable `P` becomes undefined, and the data formerly associated with `P^` are no longer accessible. The three cells that are returned to the heap can be reused later when another `New` statement is executed.

Often, more than one pointer points to the same record. For this reason, you must be careful when you return the storage occupied by a record to the heap. If cells are reallocated after they are returned, errors may result if they are later referenced by another pointer that still points to them. Make sure you have no need for a particular record before you return the storage occupied by it.

SYNTAX DISPLAY

The Dispose Procedure

Form: `Dispose (`*pvar*`)`
Example: `Dispose (P)`
Interpretation: The memory cells that make up the record whose address is stored in pointer *pvar* are returned to the heap. These cells can be reallocated when procedure `New` is called.

17.3 Linked Lists

This section introduces an important data structure called a *linked list* or, simply, *list*. You will see how to build and manipulate lists in Pascal.

Abstract Lists

An abstract list is a sequence of nodes in which each node is linked or connected to the node following it. An abstract list with three nodes follows.

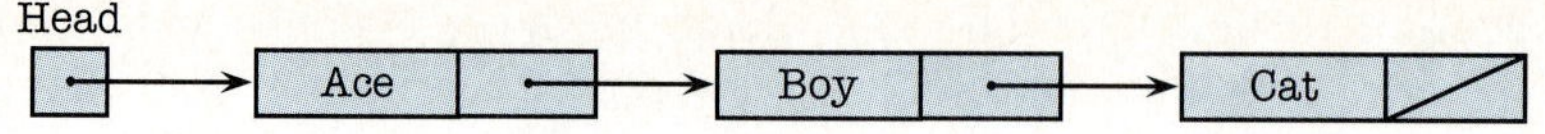

Each node in the list has two fields: the first field contains data; the second field is a pointer (represented by an arrow) to the next list element. A pointer variable (`Head`) points to the first list element, or *list head*. The last list element always has a diagonal line in its pointer field to indicate the end of the list.

Lists are an important data structure because they can be modified easily. For example, a new node containing the string `'Bye'` can be inserted between the strings `'Boy'` and `'Cat'` by changing only one pointer value (the one from `'Boy'`) and setting the pointer from the new node to point to `'Cat'`. This is true regardless of how many elements are in the list. The list shown next is after the insertion; the new pointer values are shown in color.

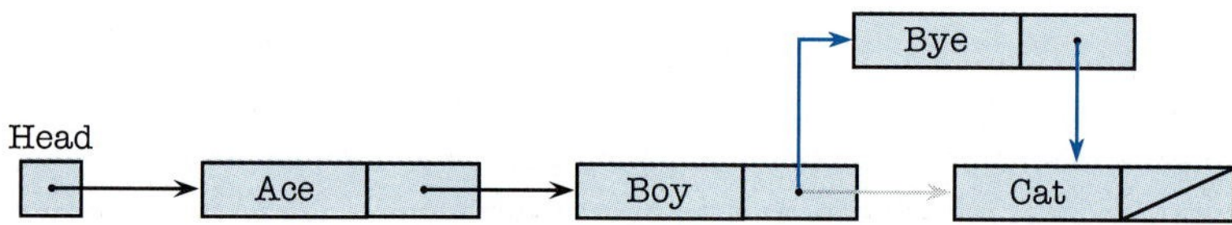

Similarly, it is quite easy to delete a list element. Only one pointer value has to be changed, the pointer that currently points to the element being deleted. The linked list is redrawn as follows after the string `'Boy'` is deleted, by changing the pointer from the node `'Ace'`. The node containing the string `'Boy'` is effectively disconnected from the list and can be returned to the heap. The new list consists of the strings `'Ace'`, `'Bye'`, `'Cat'`.

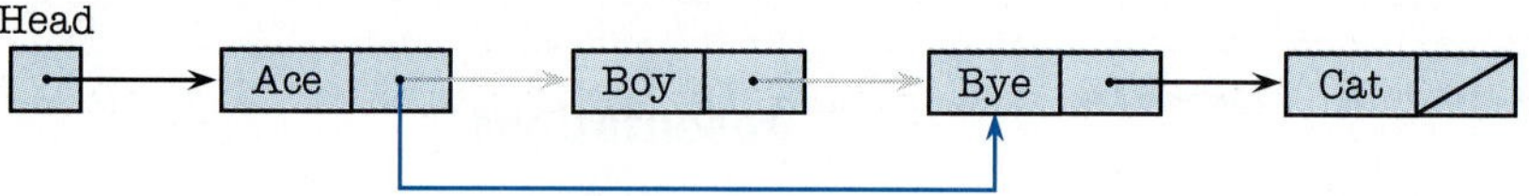

Representing Linked Lists Using Pointers

The preceding abstract list is relatively easy to create in Pascal using pointers and dynamic allocation. In Section 17.1, you saw how to connect three nodes with pointer fields. Although you didn't know it at the time, the data structure shown in Fig. 17.5 could be considered a list of three nodes with pointer variable `R` as the pointer to its head.

In Pascal, the reserved word `nil` is a predefined value that can be assigned to any pointer variable. It indicates that the pointer variable does not point to any memory cells on the heap. If `Head` is a pointer variable, we can use the assignment statement

```
Head := nil
```

to indicate that `Head` points to an *empty list*, a list with zero nodes.

Head

The pointer value `nil` is drawn as a diagonal line.

Normally, we assign the value `nil` to the pointer field of the last node in a list. After the assignment statements

```
Q^.Link := nil; Q^.Current := 'AC'; Q^.Volts := 220;
```

are executed, the data structure in Fig. 17.5 implements the following linked list. Each node has two data fields (`Current` and `Volts`) and one pointer field (`Link`).

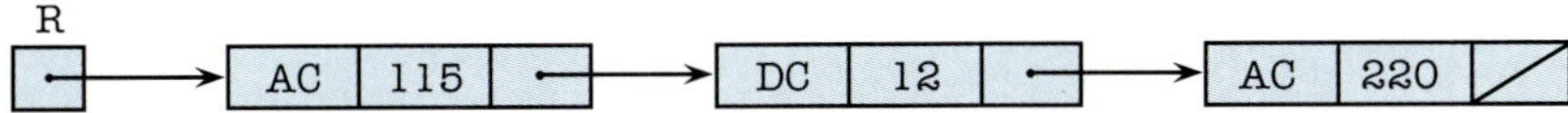

Representing Linked Lists Using Arrays

You can also represent a linked list as an array of records in which an `Integer` field stores the index of the next list element. Figure 17.7 shows the previous abstract list stored in an array (`Nodes`) whose elements are records (type `Node`). The last field of each record contains the index (subscript) of the next element. The variable `R` contains the subscript of the first list element. The three list nodes happen to be stored in array elements `2`, `4`, and `1`, in that order, although any three elements could be used. Element `1` has a link field of `0`, which indicates the end of the list.

PROGRAM STYLE

Storage Considerations for List Representations

Lists stored in arrays are just as easy to modify as lists that are created using pointer variables. To insert or delete a list element, it is necessary only to change one or more subscript values. The disadvantage, however, is that memory space for the entire array must be allocated at one time. If you create a list using pointer variables and dynamic allocation, the size of the list in memory will grow and shrink as needed, and the storage allocated to it will change accordingly. For this reason, we recommend using pointers to implement lists.

Exercises for Section 17.3

Self-Check

1. For the array `Nodes` shown in Fig. 17.7, trace the execution of the following program fragment. What is printed?

Figure 17.7 Array Representation of a Linked List

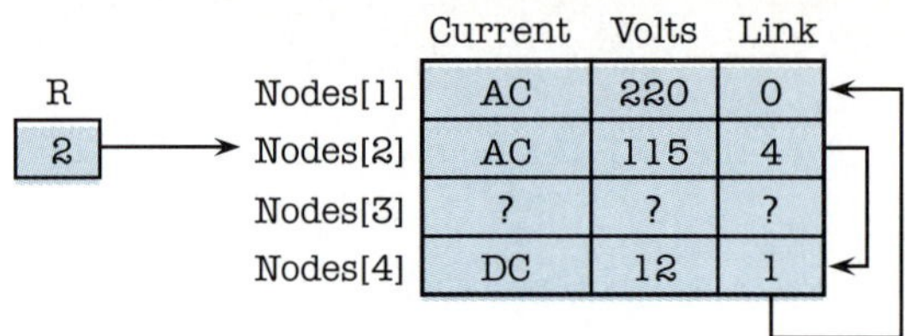


```
R := 2;
while R <> 0 do
  begin
    WriteLn (Nodes[R].Current, Nodes[R].Volts);
    R := Nodes[R].Link
  end; {while}
```

Programming

1. Solve programming exercise 1 from Section 17.1, assuming that array `Nodes` is used to store the scale.

17.4 Linked-List Operators

This section and the ones that follow consider some common list-processing operations and show how to implement them using pointer variables. We assume that the structure of each list node corresponds to type `ListNode`, declared as follows. Pointer variable `Head` points to the list head.

```
const
  StringSize = 3;

type
  StringType = string[StringSize];
  ListPointer = ^ListNode;
  ListNode = record
               Word : StringType;
               Link : ListPointer
             end; {ListNode}

var
  Head : ListPointer;          {pointer to list head}
```

Traversing a List

In many list-processing operations, we must process each node in the list in sequence; this is called *traversing* a list. To traverse a list, we must start at the list head and follow the list pointers.

One operation that we must perform on any data structure is displaying its contents. To display the contents of a list, we traverse the list and display only the values of the information fields, not the link fields. Procedure PrintList in Fig. 17.8 displays the Word field of each node (type ListNode) in the existing list whose list head is passed as a parameter (type ListPointer). If MyHead points to the list

MyHead → Hat → Boy → Cat /

the procedure call statement

```
PrintList (MyHead)
```

displays the output lines

```
Hat
Boy
Cat
```

Figure 17.8 Procedure PrintList

```
procedure PrintList (Head {input} : ListPointer);
{
  Displays the list pointed to by Head.
  Pre : Head points to a list whose last node has a pointer
        field of nil.
  Post: The Word field of each list node is displayed and
        the last value of Head is nil.
}
begin {PrintList}
  {Traverse the list until the end is reached.}
  while Head <> nil do
    {invariant:
        No prior value of Head was nil.
    }
    begin
      WriteLn (Head^.Word);
      Head := Head^.Link                {advance to next node}
    end {while}
end; {PrintList}
```

The while condition

```
Head <> nil
```

is very common in loops that process lists. If the list to be printed is an empt list, this condition is true initially and the loop body is skipped.

If the list is not empty, the loop body executes and the statement

```
Head := Head^.Link        {advance to next node}
```

advances the pointer Head to the next list element, which is pointed to by the Link field of the current list element. After the last value in the list is printed, the value nil is assigned to Head and the while loop is exited.

Because Head is a value parameter, a local copy of the pointer to the first list element is established when the procedure is entered. This local pointer is advanced, but the corresponding pointer in the calling program remains unchanged. What would happen to our list if Head was a variable parameter?

PROGRAM STYLE

Warning About Variable Parameters for Pointers

The last line in the preceding paragraph asks you to consider the effect of parameter Head being a variable parameter instead of a value parameter. We know that this would allow the procedure to change the corresponding actual parameter, regardless of our intentions. In PrintList and many similar procedures, the last value assigned to the pointer parameter is nil. If Head is a variable parameter, the corresponding actual parameter would be set to nil, thereby disconnecting it from the list that it pointed to before the procedure call.

Creating a List

Procedure CreateList in Fig. 17.9 creates a linked list by reading in a sequence of data strings that end with a sentinel ('***') and storing each string in a list. If the data lines

```
Hat
Boy
Cat
***
```

are entered, the list shown in the preceding section is created. Notice that the sentinel string is not stored in the list.

Figure 17.9 Procedure CreateList

```
procedure CreateList (var Head {output} : ListPointer);
{
  Creates a linked list of strings pointed to by Head.
  Each new string is appended to the end of the list so the
  strings will be stored in the order in which they were read.
  Pre : None
  Post: Head points to the first string entered. Head is
        set to nil if the sentinel string is the first string.
}
  const
    Sentinel = '***';

  var
    FirstWord : StringType;        {first data word}

  procedure FillRest (Last {input} : ListPointer);
  {
    Appends new nodes to the end of a list.
```

```
    Pre : Last points to the last node in a list of length n.
    Post: Last points to the last node in a list of length >= n.
          Each data string is stored in a new node in the order
          in which it was read. The last node contains the data
          string just before the sentinel.
  }
    var
      NextWord : StringType;      {next data word}

  begin {FillRest}
    ReadLn (NextWord);
    while NextWord <> Sentinel do
      {invariant:
        Last points to the last node in a list and
        the last string read is stored in node Last^ and
        no prior data string was the Sentinel
      }
      begin
        New (Last^.Link);         {attach a new node to Last^}
        Last := Last^.Link;       {reset Last to new list end}
        Last^.Word := NextWord;           {store current word}
        ReadLn (NextWord)
      end; {while}

    {assertion: The last string read was the Sentinel}
    Last^.Link := nil                     {mark end of list}
  end; {FillRest}


begin {CreateList}
  {Display instructions to user.}
  WriteLn ('Enter each data string on a line.');
  WriteLn ('Enter ', Sentinel, ' when done.');

  {Create and fill the list head with the first word.}
  ReadLn (FirstWord);
  if FirstWord = Sentinel then
    Head := nil                                 {empty list}
  else
    begin {build list}
      New (Head);                        {create the list head}
      Head^.Word := FirstWord;     {store FirstWord in list head}
      FillRest (Head)                       {fill rest of list}
    end {build list}
end; {CreateList}
```

Procedure `CreateList` first displays the user's instructions and then reads the first data word into `FirstWord`. If `FirstWord` is the sentinel, `Head` is set to `nil` to indicate an empty list. If `FirstWord` is not the sentinel, the statements

```
New (Head);                    {create the list head}
Head^.Word := FirstWord;       {store FirstWord in list head}
```

allocate a new node `Head^`, into which `FirstWord` (string `'Hat'`) is copied. The procedure call statement

```
FillRest (Head)                       {fill rest of list}
```

Figure 17.10 List after Call to FillRest

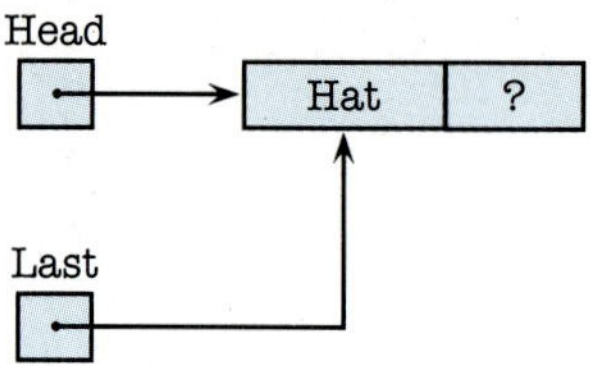

calls procedure `FillRest` to grow the rest of the list. The value of `Head` is passed into `FillRest` as the initial value of parameter `Last`. Figure 17.10 shows the partial list right after `FillRest` is called.

The `while` loop in `FillRest` is repeated until the sentinel is read. Each time the loop is repeated, the statements

```
{1} New (Last^.Link);          {attach a new node to Last^}
{2} Last := Last^.Link;        {reset Last to new list end}
    Last^.Word := NextWord;    {store last word read}
```

attach a new node to the current end of the list, reset `Last` to point to the new end of the list, and then store the data word in node `Last^`. The list after the first execution of the loop body is shown in Fig. 17.11. Each new pointer value is shown in color, along with the label of the statement that defines it; the initial value of `Last` is shown in gray.

After loop exit, the statement

```
Last^.Link := nil                          {mark end of list}
```

marks the end of the list. If the sentinel string followed `'Boy'`, the Link field of the second node in Fig. 17.11 would be set to `nil`.

Searching a List for a Target

Another common operation is searching for a target value in a list. A list search is similar to an array search in that we must examine the list elements in sequence until we find the value we are seeking or we examine all list elements without success. The latter is indicated by reaching the list node whose pointer field is `nil`.

Function `Search` in Fig. 17.12 returns a pointer to the first list node that contains the target value. If the target value is missing, `Search` returns a value

Figure 17.11 List after First Execution of while Loop

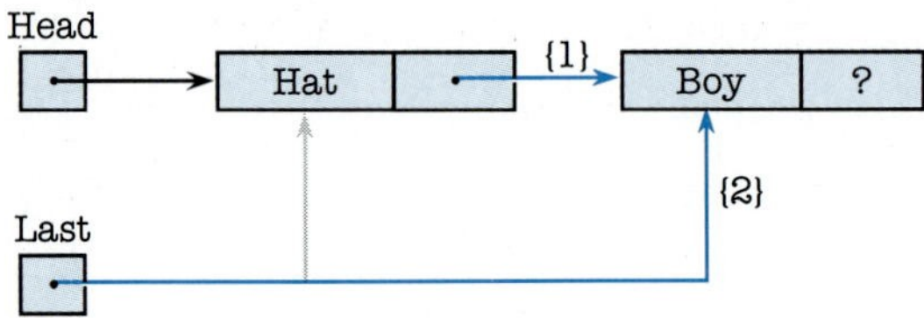

of nil. Search uses the Boolean flag Found to indicate whether the target value was found. The if statement in the while loop sets Found to True if the current list node contains the target value. The while loop exit occurs right after Found is set to True or the last list node is tested.

Figure 17.12 Function Search

```
function Search (Head : ListPointer;
                 Target : StringType) : ListPointer;
{
  Searches a list for a specified Target string.
  Pre : Head points to a list and Target is defined.
  Post: Returns a pointer to Target if found;
        otherwise, returns nil if Target is not found.
}
  var
    Found : Boolean;      {flag indicating Target found}

begin {Search}
  Found := False;         {Target not found}
  while not Found and (Head <> nil) do
    {invariant:
       no prior list node contained Target and
       no prior value of Head was nil
    }
    if Head^.Word = Target then
      Found := True
    else
      Head := Head^.Link;      {move down the list}

  {assertion: Target was found or end of list was reached.}
  if Found then
    Search := Head             {success}
  else
    Search := nil              {failure}
end; {Search}
```

PROGRAM STYLE

Avoiding Falling off the End of a List

It is tempting to eliminate the Boolean flag in Fig. 17.12 and to rewrite the while loop as

```
while (Head <> nil) and (Head^.word <> Target) do
  Head := Head^.Link;
```

The while loop exit occurs if all list elements test without success (Head is nil) or the current node contains the target value. We can then return the value of Head as the search result. Since Turbo Pascal uses short-circuit evaluation, the while loop will execute as expected. However, without short-circuit evaluation, the loop should not terminate when the target value is missing from the list because the condition Head^.Word <> Target is not defined when Head is nil. When Head is nil, Head^.Word contains garbage, and Turbo Pascal does not flag the use of nil pointers to reference garbage as a run-time error.

Exercises for Section 17.4

Self-Check

1. Trace the execution of function `Search` for the list that contains the three strings `'Hat'`, `'Boy'`, `'Cat'`. Show the value of pointer `Head` after each execution of the `while` loop. Do this for the target strings `'Boy'`, `'Cap'`, and `'Dog'`.

Programming

1. Write a function that finds the length of a list.
2. Write a recursive version of function `Search`. Your function should implement the following recursive algorithm:

```
if the list is empty then
  Target is missing - return nil
else if Target is in the list head then
  Return a pointer to the list head
else
  Search the rest of the list
```

17.5 Linked-List Representation of a Stack

Chapter 16 introduced stack and queue abstract data types and showed you how to implement them using an array for storage of the individual elements of a stack or queue. Because the number of elements in a stack or queue varies, it makes good sense to implement these data structures as dynamically allocated linked lists.

Think of a stack as a linked list in which all insertions and deletions are performed at the list head. A list representation of a stack `S` is shown on the left of Fig. 17.13. The pointer `S.Top` points to the top of stack `S`. If a new node is pushed onto the stack, it should be inserted in front of the node currently

Figure 17.13 Physical Stack S (left) and Abstract Stack (right)

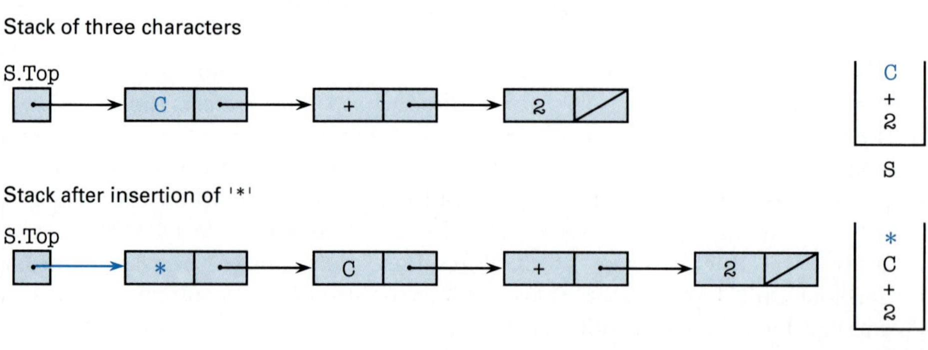

pointed to by S.Top. Stack S after the insertion of the symbol '*' is shown at the bottom of the figure.

Each element of a stack can be stored in a node with a data field (type StackElement) and a pointer field (type StackNext) that points to the next stack node (type StackNode). These data types are declared as follows:

```
type
  {Insert declaration for StackElement}

  StackNext = ^StackNode;
  StackNode = record
                 Item : StackElement;
                 Next : StackNext
               end; {StackNode}
```

The stack S can be represented by a record variable with a single pointer field, Top, that points to the top of the stack. The declarations for type Stack and record variable S (type Stack) follow.

```
type
  Stack = record
             Top : StackNext         {top of stack pointer}
           end; {stack}

var
  S : Stack;
  NextCh : Char;
  Success : Boolean;
```

■ Example 17.1

If data type StackElement is the same as Char, the assignment statement

```
S.Top := nil;
```

initializes stack S to the empty stack, as shown next.

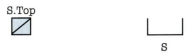

Assuming procedure Push (see Fig. 16.16) has been modified to handle the new stack declaration, the statements

```
Push (S, '+', Success);
Push (S, 'A', Success);
```

should redefine stack S, as shown next.

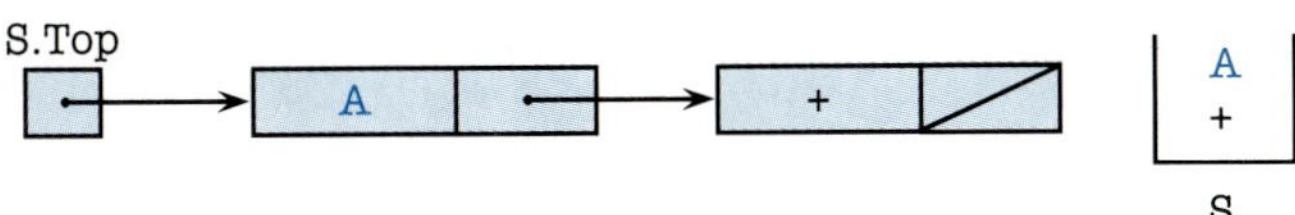

Two new nodes must be allocated to create stack S. Assuming Pop has also been modified, the statement

```
Pop (S, NextCh, Success);
```

should return the character value 'A' to NextCh (type Char) and redefine stack S as shown next. ■

Stack Operators

Each of the stack operators first shown in Fig. 16.16 is rewritten in this section assuming the previous type declaration for Stack. We begin with CreateStack, shown in Fig. 17.14. CreateStack must be called first; it creates an empty stack by intializing the top of stack pointer to nil.

Figure 17.14 Procedure CreateStack

```
procedure CreateStack (var S {output} : Stack);
{
  Creates an empty stack.
  Pre : None
  Post: S is an empty stack.
}
begin {CreateStack}
  S.Top := nil              {set top of stack pointer to nil}
end; {CreateStack}
```

Procedure Push (Fig. 17.15) must allocate a new node for storing the data item being pushed onto the stack. The node just allocated becomes the new top of the stack.

Figure 17.15 Procedure Push

```
procedure Push (var S {input/output} : Stack;
                X {input} : Char;
                var Success {output} : Boolean);
{
  Pushes X onto stack S.
  Pre : X is defined and S is a stack.
  Post: Sets Success to indicate success (True) or failure (False)
        of push operation.
}
  var OldTop : StackNext;          {pointer to old top of stack}

begin {Push}
  if IsFull(S) then
    Success := False
  else
    begin
      OldTop := S.Top;           {save old top of stack}
      New (S.Top);               {allocate new node at top of stack}
      S.Top^.Next := OldTop;     {link new node to old stack}
```

```
      S.Top^.Item := X;        {store X in new node}
      Success := True
    end {if}
end; {Push}
```

Figure 17.16 Pushing 'A' onto a Stack

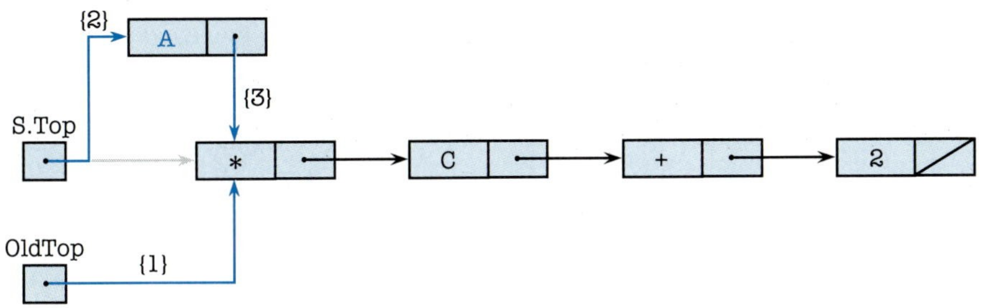

Each call to procedure Push places a new node on the stack. The statements

```
{1} OldTop := S.Top;         {save old top of stack}
{2} New (S.Top);             {allocate new node at top of stack}
{3} S.Top^.Next := OldTop;   {link new node to old stack}
```

allocate a new node (pointed to by `S.Top`) and connect this node to the former top of the stack (pointed to by `OldTop`). Figure 17.16 shows a stack before and after the letter `'A'` is pushed onto it. The original value of `S.Top` is shown in gray, and the new value is shown in color.

Procedure `Pop` (Fig. 17.17) retrieves the value at the top of the stack and returns the node in which it is stored to the heap. The node that follows the one just popped becomes the new top of the stack.

Figure 17.17 Procedure Pop

```
procedure Pop (var S {input/output} : Stack;
               var X {output} : Char;
               var Success {output} : Boolean);
{
  Pops the top of stack S into X.
  Pre : S is a stack.
  Post: Contents of X is character at top of stack S which is then
        removed from S. Sets Success to indicate success (True)
        or failure (False) of pop operation.
}
  var
    OldTop : StackNext;          {pointer to old top of stack}

begin {Pop}
  if S.Top = nil then
    Success := False
  else
    begin
      X := S.Top^.Item;           {copy top of stack into X}
      OldTop := S.Top;            {save old top of stack}
```

```
        S.Top := S.Top^.Next;         {reset top of stack}
        Dispose (OldTop);             {return top node to the heap}
        Success := True
    end {if}
end; {Pop}
```

Figure 17.18 Popping the Stack

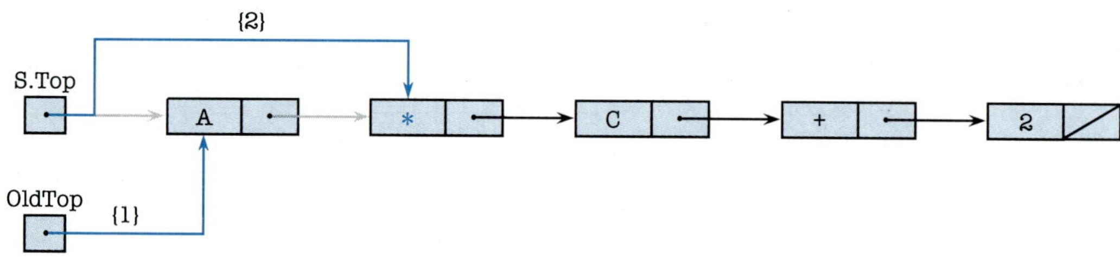

Procedure Pop first copies the value at the top of the stack into X. Next, the statement with label {2}

```
{1} OldTop := S.Top;            {save old top of stack}
{2} S.Top := S.Top^.Next;       {reset top of stack}
{3} Dispose (OldTop);           {return top node to he heap}
```

resets S.Top to point to the node following the current top node. The statement with label {3} returns the former top node to the heap so its memory cells can be reallocated. The effect of popping 'A' from the stack is shown in Fig. 17.18.

Function IsEmpty tests whether the stack is empty, and function IsFull tests whether the stack is full. The stack is considered full when there is not enough storage space left on the heap to allocate a new stack node. Turbo Pascal provides two non-standard functions that can be used to determine whether there is enough space on the heap: SizeOf and MemAvail. Function SizeOf returns the number of bytes required to store the variable or data type that is its argument. Function MemAvail returns the number of bytes left on the heap. Consequently, the condition

```
SizeOf(StackNode) > MemAvail
```

is true when there is not sufficient space on the heap to allocate a new stack node (type StackNode). Functions IsEmpty and IsFull are shown in Fig. 17.19.

Figure 17.19 Functions IsEmpty and IsFull

```
function IsEmpty (S : Stack) : Boolean;
{
  Pre : S is a stack.
  Post: Returns True if stack S is empty; otherwise, returns False.
}
begin {IsEmpty}
  IsEmpty := S.Top = nil
end; {IsEmpty}
```

```
function IsFull (S : Stack) : Boolean;
{
  Pre : S is a stack.
  Post: Returns True if stack S is full; otherwise, returns False.
}
begin {IsFull}
  IsFull := SizeOf(StackNode) > MemAvail
end; {IsFull}
```

SYNTAX DISPLAY

Function MemAvail

Form: `MemAvail`
Example: `MemAvail`
Interpretation: `MemAvail` is a function of no arguments and returns the number of bytes left on the dynamic storage heap.
Note: `MemAvail` is not available in standard Pascal.

SYNTAX DISPLAY

Function SizeOf

Form: `SizeOf(`*name*`)`
Example: `SizeOf(StackNode)`
`SizeOf(El.Item)`
Interpretation: `SizeOf` returns the number of bytes occupied in memory by a variable of data type *name*.
Note: `SizeOf` is not available in standard Pascal.

PROGRAM STYLE

Time and Space Tradeoffs for Stack Implementations

The advantage of using pointer types to implement a stack is that we can increase the size of the stack when we push on a new element and decrease its size when we pop off an element. In this way, the storage space allocated to the stack expands and contracts as needed. In the array implementation shown earlier, the entire array is allocated at once whether or not it is all needed.

This apparent saving of memory is not without cost. Each stack element requires an additional pointer field that is used for storage of the address of the next stack element. An array implementation does not require this extra field, because the elements of an array are implicitly linked together.

With respect to time, it is usually more costly for a compiler to access elements of a stack stored in an array. This is because the compiler must compute the actual memory address corresponding to a subscript value that represents the top of the stack. If the top of the stack is stored in a pointer field, no computation is required because the address of the first stack node is stored directly.

Exercises for Section 17.5

Self-Check

1. Explain why the field NumItems is not needed in the type declaration for Stack. What changes would be required to the type declaration and the stack operators if field NumItems was included?
2. Provide the algorithm for operator CopyStack that makes a copy of an existing stack.
3. What changes would have to be made to program PrintReverse (Fig. 16.6) to use the new stack data type and its operators?

Programming

1. Implement CopyStack.

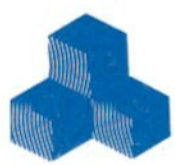

17.6 Linked-List Representation of a Queue

We can also implement a queue as a linked list that grows and shrinks as elements are inserted and deleted. We declare queue Q using the following declarations.

```
type
  {Insert declaration for QueueElement}

  QueueNext = ^QueueNode;
  QueueNode = record
                Item : QueueElement;
                Next : QueueNext
              end; {QueueNode}

  Queue = record
            Front, Rear : QueueNext;
            NumItems : Integer
          end; {Queue}

var
  Q : Queue;
  El : QueueElement:
```

The declaration for variable Q allocates storage for a record with two pointer fields, Front and Rear, and one integer field, NumItems. As shown in Fig. 17.20, Front points to the first record inserted in the queue, Rear points to the last record, and NumItems is a count of records. Each node of the queue (type QueueNode) contains storage for a queue element (type QueueElement) and a pointer to the next queue node (type QueueNext).

In a linked-list representation of a queue, the queue expands and contracts as queue elements are inserted and removed during program execution. If we store the queue elements in an array, we must allocate storage for the entire queue at compile-time.

Figure 17.20 Representing a Queue as a Linked List

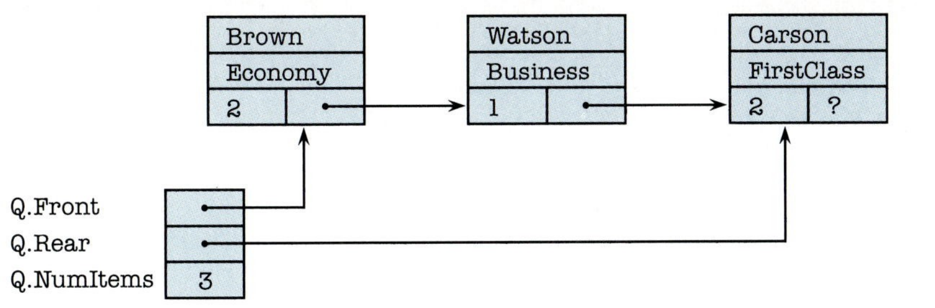

Queue Operators for Linked-List Representation

Queue operator `CreateQueue` is shown in Fig. 17.21 for a linked-list representation of a queue. Procedure `CreateQueue` initializes `NumItems` to zero and pointers `Front` and `Rear` to `nil`.

Figure 17.21 Procedure CreateQueue

```
procedure CreateQueue (var Q {output} : Queue);
{
  Creates an empty queue.
  Pre : None.
  Post: Q is initialized to a queue of zero elements.
}
begin {CreateQueue}
  Q.NumItems := 0;              {queue is empty}
  Q.Front := nil;
  Q.Rear  := nil
end; {CreateQueue}
```

In queue operator `Remove` (see Fig. 17.22), the statements

```
{1}    Temp := Q.Front;                {Point Temp to first node}
       El := Q.Front^.Item;                 {Retrieve passenger}
{2}    Q.Front := Q.Front^.Next;        {Delete passenger node}
       Dispose (Temp);                      {Deallocate storage}
```

remove the first passenger from the front of the queue, storing the passenger data in `El` (type `QueueElement`). Figure 17.23 shows the effect of these statements on the queue shown in Fig. 17.20. The `Dispose` statement returns the queue node containing the deleted passenger data to the heap.

Figure 17.22 Procedure Remove

```
procedure Remove (var Q {input/output} : Queue;
                  var El {output} : QueueElement;
                  var Success {output} : Boolean);
```

```
{
   Removes the element at the front of queue Q
   and copies it into El.
   Pre : Q has been created.
   Post: If Q is not empty, El contains its first element,
         Q.Front points to new first element,
         and Success indicates success or failure.
}
  var
     Temp : QueueNext;          {temporary pointer}

begin {Remove}
  if Q.NumItems = 0 then
    Success := False            {queue is empty}
  else
    begin
      {Remove the element at the front of the queue.}
      Temp := Q.Front;              {Point Temp to first node}
      El := Q.Front^.Item;               {Retrieve passenger}
      Q.Front := Q.Front^.Next;       {Delete passenger node}
      Dispose (Temp);                    {Deallocate storage}

      Q.NumItems := Q.NumItems - 1;
      Success := True
    end {if}
end; {Remove}
```

Figure 17.23 Removing Passenger Brown from the Queue

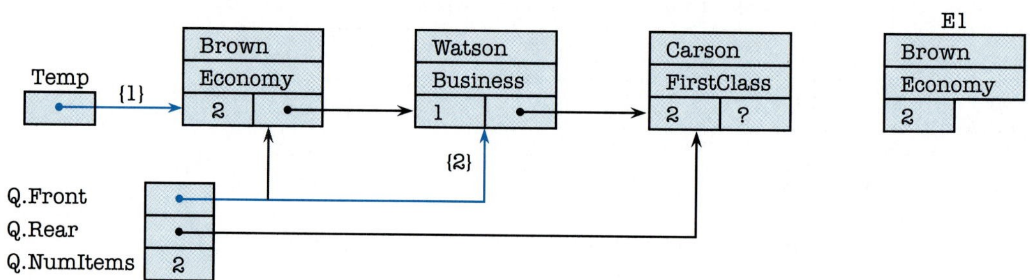

In Operator `Insert` (see Fig. 17.24), the statements

```
New (Q.Rear);                {Point Rear to first node}
Q.Front := Q.Rear           {Point Front to first node}
```

execute when the queue is empty. These statements allocate a single queue node and point `Front` and `Rear` to this node. If the queue is neither empty nor full, the statements

```
{1} New (Q.Rear^.Next);     {Attach a node at end of queue}
{2} Q.Rear := Q.Rear^.Next          {Point Rear to new Node}
```

allocate a new node at the end of the queue and point `Rear` to it. In either case, the statement

```
Q.Rear^.Item := El;            {Define new passenger node}
```

stores the contents of record El at the new end of the queue. The effect of these statements is shown in Fig. 17.25 for variable El and the queue in Fig. 17.23. By executing both the Remove and Insert procedures, we shift the element originally at the front of the queue to the rear of the queue.

Figure 17.24 Procedure Insert

```
procedure Insert (var Q {input/output} : Queue;
                  El {input} : QueueElement;
                  var Success {output} : Boolean);
{
   Inserts El in queue Q.
   Pre : Q has been created.
   Post: If Q is not full, inserts El in a new node and
         resets Rear to point to the new node.
         Sets Success to indicate success or failure.
}
begin {Insert}
  if IsFull (Q) then
    Success := False
  else
    begin {insert El}
      if Q.NumItems = 0 then
        begin {empty queue}
          New (Q.Rear);                {Point Rear to first node}
          Q.Front := Q.Rear           {Point Front to first node}
        end {empty·queue}
      else
        begin {extend queue}
          New (Q.Rear^.Next);     {Attach a node at end of queue}
          Q.Rear := Q.Rear^.Next          {Point Rear to new node}
        end; {extend queue}
      Q.Rear^.Item := El;             {Define new passenger node}
      Q.NumItems := Q.NumItems + 1;
      Success := True
    end  {insert El}
end; {Insert}
```

Figure 17.25 Reinserting Passenger Brown in the Queue

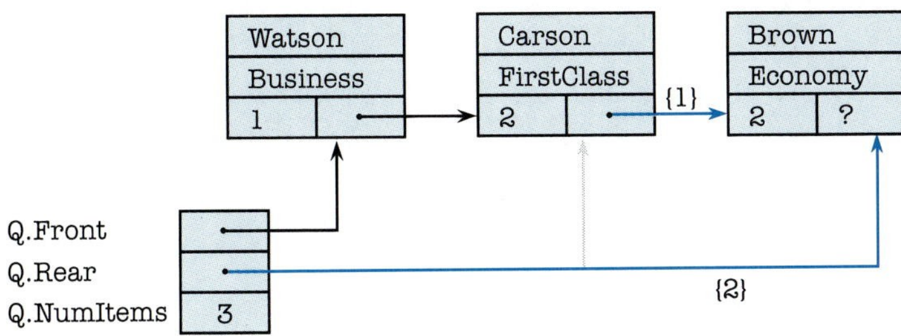

Queue as a Circular List

Section 16.7 demonstrated that a circular array was a convenient data structure for storing the elements of a queue. In this section we will see how to represent and manipulate a queue using a circular list.

Figure 17.26 shows a queue, `Q`, of three elements represented as a circular list. This is called a *circular list* because the pointer field of the last list element (passenger `Carson`) is not `nil`; instead, it points back to the first list element (passenger `Brown`). Only the pointer `Q.Rear` is required to access the queue because the pointer `Q.Rear^.Next` points to the first record in the queue (passenger `Brown`).

This enables us to eliminate the pointer field `Front` from the record type `Queue`.

The statements

```
{1} New (Temp);
{2} Temp^.Next := Q.Rear^.Next;
    Temp^.Item := El;
{3} Q.Rear^.Next := Temp;
{4} Q.Rear := Temp;
```

insert a new node in a circular queue. Statement `{1}` allocates a new node, and statements `{2}` and `{3}`insert the new node at the rear of the queue. Statement `{4}` resets `Q.Rear` to point to the new node. The effect of these statements is shown in Fig. 17.27 assuming the data for passenger `McMann` are stored in `NextPass`.

To remove a node, the pointer `Q.Rear^.Next` should be reset to point to the node following the one that is currently at the front of the queue. The statements

```
    El := Q.Rear^.Next^.Item;
{1} Q.Rear^.Next := Q.Rear^.Next^.Next;
```

store the data for passenger `Brown` in `El` and remove the first queue element. Figure 17.28 shows the effect of statement `{1}` on the queue above.

The implementation of a queue as a circular list is left as a programming project at the end of this chapter.

Figure 17.26 A Queue as a Circular List

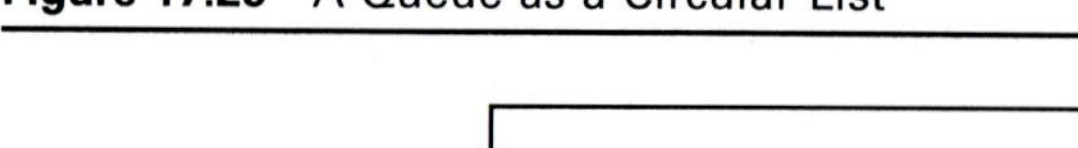
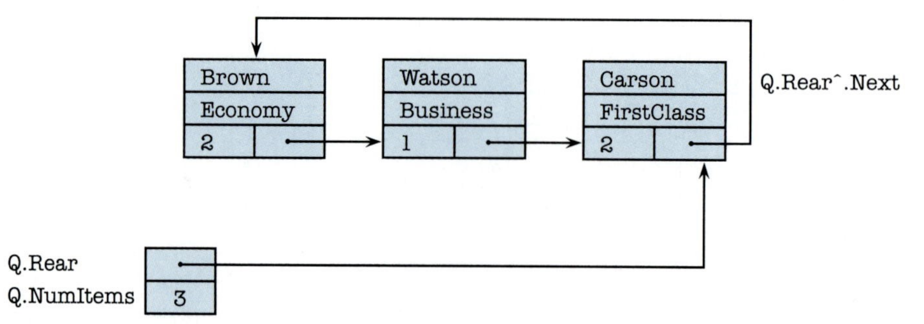

Figure 17.27 Inserting Passenger McMann in a Queue

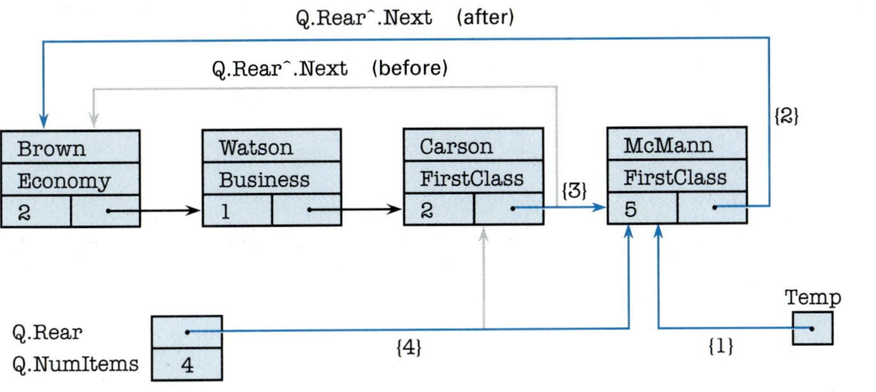

Figure 17.28 Removing Passenger Brown from a Queue

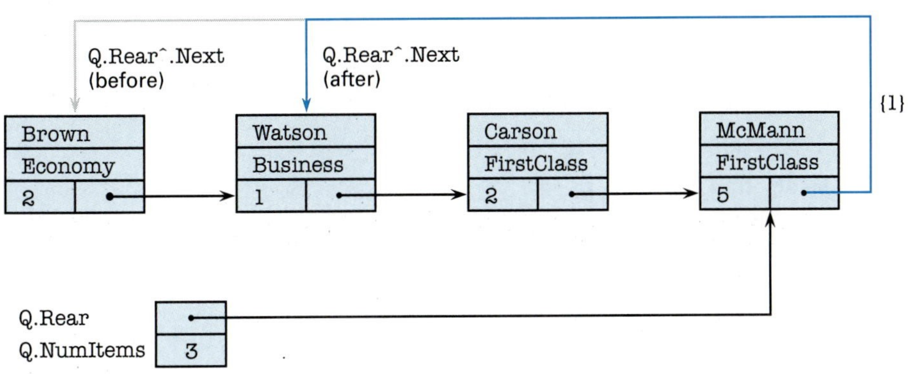

Exercises for Section 17.6

Self-Check

1. What does the following segment do to queue `Q` shown in Fig. 17.20?

```
New (Q.Rear^.Next);
Q.Rear := Q.Rear^.Next;
Q.Rear^.Name := 'Johnson';
Q.Rear^.Class := Econony;
Q.Rear^.NumSeats := 5;
Q.NumItems := Q.NumItems + 1
```

2. What does the following statement do to queue `Q` shown in Fig. 17.26?

```
Q.Rear := Q.Rear^.Next;
```

3. Insert passenger `Billingsly`, `Business` class, 2 seats in the queue of Fig. 17.26.

Programming

1. Write function SizeOfQueue for both a linked-list queue and a queue as a circular list.
2. Write procedure Retrieve for both a linked-list queue and a queue as a circular list.

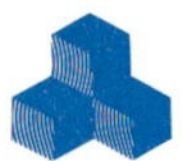

17.7 Common Programming Errors

Syntax Errors

Make sure you use the dereferencing operator ^ where it is needed. If P is a pointer variable, P^.X should be used to reference field X of the record pointed to by P.

The New and Dispose procedures allocate and deallocate storage, respectively. Both procedures require a parameter that is a pointer variable. New (P) is correct, while New (P^) is incorrect.

Run-Time Errors

Several run-time errors can occur when you are traversing linked data structures. For example, if Next is supposed to point to each node in the linked list, the while statement

```
while Next <> nil do
  Write (Next^.Word);
  Next := Next^.Link;
```

executes forever. That happens because the pointer assignment statement is not included in the loop body, so Next is not advanced down the list.

A run-time error can occur when the pointer Next is advanced too far down the list and Next takes on the value nil, indicating the end of the list. If pointer Next has the value nil, the while condition

```
while (Next <> nil) and (Next^.ID <> 9999) do
```

causes a run-time error on some systems because Next^.ID is undefined when Next is nil. The while condition should be rewritten as

```
while (Next^.Link <> nil) and (Next^.ID <> 9999) do
```

Finally, if pointer Next is a procedure parameter that corresponds to a list head pointer, make sure it is a value parameter. Otherwise, the last value assigned to Next will be returned as a procedure result. This may cause you to lose some of the elements originally in the linked list.

Problems with heap management can also cause run-time errors. If your program gets stuck in an infinite loop while you are creating a dynamic data structure, it is possible for your program to consume all memory cells on the storage heap. This situation will lead to a `heap overflow` run-time error.

Make sure your program does not attempt to reference a list node after the node is returned to the heap. All pointers to a node being returned should be assigned new values so that the node can never be accessed unless it is reallocated.

Debugging Tips

It is difficult to debug programs that manipulate pointers because the value of a pointer variable cannot be printed. If a pointer variable is displayed in the watch window, it appears as a pair of hexadecimal numbers (*segment* : *offset*) that have little meaning to anyone who is not a systems programmer. Consequently, you will often find it more informative to trace the execution of such a program by printing (or watching) an information field that uniquely identifies the list element being processed instead of the pointer value itself.

When you are writing driver programs to test and debug list operators, it is often helpful to create a sample list structure using the `New` statement to allocate several nodes and using several assignment statements to link them into a list, as we discussed in Section 17.1. You can also use assignment statements to put information into the nodes, prior to linking them.

Chapter Review

This chapter introduced several dynamic data structures. We discussed the use of pointers to reference and connect elements of a dynamic data structure. The procedure `New` was used to allocate additional elements, or nodes, of a dynamic data structure; the procedure `Dispose` returns memory cells to the storage heap.

We also covered many different aspects of manipulating linked lists. We showed how to build or create a linked list, how to traverse a linked list, and how to insert and delete elements of a linked list.

We revisited stacks and queues and showed you how to implement them as linked data structures. And we wrote new stack operators for the representation of a stack using a linked list.

New Pascal Constructs

The Pascal constructs introduced in this chapter are described in Table 17.1.

Table 17.1 New Pascal Constructs

Construct	Effect

Pointer Type Declaration
`type`
`  Pointer = ^Node:`
`  Node = record`
`           Info : Integer;`
`           Link : Pointer`
`         end; {Node}`
	The identifer `Pointer` is declared as a pointer to a record of type `Node`, where `Node` is a record type containing a field (`Link`) of type `Pointer`.

`var` `  Head : Pointer;`	`Head` is a pointer variable of type `Pointer`.
New Procedure `New (Head)`	A new record of type `Node` is allocated. This record is pointed to by `Head` and is referenced by `Head^`.
Dispose Procedure `Dispose (Head)`	The memory space occupied by the record `Head^` is returned to the storage pool.
Pointer Assignment `Head := Head^.Link`	The pointer `Head` is advanced to the next node in the dynamic data structure pointed to by `Head`.
Size Of Function `SizeOf(Node)`	Returns the number of bytes required to store an object of type `Node`.
MemAvail Function `MemAvail`	Returns the number of bytes left on the storage heap.

✓ Quick-Check Exercises

1. Procedure __________ allocates storage space for a data object that is referenced through a __________; procedure __________ returns the storage space to the __________.
2. What is the major advantage of using pointer representations of linked lists instead of array representations?
3. It is just as easy to modify a linked list that is represented as an array as one that is represented using pointers. True or false?
4. When an element is deleted from a linked list represented using pointers, it is automatically returned to the heap. True or false?
5. All pointers to a node that is returned to the heap are automatically reset to `nil` so they cannot reference the node returned to the heap. True or false?

6. Why do you need to be wary of passing a list head pointer as a variable parameter to a procedure?
7. If a linked list contains three elements with values `'Him'`, `'Her'`, and `'Its'` and `H` is a pointer to the list head, what is the effect of the following statements? Assume the data field is `Pronoun`, the link field is `Next`, and `N` and `P` are pointer variables?

```
N := H^.Next;
N^.Pronoun := 'She';
```

8. Answer exercise 7 for the following segment.

```
P := H^.Next;
N := P^.Next;
P^.Next := N^.Next;
Dispose (N);
```

9. Answer exercise 7 for the following segment.

```
N := H;
New (H);
H^.Pronoun := 'His';
H^.Next := N;
```

10. Write a single statement that will place the value `nil` in the last node of the three-element list in exercise 7.

Answers to Quick-Check Exercises

1. `New`; pointer; `Dispose`; `heap`
2. Storage space is allocated as needed and not all at once.
3. True
4. False; `Dispose` must be called.
5. False
6. The actual parameter may be advanced down a list, and in this way part of the list will be lost.
7. Replaces `'Her'` with `'She'`
8. Deletes the third list element
9. Inserts a new list with value `'His'` at the front of the list
10. `H^.Next^.Next^.Next := nil;`

Review Questions

1. Differentiate between dynamic and nondynamic data structures.
2. Define the term "linked list." Indicate how the pointers are utilized to establish a link between nodes. Also indicate any other variables that would be needed to reference the linked list.
3. Give the missing type declarations and show the effect of each of the following statements. What does it do?

```
New (P);
P^.Word := 'ABC';
New (P^.Next);
Q := P^.Next;
Q^.Word := 'abc';
Q^.Next := nil;
```

4. Assume the following type declarations for questions 4 through 9.

```
type
  StringType = string[10];
  ListPointer = ^Node;
  Node = record
           Name : StringType;
           Link : ListPointer
         end;

  HeadNode = record
               Head : ListPointer;
               NumItems : Integer
             end;

var
  List : HeadNode;
```

   Write a program segment that places the names Washington, Roosevelt, and Kennedy in successive elements of the linked list referenced by record `List`. Define `List.NumItems` accordingly.
5. Write a program segment to insert the name Eisenhower between Roosevelt and Kennedy.
6. Write an operator called `DeleteLast` that removes the last element from any list referenced by record `List`.
7. Write a procedure called `PlaceFirst` that places its second parameter value as the first node of the linked list referenced by record `List`.
8. Write a procedure called `CopyList` that creates a linked list with new nodes that contain the same data as the linked list referenced by `List`.
9. Write a procedure to delete all nodes with `Name` field `Smith` from a linked list referenced by record `List`.

Programming Projects

1. Rewrite the queue operators shown in Section 16.7 for a queue represented as a linked list.
2. Rewrite the queue operators shown in Section 16.7 for a queue represented as a circular list.
3. Do programming project 1 at the end of Chapter 16 using the queue operators from programming project 1 or 2 of this chapter.
4. Do programming project 3 at the end of Chapter 16 using the stack operators implemented in this chapter.
5. Do programming project 4 at the end of Chapter 16 using the queue operators from programming project 1 or 2 of this chapter.
6. A polynomial can be represented as a linked list, where each node contains the coefficient and the exponent of a term of the polynomial. The polynomial $4x^3 + 3x^2 - 5$ would be represented as the following linked list:

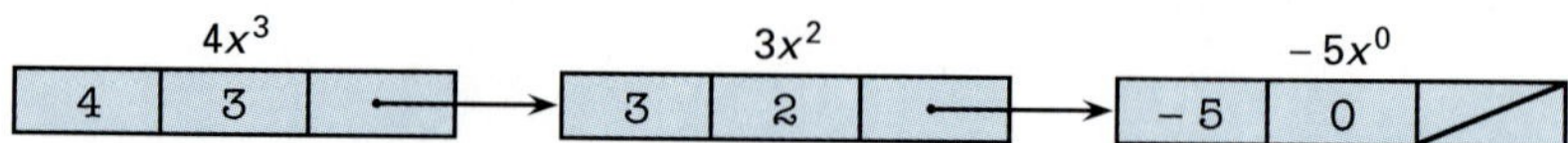

   Write an abstract data type `Polynomial` that has operators for creating a polynomial, reading a polynomial, and adding and subtracting a pair of polynomials. Hint: To add or subtract two polynomials, traverse both lists. If a particular exponent value is present in either one, it should also be present in the result polynomial unless its coefficient is zero.

7. Each student in the university takes a different number of courses, so the registrar has decided to use a linked list to store each student's class schedule and an array of records to represent the whole student body. A portion of this data structure follows.

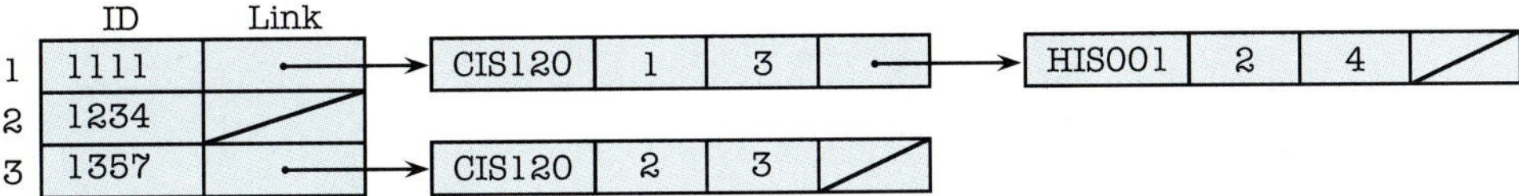

The records show that the first student (ID is 1111) is taking section 1 of CIS120 for 3 credits and section 2 of HIS001 for 4 credits; the second student (ID is 1234) is not enrolled, and so on. Write an abstract data type for this data structure. Provide operators for creating the original array of student ID numbers, inserting a student's initial class schedule, adding a course, and dropping a course. Write a menu-driven program that uses this abstract data type.

8. The `Radix` sorting algorithm uses an array of queues (numbered 0 through 9) to simulate the operation of the old card sorting machines. The algorithm requires that one pass be made for every digit of the numbers being sorted. For example, a list of 3-digit numbers would require three passes through the list. During the first pass, the least significant digit (the ones digit) of each number is examined and the number is added to the rear of the queue whose subscript matches the digit. After all numbers have been processed, the elements of each queue beginning with `queue[0]` are copied one at a time to the end of an 11th queue prior to beginning the next pass. Then the process is repeated for the next-most significant digit (the tens digit) using the order of the numbers in the 11th queue. Repeat the process again using the 3rd-most significant digit (the hundreds digit). After the final pass, the 11th queue will contain the numbers in sorted order. Write a program that implements the `Radix` sort using your `queue ADT`.

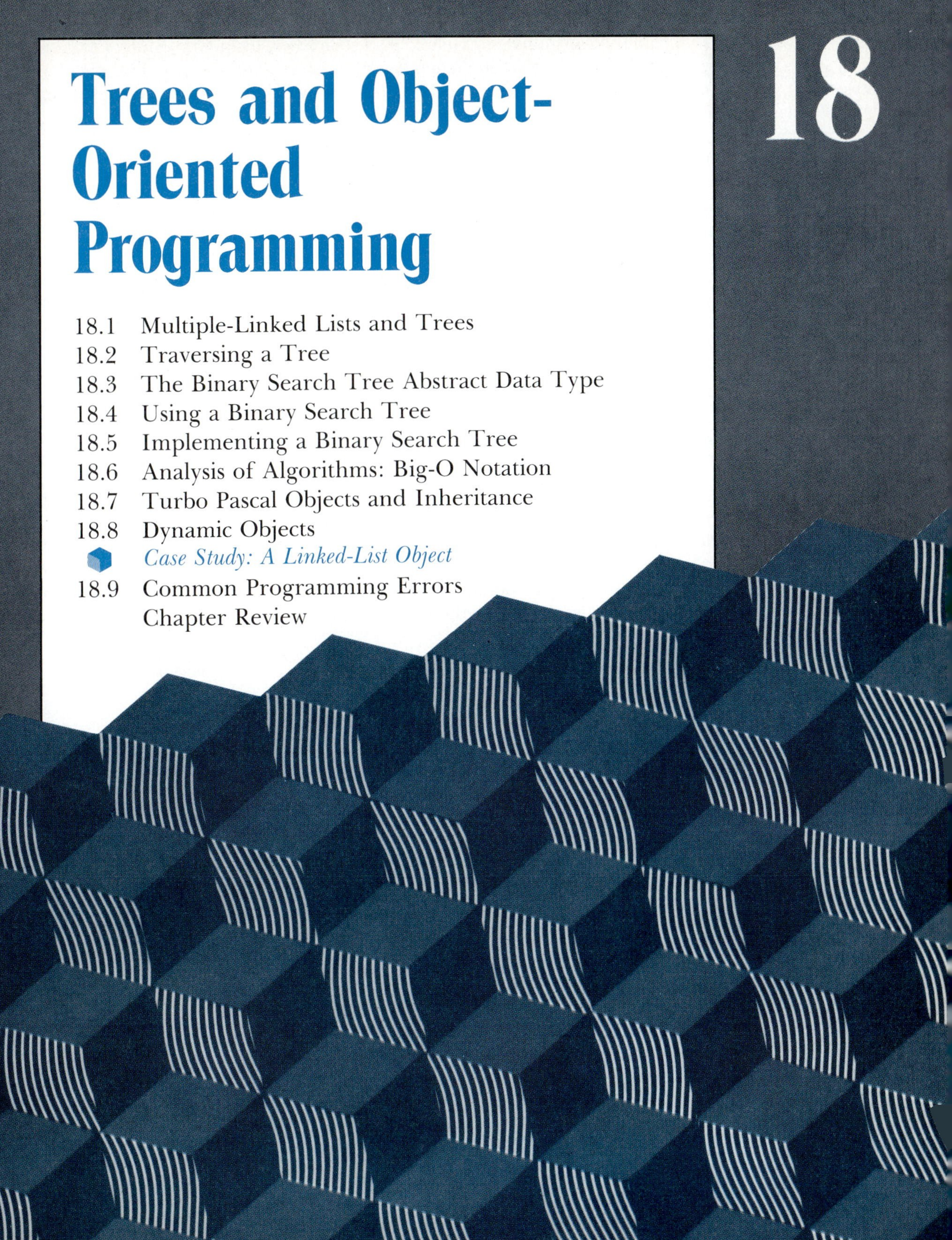

18 Trees and Object-Oriented Programming

Chapter 17 introduced dynamic data structures, including pointers, linked lists, and linked-list implementations of stacks and queues. This chapter discusses dynamic data structures that provide improved search behavior, including multiple-linked lists and binary search trees.

The binary tree has wide application in computer science. This chapter shows you how to use binary trees to represent expressions. We discuss traversing a tree and its relationship to expression evaluation. We also show you how to store information in a binary search tree and how to retrieve that information in an efficient manner.

Object-oriented programming is the second topic covered in this chapter. Turbo Pascal (version 5.5 and later) allows the programmer to encapsulate a type declaration along with declarations for operators to manipulate variables of this type into an indivisible whole known as an object. Objects may be defined in a hierarchical manner with descendant types inheriting attributes from their ancestral types. Objects are a natural means of implementing abstract data types.

18.1 Multiple-Linked Lists and Trees

All the examples of dynamic data structures you have seen so far have involved elements or nodes with a single pointer field. It is possible to have a list of elements with more than one pointer field. For example, each element in the following list has a forward pointer that points to the next list element and a backward pointer that points to the previous list element. This allows us to traverse the list in the left or the right direction.

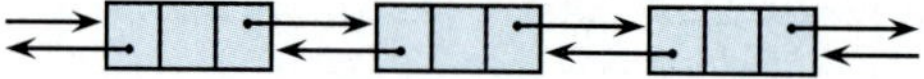

This structure is called a *doubly linked list.* The following declarations describe a general node of such a list.

```
type
  MultiLink = ^MultiNode;
  MultiNode = record
                .....
                .....   } Data Fields
                .....
                Left, Right : MultiLink
              end; {MultiNode}
```

Introduction to Trees

A special kind of multiple-linked list that has wide applicability in computer science is a data structure called a *tree.* A sample tree is drawn in Fig. 18.1.

Trees in computer science actually grow from the top down rather than from the ground up. The topmost element is called the *root of the tree.* The pointer variable Root (type Branch) points to the root of the tree in Fig. 18.1.

Figure 18.1 Tree

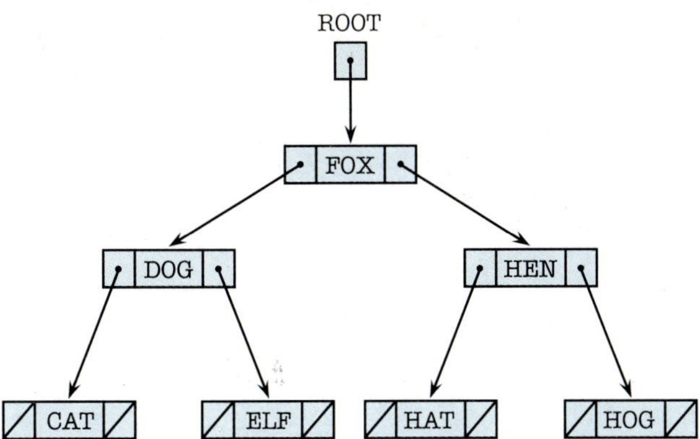

Each tree node has a single data field and two pointer fields called the *left branch* and the *right branch*.

Genealogical terminology is also used to describe computer science trees. The node that contains the string `'HEN'` is the *parent* of the nodes that contain the strings `'HAT'` and `'HOG'`. Similarly, the nodes `'HAT'` and `'HOG'` are *siblings*, because they are both *children* of the same parent node. The root of the tree is an *ancestor* of all other nodes in the tree, and they, in turn, are *descendants* of the root node.

Think of each node in a tree as the root node of its own *subtree*. Because each node has two branches, it spawns two more subtrees, a *left subtree* and a *right subtree*. One or both of these subtrees can be empty (denoted by a branch value of `nil`). A node with two empty subtrees is called a *leaf node*. The *left (right) child* of a node is the root node of its left (right) subtree. The *depth* of a tree is the length of the longest path from the root node to a leaf node.

The following statements describe the form of a tree node in Fig. 18.1. Because each node can have at most two children, such a tree is called a *binary tree*.

```
const
  StringSize = 3;

type
  StringType = string[StringSize];
  Branch = ^TreeNode;
  TreeNode = record
               Info : StringType;
               Left, Right : Branch
             end; {TreeNode}
```

Field `Info` contains the data associated with the tree node, a string of three characters.

Trees can be used to represent expressions in memory. For example, the expression

Figure 18.2 Expression Stored in a Tree

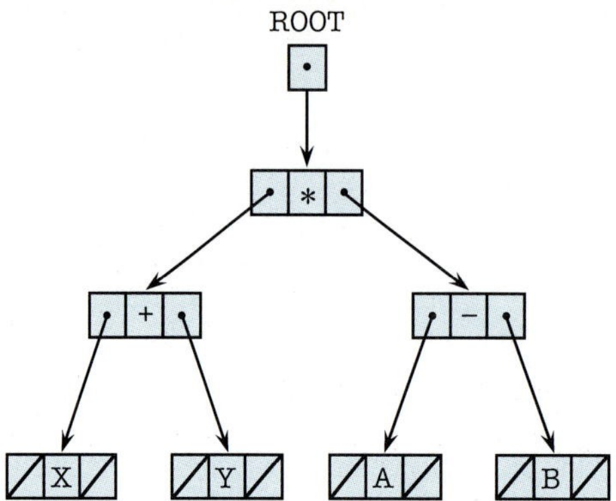


```
(X + Y) * (A - B)
```

could be represented as the tree drawn in Fig. 18.2. This tree has the same shape as the one in Fig. 18.2.

The root node contains the operator (*) that is evaluated last in the expression. Each subtree is also an expression and contains either the subexpression operator (+ or −) in its root or a variable (X, Y, A, or B). There are subtrees for the subexpressions (X + Y) and (A − B).

Exercises for Section 18.1

Self-Check

1. For the tree in Fig. 18.1, what statement can be made about the ordering of the word in a node and its left child and right child? What statement can be made regarding the relationship between the word in a node and the words in its left subtree? What about the words in its right subtree?
2. What expression is stored in the following tree?

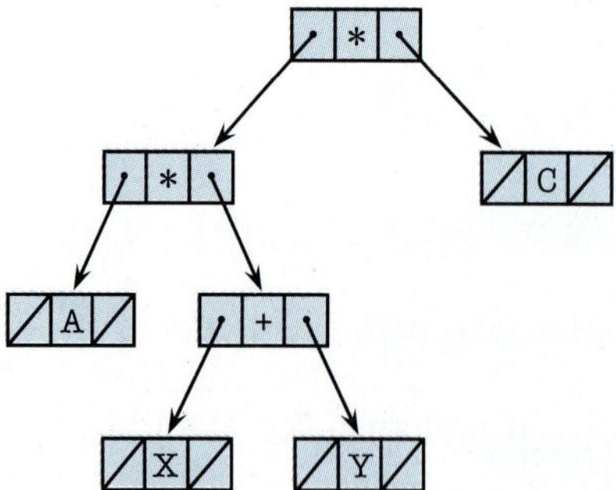

3. Draw the binary-tree representation of the following expressions. Assume the normal rules of expression evaluation.

```
X * Y / (A + B) * C
X * Y / A + B * C
```

18.2 Traversing a Tree

To process the data stored in a tree, we need to be able to traverse the tree, or visit each node in a systematic way. The first approach we illustrate is called an *inorder traversal.* The algorithm for an inorder traversal follows.

Algorithm for Inorder Traversal

1. Traverse the left subtree.
2. Visit the root node.
3. Traverse the right subtree.

You will recall that the left subtree of any node is the part of the tree whose root is the left child of that node. The inorder traversal for the tree shown in Fig. 18.1 would visit the nodes in the sequence

```
'CAT' 'DOG' 'ELF' 'FOX' 'HAT' 'HEN' 'HOG'
```

If we assume that data of each node are printed when it is visited, the strings are printed in alphabetical order, as shown.

In Fig. 18.3, a numbered circle is drawn around each subtree. The subtrees are numbered in the order that they are traversed. Subtree 1 is the left subtree of the root node. Its left subtree (numbered 2) has no left subtree (or right

Figure 18.3 Subtrees of a Tree

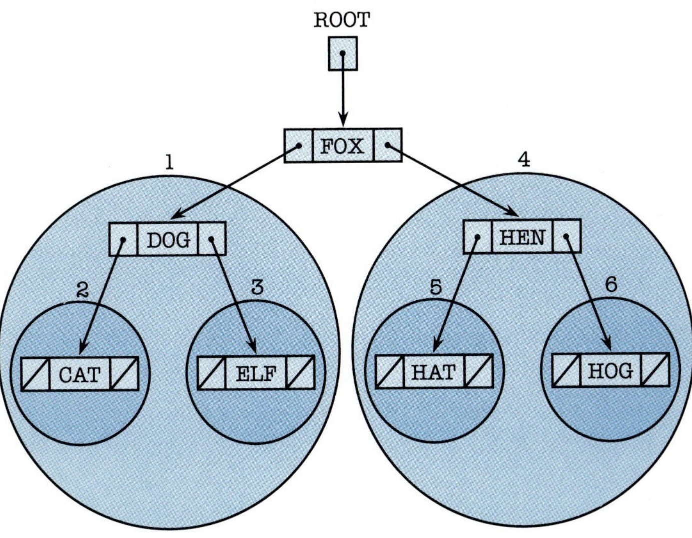

subtree); thus, the string 'CAT' would be printed first. The root node for subtree 1 would then be visited and 'DOG' would be printed. Its right subtree consists of the leaf node containing the string 'ELF' (number 3). After 'ELF' is printed, the root node for the complete tree is visited ('FOX' is printed) and the right subtree of the root node (number 4) is traversed in a like manner.

Procedure Traverse in Fig. 18.4 is a recursive procedure that performs an inorder traversal of a tree and displays each node's data. The parameter Root represents the pointer to the root node of the tree being traversed. If the tree is empty (Root = nil), an immediate return occurs. Procedure Traverse, like most procedures that process trees, can be written much more simply with recursion than without it.

Figure 18.4 Procedure Traverse

```
procedure Traverse (Root {input} : Branch);
{
  Performs an inorder traversal of a binary tree.
  Pre : Root points to a binary tree or is nil.
  Post: Displays each node visited.
}
begin {Traverse}
  if Root <> nil then
    begin {recursive step}
      Traverse (Root^.Left);      {traverse left subtree}
      WriteLn (Root^.Info);            {print root value}
      Traverse (Root^.Right)     {traverse right subtree}
    end {recursive step}
end; {Traverse}
```

The if statement in Fig. 18.4 differs from the if statements shown in earlier recursive algorithms. Those if statements had the form

if a stopping case is reached then
  Perform stopping step
else
  Perform recursive step

In a tree traversal, there is nothing to do when a stopping case is reached except unwind from the recursion. Thus, the if statement in Fig. 18.4 has the form

if a stopping case is not reached then
  Perform recursive step

As you saw earlier, an inorder traversal of the tree shown in Fig. 18.1 would visit the nodes in alphabetical sequence. If we performed an inorder traversal of the expression tree in Fig. 18.2, the nodes would be visited in the sequence

```
X + Y * A - B
```

Except for the absence of parentheses, this is the form in which we would normally write the expression. The expression is called an *infix* expression, because each operator is between its operands.

Switching the sequence of the three statements in the `if` statement shown in Fig. 18.4 produces rather different results. The sequence

```
Traverse (Root^.Left);     {traverse left subtree}
Traverse (Root^.Right);   {traverse right subtree}
WriteLn (Root^.Info)            {print root value}
```

displays the root node after traversing each of its subtrees; consequently, each root value will be printed after all the values in its subtrees. This is called a *postorder* traversal. The nodes in Fig. 18.1 would be visited in the sequence

```
CAT    ELF    DOG    HAT    HOG    HEN    FOX
```

The nodes in the expression tree in Fig. 18.2 would be visited in the sequence

```
X Y + A B - *
```

The preceding expression is called a postfix expression (see Chapter 16), because each operator follows its operands. The operands of + are X and Y; the operands of – are A and B; the operands of * are the two triples X Y + and A B –.

Finally, the sequence

```
WriteLn (Root^.Info);           {print root value}
Traverse (Root^.Left);     {traverse left subtree}
Traverse (Root^.Right)    {traverse right subtree}
```

displays the root node before traversing its subtrees; consequently, the data field of the root node will be displayed before the data fields of its subtrees. This is called a *preorder* traversal. The nodes in Fig. 18.1 would be visited in the sequence

```
FOX    DOG    CAT    ELF    HEN    HAT    HOG
```

The nodes in the expression tree in Fig. 18.2 would be visited in the sequence

```
* + X Y - A B
```

The preceding expression is called a *prefix* expression, because each operator precedes its operands. The operands of + are X and Y; the operands of – are A and B; the operands of * are the two triples + X Y and – A B.

Traversing a Tree by Tracing Its Contour

An easy way to determine the order in which the nodes of a tree are visited is to outline the contour of the tree, following all indentations as shown in Fig. 18.5. Move your finger along the tree contour, starting to the left of the root

Figure 18.5 Outlining the Contour of a Tree

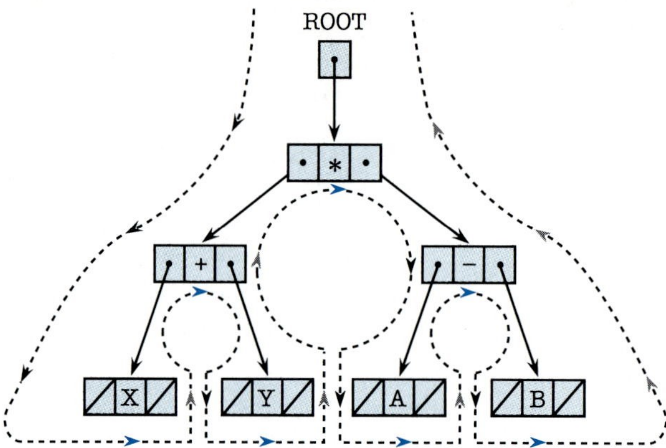

node. As your finger passes under a node (indicated by a colored arrow head), that node is visited in an inorder traversal.

As your finger passes to the right of a node (indicated by a gray arrow head), that node is visited in a postorder traversal. Your finger should be moving in an upward direction when a node is visited in a postorder traversal. As your finger passes to the left of a node (indicated by a black arrow head), that node is visited in a preorder traversal. Your finger should be moving in a downward direction when a node is visited in a preorder traversal.

Exercises for Section 18.2

Self-Check

1. Rewrite the expressions shown in exercise 3 for Section 18.1 in prefix and postfix forms.
2. What would be printed by the inorder, preorder, and postorder traversals of the tree in exercise 2 for Section 18.1?
3. What would be printed by the inorder, preorder, and postorder traversals of the tree that follows?

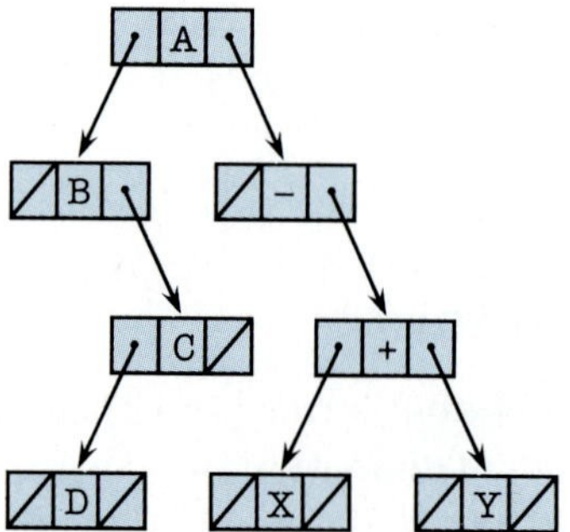

18.3 The Binary Search Tree Abstract Data Type

Trees are also used to organize related data items to facilitate efficient search for and retrieval of an item. For example, the *binary search tree* shown in Fig. 18.1 is arranged so that the left child of each node alphabetically precedes its parent and the right child alphabetically follows its parent.

A binary search tree has the property that for any node all key values less than that node's key value are in its left subtree and all key values greater than that node's key value are in its right subtree. For this reason, searching a binary search tree is a relatively efficient process. To find a particular item (the target key) at any level of the tree, we compare the target key to the key in the subtree root. If the target key is less than the key of the root node, we can eliminate the right subtree and search only the left subtree, thereby cutting the number of nodes to be searched in half. We analyze this process in more detail in Section 18.6.

Binary Search Tree Specification

The binary search tree abstract data type must include operators necessary to creating and maintaining the tree elements in key field order. The following operations must be performed: create an empty tree, search for a target key, insert a node, delete a node, retrieve a node, replace a node, display the tree, and return its size. The specification for a binary search tree and its operators follows.

Specification of Binary Search Tree Abstract Data Type

Structure: A binary search tree is a collection of elements such that each element includes among its data fields a special field called the key field. Each element of a binary tree has zero, one, or two subtrees connected to it. The key field of each element in a binary search tree is larger than all keys in its left subtree and smaller than all keys in its right subtree.
Operators: For the following descriptions, assume these parameters:

`Tree` represents the binary search tree.
`El` (pronounced el) has the same data type as the tree elements.
`Target` is a possible key field value.
`Success` is a Boolean flag indicating success (`True`) or failure (`False`) of an operation.

`CreateTree (var Tree)`: Creates an empty binary search tree; must be called before any other operators.

`SizeOfTree(Tree)`: Returns the number of elements currently in the binary search tree.

`TreeSearch (Tree, Target, var Success)`: Searches a tree to find the key `Target`. If `Target` is found, sets `Success` to `True`; otherwise, sets `Success` to `False`.

`TreeInsert (var Tree, El, var Success)`: Inserts item `El` into the binary search tree and sets `Success` to `True`. If there is already an element with the same key value as `El`, `Success` is set to `False` and no insertion is performed.

`TreeDelete (var Tree, Target, var Success)`: Deletes the element whose key value is `Target` and sets `Success` to `True`. If `Target` is not located, sets `Success` to `False`.

`TreeRetrieve (Tree, Target, var El, var Success)`: Copies the element whose key is `Target` into `El` and sets `Success` to `True`. If there is no element with key `Target`, `El` is not defined and `Success` is `False`.

`TreeReplace (var Tree, El, var Success)`: Replaces the element whose key value is the same as the key value of `El` and sets `Success` to `True`. If there is no element whose key value matches the key value of `El`, sets `Success` to `False`.

`DisplayTree (Tree)`: Displays the tree elements in sequential order by key.

We show how to use the binary search tree next; in Section 18.5, we implement operators `CreateTree`, `TreeInsert`, `TreeSearch`, and `DisplayTree`.

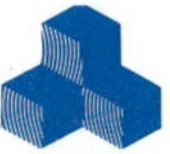 18.4 Using a Binary Search Tree

We can use the binary search tree operators in a manner analogous to the way we use the ordered list operators. The program in Fig. 18.6 stores a collection of integer data values in a binary search tree. It does this by repeatedly calling procedure `TreeInsert` to insert the node just read at its correct position in the tree. After the tree is completed, it performs a search for a target key. Finally, the program displays the keys in sequential order and displays the tree size.

Figure 18.6 Using a Binary Search Tree

```
program UseSearchTree;
{
  Builds and displays a binary search tree using ADT SearchTree.

  Import: SearchTree, TreeElement, KeyType,
          CreateTree, TreeInsert, TreeSearch, DisplayTree,
          SizeOfTree from ADT SearchTree  (see Section 18.5)
}
```

```
  uses SearchTreeADT;

  const
    Sentinel = -1;

  var
    MyTree : SearchTree;              {binary search tree}
    NextNode : TreeElement;           {each tree element}
    Target : KeyType;                 {target key}
    Success : Boolean;                {program flag}

begin {UseSearchTree}
  {Initialize the tree}
  CreateTree (MyTree);

  {Read and insert the keys in the tree.}
  WriteLn ('Enter ', Sentinel :1, ' to stop.');
  Write ('Enter next key value or ', Sentinel :1, '> ');
  ReadLn (NextNode);
  while NextNode <> Sentinel do
    {invariant:
        all prior values of NextNode that are not duplicates were
        inserted in MyTree and
        no prior value of NextNode was the sentinel
    }
    begin
      TreeInsert (MyTree, NextNode, Success);
      if Success then
        WriteLn (NextNode :1, ' inserted.')
      else
        WriteLn ('Duplicate key - no insertion.');
      Write ('Enter next key value or ', Sentinel :1, '> ');
      ReadLn (NextNode)
    end; {while}

  {assert: binary search tree completed.}
  {Perform Search operation.}
  WriteLn;
  Write ('Find record with key> ');
  ReadLn (Target);
  TreeSearch (MyTree, Target, Success);
  if Success then
    WriteLn (Target, ' found.')
  else
    WriteLn ('Not in the tree.');
  WriteLn;

  {Display the binary search tree and its size.}
  WriteLn ('The binary search tree follows.');
  DisplayTree (MyTree);
  Write ('The number of nodes in the tree is ');
  WriteLn (SizeOfTree(MyTree) :1)
end. {UseSearchTree}
```

Building a Binary Search Tree

Figure 18.7 shows a sample run of program `UseSearchTree` that builds a binary tree of seven elements with integer-valued keys. The keys are inserted in the order 4000, 2000, 1000, 5000, 6500, 4500, 3000.

Figure 18.7 Sample Run of Program UseSearchTree

```
Enter -1 to stop.
Enter next key value or -1> 4000
4000 inserted.
Enter next key value or -1> 2000
2000 inserted.
Enter next key value or -1> 1000
1000 inserted.
Enter next key value or -1> 4000
Duplicate key - no insertion.
Enter next key value or -1> 5000
5000 inserted.
Enter next key value or -1> 6500
6500 inserted.
Enter next key value or -1> 4500
4500 inserted.
Enter next key value or -1> 3000
3000 inserted.
Enter next key value or -1> -1

Find record with key> 2000
2000 found.

The binary search tree follows.
1000
2000
3000
4000
4500
5000
6500
The number of nodes in the tree is 7
```

The keys are inserted one at a time, and each insertion increases the size of the binary tree. To find the insertion point for each new key, compare each new key to the key in the root. If the new key is smaller than the root key, then compare it to the key in the left subtree root; otherwise, compare it to the key in the right subtree root. In this way, move down the tree, branching left or right, until you reach a `nil` pointer. Attach a new node to the `nil` pointer and insert the new key in this node.

Figure 18.8 shows the seven partial trees formed by inserting each element. We show the branches followed for each key insertion in color. For example, to insert the integer 4500, we first compare 4500 to 4000; 4500 is bigger, so we follow the right branch. Next, we compare 4500 to 5000; 4500 is smaller, so we follow the left branch. Because the left branch from the node with key 5000 is `nil`, we attach a new node with key 4500 to that pointer. We provide a recursive insertion algorithm in the next section.

The order in which data items are stored in a binary tree has a profound effect on the shape of the binary search tree and, as you will see later, on the efficiency of the search process. The last tree shown in Fig. 18.8 is called a *balanced binary tree*, because the left subtree and the right subtree from each node are the same depth. A tree is also considered balanced if the depth of each node's subtrees differ by at most one.

Figure 18.8 Seven Partial Trees

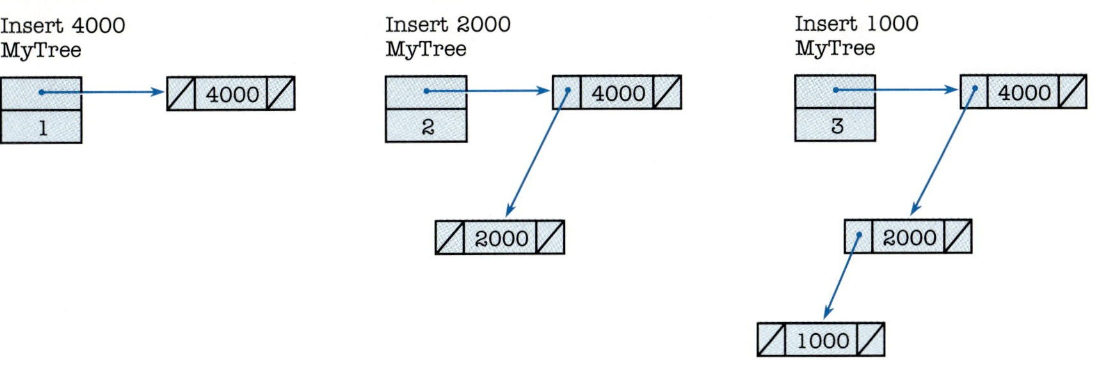

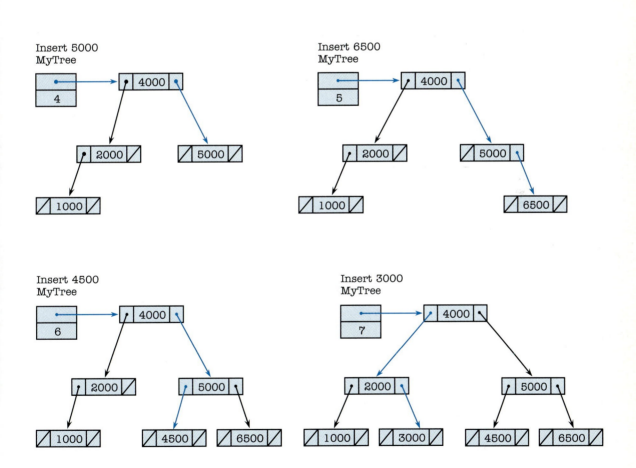

Figure 18.9 Unbalanced Binary Tree

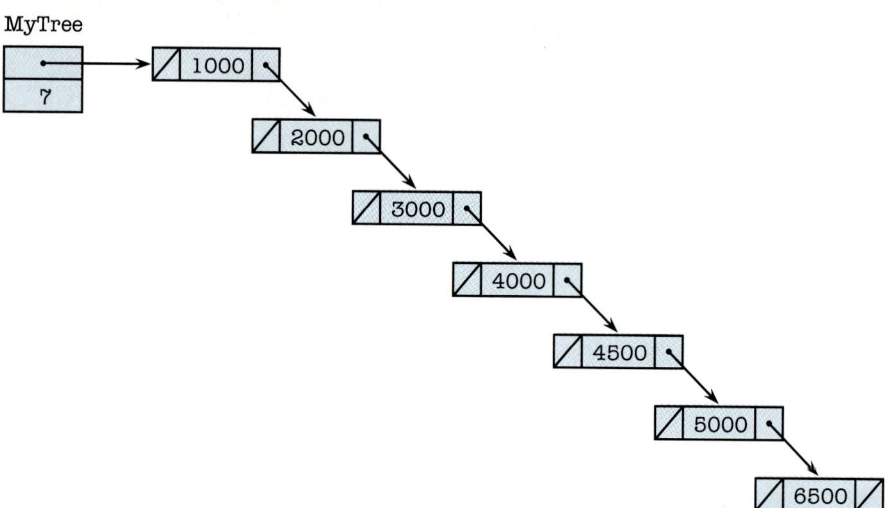

An entirely different search tree results when the data values arrive in increasing sequence (for example, `1000`, `2000`, `3000`, ...). This unbalanced tree (Fig. 18.9) actually looks more like a linked-list than a tree. Because procedure `DisplayTree` displays the tree elements in ascending order by key, the program output is the same regardless of the shape of the tree being displayed.

Exercise for Section 18.4

Self-Check

1. Explain the effect of the following program segment. Draw the tree. Is it balanced or unbalanced? If unbalanced, when does it first become unbalanced? What would be displayed by the preorder and postorder tree traversals?

```
begin
  CreateTree (MyTree);
  TreeInsert (MyTree, 3000);
  TreeInsert (MyTree, 2000);
  TreeInsert (MyTree, 4000);
  TreeInsert (MyTree, 5000);
  TreeInsert (MyTree, 2500);
  TreeInsert (MyTree, 6000);
  DisplayTree (MyTree);
  WriteLn ('Number of nodes is ', SizeOfTree(MyTree) :1)
end.
```

18.5 Implementing a Binary Search Tree

The interface section for unit `SearchTreeADT` is shown in Fig. 18.10. Each node in a binary search tree contains a data field, `Item`, and two pointers, `Left` and

Right, that connect it to its children. The data field (type TreeElement) must include a record key (type KeyType) and can be a simple type or a structured type. Data types TreeElement and KeyType must be imported into SearchTreeADT (from unit DefineTreeNode). The record type SearchTree is also declared. A variable of type SearchTree represents a header node for a binary tree. The header node contains a pointer to the root of the tree (field Root) and a count of tree items (field NumItems).

Figure 18.10 Unit SearchTreeADT

```
unit SearchTreeADT;
{
 Abstract data type SearchTree: contains declaration for data
 type SearchTree and operator procedures for an object of type
 SearchTree.

  Exports:  SearchTree, TreeElement, KeyType,
            CreateTree, SizeOfTree, TreeSearch, TreeInsert,
            TreeDelete, TreeRetrieve, TreeReplace, DisplayTree
  Imports:  InsertKey, ExtractKey, DisplayOne, TreeElement, KeyType from
            DefineTreeNode
}
 interface
   uses DefineTreeNode;

   type
     Branch = ^TreeNode;
     TreeNode = record
                  Item : TreeElement;       {Includes a key field}
                  Left, Right : Branch
                end; {TreeNode}

     SearchTree = record
                    Root : Branch;
                    NumItems : Integer
                  end; {SearchTree}

procedure CreateTree (var Tree {output} : SearchTree);
{
  Creates an empty tree. Must be called first.
  Pre : None
  Post: Tree is the header node for a binary tree.
}

procedure TreeSearch (Tree {input} : SearchTree;
                      Target {input} : KeyType;
                      var Success {output} : Boolean);
{
  Searches for Target in a binary search tree.
  Pre : Tree is the header node of a binary search tree.
  Post: If Target is located, Success is True;
        otherwise, Success is False.
}

procedure TreeInsert (var Tree {input/output} : SearchTree;
                      El {input} : TreeElement;
                      var Success {input/output} : Boolean);
{
  Inserts item El into a binary tree.
  Pre  : El is defined and Tree is the header node of a binary tree.
```

```
    Post : Success is True if the insertion is performed. If there is
           a node with the same key value as El, Success is False.
    Calls: ExtractKey
  }

  procedure DisplayTree (Tree {input} : SearchTree);
  {
    Displays the elements of a binary search tree.
    Pre : Tree is the header node of a binary search tree.
    Post: Each element of the tree is displayed. The elements
          are displayed in ascending order by key.
  }

  function SizeOfTree (Tree {input} : SearchTree) : Integer;
  {
    Returns the number of elements currently in the binary
    search tree.
    Pre : Tree is the header node of a binary search tree.
    Post: The number of elements currently in the binary search
          is returned.
  }

  procedure TreeRetrieve (var Tree {input/output} : SearchTree;
                          El {input} : TreeElement;
                          var Success {input/output} : Boolean);
  {
    Retrieves item El from a binary tree.
    Pre : El is defined and Tree is the header node of a binary tree.
    Post: Success is True if the retrieval is performed. If there is
          a node with the same key value as El, Success is False.
  }

  procedure TreeReplace (var Tree {input/output} : SearchTree;
                         El {input} : TreeElement;
                         var Success {input/output} : Boolean);
  {
    Replaces item El in a binary tree.
    Pre : El is defined and Tree is the header node of a binary tree.
    Post: Success is True if the replacement is performed. If there
          is a node with the same key value as El, Success is False.
  }

implementation
  {Insert operator procedures here.}
end. {SearchTreeADT}
```

The statement

```
uses DefineTreeNode;
```

imports several identifiers from unit `DefineTreeNode` into unit `SearchTreeADT`. For the binary search tree shown in Fig. 18.8, `TreeElement` and `KeyType` would be type `Integer`. Procedures `InsertKey`, `ExtractKey`, and `DisplayOne` will be called by the operator procedures of unit `SearchTreeADT`. We implement all the operators called in program `UseSearchTree` except for `SizeOfTree`, which is left as a programming exercise. We will discuss the operators of unit `SearchTreeADT` next and return to a discussion of unit `DefineTreeNode` later. The operators that follow would be found in the implementation section of unit `SearchTreeADT`.

Procedure CreateTree

Procedure CreateTree is shown in Fig. 18.11. It simply creates a record of type Tree with a Root field of nil and a count field (NumItems) of zero. Assuming MyTree is a variable of type SearchTree, the tree formed by

```
CreateTree (MyTree)
```

is shown next.

MyTree.Root

MyTree.NumItems 0

Figure 18.11 Procedure CreateTree

```
procedure CreateTree (var Tree {output} : SearchTree);
{
  Creates an empty tree. Must be called first.
  Pre : None
  Post: Tree is the header node for a binary tree.
}
begin {CreateTree}
  Tree.Root := nil;
  Tree.NumItems := 0
end; {CreateTree}
```

Procedure TreeSearch

It is much easier to write a recursive search algorithm than an iterative one. The recursive algorithm for searching a binary tree is shown next.

Algorithm for Binary Tree Search

1. if the tree is empty then
    2. The target key is not in the tree.
   else if the target key matches the root key then
    3. The target key is found in the root node.
   else if the target key is larger than the root key then
    4. Search the right subtree.
   else
    5. Search the left subtree.

Step 2 is an unsuccessful stopping step; step 3 is a successful stopping step. Steps 4 and 5 continue to search the right subtree and the left subtree, respectively.

Procedure TreeSearch is shown in Fig. 18.12. It starts the search at the tree root by calling DoSearch with a parameter of Tree.Root.DoSearch implements the preceding recursive search algorithm. In DoSearch, we assume that the key field is type KeyType and that procedure ExtractKey is used to extract keys.

Figure 18.12 Procedure TreeSearch

```
procedure TreeSearch (Tree {input} : SearchTree;
                      Target {input} : KeyType;
                      var Success {output} : Boolean);
{
  Searches for Target in a binary search tree.
  Pre : Tree is the header node of a binary search tree.
  Post: If Target is located, Success is True;
        otherwise, Success is False.
}

  procedure DoSearch (Parent {input} : Branch;
                      Target {input} : KeyType;
                      var Success {output} : Boolean);
  {
    Searches the subtree pointed to by Parent.
    Pre   : Target and Parent are defined.
    Post  : If Target is not found, Success is False; otherwise,
            Success is True.
    Calls: ExtractKey
  }
    var
      NextKey : KeyType;        {key of node Parent^}

  begin {DoSearch}
    if Parent = nil then
      Success := False                          {tree is empty}
    else
      begin
        ExtractKey (Parent^.Item, NextKey);
        if Target = NextKey then
          Success := True                       {Target is found}
        else if Target > NextKey then
          DoSearch (Parent^.Right, Target, Success)
        else
          DoSearch (Parent^.Left, Target, Success)
      end {if}
  end; {DoSearch}

begin {TreeSearch}
  DoSearch (Tree.Root, Target, Success)
end; {TreeSearch}
```

Procedure TreeInsert

Procedure `TreeInsert` is shown in Fig. 18.13. It stores a tree element (parameter `El`) in the tree whose header is passed as parameter `Tree`. It begins by storing the key of `El` in `ElKey`. Then it calls `DoInsert` to perform a recursive search for `ElKey`, starting at the tree root. We discussed the insertion process earlier; a recursive insertion algorithm follows.

Algorithm for DoInsert

1. `if` the pointer from the last node tested is `nil then`
   2. Attach a new node to that pointer, store `El` in this node, and set `Success` to `True`.

   `else if` the key of the current node is `ElKey then`

3. Duplicate key; set `Success` to `False`.

`else if ElKey` is greater than the key of the parent node `then`

4. Insert the node with key `ElKey` in the left subtree of the parent node.

`else`

5. Insert the node with key `ElKey` in the right subtree of the parent node.

There are two stopping states in the algorithm. If `DoInsert` is passed a pointer with value `nil` (step 1), it replaces `nil` with the address of a new node, stores `El` in the new node, and sets `Success` to `True` before returning from the recursion (step 2). If `DoInsert` finds `ElKey` in the tree, it sets `Success` to `False` and returns (step 3). Otherwise, `DoInsert` calls itself recursively to process the left subtree or the right subtree of its current tree. After the return from the original call to `DoInsert`, procedure `TreeInsert` increments the count of tree nodes if the insertion was performed.

Figure 18.13 Procedure TreeInsert

```
procedure TreeInsert (var Tree {in/out} : SearchTree;
                      El {input} : TreeElement;
                      var Success {in/out} : Boolean);
{
  Inserts item El into a binary tree.
  Pre  : El is defined and Tree is the header node of a binary tree.
  Post : Success is True if the insertion is performed. If there is
         a node with the same key value as El, Success is False.
  Calls: ExtractKey
}

  var
    ElKey : KeyType;            {key of record El}

  procedure DoInsert (var Parent {in/out} : Branch;
                      El {input} : TreeElement;
                      ElKey {input} : KeyType;
                      var Success {in/out} : Boolean);
  {
    Inserts item El in the subtree with root Parent.
    Pre  : Parent, El, and ElKey are defined.
    Post : If a node with key ElKey is found, sets Success to False.
           If a nil pointer is reached, attaches a new node
           containing El to this pointer and sets Success to True.
    Calls: ExtractKey and InsertKey
  }
    var
      NextKey : KeyType;         {key of Parent}

  begin {DoInsert}
    {Check for empty tree.}
    if Parent = nil then
      begin {Attach new node containing El to Parent}
        New (Parent);                {connect Parent to new node}
        Parent^.Left := nil;              {make new node a leaf}
        Parent^.Right := nil;
        InsertKey (Parent^.Item, El);  {insert El in node Parent^}
        Success := True
      end {attach}
```

```
        else
          begin
            ExtractKey (Parent^.Item, NextKey);
            if ElKey = NextKey then
              Success := False                  {ElKey is in tree}
            else if ElKey > NextKey then
              DoInsert (Parent^.Right, El, ElKey, Success)
            else
              DoInsert (Parent^.Left, El, ElKey, Success)
          end {if}
    end; {DoInsert}

begin {TreeInsert}
  ExtractKey (El, ElKey);                       {Get key}
  DoInsert (Tree.Root, El, ElKey, Success);
  if Success then
    Tree.NumItems := Tree.NumItems + 1          {new node is in tree}
end; {TreeInsert}
```

Procedure DisplayTree

Procedure DisplayTree (Fig. 18.14) calls procedure Traverse to perform an inorder tree traversal. Traverse then calls procedure DisplayOne to display each tree node.

Figure 18.14 Procedure DisplayTree

```
procedure DisplayTree (Tree {input} : SearchTree);
{
  Displays the elements of a binary search tree.
  Pre : Tree is the header node of a binary search tree.
  Post: Each element of the tree is displayed. The elements
        are displayed in ascending order by key.
}

  procedure Traverse (Root {input} : Branch);
  {
    Performs an inorder traversal of a binary tree.
    Pre   : Root points to a binary tree or is nil.
    Post  : Displays each node visited.
    Calls: DisplayOne
  }
  begin {Traverse}
    if Root <> nil then
      begin {recursive step}
        Traverse (Root^.Left);          {traverse left subtree}
        DisplayOne (Root^.Item);        {print root value}
        Traverse (Root^.Right)          {traverse right subtree}
      end {recursive step}
  end; {Traverse}

begin {DisplayTree}
  Traverse (Tree.Root)
end; {DisplayTree}
```

Coding Unit DefineTreeNode

Unit `DefineTreeNode` is shown in Fig. 18.15 for a binary tree containing integers. Procedure `InsertKey` stores a value in the key field of a tree node, and procedure `ExtractKey` retrieves the current contents of the key field of a tree node. Since data types `ListElement` and `KeyType` are type identical with `Integer`, the bodies of procedures `InsertKey`, `ExtractKey`, and `DisplayOne` are quite easy to write.

Figure 18.15 Unit DefineTreeNode for Integer Binary Tree

```
unit DefineTreeNode;
{
  Contains declaration for data types, and operators relevant
  to processing the data fields of a binary tree node of type
  Integer.

  Exports: TreeElement, KeyType,
           DisplayOne, InsertKey, ExtractKey
}
interface

  type
    TreeElement = Integer;
    KeyType = Integer;

  procedure InsertKey (var El {output} : TreeElement;
                      Key {input} : KeyType);
  {
    Stores Key in the key field of El.
    Pre : Key is defined and El is a binary tree element.
    Post: The key field of El becomes Key.
  }

  procedure ExtractKey (El {input} : TreeElement;
                        var Key {output} : KeyType);
  {
    Retrieves the key field of El.
    Pre : El is a binary tree element.
    Post: Key gets the key field of El.
  }

  procedure DisplayOne (El {input} : TreeElement);
  {
    Displays element El of a binary tree.
    Pre : El is defined.
    Post: Displays each data field of El.
  }

implementation

  procedure InsertKey (var El {output} : TreeElement;
                      Key {input} : KeyType);
  begin {InsertKey}
    El := Key
  end; {InsertKey}

  procedure ExtractKey (El {input} : TreeElement;
                        var Key {output} : KeyType);
```

```
  begin {ExtractKey}
    Key := El
  end; {ExtractKey}

  procedure DisplayOne (El {input} : TreeElement);
  begin {DisplayOne}
    WriteLn (El :1)
  end; {DisplayOne}

end. {DefineTreeNode}
```

It is interesting to consider what changes would be needed to maintain a list of airline passengers using a binary search tree. Unit `SearchTreeADT` would be the same as before; however, unit `DefineTreeNode` would change drastically. The new version is shown in Fig. 18.16.

Figure 18.16 Unit DefineTreeNode for Passenger Binary Tree

```
unit DefineTreeNode;
{
  Contains declaration for data types, and operators relevant
  to processing the data fields of a binary tree node of type
  Passenger.

  Exports: TreeElement, KeyType,
           DisplayOne, InsertKey, ExtractKey
}
interface

  const
    MaxSeats = 30;
    StringSize = 20;

  type
    ClassType = (FirstClass, Business, Economy, StandBy, Undesignated);
    StringType = string[StringSize];
    Passenger = record
                  Name : StringType;
                  Class : ClassType;
                  NumSeats : Integer
                end; {Passenger}

    TreeElement = Passenger;
    KeyType = StringType;

  procedure InsertKey (var El {output} : TreeElement;
                       Key {input} : KeyType);
  {
    Stores Key in the key field of El.
    Pre : Key is defined and El is a binary tree element.
    Post: The key field of El becomes Key.
  }

  procedure ExtractKey (El {input} : TreeElement;
                        var Key {output} : KeyType);
  {
    Retrieves the key field of El.
    Pre : El is a binary tree element.
    Post: Key gets the key field of El.
```

```
  }

  procedure DisplayOne (El {input} : TreeElement);
  {
    Displays element El of a binary tree.
    Pre : El is defined.
    Post: Displays each data field of El.
  }

implementation

  procedure InsertKey (var El {output} : TreeElement;
                       Key {input} : KeyType);
  begin {InsertKey}
    El.Name := Key
  end; {InsertKey}

  procedure ExtractKey (El {input} : TreeElement;
                        var Key {output} : KeyType);
  begin {ExtractKey}
    Key := El.Name
  end; {ExtractKey}

  procedure DisplayOne (El {input} : TreeElement);
  begin {DisplayOne}
    WriteLn ('Name : ', El.Name);
    WriteLn ('Seats: ', El.NumSeats)
  end; {DisplayOne}

end. {DefineTreeNode}
```

Exercises for Section 18.5

Self-Check

1. Procedure `TreeDelete` should search for the target key and then delete the node containing it from the tree. Write a recursive algorithm for `TreeDelete`, assuming that procedure `DeleteNode` performs the deletion of the node. `DeleteNode` has one parameter, which is the pointer from its parent to the node being deleted. Why is `DeleteNode` a difficult procedure to write?

Programming

1. Write function `SizeOfTree`
2. Write procedures `Retrieve` and `Replace` for the search tree abstract data type.

18.6 Analysis of Algorithms: Big-O Notation

In this chapter we have discussed storing data in a binary search tree as a technique for facilitating searching for a target item and displaying the data in order by key field. In Chapter 17 we discussed searching for a target value in a linked-list. It is possible to insert items in a linked-list in such a way so that traversing the list will always be done in key field order. This type of list is called an *ordered list.* This section discusses the merits of each method.

Big-O Notation

It is difficult to get a precise measure of the performance of an algorithm or a program. For this reason, we normally try to approximate the effect on an algorithm of a change in the number of items, N, that it processes. In this way, we can see how an algorithm's execution time increases with N, so we can compare two algorithms by examining their growth rates.

For example, if we determine that the expression

$$2N^2 + N - 5$$

expresses the relationship between processing time and N, we say that the algorithm is an $O(N^2)$ algorithm, where O stands for *order of magnitude.* This notation is called *Big-O Notation.* The reason that this is an $O(N^2)$ algorithm instead of an $O(2N^2)$ or an $O(N^2 + N - 5)$ algorithm is that we are interested only in the fastest-growing term (the one with the largest exponent) and we ignore constants.

Consider the task of searching an ordered list for a target key. If we assume that a target key is equally likely to be at the front of the list as at the end of the list, then on the average we have to examine half of the list elements to find it. This would be true whether or not the target key is in the list. If the list had N items, we would have to examine $N/2$ items on the average either to locate a given key or to determine that the key is not in the list. Consequently, searching for a data item in an ordered list is an $O(N)$ process, so the growth rate is linear.

Searching a binary search tree is more difficult to analyze. If the tree is balanced, each probe into the tree eliminates ½ of the items. Consequently, we first search a tree with N nodes, then $N/2$ nodes, then $N/4$ nodes, and so on. For example, if `N` is `1024` it requires searching ten more trees (sizes `512`, `256`, `128`, `64`, `32`, `16`, `8`, `4`, `2`, and `1`) to determine that a target is missing. It should require fewer than eleven probes to find a target in the tree. Because `1024` happens to be a power of 2 (`1024` is 2 raised to the power 10), the numbers in the preceding list are all powers of 2. Therefore, searching a balanced binary search tree is an $O(\log_2 N)$ process ($\log_2 1024$ is 10). Keep in mind that a binary search tree is not always balanced, so this is really a *best-case analysis.*

What difference does it make whether an algorithm is an $O(N)$ process or an $O(\log_2 N)$ process? Table 18.1 evaluates $\log_2 N$ for different values of N. A doubling of N causes $\log_2 N$ to increase by only 1. Because $\log_2 N$ increases much more slowly with N, the performance of an $O(\log_2 N)$ algorithm is not as adversely affected by an increase in N.

Both storage techniques enable us to easily display the data items in sequence by key field. In an ordered list, we simply advance a pointer down the list and display the data fields of the node selected by the pointer. Therefore, displaying the data in an ordered list is an $O(N)$ process.

To display the data in a binary search tree, we must perform an inorder traversal of the tree, displaying the data stored in each node as we visit it. The tree-traversal algorithm is recursive, and the number of procedure calls depends on the size of the tree. The left and the right subtrees of each tree must be traversed, so for a tree of N nodes, there are $2N$ procedure calls. Therefore, a binary search tree display is also an $O(N)$ process. Even though both algorithms are $O(N)$, it takes more time to display a binary search tree, because calling a procedure takes more time than advancing a list pointer.

Another question is the effect on memory of using an ordered list versus a binary search tree. One additional pointer field is needed for each node of a binary search tree, so the storage requirements for a tree versus a list increase linearly with N.

The memory requirements for the algorithms to search and display an ordered list are not affected by N. However, the algorithms to search and display a binary search tree are recursive, so their memory requirements increase with the depth of the tree. If the tree is balanced, its depth is related to $\log_2 N$. The worst case for an inorder traversal occurs for an unbalanced tree with all its nodes in the left subtree (why?). This tree has depth of N.

Table 18.1 Table of Values of $\log_2 N$

N	$\log_2 N$
32	5
64	6
128	7
256	8
512	9
1,024	10

18.7 Turbo Pascal Objects and Inheritance

Turbo Pascal (version 5.5 and later) allows you to encapsulate a type declaration along with declarations of operators used to manipulate variables of that type as an entity known as an *object*. Objects are a natural means of implementing abstract data types. Unlike abstract data types implemented as Turbo Pascal units, objects can be defined in a hierarchical manner with descendant types inheriting information and operators from previously declared ancestor types. The use of objects and inheritance is called *object-oriented programming*.

Object Type Declaration

In Chapter 11, we defined an abstract data type consisting of the record type `Complex` (fields `RealPart` and `ImaginaryPart`) and several operators for working with complex numbers. We could also choose to encapsulate the record fields and operators together in a Turbo Pascal object, as shown in Fig. 18.17.

Figure 18.17 Unit ComplexADT

```
unit ComplexADT;
{
  Abstract data type for initializing, displaying, and adding
  objects of type Complex.
}
interface
  type
    Complex = object
                RealPart, ImaginaryPart : Real;
                procedure Init;
                function GetReal : Real;
                function GetImaginary : Real;
                procedure SetComplex (X, Y  {input}  : Real);
                procedure AddComplex (A, B  {input}  : Complex);
                procedure WriteComplex;
              end; {Complex}

implementation

  procedure Complex.Init;
  { Initializes complex number to (0.0, 0.0) }
  begin {Init}
    RealPart := 0.0;
    ImaginaryPart := 0.0
  end; {Init}

  function Complex.GetReal : Real;
  { Returns the real part of the complex number }
  begin {GetReal}
    GetReal := RealPart
  end; {GetReal}

  function Complex.GetImaginary : Real;
  { Returns the imaginary part of the complex number }
  begin {GetImaginary}
    GetImaginary := ImaginaryPart
  end; {GetImaginary}

  procedure Complex.SetComplex (X, Y  {input} : Real);
  { Sets the complex number to (X, Y) }
  begin {SetComplex}
    RealPart := X;
    ImaginaryPart := Y
  end; {SetComplex}

  procedure Complex.AddComplex (A, B  {input}  : Complex);
  { Complex number is the sum of the complex numbers A and B }
  begin {AddComplex}
    RealPart := A.GetReal + B.GetReal;
    ImaginaryPart := A.GetImaginary + B.GetImaginary
  end; {AddComplex}

  procedure Complex.WriteComplex;
  { Displays complex number }
  begin {WriteComplex}
    Write ('(', RealPart :4:2);
    WriteLn (', ', ImaginaryPart :4:2, ')')
  end; {WriteComplex}

end. {ComplexADT}
```

Turbo Pascal object declarations are similar to those of record types. They begin with the reserved word `object` and contain information components called fields and operators called *methods*. Turbo Pascal objects can be thought of as records that inherit fields and methods from their ancestral objects. While Turbo Pascal does not require objects to be declared inside a unit, we will declare objects inside units since our examples focus on their usefulness in implementing abstract data types.

The object type `Complex` declared in the interface section of Fig. 18.17 has two fields: `RealPart` and `ImaginaryPart`. It also has six methods: `Init`, `GetReal`, `GetImaginary`, `SetComplex`, `AddComplex`, and `WriteComplex`. An object's fields must be declared before its methods. Object types and their methods must be declared in the outermost scope of any program or unit. They may not be declared locally within functions or procedures. Object types may be used anywhere that record types may be used, except that they may not be used as file components.

The declarations of the method headings that appear within the interface section are treated like forward declarations for the methods. A method's implementation appears in the implementation section. Method implementations are similar to those of ordinary functions and procedures, except that you must qualify the method identifier by prefixing it with the object type name followed by a period. Note that parameter C, which represents the complex number being defined or displayed in our ADT implementation in Chapter 11, has been omitted from the parameter lists of the methods in Fig. 18.17.

SYNTAX DISPLAY

Object Type Declaration in a Unit

Form:

```
unit unitname;

interface
  type
    obj type = object
                 field list;
                 method heading list;
               private
                 field list;
                 method heading list;
               end;

implementation
  method declarations

end.
```

Example:

```
unit FractionADT;

interface
  type
```

```
Fraction = object
             Num, Denom : Integer;
             procedure Init (N, D : Integer);
             function DecimalEquiv : Real;
           end; {Fraction}

implementation

  procedure Fraction.Init (N, D {input} : Integer);
  begin {Init}
    Num := N;
    Denom := D
  end; {Init}

  function Fraction.DecimalEquiv : Integer;
  begin {DecimalEquiv}
    DecimalEquiv := Num/Denom
  end; {DecimalEquiv}

end. {FractionADT}
```

Interpretation: When defined in a unit, the object type declaration appears in the unit interface section. Object `Fraction` has two fields (`Num` and `Denom`) declared in its *field list* and two methods (`Init` and `DecimalEquiv`) declared in its *method heading list*. The *method declarations* appear in the unit implementation section. *Method declarations* are similar to those of ordinary functions and procedures, except that the object type name followed by a period must be used to qualify each method identifier in the *method declarations*.

Notes: Although object declarations do not have to be placed in units, in object-oriented programming it is often desirable to do so. If an object is not defined in a unit, its declaration must appear in the outermost scope of the program. The use of `private` in an object type declaration is optional. If present, the fields and methods declared following `private` are visible only within the program or unit in which the object type is declared. The object's type declaration must precede its method declarations. Object types may be used anywhere that record types may be used, except that they may not be file components.

Using an Object

Program `TestComplex`, shown in Fig. 18.18, uses unit `ComplexADT`. It is a simple driver program that sets the value of a complex number, adds it to another, and displays the resulting complex value.

Figure 18.18 Program TestComplex

```
program TestComplex;

  uses ComplexADT;

  var
    A, B, C : Complex;
```

```
begin {TestComplex}
  A.Init;                     {initialize objects}
  B.Init;
  C.Init;
  B.SetComplex(5.0,-10.0);
  C.AddComplex(A,B);          {set C to sum of A and B}
  C.WriteComplex              {display value of C}
end. {TestComplex}
```

Variables declared using object types are called *instances* of these objects. In Fig. 18.18, the identifier `A` is said to be an instance of the object `Complex`. The statement

```
A.Init;
```

initializes complex number `A`. Each instance of a `Complex` type object should be initialized using method `Init` before any other reference to the object takes place. While this is not required for all object types, it is a good programming practice to follow.

Methods are called with their fully qualified names. To fully qualify a method identifier, place the instance identifier followed by a period before the method identifier (e.g., `A.Init`). Unlike ordinary functions and procedures, methods are associated with a specific instance of an object. That is why the methods in Fig. 18.17 do not need to be passed a parameter of type `Complex`. When a call to method `C.WriteComplex` is made in the program shown in Fig. 18.18, the statements within the method have direct access to the information fields of the instance `C`.

The fields `RealPart` and `ImaginaryPart` can be accessed directly, like fields of ordinary records. For example, the fields of instance `B` could be assigned values directly in program `TestComplex` using the statements

```
B.RealPart := 5.0;
B.ImaginaryPart := -10.0;
```

The `with` statement has been extended to accept object types as well as record types, so we could also write

```
with B do
  begin
     B.RealPart := 5.0;
     B.ImaginaryPart := -10.0;
   end; {with}
```

However, it is not good programming practice to manipulate the fields of an object directly. Methods should be defined to perform any operation involving an object's fields.

Object Inheritance

We can create families of objects in which a new object can be designated as a *descendant* of an earlier, more general object (its *ancestor*). Just as a child inherits certain characteristics from its parents, a descendant may inherit some of the attributes (fields and methods) of its ancestors. This inheritance enables us to simplify the definition of a new object and its methods.

In Chapter 11, we used variant records to implement an abstract data type for geometic figures. Figure 18.19 shows an object-based implementation for a similar ADT. All objects of type `Figure` and their descendants have fields `Shape`, `Perimeter`, and `Area`. They also have methods for initializing `Shape`, for computing `Area` and `Perimeter`, and for displaying those fields. Objects of types `Circle` and `Rectangle` require different algorithms for computing `Area` and `Perimeter`. To allow the computation of `Area` and `Perimeter`, `Circle` objects also need a `Radius` field and `Rectangle` objects need `Height` and `Width` fields.

Figure 18.19 Unit FigureADT

```
unit FigureADT;
{
  Abstract data type for initializing and displaying the
  attributes of objects of types Figure, Circle, and Rectangle.
}

interface

  type
    Figure = object
               Shape : string;
               Area, Perimeter : Real;
               constructor GetFigure;
               procedure ComputeArea; virtual;
               procedure ComputePerim; virtual;
               procedure DisplayFig; virtual;
             end; {Figure}

    Circle = object(Figure)
               Radius : Real;
               constructor Init (R {input} : Real);
               procedure ComputeArea; virtual;
               procedure ComputePerim; virtual;
               procedure DisplayFig; virtual;
             end; {Circle}

    Rectangle = object(Figure)
                  Height, Width : Real;
                  constructor Init (H, W {input} : Real);
                  procedure ComputeArea; virtual;
                  procedure ComputePerim; virtual;
                  procedure DisplayFig; virtual;
                end; {Rectangle}

implementation

  constructor Figure.GetFigure;
  {
    Initializes objects of type Figure.
    Pre : None.
    Post: Shape field assigned value typed from keyboard.
  }
  begin {GetFigure}
    Write ('Enter object name > ');
```

```
  ReadLn (Shape)
end; {GetFigure}

procedure Figure.ComputeArea;
{
  Computes default area for Figure objects.
  Pre : None.
  Post: Area assigned value 0.
}
begin {ComputeArea}
  Area := 0.0
end; {ComputeArea}

procedure Figure.ComputePerim;
{
  Computes default perimeter for Figure objects.
  Pre : None.
  Post: Perimeter assigned value 0.
{
begin {ComputePerim}
  Perimeter := 0.0
end; {ComputePerim}

procedure Figure.DisplayFig;
{
  Displays attributes of Figure objects.
  Pre : Object has been initialized and all fields defined.
  Post: Displays Shape, Area, Perimeter.
}
begin {DisplayFig}
  WriteLn ('Figure shape is ', Shape);
  WriteLn ('Area is ', Area :4:2);
  WriteLn ('Perimeter is ', Perimeter :4:2)
end; {DisplayFig}

constructor Circle.Init (R {input} : Real);
{
  Initializes objects of type Circle.
  Pre : R is defined.
  Post: Shape field assigned value 'Circle', Radius assigned
        value from R.
}
begin {Init}
  Shape := 'Circle';
  Radius := R
end; {Init}

procedure Circle.ComputeArea;
{
  Computes area for Circle objects.
  Pre : Object has been initialized.
  Post: Area assigned computed value.
}
begin {ComputeArea}
  Area := Pi * Radius * Radius
end; {ComputeArea}

procedure Circle.ComputePerim;
{
  Computes perimeter for Circle objects.
  Pre : Object has been initialized.
  Post: Perimeter assigned computed value.
```

```
  }
  begin {ComputePerim}
    Perimeter := 2 * Pi * Radius
  end; {ComputePerim}

  procedure Circle.DisplayFig;
  {
    Displays attributes of Circle objects.
    Pre : Object has been initialized and all fields defined.
    Post: Displays Shape, Radius, Area, Perimeter.
  }
  begin {DisplayFig}
    {
      Use inherited method to display Shape, Area, Perimeter.
    }
    Figure.DisplayFig;
    WriteLn ('Radius is ', Radius :4:2)
  end; {DisplayFig}

  constructor Rectangle.Init (H, W {input} : Real);
  {
    Initializes objects of type Rectangle.
    Pre : H and W are defined.
    Post: Shape field assigned value 'Rectangle', Height assigned
          value from H, Width assigned value from W.
  }
  begin {Init}
    Shape := 'Rectangle';
    Height := H;
    Width := W
  end; {Init}

  {
    insert method definitions for Rectangle.ComputeArea,
    Rectangle.ComputePerim and Rectangle.DisplayFig
  }
end. {FigureADT}
```

In Turbo Pascal, we can declare `Circle` and `Rectangle` to be descendant types of `Figure`. `Figure` is said to be an ancestor type of `Circle` and `Rectangle`. To declare an object as a descendant type, the ancestor's type identifier is enclosed in parentheses following the reserved word `object` in its type declaration. An object type may have any number of descendant object types, but only one immediate ancestor type.

The type `Circle` appears to have only one field and four methods. However, objects of type `Circle` inherit all fields present in their ancestor type `Figure`, in this case, fields `Shape`, `Area`, and `Perimeter`. Inherited fields cannot be removed from descendant types. Objects of type `Circle` inherit all methods not redefined by itself or its ancestors. The method `GetFigure` is the only method that has not been redefined by `Circle`.

The methods and fields inherited from `Figure` are referred to in the same way as those declared in `Circle`'s type declaration. Consequently, field `Area` (declared in type `Figure`) and `Radius` (declared in type `Circle`) are referred to in the same way by `Circle`'s methods. Methods that have been redefined by `Circle` can be accessed by `Circle`'s methods, if they are fully qualified. In Fig. 18.19, `Figure.DisplayFig` is called by `Circle.DisplayFig`.

Object methods can be declared as either static or virtual; by default, they are static. `Complex.Int` (Fig. 18.17) is an example of a static method, and `Figure.ComputeArea` (Fig. 18.19) is an example of a virtual method. Methods that are likely to be redefined by descendant types should be declared as virtual methods. Calls to static methods are resolved during program compilation, while calls to virtual methods are resolved at program run time. When static methods are redefined by descendant types, the method headings can have their parameter lists or function return types changed. Virtual methods must have identical parameter lists and function return types in all descendant object types. Furthermore, each virtual method declaration must be followed by a semicolon and the `virtual` directive in the object type declaration.

Objects containing virtual methods must be explicitly initialized at run time by calls to special methods known as *constructors*. The `{$R+}` compiler directive can be used to force each virtual method call to check the initialization status of the object instance making the call. Constructors are defined in the same way as procedures, except that the reserved word `constructor` is used in place of the reserved word `procedure`. Constructors are called in the same way as other methods. An object can have several constructors, which may be inherited. Constructors cannot be virtual.

SYNTAX DISPLAY

Descendant Object Declaration

Form:

```
type
   descendant type = object (ancestor type)
                        field list;
                        method heading list;
                     private
                        field list;
                        method heading list;
                     end;
```

Example:

```
type
   Person = object
               Name : string;
               constructor Init (N : string);
               procedure Display; virtual;
             end; {Person}

Student = object(Person)
             GPA : Real;
             constructor Init (N : string; R : Real);
             procedure Display; virtual;
           end; {Student}
```

Interpretation: The type declaration for *descendant type* must contain *ancestor type* inside parentheses following the reserved word `object`. The *ancestor type* must be a previously declared object type. The *descendant type* inherits all fields present in its *ancestor type*. Inherited fields may not be redefined in descendant objects. Object field identifiers must be unique within an object, all its descendants, and their methods.

The descendant type inherits all ancestor type methods it does not redefine. Once a method is redefined by a descendant type, its scope becomes that of the descendant type, unless the method was declared using the virtual directive. Virtual methods must contain identical method heading declarations in all subsequent descendant type declarations.

Objects containing virtual methods need to be initialized at run time by calling special methods known as constructors. An object may have more than one constructor and constructors may not be virtual. Constructor declarations are similar to those of ordinary methods, except that the reserved word constructor is used in place of either function or procedure in the method heading declaration.

Notes: The `{$R+}` compiler directive can be used to force Turbo Pascal to check the initialization status of an object before calling a virtual method. When range-checking is active, a run-time error occurs when a virtual method call is for an object not properly initialized by a constructor. As discussed earlier, `private` may be used to restrict the visibility of selected fields and methods to the program or unit in which the object type is declared.

Object Type Compatibility

The rules of assignment compatibility have been extended to allow variables declared as instances of an object to be assigned values of another instance of the same object or any of its descendant types. For example, if `F1` is a variable of type `Figure` and `C1` is of type `Circle`, the following is a valid assignment statement:

```
F1 := C1;
```

Only those fields of `C1` that were inherited from `Figure` will have their values copied to the corresponding fields of `F1`. Both `F1` and `C1` must have been initialized by appropriate constructor calls prior to this assignment. Because inheritance is a nonsymmetric relationship, `F1` cannot be assigned to `C1`.

The rules of assignment compatibility also apply to variable formal parameters that are declared as object types. Consequently, you could use either `F1` or `C1` as an actual parameter when calling a procedure that has a corresponding variable formal parameter declared to be of type `Figure`.

Use of Self

An object's field identifiers cannot be redefined as formal parameters or local identifiers in any of the object's methods. However, it is possible for identifiers that are not part of the object to be the same as the object's field identifiers. To refer to an object field that has the same name as some other identifier in the same scope, the object field identifier can be qualified by the identifier `Self`. Within a method, `Self` always refers to the object instance making the method call. For example, within the method `Figure.ComputeArea`, an assignment to the object field `Area` could be written as

```
Self.Area := 0.0;
```

Exercises for Section 8.7

Self-Check

1. What changes would need to be made to the unit `ComplexADT` shown in Fig. 18.17 to implement the remaining `ComplexNumber` operators discussed in Section 11.4?
2. Why does `ComputeArea` need to be declared as a virtual method in unit `FigureADT` (Fig. 18.19)?

Programming

1. Using the method headings from Fig. 18.19, write declarations for `Rectangle` methods `ComputeArea`, `ComputePerim`, and `DisplayFig`.
2. Add a new descendant type `RightTriangle` with fields `Base` and `Height` to `FigureADT`. Use the following formulas:

$$area = (base \times height)/2$$
$$hypotenuse = \sqrt{base^2 + height^2}$$
$$perimeter = base + height + hypotenuse$$

18.8 Dynamic Objects

Dynamic (run-time) type binding and polymorphism are two features that set object-oriented programming apart from traditional Pascal programming. *Polymorphism* means that the same operator can be used with different object types, which will respond in the appropriate way to that operator. For example, the + operator in Pascal indicates concatenation, addition, or union, depending on its operands. With objects, polymorphism allows us to use a single method call to manipulate an object regardless of whether it is an instance of an ancestor object type or one of its descendants. Inheritance and the use of virtual methods provide much of the support required to ensure that the appropriate methods are used to manipulate a given object instance. *Dynamic type binding* is the capability of deferring the binding of an object type to an instance identifier until run time. This feature provides the remainder of the support required for methods to behave in a truly polymorphic manner.

To get dynamic type binding in Turbo Pascal, we need to make use of pointer variables. Turbo Pascal allows the declaration of pointers to instances of dynamic objects. Program `PointerObjects`, shown in Fig. 18.20, declares two object pointer types, `ApplicantPrt` and `EmployeePtr`. The rules of assignment compatibility extend to object pointers, so that a variable of type `EmployeePtr` can be assigned to a variable of type `ApplicantPtr`, but not conversely. More interestingly, it is possible to have variables of type

ApplicantPtr point to instances of object type Employee. Therefore, the method call

```
Y^.Display;
```

will activate either method Applicant.Display or Employee.Display, depending on the object instance Y^. This is the essence of polymorphism.

Figure 18.20 Program PointerObjects

```
program PointerObjects;

  type
    ApplicantPtr = ^Applicant;
    Applicant = object
                  Name : string;
                  Next : ApplicantPtr;
                  constructor Init (N {input} : string);
                  procedure Display; virtual;
                  destructor Done; virtual;
                end; {Applicant}

    EmployeePtr = ^Employee;
    Employee = object(Applicant)
                 PayRate : Real;
                 constructor Init (N {input} : string;
                                   R {input} : Real);
                 procedure Display; virtual;
               end; {Employee}

  var
    X, Y : ApplicantPtr;

  constructor Applicant.Init (N {input} : string);
  {
    Initializes objects of type Applicant.
    Pre : N is defined.
    Post: Name is assigned its value from N, and Next is nil.
  }
  begin {Init}
    Name := N;
    Next := nil
  end; {Init}

  procedure Applicant.Display;
  {
    Displays Name field from object Applicant.
    Pre : Object has been initialized.
    Post: Name is displayed.
  }
  begin {Display}
    WriteLn ('Name is ', Name)
  end; {Display}

  destructor Applicant.Done;
  {
    Reclaims heap storage used by an object.
    Pre : Object has been allocated and initialized.
    Post: Object storage is reclaimed.
  }
  begin {Done}
  end; {Done}
```

```
  constructor Employee.Init (N {input} : string;
                             R {input} : Real);
  {
    Initializes objects of type Applicant.
    Pre : N and R have been defined.
    Post: Name is assigned its value from N, PayRate gets its value
          from R, and Next is nil.
  }
  begin {Init}
    Name := N;
    PayRate := R;
    Next := nil
  end; {Init}

  procedure Employee.Display;
  {
    Displays Name and PayRate fields from object Employee.
    Pre : Object has been initialized.
    Post: Name and PayRate are displayed.
  }
  begin {Display}
    WriteLn ('Name is ', Name);
    WriteLn ('Pay Rate is $', PayRate :5:2)
  end; {Display}

begin {PointerObjects}
  X := New(ApplicantPtr, Init ('John Smith'));
  Y := New(EmployeePtr, Init ('Jane Doe', 10.35));

  X^.Display;
  Y^.Display;

  Dispose (X, Done);
  Dispose (Y, Done)
end. {PointerObjects}
```

Allocating Dynamic Objects

Dynamic data objects are allocated by use of the standard identifier `New`. If the objects contain virtual methods, they also must be initialized using constuctors. To facilitate this process, the `New` operation has been extended so that it can be called with two parameters: a pointer variable as the first parameter and a constructor call as the second parameter. This means that the following forms both have the same effect.

`New (X);` `X^.Init ('John Smith);`	`New (X, Init ('John Smith'));`

Note that the object instance `X^` is not used to qualify `Init` in the extended form.

As a further extension, `New` can be called as a function that returns a pointer value. In that case, the parameter passed to `New` is the type of the pointer to an object instance rather than the pointer variable itself. Using this technique, the following statement has the same effect as the preceding ones:

```
X := New(ApplicantPtr, Init ('John Smith'));
```

The object type passed to New must be assignment compatible with the pointer variable appearing on the left side of the assignment statement. Because objects of type Employee are descendants of objects of type Applicant, the following assignment statement is valid if Y is type ApplicantPtr or EmployeePtr:

```
Y := New(EmployeePtr, Init ('John Smith'));
```

New is called as a function in Fig. 18.20, where the two preceding statements appear in the program body.

Returning Object Storage to the Heap

We can reclaim storage allocated for dynamic objects by using the standard procedure Dispose. Dispose can be passed the name of a pointer to an object as an actual parameter. However, if the object contains fields that are pointers to other dynamic variables, more work may need to be done to reclaim all the storage allocated to the object. This code typically would be collected in one or more special methods known as *destructors*. Destructors must be used to reclaim storage allocated to dynamic variables inherited from ancestor types. The object type Applicant has a method Done declared as a destructor. Destructors can be inherited. Though it is not required, destructors are usually declared as virtual methods.

A destructor is activated in one of two ways. Dispose can be called with a pointer variable as an actual parameter, followed by a call to the object's destructor, as shown below:

```
Dispose (X);
X^.Done;
```

Dispose can also be called with a pointer variable as a first parameter and a destructor call as a second parameter, as shown in Fig. 18.20:

```
Dispose (X, Done);
```

A destructor automatically returns to the heap all storage pointed to by an object's fields, including fields inherited from ancestor types. It is not necessary for the destructor to contain any calls to Dispose or any other statements to obtain this service. Calls to destructors outside a call to Dispose are treated as ordinary method calls and do not provide automatic deallocation of storage.

Case Study: A Linked-List Object

We discussed several linked-list operators in Chapter 17, but we did not present a formal specification for a linked-list abstract data type. A linked list requires operators for inserting and deleting nodes from the list and operators that allow examination of the data values stored in the list nodes. The specification for a linked-list ADT follows. The operator specifications are similar to those discussed in Section 17.4.

Specification of Linked-List ADT

Structure: A linked list is a collection of list elements or nodes, such that each element contains among its data fields a special field considered the key field. The key field values are not arranged in any particular order within the list.

Operators: For the following descriptions, assume these parameters:

> `List` represents the list.
> `Item` is a list node data item.
> `Target` is a possible key field value.

`CreateList (var List)`: Creates an empty list; must be called before any other operators.

`DeleteNode (var List, Target, var Success)`: Deletes the node whose key value is `Target` and sets `Success` to `True`. If `Target` is not located, sets `Success` to `False`.

`EmptyList (List)`: Returns `True` if `List` is nil; otherwise, returns `False`.

`InsertNode (var List, Item)`: Creates a node containing `Item` and places that node at the beginning of `List`.

`PrintList (List)`: Displays the data contents of all nodes in `List` in the same order as their nodes.

`SearchList (List, Target)`: `List` is searched for a node containing a key field matching `Target`. If such a node is found, function `Search` returns a pointer to that node; otherwise, `Search` returns nil.

`SizeOfList (List)`: Returns a count of the number of nodes in `List`.

Examples of Linked Lists

The top of Fig. 18.21 shows an instance of a linked-list object containing four integer values (`1111`, `3456`, `2345`, and `4123`). The instance identifier `MyList` contains a pointer field that points to the first node on the list and an integer field that indicates the number of nodes housed in the list. The bottom of Fig. 18.21 shows an instance (`PassList`) of an airline passenger linked-list object. In this list, the key field is the passenger name (`Adams` and `Carson`).

Using a Linked List

A program that makes use of unit `ListADT` to construct and maintain a linked list of integers appears in Fig. 18.22. It would be easy to modify this program to manipulate a linked list of airline passengers. The client program begins with a call to operator `CreateList` to create an empty list of integers. Next, the `while` loop reads each key value (an integer) into `NextNode` and calls operator

InsertNode to place the new key value at the head of the list. If NextNode were a structured type instead of a simple type, we would need to import an operator to read all node data. After loop exit, the program calls other list operators and displays the result of each operation on the linked list. The output from program TestList appears in Fig. 18.23.

Figure 18.21 Instances of Linked-List Objects

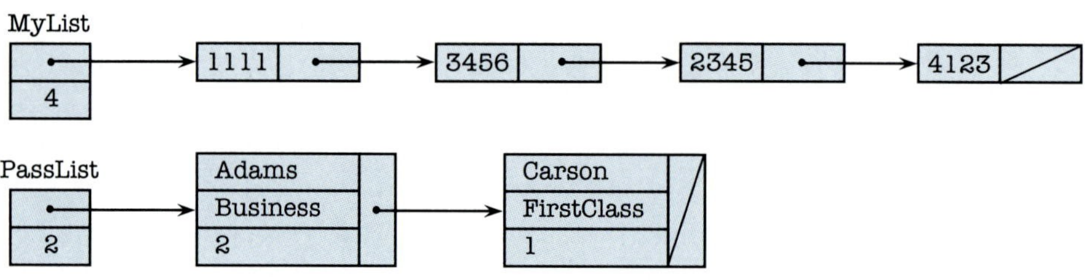

Figure 18.22 Program TestList

```
program TestList;
{
  Builds and displays a list of Integers.

  Imports: ListElement and KeyType from unit InfoADT.

           List, ListNodePtr, CreateList, Done, DeleteNode,
           InsertNode, PrintList, SearchList, and SizeOfList
           from unit ListADT.
}
  uses InfoADT, ListAdt;

  const
    Sentinel = -1;

  var
    L : List;
    NextNode : ListElement;
    Target : KeyType;
    Success : Boolean;

begin {TestList}
  L.CreateList;                              {initialize the list}

  {place nodes on the list}
  WriteLn ('Enter ', Sentinel, ' to stop.');
  WriteLn ('Enter next key or ', Sentinel, '> ');
  ReadLn (NextNode);

  while NextNode <> Sentinel do
    {invariant:
       all prior values of NextElement were inserted in L,
       and no prior value of NextElement was the sentinel
    }
```

```
    begin
      L.InsertNode (NextNode);
      WriteLn ('Enter next key or ', Sentinel, '> ');
      ReadLn (NextNode)
    end; {while}

  WriteLn;                              {display list and its size}
  WriteLn ('The list nodes contain:');
  L.PrintList;
  WriteLn ('Number of list items is ', L.SizeOfList);

  WriteLn;                              {find node with Target key}
  Write ('Find node with key> ');
  ReadLn (Target);
  if L.SearchList(Target) <> nil then
    WriteLn (Target, ' found.')
  else
    WriteLn (Target, ' not in list.');

  WriteLn;                              {delete node with Target key}
  Write ('Delete node with key> ');
  ReadLn (Target);
  L.DeleteNode (Target, Success);
  if Success then
    WriteLn (Target, ' deleted.')
  else
    WriteLn (Target, ' not found, no deletion.');

  WriteLn;                              {display list and its size}
  WriteLn ('The list nodes contain:');
  L.PrintList;
  WriteLn ('Number of list items ', L.SizeOfList);

  L.Done                                {destroy list}
end. {TestList}
```

Figure 18.23 Sample Run of TestList

```
Enter -1 to stop.
Enter next key or -1> 4123
Enter next key or -1> 2345
Enter next key or -1> 3456
Enter next key or -1> 1111
Enter next key or -1> -1

The list nodes contain:
1111
3456
2345
4123
Number of list items is 4

Find node with key> 3456
3456 found.

Delete node with key> 2345
2345 deleted.
```

```
The list nodes contain:
1111
3456
4123
Number of list items is 3
```

Implementing a Linked List

The interface section for unit ListADT is shown in Fig. 18.24. Each node in a list is implemented by a record type ListNode containing a data field, Info, and a pointer field, Link, which connects it to the next node in the list. The data field (type ListElement) must include a record key (type KeyType). ListElement and KeyType are declared in unit InfoADT and imported by unit ListADT.

The object type List is also declared in ListADT. Object List contains a pointer field Head, which points to the first node in the linked list, and an Integer field NumItems, which holds the number of nodes currently in the list. The List methods declared correspond to the linked-list operators discussed previously. Operators ExtractKey and DisplayNode are called by some List methods and must be imported from unit InfoADT. We will discuss the method implementations for our List object first and later the details of unit InfoADT.

Figure 18.24 Unit ListADT

```
unit ListADT;
{
  Declarations and methods for a linked-list object.

  Imports: ListElement, KeyType, DisplayNode, ExtractKey
           from InfoADT.

  Exports: ListNode, ListNodePtr, List, CreateList, DeleteNode,
           Done, EmptyList, InsertNode, PrintList, SearchList,
           SizeOfList
}
interface
  uses InfoADT;

  type
    ListNodePtr = ^ListNode;
    ListNode = record
                 Info : ListElement;
                 Link : ListNodePtr
               end; {ListNodePtr}

    List = object
             Head : ListNodePtr;
             NumItems : Integer;
             constructor CreateList;
             destructor Done; virtual;
             procedure DeleteNode
                (Target : KeyType; var Success : Boolean);
             function EmptyList : Boolean;
             procedure InsertNode (Item : ListElement);
```

```
          procedure PrintList;
          function SearchList
             (Target : KeyType) : ListNodePtr;
          function SizeOfList : Integer;
       end; {List}

implementation

  {Insert List method declarations here.}

end. {ListADT}
```

Constructor CreateList

Since object List has a virtual method, CreateList must be declared as a constructor, rather than a procedure. CreateList, shown in Fig. 18.25, initializes instances of List objects by assigning nil as the value of field Head and zero as the value of NumItems. Assuming L is a List object, it would be initialized using the method call

```
L.CreateList;
```

Figure 18.25 Constructor CreateList

```
constructor List.CreateList;
{
  Creates an empty linked list.
  Pre : None
  Post: List points to the header node for an ordered list.
}
begin {CreateList}
  Head := nil;
  NumItems := 0
end; {CreateList}
```

Procedure InsertNode

Because we have chosen to implement our linked list as an unordered list, the easiest place to add new nodes is at the beginning of the list. Procedure InsertNode (Fig. 18.26) allocates a new list node, places it at the beginning of the list, and adds 1 to the field NumItems. The implementation of InsertNode is much like that of the stack operator Push, discussed in Section 17.5.

Figure 18.26 Procedure InsertNode

```
procedure List.InsertNode (Item {input} : ListElement);
{
  Inserts node containing Item at beginning of a linked list.
  Pre : Linked list has been initialized.
```

```
  Post: Item becomes part of new list node El pointed to
        by Head.
}
  var
    El : ListNodePtr;                {pointer to new list node}

begin {InsertNode}
  New (El);
  El^.Info := Item;
  El^.Link := Head;
  Head := El;
  NumItems := NumItems + 1
end; {InsertNode}
```

Procedure DeleteNode

Procedure `DeleteNode` (Fig. 18.27) searches the list for a node that contains the key `Target`. If it finds such a node, the node is deleted from the list, `NumItems` is decremented, and `Success` is assigned the value `True`. If the search fails, `Success` is set to `False` and no changes are made to the list. `DeleteNode` carries out its task by saving the address of the node that precedes `Target` (`Previous`) and the address of the node containing `Target` (`Current`), as shown in Fig. 18.28. Assuming that `Target` is on the list and that the node is not the first node on the list, the statements

```
Previous^.Link := Current^.Link;    {point to next node}
Dispose (Current)
```

delete the node pointed by `Current` from the list and return its storage to the heap. If `Previous` is `nil`, the node containing `Target` is the first node on the list, and `Head` must be set to point to the following node using the statement

```
Head := Current^.Link;      {point Head to next node}
```

to avoid losing the list when the old first node is disposed.

Figure 18.27 Procedure DeleteNode

```
procedure List.DeleteNode (Target {input} : KeyType;
                           var Success {output} : Boolean);
{
  Deletes node (if any) whose data value is Target.
  Pre : Target is defined and List is not empty.
  Post: Success is True if deletion is performed;
        if no key matched Target, Success is False.
}
  var
    Current,                                {node being deleted}
    Previous : ListNodePtr; {predecessor of node being deleted}
    Found : Boolean;                                {program flag}

begin {DeleteNode}
  {Search for Target}
  Found := False;                  {Assume Target not found}
```

```
  Current := Head;
  Previous := nil;
  while not Found and (Current <> nil) do
    {invariant:
       no prior list node contained Target and
       no prior value of Current was nil
    }
    if ExtractKey(Current^.Info) = Target then
      Found := True
    else
      begin                              {move down the list}
        Previous := Current;
        Current := Current^.Link
      end; {if and while}

  {assertion: Target was found or end of list was reached.}
  if (Current = nil) or not Found then
    Success := False                       {Target not found}
  else
    begin {Delete}
      if Previous = nil then             {check for first node}
        begin
          Head := Current^.Link;     {point Head to next node}
          Dispose (Current)
        end
      else
        begin
          Previous^.Link := Current^.Link; {point to next node}
          Dispose (current)
        end; {inner if}

      Success := True;
      NumItems := NumItems - 1
    end {Delete}
end; {DeleteNode}
```

Figure 18.28 Deleting 2345

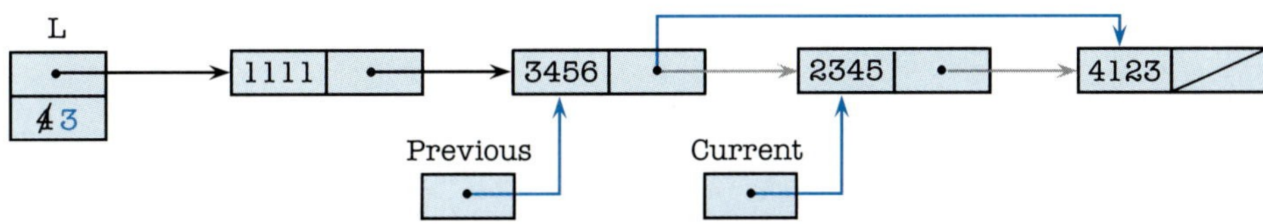

Function SearchList

In function `SearchList` (Fig. 18.29), a `while` loop is used to traverse the list to locate the node whose key field matches `Target`. Function `ExtractKey` must be imported from unit `InfoADT` to allow implementation-independent comparison of each node's key field with `Target`. If the node is present, `SearchList` returns a pointer to it; otherwise, `SearchList` returns `nil`.

Figure 18.29 Function SearchList

```
function List.SearchList (Target : KeyType) : ListNodePtr;
{
  Searches a list for a node whose key field is Target.
  Pre : List has been initialized and Target is defined.
  Post: Returns a pointer to node containing Target if found;
        otherwise, returns nil.
}
  var
    Found : Boolean;            {flag indicating Target found}
    Current : ListNodePtr;                {node being checked}

begin {SearchList}
  Found := False;                                {Target not found}
  Current := Head;
  while not Found and (Current <> nil) do
    {invariant:
       no prior list node contained Target and
       no prior value of Current was nil
    }
    if ExtractKey(Current^.Info) = Target then
      Found := True
    else
      Current := Current^.Link;           {move down the list}

  {assertion: Target was found or end of list was reached.}
  if Found then
    SearchList := Current                          {success}
  else
    SearchList := nil                              {failure}
end; {SearchList}
```

Procedure PrintList

Procedure `PrintList` (Fig. 18.30) traverses the list and displays the data contents of each node. Procedure `DisplayNode` is used to display each data element and must be imported from unit `InfoADT`.

Figure 18.30 Procedure PrintList

```
procedure List.PrintList;
{
  Repeatedly calls procedure DisplayNode to display each
  data element of the linked list.
  Pre : List has been initialized.
  Post: The data fields of each actual element are displayed.
}
  var
    Current : ListNodePtr;        {pointer to each list node}

begin {PrintList}
  Current := Head;                     {Start with first node}
  while Current <> nil do
    {invariant:
       no prior value of Current was nil.
```

```
    }
    begin
      DisplayNode (Current^.Info);                    {Display node data}
      Current := Current^.Link                          {Advance Current}
    end {while}
end; {PrintList}
```

Destructor Done

Because the implementation of List involves a linked data structure, Done (Fig. 18.31) requires more than an empty procedure body. To be sure that all nodes are returned to the heap, each is disposed of individually by traversing the list one node at a time.

Figure 18.31 Destructor Done

```
destructor List.Done;
{
  Returns all allocated list nodes to the heap.
  Pre : List has been initialized.
  Post: List is empty.
}
  var
    Current : ListNodePtr;

begin {Done}
  while Head <> nil do
    {invariant:
       no prior value of Head was nil
    }
    begin
      Current := Head;
      Head := Current^.Link;
      Dispose (Current)
    end; {while}

  NumItems := 0
end; {Done}
```

Coding Unit InfoADT

The unit InfoADT shown in Fig. 18.32 is for a linked list of integers. List-Element and KeyType are both declared to be type Integer. Since the data housed in our linked list is a simple type, function ExtractKey returns the value of its input parameter. Likewise, procedure DisplayNode has only one value to display.

It would be possible for the data housed in our linked list to be of some structured data type. In that case, ListADT could remain as it is, but InfoADT would need to be rewritten. While we will not do so, it is also possible to allow our linked list to house instances of any of the object types descended from

Figure 18.32 Unit InfoADT

```
unit InfoADT;
  {
    Contains declarations and methods for linked list node
    Info field.

    Exports: ListElement, KeyType, ExtractKey, DisplayNode
  }
interface

  type
    {Insert declarations for info data and key fields}
    ListElement = Integer;
    KeyType = Integer;

    function ExtractKey (El {input} : ListElement) : KeyType;
    }
      Retrieves key portion of list node Info field.
      Pre : El is defined.
      Post: Key gets the key field of El.
    }

    procedure DisplayNode (El {input} : ListElement);
    {
      Displays data from list node Info field.
      Pre : El is defined.
      Post: Displays each data field of El.
    }

  implementation
    function ExtractKey (El {input} : ListElement) : KeyType;
    begin {ExtractKey}
      ExtractKey := El
    end; {ExtractKey}

    procedure DisplayNode (El {input} : ListElement);
    begin {DisplayNode}
      WriteLn (El)
    end; {DisplayNode}
end. {InfoADT}
```

Figure. To do this, we would declare ListElement as a pointer type to instances of type Figure objects (or their descendants). We would also need to make some changes to both ListADT and InfoADT, but we would have a very flexible data structure (see Fig. 18.33).

Exercises for Section 18.8

Self-Check

1. What changes would be necessary to unit InfoADT if it were used with a linked list of books (Section 14.6)?
2. What changes would need to be made to the type declarations in program TestList to work with a linked list of books?

Figure 18.33 Instances of Linked-List Objects

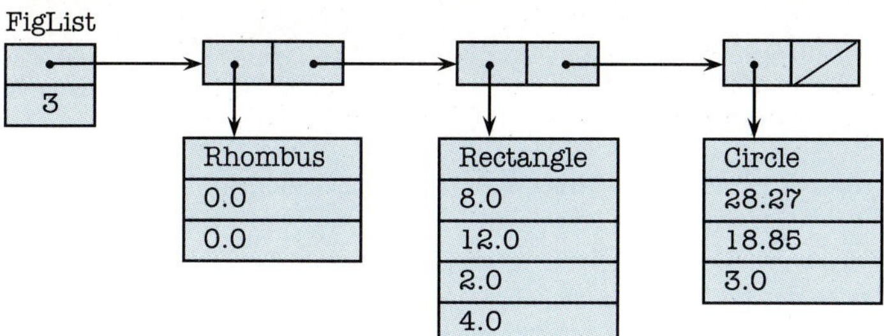

Programming

1. Write methods `SizeOfList` and `EmptyList`.
2. Write the type declaration for a `Queue` object using methods similar to those described in Chapter 17.

18.9 Common Programming Errors

The procedures in this chapter manipulate pointer fields, so review the errors described in Section 17.7. Make sure all recursive procedures do, in fact, terminate. Also, be careful when using pointers to list heads as procedure parameters. If the pointer is passed as a variable parameter and is moved down the list, you may disconnect the list head from its list. The same warning applies when using pointers to tree roots.

When working with objects having virtual methods, remember to use constructors to initialize instances of the objects or their descendants. Always define methods to manipulate object fields; avoid manipulating them directly in a client program. Make use of destructors to reclaim storage used by dynamic objects.

Chapter Review

This chapter discussed a technique for maintaining an ordered collection of records and examined a data structure for this purpose. We implemented an abstract data type for a binary search tree. This ADT included operators to search, insert, and delete records.

We discussed binary trees in general and showed how they can be used to represent expressions in memory. We discussed inorder, preorder, and postorder traversal and related these three methods to infix, prefix, and postfix expressions.

We discussed object-oriented programming in Turbo Pascal. We demonstrated how objects could be used to implement abstract data types in Turbo Pascal. We discussed the concepts of object inheritance and polymorphism and showed how they might be used to implement an object-oriented linked-list abstract data type.

New Pascal Constructs

The Turbo Pascal constructs introduced in this chapter are described in Table 18.2.

Table 18.2 New Pascal Constructs

Construct	Effect
Object Type Declaration	

`type`
`  PersonPtr = ^Person;`
`  Person = object`
`             Name : string;`
`             Next : PersonPtr;`
`             constructor Init;`
`             procedure Display; virtual;`
`             destructor Done; virtual;`
`           end; {Person}`
	The identifier `PersonPtr` is declared as a pointer to object of type `Person` containing fields `Name` and `Next`; and methods `Init`, `Display`, and `Done`.

`  StudentPtr = ^Student;`
`  Student = object(Person)`
`              GPA : Real;`
`              constructor Init;`
`              procedure Display; virtual;`
`              function GetGPA;`
`            end; {Student}`
	The identifier `StudentPtr` is declared as a pointer to an object of type `Student` descended from object type `Person`; inheriting `Person`'s fields and methods, declaring a field (`GPA`) and method (`GetGPA`) of its own, and altering inherited method `Display`.

`var` `  P: PersonPtr;`	`P` is a pointer variable of type `PersonPtr`.
New Procedure	
`New (P, Init);`	Object of type `Person` is allocated and initialized using constructor `Init`. This object is pointed to by `P` and is referenced by `P^`.
New Typecast Function	
`P := New(StudentPtr,Init);`	Object of type `Student` is allocated and initialized using constructor `Init` from object type `Stu–dent`. This object is pointed to by `P`.

Construct	Effect
Dispose Procedure	
`Dispose (P, done);`	Object storage pointed to by pointer `P` is returned to the heap and destructor `Done` is called to assist in the clean-up operation.

✓ Quick-Check Exercises

1. In what direction do computer science trees grow?
2. Name the three traversal methods and relate them to the three forms of arithmetic expressions.
3. A node in a Pascal tree can have a maximum of two children. True or false?
4. A node in a binary search tree can have a maximum of two children. True or False?
5. What is the relationship between the left child and the right child of a binary search tree? Between the left child and the parent? Between the right child and the parent?
6. When is searching a binary search tree more efficient than searching an ordered list? When isn't it?
7. How do we know if a binary tree is balanced?
8. Traverse the following tree three ways. Is this tree a binary search tree? Is it balanced or unbalanced? If it is unbalanced, why?

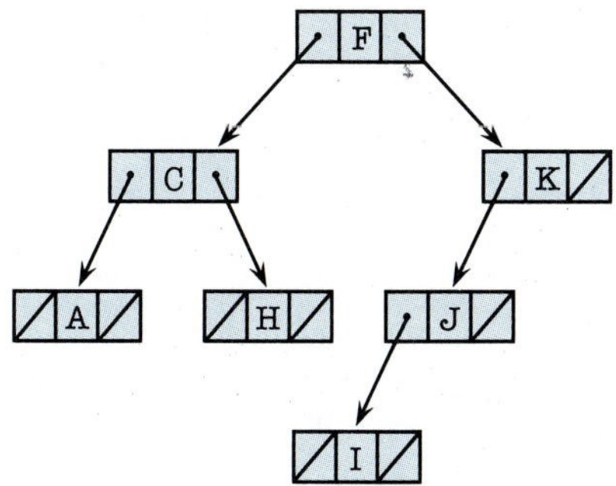

9. When should the virtual directive be used with a method?
10. What does a descendant object inherit from its ancestor?
11. Objects can be declared as local identifiers in procedures. True or False?

Answers to Quick-Check Exercises

1. From the top down
2. Inorder (infix), preorder (prefix), postorder (postfix)
3. False

4. True
5. Left child < parent < right child
6. When tree is balanced; when tree is badly unbalanced
7. The depth of the subtrees from every node differ by at most one.
8. Inorder: A C H F I J K
   Preorder: F C A H KJ I
   Postorder: A H C I J KF

   It is not a binary search tree, because H is in the wrong subtree of the root. It is not balanced, because the left subtree of K has depth 2, and the right subtree of K has depth zero.
9. Any time a method is likely to be redeclared by a descendant object and the method heading will not need to be changed.
10. The ancestor's fields and methods.
11. False.

Review Questions

1. Declare a node for a two-way, or doubly linked, list; indicate how a traversal would be made in reverse order (from the last list element to the list head). Include any variables or fields that are necessary.
2. Discuss the differences between a simple linked list and a binary tree. Consider such things as number of pointer fields per node, search technique, and insertion algorithm.
3. How can you determine if a node is a leaf?
4. Traverse the following tree in inorder, preorder, and postorder.

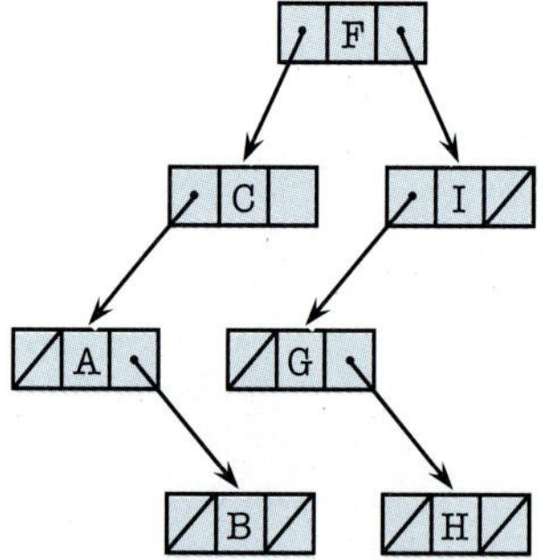

   Provide one data sequence that would create this ordered binary tree. Are there any letters that must occur before other letters?
5. Discuss how you might delete a node from a binary tree. Consider nodes with 0 or 1 child first.
6. Describe the differences in the effects of a constructor method and a destructor method.
7. Modify method `List.InsertNode` so that nodes are inserted into the linked-list in ascending key field order.
8. Modify method `List.SearchList` to take into account that the linked-list nodes have been inserted in ascending key field order and terminate unsuccessful searches as soon as possible.

Programming Projects

1. Use a binary search tree to maintain an airline passenger list. The main program should be menu driven and allow the user to display the data for a particular passenger, display the entire list, create a list, insert a node, delete a node, and replace the data for a particular passenger.
2. In this chapter, we wrote recursive procedures to perform preorder, inorder, and postorder tree traversals. A tree traversal can be written without using recursion. In that case, it is necessary to push the address of a tree node that is reached during the traversal onto a stack. The node will be popped off later when it is time to traverse the subtree rooted at this node. For example, the algorithm for a nonrecursive preorder traversal follows.

```
1. Push nil onto the stack.
2. Assign the root node as the current node.
3. while the current node is not nil do
     begin
        4. Print the current node.
        5. if the current node has a right subtree then
              Push the right subtree root onto the stack.
        6. if the current has a left subtree then
              Make it the current node.
           else
             Pop the stack and make the node removed the current node.
     end
```

In this algorithm, each right subtree pointer that is not `nil` is pushed onto the stack; the stack is popped when the current left subtree pointer is `nil`.

Implement and test a nonrecursive procedure for preorder traversal. Write a nonrecursive algorithm for inorder traversal and implement and test it as well.

3. If an arithmetic expression is written in prefix or postfix notation, there is no need to use parentheses to specify the order of operator evaluation. For this reason, some compilers translate infix expressions to postfix notation first and then evaluate the postfix string.

Write a procedure that simulates the operation of a calculator. The input will consist of an expression in postfix notation. The operands will all be single-digit numbers. Your program should print the expression value. For example, if the input string is `'54+3/'`, the result should be `((5 +) / 3)`, or 3.

To accomplish this, examine each character in the string in left-to-right order. If the character is a digit, push its numeric value onto a stack. If the character is an operator, pop the two operands, apply the operator to them, and push the result onto the stack. After the string has been completely scanned, there should be only one number on the stack, and that should be the expression value. Besides the operators `+`, `-`, `*`, and `/`, use `^` to indicate exponentiation.

4. Save each word appearing in a block of text in a binary search tree. Also save the number of occurrences of each word and the line number for each occurrence. Use a stack for the line numbers. After all words have been processed, display each word in alphabetical order. Along with each word, display the number of occurrences and the line number for each occurrence.
5. Store the Morse code (see programming project 1 for Chapter 12) in a binary tree, as shown. A dot should cause a branch to the left, and a dash should cause a branch

to the right. Each node should contain the letter represented by the code symbol formed by tracing a path from the root to that node. For example, following two left branches gives us two dots, which represents the letter I. The first two levels of the Morse-code tree are shown next.

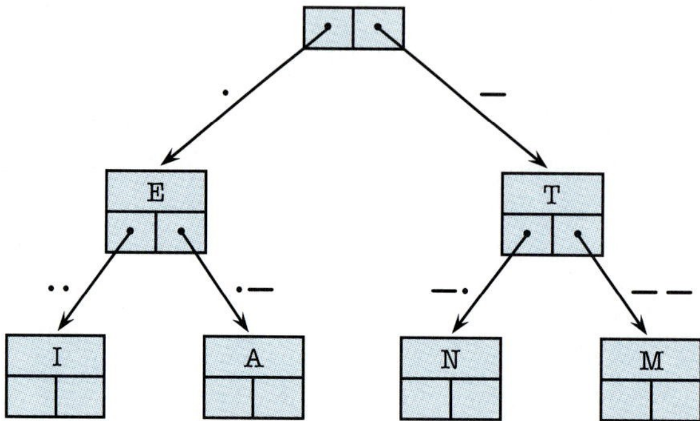

First, build an empty Morse-code tree by constructing a tree of four levels. Then read each letter, followed by its code from a data line, and insert it where it belongs in the tree. After the tree is filled, read in a coded message using a space between each letter of the message and a double space between words. Translate the message into English.

6. Pascal's set capability is limited to the number of elements that can be stored in a set. A more universal system can be implemented using a linked-list ordered by set element values to store the set.

   Write an object-oriented set ADT which includes methods for inserting and deleting integer values from the set. Also write operators necessary to implement the set difference, intersection, and union operations. Write a program to test your set operators. Display the contents of the sets before and after each operation.
7. Write a unit for a binary search tree object using the operators discussed in Section 18.4 as methods.
8. Redo programming project 1 of this chapter using the linked-list ADT discussed in Section 18.9 to maintain the airline passenger list. Unlike project 1, nodes should be removed from the list when they are deleted.

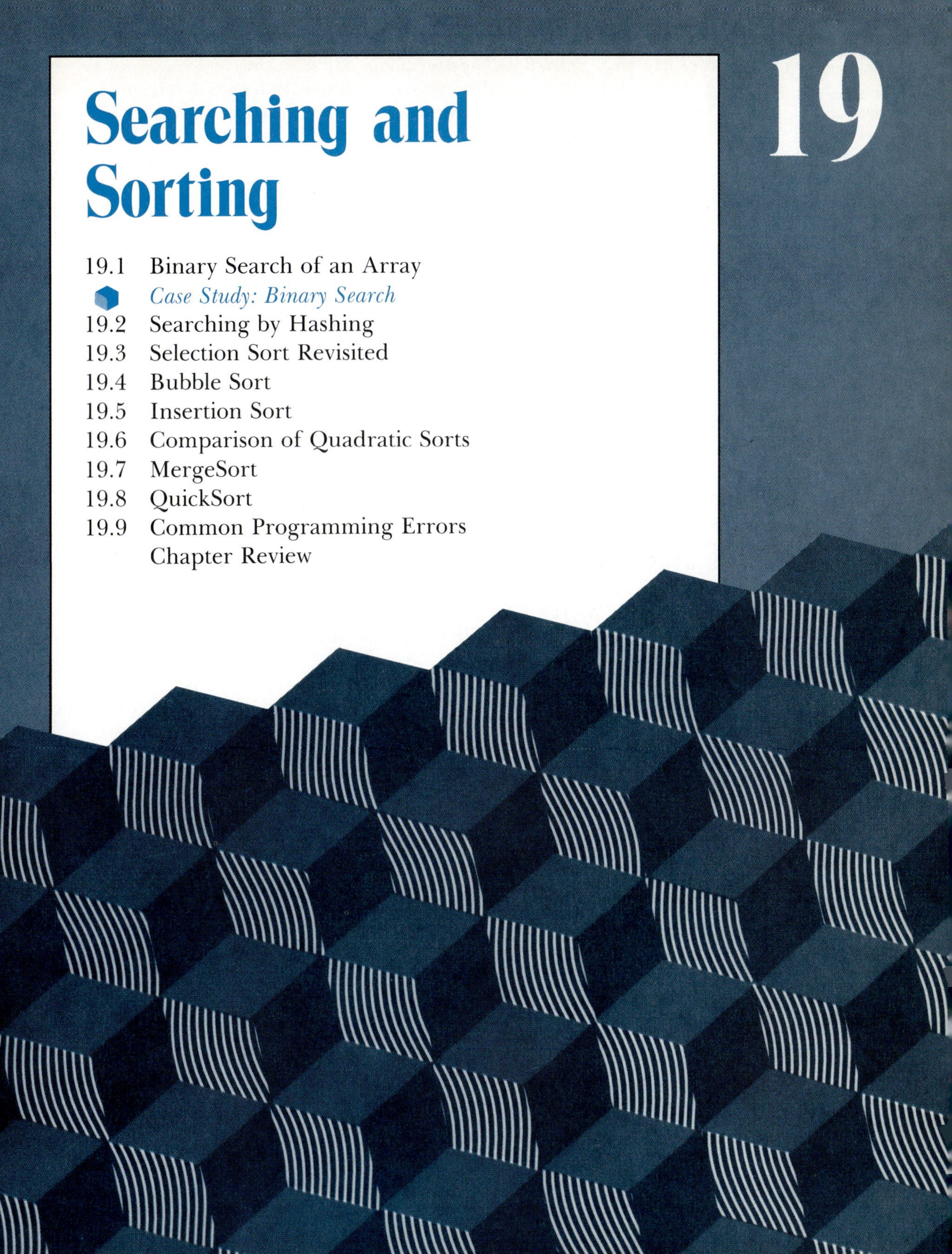

19

Searching and Sorting

Chapter 12 introduced one technique for searching an array for a target key and one technique for sorting an array. Chapter 18 considered another method of data storage (that is, using a binary search tree) that facilitates searching for a target key and eliminates the need for sorting.

Even though alternative methods are available, arrays are frequently used for data storage. Computer scientists have also spent much time and effort to devise efficient algorithms for searching and sorting arrays. This chapter discusses two techniques for searching an array and several techniques for sorting an array and compares these algorithms with respect to their efficiency.

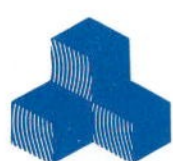

19.1 Binary Search of an Array

We discussed one technique for searching an array in Section 12.6 and wrote a function that returned the index of a target key in an array or the value 0 if the target was not present. To do this, we had to compare array element keys to the target key, starting with the first array element. The comparison process is terminated when the target key is found or the end of the array is reached. We must make N comparisons to determine that a target key is not in an array of N elements. On the average, we must make $N/2$ comparisons to locate a target key that is in the array. Because the constant 2 is ignored, array search is an $O(N)$ process.

Often, we want to search an array whose elements are arranged in order by key field. We can take advantage of the fact that the array keys are in increasing order and terminate the search when an array key greater than or equal to the target key is reached. There is no need to look any further in the array; all other keys will be larger than the target key.

Both these search techniques are called *sequential search* because we examine the array elements in sequence. The modified algorithm just discussed is a sequential search of an ordered array. On the average, a sequential search of an ordered array requires $N/2$ comparisons either to locate the target key or to determine that it is not in the array; so we still have an $O(N)$ process.

Case Study: Binary Search

The array searches described here are considered *linear searches*, because their execution time increases linearly with the number of array elements. This can be a problem when we are searching very large arrays (for example, `N > 1000`). Consequently, we often use the *binary-search algorithm* for large sorted arrays.

Problem

Your employer has a directory of customers that she keeps in alphabetical order. Because business has been very good, this list is now too large to search efficiently using a linear search. Write an improved search algorithm that takes advantage of the fact that the array is sorted.

Design Overview

The *binary-search algorithm,* like a binary-tree search, takes advantage of the fact that the array is ordered to eliminate half of the array elements with each probe into the array. Consequently, if the array has 1,000 elements, it either locates the target value or eliminates 500 elements with its first probe, 250 elements with its second probe, 125 elements with its third probe, and so on. Therefore, a binary search of an ordered array is an $O(\log_2 N)$ process. You can use the binary search algorithm to find a name in a large metropolitan telephone directory using thirty or fewer probes, so this algorithm should be suitable for your employer.

Because the array is ordered, all we have to do is compare the target value with the middle element of the subarray we are searching. If their values are the same, we are done. If the middle value is larger than the target, we should search the left half of the array next; otherwise, we should search the right half of the array.

The subarray to be searched has subscripts `First..Last`. The variable `Middle` is the subscript of the middle element in this range. The right half of the array (subscripts `Middle..Last`) is eliminated by the first probe, as shown in Fig. 19.1.

`Last` should be reset to `Middle - 1` to define the new subarray to be searched, and `Middle` should be redefined, as shown in Fig. 19.2. The target value, 35, would be found on this probe.

The binary-search algorithm can be stated clearly using recursion. The stopping cases are

- The array bounds are improper (`First > Last`).
- The middle value is the target value.

Figure 19.1 First Probe of Binary Search

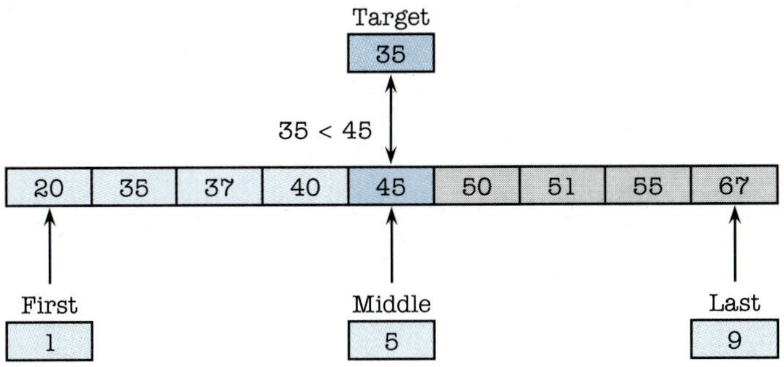

Figure 19.2 Second Probe of Binary Search

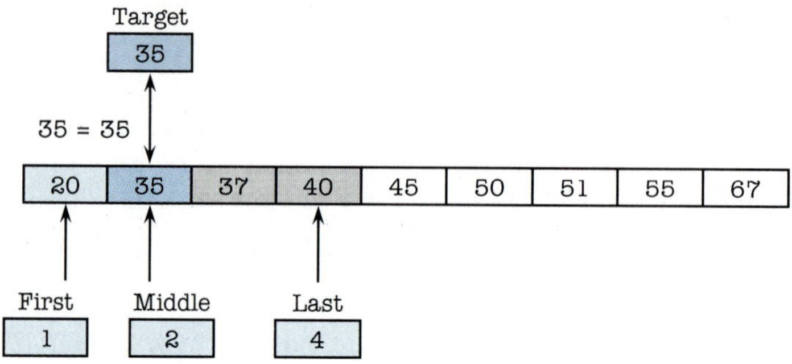

In the first case, the function result is zero; in the second case, the function result is `Middle`. The recursive step is to search the appropriate subarray.

Data Requirements

Problem Inputs

Array to be searched (`Table : SearchArray`)
Target being searched for (`Target : KeyType`)
The first subscript in the subarray (`First : Integer`)
The last subscript in the subarray (`Last : Integer`)

Problem Outputs

The location of the `Target` value or `0` if not found

Binary Search Algorithm

1. Compute the subscript of the middle element
2. `if` the array bounds are improper `then`
    3. Return a result of 0

   `else if` the target is the middle value `then`
    4. Return the subscript of the middle element

   `else if` the target is less than the middle value `then`
    5. Search the subarray with subscripts `First..Middle-1`

   `else`
    6. Search the subarray with subscripts `Middle+1..Last`

For each of the recursive steps (steps 5 and 6), the bounds of the new subarray must be listed as actual parameters in the recursive call. The actual parameters define the search limits for the next probe into the array.

Coding Binary Search

In the initial call to the recursive procedure, First and Last should be defined as the first and last elements of the entire array, respectively. For example, you could use the function designator

```
BinSearch(X, 35, 1, 9)
```

to search an array X with subscripts 1..9 for the target value 35 (assuming X has type SearchArray and KeyType is Integer). Function BinSearch is shown in Fig. 19.3.

Figure 19.3 Recursive Binary Search Function

```
function BinSearch (var Table : SearchArray;
                    Target : KeyType;
                    First, Last : Integer) : Integer;
{
  Performs a recursive binary search of an ordered array
  with subscripts First..Last.
  Pre : The elements of Table are in increasing order by
        key field and First and Last are defined.
  Post: Returns the subscript of Target if found in array Table;
        otherwise, returns a value of 0.
}
  var
    Middle : Integer;     {the subscript of the middle element}

begin {BinSearch}
  Middle := (First + Last) div 2;

  {Determine if Target is found or missing or redefine subarray.}
  if First > Last then
    BinSearch := 0                       {Target missing}
  else if Target = Table[Middle] then
    BinSearch := Middle                  {Target found}
  else if Target < Table[Middle] then
    BinSearch := BinSearch(Table, Target, First, Middle-1)
  else
    BinSearch := BinSearch(Table, Target, Middle+1, Last)
end;  {BinSearch}
```

The assignment statement

```
Middle := (First + Last) div 2;
```

computes the subscript of the middle element by finding the average of First and Last. This value has no meaning when First is greater than Last, but it does no harm to compute it.

An iterative version of the binary search function is shown in Fig. 19.4. A Boolean flag, Found, controls repetition of a search loop. Found is set to False before the while loop is reached. The while loop executes until the Target is found (Found is True) or the search array is reduced to an array of zero elements (a *null array*). The `if` statement in the loop either sets `Found` to `True` (`Target = Table[Middle]`) or resets index `First` or index `Last`. The `if` statement after the loop defines the function result.

Figure 19.4 Iterative Binary Search Function

```
function BinarySearch (var Table : SearchArray;
                       Target : KeyType;
                       First, Last : Integer) : Integer;
{
  Performs an iterative binary search of an ordered array
  with subscripts First..Last.
  Pre : The elements of Table are in ascending order by key field
        and First and Last are defined.
  Post: Returns the subscript of Target if found in array Table;
        otherwise, returns a value of 0.
}
  var
    Middle : Integer;    {the subscript of the middle element}
    Found : Boolean;     {program flag}

begin  {BinarySearch}
  Found := False;                            {Target not found}
  while (First <= Last) and (not Found) do
    {invariant:
        Last subarray searched was not null and
        Target <> Table[Middle] for all prior values of Middle
    }
    begin
      Middle := (First + Last) div 2;
      if Target = Table[Middle] then
        Found := True
      else if Target < Table[Middle] then
        Last := Middle - 1                   {search left subarray}
      else if Target > Table[Middle] then
        First := Middle + 1                  {search right subarray}
    end; {while}

  {Assert: Target is found or search subarray is null.}
  if Found then
    BinarySearch := Middle                   {Target is found}
  else
    BinarySearch := 0                        {Target not found}
end;  {BinarySearch}
```

Testing

You should test both versions of the binary search function carefully. Besides verifying that they locate target values present in the array, verify that they also determine when a target value is missing. Use target values within the range of values stored in the array, a target value less than the smallest value in the array, and a target value greater than the largest value in the array. Make sure the binary-search function terminates regardless of whether the target is missing or, if it is not missing, where it is located.

Subarrays with Subscript Zero

The result returned by the binary-search function is inconclusive if `0` is included in the subrange `First..Last`. For example, if the array being searched has subscript type `[-5..5]`, `First` is `-5` and `Last` is `5`. In this case, it would be better to convert the binary-search function to a procedure with two output parameters: the index of the target if found and a program flag indicating whether the target was found. This modification is left as an exercise.

Exercises for Section 19.1

Self-Check

1. Trace the search of the array `Table` for a `Target` of `40`. Specify the values of `First`, `Middle`, and `Last` during each recursive call.
2. Provide the algorithm for a recursive procedure that performs binary search and returns a flag as its second output parameter that indicates whether the search was successful.

Programming

1. Write the procedure for exercise 2.

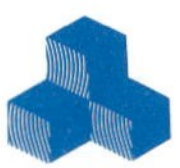

19.2 Searching by Hashing

So far, we have discussed the advantages of using the binary-search technique to retrieve information stored in a large array. Binary search can be used only when the contents of the array are ordered.

Another technique for storing data in an array so that it can be retrieved in an efficient manner is called *hashing*. Hashing consists of implementing a *hash function*, which accepts as its input a designated field of a record (called the *record key*) and returns as its output an integer *hash index*. The hash index selects the particular array element that stores the new data. To retrieve the item later, you need only to recompute the hash index and access the item in that array location. This process is illustrated in the following diagram, where the hash index is `3`.

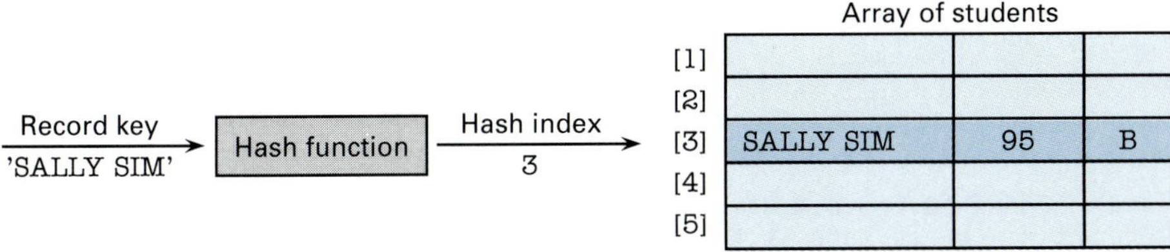

For example, let's assume that we have to maintain a collection of student records. Each record (type `Student`) has a `Name` field that is a string, an exam score, and a grade. The student data can be stored in an array with subscripts

1..MaxSlots. For reasons that will be discussed later, MaxSlots should be a prime number that is at least 20 percent larger than the number of records in the collection. Record types Student and HashArray are declared next.

```
const
  StringLen = 20;                        {length of each name string}
  BlankString = '                    ';     {string of blanks}
  MaxSlots = 97;                              {size of hash table}

type
  StringType = string[StringLen];
  Student = record                              {one student record}
              Name : StringType;
              Score : Integer;
              Grade : Char
            end; {Student}

  HashArray = array [1..MaxSlots] of Student;
```

We can use the student's name as the record key. One possible hash function would simply add up the ordinal values of each nonblank character in the student's name, then use the mod function to convert this sum to an integer in the range 1 to MaxSlots. Such a function is shown in Fig. 19.5.

Figure 19.5 Function Hash

```
function Hash (Key {input} : StringType;
               MaxSlots {input} : Integer) : Integer;
{
  Computes an integer value between 1 and MaxSlots.
  Pre : Key, MaxSlots, and StringLen are defined.
  Post: Returns an integer value between 1 and MaxSlots
        based on the nonblank characters in Key.
}
const
  Pad = ' ';                   {pad character}

var
   I,                          {loop-control variable}
   HashIndex : Integer;        {accumulated hash value}

begin {Hash}
  HashIndex := 0;                        {initialize hash sum}
  {Add ordinal values for all nonblank characters in Key.}
  for I := 1 to Length(Key) do
    if Key[I] <> Pad then
      HashIndex := HashIndex + Ord(Key[I]);

  {Assert:
     HashIndex is the sum of ordinal values for all
     nonblank characters in Key
  }
  Hash := (HashIndex mod MaxSlots) + 1     {define result}
end; {Hash}
```

Inserting a student record then becomes a matter of passing its key to function `Hash` and storing the record in the array element selected by `Hash`. After all records are stored in the array, we can retrieve a particular student's record by passing the student's name to function `Hash` and accessing the array element selected by `Hash`. The nice thing about all of this is that it usually takes only one probe into the array to get the record we are seeking. (Sometimes it does take more than one probe, as explained in the next subsection.)

A good hash function disperses the records arbitrarily throughout the hash table. If we display the records starting with the record in position 1 of the table, their keys follow no special order. Empty slots are intermixed with slots that contain actual records. For this reason, do not use hashing when it is important to display frequently the student records in order by key field.

Effect of Collisions

The hashing technique just described works fine as long as `Hash` never returns the same hash index for two different keys. However, the names `'SILLY SAM'` and `'SALLY SIM'` would both yield the same hash index because they contain the same letters. It would be an easy matter to improve the hash function so that this does not happen for these two names (see exercise 2 at the end of this section); however, regardless of the hash function used, it is always possible that two different keys will hash to the same index. Such an occurrence is called a *collision*.

One simple way to handle collisions is to insert a new record into the element selected by function `Hash` only if that slot is currently empty. If that slot is filled, advance to the next empty slot in the array and place the record in that location. The record keys can all be initialized to blank strings to indicate that they are initially empty.

Function `LocateSlot` (Fig. 19.6) uses this approach to find a desired key, `Target`, or to determine where in the array a new record with key `Target` should be placed. To indicate that there is neither a record with key `Target` nor an empty slot, the function returns zero. Function `Locate` uses the constant `BlankString`, a string of all blanks, which should be declared earlier.

Algorithm for LocateSlot

1. Start at element selected by `Hash` function.
2. Initialize number of probes to `1`.
3. `while Target` key not found and
   empty slot not found and
   all elements not examined `do`
   `begin`
      4. Advance to next slot.
      5. Increment count of probes.
   `end`
6. `if` all table entries were examined without success `then`
   7. Return `0`.

```
else
```

8. Return position of `Target` or first empty slot.

Figure 19.6 Function LocateSlot

```
function LocateSlot (var Class : HashArray;
                     MaxSlots : Integer;
                     Target : StringType) : Integer;
{
  Searches array Class for the student with key field Target.
  Pre  : Class, MaxSlots, and Key are defined.
  Post : Returns the index of the student whose name field is
         Target. Returns the location where Target should be
         inserted if missing. Returns MaxSlots + 1 if there
         are no empty slots.
  Calls: Hash
}
  var
    Index,                                    {index to array}
    Probe : Integer;                          {probe counter}

begin {LocateSlot}
   {Search for student whose name is Target.}
   Index := Hash(Target, MaxSlots); {starting point for search}
   Probe := 1;
   while(Class[Index].Name <> Target) and
        (Class[Index].Name <> BlankString) and
        (Probe <= MaxSlots) do
     {invariant:
         No prior record key matched Target and
         no prior array element was empty and
         number of probes <= MaxSlots + 1
     }
     begin
       Index := (Index mod MaxSlots) + 1;     {get next element}
       Probe := Probe + 1
     end; {while}

   {assert: Target found or empty slot found or array is full}
   if Probe > MaxSlots then
     LocateSlot := 0                           {Target not found}
   else
     LocateSlot := Index           {Target or empty slot found}
end;  {LocateSlot}
```

The assignment statement

```
Index := (Index mod MaxSlots) + 1;     {get next element}
```

increments the value of `Index`. If the current value of `Index` is `MaxSlots`, the new value will be `1`; otherwise, the new value will be one more than the current value.

The local variable `Probe` counts the number of probes into the array. If `Target` is missing and the array is completely filled, it would be possible to search forever for an empty slot. The `while` condition `(Probe <= MaxSlots)` prevents this from happening.

We can write procedures to insert and retrieve records in a hash table. Procedure `InsertHash` (Fig. 19.7) inserts a student record into a hash table. The procedure call statement

```
InsertHash (Class, MaxSlots, NextStu, Success)
```

calls `InsertHash` to store record `NextStu` in array `Class`. `InsertHash` uses `LocateSlot` to find the correct slot for the record. If an empty slot is found, the record is inserted and the Boolean flag is set to `True`. If there are no empty slots or there is already a student with the same name in the table, the Boolean flag is set to `False`.

Figure 19.7 Procedure InsertHash

```
procedure InsertHash (var Class {input/output} : HashArray;
                      MaxSlots {input} : Integer;
                      NextStu {input} : Student;
                      var Inserted {output} : Boolean);
{
  Inserts a new student record (NextStu) in the array of
  student records Class using hashing.
  Pre  : Class, MaxSlots, and NextStu are defined. An empty slot
         in Class is indicated by a record with a blank Key field.
  Post : If there is no existing record with the same key as
         NextStu, NextStu is inserted in the first empty array
         element that is nearest to the one selected by Hash.
         Inserted is set to True if the insertion was performed;
         otherwise, Inserted is set to False.
  Calls: LocateSlot
}
  var
    NewIndex : Integer;                    {insertion point}

begin {InsertHash}
   {Locate first empty slot or NextStu.}
   NewIndex := LocateSlot (Class, MaxSlots, NextStu.Name);

   {Perform insertion if slot is empty}
   if NewIndex = 0 then
     Inserted := False                              {table is full}
   else if Class[NewIndex].Name = BlankString then
     begin
       Class[NewIndex] := NextStu;          {insert new student}
       Inserted := True
     end
   else
     Inserted := False                            {duplicate entry}
end;  {InsertHash}
```

Procedure `RetrieveHash` (Fig. 19.8) is similar to `InsertHash`. If the target key is in the hash table, the procedure returns the record with that key through its fourth parameter. The procedure returns a Boolean value indicating success or failure through its last parameter.

Figure 19.8 Procedure RetrieveHash

```
procedure RetrieveHash (Class {input/output} : HashArray;
                        MaxSlots {input} : Integer;
                        Target {input} : StringType;
                        var NextStu {output} : Student;
                        var Retrieved {output} : Boolean);
{
  Retrieves the record with key Target from the array Class.
  Pre  : Class, MaxSlots, and Target are defined. An empty slot
         in Class is indicated by a record with a blank Key field.
  Post : Returns in NextStu the record with key Target.
         Retrieved is set to True if Target is present;
         otherwise, Retrieved is set to false.
  Calls: LocateSlot
}
  var
    NewIndex : Integer;                    {insertion point}

begin {RetrieveHash}
   {Locate first empty slot or NextStu.}
   NewIndex := LocateSlot (Class, MaxSlots, Target);

   {Retrieve record or display error message.}
   if NewIndex <> 0 then
     begin
       NextStu := Class[NewIndex];
       Retrieved := True
     end
   else
     Retrieved := False
end;  {RetrieveHash}
```

Analysis of Hashing

In the best case, it requires just one probe into the hash table to locate a target key or to insert a new record. The more records that are in the array, the greater the chance of one or more collisions and additional probes. To reduce the likelihood of collisions, it is a good idea to leave at least 20 percent extra capacity in the hash table. We can also reduce the chance of multiple collisions by providing better algorithms for resolving a collision than by using the simple approach of advancing to the next slot in the array. Experience shows that the latter approach causes records to be placed in adjacent slots of the hash table, which leads to bands of filled slots and increases the likelihood of multiple collisions.

The hash function should also be constructed so that it distributes the records throughout the hash table. However, we do not want a hash function that is overly complicated, which would require too much computer time to compute the initial hash index. Best results are obtained when the number of table slots is a prime number.

Exercises for Section 19.2

Self-Check

1. Assume that the ordinal number for the letter `A` is `1`, `B` is `2`, and so on; `MaxSlots` is `10` (array `Class` has ten elements). Compute the hash values for the following names and indicate where each name would be stored in the array: `'SAL'`, `'BIL'`, `'JILL'`, `'LIB'`, `'HAL'`, `'ROB'`
2. A modification to function `Hash` is proposed in which the ordinal value for each letter is multiplied by its position in the string (for example, for `'SAL'`, multiply `Ord('S')` by `1`, `Ord('A')` by `2`, and `Ord('L')` by `3`). Why is this a better hash function?
3. An improved way of handling collisions is called quadratic hashing, where 1 is added to the hash index after probe 1, 4 (2^2) is added after probe 2, 9 (3^2) is added after probe 3, and so on. Modify `LocateSlot` to use this technique.

19.3 Selection Sort Revisited

So far, we have examined a technique, the selection sort, for sorting an array. Sorting has been widely studied by computer scientists, and many other techniques are available. The remainder of this chapter introduces several sorting algorithms and compares their performance. For each sorting algorithm, we want to see how the array size (`N`) affects the number of record key comparisons and the number of exchanges performed.

Analysis of Selection Sort

The following selection sort algorithm and its refinement first appeared in Section 12.7.

Selection Sort Algorithm

```
1. for I := N downto 2 do
     begin
       2. Find the largest element in subarray 1..I
       3. if the largest element is not at subscript I then
              Switch the largest element with the one at subscript I.
     end
```

Step 2 Refinement

```
2.1. Save I as the position of the largest so far in the subarray.
2.2. for J := I-1 downto 1 do
       2.3 if the element at J is bigger than largest so far then
              Save J as the position of the largest so far.
```

Step 3 is performed $N - 1$ times and involves both a comparison of record keys and a possible exchange of records. Step 2.3 involves a comparison of record keys and is performed `I - 1` times for each value of `I`. Because `I` takes on all values between `2` and N, the following sum computes the number of executions of step 2.3.

$$1 + 2 + 3 + \ldots + (N - 1)$$

This sum is equivalent to

$$\frac{N \times (N - 1)}{2} = N^2/2 - N/2$$

Therefore, the total number of record key comparisons is

$$N^2/2 + N/2 - 1$$

and the maximum number of record exchanges is

$$N - 1$$

For very large N, we can ignore all but the most significant term in an expression, so the number of comparisons is $O(N^2)$ and the number of exchanges is $O(N)$. Because the number of comparisons increases with the square of N, the selection sort is called a *quadratic sort.*

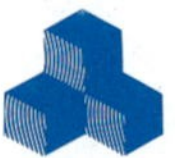

19.4 Bubble Sort

This section discusses a fairly simple (but not very efficient) algorithm called the *bubble sort.* The bubble sort compares adjacent array elements and exchanges their values if they are out of order. In this way, the smaller values "bubble" up to the top of the array (toward the first element), while the larger values sink to the bottom of the array. The bubble sort algorithm follows.

Algorithm for Bubble Sort

1. `repeat`
    2. `for` each pair of adjacent array elements `do`
    3. `if` the values in a pair are out of order `then`
        Exchange the values

    `until` the array is sorted

For example, let's trace through one execution of step 2, or one *pass* through an array being sorted. By scanning the diagrams in Fig. 19.9 from left to right, we can see the effect of each comparison. The pair of array elements being compared is shown in a darker color in each diagram. The first pair of values (`M[1]` is `60`, `M[2]` is `42`) is out of order, so the values are exchanged. The next pair of values (`M[2]` is now `60`, `M[3]` is `75`) is compared in the second array; this pair is in order, and so is the next pair (`M[3]` is `75`, `M[4]` is `83`). The last pair (`M[4]` is `83`, `M[5]` is `27`) is out of order, so the values are exchanged.

Figure 19.9 One Pass of Bubble Sort of Array M

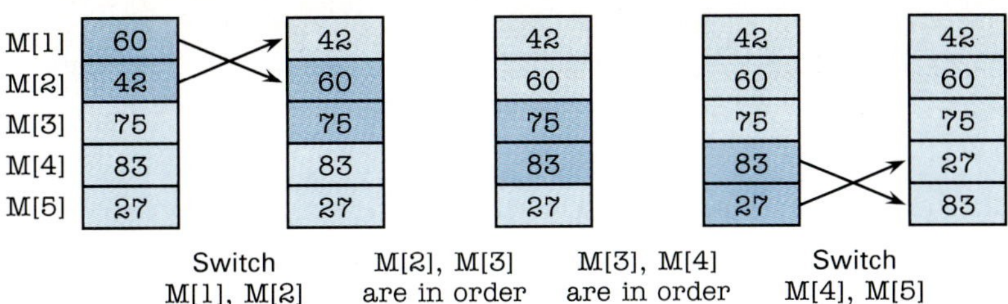

The last array shown in Fig. 19.9 is closer to being sorted than is the original. The only value out of order is the number 27 in `M[4]`. Unfortunately, it is necessary to complete three more passes through the entire array before this value bubbles up to the top of the array. In each pass, only one pair of values is out of order, so only one exchange is made. The contents of array `M` after the completion of each pass are shown in Fig. 19.10; the portion that is sorted is shown in the darker color.

We can tell by looking at the contents of the array at the end of pass 4 that the array is now sorted; however, the computer can recognize this only by making one additional pass without doing any exchanges. If no exchanges are made, then all pairs must be in order. This is the reason for the extra pass shown in Fig. 19.10 and for the Boolean flag `NoExchanges`, described next.

Local Variables for Bubble Sort

Flag to indicate whether or not any exchanges were made in a pass (`NoExchanges : Boolean`)
Loop-control variable and subscript (`First : Integer`)
Number of the current pass starting with 1 (`Pass : Integer`)

Refinement of Step 2 of Bubble Sort

2.1 Initialize `NoExchanges` to `True`
2.2 `for` each pair of adjacent array elements `do`

Figure 19.10 Array M after Completion of Each Pass

	End of pass 1	End of pass 2	End of pass 3	End of pass 4	End of pass 5
M[1]	42	42	42	27	27
M[2]	60	60	27	42	42
M[3]	75	27	60	60	60
M[4]	27	75	75	75	75
M[5]	83	83	83	83	83

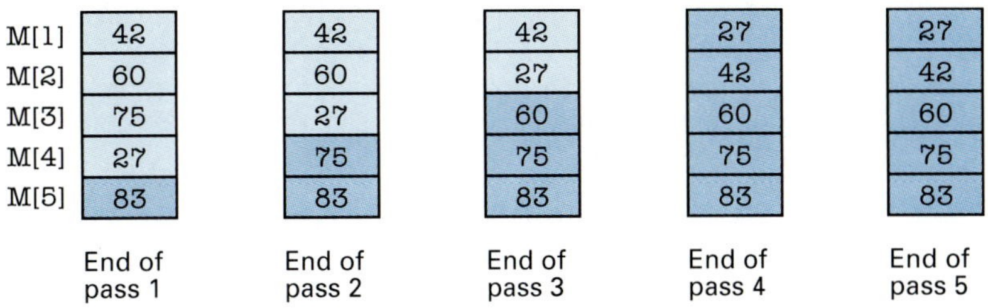

```
2.3 if the values in a pair are out of order then
      begin
        2.4 Exchange the values
        2.5 Set NoExchanges to False
      end
```

Step 2.2 is the header of a `for` statement. The `for` loop-control variable, `First`, is also the subscript of the first element in each pair; consequently, `First+1` is the subscript of the second element in each pair. During each pass, the initial value of `First` is 1. The final value of `First` must be less than the number of array elements so that `First+1` will be in range.

For an array of `N` elements, the final value of `First` can be `N-Pass`, where `Pass` is the number of the current pass, starting with `1` for the first pass. The reason for this is that at the end of pass 1 the last array element must be in its correct place, at the end of pass 2 the last two array elements must be in their correct places, and so on. There is no need to examine array elements that are already in place.

Procedure `BubbleSort` in Fig. 19.11 performs a bubble sort on an array of student records, `Class`. Each record is type `Student` as declared in Section 19.2. The array `Class` has type `StudentArray`:

```
type
  StudentArray = array [1..MaxSize] of Student;
```

`MaxSize` is a constant that determines the maximum number of student records that can be stored, and `ClassSize` is a variable that specifies the number of records actually stored (`1 <= ClassSize <= MaxSize`).

The array is being sorted on the `Name` field, so `Class[First].Name` is compared to `Class[First+1].Name`. If the student names are out of order, the statement

```
Switch (Class[First], Class[First+1]);  {Switch data}
```

calls procedure `Switch` to exchange the records of the two array elements listed as actual parameters. Notice that the entire records are switched, not just the names. When `BubbleSort` is done, the array of records will be in alphabetical order by student name.

Figure 19.11 Procedure BubbleSort

```
procedure BubbleSort (var Class {input/output} : StudentArray;
                      ClassSize {input} : Integer);
{
  Sorts the data in array Class by student name.
  Pre : Class and ClassSize are defined
        (1 <= ClassSize <= MaxSize).
  Post: Array Class is sorted.
}
  var
    NoExchanges : Boolean;      {any exchanges in current pass?}
    First,                      {first element of a pair}
    Pass    : Integer;          {number of current pass}
```

```
  procedure Switch (var Stu1, Stu2 {input/output} : Student);

  {Switches records Stu1 and Stu2.}
  var
    TempStu : Student;                {temporary student record}

  begin {Switch}
    TempStu := Stu1;  Stu1 := Stu2;  Stu2 := TempStu
  end; {Switch}


begin {BubbleSort}
  Pass := 1;                              {Start with pass 1}
  repeat
    {invariant:
       No prior array was sorted and
       elements following Class[N-Pass+1] are in place
    }
    NoExchanges := True;                {no exchanges yet}

    {Compare student names in each pair of adjacent elements}
    for First := 1 to ClassSize - Pass do
      if Class[First].Name > Class[First+1].Name then
        begin {exchange}
          Switch (Class[First], Class[First+1]); {Switch data}
          NoExchanges := False                    {Reset flag}
        end; {exchange}

    Pass := Pass + 1                    {Increment pass number}
  until NoExchanges

  {assert: array is sorted}
end; {BubbleSort}
```

Analysis of Bubble Sort

Because the actual number of comparisons and exchanges performed depends on the array being sorted, the bubble-sort algorithm provides excellent performance in some cases and horrible performance in other cases. It works best when an array is nearly sorted to begin with.

Because all adjacent pairs of elements are compared in each pass, the number of comparisons is represented by the series

$$(N - 1) + (N - 2) + \ldots 3 + 2 + 1$$

However, if the array becomes sorted early, the later passes and comparisons are not performed. In the worst case, the number of comparisons is $O(N^2)$; in the best case, the number of comparisons is $O(N)$.

Unfortunately, each comparison can lead to an exchange if the array is badly out of order. The worst case occurs when the array is *inverted* (that is, the array elements are in descending order by key) and the number of exchanges is $O(N^2)$. In the best case, only one exchange is made during each pass [($O(N)$ exchanges)], so the number of exchanges also lies between $O(N)$ and $O(N^2)$.

When estimating the performance of a sorting algorithm on a large array whose initial element values are determined arbitrarily, it is best to be pessimistic.

For this reason, bubble sort is considered a quadratic sort; its performance is usually worse than selection sort, because the number of exchanges can be $O(N^2)$.

Exercises for Section 19.4

Self-Check

1. How would you modify procedure `BubbleSort` to arrange student records in decreasing sequence by exam score? How about in increasing sequence by letter grade and then alphabetically by name (that is, all A students should be first, listed in alphabetical order; next all B students in alphabetical order; and so on).
2. How many passes of a bubble sort are needed to sort the following array of integers? How many comparisons are performed? How many exchanges? Show the array after each pass.

```
40  35  80  75  60  90  70  75
```

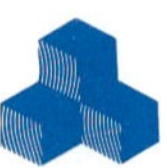

19.5 Insertion Sort

The next sorting algorithm is based on the technique used by a card player to arrange a hand of cards. The player keeps the cards picked up so far in sorted order. After picking up a new card, the player makes room for the new card and inserts it in its proper place in the hand.

The top diagram in Fig. 19.12 shows a hand of cards (ignoring suits) after three cards have been picked up. If the next card is an 8, it should be inserted between the 6 and the 10, maintaining the numerical order. If the card after that is a 7, it should be inserted between the 6 and the 8, as shown in the bottom diagram of the figure.

To adapt this *insertion algorithm* to an array that has been filled with data, we start with a sorted subarray consisting of only the first element. We then insert the second element either before or after the first element, and the sorted subarray has two elements. Next, we insert the third element where it belongs, and the sorted subarray has three elements, and so on. Figure 19.13 illustrates an insertion sort for a five-element array; the sorted portion of the array after each pass is in color.

Figure 19.12 Picking Up a Hand of Cards

Hand of 3 cards	3	6	10		
Hand of 4 cards	3	6	8	10	
Hand of 5 cards	3	6	7	8	10

Figure 19.13 Insertion Sort

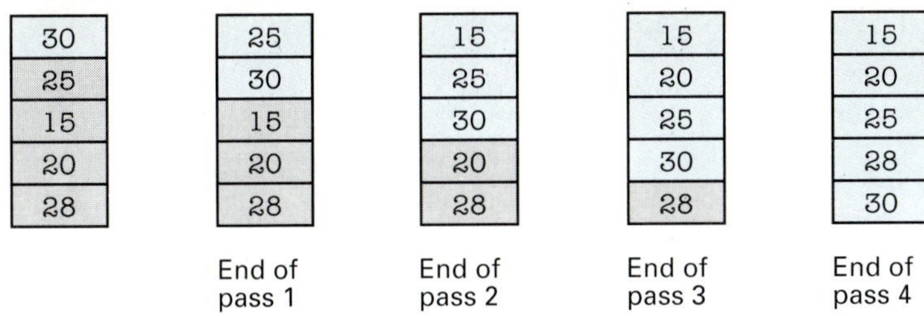

Algorithm for Insertion Sort

1. `for` each array element after the first `do`
   `begin`
   2. Save the value of this element in `NextVal`.
   3. Make room for `NextVal` by shifting all larger values down one position.
   4. Insert `NextVal` in place of the last value moved.

   `end`

Steps 3 and 4 are illustrated in Fig. 19.14. For the array shown on the left of the figure, the subarray with subscripts `1..3` is sorted, and we want to insert the next element, `20`, into its proper place. Because `30` and `25` are greater than `20`, both values are shifted down one place. After the shift occurs (middle column), there are temporarily two copies of the value `25` in the array. The first of these is erased when `20` is moved into its correct position, element 2 of the four-element sorted subarray on the right. The shift and insert operations should then be repeated to insert the new next value (`28`) where it belongs.

Procedure `InsertSort` is shown in Fig. 19.15, where `IntArray` is an array of `Integer` values. Procedure `ShiftBigger` is called to perform the shift operation and to determine the correct position for the array element currently being inserted (`NextVal`).

Figure 19.14 Inserting the Fourth Array Element

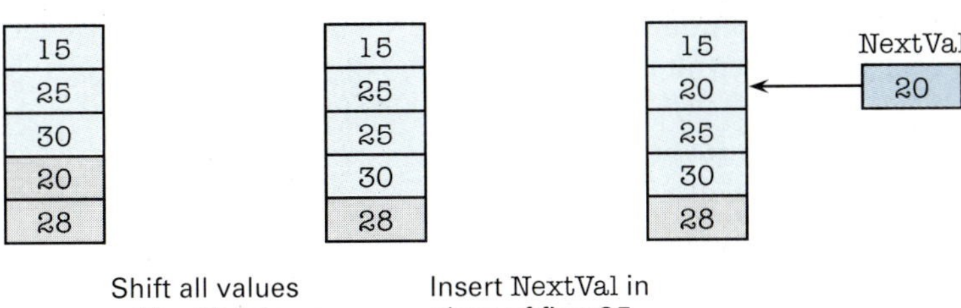

Figure 19.15 Procedure InsertSort

```
procedure InsertSort (var Table {input/output} : IntArray;
                      N {input} : Integer);
{
  Performs an insertion sort on array Table with subscripts 1..N.
  Pre : Table and N are defined.
  Post: Table is sorted.
}
  var
    NextPos,    {subscript of the next element to be inserted}
    NewPos,        {subscript of this element after insertion}
    NextVal : Integer;    {temporary storage for next element}

  {Insert ShiftBigger here.}
begin  {InsertSort}
  for NextPos := 2 to N do
    begin
      {invariant: subarray Table[1..NextPos-1] is sorted}
      NextVal := Table[NextPos];      {get next element to insert}

      {Shift all values > NextVal down one element.}
      ShiftBigger (Table, NextPos, NextVal, NewPos);

      {Insert NextVal in location NewPos.}
      Table[NewPos] := NextVal
    end  {for}
end;  {InsertSort}
```

Coding Procedure ShiftBigger

Procedure `ShiftBigger` must move all array element values larger than `NextVal`, starting with the array element at position `NextPos-1`. If `NextVal` is the smallest value so far, the shift operation terminates after all array elements are moved. If `NextVal` is not the smallest value so far, the shift operation terminates when a value less than or equal to `NextVal` is reached. `NextVal` should be inserted into the position formerly occupied by the last value that was moved. The algorithm for `ShiftBigger` follows; the procedure is shown in Fig. 19.16.

Algorithm for ShiftBigger

1. Start with the element in position `NextPos-1`.
2. `while` first element not moved and element value > `NextVal do`
   `begin`
   3. Move element value down one position.
   4. Check next smaller element value.

   `end`
5. Define `NewPos` as original position of last value moved.

Figure 19.16 Procedure ShiftBigger

```
procedure ShiftBigger (var Table {input/output} : IntArray;
                       NextPos, NextVal {input} : Integer;
                       var NewPos {output} : Integer);
{
  Makes room for NextVal in the subarray Table[1..NextPos]
  and sets NewPos as an index to the correct position of NextVal.
  Pre : Table, NextPos, and NextVal are defined.
  Post: Shifts values in subarray Table[1..NextPos-1] > NextVal
        by one position and sets NewPos to subscript of last
        element moved.
}
  var Done : Boolean;            {flag}

begin  {ShiftBigger}
  {Shift all values > NextVal. Start with element at NextPos - 1.}
  Done := False;
  while (NextPos > 1) and (not Done) do
    {invariant:
        NextVal <= each element moved so far and
        NextPos >= 1
    }
    if (Table[NextPos-1] > NextVal) then
      begin
        Table[NextPos] := Table[NextPos-1];    {shift value down}
        NextPos := NextPos - 1                 {try next element}
      end
    else
      Done := True;

  {assert: position of NextVal is found}
  NewPos := NextPos
end;  {ShiftBigger}
```

The `while` statement in Fig. 19.16 compares and shifts all values greater than `NextVal` in the subarray `Table[1..NextPos-1]`. We could attempt to eliminate the `if` statement and flag `Done` by using the compound condition

```
(NextPos > 1) and (Table[NextPos-1] > NextVal)
```

as the `while` condition. However, unless short circuit Boolean evaluation is used, the second part of this condition causes an `index out of bounds` error when `NextPos = 1 (NextPos - 1 = 0)`.

Analysis of Insertion Sort

Procedure `ShiftBigger` is called $N - 1$ times. In the worst case, `ShiftBigger` compares all elements in the subarray being processed to `NextVal`, so the maximum number of record key comparisons is represented by the series

$$1 + 2 + 3 + \ldots + (N - 1)$$

which is $O(N^2)$. In the best case, only one comparison is required for each call to `ShiftBigger` [$O(N)$]. The number of record exchanges performed by

ShiftBigger is one less than the number of comparisons or, when the new value is the smallest so far, the same as the number of comparisons. Also, each new record is copied into NextVal before the call to ShiftBigger, and NextVal is placed in the array after the return from ShiftBigger (2 more exchanges). An "exchange" in insertion sort requires the movement of only one record, whereas in bubble sort or selection sort, an exchange involves a temporary record and requires the movement of three records.

Exercises for Section 19.5

Self-Check

1. Use an insertion sort to sort the following array. How many passes are needed? How many comparisons are performed? How many exchanges? Show the array after each pass.

```
40  35  80  75  60  90  70  75
```

2. Explain how you would modify the insertion sort procedure to sort an array of student records. What changes would be needed to order the array elements as described in exercise 1 of Section 19.4?

19.6 Comparison of Quadratic Sorts

Table 19.1 summarizes the performance of the three quadratic sorts. To give you some idea of what these numbers mean, Table 19.2 shows some values of N and N^2. If N is small (say 20 or less), it really does not matter which sorting algorithm you use. However, if N is large, avoid using bubble sort unless you are certain that all arrays are nearly sorted to begin with. For most arrays, insertion sort provides better performance than selection sort. Remember that an exchange in insertion sort requires only one record assignment instead of three records assignments, as in the other sorts.

Table 19.1 Comparison of Quadratic Sorts

	Number of Comparisons		Number of Exchanges	
	Best	**Worst**	**Best**	**Worst**
Selection sort	$O(N^2)$	$O(N^2)$	$O(N)$	$O(N)$
Bubble sort	$O(N)$	$O(N^2)$	$O(N)$	$O(N^2)$
Insertion sort	$O(N)$	$O(N^2)$	$O(N)$	$O(N^2)$

Because the time required to sort an array of N elements is proportional to N^2, none of these algorithms is particularly good for large arrays (that is, N

>= 100). The sorting algorithms discussed next provide $N \times \log_2 N$ behavior and are considerably faster for large arrays. You can get a feel for the difference in behavior by comparing the last column of Table 19.2 with the middle column.

Table 19.2 Comparison of Rates of Growth

N	N^2	$N \times \log_2 N$
8	64	24
16	256	64
32	1,024	160
64	4,096	384
128	16,384	896
256	65,536	2,048
512	262,144	4,608

Exercise for Section 19.6

Self-Check

1. Indicate the best method to sort each of the following arrays in ascending order. Explain your choices.

   a. `10 20 30 50 60 80 70`
   b. `90 80 70 60 50 40 30`
   c. `20 30 40 50 60 70 10`
   d. `30 50 10 40 80 90 60`

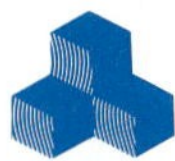

19.7 MergeSort

The next algorithm we consider is called MergeSort. Section 14.5 showed you how to merge two ordered files to generate a third ordered file. MergeSort works in a similar way. The idea is to split the array into two halves, sort each half, and then merge the halves together to get a new sorted array.

We should get an overall improvement in performance, because merging is an $O(N)$ process, and Table 19.1 shows that sorting two smaller arrays takes less effort than sorting one large array. For example, even if we use a quadratic sort to sort each half of the original array, the effort required to sort and merge would be

$$(N/2)^2 + (N/2)^2 + N$$

compared to N^2 to sort the entire array at once. For $N = 100$, the preceding equation evaluates to 5,100, while N^2 is 10,000. You will see that the improvement in performance is even more dramatic. The MergeSort algorithm follows.

Algorithm for MergeSort

1. Split the array into two halves.
2. Sort the left half.

Figure 19.17 Merging Two Sorted Subarrays

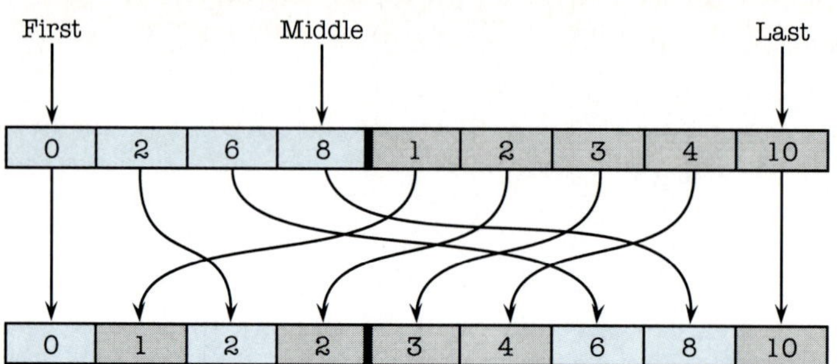

3. Sort the right half.
4. Merge the two arrays together.

Figure 19.17 illustrates this process. An array with subscript type `First..Last` has been split into a left and a right subarray, both of which are sorted. `Middle` is the index of the last element in the left subarray. The two subarrays are merged to form a sorted array.

We can reformulate this algorithm using recursion. The stopping case is an array with one element. Because an array with one element is sorted by definition, we do nothing when the stopping condition (`First = Last`) is `True`. If the array has more than one element (`First < Last`), we want to sort subarray `Table[First..Middle]` and then sort subarray `Table[Middle+1..Last]` using `MergeSort`. Next, we merge the sorted subarrays together.

Procedure Inputs

The original subarray (`Table : IntArray`)
The leftmost subscript (`First : Integer`)
The rightmost subscript (`Last : Integer`)

Procedure Outputs

The sorted array (`Table : IntArray`)

Local Variables

Index of the last element in right subarray (`Middle : Integer`)

Recursive MergeSort Algorithm

1. `if First < Last then`
   `begin`
   2. Set `Middle` to `(First + Last) div 2`
   3. MergeSort `Table[First..Middle]`.
   4. MergeSort `Table[Middle+1..Last]`

```
  5. Merge Table[First..Middle] with Table[Middle+1..Last].
end
```

Procedure MergeSort is shown in Fig. 19.18. When the recursive step executes, MergeSort calls itself first to sort the left subarray and then to sort the right subarray. Next, it calls procedure Merge (discussed next) to merge the two sorted subarrays together. Use the procedure call statement

```
MergeSort (Table, 1, N)
```

to sort the array Table (type IntArray) with subscripts 1..N.

Figure 19.18 Procedure MergeSort

```
procedure MergeSort (var Table {input/output} : IntArray;
                     First, Last {input} : Integer);
{
  Recursive procedure to sort the subarray Table[First..Last].
  Pre : Table, First, and Last are defined.
  Post: Array Table is sorted.
}
  var
    Middle : Integer;   {index of last element in right subarray}

  {Insert procedure Merge.}


begin {MergeSort}
  if First < Last then
    begin
      Middle := (First + Last) div 2;
      MergeSort (Table, First, Middle);
      MergeSort (Table, Middle+1, Last);
      Merge (Table, First, Middle, Last)
    end {if}
end; {MergeSort}
```

The two recursive calls to MergeSort in Fig. 19.18 cause the MergeSort procedure to be applied to two smaller subarrays. If any subarray contains just one element, an immediate return occurs.

Coding Procedure Merge

At the end of MergeSort, the statement

```
Merge (Table, First, Middle, Last)
```

calls procedure Merge to merge the two sorted subarrays. We stated earlier that merging two arrays is analogous to merging two files. In a file merge, two ordered files are merged to form a third file. Procedure Merge must merge two ordered subarrays that are split at Middle into a third array (Temp). The contents of array Temp are copied back into the original array (Table) after the merge. The algorithm for procedure Merge follows.

Local Variables for Merge

The result of the merge (`Temp : IntArray`)
The index to the left subarray (`NextLeft : Integer`)
The index to the right subarray (`NextRight : Integer`)

Algorithm for Merge

1. Start with the first element of each subarray.
2. `while` not finished with either subarray `do`
   3. `if` the current element of the left subarray <
      the current element of the right subarray `then`
      4. Copy the current element of the left subarray to the merged array and advance to the next element in the left subarray and the merged array.

   `else`
      5. Copy the current element of the right subarray to the merged array and advance to the next element in the right subarray and the merged array.
6. Copy the remaining elements from the unfinished array to the merged array.
7. Copy the merged array back to the original array.

Procedure `Merge` is shown in Fig. 19.19. The variables `NextLeft` and `NextRight` are indexes to the two subarrays being merged; the variable `Index` is the index to the merged array, `Temp`. `NextLeft` and `Index` are initialized to `First`; `NextRight` is initialized to `Middle + 1`, which is the first element in the right subarray.

Figure 19.19 Procedure Merge

```
procedure Merge (var Table {input/output} : IntArray;
                 First, Middle, Last {input} : Integer);
{
  Merges Table[First..Middle] with Table[Middle+1..Last].
  Pre : Table is defined and First <= Last and
        Middle = (First + Last) div 2
  Post: Array Table is sorted.
}
  var
    Temp      : IntArray;       {merger of left and right arrays}
    NextLeft,                   {next element in left subarray}
    NextRight,                  {next element in right subarray}
    Index : Integer;            {index to array Temp}

begin {Merge}
  {Start with first element of all three arrays.}
  NextLeft := First;
  NextRight := Middle + 1;
  Index := First;

  {Perform the merge until one subarray is finished.}
  while (NextLeft <= Middle) and (NextRight <= Last) do
```

```
    if Table[NextLeft] < Table[NextRight] then
      begin {copy left element}
        Temp[Index] := Table[NextLeft];
        NextLeft := NextLeft + 1;
        Index := Index + 1
      end  {copy left element}
    else
      begin {copy right element}
        Temp[Index] := Table[NextRight];
        NextRight := NextRight + 1;
        Index := Index + 1
      end;  {copy right element}

  {Copy any remaining elements in the left subarray.}
  while NextLeft <= Middle do
    begin
      Temp[Index] := Table[NextLeft];
      NextLeft := NextLeft + 1;
      Index := Index + 1
    end; {while}

  {Copy any remaining elements in the right subarray.}
  while NextRight <= Last do
    begin
      Temp[Index] := Table[NextRight];
      NextRight := NextRight + 1;
      Index := Index + 1
    end; {while}

  {Copy the merged array back into Table.}
  for Index := First to Last do
    Table[Index] := Temp[Index]
end;  {Merge}
```

Analysis of MergeSort

Our preliminary analysis indicated that MergeSort would be more efficient than a quadratic sort, but how much better is it? Procedure `Merge` copies data into two N-element arrays (array `Temp` and then `Table`). Each array copy is an $O(N)$ process, so procedure `Merge` is also an $O(N)$ process (remember, we drop the 2 from $2N$.)

The remaining question is how many times procedure `Merge` is called. The answer is that `Merge` is called once for each execution of the recursive step in `MergeSort`. The recursive step splits the array into half each time it executes. From earlier splitting processes (for example, binary search), we know that it requires $\log_2 N$ splits to reach the stopping state (N one-element subarrays). Therefore, `MergeSort` appears to be an $O(N \times \log_2 N)$ process.

Table 19.2 shows that `MergeSort` provides significant improvement over a quadratic sort for a large array. Bear in mind that this analysis does not provide the whole picture. There is quite a bit of overhead for each recursive call to `Merge`. Also, `MergeSort` requires an additional auxiliary array with the same number of elements as the original array. If the array being sorted is truly a very large array, the memory requirements of `MergeSort` could become a burden. Next, we discuss an $O(N \times \log_2 N)$ sort that moves elements around in the original array and does not require an auxiliary array.

Exercises for Section 19.7

Self-Check

1. Explain why array `Temp` is needed in `Merge`.
2. Trace the execution of `MergeSort` on the following array. Show the values of `First`, `Last`, and `Middle` for each recursive call and the array elements after returning from each call to `Merge`. How many times is `MergeSort` called? How many times is `Merge` called?

```
55  50  10  40  80  90  60  100  70  80  20
```

19.8 QuickSort

The last algorithm we will study is called QuickSort, which works in the following way. Given an array with subscripts `First..Last` to sort, QuickSort rearranges the array so that all element values smaller than a selected *pivot value* are first, followed by the pivot value, followed by all element values larger than the pivot value. After this rearrangement (called a *partition*), the pivot value is in its proper place. All element values smaller than the pivot value are closer to where they belong, because they precede the pivot value. All element values larger than the pivot value are closer to where they belong, because they follow the pivot value.

An example of this process follows. We assume that the first array element is arbitrarily selected as the pivot. A possible result of the partitioning process is shown beneath the original array.

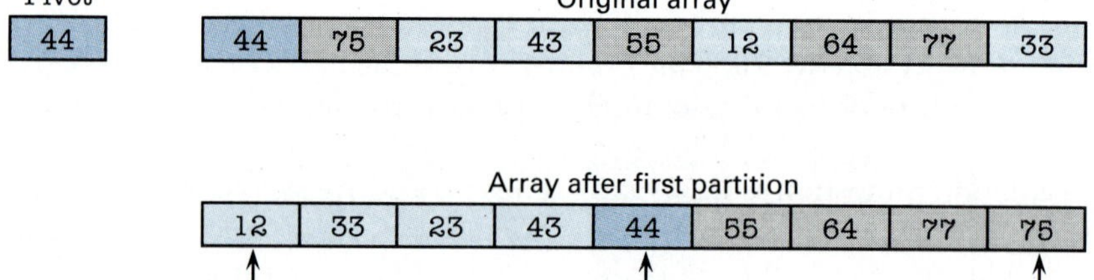

After the partitioning process, `PivIndex` is `5` and the fifth array element contains the pivot value, `44`. All values less than `44` are in the left subarray (color background); all values greater than `44` are in the right subarray (gray background). The next step would be to apply QuickSort recursively to the two subarrays on either side of the pivot value. The algorithm for QuickSort follows. We describe how to do the partitioning later.

Procedure Inputs

The array being sorted (`Table : IntArray`)
The first subscript (`First : Integer`)
The last subscript (`Last : Integer`)

Procedure Outputs

The sorted array (`Table : IntArray`)

Local Variables

The subscript of the pivot value after partitioning (`PivIndex : Integer`)

Algorithm for QuickSort

1. `if First < Last then`
   `begin`
   2. Partition the elements in the subarray `First..Last` so that the pivot value is in place (subscript is `PivIndex`)
   3. Apply QuickSort to the subarray `First..PivIndex-1`.
   4. Apply QuickSort to the subarray `PivIndex+1..Last`.

   `end`

A stopping case for QuickSort is an array of one element (`First = Last`) that is sorted by definition, so nothing is done. If `First > Last` is true, then the array bounds are improper (also a stopping case). If the array has more than one element, we partition it into two subarrays and sort the subarrays using QuickSort.

The implementation of procedure `QuickSort` is shown in Fig. 19.20. Use the procedure call statement

```
QuickSort (Table, 1, N)
```

to sort the array `Table` (type `IntArray`) with subscripts `1..N`.

Figure 19.20 Procedure QuickSort

```
procedure QuickSort (var Table {input/output} : IntArray;
                     First, Last {input} : Integer);
{
  Recursive procedure to sort the subarray Table[First..Last].
  Pre : First, Last, and array Table are defined.
  Post: Table is sorted.
}
  var
    PivIndex : Integer;        {subscript of pivot value --
                                      returned by Partition}
```

```
  {Insert Partition here.}

begin  {QuickSort}
  if First < Last then
    begin
      {Split into two subarrays separated by value at PivIndex}
      Partition (Table, First, Last, PivIndex);
      QuickSort (Table, First, PivIndex-1);
      QuickSort (Table, PivIndex+1, Last)
    end  {if}
end;  {QuickSort}
```

The two recursive calls to QuickSort in Fig. 19.20 cause the QuickSort procedure to be applied to the subarrays that are separated by the value at PivIndex. If any subarray contains just one element (or zero elements), an immediate return occurs.

Coding Procedure Partition

Procedure Partition selects the pivot and performs the partitioning operation. If the arrays are randomly ordered to begin with, it does not really matter which element we choose to be the pivot value. For simplicity, we have selected the element with subscript First. We search for the first value at the left end of the subarray that is greater than the pivot value. When we find it, we search for the first value at the right end of the subarray that is less than or equal to the pivot value. These two values are exchanged, and we repeat the search and exchange operations. This is illustrated next, with Up pointing to the first value greater than the pivot and Down pointing to the first value less than or equal to the pivot value.

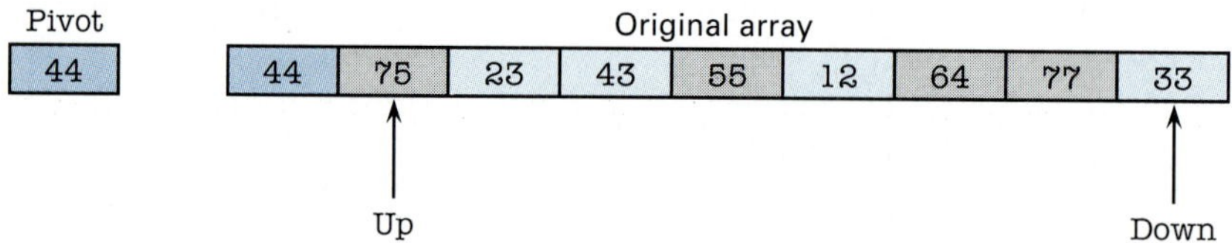

75 is the first value at the left end of the array larger than 44; 33 is the first value at the right end less than or equal to 44, so these two values are exchanged. The pointers Up and Down are then advanced from their current positions to the positions shown next.

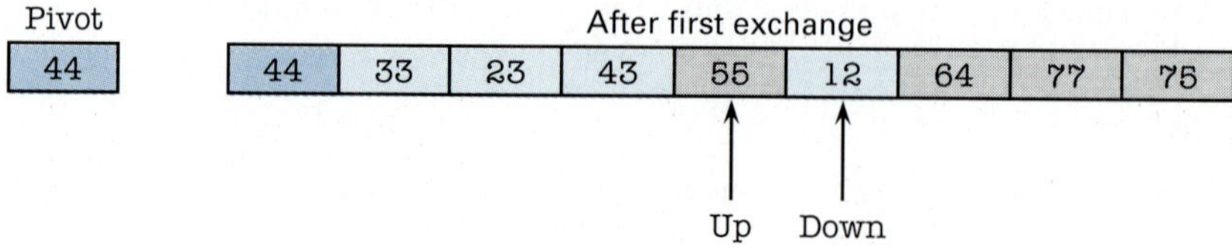

55 is the next value at the left end larger than 44; 12 is the next value at the right end less than or equal to 44, so these two values are exchanged, and Up and Down are advanced again.

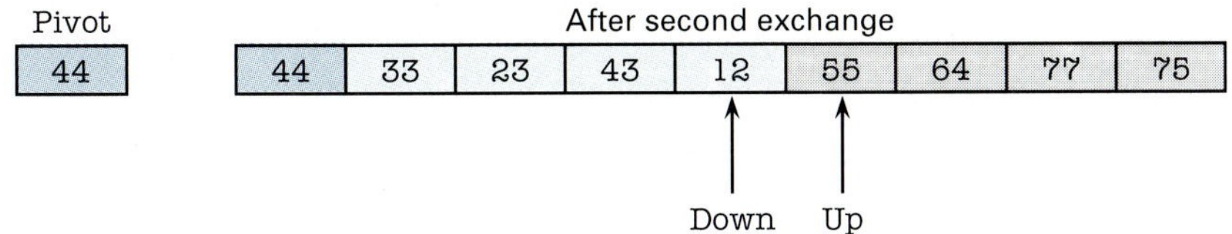

After the second exchange, the first five array elements contain the pivot value and all values less than or equal to the pivot; the last four elements contain all values larger than the pivot. 55 is selected once again by Up as the next element larger than the pivot; 12 is selected by Down as the next element less than or equal to the pivot. Because Up has now "passed" Down, these values are not exchanged. Instead, the pivot value (subscript is First) and the value at position Down are exchanged. This puts the pivot value in its proper position (new subscript is Down), as shown next.

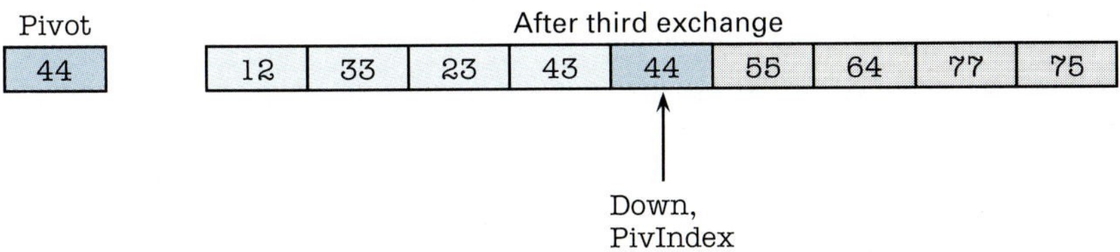

The partitioning process is now complete, and the value of Down is returned as the pivot index (PivIndex). QuickSort is called recursively to sort the left subarray and the right subarray. The algorithm for Partition follows and is implemented in Fig. 19.21.

Local Variables for Partition

The pivot value (Pivot : Integer)
Index to array elements larger than Pivot (Up : Integer)
Index to array elements less than or equal to Pivot
(Down : Integer)

Algorithm for Partition

1. Define the pivot value as the contents of Table[First].
2. Initialize Up to First and Down to Last.
3. repeat
    4. Increment Up until Up selects the first element greater than the pivot value.
    5. Decrement Down until Down selects the first element less than or equal to the pivot value.
    6. if Up < Down then

7. Exchange their values.
   until Up meets or passes Down
8. Exchange Table[First] and Table[Down].
9. Define PivIndex as Down.

Figure 19.21 Procedure Partition

```
procedure Partition (var Table {input/output} : IntArray;
                     First, Last {input} : Integer;
                     var PivIndex {output} : Integer);
{
  Partitions the subarray of Table with subscripts First..Last
  into two subarrays.
  Pre : First, Last, and array Table are defined.
  Post: PivIndex is defined such that all values
        less than or equal to Table[PivIndex] have
        subscripts <= PivIndex; all values
        greater than Table[PivIndex] have subscripts > PivIndex.
}
  var
    Pivot,                        {the pivot value}
    Up,                           {index to values > Pivot}
    Down : Integer;               {index to values <= Pivot}


  procedure Exchange (var X, Y {input/output} : Integer);

  {Switches the values in X and Y.}

    var
      Temp : Integer;              {temporary cell for exchange}

  begin {Exchange}
    Temp := X;      X := Y;       Y := Temp
  end;  {Exchange}


begin  {Partition}
  Pivot := Table[First];  {define leftmost element as the pivot}

  {Find and exchange values that are out of place.}
  Up := First;           {set Up to point to leftmost element}
  Down := Last;         {set Down to point to rightmost element}
  repeat
    {Move Up to the next value larger than Pivot.}
    while (Table[Up] <= Pivot) and (Up < Last) do
      Up := Up + 1;

    {assertion:  Table[Up] > Pivot or Up is equal to Last}
    {Move Down to the next value less than or equal to Pivot.}
    while Table[Down] > Pivot do
      Down := Down - 1;

    {assertion:  Table[Down] <= Pivot}
    {Exchange out of order values.}
    if Up < Down then
      Exchange (Table[Up], Table[Down])
  until Up >= Down;             {until Up meets or passes Down}
  {assertion:  values <= Pivot have subscripts <= Down and
               values > Pivot have subscripts > Down}
```

```
  {Put pivot value where it belongs and define PivIndex.}
  Exchange (Table[First], Table[Down]);
  PivIndex := Down
end;  {Partition}
```

The two while loops in Fig. 19.21 advance pointers Up and Down to the left and the right, respectively. Because Table[First] is equal to Pivot, the second loop stops if Down happens to reach the left end of the array (Down is First). The extra condition (Up < Last) is added to the first while loop to ensure that it also stops if Up happens to reach the right end of the array.

Analysis of QuickSort

The QuickSort procedure works better for some arrays than for others. It works best when the partitioning process splits each subarray into two subarrays of almost the same size. The worst behavior results when one of the subarrays has zero elements and the other has all the other elements except for the pivot value. Ironically, this worst-case behavior results when QuickSort is applied to an array that is already sorted. The pivot value remains in position First, and the rest of the elements are in the subarray with subscripts First+1..Last.

Procedure Partition compares each array element to the pivot value (an $O(N)$ process). If the array splits are relatively even, the number of calls to partition is $O(\log_2 N)$. Therefore, QuickSort is an $O(N \times \log_2 N)$ process in the best case. In the worst case, there are N calls to Partition and QuickSort degenerates to an $O(N^2)$ process.

Because data values are normally distributed in random order in an array, QuickSort as presented will work quite well. A possible improvement would be to use the average of two or more array elements as the pivot value. This requires more computation time and also a modification to the algorithm, because the pivot value is no longer an array element value.

Exercises for Section 19.8

Self-Check

1. Complete the trace of QuickSort for the subarrays remaining after the first partition.
2. If an array contains some values that are the same, in which subarray (left or right) will all values that are equal to the pivot value be placed?
3. Trace the execution of QuickSort on the following array. Show the values of First and Last for each recursive call and the array elements after returning from each call. Also, show the value of Pivot during each call and the value returned through PivIndex. How many times is QuickSort called? How many times is Partition called?

   ```
   55  50  10  40  80  90  60  100  70  80  20
   ```

   Which provides better performance: MergeSort or QuickSort? How would insertion sort do compared to these two?

19.9 Common Programming Errors

One problem with search and sort procedures is the possibility of going beyond the bounds of a subarray. Be sure to enable range checking using {$R+} when you are debugging any program that manipulates arrays, particularly a search or sort.

When you are debugging a search or sort procedure, it is best to use relatively small arrays (ten elements or fewer). Make sure you print the new contents of the array after each pass through a sort procedure.

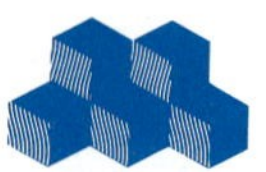

Chapter Review

This chapter discussed the binary search technique, which provides significant improvement over linear search when you are searching large arrays. A linear search is an $O(N)$ process, while binary search is an $O(\log_2 N)$ process. This means that the time required to perform a binary search increases very slowly. For example, it takes only about twice as long to perform a binary search on an array with 256 elements ($\log_2 256$ is 8) as it takes to perform a binary search on an array with 16 elements ($\log_2 16$ is 4).

We also discussed using a hash table to provide quick access to data stored in an array. The record key is passed to the hash function, which computes an index to the array. In most cases, only one probe is required to access the desired record. If there are collisions (multiple keys with same index value), the array elements following the one selected by the index are examined until the desired key is found or an empty table slot is reached.

We also analyzed several sorting algorithms. Three of these, selection sort, bubble sort, and insertion sort, are $O(N^2)$ or quadratic sorts. Two of these, MergeSort and QuickSort, are $O(N \text{ x } \log_2 N)$. For small arrays, either insertion sort or selection sort should generally be used; bubble sort is a good choice only when the array is likey to be nearly sorted. For large arrays, use MergeSort or QuickSort. Avoid MergeSort when storage space is likely to be limited. Avoid QuickSort when the array is nearly sorted.

✓ Quick-Check Exercises

1. What are three techniques for searching an array?
2. What are two techniques for searching an array whose elements are in order by key field?
3. Rate the three search algorithms in terms of time efficiency for a large array.
4. Rate the three search algorithms in terms of space efficiency for a large array.
5. Define a collision in hashing. What is one technique of resolving collisions?
6. Name three quadratic sorts.
7. Name two sorts with $N \text{ x } \log_2 N$ behavior.
8. Which algorithm is particularly good for an array that is already sorted? Which is particularly bad? Explain.
9. What determines whether you should use a quadratic sort or a logarithmic sort?

10. Which quadratic sort's performance is least affected by the ordering of the array elements? Which is most affected?

Answers to Quick-Check Exercises

1. Sequential search, binary search, hashing
2. Sequential search of an ordered array, binary search
3. Hashing, binary search, sequential search
4. Sequential search and binary search followed by hashing
5. A collision occurs when two keys have the same hash value. Linear resolution involves scanning consecutive table entries until an empty slot is found or the target is located.
6. Selection, insertion, bubble
7. MergeSort, QuickSort
8. Bubble sort and insertion sort: both require $N - 1$ comparisons with no exchanges. QuickSort is bad because the partitioning process always creates one subarray with a single element.
9. Array size
10. Selection sort; bubble sort

Review Questions

1. Show how the following keys would be stored in a hash table with five slots, assuming the linear method for resolving collisions discussed in the text. The value returned by function `Hash` is shown after each key.

   ```
   'Ace' 3, 'Boy' 4, 'Cat' 5, 'Dog' 3, 'Bye' 1
   ```

2. When does quicksort work best? When does it work worst?
3. Write a function that will recursively search a string of thirty characters and return the position of the first comma in the string. If the string does not contain a comma, the function should return 0.
4. What is the purpose of the pivot value in quicksort? How did we select it in the text? What is wrong with that approach for choosing a pivot value?
5. For the array

   ```
   30  40  20  15  60  80  75  4  20
   ```

   show the new array after each pass of insertion sort and bubble sort. How many comparisons and exchanges are performed by each?
6. For the array in exercise 5, trace the execution of mergesort and quicksort.
7. The shaker sort is an adaptation of the bubble sort that alternates the direction in which the array elements are scanned during each pass. The first pass starts its scan with the first element, moving the larger element in each pair down the array. The second pass starts its scan with the next-to-last element, moving the smaller element in each pair up the array, and so on. Indicate what the advantage of the shaker sort might be. Show how it would sort the array in exercise 5.

Programming Projects

1. Write an abstract data type called `HashTable` that consists of a declaration for a hash table and the operators in Section 19.2. Write a menu-driven program that maintains a list of passenger records in a hash table (see programming project 1 of Chapter 18). Import the necessary data types and operators.

2. Hashing can be a useful technique for maintaining information in direct-access data files. Write a new version of ADT `HashTable`, which uses a direct-access data file rather than an array as the hash table data type and redo project 1.
3. Use the random-number function `Random` to store a list of 100 random integer values in an array. Apply each of the sort procedures described in this chapter to the array and determine how long it takes each procedure to sort the array. Make sure the same array is passed to each procedure. Use the Turbo Pascal `GetTime` procedure (in the `DOS` unit) to help you compute the elapsed time for your program.
4. One technique for handling collisions in a hash table is to place all records with keys that hash to the same value in a linked list (called a *bucket*). One slot in the hash table is allocated for each hash value, and each slot consists of space for one record and a single pointer field (initially `nil`). The first record with a particular hash value is placed directly in the hash table. When a second key is encountered with that same hash value, that record is linked to the first record in the table via the pointer field. The third record with that hash value is linked to the second, and so on. Rewrite the operators in ADT `HashTable`, assuming this technique is used to resolve collisions.
5. The `Shell` sort is a sorting technique that applies insertion sort to chains of elements in an array where the elements in the chain are chosen by adding an increment value. The increment value decreases with each pass. For example, if an array has fifteen elements and the initial increment value is 5, the five chains of elements listed next would be sorted in the "first pass." Each chain would be sorted using insertion sort.

```
X[1], X[6],  X[11]
X[2], X[7],  X[12]
X[3], X[8],  X[13]
X[4], X[9],  X[14]
X[5], X[10], X[15]
```

   If the next increment is `3`, the following three chains would be sorted. Notice that the chains increase in size as the increment shrinks.

```
X[1], X[4], X[7], X[10], X[13]
X[2], X[5], X[8], X[11], X[14]
X[3], X[6], X[9], X[12], X[15]
```

   When the increment shrinks to `1`, the whole array is sorted using insertion sort.

   The initial insertion sorts involve short chains, so the sorts should be relatively quick. Normally, the performance of insertion sort degrades quickly as the length of the array being sorted increases. However, because the longer chains have had their elements presorted during earlier passes, insertion sort should be able to handle the longer chains more efficiently than would be the case without presorting.

   Implement the `Shell` sort algorithm. Read the increment values for each pass into an array `Increments` before reading in the elements of the array to be sorted.
6. The binary search is not a useful technique for searching linked lists. Searching linked lists can be done more efficiently when the items that are frequently retrieved are housed near the beginning of the list. Two techniques may be used to accomplish this: *move to front* and *transposition*. With the move to front technique, every time the sought for item is located it is removed from its present position in the list and placed in front of the first element in the list. With the transposition technique, the item sought is moved in front of its predecessor after it is located. Write a Pascal program that stores 30 random integers in a linked list and then computes the average number of comparisons required to search this list 150 times for randomly chosen integers using each of these techniques. Be sure to begin with the same list of numbers each time and to include searches for numbers that do not appear in the list.

Appendix A Using the Turbo Pascal Integrated Environment

The Main menu of the Turbo Pascal system and several of its options were discussed in section 1.6. In this appendix, we discuss more completely the Turbo Pascal 6.0 programming environment and the MS-DOS (Microsoft Disk Operating System) operating system.

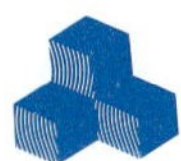

A.1 Some MS-DOS Commands

A principal function of the disk operating system is the maintenance of disk files. Before you can save a file on disk, you must *format the disk*. Assuming the operating system disk is in drive A and a new (unformatted) disk is in drive B, the command

```
A>FORMAT B:
```

formats the disk in drive B.

If the disk in drive B is not new and has been used before, you may want to see what files are currently saved on the disk. Each file name is listed in the *disk directory*. The command

```
A>DIR B:
```

displays the directory for disk drive B. Once you know the files on disk drive B, you can delete a file (using the command `ERASE`), duplicate a file (using the command `COPY`), rename a file (using the command `RENAME`), or display a file on the screen or printer (using the command `TYPE`). Table A.1 describes each of these commands.

Table A.1 MS-DOS Commands

Command	Effect
`CD C:TP`	Makes subdirectory `TP` on disk drive C the active directory.
`COPY B:AFILE.XYZ B:PAYDAY.TXT`	Makes a duplicate copy of the `AFILE.XYZ` on disk drive B; the new file has the name `PAYDAY.TXT` and its contents are identical to those of the original file.

Table A.1 *continued*

Command	Effect
`DIR`	Displays the files in the active directory.
`DIR B:`	Displays the directory for the disk in drive B.
`ERASE B:AFILE.XYZ`	Removes file `AFILE.XYZ` from disk B and frees up the storage allocated to it for use by other files.
`FORMAT B:`	Formats the disk on drive B so that it can be used for storage of files.
`RENAME B:AFILE.XYZ PAYDAY.TXT`	Changes name of `AFILE.XYZ` on disk B to `PAYDAY.TXT`.
`TYPE B:APROG.PAS`	Displays the file `B:APROG.PAS` on the screen.
`TYPE B:APROG.PAS >PRN`	Prints the file `B:APROG.PAS`.

A.2 The Turbo Pascal Integrated Environment

All Main menu items except Edit have menus of their own from which you can choose other tasks to perform or make changes in the way Turbo Pascal will compile your programs and link together previously compiled units. If a menu item is followed by ellipses (. . .), choosing that item will cause a dialog box to be displayed. Choosing a menu item followed by an arrowhead causes another menu to pop up. Unmarked commands are performed as soon as you select them. We describe each Main menu item and its associated tasks below.

The ≡ (System) Menu

You activate the system by pressing Alt-Spacebar or by using your mouse and clicking on the ≡ icon. This menu provides three system commands (`About`, `Refresh display`, `Clear Desktop`), which are described in Table A.2.

Table A.2 System Menu Choices

Command	Effect
`About`	Displays a dialog box with copyright and version information for Turbo Pascal.
`Refresh display`	Allows you to restore the integrated environment screen display in case your program accidentally overwrites it.
`Clear desktop`	Closes all windows and clears all history lists. Use this command prior to exiting the Turbo Pascal integrated environment, unless you want the desktop to contain the same set of windows in your next work session.

The File Menu

The File menu allows you to manipulate files without leaving the integrated environment. You can use the Save command to make a disk file copy of the newly created or recently modified program displayed in the active Edit window. You can use the New command to open a new Edit window. The Open command will copy an existing disk file to an Edit window. The Print command will print the program displayed in the active Edit window. You can also use the File command to exit the environment permanently (Exit) or to switch to the operating system temporarily (DOS shell). A complete list of File menu tasks appears in Table A.3.

Table A.3 The File Menu

Command	Effect
Open	Displays a file selection dialog box and copies a file from disk to an Edit window. You can use DOS directory masks to get a list of file choices, or you can type in the name of a specific file. Use the arrow keys or a mouse to select a file from the list of file names.
New	Opens a new Edit window with the default name NONAME*xx*.PAS (*xx* is in the range 00 to 99). Turbo Pascal prompts you to name a NONAME file when you try to save it.
Save	Saves the file in the active Edit window to disk. If your file is named NONAME*xx*.PAS, you will be prompted for a new name prior to the file being saved. If you do not specify an extension, the default is .PAS. A copy of the previous version of the file is also saved under the same name but with the extension .BAK.
Save as	Brings up a dialog box that allows you to save the file in the active Edit window under a different name or in a different directory or drive. The Edit window name will be changed to match the new name. If the file already exists, it will be overwritten.
Save all	Works like Save, except that all modified files in all open Edit windows are saved to disk.
Change dir	Brings up a dialog box that allows you to designate a new drive and directory to use as the current directory when Turbo Pascal saves or looks for files.
Print	Prints the contents of the active Edit window on the system printer. Use Ctrl-KP to print the contents of a selected block.
Get info	Displays a box containing information about the current .PAS file.
DOS shell	Allows temporary exit from Turbo Pascal to the DOS prompt, usually for the purpose of executing a DOS command. To return to Turbo Pascal with your previous work intact, type EXIT at the DOS prompt.
Exit	Causes complete exit from Turbo Pascal and places you at the DOS prompt. Any files not saved prior to your exit from Turbo Pascal will be lost.

The Edit Menu

The Edit menu is used to move information between Edit windows and from Help system windows to Edit windows. Most of the Edit commands require that an active text block be specified (see Section A.4). A complete list of Edit menu commands appears in Table A.4. The Clipboard is described in Section A.4.

Table A.4 The Edit Menu

Command	Effect
`Restore line`	Undoes last edit change made to a program line. Works only on last changed or deleted line.
`Cut`	Removes the selected text from the active Edit window and copies it to the Clipboard window.
`Copy`	Copies selected text from the active Edit or Help window to the Clipboard, without removing it from the active window.
`Paste`	Inserts selected text from the Clipboard at the cursor position in the active Edit window. By default, all text in the Clipboard is marked as selected. Clipboard text can be pasted in several Edit windows without needing to be reselected.
`Copy example`	Copies preselected example text from a Help window to the Clipboard.
`Show clipboard`	Opens and displays the Clipboard window. The Clipboard window can be treated like any other Edit window, except that when text is cut or copied from the Clipboard itself, the text will be appended to the bottom of the Clipboard window.
`Clear`	Removes selected text from the Clipboard or an Edit window. Text removed is not copied to the Clipboard.

The Search Menu

The Search menu allows you to search for and replace text in the active Edit window. You can also use it to locate subprogram declarations or error locations in multifile programs. The Search menu commands are discussed in Table A.5.

Table A.5 The Search Menu

Command	Effect
`Find`	Displays a dialog box that allows you to enter a text string to search for in the active Edit window. This command is discussed in more detail in section A.4.
`Replace`	Displays a dialog box that allows you to specify a text string to search for and a text string to replace it if found. Use of this command is discussed in Section A.4.
`Search again`	Repeats the last `Find` or `Replace` command.

Table A.5 *continued*

Command	Effect
`Go to line number`	Brings up a dialog box that prompts you for a line number within the active Edit window. The Edit window will be scrolled and the cursor positioned at the beginning of that line.
`Find procedure`	Available only during a debugging session. It brings up a dialog box that prompts you for the name of a procedure or function to search for. If located, the subprogram declaration will be displayed in an Edit window.
`Find error`	Displays a dialog box that allows you to find the source code location of a run-time error. It is most useful when a run-time error occurs while a program is run under DOS, since the error location is displayed as an address using hexadecimal notation (e.g., `2BE0:FFD4`).

The Run Menu

The tasks listed in the Run menu are concerned with executing a program, tracing a program, or viewing program output. A complete list of Run menu tasks appears in Table A.6. The tasks used with the debugger are discussed more completely in Chapter 5.

Table A.6. The Run Menu

Command	Effect
`Run`	Executes the program in the active Edit window; invokes the compiler if the program in the active Edit window has not been compiled.
`Program reset`	Ends the current debugging session and initializes the debugger in preparation for beginning a new debugging session.
`Go to cursor`	Starts or continues execution of a program from current execution position to the executable statement marked by Edit window cursor.
`Trace into`	Causes the next line of the program to be executed. Subroutine statements are executed one at a time.
`Step over`	Works like `Trace into`, except that subroutine calls are executed as one step.
`Parameters`	Displays a dialog box that allows you to give your running program command-line parameters exactly as if you had typed them at the DOS prompt (I/O redirection commands will be ignored).

The Compile Menu

The tasks listed in the Compile menu are concerned with translating programs to machine language, finding run-time errors, and obtaining information about the current source file. A complete list of Compile menu tasks appears in Table A.7.

The first three Compile menu options create new `.EXE` files (for programs) or `.TPU` files (for units). These tasks use one of the two rules to determine the root for the file name. The `.EXE` file name used will be derived from the Primary file name, if one was specified. If none was specified, the `.EXE` file name will be derived from the name of the file last loaded into the active Edit window.

Table A.7 The Compile Menu

Command	Effect
`Compile`	Causes the file displayed in the active Edit window to be compiled.
`Make`	Invokes Turbo Pascal's Project Manager to make an `.EXE` file. Turbo Pascal checks all files on which the current file being compiled depends. If a source file for a unit has been changed since the `.TPU` file was created, it will be recompiled. If the interface section of a unit has been modified, all units that depend on the unit are recompiled as well.
`Build`	Similar to `Make`, except that all the source files for your program are recompiled regardless of the date of the last change.
`Destination`	Specifies whether the object version of your program or unit will be stored in memory (and lost when you exit Turbo Pascal) or saved to disk.
`Primary file`	Displays a dialog box that allows you to specify which `.PAS` file to compile during a Make or Build operation.

The Debug Menu

The tasks listed in the Debug menu enable variable display or modification during a debugging session, and the setting or removal of program breakpoints. A complete list of Debug menu tasks appears in Table A.8. The debugger is discussed in greater detail in Chapter 5.

Table A.8 The Debug Menu

Command	Effect
`Evaluate/modify`	Displays a dialog box that allows you to type in any variable name or expression and display its value. New values can be typed in for variables as well.
`Watches`	Displays a pop-up menu that allows Watch expressions to be added, deleted, or removed from the Watch window.

Table A.8 *continued*

Command	Effect
`Toggle breakpoint`	Sets an unconditional breakpoint at the statement marked by the current Edit cursor position, if no breakpoint exists there. Removes breakpoint from the statement marked by the Edit cursor if one already exists.
`Breakpoints`	Displays a dialog box that allows you to control the behavior of all program breakpoints by editing, adding, or removing them.

The Options Menu

The tasks listed in the Options menu determine the manner in which the Turbo Pascal integrated environment will carry out its tasks. A complete list of Options menu tasks appears in Table A.9.

Table A.9 The Options Menu

Command	Effect
`Compiler`	Displays a dialog box that allows you to specify different compiler options, such as range checking and the generation of debugging information. These options correspond to the compiler directives described in detail in Appendix C.
`Memory sizes`	Displays a dialog box that allows you to control the default stack and heap parameters used by your program.
`Linker`	Displays a dialog box that contains several radio buttons used to set options for Turbo Pascal's built-in linker.
`Debugger`	Displays a dialog box that lets you determine whether debugging information is included in the executable program and how it will be run under Turbo Pascal.
`Directories`	Displays a dialog box that allows you to specify the location of any directories containing files to be used by Turbo Pascal.
`Environment`	Displays a pop-up menu that allows you to tailor the Turbo Pascal environment to your needs. This menu provides access to the Preferences, Editor, and Mouse dialog boxes, among others.
`Save options`	Displays a dialog box that allows you to save the settings specified in the Find and Replace dialog boxes and in the dialog boxes accessed by the items in the Options menu. Several files may be created to house this information.
`Retrieve options`	Displays a dialog box that allows you to retrieve previously saved options information from the appropriate disk files.

The Window Menu

The Window menu contains the commands necessary to manage the windows displayed on the Turbo Pascal desktop. Most of the windows opened by these menu items have all the standard window elements (scroll bars, close box, zoom box, resize corner). Use of the standard window elements is discussed in Section A.3. The Window menu commands are discussed in Table A.10.

Table A.10 The Window Menu

Command	Effect
`Size/Move`	Allows you to use the arrow cursor keys to reposition the active window on the desktop. Use the Shift key with the arrow cursor keys to change the size of the window. Press the Enter key when you are done. Equivalent mouse operations are described in Section A.3.
`Zoom`	Allows you to expand the active window to its maximum size or to shrink a window to its previous size if it is displayed at its maximum size. This is equivalent to using your mouse to click the zoom box.
`Tile`	Makes all open Edit windows the same size and displays them next to one another, without overlapping, on the desktop.
`Cascade`	Stacks all open Edit windows on top of one another. Only the topmost Edit window can be viewed fully. Only window names and numbers will be visible for the remaining windows.
`Next`	Makes the next window in the window list the active window.
`Previous`	Makes the preceding window in the window list the active window.
`Close`	Closes the active window and removes it from the desktop. This is equivalent to using your mouse to click on the close box.
`Watch`	Opens the Watch window and displays it at the bottom of the desktop.
`Register`	Opens a window containing the values of the CPU registers.
`Output`	A text window is opened at the bottom of the desktop, which allows continuous viewing of program output during a debugging session.
`Call stack`	Displays a window containing a list of the nested subprogram calls that lead to the current execution position.
`User screen`	Displays a screen containing program output.
`List`	Displays a complete list of all open windows.

The Help Menu

The Help menu provides you with access to Turbo Pascal's on-line Help system. There is information on virtually every aspect of the Turbo Pascal language and the integrated development environment. The Help screens themselves often contain keywords (highlighted text) that you can select to obtain additional information about a topic. To select a keyword, use the Tab and Enter keys or use your mouse cursor and double click the left mouse button. The Help menu items are described in Table A.11.

Table A.11 The Help Menu

Command	Effect
`Contents`	Displays a window containing the main table of contents. You can branch from this window to any other part of the Help system.
`Index`	Displays a dialog box with a full list of Help system keywords. You can scroll through this list using the cursor keys or your mouse. You can also search it incrementally by typing letters from the keyboard.
`Topic search`	Displays language help specific to the currently selected item in the active Edit window.
`Previous topic`	Returns you to the previous Help text screen.
`Help on help`	Opens a text screen explaining how to use the Help system.

A.3 Windows and Dialog Boxes

The Turbo Pascal integrated environment makes extensive use of windows and dialog boxes in its user interface. Windows are screen areas that can be moved, resized, overlapped, opened, and closed. Dialog boxes are movable screen areas that contain fields that allow options to be viewed and set. Unlike windows, which remain on the desktop even when they are not active, dialog boxes are usually removed from the desktop once their options are set.

Windows

Turbo Pascal uses several types of windows. Most have the features shown in Fig. A.1. Edit windows are opened by the `Open` or `New` command in the File menu. Many other windows are opened by a Window menu command. You can have a number of windows open in the Turbo Pascal environment, but only one window is active at any one time. Most menu commands apply only to the active window. Turbo Pascal places a double-lined border around the active window. To activate a window, either place your mouse cursor on the window and click the left button, or press the F6 key (Next window) repeatedly until the double-lined border appears around the window, or press the Alt key while typing the number of the window.

To close the active window, press Alt-F3 or position your mouse cursor on the window's close box and click the left mouse button. To change the size of the window or its location, use the Window menu `Size/Move` command or your mouse. To move a window, position the mouse cursor on the window title bar and drag it (click and hold the left mouse button while moving the mouse cursor) to the desired desktop position. The window will follow the mouse cursor. To resize a window, position the mouse cursor

Figure A.1 A typical window

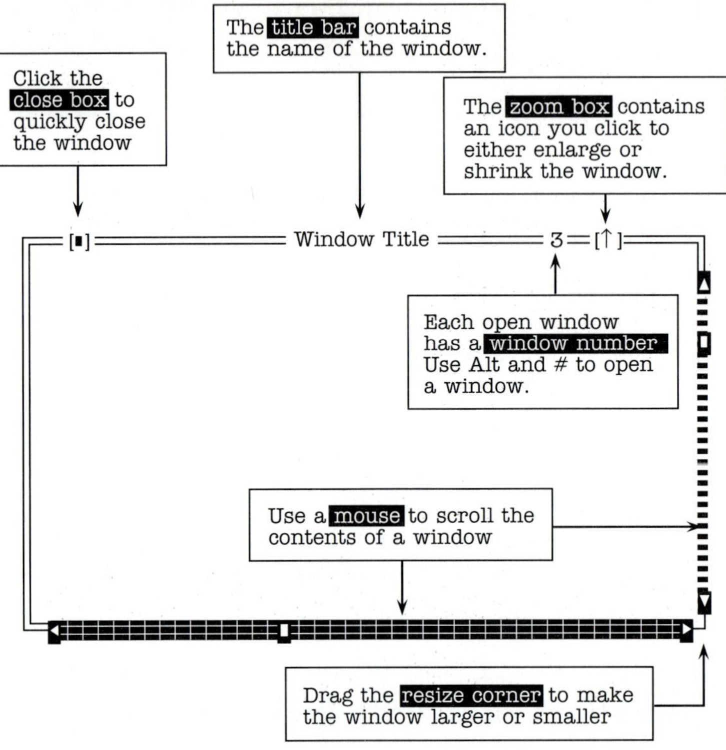
The title bar contains the name of the window.
Click the close box to quickly close the window
The zoom box contains an icon you click to either enlarge or shrink the window.
[■]
Window Title
3
[↑]
Each open window has a window number Use Alt and # to open a window.
Use a mouse to scroll the contents of a window
Drag the resize corner to make the window larger or smaller

on the lower right corner and drag the corner until the window becomes the desired size.

If a window has been resized, you can expand it to occupy the full screen by pressing the F5 key. Pressing the F5 key a second time shrinks the window back to its reduced size. You can also achieve the same effect by positioning your mouse cursor on the zoom box and clicking the left button.

You can scroll the text that appears inside a window horizontally or vertically by using the appropriate scroll bars on the sides of the window. Position the mouse cursor on one of the scroll bar arrowheads and press and hold the left button to scroll the window in the desired direction. You can also position the mouse cursor on the scroll bar box, press the left button, and drag it to some other point in the scroll bar. The text will be quickly positioned to that relative point in the window. If you do not have a mouse, use the cursor arrow keys to scroll the window text.

Dialog Boxes

A dialog box provides a convenient means of viewing and setting multiple command options. A typical dialog box appears in Fig. A.2. Five basic types of controls may be present in a dialog box: radio buttons, check boxes, action buttons, input field boxes, and list boxes. If you are using a mouse, simply position the mouse cursor on the control you want to use and press the left button. If you are not using a mouse, press the Tab key repeatedly to move one item at a time until the desired control is marked. A shortcut is to type the key corresponding to the highlighted letter in the button name.

Figure A.2 Typical Turbo Pascal Dialog Box

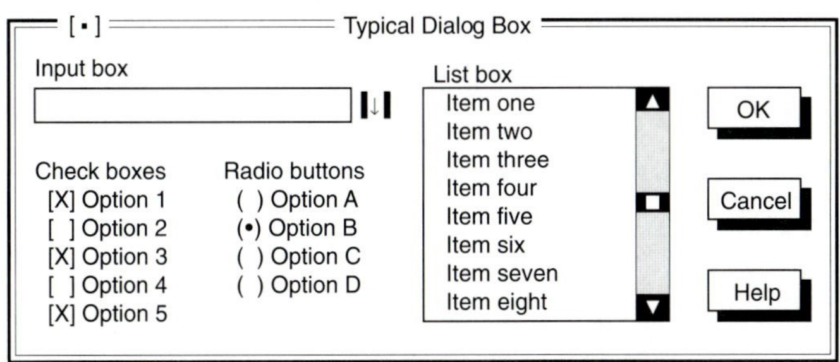

You can mark as many check boxes as you want in a dialog box. An X will appear when you activate a check box. You can have only one radio button marked as active within each group of radio buttons shown in a dialog box. To change the activation status of either a check box or a radio button, position the mouse cursor over the box or button and click the left mouse button. If you are not using a mouse, use the Tab key to select the desired check box or radio button and then press the Spacebar.

Action buttons are activated by either using your mouse or by using the Tab and Enter keys. The dialog box shown in Fig. A.2 has three action buttons: `OK`, `Cancel`, and `Help`. If you activate `OK`, the dialog box is closed and the command is executed. If you activate `Cancel` (or press the Esc key), the dialog box is closed and the command is not executed. Activating the Help button causes temporary exit to an appropriate Help screen.

Input field boxes require you to enter the appropriate text from the keyboard. If a box containing an arrow follows the input field box, a history list is associated with the input field. To access the history list, use your mouse and click on the arrow box or use the Down arrow key. You can use text that appears on the history list as your entry to the input field by using your mouse or the cursor keys to highlight and select the desired text. You can edit history list items before you make a selection.

You can make selections from a list box by using your mouse and the scroll bar or by using the cursor keys to highlight the desired item. Use the Enter key or the left mouse button to select the highlighted item.

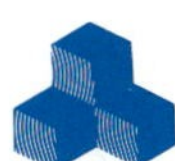

A.4 Using the Turbo Pascal Editor

The Turbo Pascal editor is invoked when you open an Edit window. Turbo Pascal 6.0 allows you to have several Edit windows displayed on the desktop at once. The editor allows you to create new programs or to change existing ones. The editor uses special commands for moving the cursor around in the Edit window, inserting text, deleting text, and searching for text. These commands are shown in Fig. A.3 and are discussed in the subsections that follow.

You can press one of the four arrow keys to move the Edit cursor. The Edit cursor can also be positioned by moving the mouse cursor to the desired character and clicking the left mouse button. Several additional commands are available to facilitate faster and more convenient movement within the Edit window. Pressing the Home key moves the cursor to column 1 of the current line. Pressing the End key moves the cursor to the last position in the current line. Typing Ctrl-Home or Ctrl-End moves the cursor to the top or bottom, respectively, of the Edit window.

As a program file grows larger, it may become too big to appear on the screen all at once. To move back to a previous page of text, press the PgUp key. To move ahead to the next page of text, press the PgDn key. To move the cursor to the beginning or end of the file, you would type Ctrl-PgUp or Ctrl-PgDn, respectively. You can also use your mouse and the Edit window scroll bars to display any portion of your program.

Figure A.3 Turbo Pascal Editor Commands

Cursor Movements			
Character left	←	or	^S
Character right	→	or	^D
Word left	^←	or	^A
Word right	^→	or	^F
Line up	↑	or	^E
Line down	↓	or	^X
Scroll up	^W		
Scroll down	^Z		
Page up	PgUp	or	^R
Page down	PgDn	or	^C
To beginning of line	Home	or	^QS
To end of line	End	or	^QD
To top of window	^Home	or	^QE
To bottom of window	^End	or	^QX
To top of file	^PgUp	or	^QR
To end of file	^PgDn	or	^QC
To beginning of block	^QB		
To end of block	^QK		
To last cursor position	^QP		
To last error position	^QW		
Insert and Delete			
Insert mode on/off	Ins	or	^V
Insert line	^N		
Insert compiler directives	^OO		
Delete line	^Y		
Delete to end of line	^QY		
Delete word right of cursor	^T		
Delete char under cursor	Del	or	^G
Delete char left of cursor	BkSp	or	^H
Block Commands			
Mark block	Shift-arrow (↑,↓,→,←)		
Mark block begin	^KB		
Mark block end	^KK		
Mark single word	^KT		
Mark single line	^KL		
Hide/display block	^KH		
Copy block	^KC		
Move block	^KV		
Delete block	^KY	or	^Del
Read block from disk	^KR		
Write block to disk	^KW		
Cut to clipboard	Shift-Ins		
Copy to clipboard	^Ins		
Paste from clipboard	Shift-Ins		
Print block	^KP		
Block indent	^KI		
Block unindent	^KU		
Misc. Editing Commands			
Abort operation	Esc		
Autoindent on/off	^OI		
Control char prefix	^P		
Pair braces forward	^Q[		
Pair braces backward	^Q]		
Find	^QF		
Find and replace	^QA		
Find place marker	^Qn		
Repeat last search	^L		
Restore line	^QL		
Save and edit	^F2		
Set place marker	^Kn		
Tab	Tab	or	^I
Tab mode	^OT		
Language help	^F1		
Invoke Main menu	F10		
Load file	F3		
Optimal fill on/off	^OF		
Unindent on/off	^OU		
Close window	Alt-F3		

^ Hold down the Ctrl key prior to typing next key
n Any integer number

Inserting or Deleting Text

Once the cursor is positioned at the error to be corrected, you can revise the text. To insert a missing letter or word, move the cursor to the first character that follows the missing text and enter the new text. For example, to insert the missing *i* in the line

```
WrteLn ('Hello');
```

move the cursor to the letter *t* and then type letter *i*. The *i* will be inserted, and the letter *t* will be moved to the right.

If you wish to insert a new line between two existing lines, you move the cursor to the beginning of the second line and press the Enter key. This opens up the text by inserting a blank line between the two existing lines. You can then enter new text on the blank line.

If a line is too long, you move the cursor to the point where you wish to split the line and press the Enter key. The cursor and the portion of the line following the cursor will move down to a new line.

All of this assumes that the editor is operating in Insert mode. In this mode, each character you type is inserted at the current cursor position, and the cursor and the existing text are advanced to the right. If the editor is not in Insert mode, each character you type replaces the character under the cursor, and the cursor advances to the right. If the editor is not in Insert mode, you can correct the line

```
WritenL ('Hello');
```

by moving the cursor to the letter *n* and then typing *Ln* over the transposed characters *nL*. Pressing the Ins key acts like a toggle to switch in and out of Insert mode.

To delete an extra character, you move the cursor just past the character to be deleted and press the backspace key as before. Or you could move the cursor to the position of the extra character and press the Del key. To delete an entire line, position the cursor anywhere within the line and type Ctrl-Y. To delete a word, move the cursor to the beginning of the word, and type Ctrl-T. To delete the remainder of the line starting at the cursor position, type Ctrl-Q Y.

If you wish to combine two lines, move the cursor to the end of the first line of the pair and type Ctrl-T. This erases the carriage return/line feed at the end of the first line and joins the two lines.

Finding and Replacing Text

Sometimes you will want to move the cursor to a word or a group of words that are somewhere in the file, but you don't know exactly where. To do this, type Ctrl-Q F or select the `Find` command from the Search menu. This brings up the Find dialog box, as shown in Fig. A.4.

First, type the characters you want to locate into the `Find` field. You can use the check boxes and the radio buttons to control the behavior of the search. If the text is located in the file, it will be highlighted and the cursor will be positioned just past it. To repeat the search and find the next occurrence of the specified text, type Ctrl-L or select the `Search again` command from the Search menu. If the text is not found, an Error dialog box will be displayed. Press the Enter key or use your mouse to close it.

Sometimes you may want to replace one identifier with another. To do this, you type Ctrl-Q A or use the `Replace` command from the Search menu. This brings up the Replace dialog box, as shown in Fig. A.5.

Figure A.4 Find Dialog Box

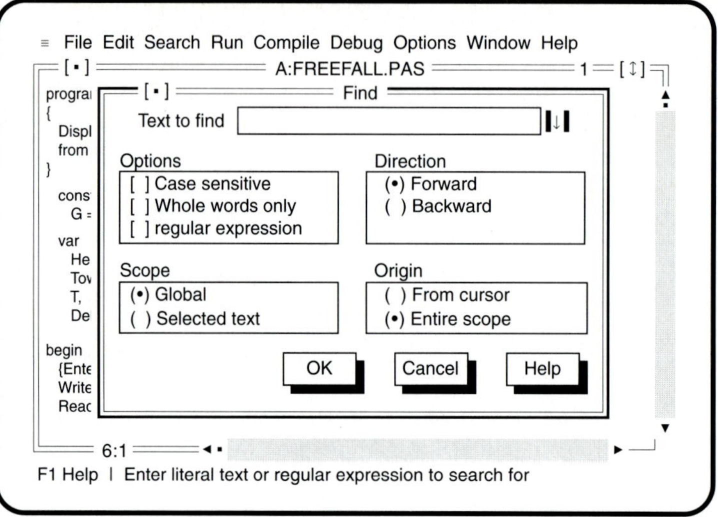

Figure A.5 Replace Dialog Box

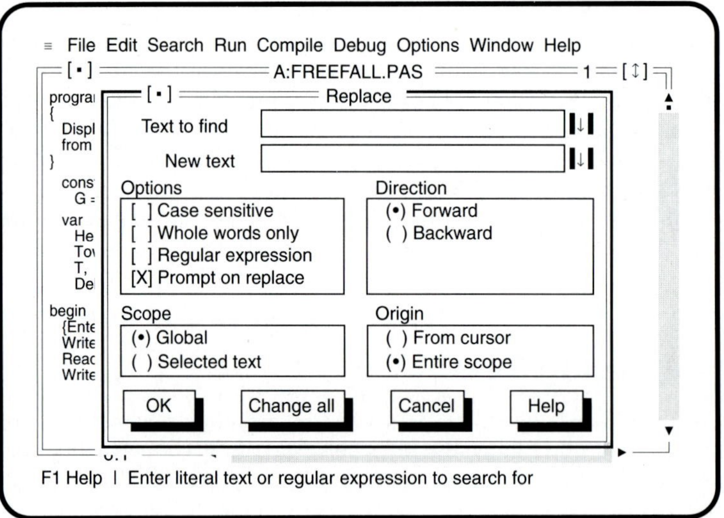

First, type the characters you want to replace into the `Find` field. Type the substitute characters into the `New text` field. You can use the check boxes and the radio buttons to control the behavior of the search. You will notice a check box (`Prompt on replace`) and a button (`Change all`) that were not present in the Find dialog box. If you mark the `Prompt on replace` check box and use the `OK` button to begin the search, the text (if located) will be highlighted, the cursor moved just past it, an Information dialog box displayed, and a prompt displayed asking if you want to replace this occurrence of the text. Using the `Yes` button causes the replacement to be made; using the `No` or `Cancel` button prevents the text replacement. You can type Ctrl-L or use the `Search again` command from the Search menu to repeat the process and replace the next occurrence of the specified text with the same replacement text. If you used the `Change all` button to initiate the replacement process, all occurrences of the search text will be replaced (as controlled by the radio buttons) without any prompting.

To cancel a command after you have begun the search or replace process, you simply press the Esc (Escape) key.

Block Operations

Several operations can be performed on an entire section of the file called a block. Most of these operations are specified by a command that begins with Ctrl-K. Before performing any of the block operations, you must first designate a particular section of your program or file as a block. To mark the beginning of the block, you move the cursor to the first character you wish to include in the block and type Ctrl-KB. To mark the end of the block, you move the cursor just past the last character you wish to include in the block and type Ctrl-KK. Once the block has been designated, the characters included in it will be displayed using inverse video (dark characters written on a lighter colored background), if your computer system has a monochrome display screen. To change the beginning or ending of an existing block, move the cursor and repeat the appropriate marking command. To use your mouse to mark a block of text, click the left button and drag the mouse cursor over the desired text. Release the left button when the entire block appears in inverse video.

You can also mark text by pressing the Shift key and using the four arrow keys to highlight text.

To delete a block of text, you type Ctrl-K Y. To move a block of text from one position to another, move the cursor to the desired position within the file and type Ctrl-K V. To make a duplicate copy of the block at another point in the file, move the cursor to the desired location and type Ctrl-K C. It is sometimes helpful after moving the cursor, and prior to initiating a block move or block copy, if you press the Enter key to open up a new line. You would then move the cursor up to the empty line and perform the move or copy operation.

Blocks of text in one file can be reused in other files. To make a copy of a block of text (for example, the declaration portion of a program) as a separate file, you type Ctrl-K W and the Write Block to File dialog box appears. You can enter the name you wish to use for the file and the block will be written to it. If you wish, you can write to an existing file by entering a DOS directory mask (a partial file name, such as `B:` or `B:*.PAS`) and then press the Enter key. A list of file names matching the directory mask will appear in the dialog box. You can then use the arrow keys or your mouse to select a file from this list. To abort the block write, you press the Esc key instead of entering a file name. The block is never removed from the current file in the Edit window. It is usually a good idea to use the extension `.PAS` with all files that will later be used as programs in the Turbo Pascal environment.

To read text from another file into the program in the active Edit window, you move the cursor to the position at which you wish to insert the new information and type Ctrl-K R. After the Read Block from File dialog box appears, you can enter the name of the file to be read. You can enter a DOS directory mask prior to pressing the Enter key and use the arrow keys or your mouse to select a file from the list of files that will appear in the dialog box. To abort the block read, press the Esc key. If your file exists, the editor will retrieve the specified file and copy the information to the current file at the current cursor position. The block read command does not alter the file it retrieves.

Using the Clipboard

You can use the Edit menu to copy blocks of text between two Edit windows. You do this by marking the desired block of text (using ^KB and ^KK or your mouse) in the first Edit window and then copying the marked block of text to the clipboard, using the `Copy` command from the Edit menu. Next, you activate the second Edit window and position the edit cursor at the location in the active window where the clipboard text is to be copied. Now you can copy the clipboard text to the active Edit window using the `Paste` command from the Edit menu.

Appendix B
Reserved Words, Standard Identifiers, Operators, Functions, Procedures, and Units

Reserved Words

Reserved words are integral parts of Turbo Pascal. They cannot be redefined and must not be declared as user-defined identifiers.

```
*absolute      *external          mod          *shr
 and            file              nil          *string
 array          for               not           then
 begin          forward          *object        to
 case           function          of            type
 const          goto              or           *unit
*constructor    if                packed        until
*destructor    *implementation    procedure    *uses
 div            in                program       var
 do            *inline            record       *virtual
 downto        *interface         repeat        while
 else          *interrupt         set           with
 end            label            *shl          *xor
```

Selected Standard Identifiers

Turbo Pascal defines a number of standard identifiers for predefined types, constants, variables, procedures, and functions. Any standard identifier may be redefined but it will mean loss of the facility offered by that identifier and may lead to confusion.

```
Units:
  Crt, Dos, Graph, Overlay, Printer, System

Constants:
  False, True, MaxInt, MaxLongInt

Types:
  Boolean, Char, Text, Integer, ShortInt, LongInt, Byte, Word, Real,
  Single, Double, Extended, Comp

Files:
  Input, Output
```

* Not reserved word in standard Pascal.

```
Functions:
  Abs, ArcTan, Chr, Cos, Concat, Copy, EOF, EOLN, Exp, FileSize,
  Frac, Int, IOResult, Ln, Length, Odd, Ord, Pi, Pos, Pred, Random,
  Round, Sin, Sqr, Sqrt, Succ, Trunc, UpCase

Procedures:
  Assign, Close, Delete, Dispose, Erase, Exit, Halt, Insert, New,
  Randomize, Read, ReadLn, Reset, Rewrite, Seek, Str, Val, Write,
  WriteLn
```

Operators

Table B.1 summarizes all operators of Turbo Pascal. The operators are grouped in order of descending precedence. If the Operand Type and Result Type columns contain `Integer`, `Real`, the result type is `Real` unless both operands are integers. *Scalar types* are all ordinal and `Real` data types.

Table B.1 Table of Operators

Operator	Operation	Operand Type(s)	Result Type
+ unary	sign identity	Integer, Real	as operand
– unary	sign inversion	Integer, Real	as operand
@	operand address	variable reference or procedure or function identifier	pointer
not	negation	Integer, Boolean	as operand
*	multiplication	Integer, Real	Integer, Real
	set intersection	any set type	as operand
/	division	Integer, Real	Real
div	integer division	Integer	Integer
mod	modulus (remainder)	Integer	Integer
and	arithmetical and	Integer	Integer
	logical and	Boolean	Boolean
shl	shift left	Integer	Integer
shr	shift right	Integer	Integer
+	addition	Integer, Real	Integer, Real
	concatenation	string or Char	string
	set union	any set type	as operand
–	subtraction	Integer, Real	Integer, Real
	set difference	any set type	as operand
or	arithmetical or	Integer	Integer
	logical or	Boolean	Boolean
xor	arithmetical xor	Integer	Integer
	logical xor	Boolean	Boolean
=	equality	any scalar type	Boolean
		string	Boolean
		any set type	Boolean
		any pointer type	Boolean
<>	inequality	any scalar type	Boolean
		string	Boolean
		any set type	Boolean
		any pointer type	Boolean

Table B.1 *continued*

Operator	Operation	Operand Type(s)	Result Type
>=	set inclusion	any set type	Boolean
	greater or equal	any scalar type	Boolean
		string	Boolean
<=	set inclusion	any set type	Boolean
	less or equal	any scalar type	Boolean
		string	Boolean
>	greater than	any scalar type	Boolean
		string	Boolean
<	less than	any scalar type	Boolean
		string	Boolean
in	set membership	see below	Boolean

The first operand of the in operator may be of any ordinal type, the second operand must be a set of that type.

Units

Turbo Pascal is distributed with several predefined units, similar to those that you might define yourself, containing a large number of additional constants, types, functions, and procedures. Some of these predefined units are described in Table B.2. All but the Graph unit are stored in the file TURBO.TPL. The details of the contents of each unit are described in the *Turbo Pascal Reference Guide* and also in the on-line help facility provided in the Turbo Pascal integrated environment.

Table B.2 Table of Standard Units

Unit	Description
Crt	Contains routines that allow you full control over the PC's screen display, keyboard, and sound.
Dos	Supports several DOS functions, including date-and-time control, directory search, and program execution.
Graph	Stored in the file GRAPH.TPU, contains a library of 50 graphics routines and device independent graphics support for several display devices: CGA, EGA, VGA, HERC, MCGA, IBM 3270 PC, and AT&T 6300.
Overlay	Contains the Turbo Pascal unit overlay management routines, which allow units to be swapped between main memory and disk storage during program execution.
Printer	Provides easy access to a printer connected to your computer system by declaring a Text file Lst and associating it with the DOS device LPT1.
System	Contains run-time support routines for all standard identifiers and is used automatically by any program or unit, without requiring a reference in a uses statement.

Functions

Some of the predefined functions of Turbo Pascal appear in Table B.3. The functions following the dashed line are not part of standard Pascal.

Table B.3 Table of Functions

Function	Returns
`Abs(num)`	Integer or real absolute value of its integer or real argument.
`ArcTan(num)`	Angle whose tangent is `num`. The result is expressed in radians.
`Chr(num)`	Character with ordinal number corresponding to the integer `num`.
`Cos(num)`	Cosine of real angle `num`, expressed in radians.
`EOF(fil)`	Boolean value indicating end of file status of file variable `fil`.
`EOLN(fil)`	Boolean value indicating end of line status of `Text` variable `fil`.
`Exp(num)`	Value of *e* (2.71828) raised to the power indicated by its real argument.
`Ln(num)`	Logarithm base *e* of its real argument.
`Odd(num)`	`True` if its integer argument is an odd number; `False` if not.
`Ord(scalar)`	Ordinal number corresponding to its ordinal type argument.
`Pred(scalar)`	Predecessor of its ordinal type argument.
`Round(num)`	Closest integer to its real argument.
`Sin(num)`	Sine of real angle num, expressed in radians.
`Sqr(num)`	Square of its integer or real argument.
`Sqrt(num)`	Real number representing the positive square root of its integer or real argument.
`Succ(scalar)`	Successor of its ordinal type argument.
`Trunc(num)`	Integer part of its real argument.
....	....
`Concat (stl, st2,...,stN)`	String formed by concatenating its argument strings in the order in which they appear.
`Copy(st, pos, num)`	Substring of `st` starting at position `pos` and consisting of `num` characters.
`FileSize(fil)`	Number of components contained in its file argument.

Table B.3 *continued*

Function	Returns
`Frac(num)`	Fractional part of its real argument `num`.
`Int(num)`	Real number representing the whole number part of its real argument.
`IOResult`	Number of input/output error or zero if no input/output error has occurred since previous call.
`Length(st)`	Number of characters in its string argument `st`.
`New(ptyp, constructor)`	A pointer to object storage is allocated on the heap.
`Pi`	Approximation to `Pi` (3.1415926536).
`Pos(subst, st)`	Starting position in `st` of first occurrence of the string contained in `subst`. Returns `0` if `subst` does not appear in `st`.
`Random or Random(int)`	Real random number between 0.0 and 1.0, if no argument given. If integer argument is given, returns random integer greater than or equal to `0` and less than `int`. The procedure `Randomize` should be called prior to the first reference to `Random`.
`UpCase(ch)`	Uppercase equivalent of `Char` argument `ch`, if one exists.

Procedures

Some of the predefined procedures of Turbo Pascal appear in Table B.4. The procedures following the dashed line are not part of standard Pascal.

Table B.4 Table of Procedures

Procedure	Effect
`Dispose (p)`	Returns dynamic storage pointed to by pointer variable `p` to heap.
`New (p)`	Creates new dynamic variable and sets pointer variable `p` to point to its memory location.
`Read (f, variables)`	Reads data from file `f` to satisfy the list variables. If `f` is not a `Text` file, only one component can be read at a time. If `f` is not specified, data is read from file `Input` (the keyboard).
`ReadLn (f, variables)`	Reads data from `Text` file `f` to satisfy the list of variables. Skips any characters at the end of the last line read.
`Reset (f)`	Opens file `f` for input and sets the file-position pointer to the beginning.

Table B.4 *continued*

Procedure	Effect
`Rewrite (f)`	Prepares file `f` for output and sets the file-position pointer to the beginning. Prior file contents are lost.
`Write (f, outputs)`	Writes data in the order specified by `outputs` to file `f`. If `f` is not a `Text` file, only one component may be written at a time. If `f` is not specified, data is written to `Output` (the screen).
`WriteLn (f, outputs)`	Writes data in order specified by `outputs` to `Text` file `f`. Writes end-of-line marker after the data.
`Assign (f, st)`	Assigns name of external file contained in the string expression `st` to file variable `f`.
`Close (f)`	Closes file `f`.
`Delete (st, pos, num)`	Removes substring of string `st` starting at position `pos` and consisting of `num` characters.
`Dispose(p, destructor);`	If called with a `destructor` as second argument, `Dispose` can be used to return object storage to heap.
`Erase (f)`	Erases external file associated with file variable `f` from disk.
`Exit`	Halts execution of current block and returns control to the calling block.
`Halt`	Stops program execution and returns control to the operating system.
`Insert (obj, targ, pos)`	Inserts string `obj` into string `targ` starting at position `pos` in `targ`.
`New (p, constructor)`	If called with a `constructor` as second argument, `New` can be used to allocate and initialize heap storage for an object.
`Randomize`	Initializes the built-in random number generator with a random value derived from the system clock.
`Seek (f, recnum)`	Moves file-position pointer for file `f` to component number indicated by `LongInt` argument `recnum`.
`Str (numval, st)`	Converts numeric value of `numval` to string stored in `st`. Form of `st` is specified by format part of `num-val`.
`Val (st, num, code)`	If successful, converts string `st` to an integer or real value as determined by the type of `num` and `code` is set to zero. If not successful, `code` will be set to the position of first offending character in `st`.

Appendix C
Compiler Directives

Some of the features of the Turbo Pascal compiler are controlled through the use of compiler directives. Compiler directives have a syntax that makes them appear like Pascal comments. Turbo Pascal allows you to place compiler directives wherever comments are allowed. This appendix describes all of the Turbo Pascal compiler directives that are relevant to the text. Consult the *Turbo Pascal Reference Guide* for information regarding other compiler directives.

Several Turbo Pascal compiler options have default values of + or –. To change its default value, the programmer must specify a new value for the compiler option. This new value is provided either in the form of a compiler directive, or by using the appropriate check box in the Options menu Compiler dialog box prior to compilation.

A compiler directive consists of an opening curly brace ({) followed by a dollar sign, followed by the option name (one or more letters), followed by the option value (+ or –) or parameters affecting the compilation of the program or unit, and is terminated by a closing curly brace (}). Spaces are not allowed before the dollar sign or between the option name and option value. At least one space must separate the option name from a parameter. Multiple compiler option specifications can be grouped within a single pair of curly braces if they are separated by commas. Examples of several compiler directives appear below.

```
{$B-}
{$R+}
{$I INCLUDE.PAS}
{$B-,$R+,$D-}
```

A plus sign as the value of a compiler option causes that option to become enabled (active), and a minus sign value causes the option to become disabled (passive).

B—Boolean Evaluation

Default: `{$B-}`

By default, Turbo Pascal uses short-circuit Boolean evaluation, that means the compiler generates code that stops evaluation of Boolean expressions containing the Boolean `and` and `or` operators as soon as the result of the entire expression becomes evident. The use of `{$B+}` causes the compiler to generate code for the complete evaluation of every operand of a Boolean expression.

D—Debug Information

Default: `{$D+}`

When the `D` option is active, the compiler generates debug information that Turbo Pascal can use to locate the source code statement that is causing a run-time error. To use the Turbo Pascal debugger on a program, the program must be compiled with the `D` option active. `{$D+}` is usually used with `{$L+}`.

E—Emulation

Default: `{$E+}`

When active, the `E` option allows a program to access a floating-point run-time library which emulates the 8087 numeric co-processor, if one is not present in the computer. When passive, the program accesses a floating-point library, which can only be used if the computer has an 8087 numeric co-processor.

I—Include File

The compiler directive `{$I PROCESS.PAS}` instructs the compiler to include the file `PROCESS.PAS` in the source program at the point where the comment occurs.

I—Input/Output Checking

Default: `{$I+}`

The `I` option controls I/O error checking. When active, all I/O operations are checked for errors. When passive, it is the programmer's responsibility to check I/O errors using the standard function `IOResult`.

L—Local Symbol Information

Default: `{$L+}`

When active, local symbol information is generated during program or unit compilation. This information is used by the Turbo Pascal debugging program to allow you to examine or modify the variables in the program or unit. Note that the `{$L+}` directive has no effect if the program or unit is compiled with the debug option passive, `{$D-}`.

N—Numeric Processing

Default: `{$N-}`

By default, the compiler generates code to perform real-type calculations using routines from the Turbo Pascal run-time library. Using the `{$N+}` state causes the compiler to generate code to perform real-type calculations using the 8087 numeric co-processor and allows you to use the extended real data types (`Single`, `Double`, `Extended`, `Comp`). Turbo Pascal allows access to the extended real data types on computers lacking 8087 co-processors if the program is compiled with both the `E` (emulation) and `N` compiler options in their active states.

R—Range Checking

Default: `{$R-}`

Turbo Pascal does not normally check for subscript range errors. The compiler directive `{$R+}` enables the generation of code for subscript range checking and should be used while debugging programs. When this option is active, all array and string-indexing expression values are checked during program execution for range errors, and all assignments to ordinal and subrange variables are checked to be within range.

S—Stack Overflow Checking

Default: `{$S+}`

In the default state, the compiler generates code that checks whether or not sufficient stack space is available for the local variables declared in a procedure or function, when the procedure or function is called. If there is not enough space, program execution will terminate and a run-time error is displayed. In the `{$S-}` state, such a call is likely to cause a system crash.

V—Var String Checking

Default: `{$V+}`

When active, the `V` option causes strict type checking to be performed on strings passed as variable parameters. Strict type checking of strings requires that formal and actual parameters are of identical string types. In the `{$V-}`state, any string type variable is allowed as an actual parameter, even if the declared capacity is not the same as that of the formal parameter.

Appendix D
Turbo Pascal Syntax Diagrams

program

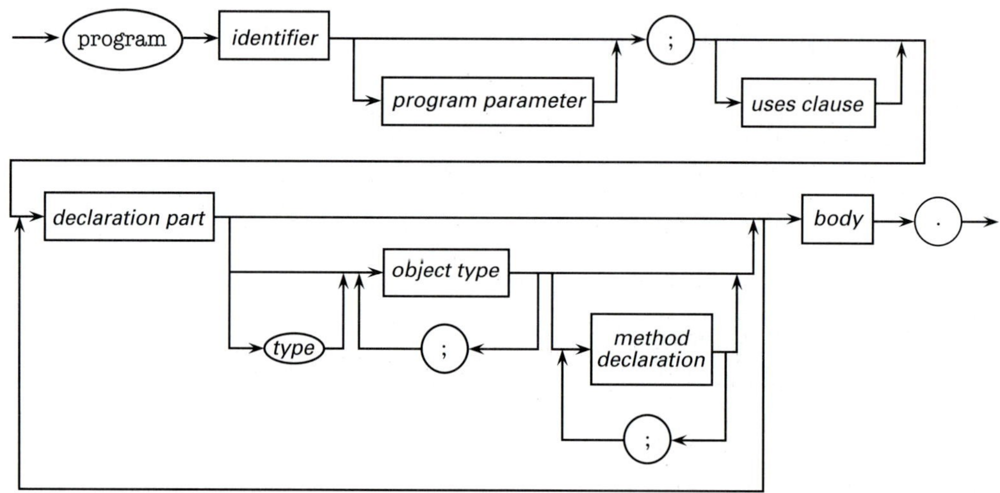

program parameters

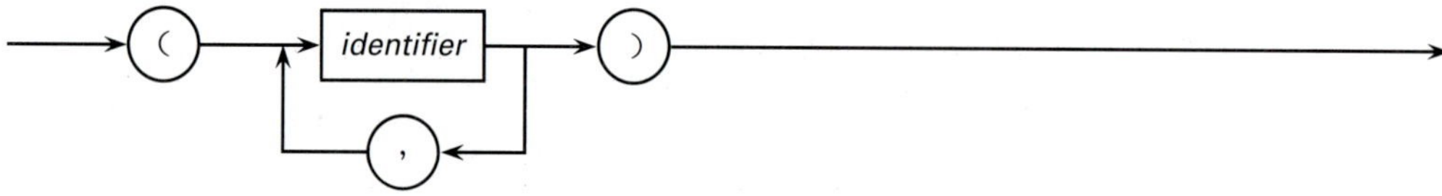

body

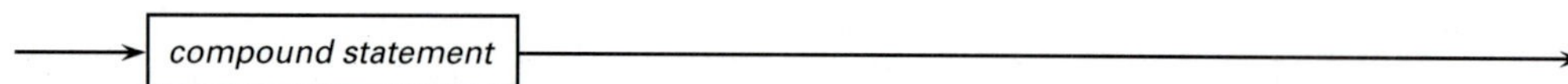

uses clause

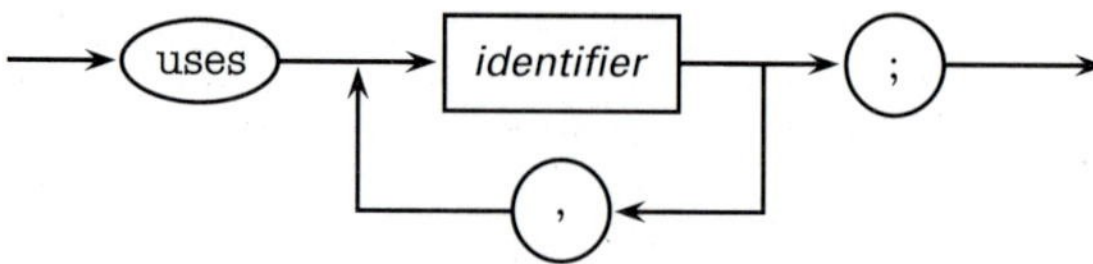

unit

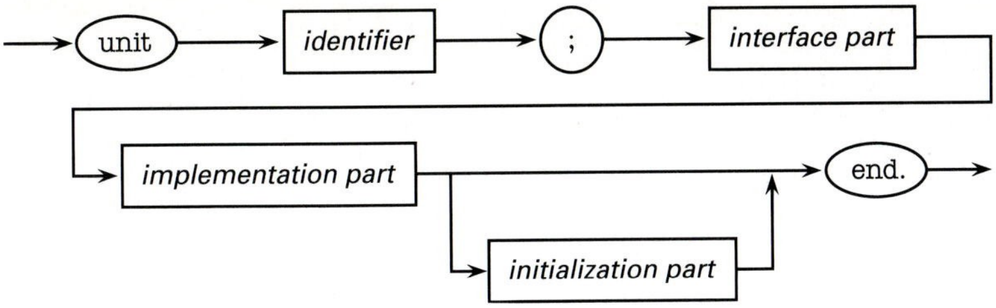

implementation part

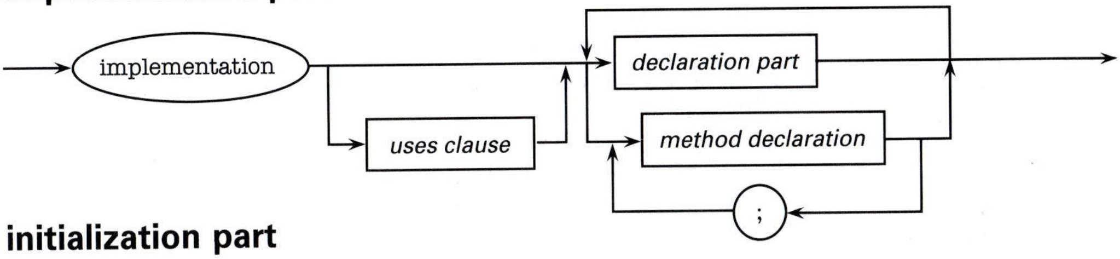

initialization part

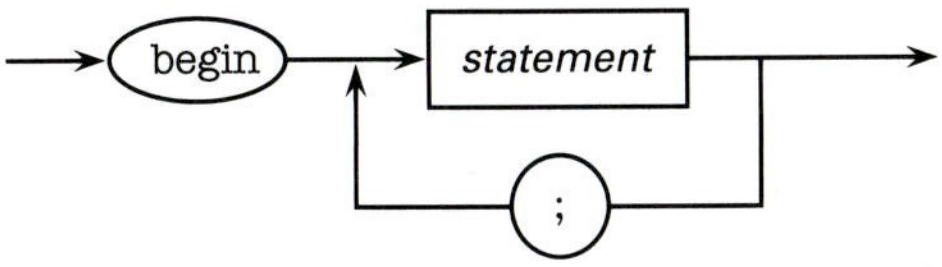

interface part

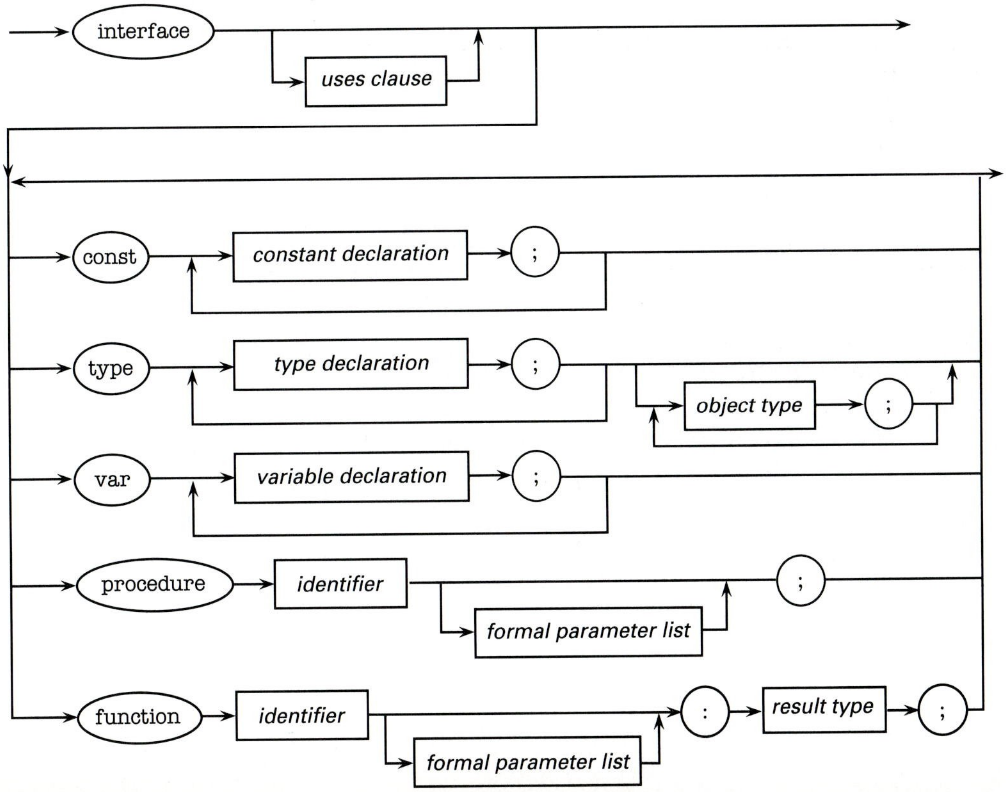

declaration part

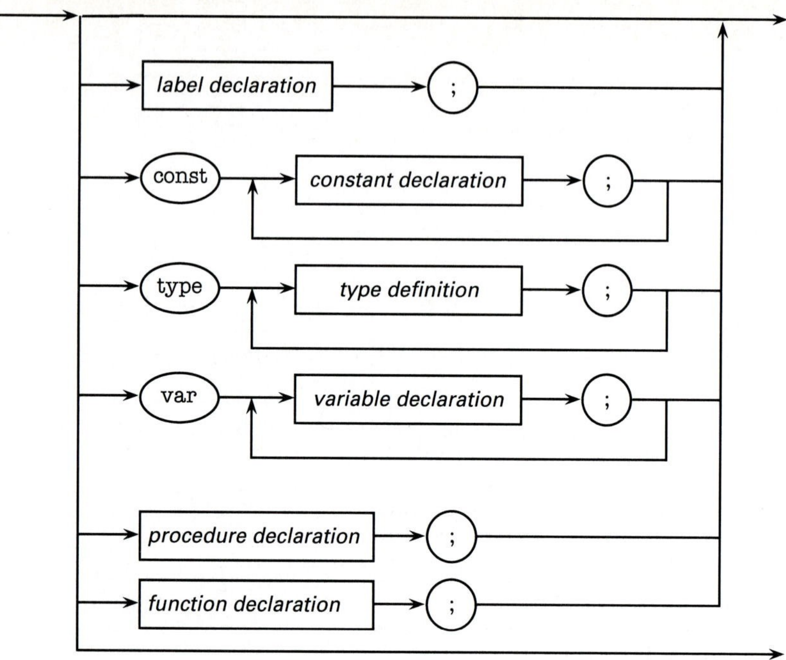

label declaration

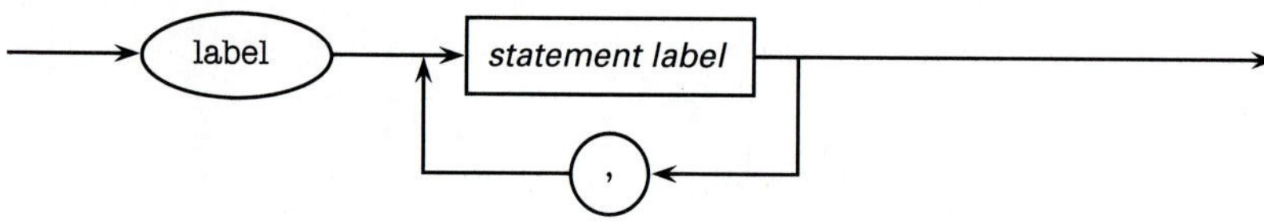

constant definition

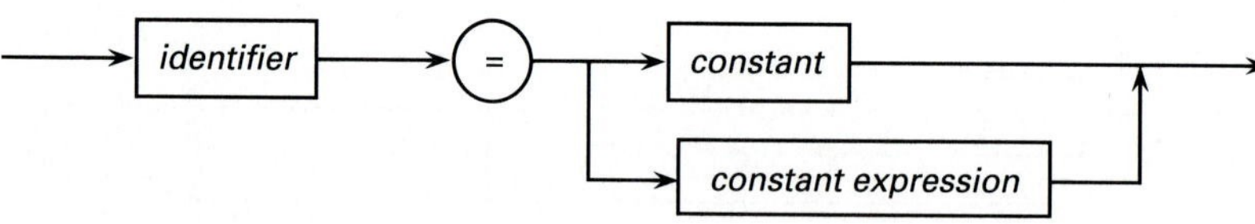

type definition

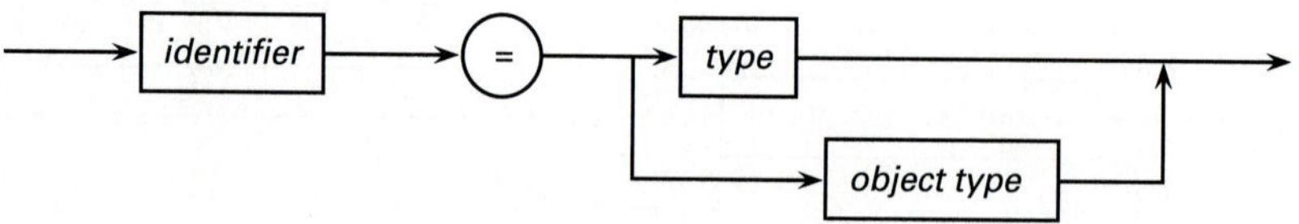

variable declaration

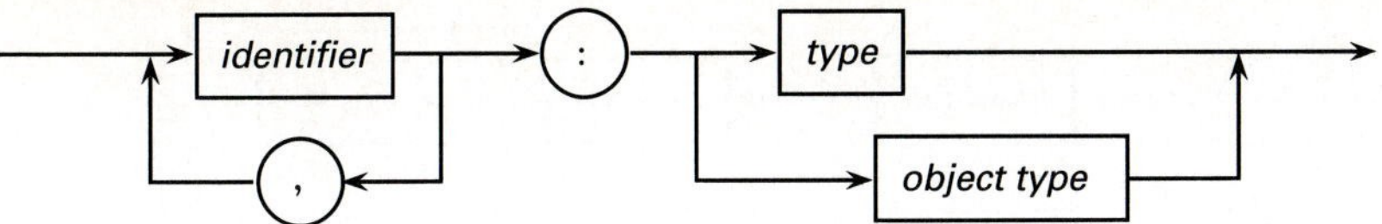

statement label

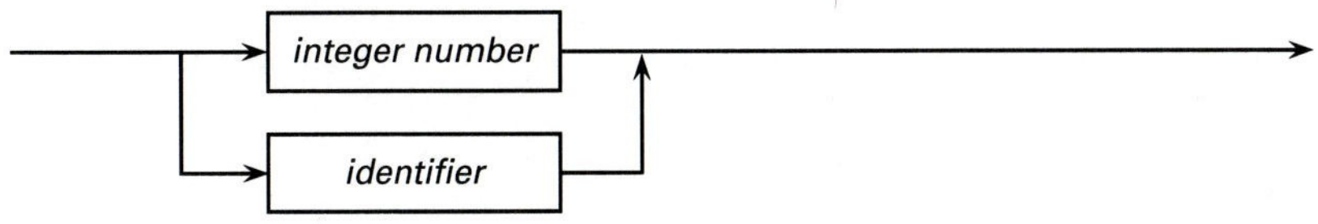

constant

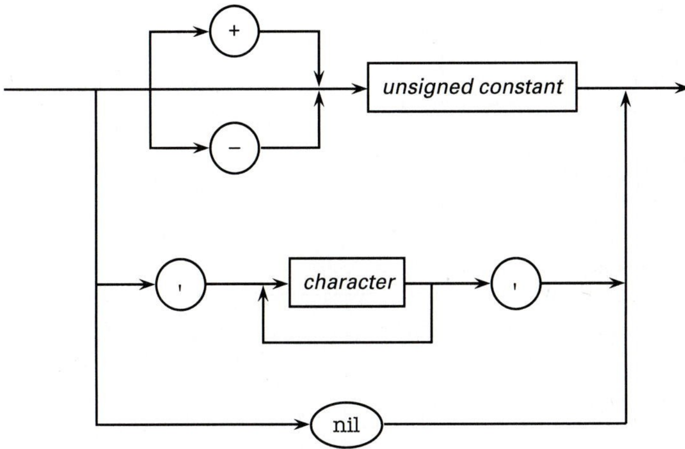

unsigned constant

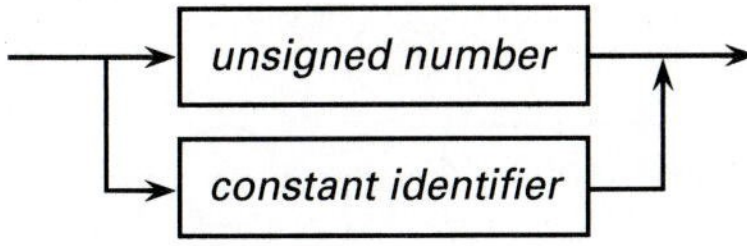

identifier

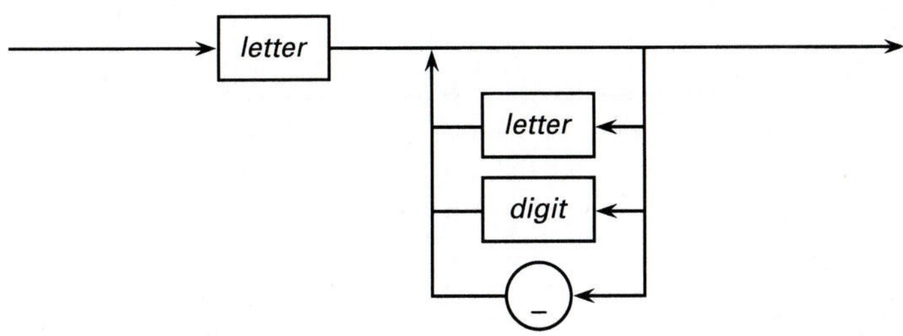

function declaration

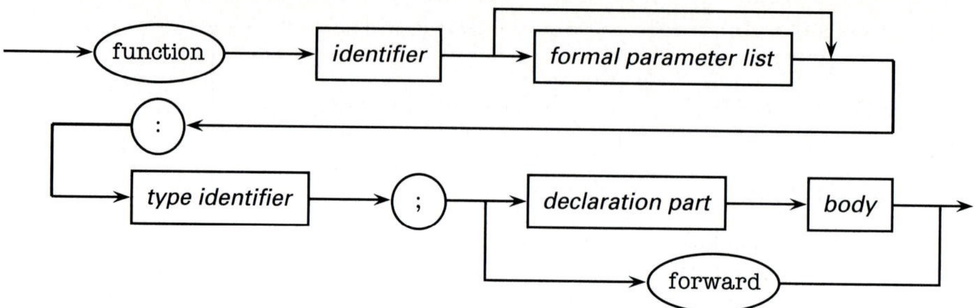

result type

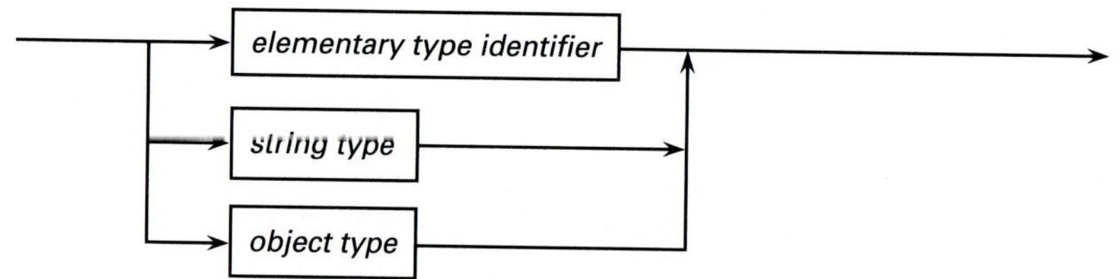

procedure declaration

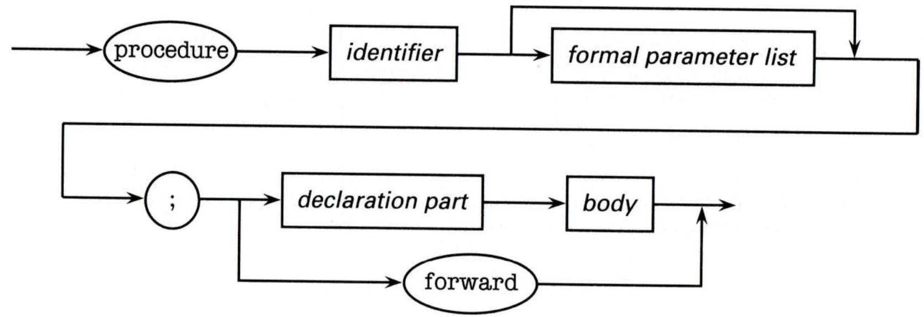

formal parameter list

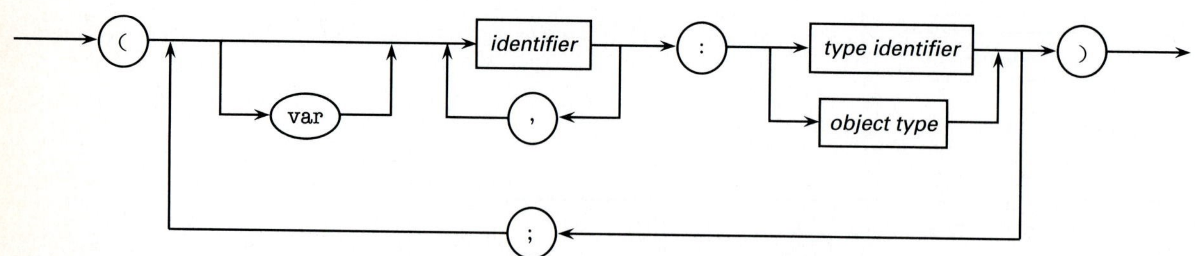

type

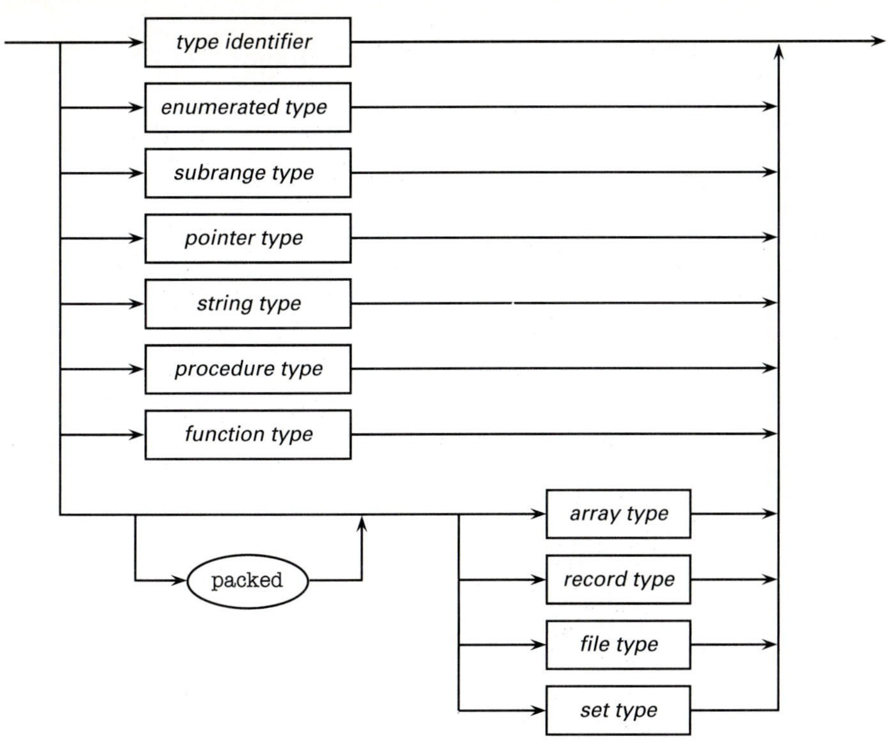

enumerated type

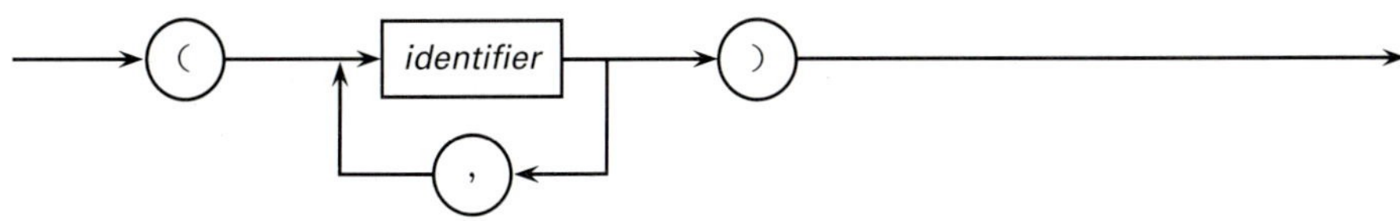

subrange type

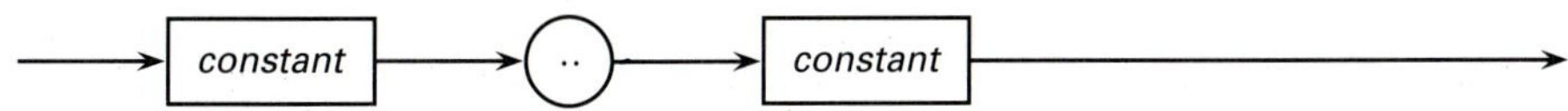

string type

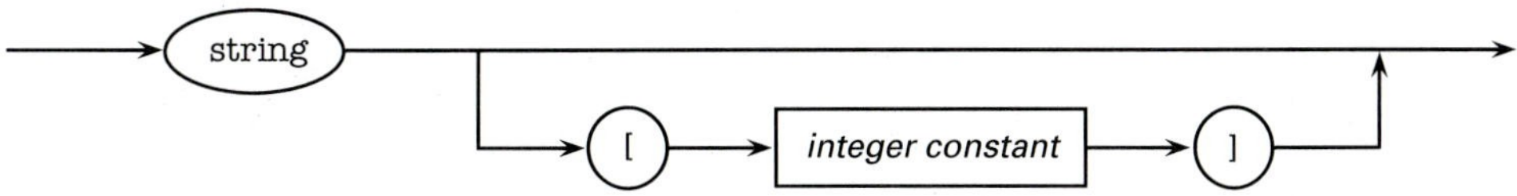

procedure type

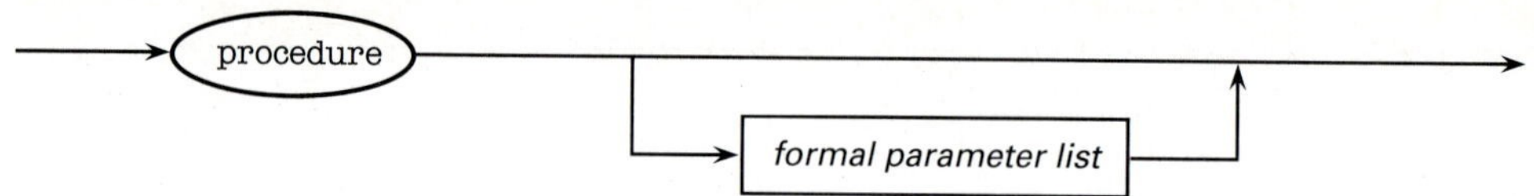

function type

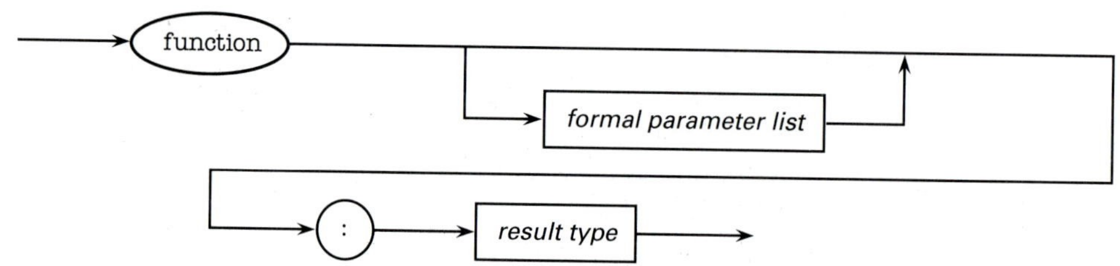

array type

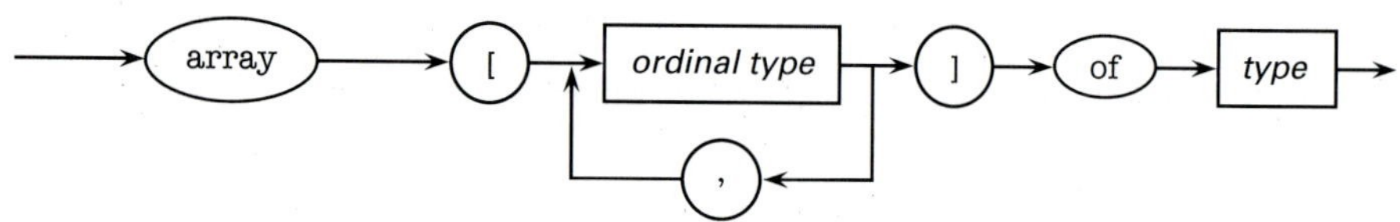

record type

field list

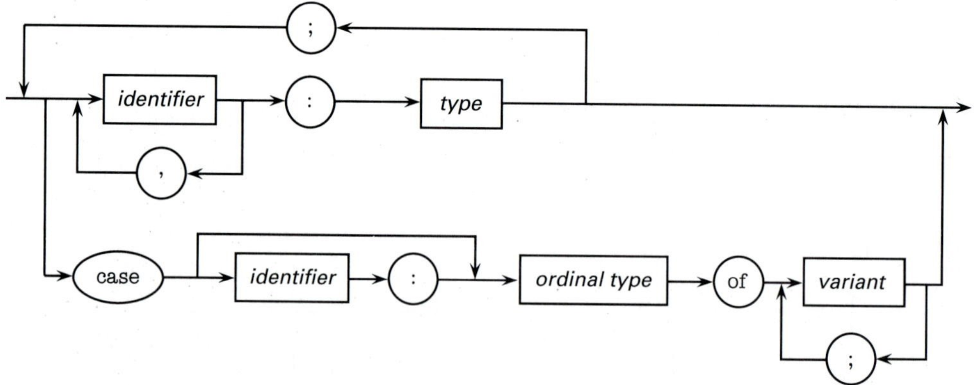

variant

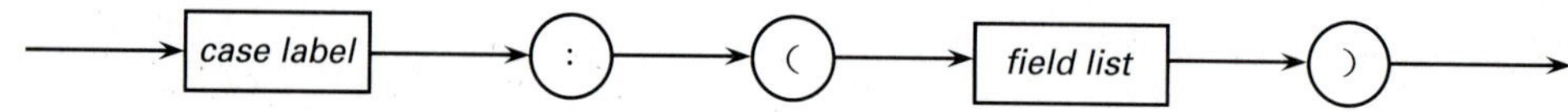

file type

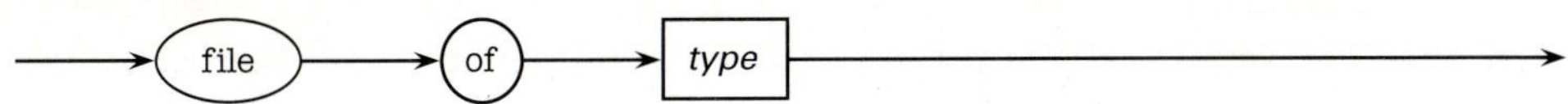

set type

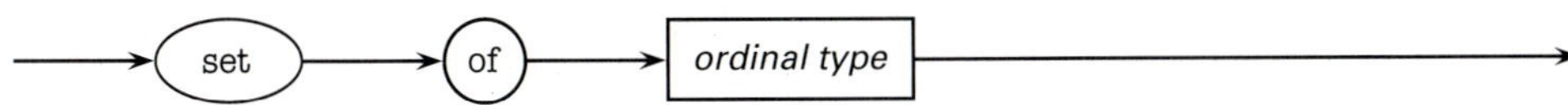

compound statement

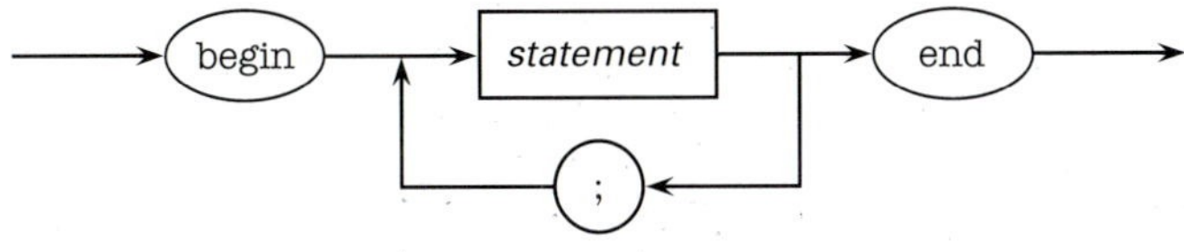

statement

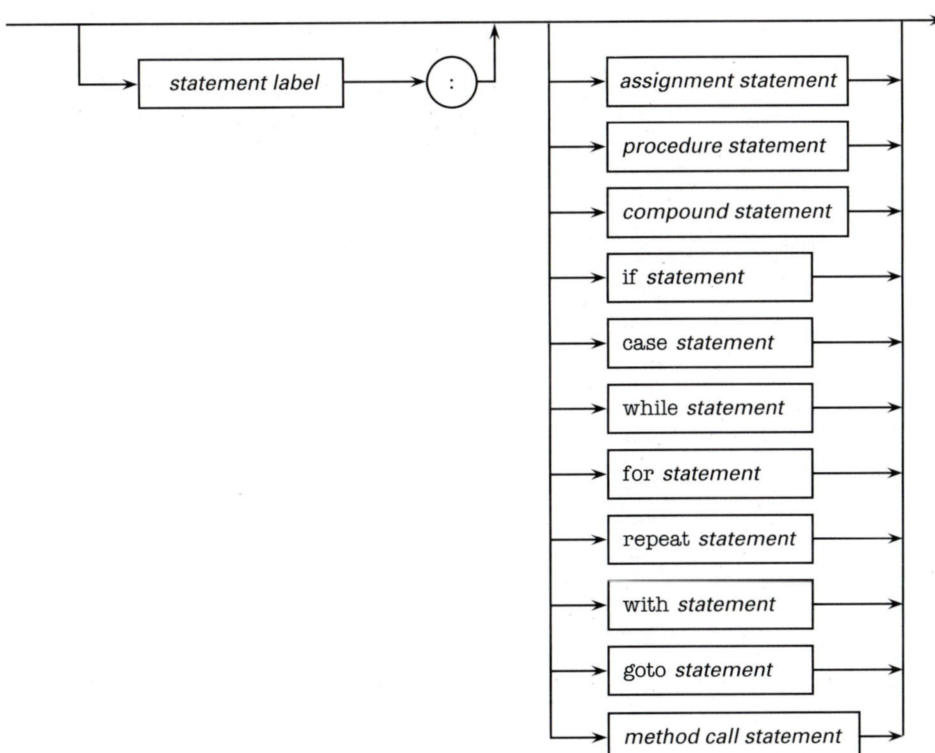

assignment statement

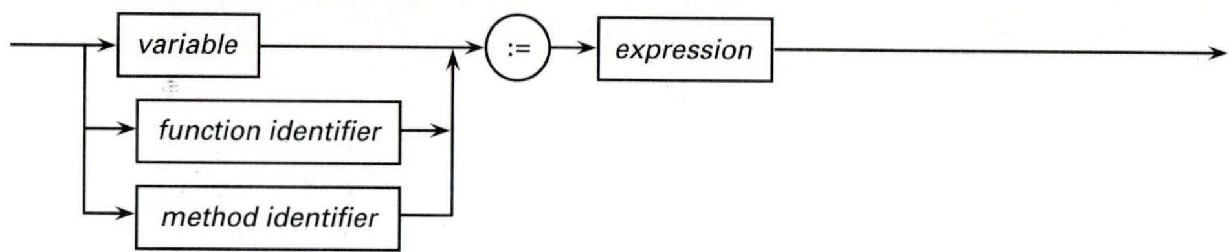

procedure call statement

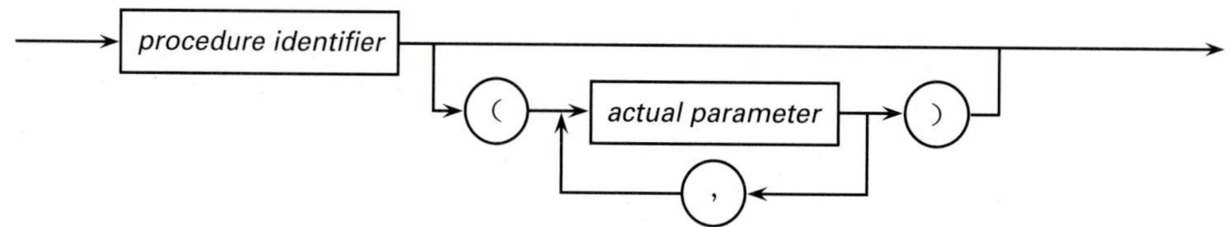

if statement

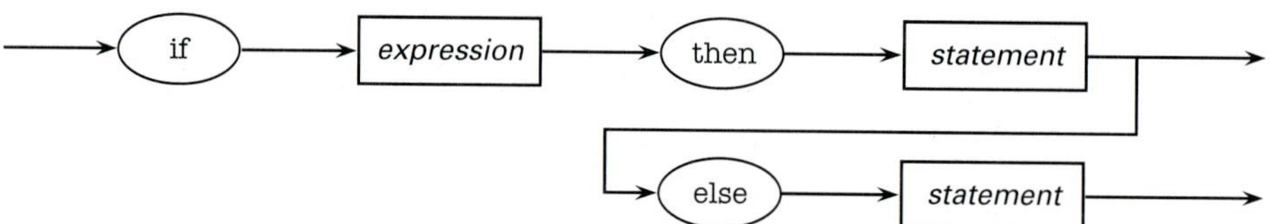

while statement

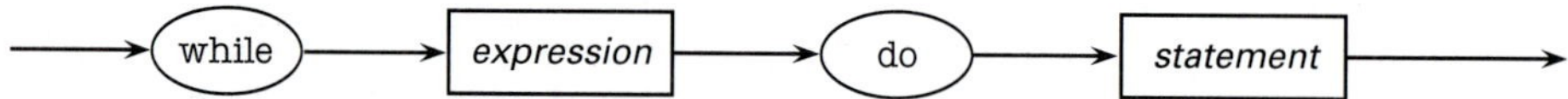

for statement

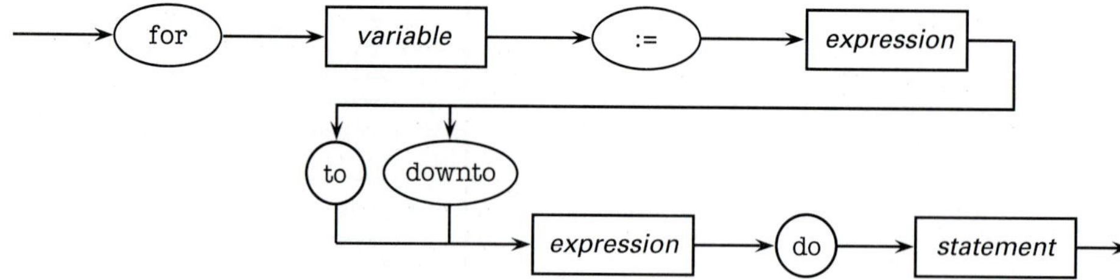

case statement

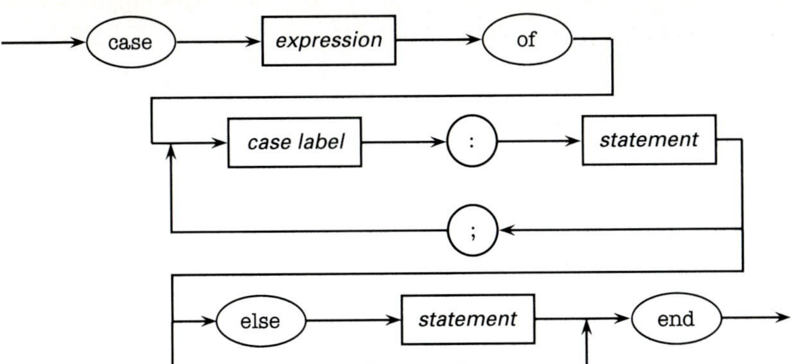

case label

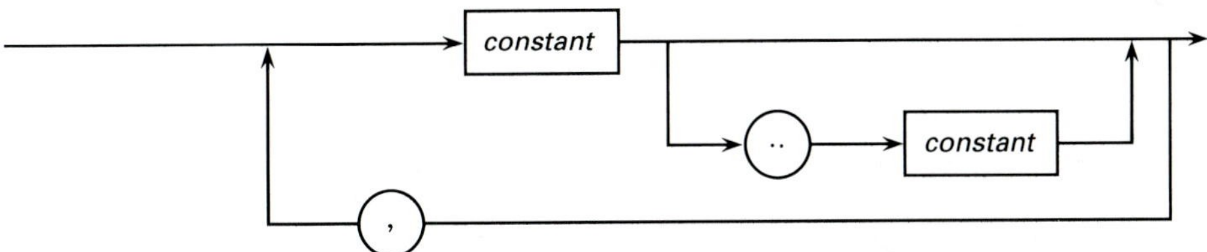

repeat statement

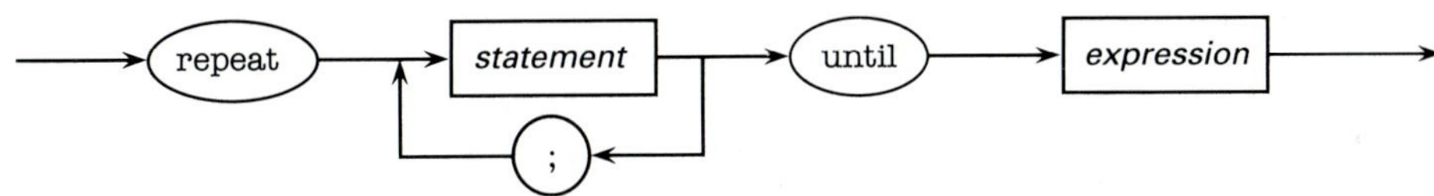

with statement

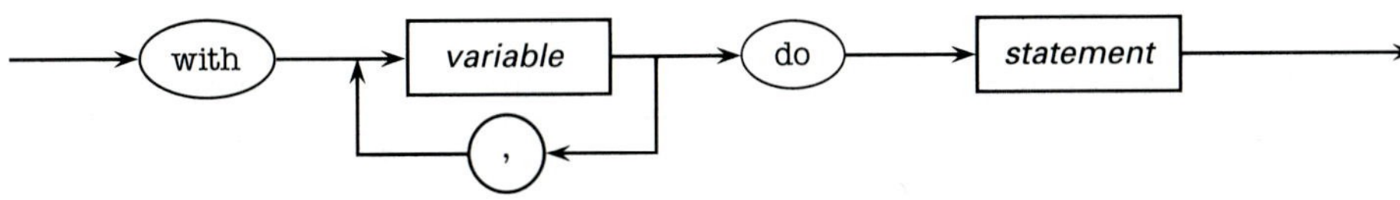

goto statement

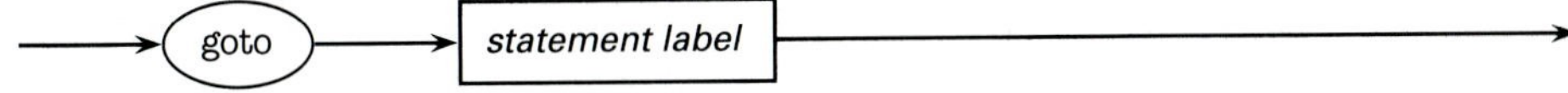

actual parameter

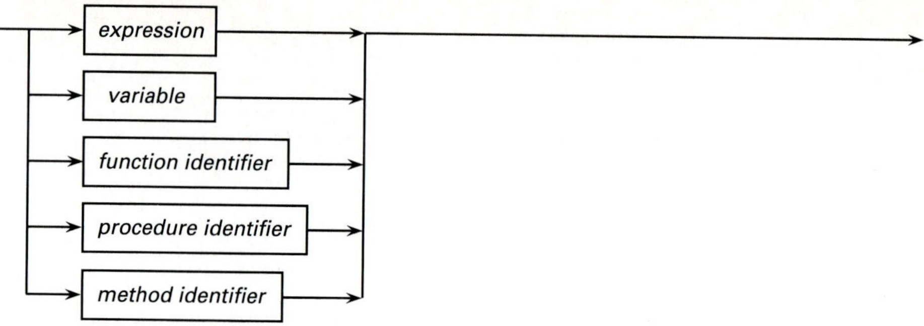

expression

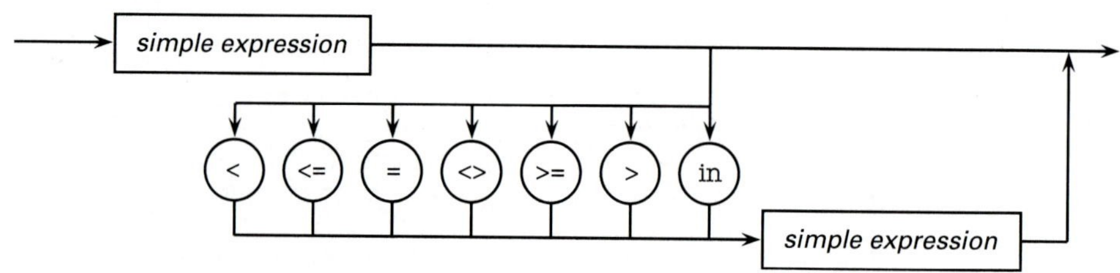

simple expression

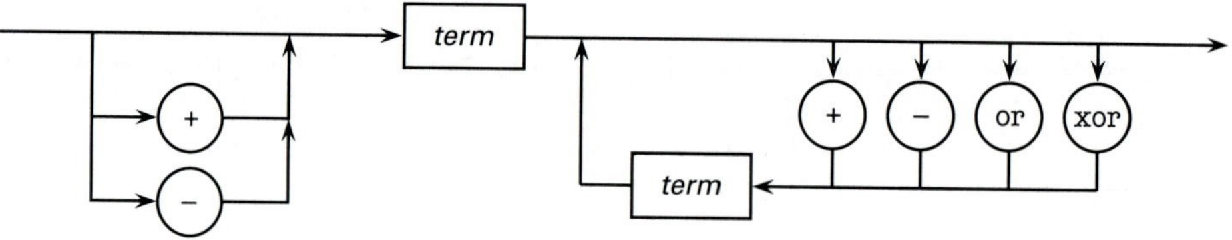

term

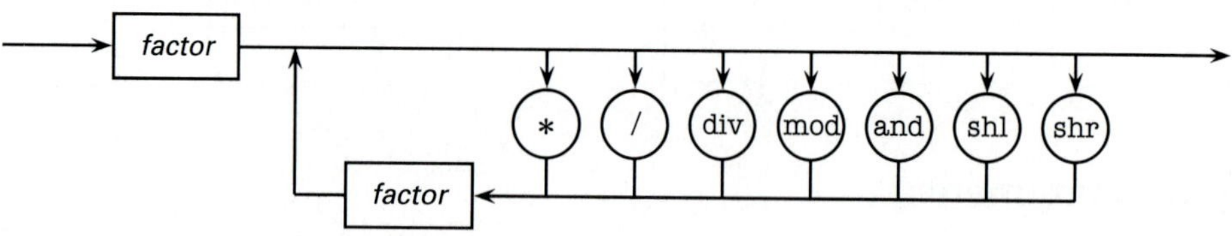

factor

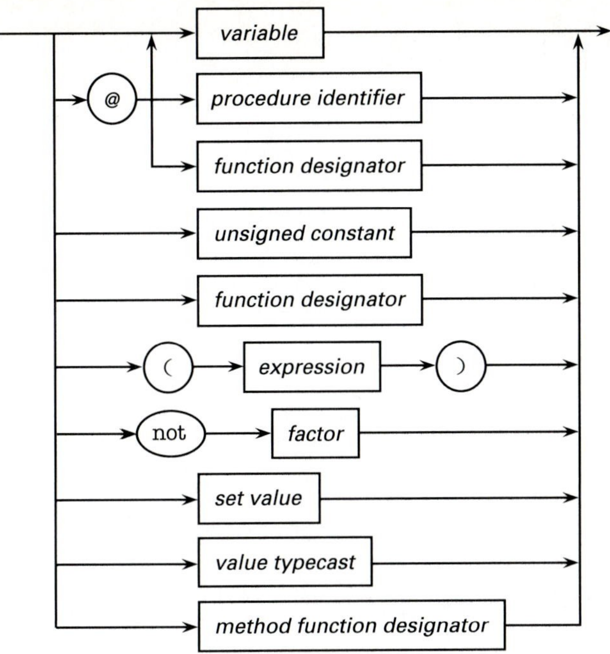

function designator

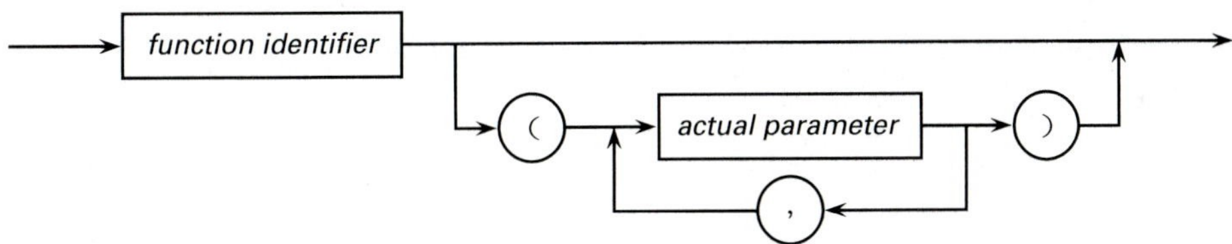

set value

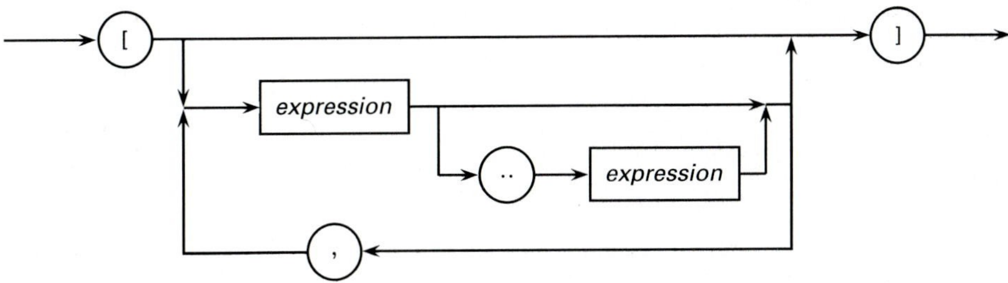

value typecast

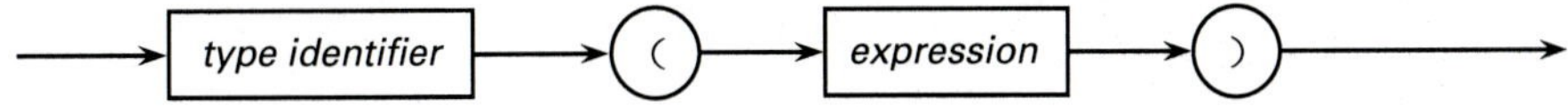

variable

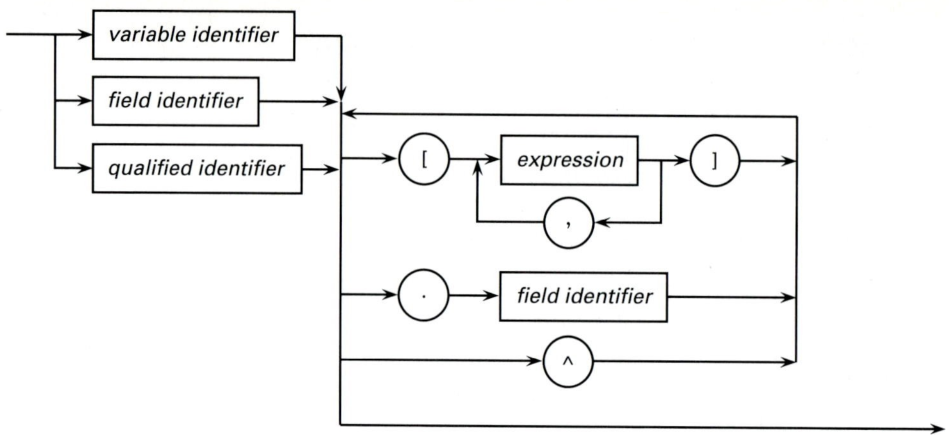

qualified identifier

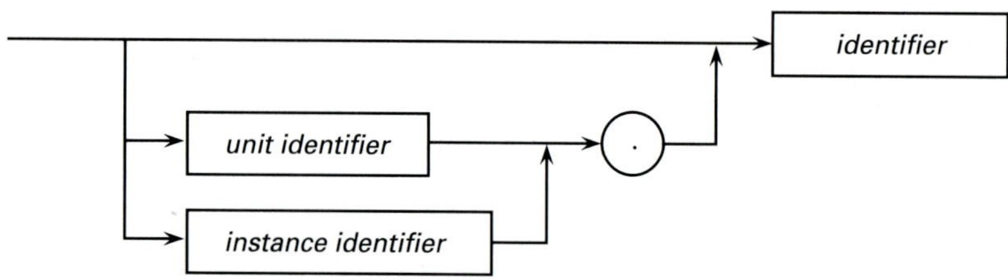

unsigned number

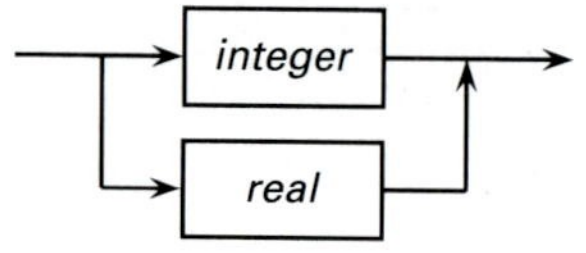

signed number

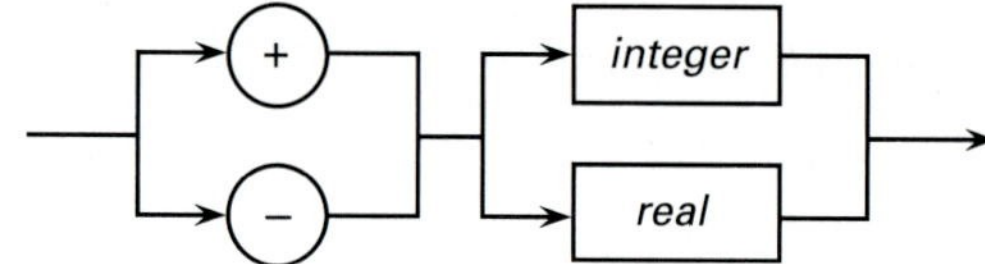

integer

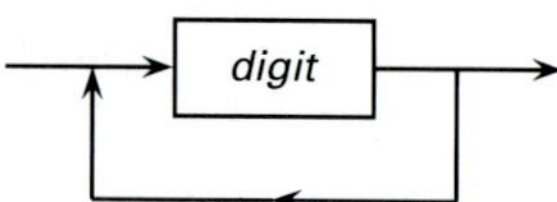

real

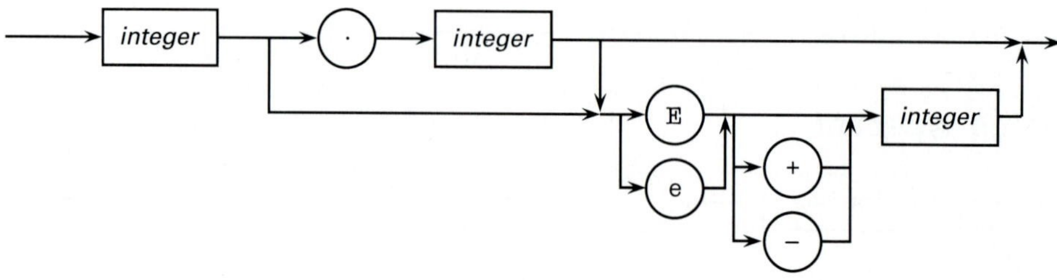

object type

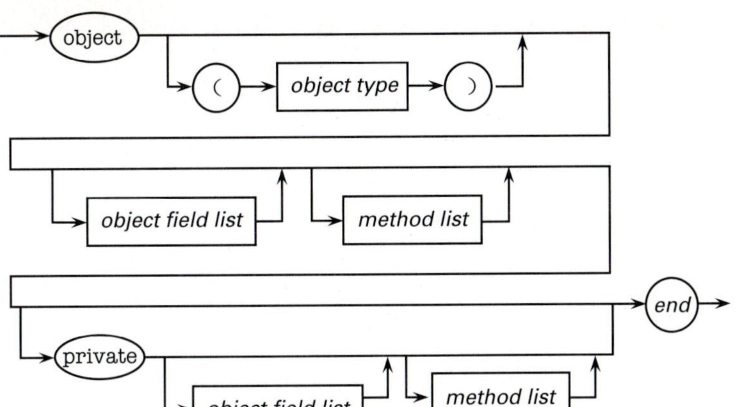

object field list

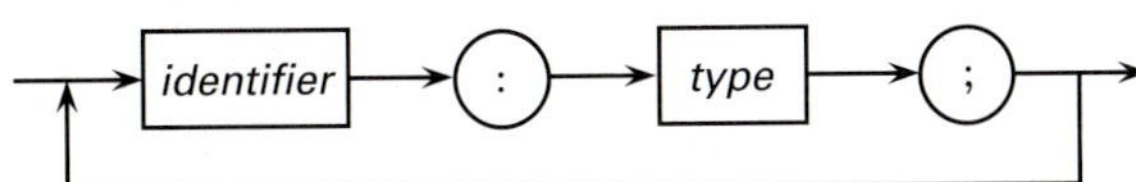

method list

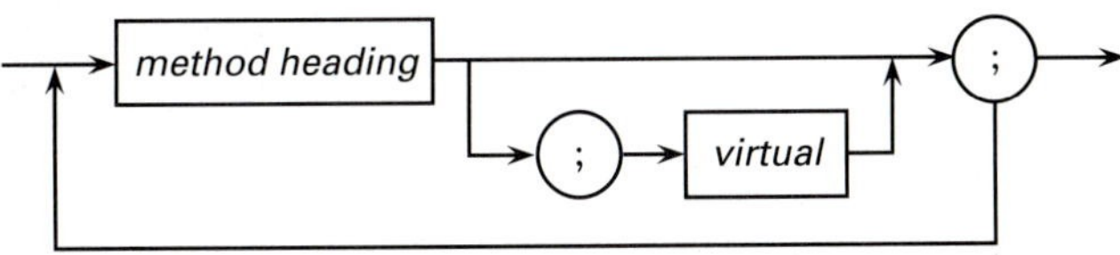

method heading

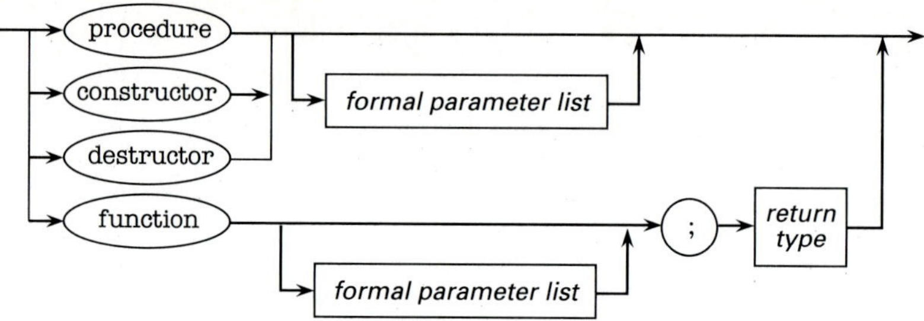

method declaration

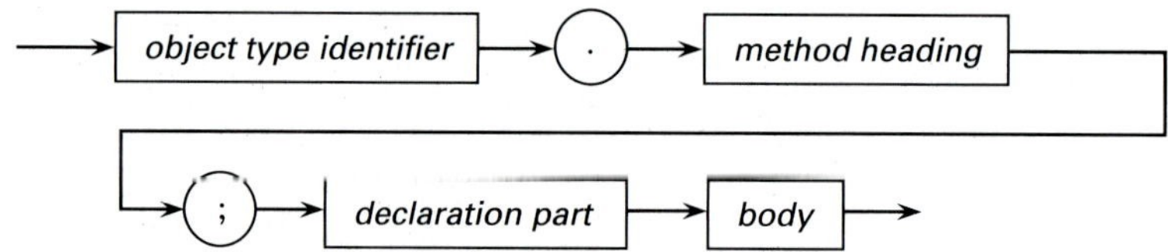

method call statement

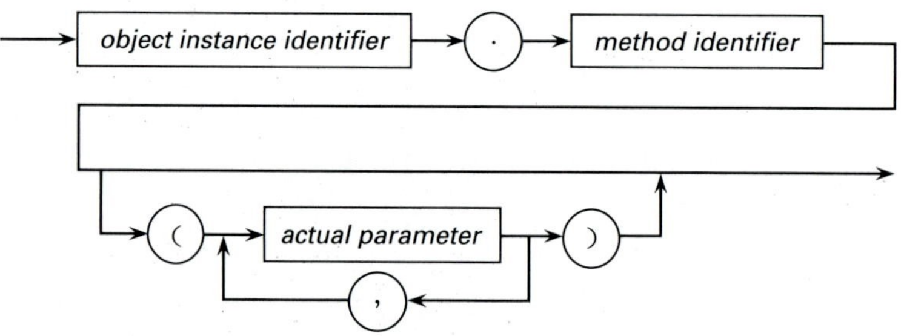

method function designator

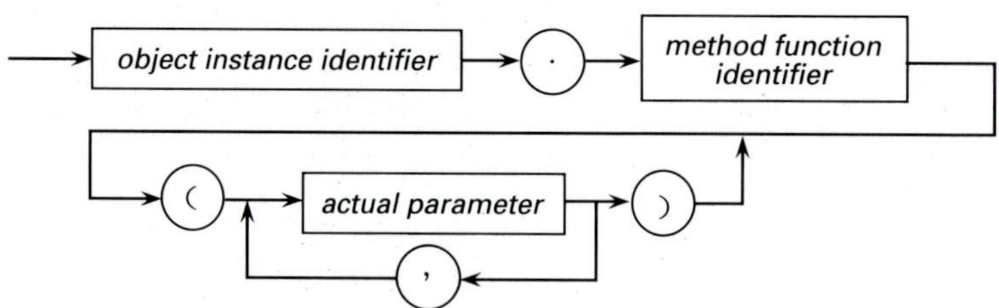

Appendix E
ASCII Character Set

Table E.1 contains the character codes from 0 to 127 for Turbo Pascal. On most computer systems, only the codes from 32 (blank or space) to 126 (symbol ~) have printable characters. The other codes represent the non-printable control characters. The IBM PC implementation of Turbo Pascal provides printable symbols for the non-printable codes as well.

Table E.1 Table of ASCII Characters

Code	Char	Code	Char	Code	Char	Code	Char
0	^@ NUL	32	□	64	@	96	'
1	^A SOH	33	!	65	A	97	a
2	^B STX	34	"	66	B	98	b
3	^C ETX	35	#	67	C	99	c
4	^D EOT	36	$	68	D	100	d
5	^E ENQ	37	%	69	E	101	e
6	^F ACK	38	&	70	F	102	f
7	^G BEL	39	'	71	G	103	g
8	^H BS	40	(	72	H	104	h
9	^I HT	41	)	73	I	105	i
10	^J LF	42	*	74	J	106	j
11	^K VT	43	+	75	K	107	k
12	^L FF	44	,	76	L	108	l
13	^M CR	45	–	77	M	109	m
14	^N SO	46	.	78	N	110	n
15	^O SI	47	/	79	O	111	o
16	^P DLE	48	0	80	P	112	p
17	^Q DC1	49	1	81	Q	113	q
18	^R DC2	50	2	82	R	114	r
19	^S DC3	51	3	83	S	115	s
20	^T DC4	52	4	84	T	116	t
21	^U NAK	53	5	85	U	117	u
22	^V SYN	54	6	86	V	118	v
23	^W ETB	55	7	87	W	119	w
24	^X CAN	56	8	88	X	120	x
25	^Y EM	57	9	89	Y	121	y
26	^Z SUB	58	:	90	Z	122	z
27	^[ESC	59	;	91	[	123	{
28	^\ FS	60	<	92	\	124	|
29	^] GS	61	=	93	]	125	}
30	^^ RS	62	>	94	^	126	~
31	^_ US	63	?	95	_	127	DEL

Appendix F
Error Messages and Codes

Compiler Error Messages

1 Out of memory.
2 Identifier expected.
3 Unknown identifier.
4 Duplicate identifier.
5 Syntax error.
6 Error in real constant.
7 Error in integer constant.
8 String constant exceeds line.
9 Too many nested files.
10 Unexpected end of file.
11 Line too long.
12 Type identifier expected.
13 Too many open files.
14 Invalid file name.
15 File not found.
16 Disk full.
17 Invalid compiler directive.
18 Too many files.
19 Undefined type in pointer definition.
20 Variable identifier expected.
21 Error in type.
22 Structure too large.
23 Set base type out of range.
24 File components may not be files or objects.
25 Invalid string length.
26 Type mismatch.
27 Invalid subrange base type.
28 Lower bound greater than upper bound.
29 Ordinal type expected.
30 Integer constant expected.
31 Constant expected.
32 Integer or real constant expected.
33 Pointer type identifier expected.
34 Invalid function result type.
35 Label identifier expected.
36 BEGIN expected.
37 END expected.
38 Integer expression expected.
39 Ordinal expression expected.
40 Boolean expression expected.
41 Operand types do not match operator.
42 Error in expression.
43 Illegal assignment.
44 Field identifier expected.
45 Object file too large.
46 Undefined external.
47 Invalid object file record.
48 Code segment too large.
49 Data segment too large.
50 DO expected.
51 Invalid PUBLIC definition.
52 Invalid EXTRN definition.
53 Too many EXTRN definitions.
54 OF expected.
55 INTERFACE expected.
56 Invalid relocatable reference.
57 THEN expected.
58 TO or DOWNTO expected.
59 Undefined forward.
60 Too many procedures.
61 Invalid typecast.
62 Division by zero.
63 Invalid file type.
64 Cannot Read or Write variables of this type.
65 Pointer variable expected.
66 String variable expected.
67 String expression expected.
68 Circular unit reference.
69 Unit name mismatch.
70 Unit version mismatch.
71 Duplicate unit name.
72 Unit file format error.
73 Implementation expected.
74 Constant and case types do not match.
75 Record variable expected.
76 Constant out of range.
77 File variable expected.
78 Pointer expression expected.
79 Integer or real expression expected.
80 Label not within current block.

Portions of Appendix F are reprinted by permission. © Borland International, Inc.

81 Label already defined.
82 Undefined label in preceding statement part.
83 Invalid @ argument.
84 UNIT expected.
85 ";" expected.
86 ":" expected.
87 "," expected.
88 "(" expected.
89 ")" expected.
90 "= " expected.
91 ":=" expected.
92 "[" or "(." expected.
93 "]" or ".)" expected.
94 "." expected.
95 ".." expected.
96 Too many variables.
97 Invalid FOR control variable.
98 Integer variable expected.
99 File and procedure types not allowed here.
100 String length mismatch.
101 Invalid ordering of fields.
102 String constant expected.
103 Integer or real variable expected.
104 Ordinal variable expected.
105 INLINE error.
106 Character expression expected.
107 Too many relocation items.
112 CASE constant out of range.
113 Error in statement.
114 Cannot call an interrupt procedure.
116 Must be in 8087 mode to compile this.
117 Target address not found.
118 Include files are not allowed here.
120 NIL expected.
121 Invalid qualifier.
122 Invalid variable reference.
123 Too many symbols.
124 Statement part too large.
126 Files must be var parameters
127 Too many conditional symbols
128 Misplaced conditional directive
129 ENDIF directive missing
130 Error in initial conditional defines
131 Header does not match previous definition
132 Critical disk error
133 Cannot evaluate this expression.
134 Expression incorrectly terminated
135 Invalid format specifier
136 Invalid indirect reference
137 Structured variables are not allowed here
138 Cannot evaluate without System unit
139 Cannot access this symbol
140 Invalid floating-point operation
141 Cannot compile overlays to memory
142 Procedure or function variable expected
143 Invalid procedure or function reference
144 Cannot overlay this unit
146 File access denied.
147 Object type expected.
148 Local object types are not allowed.
149 VIRTUAL expected.
150 Method identifier expected.
151 Virtual constructors are not allowed.
152 Constructor identifier expected.
153 Destructor identifier expected.
154 Fail only allowed within constructors.
155 Invalid combination of opcode and operands.
156 Memory reference expected.
157 Cannot add or subtract relocatable symbols.
158 Invalid register combination.
159 286/287 instructions are not enabled.
160 Invalid symbol reference.
161 Code generation error.
162 ASM expected.

Run-time Error Messages

1 Invalid function number
2 File not found.
3 Path not found.
4 Too many open files.
5 File access denied.
6 Invalid file handle.
12 Invalid file access code.
15 Invalid drive number.
16 Cannot remove current directory.
17 Cannot rename across drives.
100 Disk read error.
101 Disk write error.
102 File not assigned.
103 File not open.
104 File not open for input.
105 File not open for output.
106 Invalid numeric format.
150 Disk is write-protected.
151 Unknown unit.
152 Drive not ready.
153 Unknown command.

154 CRC error in data.
155 Bad drive request structure length.
156 Disk seek error.
157 Unknown media type.
158 Sector not found.
159 Printer out of paper.
160 Device write fault.
161 Device read fault.
162 Hardware failure.
200 Division by zero.
201 Range check error.
202 Stack overflow error.
203 Heap overflow error.
204 Invalid pointer operation.
205 Floating point overflow.
206 Floating point underflow.
207 Invalid floating point operation
208 Overlay manager not installed
209 Overlay file read error
210 Object not initialized.
211 Call to abstract method.
212 Stream registration error.
213 Collection index out of range.
214 Collection overflow error.

Appendix G
Differences Between Turbo Pascal and Standard Pascal

Assign Procedure

Standard Pascal does not require pre-initialization of file variables prior to using the procedures `Reset` and `Rewrite`. Turbo Pascal requires a file variable to be associated with an external file using the `Assign` procedure, prior to calling `Reset` or `Rewrite`.

case Statement

In standard Pascal, an error results when the `case` selector value does not match one of the `case` labels. In Turbo Pascal, an `else` clause may be present. If present, it is executed; otherwise, the next statement following the `case` statement is executed. Turbo Pascal allows constant ranges in `case` label lists (for example, `'A'..'E'`); standard Pascal does not.

Comments

In standard Pascal, a comment can begin with `{` and end with `*)`. In Turbo Pascal, comments must begin and end with a matching pair of symbols. Also, comments may be nested in Turbo Pascal, but not in standard Pascal.

Compiler Directives

A comment beginning with a `$` is recognized as a compiler directive by Turbo Pascal, but not by standard Pascal.

Constant Expressions

Turbo Pascal allows the use of expressions in constant declarations, standard Pascal does not. Constant expressions may not contain references to variables, typed constants, user-defined functions, or the address operator (@). Some standard functions (eg. `Abs`, `Chr`, `Length`, `Odd`, `Ord`, `Pred`, `Round`, `SizeOf`, `Succ`, `Trunc`) are allowed.

Data Types

Turbo Pascal implements several data types not found in standard Pascal: `ShortInt`, `LongInt`, `Byte`, `Word`, `Single`, `Double`, `Extended`, `Comp`, and `string`.

Declarations

Turbo Pascal allows label, constant, type, variable, procedure, and function declarations to occur any number of times and in any order within a block. Standard Pascal requires constant declarations to precede the type declarations within a block, type declarations to precede variable declarations, and variable declarations to precede the procedure and function declarations.

EOLN and EOF

In standard Pascal, it is an error to call `EOLN(Fil)` when `EOF(Fil)` is `True`. In Turbo Pascal, this is not an error, and `EOLN(Fil)` is `True` when `EOF(Fil)` is `True`.

for Loop Variables

In standard Pascal, statements that redefine the value of the `for` loop counter variable are not allowed. In Turbo Pascal, the counter variable may be changed within its loop, but doing so may cause an infinite loop.

Function Return Values

In standard Pascal, it is an error if there is not at least one assignment to the function identifier in the body of the function. Turbo Pascal does not detect this error.

Get and Put

The standard procedures `Get` and `Put` are not implemented in Turbo Pascal. Instead `Read` and `Write` have been extended to handle all I/O needs. Turbo Pascal does not associate a file buffer variable with a file variable, as standard Pascal does. Hence, in Turbo Pascal it is an error to write ^ after the file variable identifier.

goto Statement and Labels

Standard Pascal allows a `goto` to transfer to a label outside the block in which the `goto` statement appears. Turbo Pascal requires the use of the `Exit` procedure to transfer out of a block. Turbo Pascal allows labels to be either integers in the range 0 to 9999 or any valid identifier. Standard Pascal only allows the use of positive integers as labels.

Identifiers

In standard Pascal, identifiers can be any length and all characters are significant. In Turbo Pascal, identifiers can be of any length, but only the first 63 characters are significant. Turbo Pascal allows identifiers to contain underscore characters (_) after the first character, standard Pascal does not.

InLine Assembler

Turbo Pascal (version 6.0) allows assembly language instructions to be included in Pascal source files, standard Pascal does not.

New and Dispose Extended Syntax

In Turbo Pascal (versions 5.5 and later) the syntax of procedures `New` and `Dispose` has been modified to allow them to contain an optional second parameter (an object constructor or destructor call); this is not allowed in standard Pascal. Turbo Pascal, but not standard Pascal, allows `New` to be called as a function.

Objects

Turbo Pascal (versions 5.5 and later) allow the declaration and use of object types, standard Pascal does not.

Operators

Turbo Pascal provides support for several operators not found in standard Pascal (`xor`, `shl`, `shr`, `@`). Turbo Pascal allows its logical operators (`and`, `not`, `or`, `xor`) to be used with integers; standard Pascal does not. Turbo Pascal allows the use of + to concatenate strings; standard Pascal does not. In standard Pascal, the expression `i mod j` generates a run-time error if `j` is negative; in Turbo Pascal, this expression is always evaluated as `i - (i div j) *j`.

Packed Variables

Standard Pascal provides `Pack` and `Unpack` procedures for transferring data between a packed data structure and an equivalent structure that is not packed; Turbo Pascal does not. The reserved word `packed` has no effect in Turbo Pascal, but its use is allowed. In Turbo Pascal, packing occurs automatically whenever possible.

Page Procedure

Standard Pascal provides the `Page` procedure to initiate a new page of output. `Page` is not implemented in Turbo Pascal.

Pointer Variables

In standard Pascal, the @ symbol is an alternative for the ^ symbol. In Turbo Pascal, this is not true since the symbol @ has been defined as an operator. In standard Pascal, if `P` is a pointer variable, it is an error to reference `P^` if `P` is `nil` or undefined. Turbo Pascal does not detect either of these errors. In standard Pascal, it is an error to alter the value of `P` while a reference to `P^` exits; Turbo Pascal does not detect this error.

Procedures and Functions as Parameters

Standard Pascal permits a procedure or function name to be passed as a parameter. This is not allowed in Turbo Pascal prior to version 5.0.

Procedures and Functions as Data Types

Turbo Pascal, but not standard Pascal, allows the definition of procedure and function data types. Turbo Pascal allows both the declaration of variables using these types and the assignment of values to variables of these types during program execution. This is discussed in greater detail in Appendix H.

Program Parameters

Standard Pascal requires the identification of all input/output files used in a program as parameters of the program statement. Turbo Pascal does not require this.

Random Access Files

Turbo Pascal provides the `Seek` procedure, which enables random access to files. Random access files are not supported in standard Pascal.

Reading Text Files

In standard Pascal, reading data from a text file to a `Char` type variable when `EOLN` is `True` prior to calling `Read` causes a blank to be assigned to the variable. In Turbo Pascal, the carriage return character (ASCII 13) is assigned to the `Char` variable. In standard Pascal, reading data from a `Text` file into an `Integer` or `Real` variable stops when the next character to be read from the file is not part of a signed number. In Turbo Pascal, reading ceases only when the next character in the file is a blank or control character.

String Variables and Operators

Turbo Pascal supports the data type string along with a number of built-in procedures and functions for manipulating strings. No such facility is provided in standard Pascal. Instead, most string manipulation is performed through the use of packed arrays of characters.

Typecast

Turbo Pascal allows the type of a variable or expression to be changed from one type to another using a typecast. Standard Pascal provides no such facility.

Typed Constants

Turbo Pascal implements typed constants, which can be used to declare initialized variables of all types except file types. Typed constants are not part of standard Pascal.

Typeless Parameters

Turbo Pascal allows variable parameters to be untyped (typeless), in which case any variable reference can be used as an actual parameter when calling the procedure. Standard Pascal does not allow this.

Units

Turbo Pascal implements units to facilitate modular programming and separate compilation. Standard Pascal provides no such facility.

Appendix H Additional Features of Turbo Pascal

This appendix discusses features of Turbo Pascal that are not covered in the text. With the exception of the goto statement and procedure or function parameters, these features are not part of standard Pascal.

goto Statement and Labels

The goto statement transfers control from one program statement to another. The label indicates the statement to which control is transferred. In Turbo Pascal, a label may be either an integer in the range from 0 to 9999 or any valid identifier. In standard Pascal, only positive integers may be used as labels. Labels must be declared in a label declaration statement at the beginning of the block in which they are used. The goto statement may not be used to jump into, or out of, a procedure or function. In the function SameArray shown in Fig. H.1, the goto statement is used to exit a for loop before the maximum number of repetitions (N) are performed.

The function result is initialized to False and corresponding array elements are compared in the for loop. If an unequal pair of elements is found, the loop is exited via an immediate transfer of control to label 100. If all pairs are equal, the loop is exited after the Nth pair is tested and the function result is set to True. This function can easily be implemented without using the goto. Computer scientists generally avoid using the goto except when absolutely necessary.

Figure H.1 Function SameArray

```
function SameArray (A, B : RealArray; N : Integer) : Boolean;
{Returns True if arrays A[1..N] and B[1..N] are the same.}

  label 100;

  var I  : Integer;         {loop-control variable}
begin {SameArray}
  SameArray := False;       {assume arrays are not the same}

  {Compare elements 1..N until an unequal pair is found.}
  for I := 1 to N do
     if A[I] <> B[I] then
        goto 100;
```

```
   SameArray := True;        {assert arrays A and B are equal}
100: {return from function}
end; {SameArray}
```

Exit and Halt Procedures

The `Exit` procedure may be used to transfer out of a block and is analogous to a `goto` statement that transfers control to a label just before the block `end`. If the `Exit` procedure is called from within a procedure or function, control is returned to the calling block. If the `Exit` procedure is called directly from the main program block, program execution is terminated. Program execution terminates immediately when the `Halt` procedure is called regardless of which program block is executing.

Control Characters

Turbo Pascal allows control characters to be imbedded in strings. A control character may be designated in two ways:

- By using a pair of symbols, the first of which is the symbol `^`.
- By using the symbol # followed by the ASCII code for the character.

For example, the symbols `^G` or #7 can represent the character BEL (the terminal bell or Control-G).

The statement

```
WriteLn (' Wake up! '^G^G^G#13#10' Enter data>');
```

causes the message `' Wake up! '` to be displayed on the current output line. The symbols `^G^G^G#13#10` (BEL, BEL, BEL, carriage return, line feed) cause the bell to be "rung" three times and a new output line to be started. The message `' Enter data>'` is displayed on the new output line. Note that there are no extra spaces between the two messages and the sequence of control characters.

Another useful control character is `^L`, the form feed character. If you are using the printer as an output device and have included the `Printer` unit in your program, the statement

```
Write (Lst, ^L);
```

sends the form feed character to the printer. This causes the printer to advance to the top of a new page of paper.

Hexadecimal Constants

Turbo Pascal allows integer-type constants to be represented using a sequence of hexadecimal characters having the dollar sign ($) as a prefix. Such constants must be in the range `$00000000` to `$FFFFFFFF`. The resulting value's sign is implied by the hexadecimal characters used to represent the number.

Typed Constants

Typed constants are like variables that have initial values. A typed constant may be used to initialize a simple variable or a structured variable. The statements

```
const
  Interest    : Real = 12.67;
  NumAccounts : Integer = 0;
```

declare two typed constants as shown below.

Interest	NumAccounts
12.67	0

The value of a typed constant may be changed just like any variable. Consequently, the assignment statement

```
NumAccounts := NumAccounts + 1;
```

is valid. Typed constants may correspond to variable parameters when calling procedures or functions. Typed constants may not be used in the declaration of other constants or types. Typed constants are only initialized the first time a block is executed. Locally declared typed constants are not reinitialized on subsequent uses of a procedure or function.

Typed constants may be used to declare data structures with initial values. The declarations

```
type
  Color = (Blue, Red, Green, Black);
  Colors = array [Color] of string[5];
  Counts = array [Color] of Integer;

const
  ColorName : Colors = ('Blue', 'Red', 'Green', 'Black');
  ColorCount : Counts = (0, 0, 0, 0);
```

initialize the arrays ColorName and ColorCount as shown below.

array ColorName

[Blue]	[Red]	[Green]	[Black]
'Blue'	'Red'	'Green'	'Black'

array ColorCount

[Blue]	[Red]	[Green]	[Black]
0	0	0	0

Each element of array ColorName contains a string that corresponds to its subscript; each element of array ColorCount is initialized to zero. Note that the typed constant declaration follows the type declaration.

The declarations

```
type
  Season = (Summer, Fall, Winter, Spring);
  Book = record
           Author : string[10];
           Pages : Integer;
           Price : Real;
           Sales : array [Season] of Real
         end;
```

```
const
  MyBook : Book = (Author : 'Ludlum';
                   Pages : 355;
                   Price : 14.95;
                   Sales : (14950.0, 0.0, 0.0, 0.0));
```

initialize each field of the record variable `MyBook` as indicated above (for example, `MyBook.Author` is `'Ludlum'`, `MyBook.Pages` is 355, `MyBook.Sales[Summer]` is `14950.0`). As shown in this example, the field names in the typed constant must appear in the same order as in the type declaration.

As shown below, Turbo Pascal also allows the definition of set-type constants and pointer-type constants. Pointer-type constants may only be given the initial value of `nil`.

```
type
  Digits = set of 0..9;
  Ptr = ^Node;
  Node = record
           Name : string[10];
           Next : Ptr
         end;

const
  EvenDigits : Digits = [0, 2, 4, 6, 8];
  Vowels : set of 'a'..'z' = ['a', 'e', 'i', 'o', 'u'];
  List : Ptr = nil;
  NameRec : Node = (Name : ''
                    Next : nil);
```

Handling Input/Output Errors

Normally, program execution terminates when an input/output (I/O) error occurs. It is possible to change this using a compiler directive. If so, you must make provision for your program to handle the I/O error.

The program segment in Fig. H.2 begins with the compiler directive `{$I-}`, which disables I/O error checking. If an I/O error occurs and I/O error checking is off, all subsequent I/O operations are ignored until a call is made to `IOResult`. If an I/O error occurs, the assignment statement

```
ErrorNum := IOResult;
```

stores its error number (see Run-time Errors in Appendix E) in `ErrorNum` (type `Integer`). The standard function `IOResult` returns either the number of the I/O error or zero if there was no I/O error. In either case, the function value is updated after each call.

Calling the `Reset` procedure can cause an I/O error. If an I/O error was detected, the `if` statement in Fig. H.2 displays an error message and the loop body is repeated. When the loop is exited, the `I` compiler directive is reset to its default state (value +) and I/O checking is enabled.

Figure H.2 Handling I/O Errors

```
{$I-}
repeat
  Write ('Enter input file name>');
  ReadLn (InName);
  Assign (InFile, InName);
```

```
  Reset (InFile);
  ErrorNum := IOResult;          {save error number}
  if ErrorNum = 2 then
    WriteLn ('File ', InName, ' does not exist-try again.')
  else if ErrorNum <> 0 then
    WriteLn ('I/O error number ', ErrorNum)
until ErrorNum = 0;
{$I+}
```

Procedure and Function Types

In the programs we have discussed in this text, functions and procedures have been used as a means of encapsulating portions of algorithms for the purposes of procedural abstraction. Turbo Pascal, but not standard Pascal, also allows us to regard functions and procedures as objects of a particular data type and to manipulate them like other objects.

The syntax for a procedure or function type definition is similar to that for a procedure or function heading, with the exception that the identifier following the reserved words procedure or function is omitted. Several procedure and function type definitions appear below.

```
type
  Proc      = procedure;
  RealSwap  = procedure (var X, Y : Real);
  VisitType = procedure (Element  : string);
  Rand      = function : Real;
  Open      = function (var FileName : Text) : Boolean;
  MonteFunc = function (X, Y : integer; Z : Real) : Char;
```

These type definitions may be used to declare variables of these types. Function types may not have either function or procedures as their result types.

The declarations below

```
var
  Operation : VisitType;
  IOTest    : Open;
```

declare a procedure identifier `Operation` and a function identifier `IOTest`. The Turbo Pascal assignment operator may assign a value to a procedure or function variable. Assuming that procedures `Proc1` and `Proc2` are previously defined procedures, having a single argument of type `string`, the `if` statement

```
if Choice = 1 then
  Operation := Proc1
else
  Operation := Proc2;
```

assigns either `Proc1` or `Proc2` as the value of procedure variable `Operation`. The procedure call statement

```
Operation (OneString);
```

calls the procedure assigned to `Operation` using actual parameter `OneString` (type `string`). Similarly, assuming that `Exist` is a previously defined `Boolean` function, having a single `var` parameter of type `Text`, the assignment statement

```
IOTest := Exist;
```

makes the the function designators `IOTest(InData)` and `Exist(InData)` equivalent to one another.

In addition to being type compatible, a procedure or function must satisfy three additional requirements prior to being assigned as the value of a procedure or function variable.

- It must be compiled with the `F` compiler option enabled, `{$F+}`.
- It may not be a built-in procedure or function (that is, `WriteLn` or `Chr`).
- It may not be a nested procedure or function.

Procedures and Functions as Parameters

The use of procedure and function types also allows us to pass procedures and functions as parameters to other Pascal procedures and functions. For procedure `Traverse` having the heading

```
procedure Traverse (List {input} : ListPointer;
                    Visit {procedure} : VisitType);
```

parameter `Visit` is declared to be a procedure of type `VisitType`. Therefore, whenever procedure `Traverse` is called, it must be passed a procedure of type `VisitType`. This facility enables a different operation to be performed each time `Traverse` is called; the operation is determined by the procedure that is passed to `Traverse`.

The procedure or function passed as a parameter must conform to the same compatibility rules used for assignment to procedure and function variables. They must have been compiled using `{$F+}`, they may not be built-in procedures or functions, and they may not be nested.

Procedure and function parameters are useful in situations where the same operations need to be carried out for a set of procedures or functions. They also provide a convenient way to pass different error-handling routines to procedures or functions.

Answers to Selected Self-Check Exercises

Chapter 1

Section 1.2

1. Contents: `-27.2`, `75.62`.
   Memory cells: `998`, `2`.

Section 1.4

1. Add `A`, `B`, and `C`. Store the result in `X`.
   Divide `Y` by `Z`. Store the result in `X`.
   Subtract `B` from `C` and then add `A`. Store the result in `D`.
3. Assembly language; machine language

Section 1.5

1. A compiler attempts to translate a source file into machine language. If there are syntax errors, the compiler generates error messages. If there are no errors, it creates an object file. Syntax errors occur when statements do not follow exactly the syntax rules of the language. They are found in the source file.

Chapter 2

Section 2.1

1. It is not a good idea to use a standard identifier as the name of a memory cell because the identifier then cannot be used for its intended purpose.
   The compiler does not allow the use of reserved words as memory cell names.

Section 2.2

1. Because `MyPi` never changes, it should be stored as a constant.
3. Reserved words : `end`, `program`, `begin`, `const`
   Standard identifiers: `ReadLn`
   Identifiers: `Bill`, `Rate`, `Operate`, `Start`, `XYZ123`, `ThisIsALongOne`
   Invalid identifiers: `Sue's`, `123XYZ`, `X = Z`

Section 2.3

1. `0.0103`   `1234500.0`   `123450.0`
3. Enter two integers:
```
M = 10
N = 21
```

Section 2.4

1.

Identifier	Before Execution	After Execution
`CentPerInch`	2.54	2.54
`Inches`	?	30.00
`Cent`	?	76.20

Section 2.5

1. `WriteLn` statements used to display prompts are placed before the `ReadLn` statements and are used in interactive programs. `WriteLn` statements that echo data are placed after the `ReadLn` statements and are used in batch programs.

Section 2.6

1. `WriteLn` causes the cursor to be advanced to the next line after the output is printed. If `Write` is used, the cursor remains positioned immediately after the last character printed. You would use `WriteLn` without an output list if you wanted to print a blank line or to advance the cursor to the start of the next line.

3.
```
-15.5640
  -15.564
   -15.56
    -15.6
      -16
-1.6E+01
```

Section 2.7

1. Insert `uses Printer;` after the program heading and `Lst`, before the output list in each call to `WriteLn`.

Section 2.8

1.
```
15    , Integer     'XYZ'  , string     '*'  , Char
$     , Invalid     25.123 , Real       15.  , Invalid
-999  , Integer     .123   , Invalid    'x'  , Char
"x"   , Invalid     '9'    , Char       '-5' , string
True  , Boolean     'True' , string
```

Chapter 3

Section 3.1

1. Algorithm
   1. Put the baby's milk in the bottle.
   2. Put the bottle in a pan of water and heat on stove.
   3. Test the milk to see if it is the right temperature.
   4. Remove bottle from stove when it is the correct temperature.

   Step 3 Refinement

   3.1. Repeat step 3.2 until the milk is the right temperature.

   3.2 If it is too cold, put it back on the stove for a few minutes; if it is too warm, take it off the stove to cool for a few minutes.

Section 3.2

1. Problem Input
    Hours worked (`Hours : Real`)
    Hourly rate (`Rate : Real`)
   Problem Outputs
    Gross salary (`Salary : Real`)

   Algorithm
   1. Enter hours worked and hourly rate.
   2. Compute gross salary (`Salary`).
   3. Print gross salary (`Salary`).

Section 3.3

1. The brackets are mismatched in the first example. The second example has an embedded comment using the same delimiters, which is not allowed in Turbo Pascal.

Section 3.4

1.

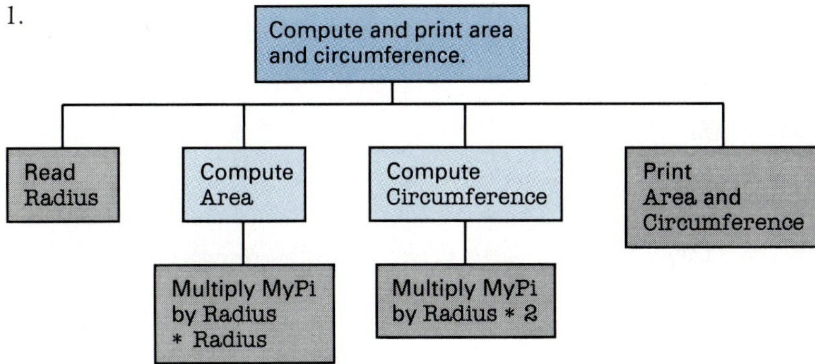

Section 3.5

1. Executing this program would display the message `OH HIM` vertically with three blank lines between words.

Chapter 4

Section 4.1

1. True, false, true, true

Section 4.2

1. a. `12.5`
   b. `30.0`

Section 4.3

1.

Case 1 (Both conditions are `True`. Data: `MUD`)

Program Statement	Ch1	Ch2	Ch3	AlphaFirst	Effect
	?	?	?	?	
`Write ('Enter three . . .')`					Prints prompt.
`ReadLn (Ch1, Ch2, Ch3)`	M	U	D		Reads data.
`if Ch1 < Ch2 then`					Is `'M' < 'U'`? Value is `True`.
`AlphaFirst := Ch1`				M	`'M'` is first so far.
`if Ch3 < AlphaFirst then`					Is `'D' < 'M'` ? Value is `True`.
`AlphaFirst := Ch3`				D	`'D'` is first.
`WriteLn (AlphaFirst . . .)`					Prints `D is the first letter . . .`.

Case 2 (First condition is `True`, second is `False`. Data: `COT`)

Program Statement	Ch1	Ch2	Ch3	AlphaFirst	Effect
	?	?	?	?	
`Write ('Enter three . . .')`					Prints prompt.
`ReadLn (Ch1, Ch2, Ch3)`	C	O	T		Reads data.
`if Ch1 < Ch2 then`					Is `'C' < 'O'`? Value is `True`.
`AlphaFirst := Ch1`				C	`'C'` is first so far.
`if Ch3 < AlphaFirst then`					Is `'T' < 'C'`? Value is `False`
`WriteLn (AlphaFirst . . .`					Prints `C is the first letter . . .`.

Case 3 (Both conditions are `False`. Data: `TOP`)

Program Statement	Ch1	Ch2	Ch3	AlphaFirst	Effect
	?	?	?	?	
`Write ('Enter three . . .')`					Prints prompt.
`ReadLn (Ch1, Ch2, Ch3)`	T	O	P		Reads data.
`if Ch1 < Ch2 then`					Is `'T' < 'O'`? Value is `False`.
`AlphaFirst := Ch2`				O	`'O'` is first so far.
`if Ch3 < AlphaFirst then`					Is `'P' < 'O'`? Value is `False`.
`WriteLn (AlphaFirst . . .`					Prints `O is the first letter . . .`.

Both conditions evaluate to `False` if all three letters are the same.

Section 4.4

1. Initial Algorithm
   1. Display user instructions.
   2. Enter hours worked and hourly rate.
   3. Compute gross salary (including overtime pay).
   4. Compute net salary.
   5. Print gross salary and net salary.

   Step 3 Refinement

   ```
   3.1 if Hours > MaxHours then
          begin
             3.2 Compute overtime pay
             3.3 Add overtime pay to base pay
          end
       else
          3.4 Compute gross salary
   ```

Section 4.5

1. `A23B`, `Alc`

Section 4.6

1.
```
if X > Y then
   begin
      X := X + 10.0;
      WriteLn ('X Bigger')
   end
else
     WriteLn ('X Smaller');
WriteLn ('Y is ', Y);
```
3. `Y` would be printed only when `X` is not greater than `Y`.
5. The `if` statement, expression, simple expression, term, factor, variable, statement and assignment statement syntax diagrams would be used to validate this `if` statement.

Section 4.7

1.

Statement Part	Salary	Tax	**Effect**
	13500.00	?	
`if Salary < 0.0`			`13500.00 < 0.00` is `False`.
`else if Salary < 1500.00`			`13500.00 < 1500.00` is `False`.
`else if Salary < 3000.00`			`13500.00 < 3000.00` is `False`.
`else if Salary < 5000.00`			`13500.00 < 5000.00` is `False`.
`else if Salary < 8000.00`			`13500.00 < 8000.00` is `False`.

Statement Part	Salary	Tax	Effect
`else if Salary <= 15000.00`			`13500.00 <= 15000.00` is `True`.
`Tax := (Salary - 8000.00)`			Evaluates to `5500.00`.
`* 0.25`			Evaluates to `1375.00`.
`+ 1425.00`		`2800.00`	Tax is `2800.00`.

Chapter 5

Section 5.1

1. The loop body will be repeated three times.
   Output: `9`
   `81`
   `6561`
3. The loop will execute forever (infinite loop) if the last statement in the loop body is omitted.

Section 5.2

1. The `WriteLn` prints a blank line between each employee's data.
3. `25`
   `125`
   `625`
   `3125`

Section 5.3

1. 0
3. Output with data value of `9.45`:

```
Enter initial distance between worm and apple: 9.45
The distance is 9.45
The distance is 4.72
The distance is 2.36
The distance is 1.18
The distance is 0.59

Final distance between the worm and apple is 0.30
The worm enters the apple.
```

Output with data value of `9.45` and order of statements in loop body reversed:

```
Enter initial distance between worm and apple: 9.45
The distance is 4.72
The distance is 2.36
The distance is 1.18
The distance is 0.59
The distance is 0.30

Final distance between the worm and apple is 0.30
The worm enters the apple.
```

Section 5.4

1. a. `CountEmp` must be `0` just before the loop is entered.
   b. `CountEmp` must be `1` more during pass `i` than it was during pass `i-1` (for `i > 1`).
   c. `CountEmp` must be `<= NumberEmp` just after loop exit.

Section 5.5

1.
```
{invariant:
    T during pass I is equal to DeltaT * (I-1) for I > 1) and
    Height is equal to Tower - 0.5 * G * T * T}
}
{assert:
    Height <= 0.0}
```

Section 5.6

1. The `else` condition will always be executed if the user enters something other than an `F` or a `V`. You can correct this problem by using a `while` loop that continually prompts the user for a letter until either an `F` or a `V` is entered.

Chapter 6

Section 6.1

1. Parameters make procedures versatile by enabling them to manipulate different data each time they are called.
3. Output: `5 cubed is 125`
   `M` would still have the value of `5` after procedure `Cube` executed. It should be declared as an integer in the calling program or procedure.

Section 6.2

1.

X	Y	Z
5	3	8
5	3	8
11	3	8
16	3	8
16	6	8

Section 6.3

1.

Actual Parameter	Formal Parameter	Description
M	A	Integer, value
MaxInt	B	Integer, value
Y	C	Real, variable
X	D	Real, variable
Next	E	Char, variable
35	A	Integer, value
M * 10	B	Integer, value

Actual Parameter	Formal Parameter	Description
Y	C	Real, variable
X	D	Real, variable
Next	E	Char, variable

3. a. Type Real of Z does not correspond to type Integer of formal parameter X.
   b. Procedure call is correct.
   c. Procedure call is correct.
   d. Type Integer of M does not correspond to type Real of formal parameter A.
   e. 25.0 and 15.0 cannot correspond to variable parameters.
   f. Procedure call is correct.
   g. Parameter names A and B have not been declared in the main program.
   h. Procedure call is correct.
   i. Expressions (X + Y) and (Y - Z) may not correspond to a variable parameter.
   j. Type Real of actual parameter X does not correspond with type Integer of formal parameter X.
   k. Four actual parameters are one too many for three formal parameters.
   l. Procedure call is correct.

Section 6.4

1. The if statement in FindTax is preferable because it allows FindTax to be highly cohesive. That is, FindTax performs only one function and passes on the result to the calling program that handles the error condition.

Section 6.5

1.

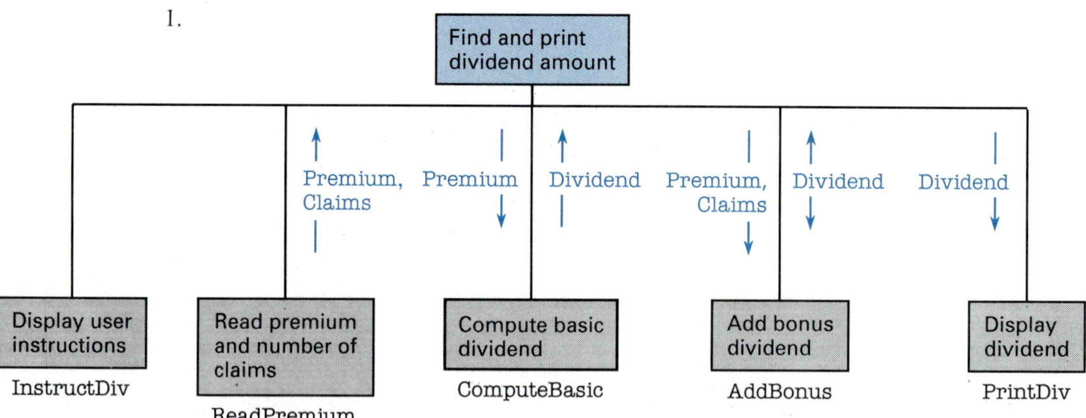


```
procedure ReadPremium (var Premium, Claims {output} : Real);

{Read number of premiums and Claims}

begin {ReadPremium}
  {Enter Premium and Claims}
  Write ('Premium amount > $');
```

```
    ReadLn (Premium);
    Write ('Number of claims> ');
    ReadLn (Claims)
  end; {ReadPremium}


  procedure ComputeBasic (Premium {input} : Real;
                          var Dividend {output} : Real);

  {Compute basic dividend}

  begin {ComputeBasic}
     Dividend := Premium * FixedRate
  end; {ComputeBasic}


  procedure AddBonus (Premium, Claims {input} : Real;
                      var Dividend {input/output} : Real);

  {Add bonus dividend for zero claims}

  begin {AddBonus}
    if Claims = 0.0 then
      Dividend := Dividend + (Premium * BonusRate)
  end; {AddBonus}


  procedure PrintDiv (Dividend {input} : Real);

  {Print dividend value}

  begin {PrintDiv}
    WriteLn ('Total dividend is $', Dividend :12:2)
  end; {PrintDiv}
```

3.
Case 1 (Num1 = 8.0, Num2 = 10.0, Num3 = 6.0).

Statement	X	Y	Temp	Effect
Order (Num3, Num2)	6.0	10.0	?	Call procedure Order.
if X > Y				Is 6.0 > 10.0? Value is False.
Order (Num3, Num1)	6.0	8.0	?	Call procedure Order.
if X > Y				Is 6.0 > 8.0? Value is False.
Order (Num2, Num1)	10.0	8.0	?	Call procedure Order.
if X > Y				Is 10.0 > 8.0? Value is True.
Temp := X			10.0	Set Temp to 10.0.
X := Y	8.0			Set X to 8.0.
Y := Temp		10.0		Set Y to 10.0.

Result: Num1 = 10.0, Num2 = 8.0, Num3 = 6.0

Section 6.6

1. The scope of variable N declared in Outer is procedure Outer. The main program body and procedure Too are not included in the scope of N. Inner is excluded because N is declared as a local variable in Inner.
3. For Outer: Parameter X is set to 5.5; global variable Y is set to 6.6; local variables M and N are set to 2 and 3, respectively; identifier O is undeclared.
   For Too and Nested: Global variables X and Y are set to 5.5 and 6.6, respectively; identifiers M, N, and O are undeclared.
5. If X is the actual parameter, the values of W, X, and Y are 5.5, 6.0 and 4.0, respectively. If Y is the actual parameter, the values of W, X, and Y are 5.5, 2.0, and 7.0, respectively. If the formal parameter is a value parameter, the values of W, X, and Y are 5.5, 2.0, and 4.0, respectively.

Chapter 7

Section 7.1

1. All are valid except:
   ```
   MinusZ = - MaxLetter
   ```

Section 7.2

1. If Base is 2 instead of base 10, a binary number is printed in reverse. When Base is 2, PrintDigits (23) displays the binary digits 1, 1, 1, 0, 1 (the binary number 10111) has the decimal value 23); PrintDigits (64) displays the binary digits 0, 0, 0, 0, 0, 0, 1 (the binary number 1000000 has the decimal value 64).
   When Base is 8, PrintDigits (23) displays 7, 2 (the octal number 27 has the decimal value 23); PrintDigits (64) displays 0, 0, 1 (the octal number 100 has the decimal value 64).
3. a. 3 b. –3 c. invalid, Real operand for mod d. –3.14159 e. invalid use of Integer division operator with Real operands f. 0.75 g. invalid assignment of Integer expression to Real variable h. invalid, division by 0 i. 3 j. 3 k. –3.0 l. invalid assignment of Real expression to Integer variable m. invalid Real operand for div operator n. 0; o. 1 p. invalid, division by 0 q. 3
5. a. White is 1.6666... b. Green is 0.6666... c. Orange is 0 d. Blue is +3.0 e. Lime is 2 f. Purple is 0.666...

Section 7.3

1. a. `Sqrt(U + V) * Sqr(W)`
   b. `Y * Ln(X)`
   c. `Sqrt(Sqr(X - Y))`
   d. `Abs((X * Y) - (W / Z))`

Section 7.4

1. True 4.0 2.0 3.0 2.0
   ```
   not (Flag or ((Y + Z) >= (X - Z)))
   ```

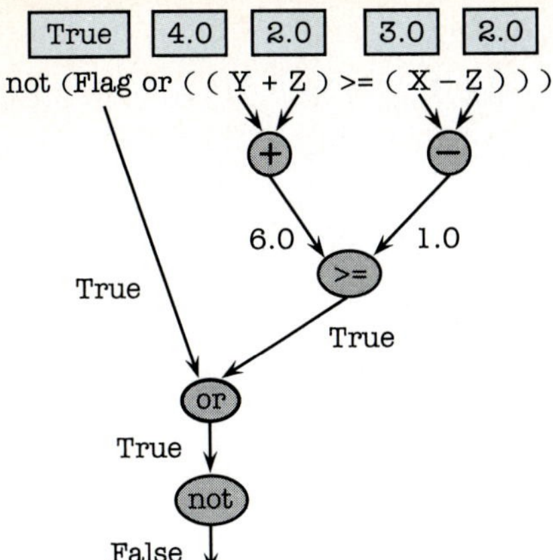

Section 7.5

1. a. `1` b. `False` c. `True` d. `1`

Section 7.7

1. Invalid subranges: f, g, h, i

Section 7.8

1. a. No constraints b. No way to avoid the error c. No constraints d. `J > 0` e. Not valid - Real result f. no constraints. g. Not valid; expression is `Real`

Chapter 8

Section 8.1

1. The six phases of the software life cycle are (1) requirements specification, (2) analysis, (3) design, (4) coding and debugging, (5) testing, and (6) operation and maintenance. The last phase, operation and maintenance, extends for the longest time.

Section 8.5

1. Insert the line

```
uses EnterData;
```

in the main program and delete the declaration of procedure `EnterInt`.

Section 8.6

1. So indentifiers declared in different modules with the same name can be referenced in the same module. Yes, `TooBuggy` could be redefined.

```
while not Errors. TooBuggy do
```

Section 8.7

1. a. 1 b. 4 c. False d. Thursday e. Thursday f. Friday g. Wednesday h. True i. undefined j. 6
3.
```
  type
    Month = (January, February, March, April, May, June, July,
             August, September, October, November, December);
var
  CurMonth : Month;

...
  if CurMonth = January then
    WriteLn ('Happy new year')
  else if CurMonth = June then
    WriteLn ('Summer begins')
  else if CurMonth = September then
    WriteLn ('Back to school')
  else if CurMonth = December then
    WriteLn ('Happy Holidays');
```

Section 8.8

1. Specifications for data type Integer
   Elements: The elements are integer numbers whose range depends on the number of bits used for storage. The standard identifier MaxInt can be used to determine this range on any system: it will always be between –MaxInt – 1 and MaxInt, inclusive.
   Operators: The arithmetic operators are +, –, *, /, div, and mod. The relational operators are <=, <, =, <>, >, and >=. The assignment operator is :=. The functions Abs, Sqr, Sqrt, Chr, Ord, Succ, and Pred can be used with type Integer arguments. Also, procedures Read, ReadLn, Write, and WriteLn can be called with type Integer parameters.

   Specifications for data type Char
   Elements: The elements are any single-character values enclosed in single quotation marks (e.g., 'A') when written in a Pascal statement; quotation marks are not used, however, when type Char data are entered at a terminal or from an input file.
   Also, procedures Read, ReadLn, Write, and WriteLn can be called with type Char parameters. The functions Ord, Succ Pred, and UpCase can be used with type Char arguments.

   Specifications for data type Boolean
   Elements: Only two values are associated with this data type, True and False.
   Operators: The assignment operator is :=. The logical operators, not, and, and or, functions Ord, Pred, and Succ can be used with type Boolean arguments. Also, procedures Write and WriteLn can be called with type Boolean parameters.

Section 8.10

1.

	X	N	C
a.	3.145	123	'3'
b.	3.145	123	' '
c.	3.145	123	'X'
d.	?	123	'3'

```
e. 123.0      5    '3'
f. 3.145     23    '3'
g. 3.145     35    '3'
h. 3.145     35    'Z'
i. 3.145    123    'Z'
```

Chapter 9

Section 9.1

1.
```
if X > Y then
  WriteLn ('X' greater')
else
  WriteLn ('Y greater or equal');
```

Section 9.2

1. a. Valid; 1, 2, 3, 4, 5
   b. Valid; '1', '2', '3', '4', '5'
   c. Invalid; mixed types
   d. Valid; '1', '3', 'A', 'B', 'C'

Section 9.3

1.
a.

Program Statement	i ?	J ?	Effect
`J := 10`		10	Set J to 10.
`for i := 1 to 5 do`	1		Initialize i to 1.
`  WriteLn (i, J)`			Display 1 and 10.
`  J := J - 2`		8	Assign 10 - 2 to J.
`increment and test i`	2		2 <= 5 is True.
`  WriteLn (i, J)`			Display 2 and 8.
`  J := J - 2`		6	Assign 8 - 2 to J.
`increment and test i`	3		3 <= 5 is True.
`  WriteLn (i, J)`			Display 3 and 6.
`  J := J - 2`		4	Assign 6 - 2 to J.
`increment and test i`	4		4 <= 5 is True.
`  WriteLn (i, J)`			Display 4 and 4.
`  J := J - 2`		2	Assign 4 - 2 to J.

`increment and test i`	5		`5 <= 5` is `True`.
`  WriteLn (i, J)`			Display 5 and 2.
`  J := J - 2`		0	Assign `2 - 2` to `J`.
`increment and test i`	5		Exit loop.

Section 9.4

1. a. `(X > Y) or (X = 15)`
   b. `((X > Y) or (X = 15)) and (Z <> 7.5)`
   c. `(X = 15) and ((Z <> 7.5) or (X > Y))`
   d. `not Flag and (X = 15.7)`
   e. `Flag or not (NextCh in ['A' .. 'H'])`
3. Twenty-six lines of output, consisting of 1 to 26 spaces followed by an * and the value of Ch

```
Ch := 'a';
while Ch <= 'Z' do
  begin
    NumSpaces := Ord(Ch) - Ord('a') H;
    WriteLn('*' : NumSpaces, Ch);
    Ch := Succ(Ch)
  end;

Ch := 'a';
repeat
  NumSpaces := Ord(Ch) - Ord('a') H;
  WriteLn('*' : NumSpaces, Ch);
  Ch := Succ(Ch)
until Ch > 'Z';
```

Section 9.5

1. a.
```
*
**
***
****
*****
```
   b.
```
***
***
***
***
***
```

Section 9.6

1. This function will not return any value to the function name and has the side effect of changing X and Y to the absolute values of X and Y. There is no need for the parameter Result, because a function always returns a single value. The function declaration should be
```
function MyTest (X, Y : Real) : Real;
```
and the second-to-last line should be
```
MyTest := Sqrt(X) + Sqrt (Y)
```

Section 9.7

1. ```
Tens := TwoDigitNum div 10;
Units := TwoDigitNum mod 10;
```

```
Ex: TwoDigitNum = 87
    Tens = 87 div 10 = 8
    Units = 87 mod 10 = 7
Ex: TwoDigitNum = 20
    Tens = 20 div 10 = 2
    Units = 20 mod 10 = 0
```

```
CheckPennies := Round(CentsPerDollar * Amount);
Dollars := CheckPennies div CentsPerDollar;
Cents := CheckPennies mod CentsPerDollar;
```

```
Ex: Amount = 36.92
    CheckPennies = Round(100 * 36.92) = Round(3692.00) = 3692
    Dollars = 3692 div 100 = 36
    Cents = 3692 mod 100 = 92

Ex: Amount = 94.13
    CheckPennies = Round(100 * 94.13) = Round(9413.00) = 9413
    Dollars = 9413 div 100 = 94
    Cents = 9413 mod 100 = 13
```

Chapter 10

Section 10.1

1. X3 is a simple variable, whereas X[3] refers to the third element of the array named X.

3. a.
```
type
  RealArray = array [Boolean] of Real;

var
  N : RealArray;
```

b.
```
type
  IntArray = array ['A'..'F'] of Integer;

var
  N : IntArray;
```

c.
```
type
  BoolArray = array [Char] of Boolean;

var
  Flags : BoolArray;
```

d. Invalid array

e.
```
type
  RealArray = array [Char] of Real;

var
  X : RealArray;
```
```

f. Invalid array

g.
```
type
  Day = (Sun, Mon, Tues, Wed, Thurs, Fri, Sat);
  RealArray = array [Day] of Real;

var
  Y : RealArray;
```

Section 10.2

1. No
3. a. `X[3] := 7.0;`
   b. `X[1] := X[5];`
   c. `X[5] := X[4] - X[1];`
   d. `X[6] := X[6] + 2;`
   e.
   ```
   Sum := 0;
   for I := 1 to 5 do
     Sum := Sum + X[I];
   ```
   f.
   ```
   for I := 1 to 6 do
     AnswerArray[I] := X[I] * 2;
   ```
   g.
   ```
   I := 2;
   while I <= 8 do
     begin
       Write (X[I] :8);
       I := I + 2
     end; {while}
   ```

Section 10.3

1. The user will be continually prompted to choose a category until a valid one is entered.

Section 10.4

1. It is better to pass the entire array of data rather than individual elements if several elements of the array are being manipulated by a procedure.
3. `I` is equal to `MaxSize` if both arrays are the same; `I` is equal to `3` if the third elements do not match.

Section 10.5

1. The `while` loop that calls `EnterInt` is exited when `MaxSize` is reached.
3.
```
repeat
  {invariant:
      No prior value read is Sentinel and
      ClassSize <= MaxSize
  }
  EnterInt (Sentinel, MaxScore, TempScore);
```

```
      case Sex of
        Female : WriteLn ('Female');
        Male   : WriteLn ('Male')
      end; {case}
      WriteLn ('Number of Dependents: ', NumDepend);
      WriteLn ('Hourly Rate: ', Rate :4:2);
      WriteLn ('Taxable Salary: ', TaxSal :4:2)
  end; {with}
```

Section 11.3

1.
```
type
  ExamStats = record
                Low, High : 0..100;
                Average, StandardDev : Real
              end; {ExamStats}

var
  Exam1, Exam2 : ExamStats;
```

This program segment prints the statistics for `Exam1`, copies `Exam1` into `Exam2`, modifies the `High` field of `Exam2`, and finally prints new statistics for `Exam2`.

Section 11.4

1.
```
(8.50, -1.50)
(7.00, 10.00)
12.21
```

Section 11.5

1. `NewAddress` must be type `Address`.

Section 11.6

1. `Married`: 22 bytes
   `Divorced`: 6 bytes
   `Single`: 1 byte

Chapter 12

Section 12.1

1.
```
type
  Day = (Sun, Mon, Tues, Wed, Thurs, Fri, Sat);
  AnArray = array ['A'..'F', 1..10, Day] of Real;
```
An array of this type can hold 420 elements (`6 * 10 * 7`).

```
  if TempScore <> Sentinel then
    begin
      ClassSize := ClassSize + 1;        {Increment ClassSize}
      Scores[ClassSize] := TempScore     {Save the score}
    end {if}
until (TempScore = Sentinel) or (ClassSize = MaxSize);
```

The `repeat-until` loop necessitates that you check twice to see whether the sentinel value has been entered, whereas it is necessary to check only once with the `while` loop. A `for` loop cannot be used in this situation because we do not know in advance how many data items are going to be entered.

Section 10.6

1. a. An array of characters with twenty elements and subscripts of one to twenty
   b. An array of `Boolean` type values with ten elements and subscripts of the digit characters `'0'` to `'9'`
   c. An array of real numbers with eleven elements and subscripts of the integers -5 to 5
   d. An array of characters with two elements and subscripts of `False` and `True`
3. Program `Cryptogram` checks to see that a letter is in the set `['A' .. 'Z']` before encoding it. Because commas and blanks are not members of this set, they are not encoded.

Section 10.7

1. The length of the string must not be less than 0 or greater than the capacity of the string variable. Nothing, extra characters will be lost.

Chapter 11

Section 11.1

1.
```
const
  StrLength = 20;

type
  StringType = string[StrLength];
  Part = record
           PartNum : Integer;
           Name : StringType;
           Quantity : Integer;
           Price : Real
         end; {Part}
```

Section 11.2

1.
```
with Clerk do
  begin
    WriteLn ('ID: ', ID);
    WriteLn ('Name: ', Name);
    Write ('Sex: ');
```

Index

Reference Guide to Turbo Pascal Constructs

(continued from inside front cover)

Construct	Page	Example of Use	
pointer	693	`ClassPointer = ^Student;`	
list node	694	`Student = record`	
		`Info : StuData;`	`{data field}`
		`Next : ClassPointer`	`{pointer}`
		`end; {Student}`	
array	381	`MajorArray = array [StudentIndex] of College;`	
file	584	`StuFile = file of StuData;`	
variable declaration	34	`var`	
record	447	`CurStu : StuData;`	`{input - student data}`
set	542	`Grades : GradeSet;`	`{allowable grades}`
text file	317	`InFile : Text;`	`{input - text file}`
file	582	`OutFile : StuFile;`	`{output - binary file}`
pointer	692	`ClassList : ClassPointer;`	`{list of classes}`
array	394	`Major : MajorArray;`	`{array of majors}`
character	57	`NextCh : Char;`	`{input - character}`
integer	48	`CountProb : Integer;`	`{counter}`
string	425	`LastName : String20;`	`{last name}`
program body	41	`begin {Guide}`	
WriteLn procedure	40	`WriteLn ('Registration for ', School);`	
assignment	36	`CountProb := 0;`	`{initialize counter}`
with statement	450	`with CurStu do`	
compound statement	111	`begin`	`{define fields of CurStu}`
string assignment	429	`Name := 'Jackson, Michael Bad';`	
display prompt	38	`Write ('Enter GPA> ');`	
ReadLn procedure	39	`ReadLn (GPA);`	
enumerated assign	302	`InCollege := Arts`	
		`end; {with}`	
case statement with	345	`case CurStu.InCollege of`	
field selection as	448	`Business : WriteLn ('Business major');`	
case selector		`Arts : WriteLn ('Arts major');`	
		`Science : WriteLn ('Science major');`	
		`General : WriteLn ('General major')`	
		`end; {case}`	
nested if	114	`if CurStu.GPA > DeansList then`	
embedded apostrophe	61	`WriteLn ('   On the Dean''s List')`	
		`else if CurStu.GPA > Probation then`	
		`WriteLn ('Satisfactory progress')`	
		`else`	
		`begin`	
format a string	52	`WriteLn ('On Probation' :21);`	
increment counter	127	`CountProb := CountProb + 1`	
		`end; {nested if}`	